BIOGRAPHICAL
DICTIONARY
OF
WORLD WAR I

BIOGRAPHICAL DICTIONARY OF WORLD WAR I

HOLGER H. HERWIG
AND NEIL M. HEYMAN

 GREENWOOD PRESS

WESTPORT, CONNECTICUT • LONDON, ENGLAND

Library of Congress Cataloging in Publication Data

Herwig, Holger H.
    Biographical dictionary of World War I.

    Bibliography: p.
    Includes index.
    1. World War, 1914-1918—Biography.   I. Heyman,
Neil M.   II. Title
D507.H47   940.3'092'2 [B]   81-4242
ISBN 0-313-21356-9 (lib. bdg.)   AACR2

Library of Congress Catalog Card Number: 81-4242
ISBN: 0-313-21356-9

First published in 1982

Greenwood Press
A division of Congressional Information Service, Inc.
88 Post Road West, Westport, Connecticut 06881

Printed in the United States of America

10 9 8 7 6 5 4 3 2 1

Copyright Acknowledgments

The epigraph is from Siegfried Sassoon's "Prelude: The Troops"
in his *Collected Poems 1908-1956*. Permission to reprint was
granted by the Trustees of the Sassoon Will Trust. Permission to
reprint in the United States was granted by Viking Penguin, Inc.
Copyright © 1961, 1964 by the Trustees of the Sassoon Will
Trust.

Four lines from a poem by J. C. Squire, which appear in *The
First World War: An Illustrated History* by A.J.P. Taylor, are
reprinted by permission of Macmillan Accounts and Administration Ltd.

Two lines from a poem by Bret Harte are reprinted
by permission of Houghton Mifflin Company.

And through some mooned Valhalla there will pass   The unreturning army that was youth;
Battalions and Battalions, scarred from hell;   The legions who have suffered and are dust.

                                          —Siegfried Sassoon
                                          from "Prelude: The Troops"

CONTENTS

MAPS

ACKNOWLEDGMENTS

A work of this scope does not come into being in a matter of two or three years; rather, it is the outgrowth of years of research on various related topics. Hence, it would be tedious to list all persons who have over the past decade contributed toward the collection and digestion of information contained herein. I would therefore like to single out for acknowledgment only a few people who have proved particularly helpful in the completion of this work. In the first place, the Alexander von Humboldt-Stiftung in Bonn-Bad Godesberg has graciously and generously supported my research since 1969. Lois V. Griest of Vanderbilt University Library over the last three years has tirelessly and cheerfully hunted down obscure or rare books essential for this project. And when all printed materials failed me, a number of ar-chivists came to my rescue: Dr. Heyl of the Bayerisches Hauptstaatsarchiv, Kriegsarchiv in Munich; Dr. Sandhofer of the Bundesarchiv-Militärarchiv in Freiburg; Dr. Obermayer-Marnach of the Österreichische Akademie der Wissenschaft in Vienna; and especially Dr. Tepperberg of the Öster-reichisches Staatsarchiv, Kriegsarchiv in Vienna. Without their expertise many entries would have remained incomplete. Finally, I owe a great debt to my wife, who not only has put up with what seemed a protracted search for minutiae and endless rewritings, but who also critically—at times caustically—worked through the entire manuscript. My daughter, Brooke, did her best to rearrange some of the entries and to add crayon comments on others!

Holger H. Herwig

I have received generous assistance from a number of kind and knowledgeable individuals. I wish to extend my warm thanks to Professor Alvin Coox, San Diego State University; Professor Glenn Torrey, Emporia State University; Professor John Bell, University of Maryland, Baltimore County; Professor Frederick Chary, Indiana University Northwest; Professor Paul Halpern, Florida State University; George Paprikoff, M.D., Chicago, Illinois; and Mr. Constantin Shopov of New York City.

The staff of the Hoover Library, Stanford University, helped to make extended stays in 1978 and 1980 pleasant and productive ventures. I am specifically grateful to Catherine Foster, Linda Thomas, and Hilja Kukk. The staff of the Inter-Library Loan Department of the Love Library, San Diego State University, helped in countless ways to obtain materials essential to this work. The difficult they did at once; the impossible merely took a little longer. My sincere thanks go to Karen Hogarth, Patricia Morrison, and Ann Wright.

My wife, Brenda, and my young son, Mark, were innocents conscripted into a long and grueling acquaintance with World War I. I want to try to thank them here for their cheerfulness, patience, and encouragement. The full measure of my gratitude goes beyond my ability to express in words.

Neil M. Heyman

A NOTE ON NAMES, PLACES, AND DATES

The areas of central and eastern Europe have witnessed especially great changes in nomenclature over the past century. Names of cities have been altered with reckless abandon. It would be sheer madness to attempt to give Czechoslovakian, German, Hungarian, Polish, Russian, or Yugoslavian equivalents for all cities cited in this multinational work—as it would be to translate all personal names into English. In the main, we have attempted merely to conform to standard English language usage: where a readily discernible English language name is in common historical use, such as with Francis Ferdinand or Nicholas II, it has been retained; the same holds true for cities such as Munich, Warsaw, or Vienna. Accents have been included wherever standard usage demands; names such as Baghdad or Bagdad, Pasha or Paşa, Bucarest or Bucharest, have merely been rendered uniform. And throughout this work all dates are according to the Gregorian rather than the Julian, or Old Style, calendar.

In the text, we have used a modified version of the Library of Congress system for transliterating Russian names. In place of "IU" and "IA" at the start of names, "Yu" and "Ya" are given; thus, Yudenich and Yanushkevich. Likewise, "ii" at the end of names has been made "y"; thus, Ruzsky, Lechitsky. Apostrophes and diacritical marks have been omitted. In the Bibliography, of course, the Russian has been transliterated according to the normal rules of the Library of Congress.

The problem of place names was most acute for Austria-Hungary and Germany. For the period before the Great War, we have throughout given the then current German language names, fully aware that these changed after 1918. Hence, appointments were to Agram, Brünn, Hermannstadt, and Pressburg, not to Zagreb, Brno, Sibiu, or Poszony-Bratislava; in the case of Germany, to Königsberg, Strassburg, Thorn, and Danzig, not Kaliningrad, Strasbourg, Torun, or Gdansk. As far as possible, we have avoided linguistic chauvinism; however, if certain place names offend, we ask the reader's forgiveness under the trying circumstances. The following list of cities is not intended to be exhaustive, but merely a rough guide to places frequently mentioned in this work:

Agram	Zagreb
Altenburg	Magyaróvár
Bozen	Bolzano
Breslau	Wroclaw
Brünn	Brno
Budweis	Budějovice
Cattaro	Boka Katorska
Czernowitz	Cernauti (Rum.), Chernovtsy (Russ.)
Danzig	Gdansk
Esseg	Osijek
Fiume	Rijeka
Flitsch	Bovec (Slov.), Plezzo (Ital.)
Gumbinnen	Gusev
Hermannstadt	Sibiu (Rum.), Nagyszeben (Hun.)
Karfreit	Caporetto
Kaschau	Kassa
Königsberg	Kaliningrad
Kronstadt	Brassó
Laibach	Ljubljana
Lemberg	Lwow (Pol.), Lvov (Russ.)
Luck	Lutsk
Marburg	Maribor
Marienburg	Malborg
Olmütz	Olomouc
Pilsen	Plžen
Pola	Pula
Posen	Poznan
Pressburg	Poszony (Hun.), Bratislava (Czech.)
Stolp	Slupsk
Strassburg	Strasbourg

Teschen	Tesin (Czech.), Cieszyn (Pol.)	Troppau	Opava
		Weichsel	Vistula
Thorn	Torun	Weissenburg	Gyulafehérvár
Trient	Trento	Zabern	Saverne

HISTORICAL
INTRODUCTION

1

ORIGINS

On Friday night, July 24, 1914, First Lord of the Admiralty Winston Churchill dined in London with Albert Ballin, head of the Hamburg-American Line and a close friend of Kaiser Wilhelm II. The German recalled that Otto von Bismarck, shortly before his death, had confided to Ballin his fears "that one day the great European War would come out of some damned foolish thing in the Balkans." That "damned foolish thing" had occurred at Sarajevo on June 28, when Gavrilo Princip, a terrorist in the service of the Serbian Colonel Dragutin Dimitrijević, murdered the heir presumptive to the Austrian Habsburg throne, Archduke Francis Ferdinand. Austria was now determined to humiliate Serbia, not only because it believed Serbia stood behind the Sarajevo assassins, but also to deflate the demands for independence of the various ethnic groups in the Dual Monarchy. What would Tsar Nicholas II do, Ballin continued, if Austria "chastized" Serbia? Ballin then laid out the scenario of probable events: "If Russia marches against Austria, we must march; and if we march, France must march, and what would England do?" It was an excellent question. When Churchill offered an evasive reply, Ballin pressed him, wanting to ascertain whether Britain would stay out of any continental war as long as Germany promised not to seize "an inch" of French territory, but "only some colonies to indemnify us." Churchill finally responded that "it would be a mistake to assume that we should stand out of it whatever happened."[1]

Here, in a nutshell, is the crux of the July crisis. Would Russia condone Austrian punitive actions against Serbia, or would Russia go to war for the "little Slav brother"? In case of the latter, would Berlin stand "shoulder to shoulder" with Vienna? Would France thereupon march with Russia? And finally, would Britain intervene in the European war on the side of the Entente, even if Germany guaranteed not to annex French territory? In less than one week, the dinner conversation between Churchill and Ballin became reality.

But how had the great powers arrived at the point where they were willing to risk a continental, if not a world, war for "some damned foolish thing in the Balkans"? Why were the Iron Chancellor's dire warnings about that region so easily dismissed in 1914? The answers to these complex questions largely revolve around the *Weltanschauung* of the various European states, dominated, to differing degrees in each, by Social Darwinism, historical determinism, and racism.

The notion of a natural life-and-death struggle among empires had by the end of the nineteenth century taken a strong hold over European statesmen. No one wanted to be left behind in either the economic or the military competition. To stand still meant to decline. Europe was experiencing a period of change, of movement, of innovation. Britain was the established world leader. But at the turn of the century, it was being challenged by Germany, Japan, and the United States. All three rivals were becoming industrial powers with their own dynamism and energy, forging ahead on a course of expansion and, if need be, confrontation. Little of the world remained to be divided: Africa had been parceled out in the 1880s; China had been forced to lease ports a decade later; and South America was "protected" by the Monroe Doctrine. Overseas rivalry had often worked as a kind of safety valve, whereby European powers could exercise their forces on the periphery, without directly endangering the Continent.

There remained the Balkans and Asia Minor. Germany sought to bring much of this area under its control through the construction of the Berlin to Baghdad Railway, but financial exhaustion as well as Anglo-French pressures eventually forced it to abandon this vast undertaking. And in 1907, Britain and Russia agreed to settle their rivalry in Asia Minor at the expense of Persia, which was neatly subdivided. The Balkans, on the other hand, seemed to afford all powers with opportunities for expansion. The Ottoman Empire, the "sick man of Europe," had over the past century slowly lost its grip on the region to the profit of Austria and Russia. The former had in 1909 annexed outright the provinces of Bosnia and Herzegovina and was seeking an alliance with Bulgaria; Russia, with French encouragement, pressed for the creation of a Balkan federation of Serbia and Montenegro, at the same time hoping to loosen the ties between Rumania and Germany. The Italians coveted Albania and Dalmatia. And the various Balkan states distrusted each other and constantly sought to play the great powers off against one another in the hopes of thereby acquiring additional territory. In 1912 and 1913, major wars occurred in the region. In 1914, Austria and Italy fell out again over Trieste, and Turkey and Greece almost went to war over several Aegean islands.

No one was more troubled over these developments than Germany. The erstwhile "New Course" of navalism and colonialism under Chancellor Bernhard von Bülow and Admiral Alfred von Tirpitz had suffered shipwreck by 1906, owing to the efforts of Admiral Sir John Fisher in London to meet the unilateral German challenge head-on by building superior dreadnought battleships and by concentrating the greater part of available forces in Europe. As a result, in 1905/06 General Alfred von Schlieffen, chief of the Prussian General Staff, had drafted memorandums that committed Germany, in case of a two-front war against France and Russia, to strike against France first by marching through Belgium to the Channel coast. Then the Germans were to swoop down behind Paris into the Seine basin. Meanwhile, Germany would fight a holding action in the east, where, in any case, its Austrian ally would have to shoulder the burden of fighting Russia. All was predicated on Germany being first, and on Russia being last, to mobilize.

General Helmuth von Moltke, "the Younger," inheriting this blueprint for victory, quickly discerned that a number of variables in Schlieffen's plan as well as time were working against him. Russia, humiliated by Japan in 1905, four years later launched a vast program of army expansion and railway building into Poland under General V. A. Sukhomlinov, to be completed by 1916/17. Could Germany still afford to denude its defenses in the east? Concurrently, Austria-Hungary was neglecting her armed forces and was beset by the centrifugal forces of nationalism among her various ethnic groups. The oft-discussed idea of the German Foreign Office for a tie with London proved to be stillborn. Germany could never aid Britain outside of Europe without at the same time surrendering her semihegemony on the Continent to France and Russia; Britain, in turn, could do nothing to help Germany in case of a two-front war on the Continent. The Ottoman Empire seemed on the verge of collapse, a course of events that would entail massive border revisions in the Danubian basin. Denied a "place in the sun," Germany retreated to the Continent as *Weltpolitik* was being scaled down to look more and more like *Balkanpolitik*.

General von Moltke became obsessed that Germany's future could only be secured through a preemptive strike against Russia. In crude, racist terms, he preached that such a showdown between "Slavs and Teutons" needed to be undertaken before reforms of the Russian army were completed by 1916/17. In Vienna, his counterpart, General Franz Baron Conrad von Hötzendorf, eagerly agreed. Conrad, hoping to arrest the national independence movements within the Habsburg Empire, had desired a strike against Serbia as early as 1909. Moreover, he shared Moltke's belief that Russia stood behind Serbia and that only war with Russia could fully stunt Pan-Slavic aspirations. In numerous written as well as verbal exchanges between 1909 and 1914, both generals agreed that it was best to strike against Russia at the first opportune moment; "to wait any longer," Moltke informed Conrad, "meant a diminishing of our chances." The Austrian also desired "to settle the inevitable conflict at an earlier date." In December 1912, Moltke went so far as to recommend war against Russia to the kaiser, "and the sooner the better."

These racist and deterministic prognoses were shared by the kaiser and his chancellor, Theobald von Bethmann Hollweg. In October 1913, at the centenary of the Battle of Nations at Leipzig, Wilhelm, clutching the hilt of his sword, assured the Austrians that he would "be ready to draw the sword whenever your actions make it necessary." Bethmann Hollweg, who greatly disliked Tirpitz's naval race with England, was likewise depressed concerning the future. The struggle between "Slavs and Teutons," he told parliament, was inevitable. Russia, he offered, "grows and grows and weighs upon us like a nightmare."[2] Above all, he was prepared to take a "calculated risk." The Entente of 1907 was informal, not a strict alliance, even though Sir Henry Wilson eagerly assured the French during his celebrated bicycle trips through their countryside that the British and French would fight together in case of war with Germany. The Cabinet, on the other hand, studiously avoided any discussion of whether intervention in France would be in Britain's interests, and the Royal Navy continued to view any future commitment to war strictly in traditional naval terms. Thus, might not Britain be won over at the last moment by a neutrality pact, or by a colonial settlement, or even by an offer to scale down the German fleet? In short, like Moltke and Conrad, Bethmann Hollweg was prepared to accept the risk of war between Germany and Austria-Hungary, on the one hand, and France and Russia, on the other, in the belief that this would solve Vienna's nationalities question and establish German hegemony over the Continent.

The events at Sarajevo must be seen against this background. For what was about to transpire was orchestrated primarily in Berlin and Vienna. Sir Edward Grey in London took a cautious insular approach to "the Serbian matter," while French President Raymond Poincaré and Premier René Viviani were on board the *France* on a visit to Russia and Sweden from July 15 through 29 and therefore were absent from the capital. Russia acted virtually in isolation and primarily in response to Austro-German initiatives. Italy was not consulted by its nominal allies, Austria and Germany, for fear that it would exploit the situation to its benefit regardless of treaty commitments. It is therefore primarily to Berlin and Vienna that we must turn in order to unravel the July crisis of 1914, which plunged Europe into its bloodiest and costliest war to date.

Austria-Hungary was fully aware that any action it took against Serbia after the regicide at Sarajevo would affect Russia. Therefore, the full support of Germany would be required before any action was undertaken: in two letters dated July 1 and 2, Foreign Minister Count Leopold von Berchtold and Emperor Francis Joseph inquired what the German position would be in the event of actions designed "to eliminate" Serbia "as a political power factor in the Balkans."[3]

Government offices in Berlin were virtually empty, as the summer holiday season was in full swing: General von Moltke was taking the waters at Karlsbad, Chancellor von Bethmann Hollweg was on his estate at Hohenfinow, Admiral von Tirpitz was in the Black Forest at St. Blasien, and Foreign Secretary Gottlieb von Jagow was on his honeymoon. But the kaiser was at Potsdam. Already on June 30 he had favored a punitive strike against Serbia, penning "now or never" on a note from his ambassador in Vienna that reported Austria as favoring a "thorough reckoning of accounts with Serbia." On July 5/6, Wilhelm II hastily recalled his chancellor, and during a series of improvised meetings—erroneously blown up later into the "Crown Council of Potsdam" by the Allies—it was decided to back whatever play the Habsburgs made in the Balkans. The kaiser assured

the Austrian ambassador, Count Ladislaus Szögény-Marich, that the Dual Monarchy could count on "Germany's full support" in the Balkans, even if "serious European complications" resulted; moreover, he counseled Vienna not to "delay the action" against Serbia. On July 6, Wilhelm pathetically assured Gustav Krupp von Bohlen und Halbach three times in the course of a brief chat: "This time I shall not give in." The following day, Bethmann Hollweg added his endorsement to the so-called blank check by assuring the Austrians that he viewed military action against Serbia as the "best and most radical solution" to Vienna's Balkan problems.[4] Both kaiser and chancellor agreed that neither France nor Russia was prepared for war and that especially Nicholas II would never condone regicide.

Armed with these assurances of German support, Berchtold on July 7 convened a Crown Council in Vienna and apprised those present of Germany's backing "even though our operations against Serbia should bring about the great war." The foreign minister, supported by Austrian Prime Minister Count Karl von Stürgkh, General Conrad von Hötzendorf, and War Minister General Alexander von Krobatin, recommended immediate military action against Serbia. Only Hungarian Prime Minister István Tisza demurred, fearing that such precipitous action would bring on "the dreadful calamity of a European war." Instead, the Magyar recommended some sort of diplomatic action, perhaps in the form of an ultimatum to Serbia to help round up the assassins. Berchtold accepted this solution as preliminary to military action, then departed for Bad Ischl in order to bring the vacationing Emperor Francis Joseph up to date; in the meantime, his staff began to prepare the note intended for Serbia. But before leaving Vienna, Berchtold had advised both Conrad and Krobatin to start their planned vacations "in order to preserve the appearance that nothing is being planned."[5] In Germany, the kaiser at about the same time left Berlin for his annual cruise off Norway.

By July 14, Count Tisza was ready to accept Berchtold's plan to present Serbia with a stringent ultimatum that would permit Austria to violate its territorial sovereignty at any time in the search for the Sarajevo murderers; Belgrade would be given forty-eight hours to accept the Austrian conditions. If it did so, Berchtold informed the emperor, Serbia would be "humiliated," and Russia would again, as in 1909, lose "prestige in the Balkans." If, on the other hand, Serbia rejected the ultimatum, Vienna would break off diplomatic relations, mobilize its army, and shell Belgrade.[6] As a concession to the powerful Tisza, Berchtold promised that Austria would annex no new Serbian territory. The Ballhausplatz also cleverly delayed sending the ultimatum until the conclusion of the visit by Poincaré and Viviani to St. Petersburg.

The Austro-German position at this point was one of a "calculated risk." Both Berchtold and Bethmann Hollweg were fully willing to risk a general European war for the twin purposes of ending "Greater Serbia" aspirations in the Balkans and Pan-Slavic agitation in Russia. And there could be no doubt about the gravity of their decision. President Poincaré on the second day of his stay in Russia tipped France's hand when he informed Austrian Ambassador Count Friedrich Szápáry: "Serbia has some very warm friends in the Russian people. And Russia has an ally, France. There are plenty of complications to be feared!"[7] With that, the two French leaders again boarded the *France* and steamed to Stockholm.

The Austrian ultimatum was delivered to Serbia on July 24. Sir Edward Grey at Whitehall termed it "the most formidable document that I have ever seen addressed by one State to another that was independent." With this burst of eloquence, he was off for his fishing lodge; the Cabinet likewise departed for the countryside for the weekend.[8] Nikola Pašić at midday on July 25 handed Austrian Ambassador Baron Giesl von Gieslingen a note stating that the Serbian government accepted all points of the ultimatum, save those permitting Austrian officials to enter Serbia in search of their suspects. The Serbian prime minister had been encouraged in his stance by assurances from Nicholas II that Russia would stand behind the "little Slav brother" in the Balkans; in fact, Pašić had ordered his army mobilized even before he handed Giesl the official answer to the ultimatum. As the Yugoslavian archives remain closed, little else is known about what transpired that day either in Belgrade or in St. Petersburg. Giesl, as prearranged, broke diplomatic relations with Serbia, picked up his already packed bags at the embassy, and, after a ten-minute train ride, arrived on Austrian soil at Semlin. Later that same day, Conrad ordered partial mobilization of his forces against Serbia, planning to announce a state of war between the two nations only after full mobilization had been completed by August 12. However, under severe pressure from Germany, the Austrians on July 28 formally declared war on Serbia; Berlin had feared that in the period between July 28 and August 12 there might exist "great danger concerning intervention of other powers."[9]

There was little reaction in the west. France's leaders were literally out at sea and were not expected back in Paris until July 29. In the meantime,

the French army recalled all officers and reservists from leave, shuttled regular units from Morocco to metropolitan France, and informed the Russians that France would honor her treaty obligations, come what may. Without Poincaré's or Viviani's backing, however, these assurances were not binding. And when the Cabinet reconvened in London, Grey found a cold reception when he raised the possibility of British intervention. He therefore fell back on Sir Arthur Nicolson's suggestion that a four-power conference be convened to discuss the Serbian matter. On July 29, the Cabinet again "decided not to decide." When the possibility that Germany might march through neutral Belgium was raised, Grey laconically replied that this would be treated as a question "of policy rather than legal obligations."[10] Nevertheless, it was becoming apparent that the issue of war or peace was shifting from the Foreign Office to the Cabinet. Grey's attempts to find a diplomatic solution to the Balkan crisis by working with Berlin, without at the same time abandoning either Paris or St. Petersburg, was foundering. At some point in the near future, the Cabinet would therefore have to wrestle with the thorny question of intervention on the Continent.

In Russia, General Sukhomlinov and General N. N. Yanushkevich, chief of the General Staff, favored a declaration of general mobilization. However, Foreign Minister Sergei Sazonov was not yet ready for such a drastic measure, preferring to do so only after Austrian troops had violated Serbian soil. But shortly before a scheduled audience with the tsar, French Ambassador Maurice Paléologue fanned the flames of war by assuring Sazonov of "the complete readiness of France to fulfill her obligations as an ally in case of necessity."[11] With this assurance, which smacked of another "blank check," Sazonov persuaded Nicholas II to mobilize the military districts Kiev, Odessa, Moscow, and Kazan, that is, those fronting Austria-Hungary only.

The German reaction was mixed. Wilhelm II had returned from his northern cruise on July 28 and, a mere sixty minutes before Vienna declared war on Serbia, was informed of the Serbian reply. He was delirious. "A brilliant performance for a deadline of only 48 hours. That is more than one could expect! A great moral triumph for Vienna, but with it every reason for war ends."[12] Admiral von Tirpitz, who knew that his fleet would not be ready to challenge the Royal Navy until the early 1920s, was also greatly relieved. Unfortunately, Bethmann Hollweg did not share this peace euphoria. He refused to relay the kaiser's sentiments to Vienna until he received official notification that a state of war existed in the Balkans.

Moreover, when he finally transmitted Wilhelm's statement, he carefully expunged from it the monarch's comment, "with it every reason for war ends." Clearly, the German chancellor was decided on war. That very day he also rejected Grey's offer of a four-power conference on the Balkan situation.

The July crisis was in its most crucial phase: the next forty-eight hours would decide whether the war would be "localized" in the Balkans, whether it would develop into a continental conflagration, or whether it would become global through the intervention of Britain and its empire. Just to be on the safe side, Admiral Prince Louis of Battenberg and Winston Churchill in London decided not to pay off the fleet after the Spithead naval review, but rather to maintain it on battle alert.

General von Moltke now intervened decisively in Berlin. Austria had already shelled Belgrade, and rumors of Russian mobilization were omnipresent. His timetable demanded mobilization before France and Russia had done so. As poet Bret Harte had advised:

Blest is the man whose cause is just;
Thrice blest is he who gets his blow in fust.

Usurping the chancellor's functions, Moltke reminded Bethmann Hollweg of the "deeply rooted sentiment of allied loyalty" between Berlin and Vienna and warned that the German people would not desert Austria now. He further demanded that the chancellor at once ascertain whether Russia and France "are disposed to go to the length of war with Germany." Under the rigors of the Schlieffen plan, for them to mobilize first would "lead to fatal consequences for us." Obviously, the army was not willing to shoulder these. Moltke concluded by arguing that "we shall never hit it again so well as we do now with France's and Russia's expansion of their armies incomplete."[13]

It was the crassest usurpation of *Staatskunst* by *Kriegshandwerk*, and it set Bethmann Hollweg into sheer panic. He knew that Germany intended to violate the neutrality of Belgium and Luxembourg and to invade France under the Schlieffen plan. But to do so brazenly and without provocation while France's leaders were out of the country would force Germany to shoulder the entire blame for provoking the war. Bethmann Hollweg wished to place this onus with Russia. That same day, July 29, he convinced Kaiser "Willy" to undertake a flurry of telegrams with Tsar "Nicky" specifically designed, "if war were to come about," to "place the guilt of Russia in the strongest light." The chancellor must have been greatly relieved later that night when he received news of Russia's *ukase* for partial mobilization. The German Social Democrats had just assured him of their support in a war against the hearth of reaction, tsarist Russia.

The chancellor now decided to play his "trump." With Wilhelm's permission, he called British Ambassador Sir Edward William Goschen to his residence shortly before midnight. For years, Bethmann Hollweg had sought a naval understanding with Britain, and he now hoped to cash in on that pool of goodwill. In addition, the kaiser's brother, Prince Henry of Prussia, had recently returned from London with the news that King George V might remain neutral in a European war. Bethmann Hollweg therefore laid out his cards before Goschen: were Britain to remain neutral in the coming war, Germany would offer her a neutrality agreement for after the war, would promise not to undertake "territorial gains at the expense of France," and would assure the future independence of Holland. Herewith, Albert Ballin's dinner conversation with Winston Churchill on July 24 was fully realized.[14] If Britain took the bait, Bethmann Hollweg's "calculated risk" would be justified.

As is well known, the chancellor's gamble failed by July 30. Grey described Bethmann Hollweg's treaty proposal as "infamous." Goschen noted: "The only comment that need be made on these astounding proposals is that they reflect discredit on the statesman who makes them." That very afternoon, Grey informed German Ambassador Prince Karl von Lichnowsky that, in case of a general European war, Britain would not remain neutral. The chancellor's house of cards had collapsed. The war between Vienna and Belgrade could not be "localized." Nor could it be limited to the Continent. In vain, Bethmann Hollweg dredged up the kaiser's earlier idea that the Austrians be asked to "halt in Belgrade" and to hold the capital as a "pledge" while the diplomats sought a solution to the Serbian matter. Thus, the very leader who for the previous three weeks had urged speed on Vienna now was attempting to apply the brakes as he had "bluffed himself into an impasse." Later that day, he informed the Prussian State Ministry that "the hope for England [was now] zero."[15]

Once again, Moltke seized the initiative. He informed the Habsburg military attaché in Berlin, Count Karl von Bienerth, that he desired immediate Austrian and German mobilization against Russia. Moreover, Moltke dashed off a cable to Conrad in Vienna: "Austria-Hungary must be preserved; mobilize also against Russia. Germany will mobilize." Coming at the same time as Bethmann Hollweg's "halt in Belgrade" *volte face*, Moltke's telegram exasperated Berchtold. "Who rules in Berlin," he asked Conrad, "Moltke or Bethmann?"[16] The answer to that rhetorical question was obvious, and orders for general mobilization were drafted at once for Francis Joseph to sign.

Center stage in the July crisis now shifted to St. Petersburg. The shelling of Belgrade by Austria on July 28 had made a great impression on Russian generals, who were united in their desire immediately to order general mobilization. Foreign Minister Sazonov preferred instead to wait until Habsburg troops had actually crossed into Serbia before decreeing full mobilization, which all knew meant war with Germany. The tsar, irresolute as ever, idled the time away. On July 29, he noted in his diary: "During the day we played tennis; the weather was magnificent." The next day he "had a delightful bathe in the sea." But on July 31, he noted: "It has been a grey day, in keeping with my mood."

The tsar's "grey" mood had developed around 4 P.M. on July 30 during a meeting with Sazonov. The foreign minister, emboldened by Generals Yanushkevich and Sukhomlinov as well as by the French envoy, Paléologue, had concluded that "it was dangerous to delay the general mobilization any longer." Sazonov ingeniously advanced the sinister argument that partial mobilizaton constituted a violation of Russian duties under the alliance with France; in addition, it would give Wilhelm II a chance to press the French for a declaration of neutrality and perhaps even prompt Paris to cut its ties with St. Petersburg and join Germany! Such utter drivel completely bowled over the indecisive Nicholas, who, while he lamented "sending thousands and thousands of men to their death," concurred that it would be "very dangerous" not to undertake "timely preparations for what was apparently an inevitable war." Sazonov at once transmitted the order for general mobilization to the waiting Yanushkevich, with the admonition: "Now you can smash your telephone."[17] The die was cast.

The mood in Berlin on the morning of July 31 was downcast and dour. The generals on the previous evening had forced the chancellor to agree to declare a military state of emergency, the necessary precondition for mobilization, to go into effect around noon on July 31. Bethmann Hollweg could only hope that Russia might yet provide him with the cherished *casus foederis*. At about 11 A.M., news began to filter through from Ambassador Count Friedrich von Pourtalès in St. Petersburg that Russia had indeed mobilized, that the bright red mobilization orders had been posted up on the walls of the capital. Bethmann Hollweg was greatly relieved. This meant

that he could still claim that Russia had forced him into war; it also meant that the Social Democrats would support the war effort. In a matter of hours, Wilhelm II signed the decree that a "threatening state of war" existed. The following day both France and Germany officially declared war against each other. And there was joy in Berlin that July 31. The Bavarian military plenipotentiary, General Karl von Wenninger, visited the Prussian War Ministry and noted: "Everywhere beaming faces, shaking of hands in the corridors; one congratulates one's self for having taken the hurdle." Admiral Georg Alexander von Müller, chief of the Navy Cabinet, reported: "The mood is brilliant. The government has managed brilliantly to make us appear the attacked." Moltke was pleased: "There was . . . an atmosphere of happiness." Only Bethmann Hollweg, always the pessimist and "Hamlet-like," worried about the German "leap into the dark."[18]

The final phase of the July crisis, from August 1 to 4, was almost anticlimactic. A chain reaction of mobilization orders and declarations of war thundered through the European capitals. Train schedules and reservist call-ups were the order of the day. These came almost as a welcome relief to the leaders who had sweated through the July crisis. Only Sir Edward Grey at Whitehall seems not to have realized that the Russian mobilization *ukase* of July 30 had made war a certainty.

Whatever doubts remained in London concerning German intentions were quickly dissipated on August 2, when Germany called on Belgium to allow its troops free passage to France. Moltke gave Brussels twelve hours to reply. That same day, his troops occupied Luxembourg. The Cabinet in London at last realized that the problem on the Continent was greater than that in Ireland (Home Rule). A German advance through Belgium would give the German navy the southern Channel coast and access to the Atlantic Ocean. Thus, the idea that a naval war would be generally acceptable began to permeate the Cabinet. However, a stubborn minority still opposed intervention in France. The logical approach seemed to be to use British sea power to augment French and Russian land power; or put more bluntly, to fight Germany "to the last Frenchman," much as Paris hoped to fight *les boches* "to the last Russian."

But the plan went awry. Conservative and insular, Grey had for years studiously evaded the conclusion that a German attack against France would involve British interests, that Britain would have to uphold the European balance of power even at the cost of a land war. The foreign secretary maintained an illusion about British intervention and refused all discussion of the matter in the Cabinet. With "an ignorance whose true name is connivance," Grey had not even informed the Cabinet back in 1911 that he had, quite on his own, authorized " military conversations" with the French General Staff. Now the Cabinet was being asked to accept the costs of a war on the Continent.[19]

Of course, no one knew what those would be. Grey tenaciously clung to his short-war illusion, somehow convincing himself that Britain would suffer hardly more if it went to war with Germany than if it stayed out! Grey, like most other leaders, had been recruited from an exclusive and sheltered elite that totally misjudged the virulent nationalism surging through central and eastern Europe and that greatly underestimated the various movements for national independence. Nor could this elite grasp the role of mass armies in modern warfare, which Léon Gambetta had foreseen in the 1870s. And few appreciated the development of new technologies, such as machine guns, howitzers, and barbed wire, that eventually rendered absurd the long-cherished dreams of a "short, cleansing thunderstorm" that would solve Europe's ills by Christmas, at the latest.

The seriousness of the European crisis was underlined by the fact that the Cabinet met at all on August 2, during the sacrosanct weekend. And when it proved no longer possible to avoid the issue of intervention, Grey was saved on August 3 by the news that Belgium intended to reject the German ultimatum for free passage for its troops—much as Bethmann Hollweg had used the Russian mobilization of July 30 to "save face." "Poor little Belgium" became the decisive moral issue that would rally the country. It would also spare the Cabinet what promised to be an unpleasant debate of whether war in France was in Britain's best interest. Bethmann Hollweg's unfortunate remark, that the treaty of 1839 was merely a "scrap of paper," and his Machiavellian pronouncement in the Reichstag on August 4, that "necessity knows no law," simply played into Grey's hand. In fact, Britain on August 3 was the only country in Europe where the crowds wildly cheered the war before it had even been declared.[20]

On the morning of August 4, German troops entered Belgium. Berlin ignored a British ultimatum that they be withdrawn, and at 11 P.M. London time, a state of war existed between Germany and Great Britain. Grey uttered his much-cited words: "The lamps are going out all over Europe; we shall not see them lit again in our life-time."[21] They not only accurately foresaw what was about to transpire in the trenches of France; in a deeper—and certainly

unintended—sense, they also offered a dismal comment on the mediocre quality of statesmanship that Europe was burdened with in 1914. Grey was no Disraeli, Sazonov no Goluchowski, Berchtold no Metternich, and Bethmann Hollweg no Bismarck. Franz Kafka was well within the mark in 1916, when he noted that the Great War had been above all else "caused by a tremendous lack of imagination."[22]

Yet few would have agreed with Kafka in early August 1914. Europe was thrilled by the news of war. The stifling peace imposed on the Continent by Bismarck's intricate alliance system was finally over. There would be honor, promotions, profits, medals, and new borders. No longer would the generation of 1914 have to listen at the local beer or wine table to worn-out tales of the great deeds of their grandfathers in the wars of 1866 and 1870/71. Instead, they now eagerly reported to their barracks and shouted "on to Paris," or "on to Berlin," or *Gott mit uns*," or "God save the tsar." Their rifles were flower-bedecked. Bands played. Women wept. They were fighting for the defense of their *Vaterland*, Holy Russia, or *la patrie*. Britain, secure behind its "moat" and the guns of the Royal Navy, was nobly doing combat for "little Belgium." And everywhere, men were secure in the knowledge that it would all be over by Christmas. Somewhere in Lorraine, or in Belgium, or in Galicia, there would be a single, decisive battle, another Cannae or Sedan. Then all could return home to "business as usual," as Churchill put it.

Of course, it was not to be. Almost exactly five years after the murder of Archduke Francis Ferdinand at Sarajevo, Germany and Austria had to accept sole guilt for the war and all its suffering (Article 231 of the Treaty of Versailles). Historians in both countries immediately set out to reject this charge, sparing no pains or tricks in their endeavors to cover tracks. A special department in the Foreign Office of the Weimar Republic systematically tampered with and in some cases destroyed documents relating to the origins of the war. This sort of "patriotic self-censorship" nearly resulted in the destruction of the diary of Kurt Riezler, Bethmann Hollweg's *intimus*, and in the publication as late as the 1950s of a carefully expunged version of Admiral von Müller's diary (see the events of August 1 above). Pressure from Prussian generals and statesmen even forced General von Moltke's widow to withdraw a posthumous edition of the soldier's memoirs; the personal papers of Moltke thereafter were so carefully "ordered" by nationalist historians that "not a single document worth reading from the pre-War period" has survived. In the case of Austria-Hungary, much of the material dealing with the July crisis either used deceptive language or was destroyed as defeat appeared imminent.[23]

In addition, major gaps in the documentation were caused by the willful destruction of diaries or by the unexpected deaths of some of the principal actors during the war. In the latter case, both the Austrian and Hungarian prime ministers, Stürgkh and Tisza, were murdered before the end of the war, while Francis Joseph died in 1916. It is known that Count Berchtold destroyed the relevant parts of his diary in 1942, that Bethmann Hollweg's papers did not survive the Russian occupation of his estate in 1945, and that Kaiser Wilhelm's diary likewise failed to survive the Nazi occupation of the Netherlands. Finally, neither War Minister von Krobatin nor Finance Minister Leon von Bilinski in Austria left papers of any relevance; the same is true for Foreign Minister von Jagow in Germany.

The memoir literature is by and large disappointing. Some, like Sukhomlinov and Paléologue, grossly falsified the record. Others, such as Bethmann Hollweg and Berchtold, left boring and terribly disappointing accounts of the July crisis. Still others, notably Nicholas II and Wilhelm II, showed in diaries and memoirs that they never fully understood the events of the summer of 1914; at best, that they were simply not up to the demands made on them by the crisis. On the positive side, there are the notes of Baron von Schilling, head of the Chancery of the Russian Ministry of Foreign Affairs, and the multivolume memoirs of Conrad von Hötzendorf, chief of the Austrian General Staff—although it should be remembered that some of these were, in fact, written not by Conrad but rather by two military historians, Edmund von Glaise-Horstenau and Rudolf Kiszling.[24] Finally, the Allied air raids of April 1945 claimed most of the records of the German army.

It is therefore all the more amazing that a number of German historians, notably Fritz Fischer and Imanuel Geiss,[25] have managed over the past two decades to uncover sufficient documentary evidence from archives in Austria, East and West Germany, and Britain to show that Berlin and Vienna purposely opted for war in July 1914 in the belief that time was running out for both of them. In the case of Austria, only a preemptive strike against Serbia could retard the centrifugal forces of nationalism within the Dual Monarchy; for Germany, only preemptive war with Russia would allow Berlin to secure continental hegemony before the Russian "Great Program" of army increases was completed by 1917. This "strike now better than later" mentality in Germany and Austria plunged Europe into the calamity of a world war.

Very few well-connected people in Germany knew the truth of the matter from the start. They communicated their intimate knowledge of events and persons to one another behind the public veil of patriotic self-censorship. One of these was Prince Philipp zu Eulenburg-Hertefeld. Once the kaiser's most trusted adviser, "Phili" had fallen from favor as a result of homosexual charges brought against him by Maximilian Harden in 1906. In September 1919, Eulenburg imparted to a friend his innermost feelings and knowledge of the July crisis, imploring the recipient of the letter to "enfold the delicate answer . . . in the thickest veil of mist that ever enshrouded your house . . . on a cold autumn morning in the North German lowlands":

Serbia *is* Russia. If Austria marches against Serbia, and *if Berlin does not prevent* Austria's *belligerent action*, then the great breaking wave of World War rolls irresistibly towards us. I repeat: Berlin *must* know that, otherwise *idiots* live in the Wilhelmstrasse. Kaiser Wilhelm *must* know that.[26]

The inescapable conclusion is that both kaiser and Foreign Office *did* know this and that along with the General Staff they purposely used the crisis to bring about a general European war. Truth is simple, refreshingly simple.

2

THE WESTERN FRONT

By August 4, the war machines of the various European states were in full gear. Millions of young men had been called off the farms and out of the factories to march to certain and quick victory. Thousands of railway cars rolled across the various lands at the then thundering speed of about twenty kilometers per hour to get companies, battalions, regiments, divisions, and armies to their appointed marshaling centers. It was much like 1870/71 all over again. "Tanks" were not yet known and automobiles not trusted; armies again moved by horse and mule. The Germans took along 4,000 horses for each army corps consisting of 17,500 officers and men, while the British shuttled nearly 6,000 horses across the Channel for every army corps of 18,000 men. The Russians confiscated 3,000 automobiles at the outbreak of the war, but most rusted in St. Petersburg because of shortages of fuel and spare parts. The Germans deployed eighty-three trucks, but most broke down in the Ardennes. As we shall see, especially in the case of Austria-Hungary, horses had a decided edge over trucks when food was scarce.

In the west, the Germans dictated the course of the war, even though their grandiose strategical concept miscarried. General Alfred von Schlieffen in 1905/06 had penned the German blueprint for victory that was set into motion eight years later: while a mere ten divisions held the Russians at bay in the east and an additional eight divisions held the French south of Metz, the main army, some fifty-three divisions, would swing like a giant revolving door through Belgium and northern France, cut south behind Paris and Rouen, and drive the disorganized French forces against the Lorraine fortresses and Switzerland; Metz-Thionville would serve as the pivot for this great wheeling action. Schlieffen, unlike the German Foreign Office, had even foreseen the landing of 100,000 British front-line troops on the Continent, but coolly planned to shut them up in Antwerp along with the regular Belgian army. German *Landwehr*

and *Ersatz* units would from the outset be used in the front line. Wherever the enemy decided to attack this "revolving door," it would be sufficiently flexible to swing around and to fall on its back. As is well known, the key to success lay in what reputedly were Schlieffen's dying words, in making "the right wing strong." All was predicated on Germany being the first to mobilize its forces and to exploit its superior railways—and on a bold, resolute, staff chief.

The French Plan XVII, like the sixteen before it, demanded for political reasons an offensive *à outrance* into Alsace-Lorraine and the German Saar. Four French armies, divided into two groups, would advance on either side of Metz and, ignoring such modern developments as machine guns, mortars, howitzers, and barbed wire, would conduct a romantic *pas de charge* as in the days of Napoleon, with banners flying and bugles blaring. French *élan* and *cran* (guts) would overcome superior German organization. It was good tonic for an army in need of self-confidence, but hardly the proper strategy in 1914. *Furor Teutonicus* would run against *Furia Francese* somewhere east of Metz.

The British, the third major participant in the war in the west, were uncertain as to whether they would enter the continental fray in the first place or, if they did, where they would deploy. The entente with France of 1904 was not a firm alliance, although General Sir Henry Wilson by 1906 had become convinced that the British Expeditionary Force (BEF) should be deployed in France as practically an appendix of the main French army. The BEF, to be sure, was a splendid little army, a "rapier among scythes," as Basil Liddell Hart called it,[1] but it was better prepared for an action in the veldt or east of Suez with its lances, khaki uniforms, and carbines. Neither howitzers, hand grenades, nor wireless equipment accompanied it to the Continent in August 1914. Indeed, Britain's political and military leaders could not even agree on a debarkation point for the BEF. At the Cabinet meeting of August 5, the BEF's commander, Sir John French, wanted to deploy at Antwerp; Wilson, supported by Sir Edward Grey and Winston Churchill, at Maubeuge; Lord H. H. Kitchener, the despotic secretary for war, at Amiens; and some even thought Liège was somewhere in the Netherlands! In the end, eighty-year-old Lord Roberts carried the day by suggesting that the French decide the matter.[2]

Given the radically different concepts of the opposing operations plans in the west, it is not surprising that the French and German armies almost went past each other in August like ships in the night. The great German *Aufmarsch* was in full swing by August 6, with 55 trains rattling across the Rhine bridges each day, for a total of 11,000 trains with 3.1 million men aboard. Two days later, every ablebodied Frenchman having plucked his trusty *chassepot* from his attic, General Joseph Joffre's armies stormed into Alsace as far as Mulhouse, encountering little or no resistance. Farther north, the French chief of staff launched his vaunted double invasion of Lorraine, but despite a decided numerical advantage, on August 20 his nineteen divisions were repulsed at Morhange-Sarrebourg. The German Fifth Army of Crown Prince Wilhelm of Prussia, ignoring Schlieffen's admonition that it hold steady and draw as many French troops as possible away from the north, abandoned its defensive posture at Metz-Thionville and mounted a difficult drive on Verdun. Crown Prince Rupprecht of Bavaria's Sixth Army, in conjunction with General Josias von Heeringen's Seventh Army, likewise neglected Schlieffen's *récipé* and charged fixed French positions in the west. Ironically, both of these precipitous acts only served to deny Joffre early and clear insight into where the major German thrust was coming.

The front gradually developed into two long opposing areas of army concentrations. The German forces, from north to south, consisted of General Alexander von Kluck's First Army (320,000 men), General Karl von Bülow's Second Army (260,000), Baron Max von Hausen's Third Army (180,000), Duke Albrecht of Württemberg's Fourth Army (200,000), Crown Prince Wilhelm's Fifth Army (200,000), Crown Prince Rupprecht's Sixth Army (220,000), and General von Heeringen's Seventh Army (125,000) in Alsace. Opposing them were the Belgian army consisting of six divisions and the BEF (four divisions) in the north as well as General Charles Lanrezac's Fifth Army (254,000), General Fernand de Langle de Cary's Fourth Army (193,000), General Pièrre-Xavier Ruffey's Third Army

(168,000), General Noel de Castelnau's Second Army, and General Auguste Dubail's First Army in the south. Seven divisions were held in reserve at Belfort and Vervins.[3]

On the morning of August 4, the main German forces had crossed the Meuse (Maas) north of Liège into Belgium. General von Kluck's First Army marched toward Brussels, while General von Bülow's Second Army headed for Namur. Overall planning rested with Helmuth von Moltke, chief of the General Staff, well behind the front, first—as in 1870—at Koblenz, and later in Luxembourg. The Belgian army, commanded by King Albert, much to Joffre's disgust fell back on Antwerp instead of linking up with the main French forces. By August 22, the French Fourth Army (Langle de Cary) as well as the Fifth Army (Lanrezac) pushed deep into the Ardennes; at Neufchâteau, they ran up against their German numerical counterparts. Mounting massed bayonet charges, the French were mowed down by German machine-gun fire in the first rude awakening of the war. Farther north, Sir John French's BEF, which had finally deployed at Maubeuge, as well as Lanrezac's Fifth Army, blindly ran into the German First, Second, and Third Armies. Lanrezac, beginning to grasp the full magnitude of the German wheeling action through Belgium, bombarded Joffre with pleas for reinforcements and for permission to withdraw and regroup—actions that would shortly cost him his command.

The four divisions of the BEF were now fully caught up in Lanrezac's retreat. French agreed to stand at Mons in order to protect the southward march of the French Fifth Army. But far removed from the fighting at St. Quentin, he grew overly pessimistic and thought of pulling his units out of the fight and perhaps embarking for England. On August 26, the anniversary of the Battle of Crécy, General Horace Smith-Dorrien fought a rear-guard action at Le Cateau, with Sir Douglas Haig's I Corps nowhere to be seen. Only Lord Kitchener's hurried arrival in Paris for a face-to-face meeting with French stiffened the BEF commander's resolve to stand with the French ally, come what may.

In the meantime, the relentless German drive continued. Joffre finally agreed with Lanrezac's assessment of where the main German thrust was coming. In less than two weeks, his grand strategy had been shattered, and his armies were in full flight in Belgium as well as in Lorraine. Northern France was in enemy hands, and Paris was threatened. On August 27, the military governor of the capital, General Joseph Gallieni, finally informed Parisians of their perilous situation, and the following day, the government departed for Bordeaux.

General von Moltke noted Lanrezac's defeat at Charleroi at the end of August and exulted: "In six weeks all this will be over." Yet with the precision of historical hindsight, one can see that the Germans were committing serious errors as they marched through Belgium. Moltke, who had long harbored deep suspicions about the accuracy of Schlieffen's concept, in mid-August rerouted six reserve divisions from the crucial right wing to the forces already lying idle in Lorraine. Furthermore, he detached seven divisions to invest the fortresses Maubeuge, Givet, and Antwerp, instead of simply bypassing them. And on August 25, panicked by the unexpectedly rapid Russian deployment in the east, he further denuded his right wing of four divisions and shuttled them across Germany to East Prussia. These critical decisions were to haunt Moltke over the next ten days.

Early in September, Kluck crossed the Aisne and Vesle rivers, driving Lanrezac behind the Oise, with the BEF on his left and Langle de Cary on his right. But Kluck became overanxious, convinced that a second Sedan awaited him if he turned in *before* Paris in order to encircle and to destroy the French forces near Meaux. On the French side, Gallieni was the first to recognize the opportunity afforded by Kluck's hasty act: on September 4, he ordered General Michel Maunoury's Sixth Army to attack the Germans, thereby initiating the so-called First Battle of the Marne. The Paris commander fully realized that if Kluck pressed on his southward course he would be caught in a trap between the retreating Anglo-French units in the north and the armies being assembled around Paris. Three days later, Maunoury's actions at the Ourcq forced Kluck to withdraw from north of the Marne—but not until Maunoury had been saved from defeat by the romantic sally of reinforcements sent him by Gallieni in Parisian taxicabs and buses.

Indeed, Kluck had been very much surprised by Maunoury's attack and as a result had to halt his southward advance and to face west to meet the new French threat. In the process, he permitted a thirty-mile-wide gap to form between his First and Bülow's Second Army. On September 8, General Louis Franchet d'Esperey, who had replaced the luckless Lanrezac as chief of the Fifth Army, discovered this gap—as did, accidentally, some British cavalry. Joffre had also recognized the flaw in the joint of the two German armies, and, calm and imperturbable, he used his lateral railways to regroup his forces at the Marne. Twenty-seven Anglo-French front-line divisions were now pitted against only thirteen German divisions at the point of decision, a full revelation of how completely Moltke had strayed away from Schlieffen's plan.

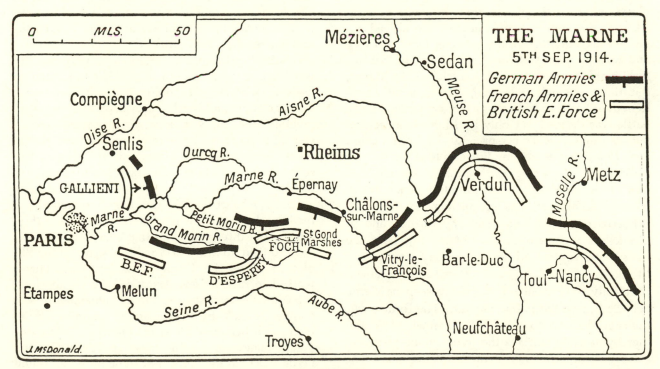

THE MARNE

From *Reputations* by Basil Liddell Hart, published by John Murray, London.

Panic now beset German headquarters at Luxembourg. Moltke received no news from the front during the critical days of September 7 through 9, and he therefore dispatched Colonel Richard Hentsch, a Saxon staff officer, on a 400-mile tour of the front with full powers to dispose of units as he saw fit. At Montmort—perhaps a fitting name—he found Bülow depressed and despondent, ready to retreat for fear of utter annihilation. And when Kluck could not assure Hentsch that he could come to Bülow's aid with all of his forces in case of an enemy assault into the gap, Moltke's deputy on September 9 ordered a retreat from the Marne behind the Aisne along the line Soissons-Fère-en-Tardenois. At the same time, the German units vainly trying to storm Verdun were also recalled from Nancy to the Vesle, thereby creating a huge salient at St. Mihiel that was to remain until September 1918.

Kluck never forgave Hentsch for allegedly depriving him of a great victory at the Marne. The charge does not sit well. It is perhaps symptomatic of the state of the German High Command that a staff colonel should be accorded the blame that properly lies with a kaiser who could not fulfill his role as supreme war lord and with a chief of General Staff who doubted his own operations plan and who lacked the resolute will and steel nerves to carry it through. To them, add one army commander (Kluck) who abandoned the blueprint for victory at the most critical phase of the battle and another (Bülow) who panicked at the approach of shadows, the alleged advance of Churchill's British marines from Antwerp and Russian armies (!) in Flanders. It later became fashionable to speak of the "miracle" of the Marne, but there was none. Instead, it was what Pierre Renouvin has termed "a victory of command."[4] The battle was decided not only by Moltke's indecision but also by Gallieni's perspicacity, by Joffre's calm, and, to a lesser degree, by French's loyalty.

On the German side, War Minister General Erich von Falkenhayn already had noted on September 5: "Our General Staff has completely lost its head. Schlieffen's notes do not help any further, and so Moltke's wits come to an end."[5] Nine days later, the clever but arrogant and sarcastic Falkenhayn replaced Moltke as chief of staff; the official announcement came only on November 3 in order to keep the Marne debacle out of the public domain. The former war minister decided to seize the Channel ports and thereby possibly outflank the French in the north and salvage some remnants of the Schlieffen plan. The two giant armies played leapfrog from September until November, as Kluck sought to outflank Joffre, who, in turn, tried to envelop Kluck. All the while,

the armies leaped toward the Channel in giant bounds in what was popularly labeled the "race to the sea." Falkenhayn declined General Wilhelm Groener's suggestion to shuttle six idle army corps from the Aisne and the Vosges to Flanders, and instead drove Crown Prince Rupprecht's exhausted Sixth Army and Duke Albrecht's Fourth Army against Ypres and Ramscapelle. The Belgians flooded their country, and furious combat ensued in the marshes of Messines and Ypres; British and German guards slew one another with reckless abandon in the Bois des Nonnes. The Germans lost 100,000 dead in Flanders, more than the combined losses of their British, Belgian, and French opponents. The war of attrition had arrived. Soon to be added to it was infanticide. On November 10, Falkenhayn threw four corps of raw and hastily trained recruits into the fray at Langemarck; and in what German nationalists euphemistically called the "march of honor to Langemarck," these boys were cut to ribbons by veteran British infantry. Chancellor Theobald von Bethmann Hollweg finally persuaded Falkenhayn to end the slaughter in the fields of Flanders, probably already determined to seize the first opportune moment to cashier the chief of staff.

The first year of the war ended with the Germans fronting Arras, Noyon, Soissons, and Reims. Neither the vaunted Schlieffen plan nor the quixotic French Plan XVII had succeeded. Instead of a war over by Christmas, the million-man armies on both sides were embedded in the blood and mud of trenches that scarred the lush countryside from the Channel to the Swiss border. For all intents and purposes, the war had been lost for both sides. There were no new leaders, with bright, bold ideas. Barbed wire, machine guns, and blockhouses deprived the war of mobility. The only alternative for most generals seemed to be to call up more young men and to hurl them against enemy lines in the hope that somewhere, somehow, someone would bend and break.

Lord Kitchener was the first major commander to realize that this war would last not three months but three years and that even Britain would have to field an army of a million men. As the BEF bled at Mons, Le Cateau, and Ypres, Kitchener worked to raise a New Army of seventy divisions: 175,000 volunteers streamed in by September 5, with another 600,000 by the end of the month. Posters with Kitchener's extended finger pointing at Britain's young males carried the message "Your Country needs YOU" to the corners of the Empire; and drew from Prime Minister Herbert Asquith's wife, Margot, the epitaph "the great poster" for Kitchener.

Indeed, Kitchener's appointment in many ways was not a happy one. Some have called it Asquith's "grave mistake." Absent from England for about forty years prior to 1914, Kitchener had ruled military affairs in India and Egypt like a despot. He did not change his ways after Lord Richard Haldane of Cloan persuaded Asquith to appoint him secretary of the War Office on August 5. Kitchener was constitutionally unable to delegate authority, nurtured a great passion for secrecy, despised the Cabinet, and made it impossible to gain access to him. He sent most staff officers with the BEF to France, then in August 1914 closed the Staff College. Moreover, Kitchener, who foresaw the German march through Belgium, never had great sympathy for new technological developments: he dismissed the tank as "a pretty mechanical toy" and thought that four machine guns per battalion were adequate. David Lloyd George later remarked: "Take Kitchener's figure. Square it. Multiply by two. Then double again for good luck."[6]

But "Kitchener's armies" could not arrive until the spring of 1916. In the meantime, that unquenchable optimist, "Papa" Joffre, decided to renew the offensive in the great winter battles of the Champagne. From December 20, 1914, until January 30, 1915, and again from February 16 to March 20, 1915, his armies were repulsed with heavy losses by General Karl von Einem's Third Army. A simultaneous British attempt to break through north of La Bassée was similarly thrown back by Crown Prince Rupprecht's Sixth Army at Neuve Chapelle. Joffre optimistically announced: "We're nibbling at them," which was, in Liddell Hart's words, like mice nibbling at a steel safe.[7]

The French were not alone in believing that a great offensive could yet save the illusion of a short war. In the Second Battle of Ypres, between April 22 and May 25, 1915, the Germans once more attempted to dislodge the Allies from their strategic cornerpost in Flanders. They failed eventually to take the town but made worldwide headlines on April 22 by releasing a strange green vapor, poison gas, against the Anglo-French lines at Steestraten-Pilkem. The Germans, however, did not as yet know how to take advantage of the resulting four-mile sector that did not contain one living defender.

Above all, the spring of 1915 was dominated by the great "shell crisis." In virtually every capital, soldiers pointed an accusing finger at politicans and trade union leaders, who, they felt, were denying the front adequate munitions. On May 17, Colonel Charles à Court Repington, the *Times*'s military correspondent, aided and abetted by Sir John French, caused a public furor with a front-page story: "Need for Shells. British Attacks Checked. Limited Supply the Cause." Repington boldly asserted that it was "certain that we can smash the German crust if we have the means."[8] Lloyd George saw his chance to advance up the political ladder and in April managed to allay the immediate uproar by heading a Cabinet Munitions of War Committee, which, in reality, was a stepping-stone to his greater ambitions.

In Germany, Walther Rathenau of German General Electric was shocked in August 1914 to learn that no provisions had been made to coordinate the supply and distribution of vital raw materials either in Germany or in occupied Belgium. Only when the short-war illusion proved fallacious did General von Falkenhayn appoint Rathenau to head a special War Raw Materials Section within the Prussian War Ministry. Rathenau quickly established a system of private stock companies to purchase, store, and distribute raw materials, and he also coordinated the allocation of raw materials to industry from one German state to another. The system worked sufficiently well by April 1915 for Rathenau to hand it over to the army. And under the energetic leadership of Major Max Bauer, the army overcame the potentially fatal loss of Chilean saltpeter resulting from the British blockade by building nitrogen-fixation plants. A special Chemicals Section was set up within the War Raw Materials Section to expedite the production of nitrates, while a War Chemicals Corporation regulated the supply of glycerine.

Thus assured an adequate supply of munitions, the armies on the western front could return to the business at hand. Verdun and other fortresses in seemingly unthreatened sectors were stripped of their heavy guns. General Joffre, ever the optimist, unleashed yet another massive assault in the Champagne against the German Third Army, arguing that it "would compel the Germans to retreat beyond the Meuse and possibly end the war."[9] Instead, between September 22 and November 3, his forces were heavily bled at Perthes, Souain, Tahure, Auberive, and Massiges. Concurrently, Sir John French from September 25 to October 13 conducted a campaign in Artois against the German Sixth Army. This assault between Arras and La Bassée climaxed in the disastrous Loos offensive in which British infantry charged through a wilderness of coal mines and hamlets, losing 50,000 men to Germany's 20,000. To make matters worse, at Loos the British for the first time used poison gas. The wind was uncertain, and although engineers advised against releasing the gas, a divisional commander overruled them; as the wind shifted, French's own troops were gassed.

Loos not only bloodied the new armies of Kitchener, but also led to a massive revamping of their command structure. Sir John French, now sixty-three years of age, was relieved of command on December 19, 1915. In his place, Sir Douglas Haig, the wealthy scion of a Scottish distillery family, used his contacts to King George V to advantage and assumed command of the thirty-six divisions now in France. "Lucky" Haig, as he was known in the service, would soon live up to the family motto, "Tyde What May." For his staff chief, Haig overlooked experienced officers in France and instead brought over from London an old friend, Sir Launcelot Kiggell. Unfortunately, "Kigg" possessed neither the ability nor the "intellectual discipline" (Foch) required; his strategic ideas were exceedingly orthodox, and he was highly subservient to Haig, agreeing with his new chief that the machine gun was "a much overrated weapon." Finally, French's former chief of staff, General Sir William Robertson, was returned to England as chief of the Imperial General Staff. "Wully" Robertson had been considered as a possible replacement for French, but as a "ranker," he obviously did not possess the "gentlemanly" qualities required of a field commander. However, his appointment brought with it two important developments. First, the General Staff, assuming the major responsibility for the war, brusquely pushed Kitchener aside and gained sole right to advise the government on all military affairs and to deal directly with field commanders in France. Second, Robertson was an avowed "Westerner," determined to get "every possible man, horse and gun" to the western front. Haig and Robertson were the new "brass hats."

"Lucky" Haig chomped at the bit to mount a major offensive in Flanders, but the Germans beat him out of the starting gate. Between February 21 and September 9, 1916, Falkenhayn before Verdun unleashed what was to become the longest single action of the war. In the process, he reduced the art of generalship to its nadir. Falkenhayn calculated that the Germans, with an excess population of 25 million, could sustain a war of attrition against France. The choice of attack was either Belfort or Verdun; in the end, the Germans chose the French salient at Verdun. "The essential question is not to take Verdun . . . but to pin down the French . . . and since they will have to defend it shoulder to shoulder, we shall bleed them white." Crown Prince Wilhelm likewise sought to destroy "the heart of France" at Verdun.

At 7:15 A.M. on the cold, dry morning of February 21, the German artillery began to transform the Verdun landscape into a pock-marked lunar scene; nine hours later, the infantry mounted the first of a myriad of senseless charges. Army Group Crown Prince Wilhelm, with General Constantin Schmidt von Knobelsdorf as chief of staff, advanced with flamethrowers against the historic, but recently stripped, forts Douaumont, Vaux, Souville, Thiaumont, Fleury, and Height 304, among others. Schmidt von Knobelsdorf had originally intended to attack only the northern and northeastern sectors of Verdun, but in time, he broadened the assault to include the entire region west of the Meuse River. On the first day of battle alone, the Germans fired 1 million shells; and throughout the summer of 1916, each side hurled about 10 million shells at each other in and around Verdun. Salients, parapets, trenches, and fox holes were often composed of dead flesh. Douaumont fell by February 25 and Vaux on June 7. Falkenhayn eventually fed forty divisions into the meat grinder along the Meuse, while the French, constantly rotating their front-line units, in the end deployed 259 of their total of 330 front-line infantry battalions at Verdun.

Falkenhayn had at least been accurate in one respect: the French accepted his basic premise for the battle. General Joffre informed Army Group Langle de Cary: "Every commander who . . . gives an order for retreat will be tried by court-martial."[10] Defense of the stone rubble was entrusted to three up and coming commanders: General Henri Pétain, the champion of the defensive who nevertheless urged his men on with the immortal cry: *"On les aura!"*; General Charles Mangin; and General Robert Nivelle, like Joffre an advocate of the offensive *à outrance*. It was Nivelle who eventually reclaimed Forts Douaumont and Vaux and in doing so captured the attention of the French nation.

The criminal destruction of young men ended primarily because Falkenhayn was pressed hard on two other fronts, by the British at the Somme and by the Russians in Galicia and the Bukovina. But not before the French had suffered 315,000 and the Germans 281,000 casualties—a rare occasion when the defenders lost more men than the attackers. Pétain held Verdun against the German fire storm by bringing in nearly every division of the French army for a brief tour. All were bloodied, but few crippled—or so it seemed. In fact, Verdun broke the French army, although this would only be revealed half a year later. It also cost Germany some of its best assault troops and a substantial number of the 116,000 noncommissioned officers who were the heart and backbone of its army.

But the Germans did not have a patent on human slaughter. As early as December 5, 1915, Haig and

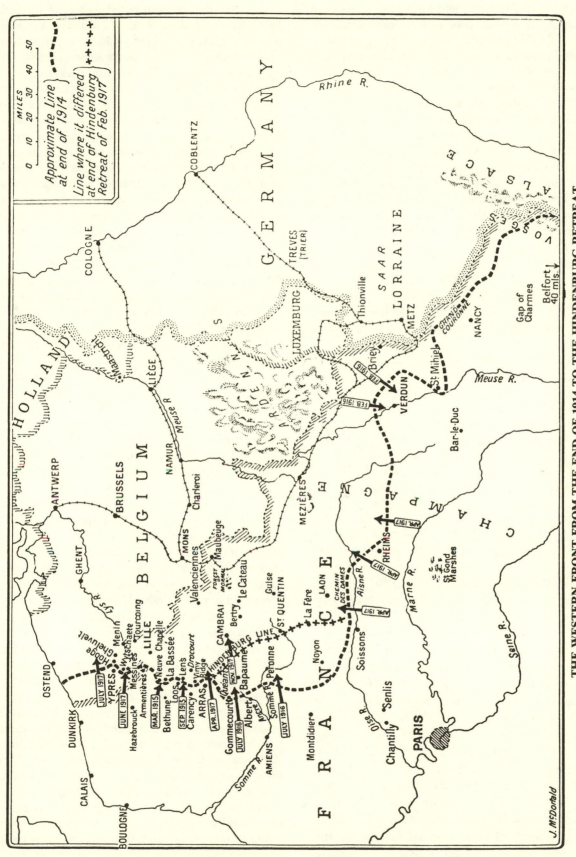

THE WESTERN FRONT FROM THE END OF 1914 TO THE HINDENBURG RETREAT

From *Reputations* by Basil Liddell Hart, published by John Murray, London.

Joffre at Chantilly had planned a massive offensive at the Somme, one that was rudely interrupted by Falkenhayn's Verdun campaign. By midsummer, Haig was determined to show the Germans "the fighting will of the British race." He had by now taken over the sector of the front stretching from Ypres to the Somme, and in the torrid heat of July 1, enjoying numerical as well as aerial superiority, thirteen British divisions went "over the top" at 7:30 A.M. Kiggell had insisted on sending his troops in waves against the German barbed wire, howitzers, and machine guns, with the result that Britain suffered its greatest loss in a single day of fighting: 19,000 men killed, or 57,000 casualties. It was also the greatest loss on a single day in the Great War by any side. Before the action of the Somme subsided, it had claimed about 1 million casualties: 420,000 British, 400,000 German, and 195,000 French. It became the graveyard of Kitchener's New Army, widely denounced by the "war poets" Siegfried Sassoon, Robert Graves, Isaac Rosenberg, and Wilfred Owen, among others.

Undaunted, Haig, the stubborn Scot, pushed his men on against Bapaume, Péronne, and Nesle. Fresh assaults were mounted on July 20 and on September 3 and 20. The artillery fired several million shells, making the landscape unrecognizable, devoid of all peaceful human and vegetable existence. Four British armies in vain sought to break the line of Generals Fritz von Below's First and Max von Gallwitz's Second Army, both part of Army Group Crown Prince Rupprecht. Below, like Joffre at Verdun, threatened courts-martial for any officer who gave up an inch of ground. By the fall of 1916, "Somme mud" brought the action to a halt, much to Haig's chagrin.

The senseless slaughter in the west in 1916 brought sweeping personnel changes with it. On August 28/29, the second anniversary of the German victory over the Russians at Tannenberg, Falkenhayn was replaced by the victorious duumvirate in the east, Field Marshal Paul von Hindenburg and General Erich Ludendorff. The costly losses in Flanders in 1914 had earned Falkenhayn the enmity of Chancellor von Bethmann Hollweg; the Verdun debacle, compounded by the British assault at the Somme and the Russian advance in Galicia, which led to Rumania's decision to enter the war on the side of the Entente, tipped the scales against the former war minister. In France, Premier Aristide Briand, a hardy perennial of French politics, early in December promoted "Papa" Joffre to marshal of France—and then installed him as technical adviser to the government, a mere figurehead. General Nivelle now cashed

in his Verdun laurels to become chief of the General Staff. Finally, in Britain, the Loos disaster brought to an end the last Liberal government in British history: on December 7, Lloyd George kissed hands at Buckingham Palace, thereby replacing Asquith with a coalition government that was run basically from the "garden suburb" in St. James's Park. Like Georges Clemenceau, Lloyd George believed that "war is too serious a matter to be left to generals." Relations between the fiery Welshman and the taciturn Scot were cool from the start. Haig despised the prime minister's lack of social graces and loathed the army of reporters and aides that customarily accompanied him on his all too frequent jaunts to the front. The army widely referred to Lloyd George as "the Goat." The prime minister, an "Easterner," considered Haig unimaginative and too much a "Westerner." After the war, Lloyd George showed a friend a full-size portrait of Haig and, placing his hands on the tops of the shiny cavalry boots, is alleged to have said: "He was brilliant up to here."[11]

But "Lucky" Haig continued to be in favor with the king and enjoyed the full backing of General Robertson, so Lloyd George could not simply cashier him. Instead, the prime minister, who greatly disliked frontal assaults in politics as well as in war, decided to circumvent Haig's powers in France. In Nivelle, he found not only an articulate general, but also one capable of good English. And Nivelle had a plan. The war, he suggested, could be won in forty-eight hours. "We can break the German front at will, provided we avoid the strongest point and attack by surprise." In London, Nivelle held out visions of Allied victory marches "to the North Sea coasts or Brussels or the Meuse or the Rhine."[12] Lloyd George was convinced, and on February 26, 1917, at Calais he not only agreed to the grand assault but also placed Haig's forces temporarily under Nivelle's command.

The Allies enjoyed numerical supremacy at the western front by the end of 1916: a total of 3.9 million effectives, of which 1.2 million were British, against 2.5 million Germans. What Nivelle did not fully know, however, was that Hindenburg and Ludendorff throughout the winter of 1916/17 had audaciously and systematically withdrawn their front line about twenty miles east to the carefully prepared defensive positions in the Siegfried line (the Allies called it the Hindenburg line). They thereby created a great defensive arc along the line Lens-Noyon-Reims, and during Operation Alberich, named after a malicious king of the dwarfs in the Nibelungen saga, totally leveled all natural as well as man-made structures, contaminated drinking wells, and planted explosive booby-traps in the rubble. It was into this void that Nivelle now prepared to hurl his forces.

On April 9, 1917, a composite Anglo-Canadian force under Sir Edmund Allenby stormed Vimy ridge, one of the few hills on the Flanders plateau. Hereafter, the British drive on Arras stalled and again degenerated into trench warfare. On a brighter note, Sir Henry Plumer's Second Army at Messines successfully conducted the only true siege warfare attack in this massive siege war: his engineers tunneled 8,000 yards under the German trenches and then exploded nineteen great mines, each containing 600 tons of explosives. Yet once again, the defenders held the upper hand as the British lost 150,000 to Germany's 100,000 men.

Nivelle launched the main attack on April 16 in the Champagne and along the Aisne with thirty divisions. He repeated the tactics that had worked for his Second Army at Verdun, that is, massive artillery barrages, followed by massed infantry assaults behind a creeping barrage. This time it failed. General Mangin's Sixth Army especially was decimated by machine-gun fire from the German subterranean blockhouses. General Henri Mazel's Fifth Army did not fare better; the two armies combined lost 40,000 dead of a total of 118,000 casualties. The heroic but misused French *poilu* finally had endured enough. Nearly half the divisions in the French army were racked by mutiny and desertions, with the Sixth Army hit most severely. Rational human beings finally tired of the endless assaults against barbed wire and machine guns, as even the simple pleasures of life accorded the men in other armies were lacking. "Food was scanty and dire, welfare and recreational facilities at a Crimean standard, sanitation and washing facilities medieval." Cold, wet, hungry, tired, and fueled with *vin ordinaire*, the men rebelled. By contrast, Nivelle maintained an excellent wine cellar, an army of chefs, and the finest silks and linens near Chantilly, where he occupied a former château of Marie Antoinette.

It is estimated that 3,427 sentences were eventually handed down by courts-martial, affecting about 10 percent of the rebels. Forty-nine of the 554 soldiers originally sentenced to death were executed. The weak government of Premier Alexandre Ribot mustered enough courage to cashier Nivelle. His replacement was a former commander at Verdun, General Henri Pétain, who on May 19 promised to abandon forever the reckless offensives that had marked the tenures of Joffre and Nivelle. Pétain managed to restore calm, discipline, and trust by visiting the trenches, listening to complaints, enhancing the quality of the food, ensuring regular leaves, and equalizing tours of duty in the trenches.[13] Fortunately for France, the Germans did not become aware of these developments.

On July 1, 1917, with order restored to the armies of France, Haig was free to undertake his pet scheme: an unlimited offensive in Flanders. His plan was to break out of the Ypres salient, march along the Belgian coast, and roll up the entire German front—preferably before the Americans, who had by now declared war against Germany, arrived in force. For fifty months, the British artillery, believing that quantity of shell, rather than surprise and concentration, was the key to victory, had pounded the drainage system in Flanders. The British attack, amidst a torrential downpour, came in three stages: the first, south of Ypres near Wytschaete, ran until July 21; the second, between Dixmuiden and Ypres, continued into mid-September; and the third, raging from September 18 to December 3, spent itself at Passchendaele. The latter, in the words of Liddell Hart, became "a synonym for military failure—a name black-bordered in the records of the British army."[14]

The major brunt of the fighting fell on Sir Hubert Gough's Second Army. Known for his dash and "cavalry spirit," Gough spurred his men on across the slimy swamps of Flanders, supported by Plumer's Second Army. "General Rain" was unrelenting. Kiggel, Haig's chief of staff, broke down because of "nervous exhaustion" after visiting the front. One million men trudged through the waist-deep mud. Their guns disappeared in the slime. Men and horses drowned. Before it was all over, in November, when British and Canadian units seized what had once been the village of Passchendaele, Britain had suffered 324,000 casualties, compared with 202,000 for the defenders. In fact, the German Fourth Army under General Sixt von Arnim, part of Army Group Crown Prince Rupprecht, for the first time effectively used mustard gas against the attackers and concentrated their machine guns in new "pill boxes." A highly placed British staff officer burst into tears after visiting the site of the Third Battle of Ypres: "Good God, did we really send men to fight in that?"[15]

The tragedy of Passchendaele, quite by accident, brought with it a single ray of hope. On November 20, Sir Julian Byng's Third Army, with the help of 381 "tanks," broke the German lines at Cambrai. Although Byng was deprived the necessary reserves to exploit the initial "tank" success, Cambrai nevertheless was a portent of things to come. The War Office in London ordered church bells to be rung for joy, the first and only time during the Great War. Flags likewise were unfurled for the first time, somewhat prematurely! On November 30, General von Marwitz launched a gas and smoke shell attack against the British and drove his Second Army to recover every inch of territory lost during Byng's "tank" offensive. Indeed, the irony of the Cambrai operation was that it had no strategic objective; instead it had been recommended by Haig on October 13 merely "to restore British prestige and strike a theatrical blow against Germany before the winter.[16]

Passchendaele energized Lloyd George. He was determined to deny Haig any opportunity for another bloody offensive and to this end, in November 1917 at Versailles, pushed to create a Supreme War Council composed of Allied political heads and their military advisers. The prime minister hoped that this would stop the wild offensive schemes of the various general staffs. However, Robertson, who already viewed the Cabinet in London as the "enemy," refused to work through the council and instead rallied the Liberal opposition at home for a great storm of isolationist rhetoric. In February 1918, Lloyd George pressed the attack, this time seeking to grant the council greater power by giving it authority to dispose of a general reserve of British and French divisions. Once again, Robertson quickly realized that without the means Haig could not undertake fresh assaults in Flanders. George V and Asquith rallied to his banner, but Lloyd George won the issue by threatening to resign. On February 18, 1918, "Wully" Robertson learned of his own "resignation" in the morning papers.

The year 1917 had been costly to Britain and France. Although at the time of the Nivelle offensive they had enjoyed a superiority of 178 Anglo-French divisions against only 129 German divisions, by early 1918 the two opposing armies had been balanced out at about 170 divisions each. The Germans had swelled their forces in the west with troops released in the east after the Bolshevik seizure of power in November 1917, while the Allies had been buttressed by about ten American divisions after the United States had declared war against Germany in April. Moreover, the supply of able-bodied reservists in Britain, France, and Germany had virtually been exhausted; all three had already reduced their divisions from twelve to nine battalions each; and all three refused to limit their commitments to side shows. The Germans maintained 1 million men in the east for fear of losing what real estate they had conquered there, the British would not scale down their Palestine front, the French refused to reduce General Maurice Sarrail's Army of the Orient in Salonika. Nor would the Italians condone the transfer of Anglo-French forces from their alpine front to France. The Entente strategy for 1918, as Pétain had earlier discerned, could only be to wait for the "tanks and Americans."

On July 4, 1917, the United States, primarily as a symbolic gesture, paraded a contingent of American troops through a delirious Paris. Colonel C. E. Stanton allegedly uttered the immortal words: "Lafayette, we are here." It was all much more show than action. When Congress declared war against Germany on April 6, the U.S. army was composed of 200,000 men, of whom 76,000 were National Guardsmen. And whereas the Allies in Europe at once requested the delivery of 16,000 airplanes early in 1918, the United States possessed only 55 craft that could fly. America had discovered what the war was like, thanks to Hearst cinema; yet as in Paris and Berlin in 1914, the doughboys marched off to war late in 1917 with flower-bedecked rifles, utterly ignorant of trench warfare, still vowing to be home by Christmas. However, through the efforts of Secretary of War Newton D. Baker and Secretary of the Treasury William G. McAdoo, over the next year the United States was to train and equip an army of nearly 4 million men, of whom 1.9 million arrived in Europe, and to deploy 3,200 fighter planes. It was also to raise, exclusive of war loans to the Allies, $24 billion in four oversubscribed Liberty Loan drives. Long before Franklin D. Roosevelt predicted it, America had become the "arsenal," if not of democracy, at least of the Entente.

General Ludendorff, first quartermaster general and the guiding brain of the German General Staff, was fully cognizant of this. Once an ardent believer in the efficacy of submarine warfare, he now realized that the great gamble had not paid off and that America's entry into the war, dismissed so lightly in January 1917, would work to Germany's detriment cumulatively with each passing day. Moreover, the general was quite aware that only a victorious outcome to the war could maintain the Hohenzollern crown and the privileged position of the Prussian Junkers, retard democratic developments at home, and permit him to maintain the vast tracts of land extorted from Russia at Brest-Litovsk and from Rumania at Bucharest. He therefore decided to gamble all on a massive assault in the west before the Americans arrived in sufficient numbers to turn the tide against him. The operation was appropriately named in honor of Germany's patron saint, Michael.

Ludendorff selected as the point of primary attack the Arras-St. Quentin area toward the Somme. Pursuing what he hoped would be the line of least resistance, he sought to part the Anglo-French armies at Amiens, roll up their flank, and drive especially the British against the Channel. Follow-up operations were planned between Arras and Lens ("Mars"), the Lys ("St. George I"), Ypres ("St. George II"), and in the Champagne ("Blücher"). New tactics also evolved. In place of the customary "waves" of long, deep assault lines going "over the top," Ludendorff's assault featured small groups of men with automatic rifles, gas and smoke shells, and mobile artillery fire. Tanks were not available, as Germany had recognized their potential too late for the spring offensive. Army Group Crown Prince Rupprecht was reinforced with the Seventeenth and Eighteenth armies and Army Group Duke Albrecht with the Nineteenth Army.

At 4:30 A.M. on the morning of March 21, 1918, 4,000 German guns announced the start of Operation Michael. On a fifty-mile-wide front Arras-St. Quentin-La Fère, the sixty-five divisions of Army Groups Crown Prince Rupprecht and Crown Prince Wilhelm overran the British front lines, whose communications had been knocked out by heavy mortar fire. When the assault was checked at Arras, Ludendorff shifted its fulcrum to the important rail center at Amiens. Although the Germans reached the outskirts of the city by the end of the month, American units, hastily inserted into the gaps at the front, stalled the drive. An urgent plea by Lloyd George directly to President Woodrow Wilson had overruled General John Pershing's stubborn insistence that the Americans deploy as a separate army.

As a result, "St. George I" commenced on April 9. The German Fourth and Sixth Armies stormed the line Armentières-La Bassée and quicky swept up the Portuguese units facing them. In violent combat, Crown Prince Rupprecht's Fourth Army seized Kemmel Hill by April 29, as the Sixth Army charged Armentières. Panic set in at Allied headquarters. General Pétain prepared to defend Paris. The British counseled a last-ditch defense of the Channel ports. Fortunately, civilian leaders kept their heads. At Allied conferences at Doullens and Beauvais, it was finally decided to entrust overall command of the western front to General Ferdinand Foch, another proponent of the offensive *à outrance*, well known since 1914 for his insane cry: "*Attaquez, attaquez, attaquez!*" Douglas Haig at the same time issued his famous order: "With our backs to the wall and believing in the justice of our cause, each one of us must fight on to the end."[17] It certainly would be interesting to know how the "Tommies" in the trenches viewed this call from a man who was enduring the rigors of war at the Château de Beaurepaire!

The German push to Amiens failed to divide the Allied armies and to push the British into the sea. Indeed, Ludendorff, as earlier at Caporetto in Italy, was allowing his strategy to be established ad hoc in reaction to tactical successes. For this reason, he overspent his reserves on Operation Michael, with the result that instead of the proposed thirty-five divisions planned for "St. George I," he could scrape together barely eleven divisions for a hastily limited and rechristened "Georgette" attack.

But Ludendorff was not finished yet. In the early morning hours of May 27, a storm of artillery fire scalded the Allied lines between Reims and Soissons. At 4:30 A.M., Crown Prince Wilhelm's First and Seventh Armies unraveled "Blücher." The celebrated Chemin des Dames was taken on May 27, and three days later, German forces had stormed over the old Aisne battlefields to the Marne, forty miles from Paris. A special railway-mounted siege gun, dubbed "Big Bertha," shelled the capital. Surprise and concentration once more carried the day. Ludendorff now attempted to expand the great bulge Reims–Château-Thierry–Soissons that he had punched into the Allied front by a drive down the narrow valley between Ourcq and Marne. But Pétain, the master of the elastic defense, allowed the German flood to overrun his front lines and to spend itself on a great semicircular arc of well-prepared defenses in rear positions.

The final German effort came on July 15 in the region of Reims as the German First, Third, and Seventh Armies desperately sought to regain the momentum that had been lost before Amiens. But once again, Pétain's tactics deflected the enemy threat in a mere three days. The *Friedenssturm* in the Champagne had exhausted itself.

The tide of war now flowed full for the Allies. By July, twenty-seven American divisions had landed in France, and Britain managed, by denuding the Palestine front and by sending the last reserves across the Channel, to enhance its forces on the Continent by about 500,000 men. On July 18, Foch unleashed a massive tank-supported offensive from the forests of Villers-Cotterêts. In what is popularly termed the Second Battle of the Marne, General Mangin's Tenth Army and General Jean Degoutte's Sixth Army, reinforced with American divisions, hurled the Germans back behind the Vesle River. In Paris, the new premier, Clemenceau, ebulliently proclaimed: "My foreign policy and my home policy are the same. At home I wage war. Abroad, I wage war. . . . I shall go on waging war."[18] The "Tiger of Lorraine" had not forgotten the humiliation of 1870/71.

The decisive Allied breakthrough came on August 8 near Amiens. Using the early morning fog to advantage, Sir Henry Rawlinson's Fourth Army followed 456 "tanks" and breached the line of General von Marwitz's Second Army, by now reduced to skeletal divisions of only about 3,000 men each. It broke the spirit and morale of the German High Command.

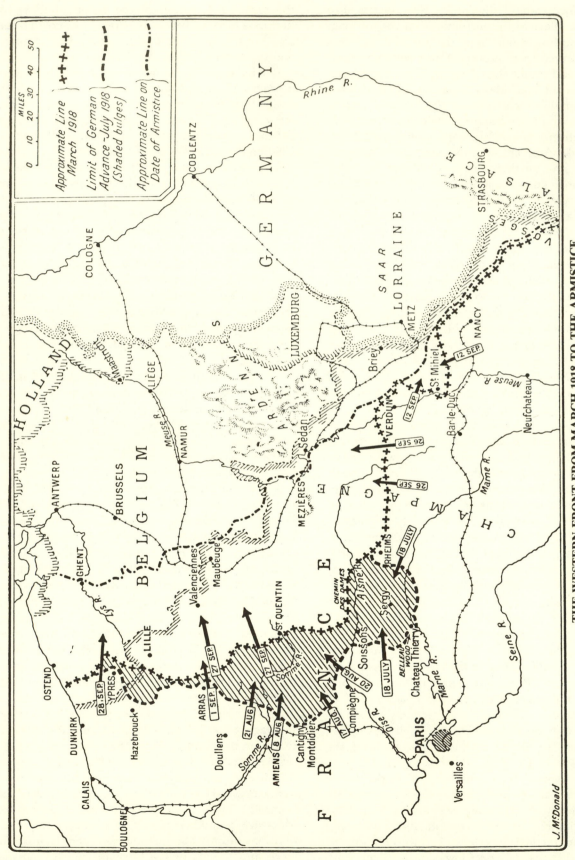

THE WESTERN FRONT FROM MARCH 1918 TO THE ARMISTICE

From *Reputations* by Basil Liddell Hart, published by John Murray, London.

Ludendorff referred to August 8 as "the black day of the German army in the war."[19] And for the first time in the war, German units capitulated without resistance. By August 21, the British First, Third, and Fourth Armies were driving on Péronne, while the French Generals Debeney, Humbert, and Mangin pressured the German Siegfried line.

The turning of the German tide, not surprisingly, revived "Black Jack" Pershing's demand that his forces be deployed in France as a separate army and not "amalgamated" with Allied units. After much interallied wrangling and ethnic slurs at the highest command levels, it was finally decided that the Americans should be accorded a certain victory. A suitable target was the St. Mihiel salient, a German bulge in the French lines that not only galled the Parisians cosmetically but that also effectively cut the rail links between the capital and Nancy as well as Verdun. On September 12, the American First Army commenced a barrage with 4,000 guns and thereafter sent nearly twenty divisions in the form of two pincers of a set of forceps against eight weary and understaffed German divisions. Moreover, since the enemy was actually in the process of evacuating the salient, it is not too far off the mark to state that the Americans "relieved the Germans."

The final campaign of the western front was an Allied push in the Meuse-Argonne sector. Based on the faulty assumption that the Ardennes forest was impenetrable, the Allies sought to hurl the Germans against this natural barrier, while at the same time sealing off all other avenues of retreat. But in 1918, as in 1940, there were decent roads as well as railways through the forest. In addition, the Germans now adopted Pétain's elastic defense—with equally devastating effect. The great American assault on September 26, supported by artillery, "tanks," and airplanes, broke against the Kriemhild sector of the Siegfried line. Recriminations set in on all sides. French commanders complained that the Americans had learned nothing of modern trench warfare. Haig pouted because Pershing had been given his way. And Clemenceau to no avail appealed to Wilson over Pershing's head for greater American vigor at the front.

"Black Jack" Pershing, in turn, blamed the stalled offensive on his commanders, replacing them en masse. On October 12, General Robert L. Bullard received command of the First Army, while General Hunter Liggett was given the new Second Army, with General Hugh Drum as the guiding brain of the American military presence in France. Deploying 3,000 guns and 189 "tanks," the Americans again failed to penetrate the enemy's elastic defense, which repeatedly drew the doughboys into woven belts of fire at the Vesle River, "death valley" as the Americans called it. But American matériel eventually gained the upper hand, and early in November, Pershing's forces broke the Siegfried line, outflanked the Bois de Bourgogne, and threw the Germans behind the Meuse. Only the American *opéra bouffe* at Sedan marred these achievements. Liggett, who had not been informed by Pershing that the Americans would attempt to deny the French the capture of this historic place, had to witness how the American First Division, Pershing's favorite, at night cut through the American Forty-second Division, taking the latter's commander prisoner! Undaunted, "Black Jack" urged his colleagues at Versailles to press on to Berlin.

But the war had run its course. On September 19, Allenby had destroyed the last Turkish army at Megiddo; ten days later, Bulgaria signed an armistice with the Allied and Associated powers. Turkey capitulated at Mudros on October 30. Austria-Hungary succumbed on November 3. Ludendorff, for his part, had realized by September 29 that Germany had reached the end of its physical and moral strength. There were no more boys to march to the trenches. The home front was near starvation and in rags. Fuel was low. His troops in the spring had ravenously charged Allied food depots rather than trenches. On October 26, the first quartermaster general fled in disguise to Sweden to pen his memoirs.

There remained the matter of an armistice. Chancellor Prince Max von Baden on October 3/4 had appealed to Wilson for an end of the war on the basis of the celebrated Fourteen Points of February 8, 1918: the right of peoples to self-determination, abolition of secret diplomacy and secret treaties, freedom of the seas, German evacuation of Belgium, the return to France of Alsace-Lorraine, reconstitution of Poland, and a supranational League of Nations, among others. The president called on Germany in his messages of October 8, 14, and 24 to evacuate all occupied territory, to end the submarine campaign, and to make no attempt to reinforce its armies. Kaiser Wilhelm II reminded his chancellor: "You have not been summoned here to make any difficulties for the Army Supreme Command."[20] Max duly agreed to Wilson's terms on November 5. Four days later in Berlin, he simply announced the kaiser's abdication. And at 11 A.M. on the eleventh day of the eleventh month of 1918, an armistice signed in the forest of Compiègne ended the Great War.

The nightmare was over. But the price had been horrendous. By estimates of the U.S. War Depart-

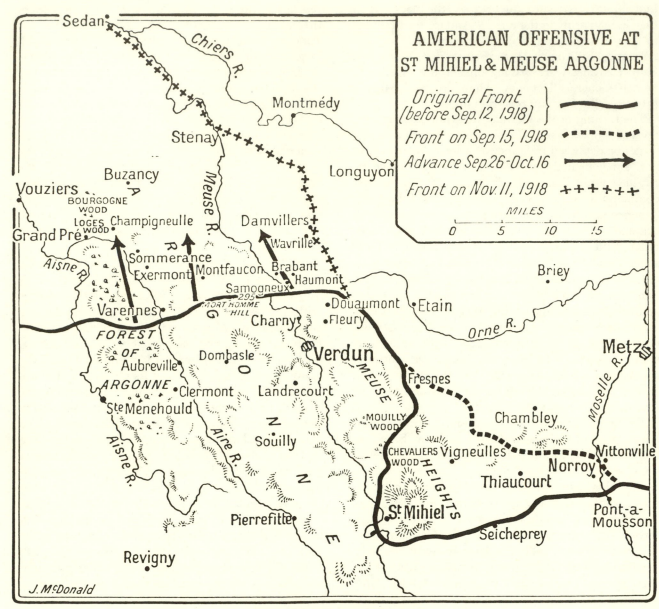

THE AMERICAN OFFENSIVE

From *Reputations* by Basil Liddell Hart, published by John Murray, London.

ment, it had cost Britain and its empire nearly 1 million men dead, 2 million wounded, and 500,000 taken prisoner. France had 1.4 million dead, 4.3 million wounded, and 500,000 taken prisoner. Germany had nearly 2 million dead, 4 million wounded, and over 1 million taken prisoner, on all fronts. The United States had sustained 126,000 men killed. And as a touch of the romantic, Allied commanders, who had spent the war touring rear echelons in motor cars, again took to horseback like medieval knights to accept the victory parades organized for them. Many collected substantial grants from grateful parliaments for jobs well done. Colonel Repington ominously foresook the contemporary term "Great War" at the time of the armistice in favor of the more suggestive title, *The First World War.*[21]

THE WAR
IN THE EAST

While the western front is well known to Americans through memoirs, novels, and films, the eastern front remained, in the words of Winston Churchill, the "unknown war." This imbalance needs to be redressed. In the east, the struggle took on truly epic proportions. Here was a war of motion involving millions of men in multinational armies; here, virtually overnight, reputations and legends were created or destroyed. Whereas the Germans forfeited their chance of victory in the west early in September at the Marne, the Russians were thwarted at Tannenberg and at the Masurian Lakes; and the Austrians at Lemberg in Galicia roughly at the same time. In the east, as in the west, commanders expected the war to be over in six weeks at most, and hence, they hastily sent their men to death in wild marches for fear that the alternative to quick victory was neutral peace. Within six months, both the Austrian and Russian military machines had been dealt crippling blows, from which they never fully recovered.

At first, all went according to plan. As the German armies marched through Belgium, the French rushed into Alsace-Lorraine, and the British embarked for Maubeuge, in the east the Russians under the auspices of "Plan 19 altered" sent two armies into East Prussia and four into Galicia. Opposing them in the north was the single German Eighth Army under General Maximilian von Prittwitz und Gaffron, known to his troops as "the rotund soldier." In the south, Field Marshal Conrad von Hötzendorf, facing Russian and Serbian armies that outnumbered his available units two to one, had devised what appeared to be a sound plan of operations: the greater part of the Habsburg armies, *A-Staffel*, would be sent against the Russians over the sprawling, flat lands of Galicia; a *Minimalgruppe Balkan*, composed of two armies, would be deployed against Serbia; and a strategic reserve of twelve divisions, *B-Staffel*, would be directed either into Galicia or into Serbia, as circumstances demanded.[1]

Unfortunately, Conrad was never quite able to stick to his operations plans or to act in accordance with his given strength. As Gunther Rothenberg put it, "On paper Conrad's plans always had an almost Napoleonic sweep, though he often lacked the resolution to carry them out and also forgot that he did not have the instruments to execute them."[2] In the first place, Conrad refused to accept the fact that Austria-Hungary was attempting to act the part of a great power with the resources and capabilities of a second-rank power. The agitation of various national groups in parliament against any strengthening of the army, combined with the penny pinching of the Vienna bureaucrats, had left the Austro-Hungarian army in a sorry state: it managed to deploy fewer battalions of infantry in 1914 than it had fielded in 1866 against Prussia and Italy—despite a twofold increase in population. Second, while he knew that the Russians by 1914 planned to send 360 troop trains per day to Galicia and would thus have about eighty divisions at the front within eighteen days of mobilization, Conrad's passionate determination to destroy Serbia blinded him to the danger in Galicia. Third, Conrad, like most men in positions of power, felt that the war would be quick, over by Christmas. This alone accounts for Vienna's social security offices' refusing to pay benefits to workers called to the colors, on the grounds that they would be home soon, and for Hungarian Finance Minister Teleszky's adamantly proclaiming that his state had sufficient credit to fight only for a month! In other words, the short-war illusion proved fallacious in the east as well. Indeed, the Russian prohibition on the use of alcohol was spawned by this same consideration—as was the state comptroller's refusal to grant funds for new typewriters for the army because "for a short war, the old ones will do."[3]

Above all, the actions of the Central Powers in the east were a classic in allied distrust and disunity. The Austro-Hungarians had not been informed of the intricate details of the Schlieffen plan, and only when

General von Moltke learned on August 1 that Conrad was sending half his army south against Serbia did he, as well as the kaiser and the Foreign Office, remonstrate and apprise Conrad that they were planning only a strategic defense in East Prussia with barely twelve divisions (against thirty Russian divisions). That same day, the German military attaché in Vienna, Count Karl von Kageneck, begged Moltke's deputy, General Georg von Waldersee, for "measures to coordinate operations against Russia" as soon as possible; only at this late hour did Kageneck discover that there existed no joint plans of operation!

Conrad, for his part, became bitter, yet resolved to humiliate Serbia, come what may. Accordingly, he pressed on with plans to send eight army corps each against Russia and Serbia; there were, it should be remembered, no trained reserves as in Germany, for both the Austrian *Landwehr* and the Hungarian *Honvéd* were part of the front line. Conrad possessed forty-eight divisions against eleven for Serbia and ninety-three for Russia. In the end, it was only the timely intervention of Hungary's Prime Minister Tisza, who had heard of Conrad's dispositions from his colleague, Foreign Minister István Burian, that brought Conrad around to reassigning at least part of the Second Army against Russia.

During the first three weeks of August, Conrad assembled in Galicia the First Army of Count Viktor Dankl, the Third Army of Rudolf Ritter von Brudermann, and the Fourth Army of Moritz Baron Auffenberg as well as two hastily assembled Army Groups under Generals Heinrich Kummer von Falkenfeld and Hermann Baron Kövess von Kövessháza. Conrad had originally intended to assemble his armies at the Russian front, but in 1913, the treason of the homosexual chief of the Prague military district, Colonel A. Redl, probably netted the Russians this information. As a result, the Habsburg forces in 1914 were deployed about 100 to 200 miles behind the border, along the Vistula River.

Instead of concentrating his forces, Conrad ordered them to fan out in order to cover the entire broad front. The Habsburg commander, for his part, remained isolated from the front at Teschen, served by uniformed lackeys and enjoying candlelit dinners and female company; he visited the front only three times in as many years. The results were not long in coming and hardly surprising. The Austro-Hungarian armies advanced northward against the enemy at the battles of Krasnik (August 23-26) and Komarów (August 26-31), but then the full impact of Russian mobilization descended on them during the titanic battle of Lemberg (August 23-September 12).

While the First and Fourth Armies were fairly successful, the Russian assault from the east totally decimated Brudermann's Third Army. Conrad was forced to withdraw, first behind the San and later the Dunajec at the gates of Hungary, some 150 miles to the rear, leaving the great fortress at Przemysl enveloped by Russian forces. As a result of this disaster, the German flank in southern Poland was fully exposed. In the first three weeks of the war, Conrad had lost one-third of his combat effectives, or 250,000 casualties and 100,000 prisoners of war. Belatedly, he recalled parts of the Second Army from Serbia, with the result that this force, as Churchill put it, left General Oskar Potiorek in Serbia "before it could win him a victory; it returned to Conrad in time to participate in his defeat."[4] Costly Austro-Hungarian counteroffensives reclaimed the Vistula-San line by October 10 and relieved Przemysl temporarily; another assault on December 3-14 halted the Russian advance at Limanowa-Lapanów. These actions reinforced Emperor Francis Joseph's reliance on his northern ally and reconfirmed the century-old saying that the Austrian Empire was always *"en retard d'une armée, d'un année et d'une idée."*[5]

The eastern front was stabilized only by developments in East Prussia. Here, too, all available evidence suggested a speedy Russian victory. Under the "Great Program" of 1913/14, Russia was strengthening her forces at the rate of 580,000 recruits per annum, and with the help of a French loan of 1.5 billion francs was extending her railroad network into Western Russia (Poland). In terms of available strength, Russia could mobilize 1,876 battalions of infantry against 1,191 for Germany—most of which would be sent against France. And whereas in Britain there were "Westerners" and "Easterners," in Russia there were similar divisions between "Northerners" and "Southerners," between those who wanted to concentrate against Germany and those against Austria-Hungary. In August, General Yury Danilov, the real power at Grand Duke Nikolai's headquarters (*Stavka*), despatched twenty-nine divisions against Germany and nearly fifty against Austria-Hungary. Those sent into East Prussia were under the overall command of General Y. G. Zhilinsky, with P. K. Rennenkampf heading the First, or Niemen, Army, and A. V. Samsonov the Second, or Narev, Army.

Initially, the Russian campaign unfolded as planned. General Hermann von François attacked the Russians precipitously at Stallupönen on August 17, and three days later, Prittwitz rushed into the fray at Gumbinnen, only to panic and retreat at first contact with superior enemy forces. Prittwitz's decision to abandon East Prussia and to withdraw to the Vistula fortresses prompted Moltke on August 22 to replace him with Generals Paul von Hindenburg and Erich Ludendorff. Zhilinsky, for his part, misinterpreted Gumbinnen as a decisive victory and ordered Samsonov to advance northward in order to cut off the "fleeing" Germans; at the same time, this incompetent staff officer allowed Rennenkampf to assume a leisurely advance on Königsberg, thereby further isolating Samsonov. Hindenburg and Ludendorff, acting on plans already drafted by Lieutenant Colonel Max Hoffmann, between August 25 and 30 concentrated against Samsonov's Second Army, inflicting over 150,000 casualties. Ludendorff, the victor of Liège, had dubbed the offensive "Frögenau," but Hoffmann persuaded him to accept the more historical name of Tannenberg, partly to erase the memory of the Teutonic knights' defeat there in 1410. Thereafter, reinforced by two army corps from the west, the Germans routed Rennenkampf's First Army at the Masurian Lakes, costing the Russians another 100,000 men. Thus were the legends of Hindenburg and Ludendorff created in the east.

But the Russian strength had not been broken. In November, the legendary "steamroller" finally got untracked as seven separate armies drove from southern Poland to the Silesian border. Ludendorff, in what Liddell Hart has termed "perhaps the finest example of his art as well as one of the classic masterpieces of all military history,"[6] used his lateral railroads to fall back upon Cracow, destroying communications as he went, until his new Ninth Army was ready to move northward up the Vistula, then to strike from Posen against the joint of the two armies guarding the Russian flank. Ludendorff's wedge, driven in at Lodz, nearly annihilated one Russian army and threw the other back on Warsaw.[7] In the process, the Russians suffered 100,000 casualties in the action of the lower Vistula. General N. V. Ruzsky, commander of the northern front, estimated that at Lodz many units had lost almost 70 percent of their effectives. The Russian threat had once again been checked, and by the end of the first year of the war, the Russian army had lost almost half of its prewar trained manpower, nearly 2 million *muzhiks*.

But in what was to become the basic pattern of the war in the east, German victories were followed—other times, preceded—by Austro-Hungarian setbacks. While massive struggles were raging in East Prussia and Galicia, General Potiorek slowly advanced against Serbia. Under his command were the Fourth and Sixth Armies as well as four divisions of the hapless Second Army; in all, about 460,000 men. Opposing Potiorek were roughly 450,000 well-armed, tough, aggressive, and battle-hardened Serbs under General Radomir Putnik as well as about 40,000 ill-trained and poorly armed Montenegrins. Potiorek crossed the Save and Drina rivers on August 12 but was repulsed with heavy losses at the battle of Jadar. Using his influence at court to acquire replacements, Potiorek on September 8 again invaded Serbia, with the same results. After yet another plea to Schönbrunn for additional troops, Potiorek on November 6 invaded a third time. Fate seemed at last to favor him: Valjevo fell and the Kolubara River was reached. On December 2, "fortress and town" Belgrade surrendered. But within twenty-four hours, King Peter and General Putnik rallied their forces and drove the invaders out of Serbia, inflicting 200,000 casualties. This "most ignominious, rankling and derisory defeat"[8] cost Potiorek his command; Archduke Eugene replaced him on December 2 and for a year assumed a defensive posture along the Save and Drina.

Conrad, ever the optimist and grand strategist, sought to reverse the tide of 1914 in the east by launching a great offensive on January 23, 1915, designed at least to relieve Przemysl, which had once again been beleaguered by the Russians. While Army Group Karl Baron Pflanzer-Baltin staged a diversionary thrust in the direction of Czernowitz, General Svetozar Boroević's Third Army and a composite German and Austro-Hungarian *Südarmee* under General Alexander von Linsingen launched a suicidal frontal assault from the Carpathian slopes. It proved an utter disaster. By February 8, Conrad had to cancel the operation after sustaining about 100,000 casualties. Przemysl was now beyond hope and surrendered on March 23 with the further loss of 125,000 officers and men. Ominous for the future was the desertion of the Czech 28th Infantry Regiment at Dukla Pass; "Soldier Schwejk"[9] was rapidly becoming a symbol of Czech resistance to Habsburg military authority. With these horrendous losses, the peacetime Habsburg army was destroyed. Almost 750,000 men had been lost, including the ablest noncommissioned as well as staff officers.

Once more, Austro-Hungarian debacles demanded immediate German countermeasures. Already in February 1915, General Hoffmann had conducted a German offensive against the Russian Tenth Army in the so-called winter battle of the Masurian Lakes; about 100,000 Russians were either killed or captured in the Augustov forest. Springtime brought a broad Russian advance southward into the Carpathians. Early in April, the hastily assembled *Beskidenkorps* was rushed to the Dukla Pass in order to stave off a Russian advance into Hungary. But the greatest Ger-

THE RUSSIAN FRONT, 1915

From *Reputations* by Basil Liddell Hart, published by John Murray, London.

man effort was launched on May 2, 1915, when General August von Mackensen's Eleventh Army, reinforced by four Habsburg divisions, broke the front of the Russian Third Army at Gorlice-Tarnów. Mackensen captured 150,000 prisoners, drove to the San River, and liberated Przemysl, while concurrently forcing the Russians to withdraw from their advanced positions in the Carpathians. The Russian "Great Retreat" rapidly developed. Lemberg fell to Mackensen on June 22, and thereafter, the Eleventh Army took Lublin, Cholm, and Brest-Litovsk; the eastern front was now secured along the line Riga-Pinsk-Tarnopol-Czernowitz. The Russian threat receded. An incredibly small force under the able commands of Generals Hindenburg, Ludendorff, Hoffmann, and Mackensen had humbled the great

Russian "steamroller." The tsar's losses included 151,000 killed, 683,000 wounded, and 895,000 prisoners of war. In the process, the Germans had saved Austria-Hungary from certain defeat and occupation. Conversely, Vienna was now totally reliant on Berlin. But amidst the jubilation engendered by Mackensen's spectacular victories, a new threat materialized: the former ally, Italy, on May 23 declared war against Austria-Hungary in the hopes of seizing a good deal of the Tyrol, Trieste, Dalmatia, Asia Minor, and Africa (Treaty of London).

In a curious way, Italy's entry into the war revitalized Austria-Hungary—despite its staggering losses to date. Here was a traditional, a hereditary enemy that had already been measured by Prince Eugene, Radetzky, and Albrecht. Here, too, was the treacherous former ally. And finally, here was an opponent that even Slav units would readily take on. Above all, Conrad sought to punish "the Italian thieves."[10] The problem was once again that the Dual Monarchy was badly outnumbered: Italy had available 850,000 men against barely half that number for Austria-Hungary. While General Luigi Cadorna favored an immediate advance along the Isonzo River, that "howling wilderness of stone," in the direction of Trieste, General Erich von Falkenhayn at German headquarters forced a purely defensive strategy on Conrad by sending him only one division, the Bavarian *Alpenkorps*, to beef up the Dolomite passes. Thereby denied his usual envelopmental strategy, Conrad grudgingly set his defenses: Archduke Eugene received overall command of the Italian front with the able General Alfred Krauss as his chief of staff; Tyrol was to be defended by Dankl, Carinthia by General Franz Rohr, and the Isonzo by Boroević.

Cadorna launched his first major assault on June 23, enjoying a numerical advantage of 460,000 to 228,000 effectives. From July 1915 to March 1916, there were to be four more indecisive Isonzo battles, in what degenerated into savage hand-to-hand fighting with frightful casualties on both sides. There can be no slights of the fighting abilities of either Austro-Hungarian or Italian infantrymen; the blame for inadequate supplies, inept staff planning, and incompetent leadership lies elsewhere.

At about the same time, yet another theater of operations was opened. Britain opted to implement what Clement Atlee, speaking some forty years later, termed "the one strategic idea of the war": an Allied assault on the Dardanelles. First Lord of the Admiralty Churchill, as early as August 31, 1914, had his eye on the Dardanelles, and the

frightful slaughter in France caused the formation of a group of "Easterners," men such as Churchill and Lloyd George who believed that victory lay in so-called side shows in the east. Sir John Fisher at the Admiralty and Lord Kitchener at the War Office were extremely leery of such a diversion of forces, but when Grand Duke Nikolai of Russia on January 2, 1915, asked for a British "demonstration" in the Straits in order to relieve the Turkish pressure on his Army of the Caucasus, London bowed to public demands for some sort of success, somewhere in this bloody war. It was hoped that the operation would force the Straits, threaten Constantinople, bring Greece into the war, and topple the Turkish government.

Admiral Sir Sackville Carden on February 19 was ordered to commence a naval bombardment of the outer forts at the Dardanelles, but the following month he broke down under the strain. In his place, Admiral Sir John De Robeck on March 18 decided to have a "real good try" at the forts: the heavy ships *Irresistible, Bouvet, Gaulois, Suffren,* and *Ocean* were rendered *hors de combat* in the process. Undaunted, the British now committed themselves to an amphibious assault. General Sir Ian Hamilton on April 25 stormed the beaches at the southern tip of Gallipoli (Cape Helles and Gaba Tepe) with his 70,000-man Mediterranean Expeditionary Force, a mixture of British, French, Australian, and New Zealand troops. It was only owing to Hamilton's courageous leadership that the landings were successful, as there existed no plan for disembarking, no reliable maps, no one with knowledge of the terrain, and insufficient medical facilities to handle the infectious diseases that plagued the invaders. In addition, the Turkish defenses had been well established by the German General Otto Liman von Sanders, commanding the Turkish Fifth Army, and his young Turkish colleague, Colonel Mustafa Kemal, in command of the Nineteenth Division. In July, Hamilton was given an additional five divisions, and in October, he secured a new beachhead at Suvla Bay. However, the Cabinet in London quickly lost confidence in the side show, and when Hamilton informed Kitchener in October of the hopelessness of the situation, the "Westerners" in London triumphed and decided on evacuation. The War Office dispatched General Sir Charles Monro to Gallipoli, and as Churchill later put it, "He came, he saw, he capitulated."[11] In fact, Kitchener diverted convoys containing winter supplies from the Dardanelles, with the result that by early November the first severe frost took the lives of about 200 and caused frost-bitten feet for 5,000 men. In the only masterful chapter of the Dardanelles campaign, about 100,000 soldiers were successfully evacuated from Gallipoli on January 8/9, 1916.

The Dardanelles campaign eventually toppled the Liberal government of Herbert Asquith and cost both Churchill and Fisher their posts. To be sure, Churchill had overplayed his hand. He overestimated naval fire power, overrode his professional staff when it differed with him, and refused to delay the amphibious assault until enough troops had been assembled to assure success. The price paid was 145,000 lives. But the plan had been audacious, even brilliant, and certainly a welcome relief from the stifling orthodoxy that crippled planners in London and Paris. Almost from the start, interallied wranglings and intraservice jealousies worked against the scheme. Sir Edward Grey's bungling diplomatic handling of the Greco-Russian rivalry in the area deprived the undertaking of the support of both powers. The Germanophile King Constantine of Greece used the occasion to "sack" his pro-Entente prime minister, Eleutherios Venizelos, who had wanted to exploit Greece's support of the Entente at Gallipoli to realize his dreams of a "Greater Greece." The Dardanelles campaign thus became perhaps the most visible graveyard for British and Greek careers, both civilian and military.

Along with Gallipoli, the spring and summer also brought Turkish military actions in the north and east. General Enver Paşa had long planned an offensive into the Caucasus, to be followed by a thrust to the Turkish populations of Central Asia. In December 1914 and January 1915, Enver personally commanded the Third Army and in a winter campaign over rugged terrain led his forces to disaster at the hands of General N. N. Yudenich at Sarikamish. As the defeated Third Army retreated through Turkish Armenia, it was mocked by rebellious Armenians at Van, Bitlis, and Sassun. The *Dashnaksutium* national party believed that the time had come to proclaim Armenia's independence. But Enver and Minister of the Interior Mehmed Talât Paşa responded on May 27, 1915, by rounding up dissident Armenians in labor battalions and marching them to Syria and Mesopotamia. Thousands died en route. Those who eventually reached Aleppo were marched into the desert to starve. Rough estimates are that about 1 million Armenians were deported, half of them dying of starvation or of torture.

In the east, the Turks faced the unpleasant prospect of major British land operations with Indian troops. In order to safeguard their oil wells in the Persian Gulf, the British in November 1914 had seized Basra; later they pushed farther inland to Amara with two Indian divisions. General Sir John Nixon was so impressed with General Sir Charles Townshend's "regatta" up the Tigris that he decided in June 1915 to drive up the Euphrates, seize Baghdad, and take over the oil wells in the region. Despite the lukewarm enthusiasm of the Cabinet for such a bold undertaking, Townshend nevertheless pushed off from Amara during the hottest time of the year without adequate medical supplies or available reinforcements. He advanced almost 200 miles inland, defeated the Turks near Kut el Amara on September 29, and in the process aroused sufficient enthusiasm in London to rally the Cabinet to support his drive on Baghdad. Britain was desperately in need of some successful feat of arms in the Moslem world, and it was decided that "Mespot" might provide the moral counterpoise to recent defeats at the Dardanelles. On October 23, Nixon finally pushed out for Baghdad, with Townshend striking out from Aziziya. An indecisive confrontation with the Turks at Ctesiphon was followed by a massed Turkish counteroffensive; Townshend was forced to fall back on Kut, which Ottoman forces surrounded on December 8. The imminent starvation of his forces compelled Townshend to surrender on April 29, 1916. A belated British offer of £2 million for the release of Townshend's army was declined at the Porte. Instead, the nearly 10,000 Anglo-Indian troops were marched to Baghdad, where they were publicly displayed, whipped, and caned. The twin disasters of Gallipoli and Kut el Amara drastically lowered the prestige of the Entente in the eyes of interested neutrals.

Bulgaria and Rumania were the major Balkan states that opted to sit on the fence, to await the outcome of the initial battles, and eventually to offer their services to the highest bidder. Rumania had been friendly toward Germany prior to the Great War, but Transylvania was the thorn between Austria-Hungary and Rumania: the Habsburgs possessed it, while King Carol coveted it. As a result, Bulgaria, which had its eyes riveted on Macedonia, was the logical ally for Berlin and Vienna, as the Central Powers could more easily offer territory that they did not possess. King Ferdinand's foreign policy was avowedly expansionist, while Prime Minister Vasil Radoslavov was an Austrophile. The upshot was an alliance concluded at German headquarters on October 6, 1915. Ferdinand, nicknamed the "Richelieu of the Balkans" for his untrustworthiness, was highly alarmed over Allied troops landing at Salonika. General von Falkenhayn greatly desired to acquire direct rail access to Constantinople at a time of intense Allied pressure at the Dardanelles.

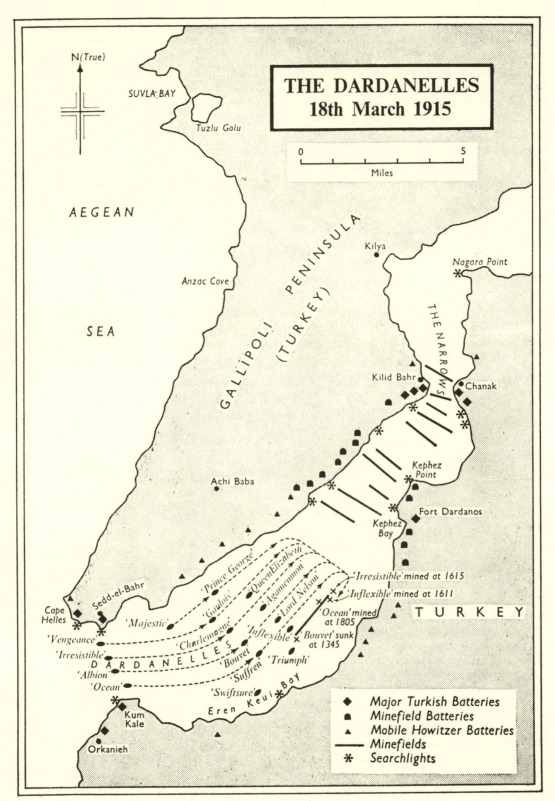

THE DARDANELLES
18th March 1915

N(True)

SUVLA BAY

Tuzlu Golu

AEGEAN

SEA

Anzac Cove

0   Miles   5

Kilya

Nagara Point

GALLIPOLI PENINSULA (TURKEY)

THE NARROWS

Kilid Bahr

Chanak

Achi Baba

Kephez Point

Kephez Bay

Fort Dardanos

TURKEY

'Prince George'

'Queen Elizabeth'

'Irresistible' mined at 1615

'Inflexible' mined at 1611

'Gaulois'

'Agamemnon'

'Lord Nelson'

'Ocean' mined at 1805

'Majestic'

'Charlemagne'

'Inflexible'

'Bouvet' sunk at 1345

'Vengeance'

'Bouvet'

'Suffren'

'Triumph'

'Irresistible'

DARDANELLES

'Albion'

'Ocean'

'Swiftsure'

Cape Helles

Sedd-el-Bahr

Eren Keui Bay

Kum Kale

Orkanieh

◆ Major Turkish Batteries
▮ Minefield Batteries
▲ Mobile Howitzer Batteries
— Minefields
✳ Searchlights

THE DARDANELLES, MARCH 18, 1915

From *Naval Battles of the First World War* by G. M. Bennett, published by
B. T. Batsford Ltd., London.

The obvious object of any German–Austro-Hungarian–Bulgarian thrust was Serbia. But once again, interallied wrangling threatened planning. Foreign Minister Burian in Vienna desired a purely Habsburg assault against Belgrade, which drew from Conrad the caustic comment, "But with what?" Indeed, the dearth of available Austro-Hungarian forces resulted in one of the finest examples of military cooperation: on October 6, 1915, a composite force commanded by Field Marshal von Mackensen, consisting of the Habsburg Third Army under Kövess and the German Eleventh Army under General Max von Gallwitz, invaded Serbia across the Danube and Save. Within the week, two Bulgarian armies under General N. T. Zhekov struck Serbia from the east. The campaign was over in six weeks: Army Group Mackensen stormed Belgrade on October 9, while the Bulgarians prevented Allied forces at Salonika from coming to King Peter's rescue. The entire country was overrun, and 150,000 prisoners were taken. But Austro-German rivalries once again flared up. While Mackensen was ordered by Falkenhayn to halt at the neutral Greek border and not to erase the Salonika salient, Conrad pushed his forces on into Montenegro, scaling the heights of Mount Lovčen and occupying the capital, Cetinje.

The fate of the Serbian army deserves comment. The only route of escape lay across the mountains through Prizren to Albania and the Adriatic Sea. Riding on ancient buffalo carts, King Peter led his remaining soldiers and thousands of refugees to Scutari, only to be viciously attacked by Albanian irregulars. Worse yet, at Valona the Italians refused to accept them and attempted to drive the Serbians back into the mountains. Finally, the French, in further violation of Greek sovereignty, seized Corfu and regrouped the remaining Serbians there. They eventually were sent to Salonika to buttress General Sarrail's army. With the Serbian threat thus eliminated and the road to the Porte secured, Conrad was free once more to turn his attention to Italy—provided, of course, that the Russians remained inactive in the east.

On May 15, 1916, Conrad swept out of the high plains of Lavarone-Folgaria and toward Padua with Dankl's Eleventh Army and Kövess' Third Army. Although reputedly an expert on mountain warfare, Conrad quickly became stalled in the deep snow and bitter cold and by June 17 had to admit defeat and break off the offensive. Meanwhile, disaster of the greatest magnitude had struck in the east. Conrad had ignored Falkenhayn's warnings not to commit his forces in the Trentino, and when denied the requested reinforcements of nine German divisions, he

had brazenly pressed ahead with his plans by denuding his forces in Galicia of some of their best divisions. He was now to pay for that foolhardy act. For the French, hard pressed at Verdun, already in March had sent an urgent appeal for help to the Russians. The latter had replied at first with an assault by General A. N. Kuropatkin's First Army against the German Baltic flank at Lake Narocz, but once again, the Russians had failed against Hindenburg and Ludendorff.

It was now General Aleksei Brusilov's turn. Still more urgent French pleas for relief prompted him on June 4/5, 1916, to attack the German–Austro-Hungarian positions from the Pripet Marshes to the Rumanian border with four separate armies of more than 600,000 soldiers: the Eighth Army under A. M. Kaledin, the Eleventh under V. V. Sakharov, the Seventh under D. G. Shcherbachev, and the Ninth under P. A. Lechitsky—at a time when German resources and manpower were tied down before Verdun and when Conrad was stuck in the ice and snow of the Trentino. Opposing the Russian commander, from north to south, were Archduke Joseph Ferdinand's Fourth Army, General Paul Puhallo's First Army, General Felix Bothmer's mixed *Südarmee*, and Pflanzer-Baltin's Seventh Army, all under the nominal command of General Alexander von Linsingen. Brusilov scored a resounding success as the Austro-Hungarian front crumbled like a piece of pastry near Luck. Only the *Südarmee* stood its ground, until its flanks had been bared by the retreating Austrians. The archduke's Fourth Army was totally decimated by Brusilov's initial assault—despite the fact that the Habsburg forces had intercepted Brusilov's orders to his troops on June 3!

The root causes for the disaster are readily discernible. Archduke Joseph Ferdinand was utterly incompetent to lead a field army and had spent much of his time before the attack hunting with aristocratic friends rather than readying his defenses. Especially Czech and Ruthenian units deserted en masse, and for the first time in the annals of Habsburg military history, the artillery galloped from the scene of fighting, leaving the infantry to its fate. There was both panic and depression at army headquarters at Teschen; Conrad evacuated his new second wife for fear that the Russians would overrun his lodgings. Linsingen saved at least the northern section of the eastern front by a clever counterstroke against the enemy at Luck, which stabilized the critical Galician sector and forced Brusilov to follow the path of least resistance to the Carpathians, beyond which lay the fertile plains of Hungary.

By June 10, Falkenhayn had realized the full magnitude of the debacle in the east. He immediately shuttled five divisions from the western front as well as five from Hindenburg's *Oberost* command to the defense of the Carpathians. Conrad, for his part, grudgingly sent five divisions north from the Italian front. His casualties in Galicia and the Bukovina had already exceeded 200,000 men. By the late summer, despite frantic Russian assaults toward Brody and Lemberg by Sakharov and against Kovel by the Guard Army, the front was stabilized by Linsingen. Brusilov was forced not only to abandon the Bukovina and Galicia but also to absorb a staggering 1 million casualties. Both the material and moral strength of the Russian army were herewith sapped. It was the last time in the Great War that the Russians sacrificed and bled for France.

The Brusilov offensive and its aftermath also had repercussions for the Dual Monarchy. General Hans von Seeckt was attached to Army Group Archduke Joseph as chief of staff; in reality, as its commander. And on September 13, Kaiser Wilhelm II became supreme commander in the east, with Hindenburg acting in his name. Austria-Hungary had, in Fritz Fischer's words for an earlier period, now truly been taken "on the leash" by the Germans. Conrad, humiliated and mocked by the Germans, spent the remainder of the winter in bitter fighting along the Italian front. Between August 6, 1916, and November 4, 1917, he was engaged in the costly sixth to ninth Isonzo battles.

Brusilov's spectacular offensive, combined with Allied pressures at the Somme and Verdun, tipped the scales for Rumania, which declared war against Germany and Austria-Hungary on August 27, 1916. The death of King Carol in October 1914 had brought to the throne the Germanophile, but pliable, Ferdinand I. Wholly under the influence of Prime Minister Ion Bratianu, Ferdinand in the late summer of 1916 believed the moment right to aggrandize Rumania at the expense of Austria-Hungary in Transylvania. Rumania's fateful decision added 550,000 soldiers to the Entente. However, its military leaders were not at all certain of the proper strategy to adopt. Nor was its army prepared to undertake modern warfare against one of the great powers. The country's geographical position was also bad, with the main part, Wallachia, sandwiched between Austria-Hungary in the north and Bulgaria in the south; only Russia could offer direct aid through Moldavia, but by the time Rumania took the plunge, Brusilov's offensive had been halted, and the Germans were everywhere advancing against the Russians. In the end, General Constantine Prezan's desire

to strengthen his Fourth Army for his planned thrust across the Carpathians into Transylvania was rejected by General Alexandru Averescu, who opted instead for a vigorous offensive in the Dobrudja with his Third Army. And in Transylvania, General Arz von Straussenburg mounted a masterful delaying action while waiting for the Germans once more to rescue the Habsburg cause.

Straussenburg did not have long to wait. On the night of September 1/2, Field Marshal von Mackensen invaded the Dobrudja with a mixed force of German, Austro-Hungarian, Bulgarian, and Turkish troops known as the Danube Army. Although outnumbered almost three to one, Mackensen stormed Tutrakan and Silistria, capturing 30,000 Rumanian troops. This drive through Rumania's "back door" in turn drew reserves away from Prezan's forces in Transylvania, and General von Falkenhayn, only recently relieved as chief of the General Staff, assembled the German Ninth Army and advanced against Hermannstadt. The two German pincers closed relentlessly on the Rumanians. Mackensen seized Constanza on the Black Sea on October 19, while Falkenhayn on November 11 stormed the mountain passes at Targu Jiu and descended into Wallachia. Mackensen next advanced westward and on November 23 crossed the Danube at Sistovo in order to turn the Rumanian flank on the Alt. A desperate attempt by Prezan to shuttle his troops east failed to relieve Averescu, and the two German commanders entered Bucharest on December 6, 1916. The remaining Rumanian forces were driven across the Sireth River into Moldavia. Mackensen was appointed commander of the German army of occupation for the remainder of the war. King Ferdinand's decision to enter the war had cost Rumania 200,000 casualties and 150,000 prisoners of war.

The prestige of the Dual Monarchy was hardly enhanced by Mackensen's triumphant campaign in Rumania. Austria-Hungary could only cling to the hope that the Germans would win the war and thereby save the shaky Habsburg throne before starvation and internal disintegration took their toll. Yet it should not be overlooked that by the end of 1916 the Dual Monarchy had mobilized nearly 5 million men. About 800,000 had been killed, and 1 million had been severely wounded or were sick. It was truly a miracle that the ramshackle empire had survived the disasters in Galicia in 1914 as well as Brusilov's massive assault two years later and that it had mounted such a substantial war effort. Indeed, the war had not been over in six weeks, and Hungary had financed the struggle for more than the one month originally estimated! Austria-Hungary by late

1916 had even managed to update its antiquated artillery: new M-14 field guns, M-15 and M-16 howitzers, and a few tractor-drawn 42cm. howitzers were introduced into the front line. Airplane production raised the original force of fewer than fifty planes in August 1914 to about 400 by the end of 1916. And in 1915, Conrad adopted the German field gray uniforms to replace his own pike gray. All in all, even the most critical German observer had to concede that *Kamerad Schnürschuh*, as the Austrians were called because of their lace-up boots, had proved himself capable of far more than anyone could have expected, or even had a right to expect.

Yet at this very moment, tragedy struck: Emperor Francis Joseph died on November 21, 1916, at the age of eighty-six. For sixty-eight years he had sat on the throne, "a cohesive force almost by sheer habit." His death quickly loosened the bonds of loyalty, tradition, and discipline. Moreover, his successor and grand-nephew, Charles, was volatile, inexperienced in politics as well as in diplomacy, unable to adhere to decisions once they were made, and all too much under the influence of his wife, Zita of Bourbon-Parma. In addition, Charles considered himself capable of military judgments and at once assumed personal command of the armies—as Francis Joseph had from 1850 to 1859, with well-known disastrous results. Charles next transferred army headquarters from Teschen to Baden, near Vienna, halted all strategic aerial bombings, abolished physical punishment in the army, canceled the September 1916 unified command agreement with the Germans, and granted amnesty to political radicals, such as the Czechs Karel Kramář, Alois Rašin, and Václav Klofač. In March 1917, Charles dismissed Conrad von Hötzendorf as chief of the General Staff and replaced him with the pliable Arz von Straussenburg, who became primarily the emperor's traveling companion; strategic planning rested with Straussenburg's deputy, General Alfred Waldstätten. The following month, Charles also cashiered War Minister Krobatin and replaced him with General Rudolf Stöger-Steiner, thereby cementing his personal control of the army.

On the diplomatic front, the new ruler opposed the German decision of January 9, 1917, to resume unrestricted submarine warfare. And in perhaps his greatest blunder, he approached the French through relatives, the Princes Sixtus and Xavier of Parma, in a vain attempt to suggest to the French that peace could be attained once France's "just demand" for the return of Alsace-Lorraine had been met. When Clemenceau published the relevant correspondence in April 1918, Charles' position vis-à-vis his German

ally was gravely undermined. All in all, not a highly auspicious beginning for the young heir to an ancient, but precarious throne.[12]

In the meantime, the eastern front had become strangely silent. The transfer of Hindenburg and Ludendorff to headquarters in the west on August 28, 1916, in the wake of Falkenhayn's bloody Verdun offensive partly accounts for this. *Oberost* was placed under the nominal command of Prince Leopold of Bavaria, but operations, such as those against Riga, were in effect planned and conducted by General Hoffmann. The most notable event of 1917 in the east was the March Revolution in Petrograd, ostensibly against the corrupt and inefficient entourage of Nicholas II, but with deeper moral causes beneath the surface. A provisional government headed by Prince George Lvov deposed the tsar, who confided to his diary that he was "sickened" by the "treason, cowardice [and] skull-duggery" that he encountered on every side. By May, a more Socialist provisional government emerged under Aleksandr Kerensky. As prime minister and war and navy minister, Kerensky championed a general peace, introduced a system of committee control into the army, and greatly underestimated the appeal of the tiny group of Bolsheviks headed by V. I. Lenin that had been secretly shuttled from Switzerland to Finland by General Ludendorff in April 1917 in the hope that it would help undermine the morale of the Russian army and home front. Above all, in a series of platform speeches, Kerensky believed that he could rally the soldiers to press on with the war. General M. V. Alekseev yielded as supreme commander of the army to Brusilov, and on July 1, the latter launched the so-called Kerensky offensive in Galicia. Brusilov's assault met with some success around Stanislau, but it failed to score the surprise breakthrough of the 1916 operation. Moreover, General Hoffmann mounted a limited counterattack that quickly drove the Russians out of Galicia and the Bukovina to the very borders of Russia itself. The appearance of Czech legionnaries in the Russian army in Galicia, on the other hand, did not bode well for the future of Emperor Charles.

There remained, of course, the Italian front. The tenth and eleventh Isonzo battles, like the previous nine, were indecisive, the eleventh lasting from May 12 to September 15, 1917. But Ludendorff had by now become convinced that Austria-Hungary could not survive a twelfth Isonzo battle and hence decided to test the Italian resolve. The problem, as usual, was that the Central Powers possessed insufficient troops even for a modest attack in the south. With the British pressure at Passchendaele and the Kerensky offensive just behind, the German lines were stretched already too thinly in both France and Russia to allow the detachment of major armies for the Italian theater. Yet Ludendorff sent his expert in mountain warfare, General Konrad Krafft von Dellmensingen, to scout the area of the Julian Alps between Flitsch and Tolmein, with Karfreit (Caporetto) in its center. The Bavarian, supported by Ludendorff's deputy, Major Georg Wetzell, recommended an assault near Tolmein with a mere six German divisions and nine Habsburg divisions, eventually assembled as the German Fourteenth Army under General Otto von Below. General Boroević was to command the Austrian units on the lower ground near the Adriatic shore. Early in October, the Germans began to bring their troops and supplies up the Julian Alps at night and by hand as well as on pack animals in order to attain the utmost surprise. Krafft planned to open his assault with only a brief artillery bombardment by 2,000 guns and an equally brief gas attack.

General Cadorna had been warned of the impending attack both by his own Intelligence Bureau as well as by Czech and Transylvanian deserters from the Austro-Hungarian army, but he refused to alter his troop deployments accordingly. In the drizzle of snow and rain on the morning of October 24, 1917, Krafft's forces, composed of twelve assault divisions, descended on the Italians. Although outnumbered, Krafft scored a complete success, taking 30,000 prisoners the first day and totally routing the Italian Second Army. By November 2, the Tagliamento River had been crossed, and five days later the Piave was reached. Italian casualties approached 600,000, of which nearly half were prisoners. Conrad von Hötzendorf, in charge of the Trentino front, on November 12 advanced with the Habsburg Tenth and Eleventh Armies, but lack of lateral railways and inadequate motor transport did not allow Ludendorff to switch troops from the Julian Alps to the Trentino fast enough to roll up the Italian flank from the west. Indeed, not even Ludendorff had envisaged such a colossal collapse of the Italian front, and his strategic concept now for the first time was belatedly drawn in the wake of a tactical plan, rather than the other way around. It was a development that he was to repeat in France early the next year.

In Italy, Cadorna yielded to General Armando Diaz as commander in chief, and Sir Henry Wilson as

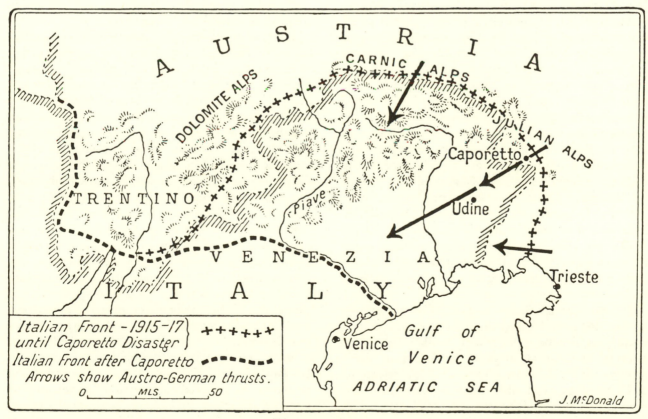

CAPORETTO

From *Reputations* by Basil Liddell Hart, published by John Murray, London.

well as General Foch rushed to the Piave to rally the Italian defenders. Eventually, and to Haig's disgust, five British divisions as well as six French divisions had to be rerouted in order to shore Italy up.

The battle of Caporetto—more accurately, Karfreit, in accordance with the custom of permitting the victor to name the battle site—did little to upgrade the Austro-Hungarian cause. Late in 1917, the Hungarians under Prime Minister Alexander Wekerle and *Honvéd* Minister Alexander Szurmay stepped up their demands for the creation of a separate army after the war. Early in 1918, widespread hunger strikes radiated out from Wiener-Neustadt and Budapest, affecting especially munitions plants. A naval rebellion broke out at Cattaro on the Adriatic Sea on February 1, 1918. By now, dried vegetables had become the staple, with little or no meat available. The fact that the army had gone into war in August 1914 with horses rather than trucks and tractors, while arousing a good deal of satire and ridicule, was now fully appreciated: many artillery batteries were down to one or three horses by the end of 1916. Domestic order was restored only when Prince Alois Schönburg-Hartenstein deployed reliable front units against the rioters (Operations Mogul and Revolver). But war weariness, hunger, want, and national as well as social agitation could not be arrested by bayonets. To compound the crisis at home, in March 1918 about 630,000 Habsburg prisoners of war were released by Russia and sent home, thereby greatly exacerbating the already acute food shortage. Many of these men had been infested with revolutionary ideas. They roamed the countryside in so-called Green Cadres, looting and robbing as best they could. Moreover, even the most reliable front-line troops were rapidly nearing the end of their endurance. Trucks were idled by lack of fuel. Artillery batteries were without horses. Shells were hard to come by. Food was in short supply. Divisions were mere skeletons with only 5,000 to 8,000 men each. Some units had uniforms only for those troops in the front trenches; reserves behind the lines often waited to move up only in their tattered underwear.

This notwithstanding, Conrad von Hötzendorf on June 6, 1918, decided to mount yet another idiotic assault against the Italians with available Tyrolean reserves. It failed. Conrad, a "broken man," was dismissed from the army on July 15. Mass desertions of Czech, Slovene, Polish, Serbian, Ruthenian, and even Croatian units followed as the Habsburg army disintegrated in front of its commanders' very eyes.

In an almost grotesque manner, German fortunes in the east mounted in direct proportion to Austro-Hungarian miseries in the south. Whereas Emperor Charles faced disintegration of his army and state, Kaiser Wilhelm II was on the verge of achieving the "sort of Napoleonic supremacy" over the Continent that in 1892 he had confided to Prince "Phili" Eulenburg was his "fundamental principle."[13]

On November 7, 1917 (October 25 in the Julian, or Old Style calendar), Lenin's Bolsheviks, with the help of the Petrograd Workers' Councils and Red Guards, seized power in Petrograd from Kerensky's provisional government. The following day, Lenin read the Soviet Congress his Decree on Peace, specifying that all conquered lands be returned to their rightful owners and that all colonies be liberated. It found an icy reception in London and Paris. With implied Allied rejection in hand, Lenin and Leon Trotsky on November 23 appealed to the Germans for an armistice, which went into effect on December 22. The Allies, outraged by what they considered to be Russian treachery, vowed to support those loyal elements in Russia willing to continue the war against Germany. Finding few, they divided Russia into zones of influence: France received the Ukraine while Britain took the Caucasus. Japanese and American units were landed at Vladivostok in eastern Siberia, while Anglo-French-American naval and land forces claimed Murmansk and Archangel.

The total collapse of the Russian army late in 1917 naturally caused a great stir in the German camp. Here, in the steppes between Poland and the Caspian Sea, was more land than most German leaders had dreamed of acquiring. New vistas of empire and colonization presented themselves to Wilhelm's military paladins. Tumultuous and often recriminatory debates quickly ensued within the German camp. Ludendorff, in the main supported by the kaiser and German industry, entertained the most utopian annexationist schemes, desiring to control the land mass in the east as far as the Caspian Sea. Russian Finland, recently liberated with German military and naval assistance, would become a German ally under its proposed new ruler, Prince Karl of Hesse. The Baltic states (Latvia, Lithuania, Estonia) would come under personal union to Prussia through the kaiser's son, Prince Oskar. Poland, promised semi-independent status as Congress Poland in the German liberation declaration of November 5, 1916, would become a reservoir of grains and manpower, as would the Ukraine under Hetman P. P. Skoropadsky. Rumania, as we shall see, would be yet another purveyor of grains and of oil. Additional German satellite states would be established in Georgia and the Caucasus—a course of events that greatly alarmed Enver Paşa at the Porte, who coveted most of southern Russia. Moreover, when General Hoff-mann, not sharing Ludendorff's utterly unattainable goals, informed the kaiser in January 1918 that only parts of Poland needed to be annexed outright by Germany, he was nearly cashiered. Hindenburg, for his part, desired the Baltic states to protect his left flank in the next war! And the German navy already envisaged bases in Finland, in the Gulf of Riga, at Murmansk, and on the Black Sea.

The German Foreign Office unsuccessfully attempted to impart a degree of reality into this macabre free-for-all. Foreign Secretary Richard von Kühlmann, while quite prepared to annex Courland and Lithuania and to create a satellite state in Poland, nevertheless suggested that it might be best to work with the Bolsheviks in the east in order to exploit their grain and oil reserves. Above all, Kühlmann feared that unrealistically harsh terms might spark a reactionary coup in Russia and lead to a resumption of the war. He was curtly dismissed on July 8. In the meantime, Trotsky's ingenious "no war, no peace" pronouncement on February 10, 1918, decided the issue.

General Hoffmann was livid, denouncing Trotsky's mental gymnastics as "disgraceful." At a hastily assembled Crown Council at Bad Homburg on February 13, Wilhelm II demanded that the Bolsheviks be "beaten to death," while Kühlmann caustically suggested that the Russians simply be allowed to "fry in their own fat."[14] Five days later, Hoffmann unleashed Operation Faustschlag, the invasion of Bolshevik Russia with fifty-two divisions. In "this strange war," as the general put it, Dünaburg fell the first day, Pskov within five days, and Kiev by March 1. Lenin agreed to German terms on February 23, and the final draft of the treaty was signed at Brest-Litovsk on March 3, 1918. It constituted a triumph for Ludendorff: Russia was to evacuate Finland, Courland, Poland, Lithuania, Estonia, Livonia, and the Ukraine; as a result, it lost about 90 percent of its coal mines, 50 percent of its industry, and 30 percent of its population.

Almost concurrently, Rumania was humbled in the Treaty of Bucharest, ratified by Germany in June 1918. King Ferdinand's country was reduced to a German vassal state. The kingdom was to be oc-cupied until "a date to be determined later," was to pay all occupation costs, was to demobilize one-third of its army, was to place its oil fields under a German banking consortium, and was to hand over to the Germans all "surplus grains." Mackensen could well crow: "This time the pen has secured what the sword has won."[15]

Yet not even these Draconian terms could satisfy Ludendorff's hunger for land. On March 31, 1918, Field Marshal Hermann von Eichhorn took command of a new army group for the occupation of both the Ukraine and the Crimea. With the able General Groener as his chief of staff, Eichhorn, "the uncrowned king of the Ukraine," dissolved the *Rada* in Kiev and encouraged noble landlords to plant their crops—until he was assassinated by a Left Social Revolutionary on July 30. The German navy had moved into Odessa and Novorossisk and was preparing to establish Constanza in Rumania as a major naval base. And in a poignant example of what sort of strange bedfellows necessity can make, the Bolsheviks on August 10, 1918, signed a pact with Germany to dislodge jointly the Allied invaders from Murmansk and Archangel! Ludendorff, for his part, probably hoped that the planned Operation *Schluß-stein* would in the process eliminate the Bolshevik "cradle of the revolution," Petrograd.

By war's end, German armies occupied Russia as far as the Black and Caspian seas, and almost 1 million German troops, albeit primarily elder reservists, stood in the east. The Romanov, Habsburg, and Hohenzollern dynasties had disappeared, and a new social order tenaciously sought to maintain its grip on at least Petrograd and its environs. In human terms, the cost of the war in the east had been staggering. Austria-Hungary had mobilized nearly 8 million men, of whom 1 million had been killed, nearly 2 million wounded, and 1.7 million taken prisoner. Russia had mobilized about 15 million men, of whom nearly 2 million had died, 5 million had been wounded, and 2.5 million taken prisoner. German losses in the east were generally less than those of Austria-Hungary. And without question, Ludendorff's vision of a new Germanic empire in the east greatly impressed at least one veteran of the Great War, the Austro-Hungarian Adolf Hitler.

4

THE WAR
AT SEA

At 11 P.M. on August 4, 1914, the British Admiralty gave the signal to commence hostilities against Germany. First Lord of the Admiralty Winston Churchill accepted the outbreak of war in a packed House of Commons the next day with tears streaming down his cheeks. A decade of intensive naval rivalry with Germany was finally at an end. The newly christened Grand Fleet, dubbed the "Crown Jewels" by Churchill, was at battle stations at Scapa Flow and its Scottish bases: 21 dreadnoughts, 4 battle cruisers, 18 light cruisers, and 225 destroyers. Admiral Sir John Jellicoe was appointed commander of this awesome armada, with the dashing Sir David Beatty as head of the Scouting Forces.

Across the North Sea, the German High Sea Fleet under Admiral Friedrich von Ingenohl consisted of 13 dreadnoughts, 3 battle cruisers, 8 light cruisers, and 152 torpedo boats. But the war had come nearly a decade too early, before Admiral Alfred von Tirpitz's battle fleet of 60 heavy units would be completed and capable of challenging Britain's naval supremacy. In vain, the German admiral had pleaded until the very last minute for the peace to be maintained at least until the early 1920s.

In terms of quality of matériel, there was not much to choose between the two sides. The German ships possessed thicker armor and were less sinkable because of more intricate and watertight hull subdivision; the British had heavier and more durable guns. With regard to tactics, both sides adhered to the rigid line of battle, which basically deprived junior admirals of initiative. Jellicoe in particular distrusted wireless communications, while Tirpitz had for years shunned submarine as well as seaplane development. Sailors on both sides were convinced that the short-war prediction would be fulfilled, at least at sea. The Germans ascribed to their foes an aggressive Trafalgar mentality, expecting the British to descend into the Helgoland Bight at the first news of war. In fact, the Reich's naval attaché on July 30 had warned

of such an "immediate attack" by the British. The burning question, "What if they do not come?" had been raised during fleet maneuvers in 1912, but its author had been hastily retired from a service utterly permeated with Tirpitz's maritime Cannae mentality. To be sure, the British press, public, and even the Royal Navy demanded spectacular and immediate results at sea.

Instead, in its own way, the war at sea became as stolid and as predictable as the trench warfare in France. The British opted not for an immediate attack but rather for a distant blockade, keeping closed Germany's two exits from the North Sea to the Atlantic, the Channel and the waters between Scotland and Norway. In a matter of months, Britain hunted down the isolated German cruiser squadrons, transported eight army divisions to France, and seized 287 German merchant ships on the high seas. Harebrained schemes for assaults against Helgoland, Flanders, Borkum, and Brunsbüttel and for landings in Pommern, Schleswig-Holstein, and Denmark were quickly shelved. Although an exasperated Churchill announced that the British would dig the Germans out "like rats from a hole," he later more rationally stated that "Jellicoe was the only man on either side who could lose the war in an afternoon."[1]

Amid mounting public pressure for naval action, Beatty on August 28 raided the waters off Helgoland, literally blowing the German light cruisers *Ariadne*, *Mainz*, and *Köln* out of the water. Ingenohl showed no inclination to take the High Sea Fleet out that day. In fact, "Fleet Order Nr. 1" of July 30 had expressly ordered him to engage only isolated portions of the British fleet under favorable circumstances by surface action. And by August 6, Kaiser Wilhelm II, Admiral Hugo von Pohl, and Chancellor von Bethmann Hollweg had further restricted the operational freedom of the fleet "in order to use it as a security at the peace table." In short, there was to be no sacrificial sortie against the entire Grand Fleet.

However, on December 16, Ingenohl began the first of a series of "tip-and-run" operations by the High Sea Fleet against the British east coast that soon degenerated into a kind of cat-and-mouse game: the Germans would dash to the English coast in the hopes of shelling it and possibly engaging Commodore Reginald Tyrwhitt's weaker Harwich Force, while Jellicoe and Beatty charged down from the Scottish anchorages at first news of the German raid in the hope of cutting the enemy off from his line of retreat. On December 16, the Germans shelled Hartlepool, Scarborough, and Whitby, drawing from Churchill the barb, "the baby-killers of Scarborough." Undaunted, Ingenohl on January 24, 1915, again steamed for England, but at the Dogger Bank, Beatty's "sea cavalry" intercepted him and destroyed the armored cruiser *Blücher*. This action had two immediate results. Pohl replaced Ingenohl as head of the High Sea Fleet, and the Germans installed "antiflash" doors at the various levels of the loading cycle as the turrets of the battle cruiser *Seydlitz* had proved vulnerable to fire; the British were to learn this lesson only after Jutland.

In the meantime, at the outbreak of war, Admiral Wilhelm Souchon in the Mediterranean decided to make for Constantinople with the battle cruiser *Goeben* and the light cruiser *Breslau*. Despite badly leaking boilers and pursuit by a formidable British armada under Sir Ernest Troubridge and Sir Archibald Milne, both ships reached the Dardanelles on August 16; their presence helped to bring Turkey into the war on the side of the Central Powers. The Germans donned fez and were incorporated into the sultan's navy.[2] Farther south, the Reich's colonies in Africa were rapidly seized by the Entente—save East Africa, where General Paul von Lettow-Vorbeck mounted a successful guerrilla struggle until war's end.

There remained the German Cruiser Squadron in the Far East. Admiral Maximilian Count von Spee realized that, with Japan's declaration of war against Germany on August 23, he could no longer tarry at Ponape in the Caroline Islands; he decided to head across the vast expanse of the Pacific to South America and from there across the Atlantic to Germany. Indeed, on November 7, precisely twenty-seven years after Kaiser Wilhelm II had seized it, Kiaochow, the German colony in China, was stormed by Japanese General Kamio Mitsuomi. Spee dispatched the light cruiser *Emden* to the Indian Ocean, where it became a legend in its time, destroying or capturing two enemy warships and seventeen merchant ships, before the Australian cruiser *Sydney* demolished it off Cocos Island.

Spee's squadron, now consisting of the armored cruisers *Gneisenau* and *Scharnhorst* and the light cruisers *Dresden*, *Leipzig*, and *Nürnberg*, on November 1 stood off Coronel, off the coast of Chile, confronted by Sir Christopher Cradock's squadron comprised of the armored cruisers *Good Hope* and *Monmouth* as well as the light cruiser *Glasgow* and the auxiliary cruiser *Otranto*. Before nightfall, both armored cruisers had been dispatched, along with Cradock and 1,600 men. First Sea Lord Sir John Fisher termed Coronel "the saddest naval action of the war." In fact, Fisher was livid. He at once ordered Jellicoe to release the battle cruisers *Invincible* and *Inflexible* to Sir Doveton Sturdee, who, reinforced by two light cruisers and four armored cruisers, made off for the Falkland Islands to intercept the German raiders. It was a classic case of overkill. At Port Stanley on December 8, Sturdee destroyed the *Scharnhorst* and *Gneisenau* along with Spee, his two sons, and 2,200 officers and men. The light cruisers were hunted down one by one. Herewith, except for the Black and Baltic seas and the waters off Helgoland, "the German flag . . . ceased to fly on any vessel in any quarter of the world." The kaiser, Admiral von Müller noted in his diary, "was very depressed."[3]

With the exception of the action at Jutland plus occasional skirmishes in the Black Sea and the Baltic, to be discussed later, the surface war at sea had ended. German leadership had proved timid and ineffective. Pohl undertook five more surface raids into the North Sea, but none of them went far beyond Helgoland or Borkum. The outrageous expenditures on battle fleets before 1914 apparently had been in vain. Schoolboys in the major German ports scrawled a cruel jingle on brick walls for all to see: "Dear Fatherland, you may rest assured; the Fleet lies in the harbors—moored!"[4] Pohl died of cancer of the liver in January 1916 and was replaced by the more energetic Vice Admiral Reinhard Scheer.

The disappointing course of the war at sea encouraged the proponents of *guerre de course* to argue vociferously that the submarine might yet alter Germany's maritime fortunes, if allowed to be used indiscriminately against enemy shipping. Indeed, these backers of *Kleinkrieg* tactics were greatly encouraged by the incredible deeds of Lieutenant Otto Weddigen's *U 9* in the Channel on September 22, 1914, when Weddigen leisurely dispatched the British armored cruisers *Aboukir*, *Cressy*, and *Hogue* (the "live-bait squadron") with the loss of nearly 1,500 men. Perhaps encouraged by this spectacular action, the Germans on February 1, 1915, decided to launch an underwater offensive with the available twenty-nine submarines. However, the sinkings of the

Lusitania (*U 20*) in May and of the *Arabic* (*U 24*) in August, both with the loss of American lives, evoked sharp notes of protest from President Wilson. The Germans halted their submarine campaign by September 18, having bagged about 748,000 tons of shipping.

On February 23, 1916, it was decided to resume U-boat warfare, this time with over sixty boats available. But when further incidents involving neutrals prompted the kaiser to order that only armed freighters be torpedoed without warning, Admiral von Tirpitz resigned on March 10, 1916. Wilhelm II curtly noted: "He is leaving the sinking ship." Four days later, *UB 29* destroyed the French steamer *Sussex* off Boulogne, again with the loss of American lives. Another sharp protest from Washington prompted the Germans to halt the undersea campaign on April 27. About 450,000 tons of shipping had been destroyed. In Britain, Admiral Sir Arthur Wilson, Fisher's successor as first sea lord, considered submarine warfare to be "underhand, unfair, and Damned unEnglish!"[5]

Unable to arrive at a consistent submarine policy, the German navy once more decided to undertake "tip-and-run" raids against the English coast. Admiral Scheer raided Lowestoft and Yarmouth on April 24/25, 1916, but he lost a golden chance to catch Commodore Tyrwhitt's weaker Harwich Force when Vice Admiral Friedrich Boedicker, fearing that Beatty was descending on him from the north, broke off the surface action too soon. After several delays due to foul weather, Scheer again put out to sea on May 31 with sixteen dreadnoughts, five battle cruisers, eleven light cruisers, and sixty-one torpedo boats in the hope of drawing the British out to the coast of Jutland. He would not have long to wait. The British, again intercepting German messages, put out to sea ahead of him. Jellicoe led twenty-four dreadnoughts, three battle cruisers, eight armored cruisers, twelve light cruisers, and fifty-one destroyers out of Scapa Flow; at the same time, Beatty dashed out of the Firth of Forth with four dreadnoughts, six battle cruisers, fourteen light cruisers, and twenty-seven destroyers. On board Jellicoe's flagship, *Iron Duke*, one of the officers growled: "Just another b—— useless sweep."[6] In fact, the only full-scale fleet encounter of the Great War was about to start.

Der Tag, for which sailors on both sides had been working for years, was at hand at last. And it was glorious at first, in the best tradition of Trafalgar or St. Vincent. By 4:48 P.M., both scouting forces had engaged in a blistering artillery duel at 15,000 meters. The noise of battle was deafening, and the naval gray paint of the gun barrels was blistering into shades of yellow and brown. Thick smoke belched from the funnels, and both sides fired salvos about every seven seconds as the ships ploughed through the heavy seas at twenty-five knots. At first, Rear Admiral Franz Hipper attempted to lure Beatty onto Scheer's High Sea Fleet, which was approaching from the south. But by 5:30 P.M., Beatty executed a battle turn of 180 degrees and now led Hipper onto the Grand Fleet, steaming down from the north. Lack of "antiflash" doors caused the British to lose the battle cruisers *Indefatigable*, *Queen Mary*, and *Invincible*. There was even a glorious destroyer melee in the oncoming darkness. In a roar of passing and exploding shells, and with missing hardly possible at incredibly close range, these light craft mauled each other. It was work in the old style at point-blank range amid a confusion of gunflashes and dazzling searchlight beams.

Around 7 P.M., Hipper informed his flag officer: "Something lurks in that soup. We would do well not to thrust into it too deeply." Indeed, what lurked in that "soup" were Jellicoe's six columns of four dreadnoughts each. In short order, Hipper's battle cruisers *Lützow*, *Derfflinger*, *Seydlitz*, and *Von der Tann* all had to leave the line. Scheer's heavy ships now also ran up against Jellicoe. As the official German history of the war at sea notes: "Suddenly the German van was faced by the belching guns of an interminable line of heavy ships . . . while salvo after salvo followed almost without intermission."[7] Half an hour after the battle had started, Scheer sought to extricate himself from certain annihilation by a battle turn away; Jellicoe had crossed his "T." But by 8 P.M., for reasons that we shall never know, Scheer again reversed his position 180 degrees. And again, Jellicoe crossed the German's "T" and mercilessly pounded Scheer's *König*-class battleships. Only a second battle turn away from Jellicoe brought Scheer relief. He had been outmaneuvered, and he knew it. "If one wants to throw me out of the navy for this, it is indifferent to me." He made for home. Nightfall was his principal hope. The two fleets by 10 P.M. passed by each other only five miles apart like the proverbial ships in the night. The murky weather perfectly suited Scheer, who later confided that he "came to the thing [the battle] as the virgin did when she had the baby." Few could fault Jellicoe's sad lament that "if it had only been about 6 P.M. instead of nearly dark, and clear instead of thick, we should have had a second Trafalgar." Yet the British had lost three battle cruisers, three light cruisers, and eight destroyers, a total of 111,000 tons, to Germany's one elderly battleship, one battle cruiser, four light cruisers, and five torpedo boats, in all 62,000 tons.

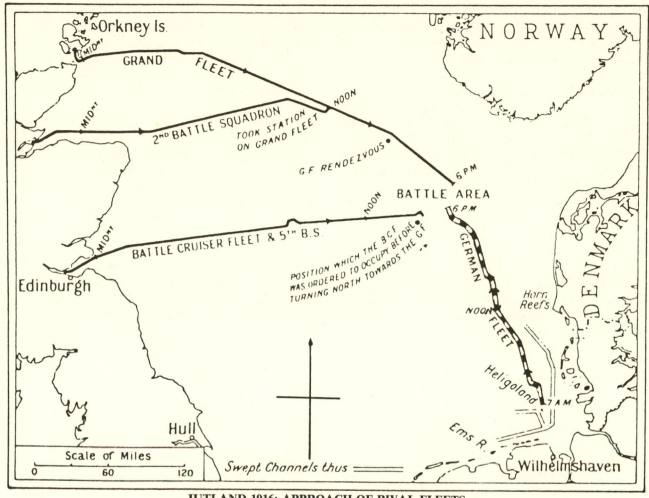

JUTLAND 1916: APPROACH OF RIVAL FLEETS

The kaiser was ecstatic: "The magic of Trafalgar has been broken." He visited the fleet on June 5, showering most captains with Iron Crosses and kisses. Scheer was promoted to admiral, and Hipper was knighted by the king of Bavaria. But the battle, which had involved 250 ships and 100,000 men, brought the Reich no strategic relief. Jutland was as decisive as Trafalgar. The Germans had been driven home, and the exits from the North Sea remained in British hands. The morning after the battle, Jellicoe waited off the German coast with his twenty-four untouched dreadnoughts and battle cruisers for Scheer to resume the action. However, the German commander preferred to keep his ten battle-ready heavy units in port. The High Sea Fleet was to put out to sea only three times more: in August and October 1916 and in April 1918. And like the French after Trafalgar, the Germans now turned to *guerre de*

course in a final attempt to throw off the steel yoke of British naval supremacy.

On July 4, 1916, Scheer presented Wilhelm II his evaluation of the battle. The crux of the matter was that "there can be no doubt that even the most successful outcome of a fleet action in this war will not *force* England to make peace." Scheer percipiently pointed to the Reich's "disadvantageous military-geographical position" and to the "enemy's great material superiority." He now returned to a theme he had already aired in November and December 1914: "the defeat of British economic life—that is, by using the U-boats against British trade.[8]

Admiral Henning von Holtzendorff, chief of the Admiralty Staff, concurred. Aided by a host of bankers and economists, Holtzendorff, in a famous memorandum of December 22, 1916, argued that Britain could be starved into submission if the

U-boats could destroy about 600,000 tons of shipping per month for six months. Such "a final and irreplaceable" loss of 40 percent of its merchant shipping would force it to the peace table. The United States was dismissed as a military factor, for the U-boats would prevent the deployment of an American army in Europe; moreover, the season's wheat rust problem would seriously deplete her harvest. On January 9, 1917, the kaiser, Generals von Hindenburg and Ludendorff, and Chancellor von Bethmann Hollweg agreed with this prognosis and opted to launch an unrestricted submarine campaign on February 1. Wilhelm "fully expected America's entry into the war" as a result, but because of Holtzendorff's assurances, stated above, he considered this "irrelevant." The United States duly declared war against Germany on April 6, 1917.

We know today that the German calculations ignored several important political factors and that they also had a narrow focus in their analysis of economic determinants. Holtzendorff greatly underestimated both the American tonnage available to Britain and the "perfidious Albion's" own merchant fleet. Moreover, he had no clear idea of how many ships were required to sustain Britain's industry and to feed her population. And owing to the British "national character," he never imagined that rationing would be instituted. Wheat was overemphasized, while other grains were readily dismissed. No account was taken of British use of previously unused land to raise crops. And American surpluses were more than sufficient to cover Allied needs for 1916 and 1917.

The German U-boat force fought a heroic, if losing, battle on the high seas. There were never sufficient boats available for the job at hand, and losses at sea continued to mount while production of new submarines lagged behind schedule. Wolf-pack tactics were never implemented because of the belief that it was best to cover as much ocean area as possible rather than to concentrate on vital shipping lanes. Most devastating of all, on April 25, 1917, Prime Minister Lloyd George undertook the unusual step of personally visiting the British Admiralty in order to force the Royal Navy to adopt the convoy system of transport. Most admirals feared stripping the Grand Fleet of its protective craft in order to assign them to escort convoys, but the prime minister carried the day. President Wilson also thought the British "ought to convoy," and through Admiral William S. Sims, he made available as many escort craft as the United States could spare—much to the distress of Chief of Naval Operations Admiral William S. Benson, who felt it was "none of our business pulling their [the

British] chestnuts out of the fire."[9] Convoy won the war against the submarines, even though the latter took a heavy toll, destroying 6,394 enemy and neutral ships of 11.9 million tons during 3,274 sorties.

The emphasis on the U-war, in turn, greatly affected the morale on board the big ships. The ablest and most energetic junior officers volunteered for U-boat duty as the fleet bobbed up and down at anchor and rusted. Idleness, compounded by abysmal food, gnawed at the spirits of the sailors. Inexperienced sea cadets took the place of seasoned front officers in the fleet; routine duties such as coaling and painting became exercises in discipline. Leave became irregular, while officers frequently took ships' stores home to their families. The slightest disturbance of the daily routine became cause for an official investigation. And when the stokers of the *Prinzregent Luitpold* had their recreational period and cinema canceled on July 31, 1917, and were instead called out for infantry drill, about fifty of them refused to return to their ship. The mood in the fleet turned ugly as word of this spread. Officers accused the men of treason and of having been subverted by the Independent Social Democratic party. The ratings, for their part, complained of food and leave inequities. Admiral Scheer on September 5 had two of the leaders of the rebellion executed after a highly suspect series of courts-martial. Tirpitz's successor, Admiral Eduard von Capelle, and Chancellor Georg Michaelis eventually were forced out of office as they attempted in the Reichstag to implicate the Independent Socialists in the revolt. Shouts of "hunger" rather than the traditional "hurrah" greeted the kaiser during a visit to the fleet.

To overcome the ebb in morale and to restore the nation's confidence in the navy, Vice Admiral Ehrhardt Schmidt was sent into the Gulf of Riga in October 1917 to seize the islands Moon, Dagö, and Oesel. It was another classic case of overkill, as no less than ten battleships and 24,000 men of the Eighth Army stormed the islands. And on February 20, 1918, a special German naval task force under Admiral Hugo Meurer transported General Rüdiger von der Goltz's "Baltic Division" to Finland, where they stormed Helsinki on April 12.

But the main theater of the war remained the west. In April 1918, Scheer took the High Sea Fleet out again, steaming as far as Bergen in the hope of intercepting Scandinavian convoys bound for England. The only noteworthy event of the sortie was the breakdown of the battle cruiser *Moltke*, which almost fell victim to a British submarine. Admiral von Holtzendorff, in turn, maintained a brave front, lamely arguing that the submarine war could yet be won if only 650,000 tons of shipping per month were destroyed. General Ludendorff asked that especially U.S. troop transports be intercepted, but the U-boats failed completely in this task. By June 1918, the United States was safely shuttling 536,000 tons of supplies to France, while nearly 1 million doughboys had arrived as well. Admiral Sims had managed to get almost 200 light craft to assist the British at convoy, and the newest American battleships, *Florida*, *Wyoming*, *New York*, *Texas*, and *Arkansas*, had been sent under Rear Admiral Hugh Rodman to augment the British Grand Fleet, now commanded by Beatty.

Only in the Mediterranean theater did interallied wrangling and jealousies prevent effective action against the warships that the Central Powers had stationed at Pola and Cattaro in the Adriatic. Not even energetic Assistant Secretary of the Navy Franklin D. Roosevelt could prompt the Italians to leave port. When he inquired of Admiral Thaon di Revel why the Italians stubbornly refused to engage Admiral Miklós Horthy's ships, the Italian replied that the currents, beaches, harbors, islands, channels, anchorages, and even the clarity of the waters favored the enemy. Further, that there was no need to undertake training exercises since the Austro-Hungarians also refrained from such activity. Roosevelt thought this "a naval classic which is hard to beat, but which perhaps should not be publicly repeated for a generation or two."[10] A projected mine barrage across the Straits of Otranto likewise never materialized.

With the failure of the German "Michael" offensive in France, the war was virtually over. By September 28/29, Ludendorff had asked for an immediate armistice, and on October 16, the submarine offensive was officially canceled in accordance with President Wilson's demands. In fact, the German navy proved surprisingly willing to cancel the U-boat campaign. As Scheer put it: "The navy does not need an armistice."[11]

The fact of the matter is that a bold new design had entered the heads of Germany's naval planners: the High Sea Fleet would be sent against the combined Anglo-American fleet in the North Sea, possibly with the kaiser on board. Scheer concluded that the "honor and existence of the navy" demanded a final sortie, even if "the course of events cannot thereby be significantly altered." Admirals von Hipper and Adolf von Trotha agreed to the suicidal sortie. On October 24, at the height of the armistice negotiations, they officially concocted "Operations Plan Nr. 19," calling for a rematch of Jutland, this time in the Hoofden, the waters between the Netherlands and Great Britain. Tirpitz's dream of a Cannae at sea

"between the Thames and Helgoland" seemed finally at hand. But news of the proposed death ride leaked out, and on October 29, many sailors refused to board their ships. Instead, they cheered Woodrow Wilson and pulled the fires out from under the boilers. Wilhelm II dismissed Scheer on November 9 with the caustic barb: "I no longer have a Navy." Two days later he crossed into the Netherlands seeking exile.

Der Tag, as it turned out, was November 21, 1918. The second largest surface fleet in the world was to be interned at Scapa Flow after the various neutrals had declined the honor of berthing the rebellious High Sea Fleet. Admiral Beatty knew perhaps better than anyone that this was not a glorious day for any sailor: "It was a pitiable sight, in fact I should say it was a horrible sight, to see these great ships" surrendered. On June 21, 1919, Admiral Ludwig von Reuter, acting on his own initiative, ordered the ships to be scuttled at Scapa Flow. About 500,000 tons of warships, estimated at a cost of 856 million Gold Mark, slipped beneath the waves that day. Once the initial shock had passed, British and American naval leaders were not at all disappointed that the Germans had scuttled their ships. Admiral Rosslyn Wemyss, the first sea lord, looked on it as "a real blessing"; the French and Italians, on the other hand, suspected British connivance in the matter in order to deprive them of their anticipated booty.

The war at sea had proved a great disappointment to both sides. There had been only one full-scale encounter on the high seas, and that one indecisive. Compared with the monumental sufferings sustained by the land forces, the contribution of the two major navies had been "inglorious and subsidiary." The Grand Fleet had not scored its cherished "second Trafalgar," and even the naval blockade, continued long after the armistice had been signed, failed to break either the will or the ability of the Germans to pursue the war. Conversely, the German fleet did not influence the outcome of the war one iota, and the U-boat campaign, while frightening in its suddenness and severity, failed either to starve England into submission or to prevent the arrival of the U.S. army in France. The naval war of 1914-18 only renewed the clash between the adherents of *guerre de course* and the "blue water school" with greater intensity and acrimony. It is yet a further testimony to the basic conservatism of the major European navies that it took a second world war for most admirals to realize that the day of the battleship had passed. For, as Paul Kennedy has noted, "it would be no exaggeration to state that the course of the First World War substantially discredited that mighty host of great grey battleships, swinging on their anchors in the distant harbour of Scapa."[12] The development of naval air power, of course, greatly accelerated this development.

Although Germany lost the war at sea in 1914-18, Britain surrendered her naval supremacy. The *Pax Britannica* died in Europe during the Great War. As ever greater quantities of British manpower and matériel were fed into the military meat grinder of the western front, the British global position declined proportionally as that of the United States and Japan increased. Greatly strapped by the exigencies of four years of bloody war, psychologically exhausted, economically sapped, Britain was in no position in 1919 to meet the twin challenges of American and Japanese naval power. Its victory at sea was truly an illusion. Sir Cecil Spring Rice, St. James's crotchety ambassador to Washington, already in October 1917 had warned that there existed in the United States "an under current of feeling that, by the end of the war, America will have all the ships and all the gold in the world, and that the hegemony probably of the world, and certainly of the Anglo-Saxon race, will pass across the Atlantic."[13] It proved to be an accurate assessment.

5

THE
HOME FRONT

The patriotic euphoria of August 1914 prompted civilian leaders in virtually all the European capitals to surrender with reckless abandon most of their powers to the military. After all, the argument went, the war would be over in six weeks, at worst by Christmas, and hence, it was only sensible to give the military a free hand to run what basically was its show. Interference in what generals considered to be their sphere of operations might hamper the chance at victory and earn the politcans the acrimonious rancor of the voters at home. Carl von Clausewitz's dictum that war was simply the extension of politics by other means and that civilian leaders needed to maintain charge of the overall situation was one of the first casualties of the Great War. And no politician could ignore the joyous rapture that the outbreak of hostilities caused among those potential voters. Many leaders were downright scared of being left out of the mainstream of public life if they failed to march in step with the festive crowds, while some were simply tired of the decades of peace forced on Europe by Bismarck. The "short, cleansing thunderstorm" would soon be over, and then one could return to "business as usual."

Especially in France, the advent of war gave the generals their first real chance since the days of military-civilian confrontation during the Boulanger and Dreyfus affairs to vent their feelings against "the Whore," the Republic. The state of siege decreed on August 2 gave the military sweeping powers to appoint judges and subprefects, to control the press and the telephone system, and to circumvent deputies and prefects under the cover of "military secrecy." President Poincaré was not told of the early defeats in Lorraine and at Charleroi, was denied knowledge of the staggering casualties, and was refused permission to tour the front near Alsace. Premier René Viviani had to learn from a flower seller that the French High Command was going to leave Chantilly. And it was not a German, but rather a French general, Hubert Lyautey, who in 1914 crowed that his country was "getting better because the politicians have shut up." Later, after parliament reconvened, he reflected, "It was so much better when all the talking and scribbling was stopped."[1]

In Britain, the military was on the verge of rebelling over Ireland, and not a few generals were relieved that the Great War had put an end—albeit, temporarily—to the vexing disturbances created by labor, suffragettes, and Home Rule. Sir William Birdwood put the generals' case best: "*What* a piece of real luck this war has been as regards Ireland—just averted Civil War and when it is over we may all be tired of fighting." And while George Dangerfield may well have underestimated the basic stability of Edwardian society, his provocative thesis of the "triple revolution" of labor, suffragettes, and Ireland cannot easily be dismissed. In fact, Sir Henry Wilson, the man most responsible for tying the British army to the French colors before 1914, utterly despised the "pestilent government" of Herbert Asquith and greatly feared that the British Expeditionary Force might be sent to Ireland rather than to France! Sir Edward Grey, dining and playing billiards at the Foreign Office in splendid isolation from the world of August 1914, tenaciously clung to the "short-war illusion" harbored in all other capitals. He had long worried that Norman Angell's prediction that a major European war would ruin the financial system might be correct; Grey's comment that Britain would hardly suffer more if it went to war with Germany than if it stayed out seemed to make sense that August as the only alternative to quick victory appeared to be neutral peace.[2]

To a degree, it was a telling sign that the various governments desperately sought to create the impression of domestic harmony and unity. In Russia, a "civil truce" was declared, while in Austria-Hungary, the nagging problem of greater autonomy for the Magyars within the Dual Monarchy was suspended for the duration of the struggle. In Britain, Andrew Bonar Law's Unionists concluded a pact of common unity of purpose and solidarity with Asquith's Liberals. France triumphantly declared a *union sacrée* to exist, while Germany countered with claims of a *Burgfrieden* as the kaiser no longer recognized political parties but only loyal citizens.

Nor were these proclamations devoid of truth. Desertions were low in August 1914, approaching only 4 percent in Russia. Moreover, men of all persuasions, long tired of peace, rallied to the defense of their nations. The avowed antimilitarist Gustave Hervé declared "the fatherland of revolution," France, to be "in danger." Ernest Lavisse, in supporting the war effort, brazenly asserted that the France of Louis XIV and Napoleon Bonaparte had never "taught the doctrine of atrocious war." Henri Bergson agreed with *La Croix*, "The History of France is the Story of God." And economist Werner Sombart declared that the world was divided between "the merchants, the British, and the heroes, the Germans."

Even Socialists were swept up by the tide, foresaking Karl Marx in favor of nationalism. German Socialists feared that they would be beaten down at the Brandenburg Gate if they pulled against the popular stream. Ramsay MacDonald in England felt that this "would be the most popular war the country had ever fought." G. V. Plekhanov, "the father of Russian Marxism," pledged his support to Tsar Nicholas II. The Italian Socialists defined their basic posture, "Oppose the war, but do not sabotage it."³ In time, Labour's Arthur Henderson joined the Cabinet in London; and Jules Guesde, Marcel Sembat, and Albert Thomas at various times sat in the French Cabinet. In Germany, General Groener effectively placated the trade unions and brought their leaders into the highest echelons of war production.

The patriotic spirit lasted for almost three months. German youths marched off to war declaring *"Gott mit uns."* At Langemarck, with the *Deutschlandlied* on their lips, they ran against seasoned British infantry. The British, for their part, tried hard to hide their German roots. The royal family changed its name from Saxe-Coburg to Windsor, while the Battenbergs became the Mountbattens. German shops in London were looted, German residents shipped off to the Isle of Man, and some even suggested banning the works of Brahms, Händel, Mendelssohn, Strauss, and Wagner, "Huns" all of them. And before the war was over, a new cult of personality had largely replaced European royalty: Hindenburg, "the saviour of the fatherland"; "Papa" Joffre, the "imperturbable" one; and Kitchener, "the organizer of victory."

But as the "short-war illusion" proved to be just that, more concrete measures were required to rally the home front behind the war effort and to explain as well as to justify the horrendous slaughter. These primarily took three major forms: the formulation of war aims to give the suffering masses something to fight for; "war socialism" to create the impression that all classes were suffering equally; and finally "information," better propaganda, to explain the need to press on to victory. The longer the war lasted, the greater became the need to manipulate the feelings (and hatreds) of the home front.

The British, with an empire that included some 50 million Africans and 250 million Indians as well as the Dominions, could not easily justify demands for more territory, and hence early in the war, the restoration of Belgium became the great moral issue behind which to rally the public. But as the nation's manpower was drained off to fight in France, there developed the need for some material gains. In time, war aims included some of Germany's African colonies, its fleet, and much of the oil-rich Ottoman Empire. The most boisterous imperialists in London even sought to realize the great dream of a Southern British World that ran from Cape Town through Cairo, across Asia Minor to Baghdad and Calcutta, and finally across the South Seas to Sydney and Wellington.⁴

France, of course, demanded the return of Alsace-Lorraine. General Joffre informed President Poincaré that he would insist on annexation of the German coal-rich Saar basin, a demand in which he was enthusiastically joined by Robert Pinot, head of the *Comité des Forges*. He also coveted French bridgeheads over the Rhine River at Strassburg and Gemersheim, which the historians Aulard, Lavisse, and Sagnac seconded, and the creation of three or four satellite states on the left bank of the Rhine. Former Foreign Minister Théophile Delcassé concurred, adding his demands that Denmark be given northern Schleswig and England her former province of Hanover. Poincaré in 1917 demanded nothing less than the dismemberment of Bismarck's empire when he suggested to the Austrians through Prince Sixtus of Parma that they take Silesia and Bavaria in return for supporting France's "just demand" for Alsace-Lorraine. Belgium would be restored to her former independence—provided there was no chance for French gains here.

The Russians, not to be outdone, signed a secret accord with Premier Aristide Briand on March 10, 1917, in which, in return for supporting French claims to Alsace-Lorraine and to the left bank of the Rhine, they would be aggrandized at Constantinople and in Poland. Hereafter, the Russians set their sights on the northern Turkish provinces of Erzerum, Trebizond, and Ardahan. In Italy, Prime Minister Antonio Salandra spoke of the nation's *sacro egoismo*, which, in the secret Treaty of London on April 26, 1915, he quickly translated into all of Cisalpine Tyrol, Trieste, and Dalmatia (*terre irredente*) in return for a declaration of war against Vienna. And when the Boselli Cabinet joined the war against Germany in 1916, Italy staked a claim to parts of Asia Minor and Africa. Well might Italian leaders have remembered Bismarck's caustic barb half a century earlier that Italy always had a ravenous appetite but, unfortunately, very rotten teeth. Serbia and Montenegro both harbored "Greater Serbia" aspirations. And finally, on the Entente side, Rumania coveted Austrian Transylvania, while Eleutherios Venizelos hoped to realize his dream of a "Greater Greece" by tying his nation's future to that of the Entente.

To confuse matters even more, in January 1916 the British and French negotiators Mark Sykes and Georges Picot signed an accord whereby Syria fell to France and Mesopotamia to Britain; in March, this pact was expanded to grant Russia Turkish Armenia. Almost concurrently, a British agent, Sir Henry McMahon, promised the Arab lands of the Ottoman Empire to Husain, sharif of Mecca. And while Sir Edward Grey and Sir Herbert Samuel gave the Cabinet's approval to this undertaking, on November 8, 1917, the new foreign secretary, Arthur James Balfour, recognized Palestine as "a national home" for the Jewish people, whose support he desired both in Europe and in the United States. It would take the great *arbiter mundi* from Washington, Woodrow Wilson, eventually to sort out and to reject most of these nefarious transactions. In the meantime, poet J. C. Squire hinted at the magnitude of the task awaiting even Him:

God heard the embattled nations sing and shout:
"Gott strafe England"—"God save the King"—
"God this"—"God that"—and "God the other thing!"
"My God," said God, "I've got my work cut out."[5]

With regard to the Central Powers, Austria-Hungary simply hoped to maintain its prewar status and to crush Serbia. Far off in the distance loomed a desire to control the grain and oil reserves of Rumania and to acquire Poland as a Habsburg satellite state. Bulgaria joined the Berlin-Vienna camp primarily in order to seize Greek Macedonia, while the Turks coveted Cyprus, Russian Armenia, Georgia, the Caucasus, Egypt, and Mesopotamia, without ever quite resolving the fact that Pan-German and Pan-Turanian ambitions in southern Russia were clearly irreconcilable.

Indeed, Germany between 1914 and 1918 worked out by far the most comprehensive and far-reaching

war aims program. Although widely known as the "September Program" of Chancellor von Bethmann Hollweg and his *intimus*, Kurt Riezler, German war aims in fact were the product of a much wider circle: Generals von Hindenburg and Ludendorff, Admirals von Tirpitz and von Holtzendorff, and Foreign Secretaries Arthur Zimmermann and Richard von Kühlmann. To them add the various pressure groups, such as the Colonial, Navy, and Pan-German leagues, as well as such leading industrialists as Krupp, Thyssen, and Stinnes. At the heart of their program lay the establishment of German hegemony over *Mitteleuropa* from Flanders to the Porte and from Belgium to Persia.

Specifically, Germany sought to annex outright Longwy-Briey, Belfort, and the French Channel coast from Dunkirk to Boulogne; Liège and Verviers in Belgium; Luxembourg; and Estonia, Latvia, Lithuania, and additional parts of Poland in the east. Belgium, the Netherlands, Scandinavia, and the remainder of Poland would come under Berlin's control, while Russia would be reduced to pre-Petrine Muscovy through the loss of Finland, the Ukraine, Georgia, and the Caucasus. A German colonial empire in central Africa would be established from the Atlantic to the Indian oceans by acquiring the Belgian Congo, French Equatorial Africa to Lake Chad, Togo and Dahomey, North Senegal, and Gambia. Austria-Hungary and Bulgaria would remain subservient allies, Rumania would become the great purveyor of grains and oil, and Turkey would fall under direct German economic and military influence. Obviously, total victory alone could realize these utopian dreams of a "bastion Central Europe," augmented by an African reservoir of raw materials.[6]

But the war cost money, lots of money. And the deprivations of the home front in time became more than discomforting. Whereas the Franco-Prussian War of 1870/71 had cost 7 million Mark per day, the Great War in 1914 cost 36 million and in 1917 a whopping 146 million Mark per day. Britain managed for the first two years of the war to keep the Entente afloat only by substantial loans: Russia received £586 million, France £434 million, and Italy £412 million—much of it covered in the end by borrowing £1 billion from the United States. It is estimated that Italy in 1916-18 spent 148 billion lire for the war effort, twice the total of all government expenditures between 1861 and 1913.

Nowhere were taxes sufficiently raised to cover even a fraction of these horrendous outlays. After all, the vanquished would be forced to pay the costs of the war. In Germany, direct income tax was barred from the federal domain, and huge loans were raised instead for future generations to pay off. In Britain, income taxes were increased to the point where, by 1917 and 1918, they accounted for about 25 percent of government revenue. In Russia, an income tax as well as an excess profits tax were introduced in 1916; combined, however, they brought in only 190 million rubles, enough to run the war for about two days. And even in the United States, where the Treasury Department raised $8 billion for the war effort, Secretary MacAdoo had to float vast loans to finance two-thirds of the cost of the war in Europe.

Even worse, and irreplaceable, was the staggering cost in human lives. Early in 1917, France had sustained 2.6 million casualties, Russia 5.8 million, Britain about 1 million, and Italy 877,000. A combination of combat, disease, starvation, and migration shrank the population of Serbia in hideous fashion. Proportionately, the tiny country lost more of its population than did any other belligerent. And the few statesmen, such as Prince Max von Baden in Germany, Lord Lansdowne in England, Joseph Caillaux in France, and Giovanni Giolitti in Italy, who appreciated that this "European civil war" would spell equal ruination for all participants, regardless of who "won" or who "lost," were denounced as defeatists, slackers, or enemy agents. Obviously, what was needed was a greater war effort on the part of the home front so that the armies could finally score the oft-promised breakthrough that would bring rich rewards in terms of additional real estate and gold, euphemistically referred to as "reparations."

"War socialism" came about as a direct result of the hideous cost of the conflagration, both in terms of manpower and matériel. Most leaders realized at least by early 1915 that the war would become, as Field Marshal Helmuth von Moltke "the Elder" had predicted in the 1890s, a struggle of peoples that might last seven years or longer. The ever-increasing reliance on industry to turn out the weapons of war brought with it the mounting importance of the very class that most ruling elites had for decades sought to exclude from the political process and to keep at the bottom of the economic ladder. Their demands for a greater share of the nation's wealth could not be denied, especially in times of national crisis.

Germany took the lead toward war socialism, in part because the strangling effects of the British naval blockade forced it to innovate and to compensate for lost imports. It has become fashionable among some historians to reject the view that the Central Powers faced starvation by the middle of the war and to argue instead that only mismanagement kept the home populace from having ample food, as production continued at prewar levels. Such speculation should best be left at historical conferences. The reality is that early in the war especially Germany

and Austria faced widespread hunger. German agricultural production between 1914 and 1917 fell 50 to 70 percent, that of Russia about 50 percent, and that of France 30 to 50 percent. Already in 1914, the Germans had issued ration cards, produced a special "K" bread from potato meal, and reduced the available quantity of fats in the diet as these were urgently needed to produce glycerine. Eventually, meat, bread, and potatoes were all rationed. A special Exports and Exemptions Office was established to enhance the flow of food and to allocate labor where it was most needed. Soaring food prices prompted farmers to slaughter their herds in order to realize maximum profits. Under Secretary of the Interior Clemens von Delbrück, an Imperial Potato Office was set up in October 1915, followed by the establishment of a national food regulatory agency under Georg Michaelis. A Wheat Corporation was also created to regulate the planting, harvesting, importing, and distribution of cereal crops, all to little avail. The terrible "turnip winter" of 1916 was followed by another bad harvest in 1917, with the result that family potato rations were reduced to seven pounds per week, meat to 250 grams per day and fat to 100 grams per day. For lack of cotton, cloth was made from paper and nettle fiber, and nearly 50 million shoes were fitted with wooden rather than with leather soles. Nor did the great hopes of 1918 for food from the "bread baskets" of the Ukraine and Rumania ever come to fruition.

Austria was perhaps even worse off. The fertile plains of Hungary continued to produce ample food, but Prime Minister Tisza jealously guarded available supplies and parsimoniously doled them out to the Austrian half of the monarchy. Within the first two years of the war, the production of cereal crops fell by half in Austria; as early as 1915, the major cities faced severe food shortages—made even more acute by the Russian invasion of the agricultural province of Galicia. Industrial workers early in January 1918 saw their daily ration of bread reduced first to 200 and then to 165 grams per day, which precipitated a wave of protest strikes.

In Russia, there were combined problems of supply, transportation, and distribution. Food riots played a substantial part in all the unrest between March and November 1917. Central Russia and Moscow received less than a third of the food required, and Petrograd only 500,000 of the 4 million poods of grain that it needed. At the same time, prices soared. Rye rose in Moscow 333 percent between 1914 and 1917, and 666 percent in the autumn of 1917. Only Great Britain, which continued its maritime supremacy, escaped the ravages of hunger. Imports of Canadian, Australian, and American grains, coupled with the cultivation of previously unused land, more than made up for the food lost on freighters destroyed by German U-boats; in fact, the island's daily needs of 15,000 tons of cereals could be delivered by four ships, and not even the supply of oats for racehorses was ever jeopardized.

Front-line troops in Austria-Hungary by 1917 were reduced to one ounce of meat per day, compared, at least in theory, with six ounces for the German army and twenty-four ounces for American doughboys. The Habsburg quartermaster general advised the troops that worms in meat, although admittedly not very appetizing, were not dangerous. In the German navy, sailors were served a nauseous concoction known as *Drahtverhau*: 75 percent water, 10 percent sausage, 3 percent potatoes, 2 percent peas, 1 percent yellow turnips, and small amounts of beef, fat, and vinegar. The Russian army late in 1916 ran out of bread altogether and instead served lentils (*chechevitsa*), widely reputed to have been a major cause of the revolution. The French, for their part, had to make do with stringy, greasy pressed beef (*singe*, or "monkey"), rubbery macaroni, cold salted fish, and a rough red wine (*le pinard*). The entire food supply system broke down in December 1915, and a subsequent committee of inquiry found that nearly half of the 300,000 field kitchens were unserviceable. And when the army's propaganda section informed the home population that the men in the trenches received two good hot meals per day, it was flooded with 200,000 letters of protest from enraged *poilus*.[7]

The other side of the coin of war socialism was enhanced production of war goods. Especially in Germany, there developed immediately a critical shortage of labor as mobilization removed 3 million men from the labor force. At first, Walther Rathenau oversaw the deportation of thousands of skilled Belgian workers to the industrial Ruhr basin in Germany, but this proved to be a one-time shot in the arm. In October 1916, General Groener was appointed head of a special War Office that was to realize mammoth armaments production increases (Hindenburg program) and the recently enacted Auxiliary Service Law. The Hindenburg program called for the supply of munitions to be doubled and the supply of machine guns and artillery to be tripled by the spring of 1917; powder output likewise was to be doubled to 12,000 tons per month and steel to 10,000 tons per month. A special Weapons and Munitions Procurement Office was created to oversee the mechanics of the program, and industrialists promised their full cooperation—provided the army could solve the acute labor shortage. The latter was partly accomplished by combing prisoner-of-war camps

and by raiding naval yards for skilled workers. And money proved to be no obstacle. Secretary of the Treasury Karl Helfferich, known as the "financial Ludendorff," simply let it be known that he intended to present Germany's enemies "at the conclusion of peace with the bill for this war that has been forced upon us."[8] The Auxiliary Service Law, on the other hand, theoretically made all Germans between the ages of sixteen and fifty-one eligible for some sort of war service. While General Groener hoped that this would make available about 200,000 additional workers, only 60,000 persons, most of them women, volunteered by April 1917, with the result that the law had to be made mandatory. However, exemptions were established for agricultural laborers, the medical professions, church personnel, and public transport workers, with the result that the law never fulfilled the hopes of its promulgators.

Germany's failure to tap the female labor supply stood in stark contrast to British endeavors. In the United Kingdom, nearly 500,000 women went to work as clerical help in the private sector, 225,000 worked on the land, and 200,000 entered government service. By far the greatest impact, both in the short and in the long run, came with the 800,000 females recruited by the engineering shops; they took well-paying jobs formerly reserved for male workers, and after the war, many of them were reluctant to abandon their lucrative trades for the home. And for the privileged, this exodus of women into the labor market spelled the loss of about 400,000 domestic servants. After all, war socialism implied equal burdens for all in this time of national emergency.

French women likewise worked in streetcars, buses, and armament factories; some even directed the small factories of their absent husbands. The millions of women who had husbands at the front for the first time in French history experienced the heady wine of financial independence as the government gave each soldier's wife one franc twenty-five centimes per day for herself and fifty centimes for each child. With regard to the men, it proved utterly demoralizing for the ordinary soldier receiving twenty-five centimes per day for his travails in the trenches to come home on leave and to see his former colleagues now working in armament plants for ten or fifteen francs per day. The gulf between the front and the rear widened with each year of the war.

Imperial Russia's efforts to arrive at "war socialism" proved to be more modest, as fully a third of her shells and guns continued to be delivered by foreigners. It was only during the great "shell crisis," early in 1915, that efforts were undertaken to streamline the production and supply of munitions. In May, a Special Council for Examination and Harmonization of Measures required for the Defence of the Country was established; its efforts proved to be as cumbersome as its title. Above all, the great industrial magnates of Petrograd (Putilov, Vyshnegradsky, Meshchersky, Plotnikov, and Davydov) refused to pass lucrative government contracts on to their counterparts in Moscow (Riabushinsky, Guchkov, Tretiakov, Poliakov, and Tereshchenko); this, in turn, prompted the Moscow industrial barons to undermine the efforts of the Special Council from within. It is estimated that the Special Council nevertheless spent 15 billion rubles on armaments, about a third of all government spending. This represented more direct government assistance between 1914 and 1917 than private industry had received in the whole of the nineteenth century! Lesser businessmen attempted to gain their share of war production through War Industries Committees, but the great captains of industry eventually brushed them aside.[9]

These incredible jumps in industrial production in the various nations at war fostered the emergence of *nouveaux riches*, variously called speculators, *pescecani* (sharks), and *Kriegsgewinnler* (war profiteers). During the first six months of the Hindenburg program alone, profits for German industrialists rose 10 billion Mark. Anglo-Persian Oil, which showed a deficit of £27,000 in 1914, three years later claimed profits of £344,000. In the United States, Washington Iron and Steel's profits tripled to nearly $2 billion, as did those of General Motors by 1917 to $11 billion. Krupp, Vickers, Zakharoff, and Schneider-Creusot, the renowned "merchants of death," found the actual business of slaughter to be much more profitable than that of simply preparing for it, as they now received lucrative and monopolistic government contracts at inflated prices. In Russia, where accurate figures are hard to come by, it is indicative that the great Putilov works in Petrograd in 1915 received an order for 113.25 million rubles worth of shells at a unit cost of 33.70 rubles, which gave a tidy return of 5.70 rubles per shell—just about the standard price of a shell manufactured by the state factories. Nor did Russian landlords (*pomeshchiki*) find it at all unrewarding to use tens of thousands of Austro-Hungarian prisoners of war of Slavic origins to till their fields.

The European middle class did not, in contrast to earlier wars and revolutions, greatly profit from the war. In fact, white-collar workers, civil servants, landlords, pensioners, and annuity holders joined in penury the unemployed army of journalists, actors, and publicists—the celebrated "crowd" in the revolutions of 1830 and 1848. As Karl Kautsky and Eduard Bernstein in Germany had foreseen, the great capitalist middle class was now "proletarianized by

parsimony." Of course, what these German Socialists could not foresee was that this middle-class army of the uprooted and impoverished would hereafter turn to right-wing extremism, be it fascism, National Socialism, or the *Croix de Feu*.

That brings us to the third great development of this war, namely, "information," as the British preferred to call it. In Prussia/Germany, the deputy commanding generals in the twenty-odd army corps districts were given sweeping powers by virtue of the Law of Siege in August 1914 to censor the press and the mail; they were officially responsible for their actions only "to God." In Austria-Hungary, the Army Supreme Command directly oversaw censorship, and special military tribunals were established to deal with all sorts of political offenses that fell under the general rubric of "national security." The suspension of the Austrian parliament (Reichsrat) for the duration of the war effectively removed the most reliable brake on the domestic power of the military. Only the emperor stood between his people and the army. In September 1915, for example, Francis Joseph refused to permit Conrad von Hötzendorf to enlarge the powers of the War Supervisory Office, created in August 1914 to deal with political agitation and domestic discontent.[10]

Initially, the military censors also attempted to shape the information received by the various nationalities in occupied territories. When the Germans in November 1916 promised to create an independent Congress Poland after the war, they also took care to rally the Polish people to their cause by publishing a special Polish-language newspaper, *Glos Stolicy*, in Warsaw. Flemish separatism, strongest at the University of Ghent, was aided by such German-sponsored papers as the *Gazet van Brussel* and the *Antwerpsche Tydingen*. French subjects in the occupied lands were served by *La Gazette des Ardennes*, while the government in Paris countered by smuggling *Die Feldpost* into German Alsace. And while the Germans conveniently failed to inform their citizens of the brutal execution of Nurse Edith Cavell on charges of espionage, the French somehow failed to report the bombing of Karlsruhe on June 26, 1916, which claimed the lives of twenty-six women and 124 children.

Much was also made of the possibility of arousing the enemy's dissident ethnic minorities, but there was to be only one national rebellion anywhere in Europe. On Easter Sunday 1916, Irish rebels seized the General Post Office in Dublin and declared their independence. And while this action greatly undermined England's claims that it was fighting this war for the independence of Belgium and the freedom of all humanity, it never enjoyed the support of Germany. Few German arms and no German soldiers

THE HOME FRONT 51

were landed in Ireland. When Sir Roger Casement was placed ashore from a German U-boat on Easter Sunday, it was with a plea to call off the planned revolt because support was lacking. It remained for President Wilson to proclaim the "liberation" of ethnic groups, but only in vanquished Central Europe.

Of far greater importance than these primitive attempts at controlling the thoughts of mankind was the establishment in Great Britain on February 10, 1918, of a Ministry of Information. Here was the forerunner of more ominous developments within the next generation. Under the leadership of William A. Aitken, Lord Beaverbrook, this "popular arm of diplomacy" became the model for future ministries of propaganda. War artists and photographers were commissioned to display their works around the country. The first war films were made to cheer the home populace. Overseas press bureaus rallied non-Europeans behind the Allied cause; one department within the ministry, under Rudyard Kipling, was entrusted with making the war popular to Americans. Beaverbrook eventually called in Alfred Harmsworth, Viscount Northcliffe, to augment his nascent efforts, and "King Alfred" of Fleet Street suspended his attacks on Prime Minister Lloyd George long enough to become director of enemy propaganda. At Crewe House, Northcliffe provided a luxurious setting for the heroic efforts of H. G. Wells and Wickham Steed against "the Huns."

The Germans, for their part, never quite managed to mount a skillful propaganda offensive, either at home or abroad. Count Johann von Bernstorff, the ambassador to Washington, often lamented the clumsiness of the German effort vis-à-vis the more glib British approach to wooing American sympathy. Nor was the German cause aided in January 1917 by the British and American interception of a cable to Bernstorff from Foreign Secretary Arthur Zimmermann, offering Mexico an alliance against the United States in return for "the lost territory in Texas, New Mexico, and Arizona."[11]

At home, "patriotic instruction" (*Vaterländischer Unterricht*) was only slightly more successful. In December 1917, in the wake of the fleet rebellion of that summer, Major Walter Nicolai and General Ludendorff sought to rally the home front as well as the fighting troops to the cause of a victorious peace with vast annexations and indemnities. Newspapers, brochures, books, films, wall posters, and public rallies were organized to popularize the war effort; pastors and professors were especially recruited to explain the need to press on to victory. At the front and on the fleet, hikes, games, sports, and theater visits were to be arranged in order to reduce the social chasm that separated ratings and enlisted men from officers.[12] In the end, it came to little. And it remained a far cry from the cynically brilliant efforts a generation later of a volunteer of 1914, rejected because of a foot deformity, Joseph Goebbels.

Finally, where was the spirit of the Prince of Peace? It still staggers the imagination that 10 million human lives could have been systematically and callously wasted before anyone seriously undertook something to end the war. And then it came only in Russia, where nearly a third of all casualties had occurred. In the main, millions of men endured the torrid heat and biting cold, the choking dust and driving rain, frostbite and gangrene, rats and lice, as though it had all somehow become natural. God's ministers, whether Catholic or Protestant, Orthodox or Moslem, praised the weapons of war and their executors. Statistics took on a numbing effect: the thousands who died each day in time were subsumed in the tables produced everywhere to show that victory was just ahead. In the madness of the Great War, it almost became a duty to die.

To be sure, there were a few signs of disillusionment. Some ethnic regiments in the Habsburg army had deserted as early as 1915, and numerous riots plagued the Russian army by the fall of 1916. But with the brief though notable rebellion in the French army in April/May 1917, the fronts by and large held beyond all expectations. Naval rebellions occurred in the German fleet at Wilhelmshaven in the summer of 1917 and in the Austro-Hungarian fleet at Cattaro in February 1918, but these were caused primarily by service inequities and by boredom, rather than by organized political protest. By the same token, the home fronts also held up well. Riots, such as those in Turin in the summer of 1917 or in Berlin, Vienna, and Budapest early in 1918, again were prompted mainly by a lack of food. Even the coal miners' strikes in southern Wales in July 1915 owed their origins not to the ravages of war but rather to closed-shop regulations. Nowhere was the outcry against the war sufficient to put a halt to the carnage.

European Socialists were perhaps most disappointed and confused by the willingness of their peoples to go to war. The International Socialist Bureau in July 1914 had refused to believe war was imminent, and the tragic death of Jean Jaurès deprived it of leadership and direction. Ramsay MacDonald could only think of "those poor German socialists" as the kaiser's armies marched through Belgium. In fact, "those poor German socialists" had closed ranks on August 4, 1914, to vote for war credits. Only at Easter 1917, after the dreadful "turnip winter," did a rival faction around Hugo Haase and Georg Ledebour break off from the Social

Democrats of Friedrich Ebert and Philipp Scheidemann to form the Independent Social Democratic party and demand an end to the war without annexations or indemnities.

International groups of Socialist women and youths met at Berne to discuss the war, and in September 1915, nearly forty European Socialists convened at Zimmerwald to denounce it. A subsequent meeting at Kienthal in 1916 passed trenchant resolutions against war once more, but a follow-up conference scheduled for Stockholm never materialized. Nor did individual peace efforts fare better. Late in 1916, the German government launched its "peace" initiative, but without taking a stand on the vital issue of Belgium's future, which effectively sabotaged the effort. President Wilson in December 1916 politely suggested "an interchange of views" among the belligerents, but especially France and Britain ridiculed the offer. Aleksandr Kerensky in Russia talked loudly of the need for a general European peace in the spring of 1917; yet at the same time, he mounted a final effort to win the war by a massive assault in Galicia. Concurrently, Emperor Charles in Vienna launched his clumsy attempt to approach France for a separate peace through his wife's brothers, the Princes Sixtus and Xavier of Parma, both officers in the Belgian army, suggesting an end to the war by honoring France's claim to Alsace-Lorraine; one wonders to what degree the French suggestion that Charles, in return, make off with German Silesia and Bavaria spurred him on. And on July 19, 1917, the German Reichstag quite heroically passed a "peace resolution" calling for an end to the war without annexations or indemnities. Unfortunately, this lost much of its impact when the army's new chancellor, Georg Michaelis, accepted it only after adding the caveat, "as I understand it."[13]

Perhaps the single most promising effort was that made public on August 15, 1917, by Pope Benedict XV. Overcoming his personal pro-Austrian sympathies, the pontiff denounced the "useless carnage" on all fronts, and called instead for a "white peace" on the basis of the status quo ante bellum. The Vatican's peace initiative received only lukewarm support in Berlin, Vienna, Paris, and London; the Russians were in turmoil in the wake of the failure of the grand offensive in Galicia, and America was pursuing its own peace plan. The Italians were greatly embarrassed by it, as Prime Minister Salandra had insisted on a provision in the Treaty of London declaring that the pope be barred from any future peace conference.[14]

V. I. Lenin's Decree on Peace in November 1917 forced the Allied and Associated Powers to renew the moral offensive on behalf of peace. President Wilson on February 8, 1918, presented Congress with his celebrated Fourteen Points, hoping to make these the basis for the universal peace that he sought to impose upon "decadent" Old Europe. At that, it did not augur well for the American leader's cause that French Premier Clemenceau proudly let it be known that he had never read the Fourteen Points. Ironically, when peace finally came in November 1918, it was accompanied by a great influenza epidemic that in the lands between England and India claimed more dead than had La Grande Guerre.

The war proved to be a milestone not only in the lemming-like destruction of mankind, but also in the daily habits of all Europeans. A. J. P. Taylor has masterfully shown how the twentieth century rudely awoke England in 1914-18. Before the war, there had been no restrictions on travel, no passports, no identity cards, and no military draft for affluent, law abiding Englishmen or even foreign residents. One could pass through life fairly unfettered by government regulations. When such existed, they generally were beneficial, regulating the quality of food, providing education for children up to the age of thirteen, and pensions for the needy over the age of seventy. Taxation was hardly burdensome, bringing in less than 10 percent of the national income.

By 1918, on the other hand, the government had fully intruded into the daily regimen of its citizens. Conscription, initiated in the spring of 1916, called 5 million men into the armed services. Trains were run by the government, and shipping insurance rates were fixed by it. An act of Parliament added an extra hour to the day during summertime (Daily Savings). Hours and conditions of work were prescribed by the government, as were wages. Bread was altered by the addition of rye, maize and even potato meal to wheat, and by late 1918 it was temporarily rationed. News was controlled by the bureaucrats. And even the neighborhood pub saw its hours of operation rigorously defined, and its beer watered down.[15] All in all, personal freedom was somehow subordinated to that mythical entity, the "general welfare," never to return in undiluted form.

In the final analysis, the Great War proved to be the "Great Folly" of the conservative ruling elites of Europe. As Allan Wildman has cogently argued, "the effort that demanded maximum mobilization of public opinion and technical and industrial resources rendered them particularly vulnerable to revolutionary liquidation as a byproduct of protracted war."[16] The conservative monarchies of Austria-Hungary, Germany, and Russia proved to be most vulnerable of all.

6

THE
PEACE

On April 28, 1919, a special train carrying 160 passengers left Berlin bound for Versailles, where only half a century earlier, the German Empire had been proclaimed. The train passed through the snow, sleet, and hoarfrost of the Rhineland and Belgium into northern France. The French intentionally slowed the train down for the greater part of the day so that its occupants could more fully view the desolate landscape. Ruined villages and bomb craters abounded. Cleanup detachments stood in stony silence as the cars rolled by. Emergency bridges spanned rivers where there had once been permanent edifices. Burned sheds, exploded munitions trains and charred ruins were omnipresent. Columns of German prisoners of war waved at the train. When it arrived at Versailles the next day, the German peace delegation on board was received with icy formality. Its luggage was rudely dumped onto the station platform. Finally, the Germans were driven to the Hôtel des Réservoirs. Wooden board fences eventually were constructed, ostensibly to protect the Germans from the crowds; in reality, to keep them isolated from the various foreign representatives.[1]

Count Ulrich von Brockdorff-Rantzau headed the German peace delegation. A *grand seigneur* of a seven-hundred-year-old Holstein family, the German minister of foreign affairs boasted ancestors who had served the kings of France and Denmark. At Versailles, when asked by a French officer whether it was true, as rumor had it, that one of his ancestors, Count Josias Rantzau, Marshal of France, was indeed the father of Louis XIV, Brockdorff-Rantzau coldly replied: "Oh yes, in my family the Bourbons have been considered bastard Rantzaus for the past three hundred years!"[2] The German diplomat was aloof, at times arrogant. But he was also egalitarian, despising most politicians and generals alike. Later at Moscow, he managed to charm G. V. Chicherin. His biting wit often offended, yet at other times he could be gentle and understanding—especially after a generous helping of champagne or, better yet, his favorite cognac.

At Versailles, he was determined not to play the role which he believed the French had designated for him on the *banc des accusés*.

On May 7, 1919, Premier Clemenceau, the "tiger" of Lorraine who had never forgotten boyhood memories of the Prussian occupation of 1870/71, opened the first and only meeting between Allied and German plenipotentiaries at Marie Antoinette's Trianon palace. *Le Tigre* read the draft of the proposed treaty to the German delegates in short, staccato sentences, wearing throughout the session his formal gray gloves. The speech was delivered in haughty disdain. Clemenceau's inexorable words, "L'heure du lourd des comptes est venue" ("The time has come for a complete reckoning of accounts"), at last brought the Germans face to face with reality; whatever illusions they had nurtured over the past five months that the peace would be on the basis of President Wilson's Fourteen Points—Clemenceau sarcastically had noted that the Lord God had been content with only ten—were now ripped away.

Brockdorff-Rantzau countered with his own prepared speech, studiously refusing to rise to his feet to address the august assembly. He refuted especially the "war guilt" clause of the treaty and fully recognized the course of events to come. "We know the intensity of the hatred which meets us, and we have heard the victors' passionate demand that as the vanquished we shall be made to pay, and as the guilty we shall be punished." Clemenceau's face became red with anger. Wilson listened in stoic silence. Lloyd George laughed. Bonar Law yawned. A German delegate, Walter Simons, termed the proposed treaty "a monument of pathological fear and pathological hatred." He was right on both counts. Brockdorff-Rantzau, perhaps imitating Bismarck at the Frankfurt Diet sixty years earlier, lit a cigarette at the end of the session as a final gesture of disdain. President Wilson, back in December 1918 on board the *George Washington* on his way to France to rearrange European affairs, in a candid moment had confided to a friend, "The picture that keeps coming before me—I hope with all my heart that it is a mistaken foreboding—is of a tragedy of disappointments."[3] The session of May 7, 1919, fully justified his earlier forebodings.

The Allied and Associated Powers were painfully aware that the peace they were about to forge would be most closely compared to that concocted a hundred years ago at Vienna; they even printed accounts of the Congress of Vienna to remind the delegates of this historic parallel. Only in one respect were their hopes fulfilled: as at Vienna, where the "Big Four" consisting of Metternich, Talleyrand, Castlereagh, and Alexander I had decided all substantial issues in closed session among themselves, so at Versailles the major decisions were hammered out by another "Big Four," this time composed of Wilson, Clemenceau, Lloyd George, and, to a lesser extent, Vittorio Orlando of Italy. Therewith the similarity ended. At Vienna, all major European powers had been represented; at Paris, Soviet Russia was glaringly absent. At Vienna, Talleyrand of defeated France had not only been allowed to move about freely, but had even helped to fashion the final draft of the treaty; at Paris, the Germans were kept behind fences and denied any influence on, or even knowledge of, the final accord. The decisions reached at Vienna remained in effect for about half a century, those at Paris less than a generation—in one case, less than three years. Not even the desire of the victors to lump the various settlements with the Central Powers into one grand "Peace of Paris" could be realized. Interminable interallied wranglings over scraps of barren real estate as well as swift political and social changes occurring in central and eastern Europe forced the victors to conclude their peace pacts with the vanquished in a series of separate accords that stretched out for more than a year.

The settlement with Hungary, long delayed by Béla Kun's Communist takeover in Budapest, was signed on June 4, 1920, at Trianon. It proved to be the harshest of all, liquidating the ancient historic state of Hungary. The country was reduced to one-third of its former size and population, losing land and subjects to Austria, Poland, Rumania, Czechoslovakia, Yugoslavia, and Italy. Its army was restricted to a militia of 35,000 men, and it was enjoined to pay war reparations, the amount to be determined at a later date. Most galling of all was the loss of the ancient capital, Pressburg or Poszony, now Bratislava, to the new state of Czechoslovakia. It is not far off the mark to state that Hungarians of all political persuasions were determined to revise the treaty at the first opportune moment.[4]

In terms of lands lost, Turkey was dealt the most severe blow in the Treaty of Sèvres. Signed on August 10, 1920, but revised only three years later on July 24 at Lausanne owing to the efforts of Mustafa Kemal, it cost Turkey her former provinces of Syria, Palestine, and Mesopotamia as well as her claims to Egypt, the Sudan, Libya, Morocco, and Tunis. The Dardanelles were to be internationalized and demilitarized, and the Turkish army was reduced to 50,000 men. Once again reverting to an onerous practice of the preceding century, the Allies placed Ottoman finances under an international financial control commission, this time made up of Britain, France and Italy.[5]

Bulgaria signed the peace at Neuilly on November 27, 1919. Similar to the accord with Austria, the Treaty of Neuilly reduced Bulgaria to its prewar size, with the notable exception of western Thrace, which was handed to Greece, and some minor border adjustments in favor of Yugoslavia. Bulgaria's army was scaled down to 33,000 men, quite insufficient to maintain order in this Balkan political hotbed. It was to pay reparations amounting to £90 million—the only time the Allies from the outset set a firm figure upon such payments.

The Allied and Associated Powers refused to recognize the Austrian Republic as a new state, and hence applied many of the terms of the German settlement in the Treaty of St. Germain, signed by Austria on September 10, 1919. Article 88 of the accord barred the desired union with the new German Republic, while Article 77 made Austria responsible for the war and saddled it with reparations, again unspecified as to final amount. The armed forces were reduced to 30,000 men, and the fleet, at first handed over to the Yugoslavs, was parceled out among the victors. Austria was reduced in size to about two-thirds of its former German territories, losing 3.5 million people to Czechoslovakia and, most odious to this day, 250,000 in South Tyrol to Italy.[6]

The most important treaty, of course, was that signed with Germany on June 28, 1919, in the Hall of Mirrors at Versailles. Clemenceau in fact referred to the accord of 1919 as "the second treaty of Versailles," thereby adding insult to injury. The first part of the Treaty of Versailles dealt with the Covenant of the League of Nations. Article 22 established "mandates" under the League to cloak the Allies' seizure of Germany's erstwhile colonies (Article 119). The second part dealt with territorial losses to be incurred by Germany. Alsace and Lorraine were returned to France, which thereby gained 2 million subjects and valuable mineral deposits (Articles

51-79). France was also given the right to exploit the coal mines of the Saar for fifteen years (Articles 45-50). The left bank of the Rhine was to be demilitarized (Articles 42-43) and occupied by the Allies for fifteen years. Belgium received Moresnet, Eupen and Malmédy (Articles 32-34), and Denmark northern Schleswig (Articles 109-114). In the east, Germany lost West Prussia and Posen to Poland (Article 87), thereby separating East Prussia from the rest of Germany as in pre-Frederican times. Danzig became a free city under the League (Articles 100-108), while Memel was eventually ceded to Lithuania (Article 99). Upper Silesia, even though it voted to remain with the Reich, later was handed to Poland (Article 88). In all, Germany lost 6 million citizens and about 13 percent of its former territory. Much more serious was the economic loss: 65 percent of its iron ore, 45 percent of its coal, 57 percent of its lead, and 72 percent of its zinc.

Articles 159 through 213 composed the military part of the treaty. The German army was to be reduced to 100,000 men, conscription was forbidden, the General Staff abolished; the navy was to maintain only six elderly battleships and to build no new vessels over 10,000 tons. Military aircraft, submarines, "tanks," and heavy artillery were proscribed. Articles 228-30 called for the trials of about one hundred so-called war criminals on charges of "acts against the laws and customs of war," whatever those were. Since the British had just conducted an election with the slogan, "Hang the Kaiser!," it is not surprising that the trial of Wilhelm II appeared in Article 227 of the list. However, the Netherlands refused to turn him over to an Allied tribunal. Another "war criminal," Paul von Hindenburg, later became the second president of the Weimar Republic.

The most galling clause of the treaty, and the one most exploited by the enemies of the republic, was that dealing with Germany's alleged "war guilt" (Article 231). The Reich was forced to accept responsibility for "all the loss and damage" caused by the war to all participants; Article 232 forced Berlin to pay all costs incurred by all victors in this war. Jan Smuts of South Africa cleverly included even Allied war pensions in this absurd demand. No final figure was given for reparations, but the French and Belgians suggested something in the neighborhood of $100 billion. Germany was to make an immediate downpayment of $5 billion in gold and kind (coal, livestock, ships, locomotives, timber, and so on). The major German rivers were to be internationalized (Danube, Elbe, Niemen, Oder, and Rhine), as was the Kiel Canal (Article 380). Moreover, the Germans had to renounce their Draconian settlements at Brest-Litovsk and Bucharest.

To the Germans, these conditions were more reminiscent of the Peace of Tilsit imposed by Napoleon in 1807 than of the Congress of Vienna in 1815. On May 12, 1919, the German Constituent Assembly had met to debate the draft treaty in the great aula of the University of Berlin, where a century earlier Johann G. Fichte had delivered his immortal "Addresses to the German Nation" at another time of national crisis. Chancellor Scheidemann of the Social Democrats refused to accept responsibility for the settlement, asking his listeners "what hand would not wither" that delivered future German generations into such bondage? He resigned on June 20. The next day, the German fleet interned at Scapa Flow was scuttled by its crews. A sharp Allied protest note and an ultimatum that the treaty be signed finally spurred the Germans to action. General Groener, once more acting for Hindenburg, who preferred to be absent during great decisions, informed the government that there was no hope of resuming the war. The Constituent Assembly decided on June 22 by a vote of 237 to 138 to accept the terms. Hermann Müller and Hans Bell signed the Treaty of Versailles six days later. Conspicuous by their absence at Versailles that day were Kaiser Wilhelm II, General von Moltke, Admiral von Tirpitz, and Chancellor von Bethmann Hollweg, the architects of July 1914. The new republic was saddled with the odium of the *Diktat* of Versailles from its birth.[7]

How does one evaluate the treaty? Obviously hundreds, if not thousands, of books have been written on the subject, and hence only a cursory assessment can be undertaken here. Clearly, the financial provisions of the settlement were utterly unrealistic, as John M. Keynes showed at the time in his influential book, *The Economic Consequences of the Peace*. The problem was not so much that Germany could not meet the staggering claims of the victors, but that over four years of war it had contracted loans of about 98 billion Gold Mark; these had now to be paid off as well. The Reich shelled out 21.6 billion Gold Mark in reparations payments between 1920 and 1931, substantially less than it received during the same period in loans, primarily from the United States. Moreover, the European Allies had borrowed over $10 billion from the United States, which now demanded repayment. From 1920 until 1932, when all payments virtually ceased, Europe repaid $2.7 billion; the rest is still owed.

The basic problem with the Treaty of Versailles is that it constituted an unhappy compromise between Wilsonian idealism and traditional European power politics. It could hardly have been otherwise, given the makeup of the Big Four. The League of Nations was created without any great enthusiasm for it. Colonies were taken from the vanquished under the guise of "mandates," yet this moral sleight of hand did not obligate the victors to free their subject peoples. Self-determination likewise was applied only in those areas where the losers possessed ethnic minorities before the war: North Schleswig, Allenstein, Marienwerder, the Saar, Upper Silesia, the South Tyrol, and Transylvania; in areas where Germans wanted to join the new republic, South Tyrol and North Bohemia, plebiscites were never permitted. Moreover, the very use of the device, made popular by Napoleon III half a century earlier, was dangerous. Might not the Germans, at a later date and under more favorable circumstances, use this ploy against others? And the promise that the military provisions of the treaty were only the preliminary to universal disarmament, while sounding noble, was never meant to be implemented.

Above all, the treaty humiliated a nation without crippling it militarily or economically. Germany remained the most populous state at the crossroads of eastern and western, northern and southern Europe. The defeats of Germany, Austria-Hungary, and Tsarist Russia had left a power vacuum in central and eastern Europe that France could not, and Britain and the United States would not, fill. And when the U.S. Senate in March 1920 refused to ratify the treaty, the settlement lost much of its substance and backbone. The world's major creditor withdrew into isolation. France lost her desperate quest for *sécurité* as a result; and Britain used the Senate's action to renege on her previous offer of an Anglo-French alliance. Marshal Foch, when apprised of the terms of the Treaty of Versailles, alleged to have said: "This is not a Peace. It is an Armistice for twenty years."[8] French military power alone became the guarantor of the peace.

The spectre of communism promised by Karl Marx finally emerged. Communist takeovers in Hungary under Béla Kun and in Bavaria under Kurt Eisner—as well as Communist uprisings in Berlin and in the Rhineland—greatly troubled the peacemakers at Paris. Might not the defeated of 1918 someday make common cause with the outcast in the east?

In all fairness, the reader needs to be reminded of the Herculean task the men at Paris faced. The borders of the European continent had to be redrawn to the satisfaction of the professor from Princeton. The British refused to hear of the doctrine of the "freedom of the seas." The United States sought repayment of war loans. The Italians demanded fulfillment of the secret Treaty of London. Japan insisted on a formal declaration of racial equality. Husain of Mecca laid claim to a united Arabia, while Zionists called upon Britain to honor the Balfour Declaration concerning a "national home" for the Jewish people. Australia and New Zealand maliciously fought for former German colonies, all the while denouncing European power politics and greed. The recently created states in the east and southeast at once fell out as a pack of thieves over the most miniscule of territories. And all the while, Clemenceau fought to satisfy France's cries of "never again."

Victory is illusion. *La Grande Guerre*, as most other major conflicts, settled little and brought with it a myriad of new problems. Europe had paid a terrible price for its "Great Folly." It had fallen from the banker of the world to its greatest debtor. Millions of human lives had been wasted. Relatively stable empires had yielded to a host of petty, ambitious, and dissatisfied nation states. Nationalism was more virulent than ever. Ethnic hatred flourished. Democracy, imposed upon Europe by the "Great Idealist," suffered a quick death, surviving only a decade in Czechoslovakia. Habsburg, Hohenzollern, and Romanov yielded to Horthy, Hitler, and Lenin. Was the world better off for it? And finally, the "war to end all wars" by 1919 was given a numerical prefix in order not to confuse it with what might come. The eloquent words used by a British historian with regard to another bloody conflict far removed in time readily come to mind.

The war solved no problems. Its effects, both immediate and indirect, were either negative or disastrous. Morally subversive, economically destructive, socially degrading, confused in its causes, devious in its course, futile in its result, it is the outstanding example in European history of meaningless conflict.[9]

NOTES

CHAPTER 1

1. Winston S. Churchill, *The World Crisis: 1911-1914* (New York, 1923), 207; B. Huldermann, *Albert Ballin* (Berlin, 1922), 301-2.

2. Conrad von Hötzendorf, *Aus Meiner Dienstzeit* (Vienna, 1925), III, 604, 670; Hugo Hantsch, *Leopold Graf Berchtold, Grand Seigneur und Staatsmann* (Graz, 1963), II, 506; K. D. Erdmann, ed., *Kurt Riezler: Tagebücher, Aufsätze, Dokumente* (Göttingen, 1972), 182-83.

3. Luigi Albertini, *The Origins of the War of 1914* (London, 1953), II, 134.

4. Fritz Fischer, *Krieg der Illusionen: Die deutsche Politik 1911-14* (Düsseldorf, 1969), 692; Imanuel Geiss, ed., *Juli 1914: Die europäische Krise und der Ausbruch des Ersten Weltkriegs* (Munich, 1965), 52.

5. Geiss, *Juli 1914*, 56-65; Albertini, *Origins of the War of 1914*, II, 165-69.

6. Geiss, *Juli 1914*, 91-94.

7. Albertini, *Origins of the War of 1914*, II, 193.

8. Zara Steiner, *Britain and the Origins of the First World War* (New York, 1977), 221-22.

9. Geiss, *Juli 1914*, 153, 211.

10. Steiner, *Britain and the Origins of the First World War*, 222-24.

11. Albertini, *Origins of the War of 1914*, II, 536-39.

12. Geiss, *Juli 1914*, 215.

13. Albertini, *Origins of the War of 1914*, II, 489; Imanuel Geiss, ed., *Julikrise und Kriegsausbruch 1914* (Hanover, 1964), II, 299.

14. Albertini, *Origins of the War of 1914*, II, 474, 506-7.

15. Geiss, ed., *Julikrise und Kriegsausbruch*, II, 333-34, 373; Volker R. Berghahn, *Germany and the Approach of War in 1914* (New York, 1973), 201.

16. Conrad von Hötzendorf, *Aus Meiner Dienstzeit*, IV, 152ff.; Geiss, *Juli 1914*, 269.

17. Albertini, *Origins of the War of 1914*, II, 569-72.

18. Bernd F. Schulte, "Neue Dokumente zu Kriegsausbruch und Kriegsverlauf 1914," *Militärgeschichtliche Mitteilungen* 1 (1979), 140; Erdmann, ed., *Kurt Riezler*, 185; Geiss, ed., *Julikrise und Kriegsausbruch*, II, document 1000c; J.C.G. Röhl, "Admiral von Müller and the Approach of War, 1911-1914," *The Historical Journal* 12 (1969), 670. These two revealing sentences are not to be found in the carefully edited version of Admiral von Müller's diary by Walter Görlitz, ed., *The Kaiser and His Court: The Diaries, Note Books and Letters of Admiral Georg Alexander von Müller Chief of the Naval Cabinet 1914-1918* (New York, 1964), 10.

19. Elie Halévy, *The Rule of Democracy, 1905-1914* (London, 1961), 438.

20. Steiner, *Britain and the Origins of the First World War*, 233-40, 254; Geiss, *Juli 1914*, 347.

21. Steiner, *Britain and the Origins of the First World War*, 245.

22. Joachim Remak, *The Origins of World War I* (New York, 1967), 148.

23. John Röhl, ed., *1914: Delusion or Design? The Testimony of Two German Diplomats* (London, 1973), 37-39; Norman Stone, "Austria-Hungary and the First Phase of War, 1914" (Paper delivered at the "Potential Enemies" Conference, Harvard University, July 1980).

24. Baron von Schilling, *How the War Began in 1914: Being the Diary of the Russian F.O. from the 3rd to the 20th July 1914* (London, 1925); Conrad von Hötzendorf, *Aus Meiner Dienstzeit 1906-1918*, 5 vols. (Vienna, 1921-25).

25. Fritz Fischer, *Griff nach der Weltmacht: Die Kriegszielpolitik des kaiserlichen Deutschland, 1914-18* (Düsseldorf, 1961), translated into English as *Germany's Aims in the First World War* (New York, 1967); and Fritz Fischer, *Krieg der Illusionen: Die deutsche Politik 1911-14* (Düsseldorf, 1969), translated into English as *War of Illusions: German Policies from 1911 to 1914* (New York, 1975). Imanuel Geiss, ed., *Julikrise und Kriegsausbruch 1914: Eine Dokumentensammlung*, 2 vols. (Hanover, 1963/64), unfortunately never translated but reprinted in a popular paper edition as *Juli 1914*.

26. Röhl, *1914: Delusion or Design?*, 128, 134.

CHAPTER 2

1. Basil Liddell Hart, *The Real War 1914-1918* (Boston, 1930), 42.

2. Zara Steiner, *Britain and the Origins of the First World War* (New York, 1977), 240.

3. Correlli Barnett, *The Swordbearers: Supreme Command in the First World War* (New York, 1964), 26-29.

4. Pierre Renouvin, *La Crise européenne et la Première*

Guerre Mondiale, Peuples et Civilisations XIX (Paris, 1962), 249.

5. Basil Liddell Hart, *Reputations: Ten Years After* (Boston, 1928), 52.

6. A.J.P. Taylor, *English History 1914-1945* (Oxford, 1965), 20, 35, 47; John Gooch, *The Plans of War: The General Staff and British Military Strategy c. 1900-1916* (New York, 1974), 299, 302.

7. Liddell Hart, *Reputations*, 29.

8. Paul Guinn, *British Strategy and Politics 1914 to 1918* (Oxford, 1965), 76-77.

9. Liddell Hart, *The Real War*, 134.

10. Ibid., 221; Liddell Hart, *Reputations*, 64-67; Renouvin, *La Crise européenne*, 352-54.

11. Frank Owen, *Tempestuous Journey: Lloyd George, His Life and Times* (London, 1954), 448.

12. Marc Ferro, *The Great War 1914-1918* (London, 1973), 82; Renouvin, *La Crise européenne*, 432.

13. Barnett, *The Swordbearers*, 212ff.

14. Liddell Hart, *The Real War*, 337.

15. Ibid., 337, 343.

16. General John Charteris, *At G.H.Q.* (London, 1931), 268; and J.F.C. Fuller, *Memoirs of an Unconventional Soldier* (London, 1936), 170.

17. Duff Cooper, *Haig* (London, 1936), II, 273. Order dated April 11, 1918.

18. Ferro, *The Great War*, 199.

19. Erich Ludendorff, *My War Memoirs 1914-18* (London, 1919), 679.

20. Prince Max von Baden, *Erinnerungen und Dokumente* (Stuttgart, 1968), 332.

21. Charles à Court Repington, *The First World War, 1914-18. Personal Experiences* (Boston, 1921), II, 291, states that he opted for the new phrase "to prevent the millenian folk from forgetting that the history of the world is the history of war."

CHAPTER 3

1. Norman Stone, *The Eastern Front 1914-1917* (New York, 1975), 73.

2. Gunther E. Rothenberg, *The Army of Francis Joseph* (West Lafayette, 1976), 178.

3. Norman Stone, "Austria-Hungary and the First Phase of War, 1914" (Paper delivered at the "Potential Enemies" Conference, Harvard University, July 1980); and Stone, *Eastern Front*, 52-53.

4. Winston S. Churchill, *The World Crisis: The Eastern Front* (London, 1931), 133.

5. Stone, *Eastern Front*, 77. This notion that the Austrian army was always "one idea and one year" behind all others was made famous by Napoleon Bonaparte.

6. Basil Liddell Hart, *Reputations: Ten Years After* (Boston, 1928), 188.

7. Ibid., 189; Allan K. Wildman, *The End of the Russian Imperial Army: The Old Army and the Soldiers' Revolt (March-April 1917)* (Princeton, 1980), 75ff.; N. N. Golovin, *The Russian Army in the World War* (New Haven, 1931), 212ff.

8. Winston S. Churchill, *The Unknown War: The Eastern Front* (London, 1931), 255.

9. Jaroslav Hašek, *The Good Soldier Schwejk* (New York, 1930). This is the classic Czech novel of enlisted men of Czech descent in the Habsburg army in World War I.

10. Marc Ferro, *The Great War 1914-1918* (London, 1973), 70.

11. Basil Liddell Hart, *The Real War 1914-1918* (Boston, 1930), 123.

12. Rothenberg, *Army of Francis Joseph*, 201-4.

13. John C. G. Röhl, ed., *Philipp Eulenburgs Politische Korrespondenz* (Boppard, 1979), II, 913. Notes on a discussion with Wilhelm II on July 11, 1892.

14. Holger H. Herwig, "German Policy in the Eastern Baltic Sea in 1918: Expansion or Anti-Bolshevik Crusade?" *Slavic Review* 32 (June 1973), 340.

15. Winfried Baumgart, *Deutsche Ostpolitik 1918: Von Brest-Litowsk bis zum Ende des Ersten Weltkrieges* (Vienna/Munich, 1966), 132ff.

CHAPTER 4

1. Winston S. Churchill, *The World Crisis: 1911-1914* (London, 1931), 232ff.; Arthur J. Marder, *From the Dreadnought to Scapa Flow: The Royal Navy in the Fisher Era, 1904-1919* (London, 1965), II, 48 and III, 80.

2. Ulrich Trumpener, "The Escape of the Goeben and Breslau: A Reassessment," *Canadian Journal of History* 6 (1971), 171-86.

3. Marder, *Dreadnought to Scapa Flow*, II, 101; Churchill, *The World Crisis: 1911-14*, 477; Walter Görlitz, ed., *The Kaiser and His Court* (New York, 1964), 49.

4. Holger H. Herwig, *"Luxury" Fleet: The Imperial German Navy, 1888-1918* (London, 1980), 177.

5. Ibid., 165; Paul M. Kennedy, *The Rise and Fall of British Naval Mastery* (New York, 1976), 245.

6. Marder, *Dreadnought to Scapa Flow*, II, 447.

7. Ibid., III, 102.

8. Herwig, *"Luxury" Fleet*, 178ff.; Marder, *Dreadnought to Scapa Flow*, III; Peter Padfield, *The Battleship Era* (London, 1972), 233-43.

9. David F. Trask, *Captains & Cabinets: Anglo-American Naval Relations, 1917-1918* (Columbia, Mo., 1972), 55, 72ff.

10. Ibid., 269; Frank Freidel, *Franklin D. Roosevelt: The Apprenticeship* (Boston, 1952), 363.

11. See Herwig, *"Luxury" Fleet*, 247-57; and Wilhelm Deist, "Die Politik der Seekriegsleitung und die Rebellion der Flotte Ende Oktober 1918," *Vierteljahrshefte für Zeitgeschichte* 14 (1966), 341-68.

12. Kennedy, *Rise and Fall of British Naval Mastery*, 259.

13. Trask, *Captains & Cabinets*, 170.

CHAPTER 5

1. Marc Ferro, *The Great War, 1914-1918* (London, 1973), 147-49; see also the splendid chapter, "Les conditions nouvelles: la guerre longue," in Pierre Renouvin, *La Crise européenne et la Première Guerre Mondiale*, Peuples et Civilisations XIX (Paris, 1962), 263-86.

2. John Gooch, *The Plans of War* (New York, 1974),

300; Zara Steiner, *Britain and the Origins of the First World War* (New York, 1977), 215ff.

3. Ferro, *The Great War*, 123; Steiner, *Britain and the Origins of the First World War*, 231-33; Denis Mack Smith, *Italy: A Modern History* (Ann Arbor, Mich., 1959), 311.

4. Prosser Gifford and Wm. Roger Louis, eds., *Britain and Germany in Africa: Imperial Rivalry and Colonial Rule* (New Haven/London, 1967), 41ff.

5. A.J.P. Taylor, *The First World War: An Illustrated History* (London, 1963), 47; A.J.P. Taylor, *English History 1914-1945* (Oxford, 1965), 50, 70-71; and Ferro, *The Great War*, 128ff.

6. See especially the seminal work by Fritz Fischer, *Griff nach der Weltmacht* (Düsseldorf, 1961), 113ff.; and, to a lesser degree, Holger H. Herwig, "Admirals *versus* Generals: The War Aims of the Imperial German Navy 1914-1918," *Central European History* 5 (September 1972), 214ff.

7. Allan K. Wildman, *The End of the Russian Imperial Army* (Princeton, 1980), 108; L. Valiani, *The End of Austria-Hungary* (New York, 1973), 177, 212-13; Ottokar v. Landwehr Pragenau, *Hunger* (Zurich/Leipzig/Vienna, 1931), 9, 167-68; Norman Stone, *The Eastern Front 1914-1917* (New York, 1975), 292-96; Holger H. Herwig, *"Luxury" Fleet: The Imperial German Navy, 1888-1918* (London, 1980), 166, 230; and John Ellis, *Eye-Deep in Hell: Trench Warfare in World War I* (New York, 1976), 125-33.

8. John G. Williamson, *Karl Helfferich, 1872-1924: Economist, Financier, Politician* (Princeton, 1971), 126; on the Hindenburg program, see the dated but still useful work by Gerald D. Feldman, *Army, Industry, and Labor in Germany 1914-1918* (Princeton, 1966), 152ff.

9. Stone, *Eastern Front*, 198-205.

10. Gunther E. Rothenberg, *The Army of Francis Joseph* (West Lafayette, 1976), 192; Wilhelm Deist, ed., *Militär und Innenpolitik im Weltkrieg 1914-1918* (Düsseldorf, 1970), I, xxxiff.

11. Barbara W. Tuchman, *The Zimmermann Telegram* (New York, 1958), 185-86. On the British Ministry of Information, see especially W.M.A. Beaverbrook, *Men and Power, 1917-1918* (New York, 1957), 82-86, 217-18, 266-78;

and David Lloyd George, *War Memoirs* (London, 1933-36), II, 1110-13.

12. Deist, ed., *Militär und Innenpolitik*, II, 894ff., 911ff.

13. On the peace efforts of the Central Powers, see Fischer, *Griff nach der Weltmacht*, 522ff.; for the Socialists, see Georges Haupt, *Socialism and the Great War: The Collapse of the Second International* (Oxford, 1972), passim.

14. Denis Mack Smith, *Italy* (Ann Arbor, Mich., 1959), 298; M. Spahn, *Die päpstliche Friedensvermittlung* (Berlin, 1919), passim. Emperor Charles is discussed by Robert A. Kann, *Die Sixtusaffäre und die geheimen Friedensverhandlungen Österreich-Ungarns im Ersten Weltkrieg* (Vienna, 1966).

15. Taylor, *English History 1914-1945*, 1-2. See also the last chapter of Renouvin, *La Crise européenne*, 634-729, entitled "la guerre et l'évolution du monde."

16. Wildman, *The End of the Russian Imperial Army*, 75.

CHAPTER 6

1. Alma Luckau, *The German Delegation at the Paris Peace Conference* (New York, 1941), 115ff.; Karl Friedrich Nowak, *Versailles* (New York, 1929), 178ff.

2. John W. Wheeler-Bennett, *The Nemesis of Power: The German Army in Politics 1918-1945* (London, 1961), 49.

3. Nowak, *Versailles*, 31; Luckau, *German Peace Delegaton*, 66, 120.

4. F. Deák, *Hungary at the Paris Peace Conference* (New York, 1942).

5. H.W.V. Temperley, ed., *A History of the Peace Conference of Paris* (London, 1924), VI.

6. Ibid. (London, 1921), IV and V.

7. *1919, The Paris Peace Conference: Papers Relating to the Foreign Relations of the United States*, 13 vols. (Washington, 1942-47). For Germany, see especially vols. V and VI.

8. Winston S. Churchill, *The Gathering Storm: The Second World War* (London, 1960), 22.

9. C. V. Wedgwood, *The Thirty Years War* (New York, 1961), 506.

THE
DICTIONARY

ADLER, Viktor (*Austria-Hungary, Foreign Minister*), was born in Prague on June 24, 1852, the son of a prosperous merchant. Adler studied medicine at Vienna University and eventually practiced this craft in the capital. Initially a Liberal, Adler in 1882 joined Schönerer, Pernerstorfer, Friedjung, and Steinwender on the Linz program, calling for the union of all German-speaking lands. However, he quickly became repulsed by Schönerer's violence as well as his anti-Semitism, and in 1883 as a Socialist he toured Germany, Switzerland, and England. He met Friedrich Engels and August Bebel on his travels.

Upon his return to Vienna, Adler edited the *Gleichheit* and then the *Arbeiter-Zeitung*, and his calm manner was responsible in 1888/89 for uniting the moderate and radical Socialists at the *Hainfelder Tag*. Adler was arrested no less than seventeen times and spent eighteen months in prison as a Socialist agitator. In 1905 he was elected to parliament, where two years later he helped pass a universal suffrage bill. Adler had worked since 1899 on a program of equal representation for all nationalities within Austrian Social Democracy, but rejection of his efforts by Czechoslovakian workers in 1911 was a bitter disappointment.

Adler worked throughout the war in behalf of peace initiatives, yet managed at the same time to promote the cause of close cooperation with the German ally. He suffered a personal tragedy on October 21, 1916, when his son Friedrich emptied a revolver into Count Karl von Stürgkh (*q.v.*) in a Viennese restaurant. As a member of the new Austrian-German Council of State, Adler rejected Emperor Charles I's (*q.v.*) attempt to shift the onus for concluding an armistice to the new body: "We did not make this war." Adler hereafter became a member of the Constituent National Assembly and was appointed foreign minister on October 31, 1918. In the latter capacity he worked in behalf of union with the nascent German republic (request to the German

chancellor on November 9, 1918), but his death on November 11, 1918, one day before the Austrian republic was established, ended his brief career in government.

Macartney, *The Habsburg Empire 1790-1918*; *Neue Österreichische Biographie*, III; *Österreichisches Biographisches Lexikon 1815-1950*, I.

AITKEN, William Maxwell (*Great Britain, Minister of Information*), first Baron Beaverbrook, was born in Maple, Ontario, Canada, on May 25, 1879, the son of a clergyman. Aitken briefly attended the University of New Brunswick, but turned to finance and business as a career. He carried through a number of mergers in banking, cement, and steel, and was sufficiently wealthy in 1910 to retire from business and to leave Montreal for London, England. For a time he served as private secretary to Canadian-born Andrew Bonar Law (*q.v.*), and from 1910 to 1916 he represented Ashton-under-Lyne in the House of Commons.

With the outbreak of war in Europe, Sir William Aitken (he had been knighted in 1911) joined the Canadian Expeditionary Force in France as an eyewitness reporter. In May 1915 he was appointed Canadian record officer and in January 1916 he created the Canadian Records Office; his biographer, A.J.P. Taylor, notes that "he became an assiduous squirrel in pursuit of contemporary records." In 1916 the Canadian government officially appointed Aitken its representative at the western front; he was created a baronet the same year. In 1917 he was appointed officer in charge of the Canadian War Records and raised to the peerage at the urging of Prime Minister David Lloyd George (*q.v.*) as Baron Beaverbrook, of New Brunswick and Cherkley, Surrey. In fact, Beaverbrook behind the scenes greatly facilitated many of Lloyd George's personnel changes during the latter part of the war.

On February 10, 1918, the prime minister appointed Lord Beaverbrook minister of information. Beaverbrook rather romantically viewed propaganda ("information" was still preferred as a gentler term) as "the popular arm of diplomacy." He took up the task with gusto. War artists were commissioned and their products displayed throughout the nation, as were the new war photographs, much of which material is now in the Imperial War Museum. A film section within the Ministry of Information turned out the first war films for viewing in the United Kingdom. Beaverbrook greatly facilitated the work of foreign press representatives and entertained them lavishly; overseas press bureaus were established under his guidance. He resigned his post on October 21, 1918, after numerous rows with the Foreign Office which, he felt, was curtailing his freedom of action too severely. Taylor concludes that Beaverbrook's stint as minister of information is important primarily as his apprenticeship for later assignments.

After the war, Beaverbrook turned to Fleet Street and acquired as part of the Beaverbrook Newspapers the *Daily Express, Sunday Express, Scottish Daily Express, Scottish Sunday Express,* and other papers. He was an avowed imperialist who continued to refer to the Commonwealth as the Empire. In 1918 he vowed that he would never enter politics again, except in time of war. Winston S. Churchill (*q.v.*) called upon Beaverbrook in 1940/41 as his minister of aircraft production; in 1941 the Canadian became minister of state, in 1941/42 minister of supply, and from September 1943 to July 1945 lord privy seal. From 1947 until 1953 he served as chancellor of the University of New Brunswick. Lord Beaverbrook died at Cherkley on June 9, 1964.

H. G. Wells once attested to Beaverbrook's varied interests when he stated that the Canadian had "a multi-track mind." When asked in 1934 what had been "the biggest thing you have ever done," Beaverbrook replied: "The destruction of the Asquith Government" in December 1916. Taylor pays Beaverbrook rare tribute with regard to the latter's two-volume account of the Great War: "The enduring merits of the book[s] are really beyond cavil."

Beaverbrook, *Politicians and the War* and *Men and Power*; Taylor, *Beaverbrook; Colombo's Canadian References; Who's Who in 1964.*

ALBERT I (*Belgium, King*), was born in Brussels, April 8, 1875. His father was Prince Philip of Saxe-Coburg, brother of King Leopold II of Belgium; his mother came from the Catholic branch of the German Hohenzollern dynasty. Albert became heir apparent to the Belgian crown in 1891 upon the death of his elder brother; Leopold's only son had died in 1869. The boy received the military education considered appropriate for a future European monarch, entering the army as a lieutenant in 1892, rising to colonel in 1901 and lieutenant general in 1907. The cultural and scientific interests of the shy young man, however, extended well beyond military affairs. He traveled widely and delved into scientific subjects, pursuits encouraged by Duchess Elizabeth of Bavaria whom he married in 1900. In December 1909, the old king died and Albert at the age of thirty-four took the crown.

The darkening international scene soon intruded. In a visit to Emperor Wilhelm II (*q.v.*) in late 1913, Albert heard his royal cousin speak about a coming war with France. That same year, the Belgian government of Baron de Broqueville (*q.v.*) met news of German military expansion by instituting general military training. This was a sharp turn from Belgian tradition, which relied on the protection offered her neutrality by international treaties dating from 1839. The Brussels government rejected the British and French approaches to aid Belgium in the event of war as infringements on its neutral status. But the army, still small and poorly trained, tried to develop plans to guard the country against invasion. Ambitiously it hoped to meet an invasion either from Germany or from Belgium's western neighbors.

On the evening of August 2, 1914, the Belgian government received Germany's ultimatum demanding free passage for the German army through the small neutral nation. Albert made a personal and unsuccessful appeal to Kaiser Wilhelm II on August 3. On August 4, the enemy struck, an event followed by Belgian pleas for aid from France and Great Britain.

Albert's dramatic speech of August 4 to both houses of the Belgian Parliament set the framework for the nation's role in World War I. The small country would fight to the limit to defend its territory. Talk that had circulated within the Belgian cabinet of offering only token resistance—or of defending only those parts of the country actually invaded—faded away. Moreover, the king stepped forward to lead the military effort. The constitution named him military commander in chief upon the outbreak of war. Albert indeed directed Belgian strategy. He barred his generals from following the repulse of the Germans at Liège (August 5) with an ill-conceived counterattack. More important, in the face of Anglo-French objections, he withdrew the Belgian army to the relative security of the port of Antwerp on August 20, although he mounted several sorties from that base to help the other nations facing the German onslaught. In early October, with the Germans mounting full-scale assaults against the port, whose prewar fortification program had never been completed, Albert ordered his army westward. Again he brushed aside offered requests from the Entente: General Joffre (*q.v.*), the French commander, wanted the Belgians to retreat southward to link up with the Allied armies racing toward the North Sea. Albert instead led his own heroic effort: a defensive stand on the Yser (October 13-30).

Much of Albert's wartime policy was foreshadowed in these early months of the conflict. He intended to command himself, would not bend to the strategic designs of France and Britain, and intended to protect his army's identity as an independent military force and to maintain it on Belgian soil. Such an approach did not make him an easy comrade in arms. Neither did his political policies endear him to the Entente. The king opposed British and French attempts to treat him as an ally. Rather, he wished to preserve Belgium's status as an innocent country, forced into the war and fighting merely to retain its territorial integrity. In April 1915, he cautioned members of the Belgian government against wavering from this stance. The king specifically opposed the growing trend among Belgium's political leaders to look to postwar territorial acquisitions and to jettison Belgium's traditional neutrality.

In practice, Albert's view of the war meant welcoming German peace feelers in the winter of 1915/16. By late 1916, the monarch and his cabinet were in open disagreement; Albert doubted prospects for a clear-cut Allied victory and urged Belgian politicians to work for a compromise peace. According to Jonathan Helmreich, ministers used the word *treason* in commenting on the royal position. Albert opposed Belgian participation in Allied offensive operations for most of the war. He rejected Allied overtures to put his army under Field Marshal Haig (*q.v.*) in order to support the British offensive at Ypres in 1917. In Albert's view, the proposed Allied attacks would wreak havoc in Belgium; moreover, the total defeat of Germany was a British and French goal, and Belgium should not pay the price for such an outcome to the war.

Opposing viewpoints in his own government gained strength. In January 1918, Charles de Broqueville was forced to abandon his brief tenure as foreign minister; this was his penalty for supporting the king's hopes for a compromise peace with Germany. By May he had to give up the premiership as well. The new tone was set by such leaders as Paul Hymans (*q.v.*), who became foreign minister in January 1918. As the war reached its final crescendo, even Albert relented and permitted the use of Belgian forces in large-scale attacks. Generalissimo Foch (*q.v.*) adroitly made Albert the commander of the Flanders Army Group in the fall of 1918. This force consisted of the Belgian army, along with French and British contingents. Under Albert's command, it thrust toward Nieuport in late September as part of Foch's series of hammer blows against the crumbling German battle front.

Albert led his army through the final weeks of the war. His immediate reward was a triumphal entry into Brussels on November 22, 1918. There his first peacetime speech to the Belgian Parliament called for sweeping reform: equal voting rights for all citizens, equal rights for all language groups, and, as a sign of how far Albert had shifted his view of Belgium's future in European affairs, an end to Belgian neutrality.

The king traveled widely in the postwar years. The crowds in the United States that hailed him in 1919 could hardly have been aware of the complex and often obstructive role he had played in the war effort. Seeing Belgium's interests imperiled, not only by invasion but also by liberation, not only by a German victory but by an unlimited Allied victory as well, Albert had walked the twisted and difficult road of a neutral at war.

The king ruled for sixteen years following World War I. His life ended in a mountain climbing accident near Namur, on February 17, 1934.

Albert I, *Les Carnets de guerre*; Aronson, *Defiant Dynasty*; Bronne, *Albert Ier*; Galet, *Albert, King of the Belgians, in the Great War*; Helmreich, *Belgium and Europe*; Kossmann, *The Low Countries*; Palo, "The Diplomacy of Belgian War Aims during the First World War"; Willequet, "Les relations entre le roi commandant en chef de l'armée, et le gouvernement belge, en 1914-1918"; *Biographie nationale*, XXIX; *Larousse mensuel*, IX.

ALBRECHT, Duke of Württemberg (*Germany, Field Marshal*), was born in Vienna on December 23, 1865, the grandson of Archduke Albrecht of Austria; as the nephew of the childless King Wilhelm II of Württemberg, Albrecht was regarded as heir apparent to the throne. The duke began studies at Tübingen in 1884, but the following year entered the military, where his career became the customary rapid royal climb up the ladder of command: by 1906 head of the XI Army Corps at Kassel, two years later command of the XIII (Württemberg) Corps, and in 1913 inspector general of the VI Army Inspectorate in the grade of colonel general. The latter post in reality placed Albrecht in charge of the Württemberg army.

On August 2, 1914, Albrecht was given command of the Fourth Army and occupied Luxembourg with this force. Thereafter he entered Belgium and on

August 22 faced the French Fourth Army near Namur; the resulting battle of Neufchâteau brought the duke his first victory in the field. Two days later his forces again defeated the French near Sedan, and on Sepbember 5, the Fourth Army reached the River Marne—only to become part of the German retreat four days later. On October 10, Duke Albrecht was given command of a newly formed Fourth Army in Flanders, which commenced a general advance between the Lys and the English Channel. Within seven days the celebrated race to the sea had started as both sides rushed toward the Channel, each attempting to outflank the other. Thousands died as the Fourth Army stood at Ypres, and when the Belgians opened the flood gates at Nieuport, Albrecht was forced to retreat to the right banks of the Yser. By mid-November the fighting in Flanders had subsided and degenerated into trench warfare. The Fourth Army failed to envelop the enemy's left flank and the year ended with yet another bitter struggle at Nieuport.

Duke Albrecht renewed the attack at Ypres on April 22, 1915, and for the first time used poisonous gas, which cost the enemy about 15,000 casualties. However, the broad assault failed to breach enemy lines and had to be called off by the end of May. In the spring, the Fourth Army again charged the British at Ypres, opening five gaps in the opposing line but failing to break through. On August 1, 1916, Duke Albrecht was promoted field marshal of the Württemberg army.

Transferred to the southern wing of the western front on February 25, 1917, as commander of the new Army Group Duke Albrecht of Württemberg with headquarters at Strassburg, this clear and independent thinker remained German military commander in the *Reichsländer* Alsace and Lorraine until the end of the war, but saw relatively little action in this theater. General Krafft von Dellmensingen (*q.v.*) ably served as his chief of staff.

Albrecht retired to Castle Altshausen after the war, and in 1921, on the death of King Wilhelm II, became head of the House of Württemberg. He died at his castle in Upper Swabia on October 29, 1939.

Liddell Hart, *The Real War*; *Geschichte der Ritter des Ordens*, II; *Neue Deutsche Biographie*, I.

ALEKSANDRA FEDOROVNA (1872-1918). *See* ALEXANDRA.

ALEKSEEV, Mikhail Vasilevich (*Russia, General of Infantry*), was born in Tver province on November 15, 1857. The son of an officer who had risen from the ranks, the younger Alekseev completed the Moscow Infantry Cadet School in 1876 and went to war against the Turks almost immediately. Like many of his contemporaries, Alekseev smoothed the path to higher command by attending the General Staff Academy, graduating in 1890. He did a turn as staff officer in the St. Petersburg Military District, then returned to the General Staff Academy to teach military history from 1898 to 1904. As a newly promoted major general, he left for the Russo-Japanese War in late 1904. There he served as deputy chief of staff of the Third Army. Apparently he survived the debacle in the Far East with his reputation intact, since, in 1908, he was named chief of staff for the important Kiev Military District. There he took the lead in opposing the plan of General Yury Danilov (*q.v.*) of the General Staff to concentrate on attacking East Prussia at the start of a future war with the Central Powers. Rallying other local military leaders who would have to face Austria-Hungary at the outbreak of war, Alekseev shaped a plan more to his liking: the main weight of the Russian army was to move against Austrian Galicia, with a subsidiary attack to be pointed at East Prussia.

At the outbreak of World War I, Alekseev was named chief of staff to General Nikolai Ivanov (*q.v.*), the ineffectual commander of the southwestern front, that is, Southwestern Army Group. In the tangled Galician campaign that followed, the Ivanov-Alekseev team proved incapable of driving forward their forces, notably the Third and Eighth Armies, advancing westward along the Carpathians. Without sufficient speed and aggressiveness, the Russians failed to cut off the exposed Austrian armies thrusting northward toward Cholm and Lublin.

The problem of lackadaisical and timid field army commanders was all too familiar to Alekseev by March 1915, when he took command of the northwestern front. He then began to exemplify the other major failing of the Russian army in World War I: the tendency of front commanders to act without regard to orders from above. Two months after assuming his new post, Alekseev received word of catastrophe to the south. General von Mackensen (*q.v.*) and an Austro-German Eleventh Army broke through Ivanov's thin defenses at Gorlice on May 2, and then drove upward into central Poland. Alekseev followed the precedent set in 1914 and only grudgingly shifted his reserves to mend the critical situation that was developing. Nonetheless, against the fading reputations of Ivanov, Grand Duke Nikolai Nikolaevich (*q.v.*), the commander in chief, and Danilov, the de facto chief of staff for the entire army, Alekseev's prospects boomed. He held the line of the Narev River against a new German offensive from East Prussia in mid-July and then retreated in good order from the perilous Polish salient. By the time the entire Russian front stabilized, in late August, the majority of the field armies had come under his direct command.

At the start of September 1915, Tsar Nicholas II (q.v.) took over as generalissimo. Alekseev was named the tsar's chief of staff; in fact, he led the entire army. Alekseev's subsequent performance has received only mild praise. A cool workaholic, he tried, in a fashion that Nikolai Nikolaevich had never done, to coordinate the army groups: the northern front, the western front, and the southwestern front. Incompetents like Ivanov were removed, although the promotion of aged officers like General Kuropatkin (q.v.), who took over the northern front in March 1916, demonstrated the shallow pool of senior talent Alekseev could tap. But the new commander mainly tried to hold the line and, at the same time, to respond to pressure from Russia's allies.

By the start of 1916 Alekseev reluctantly began to send troops to France at the urging of the Allies. The German assault on Verdun (in February) and the Austrian *Strafexpedition* against Italy (May to July) pushed Alekseev into action to promote an offensive on his side of the continent. He soon found that most of his front commanders had no desire to respond. Only the fiery new commander of the southwestern front, General Brusilov (q.v.), volunteered to undertake an early offensive to relieve the burdens on the French and Italians. Alekseev was unimpressed, however, by Brusilov's promising tactical innovations. When the southwestern front became the scene of sweeping Russian advances in June, Alekseev refused to press other front commanders to shift substantial reserves to Brusilov. General Evert (q.v.), the commander of the western front, controlled the bulk of Russia's combat divisions and artillery; Alekseev could neither push him into a vigorous offensive nor bring himself to snatch away Evert's forces for Brusilov.

As the Brusilov advance sputtered to a halt in the late summer, Alekseev again found himself pushed this way and that by Russia's partners in the war. France had insisted on drawing Rumania into the fighting. Alekseev correctly predicted that the Rumanian army could not stand up to the test of World War I; he was also on target in predicting that Russia would have to stretch her forces in order to buck up the Rumanians. Foresight made no difference. By the close of 1916 thirty-six Russian divisions had been diverted to aid the nearly defunct Rumanian army.

Throughout 1916 Alekseev found himself the object of appeals from political leaders disgruntled with the tsar and the course of the war. Any links that he

established with such figures as Aleksandr Guchkov (q.v.) were likely suspended at the close of 1916 when the tired old general suffered a heart attack. Alekseev recuperated in the Crimea, returned to duty in February 1917, and almost immediately faced the coming of the March Revolution. His actions during the days of rising unrest in Petrograd and the subsequent collapse of the monarchy have given rise to heated controversy. Katkov suggests that more vigorous action by Alekseev at the start of the bread riots might have brought the situation under control, and his timely inaction may have reflected a long held desire to promote political change. In any event, as the revolution gathered momentum, Alekseev urged the tsar on March 14 to grant parliamentary government. With the solid support of the front commanders, Alekseev arranged the tsar's abdication by March 16.

Alekseev went on to play a role in the months following the March Revolution. He accepted the post of commander in chief from the provisional government and supported Aleksandr Kerensky (q.v.) in his call for a new offensive. The general and the minister of justice (soon to be named war minister) agreed that Russian inaction gave the Central Powers a free hand first to crush the Western Allies, then to turn German and Austrian armies to the task of smashing Russia. But Alekseev disliked the rapid course of democratization Kerensky prescribed for the army and insisted on a well-planned offensive that bore some promise of success. Tagged by now as both too conservative and too pessimistic, Alekseev was dismissed in late May and replaced by Brusilov.

Following the November Revolution, the old general, whose health was rapidly failing, left for the Don. There he intended to build a new army to fight both the Germans and the Bolsheviks. By early 1918 he had formed the core of the future White military forces in the South, the so-called Volunteer Army. But Alekseev found himself with only nominal authority, as younger White leaders, notably General Lavr Kornilov (q.v.), took charge. Alekseev did not live to see the White movement reach the peak of its power and expectations. He died in Ekaterinodar on October 8, 1918.

Alekseev, "Iz dnevnika Generala M. V. Alekseeva"; Feldman, "The Russian General Staff and the June 1917 Offensive"; Katkov, *Russia 1917*; Kenez, *Civil War in South Russia, 1918*; Mayzel, *Generals and Revolutionaries*; Rostunov, *Russkii front pervoi mirovoi voiny*; Rutherford, *The Russian Army in World War I*; Stone, *The Eastern Front*; *Modern Encyclopedia of Russian and Soviet History*, I; *Sovetskaia voennaia entsiklopediia*, I; *Sovetskaia istoricheskaia entsiklopediia*, I.

ALEXANDER KARADJORDJEVIĆ (*Serbia, Prince Regent*), was born in Cetinje, Montenegro, December 16, 1888. His mother was Princess Zorka of Montenegro, his father Peter Karadjordjević (*q.v.*), the exiled pretender to the Serbian throne; in 1903 a military coup in Belgrade opened the way for Peter's return to take the crown. Alexander attended school in Geneva, and the young prince completed his education at the School for Pages in St. Petersburg. Stavrianos attributes Alexander's taste for autocracy, a departure from his father's respect for constitutional forms, to this early immersion in the Russian political environment.

In 1909 Alexander's elder brother renounced all rights to the throne, making Alexander, at the age of twenty-one, the crown prince. He served his father as a diplomatic emissary in negotiations leading to the Balkan Wars, 1912/13, and he held nominal military commands during the fighting. Serbian political life in the years before World War I was colored by the influence of irredentist groups striving for the liberation of Serbs under Habsburg rule. Albertini and Remak indicate Alexander had a brief association with the Black Hand, one of the most powerful irredentist factions. But it was the clash between military leaders from the era of the 1903 coup and Prince Peter that shaped Alexander's future. In June 1914, the quarrel over who would control the newly conquered territory in Macedonia led to bitter confrontation between civil and military leaders. In the ensuing constitutional crisis, Peter stepped down. Barely two months before the start of World War I, Alexander took over as prince regent.

During the July crisis, Alexander made a personal appeal for aid to Tsar Nicholas II (*q.v.*), but it was Premier Nikola Pašić (*q.v.*) who dominated Serbian foreign policy at this critical moment. Once Serbia was at war, Alexander stood as nominal commander in chief, with the actual responsibility of directing national defense in the capable hands of Field Marshal Radomir Putnik (*q.v.*). Not yet a shaker and mover in his own right, Alexander served as a spokesman for important ideas. His proclamation of August 4 to the army referred pointedly to Serbia's fellow South Slavs within Austria-Hungary as "our brethren." Such remarks indicated some Serbians' hopes that the war might open the way to South Slav political unification.

Alexander's stature grew during the military disasters of 1915. Suffering from appendicitis, he participated in the grim retreat through Albania to the Adriatic. Even in these dark days, he insisted the army would recover and fight again. His important role in holding the battered army together has been described as "like a campfire to a wanderer in a forest at night." As Serbian troops recovered on Corfu and prepared to embark for Salonika, Alexander and Pašić toured the Allied capitals of western Europe. They assured the Entente leaders of early 1916 that Serbia would fight on. In contrast to Pašić's caution, Alexander spoke out explicitly in favor of South Slav unity. In April 1916, for example, he met in Paris with Ante Trumbić (*q.v.*), the leading exile spokesman for South Slavs under Habsburg rule.

Alexander's serious political debut took place in the spring of 1917. In an event still cloaked in mystery, Colonel Dimitrijević-Apis (*q.v.*) and other military men linked to the Sarajevo assassinations were arrested, tried, and executed. Some historians consider Alexander the moving force behind the purge. Possibly he was clearing the way for a compromise peace with Vienna. Perhaps the recent Russian Revolution stirred him to strike immediately at potential subversives in the army. Whatever the exact cause, the result was to end the army's political restraints on the crown and on civilian leaders. Another boost for Alexander came at once: the Corfu conference of July 1917 between Pašić and South Slav exile leaders drew the outline for a united South Slav state under the Karadjordjević dynasty.

Only Pašić now stood between Alexander and a dominant role in Serbian politics. The prince regent, citing the limits of the constitution, held back from a direct attack. In mid-1918, British supporters of South Slav unity found Alexander deaf to their pleas to compel Pašić to cooperate with Trumbić's Yugoslav Committee, the voice of exiles from the South Slav provinces of Austria-Hungary. The fall of 1918, however, brought Alexander his moment. Serbian columns under Field Marshal Mišić (*q.v.*) raced northward from Salonika to liberate their homeland; they then penetrated the rebelling southern provinces of the Dual Monarchy. When representatives of Serbia, Montenegro, and the former Habsburg provinces of Croatia and Slovenia met in late November in Belgrade, Alexander dominated the proceedings. The kingdom of the Serbs, Croats, and Slovenes (subsequently renamed Yugoslavia) came into existence on December 1 with Alexander as regent. Pašić, denied the post of premier in the new state, was packed off to Paris to lead the peace delegation. On Peter's death in August 1921, Alexander became king.

The young monarch presided over an increasingly turbulent domestic scene. Throughout the 1920s other ethnic groups bridled at their heavy-handed domination by the Serbs, who controlled the central administration. In January 1929, Alexander ended parliamentary government to take on the trappings of a crowned dictator. He subsequently restored constitutional forms, but Yugoslavia remained a cauldron of ethnic and political discontent, claiming Alexander as its most prominent victim. The king was assassinated on October 9, 1934, during a state visit to France—the target of a successful plot by Croatian and Macedonian revolutionaries.

Albertini, *The Origins of the War of 1914*, 3 vols.; Dragnich, *Serbia, Pašić, and Yugoslavia*; Lederer, *Yugoslavia at the Peace Conference*; Petrovich, *History of Modern Serbia*, II; Remak, *Sarajevo*; Stavrianos, *The Balkans since 1453*; *Larousse mensuel*, X.

ALEXANDRA (*Russia, Empress*), was born in Darmstadt, Germany, June 6, 1872, the daughter of Prince Louis of Hesse-Darmstadt; her mother was a member of the British royal family. The young princess, christened Alix, found her early years punctuated by tragedy: illness struck down her mother, a sister, and a prospective fiancé, the duke of Clarence. She first met her husband to be, the future Tsar Nicholas II of Russia (*q.v.*), in 1884, when she was a child of twelve. Her marriage, which involved the requirement that she abandon her Lutheran faith to join the Russian Orthodox church, took place in grim circumstances. Tsar Alexander III died suddenly on November 1, 1894. Nicholas was obliged to mount the throne at the age of twenty-six. His young bride was given no time to adjust to her new country.

The first years of marriage produced four daughters; then, in 1904, a son was born. Tragically, the young heir to the throne was found to suffer from hemophilia. Alexis' disease was known to originate in Alexandra's family line. The empress' faith in conventional medicine had been undermined long before by physicians' inability to treat members of her family for a variety of serious ailments. She opened her doors to a parade of faith healers and assorted charlatans. Of these, the peasant holy man Rasputin (*q.v.*), who appeared around 1905, became the most durable and influential. The empress likewise immersed herself in religion. Her devotion to Russian Orthodoxy had political consequences. She took to heart the view that the power of the monarchy was divinely bestowed; if undiluted by modern reforms, it answered the deepest needs of the Russian people. Decisive and strong willed, she reinforced her vacillating husband's similar view of his office and responsibilities. In the aftermath of the revolution of 1905, the relationship between the Duma (or parliament) and the prerogatives of the monarchy constituted the nation's most pressing political concern. Alexandra, encouraged by Rasputin, threw her weight against the expansion of the Duma's area of responsibility.

The empress' combustible mixture of family and political concerns first reached a climax in 1911. Criticism of Rasputin in the Duma led to his expulsion from St. Petersburg. Even more incensed than usual at the Duma's pretentions to power, Alexandra arranged for his speedy return. The following year, Rasputin seemed to save Alexis when the child's hemophilia brought him near death during a vacation in Poland. Rasputin's baleful influence on the imperial family was now firmly established; it seemed to make no difference that the tsar was markedly less enthusiastic about the dissolute holy man than was Alexandra.

During the first year of World War I, the empress continued to strengthen the tsar's desire to limit sweeping reform. She supported the aged reactionary, Premier Ivan Goremykin (*q.v.*); meanwhile she heaped criticism on the military commander in chief, Grand Duke Nikolai Nikolaevich (*q.v.*). The latter she saw as both too liberal and a possible candidate whom other liberals might seek to place on the throne after ousting Nicholas II. In August 1915, she encouraged the tsar to dismiss the grand duke and to take personal command of the army.

The tsar's departure for supreme headquarters at the distant town of Mogilev left the day-to-day authority of the monarchy with Alexandra. The lurid view that she, guided by Rasputin, led the nation to an avoidable catastrophe is exaggerated. Russia's economic and social system was patently inadequate to face the strain of total war. Moreover, the tsar frequently returned from Mogilev for long stays in Petrograd. With some exceptions, notably the retention of the supposedly pro-German Aleksandr Protopopov (*q.v.*) as minister of the interior in the fall of 1916, Alexandra rarely threw her influence directly against the tsar's wishes. Nonetheless, within the general framework of Nicholas' preferences, Alexandra helped push out Goremykin and replaced him with an equally loyal and incompetent bureaucratic retainer, Boris Sturmer (*q.v.*). The most capable and competent ministers, like General Andrei Polivanov of the War Ministry and Foreign minister Sergei Sazonov (*qq.v.*), departed with Alexandra hastening and approving such changes.

Reaction by the public and Duma to the visible disintegration of the government during 1916 centered on the empress and Rasputin. Sturmer, with his German name and alleged bias in favor of the Central Powers, in time emerged as the symbol of doubts about the German-born empress' own loyalties. When the Duma convened in mid-

November of 1916, charges against the empress grew louder. Paul Miliukov (*q.v.*), leader of the Kadet party, cut away at Sturmer in a bitter Duma speech; he asked rhetorically whether the government was guilty of "stupidity or treason." Reading foreign newspaper articles in the original German, Miliukov voiced specific suspicions of the empress herself.

The death of Rasputin in late December at the hands of a band of aristocratic conservatives worsened the empress' reputation. She then stood alone to face the blame for the nation's woes. In January 1917, Duma leaders warned the tsar that the empress and her political activities were endangering the monarchy. Such alarums had no effect. Indeed, as the March Revolution approached, Alexandra and Protopopov were preparing a scheme to dismiss the Fourth Duma and to call new, carefully rigged elections. Even the rigged elections the two envisioned were likely to produce a less tractable Duma—but such realties of Russian politics escaped the empress completely.

When the revolution struck, Alexandra was at Tsarskoe Selo, the palace outside Petrograd; Nicholas had just left to return to Mogilev. She was arrested there with her children and soon reunited with the deposed tsar. Members of the provisional government made half-hearted efforts to send the former imperial family into exile. But Britain was reluctant to accept them and to many Russians the presence of the deposed monarchs abroad seemed certain to encourage the foreign and domestic foes of the revolution. In the end, Alexandra and the rest of the family were dispatched to Siberia shortly before the November Revolution. As civil war spread in the spring and summer of 1918, again the possibility arose that they might emerge as effective symbols for conservative forces. To prevent this, Alexandra and the rest of the family were executed by Bolshevik authorities in the Siberian city of Ekaterinburg during the night of July 16/17, 1918.

Buxhoeveden, *The Life and Tragedy of Alexandra Feodorovna*; Frankland, *Nicholas II*; *Nicky-Sunny Letters, The*; Pares, *The Fall of the Russian Monarchy*; Pearson, *The Russian Moderates and the Crisis of Tsarism*; *Modern Encyclopedia of Russian and Soviet History*, I.

ALLENBY, Edmund Henry Hynman (*Great Britain, Field Marshal*), first Viscount Allenby of Megiddo, was born at Brackenhurst, near Southwell, Nottinghamshire, on April 23, 1861, the son of a country gentleman. Allenby boasted of an ancestral link to Oliver Cromwell. After two failures to pass the entrance examinations for the Indian civil service, Allenby instead entered the Royal Military College, Sandhurst. He was promoted captain in 1888, major nine years later, and colonel in 1901. Allenby served during the Boer War; in 1905 he was promoted brigadier general, and in 1909 major general. He had a reputation for violent verbal outbursts and was universally called "the Bull."

Allenby commanded a cavalry division in the British Expeditionary Force in August 1914, and took part in the First and Second battles of Ypres. In October 1915, he received command of the new Third Army, which he led north of the Somme. Allenby took part in April 1917 in the battle of Arras, scoring a partial breakthrough between Arras and Cambrai that was never fully exploited by his commander in chief, Sir Douglas Haig (*q.v.*). Allenby's performance on the western front was not stellar: he had poor control of his troops and felt confined and stymied as merely one of numerous "Barons," as the army comanders in France were aptly styled. His antipathy towards Haig probably accounted for his transfer in June 1917 to command the Egyptian Expeditionary Force, assembled after the Turks had halted the British at the gates of Gaza.

Upon his arrival Allenby found seven infantry and three mounted divisions. He brought a fresh breeze to Egypt and on October 31, 1917, mounted an offensive on Beersheba, although an initial success was vitiated by the cavalry's tardiness in exploiting it. From Beersheba, Allenby shifted his attack on Gaza and drove the enemy northward beyond Jaffa. Next came an assault on Jerusalem, which was defended by General Erich von Falkenhayn (*q.v.*), then a marshal in the Turkish army; the ancient city fell on December 9, 1917.

The British planned a major campaign for early 1918, but it foundered not only on Allenby's cautious stance, but also on General Erich Ludendorff's (*q.v.*) great offensive in France in March. It was not until September that Allenby was ready to renew his drive beyond Jordan, this time against the German General Liman von Sanders (*q.v.*). Unmindful of casualties and supported among the Arabs by Colonel T. E. Lawrence (*q.v.*), Allenby launched his strike through Nazareth and Beisan on September 19, in what was to be the last great campaign of massed cavalry. The victory at Megiddo led to the capture of the Hejaz railroad and entry into Damascus on October 1, 1918. Tripoli fell next, and thereafter Aleppo. On October 30, the Turks signed an armistice at Mudros. Allenby had taken 75,000 prisoners at a cost of 5,666 casualties. He was confined in France, but in Palestine he was a supreme war lord; even the Arabic form of his name, Allah Nebi ("the prophet of God"), accorded him an almost mystic aura.

After the war, "the Bull" served as special high commissioner for Egypt, was promoted field marshal, ar.d was raised to the peerage as Viscount Allenby. He left Egypt in June 1925, having helped it become a sovereign state three years earlier. Allenby died in London on May 14, 1936; his ashes were deposited in Westminster Abbey. He reputedly became the model of C. S. Forester's novel *The General*.

Gardner, *Allenby of Arabia*; Liddell Hart, *Reputations*; *Dictionary of National Biography 1931-1940*.

ANDRÁSSY von CSIK-SZENT KIRÁLY und KRASZNA-HORKA, Count Julius the Younger (*Austria-Hungary, Minister of State, Foreign Minister*), was born in Budapest on June 30, 1860, the son of the elder Andrássy, Hungarian prime minister and Austro-Hungarian foreign minister. The younger Andrássy was elected to the Hungarian parliament in 1885, quickly rising up the ladder to undersecretary of state in 1893 and minister to the court one year later. An inveterate opponent of Count Kálmán Tisza, Andrássy spent the years before the outbreak of the Great War as spokesman for liberal dissidents. From 1906 to 1910 he struggled unsuccessfully as minister of the interior to create a Hungarian national army and to reform the existing suffrage.

Julius Andrássy was appointed the last Habsburg foreign minister on October 24, 1918, and it became his bitter task to terminate the German alliance, which his father had forged in 1879. After extending an offer of a separate peace to the Entente on October 28, Andrássy resigned on November 1, 1918. He was then elected to the newly constituted Hungarian National Assembly and in 1921 became leader of the Christian Democratic party. That same year he took part in Emperor Charles I's (*q.v.*) abortive attempts to regain the Crown of St. Stephen, and subsequently spent seven weeks under custody. Andrássy laid down his parliamentary mandate in 1926; he died in Budapest on June 11, 1929.

Andrássy, *Diplomatie und Weltkrieg*; Kann, *History of the Habsburg Empire 1526-1918*; *Österreichisches Biographisches Lexikon 1815-1950*, I.

ARZ von STRAUSSENBURG, Arthur Albert Baron (*Austria-Hungary, General*), was born in Hermannstadt, Transylvania, on June 11, 1857, to a Protestant pastor's family. Arz early belonged to the so-called Young Saxon party in Transylvania, which declared itself willing, unlike the "Old Saxon" faction, to work with the Magyars. A brief career in law was abandoned in June 1878 when Arz entered the army; he attended the War Academy from 1885 to 1887,

and the following year was attached to the General Staff. By the turn of the century he had risen to the grade of colonel and commanded infantry at Kaschau. From 1903 to 1908 Arz served as chief of personnel in the General Staff, and in November 1908, was promoted major general and given command of the Sixty-first Infantry Brigade in Budapest; thereafter came assignment to the Thirty-first Infantry Division.

In August 1914, Arz was given command of the Fifteenth Infantry Division; as subsequent head of the VI Army Corps he fought at Limanowa-Lapanów in 1914, and the following year saw action, in conjunction with Field Marshal August von Mackensen's (*q.v.*) German Ninth Army, during the breakthrough near Gorlice-Tarnów and the resulting capture of Brest-Litovsk. Arz distinguished himself in 1916 in his native Transylvania as head of a new First Army, fighting a model delaying action against the invading Rumanians while a mixed German–Austro-Hungarian army was being assembled by General Erich von Falkenhayn (*q.v.*).

On March 1, 1917, Colonel General Arz von Straussenburg relinquished command of the First Army and succeeded General Conrad von Hötzendorf (*q.v.*) as chief of the General Staff of the army. Arz lacked political ambition, possessed unbounded good temper, and devoted his talents to serving his imperial supreme commander, thereby reverting to the control structure prevailing in the period 1850 to 1859 under Francis Joseph I (*q.v.*). In fact, Arz has been accused of being more an adjutant general than a chief of staff. He quickly abandoned the special standing of the chief of the General Staff and reverted to the traditional role of professional military adviser to the emperor. Headquarters were removed from Teschen to Baden, near Vienna, and operational planning was left to the deptuy chief of the General Staff, General Alfred von Waldstätten (*q.v.*). For the remainder of the war, Arz supervised the Austro-Hungarian defenses in the East during General Aleksei Brusilov's (*q.v.*) offensive, and under his nominal command German–Austro-Hungarian forces broke the Italian front near Caporetto in October 1917 and occupied Venetia as far as the Piave River. Arz desired above all to preserve inviolate the Dual Monarchy and he resisted all attempts by the Hungarians to divide the army into an Austrian and a Hungarian part. Charles I (*q.v.*) raised Arz into the baronage in February 1918.

Unfortunately, Arz von Straussenburg was not a strong military leader. In June 1918, he was unable to mediate a dispute between Generals Conrad von Hötzendorf and Svetozar Boroević (*q.v.*) concerning the nature of a planned assault against the Italians in Venetia. Arz's decision to allocate equal forces to each commander and to permit each to conduct independent operations violated a cardinal tenet of military leadership, namely, concentration, and proved a disaster; by June 20, the Austro-Hungarian offensive had been blunted, the army's cohesion seriously impaired, and the morale of the fighting units destroyed. Late in October 1918, Arz offered the Italians an armistice, but they accepted it only thirty-six hours after Austro-Hungarian demobilization had begun, with the resulting "perfidious" Italian capture of hundreds of thousands of inactive veterans (Rudolf Kiszling). The armistice was finally concluded on November 3; Arz's troops, especially on the southern front, had simply melted away.

An unpolitical general, Arz von Straussenburg faithfully served his supreme commander and remained loyal to the German ally throughout the war. He died in Budapest on July 1, 1935.

Arz, *Kampf und Sturz der Mittelmächte* and *Zur Geschichte des Grossen Krieges 1914-1918*; Rothenberg, *Army of Francis Joseph*; *Neue Österreichische Biographie*, X; *Österreichisches Biographisches Lexikon 1815-1950*, I.

ASQUITH, Herbert Henry (*Great Britain, Prime Minister*), first earl of Oxford and Asquith, was born at Croft House, Morley, Lincolnshire, on September 12, 1852, the son of a nonconformist wool spinner and weaver. He went to Balliol College, Oxford, in 1870 as almost the first scholar to come from outside the ranks of the great public schools, and thereafter pursued a career in law, until his election to the House of Commons as Liberal member from East Fife in 1886. Six years later, Prime Minister William Gladstone appointed Asquith home secretary, but the Liberals were defeated in 1895 and Asquith was out of office for nearly eleven years. He broke with the Liberal leader, Sir Henry Campbell-Bannerman, over the South African War at the turn of the century; as a Liberal imperialist, Asquith objected to Campbell-Bannerman's denunciation of British farm burnings and concentration camps as "methods of barbarism." Only after the general election of January 1906, when the Liberal party was finally returned to power, did Asquith accept the post of chancellor of the Exchequer. In April 1908, the deteriorating health of Campbell-Bannerman elevated Asquith to the nation's highest office, and he took with him David Lloyd George as chancellor of the Exchequer and Winston S. Churchill (*qq.v.*) as president of the Board of Trade. Asquith's nine-year rule was to be the longest in nearly a century of British politics.

Asquith's government immediately faced a financial crisis, which quickly evolved into a constitutional question. Lloyd George's 1908 budget levied a new land tax to pay for both social programs and naval expansion. When the House of Lords rejected the budget in November, it openly challenged the 250-year-old assumption that the power of the purse belonged to the Commons. Although the Lords passed the budget in April 1910, Asquith, anxious over a projected third home rule bill for Ireland, introduced a scheme whereby a bill which had been passed in the Commons three times would, after a waiting period of two years, automatically become law even if the Lords rejected it down the line. In April 1912, the prime minister introduced his home rule bill promising to establish a Dublin parliament; this measure brought him the opposition not only of the Lords, but also of the Ulster Protestants, led by Sir Edward Carson (*q.v.*). Neither a conference of party leaders at Buckingham Palace in July 1914 nor a threat to create as many new Liberal peers as were necessary to pass the measure in the Lords could calm the political storm. In March 1914, the army camp at the Curragh had actually decided to accept dismissal rather than coerce Ulster into accepting home rule, a mutiny that forced Asquith to take over as secretary for war.

The German thrust through Belgium ended the Irish question and united the British behind Asquith on August 4, 1914, and the prime minister's appointment of Lord H. H. Kitchener (*q.v.*) as secretary of state for war was a master stroke designed to allay Conservative criticism. By December 1914, Asquith had realized that the war would not be "over before Christmas," and he turned to the more imaginative Lloyd George and Churchill, both of whom denounced the attritional tactics employed in France and called instead for a "more imaginative strategy." Specifically, in February 1915, the prime minister accepted the proposal that the navy force the Dardanelles and take Constantinople; when this failed, Asquith, still refusing to convene the War Council, agreed that the armies under Sir Ian Hamilton (*q.v.*) storm the Gallipoli Peninsula. The failure of both services to accomplish their goals at the Straits—compounded by an acute shortage of shells in France—brought about the fall of the Liberal government in May 1915.

The coalition government that succeeded it was headed by Asquith and included Andrew Bonar Law (*q.v.*) of the Conservatives and Arthur Henderson of Labour; not included were Winston Churchill and Admiral Sir John Fisher (*q.v.*) both of whom were out of favor after the Dardanelles debacle. The coalition government was not a great success. Conscription of a sort was finally forced upon Asquith as was the replacement of Sir John French by Sir Douglas Haig (*qq.v.*) as field commander in France. In October 1915, the French compelled the prime minister to support yet another "side show," this one at Salonika, and two months later the British at last gave up on the Dardanelles campaign. The slaughter in France did not add to Asquith's standing at home. In April 1916, the prime minister delineated his war-aims program, calling specifically for the "destruction of the military domination of Prussia," a perfectly nebulous phrase, and for a constitutional change in Berlin. But Asquith was losing the reins of power and becoming a passive spectator in the war that he had helped unleash. His lack of imagination, his inability to provide new ideas, his conciliation, his "wait-and-see" attitude, and his wooden personality were resented by a country whose youth was being led to the slaughter at the Somme for no apparent reason. In November and December, the Conservatives Bonar Law and Edward Carson joined with Lord Beaverbrook (*q.v.*) to champion the cause of the fiery Welshman, Lloyd George, who, on December 7, succeeded Asquith as prime minister.

Herbert Asquith was then suddenly and unexpectedly cast into the role of leader of the opposition, and he carried out his functions with only the most moderate criticism. Above all, he feared that a general election at that time would destroy the Liberal party as the country would undoubtedly rally around the national government. His fears were well-founded: in the general election of December 1918, Asquith was defeated in East Fife, which he had held for thirty-two years. In 1920, he returned to the Commons in a by-election in Paisley, and two years later he was instrumental in helping Labour form its first major government—which lasted barely eight months. In a subsequent election he was defeated at Paisley and opted to end a parliamentary career that spanned nearly four decades. In 1925 Asquith entered the House of Lords as earl of Oxford and Asquith, but further feuds with Lloyd George forced him the following year to resign as leader of the Liberals. He died at The Wharf, Sutton Courteney, Berkshire, on February 15, 1928. He made it well known that he desired no public funeral, although he was widely eulogized as "the last of the Romans." Churchill said of him that "in war he had not those qualities of resource and energy, of prevision and assiduous management, which ought to reside in the executive."

Asquith, *Memories and Reflections*, 2 vols.; Churchill, *Great Contemporaries*; Guinn, *British Strategy and Politics*; Jenkins, *Asquith*; Spender and Asquith, *Life of Herbert Henry Asquith*; *Dictionary of National Biography 1922-1930.*

AUFFENBERG von KOMARÓW, Moritz Baron (*Austria-Hungary, Field Marshal, War Minister*), was born in Troppau on May 22, 1852, the son of a circuit court president. Auffenberg attended the Theresa Military Academy as well as the War Academy (1875-77), and he saw action during the occupation of Bosnia in 1878; two years later he was attached to the General Staff in the grade of captain, being promoted major general in 1900 and field marshal in 1905. Auffenberg penned a treatise on the South Slav question for General Oskar Potiorek (*q.v.*) in 1904 in which he came out in favor of trialism and, if need be, a violent break with the Hungarian Magyars. Auffenberg's views on the minority question underwent several changes thereafter: at first he sought the creation of a South Slav state within the Dual Monarchy, but later he adhered to a utopian scheme of a legal federation of Austria-Hungary with the Kingdom of Serbia. And although he was a close personal friend of General Conrad von Hötzendorf (*q.v.*), chief of the General Staff, Auffenberg did not share Conrad's fervent desire for a preemptive strike against Serbia. By 1910 Auffenberg had fully identified himself with Archduke Francis Ferdinand's (*q.v.*) plans for a truly dynastic army and for reducing the entrenched privileges of Hungary within the empire.

In part owing to this, Auffenberg, in August 1911, was forced by the heir presumptive to accept the post of war minister. Here the soldier distinguished himself. Auffenberg carried out a much-needed rejuvenation of the army's artillery, replacing antiquated siege artillery of Uchatius design with 30.5 cm mobile mortars from the Skoda works in Bohemia; seventy-six new field batteries were created under his tutelage. However, Auffenberg's continued antipathy towards the Hungarians made him a distinct political liability, and on December 10, 1912, Emperor Francis Joseph (*q.v.*) rather brusquely ordered the war minister to submit his resignation.

Auffenberg then languished in the rather ceremonial post of inspector of the army. While in the War Ministry at the Babenberger Burg Am Hof, Auffenberg supported Conrad von Hötzendorf's desire to be rid of the alliance with the "hereditary enemy" Italy. With the outbreak of war in 1914, Auffenberg was given command of the Fourth Army, and on August 26, defeated the Russian Fifth Army at Komarów. However, in September the Fourth Army was involved in the general defeat at Lemberg as the Russians drove a wedge between Auffenberg and General Viktor Dankl (*q.v.*); Archduke Frederick (*q.v.*) took this opportunity to relieve Auffenberg of command of the Fourth Army.

On April 25, 1915, Auffenberg was raised to the baronage and given the title *von Komarów*. The former war minister had viewed the outcome of the war pessimistically since July 1914, believing that Conrad von Hötzendorf had chosen the wrong moment to humble Serbia; this state of gloom was deepened in 1916 when Auffenberg was accused of having made public secret information while defending a friend during his years as war minister. Although a special court of honor cleared him of the charges, his career in the army was beyond repair. Auffenberg retired to Vienna as a publicist and died there on May 18, 1928.

Auffenberg, *Aus Österreichs Höhe und Niedergang*; Allmayer-Beck and Lessing, *Die K. (u.) K.-Armee*; Rothenberg, *Army of Francis Joseph*; *Neue Deutsche Biographie*, I; *Neue Österreichische Biographie*, VI.

AUGAGNEUR, Jean Victor (*France, Minister of Marine*), was born at Lyons, May 16, 1855. He received his degree as a physician in 1879 and earned an international reputation in medical research and education. Politics soon became his second career. He entered the Lyons municipal council in 1888, rose to mayor of his native city in 1900, and won election as a Republican-Socialist to the Chamber of Deputies in 1904. Between 1905 and 1910 he filled still another role: governor general of Madagascar.

Augagneur returned to the National Assembly in 1910, receiving his first cabinet post in 1911 as minister of public works under Joseph Caillaux (*q.v.*). He served as vice president of the Chamber of Deputies during the first half of 1914 and entered the government of René Viviani (*q.v.*) in June as minister of public instruction. The first days of World War I drove Armand Gauthier, Viviani's minister of marine, to the brink of emotional collapse and elevated Augagneur to his most important government role. His record of success then came to an abrupt end.

Augagneur lacked any solid background for the post of navy minister. Placed at the top of a poorly defined chain of command and prone to act impulsively, he sometimes pointed the fleet in appropriate directions but more often did not. Augagneur was justified in calling on the Mediterranean commander, Admiral Boué de Lapeyrère (*q.v.*), to move energetically against the German battle cruiser *Goeben* in early August. But he had no success in subordinating Lapeyrère to his orders. Augagneur's subsequent demands for sorties into the confined waters of the Adriatic (to strike at the Austrian fleet but also to exert political pressure on Italy) threatened to expose France's battle fleet to mines, torpedo boats, and submarines. Lapeyrère resisted such pressure.

Augagneur has received scathing criticism from Cassar for his role in the Dardanelles operation. In mid-January 1915, he committed the French fleet to an unsupported naval assault on the Turkish Straits. This he did without seeing the precise battle plan, without informing the French naval commander in the Mediterranean, and without allowing word of the projected attack to reach the French war minister. According to Cassar, Augagneur was partly swayed by the glowing picture of easy success painted by his British counterpart, Winston Churchill (*q.v.*); partly he was concerned to maintain France's political presence in the eastern Mediterranean. When the naval assault failed, Augagneur like Churchill drifted into a larger commitment. By late March he was under bitter assault by members of the National Assembly.

Pliable in the face of British demands, Augagneur responded differently to the Italians. Extensive negotiations took place during the spring of 1915 over a naval convention to accompany Italy's entry into the war. Augagneur flatly opposed Rome's call for an Italian commander in chief for the Allied fleet in the Adriatic. He claimed French public opinion would not tolerate such an arrangement. His own political prospects could hardly have survived it either.

By September 1915, German submarines in the Mediterranean were active from the coast of Algeria to the Dardanelles, and Augagneur found himself attacked by his own colleagues in the cabinet. With the fall of Viviani's government in October 1915, Augagneur gave way to Admiral Lacaze (*q.v.*), a professional officer prepared to make the war against the submarine the center of French naval operations.

Augagneur returned to the less demanding role of ordinary deputy. Defeated for reelection in 1919, he resumed colonial service as governor general of French Equatorial Africa. He was reelected to the Chamber of Deputies in 1928. He died in Paris on April 23, 1931.

Cassar, *The French and the Dardanelles*; Belot and Reussner, *La Puissance navale dans l'histoire*, III; Halpern, "Anglo-French-Italian Naval Convention of 1915"; Laurens, *Le Commandement naval en Méditerranée*; Thomazi, *La Marine française dans la Grande Guerre*, II, III, IV; *Dictionnaire des parlementaires français*, I.

AVERESCU, Alexandru (*Rumania, Lieutenant General, Prime Minister*), was born into a peasant family in Ismail, Bessarabia, March 9, 1859. He enlisted in the Rumanian army in 1876 and fought in his country's war against Turkey for independence, 1877/78. When Bessarabia was annexed by Russia in the peace settlement, Averescu chose Rumanian citizenship. He served in the ranks in the 1880s, received his lieutenant's commission in 1891, and then rose quickly to the rank of captain. Like many of his contemporaries, Averescu went abroad for advanced training. He attended the Italian General Staff School in Turin and returned home with an Italian bride. Three years as military attaché in Berlin followed, 1895-98. Promoted colonel in 1901, he rose to brigadier general five years later.

In 1907 Averescu's career took a new turn. He joined the Liberal government of Ion Bratianu (*q.v.*) as minister of war. The peasant rebellion that year dominated events. Averescu, a peasant leading a peasant army, repressed the uprising with the massive use of force: flying columns armed with artillery, pitched battles against insurgent bands, large-scale reprisals. Under his control, the army remained a reliable tool even in this heated situation. A major general in 1912, Averescu served as the army's chief of staff during the Balkan Wars. Prince Ferdinand (*q.v.*) held the nominal position of commander in chief. In fact, it was Averescu who directed operations during the brief, bloodless invasion of Bulgaria in July 1913.

The outbreak of World War I did not draw Rumania into the conflict immediately, but Averescu's reputation guaranteed him a leading role once Rumania entered the hostilities. He was made commander of the Second Army in August 1916, and led a successful advance across the central Carpathians into Transylvania. When General von Mackensen (*q.v.*) responded by threatening Rumania's Black Sea province of the Dobrudja, Averescu became the leading advocate of shifting Rumanian strategy. He called for reinforcing the southern front at the expense of the Carpathians and striking boldly into Mackensen's rear. He received command of the Third Army and the forces in the Dobrudja; the former he intended to use in a daring operation across the Danube while the latter fixed Mackensen's army in position. Critics like General Prezan (*q.v.*) claimed that Rumania's poor transportation network made such an operation too risky and threatened to weaken the Carpathian front fatally.

The crossing of the Danube failed. Bad weather, the opposition of enemy river flotillas, and the fortuitous presence of strong Bulgarian units at the crossing point made it impossible to carry out the assault on Mackensen's rear. Averescu returned to the Second Army in the Carpathians to conduct a spirited resistance in the mountain passes. The inex-perienced Rumanian forces were at their best in such defensive operations, and Averescu restored his shaken military reputation. He helped cover Prezan's unsuccessful offensive on the outskirts of Bucharest, then conducted a fighting retreat northeastward to the Sireth. There Averescu and the Second Army became the only Rumanian forces in the field, as Prezan and his French advisers worked frantically to rebuild the battered Rumanian army.

The year 1917 made Averescu Rumania's greatest wartime hero. In late July he led a successful advance at Marasti against strong enemy positions. Intended to be part of a general offensive on the eastern front, the Rumanian effort was overshadowed by the accelerating collapse of the Russian army. The Central Powers responded in August with an assault aimed at capturing Jassy and driving the Rumanians out of their last bit of unoccupied territory. Averescu then distinguished himself at the battle of Marasesti, defending the salient he had won in the previous month. The Sireth line held, but Russian forces crumbled.

Averescu became Rumania's second wartime prime minister on February 8, 1918. Bratianu had resigned, intending meanwhile to supervise events from behind the scenes. He encouraged King Ferdinand to replace him with the well-known general. Averescu's acquaintance with Mackensen extended back to his years as an attaché in Berlin. Such a personal link might ease Rumania's plight. Moreover, Averescu's concern over the spread of Bolshevism and his conviction that the Central Powers would win the war made him—at least to Bratianu—the best candidate for the thankless task of negotiating peace.

Prime Minister Averescu found himself helpless. Whatever Mackensen felt, Generals von Hindenburg and Ludendorff (*qq.v.*) were intransigent. They threatened to renew hostilities unless Rumania gave in on all major issues: the surrender of the Dobrudja, open transit for German forces across Rumania to the Ukraine, the subordination of the Rumanian economy to the needs of the Central Powers. Averescu found these terms intolerable. But he insisted military resistance was futile. Bratianu shunted him aside in hopes the Germanophile Marghiloman (*q.v.*) could do better.

His political ambitions awakened, Averescu stationed himself on the edge of power. In the fall of 1918 he maneuvered unsuccessfully to replace the fading Marghiloman. In the postwar period, he founded his own political party and offered himself as a defender of order. Seton-Watson and, more recently, Victoria Brown have found him little more than a cardboard figure erected by established moderate and conservative leaders as a barrier to land reform. He served again as prime minister in the early 1920s, returned to office in the years 1926-28, and made a final effort to form a government in 1934. He was named a field marshal in 1930. Averescu died in Bucharest, October 2, 1938. He was buried at the scene of his greatest military triumph, the battlefield of Marasti.

Brown, "The Movement for Reform in Rumania after World War I"; Kiritescu, *La Roumanie dans la Guerre Mondiale*; Kitchen, "Hindenburg, Ludendorff, and Rumania"; Seton-Watson, *History of the Roumanians*; Spector, *Rumania at the Paris Peace Conference*; *Larousse mensuel*, XI.

BACHMANN, Gustav (*Germany, Admiral*), was born at Cammin in Mecklenburg on July 13, 1860, the son of a gentleman farmer. He entered the navy in 1877 and later saw service in Africa and Australia. Bachmann served as chief of staff of the East Asian Cruiser Squadron from 1901 to 1903, and in 1907 as rear admiral began a three-year stint as head of the Central Division of the Navy Office under Admiral Alfred von Tirpitz (*q.v.*). Bachmann commanded the High Sea Fleet's Scouting Forces in the grade of vice admiral from 1910 to 1913.

The outbreak of the war found Bachmann as chief of the Baltic Sea naval station at Kiel. However, on February 2, 1915, he was appointed chief of the Admiralty Staff, and one month later promoted admiral. A compromise candidate for the Admiralty, he was not known to possess a particularly strong personality; in fact, Tirpitz worked well with "the amiable, always complaisant Bachmann." Bachmann sought to obtain greater operative freedom for the fleet in both the North and Baltic seas, but Kaiser Wilhelm II (*q.v.*) instead counseled restraint and caution. But the major issue confronting Bachmann was that of unrestricted submarine warfare. Initially only a reluctant bystander, Bachmann under the influence of Tirpitz quickly came to accept the U-boat campaign as the only means available to Germany to force Britain to the peace table, and he loyally supported Tirpitz in this endeavor against Chancellor Theobald von Bethmann Hollweg (*q.v.*). Not even a sharp protest note by the United States on May 15 after the sinking of the liners *Arabic* and *Lusitania* could deter the chief of the Admiralty Staff from this course. And when the Kaiser sought to assuage the Americans by reverting to submarine warfare according to prize rules, both Tirpitz and Bachmann submitted their resignations on June 7, 1915. Wilhelm II accepted Bachmann's letter on September 3, noting that the two admirals had initiated "downright military conspiracy."

From September 1915 to October 1918, Bachmann returned to his position as head of the Kiel naval station. In the wake of the fleet revolts in the summer of 1917 he demanded energetic measures against the Independent Socialists (USPD) as well as patriotic instruction for the sailors. In vain Bachmann informed the naval command of the low morale in the ranks in October 1918, the very month in which the new Supreme Command under Admiral Reinhard Scheer (*q.v.*) retired him. Bachmann died in Kiel on August 30, 1943.

Gemzell, *Organization, Conflict, and Innovation*; Herwig, "Luxury" Fleet; *Neue Deutsche Biographie*, I.

BAKER, Newton Diehl (*United States, Secretary of War*), was born in Martinsburg, West Virginia, on December 3, 1871, the son of a physician. Endowed with a sharp mind, Baker graduated from Johns Hopkins University in 1892, having had Woodrow Wilson (*q.v.*) as one of his teachers; two years later he acquired a law degree from Washington and Lee University. Baker was brought to Cleveland by Martin A. Foran to practice law, but he quickly rose in the city administration to solicitor and in 1913 to mayor. The year before he had supported Wilson's Democratic candidacy for the presidency, but had declined the offered position of secretary of the interior.

The quiet, almost self-effacing Baker, though known as a pacifist, agreed reluctantly on March 16, 1916, to become secretary of war. Only a few days before, Pancho Villa had conducted his celebrated raid into New Mexico, and Baker ordered Brigadier General John J. Pershing (*q.v.*) to pursue the Mexican across the border.

The U.S. Army of 95,000 men was completely unprepared for war in Europe. In his first year in office Baker could do little to alter that situation owing to Wilson's strict definition of neutrality, the nation's divided soul, and the traditional military inadequacies of American peacetime forces. After April 1917, Baker supervised the creation of an army of 4 million men under the wartime conscription act. He reorganized the administration of the War Department, specifically introducing the new "G" sections, dividing the General Staff into separate departments such as supply, personnel, intelligence, and so on. Baker also made the time-saving decision to adapt the British Enfield rifle for use with American ammunition.

Nevertheless, Baker was sharply attacked by Congress for delays in creating American armies. He had also proved rather inept in handling Theodore

Roosevelt's request to raise a volunteer division, and maladroit in removing General Leonard Wood from command of a division bound for France. Above all, Baker failed to move against the "swivel-chair War Department Generals" until forced to do so by a Senate investigation in December 1917. The criticisms leveled against him concerning shortages and low-grade facilities were not always fair as the secretary straddled a delicate position between the military, who controlled operations, and a president with firm notions of his own about that military policy. Still, Baker developed a close friendship with Wilson and became one of the latter's most trusted advisers. The secretary skillfully supported his field commander in France and shared General Pershing's position that the American Expeditionary Forces not be "amalgamated" with the Allied armies. Not even the unfortunate feud between Pershing and General March (q.v.) over relocation of staff officers and promotions to the grade of general could deter Baker. General George C. Marshall said of him in the 1950s: "He rode a very difficult horse . . . between General Pershing and General March, and he did it extraordinarily well."

After the war, Baker returned to his law practice in Cleveland. In 1928 he became a member of the Permanent Court of Arbitration at The Hague. Although a supporter of Franklin D. Roosevelt (q.v.), Baker broke with the president in the 1930s over the constitutionality of the Tennessee Valley Authority. Baker died on Christmas Day 1937 in Shaker Heights, near Cleveland.

Baker, *Why We Went to War*; Beaver, *Newton D. Baker and the American War Effort*; *Dictionary of American Biography*, XXII Supplement Two.

BALFOUR, Arthur James (*Great Britain, First Lord of the Admiralty, Secretary of State for Foreign Affairs*), first earl of Balfour, was born at Whittinghame, East Lothian, on July 25, 1848, the son of a country gentleman. Educated at Eton and at Trinity College, Cambridge, he entered Westminster in 1874 at the urging of his uncle, who was later to be Prime Minister Lord Salisbury. In 1878 Balfour accompanied his uncle to the Congress of Berlin as private secretary. Balfour represented East Manchester in the House of Commons from 1885 until 1906, and in 1886 helped to defeat the first Irish Home Rule Bill; the following year he accepted the Irish chief-secretaryship under his uncle. In October 1891, Balfour assumed the Conservative leadership in the Commons and the office of first lord of the treasury. He was a staunch advocate of military action against the Boers in South Africa and ordered Sir Redvers

Buller to press on with the relief of Ladysmith, or to lay down his command and return home. In July 1902, he succeeded Salisbury as prime minister, but the issue of free trade versus protectionism quickly divided his party. In the sphere of foreign policy, Balfour established a Committee of Imperial Defence, renewed the Anglo-Japanese Agreement of 1902, and concluded the entente with France, thereby abandoning the time-honored British policy of holding the diplomatic balance in Europe. Balfour's government was swamped at the polls by the great Liberal victory in January 1906; the prime minister lost his seat for East Manchester.

A "safe" seat in the City of London brought him back to the Commons, and he worked hard to preserve the unity of the Conservative party. Balfour justified the House of Lords' rejection of David Lloyd George's (q.v.) "People's" budget of 1908, and he denounced as unconstitutional Prime Minister Herbert Asquith's (q.v.) proposal to create a sufficiency of peers to overcome the Lords' opposition to the budget as well as to Irish home rule. Balfour resigned as leader of the Conservatives in November 1911, rightly sensing that he had lost control of the party on the issue of home rule. However, he held himself ready, should King George V (q.v.) so desire, to assume the leadership in 1914 of a "ministry of Caretakers" in case the Irish issue erupted in civil war. The outbreak of war in Europe overrode such speculation.

Balfour agreed to return as a member of the Committee of Imperial Defence and, although technically a former minister in opposition, in November 1914, he even attended the meetings of Asquith's inner War Council. On May 25, 1915, after a severe shortage of shells in the British armies in France and the debacle at the Dardanelles had rocked Asquith's Liberal administration, Balfour joined the first coalition government as first lord of the Admiralty. He brought to the post a wealth of experience in government, courtly manners, personal charm, and a first-rate brain; unfortunately, these qualities were largely vitiated by his lethargy and desultory energy. Moreover, the first sea lord, Sir Henry Jackson, was utterly colorless and uninspiring, and the two, Balfour and Jackson, made a poor pair, especially coming on the heels of the dynamic duo of Winston Churchill and John Fisher (qq.v.). Lloyd George perhaps put it best: "He [Balfour] lacked the physical energy and fertility of resource, and untiring industry for the . . . Admiralty." Balfour at once became embroiled in the ongoing Dardanelles controversy, and in October he supported Sir Roger Keyes' (q.v.) plea for a renewed rush of the Straits, but only if the sea lords approved. After the battle of Jutland in May/ June 1916 he congratulated Sir John Jellicoe (q.v.) upon his "victory," but later rarely referred to it, and on at least one occasion informed Sir David Beatty (q.v.) that he considered it to have been "a missed opportunity." Above all, he adopted an utterly fatalistic attitude with regard to the German submarine menace in October 1916: "We must for the present be content with palliation." On another occasion he called the U-boat threat "an evil which unfortunately we cannot wholly cure." In November Balfour replaced Jackson with Jellicoe as first sea lord, and on December 7 Lloyd George moved Balfour to the Foreign Office. As Churchill later put it: "he passed from one Cabinet to the other . . . like a powerful graceful cat walking delicately and unsoiled across a rather muddy street."

Balfour's greatest contribution to the war began on April 14, 1917, when he sailed for the United States at the head of a diplomatic mission. He used his graceful air to charm American politicians and soldiers and convinced Washington to increase its output of antisubmarine craft and merchant shipping. The mission was made easier, in part, by Balfour's long-standing belief in the necessity of cooperation by the two Anglo-Saxon peoples. In other areas, his handling of foreign policy was less successful. Balfour badly underestimated the sincerity of Austria-Hungary's peace overtures in 1917 as well as the threat of the Bolsheviks in Russia. His declaration on November 2, 1917, viewing "with favour the establishment in Palestine of a national home for the Jewish people" was to cause Britain endless rancor and recrimination; it can perhaps best be seen as a heavy-handed attempt to keep the French out of Palestine.

In January 1919, Balfour accompanied Lloyd George to Paris; privately he informed a dear friend that "it was not so much the war as the peace that I have always dreaded." His skill and tact saved the deliberations, as Churchill put it, "from sinking into voluble fatuity"; Georges Clemenceau (q.v.) spoke openly of Balfour as the Richelieu of the conference. The Treaty of St. Germain with Austria was especially Balfour's work. Yet the strain of office took its toll and Balfour resigned as foreign secretary on October 24, 1919, retaining a place in the Cabinet as lord president of the council. In November 1921, he represented Britain at the Washington Conference on Naval Reductions; two years later he helped rehabilitate Austria financially under the auspices of the League of Nations. In 1922, he was created Earl Balfour, Viscount Traprain. He closed an illustrious career that spanned almost exactly half a century

with the so-called Balfour Definition of 1926, which redefined the freedoms of the Dominions and thereby led directly to the Statute of Westminster five years later. Balfour died at Fisher's Hill, near Woking, on March 19, 1930. He had never married.

Winston Churchill, *Great Contemporaries*; Dugdale, *Arthur James Balfour*, 2 vols.; Marder, *Dreadnought to Scapa Flow*, II, III; Young, *Arthur James Balfour*; *Dictionary of National Biography 1922-1930*.

BARDOLFF, Carl Baron (*Austria-Hungary, Colonel*), was born in Graz in the Steiermark on September 3, 1865. In the fall of 1885 Bardolff entered Graz University and earned his doctorate of jurisprudence; in 1888 he decided on a career in the army. Bardolff attended the War College in Vienna and until 1901 was attached to the General Staff. Next came service with the infantry in the Sanjak Novibazar, an instructorship at the War College, further duty with the General Staff, and finally commandant of the Nineteenth Infantry Regiment in Vienna. From 1911 to 1914 Bardolff served as chief of the military chancellery as well as adjutant to the heir presumptive, Archduke Francis Ferdinand (q.v.). In this capacity Colonel Bardolff, in January 1913, worked out a plan to move certain Czech, Magyar, Croat, and Dalmatian regiments from their home stations and to replace them with nonindigenous units because "the existence of national dissension in certain units can no longer be denied." Both Generals Conrad von Hötzendorf and Alexander von Krobatin (qq.v.) agreed to this plan to ensure a safer ethnic balance; but when it was leaked to the Vienna press in October, Emperor Francis Joseph (q.v.) cut short the proposed station changes.

Bardolff was entrusted with command of the Twenty-Ninth Infantry Brigade within the VI Corps of the Fourth Army (Auffenberg) at the outbreak of the war, and in the grade of brigadier led his unit into Komarów on August 30, 1914. Bardolff, on horseback, rallied his soldiers by swinging his cap and exhorting them in Hungarian: "Forward, long live the King!" This feat earned him a baronage as well as an appointment as chief of staff of the Second Army, later Army Group Böhm-Ermolli (q.v.), in East Galicia and the Bukovina in September 1914.

Although a military member of Francis Ferdinand's Belvedere Circle before the war, Bardolff did not transfer his unbounded enthusiasm to the new Emperor Charles (q.v.) in November 1916, even though the young ruler went out of his way to appoint numerous members of that charmed circle to his government. Bardolff was dubious about the monarch's firmness and worried about his desire for peace at almost any price; he grew apprehensive about Charles' aspirations for military command. In the wake of serious strikes in January 1918, Charles sought to appoint Prince Alois Schönburg-Hartenstein (q.v.) head of a military government at home with Bardolff as his deputy, but fortunately the wave of strikes receded and Bardolff instead was given command of the Sixtieth Infantry Regiment on the southern front. In October 1918, Charles recalled him to Vienna to serve as section chief of supply and provisioning in the War Ministry.

After the war, Bardolff returned to his law practice and served politically as head of the German Volksrat in Austria; as one of the leaders of the *völkisch* movement in Austria he was a bitter opponent of Chancellors Dollfuss and Schuschnigg. In 1938 Adolf Hitler appointed Bardolff lieutenant general in the Wehrmacht, SA Oberführer, and member of the German Reichstag; the general died in Graz on May 17, 1953.

Allmayer-Beck and Lessing, *Die K. (u.) K.-Armee*; Bardolff, *Militär-Maria Theresien-Orden* and *Soldat im alten Österreich*; Rothenberg, *Army of Francis Joseph*.

BAUER, Max Hermann (*Germany, Colonel*), was born in Quedlinburg on January 31, 1869, the son of an estate owner. Bauer entered the army in 1888 and made a career in the artillery branch: he attended the Engineer and Artillery School at Charlottenburg and from 1905 to 1908 served as artillery expert in the General Staff. In 1908 Bauer was assigned as special artillery aide to Colonel Erich Ludendorff (q.v.) in the mobilization and deployment section of the General Staff and entrusted with converting the foot artillery into heavy mobile artillery with 42 cm guns. Bauer was promoted major in 1911 and thereafter served as staff officer at Colmar.

Bauer entered the war as artillery expert in the General Staff under General Helmuth von Moltke (q.v.), and earned his military reputation by effectively deploying heavy guns during the invasion of Belgium—particularly the reduction of Liège—and by overcoming the munitions shortage during the early weeks of the war. Partly owing to this, Bauer, in July 1915, was appointed chief of Section II of the General Staff, responsible for artillery. However, Bauer's role far surpassed his technical function. A born intriguer, rabid anti-Semite and fervent antifeminist, Bauer maintained intimate ties to the captains of industry and did not shrink from using the Rhenish magnates to advance his desires for a military dictatorship. Bauer intitially also allied himself with Chancellor Theobald von Bethmann Hollweg in order in the fall of 1916 to oust the chief

of the General Staff, Erich von Falkenhayn (qq.v.); the iron-willed Bauer deplored what he termed Falkenhayn's "hand to mouth strategy" and the senseless slaughter at Verdun.

In July 1917, Bauer mobilized the new army commanders, General Ludendorff and Field Marshal Paul von Hindenburg (q.v.), to dismiss Bethmann Hollweg over the chancellor's proposed franchise reform for Prussia and his "defeatist" stance on the matter of territorial annexations. Lieutenant Colonel Bauer cleverly persuaded Crown Prince Wilhelm (q.v.) on July 12 to interview known parliamentary opponents of the chancellor while he hid in an anteroom and kept notes of the conversations; meanwhile, Bauer also spread the notion that Hindenburg and Ludendorff would resign unless the chancellor was dismissed. Within hours, Bauer reaped his reward; Bethmann Hollweg resigned.

Bauer worked diligently to fulfill the provisions of the mammoth Hindenburg Program's call for increased munitions output and to enforce the Auxiliary Service Law that made all German males between the ages of fifteen and sixty liable for "patriotic service." Neither did Bauer shrink from deploying Belgian forced labor in German industries. Throughout this period the energetic colonel continued his political intrigue, using Ludendorff's authority as cover. His list of enemies included Wilhelm Groener, Chancellor Count Georg von Hertling (qq.v.) as well as Generals Heinrich Scheuch, Hermann von Stein, and Civil Cabinet head Rudolf von Valentini (q.v.). By February 1918, Bauer's machinations reached even the House of Hohenzollern as the colonel informed the crown prince that the Kaiser had become "our doom" and slyly suggested, albeit without success, that Wilhelm II (q.v.) be replaced by his eldest son. And early in October 1918, Bauer intrigued against Ludendorff, counseling officers as well as politicians to dismiss the "silent dictator."

Colonel Bauer resigned from the military in June 1919 in order to collaborate with Ludendorff on the notorious "stab in the back" legend concerning Germany's defeat in the war as a result of "defeatist" forces on the home front. In March 1920, he took part in the right-wing Kapp *Putsch* in Berlin and consequently had to flee the country, first to Austria and later to Hungary. Bauer simply could not resist political intrigue and at times conspired against regimes in Hungary, Czechoslovakia, and Austria; he also maintained close ties to conservative forces in the Ukraine. After the failure of Adolf Hitler's beer hall *Putsch* in Munich in November 1923, Bauer embarked on an exile that took him to Russia, Madrid (1924), Argentina (1925), and China (1927) as military adviser. He returned to Germany, but in 1929 was summoned to China by Chiang Kai-Shek; Bauer died in Shanghai of smallpox on May 6, 1929.

Bauer's memoirs constituted a bitter condemnation of the entire conduct of the war. One historian has summarized the colonel's wartime aims as "a military dictatorship under Ludendorff, the exclusion of the Reichstag from active politics, and the total militarisation of the economy." It is safe to say that Bauer represented the most drastic example of the ruthless, intriguing, political "demigods" of the General Staff.

Bauer, *Der Grosse Krieg*; Feldman, *Army, Industry, and Labor in Germany*; Kitchen, *Silent Dictatorship*; Ludendorff, *Kriegführung und Politik*; *Geschichte der Ritter des Ordens*, I; *Neue Deutsche Biographie*, I.

BAUER, Otto (*Austria-Hungary, Foreign Minister*), was born in Vienna on September 5, 1882, the son of a Jewish Bohemian industrialist. Bauer obtained a doctorate of law at Vienna University and, although independently wealthy, joined the Austrian Socialist party's radical left wing. In 1907 he became editor of the *Arbeiter-Zeitung* and was regarded as the leading spokesman for the "Austro-Marxist" faction within the party.

In August 1914, Bauer was assigned to the Seventy-fifth Infantry Regiment in the grade of reserve lieutenant, and in the late fall of that year was taken prisoner on the eastern front. Bauer was sent to Siberia, where he gained contacts with numerous Russian Social Democrats; a general prisoner exchange after the October Revolution in 1917 brought him back to Vienna, where Bauer served the government first in the War Ministry and later in the Foreign Office. On November 11, 1918, he succeeded Viktor Adler (*q.v.*) as foreign minister and, like his predecessor, favored union with the German republic. Bauer resigned as foreign minister on July 26, 1919, but remained a member of the National Council until 1933. The wave of general strikes, bordering on civil war, that plagued especially Linz and Vienna in February 1934, led to proscription of radical Socialists and Bauer went into exile to Czechoslovakia and later to Paris, where he died on July 4, 1938.

Bauer, *Die österreichische Revolution*; *Neue Österreichische Biographie*, X; *Österreichisches Biographisches Lexikon 1815-1950*, I.

BEATTY, David (*Great Britain, Admiral of the Fleet*), first earl, was born at Howbeck Lodge, Stapeley, near Nantwich, Cheshire, on January 17, 1871, the second son of an army captain. Beatty entered the navy in 1884, and was quickly recognized for his energy and courage. He served Lord Kitchener (*q.v.*) 1896-98 in the naval brigade in Egypt and the Sudan, and was promoted to commander in 1898 over the heads of 395 senior lieutenants. Beatty also fought in China during the so-called Boxer rebellion, distinguishing himself through personal bravery; he was promoted to captain in 1900 at the age of twenty-nine (almost thirteen years ahead of normal procedure). In January 1910, Beatty was promoted to flag rank, the youngest officer to have been awarded this distinction for over a hundred years. The first lord of the Admiralty, Winston Churchill (*q.v.*), in 1912 chose Beatty for his naval secretary, and two years later appointed him "over the heads of all" to command the battle-cruiser squadron. Beatty was already known for his passion for victory and for being a born leader at sea.

The outbreak of war in August 1914 found Beatty on board the *Lion* as part of the Grand Fleet commanded by Sir John Jellicoe (*q.v.*). On August 28, Beatty led a British sortie into the Helgoland Bight which netted the German light cruisers *Ariadne*, *Köln*, and *Mainz*. This action showed Beatty at his best: offensive minded as well as impetuous, the vigor and determination to engage the enemy balanced by the ability to temper boldness with caution. In January 1915, he intercepted the German Reconnaissance Forces under Admiral Franz Hipper (*q.v.*) in their third attempt to shell the British coast near Whitby, Scarborough, and Hartlepool. In what is known as the battle of the Dogger Bank, Beatty's battle cruisers severely damaged the German battle cruiser *Seydlitz* and destroyed the *Blücher*. Yet it was not a great day: Beatty's flagship was disabled at the critical juncture in the battle and his second in command misunderstood his signal "attack the rear of the enemy," and instead concentrated fire on the already sinking *Blücher* and thereby permitted the rest of Hipper's squadron to withdraw safely.

During the battle of Jutland, Beatty, then in the grade of vice admiral, distinguished himself in several skirmishes with Hipper. At 3:48 P.M. on May 31, both battle-cruiser squadrons began a fierce fight, with Hipper drawing Beatty unawares onto the German High Sea Fleet steaming north up the coast of Denmark under Admiral Reinhard Scheer (*q.v.*). One hour later, Beatty sighted a forest of masts coming up from the south. Beatty the hunter now became Beatty the hunted. He reversed his position in order to draw the High Sea Fleet upon Jellicoe's battleships steaming south. At 5:35 P.M., Beatty turned eastward in order to bend back Hipper's van; this brilliant maneuver prevented the Germans from sighting Jellicoe's Grand Fleet. But the cost was high: the battle cruisers *Indefatigable*, *Queen Mary*, and *Invincible* were sunk by superior German fire which revealed British turret flash controls to have been inadequate. By 6:30 P.M. the two main battle fleets were in action. Scheer took a terrible pounding. Twice Jellicoe managed to cross the T, and the German commander extricated himself from hopeless situations by two dramatic battle turns away from the Grand Fleet. The ensuing darkness prevented Jellicoe from scoring the much-sought "Second Trafalgar." The next morning found Beatty with six battle cruisers operational against Hipper's one. Scheer chose to remain in his anchorages. Jutland was a tactical victory for the Germans who destroyed nearly twice as much tonnage as they lost, but in terms of strategy it left the Grand Fleet supreme.

At the end of 1916 Jellicoe became first sea lord and Beatty was appointed his successor with the acting rank of admiral. For the next two years he refitted the fleet on the basis of the lessons learned at Jutland, worked diligently to enhance the convoying of merchant ships, to Scandinavia especially, and rewrote the British "Battle Orders." Above all, he kept morale in the fleet high to the end of the war. On November 21, 1918, Beatty accepted the surrender of the German fleet under Admiral Reuter, and gave the famous signal: "The German flag will be hauled down at sunset, and will not be hoisted again without permission."

On January 1, 1919, David Beatty was promoted to the grade of admiral and on April 3 to that of admiral of the fleet; four days later the Grand Fleet was disbanded. Beatty served as first sea lord from 1921 to 1927 primarily in order to deal with the difficult problems concerning reducing a war fleet to a manageable peacetime navy. He represented Britain at the Washington Conference in November 1921, and retired in July 1927. Britain had rewarded her most famous sea commander in 1919 with a money grant of £100,000 and had raised him to the peerage as Early Beatty, Viscount Borodale of Borodale, Baron Beatty of the North Sea and of Brooksby. He died in London on March 11, 1936, and was buried five days later in St. Paul's Cathedral. Arthur Marder offers the view that Beatty was "a grand leader in many ways but not really at the top of the tree."

Barnes, *Beatty Papers*, I; Corbett and Newbolt, *Naval Operations*, IV, V; Marder, *Dreadnought to Scapa Flow*, I-V; *Dictionary of National Biography 1931-1940*.

BEAVERBROOK, Lord (1879-1964). See AITKEN, William Maxwell.

BELOW, Otto von (*Germany, General*), was born at Danzig on January 18, 1857, the son of a Prussian general from the Mecklenburg branch of the family. Below attended the War Academy in 1884-87 and two years later was promoted captain in the General Staff. He became battalion commander in 1897 and eight years later regimental commander in the grade of colonel; in 1909 Major General von Below was given a brigade and three years later as lieutenant general headed the Second Division at Insterburg in East Prussia.

On August 2, 1914, Below was appointed head of the I Reserve Corps, and eighteen days later fronted the Russians at Gumbinnen as the right wing of the Eighth Army. By the end of August, the I Reserve Corps had closed the ring around the Russian Narev Army; from September 5-15, Below helped defeat the Russian Second Army at the Masurian Lakes. For these twin victories that forced the enemy behind the Niemen River, Below was promoted general of infantry. He next defended East Prussia as the Eighth Army was withdrawn to Poland, and on November 7 decimated the enemy at Göritten. Below then became the youngest officer of his rank to be given command of an army, as he succeeded General Hermann von François as head of the Eighth Army. In February 1915, Below and General Hermann von Eichhorn's (*q.v.*) Tenth Army fought the bitter winter battle of the Masurian Lakes, taking 100,000 Russian prisoners at the Augustov forest; Below received the coveted order *Pour le mérite* for annihilating the Russian Tenth Army. In July Below headed a new Niemen Army and repulsed a Russian assault in eastern Poland; by December he had been returned to the Eighth Army and, in July 1916, held back another Russian offensive at Kekkau. His troops by now had taken Courland and Lithuania as far as the southern reaches of the Dvina.

On October 10, 1916, Otto von Below was appointed commander of a new Army Group Below (German Eleventh and Bulgarian First Army) in Macedonia. From November 3 to 27 he defended Monastir, but eventually abandoned it against German and Bulgarian pleas to hold it; during March 11-26, 1917, Below managed at least to stabilize the front near Monastir and to deny General Maurice Sarrail (*q.v.*) a decisive victory in Salonika. Above all, Below's holding action allowed the successful completion of the Rumanian campaign of Field Marshal August von Mackensen and General Erich von Falkenhayn (*qq.v.*) by covering the rear of the operation. Below was dispatched to the western front on April 22, 1917 to head the Sixth Army near Arras, but was recalled from this command on September 9, 1917.

Below's services were required on the Italian front. General Erich Ludendorff had entrusted his alpine expert, General Krafft von Dellmensingen (*qq.v.*), with preparing an assault over the Julian Alps against the Italians, and Below was nominally placed in command of a hastily assembled German–Austro-Hungarian Fourteenth Army consisting of twelve assault divisions. On October 24 Below's forces advanced along the line Tolmino-Flitsch-Karfreit, and three days later burst upon the Italian plain, inflicting almost 600,000 casualties and forcing the enemy behind first the Tagliamento and later the Piave rivers.

In January 1918, the much-traveled Below returned to the western front as head of a new Seventeenth Army in Artois, and he distinguished himself during the Michael offensive on March 21 in extremely heavy fighting around Arras. Unfortunately, the Seventeenth Army on August 8 was severely mauled in fighting around Arras and Albert, and the following month had to fall back upon the old Siegfried line and finally on Cambrai. On October 12 Below was given the First Army on the Aisne and ordered to hold the Hunding sector of the Hindenburg line; on November 8 he was appointed head of Home Defense West at Kassel for a final stand on German soil.

The new republican government appointed Otto von Below head of the XVII Army Corps at Danzig, but in June 1919, Below resigned from the service in opposition to the government's conciliatory policy with regard to the new Polish state. Below spent his last years in retirement working on behalf of various patriotic groups. He died at Besenhausen near Göttingen on March 9, 1944. The Allied demand of February 1920 that Below be turned over and tried on charges of war crimes was never fulfilled.

Einem, *Otto von Below*; Falls, *Caporetto*; *Geschichte der Ritter des Ordens*, I; *Neue Deutsche Biographie*, II.

BENEDICT XV (*Vatican, Pope*), was born Giacomo Della Chiesa in Genoa on November 21, 1854. His father was the Marquis Della Chiesa. After graduating from the University of Genoa, the young nobleman studied for the priesthood in Rome and was ordained in 1878. The first three decades of his life in the church were spent as a Vatican diplomat, first in Spain, then in the Papal Secretariat of State in Rome. In 1907 Pope Pius X named him archbishop of Bologna. The red hat of a cardinal came in May 1914.

A papal conclave meeting during the early weeks of World War I chose the cardinal of Bologna pope on September 3, 1914. The war inevitably dwarfed

Pope Benedict's other concerns between 1914 and 1918. He sought to mitigate the violence of the war, appealing in early 1915, for example, for an exchange of crippled prisoners of war. In his consistorial address of January 22, 1915, the new pope condemned the invasion of Belgium as a violation of justice, without, however, mentioning Germany by name.

Side by side with moral exhortations and humanitarian efforts, Benedict pursued a specific diplomatic policy. Preventing Italy from joining the belligerents became the first order of business. Italian participation in the war meant severing the Vatican from much of the Catholic population of Europe. The pope also entertained hopes of presiding over the peace conference, an impossible dream if Italy joined in the bloodshed. Thus Benedict pressed Vienna to make territorial concessions to the Italian government. During the last days of peace in May 1915, he told Italian Prime Minister Salandra (*q.v.*) that Austria would concede generously to Italy's demands, provided only that the Italian government held back a bit longer from declaring war.

Once Italy had entered the war, Benedict sought to negotiate a general peace. The uncomfortable isolation of the Vatican under wartime conditions was an obvious stimulus to action. Moreover, Benedict was particularly concerned to end the war before it destroyed the Habsburg monarchy, one of the leading Catholic powers in Europe and a long-time source of political support for the church.

By the close of 1916 the time seemed propitious for a Vatican peace initiative. Both the Central Powers and the United States had asked publicly that the belligerents state their war aims. After the particularly gruesome slaughter at Verdun and the Somme, Europe's peoples and governments seemed ready at last to lay down their weapons.

Quiet diplomacy in the spring of 1917 indicated that German Chancellor von Bethmann Hollweg (*q.v.*) might be willing to negotiate for peace, even if it meant a German evacuation of Belgium. The pope's peace appeal of August 1 was issued in part because Bethmann's fall from power seemed to be leading to a hardening of the German position. The appeal called on the belligerents to put their financial and territorial demands aside and to deal with one another on the basis of disarmament and international arbitration.

Benedict's call for a peace without victory stirred some interest in both the British and the German governments; but in the end, Germany would not make concessions to Belgium. It must be noted that, on the other side, France was hostile and the United States, just recently in April 1917 having entered the war, was uninterested. Once the war had taken on new intensity, with the Austro-German offensive at Caporetto (October 1917) and the great spring offensives of 1918, no further peace initiative was likely to get a hearing.

The greatest immediate effect of the peace appeal was felt in the Italian army. Even the common foot soldier knew that the pope had issued a condemnation of the war's "useless carnage." The partial collapse of the Italian forces in the wake of Caporetto found the army's rank and file repeating—and perhaps acting on—the pope's words.

Any hope that he would play a great role at the peace conference vanished long before the November armistice. The Vatican was not even invited to attend. Benedict himself had only a brief period to work in a Europe not torn by war. He died in Rome, January 22, 1922.

Althann, "Papal Mediation during the First World War"; Melograni, *Storia politica della grande guerra 1915-1918*; Christopher Seton-Watson, *Italy from Liberalism to Fascism*; *Dizionario biografico degli italiani*, VIII; *Larousse mensuel*, III, VI.

BENEŠ, Eduard (*Austria-Hungary, Politician*), was born at Kožlany in Bohemia on May 25, 1884, the son of a smallholder. He received his university education in France, obtaining a doctorate of law at Dijon in 1908. The following year Beneš was appointed professor of economics at the Prague Academy of Commerce, and in 1912 joined the sociology department at Prague University.

When the Great War broke out, the young Beneš was already a recognized leader of the Czechoslovakian nationalist movement, and he joined the anti-Austrian camp of T. G. Masaryk (*q.v.*). In 1915 Beneš went to Paris to work as a journalist in behalf of Czechoslovakian independence and cooperated while there with Masaryk and General Štefanik in behalf of the Entente cause. That same year Beneš was appointed general secretary in the Czechoslovakian national council, the executive body of the national movement which the Entente recognized in 1918 as the provisional government of Czechoslovakia.

On his return to Prague, Beneš became foreign minister (1918-35) and later president (1935) of Czechoslovakia. On October 5, 1938, Beneš resigned in the wake of the Munich Agreement; his travels thereafter took him to Chicago and later to London, where he led the Czechoslovakian government in exile. However, Beneš soon accepted Soviet leadership in the reconstruction of Czechoslovakia because that country promised greater force in the planned expulsion of 3 million Germans from the Sudetenland. Although reelected president in 1946, Beneš was powerless to prevent the Communist coup of February 25, 1948, and on June 7 turned over the government to Klement Gottwald. Beneš died in Sezimovo Usti, Bohemia, on September 3, 1948.

Beneš, *My War Memoir*; Mackenzie, *Dr. Beneš*; *Encyclopedia of Modern World Politics*.

BENSON, William Shepherd (*United States, Admiral*), was born in Bibb County, Georgia, on September 25, 1855, the son of a plantation owner. Benson graduated from the U.S. Naval Academy at Annapolis in 1877, and eleven years later participated in the famous cruise around the world. In 1905 he commanded the *Albany* of the Pacific Fleet, making the grade of captain four years later; from 1910 to 1913 he was commander of the battleship *Utah*. This sea duty had twice been interrupted by service as instructor at the Naval Academy. The quiet, modest, and fair Benson served after 1913 as commandant of the Philadelphia naval yard, and he was greatly surprised when Secretary of the Navy Josephus Daniels (*q.v.*) picked him to become chief of naval operations on May 10, 1915. Within the limits permitted him by the forceful Daniels, Benson began to assemble a small corps of aides, carried out a new fleet organization, and appointed a board of inspections to ascertain which merchant vessels might be used as auxiliaries by the navy in the event of war.

As early as February 1917, Benson had decreed that the U.S. Navy be developed as a "symmetrical" fleet according to the doctrines of Alfred Thayer Mahan, "with a full realization that we may eventually have to act alone." Deeply suspicious of the British, Benson was preoccupied with defense of the United States and the other Americas rather than with operations in European waters. He informed the Anglophile Admiral William S. Sims (*q.v.*) in March: "Don't let the British pull the wool over your eyes. It is none of our business pulling their chestnuts out of the fire. We would as soon fight the British as the Germans."

After this inauspicious start, relations between the navy's two chief planners in Europe and at home improved, and by October they were regularly exchanging letters. In November 1917, Benson reluctantly agreed to provide Sims with a planning section in London as well as to dispatch four coal-burning dreadnoughts to European waters. Like Sims, Benson opposed the notion of a North Sea mine barrage from Scotland to Norway, but in contrast to Sims, favored close-in blockade of German ports in the

North Sea. From October to December 1917, Benson visited London as the naval expert of the American War Commission appointed by President Wilson (q.v.) to coordinate joint plans with the Allies, and he ultimately helped establish an Interallied Naval Council. The chief of naval operations returned from London convinced of the need to lay the mine barrage in the North Sea, to close the Straits of Dover to all sea traffic, and to send a division of modern dreadnoughts to Europe.

Early in 1918 Benson struggled unsuccessfully to move the Italians to conduct an energetic offensive in the Adriatic Sea against the Austro-Hungarian fleet at Cattaro and Pola. Wilson sent Benson to Europe in October on special assignment to prepare the naval peace terms, but the admiral's stance in behalf of moderation "practically isolated me from the rest of the group at once." Although an uninspiring war leader, Benson toiled long and hard at Paris in 1919 as the U.S. representative on the committee that drafted the naval provisions of the peace treaties and as adviser to the American Peace Commissioners.

Benson retired on his birthday in 1919 in the grade of rear admiral, and in March 1920, accepted the chairmanship of the U.S. Shipping Board. He died on May 20, 1932, in Washington, D.C.

Cronon, ed., *Cabinet Diaries of Josephus Daniels*; Trask, *Captains & Cabinets*; *Dictionary of American Biography*, XXI Supplement One.

BERCHTOLD von und zu UNGARSCHITZ, FRATTING und PULLITZ, Leopold Count von (*Austria-Hungary, Foreign Minister*), was born in Vienna on April 18, 1863, the son of a wealthy estate owner in Moravia and Hungary. Berchtold served with the diplomatic corps after 1894 and became ambassador to St. Petersburg where for five years he experienced Russia's distrust and fear of Vienna. Although lacking experience in domestic affairs as well as in military matters, Berchtold was appointed foreign minister on February 19, 1912—against his will and better judgment. He was well-liked at court and possessed all the social graces required at the Hofburg; strength of character was unfortunately not one of his assets. This quickly became apparent during the three Balkan wars in 1912/13. Berchtold constantly adopted a hard line, only to draw back from intervention at the last moment. As a result, the prestige of Austria-Hungary declined precipitously and Berchtold gained the reputation of a weak and indecisive statesman.

All this changed in the wake of the assassination of Archduke Francis Ferdinand (q.v.) at Sarajevo on June 28, 1914. Berchtold seized this opportunity in order to deal Serbia a mortal blow and thereby "solve" the South Slav question by force. It was only through the moderating influence of Count István Tisza (q.v.) of Hungary that the Council of Ministers decided on July 7, 1914, to present Serbia with an ultimatum, which was transmitted to Belgrade on July 23 and amounted to a humiliation for Serbia. Nonetheless, Serbia accepted all points of the ultimatum save the one allowing Austria-Hungary to send officials to take an active part in the investigation of the assassination on Serbian soil. On July 28, 1914, Austria-Hungary declared war against Serbia.

Berchtold was unable to master the question of Italy's participation in the war. When Rome presented the Ballplatz with demands for territorial compensations in order to encourage it to honor Italy's signature on the Tripartite Pact, Berchtold felt unable to offer any Habsburg possessions, especially not in the Trentino. But when Italian Foreign Minister Sydney Sonnino (q.v.) managed to wring faint promises of compensations in South Tyrol from some German leaders, and when Berchtold informed Tisza as well as General Conrad von Hötzendorf (q.v.), chief of the General Staff, that he might accede to possible German pressures in this direction, his days as foreign minister were numbered. On January 13, 1915, Berchtold resigned his post at the urgings of Tisza and Conrad and was replaced by Count István Burian (q.v.). Berchtold retired as a grand seigneur on his estate at Peresznye/Csepreg in Hungary, where he died on November 21, 1942.

Hantsch, *Leopold, Graf Berchtold*; Kann, *History of the Habsburg Empire*; *Neue Deutsche Biographie*, I.

BERNSTORFF, Johann Heinrich Count von (*Germany, Ambassador*), was born in London on November 14, 1862, into an ancient noble family from Mecklenburg dating from around 1300; his father at the time was Prussian envoy to the Court of St. James's, having only recently relinquished the post of foreign minister to Otto von Bismarck. Bernstorff initially pursued an officer career in the prestigious guards, but in 1890, transferred to the diplomatic corps. He served at Constantinople, Belgrade, Dresden, St. Petersburg, Munich, and London, before being despatched to Cairo in 1906 as consul general. Bernstorff generally preferred an understanding with Britain over the much heralded Russian connection. In 1908 Wilhelm II (q.v.) personally picked Bernstorff as ambassador to the United States, where he was to remain for the next nine years. An intelligent and elegant man, Bernstorff's charm and candor quickly brought him acceptance in Washington, D.C.

Bernstorff grew pessimistic about the outcome of the war early, during the battle of the Marne in September 1914, and he embraced the notion of a compromise peace. This, in turn, brought him closer to President Woodrow Wilson, Colonel Edward House, and Secretary of State Robert Lansing (qq.v.), especially on the matter of unrestricted submarine warfare. The German diplomat did not share his navy's wild optimism for this weapon, and he repeatedly warned the Foreign Office that its adoption would bring the United States into the war. Germany's several flirtations with U-boat warfare in 1915/16 greatly exacerbated Bernstorf; the sinking of the liners *Lusitania* and *Arabic* in 1915 and *Sussex* in 1916 strained his relations with American leaders. Similarly, the quixotic German sabotage plans, which led to the expulsion of the military and naval attachés in the United States (Franz von Papen and Karl Boy-Ed) in December 1915, did not facilitate the ambassador's already difficult position.

Bernstorff contributed little to the German peace offer of December 12, 1916, and the decision reached at Pless on January 9, 1917, to resume unrestricted submarine warfare on February 1 regardless of the consequences finally brought his career in Washington to the abyss. The envoy's warnings about the impending American action were dismissed by Chancellor Theobald von Bethmann Hollweg (q.v.) rather curtly on January 16: "I am well aware that with this step we are running in danger of . . . war with the United States. We are decided to accept this risk." On April 6, 1917, the United States declared war against Germany.

Berstorff's return in March 1917 was anything but triumphal. He was viciously denounced by the Pan-Germans as well as by General Erich Ludendorff (q.v.) and his military paladins as a "democrat" and a "defeatist"; Wilhelm II boorishly refused to receive his ambassador. From September 1917 to the end of the war, Bernstorff served as envoy to Constantinople. During the November revolution of 1918, he supported Prince Max von Baden's (q.v.) efforts to reach a *rapprochement* with the Social Democrats, but in 1919 he declined Friedrich Ebert's (q.v.) offer of the post of foreign minister and instead retired from the diplomatic corps.

Bernstorff then turned to politics, joining the Democratic party and becoming after 1921 a parliamentary deputy for the party of Albert Einstein. A fervent supporter of the League of Nations and of Germany's entry into that world body, Bernstorff was deeply disappointed by the National Socialists' assumption of power in January 1933 and chose exile in Switzerland. He died in Geneva on October 6, 1939.

Bernstorff, *Deutschland und Amerika* and *Erinnerungen und Briefe*; May, *World War and American Isolation*; *Neue Deutsche Biographie*, II.

BESELER, Hans Hartwig von (*Germany, General*), was born at Greifswald on April 27, 1850, the son of a legal scholar. Beseler entered the army in 1868, fought in the Franco-Prussian War, then as captain attended the War Academy, and served in the War Ministry. Beseler was appointed deputy chief of the General Staff in 1899 and five years later was widely regarded as Alfred von Schlieffen's heir apparent; but the post of chief of the General Staff instead went to Helmuth von Moltke (q.v.) while Beseler was ennobled and appointed inspector general of fortresses, engineers, and sappers. Promoted lieutenant general in 1903 and general of infantry four years later, Beseler retired from active service in 1910, having passed his sixtieth birthday. In 1912 he entered the Prussian House of Lords.

On August 2, 1914, Beseler was reactivated as commander of the III Reserve Corps, and entered Belgium as part of the First Army. On September 17, he was entrusted with reducing Fortress Antwerp; Beseler attained his goal by October 10, receiving the order *Pour le mérite*. The III Reserve Corps fought along the Yser River in November, and was then shuttled east, where it stood with the Ninth Army at Lodz. As part of Army Group Gallwitz (q.v.), Beseler was ordered to capture Fortress Modlin along the Vistula; it fell on August 20, 1915, with 85,000 prisoners taken, including thirty Russian generals. Four days later General Erich von Falkenhayn (q.v.) appointed Beseler governor general of Poland at Warsaw—apparently at the suggestion of generals Paul von Hindenburg and Erich Ludendorff (qq.v.).

This was, in many ways, an unfortunate choice. Beseler was an intelligent, educated, and cultured officer, but totally unfamiliar with German politics. Neither did he possess command of the Polish language. Beseler encouraged the re-creation of Congress Poland, to be ruled through an "assembly of nobles." Above all, he saw the moment ripe for the "final phase of the Austro-Prussian historical duel," that is, for realizing a Prussian *Kleindeutsch* solution for Poland by "throwing Austria out." Ludendorff, who had initially disliked Beseler's initiative in creating an independent Polish state, in time saw merit in the proposal. His interest was mainly in the recruitment of Polish soldiers for his armies, however, and the final proclamation of Congress Poland on November 5, 1916, therefore, vividly bore his imprint. The new Poland was to be created only after the end of the war, and recruitment was to take place without direct Polish involvement. In short, Ludendorff saw the new state primarily as a satellite to serve as a manpower reservoir for the Central Powers. In time, the Poles rejected this notion and their war minister, Joseph Pilsudski (*q.v.*), was arrested by the Germans in July 1917. Therewith Beseler's original proposal failed; Ludendorff turned against the governor general when Polish recruitment failed to materialize. Beseler was promoted colonel general in January 1918, but was a physically ill and mentally broken man who, on November 12, laid down command without a farewell to his troops—an unpardonable breach of etiquette.

Violently attacked after the war by right-wing groups both for his failure to bid his soldiers farewell and for his alleged "pro-Polish" policies, the general insisted on a mock trial in 1919 and was found innocent of any wrongdoing by a court of the III Army Corps. He sought refuge at Sanatorium Loschwitz and died at Neubabelsberg on December 20, 1921.

Conze, *Polnische Nation*; Fischer, *Griff nach der Weltmacht*; *Geschichte der Ritter des Ordens*, I; *Neue Deutsche Biographie*, II.

BETHMANN HOLLWEG, Theobald von (*Germany, Chancellor*), was born at Hohenfinow on November 29, 1856, the son of an estate owner and district magistrate (*Landrat*). After studying jurisprudence at Strassburg, Leipzig, and Berlin, Bethmann entered the civil service in 1879; from 1886 to 1896 he succeeded his father as *Landrat* in Oberbarnim. Next came a spectacular career in the Prussian bureaucracy: provincial councillor at Potsdam 1896-1899, governing president of Bromberg 1899, lord lieutenant of the province of Brandenburg 1899-1905, and Prussian minister of the interior in March 1905. In the latter capacity, Bethmann in 1906 sought a basic reform of the Prussian three-class voting system of 1849, but was able only to amend some of the suffrage's most glaring inequities. In June 1907, he replaced Count Artur von Posadowsky as Reich state secretary of the interior, concurrently serving as deputy chancellor and as vice president of the Prussian state ministry. As the second most powerful administrator in the Reich, Bethmann in 1907 defended Chancellor Bernhard von Bülow during the *Daily Telegraph* affair against the Kaiser's personal "regiment," as Erich Eyck termed it; thereafter he was able to rally a new parliamentary majority consisting of Conservatives, Center, and Poles to increase federal indirect taxation. But when Bülow in 1908/09 introduced an inheritance tax in order to balance the budget especially for naval outlays, his Reichstag supporters turned against him; Bethmann succeeded Bülow as chancellor on July 7, 1909, because "'the main difficulties were with domestic affairs.'"

The new chancellor represented a change of pace from the arrogant and pliable Bülow. Tall, lanky, upright, Bethmann was more the grand seigneur than a consummate politician. In fact, he had no experience in diplomacy and his debating skills were at best modest. He possessed a degree of personal charm and warmth, but by and large remained a loner, a contemplative pessimist, a Stoic, rather than the confident "pilot" of the Bismarckian state.

Bethmann traversed a treacherous course until 1914. Although he managed to promulgate a more liberal constitution for Alsace-Lorraine in 1911, he failed to reform Reich finances. Neither did he manage to integrate the Social Democrats (SPD) into the mainstream of German politics, with the result that by 1912 one out of every three German voters rejected the Wilhelmian state; the SPD that year became the largest political party in the Reichstag with 110 seats. In the winter of 1912/13 a political storm arose over the mistreatment of civilians by Prussian officers at Zabern, and Bethmann on December 4, 1912, received the first vote of no-confidence in the German parliament. In January 1914, the Prussian Upper House also censured him, in this case for not upholding conservative principles. Hence on the eve of the Great War, the chancellor's domestic policies had suffered shipwreck.

Bethmann's foreign policy proved equally inept. He saw his main task as breaking the "iron encirclement" of Germany by the Entente that he had inherited from Bülow. Specifically, the chancellor sought an understanding with London on the matter of naval building and colonial adjustments. But by 1912, he was forced to admit defeat. Not only did France and Russia reject all German overtures, but also Admiral Alfred von Tirpitz (*q.v.*) effectively sabotaged Lord Haldane's visit to Berlin in February 1912, in an attempt to defuse the naval rivalry. Bethmann's subsequent resignation was rejected by the kaiser, and although the chancellor managed to struggle through two Balkan crises, the assassination of the Archduke Francis Ferdinand (*q.v.*) at Sarajevo on June 28, 1914, demanded of him the utmost in statesmanship.

Bethmann's performance during the July crisis has both occupied and divided historians. Some points, however, are clear. The chancellor desired the opportunity to tame Serbia, and he proved willing to accept a general war with Russia, being convinced that a war between "Slavs and Teutons" was inevitable. His hope that Britain would stay out of the fray was precisely that, and no more. His unfortunate reference to Belgian neutrality as a "scrap of paper"—signed by Prussia in 1839—as well as his reference in the Reichstag to Germany's "injustice to

Belgium" did little to enhance his statesmanship. Finally, the issuance on July 6 of the famous "blank check" to the Austro-Hungarians, assuring them that whatever policy they adopted vis-à-vis Serbia would find full support in Berlin, greatly curbed Germany's diplomatic options in July 1914. Above all, Bethmann proved utterly incapable of asserting the primacy of politics over the military that July.

As early as September 9, 1914, the chancellor prepared a detailed war aims program that reflected Friedrich List's views of the 1830s of a Central Europe dominated by Germany "for all imaginable time." France was to be reduced to secondary rank while Belgium would become a "vassal state"; Russia was to be driven as far east as possible and denied holdings in the Baltic and Balkan areas. Luxembourg was to be annexed outright along with the Franco-Belgian Channel coast, and the Netherlands were to be brought "into closer relationship with the German Empire." A central European economic union from Scandinavia to Turkey and from the Atlantic Ocean to the Caspian Sea was to have a central African colonial empire as a reservoir of raw materials.

In the ensuing two years, Bethmann's diplomacy brought Germany the support of Turkey and Bulgaria, but cost it that of Italy, Greece, Rumania, and most of the other states of the world. By agreeing, under pressure from the military, to the creation of Congress Poland in August 1916, the chancellor forever closed the connection to St. Petersburg. Bethmann further proved unable to take advantage of President Woodrow Wilson's (q.v.) peace initiatives after October 1916, and the hasty promulgation of German terms for a negotiated settlement only undermined Wilson's efforts.

Bethmann's greatest crisis came late in 1916 when the new army leaders, Paul von Hindenburg and Erich Ludendorff, concurred with Admiral Henning von Holtzendorff (qq.v.) that only an immediate resumption of unrestricted submarine warfare against all shipping bound for the British Isles could turn the tide. At a crown council at Pless on January 9, 1917, Bethmann remained "cold and pessimistic" about the U-boat gamble, but when pressed, he endorsed the action that would add the United States to the list of Germany's enemies within three months. We will probably never know why he gave in to the military on that dreary January day. Nor will we ever know why he clung to office thereafter, rather than making a clean break with a system and a policy that he could not fully endorse.

Sadly, Bethmann's domestic policies by then paralleled his diplomacy. At Easter 1917, he managed to wring from Wilhelm II (q.v.) an agreement that the three-class voting system in Prussia would finally be reformed—once the war had ended. The promise of March 7 was never fulfilled as Bethmann continued to drift between the Scylla of Prussian conservatives and the Charybdis of Reich moderates; the chancellor basically favored gradual parliamentarization for Prussia and the Reich but never managed to commit himself to such a course. In the end, his opponents, both on the right and left, in the military and in parliament, combined, though obviously for different reasons, to topple him.

On July 7, the parliamentary majority in the Reichstag consisting of Center, Progressives, and Social Democrats introduced a "peace resolution" calling for an end to the war without annexations or indemnities. Once again, Bethmann vacillated, unable to chart his own course. The military was convinced that he supported the peace initiative while parliamentarians such as Matthias Erzberger (q.v.) were equally resolved that the chancellor was unwilling to renounce his erstwhile war aims program. At the height of the crisis Bethmann attempted to persuade the kaiser to reform the Prussian suffrage and to place himself at the head of a popular monarchy. But to no avail. Ludendorff sent his alter ego, Colonel Max Bauer (q.v.), to caucus the chancellor's known parliamentary foes; Bauer was fully backed in his political offensive by Crown Prince Wilhelm of Prussia (q.v.). Bethmann's resignation on July 13, 1917, led the crown prince to crow: "This is the happiest day of my life." A colorless but energetic civil servant, Georg Michaelis (q.v.), succeeded Bethmann. With this act, Wilhelm II in effect turned political power over to Hindenburg and Ludendorff, preferring to sacrifice his chancellor in the face of threats of resignation from his military paladins. Whatever may be said of Bethmann, his dismissal proved a watershed in German affairs as with it the military fully triumphed over the political in a classic reversal of Carl von Clausewitz's dictum. Bethmann Hollweg retired to his estate at Hohenfinow to write his memoirs; he died there on January 1, 1921.

Bethmann Hollweg failed as Germany's wartime leader. The demands made on this highly competent bureaucrat by the exigencies of a world war simply were too great for his limited talents. The chancellor essentially attempted to steer a moderate course between left and right, and in the process won the support of neither and antagonized both. A Hamlet-like figure, Bethmann fell victim to indecision and half-measures, not unlike so many of the generals. He possessed neither historic nor personal greatness, as was revealed most glaringly in his pathetic performance at Pless in January 1917.

Bethmann Hollweg, *Betrachtungen zum Weltkrieg*, 2 vols.; Fischer, *Krieg der Illusionen* and *Griff nach der Weltmacht*; Jarausch, *Enigmatic Chancellor*; Riezler, *Tagebücher*; Röhl, *1914*; Vietsch, *Bethmann Hollweg*; Zmarzlik, *Bethmann Hollweg*; *Neue Deutsche Biographie*, II.

BISSOLATI, Leonida (*Italy, Politician*), was born in Cremona on February 20, 1857, the illegitimate child of Stefano Bissolati, a member of a Catholic religious order, and Paolina Caccialupi, a married woman. The elder Bissolati abandoned his religious calling in 1861, married Paolina, then a widow, and legitimized Leonida's birth through adoption. The young Bissolati studied at the universities of Pavia and Bologna. He took up journalism, and his observations of rural poverty moved him politically from the Liberal left to Socialism. He entered the Chamber of Deputies in 1897, and, by the start of the new century, led the Socialist party's reform wing.

In 1912 Bissolati was expelled from the Italian Socialist party. In domestic affairs, he had shown himself ready to join a bourgeois cabinet and to render respect to the monarchy. His sins, to an orthodox Socialist observer, were equally great in his view of foreign policy. The Bosnia-Herzegovina crisis of 1909 made him doubt the efficacy of international Socialism in general and the courage of Austrian Socialists in particular in preventing armed conflict. He began to take an active and sympathetic interest in Italy's military needs. Finally, Bissolati backed the Italian war effort against Ottoman Turkey (1911/12) and the expansion of Rome's new empire to include Libya.

Bissolati met the outbreak of World War I with renewed disgust at the impotence of Austro-Hungarian and German Socialists. He called for Italian intervention on the side of the Entente. Whereas once he had hoped to see the Habsburg Empire evolve into a democratic, multinational entity, thereby defusing the explosive question of Italy's irredentist claims on Vienna and Budapest, during the war he spoke of the need to destroy the Habsburg realm. When Bissolati spoke of trying "to prepare the spirit of the Italian proletariat for war," he saw this international involvement to be tied with the Mazzinian dream of the nineteenth century: Italy was to fight to create a freer Europe. Other interventionists, notably foreign ministers Antonio di San Giuliano and Sidney Sonnino (*qq.v.*), saw intervention as the price *Realpolitik* demanded be paid for Italian expansion.

In 1915 the fifty-eight-year-old Bissolati enlisted in the army. He divided his time between his role as a political leader and a sergeant in a combat regiment.

The following year, he entered the government of Paolo Boselli (*q.v.*). A minister without portfolio in June 1916, Bissolati worked to establish effective links between the government and the Italian army's High Command under General Luigi Cadorna (*q.v.*). Cadorna saw him as a dangerous civilian meddler, one who asked embarrassing questions about the string of military failures that had marred the first year of the war. Bissolati also called for a total national effort in support of the war, and he welcomed the declaration of war against Germany (August 28, 1916): it placed Italy on the side of justice against the power most inimical to a democratic Europe.

Bissolati's fiery patriotism and especially his idealistic visions of a postwar Europe collided repeatedly with Sonnino's conduct of foreign affairs. The minister without portfolio came close to resigning in June 1917, when Sonnino established an Italian protectorate over the whole of Albania. Whereas Sonnino saw the possible joining of South Slav nationalities into an independent Yugoslavia as a threat (he much preferred to see Austria-Hungary survive the war more or less intact), Bissolati welcomed South Slav unity. More specifically, Sonnino clung to the diplomatic pledges made in the Treaty of London (1915) that Italy would obtain the Dalmatian coast of the Adriatic. Bissolati saw Italy's interests best served by cordial relations, not land grabbing, from her Slavic neighbors to the east.

The Caporetto disaster toppled Boselli (October 1917), brought Vittorio Orlando (*q.v.*) to power, and gave Bissolati a cabinet post. He was now minister of pensions and army welfare. Along with the new minister of the treasury, Francesco Nitti (*q.v.*), Bissolati set out to boost military and civilian morale, stressing, for example, the rewards to be enjoyed by the soldiers of a victorious Italy. He underlined a parallel, but uglier, theme when he called for shooting Italian Socialists who obstructed the war effort!

The closing months of the war saw Bissolati established as Italy's foremost supporter of the ideals of American President Woodrow Wilson (*q.v.*). Italy, he insisted, must accept and welcome the emergence of new national states, even at the cost of Sonnino's territorial dreams. He resigned in late December 1918, protesting that Orlando and Sonnino were leading Italy in the opposite direction by occupying non-Italian lands like the Tyrol and Dalmatia. Bissolati soon found he could not speak publicly without facing violent protests from nationalist groups, including Benito Mussolini's new Fascist bands. Seton-Watson has called Bissolati the "true realist" of postwar Italian foreign policy. He saw that Italy, lacking both military power and the diplomatic flexibility its pre-1915 position as a neutral had conferred, could succeed only by conciliating, not bullying, its new neighbors. By April 1920, as postwar tempers cooled, Bissolati's idealism seemed to be gaining ground: Italy and the new state of Austria began to ease tensions over the Tyrol. But this was a development Bissolati could observe only briefly. He died in Rome on May 6, 1920.

Bissolati, *Diario di guerra*; Colapietra, *Leonida Bissolati*; Mayer, *Politics and Diplomacy of Peacemaking*; Melograni, *Storia politica della grande guerra*; Seton-Watson, *Italy from Liberalism to Fascism*; Whittam, *The Politics of the Italian Army*; *Dizionario biografico degli italiani*, X.

BLISS, Tasker Howard (*United States, General*), was born at Lewisburg, Pennsylvania, on December 31, 1853, the son of a classics professor. Bliss graduated from West Point in 1875, but returned to "the Point" the following year to serve as instructor until 1880. Five years later, Bliss began a three-year stint as teacher of military science at the new Naval College in Newport, and from 1888 until 1895 Captain Bliss served as an aide to General Schofield, commanding general of the army. In 1897 Bliss went to Spain as military attaché, and the following year in the grade of major participated in the campaign on Puerto Rico. Next came administrative duty in Cuba and, in the grade of brigadier general, founding president of the new Army War College. Further varied administrative tasks brought him promotion to major general in 1915 and the post of acting chief of staff in May 1917.

On September 22, 1917, Bliss replaced General Scott as chief of staff, and he served Secretary of War Newton D. Baker (*q.v.*) as an able and trusted aide; the secretary, in turn, appreciated Bliss' mind as "a comprehensive card index." The chief of staff's diplomatic and analytical skills prompted Baker to select him as the military representative on "Colonel" House's (*q.v.*) mission to London after the Italian debacle at Caporetto in order to coordinate the Allied war effort. In November 1917, Bliss was appointed the U.S. member of the new Supreme War Council, a truly statesmanlike role in view of President Wilson's (*q.v.*) absence from that body. Bliss from the start favored a unified military command under the French Marshal Foch (*q.v.*), while at the same time wholeheartedly supporting General Pershing's (*q.v.*) insistence that American land forces not be "amalgamated" with the Allied armies. Although this stance frequently earned Bliss questioning stares from Allied commanders, it greatly

facilitated his relations with the American field commander in Europe. In fact, Bliss correctly understood his subordinate role vis-à-vis Pershing and thereby precluded friction between the two from the outset. Although Bliss shared Pershing's desire for unconditional surrender of the German army, he foresaw the need to support the new German republic in its infancy through moderate peace terms. Bliss was an ardent supporter of the president's concept of a League of Nations.

The general served as a delegate to the Peace Conference in Paris in 1919, and he joined Secretary of State Robert Lansing (*q.v.*) in an unsuccessful attempt to deny Japan a mandate over the former German leasehold in Shantung. Bliss had been relieved as chief of staff on May 19, 1918; from 1920 to 1927 he served as governor of the Soldiers Home in Washington. He advocated U.S. membership on the World Court as well as a general reduction in world armaments while serving on the editorial board of *Foreign Affairs*. Bliss died on November 9, 1930.

Trask, *General Tasker Howard Bliss*; *Dictionary of American Biography*, XXI Supplement I.

BÖHM-ERMOLLI, Eduard Baron von (*Austria-Hungary, Field Marshal*), was born in Ancona on February 12, 1856, the son of an army major. After graduating from the cadet school at St. Pölten and the Theresa Military Academy in Vienna in 1875, Böhm-Ermolli joined the dragoons (Fourth Regiment). From 1880 to 1896, he was assigned to the General Staff in various capacities, and in 1911, attained the rank of general of cavalry as commander of the I Army Corps in Cracow.

The outbreak of war in August 1914 found Böhm-Ermolli head of the Second Army, originally intended for the campaign in Serbia with General Oskar Potiorek (*q.v.*), but which already in August was hastily dispatched to Galicia, where it engaged the invading Russian forces in and around Lemberg. The Second Army was deployed in defense of Silesia for the remainder of the year; in February 1915, it bridged the gap in the Carpathian front between the German South Army and the Austro-Hungarian Third Army. In June 1915, Böhm-Ermolli participated in the breakthrough at Gorlice and stormed Lemberg; in the grade of colonel general he was appointed commander of Army Group Böhm-Ermolli, composed of the Second Army and the South Army, on September 19, 1915.

For much of 1916 Army Group Böhm-Ermolli fought a tenacious defensive struggle in the east and only after repulsing General Aleksei Brusilov's (*q.v.*) offensive could it take the initiative and recapture

East Galicia and Czernowitz. Böhm-Ermolli was promoted field marshal on the last day of January 1918, and in March took part in the occupation of the Ukraine and Odessa. Emperor Charles (*q.v.*) relieved Böhm-Ermolli of his command on May 16, 1918, owing to the field marshal's inability to get along with German military leaders in the east. A plan in the summer of 1918 to appoint Böhm-Ermolli chief of staff of the army in place of General Arz von Straussenburg (*q.v.*) never reached fruition. The veteran commander of the Great War was appointed a field marshal by a fellow native of the Dual Monarchy in the army of the Greater German Empire in 1940; Böhm-Ermolli died in Troppau, Sudetenland, on December 9, 1941.

Bardolff, *Militär-Maria Theresien-Orden; Neue Deutsche Biographie*, II; *Österreichisches Biographisches Lexikon 1815-1950*, I.

BOLFRAS, Arthur Baron von (*Austria-Hungary, General*), was born in Sachsenhausen, near Frankfurt am Main, on April 16, 1838. After graduating from the Theresa Military Academy, Bolfras took part in the campaigns of 1859 and 1866 against the Italians in South Tyrol. Thereafter he served with the General Staff, in the War Ministry (1871-75), as chief of staff of the V Army Corps, and from 1889 to 1916, as adjutant general and head of Emperor Francis Joseph's (*q.v.*) military chancery.

Bolfras was becoming concerned by 1915 that the army supreme command under General Conrad von Hötzendorf (*q.v.*), chief of the General Staff, had assumed such far-reaching powers that the war was being conducted independently of the emperor: "We are being ruled by the A.O.K." In fact, military leaders assumed many political functions under the umbrella of national security, and front commanders held unlimited powers over territories behind the fighting lines. The septuagenarian Bolfras was promoted colonel general in 1916. He died at Baden, near Vienna, on December 19, 1922.

Allmayer-Beck and Lessing, *Die K. (u) K.-Armee*; Rothenberg, *Army of Francis Joseph: Österreichisches Biographisches Lexikon 1815-1950*, I.

BONAR LAW, Andrew (*Great Britain, Secretary of State for Colonial Affairs, Chancellor of the Exchequer*), was born in Kingston, New Brunswick, Canada, on September 16, 1858, the son of a Presbyterian minister. He left for Scotland at age twelve where he later began a successful career as banker and iron merchant. In the general election of 1900 Bonar Law entered the House of Commons as Unionist member from Blackfriars, Glasgow, and quickly became an exponent of Joseph Chamberlain's scheme of colonial preference and tariff reform of 1903. Six years later he denounced David Lloyd George's (*q.v.*) "People's" budget as socialism, preferring instead to pour available revenues into naval construction. At home, he defended Ulster against "the imposition of a tyranny," namely, home rule, and in November 1911, succeeded Arthur James Balfour as leader of the Conservatives, partly with the help of a fellow Canadian, W. M. Aitken (*qq.v.*). Bonar Law did not shrink from bringing the country to the verge of civil war over Irish home rule in 1912. A staunch supporter of Sir Edward Carson (*q.v.*), he assured Orangemen in July 1913 of the support of the Unionist party in their fight against home rule. However, on July 30, 1914, Bonar Law agreed to postpone the home rule Amending Bill in the face of war clouds in Europe.

On August 2, 1914, Bonar Law assured Prime Minister H. H. Asquith (*q.v.*) of the wholehearted support of the Unionist party for a war policy. For the next eight months Bonar Law loyally supported Asquith and opposed all pleas for the formation of a national government. He became deeply distressed over the naval debacles at Coronel and at the Dardanelles, blaming these setbacks on the unbalanced, eccentric, and erratic first lord of the Admiralty, Winston S. Churchill (*q.v.*), a former Tory. Churchill did not hesitate to pick up the challenge: "You dance like a will-o'-the-wisp so nimbly from one unstable foothold to another that my plodding paces can scarcely follow you." The sombre, unpretentious Bonar Law was above all a party man, and on May 17, 1915, he merely reflected the Tory position in demanding that Asquith form a coalition government.

Bonar Law accepted the post of colonial secretary in the Asquith coalition regime from May 1915 to December 1916. He pressed Lord H. H. Kitchener (*q.v.*), secretary of state for war, to improve both the quality and quantity of shells sent to the troops in France, and by the fall of 1915, counseled that the Dardanelles expedition be terminated and a new front opened up instead at Salonika, Greece. In November 1915, Bonar Law vetoed Asquith's proposal to take over the War Office permanently, and on the 23rd he voted for the evacuation of British forces from Gallipoli. In January 1916, Bonar Law ushered in the Compulsory Military Bill, being careful to exclude Ireland from its provisions. When Lord Kitchener went down with the *Hampshire* on June 5, Bonar Law was largely responsible for blocking Asquith from appointing himself Kitchener's successor and for successfully pressing the rival claim of his erstwhile enemy, Lloyd George.

On December 9, 1916, after days of intrigue and intense backstairs lobbying, Bonar Law, once again enjoying the support of his friends Max Aitken and Edward Carson, joined the new Lloyd George coalition government as chancellor of the Exchequer, leader of the House of Commons, and member of the sovereign war cabinet. The Canadian had by then abandoned his earlier mistrust of the fiery Welshman and, although a junior partner in the firm, worked well with the prime minister, who desired above all that Bonar Law "manage" the Commons while Lloyd George decided the larger issue of the so-called New Imperialism. At the Exchequer he successfully floated several war loans. Bonar Law opposed, to no avail, Sir Douglas Haig's (q.v.) plans for a massive offensive at the Somme in 1917, the very year that he lost his two elder sons, one in Palestine and the other in France. In July 1917, he vigorously, though again unsuccessfully, opposed the prime minister's choice of Churchill as minister of munitions. And in February 1918, Bonar Law, who had become disenchanted with General Sir William Robertson, chief of the Imperial General Staff, supported Lloyd George's decision to replace Wully Robertson with the more facile Sir Henry Wilson (qq.v.).

The Conservative leader agreed in December 1918 to enter the general election as coalition partner with Lloyd George's Liberals; he accepted the post of lord privy seal (1919-21) in the new cabinet. In June 1919, Bonar Law became one of the signatories of the Treaty of Versailles. Worn out by the exigencies of wartime politics, he retired to southern France in March 1921, but on October 23, 1922 returned to become the first man of colonial birth to be appointed prime minister of Great Britain, an office which he held for only 209 days. Bonar Law died in London on October 20, 1923, and was buried in Westminster Abbey. His diffident character did not inspire great enthusiasm. He was the least academically inclined of men and had greatly disliked Asquith's Balliol crowd. Bonar Law had cared for neither music nor art, and had renounced alcohol in favor of tobacco and golf.

Beaverbrook, *Men and Power* and *Politicians and the War*; Blake, *Unrepentant Tory*; *Dictionary of National Biography 1922-1930*.

BOROEVIĆ von BOJNA, Svetozar (*Austria-Hungary, Field Marshal*), was born at Umetić, Croatia, on December 13, 1856, the son of an army officer who had risen from the ranks. After graduating from cadet school in Liebenau, Boroević was commissioned in 1875. Three years later he stormed Sarajevo during the campaign in Bosnia. In 1881-83 he attended the War Academy and spent the

following decade either with the General Staff or as instructor at the Theresa Military Academy. Boroević served as chief of staff with the VIII Corps in Prague from 1898 to 1904, and the following year was raised into the Hungarian nobility. He had risen in grade from captain in 1886 to major in 1895, and from colonel in 1908 to general of infantry in 1913. Since April 1912, he commanded the VI Army Corps stationed in Kaschau.

Boroević led the VI Corps under Count Viktor Dankl (q.v.) in Galicia at the outbreak of the Great War, and soon thereafter commanded the Third Army in the victories at Komarów, Limanowa-Lapanów, and the relief of Przemysl on October 10, 1914. He also participated in the defense of the Carpathian passes as well as of Gorlice. When Italy declared war against her former ally in May 1915, Boroević, a tough and energetic commander, took charge of the hastily forming Fifth Army in the Isonzo region. He was not easy to work with and liked to ape Frederick the Great in his harshness to his troops, but Boroević got the job done. Although heavily outmanned and outgunned, his Fifth Army fought eleven battles along the Isonzo and thereby prevented the expected Italian advance into Tyrol. Not a strategist of the first order, Boroević heavily bled his Austro-Hungarian units by his insistence upon repeated frontal strikes. Finally, during the Twelfth Isonzo Battle in October and November 1917, the Fifth Army, aided by German units under General Krafft von Dellmensingen (q.v.), advanced as far as the Piave River, but a shortage of trucks and horses stalled the offensive at this line.

Boroević was promoted field marshal on January 31, 1918, but he declined the offer of a baronage, hoping after the war for a direct promotion to an earldom. Although often regarded as a possible successor to General Conrad von Hötzendorf (q.v.) as chief of the General Staff, the colorful Croat was never elevated to this post, perhaps owing to his gruff nature. Nor was he to realize his life's dream of becoming *banus* of a kingdom of Croatia, Dalmatia, and Slavonia. Instead, Boroević spent the last year of the war supervising the gradual dissolution of his multinational army behind the Tagliamento. In January 1918, he spoke out bitterly at army headquarters in Baden against Hungarian proposals to divide the army into separate Austrian and Hungarian units. In the spring of that year he opposed in vain Conrad's plans for yet another alpine battle with the Italians. The Austro-Hungarian offensive near Assiago was a disaster; Boroević managed to advance as far as Montello, but the rising waters of the Piave as well as stiff British and French resistance drove him back to his original position.

Early in November 1918, after a well-executed retreat from Italy, Boroević toyed with the notion of leading a monarchist countercoup. The idea was put to rest when Emperor Charles (*q.v.*) expressed little interest in it. Thereafter Boroević offered his services to the Croats, but Belgrade officials, fearful of his popularity, declined the offer. He died at Klagenfurt on May 23, 1920.

Bardolff, *Militär-Maria Theresien-Orden*; Rothenberg, *Army of Francis Joseph*; *Neue Deutsche Biographie*, II; *Neue Österreichische Biographie*, I.

BOSELLI, Paolo (*Italy, Prime Minister*), was born in Savona, a town west of Genoa, on June 8, 1838. The son of a notary, Boselli studied law, then taught economics at the universities of Venice and Rome. He entered the Chamber of Deputies in 1870, to begin a political career there that lasted until 1921. Identified as a Liberal, Boselli found that his skills in economics and finance brought him ministerial portfolios under a diverse succession of premiers from 1888 until the start of the twentieth century. After serving as minister of education in the cabinet of Sidney Sonnino (*q.v.*), Boselli seemed to abandon an active interest in politics in 1906. Nearing seventy years of age, he began to devote his remaining energies to the irredentist Dante Alighieri Society and its mission of promoting the spread of Italian influence and culture.

The outbreak of World War I brought Boselli back to an active interest in political affairs. He favored Italian intervention and contributed obliquely to Italy's entry into the war. In May 1915, after Premier Salandra (*q.v.*) had resigned over his policy of joining the side of the Entente, Boselli declined an invitation from King Victor Emmanuel III (*q.v.*) to form a government. This had the effect of turning the monarch back to Salandra. By the summer of 1916, however, Salandra's conduct of the war had run into the sand. Five Italian offensives on the Isonzo had won little territory at the cost of heavy casualties. The Austrians, in May 1916, had launched their *Strafexpedition* from the Trentino, threatening to cut to the south into the plains behind the Isonzo front.

Boselli, then seventy-eight years old, formed a national government. Nineteen cabinet ministers, including four without portfolios, were drawn from a multitude of political parties ranging from the Socialists to the Catholics. The strongest figure in the government was a holdover from the Salandra years, Foreign Minister Sidney Sonnino, whose policy centered around Italian territorial expansion in the Adriatic. Boselli found his prestige buoyed up at once by Italy's first great military victory of the war, the thrust to Gorizia during the Sixth Battle of the Isonzo

(August 1916). The government demonstrated its solidarity with its allies by declaring war on Germany (August 28), but Italy's military prospects soon dimmed. Three more Isonzo campaigns (September to November) brought only the usual heavy casualties; and these setbacks took place against grim news from Rumania and Russia, where the weakness of Italy's allies was all too evident.

With Boselli in tow, Sonnino continued to set the direction of foreign policy. At Rome (January 1917) and St. Jean de Maurienne (April 1917), Sonnino helped block efforts by the Western Allies to seek a compromise peace with Vienna. A moderate peace settlement with Austria-Hungary was sure to explode Sonnino's hopes for gains on the eastern shore of the Adriatic. The other major decision to come from the diplomatic gatherings of early 1917 was also a negative one: the Allies could not agree to launch a major offensive on the Italian front in 1917. When the Italians did so themselves—the Eleventh Battle of the Isonzo (August 1917)—it rattled Austro-Hungarian leaders enough to call on Berlin for military help. The result came in the form of the Austro-German breakthrough at Caporetto in October 1917.

Caporetto would have dragged down even a popular and respected premier. But by the fall of 1917, Boselli was neither. Attacked by the Right for his refusal to repress civil unrest and silence dissent, he was also assailed by the Chamber's sizable neutralist bloc as well for remaining in the war. Politicians of all persuasions found Boselli too old and feeble to meet the demands of the conflict; his oversize cabinet was compared unfavorably to the small war cabinet adopted in Great Britain. On October 25, 1917, Boselli's enemies from all sides joined to throw him out of office by a resounding vote of 314 to 96.

In the postwar era, the aged political leader wrote one last chapter in his career. In 1921 he left the Chamber of Deputies for the Senate. There he rallied to the Fascist regime of Benito Mussolini. In March 1929, at the age of ninety-one, the former premier spoke for the government in seeking approval of the Lateran Agreements with the Vatican.

Boselli died in Rome on March 10, 1932.

Melograni, *Storia politica della grande guerra*; Pieri, *L'Italia nella prima guerra mondiale*; Christopher Seton-Watson, *Italy from Liberalism to Fascism*; *Dizionario biografico degli italiani*, XIII; *Larousse mensuel*, IX.

BOTHMER, Felix Graf von (*Germany, General*), was born in Munich on December 10, 1852, the son of an army general; the family stemmed from Lower

Saxony and dated from the twelfth century. Bothmer entered the Bavarian army in 1871 and served most of his career, save a three-year stint with the General Staff in Berlin, either in the Bavarian General Staff or the War Ministry. He became battalion commander as lieutenant colonel in 1896; three years later Bothmer served as department head in the General Staff at Munich. In 1903 he was advanced to brigade commander; two years later he was promoted lieutenant general and chief of the 2nd Division; and in 1910 he became general of infantry.

On November 30, 1914, Bothmer received command of the 6th Bavarian Reserve Division at Ypres, but one month later was transferred to head the II Bavarian Reserve Corps at the western front. This position, too, proved to be short-lived: on March 22, 1915, he took over a new "Corps Bothmer," entrusted with defence of the Carpathian passes at the gates of Hungary. In May 1915, following General August von Mackensen's (q.v.) breakthrough at Gorlice-Tarnów, Bothmer was able to descend from the mountain passes at Stryi, and in extremely heavy fighting twice managed to cross the Dniester River. But on July 6, 1915, he again exchanged commands, this time becoming head of the German South Army in Galicia, where by August he managed to drive the Russians beyond Tarnopol.

Bothmer's greatest challenge came on June 4, 1916, when General Aleksei Brusilov (q.v.) unleashed a broad offensive around Luck. Outnumbered by almost fifty divisions, the German-Austro-Hungarian front in the south crumbled like a pastry shell: in three days alone, Brusilov took 200,000 prisoners, mostly from the Austrian Seventh Army in the Bukovina. Further Russian attacks in the direction of Brody, Lemberg, and Kovel forced Bothmer to fall back upon Strypa at the foot of the Carpathians; his position was secured only through a clever counterstroke by General Alexander von Linsingen (q.v.) against the northern edge of Luck. When the fighting subsided three months later, the Central Powers had lost over 350,000 men, but Brusilov had suffered more than 1 million casualties and prisoners.

General Brusilov attempted to break the southern front a final time on July 4, 1917, with an assault in the direction of Brzezany, but this time Bothmer was ready; his counteroffensive drove the Russians back over 100 kilometers. In December the new Bolshevik government sued for an armistice, and on February 3, 1918, Bothmer's South Army was dissolved.

Thereafter, Bothmer led a new Nineteenth Army in Lorraine; he was promoted colonel general in April 1918. With the collapse of the German position in France and Belgium, Bothmer on November 8 was returned to Bavaria to command the Home Defenses South in the event of a final, desperate stand on German soil against the Allies; instead, the government of Prince Max von Baden (q.v.) sued for peace. Bothmer retired from active service that same month. He died in Munich on March 18, 1937.

Liddell Hart, *The Real War*; Rothenberg, *Army of Francis Joseph*; *Geschichte der Ritter des Ordens*, I; *Neue Deutsche Biographie*, II.

BOUÉ de LAPEYRÈRE, Auguste Emmanuel Hubert Gaston Marie (*France, Vice Admiral*), was born in Cateras-Lectourois in southwestern France, January 18, 1852. He entered the Naval Training College in 1869. After two years of combat in Tonkin, 1873-75, he received his commission as ensign and spent the next years (1875-1880) on duty in the Atlantic. Promoted to lieutenant in 1881, he returned to the Far East for his first independent command in 1884. A reputation as a brave, energetic, and resourceful leader brought Lapeyrère rapid advancement. A commander in 1889, a captain in 1896, he was promoted rear admiral in 1902. In 1908, after a decade of important posts in European waters, he rose to vice admiral and took charge of the Brest maritime district. The following year, he entered the government as minister of marine under Aristide Briand (q.v.).

Lapeyrère's term as minister, 1909-11, came in the midst of a rapid naval build-up. After decades of dispute and hesitation, the government and navy were launched on a program of fleet construction centered on modern battleships. Critics like Halpern have found Lapeyrère's policies inconsistent. He slowed the pace of battleship construction, thereby implying that French efforts in a future war would be applied to the less competitive waters of the Mediterranean. At the same time, the navy minister envisioned wartime operations centered in the north, that is, against the potent German High Sea Fleet. Halpern finds Lapeyrère's characteristic optimism and aggressiveness the most plausible explanation for the inconsistency.

In late 1911 Lapeyrère returned to duty with the fleet in the Mediterranean. The division of naval responsibilities between France and Britain in 1912 brought all of France's battleships to the Mediterranean theater, where Lapeyrère was commanding the French fleet. He brought impressive qualities to his post. A proven and confident combat leader, he lifted his battleships and cruisers to a high standard of readiness, despite such problems as unreliable gunpowder. His fleet was likely to perform superbly in the great surface battles conventional wisdom anticipated. On the other hand, Lapeyrère had serious shortcomings. A war of battleships and cruisers constituted the limit of his imagination. His term as navy minister had also left its mark. He was unlikely to take orders gracefully, a fault the fuzzy lines of authority at the juncture between senior naval commanders and the minister of marine could not correct. A fine military technician, he shared the lack of sophistication in international affairs that marked France's senior admirals. Thus, he could confidently plan detailed offensives in the Mediterranean against both Italy and Austria-Hungary without concerning himself with whether both nations would in fact be his wartime opponents.

Lapeyrère's war plan received government approval in January 1914. It reflected the prevailing doctrine of the French navy, an offensive bent that is more commonly associated with the French army. The war was to begin with a vigorous offensive along the western coast of Italy. The Italian navy was to be met and defeated at once, before it could join the Austrian allies. French leadership, training, and *élan*—along with the immediate use of every available French warship—were to compensate for the numerical superiority of the Triple Alliance. With the Mediterranean turned into a French lake, the army's XIX Corps could pass safely from North Africa to fight on the continent. The insistence of General Joffre (*q.v.*) that the troops come at once, unescorted if need be, could be substantially satisfied, since the sea lanes would be swept quickly.

Events slipped out of this neat pattern. On August 2, Lapeyrère learned that Italy was not mobilizing; the war plan for a fleet action somewhere between Sicily and the Gulf of Genoa was useless. At the same time, word arrived of the dangerous German battle cruiser *Goeben*; it seemed within striking distance of the XIX Corps' sailing routes. Until August 8, in a dramatic reversal of his prewar planning, Lapeyrère guarded the troop ships. He ignored repeated orders from Paris to leave the transports and to send strong forces eastward to intercept the *Goeben* and the light cruiser *Breslau*. Lapeyrère's concern for the helpless troop ships was heightened by reports of other German war vessels off the coast of southern France and near the Canary Islands. He expected the *Goeben* to make a run for Gibraltar or the Adriatic; that it might head for Turkish waters, bringing momentous political consequences, apparently never entered his calculations.

After the dramatic opening days of hostilities, Lapeyrère remained in charge of French forces in the Mediterranean until October 1915. At least in principle, he held command over the British forces in the Mediterranean as well. It was a bitter and frustrating experience. From August 1914 to May 1915, Lapeyrère's central mission was to deal with the Austrian fleet in the Adriatic. He could not reach his enemy. The Austrians refused to come out to fight. French losses in the constricted waters of the Adriatic made proposals for a large Allied offensive unthinkable. Thus, he could only blockade and conduct limited sorties. By the spring of 1915 even a close blockade meant offering easy victims to enemy submarines, and Lapeyrère's prized battleships pulled back to Malta and Bizerte. British forces in Egyptian waters and off the Dardanelles evolved into independent squadrons. The Dardanelles served as a particular burden. French battleships under Admiral Guépratte (*q.v.*) were ordered there in September 1914 by the government. Lapeyrère was deliberately excluded from subsequent planning of the Dardanelles operation. Minister of Marine Augagneur (*q.v.*) probably expected him to object strenuously to an unsupported naval attack. When word of the plan reached Lapeyrère, he was outraged at being circumvented.

Enemy submarines, Lapeyrère's nemesis in the Adriatic, became a general danger in the Mediterranean by the fall of 1915. It was the last straw. The lack of patrol vessels and the need to regulate merchant shipping were novel problems in a novel war Lapeyrère could no longer abide. He asked to be relieved, citing his poor health and his four years in command. The next year brought his retirement. Lingering concern over the *Goeben* episode led to a new government inquiry in 1918 (the first had taken place in 1914) in which Augagneur defended the old admiral. Lapeyrère died in Pau, near his birthplace, on February 16, 1924.

Cassar, *The French and the Dardanelles*; Halpern, "Anglo-French-Italian Naval Convention of 1915" and *The Mediterranean Naval Situation, 1908-1914*; Laurens, *Le Commandement naval en Méditerranée, 1914-1918*; Thomazi, *La Marine française dans la Grande Guerre*, I, II, III; *Dictionnaire des parlementaires français*, I.

BRATIANU, Ion or **Ionel** (*Rumania, Prime Minister*), was born at his family's estate at Florica, northwest of Bucharest, August 20, 1864. His father, Ion Bratianu the elder, was the guiding figure in the founding of an independent Rumania. The Bratianu family played a commanding role in Rumanian national life well into the twentieth century. Educated in Paris as a civil engineer, the younger Bratianu returned to Bucharest for a predictably easy entry and rapid rise in Rumanian politics. He was elected a deputy to Parliament in 1895, acquired his first cabinet ministry two years later, and took over the direction of Rumanian foreign affairs in 1901. Bratianu served as minister of the interior during the repression of the peasant revolt of 1907, and he took office as prime minister for the first time in 1909. During the next eighteen years, he formally led eleven cabinets. Most governments in which he did not visibly participate he dominated from behind the scenes.

Premier almost without a break from early 1914 to the last months of 1919, Bratianu was the cardinal figure in the formation of Rumanian foreign policy during the First World War. He dominated Rumania's efforts even more spectacularly at Versailles in 1919. The prime minister brought formidable talents to his diplomatic role: cool nerves, verbal brilliance, unyielding determination, ruthlessness. He was completely self-assured in the milieu of high level negotiations.

Bratianu's cabinet of January 1914 was composed of pro-French political figures. A visit by Tsar Nicholas II and Russian Foreign Minister Sazonov (qq.v.) in June 1914 advertised Rumania's growing friendship with the eastern member of the Entente. Hostility over the status of Rumanians within the Austrian empire was growing. It combined with resentment over Austria's diplomatic support for Bulgaria in the Second Balkan War. Rumania's historic differences with Russia grew muted.

Bratianu held firm control over the cabinet and both houses of Rumania's parliament when the Great War erupted. Thus, he found it an easy task to restrain the pro-German King Carol I (q.v.). Torrey has shown that Bratianu's policy between July 1914 and August 1916 was governed by a steady desire to acquire Rumanian-inhabited lands that lay under Habsburg control. The Rumanian leader's caution and calculation outraged both sides. Nonetheless, he anticipated and desired victory for the Entente. Russia was quick to offer territorial gains at Austria's expense in return for Rumanian support. This meant that prizes like Transylvania were within reach. The Central Powers could hardly match what Russia could offer. Thus, Bratianu's prolonged negotiations with Berlin and Vienna were never interchanges the Rumanian government took seriously.

At first, time seemed to be on Rumania's side. Bratianu proceeded deliberately. He wanted written territorial and military pledges from the Entente along with time to prepare Rumania's untested army. A favorable strategic picture overall was also needed. Only with all this would he announce Rumanian belligerency. In this framework, hotheads calling for immediate intervention in the wake of Austrian military defeats early in the war required careful restraining. On October 2, Bratianu obtained a trump. A secret treaty with Russia pledged large territorial concessions without requiring Rumanian intervention. An anxious Sazonov was willing to pay dearly for mere neutrality.

Bratianu realized that active Rumanian intervention would one day be required to seal territorial pledges. The question was when. He nearly acted in the spring of 1915 when Italy declared war. The spectacular military successes of the Central Powers in Poland brought him back to a cautious stance. Meanwhile, these military blows served to make St. Petersburg even more generous in its promises. By the fall of 1915, the rewards Bratianu hoped for in return for entering the war had been largely pledged. A Russian call for immediate intervention to aid Serbia, however, struck Bratianu as premature and dangerous. He evaded it. Rumania, he declared, would move only if the hard-pressed Entente managed to invade Bulgaria. At the same time, Germany's need for Rumanian grain gave Bratianu a means to warm relations with the Central Powers.

The Russian summer offensive of 1916 under General Brusilov (q.v.) set the stage for Rumania to act. As usual, Austrian military difficulties raised a storm of interventionist feeling in Rumania. But Bratianu was not naive enough to overvalue the Russian success. Rather, delay presented different dangers. Austria might leave the war and avoid disgorging any territory. Russia might penetrate areas Rumania coveted—and St. Petersburg might become reluctant to pass them to Rumania. Moreover, the impatience of Britain and France meant that Rumania had to move, otherwise its relations with the western partners of the Entente would likely fray. The French were desperate over Verdun; leaders like Briand and Joffre (qq.v.) pushed Rumania to act.

On August 27, 1916, Bratianu led Rumania into the war. The immediate result was military catastrophe. Bratianu's splendid diplomatic skills were not matched by military insight. The Rumanians began the war with an offensive into the irredentist prize of Transylvania. It met the need to popularize the war among the Rumanian people, but it stretched Bratianu's military resources beyond the breaking point as well. The Allied pledge of strategic assistance in the form of a large-scale offensive northward from Salonika went unfilled. German, Austrian, Bulgarian, and Turkish forces pounced on the inexperienced Rumanians. By December, Bratianu's government had been driven from Bucharest to Jassy. He could only seek to broaden the political base of his Cabinet and ask more aid from Rumania's allies.

The collapse of Russia in 1917 placed Rumania in a hopeless military state. The conclusion of a separate peace meant violating Rumanian pledges to its allies. Thus it jeopardized Rumanian claims at any future peace conference. But Bratianu could apply his diplomatic wiles. He cloaked the armistice with the Germans, signed at Focsani on December 9, in confusion. It was, he claimed, merely an agreement between the Germans and the Russian forces in unoccupied Rumania. When Germany demanded a speedy conclusion to the ensuing peace talks, Bratianu resigned. He was careful to select his successors. He felt a distinguished general like Averescu or a pro-German Conservative like Marghiloman (qq.v.) could get mild peace terms. This was not the case. But to have surrogates serving as prime ministers meant Bratianu need not bear the stigma of agreeing to a harsh peace.

The failure of either side to implement fully the Peace of Bucharest (May 7, 1918) left Bratianu some latitude. He claimed, in defiance of the facts, that Rumania had never deserted the Entente. By early October, the military position of the Central Powers in the Balkans was collapsing. With it crumbled Marghiloman's government. Bratianu resumed his skilled manipulation behind the scenes. He got the pliable King Ferdinand (q.v.) to remove Marghiloman, and Rumania reentered the war one day before the armistice.

Bratianu formally reassumed office in December. He represented Rumania at Versailles with all the diplomatic resources at his command. He insisted the territorial pledges of 1916 to Rumania remained valid. Bratianu's legal case was weak, but the Big Four gradually gave in. The Rumanian army had occupied much of the disputed territory and local Rumanian populations had voted to link themselves with Bucharest. Woodrow Wilson and David Lloyd George (qq.v.) might rage at Bratianu's demands, but they lacked military forces to exert their will in eastern Europe. Italy was quick to support Bratianu's call for close adherence to wartime territorial promises; and France saw no need to offend a potentially valuable eastern European ally. Finally, the rise of a Communist regime in Hungary let Bratianu appropriate the role of defending Europe against Bolshevism.

In September 1919, Bratianu again resorted to timely resignation. He preferred to handle Rumanian foreign affairs from the shadows. By the close of 1920 his nominal successors obtained Versailles' recognition of nearly the full range of Bratianu's territorial demands. The new Rumania was twice the size it had been in 1916. The Big Four's attempt to regulate Rumania's treatment of ethnic minorities, which Bratianu had dismissed as an infringement on Rumanian sovereignty, was limited to a meaningless treaty clause.

Consistent, ambitious, and unyielding, Bratianu triumphed over wartime military defeats and peacetime efforts by the great powers to control the process of drafting a peace; he succeeded better than any other statesman in demonstrating the ability of the local powers of eastern Europe to be heard. The Versailles peace bore Bratianu's stamp as well as that of President Wilson, whom the Rumanian leader despised.

Bratianu's final years could only be an anticlimax. He returned to office as prime minister in January 1922, and remained the dominant figure in Rumanian politics until his death on November 24, 1927, in Bucharest.

Rieber, "Russian Diplomacy and Rumania"; Silberstein, *The Troubled Alliance*; Spector, *Rumania at the Peace Conference*; Torrey, "Irredentism and Diplomacy," "Romania and the Belligerents: 1914-1918," "Romania's Entry . . . The Problem of Strategy," "Rumania's Decision to Intervene," and "Rumania and the Belligerents: 1914-1916;" *Larousse mensuel*, XI.

BRIAND, Aristide (*France, Premier*), was born in Nantes, March 28, 1862. The son of an innkeeper, he trained to become a lawyer in Paris, but returned to northwestern France to practice and to enter local politics in St. Nazaire. The young Briand was a red-hot anticleric, and his advocacy of the general strike made him more of a Syndicalist than a Socialist. He moved to Paris in 1893, soon failing there as he had earlier in St. Nazaire to win election to the Chamber of Deputies. He lost for a third time in 1898. Still fiery in his radicalism at the age of forty, Briand defended the star of French anti-militarism, Gustave Hervé, in a noted trial.

Briand was elected to the Chamber of Deputies in 1902. He rose quickly. Putting aside his youthful views, he led the effort to draft a moderate law providing for the separation of church and state. This success pointed him toward bigger things. He received the ministry of public instruction and cults in 1906 and the more important position of minister of justice in 1907. A nominal Socialist since the early 1890s—he had discomfited his colleagues by his "leftist" attraction to the general strike—he now moved to the center and upward. As minister of justice under Georges Clemenceau (q.v.), Briand put down teachers' and industrial workers' strikes with a heavy hand in 1907/8. As premier himself, 1909/10, Briand continued to stand firm against labor unrest, assuring skeptics in July 1909, "a new man has been born in me." When he was taunted by his former friends in the Socialist party for crushing a railway strike by the novel means of conscripting the workers into the army, he cited the overpowering necessity to preserve social peace. Moreover, such strikes opened the door to foreign invasion. Briand's patriotic conservatism made him a natural ally for Raymond Poincaré (q.v.). Briand managed Poincaré's campaign for the French presidency and succeeded him as premier in January 1913, when Poincaré was elected. Briand subsequently played a leading role in promoting the three-year service law, a measure Poincaré saw as essential for France's security.

Briand returned to the cabinet to join the *union sacrée* government of late August 1914. He received the post of minister of justice and also served as vice-president of the council of ministers. His influence and ambition soon extended over a wide field. In the aftermath of the battle of the Marne, Briand was one of two cabinet officials entrusted with the delicate mission of sounding out General Gallieni (q.v.) on his political ambitions. With rumors spreading that he would seek to become military dictator, the old general commanding the fortified camp at Paris denied any such intentions.

Briand was an original "Easterner": an early and violent critic of France's concentration of men and energies on the western front. As early as November 1914, he identified himself with an alternative: a front in Salonika manned with an Anglo-French force of 400,000 men. It would aid France's ally Serbia, pressure neutral Greece and Rumania to join the Entente, and threaten Austria from the south. The theme was widely discussed in military circles in these early months by figures like Gallieni and Franchet d'Esperey (q.v.), but some historians credit Briand as its author. Implementing this strategy was harder. In January 1915, Briand and Premier Viviani urged Joffre (qq.v.) to implement a Balkan offensive; the French commander in chief rejected it emphatically in favor of all-out efforts in northeastern France.

The year 1915 saw Briand's skillful rise to power, aided by Viviani's political and Joffre's military ineptitude. In July Briand intervened in the case of General Sarrail (q.v.). The minister of justice used his powers of persuasion to get Sarrail to agree conditionally to command French forces at the Dardanelles. Sarrail's cooperation provided several important advantages for Briand. Good relations with him meant the vital support of his Radical party friends in the National Assembly. Moreover, Sarrail's presence in the eastern Mediterranean was a large step toward establishing a major front there. Larger interests were also at stake: leaving Sarrail on the western front, from which Joffre had fired him, meant creating a storm center within the French military system. By the fall, Briand's ambitions bore fruit. In September France's ally Serbia called for help in the face of Bulgaria's intention to enter the war. Briand led the successful fight to shift French energies from the Dardanelles to the Balkans. Joffre had to agree; after two unsuccessful offensives in France during the year, he needed Briand's backing to hang onto his post. In October Briand succeeded Viviani as premier. He also assumed the post of foreign minister.

Described by King as a hardy perennial of French politics, he brought formidable gifts to his new offices. Well-versed in domestic politics and diplomacy, suave, eloquent, composed, and resourceful, Briand was determined to play a strong role in directing the war. Determined to be a different premier from his predecessor, he found himself confronted by many of the constraints Viviani had felt. The Chamber of Deputies with its influential Radical bloc insisted on support for Sarrail, the republican hero. Briand's ministerial address underlined the need to support Serbia. Briand had to persuade the reluctant Gallieni, an "Easterner," to become war minister. But support for Sarrail had to be balanced against other considerations. Joffre remained wedded to a strategy of striking on the western front. His prestige as the victor of the Marne and his influence over allies like the British made it impossible to remove him. Neither was it possible to shift substantial resources away from the western front in the face of Joffre's opposition.

The role of President Poincaré remained a problem. Briand had been a long-standing ally of Poincaré, but the new premier was unwilling to play the secondary role Viviani had filled. Armed with his personal contacts, his prodigious energy, and his detailed information on the course of the war, Poincaré was quick to challenge the more easygoing Briand. Cabinet meetings became occasions for long, bitter wrangling. Poincaré led an anti-Briand faction within the government.

The result of these tensions was a long tenure in office but a premiership on a shaky basis for Briand. Stretched between a restive National Assembly and a jealousy self-contained High Command, Briand's political skills and flexibility alone saved the day. Critical historians have labeled Briand "an opportunist." On December 2, 1915, Briand made Joffre commander in chief of all of France's armies, Sarrail's included. The promotion apparently enlarged Joffre's position; it also served Briand well in the National

Assembly. The premier now argued that Joffre was compelled to support Sarrail and the Balkans, since he was now directly responsible for that front. Such manipulation was harder when dealing with allies like Great Britain. By early December, the British were pointing to Serbia's final defeat as reason enough to abandon the Balkans. At the Calais conference of December 4, Briand gave in to British demands backed by Lord Kitchener's (q.v.) threat to resign. Briand reversed himself at once in the face of diverse opposition from Poincaré, the Socialists, and others. He had to turn to the Russians and the Italians for diplomatic support against London; and he threatened the British with the prospect of Balkan withdrawal leading to the collapse of the French government and even a move toward a negotiated peace. The British gave in. The Balkan front was preserved. Briand survived his first great political test. Another soon followed.

In December 1915, Briand first received word—from field grade officers—that Verdun was in danger. The Verdun crisis dominated the premier's work throughout 1916, but his initial response was mild. He passed the warning on to Joffre, then soothed the French commander's outrage at this violation of the military chain of command. Gallieni took the warnings more seriously. Briand calmed him by the cynical explanation that Joffre's assurances that Verdun was secure covered the government. Briand also expressed faith in Joffre's judgment. Both articles of faith were promptly shattered.

When the Germans attacked Verdun in late February 1916, Briand rushed to Joffre's headquarters. He demanded that the fortress be held. He brushed aside military objections in light of the political peril of a withdrawal. But he also brushed aside Gallieni's official attack on Joffre the next month. Briand played his comfortable role of mediator: he supported Joffre while seeking to prevent Gallieni from embarrassing the government with a resignation. When Gallieni did leave, Joffre's recommendation that his old comrade General Roques (q.v.) succeed Gallieni was accepted.

Briand could not bring himself to fire Joffre. But in the heat of the parliamentary uproar over Verdun, the premier moved to undermine the commander in chief with press leaks. One stressed the role of de Castelnau (q.v.) as the key military personality in the early days at Verdun. Poincaré's support for Joffre made such a campaign premature; at the same time, Briand found the National Assembly could not be calmed. Thus, he acceded to demands for a secret session of the legislature. There, in June 1916, Joffre and the government as well were exposed to direct and savage attacks for their conduct of the war.

The summer of 1916 brought a myriad of problems. The Anglo-French effort on the Somme failed to produce a breakthrough. The need to replace the shopworn Joffre became pressing, but the questions how? and with whom? remained difficult to answer. In the Balkans, British resistance prevented Sarrail from installing a pro-Allied government in Greece. Rumania's entry into the war on the French side quickly led to its complete military defeat. Sarrail's failure to attack Bulgaria in timely fashion contributed to Rumania's catastrophe. Briand seemed faced with unsuccessful generals everywhere. Sarrail's victorious fall offensive and his capture of Monastir in November solved one problem. Briand solved the larger difficulty of Joffre by easing the French commander in chief out of office in stages. On December 3, Joffre was persuaded to take the post of technical adviser to the government with control over the direction of the war in France and the Balkans. When the Cabinet was reshuffled on December 8 and General Lyautey (q.v.) replaced Roques, it became clear Briand's plans were different: Joffre was to be a mere figurehead. In a typical balancing movement, Briand buttressed his position with the political Right by appointing Lyautey; the simultaneous appointment of Nivelle (q.v.) to command the western front appealed to the parliamentary Left.

Persistent difficulties remained in the Balkans, notably in Greece. In early December 1916, Allied forces clashed with Greek royalists. Briand, a sometime friend of the Greek royal family, now accepted Sarrail's call to oust the Greek king. British hesitation still barred the way to a clear resolution of the problem.

By the start of 1917 Briand realized that his position had become untenable. The tensions within the *union sacrée* were on the verge of exploding. Poincaré made it clear with parliamentary leaders that he was willing to see Briand fall. A military triumph or political success was vital to shore up Briand's cabinet; none was forthcoming. Briand had presented Nivelle as a commander who would get along with the National Assembly. He soon proved as impervious to political control and as offensively minded as Joffre. At the Rome conference of January 1917, the British refused to accede to Briand's call for major operations in the Balkans. British distrust of French ambitions in Greece grew during the remainder of Briand's term of office; the distrust was implemented by British refusal to let the French oust the Greek king. The issue was resolved only after Briand's departure. The peace mission of Prince Sixtus of Bourbon, brother-in-law of the Austrian emperor, raised hopes in Poincaré but left Briand skeptical.

Briand's fate was sealed by Lyautey's clumsiness in dealing with the Left in the Chamber of Deputies. The war minister refused to discuss technical secrets, and implied that such information was not secure in the hands of certain deputies. The consequent uproar led to the fall of Briand's government on March 18. For eighteen months, Briand had survived events; he had never dominated them.

Briand played no further role in directing the war. Between June and September 1917, however, he was approached by German emissaries to explore avenues to a compromise peace. During this "Lanck-en affair," Briand alerted Poincaré at home and set the restitution of Alsace-Lorraine as the *sine qua non* of a negotiated peace. Briand took the soundings seriously. But Foreign Minister Ribot (*q.v.*) was hostile to the project; Poincaré was equivocal; and the Germans were merely engaged in an exploratory operation. The move collapsed by the end of September.

World War I was only an interlude in Briand's remarkable political career. He returned as premier in 1921—he led ten governments in all—and he served as foreign minister for most of the period from 1925 to 1932. Harsh on the Germans concerning reparations, he soon modified his position while still premier and fell in 1922 when the Chamber of Deputies refused to go along. As foreign minister, he led in a policy of reconciliation with Germany. It featured the Locarno treaties of 1925 and the early withdrawal of French occupation troops from western Germany. Briand balanced this policy off with closer ties to the Poles and the Czechs. His wisdom in thereby weakening France's victorious postwar position has evoked continuing controversy, but Briand did not live to see the resurgent Germany of the 1930s. He died in Paris, March 7, 1932.

Cassar, *The French and the Dardanelles*; King, *Generals and Politicians*; Siebert, *Aristide Briand*; Suarez, *Briand: sa vie, son oeuvre*, III, IV; Tanenbaum, *General Maurice Sarrail*; Wright, *Raymond Poincaré and the French Presidency*; *Dictionnaire des parlementaires français*, I.

BROQUEVILLE, Charles Marie Pierre Albert, Baron de (*Belgium, Premier*), was born at Postel, his parents' estate near Moll, on December 4, 1860. De Broqueville was the descendant of a recently ennobled Belgian family of French origin. He entered local politics in 1886, and, in 1892, he was elected to the Belgian Parliament. A member of the Catholic party, dominant in Belgian politics since 1884, de Broqueville entered his first cabinet in 1910 as minister of railroads, posts, and telegraphs. The following year, he formed his own ministry and,

against expectations, led the declining Catholic party to victory in the 1912 elections. The new premier, influenced by the growing fear of a European war after the Agadir crisis of 1911, became a strong advocate of military preparedness. Long an opponent of military expansion—he had stood against the 1909 reform that instituted a limited form of national conscription—in November 1912 he took over the war minister's portfolio and began to reform and expand the army. Still, Belgium's military forces remained tiny by continental standards; and Germany, in particular, regarded the Belgian army as at most a negligible opponent in any future encounter. De Broqueville contributed to Belgium's image as a small, weak, and uncertain power by insisting with comic-opera bravado that his country would fight against invaders from any direction who tried to cross Belgian territory in time of war. Anglo-French probing about possible military cooperation against Germany met a stone wall of Belgian hostility.

When the crisis came in the form of the German ultimatum of August 2, de Broqueville joined King Albert I (*q.v.*) in telling the Parliament at Brussels that Belgium would fight with all her strength. After Albert's brief, emotional address to Belgium's political representatives on August 4, de Broqueville followed with a detailed description of the German demands. More important, he welcomed members of the Left opposition into an expanded war cabinet. For Belgium the August 1914 campaign soon reduced itself into the siege of Antwerp. The government's refusal to order the army to fight a delaying action outside Brussels led to a storm of criticism from the French. The premier adroitly responded by sending a delegation to the United States. Under Liberal leader Paul Hymans (*q.v.*), it forged a lasting practical tie to the world's most prestigious neutral nation.

With the king leading the army on the Yser, defending a small sliver of western Belgium, de Broqueville was left to run the government. The cabinet sat as guests of the French in Le Havre. Over the next two years, relations between the monarch and his premier were marked by sharp disagreement. This in turn reflected the widening chasm separating Albert and most of his ministers over several key issues. These were: the abandonment of Belgium's permanent neutrality; the effort to take territorial gains following future victory in the war; the proper response to German peace initiatives. By early 1915 the premier opposed maintaining Belgium in her prewar status of permanent neutrality. At the start of the next year, de Broqueville staunchly rejected Albert's call for seriously considering a German peace initiative; moreover, the premier was openly encouraging publicists crying for a postwar "Greater Belgium," to come mainly at the expense of Holland. But the two national leaders managed to avoid a public split; the monarch repeatedly restrained his chief minister or at least temporarily convinced him to change direction.

In October 1917, de Broqueville, who had given up the war ministry to take on the foreign minister's post, shocked his cabinet colleagues when they found him seeking a compromise peace. The prolonged military stalemate plus Albert's repeated insistence that this war could never end in an Allied victory won him over. But opinion in the cabinet had long ago shifted against the king. In 1916 some ministers had bandied the word "treason" about in discussing the king's negotiations with the Germans. Even members of de Broqueville's own party turned on him by January 1918 and forced him out from the foreign ministry. That May he was compelled to abandon the premier's post as well.

De Broqueville returned to public office at the close of World War I, serving as minister of the interior. By 1926 he was able to regain the portfolio of minister of war, and, in the last act in his political career, he led the government from 1932 to 1934. He lived long enough to see his small country overrun once again and died in Brussels, on September 5, 1940.

Jonathan Helmreich, *Belgium and Europe*; Marre, *Le Baron de Broqueville et la défense nationale*; Palo, "The Diplomacy of Belgian War Aims during the First World War"; *Biographie nationale*, XXIX.

BRUSILOV, Aleksei Alekseevich (*Russia, General of Cavalry*), was born on August 31, 1853, in Tiflis, the son of a Russian general of noble birth. In 1872 he graduated from the Corps of Pages, a military training school reserved for the aristocracy. Brusilov's first post was with a cavalry regiment near his birthplace in the Caucasus. Decorated for heroism in the Russo-Turkish War, 1877/78, he went on to attend the Officers Cavalry School in St. Petersburg from 1881 to 1883. Upon graduating, he took a teaching post at the school. Brusilov's military home for the next two decades was to be found at the cavalry school. After serving as its commandant from 1902 to 1906, he was promoted to general. A series of choice field positions in Poland followed: command of the 2nd Guards Cavalry Division, 1906-1909; command of the XIV Corps, 1909-1912; deputy commander of the Warsaw Military District, 1912-1913; promotion to general of cavalry (1912), and command of the XII Corps, 1913-1914.

The outbreak of World War I brought Brusilov command of the Eighth Army. He fought in Galicia in 1914; and, in the grim spring and summer of 1915, led his troops on a 200-mile retreat from the foothills of the Carpathians to Luck, south of the Pripet Marshes. There he turned to fight back. As Austro-Hungarian forces entered Luck in late September, Brusilov jarred them with an enthusiastic counterattack.

In March 1916, Brusilov took charge of the southwestern front, replacing the ineffectual General Nikolai Ivanov (*q.v.*). He quickly demonstrated a variety of characteristics all too rare among senior Russian commanders. As Luck had shown, Brusilov was aggressive. When the front commanders gathered at Mogilev in mid-April, Brusilov alone showed enthusiasm for the general offensive the High Command expected to launch that summer. The old cavalryman was imaginative. He set his staff to work pondering new approaches to end the stationary slugging match that had come to characterize the war in both eastern and western Europe. Moreover, Brusilov was able to bring his subordinates under effective control, no mean feat for a Russian army leader in 1916. Even a general like Shcherbachev (*q.v.*), who disagreed with Brusilov's tactical innovations, was made to adopt them. Most important of all, he was flexible. When Italy urgently called for a Russian attack on the eastern front, the Austrian *Strafexpedition* in the Trentino having reached dangerous proportions, Brusilov quickly volunteered to launch an offensive well ahead of schedule.

The Brusilov method brought striking results when he sent the southwestern front on the offensive in June 1916. Simultaneous surprise attacks battered the Austrian line over a long stretch of the front. Each of Brusilov's four field armies charged the enemy line. Artillery fire and infantry assaults worked together, another rare phenomenon in the tsar's armies. Brusilov managed to concentrate (and hide) reserves near each of his points of attack; thus, he could move to exploit one or several breakthroughs. A set of multiple crises erupting over a front 200 miles long went beyond the ability of the Austrian High Command to manage. Brusilov cut westward. Meanwhile, in France, the attack on Verdun slackened as three German divisions left the sector for Russia. In Italy, the Austrians recalled that they had drawn troops for the *Strafexpedition* from the very sector in which Brusilov was now advancing. In Bucharest, the Rumanian government moved closer to intervention on the side of the Entente.

By summer's end, however, Brusilov's promising initiative stalled. His neighbor, General Evert (*q.v.*), commanding the huge western front, refused either to launch an aggressive supporting attack or to shift large numbers of reserve units to Brusilov. General Alekseev (q.v.), commanding the Russian army, never succeeded in tightening the loose lines of authority that allowed Evert and others to go their own ways. He relied on Evert but could not move him. Brusilov's own methods had their weaknesses; reserves could be hidden close to the front, but to hide them effectively meant to keep their numbers small, hindering the full exploitation of a breakthrough. Nor did the enemy remain paralyzed by surprise and panic. By August, the German High Command had taken control of all operations on the eastern front, ending the kind of nonchalance toward Russian attacks that had helped bring the Austrians to grief.

Along with Russia's other front commanders, Brusilov accepted the March Revolution of 1917. As General Alekseev, the provisional government's commander in chief, grew pessimistic about the prospects of a new offensive, Minister of War Aleksandr Kerensky (q.v.) called on Brusilov. The July 1917 offensive, like the June attack of the previous year, met initial success. But this time the political and military environment was different; and this time the success was short-lived. The Russian army had deteriorated in the wake of the March Revolution; reliable units were in short supply, and multiple attacks over an extensive stretch of front were impossible to contrive. German reinforcements were close at hand. Brusilov faced deadly counterattacks in less than three weeks from the time his forces jumped off. Kerensky now sought a general who could restore some semblance of discipline to the routed Russian columns. Brusilov gave way to General Lavr Kornilov (q.v.).

The final brief chapter in Brusilov's military career remained to be written. The aristocratic cavalryman remained in Russia after the November Revolution. He avoided political or military activities. Then, during the Polish invasion in the spring of 1920, he rallied to the new order and joined the Red Army. His service on study commissions and the like did not equal taking a combat command against his former comrades in arms on the White side, or even fighting against the Poles. Nonetheless, Brusilov, whatever his deepest feelings about the Bolshevik Revolution, became the most visible example of the traditional Russian officer corps linking arms with the workers' and peasants' state.

Brusilov died in Moscow, March 17, 1926.

Brusilov, *Moi vospominaniia*, 5th ed.; Feldman, "The Russian General Staff and the June 1917 Offensive"; Rostunov, *General Brusilov*; Rutherford, *The Russian Army in World War I*; Stone, *The Eastern Front*; *Modern Encyclopedia of Russian and Soviet History*, V; *Sovetskaia istoricheskaia entsiklopediia*, II; *Sovetskaia voennaia entsiklopediia*, I.

BULLARD, Robert Lee (*United States, General*), was born on January 15, 1861, near Opelika, Alabama, the son of a farmer. Bullard graduated from West Point in 1885 after an undistinguished performance (twenty-seventh in a class of thirty-nine). For most of the next thirteen years he served with the Tenth Infantry, primarily in the Southwest. Slow promotion prompted him in 1898 to transfer to the Commissary Department in the grade of captain. As a commander of infantry in the Philippines in 1900/1901 he earned a reputation for determination and aggressiveness, and in 1902, he returned to the regular army in the grade of major. Further service in the Philippines brought him the support of General Leonard Wood, and after tours of duty in Cuba and Mexico, Bullard attended the Army War College in 1912. At the outbreak of the war in Europe he commanded the Twenty-sixth Infantry and throughout 1915 kept the peace in the lower Rio Grande Valley.

In June 1917, Brigadier General Bullard was appointed commander of the Second Brigade of the First Division. He accompanied it to France, where General Pershing (q.v.) transferred Bullard to command the infantry officer specialist schools of the American Expeditionary Forces (AEF) in the grade of major general in August 1917. Bullard was entrusted with the First Division in December 1917, and the following May Pershing ordered him to undertake the successful attack at Cantigny. This able and popular field commander was given the III Corps in July 1918, and he led this unit in the bloody fighting at the Vesle River ("Death Valley"). This operation formed part of the general Allied counteroffensive along the Aisne-Marne front after General Ludendorff's (q.v.) vaunted Michael offensive in France had run its course by July 1918.

Bullard next led the III Corps to the Meuse-Argonne sector. Pershing's First Army, which enjoyed a numerical superiority of eight-to-one over the Germans, had by now swelled to more than 1 million men, including 135,000 French soldiers, and had become entirely too unwieldy. Consequently, it was divided and on October 12, 1918, Bullard took charge of the American Second Army; however, his sector remained relatively quiet during the final weeks of the war.

After the war Bullard was appointed commanding general of the II Corps area at Fort Jay, Governors Island, New York, a post that he held until 1925. Politically, Bullard was isolationist and conservative;

he became an adamant opponent of the New Deal, and even suggested in 1935 that the Communists were using the relief system to undermine the United States. The general died on September 11, 1947, at Fort Jay, New York.

Bullard, *Personalities and Reminiscences of the War*; Coffman, *War to End All Wars*; Millett, *The General*; *Dictionary of American Biography*, XXIV Supplement Four.

BÜLOW, Karl von (*Germany, Field Marshal*), was born in Berlin on March 24, 1846, the son of an army officer. Bülow fought in the wars of 1866 and 1870/71 and joined the General Staff as captain in 1877. By 1894, he commanded the prestigious Fourth Foot Guards; three years later he headed the central department of the Prussian War Ministry in the grade of major general. Bülow was appointed deputy chief of the General Staff in 1902, headed the III Army Corps the following year, and in 1904 was promoted general of infantry. In 1912 he was placed in charge of the III Army Inspectorate at Hanover in the grade of colonel general.

On August 2, 1914, Bülow was given command of the Second Army which comprised mainly the Guards Corps, and he led this force in the conquest of Liège and Namur. Shortly thereafter Bülow was also given nominal command over General Alexander von Kluck's (*q.v.*) First Army. By August 23/24, Bülow's forces had defeated the French Fifth Army at the Sambre River, and followed this feat of arms with similar successes at St. Quentin. The Germans crossed the Marne River on September 4, yet Bülow grew strangely pessimistic about the war in the west. He had good reason to be apprehensive. Kluck's First Army had twice swung in toward the southwest in order to sweep through the French defenses on the near side of Paris, in the process abandoning the original plan to march around the far side of the capital. A thirty-mile wide gap developed between Bülow's Second Army and Kluck's First, which had already crossed the Marne and stood about thirty miles from Paris. Bülow was hardly a master of operative thinking and when the Allies discovered the gap between the two German armies, he panicked and became immobilized. On September 8 Colonel Richard Hentsch (*q.v.*) arrived from staff headquarters at Luxembourg and, finding only dire predictions of imminent disaster, ordered an immediate retreat from the Marne behind the Aisne River.

Briefly, Bülow was given command over the entire German right wing (First, Second and Seventh Armies) as the Entente counterattacked along the Aisne.

On October 10 he received command of a newly formed Second Army at St. Quentin. In January 1915, the kaiser promoted Bülow field marshal, but a heart attack in March forced him to seek temporary rest. Bülow's subsequent attempts to be reinstated to active duty failed, and on June 22, 1916, he resigned from the army. Bülow died in Berlin on August 31, 1921. His lack of resolution and nerve at the Marne played no small part in the decision to retire him, and the publication of his account of the battle in 1919 did little to restore his reputation.

Barnett, *The Swordbearers*; Bülow, *Mein Bericht zur Marneschlacht*; Krack, *Generalfeldmarschall von Bülow*; Liddell Hart, *The Real War*; *Neue Deutsche Biographie*, II.

BURIAN von RAJECZ, István Count (*Austria-Hungary, Foreign Minister*) was born in Stampfen, near Pressburg, on January 16, 1851, to an ancient aristocratic Hungarian family. After initial diplomatic appointments to Alexandria, Bucharest, Belgrade, and Sofia, Burian from 1882 to 1886 headed the Consulate General in Moscow. Thereafter he was envoy to Sofia (1887-1895), Stuttgart (1896), and Athens (1897). From 1903 to 1912, Burian served as Austro-Hungarian joint minister of finance. After the annexation of Bosnia-Herzegovina in 1908, Burian administered these territories with a mild hand and attempted to provide Serbs with a greater voice in the imperial administration, which merely earned him the wrath of fellow bureaucrats.

From January 1915 to December 1916, Burian served as foreign minister under his fellow Hungarian, Count István Tisza (*q.v.*). Burian attempted to preserve Austro-Hungarian dominance at least in the war against Serbia, which drew from General Conrad von Hötzendorf (*q.v.*) the sarcastic rejoinder: "But with what?" In fact, Burian was powerless to prevent the entries into the war on the side of the Entente of Italy (May 1915) and Rumania (August 1916); however, he did manage to gain Bulgaria (October 1915) for the Central Powers. Count Burian's opposition to Germany's unrestricted submarine warfare, his willingness to restore the independence of Belgium as the price of a general peace settlement, and his insistence that Austria-Hungary be paramount in Poland in the future quickly earned him the opposition of German military leaders. Burian returned to his former duties as joint minister of finance, which better suited his serious, legalistic, and unimaginative nature.

However, on April 18, 1918, he returned to the Ballplatz as foreign minister, but the empire's deteriorating military situation provided Burian little opportunity to seek an honorable end to the war. His public appeal to President Woodrow Wilson (*q.v.*) for an end to the war on September 14 went unheeded, and rather than attempt a separate peace with the Entente, Count Burian resigned his post on October 24, 1918. He died in Vienna on October 20, 1922.

Burian, *Drei Jahre: Aus der Zeit meiner Amtsführung im Kriege*; Fischer, *Griff nach der Weltmacht*; *Neue Deutsche Biographie*, III.

BYNG, Julian Hedworth George (*Great Britain, General*), was born at Wrotham Park, Barnet, on September 11, 1862, the youngest son of the earl of Strafford. Byng was educated at Eton, entered the army through the militia, and was gazetted to the Tenth Hussars in 1883; while in India he became widely known for his fine polo. The following year he took part in the Sudan campaign, and in 1894 he passed the Staff College. Three years later Byng was at Aldershot, having been promoted captain in 1889 and major in 1898. His genius for friendship and his charming personality made him popular. In November 1900, he was sent to the Cape as commander of the South African Light Horse, where Winston Churchill (*q.v.*) served as his galloper. From 1904 to 1905, Colonel Byng was commandant of the Cavalry School at Netheravon, and was promoted major general in 1909. In October 1912, he was appointed to the command in Egypt and was there when war broke out in Europe.

Byng was recalled in September 1914 and entrusted with the Third Cavalry Division, which he led during the First Battle of Ypres. Command of the Cavalry Corps followed in March 1915, but in August he was sent to the Gallipoli Peninsula to take charge of the IX Corps at Suvla Bay. Upon arrival at Gallipoli, Byng saw no alternative but to recommend the immediate evacuation of Allied troops in this area.

After brief tours of duty in Egypt and France, Byng in May 1916, took command of the Canadian Army Corps. A broad German advance in June at Mont Sorrel and Sanctuary Wood, Ypres, was checked by Byng's Corps only at great loss of lives. His finest hour came in April 1917, when the Canadian Corps, after having been heavily bled during the senseless attrition at the Somme the previous year, stormed and captured Vimy ridge. In June 1917, Byng succeeded Sir Edmund Allenby (*q.v.*) as commander of the Third Army. In this capacity he planned the Cambrai offensive, designed to capture Bourlon, Cambrai, and Valenciennes. The attack, led for the first time by almost 400 tanks, was delayed three months, thereby depriving Byng of the element of surprise; in addition, only six infantry divisions followed the

tanks. The offensive in November 1917 failed for lack of infantry and reserves, and Byng callously blamed the setback on his troops; "namely, lack of training on the part of junior officers and N.C.O.'s and men." That same year he was gazetted to the rank of general.

The German Michael offensive in France in March 1918 fell fully upon the Third Army. Byng initially vacated the Cambrai salient, but managed to halt the Germans at Arras. His forces took part in the great counteroffensive on August 21, and with the Fourth and Fifth Armies drove the enemy back to the Hindenburg line, which was breached on September 27. In eighty days, Byng advanced sixty miles and took 67,000 prisoners and 800 guns.

After the war, he was raised to the peerage as Baron Byng of Vimy, of Thorpe-le-Soken, in Essex, given the thanks of Parliament, and a grant of £30,000. Byng was appointed governor general of Canada in 1921. Unfortunately, this assignment was marred by Byng's clumsy involvement in the Canadian elections of 1926, and he returned to England that same year. In 1928 he accepted the post of chief commissioner of the London metropolitan police and set about to reform Scotland Yard until his retirement in 1931. Byng was advanced to viscountcy in 1928, and four years later received the field marshal's baton. He died at Thorpe Hall, Sussex, on June 6, 1935.

Edmonds and Davies, *History of the Great War. Military Operations: France and Belgium*, 13 vols.; Liddell Hart, *The Real War*; *Dictionary of National Biography 1931-1940*.

CADORNA, Luigi (*Italy, General*), was born in Pallanza, September 4, 1850, the son of a prominent Piedmontese military family. His father, General Raffaele Cadorna, was a distinguished military leader during the period of Italian unification. Luigi Cadorna's son was a major figure in the anti-German resistance effort in Italy during World War II.

Luigi Cadorna became an artillery officer in 1868. He passed through the General Staff Academy and, by 1898, had become a major general. Ten years later, he was offered the post of army chief of staff. Cadorna declined the honor. He could not get the government to allow him full control over the army in both peacetime and during war. He refused to share authority with the minister of war. Cadorna's father had exhibited during his own career this same distrust of civilian authority over the army. The younger Cadorna was fated to make it a major issue during World War I.

Cadorna accepted the post of chief of staff when it was offered to him a second time, in late July 1914, as

Europe hung on the edge of war. Prepared to fight alongside Germany and Austria-Hungary in accordance with the Triple Alliance, he was preparing to move troops to the Rhine and the Alpine frontier with France when Premier Salandra (q.v.) declared Italian neutrality on August 2. The next months brought repeated conflict between Cadorna and government leaders. The general saw the danger of an Austrian attack following on the heels of Italy's desertion of her diplomatic partners. Salandra refused to permit the chief of staff to mobilize fully on Italy's eastern frontier. After the battle of the Marne, when Salandra began to consider entering the war on the side of the Entente, Cadorna objected that the army was not equipped to stand up to a winter campaign. Salandra and his recently appointed foreign minister, Sidney Sonnino (q.v.), occupied Albania in late 1914. Cadorna objected that such sideshows drained forces needed to guard Italy's borders with Austria-Hungary.

The Italian entry into the war came in May 1915, and Cadorna led his troops in the first assault on the Isonzo line in June. Cadorna had used the period of preparation to plan a smooth mobilization, to bolster Italy's artillery units, and to reinforce the border fortresses. Cadorna was at his best as a military organizer, but the test of combat indicated at once that even these measures were insufficient. Between June and December 1915, Cadorna sent his armies into four offensives on the Isonzo. Each brought the same dismal results: tiny gains in the rugged mountain terrain at the cost of huge numbers of casualties. The losses in trained junior officers were particularly appalling.

Cadorna's response was to keep hammering away. His frontal tactics, which he could not pretend to support with sufficient artillery, mirrored the worst examples of fruitless slaughter on the western front. He met sinking morale with brutal discipline. Summary executions and even decimation were practices, not just threats, in the Italian army. The officer corps suffered in a parallel, if not quite equal, fashion: Cadorna fired hundreds of senior officers. Such practices might have found justification in a short, victorious war, but Cadorna, likely the least popular commander in his own army on the Allied side, sank deeper into a war of attrition. Like General Joffre (q.v.) in France, he felt he had to attack, if only to support his allies; he, like Joffre, had no solution to the problem of the attacks not working in the fashion that he conducted them.

Friction with the politicians intensified, as one might expect. Cadorna—again the parallel in France comes to mind—simply excluded political observers

from the war zone. But this wall was soon breached by such figures as Leonida Bissolati (q.v.), a member of the Chamber of Deputies who, at age fifty-eight, enlisted in a combat regiment and returned regularly to Rome to tell his colleagues what transpired at the front. Cadorna also collided with the Salandra-Sonnino team's desire to fight a war against Austria alone. More the realist than they, Cadorna saw he had to coordinate his operations with the needs of fellow belligerents like the Russians. The test of Italy's willingness to be a wartime partner with Britain and France came in the form of requests to send troops to Salonika. Cadorna favored the idea; Sonnino blocked it.

By early January 1916, Sonrino and other cabinet leaders wanted to put a halt to Cadorna's quasi-independent status. But the Italian commander curtly rejected their call for a defense council that would place him on a par with civilian authorities. The spring brought Cadorna's career to the edge of disaster. After facing repeated Italian offensives on the Isonzo, the Austrians responded with the *Strafexpedition*: this was a powerful thrust southward from the Trentino, the less active of the two Austro-Italian fighting fronts. Using veteran troops with large quantities of heavy artillery at their disposal, the Austrian Eleventh Army nearly cut into the Venetian plains. Cadorna had gotten wind of an enemy offensive, but he failed to foresee the inadequacy of the Italian defenses. As rumors ran that Cadorna might retreat to the Piave, Salandra was on the edge of firing the Italian commander. The premier's crumbling authority—he was voted out of office in early June—made him hold back. Meanwhile, Cadorna, who, according to Seton-Watson, was at his best in times of crisis, stabilized the front. The Italians enjoyed the advantage of interior lines of communication, and Cadorna called in troops from the Isonzo and from as far away as Albania to stem the Austrian tide.

The new government of Paolo Boselli (q.v.) put unsettling personalities like Bissolati into the cabinet. But Cadorna was able to begin his relationship with the new cabinet by presenting them with Italy's first great military victory of the war. In early August, his forces crossed the Isonzo to establish a bridgehead at Gorizia. But this brought dangers as well. The hero of Gorizia, the dashing General Capello (q.v.), had good political connections and the look of a potential successor to Cadorna. The chief of staff exiled him to the now quiet Trentino. This was at best a temporary solution. Cadorna's reputation now had to absorb more bad news: three new offensives on the Isonzo (September to November) restored the old pattern of bloody futility.

The year 1917 brought the Caporetto onslaught and Cadorna's downfall. Danger signals came early. At the Rome conference (January 1917), Allied leaders turned aside the Italian government's request for a grand offensive launched from Italian territory that year against Austria. New offensives on the Isonzo, notably the Eleventh (August/September 1917) were costly enough to sap Italian morale, but they were successful enough to rouse Vienna to call in German aid. Word spread of the August peace initiative announced by Pope Benedict XV (*q.v.*), with its talk of "useless carnage."

As in the case of the *Strafexpedition*, Cadorna knew danger was lurking over the nearby mountain ranges. Russia was plummeting out of the war; both German and Austro-Hungarian divisions were now freed for action against Italy. But Cadorna saw the peril approaching only in the spring of 1918; and he pictured it in the shape of a simultaneous attack on the middle Isonzo and the Trentino lines. The breakthrough on the lightly held northern sector of the Isonzo line caught him with no reserves at hand. Moreover, offensive-minded subordinates like Capello, now back on the Isonzo, had ignored his precautionary call to pull heavy artillery units west of the Isonzo just in case.

The Germans struck on October 24. The Second Army gave way and the entire front collapsed. Cadorna's conduct did not at first match his coolness under fire at the time of the *Strafexpedition*. He hesitated for two days, then (early on October 27) ordered a general retreat. As the enemy surged across the Tagliamento River, Cadorna hesitated again; then (on November 4) he ordered his battered armies back to the Piave.

Falls credits Cadorna with a good performance in directing the last stages of the Italian retreat. The army now stood on a line it could hope to hold. But Cadorna's career was in shreds. On November 3, in a pessimistic message to Rome, he hinted at the need for a separate peace. He was known to be considering a retreat beyond the Piave to the Adige-Mincio line. His open criticism of his own armies, which he accused of cowardice, and of the home front, where he saw sedition running wild, sealed his fate. On October 30, Premier Vittorio Orlando (*q.v.*) replaced Boselli and pledged to oust Cadorna. Italy's allies gathered at Rapallo on November 5 and added their voices to the demand that Cadorna depart. On November 7 he gave up his command to General Diaz (*q.v.*).

Cadorna served briefly on the inter-Allied Supreme War Council at Versailles. When the Italian Chamber of Deputies voted to investigate the Caporetto disaster, Cadorna resigned in protest and retired to private life. The parliamentary report was published only in 1919; it focused blame for the defeat on Italy's military leaders, evoking Cadorna's outrage. Mussolini eased the pain in 1924 by elevating the retired Cadorna to the rank of field marshal. The promotion came at the same time that Diaz, Cadorna's more fortunate successor, received an identical honor. Cadorna died at Bordighera, December 21, 1928.

Cadorna, *Altre pagine sulla grande guerra*; Faldella, *La grande guerra*, 2 vols.; Falls, *The Battle of Caporetto*; Melograni, *Storia politica della grande guerra*; Pieri, *L'Italia nella prima guerra mondiale*, "Les Relations entre gouvernement et commandement en Italie en 1917"; Seton-Watson, *Italy from Liberalism to Fascism*; Whittam, *The Politics of the Italian Army, 1861-1918*; *Enciclopedia italiana*, VIII.

CAILLAUX, Joseph (*France, Deputy*), was born in Le Mans, March 30, 1863, scion of a wealthy provincial family. His father, an engineer and an Orleanist deputy, served as France's minister of public works and then minister of finance between 1874 and 1877. Educated in law and economics, Joseph Caillaux entered the ministry of finance in 1886. After more than a decade as a treasury official, he was elected to the Chamber of Deputies in 1898. A moderate Republican, his closest political allies were Alexandre Ribot and Raymond Poincaré (*qq.v.*). In 1899 Caillaux took the post of minister of finance, his father's old position and one he himself was to hold in numerous cabinets. A figure of inherited wealth and aristocratic demeanor, Caillaux began to emerge as a hero to the Left in 1907 when he proposed a progressive income tax.

Caillaux became a center of national controversy during the Moroccan crisis of 1911, in which he acquired a lasting reputation as pro-German. He was chosen to be premier in June. Two months before, French troops had marched on Fez and overturned the political balance in Morocco. In July the German government demanded compensation for their lost political rights in this turbulent area of northwestern Africa. A German gunboat, the *Panther*, was dispatched to Agadir and made the crisis a serious one. Caillaux intervened in the negotiations as war fever rose on both sides of the Rhine. He was thereafter anathematized by nationalist circles for negotiating behind the back of his foreign minister and surrendering a chunk of the French Cameroons to compensate Germany.

Tactless, self-important, openly contemptuous of his colleagues and the procedures of the National

Assembly, Caillaux nonetheless found himself with a growing reputation as a republican of the Left as war approached. He was proud of avoiding war in 1911. The following year, he criticized his old friend Poincaré, who was seeking the presidency of France, as a leader who desired a collision with Germany. Caillaux led the unsuccessful fight to prevent military service from being expanded to three years. In October 1913, he was chosen president of the Radical party. The strong Radical showing in the May 1914 elections—implying the electorate's doubts about Poincaré's belligerent style in foreign policy—made Caillaux a strong candidate to become premier. An alliance with Socialist leader Jean Jaurès to form a government seemed about to take shape. Two months earlier, however, a scandal had halted Caillaux's ascent. His wife had fatally shot a newspaper editor engaged in a bitter press campaign against Caillaux. The press campaign had been attributed to Caillaux's political enemies in the National Assembly and government, notably Poincaré and Aristide Briand (q.v.). Madame Caillaux's acquittal—her husband had led her defense in court—came at the end of July and seemed to renew the Radical leader's political prospects. In less than a week, war broke out.

Jaurès was assassinated on the eve of mobilization; his killer had also tried to find Caillaux, who fled to his country home. When Caillaux tried to serve as the army's paymaster general, he was harassed by French and British officers. Minister of the Interior Malvy (q.v.), an old political ally, arranged Caillaux's release from the army. He traveled in Latin America on a food purchasing mission, lived in Italy for a time, and spent most of the next three years residing quietly in the provinces. Anticipating that he would be called to the premiership once Poincaré felt victory was impossible, Caillaux drafted his "Rubicon" project, a scheme for ruling by decree while he made peace.

Caillaux was the logical leader of a French peace movement, but he avoided treasonous contact with German emissaries. His circle of acquaintances, however, included unsavory types like Paul Bolo-Pasha who were linked to the enemy. As a symbol of a "white," that is, negotiated, peace, Caillaux was a target for the Parisian press. The new word "defeatism," with its implication of desiring a German victory, was coined by journalists to be thrown at Caillaux. He was accused of being the *de facto* interior minister, pushing Malvy to be lenient with pro-German publications. As the *union sacrée* crumbled in late 1917, Poincaré was faced with a choice between Caillaux and Clemenceau (q.v.) as premier; the one representing negotiations, the other a fight to the finish. He chose Clemenceau, who quickly launched an attack on defeatists, traitors, and pacifists.

In December 1917, Caillaux shed his parliamentary immunity and asked to be tried by the Senate. He admitted some of his wartime contacts had been imprudent. But he considered his actions innocent: his critics were castigating him for his ideas. He turned aside Clemenceau's quiet warning to leave the country and was arrested in January 1918. He was not charged until October 1918. Tried finally in 1920, Caillaux claimed again to be innocent; he insisted France would find its victory had been purchased at an exorbitant cost. The prosecution offered the "Rubicon" as evidence Caillaux had intended to commit treason. Nonetheless, Caillaux was convicted only on a minor charge, fined, and banished from France's major cities. The disillusionment with the peace settlement and the popular reaction against the Rhineland occupation of 1923 set the stage for his political rebirth. He was granted amnesty in 1924 and was back as minister of finance the following year. A fixture in the Senate from 1925 onward, he was finance minister again in 1935 and attempted to form a government that year.

Caillaux died at the age of eighty-one at his estate in Mamers, November 22, 1944.

Binion, *Defeated Leaders*; Caillaux, *Mes mémoires*, 3 vols.; Franzius, *Caillaux: Statesman of Peace*.

CAPELLE, Eduard von (*Germany, Admiral*), was born at Celle on October 10, 1855, the son of a factory owner. Capelle entered the newly formed Imperial German Navy in 1872, and after several board commands was assigned to the Navy Office. By 1897 he had become Admiral Alfred Tirpitz's (q.v.) most trusted aide and expert on budgetary matters; Capelle worked out the details of Tirpitz's Navy Bills of 1898 and 1900, being careful to make the navy as independent of parliament as possible. Capelle showed great skill in handling deputies in naval matters, plying them with a combination of flattery, statistics, and sea cruises. He was promoted captain in 1900, rear admiral four years later, and vice admiral in 1909. Capelle was rewarded for his efforts on behalf of naval expansion by being raised into the Prussian nobility in 1912; he was promoted admiral the following year.

Entering the war as chief of the Administrative Department of the Navy Office, Capelle was concurrently appointed under secretary of the Navy Office. He had from the start thought British neutrality unlikely, yet he shared Tirpitz's fears that the war had come five years too early, before the fleet stood a genuine chance of success against the Royal Navy. In August 1915, Capelle became very ill, and on November 1, at age sixty, was removed from the active list. On March 17, 1916, however, he was reactivated and replaced Tirpitz as state secretary as a result of the grand admiral's resignation over Wilhelm II's (*q.v.*) refusal to continue submarine warfare *à outrance*. Capelle's willingness to succeed his erstwhile chief brought him from fellow naval officers the nickname Judas Iscariot. Above all, Capelle was installed at the Navy Office with implicit instructions to cooperate with Chancellor Theobald von Bethmann Hollweg (*q.v.*) in the matter of submarine warfare.

The new state secretary opposed the resumption of unrestricted submarine warfare loyally throughout 1916, but on January 9, 1917, gave in to the demands of Admiral Henning von Holtzendorff and Generals Paul von Hindenburg and Erich Ludendorff (*qq.v.*). However, Capelle greatly feared the future of a navy totally devoted to *guerre de course*. As early as January 1917, he foresaw the need to create a "special cemetery" for the U-boats being built, and in October asked Holtzendorff to rescind "unlimited construction orders," since these would seriously jeopardize promotion and battleship building. Indeed, the exigencies of the war at sea forced Capelle to abandon Tirpitz's master plan of a fleet of sixty capital units and instead to divert available funds and materials to small craft, such as submarines, destroyers and cruisers.

Capelle's critical hour came in August 1917, when several hundred sailors rebelled against the fleet's failure to institute special food supervisory committees promised by him in parliament. Rather than force naval commanders to carry out his order, Capelle chose to blame the unrest in the fleet on the alleged machinations of the Independent Socialists (USPD) and to ask parliament to outlaw that party. Moreover, he demanded the death penalty for the rebellious sailors. The state secretary was only partially successful: on September 5 two of the leaders of the sailors' movement were executed, but the Reichstag refused to endorse his political stricture when Friedrich Ebert (*q.v.*) declared on behalf of the Social Democrats (SPD), "We shall be glad for every day sooner that the German people are freed from this government." Capelle bore the brunt of the resulting criticism for his blunder in the Reichstag and on October 13 drafted a letter of resignation. The kaiser refused to change command at the Navy Office and thereby to revive calls for Tirpitz's return.

The state secretary continued in office as a lame duck until the fall of 1918. On August 11, Admiral Reinhard Scheer (*q.v.*) assumed control through the newly created Supreme Command of the Navy, and Capelle was forced to retire on October 9, 1918, as part of the overall reorganization. He died in Wiesbaden on February 23, 1931. Without the charisma of Tirpitz or Scheer and with a penchant primarily for fiscal detail, Capelle proved unable to master the political furor aroused by the issues of unrestricted submarine warfare and sailors' revolts.

Berghahn, *Der Tirpitz-Plan*; Gemzell, *Organization, Conflict, and Innovation*; Herwig, *"Luxury" Fleet*; *Neue Deutsche Biographie*, III.

CAPELLO, Luigi Attilo (*Italy, General*), was born in Intra, on April 14, 1859, the son of a telegraph company official. He completed the Military Academy in 1878 and received a commission as an infantry lieutenant. Capello attended the General Staff College, 1884-1886, and in 1898, as a colonel, commanded a regiment. His relatively humble origins and his open criticism of army promotion policies based on seniority did not seem to slow his own career. Neither did his membership in the Masonic order nor his political contacts with Socialists like Leonida Bissolati (*q.v.*). Promoted major general in 1910, he led a brigade into combat against the Turks in Libya the year following. By 1914, he commanded an infantry division. Even before Italy entered the war, Capello had marked himself off from the average Italian general by his concern for his men's morale and his calls for better relations between the officer corps and the rank and file.

Capello led his division to the Carso in June 1915 as part of the Third Army. In September, having been promoted lieutenant general, he took over the VI Corps facing Gorizia. By then Capello's habit of going his own way was again on display to the displeasure of General Luigi Cadorna (*q.v.*), the commander of the Italian army. Capello put out the welcome mat for visiting politicians and journalists at his headquarters, this at a time when Cadorna was trying to wall off the army from contact with civilian authority.

In the late summer of 1916 Capello seemed the brightest star in the Italian army. His corps played a major role in the assault on Gorizia in August, the first great success for Italian arms since the start of the war. Many observers on both sides of the battlefront considered him the most capable of all Italian generals. In addition, his old friend Bissolati had become minister without portfolio in the new government of Paolo Boselli (*q.v.*). Cadorna saw Capello being groomed to take over as commander in chief of the army. He responded by exiling Capello to the quiet Trentino sector in September.

Capello returned to the Isonzo, the main front of the stalemated war in Italy, in the spring of 1917. Despite poor health, he took over command of the Second Army and, in the Eleventh Battle of the Isonzo (August/September), launched a successful night attack on the strategic Bainsizza plateau. His success there so disturbed the Austrian High Command that they called for German reinforcements with which to mount a counteroffensive.

The Austro-German breakthrough at Caporetto broke the ranks of Capello's Second Army. The debate over the parties responsible for Caporetto has always included Capello as well as Cadorna. Capello must shoulder at least some of the blame for the debacle. Word of an impending enemy attack was circulating. Capello considered it best to prepare a counterthrust from Bainsizza into the flank of the Austro-German attackers; thus he ignored Cadorna's call to pull artillery from Bainsizza back to the western bank of the Isonzo. Less explicably, he put his worst troops in the danger zone; these included recently mobilized munitions workers from Turin, the center of national antiwar sentiment.

Capello's failing health forced him to leave his troops shortly before Caporetto. He returned just in time to face the enemy onslaught on October 24 and then suffered a complete physical collapse. The following day, he urged Cadorna to withdraw at once to the strong line of the Tagliamento River, thirty miles to the rear. The senior commander refused, thus permitting the enemy attack to gather momentum and to force him beyond the Tagliamento to the distant Piave line.

Capello recovered his health but received no further command in World War I. The parliamentary committee investigating the Caporetto disaster issued its report only in 1919; it placed responsibility for the defeat on Cadorna and Capello alike.

Capello remained in the army, joining Mussolini in 1922 in full uniform for the march on Rome. In 1923, however, he resigned his membership in the Fascist party when it declared that members of the Masonic order were not welcome. He nonetheless continued to play an important role in army affairs, serving as an emissary in negotiations with Germany in 1924. He soon broke with Mussolini completely as the iron fist of the dictatorship became evident. In 1925 he was arrested and charged with complicity in a plot to murder Mussolini. He was found guilty, sentenced to thirty years of imprisonment, and stricken from the army's rolls. His serious health problems helped to get him released from confinement in 1936, although he remained forbidden from wearing the uniform of a soldier. He died in Rome, June 25, 1941.

Capello, *Caporetto, perché?*; Falls, *The Battle of Caporetto*; Pieri, *L'Italia nella prima guerra mondiale*; Seton-Watson, *Italy from Liberalism to Fascism*; Whittam, *The Politics of the Italian Army, 1861-1918*; *Dizionario biografico degli italiani*, XVIII.

CARDEN, Sir Sackville Hamilton (*Great Britain, Admiral*), was born in Templemore, county Tipperary, on May 3, 1857, the son of an army officer. Carden entered the navy in 1870, and took part in the campaigns in Egypt and the Sudan in 1882-1884 as well as in the Benin expedition in 1897. He was promoted to the grade of captain in 1899 and to rear admiral in 1908. Carden commanded the battleship *London* of the Atlantic Fleet in 1910; thereafter came duty at the Admiralty and in August 1912, the appointment of admiral superintendent of the Malta dockyard, a post usually regarded as precursor to retirement. Admiral John (Jacky) Fisher (*q.v.*) bluntly declared that Carden had been sent to Malta "to shelve him."

Events in the summer of 1914, however, radically altered these plans. The escape of the German cruisers *Goeben* and *Breslau* into Turkish waters was laid to rest at the feet of Admiral Milne (*q.v.*), who, although officially held to have been without blame by a Court of Inquiry, was deprived of further command. Vice Admiral Carden was chosen to command the British battle squadron in the Mediterranean on September 20, 1914; overall naval command in the region was then assumed by the French.

When war broke out between Great Britain and Turkey on November 5, 1914, Carden at once carried out a preliminary bombardment of the outer forts at the Dardanelles with British and French naval units. In January 1915, the first lord of the Admiralty, Winston Churchill (*q.v.*), asked Carden whether the Straits could be forced solely by naval forces. The admiral replied that the Dardanelles could not be "rushed," but agreed that the stone forts could be reduced by extended operations. Despite strenuous objections by Admiral Fisher and with the concurrence of the French and Russian governments, the War Council on January 28 adopted such a bold scheme. Carden took charge of a joint Anglo-French armada on February 19 in order to undertake the first systematic bombardment of the outer forts. The attacks, however, failed to reduce the outer forts, much less the intermediate defenses, and Carden broke down under the strain of failure. Nearly sixty years of age and without recent command of forces at sea, Carden by March 5 pessimistically evaluated his chances of success; eleven days later he relinquished command for reasons of poor health ("imminent danger of nervous breakdown") and returned to England. Admiral De Robeck (*q.v.*) succeeded Carden at the Dardanelles.

Carden was attached from April to June 1915 to the Admiralty on special service and retired in October 1917 in the grade of full admiral. He died in Lymington on May 6, 1930, without having taken any part in the acrimonious postwar debates over the value of the Dardanelles operation. Churchill acidly remarked, "I am not aware of anything that he has done which is in any way remarkable." Arthur Marder found him "utterly lacking in vigour and determination."

James, *Gallipoli*; Marder, *Dreadnought to Scapa Flow*, II; *Dictionary of National Biography 1922-1930*.

CAROL I or CHARLES I (*Rumania, King*), was born in Sigmaringen in southern Germany, April 20, 1839. The future monarch of Rumania was a prince of the southern and Catholic branch of the Hohenzollern family. A cousin to the king of Prussia, he was related as well to Emperor Napoleon III. In 1866, at the age of twenty-seven, Carol was invited to become prince of the Danubian Principalities, Wallachia and Moldavia. With war between Prussia and Austria about to erupt, he was forced to travel down the Danube to his new home in disguise. This inauspicious start notwithstanding, Carol reigned for forty-eight years, one of the most firmly entrenched monarchs in the Balkans. At first a prince under nominal Turkish sovereignty, in 1881 he became king of the fully independent state of Rumania comprising Wallachia, Moldavia, and the newly acquired Dobrudja.

Carol's years on the throne were marked by his acceptance of Rumania's agrarian order with its domination by a few large landowners. His less conciliatory predecessor had been deposed over this very issue. Foreign policy posed more of a problem for Carol. A pro-German monarch in a Francophile country, he nearly fell from power when Prussia and France went to war in 1870. He survived to fight with distinction in the Balkan War of 1877/1878, in which Rumania stood as Russia's ally against Turkey and received its independence. Russian annexation of Bessarabia at the close of the war was widely viewed by Rumanians as a betrayal. It made it possible for Carol, aided by Premier Ion Bratianu the elder, to conclude a treaty of alliance with Germany and Austria in 1883. This secret pact was known only to the king and a small number of political leaders. Nonetheless, it served as the keystone of Rumanian foreign policy through the Balkan Wars of 1912/1913.

Carol's bent toward the Central Powers began to run counter to such public opinion as existed in his country with its majority of poor, illiterate peasants. Austrian support for Bulgarian territorial claims against Rumania antagonized Carol's politically aware subjects in 1913. An even more bitter point of dispute was the mistreatment of the Rumanian population of Transylvania, a part of the Austro-Hungarian Empire under Magyar administration.

With the July crisis of 1914, Carol was placed in an untenable position. For the remaining months of his life, he tried to cope with the rising tide of interventionist fervor on the side of the Entente. On July 28 the old king warned Austria that the Transylvanian issue made it impossible for Rumania to stand beside the Central Powers. Personal appeals from the monarchs of Germany and Austria to join the war led Carol to present such a course of action to a crown council at Sinaia on August 3. The assembled political leaders and elder statesmen rejected the idea out of hand, possibly to Carol's secret relief. With an active policy in favor of the Central Powers ruled out, Carol now had to contend with groups calling for Rumania to join the Entente. Russian military successes over Austria (specifically, the Galician victories of late August and early September) encouraged Rumanian irredentists to call for the invasion of Transylvania. "For rent" signs appeared on the palace walls in Bucharest, as pro-Entente demonstrators directed their hostilities at the king.

Carol's actions in September often smacked of desperation, and he spoke of abdicating. He informed the Central Powers he might have to sanction a "preventitive occupation" of Transylvanian territory and asked Germany to obtain Austrian promises to cooperate. The Austrians refused. Some of the king's actions came close to treason. For example, he asked the Germans to stir up the Bulgarians to threaten— and thus to restrain—the Rumanian population. Moreover, he requested Berlin to send German troops to guard Transylvania and so forestall a Rumanian invasion.

As Carol's influence waned, that of Premier Ion Bratianu (*q.v.*), son of Carol's old ally, increased. Bratianu favored intervention, but only at an opportune time later in the war. During the final crucial weeks of September, the pro-Entente premier and the pro-German monarch threw their combined weight against intervention. Carol was in the last weeks of his life, and he died on October 10. Torrey speculates that if he had left the scene a few weeks earlier, irredentist circles might have been strong enough to overcome Bratianu and bring Rumania into the war. Conversely, with Carol out of the way, replaced by the more pliable Ferdinand I (*q.v.*), Bratianu could dominate events, bringing Rumania into the conflict at a time of his choosing. The crown could be expected to go passively along.

Albertini, *The Origins of the War of 1914*, 3 vols.; Lindenberg, *König Karl von Rumänien*, 2 vols.; Torrey, "Irredentism and Diplomacy" and "Rumania and the Belligerents: 1914-1916."

CARSON, Edward Henry (*Great Britain, First Lord of the Admiralty*), Baron Carson, of Duncairn, was born in Dublin to an old Protestant family on February 9, 1854, the son of a civil engineer. Carson studied law at Trinity College, Dublin, where Oscar Wilde was also a student, and in 1892, was appointed solicitor-general of Ireland; at the same time he was elected to the House of Commons for Dublin University, a post that he held for the next twenty-six years. In 1900 he was appointed solicitor-general for England and was knighted. In 1905 he became a member of the Privy Council and five years later was elected leader of the Irish unionists in Westminster. During the Parliamentary Bill debates of 1910/1911, Carson defended the veto power of the House of Lords, fearing that abolition of the veto would assure the implementation of home rule.

Elected head of the Ulster Unionist Council, Carson in Craigavon on September 23, 1911, vowed to defeat a proposal for a Dublin parliament, "the most nefarious conspiracy that has ever been hatched against a free people." He had by now earned the sobriquet uncrowned King of Ulster, and he employed his keen mind and powerful oratory to obfuscate home rule, wringing from the Conservative Andrew Bonar Law (*q.v.*) a pledge that the Tories would work to keep Ulster in the Union. On September 28, henceforth known as Ulster Day, Carson drew up a sacred covenant to exclude the Protestant counties from home rule. He denounced Prime Minister H. H. Asquith's (*q.v.*) offer of a county option for Northern Ireland as a "sentence of death." When Winston Churchill (*q.v.*) on March 14, 1914, dispatched warships to the Lamlash in the Isle of Arran, a move that provoked the Curragh incident nine days later in which army officers refused to coerce Ulster to accept home rule, Britain appeared in the throes of civil strife and only the outbreak of war in Europe apparently saved it from internecine warfare.

On September 31 Carson, the "Ulster pirate," enrolled his North Irish volunteers into the now-famous Thirty-sixth (Ulster) Division. From May to October 1915, Carson served as attorney-general in the first coalition government, but he grew restless about the delay in applying conscription, disapproved of the retreat from the Dardanelles, and denounced the British abandonment of Serbia. In the wake of the Easter Rebellion in Dublin in 1916, Carson drifted further from Asquith, and the barrister's resignation in October led two months later to the fall of the government. The new prime minister, David Lloyd George (*q.v.*), in December appointed Carson first lord of the Admiralty. Carson quickly endeared himself to the service by monthly visits to the Grand Fleet as well as by occasional inspections of naval bases. He readily admitted that he had come to the Admiralty in a state of ignorance, but assured the sea lords that he had no intention of becoming an amateur naval strategist. However, in all fairness it must be stated that although his was to be the second shortest administration at the Admiralty, Carson brought a great deal of energy to the post. He at once recalled five of eight British battleships stationed in the Mediterranean, and in his maiden speech in the Commons admitted the gravity of the German U-boat menace: "It is grave. It is serious. It has not yet been solved." While he personally favored convoy, he would not institute it against the wishes of the sea lords.

Lloyd George in the summer of 1917 decided upon a clearing of what he considered to be a stodgy and unimaginative Admiralty. In this he did not hesitate to call upon his foremost opponent, Sir Douglas Haig, the British field commander in France, who regarded Admiral John Jellicoe (*qq.v.*) as "being an old woman" and who argued that Carson was too tired for the job; on July 17, Carson was shunted off to the War Cabinet in order to make room for Sir Eric Geddes (*q.v.*) as first lord of the Admiralty.

"King" Carson was returned to the Commons in the general election of December 1918 from the newly created Duncairn division of Belfast. When the Government of Ireland Bill became law on December 23, 1920, Carson decided to step down in favor of a younger man; he resigned as leader of the Ulster unionists in February 1921. He gave up his seat in the Commons three months later and received the title Baron Carson, of Duncairn. Carson died at Cleve Court, Minster, Kent, on October 22, 1935. He received a state funeral in Belfast and was buried in St. Anne's Cathedral.

Carson, *War on German Submarines*; Colvin, *Life of Lord Carson*, III; Marder, *Dreadnought to Scapa Flow*, IV; *Dictionary of National Biography 1931-1940*.

CASTELNAU, Noel Joseph Édouard de Curières de (*France, General*), was born in Saint-Affrique,

France on December 24, 1851. He was a member of a French aristocratic family distinguished by its production of a long line of military leaders. One general de Castelnau had fought under Napoleon I; another had accompanied Napoleon III into exile in 1870 after Sedan. The family was staunchly Roman Catholic, and Castelnau's openly proclaimed religious convictions influenced his military career at several significant points.

Castelnau graduated from St. Cyr in 1870 and fought during the Franco-Prussian War. After attending the War College, he divided his service between staff and line positions, acquiring a reputation as an expert staff officer. In 1900 he was one of three officers purged from the General Staff for anti-Dreyfusard opinions. By then a colonel, he took command of an infantry regiment at Nancy.

Castelnau rose to a position of international significance in 1911 when he was chosen by General Joffre (q.v.), the army's new chief of staff, to serve as first deputy chief of staff. Joffre, a stranger to the technical side of staff work, picked Castelnau as the army's acknowledged expert in the area. The parliamentary Left objected vigorously but unsuccessfully to the appointment of a general with such an aristocratic and clerical background.

As Joffre's chief assistant, Castelnau played a major role in France's preparation for the First World War. He participated in staff talks with the British from 1911 onward, during which he was accepted as Joffre's principal adviser on strategy, and he significantly influenced the drafting of France's war plan. Castelnau rejected any suggestion that France would benefit from a strategy of parrying and counterattacking a German offensive. Instead, he helped convince Joffre to take the offensive immediately into Lorraine. The possibility of a German offensive via Belgium north of the Meuse he found unlikely. If the Germans should undertake such a move, Castelnau's estimates of their manpower indicated that they would thereby weaken the German defensive line in Lorraine, facilitating the French advance. Like most French planning for the initial stages of the war, such thinking by Castelnau erroneously predicted that the Germans, like the French, would not employ large reserve formations in combat. Thus, Germany's capability to launch an offensive would depend upon the strength of its standing army. To bolster the French standing army, Castelnau influenced Joffre to make a successful appeal in 1913 for a three-year term of service.

At the start of the war, Castelnau commanded the Second Army, with headquarters at Nancy. In accordance with the war plan he had advocated, he advanced on August 14 northeastward from the Grand Couronné, the hills east of Nancy, into German Lorraine. His immediate goal was the fortress of Morhange. An able tactician, Castelnau advanced carefully. On August 20 the Germans stopped their deliberately planned retreat, administered a bloody defeat to the attacking Second Army, and then began a counterattack. The German action was carried out prematurely, and Castelnau had a capable subordinate in the aggressive and optimistic General Foch (q.v.), in command of the Twentieth Corps. Nonetheless, the Second Army was forced into a general retreat to the Grand Couronné, and Castelnau became the first French senior commander to experience the strength of the defensive in the First World War.

Castelnau's forces held tenaciously to Nancy and the line of the Moselle, as the Germans improvised a major attack on the French position in Lorraine. During the battle, Castelnau received word of the death of a son at Morhange; he lost two more sons later in the war. Dispirited by personal tragedy and the fierce German attacks, he considered a withdrawal from Nancy several times. His subordinate, Foch, persuaded him instead to counterattack an exposed German flank on August 23, and his superior, General Joffre, personally ordered the Second Army to hold in a meeting with Castelnau on September 6. Along with Sarrail at Verdun and Dubail (qq.v.) in Alsace, Castelnau secured the eastern portion of France's defensive position and helped make the victory at the Marne possible.

During the remainder of 1914 and throughout 1915, Castelnau remained an advocate of large-scale offensives. In the aftermath of the battle of the Marne, he led five corps into the area northeast of Paris to outflank the new German defenses on the Aisne. These efforts and the German response led to the "race to the sea" and the extension of a solid defensive line from Switzerland to the North Sea. Castelnau was appointed commander of France's Center Group of Armies in June 1915. He conducted major offensive operations in Artois in the spring and Champagne in the fall. On both occasions, he clashed with his subordinate General Pétain (q.v.), who argued the futility of prolonged infantry assaults without the systematic use of overpowering artillery preparations.

At the close of 1915 Castelnau returned to general headquarters to become Joffre's chief of staff. After a full year of unsuccessful offensive campaigns, Joffre's reputation among political leaders was waning, although his public popularity made it impossible to dismiss him. General Gallieni (q.v.), the new war minister, placed Castelnau beside Joffre to aid the commander in chief but also to restrain him. Castelnau left immediately to assert Joffre's authority as commander in chief of all French armies over the maverick General Sarrail in Salonika.

In January 1916, Castelnau personally inspected the fortifications at Verdun. Alarmed at the weakened condition of the historic fortress, he ordered the construction of a new defensive line on the east bank of the Meuse. When the Germans began their major attack on Verdun in late February, Castelnau returned with plenipotentiary authority. It was he according to Horne who made the crucial decision to hold Verdun and to place Pétain in charge of the overall defense.

When Joffre fell from power in December 1916, Castelnau was considered to replace him. His ostentatious Catholicism and his long association with the discredited Joffre combined to disqualify him in favor of Nivelle (*q.v.*). He traveled to Russia at the start of 1917, and, following Nivelle's fall, took over the Eastern Group of Armies under Pétain's command. He held this post until the close of the war, when he found himself planning a climactic offensive into Lorraine, the same area in which he had begun the war.

Castelnau entered politics in the postwar period, serving in the Chamber of Deputies from 1919 to 1924. He lived to the age of ninety-seven, one of the few senior French commanders of the war who left no written memoirs. His avowed clericalism prevented him from being named marshal of France, an honor conferred on most of his peers. He died in Montastruc-la-Conseillière on March 18, 1944.

Horne, *Price of Glory: Verdun*; Isselin, *The Battle of the Marne*; King, *Generals and Politicians*; Ralston, *The Army of the Republic*; Tuchman, *The Guns of August*; Samuel Williamson, *The Politics of Grand Strategy*.

CAVID BEY, Mehmed (*Turkey, Minister of Finance*), was born in Salonika in 1875, into a Jewish merchant family that had converted to Islam. He was educated in his native city and then in Constantinople; in 1896 he graduated from the university with a degree in economics. Cavid served in the state Agricultural Bank, then in the ministry of education until his return to Salonika in 1902. There he taught economics and ran a private school. Drawn to revolutionary politics, he entered the conspiratorial circle of young officers and officials known as the Young Turks (the Committee of Union and Progress). Immediately following the Revolution of 1908, Cavid was elected to the Chamber of Deputies. He held the post of minister of finance, 1909-1911,

the first Young Turk to serve in the cabinet. At the outbreak of World War I, Cavid was back at this important station, now in a government commanded by the Young Turks.

Cavid's European travels in the cause of borrowing for the perpetually empty Ottoman treasury had equipped him for a major wartime role. He possessed extensive negotiating experience and a wide circle of diplomatic contacts. Cavid opposed aligning Turkey with the Central Powers. Reputed to be a Francophile, he was not privy to the negotiations that led to the alliance of August 2, 1914, with the Central Powers. He resigned—at least nominally—in early November when Turkey took up arms. But Cavid retained effective control of his country's finances; at the same time, he served as a busy high level negotiator and spoke with a respected voice in the formulation of Turkish policy.

Cavid's views often did not prevail. He failed to diminish Turkey's political and military participation in the war. Evidence exists to suggest that he sought a separate peace in late 1915, when the Entente closed down its operations at Gallipoli. He returned formally as minister of finance in February 1917; and he registered forceful objections to the decision to rupture relations with the United States. The young finance minister applied his negotiating skills more successfully to Constantinople's allies. German economic demands met Cavid's immovable opposition. He fended off Berlin's calls for commercial concessions, refused to liquidate Anglo-French holdings, and dodged making contributions for the Baghdad Railroad. Meanwhile, Cavid squeezed generous loans from the Central Powers to ease Turkey over one financial crisis after another. In early 1918 General Ludendorff (*q.v.*) intervened personally to press demands for postwar economic privileges. Cavid buried these ideas by asking in return that Germany's wartime loans to Turkey be forgiven. In general, Cavid's defense of Turkish interests drew the approval of his Young Turk colleagues. Historians like Trumpener have been led by these trends to revise earlier views of a weak Turkish government subservient to Germany's wartime direction.

Cavid was the only Young Turk leader to serve in the government after the collapse of the Young Turk cabinet on October 8, 1918. He remained in office until early November, when he was forced to go into hiding, then into exile. He returned to Turkey in 1922. Four years later, he was arrested and tried on charges of subverting the regime of Mustafa Kemal (*q.v.*). Along with several other figures from the Young Turk movement, Cavid was convicted and, on August 26, 1926, executed in Ankara.

Ahmad, *The Young Turks*; Shaw and Shaw, *History of the Ottoman Empire and Modern Turkey*, II; Trumpener, *Germany and the Ottoman Empire*; Weber, *Eagles on the Crescent*; *Encyclopedia of Islam, New Edition*, II.

CEMAL PAŞA, Ahmed (*Turkey, General, Navy Minister, Military Governor of Syria*), was born in Constantinople in 1872. He graduated from the War College in 1895 and received an assignment to Salonika. There, the Turkish Third Army provided a breeding ground for conspiracies among politically malcontented young officers. Cemal joined the Young Turk movement (the Committe of Union and Progress) in 1906. His posting as inspector of the Macedonian railroad system gave him a rich opportunity to promote the revolutionary cause. With his characteristic energy and efficiency, he rose quickly to a position of leadership. Following the Young Turk Revolution of 1908, Cemal entered the movement's executive committee. In 1909, then a colonel, he helped suppress a dangerous counterrevolution in Constantinople. He served as military governor in the capital and in several provincial cities, 1909-1911. The Balkan Wars of 1912/1913 brought Cemal a succession of prestigious military commands, but his political work overshadowed his career as a soldier. Elegantly mannered and charming in person, Cemal wielded a political style marked by ruthlessness and brutality. In the early months of 1913, as the Young Turks established their dictatorship, Cemal applied his talents to smashing political opposition in Constantinople.

A lieutenant general at forty, Cemal entered the cabinet in 1913. The following year he took over the post of navy minister. With British officers as advisers and with powerful warships on order from British yards, he hoped to create an effective navy. This was only one of his areas of interest. The view that the regime was controlled after 1913 by a dictatorial triumvirate of Cemal, Enver, and Talât Paşas (*qq.v.*) has been challenged by recent scholarship. But even if a wider group of Young Turk leaders held ultimate power, these three had singular influence throughout the government.

In July 1914, Cemal took on the new role of diplomat. He approached Britain and France to explore the possibility of an alliance. They refused; and the navy minister leaned toward establishing good relations with the Central Powers once World War I had broken out. But Cemal centered his attention on Turkey's needs. He was a reluctant convert to Enver's drive to enter the war. An important swing figure, Cemal had to be won over around October 10, before the Turkish government could permit German naval units to operate in the Black Sea and thereby precipitate Turkey's entry into the war.

Cemal played a variety of important roles after Turkey became a belligerent. He continued as navy minister. He commanded the Fourth Army in Syria. Most important of all, he governed the vast province of Syria, which included Palestine and the eastern shore of the Red Sea. Residing in Damascus removed him from control over the navy. On the other hand, his powerful military and administrative position in Syria made him a virtually independent potentate. After an inept assault on the Suez Canal in early 1915 had failed completely, Cemal returned to Damascus to take up other concerns. He may have negotiated with Great Britain. Weber has suggested that Cemal toyed with leaving the war and making himself ruler of an independent Syria, a plan that foundered on French opposition. In any event, suspicion of Cemal's independent intentions began to cloud his relations with Enver and Talât back in Constantinople.

Cemal moved with his characteristic ruthlessness to stifle possible Arab insurgencies. One group of Arab dignitaries went to the Damascus gallows on his orders in August 1915; a second group followed in May 1916. Cemal's heavy hand kept Syria itself tranquil. But in June 1916, the Arabs of the Hejaz rose nonetheless, and Turkish garrisons in Mecca and Medina came under siege. As British forces under General Murray and then General Allenby (*qq.v.*) advanced from Egypt into Palestine in 1917, Arab insurgents rode alongside to protect the offensive's eastern flank. As the hungry and poorly led Turkish forces in Syria and Palestine crumbled, internecine conflicts between Cemal and the front commander, General von Falkenhayn (*q.v.*), added to the problems of an effective defense. With the loss of Jerusalem to Allenby in December 1917, the Turkish leader left permanently for Constantinople.

Cemal fell from office with the collapse of the Young Turk government in early October 1918. Along with Enver and Talât, he fled his country aboard a German ship the next month. In the postwar period, Cemal, like other Young Turk leaders, remained on the stage of Near East politics. He served as an intermediary between the governments of Soviet Russia and the new Turkish republic. He also found employment as inspector general of the Afghan army. During the war, Cemal had professed to be sympathetic to the plight of Turkey's persecuted Armenians. Such claims failed to alter his fate. Vengeful Armenians hunted down Turkey's wartime leaders with no regard to such self-exculpation. An Armenian gunman ended Cemal's life in Tbilisi, July 21, 1922.

Ahmad, *Young Turks*; Djemal Pasha, *Memories of a Turkish Statesman, 1913-1919*; Shaw and Shaw, *History of the Ottoman Empire and Modern Turkey*, II; Trumpener, *Germany and the Ottoman Empire*; Weber, *Eagles on the Crescent*; *Encyclopedia of Islam, New Edition*, II.

CHARLES I (*Austria-Hungary, Emperor-King*), was born Charles Francis Joseph to Archduke Otto on August 17, 1887, in Persenbeug, Lower Austria. Educated at the Scottish High School in Vienna, Charles also attended lectures at Prague University. On October 21, 1911, he married Princess Zita of Bourbon-Parma. Charles served as cavalry officer until 1914, when the assassination of his uncle Francis Ferdinand (*q.v.*) cast him into the role of successor to the throne.

In August 1914, Charles, in the rank of colonel, was assigned to the Austro-Hungarian army in Galicia where he carried out the emperor's personal business. In the summer of 1915 he was promoted to major general and recalled to Schönbrunn to perform routine court functions. When General Conrad von Hötzendorf (*q.v.*) opted for an offensive against the Italians in South Tyrol in May 1916, Charles was given command of the XX (Edelweiss) Corps. These were among the happiest days of Charles' life, but after the Austrian defeat at Luck he was hastily dispatched to East Galicia. As commander of a new army corps, Charles was given the Prussian General Hans von Seeckt (*q.v.*) as chief of staff.

On November 21, 1916, Charles succeeded Francis Joseph (*q.v.*) as emperor of Austria, and on December 30 as king of Hungary. Charles' refusal to swear to the Austrian constitution brought about the resignation of Minister-President Ernst von Körber and his replacement with Heinrich von Clam-Martinic (*qq.v.*); after Foreign Minister Burian von Rajecz's (*q.v.*) appeal for peace on December 12, 1916, went unanswered, Charles replaced him with Count Ottokar Czernin (*q.v.*). Next Charles forced Conrad von Hötzendorf to relinquish his post as chief of staff, appointing in his place the more pliable General Arz von Straussenburg (*q.v.*). Finally, Charles moved army headquarters from Teschen to Baden, near Vienna. Francis Joseph's grand-nephew generally was a young man of humanitarian inclinations, but according to Rothenberg, "volatile, lacking in balance and experience, and strangely unable to make and stick with decisions." Most of the advisers that he sought had once belonged to the Belvedere Circle of Francis Ferdinand. And while civilian leaders were favorably inclined towards him, Austria-Hungary's military paladins were apprehensive about Charles' yearning to command the armed forces personally, to seek peace at almost any price, and to permit his wife such a powerful voice in the affairs of state.

A series of misplaced humanitarian gestures in 1917 undermined the army's morale and discipline. Charles abolished dueling in the army, ended all physical punishments for civilian and soldier alike, halted air bombings, ended the use of gas without imperial sanction, and even granted an amnesty for political crimes, thereby setting free men who had as their avowed goal the destruction of the Habsburg empire. In the realm of foreign affairs, Charles realized his almost total dependence on the Germans, but greatly resented them for it. He immediately revoked the unified command structure agreed to in September 1916, protested against the German decision to resume unrestricted submarine warfare early in 1917, and even attempted to negotiate an end to the war behind the ally's back. On March 24, 1917, Charles met with Empress Zita's brothers, Sixtus and Xavier, both officers in the Belgian army, at Laxenburg in order to plot his strategy. Little did he know that the French were cynically using the two young men simply to drive a wedge between Vienna and Berlin, and when Georges Clemenceau (*q.v.*), in April 1918, published parts of the correspondence between Charles and Sixtus, the Habsburg ruler was accused of duplicity and treachery; the result of his clumsy scheming was a greater reliance on Berlin. This became apparent in the minor role accorded the Austrians in negotiations leading to the Treaty of Brest-Litovsk on March 4, 1918, and in the forced Austro-Hungarian participation in the occupation and policing of the Ukraine.

On October 16, 1918, after two appeals for peace went unanswered, Charles issued a manifesto reorganizing Austria into a federal state with self-government for its nationalities, while at the same time assuaging the Magyars with a promise not to "disturb the integrity of the lands of the Crown of St. Stephen." This ambiguous document, which personified the emperor's pronounced inconsistencies, amounted to a death warrant of the empire, signed by its highest official. On October 31 Charles issued an order permitting his officers to accept service in the national armies then being formed, and on November 4, an armistice was formally signed. Command of the remaining forces passed to Baron Kövess von Kövessháza (*q.v.*), and on November 11, Charles stepped down as Austria's political head of government. Not even in defeat was Charles able to make a clear break with either the army or the government, and his numerous contradictory decrees in October and November 1918 brought only more confusion and rancor for the Habsburg civil service and military. In the end, Charles refused to abdicate formally and managed only with British protection to flee to Switzerland on March 24, 1919; in his Feldkirch declaration, Charles renounced his decision of November 11, 1918, as invalid.

Unlike Emperor Wilhelm II (*q.v.*), who lived in exile with the dignity he had sorely lacked as emperor-king, Charles refused to accept the historical verdict of November 1918. On Easter 1921, he attempted to return to Hungary, but passive resistance by Admiral Miklós Horthy (*q.v.*) foiled this plot. Undaunted, Charles and Zita returned by airplane on October 20, 1921, to claim the Crown of St. Stephen; this time Horthy opposed the planned coup with force. After a brief incarceration at Cloister Tihany on Lake Balaton, the imperial couple was transported aboard a British warship to Madeira. Charles died at Quinta do Monte on Portuguese Madeira on April 1, 1922, from a lung infection.

Lorenz, *Kaiser Karl und der Untergang der Donaumonarchie*; Rothenberg, *Army of Francis Joseph*; Sheperd, *The Last Habsburg*; *Neue Deutsche Biographie*, XI; *Österreichisches Biographisches Lexikon 1815-1950*, III.

CHURCHILL, Winston Leonard Spencer (*Great Britain, First Lord of the Admiralty, Minister of Munitions*), was born at Blenheim Palace on November 30, 1874, to Lord Randolph Churchill, a descendant of the duke of Marlborough. Educated at Harrow, he failed to impress his father, who decided that his son, lacking the ability for the Bar, would turn to the army. Winston failed the entrance examinations to Royal Military College, Sandhurst, several times and was able to enter only after a "crammer" in London in 1893. Two years later he was gazetted to the Fourth (Queen's Own) Hussars, and on his holidays went to Cuba as a war correspondent. Thereafter came the obligatory tour of duty in India, highlighted by the Malakand expedition, and the famous cavalry charge at Omdurman under Sir H. H. Kitchener (*q.v.*). In 1899 he went to South Africa to report on the war for the *Morning Post*, and as a member of the South African Light Horse he accompanied Ian Hamilton (*q.v.*) on his march to Pretoria as well; he was captured by Louis Botha, but managed to escape. Back in England, Churchill was elected Tory member for Oldham in the election of 1900, but four years later crossed the aisle in the House of Commons to protest Joseph Chamberlain's tariff policy. In 1906 he was elected Liberal member for Manchester and joined the government as under secretary for colonies; the next year he became a privy councillor and in 1908 was appointed president of the

Board of Trade by Prime Minister Herbert Asquith (*q.v.*). Churchill concentrated on social issues, such as unemployment insurance, hours of work, health, and pensions; he introduced the eight-hour work day in the coal mines and set up a system of labor exchanges. As home secretary in 1910/1911 he paid much attention to prison reform and quelled a general strike.

On October 25, 1911, during the height of the Anglo-German naval race, Churchill came to the Admiralty as first lord: "I accepted with alacrity." He brought Sir John Fisher (*q.v.*) out of retirement as first sea lord, created an Admiralty War Staff as well as a Royal Navy Staff College (Portsmouth), and laid down the four oil-fired *Queen Elizabeth* battleships in 1912. Churchill oversaw all facets of naval affairs with gusto. That same year, 1912, he reorganized the fleet by transferring the Mediterranean Fleet to Gibraltar and by creating a Home Fleet to deal with the mounting menace across the North Sea. In February 1912, at a time when Lord Haldane was in Berlin attempting to slow down the naval race, Churchill in Glasgow announced that the German fleet was "more in the nature of a luxury." On March 26, 1913, he proposed a "naval holiday," a notion not welcomed by the Germans who were far behind Britain in naval strength. With regard to strategy, Churchill basically favored the "seek out, hunt down, and destroy" school, and only reluctantly abandoned the notion of a close blockade in time of war in favor of a distant blockade at Scotland and the English Channel. At 11 P.M. on August 4, 1914, the signal "Commence hostilities against Germany" was flashed by the Admiralty to all ships; the following day in the Commons tears streamed down the first lord's face as Prime Minister Asquith announced that Britain was at war with Germany.

The first three months were rocky ones at the Admiralty. In August, in what Churchill termed a "fine feat of arms," British units destroyed three German light cruisers off Helgoland, and the British Expeditionary Force was ferried across the Channel without loss. Then the horizon darkened. In August the German cruisers *Goeben* and *Breslau* eluded the British in the Mediterranean and steamed to Constantinople, aided in part by Admiralty muddling and misdirection. On October 5 Churchill volunteered to take command of British troops to be sent to defend Antwerp, a notion that produced "roars of incredulous laughter" in the Cabinet; however, Lord Kitchener concurred, offering to raise the first lord to general rank. On October 10 Antwerp fell and Churchill was severely criticized for pitting raw marines against seasoned German troops. Matters then got worse.

The loss of the three elderly cruisers *Aboukir*, *Cressy*, and *Hogue* to a single German U-boat was laid at the feet of the first lord. And his speech in Liverpool, in which Churchill announced that the Royal Navy would dig the Germans out "like rats from a hole," was not calculated to enhance his statesmanship. Finally, the loss of Sir Christopher Cradock (*q.v.*) with the *Good Hope* and *Monmouth* at Coronel on November 11 constituted the nadir of Admiralty prestige.

December brought a welcome change. The new first sea lord, "Jacky" Fisher, "launched himself into this business with explosive energy," and on December 8 avenged Cradock at the Falkland Islands where Admiral Sir Frederick Sturdee defeated Count Maximilian von Spee (*qq.v.*) and destroyed the *Gneisenau*, *Scharnhorst*, *Leipzig*, and *Nürnberg*. With this action the Germans had been swept from all but the narrow seas. On January 23, 1915, the Grand Fleet caught German raiders at the Dogger Bank and destroyed the armored cruiser *Blücher*. In fact, Churchill was anxious that the fleet "do something," and he at first brought up his pet scheme of forcing the entry into the Baltic Sea and landing troops in Pomerania or Denmark; at other times he argued that the fleet should sail down the Elbe River, bomb the Kiel Canal, or seize the Dutch island Ameland and use it as an advanced base in the North Sea. On the other hand, as early as August 31, 1914, the first lord had his eye on the Dardanelles—despite Lord Nelson's dictum that "any sailor who attacked a fort was a fool." When Grand Duke Nikolai (*q.v.*) of Russia on January 2, 1915, asked for a British "demonstration" at the Straits in order to relieve the pressure on his Army of the Caucasus, Churchill seized the chance. In February and March the Anglo-French navies bombed the forts and on April 25 troops were landed at Cape Helles and Anzac Cove. By May 8 it became apparent that the soldiers would not be able to advance from their beachheads, and Churchill became the public scapegoat for what loomed as a disaster of the first magnitude.

Certainly, the first lord had miscalculated. He overestimated naval fire power, overrode his professional advisers when they differed with him, and refused to wait until sufficient troops had been assembled for the undertaking. But the plan was brilliant and even his political enemy, Clement Atlee, conceded in 1957, "Sir Winston had the one strategic idea in the war." Interallied wrangling and intraservice jealousies had worked against success at Gallipoli almost from the start, and the failure to take the peninsula in May 1915 brought about the fall of the Asquith government and the forced retirements of Churchill and Fisher, who fell out over the causes of the debacle. The press was delighted by his fall as were Admirals John Jellicoe and David Beatty (*qq.v.*), both glad to be "rid of the succubus Churchill."

Churchill accepted what he termed the "well-paid inactivity" as chancellor of the Duchy of Lancaster, but early in 1916, as lieutenant colonel he was appointed commander of the Sixth Royal Fusiliers in France. It might be pointed out that as first lord he had already supported the concept of the tank, but the military proved lukewarm to the idea, one general denouncing it as "Winston's folly." Prime Minister David Lloyd George (*q.v.*) recalled Churchill, to the great dismay of the Tories, as minister of munitions in July 1917. He enthusiastically endorsed the Zeebrugge raid in April 1918, claiming that it returned to the Royal Navy "the *panache* that was lost at Jutland."

After the war, Churchill served as secretary of state for war and for air (1918-1922) and for the colonies (1921-1922). He then wrote his four-volume *The World Crisis*, which Arthur James Balfour (*q.v.*) called "Winston's brilliant autobiography, disguised as a history of the universe." From 1924 to 1929, he was chancellor of the Exchequer under Prime Minister Stanley Baldwin. During the 1930s he cried out in vain against Germany's military resurgence and returned to politics in September 1939, for a second time as first lord of the Admiralty. On May 10, 1940, the day the Germans invaded the Netherlands, Belgium, and France, Churchill replaced Neville Chamberlain as prime minister with the sober synopsis: "I have nothing to offer but blood, toil, tears, and sweat."

His brilliant career as Britain's wartime leader lies beyond the scope of this work; suffice it to note that a less than grateful nation voted him out of office in July 1945. After six years as leader of the opposition, Churchill returned in October 1951 as prime minister for eighteen months. He was knighted in April 1953 and died on January 24, 1965, being accorded a lavish state funeral that he personally had designed and planned.

Churchill, *World Crisis*, II, III; Gretton, *Former Naval Person*; Marder, *Dreadnought to Scapa Flow*, I, II; *Current Biography 1953*.

CLAM-MARTINIC, Heinrich Jaroslav Count von (*Austria-Hungary, Minister-President*), was born in Vienna on January 1, 1863, the son of a Czechoslovakian nobleman. Clam-Martinic was active in the Bohemian Lower House as well as in the Upper House as a speaker for the Conservatives. In 1892/1893 he accompanied Archduke Francis Ferdinand (*q.v.*) on his tour around the world and became the heir apparent's close friend.

Clam-Martinic served as a company commander on the Russian and Italian fronts from August 1914 to 1916, in the process moving ever closer to the House of Habsburg, and as a result more distant from Czechoslovakian nationalists. In October 1916, he became minister of agriculture under Minister-President Ernst von Körber (*q.v.*). The new Emperor Charles (*q.v.*) in December 1916 appointed Clam-Martinic minister-president, and the Czech attempted to create a truly multinational cabinet. This endeavor failed owing especially to the opposition of the Czechs and Poles, and in the process Clam-Martinic alienated the Austrian Germans; his appeal of May 1917, "Let us above all be Austrians!" fell upon deaf ears, and Clam-Martinic resigned his post on June 19, 1917, to become military governor of Montenegro for the duration of the war. Clam-Martinic died in Clam, near Grein, on March 7, 1932.

Höglinger, *Minister Präsident Graf Clam-Martinic*; *Neue Deutsche Biographie*, III; *Österreichisches Biographisches Lexikon 1815-1950*, I.

CLEMENCEAU, Georges (*France, Premier*), was born in the small village of Mouilleron-en-Pareds in the Vendée region of western France, September 28, 1841. Like his father, he studied medicine, first at Nantes, then, 1861-1865, in Paris. In the capital, he was drawn into journalism and politics. After spending four years in the United States, Clemenceau returned to his birthplace to practice medicine briefly, then went off to Paris for a life in politics.

In 1876 Clemenceau was elected to the Chamber of Deputies. There he quickly became a powerful figure in the Radical party, a maker and breaker of premiers and cabinets. He was defeated for reelection in 1893, after being implicated in a financial scandal involving an early effort to construct a Panama canal. By 1902, however, he had returned to the National Assembly, this time to serve in the Senate until 1920. Clemenceau took his first cabinet post, minister of the interior, in 1906; the Radical leader soon alienated large sections of the French Left by his tough response to striking workers. That same year, Clemenceau formed his own cabinet, which endured until 1909. His years in office were notable for the strengthening of the informal alliance with Great Britain (established in 1904). Clemenceau fell from power in 1909, brought down by Théophile Delcassé's (*q.v.*) criticism of the state of the French navy. Nearly seventy years old, he seemed destined to become merely an influential elder statesman. In

the period before World War I, he took up the cause of military preparedness, establishing a newspaper entitled *L'Homme libre* to publish his views on the need for French military strength.

In August 1914, Clemenceau heard the offer of the ministry of justice in René Viviani's (*q.v.*) expanded wartime cabinet. He declined, and, with undisguised ambition, named the posts he would accept, including the premiership and the ministry of war. For the next three years, Clemenceau played the role of critic of the war effort and the spineless premiers who were mismanaging it. A stringent censorship restrained his public statements, but his role in the Senate provided both sources of information and a forum. From early 1915 on, he sat on both the Foreign Affairs Committee and the Army Committee of the Senate. In both he criticized specific government failings, like the "botched" army medical service and the shortages of munitions; less precisely, he spoke of the failure of French strategy. Clemenceau chided General Joffre (*q.v.*) for his fruitless offensives on the western front and War Minister Millerand (*q.v.*) for trying to shield the French generalissimo from the scrutiny of the National Assembly. But Clemenceau had little in the way of specific alternatives to offer.

As the war took the form of a bloody stalemate, Clemenceau's voice grew more influential. Joffre's failings, such as the inadequate preparations at Verdun before the German assault in February 1916, made him an obvious target. But, by June/July 1916, when the National Assembly held a secret session on the conduct of the war, Clemenceau was assaulting government ministers with equal ferocity. He now, for the first time, accused Minister of the Interior Malvy (*q.v.*) of hurting the war effort by permitting the circulation of antipatriotic propaganda.

As the war pushed on into 1917, Clemenceau came closer to the premiership. Against the alarming background of the Russian Revolution, the disastrous April offensive led by General Nivelle (*q.v.*), and an upsurge in labor unrest in France, Clemenceau took aim at Malvy. In a speech of July 22, which Geoffrey Bruun has compared to "a bugle call reforming the ranks on a stricken field," the old Radical criticized defeatism and those who permitted it. He went on to call for an all-out effort to win the war. In the fall, he spoke out against the very idea of a negotiated peace. And in November, after Socialists had abandoned the coalition cabinet and as France began to brace for the German offensive that was reckoned inevitable in 1918, President Poincaré (*q.v.*) called on Clemenceau to form a government.

The Clemenceau cabinet carried the country over the last twelve months of the war to victory. In his ministerial declaration on taking office, Clemenceau said his policy was simple: "I wage war." In contrast to earlier wartime premiers, Clemenceau struck a pose of decisiveness. Alleged defeatists like Malvy and former Premier Joseph Caillaux (q.v.) were put on trial for treason. Pacifist propaganda was repressed. The new premier installed a cabinet of competent technicians, rather than the political prima donnas of the recent past; and he kept the central position of minister of war for himself. In the most recent major study of Clemenceau, David Watson has asserted that Clemenceau succeeded when others had failed because, despite appearances, he had the nation behind him. Socialist opposition to the war was loud but not really powerful. Industrial strikes never reached the point at which they could not be settled with high wage payments, freeing the workers to express their basic patriotism.

In military affairs, Clemenceau reversed the earlier pattern of generals dominating politicians. With his personal military adviser, General Jean Mordacq, at his side, he could deal intelligently with Pétain, the French commander in chief, and Foch (qq.v.), chief of the General Staff and (after April 1918) Allied generalissimo.

As the climactic German spring offensive began in late March, Clemenceau watched with approval as the British finally came to accept the idea of a unified Allied command under the premier's old acquaintance General Foch. In the dark days of early June, when German attacks had smashed through the Chemin des Dames to approach Paris, Clemenceau defended both Foch and Pétain to the National Assembly. When Austrian Foreign Minister Count Czernin (q.v.) tried to shake French morale with reports of French moves toward a negotiated peace, Clemenceau responded with documents illustrating Austria's desperate quest for peace at the expense of her German ally. In September 1918, with Allied armies on the advance everywhere, Clemenceau made triumphant speeches in both chambers of the National Assembly.

The old premier's great success, between the grim November of 1917 and the bright one of 1918, had been twofold. First, he had been a symbol of France's commitment to fight the war to a successful conclusion. In that he was irreplaceable. Since August 1914, no political leader of national stature had spoken so loudly and so consistently of the need to prevail with victory. Second, Clemenceau succeeded in taming the very institutions that had crippled his predecessors. The High Command, a law unto itself in the era of General Joffre, responded to government direction. Internecine fighting in the cabinet ceased. The

National Assembly voted obediently to support Clemenceau's unflinching style of waging the war.

Clemenceau's story of success ended with the Peace Conference, over which he presided. The crucial goals of absolute French security against a revived Germany proved unattainable. France's allies would not grant it the Rhine frontier, nor would they sanction a permanent occupation of bridgeheads on the right bank of the river. The establishment of French puppet states in the Rhineland likewise could not be won. Clemenceau found himself in the uncomfortable position of fending off Foch's pleas for a stronger settlement with explanations that France could not realistically hope to obtain one.

By 1920 elements on both the Right and Left were lining up against Clemenceau: the latter for his alleged repression of Socialists and pacifists during the war, the former for his sins at the Versailles Peace Conference. Defeated in his effort to succeed Poincaré as president of the Republic, Clemenceau retired from public life. He died in Paris on November 24, 1929.

Clemenceau's central role in the Allied victory in World War I seems beyond dispute. Without his leadership, France's march through the war's last bloody year would have been nearly impossible. Without France still standing on the battlefield, American intervention could have had no decisive impact. The most eloquent description and judgment of Clemenceau is to be found in Winston Churchill's (q.v.) ringing phrase: "Happy the nation which when its fate quivers in the balance can find such a tyrant and such a champion."

Bruun, *Clemenceau*; Chastenet et al., *Clemenceau*; Winston Churchill, *Great Contemporaries*; Clemenceau, *Grandeur and Misery of Victory*; King, *Foch versus Clemenceau* and *Generals and Politicians*; Watson, *Georges Clemenceau: A Political Biography*; *Dictionnaire de biographie française*, VIII; *Larousse mensuel*, VIII.

CONRAD von HÖTZENDORF, Franz Count (*Austria-Hungary*, *Field Marshal*), was born in Penzing, near Vienna, on November 11, 1852, the son of an Austrian colonel. Conrad graduated from the Theresa Military Academy in 1871, and five years later was assigned to the General Staff. He took part in various campaigns in Bosnia, Herzegovina, and Dalmatia in 1878, 1879, and 1882, while officially with the army's cartography department. In 1886 he was appointed instructor in tactics at the War Academy in the grade of major. Next came field command: 1895-1899 as colonel commander of the First Infantry Regiment ("Kaiser"), 1899 as brigadier in Trieste, and 1903 as division chief in Innsbruck. It was in Trieste that Conrad, an ardent champion of the House of Habsburg, developed an intense dislike of Italian Irredentism and hence distrust of the third member of the Triple Alliance. It was also here that he met the heir apparent, Archduke Francis Ferdinand (q.v.), who helped Conrad acquire the post of chief of the General Staff in November 1906. During the next five years, Conrad sought to update the antiquated Habsburg forces, especially the artillery. His distrust of the Italians as well as his belief that the only solution to the South Slav problem rested in a preemptive strike against Serbia brought him into open conflict with Emperor Francis Joseph (q.v.) and Foreign Minister Count A. L. von Aehrenthal in 1911. When Conrad called for a preemptive strike against Italy during the Tripolitanian War that year he was asked to resign. However, new Balkan problems in 1912 again brought him the post of chief of the General Staff. In August 1910, Conrad had been raised into the nobility.

The outbreak of the war in 1914, which Conrad had desired at all costs, placed a heavy burden upon him—one that he was not able to master. His armies had to absorb the brunt of the Russian attack in Galicia in order to permit the Germans to score a quick victory in France, as dictated by the Schlieffen plan. Conrad established his headquarters at Teschen, in Austrian Silesia, far removed from the realities of battle, where his staff lived in luxurious isolation with uniformed lackeys, candlelit dinners, and female company. All this might have been forgiven a victorious commander. Conrad, on the other hand, began the war with a colossal blunder: at the last moment he ordered General Oskar Potiorek's (q.v.) Second Army from Serbia to Galicia; this force, according to Winston Churchill (q.v.), "left Potiorek before it could win him a victory; it returned to Conrad in time to participate in his defeat" at Lemberg. In fact, Conrad's forces had to retreat to the Dunajec and, in addition to suffering 350,000 casualties, had to clear almost all of Austrian Galicia, thereby seriously endangering the German flank in southern Poland. Conrad finally managed to halt the Russian "steam roller" at Limanowa-Lapanów, but only after the Germans had routed two Russian armies at Tannenberg and the Masurian Lakes. While Conrad spent the winter months of 1914 in defensive positions in the Carpathian Mountains enduring the sarcastic barbs of German commanders in the east, Potiorek in December was defeated by the Serbs.

Early in 1915 Conrad sought to extricate himself from this series of setbacks with a bold offensive, breaking the Russian lines at Gorlice-Tarnów on May 2, and regaining all the territory lost the previous fall. Yet even in victory there was little to cheer: the campaign had been only nominally under Conrad's command, with power being exercised by General Erich von Falkenhayn through Germany's eastern commanders, Field Marshal August von Mackensen and General Hans von Seeckt (qq.v.). Neither did victory over Serbia in October 1915 proceed smoothly: two strong Bulgarian armies, the German Eleventh Army (Gallwitz), and the Austro-Hungarian Third Army under General Hermann Kövess (q.v.) defeated the Serbs, while a belated Entente bid to help Belgrade by landing an expeditionary force in Salonika was checked by Bulgarian forces. Once again Conrad had been the nominal commander of the operation; and once more the Germans had bypassed him and dealt directly with Field Marshal von Mackensen.

Rebuffed by General von Falkenhayn in his bid for a knock-out blow against Italy in the Trentino, Conrad early in 1916 decided to go it alone. On May 15 two Austro-Hungarian armies attacked across the high plain of Lavarone-Folgaria; by June 17 Conrad had to admit defeat, break off the offensive, and shuttle his troops to the eastern front, where General Aleksei Brusilov (q.v.) had attacked in force on June 4. Conrad's gamble in the Trentino had enabled Brusilov to advance almost at will, and only the timely intervention of nine German divisions prevented the total collapse of the Austro-Hungarian forces. Quickly on the heels of this catastrophe came news on August 27, 1916, that Rumania had entered the war on the side of the Entente; while General Arz von Straussenburg (q.v.) held the passes in Transylvania, two German armies (Falkenhayn and Mackensen) defeated the Rumanians, occupied Bucharest, and forced the remaining enemy units to withdraw behind the Sireth River in Moldavia. These developments did little to bolster Conrad's standing: in Vienna on June 29 he was attacked for the first time in a crown council, and by September 13 the Germans had forced a unified command agreement on Austria-Hungary whereby the German emperor, acting through Field Marshal Paul von Hindenburg (q.v.), assumed command of the allied forces on all fronts. On March 1, 1917, Emperor Charles (q.v.) relieved Conrad von Hötzendorf as chief of the General Staff owing to his inability to play a subordinate role to the emperor, to his desire to pursue the war, and to his failure to achieve victory. At first set upon retirement, Conrad agreed after a personal plea by the monarch to accept appointment as commander of the South Tyrolean Army Group.

In May and June 1918, Conrad launched his last major offensive, a thrust from the South Tyrolean

Alps into the Venetian plain, designed to take the Italian army in the flank. But once again, Conrad's plans looked better on paper than in practice; British and French troops halted the advance on the Piave River, where Entente air power destroyed Conrad's pontoon bridges. Emperor Charles dismissed Conrad in July 15, 1918. In the grade of field marshal since 1916, Conrad assumed the colonelcy of the imperial guards during the last year of the war; he retired from military life on December 1, 1918, rewarded with an earldom, to write his memoirs. Conrad died in Bad Mergentheim, Württemberg, on August 25, 1925, and was laid to rest in Vienna-Hietzing.

Numerous Austrian and British historians have recognized Conrad as a resourceful and bold military leader who saved his country from much devastation by his skillful thrusts against the enemy; some have even ascribed strategic genius to him and called Conrad the best commander of the Great War. This lavish praise is unwarranted and reflects more the mediocre caliber of other field commanders than it does Conrad's abilities. His judgment of fellow human beings and of politics was not always sound, and he was never able to translate his strategic insights into practical operational planning. As Gunther Rothenberg has put it: "On paper Conrad's plans always had an almost Napoleonic sweep, though he often lacked the resolution to carry them out and also forgot that he did not have the instruments to execute them."

Conrad von Hötzendorf, *Aus meiner Dienstzeit*, 5 vols.; Regele, *Feldmarschall Conrad*; Rothenberg, *Army of Francis Joseph*; *Österreichisches Biographisches Lexikon 1815-1950*, I.

CONSTANTINE I (*Greece, King*), was born in Athens, July 12, 1868, son of the reigning Greek monarch, King George I. Despite his father's pro-British inclination, Crown Prince Constantine came quickly under German influence. Educated at Heidelberg, he graduated from the War Academy in Berlin and then served as an infantry officer in the Prussian army. His years in Germany left him with a deep admiration for the German military system and its values. His marriage in 1889 to the sister of Kaiser Wilhelm II (*q.v.*) established a comparable family tie of lasting political significance.

Trained as a soldier, Constantine had an inauspicious combat debut: he led the Greek army to disaster in the 1897 war against Turkey. This military humiliation nearly shook his father from the throne and blackened Constantine's reputation as a military leader for a decade. In 1909 he was compelled to go into exile, purged from the armed forces along with

other royal princes by a coup directed by disgruntled professional officers. Constantine returned with the advent of the Cretan revolutionary Eleutherios Venizelos (*q.v.*) to power in 1910. The prince's reputation and popularity were partly healed by his work as the army's inspector general during the military reform era, 1910-1912. His creditable role as commander in chief in the First Balkan War—this time he defeated the Turks and seized the valuable city of Salonika for Greece—made him a national hero. The assassination of George I in March 1913 brought Constantine to the throne.

With the outbreak of the Great War, Constantine and his country were plunged into a period of prolonged crises. The older view of Constantine as merely a crowned pro-German subversive no longer convinces some historians. But his concern for Greek interests had to be applied under the shadow of a conviction that Germany would win the war. Family pressures, personified by his influential wife, Queen Sophia, drew him close to Berlin, even as Greece's vulnerability to Allied naval power pulled him the other way. In Venizelos, the vacillating monarch found himself facing a partisan convinced of joining the Entente. Exacerbating their policy differences was an explosive constitutional question: did power rest with Venizelos and his mass party's parliamentary majority? Or did it center on a traditional oligarchy made up of the royal family and the General Staff?

The first round went to Venizelos. In early August 1914, Constantine rejected a personal appeal from the kaiser to join the Central Powers. Venizelos soon ousted George Streit, the Germanophile foreign minister. But Streit remained a major influence on Constantine, as did the dominant figure on the General Staff, Colonel John Metaxas (*q.v.*). In September, Constantine avoided a direct confrontation with Venizelos over joining the Entente. Bulgaria, not Greece, seemed the most promising Balkan ally to London and Paris. The Greek premier's talks with the half-interested Allies were still far from provoking crisis in Athens.

In early 1915 the issue sharpened. The focus of the war moved to the Mediterranean; and Britain offered tempting territorial concessions in return for Greek military aid at the Dardanelles. Venizelos hoped to send three army divisions, an investment that would pay rich territorial dividends in Asia Minor when the war ended. Constantine vacillated. Then, in early March, he refused, thereby provoking Venizelos to resign. Behind the facade of the new premier, Dimitrios Gounaris, Constantine and the army began to constitute "a state within a state." Constantine's private messages to the authorities in Berlin, through his wife and German diplomatic channels, made it clear that state policy would favor the Central Powers.

The smouldering constitutional issue grew into a conflagration by the autumn. Venizelos, after a convincing electoral victory in June 1915, returned to office. He soon confronted Constantine with the reality of Bulgarian mobilization and the likely invasion of Serbia. A defense treaty dating from 1913 obligated Greece to aid Serbia against a Balkan opponent. Constantine saw Venizelos' efforts to implement the treaty, especially by inviting a large Anglo-French army into Macedonia to help defend Serbia, as the certain road to general war. The monarch sanctioned Greek mobilization, and he was unable to prevent the Entente from landing in Salonika in early October. But he threw Venizelos from office; once more, the monarch took real power himself behind a parade of nonentities in the premier's chair.

The break between Constantine and Venizelos had now become a chasm. Moreover, the king's relationship to the Entente at best resembled a cold war. Constantine and Metaxas urged the Germans to invade Greek territory to throw the Anglo-French forces at Salonika into the sea! The Entente pressed the Athens regime for port facilities, communications lines, and other privileges to secure the expeditionary force. For the moment, Anglo-French naval power mediated the dispute: Constantine bowed to Allied wishes.

The year 1916 began with the Allied seizure of Corfu as a refuge for the defeated Serbian army. Further demands from London and Paris followed, evoked by Constantine's clear preference for the Central Powers. The May surrender of Fort Rupel to the Bulgarians set the final crisis in motion. Rupel guarded the main route from Bulgaria into eastern Macedonia; in Bulgarian hands, it imperiled the Anglo-French front. A new Bulgarian offensive, begun in August, led to the capture of the Aegean port of Kavalla. The Greek IV Corps surrendered without resistance and went off to internment in Germany. Rupel plus Kavalla drove Venizelos into open revolt. In late September he slipped off to form a pro-Allied government in Crete and Salonika. Allied recognition followed by the close of the year. On December 1, "the Battle of Athens" (in which a landing party of French and British sailors and marines was attacked by Greek royalist troops) blackened Constantine's reputation in London and Paris for the duration of the war. His role in the attack remains uncertain, but contemporaries considered him an accomplice to a treacherous ambush of Allied troops.

Lingering monarchist sensibilities in Britain, Russia, and Italy deferred Constantine's fall. So too did the influence of French Premier Aristide Briand (q.v.), a firm friend of the Greek royal family. By June 1917, Briand had fallen from office, and the Russian monarchy was long gone. The Greek king was forced to abdicate and depart for exile. Within two weeks, Venizelos was back as prime minister.

In Swiss exile, Constantine cherished dreams of obstructing the Greek war effort. He imagined a combined German offensive and popular insurgency driving Venizelos out and restoring royal authority. But the war had passed him by. German military and diplomatic circles based their Balkan diplomacy on the alliance with Bulgaria. To reward the Bulgarian ally meant to slice territory from Greece—more easily done with Greece on the side of the Entente. Constantine's pathetic overtures went unheard.

The exiled king played a final tragic round in Greek political life. He returned to Athens in late 1920, in the wake of Venizelos' stunning electoral defeat. A population wearied by eight years of war in the Balkans and Asia Minor had turned and repudiated the great parliamentary leader. Constantine took the throne left vacant by his son Alexander's death. By continuing the military gamble to establish Greek power in western Asia Minor, Constantine sealed his own fate. A resurgent Turkey inflicted first military defeat, then, in mid-1922, military calamity on Constantine's forces. In September 1922, he abdicated for the second time. He died in Palermo less than six months later, on January 11, 1923.

The issue of Constantine versus Venizelos has agitated Greek historians for more than five decades. Given his education, family ties, and military background, Constantine was drawn to a pro-German policy that placed him and his country under the gun muzzles of the Allied Mediterranean fleets. So long as the war remained some distance away, Constantine managed to balance his personal sympathies and strategic realities. With the defeat of Serbia and the Allied landing at Salonika, the balancing process had to end. It now seems clear that Constantine ceased to be merely a tragic figure in late 1915; rather he became virtually a participant in the war effort of the Central Powers. Popular anger at the Anglo-French landing at Salonika gave the king some fleeting support. But in the longer run, his actions probably overstepped the dim line between individual sympathy for Berlin and Vienna and open disloyalty to his people and their constitution. Nonetheless, the debate over this monarch's motives and behavior in the Great War seems destined to continue.

Leon, *Greece and the Great Powers*, "King Constantine's Policy in Exile"; Palmer, *Gardeners of Salonika*; Theodoulou, *Greece and the Entente*; Woodhouse, *Short History of Modern Greece*; *Larousse mensuel*, VI.

CRADOCK, Sir Christopher George Francis Maurice (*Great Britain, Admiral*), was born at Hartforth, Yorkshire, on July 2, 1862. He entered the navy in 1875, and ten years later took part in the campaigns in Egypt and the Sudan. Next came command of the royal yacht. In July 1900, as commander of the *Alacrity*, Cradock led the assault of the Taku Forts, and later at the head of another force relieved the Tientsin Settlement. Promotion to the grade of captain came in 1907, and to that of rear admiral three years later. In February 1913, Cradock was appointed commander of the North American and West Indies station. With his flag on board the armored cruiser *Suffolk*, he patrolled the vast expanse of ocean from Brazil to the St. Lawrence River. Of special concern to him were the German forces in this area consisting of the two light cruisers *Dresden* and *Karlsruhe*.

With the outbreak of war, Cradock was ordered to protect Britain's North Atlantic trade and to shadow German ships stopped in Atlantic ports. Specifically, the admiral raised his flag on the *Good Hope* and set out after the two German light cruisers. The Admiralty informed him early in September at Pernambuco that the German East Asia squadron under Admiral Count Spee (*q.v.*) was assumed heading eastward across the Pacific, possibly for the Falkland Islands. Cradock at once decided to intercept Spee, informing Whitehall that he would concentrate two forces, one to the east and one to the west of the Magellan Straits, each powerful enough to crush the German flotilla. Unfortunately, the Admiralty was desperately in need of warships at home and refused to reinforce Cradock, sending him only the old battleship *Canopus* to augment his contingent consisting of the armored cruisers *Good Hope* and *Monmouth*, the light cruiser *Glasgow*, and the armed merchantman *Otranto*. Moreover, the Admiralty's orders were rather ambiguous and Cradock, left to his own devices, decided to abandon his former search and protection function and to engage Spee instead.

Late in October Cradock arrived off the west coast of South America, and by October 31 had taken up station off Coronel. He assigned the slow-moving *Canopus* to protect his colliers. A newly-constituted Board of Admiralty under Admiral John Fisher (*q.v.*) ordered Cradock to delay any engagement with the Germans until the powerful battle cruiser *Defence* reached him, above all, not to do battle without the

Canopus. Apparently, the cable never reached Cradock. Hence the fuzziness of Admiralty telegrams, compounded by his impetuous nature, prompted Cradock to press the issue with Spee. In addition, he rightly discerned the black mood at Whitehall in the wake of the escape of the two German cruisers in the Mediterranean into Turkish waters: "I will take care I do not suffer the fate of poor Troubridge [(*q.v.*)]."

At 4:20 P.M. on November 1, 1914, Cradock fell in with Spee's force consisting of the armored cruisers *Scharnhorst* and *Gneisenau*, and the light cruisers *Dresden, Leipzig*, and *Nürnberg*. Although outmatched in speed, armor, and firing power, and with *Canopus* still 250 miles away, Cradock nevertheless decided to accept battle. Spee's ships were silhouetted against the dark land mass by 7:00 P.M. and were almost invisible, while the British units stood out against the bright glow of the western sky. It was all over within an hour: *Good Hope* and *Monmouth* were destroyed while the *Glasgow* managed to escape and find the *Canopus*. Cradock went down with his flagship.

The action off Coronel unleashed a storm of protest at home. British public opinion attributed the disaster solely to Cradock, specifically charging him with recklessness and with engaging a squadron superior to his own.

Marder, *Dreadnought to Scapa Flow*, II; Pitt, *Coronel and Falkland*; *Dictionary of National Biography 1912-1921*, Third Supplement.

CURZON, George Nathaniel (*Great Britain, Lord Privy Seal, Secretary of State for Foreign Affairs*), Marquess Curzon of Kedleston, was born at Kedleston Hall, Derbyshire, on January 11, 1859, the son of the rector of Kedleston. He was educated at Eton and Balliol College, Oxford. As a youth he developed a lifelong affliction of the curvature of the spine that forced him to don a steel corset. After much travel, Curzon in 1898 was appointed viceroy of India and created Baron Curzon of Kedleston in the Irish peerage. His seven years in India ended with the failure to include Tibet in the British sphere of influence and in a bitter quarrel with Lord H. H. Kitchener (*q.v.*), then commander in chief in India. In 1905 Curzon began eleven years of political isolation and disappointment. At first a "ditcher" on the issues of the Lords' veto powers, in August 1910, he reversed his position and supported the parliamentary bill upholding the Commons' power of the purse; in November 1911, he was created Earl Curzon of Kedleston, Viscount Scarsdale, and Baron Ravensdale.

On May 27, 1915, Curzon was appointed lord privy seal in Herbert Asquith's (*q.v.*) coalition government. It was a largely honorific post and Curzon received no important functions and was excluded from the War Council. He spoke out against evacuation of British troops from Gallipoli for reasons of prestige, and he strongly favored compulsory national service at home. Early in 1916 he was placed in charge of the Shipping Control Committee and in May 1916 appointed president of the Air Board; at both posts he clashed frequently with Arthur James Balfour (*q.v.*), then first lord of the Admiralty, whom he accused of having "the mind of a marshmallow." Indeed, Lord Curzon had brought to the cabinet more than the average man's fund of pomposity, and his "rotund expositions of the obvious" were often the subject of ridicule after that body had ended its daily sessions. His enemies gleefully revived the old Oxford University jingle: "My name is George Nathaniel Curzon/I am a most Superior Person. . . ."

At the end of 1916 Curzon hedged his bets as Asquith and David Lloyd George (*q.v.*) struggled for leadership of the Liberal party. The fiery Welshman's victory on December 7 brought Curzon a seat on the inner War Cabinet as well as the leadership in the House of Lords. As a spokesman of the New Imperialism, Curzon decried Balfour's "unfortunate insistence upon the Jewish National Home in Palestine," preferring instead an active British role in Persia and Mesopotamia leading ultimately to the creation of a British-controlled Arab state. Curzon accompanied Lloyd George on April 30, 1917, during the prime minister's historic visit to the Admiralty to encourage the sea lords to introduce the convoy system of merchant shipping in the wake of Germany's resumption of unrestricted submarine warfare. And Curzon shared the prime minister's pessimism concerning victory at the western front, hoping, like Lloyd George, to triumph in Palestine or Mesopotamia (the "Eastern" school).

Curzon felt betrayed by Lloyd George in July 1917, when the prime minister, breaking an earlier pledge to the Tories, installed Winston Churchill (*q.v.*) as minister of munitions. Lloyd George had correctly opted to have Churchill's parliamentary skills on his side and had sought the good offices of Lord Beaverbrook (*q.v.*) to bring Churchill back into the fold; Curzon denounced the renegade Conservative as "an ill-educated man with a great natural power of writing English." And when the House of Commons that same year accorded women the franchise ("this biological mistake"), Curzon, president of the Anti-Suffrage League, outraged his fellow Tories by deserting their cause and voting for the measure on the second reading of the bill. Shortly after the armistice, Curzon made a strong plea that the Germans be made to pay for the war and that the kaiser be brought to trial for starting it.

Curzon served as foreign minister *ad interim* from January to October 1919, while Balfour accompanied Lloyd George to Paris; on October 24, 1919, he became permanent foreign secretary. However, Curzon fell out with the prime minister over the Persian and Graeco-Turkish questions and soon denounced Lloyd George as "an evil genius." During 1922/1923, he reached the height of his career at the Lausanne Conference dealing with the crisis in Asia Minor and in denouncing the French invasion of the Ruhr. Curzon once stated that he had three ambitions in life: to be viceroy of India, to be secretary of state for foreign affairs, and to be prime minister; with regard to the latter, he was deeply offended in May 1923 when King George V (*q.v.*) overlooked him and called instead upon Stanley Baldwin to head a Conservative government. Only with great effort was Curzon persuaded to accept the post of lord privy seal in January 1924. He died in London on March 20, 1925, with the full realization that a member of the House of Lords would never again be called upon to form a government.

Mosley, *Curzon: The Glorious Fault*; Zetland and Dundas, *Life of Lord Curzon*, 3 vols.; *Dictionary of National Biography 1922-1930*.

CZERNIN von und zu CHUDENITZ, Ottokar Count (*Austria-Hungary, Foreign Minister*), was born in Dymokury on September 26, 1872, to an ancient Bohemian noble family. After graduating from the German University in Prague, Czernin served with the diplomatic corps in Paris and The Hague, but a lung infection ended this career. Since 1903 a member of the Bohemian Lower House and since 1912 also of the Upper House, Czernin became a champion of conservatism, upholding the monarchical principle and opposing universal suffrage. He regarded the nobility as the main pillar of the empire. A close friendship with Archduke Francis Ferdinand (*q.v.*) in 1913 brought Czernin back into the diplomatic corps, this time as ambassador to Bucharest, where he served until August 1916. Czernin was a leading member of the heir apparent's so-called Belvedere Circle.

Emperor Charles (*q.v.*) appointed Czernin foreign minister on December 22, 1916. More energetic, more flexible, and more original than either Count Leopold von Berchtold or Burian von Rajecz (*qq.v.*), Czernin was at the same time more unpredictable, more volatile, and also more neurasthenic than his predecessors. Although General Erich Ludendorff (q.v.) managed to convince Czernin of the necessity to resume unrestricted submarine warfare in February 1917, the foreign minister spent much of that year attempting to persuade German military leaders as well as. the emperor of the necessity of peace—even if this should mean Germany's loss of Alsace-Lorraine and restoration of Belgium's independence. Czernin hoped to wring these concessions from Berlin in return for large territorial gains in Poland. Conversely, Czernin sought to maintain inviolate the borders of Austria-Hungary, indeed, even to add Serbia and Rumania to a proposed Austrian Danubian Federation.

In April 1917, Czernin transmitted through Emperor Charles to Matthias Erzberger (q.v.) of Germany a gloomy prognostication outlining the reasons why the Dual Monarchy could not survive another winter of fighting. This document encouraged the German Parliament to pass its well-meaning but ineffective peace resolution in July 1917. Czernin climaxed his career by signing peace treaties with the Ukraine (February 9, 1918), Russia (March 3, 1918), and Rumania (April 14, 1918), although in each case bitter wrangling with the German ally preceded final accord. Czernin resigned his post on April 14, 1918, as a direct result of the notorious "Sixtus" affair. The foreign minister had been aware of Emperor Charles' secret negotiations with his brother-in-law, though not of the exact wording of the letter of March 24, 1917, in which the emperor had spoken of France's "just demand" for the return of Alsace-Lorraine. Revelation of this correspondence by Georges Clemenceau (q.v.) made Czernin's position untenable.

Ottokar Czernin retired in Austria after Czechoslovakian nationalist agrarian reforms deprived him of his lands in Bohemia. From 1920 to 1923 he served as deputy of the Democratic party in the Austrian National Council. He died in Vienna on April 4, 1932.

Czernin, *Im Weltkrieg*; Kann, *History of the Habsburg Empire*; *Neue Deutsche Biographie*, III; *Neue Österreichische Biographie*, XVII.

DALLOLIO, Alfredo (*Italy, Lieutenant General, Minister of Munitions*), was born in Bologna on June 21, 1853. He entered the Military Academy at Turin and was commissioned in the artillery. Fom 1903 until 1910 Dallolio was the commanding officer for the Italian army's artillery units in Venice; his interest was drawn to the problems of fortifying Italy's eastern border regions. Promoted general, he commanded the artillery and engineering section at the Italian ministry of war. During the 1911/1912 con-

flict with Turkey, he supervised the flow of war matériel to the troops in Libya.

Italy's declaration of neutrality at the start of August 1914 increased the need for a Dallolio. The army's stockpiles of supplies had shrunk during the Libyan War, and the cabinet under Antonio Salandra (q.v.) showed no enthusiasm for massive military expenditures before the outbreak of World War I. Nonetheless, Italy was likely to be drawn into the conflict, whose cost and dimensions were becoming evident on battlefields from Flanders to Poland. Dallolio was the obvious choice to hitch the nation's economy to the needs of its soldiers. On July 9, 1915, in what Whittam has called "one of the most crucial decisions of the war" for Italy, Dallolio was named undersecretary of state for munitions. By then, the early bloodletting on the Isonzo under General Luigi Cadorna (q.v.) had demonstrated Italy's woeful lack of the tools of war: artillery, machine guns, hand grenades, and even modern rifles were in short supply.

Dallolio set out to close the gap between what the arms factories could produce in mid-1915 and what the army needed; just as David Lloyd George and Albert Thomas (qq.v.) were attempting to meet the same problem in Britain and France. Skilled workers were shielded from conscription; some already in uniform were permitted to return to their civilian occupations. The most powerful weapon at hand was Dallolio's authority to designate industrial enterprises as essential to the war effort; these "auxiliaries" then fell under direct military control. Dallolio, who was elevated to minister of munitions in June 1917, took command of 2,000 plants in this fashion.

The ultimate test of Dallolio's work came after the Austro-German breakthrough at Caporetto (October 1917). The Italian industrial system, aided, of course, by shipments from Rome's allies, was able to reequip the battered armies for the victorious 1918 campaign. The closing year of the war saw a new candidate for control over war industry take the stage. Minister of the Treasury Francesco Nitti (q.v.) took the entire Italian economy as his proper sphere of influence. A clash with the minister of munitions was inevitable, and in May 1918, Dallolio was forced from office.

The old general's reputation as an industrial wizard endured, however, into the Fascist era. In 1935 Dallolio was named commissioner general for war production. But Dallolio was appalled at the chaotic state of Italy's economic preparation for a new European war and the government's apparent inability to remedy this situation. In August 1939, he resigned; confirmation of his fears concerning his country's lack of preparation for a modern war was quick in coming. He endured World War II and died in Rome on September 20, 1952, at the age of ninety-nine.

Clough, *The Economic History of Modern Italy*; Whittam, *The Politics of the Italian Army*; *Chi é?*, 4th ed.; *Enciclopedia italiana*, XII.

DANIELS, Josephus (*United States, Secretary of the Navy*), was born in Washington, North Carolina, on May 18, 1862. Although he passed his state's bar examination in 1885, Daniels never practiced law and instead entered into a long career as journalist and editor. He became a co-owner of the fervently progressive Raleigh *News and Observer*, which earned the nickname Nuisance and Disturber in rural and conservative North Carolina. In 1912 Daniels helped persuade North Carolina Democrats to support Woodrow Wilson's (*q.v.*) bid for the presidency, and he, in return, although lacking any previous nautical experience, was rewarded with the office of secretary of the navy. Intensely loyal to his chief, Daniels was to hold this office longer than any previous secretary but Gideon Welles, who had served under both Lincoln and Andrew Johnson.

Daniels quickly became perhaps the most controversial member of the cabinet. Officers generally distrusted his progressive beliefs and his special views on civilian-military relations; Fleet Admiral Leahy later bluntly stated that Daniels "did not like naval officers as such." His relations with the civilian supporters of the service were exacerbated by Daniels' order in 1914 to ban alcohol from officers' messes and especially by his decision to ban the Navy League from all ships. However, Daniels did undertake a number of vital reforms: he required sea duty for promotion, opened the Naval Academy to enlisted men, upgraded naval prisons, insisted on competitive bidding for contracts, and replaced the ineffective Council of Aids with a chief of Naval Operations. Plans to centralize the eight bureau heads into a general staff system, on the other hand, were brusquely denounced by Daniels in 1915 as "Prussianism." Daniels' decision to guard naval oil reserves from private exploitation led to a bitter fight with Secretary of the Interior F. K. Lane and ended in the notorious Teapot Dome scandal under President Harding.

The most damaging charge leveled against the secretary by, among others, Admiral Sims (*q.v.*) was that Daniels, a near pacifist, had failed adequately to prepare the U.S. Navy for war in 1914/1916. Nor did it help that the assistant secretary of the navy, the energetic yachtsman Franklin D. Roosevelt (*q.v.*), gave quiet encouragement to Daniels' enemies. Although an investigation by a subcommittee of the Senate Naval Affairs Committee in 1920 failed to resolve the issue, it is clear that the charges were unjust. Daniels had to maintain a balance between naval officers anxious for expansion of their service and the president who was equally determined to observe strict neutrality as long as possible. Once war was declared on April 6, 1917, Daniels did his best to help the Allies: in July he approved the immediate construction of 200 destroyers to help in the antisubmarine war, and he eventually proved willing to concentrate authority in the hands of Sims, even though he disliked this Anglophile intensely.

Daniels moved cautiously throughout the war and generally relied on the advice rendered by Admiral Benson (*q.v.*), especially that in behalf of maintaining a "symmetrical" fleet according to Mahan. The secretary "emphatically" opposed a British offer in November 1917 to appoint Benson and Sims "Honorary Lords of the Admiralty." An inveterate opponent of the North Sea mine barrage, Daniels nevertheless agreed in September 1918 to a mine barrage in the Adriatic Sea; the secretary's lack of nautical knowledge became apparent when he dismissed the concept of a barrage in the relatively narrow Straits of Otranto in favor of a mid-Adriatic barrage from Gargano Head to Curzola Island! Daniels was bitterly disappointed in November 1918, when the British refused to recognize the American principle of freedom of the seas and especially when President Wilson agreed to sacrifice this portion of the Fourteen Points in the face of British intransigence. Overall, it would be fair to state that Daniels never was able to delegate authority as freely as Secretary of War Baker (*q.v.*) owing to his basic civilian distrust of naval officers.

Secretary Daniels retired in 1921 to return to his newspaper in Raleigh, where he fought unsuccessfully in behalf of American participation on the World Court and for membership in the League of Nations. Neither was his opposition to the Ku Klux Klan popular in North Carolina. Roosevelt later appointed the man whom he continued to call "chief" as ambassador to Mexico, thereby only partially allaying Daniels' desire to return as secretary of the navy. Daniels died on January 15, 1948, in Raleigh.

Cronon, ed., *Cabinet Diaries of Josephus Daniels*; Daniels, *The Wilson Era*; Trask, *Captains & Cabinets*; *Dictionary of American Biography*, XXIV, Supplement Four.

DANILOV, Yury Nikiforovich (*Russia, Lieutenant General*), was born in the Ukraine, August 13, 1866. He graduated from the Mikhailovsky Artillery School, served briefly as a line officer, then entered the General Staff Academy. He graduated with honors in 1892, and he went on to a distinguished career as a staff officer. Danilov's first posting was to Kiev, where he specialized in mobilization problems. He soon found himself called to the General Staff in St. Petersburg; in addition to his regular duties, he taught at the General Staff Academy and helped edit the leading professional journals of the Russian army. In 1906 the rising young *Genshtabist* put the finishing touches to his preparation for higher responsibility by taking a turn in command of a field unit, the 166th Infantry Regiment. In 1908, as a colonel, he returned to the General Staff for a meteoric rise.

In the years up to 1914 Danilov served first as the chief of the General Staff's operations section and then rose to become the army's quartermaster general, that is, deputy chief of staff. Chiefs of staff came and went with bewildering speed, six in five years. It was Danilov, by 1909 promoted general, who provided an element of continuity to Russia's pre-World War I planning. With the controversial but reform-minded war minister, General Sukhomlinov (*q.v.*), Danilov developed the so-called Plan 19. This plan advocated directing Russia's initial offensive in a future conflict with the Central Powers against Germany. Such an action would strike at the more potent member of the enemy alliance and was likely to help disrupt a German offensive against France, Russia's ally. A parallel suggestion called for abandoning Russia's antiquated collection of Polish fortresses. Danilov's plans encountered massive resistance; local commanders in the southwestern provinces who expected to face an Austrian onslaught at the start of a future war howled the loudest. In the end, Danilov saw his plan reshaped. Russia would begin the war with two offensives, one against the Germans in East Prussia; the other, and stronger, against Austrian Galicia. The stage was set for a serious dispersal of Russian strength.

During the July crisis of 1914, Danilov, by his own account, played a key role. He returned from an inspection tour of the Caucasus on July 26 to throw his weight in favor of general, not partial, mobilization. Thus, his may have been the decisive voice in bringing Russia to the ultimate confrontation with Germany. As the crisis showed, a strong hand at the top of Russia's military was mandatory. Instead, confusion prevailed. Tsar Nicholas II decided at the last moment not to take the supreme command, which went to his uncle, Grand Duke Nikolai Nikolaevich (*qq.v.*). The army's youthful new chief of staff, General Yanushkevich (*q.v.*), was almost equally unfamiliar with Russia's war plans. Thus, it fell to Danilov to coordinate the widely divergent offen-

sives against Germany and Austria-Hungary. His contemporaries credited Danilov with intelligence and a huge capacity for hard work, but events quickly spun out of control.

The southwestern front (or army group) against Austria-Hungary and the northwestern front (army group) against East Prussia went their independent ways. After Plan 19 had been revised, the northwestern front under General Zhilinsky (*q.v.*) had been weakened to permit Russia to strike Austria and Germany simultaneously. Zhilinsky's remaining two armies, widely separated, could not support each other. In the last week of August, General Rennenkampf's (*q.v.*) First Army was bloodied; General Samsonov's (*q.v.*) Second Army was massacred. Meanwhile, in Galicia, a ponderous Russian advance westward along the Carpathians was too slow to cut off the Austrian armies that Conrad von Hötzendorf (*q.v.*) had boldly dispatched northward toward central Poland.

In mid-November, the slackness in the Russian command system was demonstrated anew. A German offensive southeastward from Thorn caught the exposed Russian Second Army off guard as it advanced toward Silesia. A major encounter developed at Lodz, but no one could push Rennenkampf and his First Army forward rapidly enough to cut off portions of the attacking German forces that had become dangerously exposed. By the start of the new year, Danilov, backed by the offensive-minded grand duke, was ready to attack again. A new thrust at East Prussia in February barely got off the planning board before the Germans disrupted Russian hopes by striking first at Augustovo. The Russian High Command now turned elsewhere.

During the remainder of his term as director of Russian military operations, Danilov found his attention centered in southern Poland. After the failure in February, the main Russian effort shifted to the Carpathians. By April initial advances there set a dangerous fuse burning. German reinforcements rushed in under the capable General von Mackensen (*q.v.*); and the Central Powers crashed through the Russians' thin defensive line at Gorlice in early May. The vast dimensions of the Polish salient had stretched Russian manpower and especially matériel to the limit. Effective coordination of the two great Russian fighting fronts was the only remedy, but this Danilov and Grand Duke Nikolai never achieved. As Mackensen cut northward, a strategic retreat as far as the San River promised to salvage something. Danilov refused. By June simultaneous enemy advances in Galicia and northern Poland set the stage for a grim retreat.

Not until August could the Russian forces halt. By then, all three of the top army leaders found their reputations in shreds. Grand Duke Nikolai Nikolaevich and General Yanushkevich were dispatched to the safety of the Caucasus. Danilov was ousted, but given a corps command in the main theater of operations. The British observer General Knox noted the great sense of relief that ran through the army at Danilov's demotion.

Danilov worked his way a rung or two back up the military ladder. By early 1917 he had become chief of staff of the northern front, and for a time thereafter he held command of the Fifth Army. He left his military career behind in the fall of 1917. The following year he emigrated to France, where he wrote his memoirs and a biography of Grand Duke Nikolai Nikolaevich, the commander for whom he had never been able to produce successes. Danilov died in exile in Paris on November 3, 1937.

Albertini, *The Origins of the War of 1914*, II; Danilov, *La Russie dans la guerre mondiale*; Knox, *With the Russian Army*, 2 vols.; Rostunov, *Russkii front pervoi mirovoi voiny*; Rutherford, *The Russian Army in World War I*; Stone, *The Eastern Front*.

DANKL von KRASNIK, Viktor Count (*Austria-Hungary, General*), was born at Udine, Venetia, on September 18, 1854, the son of an army captain. A descendant of Andreas Hofer, Dankl graduated from the Theresa Military Academy in 1874 and from the War Academy five years later, serving with the General Staff in 1880 before being promoted captain in 1884. Thereafter he toured various posts in the far-flung empire (Vienna, Rodymno, Agram, Komorn, Trient, Innsbruck) and rose from major general in 1903 to general of cavalry in 1912 as commandant of the XIV Army Corps in Innsbruck.

At the outbreak of the Great War, Dankl commanded the First Army, composed of the I, V, and X Corps, and in August defeated the Russian Fourth Army during a three-day battle near Krasnik. His pursuit of the enemy as far as Lublin was short-lived, however, as the First Army in September became part of the general rout of Austro-Hungarian forces at Lemberg. Dankl was forced to spend the winter months in defensive positions along the Nida River, north of Cracow.

On May 23, 1915, Dankl was appointed defender of Tyrol, and, in March 1916, given command of the Eleventh Army. In May of that year General Conrad von Hötzendorf (*q.v.*) ordered Dankl's forces to sweep out of the high plains of Lavarone-Folgaria and to take Padua. Dankl's army managed to advance as far as the Arsiero, but a stiff Italian defense,

the difficulty of terrain, and confusion at the higher-command level negated the initial gains. Moreover, a simultaneous offensive in the east by General Aleksei Brusilov (*q.v.*) forced the Austro-Hungarians to close down the Tyrolean theater of operations for the time being. Conrad attempted to shift the blame for the Italian disaster to Dankl, who on June 17, 1916, asked for and received his release from command of the Eleventh Army.

Emperor Charles (*q.v.*) in 1917 assigned Dankl the largely honorific posts of captain of the First Arciéren Leibgarde and later colonel of all Leibgarden. In December 1917, Dankl voted against a proposal to divide the common army into separate Austrian and Hungarian contingents. The general was rewarded for his services by being raised into the baronage in August 1917, in recognition of his victory at Krasnik in 1914, and by being granted an earldom in the fall of 1918. Dankl died in Innsbruck on January 8, 1941.

Bardolff, *Militär-Maria Theresien-Orden*; Rothenberg, *Army of Francis Joseph*; *Österreichisches Biographisches Lexikon 1815-1950*, I.

D'ANNUNZIO, Gabriele (*Italy, Writer, Political Agitator*), was born at Pescara, on the Adriatic coast, on March 12, 1863. His father was a wealthy landowner. D'Annunzio displayed his remarkable literary gifts at an early age, publishing his first volume of poetry in 1879. In 1888 he began to devote some of his energies to novels featuring characters modeled on Nietzschean supermen. This flamboyant *fin-de-siècle* figure served, surprisingly, as a deputy in the Italian Parliament starting in 1897. He was defeated in the next election, but in the new century his political interests blossomed in the form of violently expressed nationalism and irredentism. By 1908 his plays were lamenting Italy's lost lands in the Adriatic.

Debts forced D'Annunzio to flee to France in 1910; from there he wrote poems celebrating Italy's imperial drive into Libya. He was still more enthusiastic in welcoming World War I and urging Italian intervention. The poet turned politician returned to Italy in early May 1915. He had been pouring out interventionist propaganda while still in France, but coming face to face with his audience sent him into a frenzy of warmongering. On May 5, the day after Italy had broken off its alliance with Germany and Austria, D'Annunzio called the nation to arms in a speech at the Garibaldi monument in Genoa. Like other irredentist and interventionist leaders, such as Benito Mussolini and Filippo Corridoni, he whipped up popular emotions during the first weeks of May.

His message was: put aside the treasonous neutralism urged since the war's beginning by politicians like Giovanni Giolitti (*q.v.*). On May 12 he arrived in Rome and invited a crowd of 100,000 to take to the streets to hunt down neutralist traitors. The precise effect of this public uproar is hard to gauge, but it is likely that it helped convince neutralists like Giolitti that efforts to block Italy's entry into the conflict meant civil war.

D'Annunzio greeted the war by arranging—at the age of fifty-two—to join a cavalry division. Over the next years, he shifted to other glamorous military roles like torpedo-boat commander and combat pilot. He lost an eye in one aerial operation, but this barely restrained him. In August 1918, in his most memorable stunt, D'Annunzio led a flight of planes across the Alps to "bomb" Vienna with propaganda leaflets he had personally composed.

At the war's conclusion, D'Annunzio became a spokesman for the disgruntled nationalists and former servicemen who felt Italy was not receiving the territorial rewards it deserved. D'Annunzio himself coined the widely circulated phrase of "mutilated victory" in a newspaper piece on November 24, 1918. By the following January he had called on nationalists to seize Fiume, all of Dalmatia, and to march against Rome itself to expel the weaklings in power there. He was momentarily heartened by the departure of the Italian delegation from Versailles in April 1919, but moves to reduce the Italian garrison at Fiume, the hotly contested port on the northeastern Adriatic, pushed him into a freebooting expedition. From September 1919 until January 1921, he held Fiume with a band of personal followers swelled by deserters from the Italian army. No government dared move against him for over a year for fear the military establishment would turn to D'Annunzio.

The rise of Benito Mussolini and the Fascist movement gradually eclipsed D'Annunzio. By the close of 1922 he had given up hopes of transforming postwar discontent into a movement to put himself in power. He retired to private life and died at Lake Garda, March 1, 1938.

Ledeen, *The First Duce*; Rhodes, *The Poet as Superman: D'Annunzio*; Seton-Watson, *Italy from Liberalism to Fascism*; *Larousse mensuel*, XI.

DARTIGE du FOURNET, Louis René Charles Marie

(*France, Vice Admiral*), was born in Putanges, west of Paris, March 2, 1856. He graduated from the Naval College in 1874 at the head of his class and spent most of the next three decades in the Far East where he compiled a distinguished combat record.

Promoted rear admiral in 1909, du Fournet commanded the international fleet patrolling the waters off Constantinople during the First Balkan War (1912/1913). He advanced to vice admiral at the close of 1913, while serving as naval commander in chief at Bizerte.

Du Fournet spent the early months of World War I in North Africa, but 1915 brought him a succession of increasingly responsible sea commands. He took charge of the Third Squadron in the eastern Mediterranean in February, commanded French naval forces at the Dardanelles (May-October), and, in mid-October, replaced Admiral Boué de Lapeyrère (*q.v.*) as the ranking French naval officer in the Mediterranean.

By then, the French naval forces found their main task to be parrying the dangerous threat posed by the German submarine fleet. Du Fournet became the executor of Navy Minister Lacaze's (*q.v.*) policy of redeploying French combat ships to meet the new weapon. He champed with frustration at his inability to employ his battleships but obediently pared away at the crews of the large vessels to provide men for the fleet of small antisubmarine ships Lacaze ordered formed.

By late 1915 Lacaze and du Fournet had instituted a policy of escorting troop ships as well as patrolling the shipping lanes commonly used by merchant vessels. The need to guard the Strait of Otranto against an Austrian sortie and to support the deepening Allied commitment at Salonika meant leaving such areas as the western Mediterranean poorly guarded. By midsummer 1916, du Fournet's calls for additional patrol boats led Lacaze to reply that French resources for combating the submarine threat were now stretched to the limit. Thomazi suggests that du Fournet had by then become a partisan of well-escorted convoys to protect merchant traffic. Lacking an adequate number of suitable escorts, however, he had to content himself with attempts to patrol shipping lanes as closely as possible.

For du Fournet, Greek politics rather than German submarines emerged as the fatal challenge. In September 1916, Paris ordered him to delegate his other responsibilities in order to direct operations against the government of King Constantine (*q.v.*). The monarch's increasingly evident pro-German policies threatened the rear of the Allied forces stationed near Salonika. Notwithstanding British and Russian objections, French naval demonstrations had become the common weapon with which to hold the Greeks to their wobbling neutrality.

But du Fournet found Constantine a dangerously unpredictable antagonist. Relying on the Greek king's assurances of goodwill and pledges to surrender large quantities of artillery to the Allies as proof of his benevolence, du Fournet landed a small expedition of British and French sailors and marines at Athens on December 1. They immediately came under fire from Greek royalist forces and were extricated only with difficulty. Du Fournet now swung to a belligerent extreme and prepared to bombard Athens. The befuddled admiral was prevented by Lacaze from thus alienating the entire Greek population, and the navy minister removed him from command in mid-December. The cashiered du Fournet found himself in involuntary retirement by the start of 1917.

For the remainder of the war du Fournet sought a new command, but his active service was over. He died in Perigeux, February 17, 1940.

Laurens, *Le Commandement naval en Méditerranée, 1914-1918*; Leon, *Greece and the Great Powers, 1914-1917*; Palmer, *Gardeners of Salonika*; Thomazi, *La Marine française dans la Grande Guerre*, II, IV; *Dictionnaire de biographie française*, X.

DELBRÜCK, Clemens von (*Germany, State Secretary of the Interior*), was born in Halle on January 19, 1856, the son of a physician. Delbrück studied law and in 1882 entered the Prussian civil service. His career was meteoric: lord mayor of Danzig in 1896, lord lieutenant of the province of West Prussia six years later, and Prussian minister of trade in October 1905. In this capacity Delbrück attempted through enhanced social welfare legislation to gain the support of the workers, especially those in the mining industry, for the Wilhelmian state. In 1909 Chancellor Theobald von Bethmann Hollweg (*q.v.*) appointed Delbrück minister of the interior; four years later Delbrück also became vice-president of the Prussian ministry of state. Among his most important acts were the concentration as well as regulation of all state insurance matters in 1911 and the drafting of a new constitution for Alsace-Lorraine.

In August 1914, Delbrück was entrusted with the economic aspects of the German mobilization. It proved too much for him. Already ill and overburdened, Delbrück lapsed into inaction and was unable to meet the mounting food shortage; the Social Democrats demanded price ceilings and controls on producers in November 1914. In order to ease Delbrück's load, Georg Michaelis (*q.v.*) was entrusted with the national food supply, and in February 1915, the German Upper House (*Bundesrat*) placed wheat production under government control. By October 1915, public pressure had forced Delbrück to set up an imperial potato office.

The year 1916 proved decisive for Delbrück. Food riots increased and isolated strikes attested to the dirth of edibles. Ill and universally denounced, Delbrück resigned on May 23, 1916. However, on October 14, 1918, he accepted the post of chief of the Civil Cabinet in order to realize Wilhelm II's (*q.v.*) promise of September 30 to liberalize the constitution by introducing ministerial responsibility. But it was already too late for piecemeal reforms: the kaiser was forced to abdicate on November 9 and to yield to a republic in Berlin.

After the war, Delbrück, who had been ennobled in 1916, helped to found the German National People's party (DNVP). Unfortunately, the moderate Delbrück, who counseled support for the Weimar Republic, proved unable to lead his party; instead, the DNVP increasingly grew hostile towards the new state in general and the policy of fulfillment in particular. Delbrück died at Jena on December 17, 1921.

Delbrück, *Mobilmachung* and *Reden 1900-1916*; Feldman, *Army, Industry, and Labor in Germany*; *Neue Deutsche Biographie*, III.

DELCASSÉ, Théophile (*France, Minister of Foreign Affairs*), was born in Pamiers in the foothills of the Pyrenees, March 1, 1857. The son of a legal official, Delcassé studied at the University of Toulouse, then took up a career as a journalist. In 1889 he entered the Chamber of Deputies as a member of the Radical party. He rose quickly. He became minister of colonies in 1894/1895, and he embarked on a triumphant seven-year term as minister of foreign affairs in 1898. By 1905 Delcassé could point with pride to strengthened diplomatic links with Russia; more important, he had restored friendly relations with two formerly hostile nations, first Italy, then (in 1904) with Great Britain. Delcassé stood as a firm supporter of French imperial expansion, in particular concerning tighter control over Morocco. That view, plus his widely recognized anti-German feelings, led to his fall in June 1905. The Berlin government challenged French designs in Morocco and made it clear they preferred to deal with a more sympathetic French foreign minister. A weak premier, Maurice Rouvier, pushed him from office.

Delcassé returned to center stage in July 1909. His criticism of gross inadequacies in the French navy shook the government of Georges Clemenceau (*q.v.*) to the ground. In March 1911, Delcassé got his own chance to guide French sea power as minister of the navy. Before he left the office in January 1913, the French government had signed naval conventions with Russia (July 1912) and Great Britain (October

1912). By shifting French naval strength to the Mediterranean, Delcassé anticipated the results of the agreement with Great Britain even before it had been signed. Thus the defense of the North Sea, and the implicit obligation to join France in a future war with Germany, was pushed toward British hands. In the touchy matter of defending France against a German offensive through Belgium, Delcassé was equally daring. In February 1912, he supported General Joseph Joffre (q.v.) in calling for a preemptive French advance into the small neutral country; but Premier Raymond Poincaré (q.v.) turned the idea aside.

Delcassé became France's ambassador to Russia in February 1913, remaining until January 1914. With an eye to a coming war, he goaded the St. Petersburg government to improve the railroad system in the Russian Empire's western provinces, pledging French financial help to meet the costs. Delcassé's old friend Maurice Paléologue (q.v.) replaced him, permitting the diplomatic warhorse to return home to lead the successful fight to increase France's term of military service for its recruits to three years.

In August 1914, the war Delcassé had so long anticipated became a reality. Premier René Viviani (q.v.) called him in to take charge once again over the foreign ministry. But Delcassé could not match the great successes of his previous term in that post. In poor health, the new foreign minister carried the additional burden of knowing his son had been captured by the enemy within the first month of the war. Delcassé's straightforward policy of bolstering France's existing alliances and seeking new members for the Allied coalition aroused heated controversy.

The French foreign minister established a cordial working arrangement with Sergei Sazonov (q.v.), his Russian counterpart and a strong supporter of the wartime alliance. As early as November 1914, Delcassé backed Sazonov's call for some form of Russian control over the Turkish Straits. The following spring, Delcassé placed France alongside Britain in promising Petrograd possession of the Dardanelles and adjacent territories when the war ended in victory. Such concessions to the Russians were perhaps inescapable: Sazonov threatened otherwise to resign and to let some pro-German diplomat take his place. But Delcassé found he had aroused the concern of everyone from French businessmen worried about their economic interests in Turkey to anti-Russian Socialists who opposed any territorial gain for the tsar.

Delcassé had a less controversial success in winning Italy to the Allied side in May 1915. But the effort to create a bloc of Balkan states to fight alongside the Entente failed catastrophically. To Delcassé, Bulgaria alone could form the mainstay of such a league. If the Sofia government moved alongside France and Britain, then Rumania and Greece would have to follow. To the end, Delcassé pressed France's ally Serbia as well as neutral Greece to make territorial concessions to the Bulgars. But the Central Powers seemed better able to give Bulgaria such coveted territory as Serbian Macedonia; in October 1915, Bulgaria entered the war on the side of France's opponents. To his growing chorus of critics in the National Assembly, Delcassé seemed mistaken at every turn: too conciliatory to the Russians, too gullible vis-à-vis the Bulgars, too unsympathetic to the Serbs. The final blow came in October 1915, when Delcassé stood alone in the cabinet against landing a large French expeditonary force in Salonika. He had previously favored an Allied landing, but only if Russian and Italian units played the main role. To drain French troops from the western front was, for him, intolerable. He resigned on October 12, 1915; before the month was out, Aristide Briand (q.v.) had replaced Viviani as premier and committed France to a Balkan front.

Delcassé sat out the rest of the war quietly on the back benches, but he came alive at the news of the Versailles settlement. He demanded the Rhine frontier and nothing less as a guarantee of French security. The old architect of the 1904 Entente with Britain now claimed that London had won far more safety than Paris from success in World War I, especially the destruction of the German fleet. Delcassé bitterly refused to vote for the peace treaty in 1919; that same year he retired from political office. He died in Nice, February 22, 1923.

Beaufre, *La France de la Grande Guerre*; Cassar, *The French and the Dardanelles*; Porter, *The Career of Théophile Delcassé*; Smith, *The Russian Struggle for Power*; Samuel Williamson, *The Politics of Grand Strategy*; *Larousse mensuel*, VI.

DERBY, Seventeenth Earl of (1865-1948). See STANLEY, Edward George Villiers.

De ROBECK, Sir John Michael (*Great Britain, Admiral of the Fleet*), was born at Gowran Grange, Naas, county Kildare, on June 10, 1862, the second son of the fourth Baron De Robeck (an Irishman of Swedish descent and the only British subject holding a Swedish title of nobility). De Robeck entered the navy in 1875 and quickly became known for his dignity and charm; he was widely regarded as a strong-minded and highly talented officer. Before his promotion to the grade of commander in 1897, he served on no fewer than twenty-four warships as well as on station in China and Newfoundland. In 1902 Captain De Robeck was attached to the Mediterranean Squadron. Nine years later came promotion to the grade of rear admiral, and in 1912 the post of admiral of patrols in home waters.

August 1914 found De Robeck unemployed. He was quickly given command of the Ninth Cruiser Squadron on patrol in the mid-Atlantic area, but his gift for leadership and his ability to take subordinates into his confidence made him an ideal choice for a more senior appointment. This came early in 1915, in the form of second in command to Vice Admiral Carden (*q.v.*) of a projected naval expedition to the Dardanelles. De Robeck hoisted his flag on the battleship *Vengeance* and took part in the bombardment of the outer forts at the Straits. Carden cracked under the pressure of the command in March, and De Robeck, although junior in rank to Admiral Wemyss (*q.v.*), was entrusted with command of all naval forces at the Dardanelles. He decided to have a "real good try" at the forts again and, on March 18, resumed bombardment of the outer defenses. But Lady Luck was not with him. The battleships *Irresistible*, *Ocean*, and *Bouvet* (French) foundered upon German mines, taking 600 officers and crew down with them. De Robeck then developed serious doubts about the wisdom of the entire operation, particularly fearing that naval forces alone could not decide the issue. On April 25 he acquired the consent of Generals Sir Ian Hamilton and Sir Charles Monro (*qq.v.*) to launch a simultaneous military assault on the Turkish defenses. This, too, failed, but De Robeck's role during the massive undertaking was so highly praised by Hamilton ("the Royal Navy has been father and mother to the Army") that his was to be one of the few careers not shattered by the Dardanelles expedition. De Robeck made the right decision in calling for an early evacuation of Allied troops, and on January 8/9, 1916, over 100,000 men were successfully lifted from the beaches.

The ensuing reorganization of the Grand Fleet (the recall of Admiral Jellicoe to the Admiralty and his relief by Admiral Beatty [*qq.v.*]) brought De Robeck command of the Second Battle Squadron in the grade of vice admiral; he hoisted his flag on the *George V* on December 3, 1916. De Robeck remained at this post until the dissolution of the Grand Fleet in May 1919.

After the war, De Robeck was promoted to admiral, created baronet, given the special thanks of Parliament (as well as a grant of £10,000), and appointed commander in chief of the Mediterranean Fleet. In August 1922, he transferred to the identical command with the Atlantic Fleet, a post he held for the next two years. De Robeck was promoted to the grade of admiral of the fleet in 1925; he died on January 20, 1928, in London.

James, *Gallipoli*; Marder, *Dreadnought to Scapa Flow*, II; *Dictionary of National Biography 1922-1930*.

DIAZ, Armando (*Italy, General*), was born in Naples, December 5, 1861. Like many of his forebearers, the young Diaz chose a career as a soldier. After graduating from the Turin Military Academy in 1881, he served as an artillery officer until he entered the General Staff Academy in 1892. He graduated with distinction in 1894, and over the next seventeen years developed a reputation as one of the army's most promising young staff experts. Promoted colonel in 1910, he led one of the first combat regiments to land in Libya during the Italian-Turkish War, 1911/1912. He campaigned in Libya for nearly a year, was wounded at the battle of Zanzur (September 1912), and returned to the General Staff with the laurels of a successful field commander to speed him upward.

The outbreak of World War I put Diaz, recently advanced to major general's rank, alongside General Luigi Cadorna (*q.v.*), the army's chief of staff, to reorganize the military system in the expectation Italy might enter the fighting. With Italy's declaration of war on Austria (May 1915), Diaz took charge of the operations section of the General Staff. In late 1915, he received command of a division. He distinguished himself in the successful attack on Gorizia (August 1916) and, in the summer of 1917, as a lieutenant general in command of the XXIII Corps, he led a successful advance on the lower Isonzo.

The calamity at Caporetto (October 1917) brought the downfall of Cadorna. As the Italian armies, some driven back over seventy miles, rallied to stand on the Piave, Diaz took over as chief of staff. With King Victor Emmanuel III (*q.v.*) playing only a decorative role as generalissimo, Diaz like Cadorna before him was the real commander in chief on the Italian side.

As Cyril Falls has put it, although not a leader of genius, Diaz was "eleven years Cadorna's junior and livelier in every way." He also maintained cordial relations with key government leaders, notably his fellow southerner, Francesco Nitti (*q.v.*), the powerful minister of the treasury. Cadorna had kept himself as far from politicians as he possibly could.

Diaz rallied his troops on the Piave—Falls gives Cadorna the credit for leading the army to that line in reasonably good order—and immediately found himself under heavy enemy attack. The arrival of three British and three French combat divisions helped bolster the defenses, but Diaz also had the advantage of facing a tired and numerically depleted enemy force, dependent on overstretched lines of supply. Moreover, the German troops who had been the spearhead for the success at Caporetto, General Ludendorff (*q.v.*) was now drawing off to prepare for the 1918 spring offensive in France.

By early 1918, the Piave line was secure, and Diaz began to test his reviving army in small-scale offensives. Civil and military relations rested on a more stable basis than during the Cadorna era: a new war council brought Diaz and Premier Vittorio Orlando (*q.v.*) together for regular meetings. The most basic difference between the Cadorna approach to the war and that of the younger general was the preference Diaz demonstrated for remaining on the defensive. On the Piave, he imitated France's General Pétain (*q.v.*) and constructed a defense in depth. He resisted the departure of his Anglo-French allies for the western front in the spring of 1918 and fended off the calls (from April onward) that came from General Foch (*q.v.*), the Allied commander in chief, for a large-scale Italian offensive. Diaz fully expected the war to last into 1919, and his preparation included a futile call (in August 1918) for twenty-five American divisions to help man the line in Italy.

In June the Austro-Hungarian armies launched a last gasp offensive against the Piave. It took Diaz more than a week to mop up the last enemy bridgeheads. Even then he continued to close his ears to Foch's calls for action. Nitti helped hold the government behind Diaz, but this grew harder by the week. In the fall, Allied armies were cutting forward everywhere: in France, in the Balkans, and in the Middle East. Foreign Minister Sidney Sonnino (*q.v.*) pointed with alarm to the dangers to come if Italian armies stood quietly on their own soil facing a shaken enemy; Rome's allies would have no reason to reward such a performance when it came time for dividing the territorial spoils of war.

A reluctant Diaz attacked in late October, pushing northward toward Feltre to split the enemy's army groups from each other while his main assault went to the northeast against Vittorio Veneto. Diaz encountered some resistance for a week; but by October 29 the Italians found themselves pursuing a routed enemy. By the end of the war, Italy's resurgent armies had driven nearly sixty miles into the enemy rear.

Diaz received a title of nobility (Duke of Victory) in 1921 to reward him for his services. He also remained on the scene to play a part in the early Fascist era. Openly sympathetic to Mussolini as a senior army commander during the 1922 "march on Rome," Diaz

was named minister of war in the first Fascist cabinet. He served from 1922 to 1924, when he retired with the rank of field marshal. He died in Rome, February 29, 1928.

Faldella, *La grande guerra*, 2 vols.; Falls, *The Battle of Caporetto*; Melograni, *Storia politica della grande guerra*; Seton-Watson, *Italy from Liberalism to Fascism*; Enciclopedia italiana, XII; *Larousse mensuel*, V.

DIMITRIJEVIĆ-APIS, Dragutin (*Serbia, Colonel*),

was born to an artisan family in Belgrade, August 17, 1876. He entered the Serbian Military Academy in 1892 and compiled a glittering academic record. Thus, in 1895, though only a newly commissioned lieutenant, he was assigned to the General Staff. His schoolmates had given him the nickname Apis. Some historians claim it means "bee" and refers to the young man's constant activity, but another view connects the nickname to the ancient Egyptians' sacred bull, a symbol of strength.

The brilliant and admired officer quickly immersed himself in conspiratorial politics and assassination plots. He drafted a crude plan to murder Serbia's unpopular Austrophile King Alexander Obrenović. It failed. But Dimitrijević's tireless efforts led to grisly success in the military coup of 1903. Captain Dimitrijević then spent a decade in a series of field and staff positions, broken by a term of language study in Berlin, 1906/1907. From 1910 onward, he was a popular and influential teacher at the Belgrade Military Academy. His calls for military reform and the lasting influence his role in 1903 had given him made Dimitrijević appear to many as Serbia's invisible war minister.

Desire for military reform was only one of many interests for Dimitrijević-Apis. He also eyed Serbian expansion: a "Greater Serbia" was to be formed by slicing away at least the Serb-inhabited southern regions of Austria-Hungary and placing them under the Karadjordjević crown. In 1911 Apis organized the Black Hand. This tightly knit conspiratorial network was hidden from public view by being placed within a larger and open patriotic society, the *Narodna Odbrana* (National Defense).

Just before the First Balkan War, Apis undertook a reconnaissance mission behind the Turkish lines. This adventure into Albania set the stage for subsequent Serbian military successes. But Apis could play no role in the fighting, for while inside Albania he had contracted a serious illness that disabled him for months. In mid-1913, however, Colonel Apis was made chief of Serbian military intelligence.

In Remak's startling phrase, Dimitrijević was by now "the foremost European expert in regicide of his time." Although his exact role in the Sarajevo assassination remains a source of controversy, Apis clearly sought to promote Serbian expansion via expedient political murders. In early years, he had targeted Tsar Ferdinand of Bulgaria and Austria-Hungary's Emperor Francis Joseph (qq.v.) for assassination. The *Narodna Odbrana* and the Serbian military intelligence network were useful, if unconscious, allies for Apis and the Black Hand. Remak sees Apis as the author of the successful plot to kill Archduke Francis Ferdinand (q.v.). In Dedijer's divergent view, young Bosnian students like Gavrilo Princip (q.v.) moved the plot from inception to bloody climax with only incidental help from Apis.

Other loose threads in the story include the possible complicity of the Serbian royal family and the Serbian cabinet under Premier Nikola Pašić (q.v.). The weight of recent accounts—Remak, Jelavich, Petrovich—discounts the possibility that Apis acted in tandem with Pašić in murdering the archduke. The complicity of Russia's military attaché in Belgrade, and perhaps more weighty Russian figures in St. Petersburg, surfaces in some accounts. While access to relevant Russian and Serbian archives is closed, that line of inquiry must remain unresolved.

If Apis did plan and help implement the Sarajevo murders, the ensuing European conflagration destroyed his hopes for Serbian expansion at tolerable cost. His own career skidded downhill. The powerful colonel was removed as chief of intelligence; he served out his remaining period on active duty in the field, as a senior staff officer. With the rest of the army, he marched over the mountains to the Adriatic, rested on Corfu, and returned to action in Salonika.

In December 1916, Apis and his lieutenants were arrested by Serbian civil authorities. Charged with plotting against the Karadjordjević dynasty and with contacting the enemy, the flamboyant colonel was tried, then executed at Salonika on June 26, 1917. The mystery surrounding the Sarajevo plot is matched by, and perhaps linked to, the mystery involving Apis' arrest and execution. In late 1916, Habsburg authorities were exploring chances for a negotiated peace; some historians hold that Apis' murder was a sop to Vienna, a precondition for an Austro-Serbian settlement. Others raise the possibility that Prince Regent Alexander (q.v.) silenced Apis before the colonel could tie the crown to the Sarajevo bloodshed. Perhaps the most plausible explanation finds Alexander, then on the verge of reentering Serbian territory and no longer able to find political support in tsarist Russia, determined to extirpate independent circles in the army. These, after all, had

seemed to many Serbian leaders to form "a state within a state," harassing civil authority since 1903.

Remak has presented a useful summation of Dimitrijević-Apis' historical role: "personal magnetism, great intelligence, and utter discretion" made him a master conspirator and a figure of lasting importance. But his single-minded concern with forming a "Greater Serbia" and his ignorance of the larger stage on which he mounted his plots led Serbia and Europe to the brink of catastrophe, and beyond.

Albertini, *The Origins of the War of 1914*, II; Dedijer, *Road to Sarajevo*; Jelavich and Jelavich, *Establishment of the Balkan National States*; Palmer, *Gardeners of Salonika*; Petrovich, *History of Modern Serbia*, II; Remak, *Sarajevo*; Vucinich, *Serbia between East and West*; *Enciklopedija Jugoslavije*, II.

DJAVID BEY, Mehmed (1875-1926). See CAVID BEY, Mehmed.

DJEMAL PAŞA, Ahmed (1872-1922). See CEMAL PAŞA, Ahmed.

DRUM, Hugh Aloysius (*United States, General*), was born at Fort Brady, Michigan, on September 19, 1879, the son of an army career officer. Drum's father, a captain in the regular army, was one of the few American officers killed in action during the Spanish-American War; his son Hugh, then attending Boston College, was commissioned a second lieutenant by President McKinley in tribute to the father's sacrifice for the nation. Hugh Drum was a man of boundless ambition, a hard-driving superior; physically he was a short man with a hawklike nose. From 1910 to 1912 Drum attended the Army School of the Line and Staff College at Fort Leavenworth, Kansas, where many of the future generals of the Great War were to get much-needed tactical instruction. In 1914 Drum was assigned to the staff of the Veracruz expedition sent by President Wilson (q.v.) to avenge what he considered to have been Mexican violation of American sovereignty when they arrested several sailors of Rear Admiral Mayo's (q.v.) force at Tampico.

General Pershing (q.v.), the American field commander in France, appointed Colonel Drum to be one of the original staff officers for the American Expeditionary Forces destined for France in May 1917. Within the Operations Division of general headquarters, Drum assisted in all stages of planning, including the designation of French ports for troop debarkation, the logistics of supplies, the organization of combat units, and the rate of American troop arrivals in France. Drum was also deeply involved in the decision that the reduction of the 200-square mile St. Mihiel salient should be the major American war effort in 1918 and that it be conducted with overwhelming forces so that the first major American military action would unquestioningly be a successful one.

Pershing was impressed with Drum's efficient handling of staff matters and recognized Drummie's unbridled ambitions when he appointed him chief of staff of the newly formed American First Army on July 15, 1918. In this capacity Drum selected staff officers, worked out the First Army's organization, coordinated planning for its supply, transportation, and tactical deployment during the offensives that reduced the St. Mihiel salient as well as the subsequent thrust into the Meuse-Argonne sector. Douglas MacArthur later claimed that Drum virtually ran the army in France.

After the war, Drum fought to maintain army control over aviation and basically questioned the efficacy of air power. By 1939 he was in line to replace General Craig as chief of staff, but Drummie promoted his own cause so vigorously that the post went instead to General George C. Marshall. During the Second World War, Drum expected to become the "Pershing of World War II," but only managed to alienate both President Roosevelt (q.v.) and Secretary of War Stimson over their China policy, with the result that Drum was forced into mandatory retirement in September 1943. He died on October 3, 1951, in New York City.

Coffman, *War to End All Wars*; *Dictionary of American Biography*, XXV, Supplement Five.

DUBAIL, Auguste Yvon Edmond (*France, General*), was born in Belfort on April 15, 1851. He entered St. Cyr in 1868, fought in the Franco-Prussian War, then took part in the suppression of the Paris Commune. A graduate of the War College in 1878, Dubail held a series of choice staff and line posts that indicated he had been singled out for high responsibilities in the future. An aide to the minister of war from 1883 to 1887, then an instructor at St. Cyr, Dubail advanced rapidly to a colonel's rank and command of a regiment by 1901. Three years later he was a major general. He commanded at St. Cyr (1905-1908), led the Fourteenth Division at Belfort for three years until, in 1911, he was chosen to be the army's new chief of staff. Dubail's rapid rise owed much to his acknowledged energy and military skill; but it did not hurt him to be identified as a loyal republican in a largely conservative officer corps.

The Agadir crisis of 1911 dominated the months after Dubail took his new position. He played a ma-

jor role in solidifying France's military ties with its future wartime allies. After his discussions with the British in July, the size, shipment schedule, and continental zone of concentration for the British Expeditionary Force were specified. In August Dubail's mission to Russia led to a specific Russian timetable for an offensive against Germany in the event France faced attack from its hostile neighbor to the east. In 1912 Dubail took over the IX Corps at Tours and became a member of the Supreme War Council. His post of chief of staff had been largely superceded by the new position of chief of the General Staff given to General Joffre (q.v.).

In August 1914, Dubail led the First Army in its offensive toward Sarrebourg. He fell back on August 20 in the face of the German counteroffensive in Alsace-Lorraine. In contrast to General de Castelnau's (q.v.) leadership of the Second Army on his left, Dubail retreated reluctantly and in good order, taking up a defensive position behind the Meurthe River. There he held the eastern anchor of the French line during the battle of the Marne in early September, meanwhile sending much of his fighting strength by rail to reinforce the armies near Paris. By the close of the year, Dubail commanded the largest sector on the western front, stretching from Belfort to Verdun. Joffre drew freely on this relatively silent sector for reinforcements. Meanwhile Dubail, a general out of Joffre's own mold, conducted vigorous local attacks and counterattacks. In January 1915, Dubail formally took command of the Eastern Army Group, a role he had in fact held since September 1914.

Dubail never implemented his plans for large-scale offensive operations on his sector in 1915. Joffre continually drew both men and ammunition from the Eastern Army Group for the spring offensive in Artois and subsequent operations in Champagne. Dubail continued with local attacks and sometimes found himself the target of similar thrusts by the enemy. In July one of these German advances struck the French Third Army commanded by General Sarrail (q.v.) in the Argonne. Joffre named Dubail to investigate the affair, in which the French had been surprised and then suffered heavy losses. The commander in chief strongly intimated that he expected Dubail to recommend that Sarrail be severely punished. Joffre clearly hoped Dubail's reputation as a republican would shield the High Command from charges of taking political reprisals against the equally republican Sarrail. Dubail tried to placate both sides in the dispute. His report characterized Sarrail as a good officer with some poor qualities, and he recommended that Sarrail be transferred, not cashiered. Joffre responded by firing Sarrail, who was rescued in turn by his circle of political allies.

During 1915 Dubail strongly advanced the idea that Russian troops be brought in to fight on French territory. His own role as supplier of manpower to more active fronts convinced him that only such drastic measures could fill the gaps incurred by France's growing battle losses. By early 1916 the first Russian brigade was on its way.

Dubail's reputation was broken by the Verdun debacle. As early as July 1915, he had officially described the Verdun defenses as adequate when questioned by members of the National Assembly. The following month, his instructions to the Verdun commander specified that no siege was expected and none could be permitted. Verdun, he said, must be defended by the use of mobile forces. Like Joffre and the commander in chief's staff, Dubail considered such fortresses to be outdated. But even Dubail grew alarmed during the fall of 1915 when Joffre stripped Verdun of both artillery and machine guns to support offensives to the west. As artillery duels and German transport activity sounded louder and louder in November/December, Dubail warned Joffre with increasing urgency.

In mid-January, Dubail protested the commander in chief's plan to shift Verdun from the Eastern to the Central Army Group. An attack was imminent and the change, logical on paper, was completely ill-timed. Joffre rejected the advice.

Dubail played his usual subsidiary role in the aftermath of the German attack. His front yielded the first reserves for Verdun while the Eastern Group commander himself languished in enforced idleness. In late March, Joffre fired Dubail, making him the highest ranking member of the circle of generals ousted following the attack on Verdun. Dubail was not shunted aside completely; he received the post of military governor of Paris, which he held for the remainder of the war. He took the rear area job with bitterness, seeing himself as a scapegoat for Joffre, whom the politicians could not yet find the courage to oust. Moreover, the purge was conducted by General Roques (q.v.), Joffre's hand-picked candidate for war minister. (Roques had served with a conspicuous lack of distinction as one of Dubail's army commanders since early 1915.)

Dubail was active as an official of the Legion of Honor after the war. He died in Paris on January 7, 1934.

Contamine, *La Revanche*; Dubail, *Quatre années de commandement*; Horne, *Price of Glory: Verdun*; King, *Generals and Politicians*; Ralston, *The Army of the Republic*; Tanenbaum, *General Maurice Sarrail*; Williamson, *The Politics of Grand Strategy*; *Dictionnaire de biographie française*, XI; *Larousse mensuel*, IX.

DUKHONIN, Nikolai Nikolaevich (*Russia, Lieutenant General*), was born December 13, 1876. He received his commission after graduating from the Aleksandrovsky Military College in 1896. He completed the course at the Russian General Staff Academy in 1902, and served as an intelligence officer in the years before World War I.

Following the outbreak of hostilities in 1914, Dukhonin rose rapidly. After commanding a regiment, he returned to staff positions. By the summer of 1916, having been promoted general, he served as deputy chief of staff for the southwestern front. In August 1917, he took over as chief of staff for this portion of the Russian defense perimeter. The course of the Russian Revolution, however, elevated Dukhonin to a short-lived national prominence in the fall of 1917.

The forty-one-year-old general accepted the post of chief of staff for the entire Russian army in late September. With Aleksandr Kerensky (q.v.), the nominal commander in chief, Dukhonin stood as the effective head of the Russian army as it entered the final months of its role in World War I. Mayzel finds Dukhonin a representative of the moderate Left segment of the officer corps, especially of the elite General Staff graduates. Hoping at once to preserve the army's fighting abilities and to continue the war against the Central Powers, Dukhonin also wished to come to some accord with the revolution and its demand for democratization and reform of the military system.

The army, of course, was already changing no matter what Dukhonin chose to do. It was shrinking for one thing—partly through deliberate demobilization, more through widespread desertion. The entire basis of military service was being altered by the government. Voluntary service was becoming the norm; and the army was being reorganized into ethnically homogeneous units.

When the ultimate crisis came in early November, Dukhonin was totally in the dark. On November 5 Kerensky did not call on Dukhonin, but rather appealed to individual army commanders to come to his aid in Petrograd, where a Bolshevik move was imminent. After Lenin (q.v.) and his followers had seized power, Dukhonin called on the rank and file to stand loyal to the provisional government. His words had no effect.

The bewildered young general managed to retain the appearance of authority for a few weeks. On

November 14 he took over as commander in chief, replacing Kerensky. He avoided a direct challenge to the Bolsheviks and ordered his troops to stand fast. No more military attempts were to be made to reverse the Bolshevik Revolution, like the November 12 Kerensky-Krasnov march on Petrograd that had ended in military failure at Pulkovo, just south of Petrograd. Dukhonin could hardly have failed to realize that his troops paid little attention to anything he said.

On November 21 events reached the flashpoint. Lenin ordered Dukhonin to open truce talks with the enemy at once. The general stalled for a day. His senior officers were willing to support his refusal to obey, but the rank and file of the army was certain to explode in response to such a move. On November 22 Dukhonin received word from the new Bolshevik government that he was no longer in command.

It took over a week before Dukhonin's replacement could make his way to Mogilev. Ensign Krylenko took over as commander in chief of the Russian army. In his final hours of power, Dukhonin had permitted the release of five prominent generals held in loose custody since September. These leaders of the political Right had participated in the Kornilov (*q.v.*) coup—and they included Kornilov himself. Krylenko's entourage of revolutionary soldiers grew enraged at this news. Shortly after their arrival at Dukhonin's command post on December 3, they slipped out of Krylenko's control and murdered Dukhonin.

Kenez, *Civil War in South Russia, 1918*; Mayzel, *Generals and Revolutionaries*; *Modern Encyclopedia of Russian and Soviet History*, X; *Sovetskaia istoricheskaia entsiklopediia*, V; *Sovetskaia voennaia entsiklopediia*, III.

EBERGARD, Andrei Avgustovich (1856-1919). See EBERHARDT, Andrei Avgustovich.

EBERHARDT, Andrei Avgustovich (*Russia, Admiral*), was born on the Greek island of Patras, in November 1856, the son of a Russian diplomat of Swedish extraction. Choosing a career as a naval officer, Eberhardt completed the Naval College in St. Petersburg in 1878 and was commissioned a midshipman. The young officer saw extensive sea duty over the next twenty-five years, mainly with the Russian Pacific Fleet; he advanced to the rank of captain in 1902. In 1896-1898 Eberhardt took a break from service at sea to serve as naval attaché in Constantinople. He commanded a battleship and held a series of senior staff positions in the Far East during the Russo-Japanese War, 1904/1905. In the era of postwar reform and reconstruction, Eberhardt rose to the

peak of his profession, becoming deputy commander of the newly formed Naval General Staff in 1906. He took command of this important planning body in 1908 and remained until 1911 when he received charge of the Black Sea Fleet. Promoted rear admiral in 1907, Eberhardt rose to vice admiral two years later, and was named admiral in 1913.

Eberhardt's three years of peacetime service at the head of the Black Sea navy were colored by the rapid expansion of Turkish seapower. Russia's likely opponent in any future war in this area had purchased dreadnought battleships from Britain, and these were due to be completed in the summer of 1914. Eberhardt could not expect comparable vessels in his fleet until 1915. Moreover, the Turks were angling to buy up additional dreadnoughts, on order for various Latin American countries, in Britain and the United States. Another danger existed within the Russian fleet, illustrated by a mutiny that disturbed Eberhardt's crews in the summer of 1912. In the face of such problems, Eberhardt gained substantial success in training officers and crews. In late 1913 he accepted, with reluctance, a government plan establishing a defensive role for his fleet in a future war.

Russia's entry into a state of hostilities with the Central Powers left Eberhardt's fleet in limbo. The *Goeben* and *Breslau*, powerful German cruisers under Admiral Souchon (*q.v.*), reached Turkish waters at the outset of the war. But Russia and Turkey remained, technically, at peace. Foreign Minister Sazonov (*q.v.*) refused Eberhardt's request to be allowed to treat Souchon's war vessels, probing the Black Sea behind the shield of the Turkish flag, as fair prey. To compound the confusion, Eberhardt was burdened with contradictory instructions in the event of hostilities; told to protect Russia's Black Sea ports, he also had the chore of supporting Russian armies in the Caucasus by blocking Turkey's sea lanes. The *Goeben*'s ability to outrun and outgun any single vessel under Eberhardt's orders compounded the difficulties.

When Souchon shelled Odessa and Sevastopol in late October, Eberhardt was free to go into action. He proved himself more aggressive than his superiors. In late December 1914, the Russians drew blood. The *Goeben* struck a Russian mine near the Bosphorus with the result that the chief enemy threat in the Black Sea was crippled for months. But Eberhardt was required to use most of his limited store of mines to set up defensive fields to protect Black Sea ports. The shortage of mines plus the difficulty of laying them from destroyers in hostile waters continually frustrated Eberhardt's taste for bringing the war to the enemy.

In 1915 the Russian admiral was presented with a slightly wider field of action. With his ports now secured, Eberhardt was able to get the High Command to sanction offensive action: demonstrations to support the Anglo-French attack on the Dardanelles, action to cut the coastal coaling traffic vital to the Turkish capital, efforts to block passage of seaborne supplies to Turkey's armies in the Caucasus. Again, Eberhardt made his weight felt: summer 1915 saw Constantinople struggling with a severe coal shortage. The arrival of two Russian dreadnoughts, one in July, a second in October, seemed to tip the naval balance to the Russian side. But the appearance of German submarines in the Black Sea partly nullified this advantage. With Bulgaria fighting alongside the Central Powers, German submarines could dominate the western shores of the Black Sea.

Eberhardt did not get another chance. Short of destroyers and obligated to aid the Caucasus campaign in 1916 with amphibious operations, he failed to meet the submarine threat. He was also unable to cut off completely the important coastal routes to Constantinople. In late June the speedy German cruisers slipped through the Russian naval screen and shelled Sochi and Tuapse on the eastern coast of the Black Sea. Talk of replacing Eberhardt with a younger and more aggressive leader, heard for some months in the Russian capital and at Supreme Headquarters, was then transformed into action. Admiral Kolchak (q.v.), the rising star of the Baltic Fleet mining operations, replaced Eberhardt in July 1916. The old admiral was given the usual consolation prize of membership in the State Council. He was arrested briefly in 1918 and died in Petrograd, April 19, 1919.

Clearly an able and aggressive, if not especially imaginative, commander, he had had the misfortune to hold the Black Sea post when his forces were, at best, on a par with those of the enemy. Meanwhile, Eberhardt was loaded down with a multitude of difficult and overlapping tasks. Mitchell has called Eberhardt's displacement by Kolchak, an admiral for only two months, "highly questionable"; but it seems unlikely that Eberhardt could have mustered the energy and innovations that Kolchak brought to the Black Sea command.

Chirikov, "Admiral A. A. Ebergard"; Halpern, *Mediterranean Naval Situation, 1908-1914*; Mitchell, *History of Russian and Soviet Sea Power*; Pavlovich, ed., *The Fleet in the First World War*, I.

EBERT, Friedrich (*Germany, Politician*), was born in Heidelberg on February 4, 1871, the son of a Catholic tailor. Ebert learned the saddler's trade and in 1891 settled in Bremen; two years later he became an innkeeper as well as editor of a Social Democratic (SPD) newspaper. By the turn of the century, Ebert had entered the Bremen city assembly and become deeply embroiled in party politics in the Hanse city. No Marxist theoretician, he worked his way up in the bureaucracy and in 1905 moved to Berlin as party secretary. In 1912 Ebert entered the Reichstag and as early as September 1913 was elected successor to the venerable August Bebel. Throughout his career Ebert had shunned the radicalism of the party's left wing and had sought close ties to the trade union movement. He basically endorsed the Bismarckian state and repudiated the notion that the general strike was the workers' most potent weapon in the struggle against autocratic regime and capitalist industry.

The Great War only strengthened Ebert's patriotism. During the July crisis in 1914 he had been on holidays, and along with Otto Braun took the party's treasury to Zurich early in August for fear that the government might proscribe the SPD in time of national emergency. When this fear proved groundless, Ebert returned to Berlin on August 6—two days after the SPD had unanimously voted for war credits. Ebert shared the chairmanship of the party with Hugo Haase but left its tactics in the hands of the energetic Philipp Scheidemann (qq.v.). His position within the SPD was enhanced in December 1915 when Haase resigned as cochairman owing to the SPD's continued support of the war; Ebert, for his part, stressed that the SPD present a united front in the Reichstag, but this Lassallean tack failed in March 1916 when Haase and others voted against war credits. At Easter 1917 the Haase-led minority at Gotha convened a new party, the Independent Social Democrats (USPD).

Ebert spoke out against annexations and indemnities, but he staunchly defended the territorial integrity of the Reich, including Alsace-Lorraine, as well as the duty of every German to defend it; two of his sons died in the Great War. Deprived of the support of the USPD, Ebert moved closer to an alliance with the Progressives and the Center, forming in the process the so-called parliamentary majority bent on reform of the outdated Prussian three-class suffrage. In July 1917, he was instrumental in formulating the Reichstag's "peace resolution," which called for an end to the war on the basis of the *status quo ante bellum*. But when Chancellor Georg Michaelis (q.v.) refused to implement it and instead singled out the USPD for attack on the issue of the fleet rebellion, Ebert on October 9 led the successful assault against the former Prussian bureaucrat. Early in 1918 Ebert opposed the projected strikes in munitions plants, but when overruled by party radicals, he bowed to the will of the majority and placed himself at the head of the strike movement.

In October 1918, Ebert persuaded his colleagues to participate in the government of Prince Max von Baden (*q.v.*), and on November 9 the South German handed Ebert the reins of power after the kaiser's abdication and flight to Holland. After half a century in opposition, the erstwhile *Reichsfeinde* assumed command of the Bismarckian state. Unfortunately, Ebert was unprepared to meet the challenge. He was appalled when Scheidemann on November 9 proclaimed a republic and instead quickly reached a verbal understanding with General Wilhelm Groener (*q.v.*) to undertake no major reform of the Prussian/German military system, lamely arguing that the time was not ripe for revolution.

On November 10, 1918, Ebert and Haase cochaired the Council of People's Commissars in Berlin; in mid-December Ebert was presented by the First German Congress of Soldiers' and Workers' Councils with a clear mandate to call a constituent national assembly, to reform the officer corps, and to nationalize major industries. Ebert chose to ignore the latter two decisions. Moreover, late in 1918 and early in 1919 he empowered Gustav Noske (*q.v.*) to hurl regular army units against rebellious sailors and workers in Berlin; Haase quit the council over this brutal suppression of the revolution.

Friedrich Ebert was elected first president of the republic in Weimar on February 11, 1919; the Reichstag, in October 1922, extended his term to June 1925. Ebert served in this capacity with dignity and honor. In March 1920, he maintained order and calm during the reactionary Kapp *Putsch*, repeating this in the fall of 1923 as Communist revolts rocked Saxony and Thuringia, the French invaded the Ruhr, and the National Socialists attempted a coup in Munich. Ebert did not shy away from using Article 48 to declare a state of national emergency. His refusal to reform the officer corps in November 1918, however, returned to haunt him: General Hans von Seeckt (*q.v.*) placed himself and the army above the state and refused, as during the Kapp affair, to move against right-wing rebels. In 1924 reactionary fanatics inflicted upon the president of the republic a formal trial at Magdeburg for his participation in the munitions strikes early in 1918; although Ebert won a formal acquittal, the audacity of the legal proceedings deeply shook him and tarnished the reputation of his office. Ebert died in Berlin on February 28, 1925, as a result of an appendix operation.

Ebert obviously was not destined to become the Lenin (*q.v.*) of the German revolution. A party bureaucrat without intellectual ambitions, he had steered a middle course between Marxism and revisionism, between the trade union movement and party radicals. The events of August 1914 revealed him as a nationalist, of November 1918 as a constitutional monarchist; in the former crisis he feared the spread of tsarism, in the latter the dictatorship of the proletariat. His fateful pact with Groener and the resulting failure to enact his party's reform platform of December 1918 weighed heavily upon future developments in Germany. His eldest living son after the Second World War became a leading figure in the Communist state in East Germany.

Ebert, *Schriften, Aufzeichnungen, Reden*, 2 vols.; Groh, *Negative Integration*; Kotowski, *Friedrich Ebert*, I; Ritter and Miller, *Die deutsche Revolution*; *Neue Deutsche Biographie*, IV.

EICHHORN, Hermann von (*Germany, Field Marshal*), was born in Breslau on February 13, 1848, grandson of a Prussian minister of culture and of the philosopher Friedrich Wilhelm Schelling; his father was ennobled in 1856. Eichhorn participated in the wars of 1866 and 1870/1871, attended the War Academy, and in 1883 entered the General Staff. He was promoted major general in 1897 and lieutenant general four years later as divisional commander; in 1904 he was appointed head of the XVIII Army Corps at Frankfurt and the following year promoted general of infantry. Eichhorn became inspector general of the VII Army Inspectorate at Saarbrücken in 1912, and the next year was promoted colonel general. In case of mobilization, Eichhorn had been designated commander of the Fifth Army at Metz, but a serious equestrian injury in 1914 precluded his deployment in this capacity.

On January 26, 1915, Eichhorn was declared fit for duty and took part in the battle of Soissons; thereafter he assumed command of a new Tenth Army in East Prussia. He led this force against the Russian Tenth Army on February 8 during the winter battle of the Masurian Lakes, which ended fourteen days later with a severe rout of the Russians in the Augustov forest. In August 1915, Eichhorn stormed the fortress Kovno, for which he received the order *Pour le mérite*, and in September captured Vilna, which his Tenth Army held in bitter fighting in March and April 1916.

On July 30, 1916, the new Army Group Eichhorn was formed, consisting of the German Eighth and Tenth Armies in Courland and Lithuania. By October its commander had seized Riga and, in conjunction with the navy, had occupied the Baltic Sea islands of Ösel, Moon, and Dagö, and in December 1917 was promoted field marshal.

The year 1918 began with the occupation of Latvia and Estonia, but on March 4 Eichhorn was relieved of command of the Tenth Army as the Bolsheviks accepted German terms at Brest-Litovsk. Instead, on March 31 the field marshal was appointed head of a new army group bearing his name for the occupation of the Ukraine and the Crimea, with headquarters at Kiev. Eichhorn hoped to exploit the grain riches of the region and generally sought to circumvent the Foreign Office in this matter. "There is only one good side to the situation in the Ukraine: a firm hand by the military works wonders; there is only one diplomatic method that works: the use of money." Thus by a combination of force and bribery, the commander in time dissolved the local *Rada* ("council"), persuaded landowners to sow their crops, and appointed General Pavlo Skoropadsky *hetman*, or ruler of the Ukraine. Eichhorn was partly successful in his endeavors owing to the brilliant use of field railways made by General Wilhelm Groener (*q.v.*), his chief of staff, but in the end his harsh measures only served to drive the Ukrainians back into the arms of Russia. On July 30, 1918, the "uncrowned king of the Ukraine" was murdered by a left-wing social revolutionary in a hazy attempt to force the Bolsheviks to abandon their tenuous cooperation with the Germans.

The field marshal's remains were interned next to those of Count Alfred von Schlieffen in Berlin. Among his staff officers, Eichhorn had enjoyed the reputation of being a highly educated and cultured gentleman as well as a dashing military figure.

Baumgart, *Deutsche Ostpolitik*; Kitchen, *Silent Dictatorship*; *Geschichte der Ritter des Ordens*, I; *Neue Deutsche Biographie*, IV.

EINEM, Karl von (*Germany, General*), popularly known as Einem von Rothmaler, was born in Herzberg/Harz on January 1, 1853, to a patrician clan from Lower Saxony; his father had served as a Hanoverian army officer. Einem fought in the Franco-Prussian War, entered the General Staff in 1880 without having attended the War Academy, and was promoted captain there two years later. In 1898 he joined the Prussian War Ministry; five years later he was promoted lieutenant general and appointed Prussian war minister. As such Einem devoted his special attention not to the quantitative expansion of the army, but to the technical and tactical modernization of this force. In particular, he upgraded the field artillery and introduced the machine gun as well as the field gray uniform. Einem feared not only the escalating costs of the navy

budget, but also that any rapid expansion of the army would entail serious social and political repercussions as it would require the recruitment of officers from lower middle-class families. Einem was promoted general of cavalry in 1907; two years later he was appointed commander of the VII Army Corps at Münster.

General von Einem led the VII Corps into the Great War as part of General Karl von Bülow's (*q.v.*) Second Army. Most notably, the VII Corps on August 16 stormed the fortress of Liège, crossed the Sambre River one week later, and stood on Bülow's right wing in the ensuing victory at St. Quentin. During the critical days between September 5 and 9, Einem's units formed Bülow's right wing at the Marne and as such took part in the general retreat behind the Aisne River.

Einem was given command of the Third Army in the Champagne on September 12, 1914—a post that he held to war's end. Promoted colonel general in January 1915, Einem in February and March of that year between Reims and the Argonne fought the so-called winter battle of the Champagne. In September 1915, he was hard pressed again by fifty-two French divisions, but managed to repulse the attack and to inflict 100,000 casualties on the enemy. General Robert Nivelle's (*q.v.*) spurious offensive in April 1917 caught part of the Third Army, but Einem's forces again held the line. On July 15, 1918, after the great Michael assault in the west had failed to turn the tide, Einem's twelve divisions were ordered to attack the enemy on both sides of Reims, advancing as far as Souain and Aubérive before being driven back by the Allies. A Franco-American assault broke against the Third Army on September 26, and by October 9 Einem had retreated to positions behind the Aisne River, to the Hunding-Brunhilde sector of the Hindenburg line. Early in November he was forced to retire as far as the Antwerp-Meuse River line.

On November 12, 1918, Einem was entrusted with command of the erstwhile Army Group Crown Prince Wilhelm (*q.v.*), and he led this force home before his retirement in January 1919. General von Einem died in Mühlheim/Ruhr on April 7, 1934. Throughout his life he had enjoyed the reputation of being a completely independent military as well as political thinker. Indeed, as war minister the Hanoverian had audaciously suggested that Count von Schlieffen was not immortal; worse, that his blueprint for victory was in error.

Einem, *Ein Armeeführer erlebt den Weltkrieg* and *Erinnerungen eines Soldaten*; *Geschichte der Ritter des Ordens*, I; *Neue Deutsche Biographie*, IV.

ENVER PAŞA (*Turkey, General, Minister of War*), was born in Constantinople, November 22, 1881. Enver's father, a minor civil servant, brought the family back to his home city of Monastir in Turkish Macedonia. After completing his military training with distinction in the Ottoman capital, Enver returned to Macedonia in 1902. For three years he campaigned against local guerrilla bands. In 1906, as a young major, he was assigned to the headquarters of the politically turbulent Third Army at Monastir. Enver joined the revolutionary Young Turk movement. Two years later, on the verge of being arrested as a political criminal, he fled to the local mountains, and set off the insurgency that developed into the Young Turk Revolution of 1908.

Despite a wealth of political opportunity, Enver chose to continue with his military career. He went to Berlin as a military attaché, returning briefly to help defeat the counterrevolutionary movement of 1909. In 1911/1912 he distinguished himself in Turkey's war against Italy. The Italians drove him out of Benghazi where he commanded the local garrison, but Enver countered with a successful resistance movement in the Libyan hinterland.

During the Balkan Wars of 1912/1913 Enver rose to lasting national prominence. When the Turkish cabinet in January 1913 considered ending hostilities in the face of repeated military disasters, Enver led a small raiding party that ousted the government on January 23 and pushed the war forward. This set in motion the establishment of a full-fledged dictatorship under the Young Turks. In July 1913, during the Second Balkan War, Enver directed the advance that recaptured the Turkish stronghold of Adrianople. Promoted brigadier general, in January 1914 he took the cabinet post of war minister from the hands of Izzet Paşa (*q.v.*). His marriage to the niece of the reigning sultan added to Enver's potent ability to shape Ottoman policy.

The view that Enver along with Tâlat and Cemal Paşas (*qq.v.*) constituted a triumvirate dominating the Young Turks and controlling the Turkish government no longer commands scholarly agreement. Enver, however, enjoyed very substantial influence in Ottoman affairs. The youthful war minister helped bring Ottoman Turkey into World War I and then directed the course of his country's military policy. Although widely viewed by contemporaries and historians alike as Germany's firmest supporter among the Young Turks, Enver generally put Turkish interests first. A military planner on a grandiose scale (perhaps given confidence by his successes in smaller wars against weaker opponents) his campaign schemes turned out to be widely impractical.

His driving desire was to create a new Turkish empire based on ethnic solidarity and stretching from the Bosphorus through the Caucasus into Russian Central Asia.

In late July 1914, Enver negotiated a defensive alliance with the Central Powers almost singlehandedly. The possibility that Turkey might suffer territorial losses beyond those of 1908/1913 made it imperative to have the support of some of the Great Powers at a time of a continental war. Given Russia's designs on Turkish territory, an approach to Berlin seemed the logical option. Enver's admiration for German military power reinforced that choice.

Bringing Turkey into the hostilities required three more months. Enver's personal order allowed the German war vessels *Goeben* and *Breslau*, under the command of Admiral Souchon (*q.v.*), to enter Turkish waters on August 10/11. It was a dramatic step toward war. But other Young Turk leaders, notably Talât and Cemal Paşas, held Enver back until the close of October.

With Turkey in the conflict, Enver played a paramount role in deciding Turkish strategy. His imperial dreams required an offensive into the Caucasus, followed by a thrust eastward to the Turkish populations of Central Asia. The war minister took personal command of the Third Army facing the Russians in the Caucasus. The prospect of a sweeping advance over mountainous terrain in the dead of winter would no doubt have terrified most World War I generals. And with good reason. His attempt to outflank the Russians in December 1914/January 1915 led to the disaster of Sarikamish. Faced with able opponents like General Yudenich (*q.v.*), Enver suffered calamitous losses and exposed eastern Anatolia to the Russians.

Turkish concern over the threat to eastern Anatolia led to the controversial policy of removing the Armenian population from this region. The diffusion of authority among the Young Turk leaders has made it difficult to establish the precise responsibility for the decision—and for the savage manner in which it was implemented. The weight of Western scholarly opinion considers the deportations a form of genocide, unwarranted by military necessity. Enver and Talât are generally held to be the culprits. An important minority view, however, has come from Stanford Shaw. He points first to the serious military threat posed by Armenian subversion. Moreover, he denies that any massacre took place.

New indications that Enver's strategic ambitions outran his talents came in 1916. Word of Yudenich's capture of the stronghold at Erzurum led to more grandiose plans. Enver called for a combined offensive by two Turkish armies against the western and southern flanks of Yudenich's newly won salient. What seemed possible on Enver's maps collided with impossible realities. The terrain, the weather, and the Russian's countermoves smashed Enver's hopes. By September the Turkish army facing Yudenich from the west had been shattered; the southern force had been stopped dead in its tracks.

In March 1917, Baghdad fell to British troops led by General Maude (*q.v.*). Enver's active imagination produced the design for a bold counteroffensive. Troops from Syria and eastern Anatolia were to form a special army for the *Yilderim* ("Lightning") project—a Turkish riposte to retake the ancient city. The hard facts of geography and logistics halted the operation. No way existed to get these forces anywhere near Baghdad or, once there, to supply them. But the operation's preparatory stages served to disrupt the Turkish defense of Palestine. The other major event of 1917 shaping Turkey's war effort was the March Revolution in Russia. Enver saw it as an occasion for building the new empire: Russia's dying military machine could no longer halt Turkish ambitions.

Enver's call for shifting the war's weight to the Caucasus disturbed his Young Turk comrades. Talât for one objected strongly, but to no avail. Enver, the incompetent general, displayed by this move a parallel ineptitude as a diplomat. A thrust eastward in the political and strategic currents of 1917 meant a challenge to Berlin—this at a time when Germany was Turkey's economic lifeline. Enver had offered Turkish troops for German use in Europe in 1916; alone among the Young Turk hierarchy, he was conciliatory on economic concessions to Berlin; and in early 1917 he led the successful move to break relations with the United States. This pro-German orientation he suddenly abandoned.

In early 1918 Turkish forces trekked eastward. During March Enver's legions passed over the 1914 border with Russia; by May, they were threatening the circle of German satellite states and economic spheres set up in Transcaucasia by the Treaty of Brest-Litovsk. To make matters worse, the Turkish units that Germany needed to parry General Allenby's (*q.v.*) offensive in Palestine left instead for the Caucasus. New massacres of Armenians darkened Turkey's reputation, as Enver's forces entered Russian Armenia. By the fall of 1918 Enver's Caucasian ambitions had strained the alliance with Berlin to the point of collapse.

Turkish defeats in the south—Damascus fell on October 1 and Allenby's cavalry rode hard for Aleppo—led to the resignation of the Young Turk cabinet in mid-October. Enver and most of his colleagues left

their country with German assistance in early November. The remaining years of Enver's life were spent in colorful, but still shadowy, adventures in European and Near Eastern diplomacy. He attempted to serve as a go-between in dealings linking Soviet Russia and postwar Germany. He had hopes of returning to Turkey, perhaps to replace his former subordinate, Mustafa Kemal (*q.v.*), in leading the struggle against Greek invasion. Finally he took up the cause of the Turkic peoples of Central Asia, joining them in combat against Soviet rule. He was killed in Uzbekistan in a clash with the Red Army on August 4, 1922.

Enver seems, in sum, to have been a flawed would-be Napoleon. By 1914 only thirty-three years old, Enver occupied a nearly dominant position in Turkish affairs. Confident in his military and political gifts, he assumed a role clearly beyond his abilities and acumen. No longer adjudged by historians a mere German puppet, he still stands condemned—especially for his actions of 1917/1918—as a diplomat blind to political realities. The Armenian massacres continue to besmirch his reputation as a statesman. First and foremost a soldier, he has been subject to the harsh and lasting condemnation of scholars like Allen and Muratoff: "an incorrigible amateur."

Ahmad, *Young Turks*; Allen and Muratoff, *Caucasian Battlefields*; Shaw and Shaw, *History of the Ottoman Empire and Modern Turkey*, II; Silberstein, *Troubled Alliance*; Trumpener, *Germany and the Ottoman Empire*; Weber, *Eagles on the Crescent*; Encyclopedia of Islam, *New Edition*, III.

ERZBERGER, Matthias (*Germany, State Secretary without Portfolio*), was born in Buttenhausen, Württemberg, on September 20, 1875, the son of a tailor and mailman. He began his career as a grade school teacher, but in 1896 became editor of a Catholic newspaper at Stuttgart. Erzberger's real interests, however, lay in politics, and in 1903 he entered the Reichstag as deputy for the Center party from Biberach. His debating skills, burning ambition, vigor, and vitality quickly earned him recognition and leadership of his party's left wing. Above all, Erzberger developed into a fiscal expert; in 1905/1906 he gained national recognition by denouncing the government's colonial policy. Under Chancellor Theobald von Bethmann Hollweg (*q.v.*), Erzberger blossomed as champion of the taxation reforms of 1909 as well as of the army budget of 1913. As a South German he strove to reform the constitutional system both in Prussia and in the Reich; as a Catholic he could not bring himself before the war to cooperate with the Social Democrats (SPD).

The Great War propelled Erzberger onto the European stage. Entrusted by the chancellor with organizing German propaganda abroad, the Württemberger used his Catholic and Free Mason ties on behalf of the Reich. And as a spokesman of German heavy industry (Thyssen), Erzberger on September 2, 1914, came out in favor of sweeping annexations, including Longwy-Briey and Belgium. Finally, he worked, albeit unsuccessfully, with former Chancellor Bernhard von Bülow to prevent Italy's entry into the war on the side of the Entente.

But in time Erzberger grew more sober and realistic concerning Germany's role in the war. Specifically, he spoke out vehemently against unrestricted submarine warfare and counseled a mediated peace. Erzberger's methods were not always diplomatic: on July 6, 1917, he shocked his parliamentary colleagues by denouncing the navy's blueprint for victory over Britain by August through the U-boat war and by introducing a peace resolution calling for an end to the war without annexations or indemnities. Seven days later, vainly playing into the hands of Colonel Max Bauer and Crown Prince Wilhelm (qq.v.), Erzberger was instrumental in forcing the kaiser to dismiss Bethmann Hollweg. He had lost confidence in the chancellor and was not above allying with military intriguers for the common cause. Yet, in the end, Erzberger failed to replace Bethmann Hollweg with Bülow, and instead of the desired further parliamentarization he got the "silent dictatorship" of General Erich Ludendorff (q.v.).

On July 23, 1917, Erzberger followed with yet another political bombshell. At a confidential meeting of the Center party in Frankfurt, he read a pessimistic prognosis of the war penned by the Austro-Hungarian foreign minister, Count Ottokar Czernin, for Emperor Charles (qq.v.). This report was leaked not only to the German public but also to the Entente, and although Erzberger was not personally found liable for this indiscretion, his opponents thereafter steadfastly accused him of having committed treason.

Erzberger had little influence under Bethmann's successors. He favored the peace settlements of Brest-Litovsk and Bucharest early in 1918, and on October 3 entered the government of Chancellor Prince Max von Baden (q.v.) as state secretary without portfolio. Erzberger desired neither the kaiser's abdication nor his flight to Holland. On November 6 he was appointed a member of the German armistice commission and five days later signed the harsh terms at Compiègne.

Domestically, in January 1919, Erzberger pushed Friedrich Ebert and Hugo Haase (qq.v.) to use force to put down the Spartacist revolt in Berlin, and the following month he joined the cabinet, again as minister without portfolio. Convinced that failure to sign the Versailles Treaty would lead to further starvation and possible dissolution of the Bismarckian state, Erzberger in June worked both in his party and in the Reichstag for acceptance of the Allied terms, in the process becoming the most visible target for the right wing.

Erzberger served as deputy chancellor and finance minister in the cabinet of Gustav Bauer in the summer of 1919. In this capacity he implemented a drastic reform of the German taxation system, finally according the federal government the right to levy direct taxes such as those on income, inheritance, capital gains, and real property. In a devastating tract entitled "Away with Erzberger!" former Deputy Chancellor Karl Helfferich (q.v.) in 1920 accused the minister of personal as well as professional misconduct, of confusing private and state monies. In a celebrated trial at Berlin-Moabit in January-March 1920, Erzberger was placed in a poor light and as a result relinquished his cabinet post.

Reelected to the Reichstag in June 1920, Erzberger was most intimately associated with the armistice, the Versailles Treaty, and the Weimar Republic: on August 26, 1921, two former naval officers murdered him at Bad Griesbach in the Black Forest. The assassins, who had been recruited by Captain Manfred von Killinger of the Germanic Order, escaped to Hungary.

Matthias Erzberger had not been a politician with a grand design, but rather a shrewd and often ruthless political operator with a certain flair for the grand gesture. A man with boundless energy and ambition, he had for two decades placed his personal imprint not only upon the Center party but also on German national politics.

Epstein, *Matthias Erzberger and the Dilemma of German Democracy*; Erzberger, *Erlebnisse im Weltkrieg*; Frye, *Erzberger and German Politics*; *Neue Deutsche Biographie*, IV.

ESSEN, Nikolai Ottovich von (*Russia, Admiral*), was born on December 24, 1860, in St. Petersburg. His father was vice minister of justice under Tsar Alexander II. The young Essen chose a naval career, graduating from the Naval College in 1880 and completing the Nikolaevsky Naval Academy in 1886. Like other promising Russian naval lieutenants, Essen served long tours at sea: with the Pacific Fleet, 1892-1896, and thereafter for several years in the Mediterranean. He returned to the Far East in 1902 to command a cruiser, and the war against Japan brought him speedy promotion. After distinguishing himself in the conflict's first naval engagements, Essen received command of a battleship at the unusually tender age of forty-four. His calls for offensive strikes against the Japanese fleet went unheard, as timid and indecisive naval leaders at Port Arthur lapsed into fatal inactivity. As the enemy besieged the Russian stronghold, Essen was shifted to shore duty. He directed the defense of the crucial Tiger Peninsula, guarding the entrance to the harbor. When the Russian defense collapsed in January 1905, Essen was taken prisoner. His wartime exploits had marked him for higher command, however, and he arrived home to a hero's welcome and to promotion to the rank of captain.

By 1908 Essen was a rear admiral, his elevation in recognition of his success in leading the First Mine Division of the Baltic Fleet and his performance in the 1908 maneuvers. From 1909 until his death he commanded the entire Baltic Fleet, enjoying the reputation of the navy's most capable admiral.

Essen found his main assignment from 1909 until the outbreak of World War I to consist of preparing Russia's Baltic defenses to stand up to an assault by the superior forces of the German navy. A constant nightmare for Russia's military leaders was an enemy amphibious landing in the Gulf of Finland, followed by a lightning attack on St. Petersburg. Essen responded by placing extensive mine fields at the entrance to the gulf and within the gulf as well; the latter he combined with carefully placed coastal artillery batteries. Essen demanded and, in August 1912, received control over the coastal fortresses defending the gulf. But the energetic commander detested the passive role his fleet seemed destined to play. He insisted on training his officers and crews in offensive operations. Rather than bobbing at anchor behind mine fields, Essen's Baltic Fleet in the years before 1914 was more frequently to be found at sea for long periods, practicing its skills in all seasons and temperatures. In the midst of this prewar activity, Essen (in 1913) received his promotion to admiral.

The outbreak of World War I in August 1914 found Essen's fleet in its prepared defensive posture. Given German naval superiority, especially in battleships, this appeared inevitable. Even the German decision to concentrate in the North Sea to face Great Britain—thus narrowing the odds against Russia in the Baltic—did not strike an offensive spark in Essen's superiors. Russian inactivity seemed doubly assured when the Baltic Fleet was placed under the control of the army general commanding the area around St. Petersburg. Putting the fleet at the disposal of the Sixth Army at the start of the conflict seemed to chain Essen and his ships to the defense of the capital.

The admiral dutifully kept his large ships safe at anchor. But with the assistance of aggressive younger officers like Captain Kolchak (q.v.), Admiral von Essen set his cruisers and destroyers to work in offensive mine-laying operations. The long, dark nights of the winter, 1914/1915, permitted Essen's ships to slip southward, mining the approaches of Danzig and striking traffic between the Kiel Canal and the German Baltic ports. But for the caution imposed on him by army leaders, Essen would doubtless have moved still further; he tried, but failed, to get permission to launch cruiser raids to snap the sea link between Sweden's iron mines and German industry.

By the time of his death on May 20, 1915, Essen had established offensive mining operations as the edge of Russia's naval sword in the Baltic. Essen's immediate successors—Admiral V. A. Kanin and Admiral A. I. Nepenin—followed the same basic pattern of operations, but without Essen's driving energies and fierce aggressiveness. The March Revolution of 1917, however, turned the Baltic Fleet from a fighting unit into a storm center of political unrest. The most violent disturbances took place on shore and on the battleships that had stood for so long without an enemy to confront them. Essen's destroyers and other smaller vessels remained manned and ready for at least part of the revolutionary year. But it seems unlikely even Essen could have held the bitter, idle, and politicized crews of the capital ships in order as the revolution dismantled the Baltic Fleet.

Merkushov, "Admiral Essen vozsozdatel' flota"; Mitchell, *History of Russian and Soviet Sea Power*; Pavlovich, ed., *The Fleet in the First World War*, I; Zhitkov, "Admiral N. O. Fon Essen"; *Modern Encyclopedia of Russian and Soviet History*, X; *Sovetskaia istoricheskaia entsiklopediia*, XVI.

EUGENE (*Austria-Hungary, Archduke of Austria, Field Marshal*), was born in Gross-Seelowitz, Moravia, on May 21, 1863, to Archduke Karl Ferdinand. A passionate soldier throughout his life, Eugene, at the young age of thirty-seven was general of cavalry, commander of the XIV Army Corps, and the commanding general of Innsbruck and Vorarlberg. In 1908 he became inspector of the army and commander of Tyrol. Eugene was the only archduke to have received formal General Staff training; from 1894 to 1923 he was Hochmeister of the Deutsche Ritterorden. Needless to stress, his career was greatly enhanced by imperial favor.

Archduke Eugene was appointed nominal head of numerous Austro-Hungarian armies throughout the

Great War, though actual strategic command rested in the hands of professional soldiers, most notably General Conrad von Hötzendorf (*q.v.*), chief of the General Staff. In December 1914, Eugene was entrusted with command of all forces in the Balkan theater, and after the Italian declaration of war against the Dual Monarchy on May 23, 1915, the archduke was made commander in chief of the new southwestern front. There he was given the able General Alfred Krauss (*q.v.*) as his chief of staff; under him were the forces in Tyrol (Dankl), Carinthia (Rohr), and the Isonzo (Boroević). In May 1916, Eugene was to be in charge of a grandiose attack against the Italians, but the actual dispositions were once again made by Conrad von Hötzendorf, who did not even bother to consult with Krauss. The attack by the Eleventh (Dankl) and the Third Army (Kövess) from the plains of Lavarone-Folgaria was halted by the Italians and especially by General Aleksei Brusilov's (*q.v.*) rapid advance in the east.

Archduke Eugene was promoted field marshal in November 1916 in the wave of promotions and awards that accompanied Emperor Charles' (*q.v.*) coronation. As commander of the Italian front he was nominally in charge of the German–Austro-Hungarian breakthrough at Caporetto in October 1917, but planning and command had rested with two German generals, Otto von Below and Krafft von Dellmensingen (*qq.v.*). Thereafter it was possible to reduce the length of the Austro-Hungarian front with Italy, and in January 1918, Eugene's post as commander of the southwestern front was abolished and the venerable soldier retired from the army.

After the war, Eugene was forced to live abroad until 1934 when Chancellor Dollfuss retired the so-called Habsburg Laws, which had banished members of that house from the Austrian republic. The archduke was the center of speculation concerning a possible restoration of the monarchy for the next four years, but both his disinterest and Adolf Hitler's annexation of his homeland in 1938 put an abrupt end to such speculation. Archduke Eugene died in Meran on December 30, 1954.

Bardolff, *Militär-Maria Theresien-Orden*; Rothenberg, *Army of Francis Joseph*; *Neue Deutsche Biographie*, IV.

EVERT, Aleksei Ermolaevich (*Russia, General of Infantry*), was born on February 20, 1857, into a Russian family of German, or perhaps Swedish, background. He graduated from the Aleksandrovsky Military College in 1876, in time to serve in the Russo-Turkish War. In 1882 the young officer completed his studies at the General Staff Academy, often a way station for field grade officers heading to the top of the military ladder. The Russo-Japanese War brought Evert a series of senior staff positions with the armies in Manchuria. Following the Far Eastern conflict, he commanded a corps; then, in 1912, Evert was assigned to command the Irkutsk Military District in eastern Siberia.

In August 1914, Evert was recalled from his distant post to take over the Fourth Army, badly chopped up near Lublin in the first days of the Galician campaign. He remained with the Fourth through the fall campaign in central and southwestern Poland. At the start of the dismal spring campaign of 1915, Evert's forces stood dangerously exposed on the western extremity of the central front beyond Radom. After the Germans broke through at Gorlice to make western Poland impossible to hold, Evert led his forces in a fighting retreat that stretched over three months and 300 miles to Baranovichi and the Pripet Marshes.

In September 1915, Tsar Nicholas II took over command of the field armies with General Alekseev (*qq.v.*) as his chief of staff. Neither brilliantly successful nor hopelessly compromised by his conduct in the field, Evert surfaced as a candidate for higher command. He was perhaps considered for the post Alekseev obtained—Stone suggests that Evert's poor health and German name disqualified him—and in the end received charge of the vast western front. The old northwest front had been split into a northern front and a western front. Evert's area of responsibility now extended from Lake Narocz southward beyond Pinsk; and it included the lion's share of Russia's field artillery as well as the majority of the nation's infantry divisions.

Evert was put to a severe test of his limited abilities in 1916. From February forward, as the Germans blasted away at Verdun, French pleas for help rained down on Petrograd and Supreme Military Headquarters at Mogilev. A reluctant Evert received marching orders. He was pushed to launch a futile attack at Lake Narocz in March. The habitual failure of Russian artillery to coordinate its fire with advancing infantry was never more evident. Evert's taste for the offensive, never strong, evaporated then. In April Alekseev again passed along urgent calls from the western allies for a Russian summer offensive. In May the cries grew louder: the Austrian *Strafexpedition* in the Trentino pushed the Italians to plead for help. Evert dragged his feet throughout. His fire-eating neighbor Brusilov (*q.v.*) on the southwestern front, on the other hand, was eager to rush to the rescue.

As Brusilov advanced with unprecedented success for a Russian general assaulting Austrian defensive lines, Evert dawdled through the early summer. Ignoring his neighbor's imaginative tactical innovations, the timid commander of the western front built up his stockpiles of guns and ammunition with agonizing care, then crawled forward in bloody and ineffectual jabs at Baranovichi (July 2) and Kovel (July 27). Such a dim performance would have led to quick retirement in many an army, even in World War I. But Evert survived somehow—possibly due to Alekseev's memory that he had served as the western front commander's subordinate in the war against Japan.

In March 1917, Evert played his last turn on the national stage. Alekseev canvassed the various front commanders on their views: how should the army respond to the swelling revolution? Should it seek to support the tsar at all costs? Like his fellow senior leaders, Evert responded by refusing to back the tsar in this supreme crisis. Mayzel's analysis of the General Staff elite goes further; he suggests that Evert, an ultra-conservative even by the measure of the senior officer corps, was willing to launch a military coup to oust the tsar and to open the way to more effective national leadership.

Evert did not survive the monarchy for long. He was dismissed from his post in the spring of 1917 and passed into obscurity. He apparently died sometime in 1918 in a location that has never been precisely identified.

Mayzel, *Generals and Revolutionaries*; Rostunov, *Russkii front pervoi mirovoi voiny*; Rutherford, *The Russian Army in World War I*; Stone, *The Eastern Front*; *Sovetskaia istoricheskaia entsiklopediia*, XVI.

FALKENHAYN, Erich von (*Germany, General*), was born at Castle Belchau near Thorn in West Prussia on September 11, 1861, the son of a moneyless Junker estate owner; the family was of ancient nobility and stemmed from Meissen. Falkenhayn was raised in the Cadet School and in 1890 graduated from the War Academy third in his class. In 1896 he toured China as a captain in the General Staff and three years later as major and instructor at the Chinese Military School at Nankow, he was ordered to serve as second staff officer in the suppression of the Boxer Rebellion. His reports from China found favor with Wilhelm II (*q.v.*) and Falkenhayn's career was assured: in 1905 he was promoted lieutenant colonel, three years later colonel, and after staff work with the XVI and IV Army Corps, commander of the Fourth Foot Guards in 1911. The next year came promotion to major

general and, in July 1913, to lieutenant general as Prussian war minister at the young age of fifty-one. During the Zabern (Saverne) Affair he staunchly defended army officers against Reichstag critics for their harsh treatment of civilians in the *Reichsländer* Alsace-Lorraine. In the officer corps Falkenhayn had earned the reputation of being a pusher, a careerist, yet he unflinchingly continued to defend matters such as the duel, officer honor, and the institution of the military cabinet against parliamentary critics.

On September 3, 1914, Falkenhayn urged the chief of the General Staff, Helmuth von Moltke (*q.v.*), to take the Channel ports and to halt the German advance at the Marne, but his advice was rejected. Two days later the hasty retreat from the Marne began and Falkenhayn caustically noted: "Our General Staff has completely lost its head. Schlieffen's notes do not help any further, and so Moltke's wits come to an end." On September 14 Falkenhayn replaced the broken Moltke as head of the General Staff—an appointment not made public until November 3 in order to spare Moltke humiliation; Falkenhayn concurrently served as Prussian war minister until February 1915, one month after his promotion to general of infantry.

Tall, slender, aloof, Falkenhayn seemed the epitome of a Prussian staff officer. His closely cropped hair and his "clever but sarcastic eyes" conjured up visions of precision, sharpness, and action. Unfortunately, his military strategy was precisely the opposite: security dominated all his thoughts and deeds.

Falkenhayn's tenure as staff chief began on an unfortunate note. The costly drive to the sea in September and October was followed in October and November by massive assaults against Ypres with raw recruits—at a time when battle-tested veterans lay idle between the Aisne and the Vosges. Worse, Falkenhayn rejected out of hand General Wilhelm Groener's (*q.v.*) proposal to shuttle six army corps to Ypres in order to turn the tide against the Allies. Nor did Falkenhayn have a successful hand in the east. After the twin victories of Generals Paul von Hindenburg and Erich Ludendorff (*qq.v.*) at Tannenberg and at the Masurian Lakes, the staff chief could not bring himself to release sufficient units from France for a planned breakthrough at Lodz.

Indeed, Falkenhayn was hardly in an enviable position. He had at all times to balance men and supplies among three major fronts, and to steer a clear course between Reichstag and kaiser. In the west, Falkenhayn early in 1915 accepted the stalemate and prepared for a long entrenchment by expanding military railways and increasing munitions supplies.

In the south, his hopes that the entry of Turkey into the war on the side of the Central Powers would help turn the tide proved illusory. And in the east, there rapidly developed a vicious power struggle between Falkenhayn and Ludendorff. While the former sought to dole out sufficient troops to the eastern command to keep the Austro-Hungarian ally in control of the Carpathians, the latter demanded a grand sweep through Poland and a knock-out blow against the Russian armies near Vilna.

In the end, Falkenhayn compromised: the German breakthrough at Gorlice-Tarnów on May 2, 1915, by General August von Mackensen (*q.v.*) netted 400,000 Russian soldiers as well as Lemberg and Przemysl, but there were insufficient reserves to exploit the breach in the enemy lines. By September the eastern front had again been stabilized from Riga to Czernowitz. Next, the Austrian commander, Field Marshal Baron Franz Conrad von Hötzendorf (*q.v.*) insisted on a major operation against Italy; Crown Prince Wilhelm of Prussia (*q.v.*) countered with demands that Russia be accorded primary emphasis. Falkenhayn temporarily escaped a basic decision because of Bulgaria's entry into the war in the fall of 1915: after Serbia was overrun by Austro-German-Bulgarian forces, the Allies fell back upon Salonika with 500,000 men. But again relations with the ally at Vienna soured as Conrad demanded the elimination of the Salonika pocket, while Falkenhayn successfully countered with shifting the fulcrum of the war back to France. A fervent adherent of the strategy of attrition (*Ermattung*), Falkenhayn, in December 1915, persuaded the kaiser to adopt the limited objective of bleeding the French white near the historic fortress of Verdun.

On February 21, 1916, the monstrous German action at Verdun unfolded as a series of limited advances designed to draw the French into German artillery fire. Falkenhayn had correctly assessed the French temperament as Paris committed division after division to hold the stone forts at any cost. Unfortunately, as the German armies hurled themselves against French units at Verdun, General Aleksei Brusilov (*q.v.*) unleashed a broad assault against the entire Austro-Hungarian front in the east. The initial attack between June 5 and 8 quickly turned into a rout as over 200,000 troops were taken by Brusilov. At the same time, the British opened a major effort at the Somme, and when Rumania in August declared for the Entente, Falkenhayn's position became untenable. Too many powerful agencies joined forces to oust him. The Prussian war minister, General Wild von Hohenborn, regarded the staff chief as a "weakling." Chancellor Theobald von Bethmann Hollweg feared Falkenhayn's rumored political ambitions, while Foreign Secretary Gottlieb von Jagow (*qq.v.*) was solidly in Ludendorff's camp. Crown Prince Rupprecht of Bavaria (*q.v.*) went so far as to state that Falkenhayn's continued stay at the General Staff meant certain defeat for Germany. Above all, Falkenhayn was viciously denounced by Ludendorff and Hindenburg, and he yielded to this duumvirate on August 29, 1916.

Falkenhayn declined the offer of an ambassadorship to the Porte, and instead, on September 16, took command of the Ninth Army against Rumania. He was completely successful in the field. The enemy was dislodged from Hermannstadt and Transylvania, and on November 11 Falkenhayn's forces captured the mountain passes leading into Wallachia hours before the major snows arrived; in conjunction with Mackensen, Falkenhayn, in December 1916, victoriously entered Bucharest.

Early in 1917 Falkenhayn arrived in Turkey at the head of the so-called Asiatic Corps in order to regain Mesopotamia, but the scheme had to be abandoned. In July he was sent to Palestine as chief of Army Group F to shore up the Ottoman front; but the German arrived in Jerusalem the day after Field Marshal Edmund Allenby's (*q.v.*) drive on Beersheba. A series of counterattacks failed to halt the British advance and, in February 1918, General Liman von Sanders (*q.v.*) replaced Falkenhayn as commander in Palestine. Promoted a Turkish marshal, Falkenhayn returned to Germany in March to assume command of the Tenth Army in Lithuania. He brought this unit home in February 1919, retired in June of that year, and died at Castle Lindstedt near Potsdam on April 8, 1922.

Falkenhayn was certainly not one of the great military captains. Two verdicts, one of his day, and the other more recent, must suffice. Colonel Max Bauer (*q.v.*) noted that Falkenhayn possessed nearly every gift of nature "except the intuition of a commander. His decisions were half measures and he wavered even over these." Sir Basil Liddell Hart concurred, castigating Falkenhayn's strategy as "history's latest example of the folly of half measures."

Falkenhayn, *Der Feldzug der IX Armee* and *Die Oberste Heeresleitung*; Janssen, *Kanzler und General*; Liddell Hart, *Reputations*; Zwehl, *Falkenhayn*; *Geschichte der Ritter des Ordens*, I; *Neue Deutsche Biographie*, V.

FAYOLLE, Marie-Émile (*France, General*), was born in Puy, May 14, 1852, the son of a lace manufacturer. The young man was educated at the École polytechnique and commissioned in the artillery in

1877. His career before World War I was a varied one, combining regimental duties, staff assignments, and a long turn teaching at the War College. Fayolle fought in Tunisia in 1881 and advanced to captain in 1883. He completed the War College with distinction in 1891, held a series of staff positions in Paris, then returned to the War College in 1894 as assistant professor of artillery. He became the chief professor in the artillery course in 1897, a position that he held until 1908. His fellow instructors included Pétain, who taught tactics, and Foch who taught the infantry course (qq.v.). Following his term at the War College, Fayolle took a series of line commands. He led a regiment and then a brigade, the latter position apparently marking the close of his career: he retired in early 1914 after reaching the age limit for a brigadier general. A reserved and modest personality, a devout Catholic without spectacular colonial service on his record, Fayolle had found no chance for rapid advancement in the peacetime military.

In August 1914, Fayolle was recalled to active duty to assume command of the Seventieth Infantry Division, a force made up largely of reservists. His unit advanced as part of Foch's XX Corps toward Morhange, then took part in the subsequent retreat and bitter defensive battles east of Nancy in late August and early September. At the close of September Fayolle's men joined in the race to the sea and ended in a defensive position north of Arras. There Pétain became his corps commander. Much of Fayolle's wartime service was thereafter dominated by his role as Pétain's military workhorse and key subordinate.

The two former teachers at the War College agreed from the start of hostilities on the futility of ambitious infantry assaults unsupported by adequate artillery fire. Both pessimistically foresaw a long war dominated by defensive tools: the trench, the machine gun, and barbed wire. In June 1915, Fayolle was promoted; he succeeded Pétain as commander of the XXXIII Corps during the limited but costly success of the Artois offensive.

Fayolle increasingly criticized Foch and Joffre, the ranking commanders of the French army in 1915, for demanding such attacks without sufficient resources. As an artilleryman himself, Fayolle saw the necessity for superior strength in this arm of the service: the enemy's artillery had to be overwhelmed in order to permit limited and methodical advances by French troops. Like Pétain, he believed that successful attacks must be halted periodically so that the artillery could be brought up in force to prepare for the next step forward. In the existing military framework, ambitious hopes for a breakthrough were illusions.

Moreover, he hoped that economic pressure, or perhaps a breakthrough in the Balkans, would end the hopeless deadlock in France.

Fayolle was promoted to command the Sixth Army in February 1916, and he conducted limited advances between the Somme and the Aisne to relieve the pressure on Verdun. He led his army on the southern flank of the British Expeditionary Force (BEF) during the huge offensive on the Somme (July-September 1916). His advance far outstripped that of his British neighbors, whom he criticized for employing "infantile tactics." These months were also marked by growing friction with Foch, whom Fayolle reviled for "scratching out" meaningless gains at heavy cost in French lives. Marked down as too cautious and prudent, Fayolle was moved from command of the Sixth to the First Army in early 1917. Joffre's successor, General Nivelle, wanted his protégé, General Mangin (qq.v.), to spearhead the coming spring offensive with the Sixth Army. Following the debacle of April 1917, Fayolle again filled Pétain's shoes, taking command of the Center Army Group as Pétain rose to become commander in chief. Fayolle's forces attacked with success at Verdun in late August; this was the first of Pétain's cautious and limited offensive operations following the spring mutinies.

The Italian defeat at Caporetto in October 1917 led to Fayolle's departure over the Alps in mid-November. Foch was already on the scene, and the French troops in Italy repeatedly became a bone of contention between him and Pétain. Fayolle's Tenth Army in Italy, along with the British forces under General Plumer (q.v.), held the mountain passes protecting the northern flank of the Piave line, and the shaken Italian army was able to pull itself together by the close of 1917.

Fayolle returned to France in March 1918 to take command of a multinational reserve army of forty divisions under Foch's direction. Fayolle was to hold the crucial sector of the western front stretching from the Oise northward to Péronne, that is, the hinge where the French and the British armies met. The final months of the war saw Fayolle tugged back and forth by Foch, the supreme Allied commander, and Pétain, the French commander in chief, as the Allies first struggled to parry a series of German offensives, then began to take the war to the enemy. In the final week of March, as Ludendorff (q.v.) threatened to seize Amiens and to push apart the French forces and the BEF, Foch called on Fayolle to hold Amiens at all cost; meanwhile, Pétain encouraged his old friend to keep open the option of retreating southward to cover Paris. Luckily, by March 27/28, the German offensive bogged down after opening a small gap between Fayolle and the British.

In May Foch ordered Fayolle to hold every foot of territory against new German onslaughts; Pétain countered with a demand for a defense in depth. To Fayolle, his old friend Pétain seemed to be shaken psychologically by this time; sometimes the French commander radiated optimism, but more often seemed plunged into a paralysis of pessimism. As the way opened for French counterattacks, Fayolle came to put aside old quarrels to accept as a virtue Foch's single-minded aggressiveness. In mid-July, for example, Fayolle prepared to counterattack the western edge of the enemy's Marne salient. Pétain intervened to call off the operation, and a delighted Fayolle received word on July 16 that Foch had overruled the French commander in chief.

By the close of September, Fayolle had fulfilled Foch's directive to the Allied armies to destroy all enemy salients in his sector, just as the BEF north of the Somme and General Maistre (q.v.) and his Central Army Group on Fayolle's right had done. Fayolle drove his troops steadily forward until the November armistice. He then led the Army of Occupation to its headquarters at Mainz on December 14. At the peak of the action during the final summer of the war, Fayolle had controlled fifty-five divisions, one-half the total fighting strength of the French army. But in October 1919, he quietly gave up his command of the occupation forces on the Rhine and, the year following, went into retirement.

A public clamor, stirred up by the press, brought Fayolle back into service. Still only a brigadier general on the official army records, Fayolle was promoted marshal of France in 1921. He went on special missions to Canada and Italy, then remained at least nominally on active duty as a member of the Supreme War Council until his death, August 27, 1928, in Paris.

The quiet and self-effacing general left a remarkable written record of his experience. In 1964 his *Cahiers secrets* were published. These turned out to be an invaluable day-to-day record of the war from the vantage point of an informed—and deeply disillusioned—senior officer.

Barnett, *The Swordbearers*; Edmonds and Davies, *History of the Great War. Military Operations: Italy, 1915-1919*; Fayolle, *Cahiers secrets de la Grande Guerre*; Griffiths, *Pétain*; Pedroncini, *Pétain: général en chef*; Ryan, *Pétain the Soldier*; *Dictionnaire de biographie française*, XIII.

FERDINAND (*Bulgaria, Tsar*), was born in Vienna, February 26, 1861, the scion of European royalty. His father was Prince Augustus of the German house of Saxe-Coburg; his mother was the daughter of the former French king, Louis-Philippe. Ferdinand served in the Austrian army and, in 1887, the Bulgarian National Assembly chose him to become Bulgaria's monarch. The former ruler, Prince Alexander of Battenberg, had been overthrown and the crown had gone begging. Ferdinand accepted it in the face of disapproval by the great powers. It was years before he was formally recognized by his fellow monarchs. At home, the young prince was at first under the thumb of the Bulgarian politician Alexander Stambulov. By 1895, however, Ferdinand forced Stambulov out of office and probably conspired to have his former leading minister murdered.

Ferdinand then dominated Bulgarian politics. He encouraged the fragmentation of the party system, played one set of venal political leaders off against another, and showed a preference for appointing ministers whose clouded reputations made them his personal dependents. In R. W. Seton-Watson's often quoted words, Ferdinand managed the course of affairs in Bulgaria with "his skill in calculating the psychological moment for driving each batch of swine from the trough of power."

Ferdinand's foreign policy was avowedly expansionist. It centered on the acquisition of the Turkish province of Macedonia, to which Bulgaria could make ethnic and historical claims. In October 1908, Ferdinand took advantage of the Young Turk revolt to throw off the vestiges of foreign sovereignty, declaring Bulgaria legally independent of Turkey. His old title of "prince" he replaced with the ambitious, medieval one of "tsar."

Ferdinand led his country into the First Balkan War in October 1912. Already widely distrusted by European leaders, Ferdinand's policies heightened concern about his lack of principle and sweeping territorial ambitions. Bulgarian armies won impressive initial victories but failed to carry Ferdinand, as he had dreamed, all the way to Constantinople. Relations between Bulgaria and its allies Greece and Serbia deteriorated in the spring of 1913. The division of the war spoils, especially the contested region of Macedonia, proved unachievable.

In late June the Bulgarian army suddenly attacked the Serbs, and therewith set off the Second Balkan War. Ferdinand's role in the attack has remained a center of controversy. Ernst Christian Helmreich claims that the tsar himself ordered the attack, without bothering to inform most of the Bulgarian government. Ferdinand was doubtless swayed by the wishes of the army and public opinion, not to mention Macedonian revolutionaries who threatened to assassinate him if he failed to unite their homeland with Bulgaria. The war brought first military, then diplomatic disaster. The peace treaty, signed at

Bucharest on August 10, 1913, cost Bulgaria most of its wartime gains. Rumors circulated that Ferdinand might be forced to abdicate. Instead he changed course.

Even before the fighting ended, Ferdinand had appointed the Austrophile Vasil Radoslavov (q.v.) to form a new government. This indicated a shift in foreign policy from friendship with Russia to a set of links with the Central Powers. In November 1913, Ferdinand traveled to central Europe shopping for an alliance. He found a cool reception in Vienna and a frigid one in Berlin. His attack on Serbia had confirmed the widespread view that—even by the standards of the time for Balkan political leaders—Ferdinand, "the Richelieu of the Balkans," was utterly untrustworthy.

The outbreak of World War I placed Ferdinand in the more comfortable role of receiving a crowd of diplomatic suitors. The tsar saw the advantages of waiting, since Bulgaria was certain to receive competing offers from both sides. A clear delineation of his relationship with Radoslavov is difficult to draw. Ferdinand held and apparently exercised final control over Bulgarian policies; Radoslavov stood beside him as a trusted adviser and skillful executor. Since the final decision to enter the war had to come from the monarch, Radoslavov could use one of Ferdinand's timely "illnesses" to evade pressing foreign demands.

By the summer of 1915 Radoslavov's adroit diplomacy had drawn the Central Powers into sweeping territorial concessions, notably concerning the future of Macedonia. The German victories on the eastern front following the May breakthrough at Gorlice allayed Ferdinand's fears of a vengeful Russia. In September 1915, Bulgaria agreed to throw its military weight onto the scales. Ferdinand immediately faced bitter domestic opposition; critics like the Agrarian party leader Stamboliski (q.v.) were jailed. Initial military successes held dissidents in check, but the victories became fewer after 1915.

During the years 1916/1917 Ferdinand found himself reduced to the ruler of a satellite kingdom. Bulgaria was picked clean of its food reserves and left to shift for itself on the battlefield. Although rumors often flew concerning a separate peace, Ferdinand saw no choice for himself but to remain alongside Germany and Austria. In a gesture to muffle domestic unrest, he ousted Radoslavov in June 1918; but the new minister-president, Alexander Malinov (q.v.), was not permitted to alter the main lines of foreign policy. When the Macedonian front collapsed in September 1918, mutiny struck the army and Malinov moved to obtain an armistice. Ferdinand called in German troops to help save his throne, but

he won only a few more days. At the insistence of the victorious Entente, Ferdinand was forced into exile and departed for Germany. The former "Balkan Richelieu" spent the remaining years of his life immersed in his old hobbies of ornithology and entomology. He died in Berlin, September 10, 1948.

Bell, *Peasants in Power*; Helmreich, *Diplomacy of the Balkan Wars*; Holden, "Bulgaria's Entry into the First World War"; Seton-Watson, *History of the Roumanians*; Silberstein, *Troubled Alliance*; Stavrianos, *Balkans since 1453*; *Bulgarska Entsiklopediia*; *Larousse mensuel*, IV.

FERDINAND (*Rumania, King*), was born August 24, 1865, in Sigmaringen, Germany. The nephew of the childless King Carol of Rumania (q.v.), Ferdinand was adopted and declared heir presumptive to his uncle's throne in 1889. He brought a thoroughly German background to his duties in Bucharest. The young prince was a member of the Swabian branch of the Hohenzollern family. He had been educated at the universities of Tübingen and Leipzig, and then performed military service at Kassel. Wilhelm II of Germany was his cousin; Francis Joseph of Austria-Hungary (qq.v.) was a personal friend.

In 1893 a countervailing influence entered Ferdinand's life. He married Princess Marie of Great Britain, daughter of the duke of Edinburgh and granddaughter of Queen Victoria. In her memoirs, Marie called herself "the joyful warrior" of the family. She described her husband as "modest, timid, doubting, but honest and unselfish." Contemporary observers and historians alike have agreed with her assessment. Ferdinand was barely visible during his twenty-five years as heir apparent, although he served as nominal commander in chief of the Rumanian army during the Second Balkan War in 1913.

The death of Carol in early October 1914 made Ferdinand king of Rumania. His personal sympathies lay with the Central Powers. Two of his brothers served with the German army, and he was convinced Germany would win the war. Nonetheless, he first disappointed and then outraged those who looked to him to forge a close political link connecting Rumania and the Central Powers. He supported Premier Ion Bratianu's (q.v.) policy of neutrality; then, in mid-1916, the king backed Bratianu's decision that the opportune moment had come to enter the war on the side of the Entente. The queen's vigorous preference for Great Britain and France made itself felt on Ferdinand throughout the war. So too did the powerful currents of concern in Rumania for Rumanians under Habsburg control in Transylvania. Irredentist feeling swelled once word arrived of Austrian military defeats in Galicia and Serbia in the fall of 1914. Ferdinand knew any attempt to bend Rumanian policy to favor the Central Powers meant risking his crown. German and Austrian diplomats repeatedly approached the timid king but Ferdinand remained firmly in tow behind the confident Bratianu.

When Rumania entered the war in August 1916, Ferdinand appealed to the nation's assembled political leaders to support intervention. Berlin rumbled about the "degenerate Hohenzollern" in Bucharest, contrasting him with the pro-German King Constantine of Greece (q.v.). Ferdinand was nominal commander in chief of the Rumanian forces during the catastrophic campaign of 1916. By midwinter, he had seen his forces badly battered and driven into the northeastern corner of his country. Surrounded by the disintegrating Russian army, the Rumanian units seemed in danger of imminent collapse.

Fedinand gave a rare display of decisiveness. He took the lead in April 1917 in pledging land reform and an expanded suffrage for his peasants, who formed most of the army's rank and file. In June the Rumanian constitution was amended to permit the expropriation of landed estates. That the Rumanian army remained a cohesive and effective force owed much to Ferdinand and like-minded politicians such as Bratianu. But the collapse of the Russians made the Rumanian position hopeless. Ferdinand resigned his role as military figurehead in December 1917 to facilitate the inevitable armistice. The whirlwind of 1918 pulled him passively along. Bratianu stage-managed the appointment of Averescu, then Marghiloman (qq.v.) as premier. For a time it seemed that Germany would replace Ferdinand, a step Marghiloman's intervention helped to prevent. The king's most important action was a negative one: he avoided signing the Peace of Bucharest (May 1918), in which Rumania agreed to leave the war. Subsequently, this omission helped Bratianu to reassert Rumanian territorial demands at Versailles, claiming that Rumania had never severed fully its tie with the Entente.

Bratianu's power revived as the position of the Central Powers crumbled in the Balkans in the early fall of 1918. Under his urging, Ferdinand replaced the pro-German Marghiloman on November 6 and reopened hostilities against the Central Powers on November 10. Three weeks later, the royal family returned in triumph to Bucharest.

Ferdinand played a minor part in the Versailles negotiations. Apparently under Bratianu's direction, he addressed a letter to his fellow heads of state in France, Britain, and Italy in November 1919 to plead Rumania's cause. Thanks essentially to Bratianu's stubborn diplomacy, Ferdinand's kingdom more than doubled in size with the territorial fruits of standing on the winning side. In October 1922, Ferdinand and Marie were crowned monarchs of Greater Rumania.

Ferdinand's wartime pledge of generous land reform went unfulfilled. The influence of large estate owners combined with Ferdinand's own conservatism to lead only to the limited land reform of 1922. Much of the postwar period saw Ferdinand under the familiar influence of his mentor Bratianu, and Bratianu was serving as premier when Ferdinand died at the royal retreat of Sinaia on July 20, 1927.

Brown, "The Movement for Reform in Rumania after World War I"; Marie, Queen of Romania, *The Story of My Life*, 2 vols.; Seton-Watson, *History of the Roumanians*; Silberstein, *Troubled Alliance*; Spector, *Rumania at the Paris Peace Conference*; Torrey, "Rumania and the Belligerents, 1914-1916"; *Larousse mensuel*, VII.

FISHER, John Arbuthnot (*Great Britain, Admiral of the Fleet*), first Baron Fisher, of Kilverstone, was born in Ceylon on January 25, 1841, the son of an army captain. Fisher entered the navy at age thirteen, and served in the Crimean War as well as in the China War 1859/1860. After command of the battleship *Inflexible* in Egypt in 1882 came almost fourteen years of uninterrupted service ashore as gunnery and torpedo expert. As controller of the navy, Fisher was responsible for executing the Naval Defence Act of 1889; he was promoted to the grade of rear admiral in 1890 and vice admiral six years later. In 1897 Fisher was appointed commander in chief, North America and West Indies station; thereafter he was sent as Britain's delegate to the First Hague Conference, followed by command of the Mediterranean Fleet and promotion to the grade of admiral in 1901. In the Mediterranean, Fisher applied modern scientific advances to the fleet: telegraphy was introduced, longer firing ranges inaugurated, routine dismantled, and reform introduced for the lower deck. Fisher met the earl of Selborne, first lord of the Admiralty, in the summer of 1901 in Malta, and at Selborne's suggestion transferred to Whitehall as second sea lord in charge of personnel.

The team of Fisher and Selborne moved with alacrity. On Christmas Day 1902 a revolutionary scheme of training was announced: executive, engineer, and marine officers were to be trained under one common system for four years before specialization; new naval colleges were established at Dartmouth and Osborne; and selection was preceded by personal interviews. On Trafalgar Day (October 21) 1904, Fisher was appointed first sea lord. In this capacity he pushed through a redistribution of the fleet, concentrating the main fighting strength of the Royal Navy in the North Sea, striking down numerous foreign ports, and retiring 150 old ships. Under the nucleus crew system, ships in the reserve maintained part of their crew on board at all times; during active service, the remainder of the crew was quickly augmented from the available personnel reserves.

Perhaps most revolutionary of all, Fisher in 1905 introduced the world's first "all big gun" battleship, the *Dreadnought*. Turbine-driven, it possessed greater speed and vastly enhanced firing power over conventional warships. Navies, especially of Japan and the United States, were experimenting with similar vessels; therefore, Fisher had no choice but to proceed with this radical design change. Of course, such feverish activity did not sit well with everyone. The first sea lord's one-sidedness produced rancor and vindictiveness, especially from those not in the "Fishpond" (Fisher's circle of admirers); a bitter dispute with the popular commander of the Channel Fleet, Lord Charles Beresford, after 1907 exacerbated personality rifts in the service. Fisher managed to persevere partly because of his close friendship with King Edward VII between 1904 and 1910, serving as the monarch's first and principal naval aide-de-camp.

Fisher was greatly annoyed with the Liberal government after 1906, especially with its reduction in the ship-building program and its cancellation of a dockyard at Rosyth. By 1909/1910, however, the German "danger" was sufficient to hasten construction of the facility at Rosyth and to pass the famous program laying down eight battleships in a single year. In 1909 Fisher was raised to the peerage with the title of Baron Fisher, of Kilverstone, an estate in Norfolk. Jacky Fisher retired as first sea lord in January 1910, but two years later, as chairman of the royal commission on oil fuel, he recommended its adoption for the fleet; hence the Oil Maniac, as he was nicknamed in the fleet, not only encouraged the government's purchase of the Anglo-Iranian Oil Company, but also pioneered the building of the *Queen Elizabeth* class of oil-fired dreadnoughts.

In October 1914, the first lord of the Admiralty, Winston Churchill (*q.v.*), invited Fisher to return as firt sea lord. He accepted at once. The combination of Churchill and Fisher worked well at first; indeed, Fisher had also strongly recommended that Admiral Sir John Jellicoe (*q.v.*) be entrusted with command of the newly formed Grand Fleet. Fisher's first act in office was to dispatch Sir Doveton Sturdee with two fast, powerful battle cruisers from the Grand Fleet to the South Atlantic, in order to redress the loss of Sir Christopher Cradock (*qq.v.*) at Coronel. Sturdee's complete triumph seemed to vindicate Fisher's firm faith in that type of warship. The first sea lord next turned his fertile mind to a pet scheme: to force the entry of the Baltic Sea and to land a military force in Pomerania by use of special troop barges. Before this scheme could progress further, however, Fisher's attention was diverted to the Dardanelles.

While he could never share fully Churchill's enthusiasm for this operation, Fisher nevertheless backed his chief in the cabinet in calling for a naval attempt to force passage of the Straits. Well might he have remembered his hero Nelson's warning that "any sailor who attacked a fort was a fool." The naval operations in the spring and summer of 1915 failed, and the ensuing retreat from the Dardanelles caused the government to fall. Arthur James Balfour (*q.v.*) accepted the post of first lord of the Admiralty in the new coalition ministry, but did not ask Fisher to stay on as first sea lord. Fisher, who had behaved rather undiplomatically at the end, was instead pushed off to the post of chairman of the Admiralty inventions board.

Jacky Fisher published two volumes of reminiscences after the armistice. He died on July 10, 1920, and after a public funeral at Westminster Abbey was buried at Kilverstone. Arthur Marder has described Fisher as a genius. His was a most remarkable personality: he combined a singular clarity of vision with a quick grasp of the essentials, demonic energy, a burning patriotism, and a firm belief in the superiority of the English race. He rewarded those who helped him. He was vindictive to those he believed opposed him. Above all, he was a devoted reader of the Bible, especially of the Old Testament.

Fisher, *Memories, Records*; Mackay, *Fisher of Kilverstone*; Marder, *Dreadnought to Scapa Flow*, I, II; *Dictionary of National Biography 1912-1921*.

FOCH, Ferdinand (*France, Field Marshal*), was born in Tarbes in southwestern France, on October 2, 1851. The son of a civil servant, Foch interrupted his education and preparation for the École Polytechnique to enlist as a private during the Franco-Prussian War, 1870/1871. The future Allied supreme commander saw no action in this first tour in uniform. He entered the École Polytechnique in 1871; three years later he left for his first assignment as a lieutenant in the artillery. Foch advanced with some speed, due partly to the shortage of officers during this gloomy era for the French army. Attendance at the War College, 1885-1887, marked him for future military stardom. He graduated near the top of his class, and his rewards included a choice position in General Staff headquarters in Paris (1890). Then, in 1895, he was called back to the War College to teach military history, strategy, and applied tactics. In his next five years of teaching, Foch's lectures gained him a reputation as a leading military thinker. His first book, *The Principles of War*, appeared in 1903. Foch's military analyses were based on a study of Napoleonic warfare as well as the German performance in the Franco-Prussian War. Several themes ran through his writing: the importance of the commander's will and determination on shaping the outcome of battle; a heavy emphasis on the advantages of waging offensive operations. Critics like Colonel Hunter have denied that Foch was an offensive fanatic on the pattern of Colonel Loyzeaux de Grandmaison, the father of the *offensive à outrance* school. But Foch stood in marked contrast to his cautious colleague at the War College, Henri-Philippe Pétain (*q.v.*), who emphasized the hitting power that modern weapons gave to the defensive side.

In 1900 Foch left his academic post for a minor field command. His undisguised Catholicism—his brother was a Jesuit priest—clearly contributed to this pause in his career. But his obvious abilities and the growing popularity of his books in professional circles allowed him to renew his march upward. In 1907, after his appointment as chief of staff to the V Corps, Foch became a brigadier general. The following year, Premier Georges Clemenceau handpicked Foch over the more prosaic alternative of Charles Lanrezac (*qq.v.*) to direct the War College. In 1911, as a major general, he received command of a division; in 1913 Foch approached the top of the military ladder when he took charge of the VIII, then the XX Corps. The latter was an elite formation; it had the vital mission of guarding the Lorraine sector of the frontier against Germany.

The first campaign of World War I brought Foch speedy advancement. In little more than two months the promising corps commander climbed to become chief assistant to General Joffre (*q.v.*), the French generalissimo. Foch first saw action in the Second Army's advance on Morhange, an attack that went into reverse on August 20 in the face of fierce German counterassaults. By August 28 the XX Corps was back at Nancy, its jumping-off point. Foch distinguished himself by his skill in both the drive on Morhange and in his fighting retreat. On August 28 Joffre called him to take command of the Ninth Army, then forming to fill the gap between Franchet d'Esperey's Fifth Army and Langle de Cary's Fourth Army (*qq.v.*). Before leaving for his new command,

Foch was joined by Lieutenant Colonel Maxime Weygand (*q.v.*), who was to serve him as chief of staff and military alter ego for the next four years.

At the battle of the Marne Foch held a crucial defensive sector in the face of desperate German attacks from September 4 to September 9. Despite his defensive mission, he attracted Joffre's eye with his exhortations to subordinates to launch constant counterattacks, as well as by his explosive optimism. There Foch practiced loudly and visibly the lessons of aggressiveness and willpower he had preached at the War College. As both Allied and German armies raced toward the North Sea, the center of the war shifted to Flanders. On October 4 Joffre named Foch his assistant and put him in charge of all French forces in the north; in January 1915, Foch received the formal title of commander of France's Northern Army Group. His task from the start was to coordinate French efforts in Flanders with the British and Belgian defensive actions. In part a high level military diplomat, Foch possessed the powerful tool of controlling French military reserves in the region. He used both his diplomatic skills and his powers of persuasion to stiffen the will to fight of such diverse personalities as King Albert I of Belgium and French General de Castelnau (*qq.v.*). As at the Marne, Foch demanded that even defensive operations rely on spirited counterattacks.

By the close of 1914 Foch's power within the French command system was second only to that of Joffre. Therein lay both opportunity and danger. Joffre's continued tenure as commander in chief meant a secure position for Foch; Joffre's fall likely meant Foch would be retired as well. The unique shape of Foch's career in World War I—his initial speedy rise, his near fatal decline, and his subsequent ascent to the top—had its roots in this relationship. Foch directed fruitless offensives in Artois during May and September 1915. By the close of the year, the second characteristic of Foch's World War I leadership was taking shape. The former War College professor no longer clung to the simple ideal of an aggressive commander imposing his will on the enemy by a vigorous offensive. In his memo to Joffre at the end of the year, Foch wrote of the realities of trench warfare; one must abandon, he said, the hope of a decisive breakthrough and replace it with plans for a series of attacks on different sectors in order to wear the enemy down gradually. The old, aggressive Foch lived on, but tempered by the harsh lessons of 1915.

Next came the fall from grace. Joffre's plans for a powerful Anglo-French offensive along the Somme in 1916 were thwarted by the German attack at Verdun (February 1916). Foch fought alongside the British, but he had fewer troops and fewer guns than scheduled. While his forces advanced farther and at smaller cost in lives than his British neighbors', the advance was nevertheless limited and the cost in lives very high. His prospects were already dimming when Joffre fell from power in mid-December 1916 to be replaced by General Robert Nivelle (*q.v.*).

Foch became a peripatetic military consultant throughout 1917. In the wake of Joffre's professional demise, his leading assistant was assigned to a study commission at Senlis and told to busy himself planning for emergencies that might never arise. In early 1917 Foch examined the defenses at Belfort in anticipation of a German outflanking attack on France through Switzerland. In March/April, he traveled to Italy to meet General Luigi Cadorna (*q.v.*). They discussed how France might aid her ally to the south in the event Germany shifted its strategy to institute an offensive against Italy. The reshuffling of seats at the top of the French military system as Nivelle fell to oblivion and Pétain took over as commander in chief brought Foch in as chief of the General Staff. It signaled his partial rehabilitation, but command authority still rested with Pétain.

The Austro-German breakthrough at Caporetto (October 1917) brightened Foch's future. He rushed to Italy as he had three years earlier to Flanders. He bombarded his hosts with optimism and determination; Verdun, he reminded them, had shown what a determined army could do in a defensive battle. He helped get French and British divisions to Italy, although far fewer than the fifteen Italian Premier Vittorio Orlando (*q.v.*) requested.

While the Caporetto crisis aided Foch in displaying his talents as a high level Allied coordinator, events outside his control were working to his advantage. On November 16, 1917, Georges Clemenceau became France's premier, and Foch then had a powerful ally at the highest levels of power. Caporetto had moved Clemenceau's predecessor, Paul Painlevé (*q.v.*), to erect the framework for permanent inter-Allied military cooperation: the Supreme War Council at Versailles.

When the Germans launched their final series of offensives in France in late March 1918, the issue of coordinated Allied operations became crucial. As Ludendorff (*q.v.*) threatened to split the French and British armies by his thrust toward Amiens—Pétain was considering pulling the French armies southward to guard Paris—Foch was named to "coordinate" the operations of the French and British armies. On April 3 the power to give "strategic direction" to the armies was his, although the French and British generalissimos retained the right to appeal to their respective governments. On April 14 the process was completed: Foch became Allied commander in chief. At first this meant control over French, British, and American forces. In June his authority was extended, in a limited form, over the Italians; and, in September, he finally got to supervise Belgian operations.

Most immediately, Foch had control over France's forces. In June Pétain lost his right to appeal to Clemenceau to protest Foch's orders. This shifted the emphasis in French leadership, since Foch saw Pétain as an excessively cautious and pessimistic commander, out of step with Foch's own resurgent devotion to the offensive.

By mid-July, the German attack had run its course, and Foch, as optimistic and aggressive as ever, orchestrated an Allied offensive that continued for three months until victory was achieved. As Hunter has pointed out, Foch had by then put aside hopes for a spectacular breakthrough. Rather he confronted the Germans with a steady succession of offensives over vast stretches of the western front. On August 6 Clemenceau awarded him the rank of marshal of France, partly in gratitude for repelling the German July offensive east of Paris (Second Battle of the Marne), more to augment Foch's authority in dealing with various Allied commanders.

By October Foch's steady advance had made victory only a question of time. In response to the first German requests for an armistice, Foch drafted terms designed to cripple Germany's ability to renew the war: among other provisions, Foch demanded the surrender of vast quantities of heavy weapons, a German retreat to the Rhine, and the establishment of Allied bridgeheads on that river's eastern bank.

In November 1918, with the armistice achieved, Foch's influence began to diminish. This was not merely the predictable story of a battlefield hero ignored in quieter times. Rather Foch launched himself on a political crusade to influence the peace negotiations. To secure France's future security meant to him to make the Rhine France's eastern frontier. Even before the shooting stopped, Foch and Clemenceau were at loggerheads over issues of grand strategy. Foch's attempt to invade the precincts of diplomacy—he pressed his demands on the French government and foreign leaders at Versailles until May 1919—aroused Clemenceau's implacable opposition. The premier saw what the field marshal could not: Paris' allies would not let France thus sow the seeds of a future war.

The postwar years saw Foch heaped with honors. He was named a British field marshal in 1920. The year before, he had been called to membership in the

Académie française. Despite his disappointment at Clemenceau's political leadership, Foch refused to seek a forum for his opinions by running for the National Assembly. He died in Paris, March 20, 1929.

Judged alongside his French contemporaries, Foch stands as his nation's military giant of World War I: more optimistic and aggressive than Pétain, more realistic and flexible than Nivelle, more resilient and imaginative than Joffre. As Winston Churchill (*q.v.*) put it in *Great Contemporaries*: "In 1914 he had saved the day by refusing to recognize defeat. In 1915 and in 1916 he broke his teeth upon the Impossible. But 1918 was created for him."

Foch, *The Memoirs of Marshal Foch*; Hunter, *Marshal Foch: A Study in Leadership*; King, *Foch versus Clemenceau* and *Generals and Politicians*; Laffargue, *Foch et la bataille de 1918*; Liddell Hart, *Reputations*; Marshall-Cornwall, *Foch as Military Commander*; *Dictionnaire de biographie française*, XIV; *Larousse mensuel*, VIII.

FON ESSEN, Nikolai Ottovich (1860-1915). See ESSEN, Nikolai Ottovich von.

FRANCHET D'ESPEREY, Louis Felix François (*France, General*), was born in Mostaganem, Algeria, on May 25, 1856. A practicing Catholic, he came from a family with royalist political connections. He entered St. Cyr in 1874, graduating as a lieutenant of infantry in 1876. D'Esperey spent much of his early career outside of metropolitan France, becoming one of the army's best traveled younger officers. He served as a line officer in Algeria and Tunisia from 1876 to 1881, attended the General Staff School, 1882-1884, following which he saw combat in Indo-China. Between 1886 and 1900 he held a variety of staff and line appointments in metropolitan France, including service as an instructor at St. Cyr.

In 1900 d'Esperey participated in the suppression of the Boxer Rebellion and returned to France to command first a regiment, then a brigade. The two years preceding the First World War he spent under General Lyautey (*q.v.*) in the pacification of Morocco. In addition to his official travel, d'Esperey made extensive private tours of the Balkans and eastern Europe, including areas of subsequent strategic significance like the Greek and Dalmatian coasts. Fifty-eight years old in 1914, he struck colleagues and acquaintances as a particularly energetic and resolute officer—a man who retained some of the unsophisticated manner and hotheadedness of a lieutenant on African service.

D'Esperey led the I Corps of the Fifth Army during the opening weeks of the war, holding his battered units together during the retreat from Charleroi and taking the lead in the important counterattack at Guise on August 29, 1914. Promoted to command the Fifth Army on the eve of the battle of the Marne, he adopted the innovative artillery tactics of his talented subordinate, General Pétain (*q.v.*), in preparing the way for a speedy advance. His army played a crucial role at the Marne, liberating Reims and establishing d'Esperey as a senior commander for the remainder of the war. In October 1914, as the western front was degenerating into stalemate, he used the occasion of a visit by President Raymond Poincaré (*q.v.*) to suggest that a major Allied offensive take place in the Balkans. D'Esperey envisioned a thrust up the Vardar valley to Belgrade and on to Budapest. The idea was quietly turned aside.

By 1916 d'Esperey was an army group commander and was considered as a candidate to succeed General Joffre (*q.v.*) as commander in chief, but his political orientation and religious affiliations removed him from serious contention. He distinguished himself once again in October 1917, leading the first major offensive by French troops in the period following the spring and summer mutinies, the politically and militarily sensitive offensive at Malmaison. In May 1918, however, d'Esperey's Northern Army Group was the victim of a successful German advance of thirty miles from the Chemin des Dames southward to the Marne. He was "demoted upward" and sent to command the diverse Allied units gathered in Macedonia.

In September 1918, d'Esperey launched an offensive with his force of French, British, and Serbian units that advanced to Skopje, Belgrade, and on into Hungary. Alert to the strategic possibilities that his successes had brought—he had among other things forced the Bulgarians to sue for an armistice—d'Esperey urged the Supreme War Council at Versailles to permit an advance to Vienna, Prague, and Dresden. Marshal Foch (*q.v.*) remained wedded to the need to maintain the bulk of the Allied armies on the western front, however, and the November 1918 armistice put an end to these ambitious strategic musings.

D'Esperey remained in the Balkans for two years in the de facto role of Allied pro-consul in southeastern Europe. He supported extensive Yugoslav territorial claims at the Versailles peace negotiations, and aided in the suppression of Béla Kun's Soviet government in Hungary. He returned to North Africa in 1920 and was promoted from general to marshal of France in 1922. He was severely injured in an automobile accident in 1933, still on active duty in Tunisia at the age of seventy-seven. He died at Albi in southern France on July 8, 1942.

Azan, *Franchet D'Esperey*; Isselin, *The Battle of the Marne*; Palmer, *Gardeners of Salonika*; Ryan, *Pétain the Soldier*.

FRANCIS FERDINAND (*Austria-Hungary, Archduke of Austria-Este*), was born in Graz on December 18, 1863, to Archduke Karl Ludwig. After the customary court education, Francis Ferdinand served with the infantry and the cavalry; since 1890 he was colonel of the Ninth (Hungarian) Husarenregiment. After the suicide of Crown Prince Rudolf in 1889, Francis Ferdinand was generally regarded as heir to the throne, although never formally installed as such by Emperor Francis Joseph (*q.v.*). Lung disease compelled the archduke in 1892/1893 to undertake a trip around the world, and upon his return he commanded the Thirty-eighth Infantry Brigade in Budweis in the grade of major general. Lung problems continued to plague him, and, in order not to be precluded from inheriting the throne, Francis Ferdinand for four years vacationed in the Tyrol and in Mediterranean spas. In 1896 he was promoted field marshal and on March 29, 1898, placed "at the disposition" of the imperial supreme commander; in 1899 he was promoted general of cavalry. The heir presumptive concluded a morganatic marriage on July 1, 1900, with Sophie Chotek, a lady-in-waiting promoted Duchess of Hohenberg; the couple had one daughter and two sons born to them. The latter, according to a Habsburg family statute of 1839, would have been precluded from imperial succession and Sophie from the title of empress had Francis Ferdinand lived long enough to succeed Francis Joseph. The archduke has been depicted as being self-willed, autocratic, reactionary, clerical, and abrasive; at Castle Belvedere he gathered about him a little brain trust (according to some, a shadow government) composed of men who ultimately were to serve Emperor Charles (*q.v.*).

Francis Ferdinand busied himself with military matters, and gained credit especially after his promotion to admiral in 1902 for his work with Admiral Rudolf von Montecuccoli (*q.v.*) in behalf of the navy. In politics, the archduke stood close to the Christian-Socialists at home, and distinctly disliked the Pan-Germans. His special animosity was reserved for the Magyars, although neither the Czechs nor the Poles enjoyed his favor; alone the Rumanians and the Slovaks consistently could count on his support. Initially Francis Ferdinand favored reorganization of the empire on the basis of Vienna-Budapest-Agram trialism, but a falling out with the Croats over their role in the future empire scrapped this project in favor of a plan to divide the monarchy along strictly linguistic lines. This, in turn, yielded to a proposal to accord each of the historic Crown Lands an equal voice in the administration of the empire; finally, the heir presumptive arrived back at dualism, albeit with reform of the excessive rights that he felt the Magyars had been granted in 1867. In terms of foreign policy, Francis Ferdinand distrusted the Italians and generally preferred the resurrection of the Three Emperors' League of 1873.

The archduke spoke out between 1908 and 1911 against General Conrad von Hötzendorf's (*q.v.*) desire for a preemptive strike against Serbia as the only solution to the South Slav problem; ironically, it was this issue that was to cost him his life. Francis Ferdinand had been appointed inspector general of all Habsburg armed forces on August 17, 1913, and in this capacity he decided to tour Bosnia with his wife in June 1914. The assassination of the imperial couple in the streets of Sarajevo by Gavrilo Princip (*q.v.*) on June 28 set in motion the chain of events that culminated in the First World War.

A number of recent Habsburg apologists have attempted to make Francis Ferdinand an enlightened ruler who, had he been given the chance, might have solved the nationalities question and in the process transformed the Dual Monarchy into a truly supranational community. Gunther Rothenberg has suggested instead that Francis Ferdinand's foremost aim was to resurrect the centralized monarchy created by Prince Felix zu Schwarzenberg and the army after 1848—a more realistic appraisal by far.

Kiszling, *Erzherzog Franz Ferdinand von Österreich-Este*; Rothenberg, *Army of Francis Joseph*; *Neue Österreichische Biographie*, III; *Österreichisches Biographisches Lexikon 1815-1950*, I.

FRANCIS JOSEPH I (*Austria-Hungary, Emperor of Austria, King of Hungary*), was born at Castle Schönbrunn in Vienna on August 18, 1830, the son of Archduke Franz Karl. Francis Joseph received a careful education especially from Cardinal Rauscher to prepare him to rule his people. The events of 1848 proved central to his subsequent career: at first Francis Joseph took part in the campaign in Italy, but on December 2, 1848, he replaced his weak and mentally unstable uncle Ferdinand I as ruler of the Habsburg Empire. Thereafter, the young ruler personally took part in the campaign to quell the Hungarian revolt; he viewed the army as the main pillar of his rule. Prince Felix zu Schwarzenberg counseled the emperor to crush the Italian nationalist movement, to reject Prussia's attempts to unite the German states, and, in 1851, to suspend the constitution and to rule in a clerical, absolutist, centralized manner. Unfortunately, his foreign adviser Count Buol-Schauenstein had a more disastrous effect on the monarch: Austria's participation in the Crimean War on the side of England and France cost it Russia's friendship, and the unfortunate defeat at Solferino in 1859 cost it the Lombardy. In fact, from 1850 to 1859, Francis Joseph, under the influence of General Grünne, attempted to gain firm control over the army and to command it in person—which no Habsburg other than Joseph II had ever done.

These foreign policy setbacks, in turn, evoked demands for internal reform, especially by the Magyars. Further setbacks came through a series of decrees (1860, 1861, 1865) in which Francis Joseph was forced to abandon his neoabsolutism in favor of constitutional monarchy; in this the emperor was ably assisted by Anton von Schmerling. Later, the crushing defeat at Königgrätz at the hands of Prussia in 1866/1867 not only cost him Venetia, but also compelled Francis Joseph through Baron Friedrich von Beust to seek an *Ausgleich* ("compromise") with Hungary (1867). The monarch was forced to grant self-rule to the Magyars and to have himself crowned king of Hungary at Ofen; in army affairs Francis Joseph remained adamant, however, preserving the armed forces as a single unified entity, and retaining control over it (army order at Chlopy on September 18, 1903).

Francis Joseph redirected his foreign policy toward the southeast. The Dual Monarchy under the leadership of Count Andrássy the Elder in 1873 concluded the Three Emperors' Convention, followed in 1879 by the alliance with Germany, and three years later with Italy (Triple Alliance). At the Congress of Berlin in 1878 Austria-Hungary received the administration of Bosnia-Herzegovina; precisely thirty years later these two territories were annexed under Count A. L. von Aehrenthal. In 1908, 1911, and again in 1912 Francis Joseph firmly rejected the plans of his chief of the General Staff to strike against Serbia in order to solve the South Slav problem.

At home, Francis Joseph opposed all attempts, especially those of the Czechs, to attain equality within the empire and clung to his commitment to Hungary in 1867. Galicia alone managed to acquire special standing within the Dual Monarchy. The emperor in 1907 agreed to the introduction of universal suffrage in the misplaced hope that this would retard the centrifugal forces of nationalism among the thirteen ethnic groups that comprised the empire.

Privately, Francis Joseph was reserved yet warm. He kept family affairs out of the public eye and conducted the court with a rigid, formal etiquette. His self-discipline was remarkable, and his daily work load became legendary. Unfortunately, the last years of his reign were to betray all the optimism that had

accompanied his accession to power at Olmütz in 1848. Francis Joseph was forced to witness the suicide of his only son, Rudolf, in 1889 and, in 1898, the murder of his wife Elizabeth, duchess of Bavaria, whom he had married in 1854; his brother Maximilian had been executed in Mexico in 1867. These personal tragedies drove Francis Joseph into increasing isolation, and he sought comfort only in alpine hunting and, after 1885, with Katharina Schratt.

The assassination of the heir presumptive, Francis Ferdinand (*q.v.*), at Sarajevo on June 28, 1914, prompted the monarch to "put my faith in the Austro-Hungarian army, in its bravery and dedicated loyalty." Francis Joseph followed, rather than directed, Foreign Minister Count Leopold von Berchtold (*q.v.*) to inaugurate hostilities against Serbia; his memories of Solferino and Königgrätz gave him nagging doubts about the fortunes of war. However, the ruler suffered the numerous Austro-Hungarian setbacks stoically "because today's unlucky commander may well be victorious tomorrow." Unfortunately, this prediction went unfulfilled: Francis Joseph died on November 21, 1916, having lost all hope for a military victory and resigned simply to "see if we can last out the winter."

The emperor's death was a mortal blow to the Dual Monarchy. Alive, Francis Joseph had been a strong—perhaps the only—cohesive force almost by longevity and habit alone; when he passed away, affection for the venerable old man was replaced by the long-pent-up forces of nationalism manifest in the numerous ethnic groups that composed the empire. With military victory apparently out of reach and the loyalty of his diverse subjects suspect, Francis Joseph died knowing that his life's work, the preservation and consolidation of the Dual Monarchy, was seriously in jeopardy. It remained for the new Emperor Charles (*q.v.*) to initiate the dissolution of the multinational empire.

Redlich, *Kaiser Franz Joseph von Österreich*; Rothenberg, *Army of Francis Joseph*; *Neue Deutsche Biographie*, V; *Neue Österreichische Biographie*, I.

FREDERICK (*Austria-Hungary, Archduke of Austria, Duke of Teschen, Field Marshal*), was born Friedrich Maria Albrecht in Gross-Seelowitz, Moravia, on April 4, 1856, to Archduke Karl Ferdinand. Frederick began his military career in 1871 with the Tyrolean Kaiserjägerregiment and quickly rose to the grade of major general (1882); in September 1889 he was given command of the V Army Corps in Pressburg and by 1900 had risen to the post of inspector of the army. Frederick was especially active in upgrading the Austrian Landwehr and in building the alpine troops into first-rate fighting units.

Archduke Frederick, in the grade of general of infantry, was appointed commander of the army (*Armee-Oberkommando*) at the outbreak of the war, but all major operational decisions were made by the chief of the General Staff, General Conrad von Hötzendorf (*q.v.*). Frederick became enraged in April 1915 when the Twenty-eighth Infantry Regiment, home garrison Prague, surrendered almost to a man to the Russians at the battle for Dukla Pass, and he requested and received permission from Emperor Francis Joseph (*q.v.*) to dissolve the unit on April 17, 1915. This action not only exacerbated the problem of Czech loyalty, but it also prompted the army to assume control over the civilian administration in Bohemia.

The archduke's primary contribution to the war effort appears to have been his patience and steadying influence on his more mercurial military commanders. These traits served Frederick well not only in his dealings with the volatile German Emperor Wilhelm II (*q.v.*) and with Conrad von Hötzendorf, but also in smoothing numerous petty clashes between his chief of the General Staff and the various German chiefs of the General Staff. Frederick held the grade of field marshal as the only Habsburg soldier from 1895 until November 1916; that same month the new Emperor Charles (*q.v.*) appointed the archduke his personal deputy at army headquarters in Baden—a post which Frederick was relieved of one month later because Charles believed himself capable of strategic planning. Frederick retired from the army in 1917, and apart from a critique of the disastrous campaigns in the summer of 1918, retired from public life. Once among the richest members of his house, Frederick after 1918 lost most of his inheritance to the national states then emerging, and after a short period of exile in Switzerland retired to Hungary, where he died at Altenburg (Magyaróvár) on December 30, 1936.

Bardolff, *Militär-Maria Theresien-Orden*; Pitreich, *Der österreich-ungarische Bundesgenosse im Sperrfeuer*; *Neue Deutsche Biographie*, V; *Österreichisches Biographisches Lexikon 1815-1950*, I.

FRENCH, John Denton Pinkstone (*Great Britain, Field Marshal*), first earl of Ypres, was born in Ripple, Kent, on September 28, 1852, the son of a navy commander. French entered the Royal Navy in 1866, but four years later joined the Suffolk Artillery Militia; in 1874 he was gazetted to the Eighth Hussars. He was promoted captain in 1880 and major

three years later, seeing service in Egypt, the Sudan, and India. After assignment to the War Office, French in September 1899 fought during the Boer War in the rank of major general. Thereafter, Lieutenant General French was commander in chief at Aldershot and promoted general in 1907. In March 1912, he was appointed chief of the Imperial General Staff, and the next year promoted field marshal. However, in 1914 French was forced to resign his post in the wake of the Curragh mutiny, in which the chief of the Imperial General Staff agreed that officers stationed at the Curragh in county Kildare would not have to participate in any armed coercion of Ulster into the acceptance of home rule for Ireland.

On August 4, 1914, at nearly sixty-two years of age, French was appointed commander in chief of the British Expeditionary Force to France. Ten days later he landed at Boulogne, and on August 23 the German First Army engaged French's forces near Mons. The British were almost totally enveloped within twenty-four hours and had no choice but to retreat. In the process, French's army was divided between Sir Douglas Haig's I Corps and Sir Horace Smith-Dorrien's (*qq.v.*) II Corps because the commander in chief was too far removed from the front at St. Quentin. In fact, French then panicked and grew overly pessimistic; convinced that disaster was inevitable, he ordered a retreat from Mons and only a hasty visit by the secretary of state for war, Lord H. H. Kitchener (*q.v.*), to France on September 1 brought the retreat to a halt. French later blamed the disaster at Mons on Smith-Dorrien, who had made a stand a Le Cateau after having lost contact with headquarters and with Haig's I Corps. The overall situation was saved when General Joseph Joffre (*q.v.*), the French commander in chief, advanced with the new Sixth Army from Amiens on September 5-6, crossed the River Marne three days later, and on September 15 had forced the Germans to withdraw to a strong line of defense on the River Aisne.

The British Expeditionary Force was next transferred to Flanders, and late in October French grew so optimistic as to report to Kitchener that the enemy was "playing their last card" in Flanders. On October 31 the British made a stand in the First Battle of Ypres, which ushered in trench warfare after fierce fighting. French felt that he could break the enemy lines if given sufficient forces and, in March 1915, tried at Neuve Chapelle, but to no avail. Late in April the Germans counterattacked, using chlorine gas for the first time, and French's belated efforts to storm the Aubers ridge came to nought. On September 25, 1915, the British attacked in force in Artois, only to be beaten back again at twice the casualty rate they had inflicted upon the enemy. It was a bad case of reverse attrition, and not even the British use of gas at the battle of Loos brought relief; the operation was broken off on October 14. French had not been mentally or physically up to the strains of high command and on December 4, 1915, resigned; fifteen days later Haig replaced him as commander in chief in France.

In January 1916, French was created viscount of Ypres and of the High Lake, county Roscommon, and appointed commander in chief of home forces. He was faced by a severe crisis at Easter 1916, when the Sinn Fein party rose in arms in Ireland and proclaimed a republic. French dispatched two territorial divisions to Dublin and eventually quelled the uprising. In May 1918, Viscount French was appointed lord-lieutenant of Ireland and his tenure in that unhappy land was highlighted only by an unsuccessful attempt on his life in December 1919. He retired in April 1921. French was created earl of Ypres the following year, and he died at Deal Castle on May 22, 1925.

Edmonds and Davies, *History of the Great War. Military Operations: France and Belgium*, 13 vols.; French, *1914*; Keegan and Wheatcroft, *Who's Who in Military History*; Liddell Hart, *The Real War*; *Dictionary of National Biography 1922-1930*.

GALLIENI, Joseph Simon (*France, General, Minister of War*), was born in St. Béat in southwestern France, April 24, 1849. His ancestors had emigrated to France from Corsica at the start of the nineteenth century. Gallieni entered St. Cyr in 1868, graduating in time to participate as an infantry officer in the Franco-Prussian War. That conflict brought him his first war wound and a period as a prisoner of the enemy. In 1876 Gallieni began thirty years of distinguished service in France's colonies. The young officer served in Senegal until 1879, then led an important expedition to the upper Niger. In 1886 Gallieni, then a major, governed the French Sudan. A tour of duty at the War College followed in 1888, but Gallieni soon returned to the colonies. He took command of a military district in Tonkin in 1893, and his service in Indo-China led to a promotion to the rank of general in 1896. Between 1896 and 1905 Gallieni governed Madagascar. He stamped out indigenous resistance in this new French possession, then established a model colonial administration. By now France's most renowned colonial commander, the governor general of Madagascar helped advance the careers of able subordinates like Joseph Joffre and Hubert Lyautey (*qq.v.*).

Gallieni's military career took a sharply different turn in 1905. He returned to metropolitan France to assume command of the XIV Corps at Lyons. The new military environment led the old colonial soldier to rely heavily on young staff officers to help him adjust. Gallieni was offered the post of chief of the General Staff, the senior position in the peacetime army, in 1911. He declined, pointing to his impending retirement and relative inexperience in the *métropole*. He offered the names of Pau and Joffre.

The outbreak of the First World War came three months after Gallieni's retirement. He was recalled to active duty, named Joffre's deputy, and designated to take over as commander in chief if Joffre were killed or disabled. His former subordinate saw Gallieni as a threat as well as an unwelcome ambassador for the war ministry. Gallieni became alarmed at the German attack on Liège, but Joffre rejected his warnings and refused to allow Gallieni at French general headquarters. On August 26 the energetic and frustrated Gallieni was appointed military governor of Paris by the War Ministry. With an outlet for his untapped abilities, he threw himself into preparing the city's decrepit fortifications for an impending siege. Gallieni commanded the city and its garrison during the crucial period that followed, his authority enhanced by the government's hasty departure to Bordeaux on September 2. The Sixth Army, General Maunoury (*q.v.*) commanding, had been formed by Joffre for a blow against the German flank in late August. But the rapid enemy advance pushed it southward from Amiens. It came under Gallieni's control on September 1, but Joffre convinced the War Ministry to put the Paris garrison, along with Gallieni's newly acquired field army, under Joffre's supervision the following day.

Gallieni exchanged messages with his former subordinate on September 3. The Paris commander stressed the need to defend the capital and the difficulty of conducting field operations with the territorial forces that constituted much of the city's garrison. Joffre responded by suggesting that the more reliable units of the Paris forces be used to attack eastward when the French army resumed the offensive. Gallieni seized on this still vague intention. He alerted Maunoury and, on September 4, ordered the Sixth Army to move eastward toward Meaux the next day. The crucial interchange took place between Gallieni and Joffre on the evening of September 4. Aerial and cavalry reports had confirmed that the Germans were crossing the Marne to the east of Paris. The German right flank stood open to Gallieni. Joffre intended to order a general offensive on September 7, but he had not yet issued corresponding orders. To Gallieni, this was intolerable vacillation. He telephoned Joffre to urge an attack on September 6; the Paris garrison would strike the Germans north of the Marne; the British army was to attack northward from its positions south of the river. Joffre agreed. That night his staff issued orders calling for a general offensive on the date Gallieni had demanded. Joffre took direct control of the Sixth Army on September 8. Deprived of his field command, Gallieni continued his efforts to fortify Paris. Meanwhile, he rushed all available forces to help the hard-pressed Maunoury hold on the Ourcq. One division arrived by way of the famous "taxicabs of the Marne," a fleet of Parisian vehicles commandeered by Gallieni. Pinned down by the Sixth Army and threatened by the advance of the British and French armies south of the Marne, the Germans went into a general retreat on September 9. Gallieni later claimed that a strategic triumph would have been in hand had he been allowed to retain the Sixth Army to outflank the German right north of the Marne.

Partisans of Gallieni, notably B. H. Liddell Hart, have called for the old colonial general to receive the lion's share of credit for the German defeat. They laud Gallieni for pushing an indecisive Joffre into the offensive that destroyed Germany's hopes for a quick victory over France and an early end to the war. Gallieni himself argues that Joffre's intention of retreating to the Seine and then turning to attack the Germans was unrealistic: the French forces would have become even more disorganized; the Germans would have smashed them before a position on the Seine could be set up. Joffre's partisans reply that Gallieni's premature attack saved the German army from complete catastrophe: the Germans were entering a hopeless trap south of the Marne when Gallieni, in effect, warned them of their peril. Neither scenario was played out. Gallieni's supporters have the undeniable advantage of pointing to at least a partial victory—the German retreat from the Marne—which was the result of Gallieni's initiative.

Gallieni remained military governor of Paris for another year. Rumors circulated within the government that he had ambitions to take over as a military dictator. The cabinet's unseemly flight to Bordeaux and Gallieni's popularity with the Parisian population gave these murmurings some plausibility. Gallieni heatedly denied them. His interests focused on the military conduct of the war, and his restless interlude away from the fighting was marked by friction with Joffre. Gallieni spoke out as early as November 1914 on the dismal prospects for a strategic victory on the western front. A Balkan campaign offered more promise. Both views were anathema to the commander in chief. Gallieni had friends in high places, notably the vice premier, Aristide Briand (q.v.). Their efforts to gain him a

suitable field command met Joffre's immovable opposition. Gallieni wanted an army group, either the northern one or the one at the center of the fighting front. These went instead to Generals Foch and de Castelnau (qq.v.), respectively.

When Briand took over as premier in October 1915, he offered the War Ministry to Gallieni. Briand had to overcome Gallieni's poor health and reluctance to serve in a civil position. Briand, the "Easterner," persisted; he needed a popular and like-minded war minister. Gallieni, in turn, hoped to reshape the French military effort and perhaps to become de facto commander in chief. He succeeded in removing a number of Joffre's subordinates; and de Castelnau was dispatched to general headquarters to serve as Joffre's deputy. In reality de Castelnau was expected to restrain the commander in chief's penchant for futile offensives on the western front. Briand and Gallieni inherited a disintegrating situation in the Balkans: Anglo-French forces reached Macedonia in October 1915, but too late to meet their aim of bolstering Serbia. Gallieni's military expertise had to give way to political exigencies. He supported Briand's policy of maintaining a force of 150,000 troops at Salonika—too few to have a strategic effect but a sop to the parliamentary critics of concentrating all resources in the west.

In December 1915, Gallieni attempted to reshape the French High Command: Joffre was to be pushed aside; de Castelnau was to control field operations while Gallieni combined the roles of war minister and commander in chief. This ambitious undertaking ran into opposition from Briand and President Poincaré (q.v.). Whatever Joffre's failings, his popularity in France and his prestige among the British government and army commanders made him indispensable. Moreover, Gallieni was sixty-six years old and in poor health. He seemed no candidate for this overwhelming set of responsibilities.

Gallieni's diaries (an invaluable and candid record of the government through military eyes) reflected a steady disillusionment with Briand. The Verdun crisis brought Gallieni's dissatisfaction to a head. First, he found himself situated uncomfortably between the contending parties. Government leaders, warned in late 1915 by field officers of Verdun's weakness, urged corrective action. Joffre responded with an uproar over this violation of the military chain of command. The German avalanche struck on February 21, 1916. Two weeks later Gallieni presented his cabinet colleagues with a sharp attack on Joffre's negligence at Verdun. This he placed into the larger framework of Joffre's unwillingness to accept direction from the government. Gallieni called for bringing the military leaders under effective control. True, some would object; but these were to be dismissed.

Briand realized an open repudiation of Joffre would destroy the government. He swung momentarily to Joffre's defense. Gallieni offered his resignation. At the urging of Briand and Poincaré, he agreed to hang on briefly to preserve the illusion of a united government. But in mid-March, he was ready to resign, his health in ruins. He endured two surgical operations, then died in Paris on May 27, 1916. The last news he received from the front reported the German capture of Fort Douaumont at Verdun. Gallieni was posthumously promoted marshal of France on May 7, 1921.

Gallieni's reputation has risen and fallen in inverse relation to Joffre's. The phlegmatic, quiet, well-fed Joffre with his faith in heavy offensives in the Champagne and Artois stands in sharp contrast to Gallieni—insomniac, vegetarian, and military skeptic. Without the intervention of his poor health, Gallieni might have used the prolonged Verdun crisis to gather the direction of the war into his own hands. Perhaps the authoritarian Gallieni, not the Republican General Sarrail (q.v.), constituted the greatest challenge to Joffre's continued direction of the war.

Esmenard, *Galliéni*; Gallieni, *Mémoires: Défense de Paris, Les Carnets de Gallieni*; Horne, *Price of Glory: Verdun*; Isselin, *The Battle of the Marne*; King, *Generals and Politicians*; Liddell Hart, *Reputations*; Varillon, *Joffre*.

GALLWITZ, Max von (*Germany, General*), was born in Breslau on May 2, 1852, the son of a commoner, a county tax collector. Gallwitz volunteered for the war against France in 1870 and later served in the General Staff as well as the Prussian War Ministry; he was promoted major in 1890 and colonel six years later as chief of field artillery in the War Ministry. Gallwitz was promoted major general in 1902 and appointed department head in the War Ministry as well as deputy chief to the German *Bundesrat*. Three years later, Lieutenant General Gallwitz commanded the Sixteenth Division and in 1911 became inspector of field artillery in the grade of general of artillery. The kaiser raised him into the Prussian nobility in 1913.

Gallwitz entered the Great War as commander of the Guards Reserve Corps as part of the Second Army, and General Karl von Bülow (q.v.) on August 18 ordered him to storm Namur. Thereafter, Gallwitz's Corps was transferred to the east, arriving too late for the battle of Tannenberg but in time on September 9-12 to form the left wing of the Eighth Army at the Masurian Lakes as it enveloped the Russian Second Army. Next came service with the Ninth Army in Silesia and Poland (Ivangorod), then with Army Group Woyrsch (q.v.) near Cracow, and finally as leader of Austro-Hungarian units at the Pilica River.

On February 9, 1915, Gallwitz became head of an army group bearing his name in southeastern Poland and engaged in heavy fighting near Przasnysz. In July Army Group Gallwitz accompanied Field Marshal August von Mackensen (q.v.) during the latter's campaign in Galicia, and thereafter Gallwitz crossed the Narev River and occupied Pultusk, Rozan and Ostrolenka with a newly formed Twelfth Army; in the process he took 111,111 Russian prisoners of war.

On September 30, 1915, Mackensen placed Gallwitz at the head of the Eleventh Army for the campaign in Serbia. The Germans crossed the Danube on October 7, and by the end of November the greater part of the country had been conquered in conjunction with the Austro-Hungarian Third Army. While planning an assault against the Allies at Salonika, Gallwitz, on March 29, 1916, instead was appointed commander of a special Meuse Group West at Verdun. However, General Erich von Falkenhayn (q.v.) next transferred this veteran commander to the Somme, first as head of the Second Army and later as commander of yet another army group bearing his name (German First and Second Armies).

The new army commanders, Field Marshal Paul von Hindenburg and General Erich Ludendorff (qq.v.), in December 1916, appointed Gallwitz head of the Fifth Army before Verdun with the task of stabilizing this sector after the French had retaken Fort Douaumont. In January 1918, Gallwitz's Fifth Army was reinforced with Army Division C and reconstituted as Army Group Gallwitz to the end of the war. In this capacity, Gallwitz absorbed the brunt of American charges in the Meuse-Moselle theater in the fall of 1918. Specifically, his forces blunted the American thrust into the St. Mihiel salient and held the fortified Michel line. The general counseled against an armistice early in November, and instead called for an appeal to the nation to rally in defense of the homeland. Gallwitz resigned on December 6, 1918; from 1920 to 1924 he served in the Reichstag as deputy for the German National People's party.

Gallwitz on several occasions narrowly missed higher appointments. Before the war he had been considered for the posts of Prussian war minister and chief of a military mission to Turkey; from 1914 to 1918 he was twice mentioned as a possible chancellor, and in November 1918, he almost became Hindenburg's successor. These honors attest to his self-confidence, education, and great sense of duty. Gallwitz died in Naples on April 17, 1937.

Gallwitz, *Erleben im Westen* and *Führertätigkeit im Weltkriege; Geschichte der Ritter des Ordens*, I; *Neue Deutsche Biographie*, VI.

GAUCHET, Dominique Marie (*France, Vice Admiral*), was born on August 14, 1853, at Vains, near the English Channel. He was commissioned in the navy in 1879 and, like many of his contemporaries, saw extensive duty at sea in the Far East. Promoted rear admiral in 1910, Gauchet advanced to vice admiral in 1914; at the outbreak of war in 1914, he commanded the navy's department of administration and supply.

In the reshuffling of commanders following the retirement of Admiral Boué de Lapeyrère (*q.v.*), Gauchet took command of the French squadron at the Dardanelles (October 1915). When Admiral Dartige du Fournet (*q.v.*) was relieved in December 1916, following his misadventure in landing an expedition at Athens, Gauchet replaced him as commander in chief of the French fleet in the Mediterranean and nominal director over all Allied naval operations in that theater.

Gauchet proved to be little more than a passive observer of events. In Laurens' vivid description, he saw himself above all as a squadron commander: he busied himself preparing his fleet at Corfu for a grand encounter with the Austrian fleet that, in the end, never materialized. He delegated the touchy political and military task of pressing the Greek royalist government to a subordinate; the more explosive problem of dealing with the enemy submarine offensive he left to the hands of an interallied naval commission. Despite his narrow conception of his sphere of action, he was permitted to remain at his post until the November armistice. The conclusion of the Mudros armistice (October 30, 1918) with Turkey by Admiral Calthorpe of the Royal Navy bound France as well as Great Britain but, given Gauchet's limited inclination to act forcefully on the wider stage of Mediterranean affairs, scarcely involved the French commander.

Gauchet retired from active duty in 1919. He died, at his birthplace, on February 4, 1931.

Laurens, *Le Commandement naval en Méditerranée, 1914-1918*; Taillemite, *Dictionnaire de la Marine*; Thomazi, *La Marine française dans la Grande Guerre*, IV.

GEDDES, Sir Eric Campbell (*Great Britain, First Lord of the Admiralty*), was born in Agra, India, on Sep-

tember 26, 1875, the son of a civil engineer. After graduation from the Oxford Military College, Cowley, Geddes spurned a career in the Royal Engineers and instead departed for the United States in 1891. He returned after four unspectacular years to Scotland, but quickly headed out to India to manage a forestry estate. Geddes returned to England in 1906 in order to work for the North Eastern Railway.

In August 1914, Geddes raised a battalion from the employees of the North Eastern, later known as the Seventeenth Royal Northumberland Fusiliers. The following year he served as deputy director-general of munitions supply, and was asked to investigate the obstacles that impeded the flow of arms to the front in France. In this capacity he won the complete trust of David Lloyd George (*q.v.*), and in 1916 he was appointed director-general of transportation on the staff of the commander in chief, British Army in France, Sir Douglas Haig (*q.v.*), and knighted. Next came the post of inspector-general of transport for all theaters of the war, with the honorary rank of major general. In May 1917, Geddes began a relatively new career as controller of the navy and an additional member of the Board of Admiralty with the temporary and honorary rank of vice admiral. On July 20, 1917, Geddes brought his enormous energy, courage, and initiative to the post of first lord of the Admiralty. He was quickly elected Unionist member of Parliament for the borough of Cambridge in a special by-election; in 1918 he was reelected in the general elections.

Geddes at first was treated with suspicion at the Admiralty. His insistence on appearing in full naval uniform did not sit well with other members of the board: Lord Esher thought it to be right out of Gilbert and Sullivan, "a general to-day, and an admiral to-morrow." In all fairness, it must be said that Geddes simply "loathed" the idea of going to the Admiralty, and that he did so only because of the pressure applied to him by Lloyd George and Sir John Jellicoe (*q.v.*). Geddes proved an able administrator. Specifically, he pushed for the adoption of the convoy system against the advice of most admirals; by September 1917, he could announce that "the convoy system has undoubtedly been a success." Unfortunately, in December 1917, there came a parting of the ways with Jellicoe over the organization of the naval staff and personnel appointments. Moreover, as Geddes put it, "Lord Jellicoe did not evidence progressive adaptability and effectiveness in decision." In a rather clumsy display of lack of tact, Geddes forced Jellicoe's dismissal through a curt letter on Christmas Eve, 1917. Jellicoe, not without pique, believed "that the true reason is that I will not agree to the Navy being run by an autocrat like a Railway!!" And although Jellicoe's successor, Admiral David Beatty (*q.v.*), favored retaining Geddes at his post, it was not to be: Lloyd George transferred the former first lord to the Imperial War Cabinet instead.

Geddes retired from government service on December 11, 1918, but returned in January 1919 as minister of transport, where he was instrumental in the amalgamation of Britain's railroads into four major groups. As chairman of the committee on national expenditure, Geddes recommended a drastic reduction in government spending of almost £87 million ("Geddes Axe"). He left politics in 1922 for the chairmanship of the Dunlop Rubber Company; later he was to pioneer civilian aviation as the first chairman of Imperial Airways. The hard-driving Geddes died on June 22, 1937, on Albourne Place, Hassocks, Sussex.

Marder, *Dreadnought to Scapa Flow*, IV, V; Trask, *Captains & Cabinets*; *Dictionary of National Biography 1931-1940*.

GEORGE V (*Great Britain, King-Emperor*), was born George Frederick Ernest Albert at Marlborough House, London, on June 3, 1865, the second son of the Prince of Wales, later King Edward VII. Prince George joined the navy in 1877 and there befriended Rosslyn Wemyss (*q.v.*). In 1884 the prince attended the Royal Naval College, Greenwich, and seven years later was promoted commander. His naval career was abruptly terminated, however, in 1892 when his older brother, Prince Eddy, Duke of Clarence, died of pneumonia, leaving Prince George (now Duke of York) second in succession to the throne. The following year he married Princess Victoria Mary (May) of Teck, a member of the royal house of Württemberg. Upon the death of Queen Victoria in January 1901, George became Duke of Cornwall; in November of that year he was invested as Prince of Wales. On May 6, 1910, Edward VII died and George V became king of Great Britain, Ireland, and the British dominions beyond the seas, emperor of India.

The new monarch was beset with a host of nagging domestic problems, most notably the veto power of the House of Lords and Irish home rule. In November 1910, Prime Minister H. H. Asquith (*q.v.*) managed to extricate from the king assurances that if the Lords continued to veto the budget sent up by the Commons, sufficient new peers would be created to swing the vote for the government. In the end, the Lords in August 1911 accepted the parliamentary bill which curtailed their veto power. The center of attention

then shifted to Ireland. In January and again in July 1913, the Lords rejected a home rule bill for that unhappy land, and on July 21, 1914, George V called a meeting of leading politicians at Buckingham Palace in an attempt to find a solution to the vexing problem of home rule and the Ulster Unionists. To no avail: four conferences failed to break the deadlock. The king later noted: "For me, the most difficult was the constitutional crisis. In the War we were all united, we should sink or swim together. But then, in my first year, half the nation was one way and half the other."

George V spent much of the war at Buckingham Palace. Early in 1915 he made a gift of £100,000 to the Exchequer and forbade the consumption of alcohol for the duration of the war in his household; in February 1917, rationing was introduced at the palace. The king was deeply saddened by the dismissal of his cousin, Prince Louis of Battenberg, the first sea lord, as a result of scurrilous press attacks on Louis' German ancestry. Moreover, he viewed the loss of the secretary of state for war, Lord H. H. Kitchener (*q.v.*), in June 1916, as a national tragedy. The ruler was extremely fond of Asquith, and thus was saddened to see the prime minister depart in December 1916; George V was outwardly correct towards the new head of government, David Lloyd George (*q.v.*), but he feared the Welshman and especially disliked the running feud the prime minister maintained with the British field commander in France, Sir Douglas Haig (*q.v.*), with whom the monarch maintained a warm correspondence.

On June 20, 1917, George V ordered all princes of his family bearing German names and titles to relinquish them. He took the name Windsor, Battenberg became Mountbatten (marquesses of Milford Haven and Carisbrooke), and Teck became Cambridge (marquesses of Cambridge and earls of Athlone). On a more positive note, George V visited the Grand Fleet five times during the war and paid no less than seven calls to his armies in France. He also made over 300 pilgrimages to hospitals during the war, thereby greatly enhancing morale both at home and at the front. One of his sons (afterwards King Edward VIII) fought with the army in France; another (later King George VI) was with the navy at Jutland.

After the war the vexing problem of Ireland returned. The Home Rule Act was finally passed in December 1920, and in June of the following year George V opened the parliament at Belfast; the Irish Free State was voted into being in December 1921. Three years later the king called upon Ramsay MacDonald to form the first Labour government of Britain—an important chapter in George's kingcraft. In

1926 Arthur James Balfour (*q.v.*) devised the Nicene Creed of the Commonwealth, which five years later led to the Statute of Westminster, according the dominions a greater degree of political autonomy. One of the king's most disputable acts, according to Winston Churchill (*q.v.*), was his bringing about the formation of a national government under Ramsay MacDonald and Stanley Baldwin in 1931, at a time when the depression had crippled the British economy.

George V received the tumultuous acclaim of his subjects during the silver jubilee celebrations in 1935. He died in Sandringham on January 30, 1936. His eldest son reigned as Edward VIII for less than one year, but his second son as George VI guided the nation calmly and safely through the Second World War.

Churchill, *Great Contemporaries*; Guinn, *British Strategy and Politics*; Nicolson, *King George the Fifth*; *Dictionary of National Biography 1931-1940*.

GERARD, James Watson (*United States, Ambassador*), was born in Geneseo, New York, on August 25, 1867, the son of a lawyer. Gerard graduated from Columbia University in 1890, and received a master's degree the following year. From 1892 to 1941 he worked in his paternal grandfather's law firm with only a few interruptions. Gerard sat on the New York Supreme Court from 1908 to 1913. During the presidential campaign in 1912 he had given generously to the Democratic party and in return expected an ambassadorship. Woodrow Wilson (*q.v.*) duly appointed Gerard envoy to Madrid, but in 1913 transferred the barrister to the more important post at Berlin. Without any diplomatic training, Gerard spent his first year at the court of Emperor Wilhelm II (*q.v.*) attempting to learn the rudiments of the language as well as to master the intricacies of court etiquette. For the first two years of the European war, Gerard worked diligently in behalf of Allied prisoners of war and British subjects stranded in Germany.

Ambassador Gerard regularly reported to Washington Germany's hostility concerning American arms sales to the Allies, arguing that the Reich regarded this activity as patently "un"-neutral and that it would seek revenge on the American republic after the war in Europe had ended; South America was singled out as the most likely victim of such German action. Gerard cautioned the State Department to be ready after the European war to counteract expected German offensives in the southern hemisphere. President Wilson generally considered Gerard to be highly gullible and

unreliable, but Colonel House (*q.v.*) thought well of him. The ambassador was somewhat sympathetic to Germany's plight in 1915, and he discerned an element of reason in the German argument that Great Britain's distant naval blockade of the North Sea could be countered only with an equally harsh submarine blockade. In fact, Gerard took the rather unusual step on July 8, 1915, of suggesting to the German government compromise language in their note to President Wilson at the height of the crisis precipitated by the sinking of the liner *Lusitania*. The envoy was to be painfully embarrassed when Wilson flatly rejected the German note, and his relations with the German government soured. In a last-ditch attempt to avoid a break between the two nations, Gerard, in April and May 1916, went to German army headquarters in Charleville to impress upon German leaders the president's firmness over the issue of unrestricted submarine warfare during the *Sussex* crisis. And it was at the suggestion of the German government that Gerard returned to the United States in the fall of 1916 in order to urge Wilson to undertake an early bid for peace in Europe. Upon his arrival in New York City, the diplomat gave a sensational interview to the New York *World* in which he predicted that Germany would resume unrestricted submarine warfare in the near future if the war could not be ended quickly. Gerard's prophecy was fulfilled on February 1, 1917. At the time the ambassador opined that Geman leaders regarded Americans as "a fat, rich race without sense of humor and ready to stand for anything in order to keep out of the war."

After the Great War, Gerard entered a career as Democratic party fund raiser that spanned three decades. He died on September 6, 1951, in Southampton, Long Island.

Gerard, *My Four Years in Germany*; Trask, *Captains & Cabinets*; *Dictionary of American Biography*, XXV Supplement Five.

GIOLITTI, Giovanni (*Italy, Politician*), was born in Mondovì in the kingdom of Piedmont on October 27, 1842. Following in the footsteps of generations of his middle-class family, he obtained a law degree (at the University of Turin in 1860), then entered the civil service. Giolitti carved out a reputation as a rising young talent in the ministry of finance and the ministry of justice in the newly founded kingdom of Italy. In 1882 he was elected to the Chamber of Deputies, and in 1889 he first entered the government as minister of the treasury. In 1892, Giolitti formed his first cabinet—he was to serve five times as Italy's prime minister—and, despite a financial scandal that momentarily disrupted his career, he went on to dominate Italian parliamentary politics in the first decade of the twentieth century. He combined careful "management" of elections, an eclectic willingness to draw support from parties of the Right and Left, and such timely reforms as the establishment of universal suffrage (1912). Even when sometimes out of office during the years from 1903 to 1914, he continued to tower over the political scene.

The expansion of the suffrage led to new elements, such as Nationalists and an enlarged contingent of Socialists, entering the parliamentary scene. Giolitti's ability to twist the Chamber of Deputies to his will weakened in the aftermath of the war with Turkey over Libya, 1911/1912, an expensive venture into which he had been led by Foreign Minister San Giuliano (q.v.). With his parliamentary majority in place but crumbling, Giolitti resigned in March 1914. His successor was Antonio Salandra (q.v.), a Conservative whose cabinet was expected to last a few months, then to give way to Giolitti's return.

When World War I broke out, Giolitti, the logical figure to lead the government, merely stood by. He backed Salandra's initial declaration of neutrality. Unlike the prime minister, Giolitti remained convinced that it would be perilous to depart from neutrality. For one thing, he was pessimistic about Italian military strength—he pictured an enemy army marching into Milan. The nation's continuing economic problems seemed to demand a period of peaceful growth, not the strain of war. Moreover, he thought that Italy could gain territory from the war by means of adroit diplomacy, that is, as the price for its continued neutrality.

In the winter of 1914/1915, interventionists waged an intense press campaign against Giolitti. His neutralism, they alleged, was a disguise for pro-Austrian sympathies. Giolitti's supporters countered by publishing a letter he had written in early January 1915, in which he stated that Italy could expect "quite a lot" (parecchio) from Austria in return for pledges to stay out of the war. Giolitti stood as the recognized spokesman for the neutralist side. Seton-Watson has suggested that this served to strengthen Salandra's personal interest in bringing Italy into the war: the premier could use interventionist supporters to make him a political leader independent of the Giolittian majority in the Chamber of Deputies.

Giolitti met with Salandra in early March and left with the assurance that Italy would remain neutral; this came at a time when Rome's negotiations with both sides in the war proceeded furiously. When Italy severed its ties with Austria and Germany from the prewar Triple Alliance (May 4, 1915), Giolitti came out of seclusion in Piedmont to wage a campaign against intervention.

A string of Allied failures combined with successes for the Central Powers seemed to favor Giolitti. Allied hopes for a quick victory at Gallipoli were fading, for example, at just the time that Austro-German armies were pouring into the Russian rear in Poland. The Cabinet wavered, and Salandra still confronted a solid bloc of Giolitti's supporters dominating the Chamber of Deputies. But Salandra's resignation (May 13) did not lead to Giolitti's accession to power. Offered the chance to form a government, he declined, paving the way for Salandra's return and Italy's entry into the war. His motives, at this turning point in Italy's history, appear uncertain. They probably included fear of provoking civil war, along with concern that his known neutralist convictions would prevent him from drawing territorial concessions from Vienna. Possibly he feared for his life; interventionist demonstrations were causing an uproar in the cities of northern and central Italy.

Giolitti spent most of the war in seclusion. It was not until August 1917 that he made a public political statement—and that dealt with new initiatives in foreign policy and domestic reform to be launched only after the war had ended. In the crisis that followed the Italian military debacle at Caporetto (October 1917), Giolitti took care not to encourage recriminations against the interventionists of 1915.

In 1920, then seventy-eight years old, Giolitti formed his last government. He helped candidates of Mussolini's new Fascist party to get elected, seeing in fascism an antidote to Italy's postwar chaos. In 1924, as the dictatorship tightened its grip, Giolitti broke with Mussolini, joining with Salandra after a decade of political hard feelings had separated the two. Giolitti then faded from the scene. He died in Cavour in Piedmont, July 17, 1928.

Askew, "Italy and the Great Powers Before the First World War"; Bosworth, Italy, the Least of the Great Powers; Giolitti, Memoirs of My Life; Christopher Seton-Watson, Italy from Liberalism to Fascism; Enciclopedia italiana, XVII; Larousse mensuel, VII.

GOLTZ, Colmar Baron von der (*Germany, Field Marshal*), was born in Bielkenfeld, East Prussia, on August 12, 1843, the son of an estate owner. Goltz entered the army in 1861 and took part in the campaigns of 1866 and 1870/1871; next came almost a decade in the military-historical section of the General Staff. Goltz quit the army as major in 1883 in order to reorganize the Turkish military's training centers and eventually the Turkish army. He served first as pasha and later as marshal. Goltz returned to Germany in 1896 as lieutenant general, and two years later was appointed head of fortresses, engineers, and sappers. In 1902 he took command of the I Army Corps in East Prussia, and later became inspector general of the VI and then the II Army Inspectorate. In 1905 many generals favored Goltz as possible successor to Count Alfred von Schlieffen. Instead, the East Prussian in 1909 returned to the Porte; two years later he was promoted Prussian field marshal. In his numerous writings Goltz praised Léon Gambetta's people's army of 1871 and favored two-year enlistments over the prevalent three-year service (neither position earned Goltz the amity of Generals von Schlieffen or Helmuth von Moltke [q.v.]). Above all, Goltz saw future wars involving million-men armies being conducted as national wars, requiring combined land-sea strategies.

Perhaps because of the mediocre performance of Turkish forces in the First Balkan War in 1912, Goltz in August 1914 was given only the administrative post of governor general of occupied Belgium. As early as November 28, 1914, however, he was ordered to Constantinople to serve as the sultan's "adjutant general," a highly nebulous post. Goltz arrived at the Porte on December 12 and was received with icy formality by General Otto Liman von Sanders (q.v.), head of the German military mission to Turkey. The impasse was resolved in mid-May 1915, when Liman assumed command of a new Turkish Fifth Army at the Dardanelles and grudgingly surrendered command of the First Army at the Bosphorus to Goltz. Goltz enjoyed great respect among Turkish army officers, but the minister of war, Enver Paşa (q.v.), viewed the Prussian as being "too old, too soft, a poor judge of men" and generally ignored him. Goltz, for his part, turned his attention to matters of grand strategy and counseled army command at home to consider a German thrust against the British either at Egypt, or, preferably, at India. While this notion was quickly dismissed as quixotic in Germany, Goltz, in October 1915, nevertheless was given command of the Turkish Sixth Army in Iraq and provided a chance to realize at least part of his scheme. General Sir Charles Townshend's (q.v.) army had advanced up the Tigris River in Mesopotamia in a hasty and ill-planned attempt to seize Baghdad, but on December 8, 1915, Goltz's Turkish forces invested Townshend's 12,000 soldiers at Kut el Amara; the British garrison surrendered on April 29, 1916, ten days after "Goltz-Pasha" had died at Baghdad, either of spotted fever or of having been poisoned by the Young Turks.

Colmar von der Goltz, *Denkwürdigkeiten*; Liddell Hart, *The Real War*; Trumpener, *Germany and the Ottoman Empire*; *Neue Deutsche Biographie*, VI.

GOLTZ, Rüdiger Count von der (*Germany, General*), was born in Züllichau in Brandenburg on December 8, 1865, into a noble clan that dated from the thirteenth century and stemmed from the Uckermark. Goltz entered the army in 1885, attended the War Academy, and served as captain in the General Staff. By 1906 he had been promoted major and five years later lieutenant colonel in the General Staff and then at the War Academy. Promoted colonel in 1913, Goltz in March 1914 became regimental commander.

In August 1914, Count von der Goltz led a Hamburg infantry regiment at the battle of Mons. Next came command of the Mecklenburg Thirty-fourth Infantry Regiment at the winter battle of the Masurian Lakes in February 1915; three months later he led the Fifth Guards Infantry Regiment in northern Poland. Goltz in July broke through the Russian lines south of Vilna with this unit, but in October 1915 returned to the western front near Cambrai. In May 1916, Goltz took over the First Guards Infantry Brigade in heavy fighting at the Somme, and in August of that year was promoted major general. In the spring of 1917 he fought with this outfit at the Chemin des Dames, then at the Argonne forest, and in June 1917 he was back at the Chemin des Dames—this time with the Thirty-seventh Infantry Division.

Goltz's career changed dramatically on February 26, 1918, when he was given the Twelfth Landwehr Division—the so-called Baltic Division—for a projected invasion of Finland. Although Chancellor Count Georg von Hertling objected to this undertaking because it would expand the war still further, Field Marshal Paul von Hindenburg (qq.v.) on March 12 persuaded the kaiser to launch the invasion in order to exert "healthy pressure" on the Bolshevik government at Petrograd. On April 1, Goltz moved his 12,000 men across the Baltic Sea. Two days later he landed at Hangö and, meeting with very little Russian resistance, entered Helsingfors (Helsinki) on April 13. Later, at Lahti, his Baltic Division captured 25,000 Russian soldiers. Goltz was appointed "German General in Finland" to the end of the war.

In January 1919, Goltz stood at the Czechoslovakian border, but the next month was sent to Libau as German governor in the Baltic region. His forces captured Riga and Courland from the Bolsheviks in May, a move that aroused suspicion among the Allies in Paris that Goltz might use his VI Reserve Corps to support conservative and reactionary movements in Germany as well as in Russia. Hence the Berlin government on October 3, 1919, recalled and retired Goltz. In fact, his forces (*Das Baltikum*) took part in the right-wing Kapp Putsch in Berlin in March 1920, and were only with great difficulty demobilized. Thereafter, Goltz became active in the youth movement and in officer clubs; in 1924 he was elected president of the United Patriotic Associations. In October 1931, Goltz participated in the right-wing Harzburger front. He died in Kinsegg in Bavaria on November 4, 1946.

Baumgart, *Deutsche Ostpolitik*; Goltz, *Meine Sendung in Finnland* and *Politischer General im Osten*; *Neue Deutsche Biographie*, VI.

GOREMYKIN, Ivan Logginovich (*Russia, Chairman of the Council of Ministers*), was born to a noble family in Novgorod, November 8, 1839. Educated as a lawyer, Goremykin entered government service in 1860 in the era of Alexander II; he was to serve three tsars in all, during a career that spanned fifty-six years. His reputation as an expert on the Russian peasantry helped his ascent to high positions in the Ministry of Justice and the Ministry of the Interior. He rose to minister of the interior (1895), with responsibility for a wide range of police and internal security functions. But friction with a powerful rival, Finance Minister Sergei Witte, led to Goremykin's temporary eclipse. He resigned his office in late 1899 and received membership in the State Council, the customary consolation prize for outworn bureaucrats. In the spring of 1906, however, Goremykin had his revenge: Tsar Nicholas II (*q.v.*) dismissed Witte from the premiership, as he seemed to be overly enthusiastic in welcoming the constitutional shifts brought about by the revolution of 1905. Goremykin, by then recognized as a stalwart of the *ancien régime*, was called back, only to fall after a scant three months in office. Too reactionary to meet the demands of liberal politicians, and seemingly too weak and decrepit to repress them effectively, Goremykin seemed finished.

In early 1914 the old man found himself again in demand to preside over the tsar's council of ministers. At seventy-four years of age, he struck Nicholas II as the perfect antidote to ambitious (and capable) political leaders who might choose to govern at the expense of the monarch's prerogatives.

Goremykin had no voice in the discussions that brought Russia into World War I. But his wartime career—he was Nicholas' premier for the first eighteen months of the conflict—made clear the dangers of ruling Russia through old, faithful retainers. Goremykin was an inadequate leader at a time of grave national peril; his weakness led to the rise of ambitious figures like Nikolai Maklakov inside the cabinet and Grigory Rasputin outside (*qq.v.*). Moreover, an incompetent reactionary as head of the government served as both goad and temptation to Duma leaders anxious for instituting sweeping political reform.

Until the first days of August 1914, the tsar expected to lead his troops personally into battle. Thus, Goremykin began the war with his already considerable powers augmented to let him fill the monarch's shoes. These powers he used to keep Duma sessions short and to administer the government without much regard to growing public discontent. Such a course could prosper, or at least survive, against a background of success; it could not surmount failure. By the summer of 1915, Russia's poorly equipped armies were in headlong retreat from Poland; the civilian population tottered under the stresses of inflation, food and fuel shortages, and the breakdown of the nation's railroads. The tsar revamped the cabinet in the spring of 1915, and, by summer, some of Goremykin's new colleagues taunted the old man for his patent inadequacies as a wartime leader. But the aged premier could still fight back on a narrow front. Almost alone among the ministers, he supported the tsar's decision to take direct command over the armies in the late summer. He encouraged Nicholas to prorogue the Duma in September 1915; and when his cabinet colleagues revolted, Goremykin encouraged the tsar to send the most outspoken of them packing.

Goremykin fell victim, however, to his own success. When the tsar was happily ensconced at Supreme Headquarters in the distant town of Mogilev, sweeping authority was left in the hands of Empress Alexandra (*q.v.*). She found the old man ineffective. At the same time, Duma leaders saw in him a sworn enemy, out to crush the fledgling Russian parliamentary body. Worst of all, the tsar was not yet ready to abandon hopes for a show of support from the Duma. Thus, Goremykin had to go. In February 1916, he left his post at the tsar's request, to be succeeded by a like-minded but smoother figure, Boris Sturmer (*q.v.*).

Goremykin played no further role in the war. He fled to the Caucasus during the March Revolution that followed his resignation by a year and a month. He died there—murdered by a mob according to some accounts—on December 24, 1917.

Florinsky, *The End of the Russian Empire*; Gurko, *Features and Figures of the Past*; Oldenburg, *Last Tsar*, 4 vols.; Pearson, *The Russian Moderates and the Crisis of Tsarism*; Thomson, "Boris Stürmer and the Imperial Russian Government"; *Modern Encyclopedia of Russian and Soviet History*, XIII.

GOTŌ, Shimpei (*Japan, Minister of Foreign Affairs*), was born on the island of Honshu, June 4, 1857, the son of a poor samurai family. He chose a career as a physician, receiving his initial training in Japan followed by advanced study in Germany. Gotō began government service in 1882. By the outbreak of the Sino-Japanese War in 1894, he was director of the Health Bureau of the Home Ministry. The young doctor rose to prominence in establishing a wartime quarantine system to guard the civilian population from diseases carried home by members of the armed forces. In 1898 Gotō accepted appointment as a colonial administrator in Formosa. A notable career in politics followed, marked by Gotō's selection as Japan's minister of communications in 1908, a post he held until 1911. Meanwhile, the physician-turned-politician maintained an active interest in colonial affairs, directing the South Manchurian Railroad Company and serving as vice-president of the government's Colonization Bureau.

In October 1916, Gotō reentered the government to become home minister under General Terauchi Masatake. Gotō was widely considered by contemporaries to be "the power behind the Terauchi cabinet." His interests included foreign affairs, and, in June 1917, he joined the influential Advisory Council on Foreign Policy, composed of military, political, and parliamentary leaders.

The last months of 1917 and the early months of 1918 were a critical period in Japanese foreign affairs. Russia's eastern Siberian provinces were close to anarchy as the effects of the 1917 revolutions spread. Members of the Entente, notably Britain, urged Japan to land an expeditionary force in Vladivostok and proceed westward. London fantasized that such Japanese action might revitalize—or even restore—the eastern front against Germany. Some leaders, including Foreign Minister Motono, were willing, but the necessary consensus did not materialize. Gotō for one insisted that an invitation from the Entente was insufficient. He deprecated the fading power of countries like Britain. Like the *genro*, Japan's influential group of elder statesmen, Gotō insisted that the United States must join in any such expedition. This guaranteed that Japan would not lose the vital financial and material support only the United States could provide. It also shielded Japan from the possibility of a debilitating campaign in Siberia while the Americans stood aside, growing both stronger and more hostile. With the broad consent of diplomatic, political, and military circles, Gotō assumed the post of foreign minister in late April 1918.

Chaos in Siberia deepened. In May the Czech legion, passing through to join Entente forces on the western front, revolted against the Bolsheviks. The Czechs seized the Trans-Siberian Railroad and advanced to the port of Vladivostok. Under intense pressure from Britain and France to aid the Czechs and to support Russian anti-Bolshevik elements,

Woodrow Wilson (*q.v.*) ended American opposition to a Japanese landing. On July 8 Gotō received an invitation to cooperate with the United States in landing limited forces in the area around Vladivostok.

Gotō had larger ambitions. Proposals and counterproposals passed between Tokyo and Washington over the next month. Gotō could not obtain American assent to a large Japanese expedition permitted to occupy the entire Amur valley. Nonetheless, his authoritative statement of Japanese policy, promulgated on August 2, evaded the precise territorial and numerical limits the United States hoped to impose. Interventionist elements in the Japanese military were disappointed, but Japan's Siberian intervention could then begin. To Hayase, Gotō was "its chief architect." When the Terauchi cabinet fell in September 1918, Japan was firmly entrenched in eastern Siberia, with the army providing a powerful impetus for future expansion.

Gotō continued his political career in the 1920s, serving as mayor of Tokyo and returning to his wartime office of home minister. He died in Kyoto, April 13, 1929.

Hayase, "The Career of Gotō Shinpei"; Kennan, *Soviet-American Relations, 1917-1920*, I; Morley, *The Japanese Thrust into Siberia, 1918*; *Biographical Dictionary of Japanese History*.

GOUGH, Sir Hubert de la Poer (*Great Britain, General*), was born in London on August 12, 1870, the son of Sir Charles J. S. Gough, a Victoria Cross winner. He was educated at Eton and at the Royal Military College, Sandhurst, joining the Sixteenth Lancers in 1889. Gough served with the Tirah expedition in 1897/1898, and was severely wounded during the Boer War. From 1904 to 1906 he was assigned a professorship at the Staff College, Camberley, and in 1907 he began four years service as commander of the Sixteenth Lancers. Early in 1914 he headed the Third Cavalry Brigade and during the Curragh mutiny expressed to Prime Minister Herbert Asquith (*q.v.*) his and his officers' unwillingness to compel Ulster to accept home rule for Ireland. Gough was widely unpopular in the army, being known especially for his arrogant manner.

In France in 1914 Gough commanded first the Third Division and in 1915 was given the Second Cavalry Division; later that year he was transferred to head the Seventh Division. Early in 1916 Gough was entrusted with the I Army Corps, Sir Douglas Haig's (*q.v.*) old unit, and then rapidly promoted to command the new British Fifth Army. In July 1916, Gough's forces were heavily blooded in the war of attrition at the Somme. Gough, noted for his dash and "cavalry spirit," (Liddell Hart), desired quick results regardless of the cost, and he launched his army against the enemy at Pozières. Heavy rains combined with bombardments to turn the battlefield into a giant morass over which even the lightly armed infantry could move only with difficulty, but the Germans were finally displaced from the high ground at the Somme. The British frivolously gambled away this temporary advantage by foresaking the high ground and pursuing the Germans down the ridge into the valley beyond, where the troops were to spend the winter of 1916 in flooded trenches. Even so, Gough was knighted in 1916.

On July 31, 1917, General Haig launched another massive attack against the enemy at Ypres and, as in 1916, once again the slapdash work of his staff greatly exacerbated Gough's task. Moreover, the commander's persistence that the quantity of shell was the key to success vitiated any initial successes scored: the British bombardment ruined the drainage system at Ypres, which, compounded by heavy rains, turned the field of battle into a swamp, in which countless soldiers drowned. By November the British had bogged down near Passchendaele, having lost almost 400,000 casualties. General Herbert Plumer's (q.v.) Second Army finally took over the Ypres sector of the front in what was the one bright spot in the British picture.

General Erich Ludendorff's (q.v.) so-called Michael offensive in France broke against Gough's Fifth Army on March 21, 1918, dangerously stretched thin in the Somme sector. Forced to yield ground at considerable loss, Gough's forces retreated over the old battlefields at the Somme, and the cabinet in London laid the blame solely on Gough, forcing his removal from command of the Fifth Army.

General Gough was appointed chief of an Allied mission to the Baltic in 1919, and he retired from active service in 1922 with the rank of general to become chairman of Siemens Bros. During the Second World War, Gough was appointed colonel and zone commander, Home Guard, to 1942. He died in London on March 18, 1963, at age ninety-two.

Gough, *The Fifth Army*; Keegan and Wheatcroft, *Who's Who in Military History*; Liddell Hart, *The Real War*.

GRAVES, William Sidney (*United States, General*), was born in Mount Calm, Texas, on March 27, 1865, the son of a Baptist minister. Graves graduated from "the Point" in 1889 and for the next ten years was attached to the Seventh Infantry. He saw service in the Philippines during the Spanish-American War, and from 1909 to the end of the First World War served with only a few interruptions in the General Staff,

first as its secretary and later as an assistant to the chief of staff.

In June 1918, Graves was promoted to the grade of major general and given command of the Eighth Infantry Division in California. This assignment proved to be of short duration, however, for on August 2, he received secret orders to meet Secretary of War Baker (q.v.) in Kansas City; the secretary met Graves at the railway station and informed the general that he was to proceed immediately to Siberia to command an American Expeditionary Force (AEF) which was being sent there. Baker admonished Graves: "Watch your step; you will be walking on eggs loaded with dynamite. God bless you and good-bye."

Graves never really understood the nature of his mission. He was unaware that President Wilson (q.v.) had agreed to this quixotic adventure only at the insistent pleas of the British and the French. Indeed, the assignment was hopeless. Siberia was racked by a vicious civil war between Bolshevik and White armies; widespread starvation existed; and British, French, and Japanese forces roamed the area at will—as did almost 90,000 soldiers of the so-called Czech legion, deserters from the Austro-Hungarian army. Graves found upon his arrival that he had barely 9,000 men of the Twenty-seventh and Thirty-first Infantry Regiments under his command. The Czech troops hoped eventually to reach the western front by way of Siberia and the sea passage, but they had in the meantime become hopelessly embroiled in fighting with Bolshevik units. Moreover, Wilson's instructions to Graves had been purposely kept ambiguous: the American commander was instructed to protect Allied military stores in Vladivostok, to render aid to the Czechs, and to help the "Russian people" (whoever they were) to determine freely their own destiny. Wilson had not included a further aim, namely to prevent the Japanese from annexing parts of Siberia. Despite pressure from the British and French, Graves heroically stuck to the letter of his instructions and refused to become involved in fighting the Red forces; he had rightly surmised that the president did not desire military operations with the aim of overthrowing the Bolshevik government. Both Secretary of War Baker and General March (q.v.), chief of the General Staff, had opposed the Siberian venture, but the president had overruled them because of the British and French.

Graves finally managed to extricate his troops from Siberia on April 1, 1920. He retired from the army eight years later and died in Shrewsbury, New York, on February 27, 1940.

Graves, *America's Siberian Adventure*; *Dictionary of American Biography*, XXII Supplement Two.

GREY, Sir Edward (*Great Britain, Secretary of State for Foreign Affairs*), third Baronet, Viscount of Fallodon, was born in London on April 25, 1862, the son of an army officer and country gentleman. Educated at Winchester and Balliol College, Oxford, Grey in 1885 was elected Liberal member for Berwick-on-Tweed to the House of Commons; he held this seat throughout his political career. In 1892 Grey became undersecretary of the Foreign Office under Lord Rosebery and later under Lord Kimberley. In March 1895, he gave the so-called Grey declaration in the Commons that French activity in the Upper Nile would be viewed in London as an "unfriendly act." As an avowed imperialist he supported the Boer War, and as a Liberal he favored free trade. As early as 1904, Grey had come out in favor of alignment with Paris, fearing German expansion. In December 1905, he became minister for foreign affairs in the cabinet of Sir Henry Campbell-Bannerman, and three months later at Algeciras upheld the French claim to Morocco. Grey was the principal author of the Anglo-Russian agreement of August 1907, whereby Tibet was declared neutral, Russia abandoned Afghanistan, and both nations agreed to separate spheres of influence in Persia. In 1911 Grey renewed Britain's agreement with Japan and two years later acknowledged Berlin's interests in Turkey. Until 1914 Grey, a man of portentous gravity, eschewed all secret treaties suggested by Germany for the eventual division of European, and especially Portuguese, colonies in Africa. His attempt to mediate the Vienna-St. Petersburg feud arising out of Austria-Hungary's seizure of Bosnia and Herzegovina in 1908 was rejected. Grey was more successful three years later in getting Berlin to recognize the French position in Morocco in return for two strips of the French Congo. In 1912, however, he was to be bitterly disappointed over the failure of Lord Haldane's mission to Berlin to bring about mutual reductions in naval armaments.

The assassination of the Austro-Hungarian heir presumptive, Archduke Francis Ferdinand (*q.v.*), at Sarajevo on June 28, 1914, ushered in Grey's gravest hour: the state secretary's efforts to convene a European conference to deal with the matter were rebuffed in Vienna and Berlin. A pessimistic Grey stood at the windows of Whitehall on August 3 and sadly commented: "The lamps are going out all over Europe. We shall not see them lit again in our lifetime." The next day he witnessed Germany's refusal to recall its troops from Belgium and the resulting British declaration of war. Grey was no longer at the height of events. As one British historian, Paul Guinn, has noted: "The advent of war was to Grey, as to Neville Chamberlain twenty-five years later, a personal disaster to the conduct of which it was impossible to devote a whole-hearted participation."

Grey's bungling diplomacy in 1914/1915 cost the Entente Greece's entry into the war; instead, Grey pursued the mirage of Bulgarian support against the Central Powers and steadfastly refused to guarantee Greece's northern borders for fear of thereby jeopardizing Bulgaria's claims to Greek Macedonia. The implications of this stubbornness for Britain's Dardanelles venture are obvious. On April 26, 1915, Grey signed the secret Treaty of London with Baron Sidney Sonnino (*q.v.*) in which Rome extorted promises of large parts of Dalmatia, North Africa, south Austria, and the Middle East in return for its willingness to join the Entente. By the end of that year, Grey was still, as he put it, "trying at Sofia," but his dilatory efforts were rejected not only by the Bulgars, but also by the Greeks and the Rumanians, with the result that Britain abandoned Serbia and virtually wrote off southeast Europe by October 1915.

In November 1915, Prime Minister Herbert Asquith (*q.v.*) declined to make Grey a member of the new War Committee owing to the state secretary's Balkan disasters, thereby clearly divorcing diplomacy from strategy in Britain's conduct of the war. In fact, Grey was quite isolated even on the matter of British war aims. The state secretary favored the restoration of Belgium's independence, but early in 1916 Asquith went much further in demanding an end to "Prussian militarism" and to "German domination," that is, a crushing military victory over Berlin. Grey, who had close ties to "Colonel" Edward M. House as well as to U.S. Ambassador Walter Hines Page (*qq.v.*), on February 22, 1916, signed the so-called Grey-House agreement, whereby Washington agreed to call a conference to end the war in Europe. The document bluntly stated: "Should the Allies accept this proposal, and should Germany refuse it, the United States would probably enter the war against Germany." Specifically, Grey and House promised to restore Belgian independence and to give Alsace-Lorraine to France. But the political power of the state secretary had ebbed so low by September that he could do little more than register a protest when David Lloyd George, then secretary of state for war, issued a public warning to President Woodrow Wilson (*qq.v.*) that Britain would tolerate no intervention "now that she is prepared until the Prussian military despotism is broken beyond repair." When Lloyd George became prime minister on December 7, 1916, with a clear mandate to win the war, he did not retain Grey at the Foreign Office.

In fact, Grey's health had deteriorated steadily during the war and he was almost blind by the end of his tenure at Whitehall. As early as July 1916 his physical inability to stand up to the rigors of debate in the Commons had led to his creation as Viscount Grey of Fallodon and transfer to the House of Lords. Like Asquith, he simply was not up to the task of running a wartime government or of leading a multinational coalition. As a final service to his country, Grey in September 1919 traveled to Washington in order to persuade the American leader to compromise with the Senate on the issue of the League of Nations and the Versailles Treaty; Wilson refused even to see Grey. Grey died at Fallodon on September 7, 1933.

Birkenhead, *Contemporary Personalities*; Grey, *Twenty-five Years*; Guinn, *British Strategy and Politics*; Robbins, *Sir Edward Grey*; Steiner, *Britain and the Origins of the First World War*; *Dictionary of National Biography 1931-1940*.

GRIGOROVICH, Ivan Konstantinovich (*Russia, Admiral, Minister of the Navy*), was born on February 7, 1853. He graduated from the Naval College in 1874 and served in the Russo-Turkish War, 1877/1878. He then embarked on a steady climb through the navy's officer corps in a succession of sea commands in the Baltic and Far East. Grigorovich took one notable break from sea duty, serving as naval attaché in Great Britain, 1896-1898. In 1903 he took command of the newly constructed battleship *Tsarevich*, built in France, and sailed it from Toulon to the Far East. He was decorated for heroism at the start of the Russo-Japanese War; then, as a newly promoted rear admiral in March 1904, he was placed in command of the shore installations at Port Arthur. He held this post through the siege of Russia's Far Eastern stronghold, and he was decorated again, this time in recognition of his growing reputation as an administrator.

The years of rebuilding Russian naval strength after the debacle against Japan brought new luster to Grigorovich's reputation. Appointed chief of staff for the Black Sea Fleet in 1905, he left to take command of the Baltic port of Libau in 1906. In 1908 he took charge of Kronstadt, the most important of Russia's naval bases. The next year Grigorovich began service as assistant to the minister of the navy. In 1911, promoted admiral, he became minister of the navy.

Grigorovich proved to be both an able administrator and a skilled cabinet bureaucrat. He enjoyed good relations with Duma deputies (notably Octobrists) interested in expanding the navy; at the same time, he managed to retain the support of Tsar Nicholas II (*q.v.*). The admiral quickly won the Duma's approval for a massive building program, which would provide Russia with seven new battleships and a comparable number of cruisers and destroyers; the program was to last until 1930. An even more impressive show of his political skill can be found in Grigorovich's ability, unique among the ministers serving in July 1914, to remain in office until the March Revolution in 1917.

Grigorovich's policies called for concentrating Russian naval strength in the Baltic, bolstering the fleet there with expanded and modernized bases such as Reval. In Admiral von Essen (*q.v.*), Grigorovich had a Baltic Fleet commander more than able to put Russian resources to maximum use. But even this dynamic team could not offset the superiority of German naval resources. Fear of a German offensive strike into the Gulf of Finland, followed perhaps by an amphibious landing near St. Petersburg, dictated a defensive strategy based on massive mine fields. In the Black Sea the picture was similarly cloudy before 1914. Turkey threatened to tip the balance away from Russia by acquiring foreign built battleships. In the summer of 1912 mutinies broke out in the Black Sea Fleet, and these echoes of the revolution of 1905 brought Grigorovich personally to the scene to deal with this internal menace.

The outbreak of World War I blurred Grigorovich's role. The navy came under the supervision of Grand Duke Nikolai Nikolaevich (*q.v.*), Russia's generalissimo. And the potent Baltic Fleet, with a view to possible German amphibious landings in the Finnish gulf, was placed directly under the command of the local Sixth Army. Essen bridled at the consequent restrictions placed on his offensive tendencies; until his death in 1915, he sent his smaller war vessels off on offensive mining operations. His successors, Kanin and Nepenin, pursued this policy, but with diminished verve. In the Black Sea the presence of the German battle cruiser *Goeben* and the light cruiser *Breslau* tipped the scales in favor of the enemy in 1914. The following year, German submarines appeared to keep the Russians insecure. The Black Sea force found itself saddled with a variety of missions: from cutting off Constantinople from coastal vessels delivering fuel to interdicting Turkish seaborne supplies for the armies in the Caucasus to mounting naval demonstrations to the north of the Dardanelles. Not until the arrival of the young Admiral Kolchak (*q.v.*) in the summer of 1916 did Russia begin to dominate the Black Sea. In all this, Grigorovich found himself in a tangle of conflicting interests: a military High Command that looked almost exclusively to land operations and a diverse set of admirals, some of whom welcomed a passive posture and others who bridled at it.

As a cabinet member Grigorovich is credited with quiet and effective support of the needs of the navy. He avoided the bitter ministerial infighting that seriously disrupted the Russian government. To his friends in the Duma, he seemed a liberal, and in the summer of 1915 their trial balloons raised his name as an alternative to the aged reactionary premier, Ivan Goremykin (q.v.). Nonetheless, Grigorovich carefully skirted direct clashes with the crown. In September 1915, citing his military oath of loyalty to the tsar, he joined Goremykin in refusing to sign the protest launched by most cabinet members against Nicholas' decision to take direct command of the armies.

Additional indications that Grigorovich sought to arrest, and perhaps reverse, the disastrous course of Russian affairs were evident in 1916. He opposed the plan of Minister of the Interior Aleksandr Protopopov (q.v.) to concentrate most essential government functions under that incompetent reactionary. In the tumultuous Duma session of November 14, Kadet leader Paul Miliukov had attacked Premier Sturmer and, by implication, Empress Alexandra (qq.v.). Along with the war minister, General D. S. Shuvaiev, Grigorovich visited the Duma at once to ask for continued support for their efforts. In the judgment of some historians, he thus deliberately distanced himself from the hidebound conservatism of Sturmer. Grigorovich also visited the tsar to warn of the growing unrest to be found in the Russian fleet and in the shipyards. The tsar did not respond.

As the March Revolution exploded, Grigorovich tried to confine his volatile naval units to their barracks in Petrograd. But the situation was beyond this last minute effort at repair. In the final hours of the old order, the admiral stood with moderates in the cabinet against Protopopov's inflammatory call for proroguing the Duma.

Grigorovich remained in Russia following the November Revolution. In 1923 he received permission to emigrate to France. He died in exile, March 3, 1930.

Gurko, *Features and Figures of the Past*; Halpern, *The Mediterranean Naval Situation, 1908-1914*; Mawdsley, *The Russian Revolution and the Baltic Fleet*; Pavlovich, *The Fleet in the First World War*, I; Pearson, *The Russian Moderates and the Crisis of Tsarism*; Saul, *Sailors in Revolt*; Thomson, "Boris Stürmer and the Imperial Russian Government"; *Modern Encyclopedia of Russian and Soviet History*, XIII; *Voennaia entsiklopediia*, VIII.

GROENER, Wilhelm (*Germany, General*), was born in Ludwigsburg, Württemberg, on November 22, 1867, the son of a regimental paymaster. He entered the Württemberg army in 1884, attended the Prussian War Academy in 1893-1896, and in the grade of captain entered the General Staff at Berlin in 1899. He was promoted major in 1906 and six years later as lieutenant colonel headed the field railway section in the General Staff. In this capacity Groener was largely responsible for the mobilization of August 1914.

Colonel Groener, by September 1914, had transported 3.1 million men and 860,000 horses to the front. He continued to coordinate the German field railways throughout 1915, received the order *Pour le mérite* and was promoted major general in June 1915 after the capture of Lemberg. Often critical of the strategy of General Erich von Falkenhayn (q.v.), Groener nevertheless was entrusted with a new War Supplies (Food) Office on May 26, 1916; his primary task was to facilitate the import of wheat from Rumania.

On October 29, 1916, Groener was appointed chief of a new War Office within the Prussian War Ministry as well as deputy war minister; the next month he resigned as head of field railways and was promoted lieutenant general. Groener was then in charge of supervising the fulfillment of the monstrous Hindenburg Program's munitions quotas as well as execution of the Auxiliary Service Law, which theoretically made all males draft eligible until their sixtieth birthday. As a pragmatist and as a South German with less of the caste mentality than his Prussian colleagues, Groener fully realized that the German economy could be placed on a war footing only with the cooperation of the trade unions and the Social Democrats (SPD). This meant, in effect, stabilizing inflation through wage and price controls (summer 1917), allowing worker participation on economic planning committees, and generally enhancing the financial lot of the workers. And while Groener denounced strikers in the spring of 1917 as "dirty dogs," his alleged pro-Socialist policies quickly earned him the opposition not only of German industrialists, such as Hugo Stinnes and Carl Duisberg, but also of Colonel Max Bauer who, in turn, mobilized General Erich Ludendorff (qq.v.) against the "brave Swabian."

On August 16, 1917, Groener was transferred to the Thirty-third Infantry Division first at Verdun and later in the Champagne; after this he commanded the XXV Reserve Corps of the Seventh Army at the Aillette River. On February 25, 1918, Groener was sent to the east as head of the I Army Corps under

General Alexander von Linsingen (*q.v.*) in the Ukraine, but on March 28 the Württemberger became chief of staff for Army Group Eichhorn (*q.v.*) at Kiev. Once again, Groener's mastery of field railways was required to exploit the grain reserves of the Ukraine. He enjoyed the reputation of being a brilliant staff officer—provided that the plans were his own creation and not the work of others. On October 29, 1918, Groener succeeded General Ludendorff as deputy chief of the General Staff. He accepted his role stoically: "What transpires now will take its unalterable course, and I must be its whipping-boy."

Groener immediately withdrew the German armies to the Antwerp-Meuse line and by November 6 demanded that the government of Prince Max von Baden (*q.v.*) conclude an armistice. As early as November 2 he had proposed that Wilhelm II (*q.v.*) seek a heroic death at the front at the head of his troops but opposed the notion of abdication as well as the proposed flight to the Netherlands. It was Groener's unenviable task on November 9 to reject the kaiser's plan to deploy force to suppress the revolution in Germany and instead to inform the monarch that the army "no longer stands behind Your Majesty." That same day, Groener concluded a pact with Friedrich Ebert (*q.v.*), whereby the general promised to support the new Social Democratic government, provided that it did not drastically reform the officer corps. Thereafter Groener supervised the return and demobilization of the German armies. After counseling acceptance of the Versailles Treaty in June 1919, Groener retired from active service on September 30, 1919, against the express wishes of President Ebert. He recommended that General Hans von Seeckt (*q.v.*) succeed him.

In retirement Groener gravitated towards the German Democratic party and from July 1920 to August 1923 served as minister of transport, mainly rebuilding the national railway system. Although a staunch monarchist, Groener, unlike many of his colleagues, was nevertheless willing to accept the Weimar Republic and to bring army and nation closer together. Consequently, in January 1928 he agreed to become defense minister; in October 1931 he concurrently served as minister of the interior. Groener's moderate policies might have been successful at another time, but in the tumultuous years that he served they failed to master the situation. The death of Gustav Stresemann (*q.v.*) and the financial collapse of 1929 were followed by brutal street battles between Communists and Nazis. When the latter viciously denounced President Paul von Hindenburg (*q.v.*) during the presidential election of 1932,

Groener was forced to impose a ban on the NSDAP's paramilitary formations (SA and SS), thus vitiating his plans to incorporate these formations into army sports clubs. The right wing vilified him as the man who had forced the kaiser into exile and General Kurt von Schleicher brutally informed Groener, his former patron, that the army no longer possessed confidence in him; Groener resigned his cabinet posts in May 1932. He died in quiet seclusion at Bornstedt near Potsdam on May 3, 1939.

Baumgart, *Deutsche Ostpolitik*; Groener, *Lebenserinnerungen* and *Politik und Kriegführung*; Groener-Geyer, *General Groener*; *Geschichte der Ritter des Ordens*, I; *Neue Deutsche Biographie*, VII.

GUCHKOV, Aleksandr Ivanovich (*Russia, Politician*), was born in Moscow on October 14, 1862. The heir to an industrial fortune, Guchkov studied at Moscow University, then continued his education in Germany. By 1891 he was back in Russia, where he undertook to provide relief to the victims of the famine ravaging large parts of the country. His taste for adventure took him all over the world. Guchkov went to Siberia to help construct the Trans-Siberian Railroad, and, in 1900, he volunteered to fight against the British during the Boer War. He directed the Russian Red Cross in Manchuria in the course of the Russo-Japanese War, 1904/1905, and returned home to launch a political career in the wake of the revolution of 1905. A leader of the Octobrist party, founded as a group of constitutional moderates devoted to the preservation of the monarchy, Guchkov was elected to the Third Duma in 1907.

Guchkov's five years as a Duma deputy—he was defeated for reelection in 1912—set his course for the later years of World War I. He led the Duma's defense committee and developed an interest in modernizing the Russian armed forces. Rising young military officers like Vasily Gurko became his close associates, as did more established figures like General Andrei Polivanov (*qq.v.*), assistant war minister. Guchkov openly criticized Rasputin (*q.v.*), confidant to the imperial family. In December 1913, Guchkov precipitated a split in the Octobrist ranks by opposing support for the increasingly reactionary cabinet ministers being selected by Tsar Nicholas II (*q.v.*). Guchkov then led one Octobrist faction; the other was dominated by Mikhail Rodzianko (*q.v.*), chairman of the Duma.

The outbreak of World War I reunited the Octobrists and returned Guchkov to national prominence. He directed the Russian Red Cross and, in the spring of 1915, took charge of the new war industries committees. These committees brought together

Duma, industrial, and government leaders to solve the bottlenecks in military production that were crippling Russia's war effort. But the tsar's flirtation with political moderation ended by the beginning of the new year. Guchkov, then a member of the State Council, entered the shadow world of political conspiracy. Removing the tsar, perhaps to install the monarch's uncle, Grand Duke Nikolai Nikolaevich (q.v.), became the goal; to do so it was necessary to draw sympathetic military leaders into the plot. But Guchkov suffered a serious heart attack in the first months of 1916. He fell ill again toward the close of the year. General Alekseev (q.v.), chief of staff and a principal target of Guchkov's wooing, was also removed from the scene in late 1916 by failing health.

The coming year brought changes in a less manageable form. Spontaneous revolution exploded in early March, and palace coups were no longer a serious political tool. Guchkov remained a monarchist, however, and he made a vain effort to save the crown, if not the present monarch, by arranging a timely abdication. This failing, Guchkov took the post of minister of war in the new provisional government.

The military expert of the Third Duma could not ride the rapid course of events in the revolutionary spring months. He found himself wedged between the conservative generals at the top of the military hierarchy and the radicals of the Petrograd Soviet. Guchkov tried to slow down the democratization of the army, calling in his friend from the days of the Third Duma, General Polivanov, to lead a study commission on proposed changes in military regulations. Such moves were doomed efforts to dam the tide. Foreign Minister Paul Miliukov (q.v.) attempted to maintain Russia's pre-1917 link to its allies, a step that would bring sizable territorial gains at the close of the war. This sent angry revolutionary crowds into the street calling for the ouster of both Miliukov and Guchkov. The two were driven from office in mid-May 1917.

Guchkov left Russia after the Bolshevik Revolution to settle in western Europe. He made his new home in Paris, where he entered the world of anti-Soviet exile politics. But years of involvement in assassination and sabotage plots could not open the way home. Guchkov died in Paris on February 14, 1936.

Gurko, *Features and Figures of the Past*; Hosking, *The Russian Constitutional Experiment*; Katkov, *Russia 1917*; Menashe, "A Liberal with Spurs"; Pearson, *The Russian Moderates and the Crisis of Tsarism*; Siegelbaum, "The War-Industries Committees and the Politics of Industrial Mobilization in Russia"; Wildman, *The End of the Russian Imperial Army*; *Modern Encyclopedia of Russian and Soviet History*, XIII.

GUÉPRATTE, Émile Paul Aimable (*France, Vice Admiral*), was born in Granville, near Cherbourg, August 30, 1856. The son of a naval officer, Guépratte entered the Naval Training College in 1871 and was commissioned an ensign in 1876. The leader whom his British colleagues later named The Fire-Eater rose quickly. He saw service in the Far East, was promoted captain in 1904, and entered World War I as a rear admiral.

August 1914 found Guépratte in the Mediterranean in command of the *division de complément*, a squadron of aged battleships assigned to guard transports carrying the XIX Corps from North Africa to France. His force became the center of a quarrel between Admiral Lapeyrère, the French naval commander in the Mediterranean, and Minister of Marine Augagneur (qq.v.). Lapeyrère ordered Guépratte to protect the transports; Augagneur ordered him to move eastward to an offensive station off Cape Bon.

In late September Guépratte again found himself in the midst of a dispute between Paris and the Mediterranean command. Over Lapeyrère's objections, Augagneur sent Guépratte and two battleships to strengthen the British forces guarding the Dardanelles, where the powerful German battle cruiser *Goeben* had taken refuge.

Guépratte placed his forces under British authority with no apparent reservations. Augagneur's decision of January 1915 to use French forces in the forthcoming assault on the Dardanelles meant Guépratte would attack under Admiral Carden (q.v.). Lapeyrère learned of the proposed operation only when his nominal subordinate asked for supplies. Guépratte expressed his "absolute confidence in the success" of the coming naval assault on the narrows. His enthusiasm was genuine. At Guépratte's request, his squadron—four battleships strong—received the dangerous task of passing through the British line on March 18 to engage Turkish shore batteries at close range. The initial failure left Guépratte undaunted. He pulled gunners from his battleships to support the ensuing land operations on Gallipoli and called for carrying the army's attacks to the Asiatic side of the Straits. He then became a prominent advocate for a new naval assault: high speed mine sweepers, night operations, the deliberate sacrifice of old battleships manned with volunteers—all seemed promising tools for a naval breakthrough. This endeared him to like-minded British leaders such as Commodore Keyes (*q.v.*). Back in Paris, such ideas terrified Augagneur, whose political career was already fatally compromised by the Dardanelles involvement. He removed Guépratte as quickly as possible to shore duty.

Promoted vice admiral, Guépratte took over the maritime district at Brest and sat out the rest of the war at Bizerte. In his postwar writings he rejected the label "dangerous hothead" he felt Augagneur had given him. Guépratte's allies appreciated him to the end. In November 1915, Lord Kitchener (*q.v.*) considered a final proposal for a naval assault on the Dardanelles and asked that Guépratte command the French contingent; instead, evacuation was agreed upon in London on November 23.

Guépratte retired in 1918 and served in the Chamber of Deputies from 1919 to 1924. He died in Brest, November 21, 1939.

Cassar, *The French and the Dardanelles*; Guépratte, *L'Expédition des Dardanelles*; James, *Gallipoli*; Thomazi, *La Marine française dans la Grande Guerre*, II, III, IV; *Dictionnaire des parlementaires française*, V.

GUILLAUMAT, Marie-Louis Adolfe (*France, General*), was born in Bourgneuf in southwestern France on January 4, 1863. Commissioned as an infantry officer after completing St. Cyr in 1884, he served with distinction in several capacities before August 1914. Guillaumat fought in twelve colonial campaigns including the Boxer Rebellion. The rising young officer taught at the War College in 1907, and, two years later, commanded the La Flèche School for the sons of French soldiers. He directed the infantry office at the War Ministry, and, for a brief period in mid-1914, was *chef de cabinet* to the minister of war.

The course of World War I brought Guillaumat additional opportunities to add to his already bright reputation in the officer corps. He led a division at the battle of the Marne, rose to corps command in 1915, and was clearly marked to go higher still. At the close of 1916, in the reshuffling of high level posts that followed the ouster of General Joffre (*q.v.*) as commander in chief, Guillaumat received the Second Army. In the precarious conditions of mid-1917, he convinced General Pétain (*q.v.*), the new French generalissimo, that the Second Army could stage a successful offensive at Verdun. Guillaumat's August assault on Mort 'Homme and Hill 304 was the first of Pétain's carefully managed offensives designed to restore the confidence of the badly shaken French forces. A failure would have had incalculable consequences for the entire western front, but Guillaumat did not fail. Using a massive artillery preparation and a two-day advance, he gave Pétain precisely the victory the commander in chief needed.

As reward, Pétain named Guillaumat to lead the Army of the Orient in Macedonia. Guillaumat left in December 1917 to reorder the Balkan tangle created by his cashiered predecessor, General Sarrail (*q.v.*). A proven combat leader, well regarded in the National Assembly but free of embarrassing close links to any political party, Guillaumat turned out to be the ideal man for the task. He moved at once to restore good relations with France's allies on the multinational Balkan front and began to prepare for a vigorous offensive—two areas in which Sarrail had been notably deficient. No troops were available from the western front, of course, but Guillaumat had a solution there as well. He welcomed several Greek divisions into his force; Prime Minister Venizelos (*q.v.*) had brought Greece into the war in July 1917. Guillaumat bolstered the morale of the untested Greek units by encouraging their assault on the Bulgar stronghold at Skra di Legen (May 1918), a success upon which the Greeks prided themselves for the remainder of the war.

The crisis on the western front led Pétain to recall Guillaumat; he was replaced by General Franchet d'Esperey (*q.v.*), whose brilliant career had received a potentially fatal setback during the Second Battle of the Marne. Guillaumat took over as military governor of Paris and served as the French representative to the Supreme War Council at Versailles. But he had a lasting interest in the Balkans. With most eyes turned to the crisis on the western front, Guillaumat became d'Esperey's leading supporter in the highest councils at home on the possibility of a fall offensive in the Balkans. He won over the Supreme War Council in July; in a personal visit to London (September 1918), the enthusiastic Guillaumat convinced the British government to back a major effort in Macedonia. Having thus set the stage for d'Esperey's great march from Macedonia to Hungary, Guillaumat spent the final weeks of the war in the field at the head of the Fifth Army driving into the Ardennes.

Guillaumat's wartime exploits made him a major figure in the postwar army: member of the Supreme War Council, army inspector general, and commander of French occupation forces in Germany (1924-1930). In 1926 he served briefly as minister of war under Aristide Briand (*q.v.*). He died at Nantes, in June 1940.

Beaufre, *La France de la Grande Guerre*; King, *Generals and Politicians*; Palmer, *The Gardeners of Salonika*.

GURKO, Vasily Iosifovich (*Russia, General*), was born May 8, 1864, to a family in the Russian nobility. He was still a teenager when his father, Iosif Vladimirovich Gurko, covered himself with glory as a high-ranking commander in the 1877/1878 conflict with Turkey. The younger Gurko followed in these distinguished footsteps. He graduated from the aristocratic Corps of Pages in 1885 and took a suitable command in a regiment of the Imperial Guards. In 1892 he completed the General Staff Academy. Thus, the young officer was primed, both by birth and military education, for a rapid ascent in his profession. Neither were his prospects hurt by having an elder brother, Vladimir Iosifovich Gurko, rising to high position in the Imperial Chancellery and the Ministry of the Interior.

By 1900 Gurko had advanced to colonel, after serving as a military attaché with the forces of the Orange Free State during the Boer War, 1899/1900. He acquitted himself well in the Russo-Japanese conflict: in a befitting course for a properly rounded *Genshtabist*, he served as chief of staff for the I Siberian Army Corps, then turned to command a Cossack cavalry brigade.

Between 1906 and 1911 Gurko emerged as a leading advocate of army reform. He chaired the military commission investigating the Russian combat performance in the war with Japan. He also developed political ties with sympathetic members of the Duma, Russia's new parliamentary body. Particularly close to Octobrist leader Aleksandr Guchkov (*q.v.*), whom he first encountered when Guchkov fought as a volunteer with the Boers, Gurko was one of a circle of young officers whom Guchkov recruited to advise Duma leaders on proposals for revamping Russia's discredited military system. In 1911 Gurko returned to duty with troops, taking command of the First Cavalry Division.

The wartime years saw Gurko rise with astonishing speed. In August 1914, he was leading his division as part of General Rennenkampf's (*q.v.*) First Army in East Prussia. Little more than two years later, Gurko was acting chief of staff for the Russian army, filling in for the ailing General Alekseev (*q.v.*). Gurko fought as a division commander at Lodz in November 1914, then advanced in January of the following year to take charge of the VI Army Corps.

In mid-1916, Gurko was the logical choice to rescue and restore the battered Guards Army. This force had been formed from the army's elite guards units the previous winter and specially trained as a reserve to be thrown into combat at a decisive time. The summer of 1916 brought it to the brink of disaster: the incompetent General Bezobrazov led the

guards to be mauled in the marshes east of Kovel. By September Gurko's force—renamed the Special Army—was back on the line, and it participated in the last stages of General Brusilov's (*q.v.*) offensive in mid-October. Shortly thereafter, Gurko was called upon to take Alekseev's place, in effect commanding the entire Russian army.

Gurko's major accomplishment in his tenure as acting commander was to draft a reorganization plan for the entire Russian front. The controversial proposal called for reducing the size of Russia's combat divisions, thereby opening the way to create as many as sixty new divisions. Gurko apparently hoped to distribute artillery and other heavy equipment more equitably and, in general, to improve the efficiency of the faltering military system. Critics have suggested that the scheme was doomed to fail: no reshuffling of masses of conscripts could make up for the intolerable shortages of weapons and trained cadres. Politics formed a more shadowy facet of Gurko's activities. At least since early 1916, his old associate Guchkov had been approaching top generals like Alekseev, seeking to form a united front against the monarchy. According to Katkov, Gurko continued this subversive work, first established between the Octobrist leader and the army chief of staff.

Alekseev returned to duty in early 1917 to lead the army through the crisis of the March Revolution. In the wake of that event, Gurko rose to command the western front, replacing General Evert (*q.v.*). Gurko's efforts to cooperate with the provisional government soon became overshadowed by the latter's desire to democratize the military system. The distinguished general tried to channel, and thus to moderate, the action of soldiers' committees and other outgrowths of the revolutionary era on his front. But by May, Gurko and most of the other senior army commanders were on their way out. Opposed to the projected summer 1917 offensive, and disturbed by sweeping official declarations on "soldiers' rights," Gurko made one last effort to sway War Minister Kerensky (*q.v.*) in mid-May. At a meeting of Kerensky and the senior commanders, Gurko found his call for caution in revamping the army rejected. Gurko had combined his warning with pointed suggestions that the army High Command might abandon the provisional government and perhaps restore military discipline on its own initiative. Kerensky turned at once to more conciliatory generals like Brusilov.

Gurko was relieved in June. To compound his humiliation, Kerensky assigned the senior general to command a division in Kazan, hundreds of miles from the fighting front. Gurko resigned. The cashiered general was arrested in August for writing a letter of sympathy to the deposed Tsar Nicholas II (*q.v.*), then banished to live abroad. He spent the rest of his life in exile and died in Rome, February 11, 1937.

Gerua, "General-rytsar' "; Gurko, *War and Revolution in Russia*; Katkov, *Russia 1917*; Mayzel, *Generals and Revolutionaries*; Rutherford, *The Russian Army in World War I*; *Modern Encyclopedia of Russian and Soviet History*, XIII; *Sovetskaia istoricheskaia entsiklopediia*, IV; *Voennaia entsiklopediia*, VIII.

HAASE, Hugo (*Germany, Politician*), was born at Allenstein, East Prussia, on September 29, 1863, the son of a Jewish cobbler. Haase studied law and first practiced at Königsberg as the only Social Democratic lawyer in East Prussia; he rapidly made a name for himself throughout the land, defending Otto Braun in 1904 and Karl Liebknecht three years later. But Haase was also deeply interested in politics. As a lad he had already joined the Social Democratic party (SPD) during the period of Otto von Bismarck's anti-Socialist laws; in 1894 he became the first SPD deputy elected to Königsberg's city parliament, and in 1897-1906 and 1912-1919 he served his party in the Reichstag. A soft-spoken man devoid of personal ambitions and histrionics, Haase in 1911 succeeded Paul Singer as deputy leader of the party and two years later, after the death of August Bebel, joined Friedrich Ebert (*q.v.*) as cochairman of the SPD. Haase continued to nourish a deep sense of justice and right and from his office in Berlin became a renowned defender of workers in court, never charging for his legal services. Although he mastered Marxist rhetoric, Haase in spirit remained closer to the humanism and cosmopolitanism of his fellow Königsberger, Immanuel Kant.

Unlike Ebert and Philipp Scheidemann (*q.v.*), Haase did not rise through the party bureaucracy; rather, he remained an outsider, a left-wing intellectual. Haase spoke out against militarism and imperialism and in favor of pacifism. On the eve of the Great War he opposed the demands of South German (Baden) Socialists that the SPD cooperate with middle-class parties in the Reichstag.

August 1914 proved a bitter experience for Haase. During the July crisis he stood almost alone in denouncing the approach of war, and his public utterances raised for the government the prospect that the SPD might not vote for war credits. During the decisive party caucus on August 3, however, only 12 of the 110 SPD deputies joined Haase in opposing the war; as caucus leader he was forced by party discipline to bow to the will of the majority and next day in the Reichstag to read his party's unanimous vote on behalf of war credits. In his heart, however, Haase knew that the decision had been wrong. On June 19, 1915, he joined Karl Kautsky and Eduard Bernstein in a famous Demand of the Hour, which denounced the government's annexationist war aims program. In March 1916, Haase formed a Social Democratic Working Union and formally voted against war credits; as a result, he was forced to relinquish coleadership of the SPD. Although suffering from frayed nerves and bouts of depression, Haase continued to campaign against censorship, the state of siege, and the lack of political and social equality in imperial Germany. Easter 1917 brought the final split in the party when Haase was elected head of a new Independent Social Democratic party (USPD) at Gotha—the very place where over a half century earlier the various factions of German socialism had united. In place of the victor's peace demanded especially by the vociferous Pan-Germans, the USPD offered the notion of a peace without victors or vanquished.

Haase proved his vision and statesmanship during the revolution of November 1918. Curbing the romantic revolutionaries within the USPD, he counseled cooperation with Ebert's SPD in directing Germany towards a democratic, republican future. Haase joined Ebert on November 10 as coleader of the Council of People's Commissars, and one month later, during the First German Congress of Workers' and Soldiers' Councils, opted against the dictatorship of the proletariat in favor of a constituent national assembly, reform of the officer corps, and nationalization of heavy industry. Unfortunately, Ebert preferred to cling to his secret pact with General Wilhelm Groener (*q.v.*) in which the head of the German labor movement had promised not to reform the aristocratic Prussian officer corps. And when at the end of the year Ebert ordered army units to dislodge radical sailors from the former royal stables in Berlin, Haase protested the blood spilled by resigning from the Council of People's Commissars.

Yet the level-headed Haase refused to bolt to the extreme left. Despite the bloody suppression of the Spartacist uprising in January 1919 and the cowardly murders of Rosa Luxemburg and Karl Liebknecht, Haase in March 1919 urged the USPD to support the SPD. His pleas on behalf of a "unified Socialist party"—excluding the newly founded Communist party—were to remain stillborn for him: Haase died on November 7, 1919, four weeks after a psychotic shot him with a revolver.

Groh, *Negative Integration*; Haase, *Hugo Haase*; Ritter and Miller, *Die deutsche Revolution*; Schorske, *German Social Democracy*; *Neue Deutsche Biographie*, VII.

HAIG, Sir Douglas (*Great Britain, Field Marshal*), first Earl Haig, was born in Edinburgh on June 19, 1861, the son of a Scottish distiller. The family motto later proved most apt: "Tyde What May." Haig was admitted to the Royal Military College, Sandhurst, by patronage in 1883, and was subsequently gazetted to the Seventh Hussars in India, where he excelled at polo. He was promoted captain in 1891 and five years later attended the Staff College. After service with Lord H. H. Kitchener in the Sudan, he returned as major in the cavalry at Aldershot under Sir John French (*qq.v.*), and later accompanied French to South Africa as his staff officer during the Boer War. From 1906 to 1909 Lucky Haig, as he was commonly called, was attached to the War Office in order to draft the first British field service regulations and to lay the foundations for the creation of an Imperial General Staff. After another brief tour of India, Haig in 1911 returned to the blue ribbon of home commands, Aldershot, and was promoted lieutenant general. Hence, when he took the I Army Corps to France in August 1914 it was composed primarily of his Aldershot troops. Liddell Hart has called Haig the "distilled essence of Britain," an officer dominated by determination "which when beneficial is called tenacity, and when harmful called obstinacy."

Haig did not share General French's cheerful optimism about the war, and instead urged Lord Kitchener, then state secretary for war, to plan for a prolonged struggle. He fully expected the German march through Belgium and, therefore, was prepared for the retreat from Mons at the end of August. His end of the operation left much to be desired: by retreating south instead of southwest as ordered, Haig exposed the flank of Sir Horace Smith-Dorrien's (*q.v.*) II Army Corps, forcing Smith-Dorrien to make a stand at Le Cateau. Haig's I Corps joined the French counterattack on September 9 and crossed the River Marne. Lucky had a splendid opportunity to separate the German First Army (Kluck) from the Second (Bülow), but an inaccurate aerial report urged caution rather than action upon him. Several days later Haig crossed the River Aisne, but stubborn German resistance denied him the important Chemin des Dames.

Generals French and Joffre (*q.v.*) moved the British Expeditionary Force from the Aisne to Flanders at the end of September 1914, and Haig's I Corps joined General Henry Rawlinson's (*q.v.*) forces at Ypres on October 19. In the ensuing First Battle of Ypres, Haig's stout defense and his imperturbable calm saved the day against four attacking enemy corps; Sir John French had been ready once

again to retreat. Early in 1915, when the British Expeditionary Force was reorganized into two armies, Haig received command of the First Army, composed of the Indian Corps, the IV Corps, and his own I Corps. In March Lucky Haig went on the attack at Neuve Chapelle "regardless of loss," as he put it. Several abortive attempts to break through the German trench barrier and to storm enemy machine gun fire failed miserably; in fact, Haig viewed the machine gun as "a much overrated weapon." Matters went from bad to worse. General Joffre planned a massive offensive in Artois for May, to be commanded by General Ferdinand Foch (*q.v.*); Haig, for his part, stormed the Aubers ridge, to no avail. Undaunted, the ever optimistic Joffre decided to send Foch on yet another charge at Artois and in Champagne. When Generals French, Haig, and Rawlinson objected, the French government appealed directly to the British cabinet. The resulting battle of Loos on September 25 proved a costly failure. Although supported for the first time by gas, the attack quickly degenerated into trench warfare; British casualties of nearly 60,000 were double those of the enemy. General French was relieved of command, and on December 19, 1915, Haig succeeded him as commander in chief of British forces in France—a turn of events aided no doubt by Haig's secret dispatches to King George V (*q.v.*) concerning French's military leadership.

The British by 1916 had three armies in France, and when General Erich von Falkenhayn (*q.v.*) began the siege struggle for Verdun in February, Haig went on the attack at the Somme in order to relieve the pressure on the French. It proved to be, as Liddell Hart noted, the glory as well as the graveyard of "Kitchener's Army"—the citizen volunteers who in 1914 had formed the first national army of Britain. On July 1, 1916, reinforced by a fourth army, Haig formally began the battle of the Somme. On the first day alone, 60,000 men were lost and before the struggle was broken off in November, Britain had lost almost 400,000 casualties on the field of battle. These attritional tactics were the nadir of infantry tactics, and the governments both in London and in Paris vetoed demands by Haig and Joffre to renew the attack in mid-November.

In January 1917, Haig was ordered by Prime Minister David Lloyd George at Calais to support an offensive by the new French commander in chief, General Robert Nivelle (*qq.v.*). It, too, proved an utter disaster and resulted in a series of mutinies in the French armies. As for Haig, the Germans had in the meantime abandoned their positions along the Somme for the Hindenburg line, with the result that the British advance at Vimy Ridge and at Arras in April was directed into a void. However, the new French commander in chief, General Henri Pétain (*q.v.*), urged Haig to keep the pressure on the Germans while he restored order and morale to the French armies. Haig accordingly ordered the Second Army of General Herbert Plumer (*q.v.*) in Flanders to attack Messines, and himself planned a great demonstration at Ypres. Once again disdaining the "old master keys of concentration and surprise," Haig on July 31 launched the Third Battle of Ypres, better known as Passchendaele—the last phase of what Liddell Hart termed "the gloomiest drama in British military history." A lengthy bombardment not only tipped the Germans to the coming assault but also destroyed the drainage system and turned the fields into swamps even before the rains came; the British lost a further 400,000 casualties at Ypres. It was but slight consolation that a tank offensive at Cambrai on November 20 foreshadowed the events of the next fall. But late in 1917 the Italian collapse at Caporetto and the Bolshevik seizure of power in Russia convinced Haig that the great German offensive would come in the spring of 1918.

The expected storm broke against the British Third and Fifth Armies on March 21, 1918. Haig, who up to now chose to rely on his friendship with Pétain for mutual support, at last consented to the appointment of General Foch as generalissimo. "I can deal with a man, but not with a committee," an obvious reference to his opposition to the creation of the Supreme War Council late in 1917. Foch duly set about to repair the threatened rupture between the French and British armies at Amiens, but further German attacks at Arras and on April 9 in Flanders near Neuve Chapelle brought Haig to the point of despair. No fewer than twenty-four British divisions had been broken up and reinforcements rushed to France from Palestine and Salonika. On April 10 Haig fully acknowledged the gravity of the situation in his historic order of the day: "There is no other course open to us but to fight it out. Every position must be held to the last man. . . . With our backs to the wall and believing in the justice of our cause, each one of us must fight to the end." Relief came on July 18, when Foch mounted his great counterattack along the Marne. Haig also went on the offensive, most notably on August 8 on the Amiens front with 450 tanks, the "black day of the German army" according to General Erich Ludendorff (*q.v.*). Method and determination, Haig's greatest assets, now were rewarded. On August 21 he sent his Third Army across the Somme battlefields of 1916, and by the third week in September the Germans had withdrawn

to the shelter of their Hindenburg line; by October 12 even this great defensive system had been broken and the enemy thrown back behind Lille. On November 11, 1918, it was all over.

Haig came home in July 1919 to take command of the home forces. He received the thanks of Parliament, a grant of £100,000, and was created Earl Haig by the king. He retired from the home forces in January 1921, and devoted his remaining years to the cause of those who had fought in the Great War. Haig died in London on January 30, 1928, and was accorded a national funeral. He was buried near the ancestral home of the Haigs at Bemersyde, which had been purchased by national subscription in 1921.

Haig was not one of the great captains of military history. As a person, he was cold and self-seeking. As a military commander, he was unimaginative. Haig was not receptive to creative inventions, refusing in 1915 to acknowledge the importance of the machine gun and cancelling construction of tanks, owing to their alleged low military value. He displayed throughout the war an obstinacy in adhering to fixed plans regardless of the facts; the battles of Arras and Passchendaele in 1917 especially showed Haig pursuing unattainable goals, even at the price of destroying his own armies. His choice of an old friend without experience in France, General Sir Launcelot Kiggell (*q.v.*), as chief of staff in December 1916, proved unfortunate. And Haig's unbounding faith that he was the only man in Britain for the job did not bode well either for his relations with the government in London or with the French command. The frequent comment that he was no worse than any of the other British military "Barons" in the Great War reflects only upon the mediocre stable of military leaders available to Britain in 1914.

Edmonds and Davies, *History of the Great War. Military Operations: France and Belgium*, 13 vols.; Keegan and Wheatcroft, *Who's Who in Military History*; Liddell Hart, *Reputations* and *The Real War*; Marshall-Cornwall, *Haig as Military Commander*; *Dictionary of National Biography 1922-1930*.

HAMILTON, Sir Ian Standish Monteith (*Great Britain, General*), was born on Corfu on January 16, 1853, the son of an army captain. He attended the Royal Military College, Sandhurst, and in 1872 was posted to the Twelfth Foot in Ireland. Next came duty in India, where the charming, intelligent Johnny Hamilton blossomed; he took part in campaigns in Afghanistan, Natal, Egypt, and Burma, being promoted major in 1885 and colonel six years later. Hamilton came home in 1898 to command the Musketry School at Hythe, but the following year left for South Africa, where he took part in the relief of Ladysmith and the march on Pretoria. By then he prided himself on being a protégé of both Lord Roberts and Sir H. H. Kitchener (*q.v.*). His career was secure: after serving as chief of a military mission with the Japanese army in 1904, he headed the Southern Command at home from 1905 to 1909, was promoted general in 1907, and from 1910 to 1914 had the Mediterranean Command at Malta.

The outbreak of war in Europe found Johnny Hamilton as aide-de-camp to King George V (*q.v.*). Lord Kitchener, then state secretary for war, appointed Hamilton to head the Central Force, responsible for the defense of England in the event of invasion. Hamilton's fortunes turned on March 12, 1915, when Kitchener ordered him to his great surprise to depart at once for Mudros to take command of an Anglo-French force at the Dardanelles. It was fully expected in London that the navy could do the job unaided and hence Hamilton's orders were most vague; only in the unlikely event that the naval action failed, would he engage his entire force to open the way for the fleet.

Hamilton's Utopian dreams of an easy entry into Constantinople faded rapidly on March 18 as he witnessed the loss of several battleships in the first unsuccessful attempt by Admiral Sir Sackville Carden (*q.v.*) to force the Straits. When the admiral's successor, Sir John De Robeck (*q.v.*), informed Hamilton that the navy could not renew the attack until the army had seized the craggy peninsula, Hamilton agreed; on March 27 he received the official go-ahead. His maps were woefully outdated and his knowledge of the rugged terrain nil. The element of surprise had been lost when lack of facilities at Mudros forced Hamilton to outfit his 75,000-man Mediterranean Expeditionary Force at Alexandria. Last but not least, the bungling diplomacy of the Foreign Minister, Sir Edward Grey (*q.v.*), had cost the Allies the support of Greece and Russia at the Straits.

This notwithstanding, Hamilton stormed the beaches at the southern tip of the peninsula at Cape Helles and Gaba Tepe, and it was primarily due to his courageous leadership that the landings were at all a success. With the Turks commanding the heights, the struggle quickly degenerated into trench warfare and Hamilton's plight became acute; repeated pleas for reinforcements went unanswered, but national prestige demanded a victory. In July the government at last sent him an additional five divisions—but the Turks had also been reinforced. Hamilton secured a new beachhead at Suvla Bay on August 6, but once again the initial surprise was vitiated by defensive deployment on the beaches rather than storming the heights. The cabinet then lost confidence in Hamilton, and when he informed Kitchener in October that evacuation of Gallipoli would cost at best half, at worst all, of the force, it was decided to change commanders in Asia Minor. General Charles Monro (*q.v.*) replaced Hamilton and upon visiting all three beaches, advised immediate evacuation. As Winston Churchill (*q.v.*) put it: "He came, he saw, he capitulated."

Johnny Hamilton received no further command during the Great War. He published his account of the operation in 1920, and died in London on October 12, 1947.

Aspinall-Oglander, *Military Operations: Gallipoli*, 2 vols.; Hamilton, *Gallipoli Diary*, 2 vols.; Liddell Hart, *The Real War*; *Dictionary of National Biography 1941-1950*.

HARBORD, James Guthrie (*United States, General*), was born the son of a farmer near Bloomington, Illinois, on March 21, 1866. Harbord received a Bachelor of Science degree from Kansas State Agricultural College in 1886; three years later he was unsuccessful in his application to West Point and instead entered the army as a private. In 1895 Harbord graduated from the Infantry and Cavalry School and was awarded a Master of Science degree. While with the Tenth Cavalry in the fall of 1899 he met John J. Pershing (*q.v.*). Harbord served from 1902 to January 1914 in the Philippines, initially in the grade of captain; from January 1914 to April 1917 he was a student at the Army War College.

On May 15, 1917, Harbord was appointed chief of staff to his old friend General Pershing, and for the next twelve months he helped the American field commander to pick and to organize a staff for the projected American Expeditionary Forces. Harbord was decisive, frank, and completely loyal to Pershing, who appointed Harbord in May 1918 as commanding brigadier general of the marine brigade in the Second Division. Sixty days later Harbord was given command of the Second Division and promoted to the grade of major general, and in this capacity he led the Second Division at Soissons in the wake of General Ludendorff's (*q.v.*) Michael offensive in the west. Harbord's success was often due more to the raw courage of his men than to his tactical brilliance; in fact, it has been charged that the general often failed to have complete control over his troops during combat. Harbord also overestimated the role of the rifle and the machine gun in modern warfare at the expense of artillery—in short, he did not fully grasp the concept of superior concentrated fire power. Some critics have claimed that Harbord at times expected his men to fight beyond a reasonable threshold of endurance.

Above all, Harbord's unbending loyalty to his chief was to place him in the center of the celebrated "Pershing-March Feud." During the summer of 1918 Pershing got wind of a plan in the War Department by General March (q.v.), army chief of staff, to send General Goethals to France as senior supply officer. Pershing fended this scheme off by appointing Harbord head of the Services of Supply on July 28, 1918. Harbord's adept handling of the logistical forces helped expedite the transport of 3 million soldiers to Europe, and by the war's end Harbord had under him a force of 386,000 soldiers as well as a host of civilian aides and German prisoners. Unfortunately, Harbord had not been as adept in his dealings with March. He fueled the "Pershing-March Feud" by completely rejecting any good intentions on the part of the chief of staff, whom he accused of a "distinctly unfriendly act" when March sought to establish an exchange of staff officers between his office and Pershing's headquarters in France. Harbord informed Pershing that this proposal "shows no consideration for your needs, and undermines your well-laid foundation, with what wild ambition in mind we can only guess."

Harbord continued to serve Pershing in various capacities after the Great War, and he retired in December 1922. Owen D. Young and David Sarnoff brought the retired general to the Radio Corporation of America as president, a post that Harbord held for the next twenty-five years. He died on August 20, 1947, at Rye, New York. Not surprisingly, Pershing spoke of him in an efficiency report in 1922 as "the ablest officer I know."

Coffman, *War to End All Wars*; Harbord, *The American Army in France* and *Leaves from a War Diary*; Penrose, *James G. Harbord*; *Dictionary of American Biography*, XXIV Supplement Four.

HARMSWORTH, Alfred Charles William (*Great Britain, Director of Enemy Propaganda*), Viscount Northcliffe, was born in Chapelizod, near Dublin, on July 15, 1865, the son of a barrister. Largely self-educated, he devoted his youth to free-lance journalism. In 1887 he formed a general publishing business in London for several journals, most notably *Answers*. Harmsworth's Amalgamated Press soon tallied annual profits of £50,000, which he used to purchase newspapers: in 1894 the *Evening News*, 1896 the *Daily Mail* for the "man in the street," 1903 the *Daily Mirror*, and in 1905 the *Observer*. He even

began his own logging and papermaking enterprise in Newfoundland to supply his press with paper. Harmsworth was created a baronet in 1903 and two years later was raised to the peerage as Baron Northcliffe, of the Isle of Thanet—in each case upon the recommendation of Arthur James Balfour (q.v.). He reached the zenith of his ambitions in 1908 when he became the chief proprietor of *The Times*, designed for those of "quality." It is estimated that the Northcliffe stable accounted for half the circulation in London during the Great War.

The First World War thrust "King Alfred," as many called him, into the public limelight. He had for some time predicted that war would break out on the Continent, and in December 1914 the *Daily Mail* crowed that it was "the paper that foretold the War." Northcliffe generally championed the cause of the generals against the politicians, whose careers he claimed he had made. In August 1914, his press clamored for the immediate dispatch of the British Expeditionary Force to France; the following year it incited the public outcry that forced the resignation of Lord Haldane from the government. Through *The Times* Northcliffe raised about £17 million for the care of the sick and the wounded. Although, in August 1914, he had demanded the appointment of Lord H. H. Kitchener (q.v.) as secretary of state for war, early in 1915 Northcliffe turned his newspapers against the venerable soldier, bitterly attacking him for supplying deficient and obsolete shells to the armies in France. Dictatorial, capricious, and distrustful, Northcliffe supported, and then denounced, the coalition governments of Herbert Asquith in May 1915 and of David Lloyd George (qq.v.) in December 1916. He campaigned for the introduction of compulsory military service and visited the western front several times, most notably at Verdun in March 1916.

Prime Minister Lloyd George dispatched Northcliffe to the United States from June to November 1917 as head of a British war mission. The press lord mainly toured the Midwest, as well as Canada, but managed to send off occasional advice on how to deal with Washington: "Nothing can be gained here by threats, much by flattering and self-abnegation." Upon his return, Northcliffe was created a viscount, but he turned down an offer of secretary of state for air. In February 1918 Lloyd George, who viewed the great press lords as modern-day equivalents of the great territorial magnates of the eighteenth century, appointed Northcliffe director of enemy propaganda, thereby bringing the Northcliffe press over to his side.

After the war, the *Daily Mail* engaged in vituperative attacks against the former secretary of state for war, Alfred Lord Milner (*q.v.*), and against Lloyd George, who had refused to take King Alfred to Paris as an official member of the British peace delegation. At home, Northcliffe demanded that the kaiser be brought to trial for war crimes and that the Germans be made to pay for the war. He viewed himself as the principal director of the empire's destiny and in 1921 set out to visit the various far-flung British possessions. Although he returned a sick man, early in 1922 he visited Germany and promptly declared that his former enemies had poisoned him. Northcliffe died in London on August 14, 1922. He had been the undisputed press lord of Fleet Street for nearly two decades, but, as one critic aptly put it, "he never quite understood the rooted objection of his countrymen to the exercise of power without responsibility."

Guinn, *British Strategy and Politics*; Pound and Harmsworth, *Northcliffe*; Trask, *Captains & Cabinets*; *Dictionary of National Biography 1922-1930*.

HAUS, Anton Baron von (*Austria-Hungary, Grand Admiral*), was born in Tolmein, Slovakia, on June 13, 1851, the son of a tavern owner. Haus originally wanted to study natural science, but owing to financial stringency instead entered the navy in 1869. A master of six languages, he taught oceanography for four years at the Naval Academy in Fiume; in 1890-1892 he sailed around the world on the *Saida*. Thereafter, Haus was assigned to the torpedo service and in 1901 as captain took part in the expedition to quell the so-called Boxer Rebellion in China on board the cruiser *Maria Theresia*. For the next three years he served in the Naval Section of the War Ministry, and in 1902 befriended the heir presumptive, Archduke Francis Ferdinand (*q.v.*), an ardent supporter of a modern battle fleet. Rear Admiral Haus represented the Dual Monarchy at the Second Peace Conference at The Hague in 1907, and for the next three years commanded the Active Fleet; he was promoted vice admiral in 1911 and one year later the special post of inspector of the navy was created for him. Upon the retirement of Admiral Rudolf von Montecuccoli (*q.v.*) in February 1913, Haus was promoted full admiral and appointed head of the navy as well as chief of the Naval Section. He abandoned Vienna in favor of Pola on the Adriatic Sea in order to be closer to the fleet.

At the outbreak of the war, Haus made the fateful mistake of halting all ship construction and releasing highly skilled workers to the army, since he felt, along with so many others, that the war would not last long. The admiral concentrated his forces at Pola and saw his primary objective as the blockade of the Montenegrin coast. When Italy declared war against Austria-Hungary, however, Haus on May 24, 1915, ordered a raid on the eastern seaboard of Italy from north of the Po River as far south as Ancona. A flotilla including ten capital ships shelled the Italian coast from Barletta to Rimini, catching the Italians completely off guard and delaying the assembly and transport of ground forces in Venetia for several weeks. In May 1916, Haus was promoted grand admiral—the only officer of the Austro-Hungarian navy ever to reach that grade.

Haus was initially opposed to the concept of German unrestricted submarine warfare, but in time came to champion this new weapon of *guerre de course*. At the crown council on January 20, 1917, he was the only high-ranking government official save General Conrad von Hötzendorf (*q.v.*) to support unconditionally Germany's decision to resume unrestricted submarine warfare.

Lung disease cut short his career; the grand admiral died on board the dreadnought *Viribus Unitis* on February 8, 1917. Haus had several times rejected offers of ennoblement.

Bardolff, *Militär-Maria Theresien-Orden*; Sokol, *Österreich-Ungarns Seekrieg 1914-1918*, 4 vols.; *Neue Österreichische Biographie*, I.

HELFFERICH, Karl (*Germany, Deputy Chancellor*), was born in Neustadt/Haardt on July 22, 1872, the son of a textile factory owner. Helfferich studied economics in Berlin, Munich, and Strassburg and in 1899 accepted a post at Berlin University; he lectured there for the next seven years, arguing for the need to adhere to the gold standard. Concurrently, beginning in 1901, Helfferich joined the Colonial Office, where by 1904 he helped to establish the German mark as the currency in Berlin's colonies (save East Africa, where the following year a reformed Indian rupee was introduced). In 1906 Helfferich quit government service and moved to Constantinople as director of the famous Baghdad Railroad; two years later he became director of the Deutsche Bank in Berlin. Helfferich thus closely personified the expansionist, exuberant Wilhelmian entrepreneur.

On January 31, 1915, Helfferich was appointed state secretary of the treasury. He rejected the British method of paying for the war by sharply increased taxation and instead opted to finance war production by floating mammoth loans, to be repaid either by the vanquished or by future German generations. This highly inflationary course was only partially offset in 1916 by new consumer, transport, and war profits taxes.

Helfferich on May 22, 1916, also assumed leadership of the Ministry of the Interior and became deputy chancellor to Theobald von Bethmann Hollweg (*q.v.*). In this capacity he was largely responsible for carrying out the Hindenburg Program of increased armaments production as well as the Auxiliary Service Law—both drafted by Colonel Max Bauer (*q.v.*). When several left-wing leaders of the Social Democratic party opposed Helfferich's heavy-handed enforcement of the Service Law, the state secretary responded by jailing them. "It is better that one or another innocent person suffer than that a guilty one be left at large to create harm for the Fatherland."

Early in the war Helfferich opposed unrestricted submarine warfare fearing that it would lead to a clash with the United States. He was not present at the crown council at Pless on January 9, 1917, which adopted U-boat warfare *à outrance* regardless of the consequences; one month earlier Helfferich had convinced Bethmann Hollweg of the need to put out peace feelers after the disastrous Verdun campaign, but the combined army-navy submarine initiative easily carried the day instead.

In 1917 Helfferich gravitated toward the army's new commanders, Paul von Hindenburg and Erich Ludendorff (*qq.v.*); the deputy chancellor then endorsed the U-boat gamble, opposed the Reichstag's "peace resolution" calling for an end to the war without annexations or indemnities, and flatly came out against Bethmann Hollweg's promised reform of the antiquated Prussian three-class suffrage. Neither did the deputy chancellor attempt a major effort to support his chief against the vicious attacks of Bauer, Ludendorff, and Crown Prince Wilhelm (*q.v.*) in July 1917. Helfferich resigned as secretary of the interior after Bethmann's fall, but clung to his other two cabinet posts under the army's chancellor, Georg Michaelis (*q.v.*), until the latter's dismissal in October 1917 over his inept handling in Parliament of the naval rebellions of that summer.

In July 1918, Helfferich succeeded the murdered Count Wilhelm von Mirbach-Harff as ambassador to Russia. In contrast to the state secretary for foreign affairs, Paul von Hintze (*q.v.*), who favored cooperation with the Bolsheviks, Helfferich worked actively on behalf of the counterrevolution and in August had to be recalled.

Throughout the war, Helfferich had opposed the parties of the Reichstag majority, and in 1919 he joined the German National People's party as an avowed enemy of the Weimar Republic and the policy of fulfillment. Helfferich's caustic diatribes against the republic's supporters led Chancellor Joseph Wirth after the assassinations of Matthias Erzberger and Walther Rathenau (*qq.v.*) to point to Helfferich in the Reichstag and to state, "The enemy stands on the right," thereby publicly associating Helfferich with the assassins. Although the directors of the Reichsbank unanimously endorsed Helfferich's candidacy for the presidency of the central bank, neither President Friedrich Ebert nor Chancellor Gustav Stresemann (*qq.v.*) was willing to underwrite the reactionary former deputy chancellor; instead, the appointment went to Hjalmar Schacht. To the open relief of many, Helfferich was fatally injured in a train accident in Bellinzona, Switzerland, on April 23, 1924.

Ambitious, arrogant, a tenacious "clinger" to office, Helfferich had struggled for the greater glory of the German Empire, and when this creation died in 1918, he lashed out in blind fury at those he considered most responsible, particularly Erzberger. Perhaps because of his Calvinist temperament, Helfferich was always inclined to view himself as one of the elect and apt to confuse his own interests with those of the nation.

Fischer, *Karl Helfferich*; Helfferich, *Der Weltkrieg*, 3 vols.; Williamson, *Karl Helfferich*; *Neue Deutsche Biographie*, VIII.

HENRY, Prince of Prussia (*Germany, Grand Admiral*), was born in Potsdam on August 14, 1862, the second son of the future Kaiser Frederick III. According to Hohenzollern tradition, Henry at age ten became a second lieutenant in the First Guards Regiment. In 1877, however, he switched to the navy. After travels to South America, Asia, and Africa, Henry was posted to the Navy Academy and, in 1887, became chief of a division of torpedo boats. A host of ship commands followed, and in 1897 Rear Admiral Prince Henry was assigned to the Cruiser Squadron in East Asia, which he commanded as vice admiral two years later. In 1900 the prince led German naval units to China in the wake of the so-called Boxer Rebellion with explicit orders from his imperial brother to crush the Chinese. Promoted admiral in 1901, Henry returned to head the Baltic Sea naval station at Kiel in 1903. Three years later he was appointed chief of the High Sea Fleet, a post Henry held until 1909 when quarrels with Admiral Alfred von Tirpitz (*q.v.*) over naval strategy forced the kaiser to choose between the two; Prince Henry was promoted grand admiral and given the largely honorific title of inspector general of the navy.

As early as July 30, 1914, Grand Admiral Prince Henry was appointed commander in chief, Baltic Forces. The post had been created specifically for this senior royal commander, whose deployment in the main theater of the war was not desired. For three years, Henry held the Baltic Sea lanes to Sweden open for vital ore shipments; occasional sorties against Russian units at times ended with the loss of German cruisers owing to mines or to British submarines. In November 1916, Henry lost seven of the most modern torpedo boats during a senseless raid into the Gulf of Finland. Above all, the prince was an enthusiastic advocate of a German invasion and annexation of Denmark ("Case N") should the chance present itself, so that the navy would command Jutland and thereby gain access to the northern approaches of the North Sea to the Atlantic Ocean. In October 1917, a German flotilla under Vice Admiral Ehrhardt Schmidt—and nominally under Prince Henry's command—occupied the Baltic islands Ösel, Moon, and Dagö in the Gulf of Riga; the Russian battleship *Slava* was severely crippled by German naval fire. The Bolshevik Revolution ended operations in the Baltic Sea, however, and on February 1, 1918, Henry's Baltic Sea command was dissolved. The prince virtually retired to his estate at Hemmelsmark near Eckernförde for the rest of the war. In November 1918, he managed to escape, in disguise and flying the red flag, from rebelling sailors in Kiel.

After the war Prince Henry maintained naval traditions and connections, became an avid flyer and car driver, and was one of the few Hohenzollerns to be allowed to remain on German soil. The kaiser's brother died at Hemmelsmark on April 20, 1929, of cancer of the throat, the same disease that had claimed his father in 1888.

Gemzell, *Organization, Conflict, and Innovation*; Herwig, *"Luxury" Fleet*; *Geschichte der Ritter des Ordens*, II.

HENTSCH, Richard (*Germany, Colonel*), was born in Köln on December 18, 1869, the son of an army sergeant. Hentsch entered the Saxon army in 1888, attended the Prussian War Academy, and was attached to the Prussian General Staff where he was promoted captain in 1901. Thereafter, Hentsch served on the Saxon army's General Staff and was given several infantry commands; in 1906, however, he returned to the Prussian General Staff where he was promoted major three years later. In 1912 Hentsch served as staff officer with the XII Army Corps and, in April 1914, received his third appointment to the Prussian General Staff in the grade of lieutenant colonel.

In August 1914, Hentsch was head of the Foreign Armies (Intelligence) Department of the General Staff. Helmuth von Moltke (*q.v.*) had great confidence in Hentsch and often used him to relay messages to front commanders—as was to be the case in September 1914 at the River Marne. In the general advance on Paris, General Alexander von Kluck's (*q.v.*) First Army had precipitously turned southwest near Amiens-Péronne, and in the process a wide gap developed between the inner wings of this force and General Karl von Bülow's (*q.v.*) Second Army. The French and British threatened to exploit it. Moltke, at German headquarters in Luxembourg, dispatched Hentsch on a 400-mile tour of the front with sweeping powers to make adjustments to the deployment of armies as he saw fit. At Montmort on September 8, Hentsch found a deeply pessimistic Bülow, convinced that he was on the brink of annihilation unless ordered to retreat at once. When Kluck could not assure Hentsch that he would be able to support Bülow with all available forces immediately upon the heels of a French thrust into the gap, Hentsch felt no choice but to order on September 9 a general retreat from the Marne behind the Aisne along the line Soissons-Fère-en-Tardenois. The battle of the Marne had thus been won by the Entente.

In May 1915, Hentsch was attached to an Austro-Hungarian Army Corps and during the summer of that year planned the invasion of Serbia. On September 12, 1915, Hentsch became deputy chief of staff of the Eleventh Army, part of Army Group Mackensen (*q.v.*), and received credit for the successful crossing of the Danube and Save rivers. Promoted colonel in January 1916, Hentsch served under Mackensen during the ensuing Rumanian campaign in the fall and winter of 1916 and, on March 1, 1917, was appointed staff chief of the military occupation of Rumania at Bucharest. He died there on February 13, 1918. Hentsch maintained to the end that his decision at the Marne had been the proper one.

Indeed, Hentsch's action of September 8/9, 1914, is probably the most debated single event of the Great War. General Oskar von Hutier spoke for many when he accused the staff officer of having "cheated the troops of victory" on that day. There is near consensus in the memoir literature of German generals that Hentsch's actions deprived an apparently victorious army of the fruits of their labors and thereby frustrated the Schlieffen plan. The charge does not sit well. It is perhaps symptomatic of the state of the German military in 1914 that a staff colonel should be accorded the blame that properly rests with a kaiser who could not fulfill his chosen role, with a General Staff chief who doubted the master plan and who lacked resolute will as well as steel nerves, and an army commander (Bülow) who was overly pessimistic at the approach of shadows, the alleged movement of British marines and Russian armies (!) in Flanders.

Barnett, *The Swordbearers*; Baumgarten-Crusius, *Deutsche Heerführung im Marnefeldzug*; Liddell Hart, *The Real War*; *Geschichte der Ritter des Ordens*, I; *Neue Deutsche Biographie*, VIII.

HERTLING, Georg Count von (*Germany, Chancellor*), was born in Darmstadt on August 31, 1843, the son of a Hessian privy councillor; the family had been ennobled in 1745 in the Rhenish Palatinate. For a time Hertling considered entering the priesthood, but instead, he turned to philosophy at Münster, Munich, and Berlin. In 1867 he accepted a position at Bonn University, but was denied promotion owing to his defense of the Catholic Church during Bismarck's struggle with Rome (*Kulturkampf*). In that same year Hertling founded the Görres Society for the advancement of learning in Catholic Germany; he remained its head until his death in 1919. In 1882 Hertling received a politically motivated appointment as professor of philosophy at Munich University.

Hertling became increasingly active in politics. In 1877-1890 and again in 1896-1912 he represented the Center party in the Reichstag, leading his party's parliamentary caucus from 1909 to 1912. Hertling had been a passionate protagonist of Ludwig Windthorst, but in time he sought to bring the Center party into the mainstream of German national politics. Specifically, he was the only Bavarian Center delegate who voted for Admiral Alfred Tirpitz's (*q.v.*) first navy bill in 1898.

Hertling's career entered yet another phase on February 9, 1912, when he accepted the post of Bavarian minister president under Prince Regent Luitpold, thereby ushering in a parliamentary regime at Munich. Hertling was instrumental in persuading Prince Regent Luitpold to accept the Bavarian Crown as King Ludwig III in November 1913. The minister president played no role during Germany's decision to go to war in July 1914, and he staunchly defended Chancellor Theobald von Bethmann Hollweg (*q.v.*) in July 1917 against attacks from both the military and the Reichstag.

Hertling was mentioned as possible successor to Bethmann Hollweg in July 1917, mainly owing to the astute lobbying efforts of the Bavarian envoy to Berlin, Count Hugo Lerchenfeld-Köfering. The Bavarian minister president refused to leave Munich.

Only after the abysmal failure of Chancellor Georg Michaelis (*q.v.*) to steer an independent course between generals and the parliamentary majority did Hertling agree on November 1, 1917, to accept the nation's highest political office; he served concurrently as Prussian prime minister.

Hertling's one-year stint as chancellor was not a success. He was already seventy-four years old and plagued by ill health. Moreover, his own party under the leadership of Matthias Erzberger (*q.v.*) provided little support. Hertling did not view favorably the development of a parliamentary majority bent on reforming the iniquitous Prussian three-class voting system. The chancellor also proved utterly unable to assert his will against General Erich Ludendorff's (*q.v.*) vast annexationist schemes in the east, embodied in the Draconian settlements of Brest-Litovsk and Bucharest. Never certain that he was the right man for the job, Hertling seized upon the military setbacks in the west to resign on October 3, 1918, in favor of a fellow South German, Prince Max von Baden (*q.v.*). Hertling retired to his estate in Ruhpolding, Upper Bavaria, to write his memoirs, but died on January 4, 1919.

Baden, *Erinnerungen und Dokumente*; Hertling, *Ein Jahr in der Reichskanzlei*; *Neue Deutsche Biographie*, VIII.

HINDENBURG, Paul von Beneckendorf und von (*Germany, Field Marshal*), was born in Posen on October 2, 1847, the son of an army officer; both sides of his family had once possessed estates in East Prussia. At age twelve Hindenburg entered the cadet corps at Liegnitz/Silesia and later at Berlin. He fought with the Prussian army at Königgrätz in 1866 and against France in 1870/1871. Next came studies at the War Academy in 1873-1876 and thereafter service in the General Staff as captain; Hindenburg was promoted colonel in 1894, major general three years later, and lieutenant general in 1900. He became regimental commander at Oldenburg in 1893, staff chief of the VIII Army Corps at Koblenz in 1896, divisional commander at Karlsruhe by the turn of the century, and chief of the IV Army Corps at Magdeburg from 1903 to 1911. Hindenburg had been considered as possible successor to Count Alfred von Schlieffen at the General Staff and later as Prussian war minister, but each time without success. He had not helped his cause in 1909 when he made the colossal blunder of allowing the kaiser to lose a sham battle during fall maneuvers. He retired to Hanover on January 9, 1911, seeing little prospect for war in the near future. A man of solid, simple strength, Hindenburg had been sure, steady, and faithful as an officer. He was slow moving and slow thinking, but surrounded by an aura of imperturbable calm. Tall and thickset, his brush-cut hair and beetling brows defined his physical features.

General of Infantry von Hindenburg was reactivated on August 22, 1914, after General Max von Prittwitz und Gaffron (q.v.) had ordered a German retreat in the east behind the Vistula. He was told to meet his chief of staff, General Erich Ludendorff (q.v.), at the train station in Hanover, and in this unorthodox manner Germany's most influential and fateful team was hastily assembled to halt the Russian "steamroller" in the east. Hindenburg was quickly promoted colonel general.

Acting upon plans already largely drawn up by Prittwitz's first staff officer, Colonel Max Hoffmann (q.v.), Ludendorff and Hindenburg on August 23-30 routed the Russian Second Army at Tannenberg, and then at the Masurian Lakes on September 5-15 inflicted a severe defeat upon the tsar's First Army; Hindenburg's primary contribution to victory had been to steady, as the battle unfolded, the brilliant but flighty Ludendorff. Hindenburg was then widely celebrated as the "savior of East Prussia," and, in November 1914, was promoted field marshal as commander in chief of the eastern front. His name became a household word. With the Eighth and Ninth Armies, Hindenburg engaged the Russians around Lemberg and Warsaw and defeated them near Brzeziny. And in February 1915, he led the Eighth and Tenth Armies at the bitter winter battle of the Masurian Lakes, in which the Russian Tenth Army was virtually annihilated and East Prussia again cleared of enemy troops. Hindenburg was hailed as the true pupil of Schlieffen, as the one soldier who properly understood the concept of battle of annihilation à la Cannae and Sedan.

No new envelopments came in the east in 1915. Though Ludendorff and Hindenburg had planned to deploy six or eight army corps in a great left-handed turning movement from the north (East Prussia), designed to scoop up the 1 million Russian troops in the Warsaw salient, General Erich von Falkenhayn (q.v.), however, refused to release the requisite forces from the western front. Falkenhayn instead stormed Armentières and raced the enemy to the Channel ports; in the east, the frustrated duumvirate of Ludendorff and Hindenburg twice failed to take Warsaw, and General August von Mackensen's (q.v.) breakthrough at Gorlice-Tarnów on May 2 could not properly be exploited owing to lack of reserves. Not surprisingly, relations between Falkenhayn and Ludendorff and Hindenburg soured, and bitter recriminations became the order of the day. For the moment, Falkenhayn's strategy of

winning over Bulgaria, defeating Serbia, and establishing a direct link with Turkey won the day. But then in February 1916, the chief of the General Staff gambled almost 300,000 of his best assault troops against Verdun and the tide quickly turned against him. The British counterattacked at the Somme and the Russians in Galicia, Rumania joined the Entente, and Verdun remained in French hands. Chancellor Theobald von Bethmann Hollweg joined with Colonel Max Bauer (qq.v.) to depose Falkenhayn, and on August 28, 1916, Wilhelm II (q.v.), to the utter surprise of his chancellor, received Hindenburg at Pless as the new chief of the General Staff and Ludendorff as his first quartermaster general.

The appointment of the duumvirate of Tannenberg fame marked a turning point in German history. The powers of the kaiser rapidly ebbed and those of politicians were openly questioned by the military. Ludendorff and Bauer especially usurped the civilian domain; Hindenburg lent his national reputation to these efforts, often agreeing to tender his resignation when Ludendorff ran up against stiff opposition. Many of Hindenburg's decrees and letters were actually written by Ludendorff, who cleverly rallied the venerable old soldier against the kaiser and cabinet.

The Third Army Supreme Command got off on the right foot. In December 1916, Rumania was defeated, the eastern front was stabilized by General Hoffmann, the armies in the west were safely withdrawn behind the so-called Hindenburg line, and a massive program of munitions production as well as an Auxiliary Service Law were promulgated under Hindenburg's name. In Berlin a massive wooden statue attested to the field marshal's stature.

Unfortunately, Hindenburg agreed with naval experts that Great Britain could be forced to the peace table within six months if the U-boats were allowed to sink Allied ships without constraint; unrestricted submarine warfare commenced on February 1, 1917, but failed to attain its promised goal. When Parliament approved a peace resolution calling for an end to the war without annexations or indemnities, and when Bethmann Hollweg opened up the Pandora's box of Prussian suffrage reform, Hindenburg and Ludendorff, on July 13, 1917, forced the chancellor's resignation, against the kaiser's wishes. As successor they chose an unknown, petty bureaucrat, Georg Michaelis (q.v.), who promised to be a submissive figurehead.

On the military side, Italy was severely crippled at the battle of Caporetto in October 1917, and the Russian front collapsed in the wake of the Bolshevik takeover in November 1917, even though peace negotiations were to drag on until March 1918. Hindenburg shared most of Ludendorff's utterly unrealistic war aims and lent his name to the outrageous demands made upon Rumania and Russia in 1917/1918 that would have extended German influence in the east to Finland, the Baltic states, the Ukraine, and the Crimea as far as the Caspian Sea. The main decision, however, was still to come on the battlefields in France.

In March 1918, Ludendorff and Hindenburg gambled on a massive assault near St. Quentin, designed to break the Allied line where British and French units were joined. Over fifty divisions were hurled against the enemy from March to June, and although the Marne was again reached, German resources of manpower and material had been utterly sapped and Marshal Ferdinand Foch's (*q.v.*) counterattack during the Second Battle of the Marne broke the German front by August 8. Ludendorff resigned on October 26 and fled to Sweden, deeply offended that Hindenburg had not also resigned. On November 9, 1918, Hindenburg agreed with Ludendorff's successor, General Wilhelm Groener (*q.v.*), that the army no longer stood behind the kaiser, who, upon hearing this, fled to the Netherlands. The following day Hindenburg asked the government to conclude an immediate armistice, oversaw the return of the armies to Germany, and retired from active service after the Versailles Treaty had been signed. At Hanover he began work on his memoirs, taking time out in November 1919, to join Ludendorff in Berlin in order to concoct the infamous "stab in the back" legend, namely, that the German armies had never been defeated in the field but rather "stabbed in the back" by the defeatists, Socialists, and Jews at home.

On April 26, 1925, yet a third major career was launched for Hindenburg when, acting on the advice of Admiral Alfred von Tirpitz (*q.v.*), he successfully ran for the office of president of the Weimar Republic. It was a strange turn of affairs as the staunch monarchist swore to uphold a republic, while inwardly he yearned for the day when Wilhelm II could return from Doorn. Instead, on January 30, 1933, after years of intrigue by his son Oskar, Hindenburg appointed Adolf Hitler chancellor of Germany. Thereafter, Hindenburg mainly retired to his estate Neudeck in East Prussia, a gift of the Prussian government to him in 1927. He lent his public support to the Nazis and openly embraced their leader over the grave of Frederick the Great at the Garrison Church in Potsdam on March 21, 1933. Hindenburg died at Neudeck on August 2, 1934, and

was interred at the national monument at Tannenberg; after the Second World War, his remains were removed to Marburg. A simple soldier, Hindenburg was neither mentally nor intellectually fit for the heavy demands made upon him as military dictator in 1916-1918 and as president of the Weimar Republic.

Görlitz, *Hindenburg*; Hindenburg, *Aus meinem Leben*; Wheeler-Bennett, *Wooden Titan*; *Geschichte der Ritter des Ordens*, I; *Neue Deutsche Biographie*, IX.

HINTZE, Paul von (*Germany, State Secretary of the Foreign Office*), was born in Schwedt on the Oder River on February 13, 1864, the son of a tobacco merchant. He entered the navy in 1882 and attended the Navy Academy in 1894-1896; two years later he served as adjutant to Admiral Otto von Diederichs while the latter shadowed Commodore George Dewey's forces at Manila. Hintze was appointed naval attaché to St. Petersburg in 1903 and his clever, if not always accurate, reports quickly caught the eye of Wilhelm II, who asked the young officer to accompany him to his historic meeting with Tsar Nicholas II (*qq.v.*) at Björkö in 1905. Hintze was promoted captain in 1907, ennobled one year later, and in 1911 retired from the navy in the grade of rear admiral. His career then continued in the foreign service as ambassador to Mexico (1911-1914), to China (1914-1917), and to Norway (1917/1918).

In June 1918, the vain and ambitious Hintze succeeded Richard von Kühlmann (*q.v.*) as state secretary of the Foreign Office. To the surprise of many, Hintze favored a policy of cooperation with the Bolsheviks, thereby antagonizing General Erich Ludendorff and former Deputy Chancellor Karl Helfferich (*qq.v.*). Although he favored the Draconian peace of Brest-Litovsk, he counseled against further military operations in Russia, and eventually succeeded in preventing Ludendorff from overturning the Brest-Litovsk peace and imposing even harsher terms on the Bolsheviks. On September 29, 1918, after Wilhelm's military paladins had declared the war to be lost, Hintze persuaded the kaiser to introduce a pseudoparliamentary government. Hintze resigned as state secretary on October 3, but remained at army headquarters as the Foreign Office's representative; in this capacity he, along with Generals Wilhelm Groener (*q.v.*) and Count von der Schulenburg, advised the monarch on November 1/2 to seek an honorable death at the front at the head of his troops. When Wilhelm rejected the suggestion, Hintze advised exile and helped to prepare the way for the kaiser's flight to the Netherlands.

After the war, Hintze headed the German People's party in Silesia; later he guided the "League of Overseas Germans" as well as the "German Overseas Institute" in Stuttgart. Hintze died in Merano on August 19, 1941.

Baden, *Erinnerungen und Dokumente*; Niemann, *Revolution von Oben*; *Biographisches Wörterbuch zur Deutschen Geschichte*, I; *Neue Deutsche Biographie*, IX.

HIPPER, Franz Ritter von (*Germany, Admiral*), was born in Weilheim in Upper Bavaria on September 13, 1863, to a family of beer brewers and innkeepers. He entered the navy in 1881 and saw service on torpedo boats as well as the imperial yacht. After 1903 Hipper commanded mainly light and heavy cruisers. He was promoted captain in 1908 and rear admiral four years later; on the eve of the Great War, Hipper served as chief of Scouting Forces with the High Sea Fleet.

The outbreak of the war found Hipper unprepared: on August 28, 1914, the British surprised his forces in the Helgoland Bight, destroying the light cruisers *Ariadne*, *Mainz*, and *Köln* while Hipper tarried in port. Thereafter the chief of the Scouting Forces undertook several raids against the English east coast, shelling Yarmouth and Lowestoft on November 2/3 and Hartlepool, Scarborough, and Whitby on December 15/16, 1914. A further raid on January 24, 1915, cost Hipper the armored cruiser *Blücher* at the Dogger Bank, while the battle cruiser *Seydlitz* was severely damaged. This disastrous action curtailed offensive sorties until April 1916, when Hipper's units again shelled Great Yarmouth and Lowestoft. The Bavarian was promoted vice admiral in June 1915.

Hipper opposed a decisive fleet encounter with the British throughout 1914/1915, arguing that Admiral Alfred von Tirpitz's (*q.v.*) public call for such a thrust was designed merely to assuage his Reichstag critics on this matter. But by 1916 Hipper began to fear that an idle fleet would have no future and he yearned "to do battle." He got his wish at the end of May 1916. Admiral Reinhard Scheer (*q.v.*) left port on May 31 in order to intercept isolated units of the Grand Fleet in the Skagerrak; at about 3:30 P.M. that afternoon, Hipper on *Lützow* sighted Admiral David Beatty's (*q.v.*) battle cruisers and within an hour engaged the enemy. Hipper proved himself a cold-blooded tactician that day as he outmaneuvered Beatty and with deadly accurate fire destroyed the British battle cruisers *Indefatigable*, *Queen Mary*, and *Invincible*. By about 7 P.M., however, Admiral John Jellicoe (*q.v.*) was bearing down hard upon the Germans with the entire Grand Fleet, and Scheer twice managed to avoid annihilation only by

desperate 180-degree turns; Hipper's ships took a terrible pounding while attempting to cover these evolutions with smoke and fire. At 8:13 P.M., Hipper received Scheer's order "Attack the enemy!" and he hurled his remaining forces against the entire Grand Fleet as Scheer once again found that Jellicoe had crossed his T; the *Lützow* was destroyed and only the *Moltke* remained seaworthy and served as Hipper's flagship that night. Scheer and Hipper managed to reach port safely. They refused on the morning of June 1 to offer the British battle in the Helgoland Bight. For his actions, Hipper received the Prussian order *Pour le mérite* and was raised into the Bavarian nobility.

The next year brought not further fleet action but rebellion on many capital ships. Hipper denounced his sailors' complaints for food quality improvement and supervision as an "anarchist movement" and counseled that several leaders of the action "ruthlessly" be "put against the wall." Moreover, Hipper saw the time ripe for a major political change in Germany: "Send the Reichstag home [and] appoint a dictator." In the end, several leaders of the rebellion were summarily executed, but the unrest and low morale of the sailors continued unabated.

In April 1918, Scheer decided to advance with the High Sea Fleet as far north as Bergen in order to intercept Scandinavian convoys bound for the British Isles, and Hipper covered this advance with his Scouting Forces. The last major sortie by the Germans was highlighted only by the mechanical breakdown of the *Moltke*; Hipper, well remembering the plight of the *Blücher* at the Dogger Bank, favored cancellation of the operation rather than risk the loss of another heavy unit. On August 11, 1918, Hipper was promoted admiral and appointed chief of the High Sea Fleet as Scheer accepted the new post of head of a Supreme Command of the Navy.

Early in October 1918, as the German armies were being driven back in France, Hipper and his staff decided upon "an honorable fleet engagement, even if it should become a death struggle." With the assistance of Rear Admiral Adolf von Trotha and Commodore Magnus von Levetzow (*qq.v.*), Hipper on October 24 formally endorsed Operations Plan Nr. 19, which called for a sortie by the entire High Sea Fleet against the British on October 30. Instead, the sailors of the fleet got wind of the planned death ride and refused to get up steam. A belated attempt to attribute the planned assault to the government of Prince Max von Baden (*q.v.*) failed, and on November 9 the sailors raised the red flag on Hipper's flagship. The last commander of the High Sea Fleet retired on December 13 after having witnessed the surrender of the ships to the British ("My heart is breaking"). Hipper died at Altona-Othmarschen near Hamburg on May 25, 1932.

Herwig, "Luxury" Fleet; Waldeyer-Hartz, Admiral von Hipper; Geschichte der Ritter des Ordens, I; Neue Deutsche Biographie, IX.

HOFFMANN, Max (*Germany, General*), was born in Homberg near Kassel on January 25, 1869, the son of a county court judge. Hoffmann entered the army in 1887, attended the War Academy, and served in the General Staff, where in 1899 he settled into the Russian department. Thereafter, Hoffmann was firmly established as the General Staff's eastern expert, and in 1904/1905 he accompanied the Japanese army as military observer in the war against Russia. In 1905 at the railway station in Mukden Captain Hoffmann witnessed two Russian officers, A. V. Samsonov and P. K. Rennenkampf (*qq.v.*), blaming each other for the Russian debacle, rolling on the ground in front of the troops, and vowing never to aid one another; Hoffmann was to remember the incident in August 1914. After the Russo-Japanese War, Hoffmann returned to the General Staff and was then given command of the 112th Infantry Regiment as well as promotion to lieutenant colonel in January 1914.

In August 1914, Hoffmann was appointed first staff officer to the Eighth Army under General Max von Prittwitz und Gaffron (*q.v.*) in East Prussia. Hoffmann bitterly opposed his commander's decision on August 20, after the costly battle of Gumbinnen, to withdraw behind the Vistula River and to abandon East Prussia to the Russians, but in his memoirs he credited Prittwitz with revoking the order shortly after he had given it. Unfortunately, German headquarters at Koblenz had already replaced Prittwitz with Generals Paul von Hindenburg, whom Hoffmann dubbed a "pathetic figure," and Erich Ludendorff (*qq.v.*); Hoffmann remained at his post as first staff officer. On August 29, 1914, the Germans, using Hoffmann's plans, encircled the Russian Second Army under Samsonov at Tannenberg and inflicted over 200,000 casualties upon the enemy; next, reinforced by two army corps from the western front, the Germans turned north and at the Masurian Lakes inflicted a severe defeat on Rennenkampf's First Army in September. The legends of Hindenburg and Ludendorff had been created. The two Russian commanders, personal foes since Mukden in 1905, had refused to join forces and to coordinate their efforts. While Hindenburg does not even mention Hoffmann's name in his bulky memoirs, the Hessian staff officer later stated that "if the battle of

Waterloo was won on the playing-fields of Eton, that battle of Tannenberg was lost on the railway platform at Mukden." Indeed, Hoffmann's physical appearance belied his intellect: behind the stocky figure and the great shaven head reposed one of the most brilliant minds of the General Staff; patience and nerves of steel further enhanced his qualifications for high military office.

Hoffmann planned the winter battle of the Masurian Lakes in February 1915 in which about 100,000 Russians were captured in the Augustov forest, and throughout the summer and fall of 1916 he worked to secure the German position in Poland against heavy Russian attacks. Hoffmann was promoted colonel in August 1916, and when Hindenburg and Ludendorff assumed direction of the Third Army Supreme Command, Hoffmann became chief of staff to the new commander in the east, Field Marshal Prince Leopold of Bavaria (*q.v.*), with whom he enjoyed amicable relations. After halting the massive offensive by General Aleksei Brusilov (*q.v.*) in July 1917, Hoffmann counterattacked in Galicia and defeated the Russians near Zloczov; on September 1 he orchestrated the attack on Riga and supervised the seizure of the Baltic islands Moon, Ösel, and Dagö in October, at which time he was promoted major general.

Hoffmann concluded an armistice with the Bolsheviks in December 1917 and represented Hindenburg and Ludendorff at the peace talks in Brest-Litovsk. It was not an enviable task for this bluff and direct officer as he constantly had to balance the grandiose and unrealistic expansionist plans, especially Ludendorff's, against German capabilities as well as against the wishes of the state secretary of the Foreign Office, Richard von Kühlmann (*q.v.*). In time, Hoffmann was accused by Ludendorff's toadies of being influenced by "Semitic circles," and when, in January 1918, this capable officer dared to suggest to the kaiser modified demands for Polish territory, he was vilified in army and right-wing circles. In truth, Hoffmann had brusquely informed the Russians, in December 1917, that they would have to cede Courland, Lithuania, and parts of Poland to Germany, and after Leon Trotsky (*q.v.*) announced his famous "no war, no peace" resolution and demobilized the Russian army, Hoffmann had termed this tack "disgraceful." On February 18, 1918, he hurled fifty-two divisions against a disorganized Russian army. Dünaburg fell the first day, Pskov within five days, and Kiev by March 1, forcing the Bolsheviks to agree to German terms at Brest-Litovsk. Hoffmann brought much of the German army in the east home after November 1918, and retired from active service on March 31, 1920.

Hoffmann sharply criticized Hindenburg and Ludendorff in his postwar writings. He also favored in 1922 a cooperative effort by the victorious Allies designed to tumble the Bolsheviks in Russia from power. Hoffmann died at Bad Reichenhall on July 8, 1927, of heart trouble.

Hoffmann, *Aufzeichnungen*, 2 vols., *Der Krieg der versäumten Gelegenheiten*, and *Tannenberg*; Kitchen, *Silent Dictatorship*; Wheeler-Bennett, *Wooden Titan*; *Geschichte der Ritter des Ordens*, I; *Neue Deutsche Biographie*, IX.

HOHENLOHE-SCHILLINGSFÜRST, Gottfried Prince zu (*Austria-Hungary, General*), was born in Vienna on November 8, 1867, to Lord High Steward Konstantin Prince zu Hohenlohe-Schillingsfürst. Gottfried graduated from the Scottish Gymnasium and in 1887 entered the army as a hussar. From 1893 to 1895 he attended the War Academy, followed by duty with the General Staff. Gottfried was sent to St. Petersburg as captain and military attaché in 1902; five years later he retired in the grade of major from the army.

Emperor Francis Joseph (*q.v.*), in February 1913, entrusted Hohenlohe-Schillingsfürst with a special mission to St. Petersburg designed to alleviate the strained relations arising out of the Balkan crisis in the winter of 1912/1913. The prince thereupon entered the Austro-Hungarian diplomatic corps, and on August 4, 1914, the emperor dispatched him to Berlin as ambassador. The forty-seven-year-old diplomat worked in the German capital as an enthusiastic supporter of the alliance of 1879, and he attempted to the best of his ability to maintain the alliance on the basis of equality. The deteriorating military fortunes of the Dual Monarchy greatly hampered his endeavors, however, and, in September 1916, the Germans forced Vienna to surrender to them strategic control over all the fronts. Hohenlohe-Schillingsfürst was convinced by 1917 that military victory was out of reach, and he supported the clumsy attempts of Emperor Charles (*q.v.*) to bring about a separate peace. The ambassador retired from public service in 1918 and devoted his remaining years to horse racing. He died in Vienna on November 7, 1932.

Pitreich, *Der österreich-ungarische Bundesgenosse im Sperrfeuer*; Silberstein, *The Troubled Alliance*; *Österreichisches Biographisches Lexikon 1815-1950*, II.

HOLTZENDORFF, Henning von (*Germany, Grand Admiral*), was born in Prenzlau on January 9, 1853, the son of a superior court judge; the family was of ancient noble stock from the Mark. Holtzendorff entered the navy of the North German Confederation in 1869 and saw action in the North Sea during the war against France in 1870/1871. Thereafter came duty with the newly created Imperial German Navy in the Cameroons and in China during the Boxer Rebellion as battleship commandant. Promoted captain in 1897 and rear admiral in 1904, Holtzendorff served with the East Asian Cruiser Squadron during the Russo-Japanese War in 1905/1906; from 1906 to 1909 Vice Admiral von Holtzendorff commanded the First Squadron of the High Sea Fleet in home waters. In October 1909, Holtzendorff succeeded Prince Henry (*q.v.*) as chief of the High Sea Fleet; Reinhard Scheer (*q.v.*) served as his chief of staff. In the fall of 1912 fleet maneuvers proved a bitter experience for Admiral von Holtzendorff. He recommended a German posture in the waters between Denmark and Norway in case of war with England, but the chief of the Admiralty Staff, August von Heeringen, and especially the kaiser vetoed this plan in favor of "great emphasis on the North Sea as our battlefield." Moreover, Holtzendorff was alarmed over Admiral Alfred von Tirpitz's (*q.v.*) expansion of the navy at what he felt to be too rapid a pace, and instead favored a slowdown in construction and consolidation of available matériel. As a result, Holtzendorff was forced to resign in the spring of 1913 and to accept forced retirement.

In the spring of 1915, however, Holtzendorff was reactivated and replaced Admiral Gustav Bachmann (*q.v.*) as head of the Admiralty Staff. Initially not an advocate of unrestricted submarine warfare, Holtzendorff nevertheless came to support it by December 1915. Unfortunately, he never developed a consistent stand on the issue. A brief campaign of U-boat warfare *à outrance* was called off in April 1916 after sharp American protests over the sinking of the liner *Sussex*. Throughout 1916 Holtzendorff wavered in his position concerning the underwater offensive, so that in naval circles he gradually was accorded the nickname Inventor of the Lie. This notwithstanding, Holtzendorff on December 22, 1916, penned a memorandum in which he predicted German victory over England as a result of submarine warfare; if the U-boats could destroy about 600,000 tons of shipping bound for Britain each month for six months and if a significant number of neutrals could be driven from the seas, London would be forced to the peace table by August 1917, if the campaign began on February 1, 1917. This mathematical wizardry prompted German leaders on January 9, 1917, in Pless to gamble the future on the U-boats; kaiser, chancellor, and generals all endorsed the naval initiative, believing that the submarines would force a decision in Europe before the resulting (and expected) American intervention could alter the delicate balance on the Continent.

Almost concurrently, in November and December 1916, Holtzendorff worked out an elaborate list of German war aims. These included the coasts of Belgium and Courland, the Faeroe Islands, and naval bases in the Atlantic, Indian, and Pacific oceans. In May 1917, flushed with the early successes of the U-boat campaign, Holtzendorff presented these proposals to Wilhelm II (*q.v.*), who enthusiastically endorsed them, especially the notion of creating a German colonial empire in central Africa. But the dream was to be short-lived. The British Admiralty, spurred on by Prime Minister David Lloyd George (*q.v.*), finally adopted the convoy system of transport and the August 1917 deadline for British surrender passed without the anticipated demise. Moreover, early in 1918 American troops began to arrive in France in force—despite the German navy's promise that not a single doughboy would ever set foot in Europe. General Erich Ludendorff (*q.v.*) fell out with Holtzendorff, who had accused the quartermaster general of possessing an insatiable "hunger for power," while Ludendorff "declared war" on the head of the Admiralty Staff over Holtzendorff's refusal to endorse the army's vast annexation schemes in the east. In the end, Holtzendorff was forced to yield after Admiral Scheer early in August had taken command of a newly created centralized naval headquarters and personally succeeded Holtzendorff. The latter was promoted grand admiral on July 31, 1918. Already an ill man, Holtzendorff died in Jagow in the Uckermark on June 7, 1919. He was the last imperial naval officer to be promoted grand admiral, and the only head of the Admiralty Staff to receive the order *Pour le mérite* (March 1917).

Gemzell, *Organization, Conflict, and Innovation*; Herwig, *"Luxury" Fleet*; Stegemann, *Deutsche Marinepolitik*; *Geschichte der Ritter des Ordens*, I; *Neue Deutsche Biographie*, IX.

HOLUB, Franz von (*Austria-Hungary, Admiral*), was born in Prague in 1865. Holub graduated from the Naval Academy in Fiume in 1882 and devoted his early career to the development of mines and torpedoes; later he transferred to the artillery branch and until 1905 taught courses for both officers and men at the Artillery School of the fleet. This activity

brought Holub the post of chief artillery officer in the Adriatic Fleet in 1909. The following year he was reassigned to the Naval Section of the War Ministry in Vienna, and in 1911 he was promoted captain. Holub next headed the second, or technical, department of the Naval Section in 1912, but one year later returned to the fleet as commander of the dreadnought *Viribus Unitis*.

Holub's steady work at Pola did not go unrecognized: in May 1915, he was promoted to the grade of rear admiral, and in 1916 raised into the Austrian nobility and assigned chief of staff to fleet commander Admiral Maximilian Njegovan (*q.v.*). It was not a particularly rewarding experience for Holub who, like his chief, was relieved of command on March 1, 1918, in the wake of serious riots in the Dual Monarchy's Adriatic sea ports. When Rear Admiral Miklós Horthy (*q.v.*) was given command of the fleet, Holub returned to Vienna to take charge of the Naval Section of the War Ministry, a post that he held until the end of the war. Holub died in Vienna on October 28, 1924.

Sokol, *Österreich-Ungarns Seekrieg 1914-1918*, 4 vols.; Veltzé, "Unsere Flottenführer."

HORTHY de NAGYBÁNYA, Miklós (*Austria-Hungary, Vice Admiral*), was born in Konderes, Hungary, on June 18, 1868, to an ancient Protestant noble family. Horthy graduated from the Naval Academy at Fiume in 1886 and was assigned various commands, including service with the torpedo branch and escort duty to the South Seas. In 1908 the Hungarian was given command of the *Taurus* at Constantinople, and he distinguished himself by submitting prescient reports on the Young Turk rebellion then in progress; Emperor Francis Joseph (*q.v.*) rewarded the magnate with the post of naval aide-de-camp (1909-1914). Horthy was promoted captain and appointed chamberlain in 1913; he was posted to the emperor's naval chancellery as well as to the Naval Section of the War Ministry.

At the outbreak of the Great War, Horthy commanded the battleship *Habsburg*, but after ten months was transferred to the new cruiser *Novarra*. During the night of May 23/24, 1915, he took part in the Austro-Hungarian sea raid against the Italian east coast between Bonletta and Venice; Horthy commanded the daring raid against Porto Corsini, the outer harbor of Ravenna. On December 6 the *Novarra* managed to intercept and to destroy transports bound for the relief of Montenegro in the port of San Giovanni di Medua. And when the Entente in 1917 began to bottle up the Dual Monarchy's fleet with a mine barrage across the Straits of Otranto, Horthy induced his superiors to undertake a cruiser raid against this barrier. On May 15, 1917, Captain Horthy commanded what was to become Austria-Hungary's most daring naval action of the war when he led three cruisers and two destroyers into the Straits. Superior forces attacked the flotilla and Horthy, severely wounded in both legs, barely managed to escape and, under cover of heavy units hastily dispatched from home, to reach port safely. This daring sortie made Horthy somewhat of a national hero.

The new Emperor Charles (q.v.) raised Horthy to the grade of rear admiral. After naval unrest in October 1917 and February 1918 had severely undermined Admiral Maximilian Njegovan's (q.v.) command, Horthy on March 1, 1918 was made fleet commander over several more senior admirals. Charles completed the fragmentation of the naval command by appointing Vice Admiral Franz von Holub (q.v.) head of the Naval Section in the War Ministry. Moreover, all operations now had to be cleared with the emperor. It is hardly surprising, given this cumbersome chain of command, that no further naval action took place. Horthy was promoted vice admiral shortly before the end of the war and it became his bitter task to supervise the end of the Imperial Navy. On October 30, 1918, Charles transferred the entire fleet to the new Yugoslav National Council, and one day later Horthy hauled down the Habsburg banner for the last time, turning the ships under his command over to Rear Admiral Dragutin Prica. This rear admiral promptly managed to run his flagship *Yugoslavia* (formerly *Viribus Unitis*) onto an Italian mobile mine as he sailed out of Cattaro on November 1. In the end, Yugoslavia was cheated of the spoils as all but eleven torpedo boats were taken from it and distributed among the Allies.

In November 1919, Horthy abandoned retirement at Konderes in order to take part in suppressing the Communist rebellion of Béla Kun in Budapest; a grateful National Assembly elected him regent governor for life on March 1, 1920. The admiral managed to frustrate Emperor Charles' attempts at restoration in March and October 1921. Twenty years later, Horthy joined Adolf Hitler's crusade against the Soviet Union, but differences of opinion between the two former Habsburg subjects led to the deposition of Horthy on March 19, 1944. When the admiral appealed to Joseph Stalin in October for an armistice and ordered Hungarian soldiers to lay down their guns, he was promptly arrested on October 15 and power turned over to the Nazi-controlled Arrow Cross movement. U.S. troops found Horthy in Bavaria on May 1, 1945, and the Hungarian retired to private life at Estoril, Portugal, where he died on February 9, 1957.

Bardolff, *Militär-Maria Theresien-Orden*; Horthy, *Memoirs*; Sokol, *Österreich-Ungarns Seekrieg 1914-1918*, 4 vols.; Veltzé, "Unsere Flottenführer"; *Current Biography 1940*.

HOUSE, Edward Mandell (*United States, Presidential Adviser*), was born in Houston, Texas, on July 26, 1858, the son of a prosperous planter and overseas trader. House managed the family plantations for a while and then sold them for a tidy profit. As a Texas Democrat he helped to elect Governor James S. Hogg, who bestowed upon House the title of colonel, which stayed with him. In November 1911, House met Woodrow Wilson (q.v.) and the so-called colonel not only helped to swing the support of Texas Democrats behind the professor, but also was instrumental in securing William Jennings Bryan's support for him. Wilson, in turn, was impressed by House's moderating influence and looked to him for the selection of the cabinet and for intimate advice. In 1913 House met Sir Edward Grey (q.v.) and the following year persuaded the British foreign secretary to withdraw support from Mexico's dictator Victoriano Huerta.

For the first two years of the Great War, House loyally supported the president's strict neutrality, but earlier than Wilson he urged "preparedness" upon the nation. Early in 1915 and again in 1916 House visited London, Paris, and Berlin in efforts to bring about a negotiated peace. With Grey he drafted a memorandum, in February 1916, proposing American mediation of the conflict and threatening American intervention on the side of the Entente should Germany refuse to sit at the peace table; Wilson approved the action, but the London government rejected it. Thus House's attempts to pave the way for "peace without victory" fell by the way.

In 1917/1918 House was the president's chief agent in all negotiations with the Allies. Specifically, the "colonel" was appointed chief of the American mission to London and Paris in December 1917, and at the Interallied Conference House provided for effective coordination of American war efforts with the critical needs of the Allies. He reported to Wilson the startling "lack of unity of control and action" among the Entente partners: "None of them at heart like each other, and I doubt whether any of them like us." That same fall, House helped to establish an agency known as The Inquiry to gather facts and to formulate policies relative to the future peace settlement. This agency came up with the final draft of the later Fourteen Points, and in the spring of 1918 Wilson asked House to put together a tentative "Covenant" of a proposed League of Nations.

The Pre-Armistice Agreement of October 1918 proved to be House's ultimate triumph. While many members of the Entente opposed the Fourteen Points, especially Clemenceau (q.v.) of France who claimed never to have read them, House also ran into trouble with the British over the old American principle of "freedom of the seas." In fact, at one point House threatened the British that, if need be, the United States would build a navy and an army second to none: "We had more money, we had more men, and our natural resources were greater." The British ultimately accepted the logic of this argument, if not the principle of the "freedom of the seas." Throughout the peace discussions, House was Wilson's chief deputy in Europe and, more a realist than Wilson, urged compromise with Great Britain and France. House managed to survive General Pershing's (q.v.) unexpected demand for "unconditional surrender" by Germany at the Supreme War Council, but he began to drift away from Wilson. The colonel in particular urged the president in the summer of 1919 to approach the Senate in a spirit of compromise and to allay the fears and suspicions of Henry Cabot Lodge (q.v.), the powerful chairman of the foreign relations committee; Wilson refused and, in June 1919, saw House for the last time. No public rupture ever took place and House, discreet to the point of taciturnity, died on March 28, 1938, in New York City as a staunch supporter and admirer of Woodrow Wilson.

Seymour, *Intimate Papers of Colonel House*, 4 vols.; Trask, *Captains & Cabinets*; *Dictionary of American Biography*, XXII Supplement Two.

HUSSAREK von HEINLEIN, Max Baron (*Austria-Hungary, Minister-President*), was born in Pressburg on May 3, 1865, the son of a field marshal. Hussarek acquired a doctorate of law at Vienna University in 1889 and thereafter taught canon law at several schools; in 1893 he began what was to become a long and fruitful career at the law school of Vienna University. A full professor by the turn of the century, Hussarek from 1911 to 1917 also served as minister of culture and education in the cabinets of Karl von Stürgkh, Ernst von Körber, and Heinrich von Clam-Martinic (*qq.v.*).

Emperor Charles (*q.v.*) appointed Hussarek minister-president of the Dual Monarchy on July 25, 1917. The law professor regarded federalism as the sole alternative to dissolution; specifically, he strove for a trialistic solution to the Croatian question by seeking to unite Croatia and Dalmatia with Bosnia-Herzegovina in order to form a third equal partner in the empire. Hussarek initiated the so-called October Manifesto on October 16, 1918, which sought to transform the Austrian part of the empire into a federation of nationalities while maintaining inviolate the lands of the Crown of St. Stephen. The latter pledge in effect meant that Croatian, German, Rumanian, Serbian, and Ruthenian territory would remain divided; Robert Kann has denounced the manifesto as "a farce." The Hungarian prime minister, Alexander Wekerle (*q.v.*), informed Charles that the manifesto violated the Compromise of 1867, and this opposition sufficed to defeat it. Hussarek thereupon resigned his post on October 27, 1918, and returned to his professorship at Vienna University. Regarded by many as the founder of the department of legal church history at Vienna University, Hussarek died in Vienna on March 6, 1935.

Kann, *History of the Habsburg Empire*; Rumpler, *Max Hussarek*; *Österreichisches Biographisches Lexikon 1815-1950*, III.

HYMANS, Paul (*Belgium, Minister of Foreign Affairs*), was born in Ixelles on March 23, 1865. The son of a prosperous Protestant family of Dutch descent, Hymans was educated in law and history at the University of Brussels, where he joined the faculty in 1897. He was elected to Parliament in 1894. As a Liberal during an era dominated politically by Belgium's Catholic party, he had no prospects for a cabinet seat, but he promoted such successful initiatives as the end to the king's personal control over the Congo (1908) and the reform of Belgium's system of conscription (1909).

World War I opened the door to national office. Hymans led a successful diplomatic mission to the United States in August/September 1914. There he made a direct appeal to President Woodrow Wilson (*q.v.*) for food and moral support. In February 1915 he took the post of ambassador to Great Britain. When the Belgian government in exile refused to link itself formally to the Entente, Hymans' concern over Belgium's diplomatic isolation led him to work toward an alternative. His efforts produced the Declaration of Sainte-Addresse (February 1916): in this, Britain, France, and Russia pledged to include Belgium in the peace negotiations. The Belgians also received a promise that the future settlement would include a restoration of Belgium's independence, as well as monetary compensation from Germany for the ravaged nation. In October 1917 Hymans joined the government in exile in Le Havre as minister of economic affairs. In January 1918, he became Belgium's new foreign minister. By the closing months of the war, Hymans had become the spokesman for basic changes in Belgian foreign policy.

It was Hymans who led Belgium's delegation to the Peace Conference at Versailles. He was, first of all, determined to end Belgium's neutral status; imposed in 1839 and guaranteed by the great powers, it had been a useless paper shield in 1914. He also sought to place Belgium first in line to receive reparations payments from Germany. In these areas Hymans emerged victorious. Other ambitions went unfulfilled. Belgium did not obtain substantial territorial additions, only the small enclaves of Eupen and Malmédy along with a number of protectorates in Africa. Hymans had hoped to annex substantial portions of Holland and all of Luxembourg. Skilled Dutch diplomacy blocked the former goal; France's own ambitions toward Luxembourg killed the latter. As the Luxembourg issue illustrated, Hymans found his country's wartime associates willing to pursue their ambitions with minimal regard for Belgian expectations. He was even more disappointed to find the great powers in the Council of Five shaping the peace settlement to the exclusion of the smaller nations.

Hymans emerged as a spokesman for the minor powers at Versailles. This in turn led to his selection as president of the first assembly of the League of Nations. He went on to direct the Belgian Foreign Ministry almost without a break from 1924 to 1935, a period marked by the successful negotiation of the Locarno Treaties. In 1940, however, Hymans fled the second German invasion of his country in his own lifetime. He did not survive to see the liberation but died in Nice, March 6, 1941.

Fenaux, *Paul Hymans*; Helmreich, *Belgium and Europe*; Hymans, *Mémoires*, 2 vols.; Kossmann, *The Low Countries*; Palo, "The Diplomacy of Belgian War Aims during the First World War"; *Biographie nationale*, XXIX; *Larousse mensuel*, XI.

IVANOV, Nikolai Yudovich (*Russia, General of Artillery*), was born August 3, 1851. Some scholars (for example, Stone, Wildman) and most of his contemporaries identify Ivanov as one of the few Russian generals to come from a peasant background. Other sources indicate aristocratic birth and cite, in support, an early posting to a guards unit after graduation from the Mikhailovsky Artillery College in 1869. All sources agree on Ivanov's rapport with the peasant rank and file of the army. He saw action in the 1877/1878 war against Turkey and rose during the Russo-Japanese War to command a corps. Close ties to the imperial family helped Ivanov to climb rapidly. Following the war in the Far East, Ivanov was governor general of Kronstadt; in 1906 he suppressed a military mutiny in the important base near St. Petersburg. It was the kind of service that made him a lasting favorite of Tsar Nicholas II (*q.v.*). Promoted general of artillery in 1908, Ivanov spent the next six years in charge of the Kiev Military District, one of the stellar field posts in the Russian army. At the outbreak of World War I, he moved, according to prewar preparations, to command the southwestern front facing Austria-Hungary.

A modest talent at best, Ivanov's year-long tenure in this crucial position brought him little glory. At the very start, the complex and rapidly evolving Galician campaign (August/September 1914) gave evidence of Ivanov's failings. The weight of the Austrian armies facing Russia began the campaign by advancing northward toward the line Lublin-Cholm. The Austrian First Army under Dankl (*q.v.*) defeated the Russians at Krasnik on August 23 sending Ivanov into panic; he nearly conceded the field to the enemy by ordering a withdrawal to Brest-Litovsk. The Russian commander's next major decision was similarly to raise doubts about his grasp of events. Ivanov called on General Pleve (*q.v.*) to wheel the Fifth Army westward into the Austrians' right flank. As fresh enemy forces arrived, Pleve found himself strung out over fifty miles of countryside and in danger of being cut off from his neighbors. Patching the crisis in the north depended in the end on Pleve's fighting qualities and his independent decision of August 30 to retreat from the pocket into which Ivanov had drawn him. Meanwhile, Ivanov's main forces, the Third and Eighth Armies, advanced only sluggishly toward Lemberg in the face of notably inferior numbers of Austrians. When the overextended Habsburg armies pulled back to the southwest in mid-September, in a retreat that soon degenerated into a rout, Ivanov rested his troops, then pushed lackadaisically forward.

Ivanov's modest capabilities were stretched beyond their bounds in 1915. His huge southwestern front rimmed the Carpathians, then turned northward into the central plains of the Weichsel valley. In late March Ivanov got orders from the Russian High Command (*Stavka*) to push into the Carpathians and thus to threaten the Hungarian plain. In combination with the Allied assault on the Dardanelles, such an advance seemed to promise Balkan hegemony for the Entente. But Vienna responded to Ivanov's advance with a call for German aid. It came in a trickle at first, then in a stream of German troops for the Carpathians. In early May disaster struck. General von

Mackensen (q.v.) smashed Ivanov's thin line at Gorlice, cut into open country, and headed northward. Ivanov's armies reeled backward to stand briefly on the San River. Then, the shattered forces of the southwestern front retreated for nearly four months. Only in August was Ivanov able to establish a stable line near Luck. Throughout this fiasco, Ivanov's failings were matched by those of the *Stavka*. The old artilleryman's fellow front commanders were able to brush aside orders to send reserves southward. Meanwhile, Mackensen's advance made all of Russian Poland a German prize.

Ivanov was permitted a pathetic encore. In November the *Stavka* ordered him to advance in eastern Galicia, in the feathery hope this might relieve the collapsing Serbs. Ivanov reshuffled his senior officers on the eve of battle. The fighting presented a classic example of the failure of Russian artillery to support advancing infantry with well-coordinated fire. Stone has called this futile action on the Strypa "one of Ivanov's perfect little jewels of ineptitude." It apparently sealed his fate, and in March 1916, Ivanov was relieved. But the shift took place with a solicitude befitting an imperial favorite. Ivanov was transferred to the *Stavka* at Mogilev to be a military adviser to the tsar.

The old general thus found himself at the monarch's side when the March Revolution struck. On March 12, 1917, Ivanov received charge of a force of 800 decorated war heroes. With this imposing band, he was to move on Petrograd to restore order. Other troops, he was assured, would join him on the way. The expedition was stymied at every turn. Rail workers sympathetic to the revolution blocked the line. Reinforcements destined for Ivanov melted away as they moved from the front to the turmoil of rear areas. Ivanov was given one final humiliation. In October 1918, he was persuaded to take nominal command of the White "Southern Army" on the Don. This rag-tag collection of reactionary officers and rank-and-file criminals soon dissolved, its militarily sound elements drawn to the more promising leaders on the White side. Ivanov died of typhus in southern Russia, January 27, 1919.

Heyman, "Gorlice-Tarnow"; Kenez, *Civil War in South Russia, 1918*; Rostunov, ed., *Istoriia pervoi mirovoi voiny*, 2 vols.; Rutherford, *The Russian Army in World War I*; Stone, *The Eastern Front*; Wildman, *The End of the Russian Imperial Army*; *Modern Encyclopedia of Russian and Soviet History*, XV; *Sovetskaia istoricheskaia entsiklopediia*, V.

IZZET PAŞA, Ahmed (*Turkey, General, Grand Vizier*), was born in Monastir in Turkish Macedonia in 1864, the son of a prominent civil servant. He chose a military career. After graduating in 1887 from the Ottoman Military Academy in Constantinople, where he had passed the General Staff course in addition to the regular training for officers, the young captain rose rapidly. He took advanced training in Germany, 1891-1894, fought in the 1897 war against Greece, and was promoted to the rank of colonel at the age of thirty-seven. The next few years saw him campaigning in Yemen. There he was promoted brigadier general in 1905. By the time he had been called back to Constantinople in 1908 to take over as the army's chief of staff, he had been promoted twice: to lieutenant general in 1907 and to full general's rank the next year.

As chief of staff, he tapped the talents of German military advisers to plan for a future Balkan war. Izzet feared that Turkey might soon face a hostile Balkan coalition. He also tried to avoid political involvement—an impossible undertaking in the years after the Young Turk Revolution of 1908. In 1911/1912 he was again sent to subdue insurrection in Yemen—this time it was a form of political exile. He was still nominally chief of staff, but he had lost central control over the army. His warnings to avoid a Balkan war at all cost were ignored. His well-founded plans for such a conflict called for a defensive posture until reinforcements could arrive from Asiatic Turkey. They too were cast aside, and the opening weeks of the First Balkan War in October 1912 brought the disaster he had feared. They also brought political turmoil, culminating in the establishment of the Young Turk dictatorship in the first half of 1913.

Following his sense of duty, Izzet served in several crucial posts during the first year in which the Young Turks were in power, notably as minister of war. He apparently feared that less-experienced figures from the Young Turk circle would botch such responsibilities unless he agreed to serve. Nonetheless, despite the shortcomings revealed by the Balkan Wars, he balked at purging the officer corps. That meant turning on his long-time comrades. He passed his post—temporarily, he thought—to the flamboyant Young Turk leader Enver Paşa (q.v.) in January 1914. Two years of semiretirement followed, as Enver used the War Ministry to establish himself as one of the commanding figures in the Turkish government.

After the outbreak of World War I, Izzet, then on the sidelines, opposed undertaking offensive operations in the Balkans or the Caucasus. Turkey's wartime role could only be a defensive one: barring the lines of communication between Russia and western

Europe. As in 1912, his strategic insight failed to carry the day.

In April 1916, Izzet renewed his military career by taking command of the Second Army in eastern Anatolia. Under the spirited leadership of General Yudenich (q.v.), the Russians had seized the Turkish stronghold at Erzurum. Enver put forth a grandiose scheme for a counterattack. The Turkish Third Army was to strike Yudenich from the west, while Izzet's forces advanced from the south. Such happy visions ignored hard realities: spring floods, difficult mountain terrain, and Yudenich's habit of striking first.

By the time Izzet could begin his offensive in August, the Second Army had to attack alone. Yudenich had launched a preemptive attack and shattered the Third Army. Critics have accused Izzet of making a mediocre situation worse. He dispersed his forces widely; he advanced in three separate directions; and he pushed into impassable mountainous terrain in some sectors, while moving with excessive caution elsewhere. Talented subordinates like General Mustafa Kemal (q.v.) could not save the situation. By the start of September Izzet was back at his starting line. His campaigning days were over.

Izzet served as Turkey's military representative at the peace negotiations with Soviet Russia and Rumania. And in October/November 1918, after the collapse of the Young Turk government, he took office as grand vizier. Using the captive British general, Charles Townshend (q.v.), as go-between, Izzet's cabinet concluded the Mudros armistice. Turkey left the war on October 30; the Straits opened to allow Allied ships into the Black Sea. As Turkish forces were demobilized, the Allies took over key areas and lines of communication. On November 2 a German ship spirited away most of the Young Turk leaders. Izzet may have helped arrange their departure. In any event, he was blamed for the escape both inside and outside Turkey and fell from power on November 11.

During the declining years of the sultanate, 1918-1922, Izzet served in several cabinet positions. With the birth of the Turkish republic, the old soldier went into lasting retirement. He died in Istanbul, April 1, 1937.

Ahmad, *Young Turks*; Allen and Muratoff, *Caucasian Battlefields*; Helmreich, *Diplomacy of the Balkan Wars*; Trumpener, *Germany and the Ottoman Empire*; *Encyclopedia of Islam*, New Edition, IV.

JACKSON, Sir Henry Bradwardine (*Great Britain, Admiral of the Fleet*), was born in Barnsley on January 21, 1855, the son of a farmer. Jackson joined the navy in 1868, and later took part in the Zulu War; he was promoted to the grade of commander in 1890

and to captain in 1896. That year he met Guglielmo Marconi at the War Office, and the Italian encouraged Jackson to continue his research into wireless communication. In 1897 Jackson was sent as naval attaché to Paris. As an officer he was modest and no inspirer of men; as a person he was reserved, at times morose. Jackson was most happy in 1900 when the Marconi Company was instructed to supply many Royal Navy ships with wireless installations; the following year this able pioneer of wireless telegraphy was appointed a Fellow of the Royal Society. In 1904 Jackson went to sea as commander of the *Vernon*, but returned to land the following year as third sea lord and controller of the navy. Jackson encouraged the development of the world's first turbine-driven battleship, the *Dreadnought*, and the battle cruiser *Invincible*. In 1908 he was entrusted with command of the Third (later Sixth) Cruiser Squadron in the Mediterranean; three years later he was back in England as director of the newly created Royal Naval War College at Portsmouth, where he trained the first War Staff officers. One year before the outbreak of the European war, the sensible, level-headed Jackson was appointed chief of the War Staff of the Admiralty.

In August 1914, Jackson was nominated to be commander in chief in the Mediterranean, but at the last minute was retained at the Admiralty, partly to coordinate attacks on Germany's colonial possessions. Upon the forced retirement of John (Jacky) Fisher in 1915, Arthur James Balfour (qq.v.), the new first lord of the Admiralty, selected Jackson to succeed Fisher as first sea lord. It was, in many ways, a strange choice. Jackson had neither commanded heavy squadrons at sea nor displayed any leadership qualities or fertile imagination. Yet perhaps his solid scientific background in weapons development made him an attractive candidate at a time when the German submarine menace was paramount. In any case, Jackson quickly initiated new mining policies designed to bottle the U-boats up in the North Sea. But the job proved too much for him. The first lord's staff quickly bogged down in red tape and excessive centralization; Jackson simply spent too much time on trivia. Moreover, the combination of Balfour and Jackson lacked drive and energy, and when Admiral John Jellicoe (q.v.), in December 1916, was "kicked upstairs" as first sea lord, a physically tired Jackson seized the chance to leave the jungle at Whitehall in order to accept the less prestigious but more rewarding post of president of the Royal Naval College at Greenwich.

In July 1919, Jackson was promoted to the grade of admiral of the fleet, having served since 1917 as the first and principal naval aide-de-camp to King George V (*q.v.*). The former first lord retired from the service in July 1924; he died on December 14, 1929, at Salterns House, Hayling Island.

Marder, *Dreadnought to Scapa Flow*, II, III; *Dictionary of National Biography 1922-1930*.

JAGOW, Gottlieb von (*Germany, Foreign Secretary*), was born in Berlin on June 22, 1863, the son of an army officer and estate owner; the family belonged to ancient Mark Brandenburg nobility. Jagow studied law and then entered the Prussian bureaucracy, but in 1895 his patron, Bernhard von Bülow, convinced Jagow to transfer to the diplomatic corps. By 1907 Jagow was envoy to Luxembourg; two years later he served in similar capacity in Rome. Chancellor Theobald von Bethmann Hollweg (*q.v.*) appointed Jagow state secretary of the Foreign Office in January 1913. The diminutive aristocrat reluctantly accepted the call, plaintively writing Bülow: "Nothing has helped, I am appointed." Wilhelm II (*q.v.*) accepted the "little man" partly because of Jagow's self-effacing blandness and partly because he was the kaiser's fraternity brother in the Bonn *Borussen*.

Jagow was thoroughly convinced that a clash with Russia was inevitable, that a natural antagonism existed between the Germanic and Slavic peoples, and hence he encouraged Austria-Hungary against Russia while desiring an accommodation with England. This policy quickly brought Jagow into conflict with Admiral Alfred von Tirpitz's (*q.v.*) vast fleet plans and led the foreign secretary to doubt the wisdom of the Schlieffen plan—that called for violation of Belgian neutrality, guaranteed by both London and Berlin in 1839. However, Jagow's attempt to rethink the matter early in 1913 was hastily shelved. On the eve of the Great War, the state secretary still hoped to reach a colonial agreement with Britain, especially over Portugal's African possessions, and he worked hard to localize the Second Balkan War in 1913.

News of the assassination of Archduke Francis Ferdinand (*q.v.*) reached Jagow during his honeymoon, and he returned to Berlin on July 6, 1914, only to learn that Wilhelm II and Bethmann Hollweg had already presented Count Leopold Berchtold (*q.v.*) in Vienna the famous "blank check," offering the Dual Monarchy full German backing in any European conflict arising from the Serbian question. Jagow was sufficiently realistic to see that Britain would not remain neutral in a general European war, but he hoped that Russia might at the last moment back down and allow Austria-Hungary to strengthen its position in the Balkans. While convinced that war

with Russia was unavoidable, Jagow nevertheless did not believe that the summer of 1914 was the most propitious moment in which to strike. In the end, he bowed to the dictates of military mobilization.

Jagow became pessimistic about the outcome of the war as early as mid-September 1914, after the First Battle of the Marne. Thereafter, he counseled a moderate peace in the west and worked against those elements that desired the outright annexation of Belgium, the Channel coast, and Longwy-Briey. In the east, on the other hand, Jagow favored the creation of a satellite German Polish state and sought annexation of Courland and Lithuania. Generally speaking, the foreign secretary favored Bethmann Hollweg's *Mitteleuropa* concept, that is, the notion of a Central Europe dominated by Germany economically and politically from the North Sea to the Black Sea, and from Flanders to the Ukraine. But when Jagow opposed the resumption of unrestricted submarine warfare in November 1916 because it would lead to America's entry into the war, he was dismissed. Jagow regarded the decision of January 9, 1917, to resume the undersea campaign as the cardinal error of the war.

Gottlieb von Jagow was hardly a statesman of the Bismarckian mold. He accepted the post only reluctantly in 1913, aware that a frail constitution, precarious health, lack of parliamentary experience, and poor debating skills would greatly inhibit his effectiveness. The July crisis of 1914 fully revealed these shortcomings as Jagow proved unable to master the situation; above all, he failed miserably to uphold the primacy of politics. On the positive side, it should be noted that he faithfully supported the chancellor. The distorted negative portrait sketched of Jagow by Bülow and Tirpitz in their memoirs is unjust. Jagow died in Potsdam on January 11, 1935.

Cecil, *German Diplomatic Service*; Fischer, *Griff nach der Weltmacht* and *Krieg der Illusionen*; Jagow, *Ursachen und Ausbruch des Weltkrieges*; Ritter, *Staatskunst und Kriegshandwerk*, III; *Neue Deutsche Biographie*, X.

JEKOV, Nicholas (1864-1946). See ZHEKOV, Nikola.

JELLICOE, John Rushworth (*Great Britain, Admiral of the Fleet*), first Earl Jellicoe, was born in Southampton on December 5, 1859, the son of a merchant marine captain. Jellicoe entered the navy in 1872 and saw action with the British squadron at the Dardanelles during the Russo-Turkish War in 1877 as well as in the campaign in Egypt (1882). Already at this early juncture, Jellicoe was known for his charming and happy disposition as well as for his great self-control. Courses in gunnery and torpedo development on the *Excellent* brought him into contact with John Fisher (*q.v.*); when Fisher moved to the Admiralty as director of naval ordnance under the auspices of the Naval Defence Act of 1889, Jellicoe joined him in revamping fifty-two warships. Jellicoe was promoted to the grade of commander in 1891, and the following year was an invalid for a period when his ship, the *Victoria*, was rammed by the *Camperdown* in the Mediterranean; after recovering, Jellicoe commanded the *Ramilles* from 1893 to 1896, making captain the following year. In 1898 he participated in the British seizure of Wei-hai-wei, and two years later was seriously wounded during the so-called Boxer Rebellion.

Fisher appointed Jellicoe director of naval ordnance in February 1905, and in this capacity Jellicoe assisted in the design of the *Dreadnought*; two years later he was promoted to rear admiral and knighted by King Edward VII. Jellicoe was securely in the "Fishpond," and in October 1908 was appointed third sea lord; as such he was instrumental in securing the eight battleships in the 1909/1910 naval estimates. Promoted to the grade of vice admiral, Jellicoe, in December 1910, commanded the Atlantic Fleet, and in 1911 the second division of the Home Fleet. Next came another stint at the Admiralty, this time as second sea lord, and finally on August 4, 1914, the post of commander in chief of the newly created Grand Fleet, with his flag aboard the *Iron Duke*.

Vice Admiral Jellicoe commanded 60,000 officers and men and in his hands rested the security of the British Isles. If he had a fault, it was that he could not easily delegate authority, preferring to shackle his time with routine administrative duties. The first few months of the war brought little action for the Grand Fleet. The Germans remained in port and the British distant blockade forced inaction on the war at sea. The new lair at Scapa Flow was made safe against torpedo attacks and Cromarty and Rosyth were put into full use. Jellicoe was promoted to the grade of admiral in 1915, but the few German "tip-and-run" raids on the English east coast involved primarily Admiral David Beatty's cruisers and Commodore Tyrwhitt's (*qq.v.*) Harwich Force; the Germans made no attempt to break the British stranglehold on the exits of the North Sea.

All this changed for one brief moment on May 31, 1916, when the British light cruiser *Galatae* sighted the German light cruisers under Admiral Franz Hipper (*q.v.*) off the coast of Denmark in the Skagerrak at 2:20 P.M. The German High Sea Fleet under Admiral Reinhard Scheer (*q.v.*) had put out to sea for another routine search of the waters north of Jutland, but British intelligence had intercepted their signal to get up steam, and hence the Grand Fleet left Scapa Flow to intercept the Germans even before the latter left port. Shortly before 3:00 P.M. on May 31, Beatty's battle cruisers sighted Hipper's Scouting Forces. Beatty at once gave chase, but by 4:33 P.M. sighted the masts of the High Sea Fleet coming up from the south and put about to the north. Beatty became the prey: he hoped to lure the Germans northward onto the mighty columns of the Grand Fleet. Jellicoe got word of Scheer's approach about 6:14 P.M., and deployed his forces on his right wing; however, as the six columns of twenty-four dreadnoughts and accompanying craft drew into a long battle line, his vision was temporarily blurred and his ships silhouetted against the glare of the setting sun. But at 6:23 P.M. he crossed Scheer's T. Nine British battleships opened fire at that moment. Outgunned and outmaneuvered, Scheer wheeled 180 degrees, thereby allowing Jellicoe to assume position between the High Sea Fleet and the mainland. At 7:10 P.M., Scheer wheeled his forces about and came at the British once again in line ahead; for a second time his fleet took a terrible pounding from Jellicoe's dreadnoughts and only a second 180-degree turn extricated his forces from certain annihilation. To ward off a massed attack by German torpedo boats, Jellicoe turned 45 degrees to the east and, as night descended, was still in position between Scheer and his home bases. Scheer, however, managed to reach his sanctuary under cover of darkness. Next morning the Grand Fleet stood off the Elbe estuary in vain awaiting the renewal of battle with the High Sea Fleet.

The British public, when apprised of the heavy losses—especially of the battle cruisers *Indefatigable*, *Invincible*, and *Queen Mary*—blamed the drawn battle on Jellicoe's temerity and lack of Nelsonian stature. Yet Winston Churchill (*q.v.*) put the battle of Jutland into proper perspective: "Jellicoe was the only man on either side who could lose the war in an afternoon." In November 1916, Jellicoe was "kicked upstairs" as first sea lord and devoted his attention to the German submarine menace. He had serious doubts about the efficacy of the convoy system, which drew from David Lloyd George (*q.v.*) the ringing rejoinder that Jellicoe was the embodiment of Admiralty maladministration; the new first lord of the Admiralty, Sir Eric Geddes (*q.v.*), hardly calmed a charged atmosphere by seconding the prime minister's stance. Jellicoe's obfuscation over the convoy issue brought forth charges that he had a "tendency to be absorbed in detail" and that he "attempted to do too much himself." Finally, on Christmas Eve 1917, Geddes rather curtly dismissed Jellicoe as first sea lord. In January 1918, he was raised to the peerage as Viscount Jellicoe, of Scapa, and in 1919 received the thanks of both Houses of Parliament, a grant of £50,000, and promotion to the grade of admiral of the fleet.

Early in 1919, Jellicoe left on an inspection cruise to India, Australia, New Zealand, and Canada. In August 1920, he was appointed governor general of New Zealand, retiring from this post as well as from the service in 1924. In June of the following year he was advanced to the rank of Earl Jellicoe. The former commander in chief of the Grand Fleet died in Kensington on November 20, 1935, and was buried in St. Paul's Cathedral alongside Nelson.

Jellicoe's strengths had been his selflessness, his "instinctive ability which practice gives to size up a situation" (Marder) quickly, his imperturbable calm, and the utter lack of recriminatory actions. His detractors claim that he was overly confident, that pride often interfered with decision making.

Corbett and Newbolt, *Naval Operations*, III; Jellicoe, *The Grand Fleet 1914-1916*; Marder, *Dreadnought to Scapa Flow*, II, III, IV; Patterson, *Jellicoe: A Biography*; *Dictionary of National Biography 1931-1940*.

JOFFRE, Joseph Jacques Césaire (*France, Field Marshal*), was born, the son of a barrel maker, at Rivesaltes in southwestern France, January 12, 1852. He interrupted his training at the École polytechnique to serve as an officer in the Franco-Prussian War, 1870/1871, then returned to graduate and to enter the regular army. Commissioned in the engineers, Joffre served in metropolitan France until 1885, when he requested duty with the colonial army. He spent most of the next fifteen years in Indo-China, West Africa, and Madagascar. He acquired a burst of publicity in 1894 by leading an expedition through West Africa to reach the fabled city of Timbuktu; and his construction work in fortifying Madagascar developed his reputation as one of the army's leading engineers.

In 1900, then a brigadier general, Joffre returned to France. He advanced to major general in 1905, and the year following received command of an infantry division. By 1910 he was a corps commander and member of the Supreme War Council. Nonetheless, he was a surprise choice for the post of chief of the General Staff to which he was appointed in July 1911. Joffre lacked the General Staff training deemed essential for the job and did not have extensive combat experience, but he was free of embarrassing political links or religious affiliations. His promotions had come in the colonial service, where rapid advancement due to merit, not connections, was the norm. Finally, he was fifty-nine years old, and thus able to serve long enough before reaching mandatory retirement age to provide some stability and continuity at the top of the army's command system.

Joffre explicitly recognized the weaknesses in his own preparation for the post by requesting that General Castelnau (*q.v.*), the army's most renowned staff officer, be named as deputy. The most important product of the Joffre-Castelnau team over the next three years was Plan XVII, outlining French strategy in the event of war with Germany. In its final form, it centered on a French offensive into Lorraine, in tune with the offensive tenor of French military thought in the pre-1914 period. Joffre and Castelnau were aware that a German invasion might come through Belgium. In early 1912 Joffre sought permission to move French forces into Belgium to forestall such a German move. This was unacceptable to both the Belgians and the British. Plan XVII thus provided for sufficient French strength around Sedan to parry a German thrust through Belgium. But it assumed, incorrectly it turned out, that Germany lacked the manpower to conduct a sweeping invasion of Belgium west of the Meuse. Nonetheless, Plan XVII expected the French offensive into Lorraine, which could be varied by wheeling two of the French armies northeastward into the Ardennes, to disrupt any German offensive effort.

By mid-August 1914, Joffre had launched his Lorraine offensive. Moreover, in response to news of the German assault on Belgium, General Lanrezac (*q.v.*) and the French Fifth Army moved northward into Belgium to hold the angle formed by the Meuse and Sambre rivers. As Lanrezac found himself overwhelmed by a German tide and the armies striking into Lorraine met heavy resistance, then counterattacks, Plan XVII collapsed. The French armies were thrown into headlong retreat. To Joffre's partisans, the French commander in chief then took charge of the situation, holding his armies together with imperturbable calm while he launched a long-planned counterattack against the right flank of the enemy in early September. To equally bitter critics of Joffre, of whom Liddell Hart is representative, Joffre merely drew his armies blindly backward until the intervention of General Gallieni (*q.v.*), military governor of Paris, sparked the successful French counterattack and stopped the Germans on the Marne. Recent authors like Isselin have taken a middle position: Joffre had much of the situation in hand, moving his forces westward from the First and

Second Armies in Alsace and Lorraine to hold at the Marne, even if Gallieni's initiative determined the exact timing of the counterblow.

The Marne was Joffre's greatest success. Thereafter, the war on the western front settled into bloody stalemate. Joffre tried, with meager results, to force a breakthrough in Artois (May 1915) and Champagne (September 1915). Meanwhile, criticism of his heavy losses and insignificant results mounted in the National Assembly. Deputies were angered at being barred from the war zone, and many were outraged when Joffre fired General Sarrail (*q.v.*), a particular favorite of the Radical party.

In December 1915, after Joffre's docile Minister of War Millerand (*q.v.*) had been replaced by the more independent Gallieni, government leaders attempted to restrain Joffre. Castelnau was brought in to assist—that is, to watch over—the French commander. Moreover, Joffre was given the responsibility of supporting Sarrail, dispatched at the behest of political circles to create a new front in the Balkans.

In 1916 the calamities mounted up. A prolonged German assault on Verdun started in late February; Joffre had stripped the fortress of its heavy artillery to support his 1915 offensives in Artois and Champagne. In July the French joined the British in attacking on the Somme. For both countries, this soon turned into a prolonged bloodletting for miniscule gains in territory. By December Premier Aristide Briand (*q.v.*) responded to Joffre's persistent failures. To save his own government he ousted the general, by pretending to promote him to a more responsible position, and then rewarded him with the title of marshal of France.

Joffre played a largely ceremonial role for the remainder of the war, visiting the United States in 1917, for example, to greet France's new ally. He died in Paris, January 3, 1931.

Liddell Hart's acid characterization of Joffre as the false hero of the Marne, "a national nerve sedative," has not stood the test of time. Joffre handled a difficult situation at the start of the war with calm, in sharp contrast to his German counterpart, General von Moltke (*q.v.*). But with the Marne victory behind him, he had little to offer France. Like General Cadorna (*q.v.*) in Italy, he justified one bloody offensive after another by the need to support his allies or to nibble away at the enemy. But in the absence of either imagination or great quantities of heavy artillery, such narrow vision simply led to a prolonged national tragedy and, in the not too distant future, the near collapse of the French army.

Cassar, *The French and the Dardanelles*; Horne, *The Price of Glory: Verdun*; Isselin, *The Battle of the Marne*; Joffre, *The Personal Memoirs of Joffre*, 2 vols.; King, *Generals and Politicians*; Liddell Hart, *Reputations*; Ralston, *The Army of the Republic*; Varillon, *Joffre*; Williamson, *The Politics of Grand Strategy*; Larousse mensuel, V.

JOSEPH (*Austria-Hungary, Archduke, General*), was born at the château of Alcsuth, Hungary, on August 9, 1872, the son of Archduke Joseph, commandant of the Hungarian Honvédség. Joseph belonged to the so-called Hungarian branch of the House of Habsburg-Lorraine. Upon entry into the First Infantry Regiment ("Kaiser") in 1890, he became the third archduke bearing the name Joseph to have done so. In May 1902, he was assigned to the Hungarian First Regiment, where he rose to the grade of colonel before being given the Seventy-ninth Honvédség Infantry Brigade as major general in 1908.

At the outbreak of the war, Joseph commanded the Thirty-first Infantry Division and was initially ordered to the Serbian front; however, the unexpected rapid Russian advance brought him to Galicia. In November 1914, General of Cavalry Joseph was entrusted with the VII (Temesvár) Corps during the tenacious defense of the Carpathian passes. On July 8, 1915, after Italy entered the war against Austria-Hungary, Joseph's VII Corps was assigned to army command Boroević (*q.v.*) at Laibach and ordered to hold the southern Isonzo front near Doberdó "at all costs." In what became known as the Second, Third, and Fourth Isonzo battles, the VII Corps held off the Italians under the Duke of Aosta in costly hand-to-hand fighting. Joseph remained at the Italian front through the Ninth Isonzo battle during October and November 1916, and then in the grade of colonel general was appointed commander of the eastern front against Russian and Rumanian units. The archduke was credited by army headquarters with the successful repulse of a major Russian-Rumanian attack in the winter of 1916, with the advance of mixed allied units under the Württemberg General von Gerok into Rumania early in 1917, with the offensive of the Seventh Army under General Hermann Kövess from the Carpathian passes into the Bukovina in July 1917, and finally with the triumphant German-Austro-Hungarian advance from Transylvania over the Ojtoz Pass into Rumania under Field Marshal August von Mackensen (*qq.v.*). Joseph displayed personal bravery on several occasions and was able to relate to his men in a remarkable degree.

Unfortunately, the archduke's career then took a turn for the worse. Early in January 1918, as head of the Sixth Army in Venetia, he took part in a council of marshals convened at army headquarters in Baden and voted as the only one of twelve military commanders for the division of the common army into separate Austrian and Hungarian armies. In July Joseph was entrusted with his last field command: he succeeded General Conrad von Hötzendorf (*q.v.*) as army group commander of the Tyrolean front in Bozen. Late in October the archduke's headquarters informed Vienna that "only an unconditional cessation of hostilities . . . can avoid a catastrophe."

After the war Joseph assumed the leadership of the counterrevolution in Budapest and conducted negotiations as *homo regius* between Emperor Charles and Prime Minister Mihály Károlyi (*qq.v.*). Immediately after the fall of Béla Kun's Soviet Republic, the archduke was made Regent of Hungary (August/September 1919), but was forced to retire by the Entente powers, which would not tolerate a Habsburg as head of state in Hungary; they accepted instead the dictatorship of Admiral Miklós Horthy (*q.v.*). Joseph died in Regensburg, Federal Republic of Germany, on July 7, 1962.

Bardolff, *Militär-Maria Theresien-Orden*; Rothenberg, *Army of Francis Joseph*.

JOSEPH FERDINAND (*Austria-Hungary, Archduke, General*), was born in Salzburg, Austria, on May 24, 1872, as Joseph Ferdinand Salvator. Upon graduation from the Theresa Military Academy, he entered the Kaiserjäger in 1892 and from 1895 to 1897 attended the War Academy. Joseph Ferdinand attained the grade captain in 1897; he was promoted colonel in 1905, and three years later commanded the Fifth Infantry Brigade as major general. In 1911 the archduke was entrusted with the Third Infantry Division at Linz.

General of Infantry Joseph Ferdinand at the outbreak of the Great War led the XIV Army Corps under General Moritz von Auffenberg (*q.v.*) near the Bug River, seeing action at Komarów, Zamość, and Rawaruska. Joseph Ferdinand spent the winter of 1914 as head of the Fourth Army defending the snowy Carpathian passes. Early in 1915 he led this force at Bochina and Limanowa, taking part in the overall advance from Cracow to the Dunajec. The archduke was especially active during the capture of Krasnik, Lublin, and Volhynia. On June 4, 1916, however, General Aleksei Brusilov (*q.v.*) mounted his massive offensive against the Dual Monarchy's forces on a broad front stretching from south of the Pripet Marshes to the Rumanian frontier. The mixed German–Austro-Hungarian troops were under the command of the German General Alexander von Linsingen and consisted of the Austro-Hungarian

Fourth Army (Joseph Ferdinand), the First Army (Puhallo), the Seventh Army (Pflanzer-Baltin), and a composite force under General Felix von Bothmer (*qq.v.*). When the offensive finally ground to a halt in September, Brusilov had taken Austrian Galicia, the entire Bukovina, and was encamped on the slopes of the Carpathians; beyond lay the Carpathian passes and the very heart of the Dual Monarchy.

Joseph Ferdinand had been badly defeated at Luck, and the archduke had to witness the ignominious desertion of numerous Czech and Ruthene units. Nor had he helped his cause by spending the days hunting with aristocratic friends and permitting morale and discipline to decline precipitously. In fact, Joseph Ferdinand was a poor commander and after Luck was relieved as head of the Fourth Army. However, the new Emperor Charles (*q.v.*) exercised imperial prerogative and appointed the archduke, one of the empire's first balloonists, inspector general of air forces in 1917. Joseph Ferdinand died in Vienna on August 26, 1942.

Rothenberg, *Army of Francis Joseph*; Veltzé, *Unsere Heerführer*; *Österreichisches Biographisches Lexikon 1815-1950*, III.

KAMIO, Mitsuomi (*Japan, General*), was born in 1856, the second son of a samurai family. Graduating from military school in 1876, before Japan adopted Western-style cadet training, Kamio like many of his contemporaries began service as a sergeant. He fought against the Satsuma Rebellion of 1877 and was commissioned a lieutenant in 1879. His career over the next twenty years brought a rotation between staff and line positions, including command of first a company, then in 1897 a regiment. In 1888, while assigned to the army General Staff, Kamio along with a coterie of other rising young officers was exposed to the ideas of Major Jacob Meckel. On leave from the Prussian army, Meckel was serving as an instructor and adviser to the Japanese forces. He immersed his students in the need for methodical logistical preparation for battle; then he demanded aggressive offensive tactics using the natural cover offered by the terrain of the battlefield. Meckel taught that the Japanese army must look to future operations on the Asian continent. Kamio proved an apt pupil.

Kamio's career was marked by extensive tours in China: in 1882-1886 as a lieutenant; in 1892-1896 as a field grade officer, including duty as a military attaché; then as a staff officer during the Sino-Japanese War. He visited Europe in 1899, advanced to the rank of major general in 1902, and went on to serve in the Russo-Japanese War. By 1914 he had commanded the Eighteenth Division for two years. On August 16 he received orders to move his forces from Japan to the Chinese mainland.

Kamio conducted a model campaign against Germany's prize possession in the Far East, the leased territory of Kiaochow and its important port of Tsingtao. At the start of September, his two brigades landed at Lungkow in northern Shantung province, then moved southward to bottle up the entire German leasehold and its garrison of 4,000 men. Storms and floods impeded the Japanese land and naval forces more than did German opposition. To these difficulties was added the need to integrate a token British contingent, a reinforced battalion of the South Wales Borderers, into the expedition. Kamio had the historic distinction of commanding regular European troops—the first Asian military leader in modern times to do so.

By late September the Germans had been pushed back into the city of Tsingtao. Kamio assembled an overwhelming superiority in heavy artillery during a methodical siege that lasted throughout October. The need to divert troops for an advance into western Shantung—as the Japanese government used the war to cover its larger goal of expanded influence in northern China—slowed Kamio down. So too did unseasonable rains that swept away Japanese landing facilities and turned the field of operations into a sea of mud. Artillery barrages and naval gunfire smashed the city's defenses in early November. The novel tool of aerial reconnaissance was only one of the remarkable features of the campaign; it served to map out and then to coordinate the work of the heavy guns. A final night assault carried the city's defenses. It surrendered on November 7.

With a force of over 30,000 men, the Japanese High Command was certain of victory from the start. But Kamio brought notable elements to the campaign. His stress on limiting Japanese casualties through a series of short advances preceded by devastating artillery fire is strongly reminiscent of his contemporary in the French army, General Henri-Philippe Pétain (q.v.). His knowledge of German military practice proved valuable. German regulations stressed the likelihood of enemy attacks at dawn. Kamio's climactic assault was accordingly carried out at night.

The victorious general commanded the Tsingtao garrison and became the first Japanese governor general of Kiaochow. In 1915 he took command of the Tokyo garrison. Additional rewards came in the following year: elevation to the nobility and advancement to the rank of general. Kamio retired from the army in 1925 and died two years later.

Burdick, *The Japanese Siege of Tsingtau*; *Nihon Riku-Kaigun no Seido: Soshiki Jinji* (through the courtesy of Professor Alvin D. Coox); Nish, *Alliance in Decline*; Presseisen, *Before Aggression*.

KÁROLYI von NAGYKÁROLY, Mihály Count

(*Austria-Hungary, Prime Minister*), was born to an ancient Magyar family in Hungary in 1875. Károlyi began his political career as a Liberal, but in 1906 declared his "independence" and six years later became chairman of the Independence party.

In the summer of 1916 Károlyi broke with Count Julius Andrássy's (q.v.) Independence party in order to establish his own left-wing party club. This aristocratic *frondeur* demanded national autonomy for Hungary, the introduction of general suffrage, and the breaking up of large landed estates. In doing so, he incurred the wrath of Count István Tisza (q.v.), who felt that Károlyi had betrayed his class. In October 1918, Károlyi headed the Hungarian National Council, and on October 31 Emperor Charles (q.v.), ill advised once more, appointed him prime minister of Hungary in the hope that Károlyi's tenure in office would head off a national revolt in Hungary. In fact, the appointment merely accelerated the revolt and Red Guards murdered Tisza the same day that Károlyi took office. The Magyar *frondeur* asked Emperor Charles on November 1 to be absolved of his oath of allegiance; Charles complied and Károlyi was then responsible only to the nation. On November 11 the prime minister proclaimed the Hungarian republic and from January to March 1919 was head of state. A Communist revolution led by Béla Kun drove him out of office, and Károlyi spent most of the following thirty-six years in exile, where he died in 1955.

Kann, *History of the Habsburg Empire*; Károlyi, *Fighting the World*; Pamlényi, *History of Hungary*.

KATŌ, Takaaki

(*Japan, Minister of Foreign Affairs*), was born to a provincial samurai family in Owari in 1860. He completed his training as a lawyer at Tokyo Imperial University in 1881 where he ranked first in his class. Katō then took an unusual step: he joined the Mitsubishi Company rather than follow the traditional career pattern of promising university graduates who entered the government at once. He rose quickly. The future Anglophile statesman spent two years working in London and Liverpool, then returned to Japan to marry the daughter of Mitsubishi's director. In 1886 Katō became private secretary to the minister of foreign affairs. It was the start of a brilliant political career. By 1895 the young lawyer was Japan's minister to Great Britain, a post he held until 1899. He strongly favored a diplomatic link with the British; and, unlike the passive Japanese diplomat typical for that time, he urged his own policy on his home government. Elevated to the rank of foreign minister in 1900, Katō led the opposition to Russian expansionism and set the stage for the Anglo-Japanese alliance of 1902.

Katō returned to Britain as Japan's minister in 1909. His tour was marked by his successful support for the renewal, in 1911, of the Anglo-Japanese alliance. Before returning home two years later, he held informal discussions with Sir Edward Grey (q.v.) on Japan's long-range interests in China. Grey was noncommittal, but he seemed to indicate Britain's approval for Japanese expansion in areas such as southern Manchuria.

The outbreak of World War I found Katō back in the post of foreign minister. German naval strength in the Far East impelled London to call on Japan for a limited degree of military aid: the British wanted the Japanese navy to help in hunting down German commerce raiders. Katō argued for wider Japanese participation. He looked to the seizure of German holdings in China's Kiaochow province; German islands in the Pacific were also tempting and vulnerable. On August 7 Katō passed his first test when the Japanese cabinet agreed to enter the war. Japanese military circles likewise assented. On August 8 Katō won over the group of *genro* ("elder statesmen") who played a crucial role in approving major policies. Thus, in less than two days of frantic discussion, the energetic foreign minister brought Japan into the war. The British, much to their surprise and discomfort, found themselves saddled with an ambitious Japanese ally out to use the European war as occasion for a burst of expansion. Grey's efforts to place clear geographic limits on Japanese military activities were firmly turned aside.

The withdrawal of European power and attention from the Far East encouraged Katō to go further. In January 1915, he presented the Chinese government with the so-called Twenty-one Demands. These sought to establish or confirm broad Japanese controls over China's politics and economic life. The Chinese agreed to much of the list of demands by May. But by then a wave of anti-Japanese demonstrations had swept China. More ominously, Anglo-American objections to Tokyo's demands—some of which Katō had tried to keep secret—created a serious diplomatic crisis. The *genro* were outraged. The consensus Katō managed to construct in the summer of 1914 then dissolved. He was forced from office in July 1915 and played no important role during the remainder of the war.

Katō returned to high position in 1924 at the head of a coalition government. He died in Tokyo, January 28, 1926, while serving as prime minster.

Chi, *China Diplomacy, 1914-1918*; Duus, *Party Rivalry and Political Change in Taishō Japan*; Lowe, *Great Britain and Japan, 1911-1915*; Nish, *Alliance in Decline* and *The Anglo-Japanese Alliance*; *Biographical Dictionary of Japanese History*.

KEIL, Franz Ritter von (*Austria-Hungary, Admiral*), was born the son of an Austrian army officer at the federal fortress of Mainz, Germany, on September 15, 1862. Keil entered the navy in 1881 after successful completion of studies at the Naval Academy at Fiume. He was promoted captain in 1910, rear admiral three years later, and vice admiral in 1917. Keil served as instructor at the Torpedo School in Pola from 1896 to 1900, and it was largely owing to his urgings that the Dual Monarchy bought its first torpedo boat, the *Huszar*, from Great Britain. In 1907 Keil was placed in charge of the cruiser squadron that was sent to North America. Five years later he was recalled to Vienna to serve as head of the Präsidialkanzlei in the War Ministry, and in 1913 he was the ranking flag officer in the Naval Section of the War Ministry.

Rear Admiral Keil entered the war as naval commandant of the port of Pola on the Adriatic Sea, a post which he held until February 1917, when he took command of the Second Battleship Division. Promotion to vice admiral came in August 1917, and on March 1, 1918, when the new Emperor Charles divided the naval command, making Rear Admiral Miklós Horthy fleet commander and Vice Admiral Franz von Holub (qq.v.) head of the Naval Section, Keil was appointed naval adviser to the emperor. This proved to be a meaningless assignment as Charles required all naval chiefs to seek his personal approval before any major operations could be undertaken. In May 1918, Keil was promoted full admiral and that year appointed chief of the Naval Officer Corps. The last naval adviser to the Habsburgs died in Vienna on November 22, 1945.

Sokol, *Österreich-Ungarns Seekrieg 1914-1918*, 4 vols.; Veltzé, "Unsere Flottenführer"; *Österreichisches Biographisches Lexikon 1815-1950*, III.

KEMAL PAŞA, Mustafa (*Turkey, General*), was born in Salonika in 1881, the son of a low-ranking Ottoman bureaucrat. At the age of twelve, he began a decade of military schooling in Salonika, Monastir, and finally Constantinople. The young cadet struck contemporaries with both his academic brilliance and his arrogant personality. One of his first instructors gave him the lasting nickname Kemal, the Turkish word for "perfection." Like many young officers, Kemal was drawn into conspiratorial politics. His first duty after completing the War Academy in 1905 was a post in the remote city of Damascus; it was punishment for his subversive interests. The young captain responded by founding a revolutionary political group. In 1906 he took unauthorized leave to form a second branch of his group in the strategic and centrally located city of Salonika. The movement grew speedily. When Kemal, by then a major, returned to Salonika in 1907, he discovered other leaders had pushed him aside. These men, notably Enver (q.v.), sparked the Young Turk Revolution of 1908.

Kemal immersed himself in his military career. During the Italo-Turkish War of 1911/12, he led Turkish forces in eastern Libya; there his desert bands pinned Italian soldiers and marines to the coastal cities of Cyrenaica. Kemal's success in mobile warfare did not blind him to a more useful lesson: Italian naval gunnery exposed the entire Libyan littoral to new landings. For the immediate future, however, Kemal's prickly personality combined with the spectacular political rise of his rival Enver to ensure the young colonel a quiet career. After brief service in the Balkan Wars of 1912/13, Kemal was packed off to Bulgaria as Turkish military attaché. He rusticated there until the final months of 1914.

Kemal opposed Turkey's entry in the Great War alongside the Central Powers; but the conflict soon elevated him to national prominence. His great military gifts came to the fore in early 1915. The Allied attack on the Dardanelles found Kemal in command of the Nineteenth Division, the main Turkish reserve on the Gallipoli Peninsula. German military commanders anticipated an Allied landing on the Asiatic side of the Straits; and most Turkish commanders saw the western shores of Gallipoli to be effectively guarded by barbed wire emplacements. The confident young Kemal—he was only thirty-four years old—rejected such ideas. He expected the assault to the south at Cape Helles and on the western shore near Gaba Tepe. Cyrenaica had taught him that barbed wire constituted no barrier to a determined assault with heavy naval guns. Those guns woke him on April 25, 1915. He threw all available reserves into headlong counterattacks. Australian infantry advancing from the beaches near Gaba Tepe were overwhelmed. This lightning response contained the Allied landing, saved the day, and perhaps decided the entire Gallipoli campaign in favor of the Turks. By July Kemal was arguing the probability of a new landing to the north at Suvla

Bay. He was ignored. When his predictions proved on the mark, he was advanced to a corps command and assigned to meet the threat. Once again his fierce counterattacks—with little view to the cost in Turkish lives—dashed British hopes.

In 1916 Kemal commanded first a corps, then an army against the Russians in eastern Anatolia. With these responsibilities, he finally reached the rank of general. The poorly conceived Turkish summer offensive involved two field armies, vainly trying to cooperate with each other. Weather, logistical problems, and the harassment conducted by skilled Russian opponents destroyed any chance of success. Kemal alone emerged with any credit. His reward was an army command in Syria for the 1917 *Yilderim* offensive. This imaginative plan envisioned a sweeping advance eastward from Aleppo to recapture Baghdad from the British. Kemal considered it absurd. When his army was diverted to Palestine instead to meet the menacing British offensive out of Egypt, Kemal stayed with it briefly, then sent a blistering letter to the government in September 1917. Economic decay, government corruption, and plummeting morale—such factors dictated a defensive strategy centered on Turkey's Anatolian provinces. To leave Turkish troops to fight in Europe was as dangerous as trying to retain the indefensible Arab provinces of the empire. This sage advice ignored, Kemal resigned.

In the closing months of the war, the young general gave a final display of his skills on behalf of the Young Turk regime. In August 1918, he took charge of the skeletal remains of the Seventh Army in Palestine. Harried by Arab insurgents and British cavalry, Kemal conducted a fighting retreat from central Palestine to Damascus, and finally to Aleppo. By the close of the war, Kemal, then an army group commander, held the southern gateway to Anatolia. A recent historian's judgment has him "the greatest Ottoman military hero to emerge from the war."

Kemal's subsequent career was more spectacular still. The Young Turks were gone. The absence of any potent political authority offered Kemal a free stage on which to demonstrate his gifts as a leader. With Turkey close to partition at the hands of the war's victors, Kemal set out to defend the nation. Between 1920 and the start of 1923, he defeated Greek efforts to slice away parts of Asia Minor, drew internationally respected borders, and abolished the sultanate. Turkey then became a republic, with Kemal its first president, 1924-38. He prodded his nation into modernization and secularization. In 1934 Kemal required all Turks to adopt Western style surnames. For himself, he chose "Atatürk," father of the

Turks. He died in Istanbul (the name Constantinople had been discarded in 1930) on November 10, 1938.

Allen and Muratoff, *Caucasian Battlefields*; Falls, *Armageddon: 1918*; James, *Gallipoli*; Kinross, *Atatürk*; Shaw and Shaw, *History of the Ottoman Empire and Modern Turkey*, II; Windrow and Mason, *Concise Dictionary of Military Biography*; *Encyclopedia of Islam, New Edition*, I.

KERENSKY, Aleksandr Fedorovich (*Russia, Politician*), was born May 4, 1881, the son of a school administrator in the town of Simbirsk on the Volga. He graduated from the law faculty at St. Petersburg University in 1904. Rather than taking the conventional step of entering the government bureaucracy, the young attorney began a private practice in which he specialized in defending the accused in political trials. He flirted with a violent brand of political activity himself, and, in early 1906, he was jailed briefly for joining a Socialist Revolutionary party plot to assassinate Tsar Nicholas II (*q.v.*). His family connections—his wife was the daughter of a colonel on the General Staff—and the comparatively lenient political atmosphere of the time helped get his sentence annulled; in return, Kerensky departed for temporary residence in Central Asia. In 1912 the *Trudoviks*, a small peasant party that abjured political violence, asked him to run as a candidate for the Fourth Duma. The charismatic young defense lawyer used his seat in Russia's legislative body to act as the tribune of the people. Brilliant rhetorical talent plus his scorn for the moderate conservatives who dominated the last Duma made him the outstanding radical figure in the public eye.

World War I saw Kerensky shift his position only slightly. He had contempt for the moderates like Duma President Rodzianko (*q.v.*) who rallied without condition to the side of the monarchy. He refused to vote for the war credits, claiming they set the conflict's burdens on the working class, and he condemned the government's action in arresting the Duma's Bolshevik delegation in early November 1914. In the fall of 1915 Kerensky refused to support the "Progressive Bloc," the multiparty coalition formed as a result of the gradual, cautious leftward drift of the Duma's majority. He demanded, in September 1915, that attempts to prorogue the Duma be ignored. With an apparent eye to 1789, Kerensky proclaimed that the Russian legislative body should declare itself to be a constituent assembly. Withal, Kerensky defended the war effort against Germany, not as a coalition with the tsar, but, as he put it with a typical lack of clarity in a speech on August 7, 1914, as the work of the "great elemental force of Russian democracy."

From late 1915 until mid-1916 Kerensky was removed from the political scene by serious illness. When his recuperation in Finland ended, he returned to a sour atmosphere in which even Duma moderates like Paul Miliukov (*q.v.*) spoke bitterly about the abuses of the imperial family. Kerensky added fuel to the flames. In December 1916, he again cited the French Revolution to stress how events could push the Duma reluctantly toward a political explosion. On February 28, 1917, on the eve of the upheaval, Kerensky called for an end to Russia's "medieval regime"; it had been futile, he remarked, to assassinate Rasputin (*q.v.*), the imperial family's confidant, but hinted that assassinating the tsar would be more productive. Such rhetoric seemed designed to land him, at best, in a jail cell. But instead it set the stage for the fiery young politician to play a starring role in the revolution that was about to unfold.

Kerensky quickly saw the opportunities the expanding bread riots and military mutinies offered. He advised his fellow Duma deputies not to accept the prorogation decree of March 12, but rather to place the Duma on the side of the revolution. Anticipating his subsequent appointment as the provisional government's minister of justice, he hunted down and arrested members of the tsar's last cabinet. As both a member of the provisional government and a leading figure in the more radical Petrograd Soviet, Kerensky alone bridged the gap between the two rival authorities that had sprung up after the demise of the monarchy.

Kerensky's role soon went beyond the bounds of his portfolio as minister of justice. Having forced Miliukov's departure from the post of foreign minister in mid-May, Kerensky stood as the strongman of the provisional government until its fall in November. He likewise became the most audible spokesman for early revolutionary Russia on the question of the war. He took on the role of minister of war in May, then formally undertook the responsibilities of premier in July. Kerensky rejected the Miliukov view of fighting the war to victory for the sake of territorial gains pledged to the prerevolutionary regime. But the young firebrand found compelling reasons for continuing the war effort; more strongly still, he called for a new Russian offensive. To stop fighting meant to let Germany defeat the western Allies, then inevitably turn against revolutionary Russia. To stop fighting meant to forfeit Russia's role as a great power, and thus to nullify its ability to influence its allies to make a democratic peace without annexations. Such views were at least arguable; indeed, Russian military leaders like General M. Alekseev (*q.v.*) agreed on the strategic necessity to prevent the Germans from picking off Britain and France first, then crushing the Russians. But Kerensky went further: the March Revolution had been, in part, a protest against tsarism's flirtation with a separate peace. The revolution must therefore produce victory, he proclaimed. Russia's peasant soldiery saw matters differently. Kerensky's July offensive collapsed; the disintegration of the army, well under way by early summer, speeded up.

Kerensky's last months in power saw him strike ineffectually at enemies on the Right and Left. He repressed with loyal military forces the widespread unrest following the July offensive. Bolshevik leaders like V. I. Lenin and Leon Trotsky (qq.v.) were driven underground or jailed, but an effort to use the army for full-scale repression of the Left failed in September. Kerensky had encouraged Russia's commander in chief, General Lavr Kornilov (q.v.), to move on Petrograd. But fearing the general's own ambitions, Kerensky reversed himself, then called on the Bolsheviks to help defeat Kornilov's troops.

Bolshevik influence swelled. In large measure, this was due to Lenin's clear promise of an early peace. By the start of November, Kerensky could make only ineffectual moves to close down Bolshevik printing shops and to arrest Bolshevik leaders. These may have served to rally the Bolshevik party's rank and file on November 6/7 behind Lenin's controversial call for an armed uprising in the name of the Soviets, the councils of soldiers', workers', and peasants' representatives. Kerensky gathered a scratch military force and tried to retake Petrograd; his defeat at Pulkovo on November 12 left the capital, and eventually control of the nation, in Bolshevik hands.

Kerensky's talents as a speaker and inspirational war leader had briefly reinvigorated Russia's military effort in the spring of 1917. By insisting that the country could—indeed, must—fight on, however, he widened the cracks in Russian society. The political revolution of March was perhaps destined to become a social whirlwind; Kerensky's misreading of the national temper and his insistence on forcing the military pace of the war opened the way for Lenin's complete break with the war effort.

All this was the work of a young man. Kerensky left power when he was barely thirty-six years of age. The failed political leader spent over five decades sifting through his memories to justify his conduct in 1917. He lived in Europe as a political exile until the start of World War II, then left for the United States. He died in New York City, June 11, 1970.

Fontenot, "Alexander F. Kerensky: The Political Career of a Russian Nationalist"; Kerensky, *Russia and History's Turning Point*; Rabinowitch, *The Bolsheviks Come to Power*; Smith, *The Russian Struggle for Power*; Wade, *The Russian Search for Peace*; *Modern Encyclopedia of Russian and Soviet History*, XVI; *Sovetskaia istoricheskaia entsiklopediia*, VII.

KEYES, Roger John Brownlow (*Great Britain, Admiral of the Fleet*), first baron, was born in Tundiani, India, on October 4, 1872, the son of an army colonel. Keyes was particularly proud of his direct descent from the Norman house of Guiz or Gyse. He entered the navy in 1885 and saw service during the so-called Boxer Rebellion in China, where he was promoted to the grade of commander in 1900. A born leader and fighter, full of dash, aggressive and fearless almost to the point of endangering sound judgment, Keyes quickly earned the devotion of all who served under him. From 1905 to 1908 he was stationed in Rome as naval attaché in the grade of captain; five years later, he was inspecting captain of submarines and in August 1912, commodore in charge of the submarine service.

For the first six months of the Great War, Keyes was responsible for submarine warfare in the North Sea, and late in August 1914, he took part in the action in the Helgoland Bight in which Admiral David Beatty's (q.v.) battle cruisers surprised and destroyed three German light cruisers off Helgoland Island; Keyes rescued 220 of the crew of the *Mainz* during that action.

In February 1915, Keyes was assigned chief of staff to Admiral Sackville Carden (q.v.) in command of the naval squadron at the Dardanelles, and one month later, after Carden's retirement owing to ill health, he became chief of staff to Carden's successor, Admiral De Robeck (q.v.). In this capacity Keyes played a prominent role in planning the naval as well as the military operations in this theater of the war. Although the great naval attempt to force the Straits on March 18 failed, Keyes remained "coldly confident" that the operation could yet be brought to a swift and successful conclusion. When army General Sir Charles Monro (q.v.) in October 1916 counseled immediate evacuation of the Allied troops beached at Gallipoli, Keyes urged De Robeck to attempt yet another naval assault upon the Straits. De Robeck, however, regarded the risks of further naval operations as out of all proportion to the possible gains. This notwithstanding, he allowed his chief of staff to plead his case in London. Lord Kitchener (q.v.) found Keyes to be "a very pertinacious young man," and agreed at the request of the government to undertake a personal tour of the Dardanelles and to report on the situation at the narrows. Kitchener's negative evaluation ended all further offensive actions in this theater. According to De Robeck, the soldiers at Gallipoli referred to Keyes openly as the "lunatic sailor."

From June 1916 to June 1917, Keyes commanded the battleship *Centurion* in the Grand Fleet and, upon promotion to the grade of rear admiral, was placed in charge of the fourth battle squadron. In October 1917, he was recalled to the Admiralty as director of plans, and in this capacity turned his attention to possible naval operations against the enemy submarine lairs at Zeebrugge and Ostend. Keyes got the chance to put his theory into practice in January 1918 when, after promotion to vice admiral, Dover Patrol, this master of narrow-seas warfare came up with a bold design to block the two captured Belgian ports. Specifically, Keyes planned to block Ostend by sinking two old cruisers in the channel under cover of a smoke screen; at Zeebrugge, where a mole housed powerful shore batteries, he opted to land a party of marines under cover of smoke to silence the German guns, and to blow up an old submarine loaded with explosives under the viaduct leading to the mole, thus preventing the enemy from bringing up reserves, while another three superannuated cruisers would be sunk in the canal entrance. The operation was carried out on April 22, 1918, with Keyes on board the *Warwick*. Zeebrugge was a complete success, but at Ostend the blockships failed to reach their destination because the Germans had moved a buoy. Nevertheless, the audacity of the plan received worldwide attention—even though the Germans cleared the channel in a few hours. As Marder has aptly put it: "The psychological effect was considerable; the strategic, almost nil."

After the war, Keyes was created a baronet and given a grant of £10,000. He commanded the battle cruiser squadron in 1919-21, and next served as deputy chief of the naval staff in the Admiralty in the grade of vice admiral. In 1925 he was appointed commander in chief, Mediterranean Fleet, reaching the grade of admiral the following year; in 1929 he was commander in chief, Portsmouth, and promoted to admiral of the fleet. Keyes was placed on the retirement list in May 1935. On May 7, 1940, he took a decisive role in the debate in the House of Commons that led to the resignation of Prime Minister Neville Chamberlain. Next came duty as liaison officer to King Leopold III of Belgium, and in 1940 Keyes was instrumental in the creation of the famous "commandos." In 1943 he was raised to the peerage as Baron Keyes, of Zeebrugge and of Dover. He died on December 26, 1945, at Buckingham. Winston Churchill (*q.v.*) said of him: "In many ways his spirit and example seemed to revive in our stern and tragic age the

vivid personality and unconquerable dauntless soul of Nelson himself."

Aspinall-Oglander, *Roger Keyes*; Halpern, ed., *The Keyes Papers*, I; Keyes, *Naval Memoirs*, 2 vols.; Marder, *Dreadnought to Scapa Flow*, II, V; *Dictionary of National Biography 1941-1950*.

KIGGELL, Sir Launcelot Edward (*Great Britain, General*), was born in Ballingary, county Limerick, on October 2, 1862, the son of an army officer and justice of the peace. He was educated at Sandhurst, and in 1882 posted to the Royal Warwickshire Regiment, serving as adjutant from 1886 to 1890. Kiggell left the Staff College in 1894, and for the next three years served as instructor at Sandhurst. Kigg, as he was commonly called, spent most of his duty thereafter in staff assignments. He saw action during the Boer War and in 1913/14 was commandant of the Staff College; he was promoted major general in 1914. His military ideas were exceedingly orthodox and plodding, but in an army where wealth and connection dominated, Kiggell had no choice as a man of only modest means but to work his way up in the staff in lieu of choice field commands.

Kigg served at the War Office during the first year of the Great War, and, in November 1915, was appointed assistant to the chief of the Imperial General Staff. The next month, however, his good friend Sir Douglas Haig (*q.v.*), the new British commander in chief, brought Kiggell over to France as chief of the General Staff. It was a curious appointment since Kiggell had no experience in modern large-scale warfare since August 1914, having spent the early war years in England. Unfortunately, Kiggell and his staff proved to be not only generally mediocre but also highly subservient to Haig. It is perhaps ironic that in July 1916, in a fatal moment of independence, Kigg persuaded Haig to abandon small group attacks at the Somme in favor of assaults in successive waves, which were mercilessly cut down by enemy machine-gun fire.

Kiggell was serenely optimistic as late as August 1917 that the Germans could be displaced from the Belgian coast, and he pushed Haig to maintain the offensive during the Third Battle of Ypres to the point of canceling a planned tank offensive in the direction of Cambrai with General Julian Byng's (*q.v.*) Third Army for fear that this would divert forces and equipment from the vital Ypres sector. Despite flooded battlefields, heavy downpours, fields of mud, and the utter exhaustion of the British troops, Kiggell throughout October 1917 forced the drive on Passchendaele to continue. The slaughter of the campaigns of 1917 (400,000 British casualties alone at

Ypres) resulted in pressure to remove Kiggell as chief of the General Staff in France; indeed, Kigg broke down owing to "nervous exhaustion" after visiting the Passchendaele front late in 1917 (after the fighting had ended). Early in 1918 he was sent to Guernsey as lieutenant governor and military head. Haig incredibly lamented his departure: "I am very loth [sic] to part with Kigg's help and sound advice." Kiggell was promoted lieutenant general in 1917; he died at Felixstowe on February 23, 1954. Generals Sir Henry Rawlinson and Sir Hubert Gough (qq.v.) concurred that Kigg was well below standard as a staff chief.

Guinn, *British Strategy and Politics*; Liddell Hart, *The Real War*; *Dictionary of National Biography 1951-1960*.

KITCHENER, Horatio Herbert (*Great Britain, Field Marshal*), first Earl Kitchener, of Khartoum and of Broome, was born in Crotter House on June 24, 1850, the son of an army officer. He graduated from the Royal Military Academy, Woolwich, in 1870, and the following year was gazetted to the Royal Engineers. Kitchener was assigned to tours of duty in Palestine, Cyprus, and Egypt, coming home in 1885—only to be sent out the following year as governor general of the eastern Sudan. From 1892 to 1900 Kitchener was sirdar of the Egyptian army; in this capacity he defeated the Mahdi's army of 50,000 at Omdurman with half the force in September 1897. He proceeded thereafter to Fashoda in order to forestall the attempt by Major Marchand to claim the Sudan for France. Kitchener was rewarded by being appointed governor general of the Sudan and by being raised to the peerage as Baron Kitchener, of Khartoum. In December 1899, he joined Lord Roberts at Gibraltar as chief of staff, and for much of the Boer War served virtually as second in command. Kitchener's policy of gutting Boer farms, taking their grain and herds, and rounding their women and children up in concentration camps was severely criticized in many quarters; even so, in 1902 he received a viscountcy for his efforts. General Kitchener next served as commander in chief in India to 1909. The following year he returned to Egypt as field marshal, and in June 1914, received an earldom.

On August 3, 1914, Prime Minister Herbert Asquith (q.v.) literally had Kitchener snatched off a Channel boat and appointed him state secretary for war. Kitchener not only foresaw the German march through Belgium and tried, albeit unsuccessfully, to get the British Expeditionary Force to deploy near Amiens, but also concluded that the war would last at least three years. Accordingly, he set out to create "New Armies" comprising a total of seventy divisions (as compared to the twenty available in August

1914); in the meantime, he counseled utmost support of the French command, personally traveling to Paris on September 1 to stiffen the resolve of Sir John French (q.v.) to reverse the retreat from Mons. The state secretary for war was bitterly attacked in May 1915 for the failure to supply units in France with high explosive shells, and he weathered the storm only by creating a special Ministry of Munitions in June of that year.

A greater crisis faced Kitchener in the eastern Mediterranean in 1915, however. As early as January 2 he had informed General French of his view that "the German lines in France may be looked upon as a fortress that cannot be carried by assault," and had asked the field commander "*where* anything effective can be accomplished"? The answer came instead that same day from Grand Duke Nikolai (q.v.), commander of the Russian armies, who requested a British "demonstration" at the Dardanelles in order to relieve the pressure upon his forces in the Caucasus. Winston Churchill (q.v.) at the Admiralty endorsed with alacrity a British rush of the Straits and assured Kitchener that the Royal Navy could force the Straits; the army was to supply only occupation troops for Constantinople. On March 12 Sir Ian Hamilton (q.v.) was appointed commander of the Mediterranean Expeditionary Force of about 80,000 men.

Although the naval attempt to force the Straits failed badly on March 18, British prestige, emotional commitment, and the hope of acquiring two new allies (Italy and Rumania) by a swift victory over Turkey carried the day: the army was to take the Gallipoli Peninsula alone. Sir Edward Grey (q.v.), state secretary for foreign affairs, at the last moment botched negotiations that might have led Greece and Russia to join the assault at the Straits, but nothing daunted London's determination to rush the Dardanelles. On April 25 Sir Ian Hamilton's forces stormed the beaches at Cape Helles and Anzac Cove, and by May 3 Kitchener assured the cabinet that there was "no doubt that we shall break through." However, the Turks held the Sari Bair heights, and even a later diversionary landing at Suvla Bay did not change the course of the campaign at Gallipoli. Kitchener in October sent a western front infantry general, Sir Charles C. Monro (q.v.), to Gallipoli, but refused to accept this officer's recommendation that the evacuation of British forces commence at once. Instead, Kitchener departed for the Peninsula on November 4, returning by December 1 convinced that General Monro had been correct in his analysis of the situation; on December 7 the cabinet recommended evacuation. Kitchener, whose prestige was closely associated with the Dardanelles campaign, tendered his resignation, but Herbert Asquith refused the offer.

In the general political and military realignment following the debacle at the Straits, Kitchener appointed Sir Douglas Haig as General French's replacement as commander in chief in France, and brought Sir William Robertson (qq.v.) home from France as chief of the Imperial General Staff. With his prestige at low ebb at home, Kitchener early in 1916 managed to extract from the tsar of Russia an invitation to visit that country and to get away from London. On June 5, four days after the battle of Jutland, Kitchener boarded the cruiser Hampshire at Scapa Flow bound for Archangel; the ship struck a mine off the Orkneys, taking Kitchener down with it. He received a splendid funeral service and a memorial chapter in St. Paul's Cathedral.

Kitchener's performance at the War Office has to be judged a failure. He proved unable to delegate authority, isolating himself by overwork, and refusing to seek counsel from either the chief of the Imperial General Staff or from the director of military operations. The few people he corresponded with were mainly still in India and Egypt; in fact, Kitchener had not resided in England since his boyhood. He was contemptuous of his political colleagues, a prima donna who sought to run the war as a personal undertaking. As a result, army headquarters in France became virtually autonomous and it took Prime Minister David Lloyd George (q.v.) nearly two years to reassert civilian control over strategy. Some have even suggested that Kitchener's loss was not much regretted by anyone.

Gooch, The Plans of War; Guinn, British Strategy and Politics; Keegan and Wheatcroft, Who's Who in Military History; Magnus, Kitchener; Dictionary of National Biography 1912-1921.

KLUCK, Alexander von (Germany, General), was born at Münster on May 20, 1846, the son of a master builder. He entered the Prussian army in 1865, took part in the campaigns of 1866 and 1870/71, and was promoted colonel in 1896. Kluck was advanced major general in 1899 and general of infantry in 1906; the family was raised into the Prussian nobility in 1909. Head of the V Army Corps in 1906, Kluck the next year commanded the I Army Corps in East Prussia. In 1913 he was appointed inspector general of the VIII Army Inspectorate in Berlin, and the following year was promoted colonel general and placed in charge of the First Army.

Kluck assembled the First Army near Aachen between August 7 and 15, 1914, as the right wing of the projected great wheeling movement through Belgium, which was thereafter to advance along the Channel coast and to swoop down upon and envelop French forces behind Paris. At first, all went according to plan. Kluck's units surrounded Brussels and defeated the British Expeditionary Force near Mons on August 23; three days later Kluck defeated the British again at Le Cateau. Obsessed with the notion of a new Sedan, the commander of the First Army abandoned the original plan of advance and wheeled inwards prematurely east of Paris, in the process exposing the German right to envelopment. Indeed, Kluck then headed toward the south and Compiègne, defeated the French near Amiens, but in the process failed to cover the flank of General Karl von Bülow's (q.v.) Second Army and instead crossed the Marne on September 3. A thirty-mile wide gap developed between the inner flanks of the First and Second Armies and within two days the First Battle of the Marne was in full swing from Paris to Verdun. Although his troops were plagued by hunger and exhaustion, they nevertheless defeated the French at the battle of Ourcq as Kluck successfully threw his right wing against the French Sixth Army. However, German headquarters far distant in Luxembourg feared that the French and British might exploit the gap between Kluck and Bülow, and on September 9 Colonel Richard Hentsch (q.v.) advised Kluck to withdraw his forces behind the Aisne River rather than risk French counterattacks against his flank. Thus the battle of the Marne was handed the French by the panic of German staff headquarters. And by Kluck's premature inward wheeling motion before Paris.

On March 28, 1915, Kluck was severely wounded in the leg by shrapnel near Vailly. He turned seventy years of age while recuperating and in October 1916 was retired; his eldest son died in Flanders. Kluck was the only German commander of the Great War who had never served in the General Staff. He died in Berlin-Grunewald on October 19, 1934, convinced that staff headquarters had deprived him of a decisive victory at the Marne in September 1914.

Baumgarten-Crusius, Deutsche Heerführung im Marnefeldzug; Kluck, Marsch auf Paris; Liddell Hart, The Real War; Biographisches Wörterbuch zur Deutschen Geschichte, II; Geschichte der Ritter des Ordens, I.

KOLCHAK, Aleksandr Vasilevich (Russia, Vice Admiral), was born in St. Petersburg, November 16, 1874. His father was a high-ranking naval officer, and the Kolchak family was of Turkish origin, the descendants of a Turkish prisoner of war brought to Russia in the 1730s. The young Kolchak chose a naval career and completed the Naval College, second in his class, in 1894. He received his first assignment with the Pacific Fleet. In 1900 the talented young lieutenant was invited to join an expedition to the North Pole, and he soon made a reputation for himself as an explorer. He fought with distinction at Port Arthur in the Russo-Japanese War, 1904/1905, commanding a destroyer, then a shore battery. After a stint as a Japanese prisoner of war, Kolchak returned to Russia to serve in the newly established Naval General Staff. This body, designed to reform the navy and to prepare for a future war, became home for a number of young military innovators. Kolchak's work there, along with new polar explorations, 1910/1911, marked him as an officer with a bright future. In 1912, then a commander, he requested sea duty and received charge of a destroyer in the Baltic Fleet under Admiral von Essen (*q.v.*).

In World War I Kolchak received rapid and well deserved promotion. Essen set the stage. The admiral refused to accept the High Command's call to float passively behind mine barriers in the face of the superior German navy. Kolchak played a leading role, both as a staff and line officer, in implementing Essen's orders to cut away at German naval traffic in the Baltic. As a staff officer, Kolchak directed the Baltic Fleet's operations section; by the fall of 1915 he was the commanding officer of the crack Mine Division, the most active segment of the fleet. In the spring of 1916 Kolchak, at age forty-one, was a rear admiral. His reputation for efficiency joined with daring was well established; as early as February 1915 he had personally led a squadron of destroyers to mine the approaches to Danzig.

In July 1916, promoted vice admiral, Kolchak took command of the Black Sea Fleet. The Russians enjoyed a rough balance with their foes there, and Kolchak found even greater scope than in the Baltic for his energy and imagination. Using combined submarine and destroyer squadrons, he applied new techniques for the rapid deployment of mines. Such offensive operations obstructed enemy naval traffic between the Bosphorus and the Black Sea and constituted a severe blow to Turkish and German cruisers and submarines. In August the Russians mounted an imaginative offensive comparable to the air-sea strikes of World War II; leading a force of cruisers, destroyers, and sea plane carriers, Kolchak tried to attack the Bulgarian port of Varna. As the year ended, the Black Sea naval leader was looking forward to an assault on the Dardanelles the following spring.

Even in the adverse conditions following the March Revolution, Kolchak performed well. His fleet was well removed from the urban storm centers of northern Russia, and Kolchak himself quickly accepted the fall of the monarchy and the establishment of the provisional government. For months, he was able to negotiate with the fleet's revolutionary committees to maintain order and discipline. By June, however, the sailors of the Black Sea command were moving rapidly to the political left and Kolchak abandoned his command. The provisional government sent him to Washington to discuss future joint operations with the U.S. navy. Kolchak was returning from this disguised form of political exile by way of Japan when he received word of the November Revolution.

The distinguished young admiral, totally lacking any political experience, was determined to hold his country in the war against Germany. This dedication proved the road to personal and national tragedy. By November 1918, Kolchak had taken nominal command over anti-Bolshevik forces in Siberia. Although more than a figurehead, Kolchak found his power severely constricted. The admiral was dependent upon Czech and Allied, notably British, military power. A leader of political brilliance might have transformed the situation; but Kolchak had no appealing program to offer the Russian population in place of Bolshevism. The main effect of his rise to power was to stamp the White cause as one dominated by nationalist-minded military men, uninterested in political and social reform. Neither were Kolchak's substantial military talents at home in a war in which cavalry divisions rather than torpedo boats and mine sweepers were the crucial weapons. His spring advance westward in 1919 collapsed, went into reverse, then turned into a rout. In early 1920 the luckless admiral fell into the hands of the local government in the Siberian city of Irkutsk, then faced a tribunal dominated by the area's Bolsheviks. Russia's greatest naval hero of World War I was executed by firing squad outside Irkutsk, February 7, 1920.

Chirikov, "Verkhovnyi pravitel' admiral A. V. Kolchak"; Footman, *Civil War in Russia*; Khoroshavin, "Admiral A. V. Kolchak"; Mitchell, *History of Russian and Soviet Sea Power*; Pavlovich, ed., *The Fleet in the First World War*, I; *Modern Encyclopedia of Russian and Soviet History*, XVII; *Sovetskaia istoricheskaia entsiklopediia*, VII; *Sovetskaia voennaia entsiklopediia*, IV.

KÖRBER, Ernst von (*Austria-Hungary, Minister-President*), was born in Trient on November 6, 1850, the son of an army colonel. In 1872 he attained his doctorate of law at Vienna University and commenced a long career closely associated with the departments of commerce and the interior, which he headed 1897/98 and 1899 respectively. On January 18, 1900, Körber was appointed minister-president as well as interior minister; in 1902 he added to this minister of justice. Körber, an experienced civil servant, was brought in to quell riots in Prague and to allay deteriorating relations between Emperor Francis Joseph (q.v.) and the Reichsrat. In June 1900, he launched a massive program of domestic spending (Danube-Oder Canal, expansion of the harbor at Trieste, Tauern-Wochein railroad) designed to stimulate the sluggish economy. His relations with the Hungarians were never the best, however. Körber's proposals in 1902 for the renewal of the Compromise of 1867 were flatly rejected in Budapest, and the minister-president's opposition to Hungarian plans to divide the common army into two separate Austrian and Hungarian armies was well known. Moreover, Körber was unable to convince the Czechs to go along with his plans to use German as the language of administration only in districts where this was warranted; the Young Czechs sought to abolish completely the use of German as the official language. Körber resigned his posts on December 31, 1904, and totally withdrew from public life for the next eleven years.

On February 7, 1915, he agreed to return as joint minister of finance and as administrator of Bosnia, and after the assassination of Count Karl von Stürgkh (q.v.) on October 28, 1916, Körber accepted the minister-presidency for a second time. His candidacy led many to expect a modification of the system of wartime absolutism, but Körber was not up to the task. He was deeply pessimistic about the future of the Dual Monarchy, and when the new Emperor Charles sent Count Leopold von Berchtold (qq.v.) to confront Körber with the alternative either to accept a moderate Compromise with Hungary or to resign, the minister-president opted for the latter on December 14, 1916. His relations with Charles had been strained for some time. The experienced bureaucrat Körber objected to the monarch's refusal to take the coronation oath, while Charles disliked the elder statesman's strong stand on renegotiating a new ten-year Compromise with the Magyars. For the last two years of the war, Körber became an inveterate opponent of what he termed Charles' "experimental policies." He died at Baden, near Vienna, on March 5, 1919.

Kann, *History of the Habsburg Empire*; *Neue Österreichische Biographie*, I; *Österreichisches Biographisches Lexikon 1815-1950*, IV.

KORNILOV, Lavr Georgievich (*Russia, General of Infantry*), was born in Ust Kamenogorsk in eastern Siberia, August 30, 1870. He was the son of a retired junior officer in a Cossack regiment. He graduated from the Mikhailovsky Artillery College in 1892 and completed the General Staff Academy in 1898. Following his staff training, Kornilov participated in mapping expeditions to Chinese Turkestan and eastern Persia. He served as an intelligence officer in Manchuria during the Russo-Japanese War, remaining in Asia as a military attaché in Peking, 1907-11.

At the beginning of World War I, Kornilov was a brigade commander in the Eighth Army under General Brusilov (q.v.). He soon acquired a reputation for toughness and personal bravery, but his superior officers also noted Kornilov's clumsiness and frequent insubordination in responding to orders from above. During the Austro-German offensive at Gorlice (May 1915), Kornilov, as commander of the Forty-eighth Infantry Division, failed to withdraw from his position east of the enemy breakthrough and was trapped in the Carpathians. The rash young general spent over a year as a prisoner of war. He escaped from his confinement in Hungary in the summer of 1916, made his way back to Russia, and found himself welcomed as a hero by the public and the imperial court. In a country starved for military victories, the first Russian general to escape from enemy hands qualified as an instant celebrity. He was rewarded with command of an army corps.

While in his prisoner-of-war camp, Kornilov had railed against liberal parliamentary leaders like Miliukov and Guchkov (qq.v.), who he thought were undercutting the nation's war effort. Nonetheless, he initially accepted the March 1917 Revolution, along with many other army leaders, hoping the ouster of the monarchy would energize both the army and the home front. Kornilov was chosen by leaders of the provisional government to command the Petrograd Military District. It was an unhappy appointment. They wanted an authoritative figure to calm the city's radicalized garrison; Kornilov wanted to use methods a liberal regime could not tolerate. He soon resigned in disgust when he was not allowed to use heavy weapons to end popular demonstrations against Miliukov. Embittered with weak parliamentarians who could not contain the revolution, he departed to resume active duty on the southwestern front.

Kornilov's Eighth Army performed creditably in the unsuccessful July offensive, and he was rewarded with meteoric advancement. Now promoted a general of infantry, he barely had time to settle in as the new front commander when Premier Kerensky (*q.v.*) elevated him in early August to supreme commander. Kornilov's advancement was due less to his abilities as a strategist and director of military operations than to his vocal insistence that discipline in the crumbling armies be rebuilt at any cost. He called for the restoration of the death penalty in the army, and, meanwhile, ordered machine guns and artillery fire turned on troops who retreated without orders. Kornilov was soon calling for martial law on Russia's railroads as part of a sweeping program to restore national order for the sake of the war effort.

Kornilov's political naiveté soon led him into a complex confrontation with Kerensky, whose own authority was crumbling. By late August both hoped to reconstitute the Russian government on authoritarian lines; each expected to be the strongman of the new regime. Kornilov massed troops near Petrograd with Kerensky's consent; but, against the prime minister's wishes, the general marched on the capital in early September. Kerensky turned to the political Left, notably the antiwar Bolsheviks, for aid, a move that seriously undermined his own government. Kornilov found his forces collapsing as they tried to advance; railroad workers held up their trains; Bolshevik agitators surrounded the troops and dissolved the discipline that held Kornilov's own forces together. The renegade general was arrested in mid-September, and the decline of the provisional government continued.

Sympathetic military leaders released Kornilov from confinement at Bykhov near Supreme Headquarters at Mogilev, fearing that the rebel general would fall into the hands of the Bolsheviks, who held control of the government after the November Revolution. Kornilov fled to the Don in early December. There he intended to raise a new army; with it, he hoped to throw the Bolsheviks from power and to lead Russia anew into battle against the Germans. He helped create the nucleus of a potent White movement, but the young general did not live to see it develop. Kornilov was killed at Ekaterinodar, to the northeast of the Black Sea, April 13, 1918, during an early skirmish between his White force and pro-Bolshevik Red Guards.

Chamberlin, *The Russian Revolution*, 2 vols.; Kenez, *Civil War in South Russia, 1918*; Rabinowitch, *The Bolsheviks Come to Power*; Rostunov, ed., *Istoriia pervoi mirovoi voiny*, II; *Modern Encyclopedia of Russian and Soviet History*, XVII; *Sovetskaia istoricheskaia entsiklopediia*, VII; *Sovetskaia voennaia entsiklopediia*, IV.

KÖVESS von KÖVESSHÁZA, Hermann Baron

(*Austria-Hungary, Field Marshal*), was born in Temesvár, Banat, on March 30, 1854, the son of an army general. Kövess entered the army in 1872 after attending the Technical Military Academy. Completion of studies at the War Academy was followed by a long tenure in the General Staff, capped in 1882 by a campaign to quell a native uprising in Herzegovina. Kövess failed his examinations for promotion to the grade of major in the General Staff, and he then turned to the infantry; rapid promotions followed to major general in 1902, inspector of Tyrolean fortifications in 1910, and chief of the XII Army Corps and commanding general in Hermannstadt, Transylvania, in 1911. But once again qualification reports negated his talents, and Kövess was scheduled to retire late in 1914 owing to lack of offensive spirit.

Instead, the outbreak of war confirmed his command of the XII Corps, which he led into east Galicia, taking up positions south of Przemysl in October 1914. While junior generals such as Baron Eduard Böhm-Ermolli, Count Viktor Dankl, and Svetozar Boroević (*qq.v.*) were given command of armies, Kövess continued to head the XII Corps; late in 1914 he became involved in the general rout of Austro-Hungarian forces at Lemberg, and spent the winter months defending Silesia as part of General von Woyrsch's (*q.v.*) forces. Kövess' fortunes then turned for the better. During the breakthrough at Gorlice, he stormed the fortress Ivangorod on August 4, 1915, and, as commander of the Third Army attached to Army Group Mackensen (*q.v.*), captured Belgrade on October 9, 1915. Kövess capped his string of successes in January 1916 by taking Montenegro; in February he conquered most of north and central Albania.

On May 15, 1916, Kövess led his Third Army as part of General Conrad von Hötzendorf's (*q.v.*) design to sweep down upon the Italians from the high plain of Lavarone-Folgaria and to capture the key rail center of Padua. Kövess managed to take Asiago, but stiff enemy resistance, the difficulty of terrain, and General Aleksei Brusilov's (*q.v.*) offensive in the east forced cancellation of the Tyrolean operation; Kövess was hastily sent back to Galicia. In October 1916, he was placed in charge of the Seventh Army in Mármaros-Sziget. Kövess helped to drive the Russians from east Galicia in the summer of 1917, and in August liberated the Bukovina and Czernowitz. Emperor Charles (*q.v.*) promoted him field marshal in August 1917 and raised him into the Hungarian baronage.

From January to April 1918, Kövess headed an army group comprised of the First and Seventh Army spanning the eastern front from Kronstadt to Czernowitz, but the conclusion of a separate peace with

Russia in March left him temporarily unemployed. At a crown council on September 27, 1918, General Arz von Straussenburg (*q.v.*) suggested the formation of an army group, "West Balkans," under Kövess along the line Danube-Save-Drina in order to stem the Entente advance from the southwest in the wake of Bulgaria's collapse. Mass desertions by various ethnic formations rendered this proposal unfeasible. Kövess, as senior commanding general, was given supreme command of the army on November 3, 1918, by then an utterly meaningless appointment. He died in Vienna on September 22, 1924.

Bardolff, *Militär-Maria Theresien-Orden*; Rothenberg, *Army of Francis Joseph*; *Neue Österreichische Biographie*, II; *Österreichisches Biographisches Lexikon 1815-1950*, IV.

KRAFFT von DELLMENSINGEN, Konrad (*Germany, General*),

was born in Laufen, Bavaria, on November 24, 1862, into an ancient Bavarian noble clan. Krafft entered the Bavarian army in 1881, attended the War Academy, and was assigned to the General Staff. Next came various regimental and divisional commands as well as further duty in the Bavarian General Staff. In 1912 Krafft was promoted major general and appointed chief of the Bavarian General Staff, which would according to the treaty of 1871, yield to its Prussian counterpart in time of war.

In August 1914, Krafft was assigned chief of staff of the German Sixth Army commanded by Crown Prince Rupprecht of Bavaria (*q.v.*). Along with the Seventh Army of General Josias von Heeringen, Rupprecht was supposed to conduct a yielding and "enticing" defensive on the German southern flank, according to the Schlieffen plan. General Helmuth von Moltke (*q.v.*), however, not only doubled the size of his forces in Alsace-Lorraine, but even diverted six reserve divisions to Lorraine that should have been attached to the right wing marching through Belgium. This tactic only brought confusion, and Krafft and Rupprecht were left without clear orders; their attack against the French line Morhange-Sarrebourg on August 20 was sufficiently strong to force a French withdrawal, but too weak to envelop the French right flank. Krafft initially demurred when ordered by German headquarters to pursue the fleeing French; his forebodings proved correct when the French fought the Germans to a standstill at Nancy-Epinal in mid-September.

Next came a bewildering plethora of commands. At the end of September Krafft was assigned staff chief to a new Sixth Army, first at the Somme, then at Arras and Lille, and finally at Ypres; by December 1914, he stood with the Sixth Army in Flanders. This force fought in March 1915 at Neuve Chapelle and in May at La Bassée and Arras. Thereafter Krafft was appointed commander of the German Alpine Corps and sent to the Serbian border. In October 1915, Krafft accompanied Field Marshal August von Mackensen (*q.v.*) into Serbia, reaching the Greek frontier by March 1916. Reassignment to the western front in the Champagne followed in the spring, and for much of the summer he fought before Verdun.

In the fall of 1916 Krafft returned to the Balkan theater after Rumania had declared war against the Central Powers. His Alpine Corps was placed under General Erich von Falkenhayn's (*q.v.*) Ninth Army and fought at the battle of Hermannstadt. From October 17 to November 27, it forced the passes through the Transylvanian mountains; this allowed the Germans to storm Targu Jiu in Wallachia, to cross the Arges, and to occupy Bucharest on December 6, 1916. In March 1917, Krafft was briefly assigned yet again to the western front as chief of staff to Army Group Duke Albrecht of Württemberg (*q.v.*) at Strassburg, but in August was ordered to the Italian front.

General Erich Ludendorff (*q.v.*) had sent Krafft, his expert in mountain warfare, to scout the Julian Alps near Tolmino and Flitsch, and he recommended an assault by six German and nine Austrian divisions (the hastily formed German Fourteenth Army) at Tolmino. General Otto von Below was formally in command, while General Svetozar Boroević (*qq.v.*) led two Austrian armies on the lower ground near the Adriatic shore. The Germans had brought their troops and supplies up the Julian Alps by night and on pack animals to attain the utmost surprise, and they were greatly aided in this when the Italian commander, Count Luigi Cadorna (*q.v.*), refused to believe reports of the impending attack. On October 24, 1917, Lieutenant General Krafft attained a smashing victory as the mixed German-Austro-Hungarian forces broke the Italian line at Caporetto (Tolmein-Flitsch) and forced Cadorna to retreat, first behind the Tagliamento and finally behind the Piave; the Italian Second Army was utterly destroyed and Rome lost nearly 600,000 men. Only with British and French reinforcements were the Italians able to stabilize their northern frontier.

Krafft on February 1, 1918, became chief of staff of the Seventeenth Army in Artois. On March 21-23 he fought the battle of Monchy-Cambrai and on March 25 he defeated the French at Bapaume; however, early in April Krafft failed to advance at Scarpe and his sector of the front degenerated into trench warfare along the line Arras-Albert. On April 19 Krafft became commander of the II Bavarian Army Corps;

on August 8 he was promoted general of artillery. The Allied advance on August 26 forced Krafft to abandon Arras and his units rapidly fell back upon Cambrai and St. Quentin, finally reaching the Hermann portion of the Hindenburg line. At the end of August, following the collapse of the Austro-Hungarian front, Krafft was rushed to the Bavarian-Tyrolean sector in order to keep the Italians out of southern Germany; instead, the Germans concluded an armistice on November 11, 1918. Krafft retired from the army on December 4, 1918; he died at Seeshaupt in Upper Bavaria on February 22, 1953.

Falls, *Battle of Caporetto*; Krafft, *Der Durchbruch am Isonzo*; Liddell Hart, *The Real War*; *Geschichte der Ritter des Ordens*, I.

KRAMÁŘ, Karel (*Austria-Hungary, Politician*), was born in Hochstadt, Bohemia, on December 27, 1860, the son of a master builder. Studies in Prague, Strassburg, Berlin, and Paris led to his receiving a doctorate of law in 1884. Independently wealthy, Kramář entered politics on the side of the "Realists" of T. G. Masaryk (*q.v.*) and was elected to the Reichsrat in 1891 and to the Bohemian Landtag three years later. As a member of the so-called Young Czechs, Kramář at first avoided radical nationalist programs and sought instead to work for a compromise solution to the Slav question. In terms of foreign policies he denounced the Triple Alliance and called instead for closer ties with Russia.

In May 1915, Kramář was arrested and charged with high treason by the Austro-Hungarian army in the wake of desertion by several Czech units in the east. In a lengthy secret trial in Vienna lasting until November 1916, Kramář defended himself brilliantly; nevertheless, the army court found him guilty and sentenced him to death by hanging. Although the sentence was later commuted to fifteen years of hard labor, Kramář emerged as a determined enemy of the Habsburgs. Not even the clumsy attempt by Emperor Charles (*q.v.*), in July 1917, to widen the basis of support for his policies by granting a general amnesty could bring Kramář back into the fold.

Ironically, Kramář was not destined to play a decisive role in the creation of the new Czechoslovakian state. He served as the Czechoslovakian representative at the Paris Peace Conference in 1919, but subsequently fell out with the pro-Soviet Eduard Beneš (*q.v.*) over the issue of intervention in Russia's civil war on the side of the Whites. Kramář died in Prague on May 26, 1937.

Kann, *History of the Habsburg Empire*; *Österreichisches Biographisches Lexikon 1815-1950*, IV.

KRAUSS, Alfred (*Austria-Hungary, Field Marshal*), was born in Zara (Zadar), Dalmatia, on April 26, 1862. He attended the Military Academy from 1881 to 1883, and in 1891 in the grade of captain was assigned to the V Army Corps in Pressburg as General Staff officer. Next came four years with the infantry in Graz, and by 1904 Colonel Krauss went to work to improve Austro-Hungarian field kitchens, mechanized vehicles, and infantry battle gear. In 1910 he was appointed commandant of the War Academy and promoted major general.

On August 28, 1914, Krauss was given command of the Twenty-ninth Infantry Division in Serbia, and on September 6 he defeated the Serb Timok Division near Sasinci. At that time Krauss criticized General Conrad von Hötzendorf's (*q.v.*) decision to launch an all-out strike against Serbia, blaming this dilution of strength for the overall lack of preparedness against Russia in the east. And when Archduke Eugene took over command of the southeastern front after General Oskar Potiorek's (*qq.v.*) disastrous campaign in Serbia, Krauss joined the archduke on December 23, 1914, as chief of staff. Again, when Eugene was given command of the southwestern front on May 27, 1915, Krauss followed him to Marburg as chief of staff. Throughout this period the able Krauss built up the Austro-Hungarian defensive positions along the Isonzo front as well as in the Dolomites. Early in 1916 Archduke Eugene entrusted Krauss with the planning of a projected strike against the key railroad center at Padua; Krauss recommended an assault through the alpine passes, but Conrad brushed that aside in favor of a sweep from the high plains of Lavarone-Folgaria. The offensive, launched on May 15, proved a disaster and was compounded by General Aleksei Brusilov's (*q.v.*) offensive in the east.

Krauss was relieved as chief of staff of Army Group Archduke Eugene on February 28, 1917, and in mid-March was given command of the I Army Corps as part of General Hermann Kövess' (*q.v.*) Seventh Army in the Carpathians, the Bukovina, and Galicia. Krauss was promoted general of infantry on August 1, and midway through the following month was again transferred to the southwestern front as part of the right wing of the German Fourteenth Army. On October 25, 1917, Krauss finally got his chance to storm the alpine passes, breaking the Italian lines at Flitsch and rolling the enemy units up as far as Feltre and Monte Grappa in what became known as the battle of Caporetto. Krauss felt that the victory could have been even greater had General Svetozar Boroević (*q.v.*) closed the trap on the fleeing Italians from the south.

Krauss was next considered for several administrative posts, including minister of food and agriculture, but on May 16, 1918, was given command of the East Army in the Ukraine and entrusted with the job of exploiting the food resources of this area. Not even the talented Krauss, however, could master this impossible task, and he was recalled to Vienna at the end of November 1918. In numerous writings Krauss became a sharp critic of the Austro-Hungarian conduct of the war. He died in Bad Goisern, Upper Austria, on September 29, 1938.

Krauss, *Die Ursachen unserer Niederlage, Das Wunder von Karfreit*; *Österreichisches Biographisches Lexikon 1815-1950*, IV.

KRIVOSHEIN, Aleksandr Vasilevich (*Russia, Minister of Agriculture*), was born in 1858, received his education as an attorney at St. Petersburg University, and entered government service in 1884. During the next twelve years, he served in both the ministry of justice and the ministry of the interior. In 1896 Krivoshein advanced to become assistant director of the Interior Ministry's department of peasant colonization; in 1904 he took over as director. During the revolution of 1905 and its aftermath the astute agricultural expert emerged as a spokesman for land reform. Encouraging peasants to leave their traditional communes to stand as independent proprietors, Krivoshein found his ideas adopted and implemented by Petr Stolypin, Russia's premier, 1906-1911.

In 1908 Krivoshein was made minister of agriculture. He stood apart from the backward-looking ranks of ministers who usually served Tsar Nicholas II (*q.v.*) after 1905. Reaching out to local governing bodies, establishing cordial contacts with Duma deputies, he was a domestic diplomat among political leaders who preferred the bludgeon. In a widely noted speech of July 1913, Krivoshein called for building bridges between the nation's aloof government and Russian society. To a sympathetic contemporary like Vladimir Gurko, a fellow agrarian reformer, Krivoshein was more than just a fine administrator; he was a leader with "a power of thought worthy of a real statesman."

World War I brought Krivoshein an expanded influence in national affairs. Under the weak hand of Premier Ivan Goremykin (*q.v.*), the tsar's ministers struggled among themselves in an effort to shape government policy in wildly differing ways. Krivoshein and Foreign Minister Sergei Sazonov (*q.v.*) called for the Duma to play a continuing role in Russian political life, even in wartime circumstances. Such moderates managed to restrain the schemes of Interior Minister Nikolai Maklakov (*q.v.*) for reducing Russia's infant parliamentary body to a ceremonial role. Thus Maklakov could only try in vain to get the tsar to dismiss the Duma until November 1915, by which time, it was thought, the war would be long past. Krivoshein's moves were doubtless influenced by his hopes of becoming premier himself, with the aid of a friendly body of supporters in the Duma.

Krivoshein's ambitions advanced after the military disasters of 1915 in which a German-Austrian offensive snatched all of Poland from Russian control. Krivoshein and his colleagues pushed from office cabinet reactionaries like Maklakov, although Goremykin, supported by Empress Alexandra (*q.v.*), managed to weather the assault. Krivoshein unsuccessfully urged a full reorganization of the war effort: a Supreme War Council would run the nation's affairs, with Krivoshein taking charge of civil government and the highly regarded war minister, General Aleksei Polivanov (*q.v.*), directing the military effort.

But events slid in another direction. The tsar chose, in August 1915, to take direct command of the armies in the field, thereby uniting in himself civil and military leadership. Krivoshein joined the majority of the cabinet in protesting this move; but he found the tsar, staunchly backed by Goremykin, to be beyond such arguments. Krivoshein's hopes to become premier then evaporated. In the heat of the monarch's resentment at the brief cabinet rebellion, Nicholas launched a purge; Krivoshein was one of the first to lose his portfolio. The government went on to stagnate under Goremykin.

Even in the fall of 1915 events may have outpaced Krivoshein's hopes for an effective wartime government backed by the goodwill of the Duma. Krivoshein, a monarchist, did not envision a British-style government supported by a formal legislative majority. As tempers rose in the Duma, such mildly enlightened monarchism was rapidly losing its appeal. Tsar Nicholas was, true to form, the last to understand this. On March 14, 1917, with the monarchy reduced to rubble and the provisional government about to take shape, Nicholas entertained visions of calming the situation by calling Krivoshein back to become his premier.

The former agricultural minister supported the White side in the emerging civil war, becoming a leader in Baron Wrangel's anti-Bolshevik government in the south of Russia in 1920. With the collapse of this last White effort, Krivoshein emigrated to France where he died in 1921.

Gurko, *Features and Figures of the Past*; Hosking, *The Russian Constitutional Experiment*; Krivoshein, *A. V. Krivoshein (1857-1921)*; Pearson, *The Russian Moderates and the Crisis of Tsarism*; *Sovetskaia istoricheskaia entsiklopediia*, VIII.

KROBATIN, Alexander Baron von (*Austria-Hungary, Field Marshal*), was born in Olmütz, Moravia, on September 12, 1849, the son of an artillery major. Krobatin graduated from the Artillery Academy in Moravia-Weisskirchen in 1869 and subsequently undertook further education in applied chemistry and artillery that qualified him to teach at the Technical Military Academy (1877-1882). Thereafter, in the grade of major, Krobatin headed the Artillery Cadet School in Vienna; after 1896 he served in the grade of colonel in the War Ministry, being promoted major general in 1900. Krobatin, a close friend of General Conrad von Hötzendorf, in 1912 succeeded Baron Moritz Auffenberg (*qq.v.*) as war minister, and under his guidance the Austro-Hungarian army adopted the rapid-fire 8-cm gun M. 5/8 for field artillery, a new 10-cm alpine howitzer, and the new 30.5-cm mortar developed by Skoda in Pilsen.

In the aftermath of the assassination of Archduke Francis Ferdinand (*q.v.*) in Sarajevo on June 28, 1914, Krobatin vigorously supported Conrad's stance for an immediate strike against Serbia. For the first two years of the Great War, Krobatin struggled tirelessly to supply machine guns to the infantry and to introduce flame throwers into the army; his efforts largely accounted for the tripling of the artillery at the divisional level. After repeated requests for front duty, the new Emperor Charles (*q.v.*) appointed Krobatin commander of the Tenth Army in Kärnten on April 12, 1917. The Moravian had been a military member of Francis Ferdinand's Belvedere Circle, but unlike the civilian members of that body he did not view Charles' coming to power as a blessing owing to the ruler's aspirations for personal military command and his lack of firmness. General Rudolf Stöger-Steiner (*q.v.*) succeeded Krobatin as war minister.

The sixty-eight-year-old Krobatin took part in the assault against the Italians in October 1917. While the main thrust of the German Fourteenth Army was set for the sector in and around Flitsch and Tolmino, Krobatin undertook several minor raids designed to hide the main thrust. After the German breakthrough, Krobatin along with Archduke Eugene (*q.v.*) stormed the Tagliamento Valley and advanced as far as Cadore by November 4; in the process, Krobatin captured two Italian divisions near Tolmezzo. For his part in the victory, Krobatin was promoted field marshal on November 5. The great triumph at Caporetto had its disappointing side. It meant that the Tenth Army had become superfluous because the front with Italy could now be greatly reduced, and the Moravian had to witness the dissolution of his army and a transfer to the southwestern front in Tyrol with headquarters at Trient.

As the Dual Monarchy mounted its last major offensive in the summer of 1918, Krobatin was ordered on June 13 to conduct a feint down the Tonale Pass to camouflage the main thrust of the Eleventh Army south of Asiago. Unfortunately, both the feint and the main attack failed, and by late October 1918 the Eleventh Army was in full revolt. Croatian and Hungarian units mutinied and threatened the life of Archduke Joseph (*q.v.*), commander of Army Group Tyrol. Joseph left the front on October 26 for Budapest and turned the Eleventh Army over to Krobatin. The latter asked the Italians for an armistice on October 31, but had to watch the Italians storm the defenseless remnants of the erstwhile Habsburg army between November 1 and 4 in what is termed the "victory" at Vittorio Veneto. Krobatin retired to private life after the war; he died in Vienna on December 27, 1933.

Rothenberg, *Army of Francis Joseph*; *Neue Österreichische Biographie*, XVII; *Österreichisches Biographisches Lexikon 1815-1950*, IV.

KÜHLMANN, Richard von (*Germany, Foreign Secretary*), was born in Constantinople on May 3, 1873, the son of the director general of the Anatolian Railway and an estate owner; he later married a daughter of the Saarland magnate Baron von Stumm. After studying jurisprudence, Kühlmann used his contacts with Chancellor Prince Hohenlohe to procure entry into the foreign service; he served as legation counselor in St. Petersburg, Teheran, London, Morocco, Washington, and The Hague. In London at the turn of the century, Kühlmann sought a *rapprochement* with Britain over the Berlin-Baghdad Railroad, the Portuguese African colonies, and oil reserves in Asia Minor. He almost challenged the German naval attaché, Wilhelm Widenmann, to a duel owing to the captain's insistence that the Anglo-German trade rivalry was the tap root of the naval race developing between Berlin and London. From 1909 to 1914 Kühlmann served in London as embassy counselor and attempted, albeit unsuccessfully, to defuse the Anglo-German rivalry.

After the outbreak of the war, Kühlmann was given special diplomatic missions to Stockholm and Constantinople; thereafter he was appointed ambassador to the Netherlands and in 1916 envoy to the Porte.

On August 7, 1917, he became state secretary of the Foreign Office under Chancellor Georg Michaelis (q.v.). It was hardly an enviable task in the fall of 1917 as three major areas of contention opened between the Foreign Office and the General Staff: Poland, Rumania, and Russia.

Overall, Kühlmann can be depicted as a moderate on the issue of German war aims, that is, he basically endorsed Chancellor Theobald von Bethmann Hollweg's (q.v.) *Mitteleuropa* scheme of September 1914 calling for German economic and political control over Europe from Scandinavia to Turkey, from the Atlantic Ocean to the Caspian Sea. Thus the foreign secretary on November 5, 1917, was able to convince the kaiser to adopt the so-called Austro-Polish solution, while General Erich Ludendorff (q.v.) vehemently demanded direct German control of Poland and at one point even recommended the outright *Anschluss* of that land. The matter was tabled at the crown council of November 5 because Wilhelm II (q.v.) was interested only in the future of Rumania, likening Poland to "the Jüterbog artillery ground."

Russia posed an even greater challenge. Peace talks with the Bolsheviks opened at Brest-Litovsk on December 22, 1917, and dragged on until March 1918. Kühlmann basically desired the outright annexation of Courland and Lithuania as well as Russian evacuation from Poland; beyond that, he hoped to work with the Bolsheviks to stabilize the east as quickly as possible in order to draw on its alleged reserves of grain and oil. Above all, he feared that unrealistically harsh terms might bring about a reactionary coup and hence a reopening of the war with Russia. One could not, he counseled, conduct a policy in the east "with the pen in the left and the sword in the right" hand. Ludendorff, on the other hand, entertained the most Utopian annexationist schemes, desiring to control the land mass in the east as far as the Caspian Sea. The final draft signed on March 3, indeed, represented the triumph of Ludendorff's direct, over Kühlmann's indirect, imperialism: Russia was to evacuate Finland, Courland, Poland, Lithuania, Estonia, Livonia, and the Ukraine; as a result, it lost about 90 percent of its coal mines, 50 percent of its industry, and about 30 percent of its population.

While the Bolsheviks signed the German terms at Brest-Litovsk, Kühlmann was dictating similarly harsh terms to the Rumanians. The Treaty of Bucharest, ratified by the Reichstag in June 1918, virtually reduced Rumania to a vassal state. The country was to be occupied until "a date to be determined later," was to pay all occupation costs, one-third of its army was to be demobilized, its oilfields were to be placed under a German banking consortium for thirty years, and all "surplus" grains were to be handed over to the Germans. Field Marshal August von Mackensen (q.v.), who was to head the German occupation, reflected the mood of the Prussian military: "This time the pen has secured what the sword has won."

Incredibly, the General Staff was dissatisfied with these Draconian settlements in the east and immediately after the signing of terms at Bucharest set out to remove Kühlmann from office. The generals got their chance on June 14, when Kühlmann in a speech in the Reichstag pointed to the "incredible magnitude" of the global coalition lined up against Germany and concluded that "a purely military decision" was beyond Germany's reach. The speech proved a veritable bombshell. It earned him the implacable hatred of the Army Supreme Command and the Pan-Germans, and on July 8 Wilhelm II informed his foreign secretary at Spa that he would have to go. Kühlmann, ever the suave aristocrat, kissed the kaiser's hand, and with this archaic gesture departed from the Wilhelmstrasse. His evaluation of the military situation in June 1918, had, of course, been accurate, although such a public confession proved highly embarrassing to the German government. In many ways Kühlmann had been too subtle, too clever; and much underestimated by the military. Kühlmann retired to his numerous industrial interests and died in Ohlstadt near Neuenahr on February 6, 1948.

Baumgart, *Deutsche Ostpolitik*; Fritz Fischer, *Griff nach der Weltmacht* and *Krieg der Illusionen*; Kitchen, *Silent Dictatorship*; Kühlmann, *Erinnerungen*; *Biographisches Wörterbuch zur Deutschen Geschichte*, II.

KUMMER von FALKENFELD, Heinrich Baron (*Austria-Hungary, General*), was born in Pressburg on April 22, 1852. Kummer graduated from the Theresa Military Academy in 1872; the years from 1876 to 1878 were spent at the War Academy, followed by two years with the General Staff. In 1882 Kummer participated in quelling revolts in Bosnia, and for the next five years he served in the railroad division of the General Staff. Next came a series of appointments to various infantry units. In 1888 he was appointed chief of staff of the Eighteenth Infantry Division in Mostar in the grade of major, in 1894 chief of staff of the X Army Corps in Przemysl in the grade of colonel, 1900 major general and commander of the Thirtieth Infantry Brigade in Miskolcz, then command of the Thirty-ninth Infantry Brigade in Dolnja Tuzla, and until 1910 commander of the Nineteenth Infantry Division in Pilsen. That same year Kummer was promoted general of cavalry and saw service with the Landwehr command.

Early in August 1914, Kummer headed an army group bearing his name at the eastern front in Galicia. His forces were placed on the extreme left of the Austro-Hungarian armies, next to those commanded by Count Viktor Dankl (q.v.), and assigned the advance from Cracow to the Weichsel (Vistula) and Bug rivers. Initial victories at Krasnik and Lublin were erased by the Russian advance in September through Lemberg; by the end of that year, much of Austrian Galicia was in enemy hands. The resulting reorganization of the armies of the Dual Monarchy entailed dissolution of Army Group Kummer, and its erstwhile commander was assigned to the War Ministry in Vienna as an expert on military-scientific developments. Early in August 1915, Kummer was given the thankless task of preparing the army's case against former War Minister General Moritz Auffenberg (q.v.), charged with releasing secret documents to the public; Kummer retired from active service the following year and died in Salzburg-Aigen on December 8, 1929.

Österreichisches Biographisches Lexikon 1815-1950, IV.

KUROPATKIN, Aleksei Nikolaevich (*Russia, General of Infantry*), was born in Pskov, March 29, 1848, the son of a retired officer. He graduated from the Pavlovsky Military School in 1866, completed the General Staff Academy in 1874, and served with distinction as chief of staff in an infantry division during the Russo-Turkish War, 1877/78. The bulk of Kuropatkin's first two decades of service, however, was spent in Central Asia. There he built a glittering reputation as diplomat, soldier, and colonial administrator. By 1882, at the age of thirty-four, he was a major general. His career continued its spectacular upward curve. Kuropatkin served with the General Staff, 1883-90, commanded the Trans-Caspian Military District, 1890-97, and then became Russia's minister of war. He remained in this post for six years, with appropriate elevations in rank: to general of infantry in 1901 and to the honorific title of general adjutant the following year.

The Russo-Japanese War shattered his brilliant line of successes. Kuropatkin took over command of the Manchurian Army in early 1904. By October he was in charge of all Russian forces in the Far East. The Japanese, however, proved a less tractable foe than the Turks or the tribes of Central Asia. Soviet historians have castigated his performance as indecisive and marked by an inability to coordinate large armies in the field—characteristics that were to become even more evident in World War I. Following the Russian defeat at Mukden, Kuropatkin was demoted; he went down the ladder of command to take charge of the First Army. The end of the war

saw him given the consolation prize of membership in Russia's State Council. Prospects for further combat command seemed nonexistent; the aging general took up the pen to defend his policies as war minister and his combat performance.

World War I gave Kuropatkin a second chance. He besieged the War Ministry, pressed his influential former subordinate General Alekseev (q.v.), and in late 1915 received a corps for his troubles. That Kuropatkin was returned to duty tells volumes about the shortage of promising senior commanders in the Russian army. Tsar Nicholas II (q.v.) was stirred to hope that the old general would be carefully supervised. Kuropatkin at once bloodied his corps in a futile night attack; using searchlights to illuminate the battlefield, he made 8,000 of his men into perfect targets, then corpses. He moved upward. By February 1916, the old warhorse had received charge of the northern front, after a brief stint as commander of the Fifth Army. He thus supervised a front stretching from the Gulf of Riga southward to Lake Narocz.

Kuropatkin's characteristic indecisiveness was joined to a fatal pessimism about Russian prospects against the Central Powers. Together with his like-minded neighbor General Evert (q.v.), commander of the western front, Kuropatkin fended off repeated calls to attack in aid of the French at Verdun. Kuropatkin scarcely budged to support Evert's reluctant, botched offensive at Lake Narocz in mid-March. When French calls grew louder in April, it was the fiery Brusilov (q.v.), commanding the southwestern front, who begged for a chance to move. Kuropatkin icily dismissed the chances for a Russian advance. He was predictably passive when Brusilov successfully challenged such predictions on the battlefield in early June. Rutherford claims that Alekseev was partly to blame. The Russian chief of staff may have lacked the will to push Kuropatkin, his former superior in the Far East, into action. Some reserves did move southward as Kuropatkin responded to Brusilov's pleas for more men, but the northern front remained rich in resources, passive in posture.

In July Kuropatkin resigned, doubtless to avoid outright dismissal. He returned to Central Asia, where he served as governor general of Turkestan until early 1917. There he found local insurgents easier to fight than the field armies of the Central Powers. The aged commander stayed on in Russia despite the revolution. He was arrested briefly in April 1917, and transported from Central Asia to Petrograd; but the provisional government set him free to return to his old estate near Pskov. He refused French offers to help him emigrate and passed the last years of his life as a local schoolteacher. He died in the village of Sheshurino, near the estate he had once owned, on January 16, 1925.

Gurko, *Features and Figures of the Past*; Rutherford, *The Russian Army in World War I*; Stone, *The Eastern Front*; *Sovetskaia istoricheskaia entsiklopediia*, VIII; *Sovetskaia voennaia entsiklopediia*, IV.

LACAZE, Marie Jean Lucien (*France, Vice Admiral, Minister of Marine*), was born in Pierrefonds near Paris, June 22, 1860. He graduated from the Naval College in 1882 and saw extensive sea duty over the next two decades, serving in Tunisia, Madagascar, West Africa, and Indo-China. In 1898 Lacaze returned to Paris as an assistant to the minister of marine. In 1906, by then a captain, he held the post of French naval attaché in Rome. In the years immediately preceding World War I, Lacaze served as a senior staff officer in the Mediterranean, then, in 1911/12, as *chef de cabinet* to Minister of Marine Théophile Delcassé (*q.v.*).

The outbreak of war in 1914 found Rear Admiral Lacaze in command of a squadron of battleships in the Mediterranean. His criticism of Admiral Boué de Lapeyrère (*q.v.*), the French naval commander in the Mediterranean, led to Lacaze's transfer to shore duty at Marseilles in early 1915.

In October 1915, Lacaze was named minister of marine in the new cabinet led by Aristide Briand (*q.v.*). By this time, the German submarine campaign in the Mediterranean had become the main concern for the French navy. Lacaze met the new threat by drawing men and small vessels from France's northern ports. The crews of French battleships, huddled in ports like Malta and Bizerte, were tapped for duty with the antisubmarine forces. Lacaze also advocated, but could not yet establish, a convoy system to protect merchant traffic.

The establishment of an Allied base at Salonika (October 1915) sharpened divisions in Greek politics between factions led by King Constantine and former premier Eleutherios Venizelos (*qq.v.*). French naval forces in the seas near Greece were the handiest weapon with which to pressure the pro-German monarch. By June 1916, Lacaze was ordering his Mediterranean commander, Admiral Dartige du Fournet (*q.v.*), to take a firm line against the Greek government. Lacaze's demands (October/November 1916) for securing firm guarantees from Athens to protect the Allied Army of the Orient helped precipitate the final split between Constantine and the Entente. When du Fournet's forces landed at Athens on December 1 only to be met by hostile gunfire, Lacaze stripped the admiral of his command.

The Greek king had by then become openly in favor of the Central Powers but it took until the summer of 1917 before he could be removed from the scene.

Lacaze meanwhile survived the fall of the Briand government (March 1917) and, serving under Premier Alexandre Ribot (*q.v.*), continued to focus his energies on the escalating submarine threat. By summer Allied countermeasures (including convoys) were reducing the grim toll of lost merchant ships. Lacaze, however, had become a prime target for critics in the National Assembly. When Ribot refused to block a proposal to form a committee of inquiry on the antisubmarine effort, Lacaze abandoned his cabinet post in August 1917.

The following month, having been promoted vice admiral, Lacaze took command of the Toulon Naval District and remained there for the concluding year of the war. He retired from active duty in 1922 and died in Paris, March 23, 1955.

Laurens, *Le Commandement naval en Méditerranée, 1914-1918*; Thomazi, *La Marine française dans la Grande Guerre*, I, II, IV; Taillemite, *Dictionnaire de la Marine*; *Larousse mensuel*, XI.

LAMMASCH, Heinrich (*Austria-Hungary, Minister-President*), was born in Seitenstetten, Lower Austria, on May 21, 1853, the son of a notary. Lammasch received his doctorate of law from Vienna University in 1879, and for the next two decades taught criminal and international law at Innsbruck and Vienna. He became a member of the Austrian Upper House in 1899 and was legal adviser to the First and Second Peace Conferences at The Hague in 1899 and 1907; Lammasch was a member of the Cour internationale d'arbitrage since 1899. At home he was a Conservative and opposed to the introduction of universal suffrage.

Lammasch retired from his law practice early in 1914 and, as a well-known pacifist, escaped arrest in August only through the last-minute intervention of Emperor Francis Joseph (*q.v.*). Lammasch hoped to end the war on the basis of ideals espoused by Woodrow Wilson (*q.v.*), and to this end he gave a number of speeches in the Upper House calling for a negotiated peace. Lammasch especially disliked the German ally and had in the past worked to reorient the Dual Monarchy's foreign policy towards a shift to the West (Britain and France). His sincere and courageous personality appealed to the new Emperor Charles (*q.v.*) and, after twice rejecting offers to head the government, Lammasch accepted the minister-presidency on October 25, 1918. Charles hoped to use Lammasch's publicized stand in behalf of peace, but the chance for a negotiated end to the war had long since evaporated. When Charles announced his withdrawal from participating in the government of Austria-Germany on November 11, 1918, Lammasch took the opportunity to resign as head of the last imperial cabinet.

Heinrich Lammasch was the first politician to suggest that Austria in the future should chart a course of strict neutrality. He represented Austria at the Treaty of St. Germain, where he had to accept the humiliating clauses pertaining to war reparations and loss of South Tyrol. Lammasch died shortly thereafter in Salzburg on January 6, 1920.

Lammasch, *Seine Aufzeichnungen, sein Wirken, und seine Politik*; Valiani, *The End of Austria-Hungary*; *Neue Österreichische Biographie*, I.

LANGLE de CARY, Fernand Armand Marie de (*France, General*), was born in Lorient on July 4, 1849. He entered St. Cyr in 1867 and graduated as a cavalry officer in 1869. De Cary fought in the Franco-Prussian War, 1870/71, distinguishing himself during the siege of Paris. He advanced steadily over the next two decades; then, after a tour of teaching at the War College, his career sped forward. A colonel in 1895, de Cary rose to brigadier general five years later and led a cavalry brigade in Algeria. He returned to France to take over an infantry brigade in 1903, and, three years later, as a major general, commanded a division. The former cavalryman was awarded a corps in 1908, and, from 1912 until his retirement two years later, he sat in the select circle of France's senior generals designated to command field armies in case of war, the Supreme War Council.

Langle de Cary barely had a chance to remove his uniform after leaving the service in July 1914. He was recalled to command the Fourth Army, three corps and a cavalry division, 160,000 men in all. With this force, he entered Belgium in mid-August on the eastern flank of General Charles Lanrezac's (*q.v.*) Fifth Army. By August 25, his forces were retreating southeastward, after a bloody encounter with the German Fourth Army in the Ardennes. De Cary retreated in good order to a line stretching, in early September, from Vitry-le-François to Bar-le-Duc. As the Germans had rolled forward, the French field armies threatened to pull apart from one another. General Foch (*q.v.*) and his newly formed Ninth Army were placed alongside Langle de Cary to help ease the strain. The latter's task during the fierce battle of the Marne was to hold tight to Foch on the left and General Sarrail's (*q.v.*) Third Army on the right. De Cary coolly held his line; at times, portions of two German field armies converged on his battered forces.

On September 8, he surmounted a final crisis only with the help of the XV Corps, just arrived that day from General Dubail's (*q.v.*) First Army in the Vosges.

De Cary followed orders from General Joffre (*q.v.*) to pursue the retreating Germans from September 11 onward. By September 14 the Fourth Army bogged down north of St. Menehould, just as other French armies were halting in the face of well-prepared German defenses. There de Cary remained for the better part of a year of futile fighting, brightened by some advances during the offensive that took place in the autumn of 1915.

On December 11, 1915, de Cary was rewarded with command of the Center Army Group, stretching from the fortress of Verdun through Champagne. In January he received specific operational control over Verdun. In his bitter set of memoirs, he claimed that Joffre gave him the fortress because the commander in chief no longer trusted Dubail, commander of the Eastern Army Group, to defend it. But blame for the much-neglected fortress—which Joffre himself had stripped of its heavy guns to support offensives elsewhere in 1915—fell on de Cary. Two days after the massive German attack on Verdun began on February 21, 1916, he suggested a massive withdrawal from the Plain of Woevre on Verdun's eastern flank. He soon found both Verdun and the nearby field armies pulled from his control and placed under the new arrival, General Pétain (*q.v.*). In late March de Cary was relieved. Ostensibly withdrawn from active duty because of his age, he was one of a coterie of senior commanders, Dubail included, whom Joffre sacrificed as questions began to fly about the neglected fortress that was costing so much French blood to defend.

Langle de Cary was given a meaningless mission to inspect French forces in North Africa. Then, in December 1917, he was removed completely from active service. He retired to write his memoirs, pointing his pen at Joffre and Dubail in particular to explain his misfortunes over the course of a year and a half in the field. He died in Point-Scorff on January 19, 1927.

Horne, *The Price of Glory: Verdun*; Isselin, *The Battle of the Marne*; King, *Generals and Politicians*; Langle de Cary, *Souvenirs de commandement*; *Larousse mensuel*, VII.

LANREZAC, Charles Louis Marie (*France, General*), was born July 31, 1852, at Pointe-à-Pitre in the French colony of Guadeloupe. He left St. Cyr in 1870 to fight as an infantry officer. Recognized as a gifted military intellectual, a brilliant teacher, and a capable leader, Lanrezac rose steadily to senior rank. He was promoted a colonel in 1902, took the post of professor of history and tactics at the Supreme War College, and was made a brigadier general in 1906.

Lanrezac became a protégé of the new chief of staff, General Joffre (*q.v.*), who considered Lanrezac a candidate for deputy chief of staff. Instead, Lanrezac received command of a division in 1911 and a corps command the following year. He reached the upper stratum of the peacetime officer corps in the spring of 1914 when he was selected for the Supreme War Council and made commander designate of the Fifth Army in the event of war. In May 1914, Lanrezac received the details of the Fifth Army's wartime mission under Plan XVII: (1) to guard the northern sector of the French line against an anticipated weak German attack through southern Belgium, and (2) to hit the northern flank of that German offensive forecast for the region of the Ardennes. Lanrezac immediately expressed concern about his dangerously isolated position in a war plan that discounted a major German attack across Belgium.

During the first week of August 1914, Lanrezac became increasingly alarmed about a sweeping German offensive through Belgium north of the Meuse, signalled by the strong German attack on Liège. After a week of pleading, he got permission from Joffre to deploy his army northwestward into the angle of the Sambre and the Meuse. He hoped this defensive position would secure the French left from a German outflanking maneuver. Lanrezac linked up with the British Expeditionary Force on his left on August 17, but his subsequent inability to cooperate with its commander, General Sir John French (*q.v.*), endangered both armies.

The Fifth Army barely held the Germans on the Sambre at the battle of Charleroi on August 22/23, and on August 24 it began a retreat that pulled the entire French defensive line back to the Marne. With the Germans pressing him southward from the Sambre while they established bridgeheads across the Meuse in his rear, Lanrezac had no choice but to retreat, cutting loose from the British engaged at Mons. The accelerating speed of the retreat by Lanrezac and the British led Joffre to insist in increasingly strong terms on an offensive by the Fifth Army. On August 29, with Joffre present to supervise, Lanrezac achieved an important tactical success at Guise, striking northwest into the flank of the German First Army, then wheeling northward against the approaching German Second Army. The Germans recoiled and reacted to this show of French boldness with caution: they abandoned the wide sweeping movement planned to bring the German First Army west of Paris.

During the remainder of the retreat to the Marne, the exhausted Fifth Army began to disintegrate, its morale collapsing, and many of its leaders infected with Lanrezac's pessimistic conviction that Plan XVII had fatally compromised France's military position.

On September 5, as the French forces prepared to counterattack on the Marne, Joffre relieved Lanrezac, and replaced him with the Fifth Army's most colorful and aggressive corps commander, Franchet d'Esperey (*q.v.*). Lanrezac joined the scores of senior French officers retired by Joffre for unsatisfactory performance to the quiet provincial city of Limoges. Joffre claimed his decision was based on Lanrezac's obvious exhaustion and pessimism, and, more important, his inability to deal productively with the British.

Lanrezac refused the offer of a new military post in 1917. In 1920 he published a scathing critique of Joffre's conduct during the August 1914 campaign. In 1924 Marshal Pétain (*q.v.*) decorated Lanrezac and in the eyes of many Frenchmen vindicated Lanrezac's conduct in the early months of the war.

Lanrezac remains one of the great enigmas of the war, painted by his friends as a capable and farsighted leader, victimized by blind and stubborn superiors; his detractors portray him as a fine peacetime leader, not up to the strain of real combat. In all, he can claim strategic gifts and foresight, and his conduct of the battle of Guise attests to his battlefield skill. In the day-to-day strain of controlling a shaken and retreating army and maintaining a working alliance with an untested ally, he was clearly inadequate. His contagious pessimism—justified in the short run and invaluable in moving him to action in early August—was a serious liability by early September.

He died in Paris on January 18, 1925.

Barnett, *The Swordbearers*; Isselin, *The Battle of the Marne*; Lanrezac, *Le Plan de campagne français et le premier mois de la guerre*; Spears, *Liaison, 1914*; Terraine, *Mons*; Tuchman, *The Guns of August*.

LANSING, Robert (*United States, Secretary of State*), was born in Watertown, New York, on October 17, 1864, the son of a lawyer. Lansing graduated from Amherst College in 1886 and joined his father's law firm; from 1892 until 1914 he rendered frequent service as counsel or agent of the U.S. government before international arbitration tribunals. Also, Lansing for years acted as counsel for the Chinese and the Mexican legations in Washington, D.C. In April 1914, he accepted a post as counselor for the Department of State, and in August of that year was promoted to acting secretary of state under William Jennings Bryan. When Bryan, the Great Commoner, resigned owing to President Wilson's (q.v.) sharp protest note over the German sinking of the *Lusitania*, Lansing replaced him as secretary of state *ad interim*; on June 23, 1915, Lansing was appointed as official head of that office. In effect, Wilson decided most foreign policy issues and entrusted the conduct of delicate negotiations to "Colonel" House, with the result that the German ambassador, Count Bernstorff (qq.v.), viewed exchanges with Lansing as a "mere matter of form."

Lansing, before Wilson, foresaw the eventual entry of the United States into the war and for that reason urged American recognition of the Carranza regime in Mexico in order to keep the U.S.'s hands free for possible intervention in the European war. While the President handled all correspondence concerning the German sinkings of the *Lusitania, Arabic*, and *Sussex*, Lansing was entrusted with the task of protesting the British blockade of the North Sea and especially of the British contraband controls. Lansing's language was often so strong in these exchanges that the Anglophile Ambassador W. H. Page (q.v.) described one of the notes as "an uncourteous monster of 35 heads and 3 appendices." This notwithstanding, the secretary of state as early as March 1917 counseled the entry of the United States into the war on the side of the Entente.

Lansing seized the chance to conduct his own diplomacy late in 1917. On November 2, he signed an agreement with Viscount Ishii of Japan that, while upholding the principle of the "open door" in China, recognized special Japanese interests there. This indiscretion cost the United States China's trust; it was, no doubt, motivated by the Allied desire to rally all possible support against the Central Powers.

Lansing and Wilson began to part ways at the Peace Conference in Paris in 1919. The secretary's legalistic and realistic views clashed with the president's idealistic and imaginative proposals: the former viewed the League of Nations as an unimportant appanage to the overall peace settlement, while the latter regarded it as paramount. Lansing was responsible for the unfortunate "sole war guilt" clause of the peace treaties, which laid the blame for the Great War totally upon Germany and Austria-Hungary, and which was exploited ruthlessly by the enemies of the Weimar Republic throughout the 1920s and early 1930s. In the end, Lansing signed the Versailles Treaty and advocated ratification by the Senate, arguing that it was better than no treaty at all. A final break with the president came on February 12, 1920, when Lansing called a cabinet meeting during Wilson's illness; the ailing leader forced the secretary of state to tender his resignation for this alleged slight.

A man of extreme courtesy and tact, Lansing returned to his private law practice in Washington until his death on October 30, 1928.

Lansing, *War Memoirs*; Livermore, *Politics Is Adjourned*; *Dictionary of American Biography*, X.

LAWRENCE, Thomas Edward (*Great Britain, Colonel*), known as Lawrence of Arabia, was born in Tremadoc, North Wales, on August 15, 1888, the illegitimate son of an Anglo-Irish landowning family originally named Chapman. Lawrence received his education at Jesus College, Oxford, traveled extensively in France, Syria, Palestine, and Turkey, and in 1910 received a senior demyship for travel from Magdalen College, which he used in 1911 to accompany a British Museum expedition to the Hittite city of Carchemish.

In August 1914, Lawrence failed to join the army because he could not meet the standard height of five feet, five inches, and instead was assigned to the Geographical Section of the War Office. When Turkey joined the war on the side of the Central Powers, Lawrence was dispatched for two years to military intelligence in Egypt, later called the Arab Bureau. At Jidda in October 1916, Lawrence met Sharif Abdullah, second son of Husain, Grand Sharif of Mecca, and later also was introduced to Husain's third son, Faisal, who was then retreating before the Turks' march on Medina. Shortly thereafter, he was appointed liaison officer and adviser to Faisal.

Lawrence at once encouraged Faisal to raid the Turkish Hejaz rail link, while he contained the enemy's garrison of 10,000 men at Medina. Thereafter taking the port of Wajh and leaving Faisal in command there, Lawrence headed north as far as Syria in order to raise the tribes against the Turks. Returning, he routed the enemy near Ma'an, and in August 1917, captured Aqaba for Faisal.

Lawrence convinced the new British commander in Egypt, General Edmund Allenby (q.v.), to finance Arab levies and to brigade them with regulars from the British Expeditionary Force in Egypt. He defeated the Turks at Tafila, and then isolated Medina by systematic destruction of their train connections. Toward the end of that year he was captured, though not recognized, and beaten senseless by the Turks, but he managed to escape the day after his capture.

During the summer of 1918 Lawrence persuaded Faisal to leave Aqaba and to advance on Damascus. El-Orens, as he was called by the Arabs, defeated the Turkish Fourth Army east of Jordan, and on October 1, 1918, entered Damascus three hours ahead of Allenby. In the campaign Lawrence's force of fewer than 3,000 Arabs had paralyzed almost 15,000 Turkish troops stationed south of Damascus. He viewed his Arabs as "an idea, a thing invulnerable, intangible, without front or back, drifting about like a gas, a vapour, blowing where we listed." His task having been accomplished, he came home on Armistice Day 1918 with the comment: "Never outstay a climax."

The peace in 1919 proved a bitter disappointment. The surrender of Syria to France was a betrayal to him, and with a sense of remorse for his part in arousing Arab nationalism, he abandoned politics and set out to write his memoirs. After a brief stint at All Souls College and at the Colonial Office, he enlisted in the Royal Air Force and the Tank Corps (1923-1935) under the ostentatious obscurity of several pseudonyms (J. H. Ross and T. E. Shaw). He died at Bovington Camp Hospital on May 19, 1935, after a motorcycle accident. His exploits were posthumously published as *The Revolt in the Desert* (1927) and *Seven Pillars of Wisdom* (1935). Liddell Hart regarded Lawrence as a master of guerrilla tactics.

Liddell Hart, *T. E. Lawrence*; Mack, *Prince of Our Disorder*; *Dictionary of National Biography 1931-1940*.

LENIN, Vladimir Ilich (*Russia, Politician*), was born in the provincial town of Simbirsk on the Volga on April 22, 1870. He was the son of Ilia Ulianov, an upwardly mobile school administrator who eventually earned the status of a hereditary nobleman. Young Vladimir, who took the revolutionary pseudonym "Lenin" as an adult, had an uneventful childhood until 1887. In that year, his older brother, a university student, was executed for conspiring to murder Tsar Alexander III. Vladimir was permitted to complete his schooling and he moved on to Kazan University. There Lenin was drawn into student radical circles and, expelled for his activities, had to complete his legal training on his own. By the mid-1890s, he had moved to St. Petersburg, immersed himself in Marxist political ideas, and begun work as a full-fledged revolutionary. He was arrested in 1895 and dispatched to Siberia where he wrote his first major treatise, *The Development of Capitalism in Russia*. He was released in 1900 and left his homeland for a period of exile that stretched, with a brief break in 1905, for nearly two decades.

By the time Russian Marxists gathered for their Second Congress in Brussels and London in 1903, Lenin had emerged as one of the notables of the Russian revolutionary movement. He offered his fellow Marxists a blueprint for an underground party of revolutionary professionals; outvoted on this issue, he seized his victory over a lesser question to dub his faction the Bolsheviks (the majority). In 1912, after a decade of wrangling with Marxists of other temperaments and viewpoints, Lenin marched away from other notables in the loosely knit Russian Marxist movement and formally declared his faction to represent the true Russian Marxist party of the revolution.

Despite Lenin's dramatic step in 1912, he remained merely one of several respected leaders in Russian Marxist circles. He had let the opportunities presented by the revolution of 1905 slip by; Lenin returned to Russia, but it was the fiery young Leon Trotsky (*q.v.*) who had seized the reins of the St. Petersburg Soviet and ridden the chaotic political tide of 1905 to national prominence. Apart from Lenin's call for an elite party of dedicated professionals, he was marked off from his contemporaries by his interest (unusual for a Russian Marxist) in the peasantry as a revolutionary force. World War I opened the way, however, for Lenin's personal and political triumph.

The outbreak of hostilities found the Russian exile in Cracow, a city in Austrian Galicia. The authorities promptly interned him as an enemy alien. Austrian and Polish Socialists, most of whom Lenin later marked as bitter enemies, interceded with Vienna to release Lenin from prison, and he departed for Switzerland. He remained there until early 1917. From the first, Lenin elaborated a position on the war that was foreshadowed by his pre-1914 writings. Marxist revolutionaries, he maintained, ought not to seek to prevent war or to limit it; rather they must use the dislocation a great war was likely to bring in order to pull down the existing order. Even more dramatically, he advocated the defeat of the tsarist armies as the first step toward revolution in Russia. Such an extreme position found few supporters; even Trotsky, who viewed the conflict in the same general way, would not support Lenin's manifestos at the Zimmerwald (September 1915) and Kienthal (April 1916) gatherings of international Socialist leaders. In early 1917 Lenin told a Swiss youth group that they, not he, might be the ones to witness "the decisive struggles of the coming revolution."

Word of bread riots in March soon gave way to exhilarating news that the monarchy had fallen. Lenin succeeded, only after an agonizing delay of a month, in getting back to Petrograd by way of Germany and Scandinavia. His trip through Germany in the famous "sealed train" gave his foes in Russia powerful evidence to use in condemning Lenin as a German agent. The weight of recent scholarship (Zeman, Senn, Rabinowitch) supports the view that Lenin received German financial aid during 1917 and probably in earlier years. But the Germans were spending lavish amounts of cash to support a broad range of potential saboteurs of the Russian war effort. There is no evidence to indicate Lenin pursued anything other than his own plans, although he was doubtless delighted to use any aid Berlin chose to supply.

Even before Lenin returned to Russia, he assaulted the provisional government and lashed out at Russian Marxists, including some of his own Bolsheviks, who backed the provisional government's policy of continuing the war. Lenin called for accelerating and deepening the March Revolution, pushing bourgeois elements and moderate Socialists aside. He offered land to the peasants, the vast group that the provisional government had asked to remain patient until orderly land reform could take place, probably after the war.

After an abortive effort in the so-called July days, Lenin led his Bolshevik party (then renamed the Communist party) to power in November 1917. Trotsky, a newly hatched Bolshevik, served as his leading lieutenant. Both Lenin and Trotsky anticipated that a Russian revolution would spark comparable upheavals in the other warring nations, in particular in Germany. This would, at the least, bring the belligerents to a Russian-sponsored peace conference. Perhaps, they went on to dream, it would mean workers' governments elsewhere rushing to aid the beleaguered Bolsheviks, a small workers' party in the midst of an underdeveloped peasant nation.

When Russian calls for a peace conference drew no response, Lenin and Trotsky began negotiations with the Central Powers alone in mid-December at Brest-Litovsk. Lenin was quicker than his younger colleague to abandon the dream of a German revolution. The generals who dominated German foreign policy insisted on a victors' peace, featuring territorial expansion in eastern Europe at Russia's expense. Trotsky's delaying tactics and his dramatic declaration of "no war, no peace" failed by mid-February. German armies drove eastward in an eleven-day push, unopposed by any organized Russian military force. And Lenin stepped in to accept Berlin's terms. Debo suggests that Lenin had deliberately distanced himself from Trotsky's flamboyant approach to the peace talks; and, in the end, he won over Trotsky and the leading lights of the Communist party to peace. It was close to peace at any price, and it left revolutions in Central Europe to rise or fall on their own. But it saved the Russian Revolution from an early demise at the hands of the German army.

Between the Treaty of Brest-Litovsk on March 3, 1918, and the armistice of November 11, Lenin continued his policy of survival at any cost. He quietly accepted German thrusts into the Ukraine and Finland, beyond anything permitted by Brest-Litovsk. At the same time, Lenin and Trotsky, then commissar of war, spoke of getting help from "the brigands of French imperialism" to fight "German brigands." By summer the greater danger seemed to come from the Entente, whose members were landing troops in northern Russia and at Vladivostok. In August Lenin spoke of calling on "the German imperialist vultures" for help in fighting off these Anglo-French and Japanese-American assaults.

The November armistice deprived revolutionary Russia of the chance to maneuver between the opposing camps. The next stage of Lenin's career saw him consumed by the ordeal of civil war, already under way by early 1918. There several Entente nations offered support in varying degrees to anti-Communist White forces. The fate of the revolution was contested on the battlefield until the close of 1920.

Lenin had little time thereafter to shape the future of his Soviet republic. In early 1921 he launched the "New Economic Policy," reversing the radical policy of agrarian and industrial expropriations that had been applied during the civil war. At the close of his life, he showed signs of dissatisfaction with the fruits of the revolution: the bureaucratic dictatorship that Communist party rule had established, the bullying of non-Russian ethnic groups represented by the armed takeover of the independent Georgian republic in 1921. Beginning in early 1922 the revolution's founder suffered a series of disabling strokes. He died, still a relatively young man of fifty-four, in Moscow on January 21, 1924.

Debo, *Revolution and Survival*; Louis Fischer, *The Life of Lenin*; Lenin, *O voine, armii i voennoi nauke*, 2 vols.; Rabinowitch, *The Bolsheviks Come to Power* and *Prelude to Revolution*; Schapiro and Reddaway, eds., *Lenin: The Man, the Theorist, the Leader*; Senn, *The Russian Revolution in Switzerland*; Ulam, *The Bolsheviks*; Zeman, ed., *Germany and the Revolution in Russia*.

LEOPOLD, Prince of Bavaria (*Germany, Field Marshal*), was born in Munich on February 9, 1846, the second son of Prince Regent Luitpold; he later became a son-in-law of Emperor Francis Joseph (*q.v.*) of Austria-Hungary. Leopold fought with the Bavarian army against Prussia in 1866, but four years later accompanied the Prussians to Sedan in the war against France. His career was marked by the customary rapid royal promotions: general in 1887 as head of the I Army Corps, inspector general in 1892 of the IV Army Inspectorate, which included Bavarian as well as Prussian corps, colonel general three years later, and field marshal in 1905. The prince was retired from active service in 1912 and was, therefore, without a command when the Great War began.

On April 16, 1915, Prince Leopold was reactivated as head of the German Ninth Army in the east, and he led this force into Warsaw on August 5. The prince then took over the Army Group Woyrsch (*q.v.*) as the new Army Group Prince Leopold of Bavaria, and with this force drove the Russians back upon Minsk. Throughout the summer and fall of 1916 Leopold attempted to shore up the Austro-Hungarian front in the wake of General Aleksei Brusilov's (*q.v.*) successful offensive in the direction of the Carpathians; the Germans finally brought the Russians to a halt near Baranovichi. On August 29 Prince Leopold succeeded Field Marshal Paul von Hindenburg as military leader in the east, taking Colonel Max Hoffmann (*qq.v.*) as his chief of staff. His forces were spread from the Baltic Sea to the Carpathians and included two Austro-Hungarian armies.

Leopold in April 1917 mounted a successful offensive across the Stokhod near Toboly; on July 19 he began a further offensive that within a month had driven the Russians out of Galicia and the Bukovina. In September the Germans captured Riga and in October the Baltic islands Ösel, Moon, and Dagö. On November 26, 1917, the Bolsheviks ended hostilities and a temporary armistice in the east was concluded on December 17. In February the peace was broken, however, and General Hoffmann launched a powerful drive that netted the Germans Estonia and Lithuania. Another assault drove the Russians across the Narva and out of Minsk, beyond the Dnepr; both the Ukraine and the Crimea later fell into German hands. On March 3, 1918, Leon Trotsky (*q.v.*) agreed to German terms at Prince Leopold's headquarters, and the war in the east finally ended. Leopold retired from the army in January 1919, and returned to his native Bavaria, where he died at Munich on September 28, 1930.

Baumgart, *Deutsche Ostpolitik*; Wolbe, *Leopold von Bayern*; *Biographisches Wörterbuch zur Deutschen Geschichte*, II; *Geschichte der Ritter des Ordens*, I.

LETTOW-VORBECK, Paul von (*Germany, General*), was born in Saarlouis on March 20, 1870, to an ancient noble clan of Pomeranian ancestry. Lettow-Vorbeck entered the army in 1888, attended the War Academy and served in the General Staff, where he was promoted captain in 1901. That same year he became adjutant to Field Marshal Alfred von Waldersee during the China Expedition; from 1904 to 1907 he assisted General Lothar von Trotha to suppress the Herero and Hottentot uprising in German South-West Africa, at the end of which he was promoted major. In 1913 Lieutenant Colonel von Lettow-Vorbeck was placed in charge of German troops in East Africa, and in January 1914, was appointed military commander in the colony.

Lettow-Vorbeck defended German East Africa during the Great War with consummate energy and skill, but with only a force of at best 3,000 whites and 11,000 Askaris against at times 300,000 British, Belgian, and Portuguese troops. He was twice wounded in the field and dubbed "the African Hindenburg" by his enemies. In November 1914, Lettow-Vorbeck led 1,000 men against 8,000 British and Indian troops at the battle of Tanga; he followed this initial victory with another in January 1915, at Jassini, and in August was promoted colonel. In March 1916, his enemies pressed him hard at Reata, and Lettow-Vorbeck began a series of strategic retreats: after the loss of Kilimanjaro, the British in September captured Dar-es-Salaam. In November his chivalrous enemy, General Jan Smuts (*q.v.*) of South Africa, informed Lettow-Vorbeck that he had been awarded the order *Pour le mérite*.

A turn in fortune came to Lettow-Vorbeck in 1917. After defeating 6,000 enemy soldiers with barely 1,500 men at Lindi in October, the odds against him became very great. By the end of the year Smuts had secured the colony's only rail link between Dar-es-Salaam and Ujiji on Lake Tanganyika, thereby forcing the German commander first into the Uluguru Mountains and finally across the border into Portuguese Africa. From November 1917 until the end of the war, Lettow-Vorbeck conducted a guerrilla campaign there with a force of scarcely 3,000 soldiers, and in the process won the admiration of friend and foe alike. Back in the German colony late in 1918, the German heard of the armistice only on November 13; twelve days later he surrendered at Abercorn.

Lettow-Vorbeck returned to Germany in March 1919 and at once led Free Corps units carrying his name against the Spartacists in Berlin. In March 1920, he placed his brigade at Schwerin at the disposal of right-wing reactionaries during the Kapp *Putsch* and as a result was forced to retire in May 1920. Thereafter he turned to politics as a parliamentary deputy for the German National People's party (1928-1930). He died in Hamburg on March 9, 1964.

Lettow-Vorbeck, *Meine Erinnerungen aus Ostafrika* and *Mein Leben*; Louis, *Great Britain and Germany's Lost Colonies*; *Biographisches Wörterbuch zur Deutschen Geschichte*, II; *Geschichte der Ritter des Ordens*, I.

LEVETZOW, Magnus von (*Germany, Commodore*), was born in Flensburg on January 8, 1871, to a noble clan that had settled in Mecklenburg around 1300. Levetzow entered the navy in 1889 and attended the War Academy in 1900-1902. The following year he served as Admiralty staff officer during the German blockade of Venezuela, and from 1906 to 1918 was attached to the High Sea Fleet in various capacities. From 1909 to 1912 Levetzow was first Admiralty officer in the fleet command; in 1912 he commanded the light cruiser *Stralsund* and the following year in the grade of captain the battle cruiser *Moltke*.

Captain von Levetzow led the *Moltke* to the coast of England on December 16, 1914, and bombarded Hartlepool. On January 24, 1915, he stood off the Dogger Bank as the British demolished the armored cruiser *Blücher*. One year later Levetzow joined the High Sea Fleet as chief of the Operations Division immediately under Captain Adolf von Trotha; Vice Admiral Reinhard Scheer (*qq.v.*) served as fleet commander. This triumvirate directed the fleet at Jutland on May 31/June 1, 1916, and inflicted serious material losses upon the British Grand Fleet, while twice facing annihilation by Sir John Jellicoe's (*q.v.*) dreadnoughts as the latter crossed Scheer's T.

In September 1917, Levetzow was temporarily appointed chief of staff to Vice Admiral Ehrhardt Schmidt's squadron for the conquest of the Baltic islands of Ösel, Moon, and Dagö in the Gulf of Riga, which also netted the Russian battleship *Slava*. Levetzow received the order *Pour le mérite* in October 1917.

In November 1917, Levetzow returned to the High Sea Fleet, and by January 1918, was promoted commodore and given command of the Second Division, Scouting Forces, under Admiral Franz von Hipper (*q.v.*). In August 1918, the restless Levetzow became chief of staff of the new Supreme Command of the navy under Admiral Scheer, and in this capacity actively planned the fatal Operations Plan Nr. 19, which called for a suicide sortie against the British Grand Fleet on October 30, 1918. The sailors of the fleet instead rebelled.

Levetzow was a highly political creature. A fanatical follower of Admiral Alfred von Tirpitz (*q.v.*), Levetzow had spared no effort to propagate the state secretary's views in the navy—and beyond. Levetzow recruited members of the Court and of other ruling houses to uphold the Tirpitz line, and he used the same channels to drum up support for a fleet engagement as well as for unrestricted submarine warfare. With the wily Trotha, Levetzow worked diligently to undermine the positions of Georg A. von Müller of the Navy Cabinet, Henning von Holtzendorff of the Admiralty Staff, and Chancellor Theobald von Bethmann Hollweg (*qq.v.*) with the kaiser, the politicians, and the nation. Levetzow favored sweeping territorial annexations by Germany in Europe, Asia Minor, and Africa as late as September 1918, and he encouraged fellow naval officers to pursue these aims through Tirpitz's rightwing Fatherland party.

Levetzow survived the reduction of the German navy to 10,000 officers and men under the Versailles Treaty and in January 1920, was promoted rear admiral and given command of the Baltic Sea naval station at Kiel. In this capacity he supported the Kapp *Putsch* in March 1920 and was forced to resign from the service. For a time, Levetzow hoped to establish close contacts between the exiled Kaiser Wilhelm II (*q.v.*) in Doorn and Hermann Göring and Adolf Hitler of the NSDAP; however, by 1932 Levetzow accepted the kaiser's refusal to become embroiled with the Nazis and was elected an NSDAP member of parliament. Hitler rewarded the admiral, who had helped to bring naval support to the Nazis, by appointing him police president of Berlin on February 15, 1933; for the next two years Levetzow energetically purged the Ministry of the Interior of republicans. He withdrew from politics in July 1935 and died in Berlin on March 13, 1939.

Gemzell, *Organization, Conflict, and Innovation*; Herwig, *"Luxury" Fleet*, "From Kaiser to Führer"; *Geschichte der Ritter des Ordens*, I.

LIGGETT, Hunter (*United States, General*), was born in Reading, Pennsylvania, on March 21, 1857, the son of a tailor and politician. Liggett graduated from "the Point" in 1879, and for the next decade served at frontier posts. He rose to the grade of captain in 1897, being appointed to various commands in Texas, Florida, and Georgia. Liggett was posted to the Philippines from 1899 to 1901; he attended the Army War College in 1909/1910, and in 1912 became president of that institution in the grade of colonel. A universally admired soldier, Liggett was promoted to the grade of major general one month before the United States entered the First World War. By then he had established a reputation as trustworthy and loyal to superiors and subordinates alike.

In October 1917, Liggett arrived in France to take command of the Forty-first (Sunset) Division. After a period of observation duty at the front, he was given command of the I Army Corps in January 1918. The appointment came as a surprise to many. Although Liggett was well known for his moral courage and his tact as well as lack of self-centeredness, it was widely known that General Pershing (*q.v.*) despised field commanders who were fat. Liggett typically answered his enemies by stating that this was "the more serious if the fat is above the collar."

As part of the French Sixth Army, the American I Army Corps saw action near Château-Thierry early in July 1918. The doughboys helped blunt the German Michael offensive in France, and between July 15 and 18, stood firm at the front from the Argonne Forest to Château-Thierry. After securing his sector during the Champagne-Marne operation, Liggett counterattacked between July 18 and August 6, in what is known as the Second Battle of the Marne, driving the Germans across the Ourcq and Vesle Rivers in bloody hand-to-hand combat. On August 10 his I Army Corps became part of Pershing's First Army and occupied the right of the line during the celebrated St. Mihiel operation between September 12 and 16. His four divisions in four days of heavy fighting reduced the St. Mihiel salient and scored the Americans' first victory in Europe against a much smaller and demoralized foe. Liggett next stormed the Argonne Forest between September 26 and October 12 with his I Army Corps, advancing ten miles. This operation, supported by 2,700 guns and 189 small tanks, was designed to break the German Kriemhilde line, but the slow advance of the V Army Corps and the opponent's elastic defense, which drew the American troops into woven belts of fire, worked against its success. On October 16, 1918, General Pershing entrusted command of the First Army consisting of 1 million men and 4,000 guns to Liggett; Hugh Drum (q.v.) served as Liggett's chief of staff. During the Meuse-Argonne offensive to November 11, the First Army managed to break the Hindenburg line, outflank the Bois de Bourgogne, and force a German retreat behind the Meuse River. Alone the American burlesque at Sedan marred these impressive achievements: Liggett, who had not been informed of Pershing's order to take Sedan, had to witness how the American First Division, Pershing's favorite, cut through the American Forty-second Division at night, taking prisoner the latter's commander!

After the armistice, General Liggett remained in Germany in various occupation commands until July 1919. He returned home to assume command of the IX Corps Area (San Francisco) until his retirement on March 21, 1921. Liggett died in San Francisco on December 30, 1935. The general was known as a man of shrewd character judgment, of quiet simplicity and fair-mindedness; he is credited with the comment that "War provokes more muddled thinking than any human activity I know of." Liddell Hart called him "the soundest reasoner and strongest realist in the American Army."

Liddell Hart, *The Real War*; Liggett, *A.E.F. Ten Years Ago in France*; Stallings, *The Doughboys*; *Dictionary of American Biography*, XXI Supplement One.

LIMAN von SANDERS, Otto (*Germany, General*), was born in Schwessin near Stolp in Prussia on February 18, 1855, the son of a Pomeranian estate owner and the grandson of a baptized Jewish banker. Otto Liman entered the army in 1874 and five years later was attached to the cavalry; in 1887 he entered the General Staff. He was appointed brigade commander as major general in 1906, and five years later was in Kassel as lieutenant general and commander of the Twenty-second Division. Ennobled in July 1913, Liman added his wife's Scottish name to his own. In December 1913, he was dispatched to Turkey as chief of a German military mission, and in January 1914, was promoted Turkish field marshal, inspector general of all Ottoman forces as well as Prussian general of cavalry.

In August 1914, Liman worked diligently to bring about Turkey's entry into the war and he grew bitter and cantankerous as the Turks agonized over their position—to the point where Liman considered challenging both the Turkish war minister and navy minister to a duel, and asked Wilhelm II (q.v.) to recall the mission. Instead, he was appointed commander of the Turkish First Army at the Bosphorus in August 1914, all the while quarrelling over jurisdiction with Ambassador Hans von Wangenheim. Liman gained world recognition after March 1915 when General Enver Paşa (q.v.) appointed him head of the new Turkish Fifth Army entrusted with defense of Gallipoli against expected Allied assaults. Especially in May and June Liman capably handled the defenses against overwhelming enemy naval and material superiority; only the successful Allied evacuations of 500,000 troops in December 1915 tarnished Liman's image both at Constantinople and at Berlin. It was over the general's bitter objections that Germany and Turkey in October 1917 concluded a new ten-year military convention, to take effect after the war, which gave the Turks ultimate command over all German officers attached to their forces.

On February 27, 1918, Liman was given the thankless and impossible task of shoring up the Turkish front in Palestine as commander of Army Group F in Syria. Twice he repelled British attacks in Jordan but, denied supplies and reinforcements by Enver and General Hans von Seeckt (q.v.), the new chief of staff at Ottoman headquarters, the front soon collapsed. On September 20 General Sir Edmund Allenby's (q.v.) troops captured Nazareth, barely failing to seize the German commander. Liman fell back upon Damascus in October 1918, but the armistice of Mudros precluded further disasters for the Turkish forces. Liman returned to Constantinople until January 1919 in order to oversee the repatriation of German troops in Asia Minor. On his way home in February, the British held "Pasha Liman" at Malta for six months as a suspected war criminal; finally released in August, he was permitted to return home. Field Marshal Liman von Sanders retired from the army in October 1919 to write his memoirs, and he died in Munich on August 22, 1929. Liman was, in the words of Ulrich Trumpener, "one of the most capable field commanders the Turks had during the war." It should not be overlooked that in November 1916 he energetically—albeit, unsuccessfully—attempted to halt the Armenian deportations to Smyrna.

Liman, *Five Years in Turkey*; Trumpener, *Germany and the Ottoman Empire*; *Biographisches Wörterbuch zur Deutschen Geschichte*, II; *Geschichte der Ritter des Ordens*, I.

LINSINGEN, Alexander von (*Germany, General*), was born in Hildesheim on February 10, 1850. He entered the army in 1868 and took part in the war against France in 1870/1871. By 1890 Linsingen had been promoted major as battalion commander; five years later he rose to regimental chief in the grade of colonel, and in 1901 was advanced to major general as head of the Eighty-first Infantry Regiment. Next came command of the Twenty-seventh Division in the grade of lieutenant general, and from 1909 to 1914 General of Infantry von Linsingen was chief of the II Army Corps.

At the outbreak of the war, the Pomeranian II Corps was attached to General Alexander von Kluck's (*q.v.*) First Army and received its baptism of fire at Mons on August 22/23 against the British Expeditionary Corps. Several days later it again drove the British back at Le Cateau, and on September 5, at the onset of the battle of the Marne, the II Corps was rushed to the Ourcq River to assist the hard-pressed IV Reserve Corps. Colonel Richard Hentsch (*q.v.*), however, ordered a German retreat from the Marne on September 9, and Linsingen withdrew behind the Aisne River. On November 8 he was ordered to Flanders as head of an army group between the Fourth and Sixth Army with instructions to take Ypres. Failing to accomplish this, he was transferred to the eastern front late in November 1914, in time to participate in the battles around Lodz.

On January 9, 1915, Linsingen was given command of a composite German-Austro-Hungarian force known as the German South Army in the Carpathians. This unit managed to advance from the mountain passes as far as Stryi on January 22, but snow halted any further actions. The breakthrough of General August von Mackensen's (*q.v.*) Eleventh Army at Gorlice-Tarnów on May 2, however, heralded a general advance in the east, and Linsingen marched into Galicia as far as the Dnjestr River, and on May 31 took 60,000 prisoners at the battle of Stryi. There the offensive ground to a halt as the Russians reinforced their units around Stryi and Zuravno; Linsingen was rewarded for his efforts in the south with the coveted *Pour le mérite*.

Mackensen's army had gradually swelled to such proportions that in July 1915, it was divided into two units; Linsingen received command over a new Bug Army. On August 26 he took Brest-Litovsk with this force and drove the Russians back upon Pskov. The next month Linsingen was reinforced with the Austro-Hungarian Fourth Army and became head of a new Army Group Linsingen, with orders to stabilize the southern sector of the eastern front. Linsingen's darkest hour came on June 5, 1916, when General Aleksei Brusilov (*q.v.*), attempting to relieve the pressure on Verdun, unleashed a massive attack directly against Army Group Linsingen. The Habsburg Fourth Army under Archduke Joseph Ferdinand (*q.v.*) collapsed totally and its headquarters at Luck were overrun by the Russians. By July Linsingen had managed to regroup his forces behind Luck and to halt the Russian drive near Kovel, but not before over 200,000 Austro-Hungarian soldiers had been lost. Brusilov, for his part, absorbed a horrendous 1 million casualties. Linsingen's sector of the front thereafter remained relatively quiet.

In February/March 1918, after the Bolsheviks had broken off peace talks at Brest-Litovsk, Linsingen led the German drive into the Ukraine and the Crimea, taking Odessa and Poltava. The Bolsheviks then agreed to German terms and Army Group Linsingen was officially disbanded; in April Linsingen was promoted colonel general.

In addition, General Wilhelm Groener had found it impossible to work with Linsingen and had replaced him with General Hermann von Eichhorn (*qq.v.*); on June 1, 1918, Linsingen was shunted off to become commander in chief in the Mark and governor of Berlin. He retired from the army on November 17, 1918, after his troops had made common cause with the revolution in Berlin. Linsingen died in Hanover on June 5, 1935.

Barnett, *Swordbearers*; Baumgart, *Deutsche Ostpolitik*; Liddell Hart, *The Real War*; *Geschichte der Ritter des Ordens*, I.

LLOYD GEORGE, David (*Great Britain, Prime Minister*), first Earl Lloyd-George of Dwyfor, was born in Manchester on January 17, 1863, the son of a schoolmaster. He took an intense pride in his national heritage, and early in life already possessed that steely resolution, restless energy, and dogged industry that were to take him to the top. In 1884 Lloyd George started a law practice; six years later he entered the House of Commons as Liberal member for Caernarvon Boroughs. He bitterly decried the war in South Africa as unworthy of a great empire and consistently throughout his life championed the cause of small countries, especially if they were small farming nations. His incomparable platform rhetoric brought him national acclaim, and in December 1905, Sir Henry Campbell-Bannerman appointed him president of the Board of Trade. Three years later, Lloyd George served Herbert Asquith (q.v.) as chancellor of the Exchequer when Asquith became Liberal prime minister. It was in this capacity that Lloyd George drew up the famous "People's" budget of 1908/1909, which proposed a land tax to pay for social services such as insurance covering health and unemployment, as well as dreadnought building. It was the fiery Welshman who took the budget to the country as a crusade against "those Dukes," and who transformed the whole field of politics with the Parliamentary Bill curtailing the veto power of the House of Lords. By 1914 he was one of the most profound political strategists in England, endowed with an uncanny gift for being able to discern at once the moods of an assembly or the thoughts of an individual.

Late in July 1914, Lloyd George stood with the nonintervention group in a divided Cabinet until Germany's invasion of Belgium once again aroused this champion of small nations. In November 1914, he drew up the first war budget, doubling the income tax and increasing consumer levies especially on tea and beer. In fact, he railed against the evils of drink. "Drink," he stated in February 1915, "is doing more damage in this war than all the German submarines put together"; while he could not separate Englishmen from their ale, he did curtail their hours of imbibing and watered down their libations. That same spring he was at daggers drawn with Prime Minister Asquith. "The P.M. is treating the war as if it were Home Rule. . . . He does not recognize that the nation is fighting for its life." Specifically, the chancellor of the Exchequer opposed the massive offensives in France, and called instead for a "southern flank" against Austria and Turkey; as a diehard "Easterner," he repeatedly urged a strike from Salonika, Greece, in conjunction with Serbia, Rumania, and Greece, against Vienna. His chance to be heard came as a result of a severe shortage of high explosive shells with the armies in France, and Lloyd George mercilessly castigated Lord H. H. Kitchener (q.v.), then secretary of state for war, as the single cause of the shortage. As a result of this as well as of the debacle at the Dardanelles, Asquith, in May 1915, was forced to form a coalition government; Lloyd George was appointed minister of munitions and worked tirelessly and successfully to increase the supply of shells to the various fronts. One of his innovations was to employ women in Britain's war industries.

Scheduled to accompany Kitchener to Russia on June 5, 1916, Lloyd George was kept in London by continuing troubles arising out of the Easter rebellion in Dublin; when Kitchener went down with the *Hampshire* in the North Sea, the Welshman succeeded him as state secretary for war for the next five months. At the War Office Lloyd George chafed and fretted over his inability to decide major strategy. In particular, he differed radically with Sir William Robertson (q.v.), chief of the Imperial General Staff, over the conduct of the war in France; Lloyd George continued to cherish operations emanating from Greece in the direction of Laibach and Vienna. In September 1916, the head of the War Office accorded Roy Howard of the United Press Association an interview in which he called for the famous "knock-out blow" against Germany. Indeed, "the Goat," as he was called especially in army circles, felt that Asquith lacked the requisite vigor to pursue victory, and in December 1916 set out with the help of Andrew Bonar Law, Sir Edward Carson, and Sir Max Aitken (qq.v.) "to get rid of the Asquith incubus." With this combination of Conservatives, the press, public opinion, and army headquarters in France, Lloyd George brought down the Asquith government. On December 7 "the Goat" formed the second coalition government with Bonar Law and Labour's Arthur Henderson. Lloyd George was fifty-four years of age at the time. He at once replaced the cumbersome Cabinet of twenty-three with an inner War Cabinet of five that met daily to decide major policies; at No. 10 Downing Street he maintained a retinue of trusted aides, popularly dubbed "the garden suburb."

Lloyd George's tenure as prime minister had a most tempestuous beginning: on February 1, 1917, Germany resumed unrestricted submarine warfare; on April 6 the United States as a result entered the war as an Associated Power; and on March 12 Russia was rocked by revolution. By April 1917, Britain was losing ten freighters daily while the Admiralty dithered and refused to implement convoy. It was an irate prime minister who on April 30 took the unprecedented step of visiting the Admiralty with clear instructions, as Winston Churchill (q.v.) put it, to "act or go." Act they did, and by August the submarine menace had been largely overcome.

The "little Welsh wizard," as Alfred Harmsworth, Lord Northcliffe (q.v.) called him, had his greatest problems with the generals. Perhaps it was as much a clash of personalities and outlook as it was of strategy. Most general officers had aristocratic lineage or connections, had been educated at the finest schools and at Sandhurst, had married well or possessed their own financial independence, and, in short, were of a different Britain than the struggling, tempestuous Welshman who, as Sir Douglas Haig (q.v.) lamented, was late for appointments and sat with his arms on the table. In fact, Haig was terribly disappointed with Lloyd George and especially despised the large retinue of aides and the press that accompanied the prime minister to the front. Lloyd George, for his part, after the war once showed a friend a full-size portrait of Haig and, placing his hands on the top of the shiny cavalry boots, stated: "He was brilliant up to here."

An open rupture came almost immediately. On January 5-7, 1917, Lloyd George at Rome proposed an Allied offensive through the Julian Alps to Laibach and Vienna. The generals, instead, on January 15/16 counseled a major offensive at the western front. In the end, the generals won the day, but with a stunning caveat: Haig's troops were temporarily placed under the nominal command of the French General Robert Nivelle (q.v.). In the spring of 1917 Lloyd George developed a defensive military posture: he desired to keep Russia in the war against Germany, he wished to await the arrival of American troops before launching further offensives in France, and he hoped to seek a decisive military victory in the east. Instead he got Haig's attritional tactics at Ypres in 1917, after the failure of Nivelle's charge had resulted in widespread revolts in the French armies. The prime minister had let himself be overruled in his misgivings about a third Ypres by British generals and admirals alike, but all his forebodings were to be fully realized. That summer one million British men trod through the yellow, slimy swamps of Ypres towards Passchendaele; the terrain had been ripped up by 24 million shells fired in one month alone, and by November 10 it was all over, Britain having suffered 400,000 casualties. Lloyd George was boiling with rage. In October, moreover, the Italians had been routed at Caporetto and the Bolshevik Revolution had irrevocably taken Russia out of the war. A depressed Lloyd George took a holiday in his native Wales. The Conservatives directed their insensate fury at him for having appointed Churchill minister

of munitions that summer, and the generals abhorred his unending calls for knocking away the props in the east.

Late in 1917 the prime minister emerged with new-found vitality. He summoned the Dominion ministers to an Imperial Conference and Cabinet in London, and even appointed one of them, J. C. Smuts (q.v.) of South Africa, to the British War Cabinet. At Rapallo on November 7 Lloyd George won acceptance of his scheme to create a Supreme War Council in Versailles to coordinate Allied strategy. Wully Robertson stormed out of the meeting in protest, but the prime minister was in full stride. On January 5, 1918, he announced his war aims: the complete restoration of the independence of Belgium, Serbia, Montenegro, and the occupied parts of France, Italy, and Rumania. This plan was endorsed three days later in President Woodrow Wilson's (q.v.) celebrated Fourteen Points. The prime minister had also enthusiastically endorsed Foreign Secretary Arthur James Balfour's (q.v.) earlier declaration of a national home for the Jews in Palestine.

Lloyd George brought the press into his camp early in 1918 by appointing Aitken, then Lord Beaverbrook, minister of information, and Lord Northcliffe director of enemy propaganda. With this backing, the prime minister on February 18 was able do dismiss the truculent Robertson, who opposed the creation by the Supreme War Council of an Allied strategic reserve, and to replace him with the more facile Sir Henry Wilson (q.v.) as chief of the Imperial General Staff. Lloyd George thereby reclaimed strategic leadership of the war from army headquarters.

And not a moment too soon. On March 21 the German Michael offensive broke against the British Fifth Army at Amiens. Haig at last removed his tenacious objections to the creation of an Allied overall commander at a conference at Doullens on March 26; on April 3 at Beauvais the American Generals John J. Pershing and Howard Tasker Bliss gave their approval to the scheme, and on April 14 General Ferdinand Foch (qq.v.) was duly appointed général-en-chef des armées alliées en France, thereby realizing Lloyd George's fondest hopes. The prime minister propped up the western front by recalling troops from Egypt, Salonika, and Italy, and supported Foch's demand that American troops be sent out as infantry units and merged with Allied divisions in France. These policies bore fruit on November 11, 1918.

The first postwar general election was held in December 1918, with the slogans "trial of the kaiser" and "make the Germans pay." This immense, and unfortunate, demagogic election brought the coalition government 526 of 707 seats, but Lloyd George's Liberals only 133 of these. On January 18, 1919, he went to Paris with Balfour to draft the peace. The prime minister successfully opposed American demands for the "freedom of the seas"; his particular contribution to the Treaty of Versailles was placing Danzig under the League of Nations and demanding plebiscites in Upper Silesia and the Saar basin. The concept of a League of Nations never received his wholehearted support, but he compromised continuously between the hard-line stance of Georges Clemenceau (q.v.) and the idealism of Woodrow Wilson.

At home, Lloyd George at first opposed the Sinn Feiners with his "Black and Tans" shock troops, but on December 6, 1921, agreed to the creation of an Irish Free State. He resigned as prime minister in October 1922, when Mustafa Kemal (q.v.) invaded the neutral zone at Chanak in the hopes of thereby retrieving Smyrna, which Lloyd George had given Greece. Thereafter came a decade of isolation and impotence in British politics. By the early 1930s Lloyd George regretted the harsh treatment meted out to the Germans at Versailles and grew hostile toward France. He visited Adolf Hitler at Berchtesgaden in 1936 and admired the Führer's New Deal economics. In June 1940, Lloyd George refused Churchill's offer to join the coalition government; six months later he likewise declined an offer of an ambassadorship to Washington. On New Year's Day 1945 he was elevated to the peerage as Earl Lloyd-George of Dwyfor, Viscount Gwynedd of Dwyfor. The wartime leader died at Ty Newydd on March 26, 1945, and was buried on the banks of his favorite stream, the Dwyfor. His biographer, Frank Owen, called him simply the greatest British war minister since Pitt, the Earl of Chatham.

Beaverbrook, *Men and Power*; Hankey, *Supreme Command*, 2 vols.; Lloyd George, *War Memoirs*, 6 vols.; Owen, *Tempestuous Journey*; *Dictionary of National Biography 1941-1950.*

LODGE, Henry Cabot (*United States, Senator*), was born in Boston, Massachusetts, on May 12, 1850, the son of a prosperous merchant and owner of clipper ships. Lodge graduated from Harvard University in 1871 and three years later obtained a law degree; in 1876 he was awarded the first degree of Ph.D. in political science at Harvard. Lodge wrote a number of biographies during the 1880s and from 1887 to 1893 served in the House of Representatives. He entered the Senate in January 1893 and stayed there until his death.

Senator Lodge helped draft several important pieces of legislation, such as the Sherman Anti-Trust Law of 1890, the Pure Food and Drugs Law and, as a protectionist, the tariff measures of 1909. He stood fast against free silver from 1894 to 1900, against all disarmament proposals, and against women's suffrage. Lodge became an ardent supporter of the navy, favored the acquisition of the Philippines, and supported President Theodore Roosevelt's Panama venture. In fact, from 1901 to 1909 Lodge was a firm supporter of the president, especially backing the Roughrider's foreign policy. Both men feared German violation of the Monroe Doctrine in the southern hemisphere and worked hard to guard against such action.

Senator Lodge's great moment in history, however, was not to come until 1919. In what was billed as the most important Senate decision in half a century, Lodge as chairman of the foreign relations committee led the fight against ratification of the Versailles Treaty and the Covenant of the League of Nations. The senator from Massachusetts from the start had favored harsh terms for the vanquished Central Powers, and specifically advocated a heavy indemnity for Germany. Moreover, Lodge opposed President Wilson's (q.v.) decision to couple the peace treaty with the Covenant of the League of Nations. In speeches that were widely quoted in Europe, the senator warned against Wilson's tactics; the president, in turn, refused to include members of either the Republican party or the Senate in his negotiations in Paris, thereby exacerbating an already tense atmosphere. Lodge made his position well known when he was joined by thirty-six Republican senators in a public denunciation of the Versailles Treaty and the Covenant of the League of Nations. A meeting with Wilson early in 1919 failed to erase their differences: both strong-willed men refused last-minute compromise proposals. In July 1919, the treaty and the covenant were officially sent to the Senate in final form. Lodge used his powers as chairman of the foreign relations committee to add several reservations. The president rejected out of hand any tampering with the original draft of the two documents and, rather than bow to Senate pressure, assured their defeat by ordering Democratic senators to vote against the documents as revised by Lodge. On March 19, 1920, the treaty failed by seven votes to secure the necessary two-thirds vote of the Senate.

In 1920 Lodge supported Warren Harding, and both men opposed the entry of the United States into the League of Nations; Harding's victory in the presidential election was to Lodge a vindication of his actions with regard to the Versailles Treaty. The

Senator died on November 9, 1924, at Cambridge, Mass., as senior member of the Senate, titular leader of the Republican majority there, and chairman of the foreign relations committee. Lodge has been credited with literary as well as oratorical skills, and with loyalty toward his friends. His enemies, however, charged that he was ruthlessly vindictive towards them, that he was not always frank in his dealings, that he nurtured personal grudges much too long, and that as a Conservative he was opposed to almost all reforms.

Garraty, *Henry Cabot Lodge*; Lodge, *The Senate and the League of Nations*; *Dictionary of American Biography*, XI.

LUDENDORFF, Erich (*Germany, General*), was born in Kruszevnia near Posen on April 9, 1865, the son of a rural estate agent; the family of merchants had resided in Polish Prussia since 1600. Ludendorff entered the army in 1883, and in 1895 joined the General Staff as captain. In 1908, after a brief period as company commander, he was appointed head of the mobilization and deployment section of the General Staff, that is, of the section responsible for the ultimate material preparations for the Schlieffen plan in case of war. Ludendorff drafted the Army Bill of 1913 that called for upgrading the heavy artillery, enhancing production of munitions, and expanding the peacetime army by three army corps (300,000 men). The Prussian War Ministry was unwilling to adopt such a bold design and instead transferred Colonel Ludendorff, in January 1913, to the relative obscurity of the Thirty-ninth Fusiliers Regiment at Düsseldorf; the following year he was promoted major general as chief of the Eighty-fifth Infantry Regiment at Strassburg. A man of enormous powers of concentration and energy, Ludendorff was also a narrow technical specialist with a limited horizon. He possessed the mental arrogance of the self-made man. His stocky figure with its close-shaven head and omnipresent monocle was to become a national symbol.

Erich Ludendorff was appointed deputy chief of staff to General Karl van Bülow's (*q.v.*) Second Army on August 2, 1914. Six days later he won fame, and the order *Pour le mérite*, for his daring seizure of the Belgian fortress Liège with only a brigade at his disposal; by August 21 Ludendorff had crossed the Sambre River. Events in the east were then to shape his future. The Russian First Army under General P. K. Rennenkampf fronted the German Eighth Army of General Max von Prittwitz und Gaffron at Gumbinnen, while the Second Army under General A. V. Samsonov (*qq.v.*) threatened Prittwitz from the south; as a result, Prittwitz panicked and ordered a

withdrawal behind the Vistula River, thereby possibly abandoning all of East Prussia to the enemy. General Helmuth von Moltke (*q.v.*) at Koblenz instead summarily dismissed Prittwitz and on August 22 appointed Ludendorff chief of staff of the Eighth Army; almost as an afterthought, General Paul von Hindenburg (*q.v.*) was brought out of retirement and ordered to board Ludendorff's train at Hanover.

At headquarters in Marienburg, the new duumvirate adopted plans already prepared by Prittwitz's first staff officer, Colonel Max Hoffmann (*q.v.*), to score the desired Cannae. Six divisions were deployed against Samsonov's left wing and most of the troops fronting Rennenkampf were secretly withdrawn and hurled against Samsonov's left wing, with the result that the entire Army of the Narev caved in with the loss of nearly 150,000 men at Tannenberg (where in 1410 the Teutonic knights had suffered a historic defeat). Again relying upon intercepted unciphered Russian wireless messages and reinforced by two fresh army corps, the Eighth Army turned against Rennenkampf in mid-September and at the battle of the Masurian Lakes drove the Army of the Niemen out of East Prussia with the loss of over 100,000 men.

Ludendorff next proposed to break out of the Cracow area and to advance against Warsaw, but in November 1914 the legendary Russian "steamroller" finally got under way as seven separate armies drove from southern Poland to the Silesian border. In what Liddell Hart termed "perhaps the finest example of his art as well as one of the classic masterpieces of all military history," Ludendorff used his lateral railways to fall back of Cracow, all the while systematically destroying communications, until his new Ninth Army was ready to move up the Vistula against the joint of the two armies guarding the Russian flank. Thus Ludendorff's wedge, driven into the Russians at Lodz against overwhelming numerical odds, nearly annihilated one army and drove the other back to Warsaw. It was the classic example of concentration and mobility designed to paralyze a much larger force. In fact, General Erich von Falkenhayn (*q.v.*) had denied Ludendorff sufficient troops for a decisive victory; German reserves either rested idly in Lorraine or were being bled senselessly at Ypres.

In November 1914, Ludendorff was promoted lieutenant general and appointed staff chief of a new supreme command in the east under Hindenburg. In February 1915, the German Eighth and Ninth Armies routed the Russian Tenth Army of Baron Sievers at the winter battle of the Masurian Lakes, taking 92,000 prisoners in the Augustov forest. But once again, Ludendorff and Falkenhayn fell out over strategy. While the chief of the General Staff desired a frontal attack against the Russians near Gorlice, Ludendorff had developed a plan for a huge sweep from East Prussia into Poland through Kovno and Vilna; these movements were designed to envelop the enemy's northern flank near Minsk and thereby to knock Russia completely out of the war. Of course, Falkenhayn won the day and as a result General August von Mackensen's (q.v.) victory at Gorlice-Tarnów on May 2, though great, was indecisive. Relations between Ludendorff and Falkenhayn degenerated into a state of cold war and both sides tried to rally press, industry, and politicians to their banners. On September 9 Ludendorff was finally allowed to commence his drive on Vilna—four months too late—and although the armies of Generals Otto von Below and Hermann von Eichhorn (qq.v.) drove on Dvinsk and Vilna while the cavalry scouted as far as the Minsk railyards, the front was too extended, and winter forced the Germans to withdraw to more secure positions. The moment for a knockout blow in the east had passed.

Falkenhayn's position had rapidly deteriorated in the meantime. Rumania joined the war against Germany, Verdun refused to fall, and the British and Russians counterattacked at the Somme and in Galicia in order to relieve the pressure on the French along the Meuse. On August 29, 1916, Falkenhayn yielded as chief of the General Staff to Hindenburg; Ludendorff was promoted general of infantry and appointed first quartermaster general of the armies, or deputy staff chief. With Hindenburg little more than a figurehead and Wilhelm II (q.v.) unable to perform his vast constitutional powers, Ludendorff virtually ruled as "silent dictator" for the remainder of the war. The energetic Colonel Max Bauer (q.v.) helped to enact a program of industrial expansion and enhanced munitions output under the venerable field marshal's name; an Auxiliary Service Law was promulgated, Belgian forced labor was transported to Germany, and skilled workers were assigned to special military priorities. Hoffmann was instructed to stabilize the eastern front in the wake of General Aleksei Brusilov's (q.v.) June offensive, and Generals Falkenhayn and Mackensen by December had defeated Rumania and occupied Bucharest. In the west, where Ludendorff expected a massive British assault along the Somme in the spring of 1917, great artificial defenses were constructed along the arc Lens-Noyon-Reims; step-by-step the Germans withdrew behind this "Siegfried line" (the Allies dubbed it the "Hindenburg line"), thereby dislocating the enemy's plans for the following spring.

Unfortunately, these constructive measures were vitiated on January 9, 1917, when Ludendorff endorsed the navy's blueprint for victory in six months over Britain through unrestricted submarine warfare. The latter failed to achieve its desired result, and on April 6 the United States entered the war against Germany. Ludendorff had fully counted on this turn of events, arguing that he could win the war before the United States could deploy its troops in France.

On the domestic scene, Ludendorff, in July 1917, was primarily responsible for forcing the dismissal of Chancellor Theobald von Bethmann Hollweg (q.v.). The general regarded the chancellor as a "defeatist" on the issue of the U-boat war and spied his chance to move against Bethmann after the Reichstag had drafted a peace resolution calling for an end to the war without annexations or indemnities and after the chancellor had promised suffrage reform for Prussia. This overt political act, culminating in Bethmann's removal from office on July 13, above all others firmly propelled Ludendorff onto the center stage of domestic politics. The appointment of the colorless bureaucrat, Georg Michaelis (q.v.), as chancellor temporarily allowed Ludendorff to turn his energies once again to the military situation.

In October 1917, the first quartermaster general dispatched six divisions under General von Below to the Julian Alps where, together with nine Austrian divisions, the new Fourteenth Army on October 24 routed the Italians near Tolmino-Flitsch at the battle of Caporetto. The enemy suffered almost 600,000 casualties, prisoners, and deserters and had to fall behind first the Tagliamento and ultimately the Piave rivers before Anglo-French reinforcements could stem the German-Austro-Hungarian advance. Ludendorff had not envisaged such a colossal collapse of the Italian front, and was, therefore, unable after Caporetto to switch his troops to his right wing and thereby to envelop the fleeing Italians totally. For the first time, Ludendorff's strategic concept was drawn in the wake of a tactical plan, rather than vice versa.

That same month the Bolshevik seizure of power in Petrograd marked the end of fighting in the east. Ludendorff had helped to shuttle V. I. Lenin (q.v.) in April 1917 from Berne, Switzerland, to Finland, and at Brest-Litovsk in December he demanded payment: German control over Finland, the Baltic states, the Ukraine, and the Crimea as far as the Caspian Sea. These demands were largely realized in March 1918, and, coupled with similar Draconian terms imposed upon Rumania, gave Germany legal control over most of European Russia and the Balkans. There is no question that Ludendorff was motivated by greed and that he insisted on terms that were far beyond Germany's capability to enforce.

The main decision, however, was yet to be sought in the west. For the spring of 1918 Ludendorff selected the Arras-St. Quentin sector toward the Somme and Amiens as the point of primary attack for the Michael offensive, viewing this as the line of least resistance; follow-up operations were planned between Arras and Lens (code name: Mars), the Lys (St. George I), Ypres (St. George II), and in the Champagne (Blücher). Above all, in place of the customary long, deep assault lines that went over the top, Ludendorff deployed new infantry tactics featuring small groups of automatic riflemen, gas and smoke shells, and mobile artillery fire. The Michael offensive was launched on March 21 along the fifty-mile front of Arras-St. Quentin-La Fère, but the original idea of driving the British against the Channel coast had to be abandoned as the attack was checked at Arras; instead, Ludendorff sought a concentration against Amiens and by the end of the month had reached the outworks of this vital rail center. On April 9 the Germans launched the so-called St. George I offensive against Lys, and its rapid success encouraged Ludendorff to exploit a tactical gain and to turn it into a major operation, as he had done at Caporetto. By May 27 the Blücher assault was unleashed between Soissons and Reims, quickly sweeping across the Aisne as far as the Marne by May 30, where an American counterattack at Château-Thierry brought it to a halt. Ludendorff had driven three large bulges in the Allied line by then, but had been denied the decisive breakthrough. A final two-handed punch at Reims failed early in July, and on July 18 the Allies riposted. The German front, extended, indented, and susceptible to flanking counterstrokes, reeled thereafter as the Allies relentlessly attacked. Ludendorff, who held little esteem for the tank, witnessed the British tank attack from Amiens on August 8; he termed it the "black day of the German Army" as over 30,000 troops were lost on that one day. Moreover, Ludendorff had been too slow to see the utter exhaustion of the nation; as army leader he was now too anxious to demand peace, and losing his nerve on September 29, he counseled for the immediate cessation of hostilities regardless of the consequences. Then, too late again, he regretted his earlier haste and, in vain, argued for continuation of the war. Instead, the government of Prince Max von Baden (q.v.) forced his resignation on October 26, and an embittered Ludendorff fled to Sweden, where he was to begin immediately to write his memoirs.

After the war Ludendorff continued in politics, and along with Colonel Bauer became the focal point of the national and racial *völkisch* movement. In March 1920, he participated in the right-wing Kapp *Putsch* in Berlin and, in November 1923, joined Adolf Hitler's aborted beerhall *Putsch* in Munich—each time his wartime reputation spared him incarceration. In May 1924, Ludendorff became parliamentary leader of the Nazi contingent in the Reichstag, and the following year he received 1 percent of the total vote as NSDAP candidate for the presidency of the Weimar Republic. Thereafter, under the influence of his second wife, Mathilde, Ludendorff crusaded against Jesuits and Free Masons and called for a special Germanic religious revival. He died in Tutzing in Bavaria on December 20, 1937.

Liddell Hart called Ludendorff "the robot Napoleon" and ranked him as "perhaps the greatest of all among the leaders of the War of 1914-1918." This was primarily for the clearness and the vision of the master strategist in the east in 1914-1916; in the west by 1918 he had been reduced to a brilliant tactician and had felt the strain of too many operations at once. Moreover, his greed in the east probably cost him the requisite reserves to attain an outright decision in the west. Although a man of brilliant intelligence and prodigious energy, Ludendorff lacked a wider outlook. His position as demigod in the General Staff was secure, but as political and diplomatic leader of the nation in 1916-1918 he lacked vision and above all a sense of *Realpolitik*.

Foerster, *Feldherr Ludendorff*; Goodspeed, *Ludendorff*; Liddell Hart, *Reputations*; Ludendorff, *Meine Kriegserinnerungen*, *Kriegführung und Politik*, *Urkunden der Obersten Heeresleitung*; *Biographisches Wörterbuch zur Deutschen Geschichte*, II, *Geschichte der Ritter des Ordens*, I.

LYAUTEY, Hubert (*France, General, Minister of War*), was born in Nancy, November 17, 1854, the son of a civil engineer. The young Lyautey's future military vocation and his royalist politics were rooted in a distinguished family background. On his father's side, he could claim ancestors who included three generals. His mother was the offspring of aristocratic families from Normandy and Lorraine. Lyautey graduated from St. Cyr in 1875, entered the cavalry, and served unhappily in a succession of line and staff positions for the next nineteen years. His early years were marked by religious crises; by the late 1880s, he was involved in such uncharacteristic pursuits as participation in a literary circle that included Marcel Proust. In defiance of army orders, he published schemes for army reform in the *Revue des* *deux mondes*, a civilian journal. When the War Ministry learned the identify of the anonymous author, Lyautey found himself exiled to Indo-China. There he entered the orbit of General Joseph Gallieni (*q.v.*) and found his own role as a brilliant colonial administrator. He served under Gallieni for eight years, 1894-1902, first in Indo-China, then in Madagascar. In 1900 he was advanced to full colonel. Three years later, he was assigned to Algeria and promoted brigadier general. Wearing his military insignia on a black bournous, Lyautey cut a colorful figure, but his eccentricities were accompanied by substantial achievements. He distinguished himself in pacifying the Moroccan-Algerian frontier and reached the rank of major general in 1906. He received the X Corps in France in 1911, but the establishment of the French protectorate over Morocco the following year led to Lyautey's appointment as resident general.

In his new role, Lyautey answered only to the French foreign minister, and in effect governed Morocco with nearly unlimited authority. After restoring order with the help of subordinates like Charles Mangin and Louis Franchet d'Esperey (*qq.v.*), he applied Gallieni's maxims for effective colonial rule: respect for local social and political hierarchies; the establishment of economic and military security for the indigenous population. To develop and modernize the Moroccan economy while limiting actual French settlement in Morocco became his main goal. He remained in North Africa for more than two years after the outbreak of World War I. Rejecting orders that he withdraw his reduced garrison to the coast, he continued the military pacification of the Moroccan interior. German submarines off the coast and German agents stirring up tribal rebellions brought the war closer, but Lyautey felt forgotten and bitter at his failure to get a command in France.

In December 1916, Premier Briand (*q.v.*) reshaped his cabinet and offered Lyautey the War Ministry. Despite the pull of his Moroccan duties, the resident general accepted the new post. The lack of firm direction over the French war effort had disturbed him for years, and he left for Paris expecting to serve as a strong war minister. Disappointment and frustration followed at once. A new commander in chief, General Nivelle (*q.v.*), had been chosen without consultation with Lyautey. Moreover, the new war minister found his role diminished at once: the government shifted military transportation and arms production to new and independent ministries in late 1916.

Lyautey proved unequipped for his political duties. An efficient authoritarian in Morocco, he despised equally administrative details and political infighting. Lyautey's doubts about the forthcoming Nivelle spring offensive developed early. Tours of the front brought him into contact with the skeptical commanders of France's field armies. The operations officer who coolly presented Nivelle's detailed scheme to the war minister was a former subordinate from North Africa. Under Lyautey's probing, the unhappy colonel broke down and confessed his own doubts. Lyautey called Nivelle's project "a plan [fit] for the Grand Duchess of Gerolstein." His cabinet post, his military expertise, and his personal reputation made Lyautey the best-situated critic to halt the slide to calamity in April. In the face of Nivelle's confidence and the backing of government leaders like President Poincaré (*q.v.*), however, even he could not stop it.

Lyautey was removed from office before the offensive began. A squabble with the Parliamentary Left over discussing military secrets before the Chamber of Deputies led to the war minister's resignation on March 14. The fall of Briand's entire government came two days later. Lyautey returned to Morocco to serve eight more years as resident general. Forced from that office in 1925, he retired to Thorey in Lorraine. He died there, July 27, 1934.

King, *Generals and Politicians*; Ormesson, *Auprès de Lyautey*; Scham, *Lyautey in Morocco*.

McADOO, William Gibbs (*United States, Secretary of the Treasury*), was born in Marietta, Georgia, on October 31, 1863, the son of a lawyer and professor. McAdoo graduated from the University of Tennessee and, after a brief career as barrister, ventured to New York City where he became involved in the construction of four tunnels under the Hudson River linking New York to New Jersey by 1909. In the following year he supported Woodrow Wilson's (*q.v.*) gubernatorial campaign in New Jersey, and in 1912 became campaign manager for the Princeton professor in his bid for the presidency. Wilson rewarded McAdoo with the post of secretary of the treasury, and the Georgian became the most able and most energetic member of the Wilson cabinet. In May 1914 he married one of Wilson's daughters.

McAdoo rendered candid, forceful, and often unorthodox advice to the president. From 1914 to 1916 McAdoo pressed Wilson for a declaration of war rather than to acquiesce in the German destruction of American shipping. The secretary was especially upset over the government's decision to instruct U.S. shippers not to risk the high seas.

When the United States finally entered the war in April 1917, McAdoo worked energetically over the next seventeen months to raise $24 billion—exclusive of American loans to the Allies—by four Liberty Loan drives. The secretary's patriotic appeals were so successful that each loan was oversubscribed. In addition to his post at the Treasury Department, McAdoo also assumed the chairmanship of the Federal Reserve Board, the Federal Farm Loan Board, and the War Finance Corporation; in December 1917, he became director general of the nation's railways after their takeover by the government. On the issue of taxation, McAdoo rejected proposals by Claude Kitchin and Robert LaFollette for a high tax-loan ratio; on the other hand, he also kept clear of conservative proposals for higher consumption taxes and bond issues. The secretary favored instead a compromise: a one-to-three tax-loan ratio in all war-time financing. And although fewer than eight billion dollars were raised in taxes by the Treasury, the incredible Liberty Loan drives mobilized America's wealth, while permitting the secretary to maintain his cherished ideological neutrality.

The war effort drained McAdoo's strength, and in January 1919, he laid down his offices owing to sheer exhaustion. Subsequent aspirations for high political office were dashed in 1924 when he was linked to the Teapot Dome scandal; in fact, McAdoo lost his party's presidential nomination that very year. From 1932 to 1938 he served as Democratic senator from California and supported Franklin D. Roosevelt's (q.v.) New Deal. McAdoo died on February 1, 1941, in Washington, D.C.

Broesamle, *William Gibbs McAdoo*; McAdoo, *Crowded Years*; *Dictionary of American Biography*, XXIII Supplement Three.

MACKENSEN, August von (*Germany, Field Marshal*), was born in Schmiedeberg in Saxony on December 6, 1849, the son of an estate owner. Mackensen entered the army in 1869 and fought in the war against France; in 1871 he enrolled at the University of Halle, only to return two years later to the army. In 1880, without having attended the War Academy, he was assigned to the General Staff, where eight years later he was promoted major; in 1891 Mackensen was appointed Count Alfred von Schlieffen's adjutant. By the turn of the century, Mackensen had been promoted colonel, raised into the Prussian nobility (1899), and appointed adjutant to Wilhelm II (q.v.). Lieutenant General von Mackensen was given the Thirty-six Division in 1903; five years later as general of cavalry he headed the XVII Army Corps at Danzig. Mackensen's repeated commands of the prestigious horse guards had caught the kaiser's attention on several occasions.

On August 4, 1914, the XVII Army Corps was transformed into the Eighth Army with Mackensen in command. Sixteen days later, this force fronted the Russians at Gumbinnen, but withdrew after suffering 8,000 casualties that day; on August 21 Mackensen led his army behind the Vistula as part of the retreat ordered by General Max von Prittwitz und Gaffron (q.v.). Under the new commanders in the east, Generals Paul von Hindenburg and Erich Ludendorff (qq.v.), Mackensen resumed the offensive: on August 26 his army rolled up the Russian right wing of General A. V. Samsonov's (q.v.) Second Army, and on September 9 the Eighth Army successfully attacked General P. K. Rennenkampf's (q.v.) Niemen Army at the Masurian Lakes, throwing the enemy back upon Kovno. The former XVII Army Corps was next transferred to Silesia as part of a new Ninth Army. Mackensen entered Poland and on October 8 received orders to move against Warsaw. The order was ill advised and on October 13 Grand Duke Nikolai (q.v.), enjoying a numerical advantage of fourteen to five divisions, repulsed the German attack and chased the invaders back over Lodz to Wartha by October 20.

The Germans on November 1, 1914, totally reorganized their eastern front. Hindenburg became eastern commander in chief and Mackensen was given the Ninth Army, now strengthened by eight new divisions. Mackensen reclaimed Lodz on December 6 and forced the Russians to fall back upon Warsaw with the loss of 80,000 prisoners of war; he was promoted colonel general and given the order *Pour le mérite* for the triumph at Lodz. With this action, Germany's eastern borders were secured.

On April 16, 1915, Mackensen was given a new Eleventh Army (including the Austro-Hungarian Third and Fourth Armies) and ordered to free Galicia of Russians. The great German breakthrough at Gorlice-Tarnów on May 2 brought Mackensen prestige second only to that enjoyed by Hindenburg. By mid-May the Germans had taken 150,000 prisoners and had reached the San River; the great fortress of Przemysl was retaken on June 2 and later that month the Russians were again defeated at Lubaczov and at Grodek-Magierov. Mackensen was promoted field marshal when his troops stormed Lemberg on June 22. On July 4, 1915, this dashing cavalryman was placed at the head of Army Group Mackensen, consisting of the German Eleventh Army and the Bug Army as well as of the Austro-Hungarian Fourth Army. In rapid succession the Russians were driven out of Lublin, Cholm, and Brest-Litovsk (August 26), and as far back as the Pripet Marshes.

Mackensen was at the height of his military career when he received command of a new Army Group Mackensen (German Ninth, Austro-Hungarian Third, and Bulgarian First Armies) on September 16, 1915, against Serbia. He crossed the Danube and Save rivers on October 6, and three days later Belgrade fell. The entire country was overrun by November and 150,000 prisoners taken; Mackensen's forces halted at the border of neutral Greece and hence left an Allied army bottled up at Salonika.

On August 28, 1916, after Rumania had declared war against the Central Powers, Mackensen was given a mixed force of German, Bulgarian, Austro-Hungarian, and Turkish troops, with which he invaded the Dobrudja during the night of September 1/2. The Rumanians, although enjoying almost a three-to-one numerical advantage, lost Tutrakan and Silistria along with 30,000 men. By October 19 Mackensen had seized the important port of Costanza, while General Erich von Falkenhayn's (q.v.) Ninth Army advanced across the Transylvanian mountains at Targu Jiu. Mackensen crossed the Danube at Sistovo on November 23, turned the Rumanian flank on the Alt, and advanced upon Bucharest, which he entered on December 6, 1916. By January of the following year the greater part of the country was in German hands; Mackensen headed the army of occupation until the end of the war.

On November 10, 1918, the field marshal began to clear his units out of Rumania, by way of Transylvania, into Hungary. On December 16 the government of Count Mihály Károlyi (q.v.), acting on orders from the Entente, arrested Mackensen in Budapest and turned him over to French authorities. Interned at Neusatz, the general was finally allowed to return home in December 1919; he retired from the army in January 1920.

Mackensen settled on his estate near Stettin and in August 1933 was made a member of the Prussian Council of State by Hermann Göring. The field marshal frequently appeared at Adolf Hitler's side in public wearing the uniform of the famous "Death's Head Hussars," with which he had commenced his illustrious career as a cavalryman. He was most proud that his waistline had not expanded from subaltern to field marshal. Mackensen died in Burghorn, near Celle, on November 8, 1945, at the age of ninety-six. During the war, he had displayed judicious and independent political as well as military judgment, not at all the "court general" he was often accused of being. Though it should be noted that much of his military prowess had stemmed from his brilliant staff chief, General Hans von Seeckt (q.v.)

François, *Gorlice*; Mackensen, *Briefe und Aufzeichnungen*; Ruedt von Collenberg, *Mackensen*; *Biographisches Wörterbuch zur Deutschen Geschichte*, II; *Geschichte der Ritter des Ordens*, II.

MAISTRE, Paul (*France, General*), was born in Joinville on June 20, 1858. The son of a tax collector, Maistre graduated from St. Cyr, completed the course at the War College, and launched a distinguished career as an infantry officer. He rotated through a succession of staff, line, and teaching posts. As a young major, he taught tactics at the War College under the direction of Ferdinand Foch (q.v.). In 1909, by then a colonel, he received his own regiment, and a brigade command followed shortly. By 1914 Maistre was chief of staff to General Langle de Cary (q.v.), the commander of the Fourth Army.

Maistre followed Langle and the Fourth Army from the Ardennes to the Marne in August/September 1914. His service at the battle of the Marne won him command of the XXI Corps, having skipped the usual step of holding a divisional command. He led the XXI Corps in the race to the sea. By November 1914, Maistre was entrenched near Armentières, where he remained for over a year. The XXI Corps felt the weight of both the major French campaigns of 1916. It did its turn at Verdun in the early months of the year; then Maistre led it to the Somme for the last phase of the offensive on that hot corner of the western front. Maistre's troops were a reserve formation in April 1917, and were, therefore, spared General Nivelle's (q.v.) bloodbath at the Chemin des Dames.

On May 1, 1917, Maistre received command of the Sixth Army, which Nivelle's pet commander, General Mangin (q.v.), had shattered during the futile April attacks. He quickly informed General Pétain (q.v.), Nivelle's successor as commander in chief, to have "no illusions" about sending this force into new combat operations: the men would simply refuse to leave their trenches! Maistre's work in restoring his army into a formidable instrument of war was complete within five months. He convinced Pétain to use this force for a limited and carefully planned attack at Malmaison, where Nivelle had recently met a bloody repulse. Maistre succeeded (October 23-25) and Malmaison stands as the most impressive in Pétain's series of meticulous attacks designed to restore the fighting confidence of the French army by winning successes at small cost in French lives. It also displayed Maistre's skillful use of tanks, accompanying Pétain's favorite tool of massive artillery concentrations.

Maistre soon left for a tour in Italy. He commanded the French Tenth Army, bolstering the Italian forces after the Austro-German breakthrough at Caporetto. But he was soon needed in France to help meet the climactic German offensives in the spring of 1918. By June Maistre advanced to command the Center Army Group, stretching from Soissons to the Argonne. With the American Expeditionary Forces (AEF) on his right, he advanced northward. By the November 11 armistice, Maistre had reached Sedan and Charleville, the same familiar ground where Langle de Cary's old Fourth Army had first encountered the enemy in August 1914.

Maistre served briefly in the postwar army as a member of the Supreme War Council and inspector general of infantry. He died in 1922.

Beaufre, *La France de la Grande Guerre*; Pedroncini, *Pétain: général en chef*; Ryan, *Pétain the Soldier*.

MAKLAKOV, Nikolai Alekseevich (*Russia, Minister of the Interior*), was born in Russia in 1871. He graduated from Moscow University and entered the state treasury bureaucracy in 1892. Twenty years later, he rose to the uppermost rung of the ladder for the tsar's functionaries, becoming acting minister of the interior in December 1912 and taking formal control of the ministry in early 1913. His predecessor had failed to meet the expectations of Tsar Nicholas II (*q.v.*) in the crucial areas of muzzling the Russian press and manipulating elections to the Fourth Duma in 1912. More was expected of Maklakov, a convinced monarchist who saw the Duma merely as a troublesome and ambitious set of political meddlers with no independent authority. His ministry had, by tradition, been the most important of the monarch's political instruments. Maklakov promised a strong hand, and his views were compatible with—and sometimes even more extreme than—those of the tsar.

The outbreak of World War I made Maklakov, for nearly a year, one of the weighty figures in the council of ministers. Under the aged, reactionary premier, Ivan Goremykin (*q.v.*), Maklakov had a clear field of action. After it had met for a single day, he urged that the Duma be prorogued until late 1915. He expected the war to be over by then. He instituted close surveillance over the country's fledgling political parties; he saw the Western-style Kadets (Constitutional Democrats) as particularly dangerous in an era marked by a diplomatic alliance with Britain and France. He threw his considerable authority against efforts by Foreign Minister Sergei Sazonov (*q.v.*) to win the loyalty of Russia's Polish population by pledging to reconstitute a unified Polish state under the tsar's authority at the war's end.

Maklakov quickly became the most visible of the reactionary ministers who dominated the cabinet for most of the first year of hostilities. In reality, he was less than victorious. Tsar Nicholas prorogued the Duma, but only until early 1915. Russia's political representatives (the five Bolshevik deputies in the Duma were the most noisy exceptions) supported the war effort. Maklakov's hopes of provoking a premature demand for power from Duma leaders, to be followed by a harsh crackdown on all Duma pretentions, did not reach fruition. On the other hand, his insistence that the government's Polish policy aim at "serving the interests of Russia exclusively" forestalled Sazonov's hopes of quickly winning over the Poles. The interior minister mobilized his powers as Russia's censor to see to it the issue got no public exposure in the nation's press. Hopes for a broadly based war effort, employing rural and urban *zemstvos* ("local government bodies") bogged down in the face of Maklakov's fierce opposition.

Maklakov and most of the other leading reactionaries departed the cabinet, however, in the spring and early summer of 1915. Maklakov himself had been partly immobilized by illness in 1915. But more important, military catastrophe in Poland cut away at the credibility of the cabinet; the group's liberal faction, led by Minister of Agriculture Krivoshein (*q.v.*), temporarily enjoyed the tsar's attention, if not his affection.

In January 1917, Maklakov seemed on the road back to power. His new assignment was to gerrymander districts and otherwise to manipulate forthcoming elections to the Fifth Duma in order to insure a conservative majority; the March Revolution made this just a paper exercise. Maklakov never regained office, and, predictably enough, the Bolsheviks shot him in 1918. His brother, Vasily Alekseevich Maklakov, a conservative Kadet and ranking official in the provisional government with whom Nikolai Alekseevich is sometimes confused, was more fortunate. He left Russia in 1917 and lived on in exile to die peacefully in 1957.

Dallin, "The Future of Poland"; Gurko, *Features and Figures of the Past*; Hosking, *The Russian Constitutional Experiment*; Pearson, *The Russian Moderates and the Crisis of Tsarism*; Smith, *The Russian Struggle for Power*; *Sovetskaia istoricheskaia entsiklopediia*, VIII.

MALINOV, Alexander (*Bulgaria, Minister-President*), was born to a Bulgarian family in Russian Bessarabia, April 21, 1867. His early life was spent in Russia, and he received his education as a lawyer at the University of Kiev. In 1887 Malinov took up residence in Bulgaria. He entered the National Assembly (*Sobranie*) in 1901 and became head of the Democratic party. Malinov first served as minister-president in the years 1908-1911. Once in power, he quickly abandoned the reformist zeal he had once displayed, becoming a docile executive for the real director of Bulgarian affairs, Prince Ferdinand (*q.v.*). Unlike Rumanian politicians such as Ion Bratianu (*q.v.*), party leaders in Bulgaria were more the symbols of the drift in foreign and domestic policies than the shapers of government decisions. Malinov came to be known as staunchly pro-Russian. In 1913, as Bulgaria suffered defeat in the Second Balkan War, rumors spread that Malinov would be called upon to form a new government. The post went instead to the pro-Austrian Radoslavov (*q.v.*). Malinov's name circulated once again in early 1914, when Radoslavov aroused controversy by actively seeking a tie with the Central Powers.

With the outbreak of World War I, Malinov urged that Bulgaria remain neutral. The Entente's assault on the Dardanelles temporarily displaced Ferdinand's alignment with the Central Powers. New rumors ran that Malinov might return to lead a cabinet. In September 1915, however, Ferdinand called all party leaders together to announce his decision to fight alongside Germany and Austria. Malinov remained a firm spokesman for continued neutrality. Ferdinand asked him to join the Radoslavov cabinet in a show of national unity. Malinov refused, but his moderate and conventional opposition stood in sharp contrast to the violent protests of the leader of the Agrarian party, Alexander Stamboliski (*q.v.*). The following summer, Malinov argued, again without success, against a Bulgarian declaration of war on Rumania.

During the first three years of the war, a government led by Malinov had become a symbol for loosening Bulgaria's ties to the Central Powers. In the spring of 1918 Malinov was at the edge of power. Bulgaria had been picked clean of food by her allies. Bread riots spread at home. A broad opposition bloc had formed in the *Sobranie*. Mutinies threatened to cripple the thinly stretched and isolated Bulgarian armies defending the Macedonian front. In June Ferdinand called on Malinov to form a new government. The Democratic party leader was widely expected to seek a separate peace. Radoslavov himself had held back from declaring war on the United States. The mediation of Woodrow Wilson (*q.v.*) seemed a likely route by which Bulgaria could depart from the war. Such expectations were soon disappointed.

Malinov failed to form the broad coalition government he desired. Ferdinand refused to countenance the release of Agrarian leaders from prison. Their

followers in the *Sobranie* responded by refusing to back Malinov's government. The monarch remained firmly linked to the Central Powers and barred the way to a new foreign policy. Bulgaria put out peace feelers in late June. In Mamatey's view, these were largely intended to put pressure on Germany to treat Bulgaria more equitably in dividing the war spoils from the conquest of Rumania. Moreover, in the event of future defeat, early peace inquiries might provide Bulgaria with a favorable background for dealing with the Entente. The British government suspected as much and helped to hold the United States back.

In August 1918, Malinov protested the precarious military situation in Macedonia to Ferdinand and the German High Command. His messages had no effect. The catastrophe arrived in mid-September. Franchet d'Esperey (*q.v.*) and his multinational army broke the Bulgarian defenses at Dobro Pole. The entire Macedonian front collapsed within a week. For once, Malinov and his government ignored Ferdinand. The cabinet asked for an armistice. Hostilities ended on September 30.

Malinov remained in power until the end of the European war, surviving a radical uprising by the troops at Radomir as well as Ferdinand's last efforts to keep Bulgaria in the fighting by calling German troops to Sofia. At the insistence of the Entente, Ferdinand abdicated in early October. Malinov resigned in late November, an act intended to protest the Rumanian occupation of the southern Dobrudja.

Postwar Bulgarian politics saw Malinov playing a continuing role. Along with other moderate leaders, he first refused to participate in Stamboliski's government, then actively opposed the Agrarian leader. Imprisoned from the fall of 1922 until June 1923, Malinov publicly praised the military coup that ousted Stamboliski. Malinov formed a new government in 1931, but poor health made it impossible for him to retain the office. He died in the midst of a new election campaign, March 20, 1938.

Bell, *Peasants in Power*; Buchan, ed., *Nations of Today: Bulgaria and Romania*; Holden, "Bulgaria's Entry into the First World War"; Mamatey, "The United States and Bulgaria in World War I"; Rothschild, *The Communist Party of Bulgaria*.

MALVY, Louis Jean (*France, Minister of the Interior*), was born in Figeac in southern France, December 1, 1875. By 1906 he had obtained a law degree and, after several unsuccessful attempts, won a seat as a Radical in the Chamber of Deputies. In 1911/1912, by then a well-known anticlerical, his political career gathered momentum as he served as an undersecretary, first in the ministry of justice, then in the ministry of the interior. More important, he formed a close political alliance with Joseph Caillaux (*q.v.*), minister of the interior and one of the commanding figures in the National Assembly. Association with Caillaux brought with it murmurs of being pro-German, since Caillaux had aroused a storm of protest by supposedly appeasing the Germans during the Agadir crisis of 1911/1912. In 1913, at the age of only thirty-eight, Malvy took office as minister of commerce. In March 1914, he assumed the powerful post of minister of the interior. Few felt he had attained such preeminence by his own talents. Rather Caillaux seemed to be working through Malvy, since a personal scandal—Caillaux's wife had gunned down a newspaper editor who had been attacking her husband—had momentarily neutralized Caillaux's ambitions.

At the outbreak of World War I, Minister of the Interior Malvy argued successfully against a roundup of subversive leaders. Some 3,000 syndicalists, pacifists, and the like had been named on *Carnet B*—to be arrested upon news of war. As a Radical of the Left, Malvy had no taste for enforcing *Carnet B*. Moreover, in the first days of mobilization, even syndicalist leaders pledged not to interfere with the war effort. With the knowledge of his cabinet colleagues, Malvy embarked on another venture that contained some risk: subsidizing workers' newspapers that were willing to praise the war and rouse the working class to support the war effort. These measures seemed to bring substantial success. Strikes and labor unrest remained far below prewar expectations.

Governments came and went, but Malvy lingered on. When Aristide Briand replaced René Viviani (*qq.v.*) at the head of the government in October 1915, Malvy found himself charged with being too lenient toward the workers to be an effective minister of the interior. He rejected the criticism and refused to take a different cabinet post. Backed by the Radical bloc in the Chamber of Deputies, he could not be ousted. But danger signs were evident even in 1915. Malvy had to halt some newspaper subsidies; publications like the infamous *Bonnet rouge* shifted their editorial line toward pacifism. Malvy came under direct attack by Georges Clemenceau (*q.v.*) in the summer of 1916. The so-called Tiger accused Malvy of tolerating the circulation of defeatist propaganda.

In 1917 criticism arrived frequently and heatedly. In the aftermath of General Robert Nivelle's (*q.v.*) offensive, which Malvy had vigorously supported, the temper in the National Assembly shifted sharply. Mutinies crippled the army, industrial unrest was growing, and, in the east one saw the ominous example of the March Revolution in Russia. All this combined to erode Malvy's political support. Clemenceau continued to be critical; but his castigation of Malvy for excessive weakness toward strikers and dissenters did not alter Malvy's actions. In May 1917, the interior minister settled a wave of strikes in the metals industry through negotiations, even though some strikers had adopted "down with the war" as a slogan and some Nationalist leaders in the National Assembly called for repressive measures. Similarly, Malvy argued, albeit unsuccessfully, that French Socialist leaders should be permitted to attend the controversial international conference of Socialists supposed to meet in Stockholm. Such actions provoked controversy, but the worst blow to Malvy's position came in the summer when members of the *Bonnet rouge* staff were arrested and faced strong evidence of being in German pay.

Malvy was compelled to resign from Alexandre Ribot's (*q.v.*) cabinet (August 31, 1917), and Ribot soon fell himself. But the attacks in the National Assembly continued; the former interior minister was even accused of selling the plans of the Nivelle offensive to the enemy. When Clemenceau took office (November 1917), having pledged to crush defeatism, Malvy demanded to be tried by the National Assembly. Thus he apparently hoped to avoid the perilous alternative of a court-martial. After a lengthy investigation, Malvy was acquitted of treason in August 1918, but at the same time found guilty of criminal negligence in performing his duties. The penalty was five years in exile.

Malvy returned from Spain in 1924, succeeded in obtaining a seat in the Chamber of Deputies, and in March 1926 Briand recalled him to his wartime post of minister of the interior. The passage of time had not yet cooled tempers enough to permit this reminder of a bitter past to go unopposed. In the face of an uproar in the National Assembly, Malvy quickly stepped down. He continued to serve on the back benches until 1940, and he died in Paris, June 9, 1949.

Chastenet, *Histoire de la troisième république*, IV; King, *Generals and Politicians*; Malvy, *Mon crime*; Watson, *Georges Clemenceau*; Weber, *Action Française*; *Dictionnaire des parlementaires français*, VII.

MANGIN, Charles (*France, General*), was born on July 6, 1866, in Sarrebourg, France, a town included in the portion of Lorraine annexed by Germany in 1871. Mangin, however, remained French and graduated from St. Cyr in 1888; he began a long period of active duty as an infantry officer in France's colonial forces. He was wounded in action on three occasions. Mangin saw service in the Sudan, 1890-1894, and he commanded the advance guard in the Marchand expedition that transversed Africa from west to east in the years 1895-1898. Service in Indo-China, 1901-1904, was followed by a tour in West Africa, 1907-1911. Mangin capped his distinguished career as a colonial soldier by defeating the Moroccan pretender Al-Hiba and expelling him from Marrakesh in 1912.

Mangin, promoted to general, led a brigade in General Lanrezac's (q.v.) Fifth Army in the opening weeks of the war and received a divisional command in late August 1914. He participated in the Artois offensive of 1915. By the beginning of 1916, General Mangin had a widespread reputation for technical competence and bravery, combined with optimism, fierce aggressiveness, and a willingness to accept heavy losses. He frequently commanded troops from French West Africa, and his reputation was clouded in early 1916 by the collapse of one of these units under the strain of prolonged combat. Only the intervention of General Nivelle (q.v.) saved his career.

Mangin commanded the Fifth Infantry Division in Nivelle's corps at Verdun during the first phase of the battle. In early April 1916, Mangin launched a series of bloody and futile counterattacks against the Germans along the flanks of Fort Douaumont. In late May he succeeded at enormous cost in retaking Douaumont briefly, but his forces were by then too weak to hold that symbolic and powerful set of fortifications. Mangin was temporarily relieved, but he returned to command a corps on the right bank of the Meuse in June. His fierce frontal assaults, backed by only poorly coordinated artillery support, failed in June and July, earning him a personal rebuke from General Pétain (q.v.), the supreme commander at Verdun.

Established as Nivelle's protégé, Mangin carried out successful Verdun counteroffensives from October to December 1916. His forces, adequately supported by artillery using Nivelle's innovative "rolling barrage," retook Douaumont. In late December Mangin took over the Sixth Army, which Nivelle, now France's generalissimo, had designated for the crucial role in the coming spring offensive on the Aisne.

Mangin's enthusiasm helped stifle doubts in Prime Minister Ribot's (q.v.) government concerning the planned Nivelle offensive. When the Reserve Army Group commander General Micheler (q.v.) began to develop doubts, Nivelle circumvented the chain of command to deal directly with Mangin. Mangin's Sixth Army suffered bloody losses in the calamity of

April 1917 against the Germans' powerful defenses at the Chemin des Dames. The Sixth Army became a center for the ensuing mutinies. Mangin was relieved of command and went into involuntary retirement until the close of 1917. He was rehabilitated under the patronage of the offensive-minded General Foch (q.v.), who sought to counterattack Pétain's preference for defensive actions by installing as his subordinates such figures as Mangin. Mangin received a corps at first and then, in the summer of 1918, the Tenth Army. His forces attacked the western flank of the Marne salient at Soissons in July 1918, and Mangin's boldness and optimism (questionable assets on the constricted battlefields of 1916 and 1917) shone in the conditions of more mobile warfare. At the time of the armistice, Mangin was preparing an offensive into his native Lorraine, and he subsequently returned in triumph to Metz. He became a public hero and Prime Minister Clemenceau (q.v.) expressed concerns about Mangin's political ambitions.

Mangin's Tenth Army stood occupation duty on the Rhine with headquarters at Mainz, and Mangin became a patron to Rhenish separatist movements in 1919, favoring an independent republic and French client state on the west bank of the Rhine. He was relieved by Clemenceau in October 1919 but remained on active duty and saw extensive service in North Africa. He died in Paris on May 12, 1925.

Horne, *Price of Glory: Verdun*; King, *Foch versus Clemenceau* and *Generals and Politicians*; Mangin, *Lettres de guerre, 1914-1918*; Spears, *Prelude to Victory*.

MARCH, Peyton Conway (*United States, General*), was born at Easton, Pennsylvania, on December 27, 1864, the son of a philologist. March graduated from Lafayette College in 1884 and from West Point four years later. He gained prominence during the Spanish-American War as commander of the privately raised Astor Battery during the battle of Manila. From 1901 to 1917 March received various assignments as battery, battalion, and regimental commander; his staff tours included that of military observer with the Japanese First Army during the Russo-Japanese War.

A forceful and decisive officer, Colonel March in April 1917 was chief of the Eighth Field Artillery Regiment, and three months later was sent to France in the grade of brigadier general to command the artillery brigade of the First Division. In August 1917, he was promoted to the grade of major general and still later that year appointed head of all artillery for the American Expeditionary Forces. During the winter of 1917/1918, Secretary of War Baker (q.v.)

came under intensive fire from Congress for alleged inadequacies in his office's logistical efforts, and the secretary appointed March acting chief of staff on March 4, 1918, in order to allay such fears and suspicions; two months later March was officially appointed army chief of staff. He approached his job with a single-minded, ruthless drive for efficiency. March's cold, tactless manner may have upset congressional leaders, but he got the job done, first by reducing the power of the entrenched bureau chiefs. Specifically, March deployed his assistant chief of staff, General Goethals, the builder of the Panama Canal, as a trouble-shooter endowed with sweeping powers to streamline all phases of production. In Bernard Baruch March found an able civilian economic planner and coordinator. The new chief inherited a staff of fewer than twenty officers in April 1917; by November the General Staff had swelled to more than 1,000 members.

March introduced grand reforms for his office: weekly press conferences became routine, training at "the Point" was reduced to one year for the duration of the war, the special branches of Air Service, Tank Corps, and Chemical Warfare Service were created, the distinctions between Regular Army, National Guard, and National Army were abolished, and March succeeded in elevating his position to that of the highest-ranking officer in the army and the immediate military adviser to the civilian authority. This brilliant, hard-driving officer "lived, breathed, and slept efficiency." He also understood his task in Washington: "My position was that under the war power of the President I could do anything necessary to carry out the military program, and I invariably acted on that assumption." Between March and November 1918, General March helped swell the U.S. forces in France from 250,000 to 2,000,000—at a crucial time when Allied fortunes were at full ebb after the Italian defeat at Caporetto and Russia's withdrawal from the war. Secretary of War Baker unequivocably supported the endeavors of his chief of staff.

March's hard manner and cold efficiency naturally aroused fears among other military leaders. Generals Pershing and Harbord (qq.v.) especially disliked the manner in which March had increased the powers of his office, and the American field commander in France was apprehensive that March might seek to replace him. The army's top field commander and its chief of staff feuded in 1918 over a proposal to exchange staff officers regularly as well as over the right of promotions to general rank. Pershing desired control over the latter, hoping to reserve such

distinction for officers in France; March, on the other hand, had to consider the entire army in this regard. Finally, Pershing objected to March's decision to send Goethals to France as logistics chief, and he countered this feared move by appointing his friend Harbord to that position. March's memoirs, published in 1932, constituted an acid criticism of Pershing's writings of the war experience, and greatly fueled the so-called Pershing-March Feud.

General March retired as chief of staff on June 30, 1921. He died on April 13, 1955, in Washington, D.C.

Coffman, *Hilt of the Sword*; March, *The Nation at War*; *Dictionary of American Biography*, XXV Supplement Five.

MARGHILOMAN, Alexandru (*Rumania, Prime Minister*), was born in Buzau, Wallachia, July 4, 1854. In 1859 Wallachia and Moldavia, while nominally under Turkish sovereignty, joined to form a united and autonomous Rumanian state. After studying law and political science in Paris, Marghiloman returned to Rumania to begin an important career in that country's Conservative party in 1884.

At the outbreak of the war in 1914 Marghiloman was the leader of his party. The Conservatives soon split over whether to support the Entente or the Central Powers. To Marghiloman, an outspoken advocate of a tie with Germany, the best to be expected in a Francophile country was continued neutrality. He advocated this policy at the August 3, 1914, crown council at Sinaia, which decisively rejected implementing Rumania's secret defensive treaty with the Triple Alliance. As irredentist and pro-Entente fever rose in September, Marghiloman aligned himself with King Carol and Premier Bratianu (qq.v.) to urge continued neutrality. Far from being a ready collaborator with the Central Powers, Marghiloman pushed Carol to use Austria's plight to gain better treatment for Rumanians within the Austro-Hungarian empire. Bratianu apparently thought he could safeguard Rumania's interest, assuming victory for the Entente. On the other hand, as he told Marghiloman, the Conservative leader could take over and serve the same purpose in the event the Central Powers prevailed.

Marghiloman saw his party split in May 1915: pro-Entente figures like Filipescu demanded Rumania follow Italy's lead into the war. The German and Austrian victories of the following months raised rumors Marghiloman might replace Bratianu—a change the Central Powers urged—but the premier continued to dominate both Rumania's monarch and parliament. So long as Bratianu felt the time was not ripe for war, Rumania retained a friendly neutral stance toward the Entente, Marghiloman's will notwithstanding.

The summer of 1916 set Marghiloman on the road to power. He opposed Bratianu's decision to intervene in the hostilities, but agreed to remain silent to preserve the appearance of national unity. Nonetheless, he saw defeat as certain and hinted he would be there for the country to fall back upon. Autumn 1916 brought the military calamity he had foreseen. With a coterie of pro-German leaders, Marghiloman remained in Bucharest to perform what Seton-Watson called "the ungrateful but useful function" of dealing with the Germans. As president of the Rumanian Red Cross and a political leader of stature, he enjoyed a good relationship with the Germans. This he used during 1917 to warn off German and Rumanian leaders who advocated dethroning King Ferdinand (q.v.).

Russia's departure from the war made continued Rumanian participation impossible. During the first months of 1918, Austrian diplomats suggested that a Marghiloman ministry might mean lighter peace terms than those available to Bratianu's successor, General Averescu (q.v.). Bratianu agreed. Marghiloman was expendable if the fortunes of war were to turn, and Bratianu arranged his appointment.

Marghiloman took office on March 18, 1918. One of his desires was achieved quickly: Rumania was permitted by the Central Powers to annex Bessarabia, a territory it had long disputed with Russia. But otherwise Marghiloman failed to obtain mild peace terms. He continued to expect a German victory and sought substantial cooperation with the Central Powers, although it is unlikely he would have stood voluntarily aside for the direct military government the German High Command considered imposing in the spring of 1918. Marghiloman secured his domestic position by constructing a working relationship with King Ferdinand and contriving a parliamentary majority in blatantly rigged elections. Bratianu's Liberals were persecuted and several forced into exile.

The victorious Allied push in the Balkans (September/October 1918) made all of this futile. By early November the Germans had begun to evacuate their troops from Rumania. Alert diplomacy by the United States raised hopes in Bucharest for territorial gains in return for renewing hostilities. Bratianu persuaded the king that Marghiloman had served his purpose, and Ferdinand installed a new government on November 6.

Marghiloman remained an active figure in Rumanian politics during the years following the war, but he and his Conservative party were fatally compromised by their actions during the German occupation. Marghiloman justified his conduct by pointing to the annexation of Bessarabia, as well as his country's success in maintaining its dynasty and even part of its army in the aftermath of military disaster. Seton-Watson added a historian's endorsement to Marghiloman's self-justification, calling him Rumania's "one man in occupied territory who showed a gleam of statesmanship" in helping to save the dynasty, and overall a patriot who served his country well.

Marghiloman died at his birthplace, Buzau, on May 10, 1925. His five volumes of memoirs, *Notice Politice, 1897-1924*, appeared in Rumanian shortly after his death.

Kitchen, "Hindenburg, Ludendorff, and Rumania"; Seton-Watson, *History of the Roumanians*; Spector, *Rumania at the Peace Conference*; Torrey, "Irredentism and Diplomacy" and "Rumania's Decision to Intervene."

MARSHALL, Sir William Raine (*Great Britain, General*), was born in Stranton, near Hartlepool, on October 29, 1865, the son of a solicitor. He graduated from the Royal Military College, Sandhurst, in 1885, and thereafter saw service mostly in Ireland with the Sherwood Foresters. He was promoted captain in India in 1893 and four years later took part in the Malakand campaign. Marshall was sent to Malta in 1899, and from there went to South Africa to join the Seventh Mounted Infantry Battalion; he was cited for valor in the fighting around Bothaville. Marshall was promoted major in 1908 and four years later as colonel took command of the First Battalion of the Sherwood Foresters in India.

Sir William Marshall was ordered home in October 1914, and during the winter of 1914/1915 his battalion engaged as part of the Eighth Division in the fighting at Neuve Chapelle on the western front in water-logged trenches. In January 1915, Marshall was given the Eighty-seventh Brigade of the Twenty-ninth Division, then being formed for the projected Gallipoli campaign; on April 25 he led this unit during the landing at the so-called X beach. He proved to be cool under fire, and was promoted major general in June 1915. Toward the end of that year he took an active part in the evacuation of British forces from Cape Helles and Suvla Bay under Sir Charles Monro (q.v.).

From January to September 1916, Marshall commanded the Twenty-seventh Division at Salonika, but saw little action on the Macedonian front in this period. He was next entrusted with command of the III (Indian) Corps in Mesopotamia, and on February 24, 1917, led this unit in retaking Kut el Amara; this success was exploited on March 11 by the capture of Baghdad. In fact, the chief of the Imperial General Staff, Sir William Robertson, had admonished the local commander in "Mespot," Sir Stanley Maude (qq.v.), to press on towards Baghdad. It was feared in London that Grand Duke Nikolai (q.v.) of Russia, commanding the Army of the Caucasus, might take the fabled city on the River Tigris before the British.

When General Maude died of cholera in November 1917, Marshall replaced him as commander in chief of the Mesopotamia Expeditionary Force. Although the Seventh Division was taken from him and sent to General Edmund Allenby (q.v.) in Egypt, Marshall managed not only to hold his own in Mesopotamia, but also to force the surrender of the Turkish army on the Upper Tigris in October 1918, and to occupy the entire Mosul *vilayet*, or administrative district. In effect, the dream of a "Southern British World" was a reality: a semicircle including the entire Indian Ocean and passing through Africa from the Cape to Cairo, from Palestine through India to Australia, patrolled by British sea power.

Marshall was promoted lieutenant general in January 1919, and given the Southern Command, India, in August of that year. He retired in 1924, and died at Bagnoles de l'Orne, France, on May 29, 1939. Marshall had not been a theorist, much less a student of war, but a natural leader endowed with imperturbable courage and a gift for making the right decision quickly.

Guinn, *British Strategy and Politics*; Marshall, *Memories of Four Fronts*; *Dictionary of National Biography 1931-1940*.

MARTERER, Ferdinand Baron von (*Austria-Hungary, Field Marshal*), was born in Prague on October 30, 1862, to middle-class parents. He enrolled at the Infantry Cadet School in Prague in 1879 and served with the infantry in Bohemia and Moravia before attending the War Academy in 1887-1889. Next came a tour of duty with the General Staff and promotion to captain in 1892. Marterer again returned to the infantry, this time in Prague with the Ninety-first Infantry Regiment and in Vienna with the Thirteenth Infantry Division. In 1904 Emperor Francis Joseph (q.v.) appointed Marterer to his military chancellery and advancement and awards came quickly: promotion to colonel in 1905, ennoblement three years later, deputy to chancellery head Baron Arthur von Bolfras (q.v.) in 1910, and promotion to major general that same year.

During the first three years of the Great War,

Marterer was entrusted by the military chancellery with various missions between Schönbrunn and the front. Marterer, who before the war had belonged to the Belvedere Circle of Archduke Francis Ferdinand, was appointed adjutant general and chief of the military chancellery in the fall of 1916 by Emperor Charles (qq.v.). In this capacity Marterer has often been named in close connection with Charles' decision on March 1, 1917, to relieve General Conrad von Hötzendorf (q.v.) of his post of chief of the General Staff of the army. Marterer was promoted general of infantry in 1917 and although among the ruler's closest military advisers, his influence was marginal on the emperor, who fancied himself gifted in matters of military operations. In any case, Marterer had spent nearly two decades by now at the military chancellery and was far removed from the realities of the front. Charles raised him into the baronage in 1917, and the following year Marterer retired owing to ill health. He died in Vienna on January 29, 1919.

Führ, *Das K. u. K. Armeeoberkommando und die Innenpolitik in Österreich 1914-1917*; *Österreichisches Biographisches Lexikon 1815-1950*, VI.

MARWITZ, Georg von der (*Germany, General*), was born near Stolp/Pomerania on July 3, 1856, into an ancient Neumark noble clan with a long-standing record of military service. Marwitz entered the army in 1875 and spent many years of service in the General Staff. From 1900 until 1905 he commanded the prestigious Third Guards Cavalry Regiment; next he was appointed staff chief of the XVIII Army Corps, after which he returned to the guards cavalry, this time commanding the First Brigade. Marwitz was promoted major general in 1908 and lieutenant general three years later as chief of the Third Division. One year before the war he became inspector general of all cavalry.

On August 4, 1914, Marwitz commanded the German cavalry west of Aachen and led it into Belgium as far as Lille and Senlis in order to decoy the advance of the First and Second Armies. He was promoted general of cavalry on August 19, and fought with General Alexander von Kluck's (q.v.) First Army against the British at Le Cateau. Marwitz was rushed to the Ourcq River on September 5-9 and ordered to cover the exposed left wing of the First Army during the battle of the Marne; thereafter as part of the German retreat ordered by Colonel Richard Hentsch (q.v.), Marwitz withdrew behind the Aisne. By the end of September his cavalry stood at the Somme as part of Crown Prince Rupprecht's (q.v.) Sixth Army and fought at the battle of Arras the following month. Sent to Flanders and Artois in December, Marwitz, who was commanding eight cavalry divisions, took part in the race to the Channel and fought bloody engagements at Lille and Ypres. The advent of the machine gun, barbed wire, and poisonous gas greatly inhibited a force that still relied mainly on saber and lance.

On December 24, 1914, Marwitz was appointed head of the XXXVIII Reserve Corps, but soon was transferred to the eastern front where, in mid-February 1915, he took part in the winter battle of the Masurian Lakes as the right wing of General Hermann von Eichhorn's (q.v.) Tenth Army, which routed its Russian numerical counterpart. Marwitz next trapped the Russian XXII Army Corps at the Augustov forest and received the order *Pour le mérite* for this daring feat of midwinter cavalry action.

In March 1915, Marwitz was dispatched to Hungary to assume comand of the Beskiden Corps in an attempt to shore up the weak southern front. In April he repulsed the Russians in the Laborcza Valley in the Carpathians, and when General August von Mackensen (q.v.) broke the enemy's lines at Gorlice-Tarnów on May 2, Marwitz was able to join the broad advance and drive the Russians beyond Lemberg. Illness in July, however, forced him to rest.

By November 1915, Marwitz had sufficiently recuperated to assume command of the VI Army Corps at Péronne, where he engaged the British in trench warfare until June 1916. General Aleksei Brusilov's (q.v.) massive thrust against the Austro-Hungarians that same month brought Marwitz's VI Army Corps to the Carpathians in yet another attempt to hold the mountain passes and to prevent the enemy from deploying on the Hungarian plain. At Kovel, having received command of an army group, Marwitz managed not only to blunt Brusilov's attack, but also to regroup the beaten Fourth Army of Archduke Joseph Ferdinand (q.v.).

Marwitz returned to the western front on December 17, 1916, as head of the Second Army near St. Quentin, where he conducted trench warfare until March 1917. That month his troops were successfully withdrawn behind the Siegfried line in a defensive posture, but on November 20, 1917, Marwitz had the dubious honor of first experiencing mechanized warfare during the tank battle at Cambrai. By November 30 he had managed to counterattack and to force the enemy behind Cambrai.

On March 21, 1918, the Second Army advanced against Péronne as part of the overall Michael offensive. Marwitz next struck out for Amiens, the vital rail link where the British and French armies were joined, but he was forced to halt along the line Albert-Villers-Bretonneux. In April the Second Army engaged in bloody combat at the Somme as well as at the Ancre and Avre rivers. On August 8, in what General Erich Ludendorff (q.v.) termed the "black day of the German Army," Marwitz's units were mauled by enemy tank and infantry advancing under the cover of fog along the broad line Albert-Villers-Bretonneux; several divisions were totally destroyed —nearly 30,000 men were lost that day—in what became the worst German defeat in the Great War. Thereafter Marwitz was dispatched to Verdun to assume command of the Fifth Army in the Champagne, where he faced mainly American units. He retired from the army in December 1918. After the war, Marwitz became active in various officer clubs; he died of a heart attack in Wundichow on October 27, 1929.

Barnett, *Swordbearers*; Tschiwitz, *Marwitz*; *Geschichte der Ritter des Ordens*, II.

MASARYK, Thomas Garrigue (*Austria-Hungary, President*), was born in Hodonin, Moravia, on March 7, 1850, the son of a Slovakian coachman. After a brief apprenticeship as blacksmith, Masaryk studied at universities in Brünn and Vienna, where he attained the doctorate of philosophy in 1876. Six years later, when the University of Prague was divided into two sections, one German and the other Czech, Masaryk was appointed to a Czech professorship. He was extremely receptive to western trends in sociology and political science, and his journals, *Athenäum* and *Čas* especially, worked to counteract Czech romanticism. Masaryk never developed a philosophical system of his own; rather, he sought to synthesize German idealism and West European positivism. He also wrote widely on Marxism (which he opposed) and Russian history, religion, and philosophy. Pan-Slav ideals did not appeal to him.

From 1891 to 1893 Masaryk served as deputy of the Young Czech (Liberal) party in the Austrian Reichsrat as well as in the Bohemian Landtag. He returned to active politics in 1907 as deputy for the moderately left liberalist Realist party, and bitterly opposed the Dual Monarchy's alliance with Germany and its annexation of Bosnia-Herzegovina in 1908. Masaryk in 1880 had formally abandoned Catholicism for Protestantism, but soon embraced agnosticism.

At the outbreak of the war he at once came out for a western orientation as the solution to the question of Czech statehood. Specifically, Masaryk, in December 1914, fled Vienna and spent the next four years arguing for Czech independence in Switzerland, France, Britain, Italy, Russia, and the United States. He was ably assisted in his propagandistic efforts by Eduard Beneš (*q.v.*), secretary of the Czechoslovakian National Council of which Masaryk was president.

The Russian Revolution in 1917 gave Masaryk the opportunity to go to that country, and he successfully negotiated with Bolshevik leaders the formation of a Czech Legion, comprised of about 92,000 Czech deserters from the Austro-Hungarian army. In May 1918, Masaryk went to the United States, where he was to achieve his greatest publicity triumphs. On May 29, 1918, he persuaded Secretary of State Robert Lansing (*q.v.*) to issue a declaration of sympathy with the cause of Czech and Yugoslav independence; the Lansing declaration was approved by the Allied governments on June 3, 1918. Moreover, on June 30 in the so-called Pittsburgh Declaration, Masaryk attained the acceptance of American-Slovak leaders to the notion of a joint Czecho-Slovakian state. A realist, Masaryk credited the American actions more than the official proclamations of statehood by the Czech National Council on October 28 and the Slovak Council one day later for the founding of the new state. On November 14, 1918, Masaryk was elected "president and liberator" at Prague, and in 1920, 1927, and 1934 was reelected president of the Czechoslovakian republic. He retired in 1935 at the age of eighty-five, leaving the government in the hands of his beloved pupil, Beneš. Masaryk died in Castle Lana, near Prague, on September 14, 1937. Eleven years later his son Jan committed suicide rather than see his father's creation pass into Joseph Stalin's rule.

Herben, *Masaryk's Path and Legacy*, 3 vols.; Mamatey, *The United States and Eastern Central Europe 1914-1918*; Masaryk, *Die Weltrevolution*; *Österreichisches Biographisches Lexikon 1815-1950*, VI.

MAUDE, Sir Frederick Stanley (*Great Britain, General*), was born in Gibraltar on June 24, 1864, the younger son of General Sir Frederick Francis Maude. He was educated at Eton and Sandhurst, and in 1884 joined the Coldstream Guards, seeing action in the Sudan the following year. In 1895 Maude was at the Staff College, Camberley, and four years later accompanied the guards to South Africa. From 1901 to 1905 he was military secretary to the earl of Minto, governor general of Canada. Maude spent the next three years in secretarial appointments, and from 1908 until 1914 held staff assignments in England and in Ireland.

Early in August 1914, Maude joined the staff of General William Pulteney of the III Army Corps during the retreat from Mons, and took an active role in the ensuing battles of the Marne, the Aisne, Armentières, and the Lys. In October he was appointed brigadier general of the Thirteenth Brigade, and he led this unit in the counterattack at Neuve Chapelle. Maude was wounded at St. Eloi and came home in November. In May 1915, he rejoined his brigade, was promoted major general six weeks later as head of the Thirty-first Division, and in August was sent to the Dardanelles to command the Thirteenth Division. Maude found his unit at Anzac Cove badly mutilated: barely a single brigade remained after the battles for the Sari Bair heights. The division was transferred to Suvla Bay by Sir Ian Hamilton (*q.v.*), but in December Maude received instructions to prepare for the evacuation of his forces. The Thirteenth Division briefly made a stand at Cape Helles until this position, too, was evacuated in January 1916.

After a brief stay in Egypt, Maude's forces were ordered to Mesopotamia in February to reinforce the Tigris Corps in an attempt to relieve Sir Charles Townshend (*q.v.*), besieged at Kut el Amara by the Turks. But to no avail; the Ottoman forces could not be budged, and Kut fell on April 29, 1916. In July Maude received command of the Tigris Corps and the following month of the Army of Mesopotamia. For more than three months he carefully prepared his weary and disheartened troops for the eventual advance on Baghdad that had been promised as early as September 28, 1916 by Sir William Robertson (*q.v.*), chief of the Imperial General Staff. On December 12, Maude began a series of cautious siege operations that slowly evicted the Turks from their positions along the Tigris and its tributary, the Hai, with the result that on February 24, 1917, Kut el Amara was recaptured by the British. Enjoying a numerical superiority of at least four-to-one, Maude pushed on to Baghdad and on March 11, 1917, entered the legendary capital of Mesopotamia; ten days later he was promoted lieutenant general. But his victory was to be short-lived: on November 18, 1917, Maude died of cholera in Baghdad after drinking milk. He was a grand soldier, able and energetic, a born fighter who prided himself on being punctual and methodical.

Callwell, *Life of Sir Stanley Maude*; Guinn, *British Strategy and Politics*; Liddell Hart, *The Real War*; *Dictionary of National Biography 1912-1921*, Third Supplement.

MAUNOURY, Michel Joseph (*France, General*), was born on December 17, 1847, in Maintenon, southwest of Paris. He graduated from the École polytechnique and, as a young artillery lieutenant, fought with distinction in the defense of Paris during the Franco-Prussian War, 1870/1871. The next decades saw his steady climb from captain in 1874 to brigadier general in 1901. En route, he had served as an artillery instructor at St. Cyr and completed the War College (École supérieure de guerre) with honors. In 1905, promoted major general, Maunoury took command at the War College. Then came two tours as a corps commander and, at the apparent close of a distinguished career, a term as military governor of Paris (1910-1912) and membership on the Supreme War Council. In 1912 Maunoury reached retirement age and returned to his family home. The outbreak of World War I ended his quiet life as a gentleman farmer.

In the confused days of mid-August 1914, Maunoury was first sent to defend the area north of Verdun. His immediate task was to mold a collection of reservists and units lifted from other field armies into a new "Army of Lorraine." On August 26 the old artilleryman was given a more exciting mission. He was ordered to take command of another scratch force of reservists stiffened by units detached from various field armies; with these he set out to form a new Sixth Army on the Somme. General Joseph Joffre (q.v.), the commander in chief, intended to launch this force in a counterattack against the right flank of the wheeling German First Army near Amiens. That possibility vanished in the face of the rapid enemy advance. The aggressive Maunoury retreated reluctantly, meanwhile urging Joffre to let him attack at the first opportunity.

On September 4 the Sixth Army took up positions northeast of Paris. Maunoury was told to prepare for a counterattack on September 7. But General Gallieni (q.v.), military governor of Paris, convinced Joffre to move the offensive up to strike the exposed right flank of the German First Army east of Paris. On September 5 Maunoury hurriedly wheeled to his right, advanced blindly, and by early afternoon stumbled into the German flank defenses. Both Gallieni and Maunoury had expected to encounter the enemy only the following day.

Maunoury faced deep trouble, even as his blow knocked the overall German advance off stride. General von Kluck (q.v.) recalled his III and IX Corps from their advance south of the Marne to hurl these reinforcements at Manoury. Gallieni rushed reinforcements to the Sixth Army, the western anchor for a huge battle of the Marne that stretched from Paris to Verdun. One division arrived on the Ourcq to aid Maunoury via the famous fleet of Parisian taxi cabs. The hard-pressed Maunoury barely held on until September 9, when Kluck was ordered to retire to the Aisne. Maunoury and his exhausted troops pursued in the rain, trying unsuccessfully to outflank an enemy retreating in good order.

Maunoury's field service was cut short at the start of the spring campaign on the Aisne. In March 1915, while observing the enemy from the French forward line, the old general was severely wounded. Partially blinded, he managed to serve as military governor of Paris until 1916, then left active duty. He died on March 28, 1923. For his tenacious defense on the Ourcq in September 1914, Maunoury was named a marshal of France shortly after his death.

Beaufre, *La France de la Grande Guerre*; Isselin, *The Battle of the Marne*; *Larousse mensuel*, VI.

MAX, Prince of Baden (*Germany, Chancellor*), was born in Karlsruhe on July 10, 1867, cousin of the childless Grandduke Frederick II of Baden. Max embarked upon a military career, but in 1911 quit the service as brigade commander and instead pursued a doctorate of jurisprudence. In 1907 he became the heir presumptive to the throne of Baden; as such he automatically served as president of the Upper House at Karlsruhe. Concurrently, Max was a frequent guest of the Wagners in Bayreuth, and he greatly treasured their son-in-law, Houston Stewart Chamberlain.

Max von Baden, like other German princes, had virtually no influence upon the course of events in July 1914. He basically believed in Germany's innocence, arguing that Serbian complicity in the assassination of Archduke Francis Ferdinand (q.v.) as well as the precipitous Russian general mobilization had forced war upon Berlin. Once the fighting started, Max worked diligently to alleviate the plight of thousands of prisoners of war in Germany. Early in 1915 he began to recognize the need for a conciliatory peace. Influenced by men such as Paul Rohrbach, Kurt Hahn, and Johannes Müller, the prince opposed the resumption of unrestricted submarine warfare in February 1917 for fear that it would bring the United States into the conflict. On the other hand, he was, not surprisingly, a staunch monarchist and an opponent of democratic, parliamentary government for Germany.

After the fall of Chancellor Theobald von Bethmann Hollweg (q.v.) in July 1917, Max was considered a possible successor, but the highest political office in the land came to him only on October 3, 1918, after the dismissal of the inept Count Georg von Hertling (q.v.), a fellow south German. It is not unfair to state that Max was appointed chancellor because neither the kaiser, nor the generals, nor the parliamentary majority (Center, Progressives, Social Democrats) could agree on a rival candidate.

Rarely has a politician been appointed in more trying circumstances. The great spring offensive in France had been repulsed, the army's morale was rapidly deteriorating, the home front was racked by strikes and plagued by hunger, and the issue of parliamentary reform for Prussia continued to divide the political parties. Ironically, Max, a prince of the blood, on October 28 was to become the head of the first parliamentary government in German history after Wilhelm II (q.v.) agreed to institute cabinet responsibility and to curb his own powers in foreign and military affairs. Above all, Max's rhetoric was conventional and pale; as a wartime leader he was not of the same cut as the fiery David Lloyd George or Georges Clemenceau (qq.v.).

Already on the day before he was officially installed as chancellor, Prince Max had been brutally informed by the kaiser: "The Army Supreme Command considers it [an armistice] necessary, and you have not been summoned here to make any difficulties for the Army Supreme Command." Dutifully, on October 3/4 the chancellor appealed to President Woodrow Wilson (q.v.) for an end to the war on the basis of the Fourteen Points. In notes dated October 8, 14, and 24, the U.S. president called on Germany to evacuate all occupied territories, to curtail the submarine offensive, and to make no effort to reinforce her armies. Unfortunately, the prince's frail constitution failed him during these perilous days: he was bedridden from October 22 to 29. Yet surprisingly, on October 26 the kaiser concurred with his chancellor and forced the resignation of General Erich Ludendorff (q.v.), Germany's "silent dictator" since the fall of 1916. But three days later, Wilhelm took advantage of Max's illness to slip out of Berlin and to join army headquarters at Spa.

Max on November 1 completely broke down physically and mentally for thirty-six hours after a bitter telephone exchange with the kaiser concerning that leader's future as German emperor and Prussian king. When the chancellor recovered on November 3, he was a changed man, no longer directing but merely observing the course of German affairs. On November 5 Wilson finally agreed to accord Germany the needed armistice, but the following day Friedrich Ebert (q.v.) of the Social Democrats informed Max that his party demanded the kaiser's abdication by the morning of November 9. Every day, every hour then became crucial. As successor to the throne of Baden, Max felt hesitant to call upon Wilhelm to abdicate; a belated attempt to force this role upon Prince Friedrich Karl of Hesse failed for similar reasons. Still, Max hoped that a timely abdication might at least secure the throne for Wilhelm's eldest grandson under a regent, but the monarch refused to consider this alternative. By now even the military commanders, Field Marshal Paul

von Hindenburg and General Wilhelm Groener (qq.v.), were counseling abdication and exile, as the army no longer stood behind the emperor.

Wilhelm dawdled. In Berlin workers on the morning of November 9 poured into the streets to demand an end to the war. At noon on that day, having only vague hints from the army that Wilhelm would indeed abdicate, Max publicly announced the abdication of both Wilhelm II and Crown Prince Wilhelm (q.v.) for Prussia and Germany, and that a regency would be established for the crown prince's eldest son. Later that afternoon Philipp Scheidemann (q.v.) of the Social Democrats proclaimed the birth of the German republic, thereby frustrating Max's plans for a constitutional monarchy. In the end, the prince turned the reins of government over to Ebert and declined to assume the proposed regency.

Max's actions of November 9 later earned him the enmity not only of Wilhelm II and Crown Prince Wilhelm but also of army leaders, Conservatives, fellow princes, and Pan-Germans. Their denunciations were extremely unfair. When Max finally acted, it was not only with the greatest reluctance but also with the full knowledge that the fleet had mutinied, that rebellious sailors had seized the major ports, and that the ruling princes of Braunschweig and Bavaria had already abdicated in the face of revolution. If anything, Max's pronouncement constituted a simple recognition of existing conditions. He retired to his castle at Salem to write his memoirs. Prince Max died there on November 6, 1929, at the age of sixty-two.

Max von Baden was not a man of action, not a great statesman. Sensible, decent, honest, straightforward, he administered the six-week transition period in German history from the Hohenzollern Empire to the Weimar Republic. Neither his physical constitution nor the military situation permitted any other course.

Max von Baden, *Erinnerungen und Dokumente*; Morsey and Matthias, *Regierung des Prinzen Max*; Ritter and Miller, *Die deutsche Revolution*; *Biographisches Wörterbuch zur Deutschen Geschichte*, II.

MAYO, Henry Thomas (*United States, Admiral*), was born in Burlington, Vermont, on December 8, 1856, the son of a steamboat captain. Mayo graduated from the Naval Academy in 1876 and was assigned to the Pacific Station. He rose in rank from commander in 1905 to captain in 1908, and during this period commanded the cruisers *Albany* and *California*. In 1913 Rear Admiral Mayo was assigned to the Navy Department as personnel aide to Secretary of the Navy Josephus Daniels (q.v.); thereafter came command of the Fourth Division,

Atlantic Fleet. In April 1914, Mayo became the center of the "Tampico Incident" when Mexican authorities arrested a boat's crew unwarrantedly. Mayo demanded disciplinary action against those responsible, a public apology, and a twenty-one gun salute to the U.S. flag. The latter request was refused by the Mexican government; President Wilson (q.v.) fully backed his naval commander, afterwards ordering the occupation of Veracruz. In 1915 Mayo was promoted to the grade of vice admiral, and on June 16, 1916, appointed commander in chief, Atlantic Fleet, with the rank of admiral.

President Wilson sent Mayo to Europe in August 1917 "to go over and find a way to break up the hornet's nest and not to try to kill individual hornets over a forty-acre lot." Mayo relayed the president's homely analogy concerning the German submarine menace to the first lord of the Admiralty, Sir Eric Geddes (q.v.), by informing him "you cannot make omelettes without breaking eggs, and . . . war is made up of taking risks." At the root of this obtuse language lay the president's conviction that the Allies "ought to convoy" merchant shipping. Mayo was not impressed by Admiral Jellicoe's (q.v.) proposal to sink eighty-three old battleships and cruisers filled with concrete in the Helgoland Bight in order to pen up the German fleet in its North Sea lairs. In general, Mayo was disappointed over the nature of his discussions in London, feeling that too much time was being frittered away on generalities. Upon his return to Washington, the admiral recommended emphasis on production of antisubmarine forces rather than improvement of existing naval equipment. In particular, Mayo favored a North Sea mine barrage from Scotland to Norway; the General Board agreed in October 1917 that this was "the only big thing the combined navies could do."

After the war, Mayo was entrusted with command of the redesignated U.S. Fleet, a position that he held from January to June 30, 1919. Mayo died on February 23, 1937, at Portsmouth, New Hampshire. His single-mindedness and almost self-obliterating devotion to the navy greatly facilitated its efficiency during the war. Fleet Admiral Ernest J. King characterized Mayo as "the best, the ablest, and the most competent of all the flag officers of the United States Navy down to the end of World War I."

Trask, *Captains & Cabinets*; *Dictionary of American Biography*, XXII Supplement Two.

MERCIER, Désiré Joseph (*Belgium, Cardinal*), was born on November 22, 1851, in the village of Braine l'Alleud, south of Brussels. The son of a tanner, Mercier was ordained a priest in 1874. The young cleric distinguished himself early as a talented theologian and philosopher. At thirty-one years of age, Mercier was awarded the newly founded chair in Thomistic theology at the University of Louvain. In his writing, the young Mercier sought a synthesis between Thomistic philosophy and modern scientific ideas. He established (in 1894) an autonomous Institute of Philosophy within the university and founded his own philosophical journal.

In 1906 Mercier saw his life take an abrupt turn when Pope Pius X named him archbishop of Malines, the largest diocese in Belgium. The following year he received the red hat of a cardinal. As primate of Belgium, Cardinal Mercier stood alongside King Leopold II and, after 1909, young King Albert I (q.v.) as a symbol of unity in a deeply divided country. Aside from its linguistic squabbles, Belgium was seriously split over the issue of compulsory military service, the establishment of undiluted universal suffrage, and the role of the Catholic church in primary education. Mercier's political weight went on the scales in the debate over all such national issues. He backed the establishment of general military service and vocally took his stand as a fiery Belgian patriot even before 1914.

When World War I overwhelmed the small country and sent the king and government fleeing to Belgium's remote northwestern corner, Mercier gladly inherited the role of spokesman for the nation. The death of Pope Pius X in late August 1914 compelled Mercier to travel to Rome for the conclave. He returned to Louvain to find his university in flames and nearly the entire country under military occupation. Pastoral letters served as his vehicle for promoting resistance. He began with his Christmas letter of 1914, "Patriotism and Endurance," in which he reminded Belgian churchgoers that their loyalty still belonged to the king and the Belgian government. "There can be no perfect Christian," he wrote, "who is not a perfect patriot." By July 1916, in his Independence Day sermon, he was telling his listeners to find "austere beauty" in this "just war."

German military authorities would gladly have deported Mercier, as they did many less visible Belgian clerics. To do this, however, meant stirring anti-German feeling in neutral countries, as well as troubling Germany's own Catholic population. From October 1916 to February 1917, Mercier conducted a campaign opposing the forced deportation of Belgian workers to Germany. Appealing to Pope Benedict XV (q.v.), to neutral powers, and to local German military commanders as well, Mercier saw the pressure on Berlin become intolerable. By mid-1917, the deportees had returned.

The cardinal likewise criticized German efforts to split the Belgian population by promoting Flemish nationalism. In 1917 he wrote Premier Charles de Broqueville (q.v.), heading the exiled government in residence in Le Havre, to castigate the "treason" of Flemish notables who accepted the blandishments of the enemy.

Mercier applied his powerful pen to the debate over the peace settlement in 1919. In particular, the church leader opposed the enthusiasm of some political figures for the annexation of Dutch border regions. That same year, he toured the United States and Canada to find himself received as a wartime hero. During his last years, he took up the cause of ecumenism, meeting with Anglican leaders to begin to bridge the centuries-old divisions in European Christianity. In 1925 Mercier was discovered to be suffering from cancer; he died in Brussels on May 23, 1926.

Paul Hymans (q.v.), Belgian foreign minister in the last year of the war, called Mercier "the symbol of patriotism." Indeed, no other leader in the occupied nations of World War I acted with such force and effectiveness as the theology professor turned cardinal.

Beauduin, *Le Cardinal Mercier*; Gade, *The Life of Cardinal Mercier*; Kossmann, *The Low Countries*; *Biographie nationale*, XXX; *Larousse mensuel*, VII.

METAXAS, John (*Greece, Colonel*), was born in Ithaca, April 12, 1871, the son of a member of the Greek Parliament. After graduating from the Athens Military Academy with a commission in the engineers, he fought with distinction in Greece's unsuccessful war against Turkey in 1897. He continued an exemplary military career by compiling a brilliant record at the War Academy in Berlin, 1899-1903. As a General Staff officer during the Balkan Wars, 1912/1913, he drafted plans for a future seizure of the Dardanelles by the Greek army.

At the outbreak of World War I Colonel Metaxas was deputy chief of staff of the Greek army. Greek foreign policy soon became a contest of wills between Prime Minister Venizelos and King Constantine (qq.v.); the circle of military advisers close to the monarch played a crucial role. In Leon's view, Metaxas soon became "the most influential military man in the king's immediate entourage." At critical moments, Metaxas reinforced Constantine's long-standing respect and sympathy for the Central Powers. The brilliant young officer saw a clear-cut Entente victory as unlikely. On the contrary, he assumed German military power was going to determine the outcome of the war and German culture was destined to dominate Europe's future.

Metaxas opposed cooperation with a British move against the Dardanelles when London first approached the Greek government in early September 1914. Allied pressure intensified in early 1915, and Venizelos urged the king to accept proferred rewards of territory in Asia Minor. Along with diplomatic advisers like George Streit, Metaxas held Constantine to a neutral course. Metaxas pointed to the difficulties in establishing and maintaining military control over the areas the Entente held out. When Venizelos seemed about to win Constantine over in early March, Metaxas again used telling military arguments to halt the king: Constantine heard his trusted military adviser state that hopes of effective army operations at Gallipoli were unfounded. Venizelos resigned.

As Bulgaria mobilized in late September 1915 and Anglo-French forces prepared to land at Salonika, Metaxas provided Constantine with the usual cogent military arguments to protest this Allied presence. Athens, he noted, had made no plans for joint operations with Britain and France to aid Serbia. Moreover, Greek mobilization, to comply with the Greco-Serb defense treaty of 1913, would be disrupted by improvised attempts to cooperate with the Entente.

The successful offensive of the Central Powers against Serbia brought the war to Greece's northern borders. Metaxas now acted as Constantine's link to the German High Command, pledging to intern the retreating Serbs and to "neutralize" the Anglo-French forces now established in Macedonia. Metaxas pushed Constantine to draw closer to Berlin. Along with other influential army officers, Metaxas pictured a German advance against Salonika as a means of liberating Greek territory from an Anglo-French invasion. In January 1916, he urged Constantine to slip off to northern Greece, where the monarch could rally Greek troops to fight alongside the Central Powers. The hesitant king rejected such suggestions. But Metaxas and the General Staff provided intelligence information for the Bulgarian army, purged Venizelist officers from the Greek army, and, in May 1916, permitted the Bulgars to seize the strategic border position of Fort Rupel.

Allied demands for the demobilizaton of the Greek army led Metaxas to organize the Reservist Leagues, powerful paramilitary organizations devoted to the king. Allied pressure led to a nominal purge of the General Staff in August. Packed off to run an officers school, Metaxas nonetheless continued his role as adviser to Constantine. In November 1916, he helped reverse Constantine's drift to conciliate the Entente by surrendering a large number of heavy guns. The ensuing "Battle of Athens" in early December saw royalist troops fighting French and British marines. Constantine's days were numbered. Metaxas helped organize guerrilla units in Macedonia, and he called again for Constantine to flee northward to lead the Greek army into battle side by side with the Germans. When Constantine was deposed and exiled in June 1917, Metaxas and his like-minded colleagues of the General Staff were exiled to Corsica.

World War I merely marked Metaxas' debut as a major Greek figure. He continued to play a leading role as a monarchist politician and antirepublican revolutionary. In 1936 a military coup made him dictator of Greece. Despite his creation of a regime that borrowed freely from Fascist political practice, Metaxas saw no ally in Italy. His military talents intact, he led the Greek army in humiliating Mussolini's forces in the fall of 1940. His death in Athens on January 29, 1941, spared him the need to fight against German forces the following spring.

Leon, *Greece and the Great Powers*; Stavrianos, *Balkans since 1453*; Theodoulou, *Greece and the Entente*; *Larousse mensuel*, XI.

MICHAELIS, Georg (*Germany, Chancellor*), was born into an old Prussian civil service family on September 8, 1857, at Haynau, Silesia; one of his ancestors had been Frederick the Great's first bourgeois finance minister. Upon completion of theological and juridical studies, Michaelis entered the Prussian justice ministry in 1879; from 1885 to 1889 he served as instructor at the German Law School in Tokyo. In 1892, upon his return from Japan, he joined the Prussian administration as counselor at Trier and in 1895 at Arnsberg; three years later he was director for schools and churches in the Ministry of Culture. In 1900 Michaelis became deputy to the administrative president in Liegnitz, and two years thereafter lord lieutenant in Breslau. By 1905 Michaelis had returned to Berlin as privy councillor and four years later assumed the post of undersecretary in the Prussian Ministry of Finance.

Immediately after the outbreak of war in August 1914, Michaelis became head of a newly created war grain trade society; the following year he was named director of the imperial department for the control of the grain trade. In February 1917, Michaelis was appointed state commissioner for the national food supply, therewith apparently capping a long career in the Prussian civil service.

To almost everyone's surprise, Michaelis was selected by General Erich Ludendorff on July 14, 1917, to succeed Theobald von Bethmann Hollweg (*qq.v.*) as imperial chancellor and Prussian minister president. It apparently was Ludendorff's hope that this colorless but hard-working bureaucrat could calm the troubled waters lapping at the very base of the Prussian/German constitutional system. In this the general was to be disappointed. Not familiar with the world of politics, Michaelis was unable to control the parliamentary majority, against whose will he had been appointed, and equally unable to exert any moderating influence over Ludendorff. The chancellor was forced to accept the Reichstag's "peace resolution" of July 19, 1917, which demanded an end to the war without annexations or indemnities. He did so only by attaching to it the caveat "as I understand it." Thereafter, Michaelis' fortunes ebbed rapidly. He proved unwilling to articulate a clear stand on Germany's policy vis-à-vis Belgium during the Vatican peace initiative that year. As Prussian minister president he failed to draft reform proposals of the innocuous three-class voting system as promised in the kaiser's Easter message. In October the chancellor was further compromised when he attempted to uphold Admiral Eduard von Capelle's (*q.v.*) unfounded assertion that members of the Independent Social Democratic party had instigated a mutiny in the fleet. His subsequent inability to prevent the formation of a solid Reichstag front from Center to Social Democrats clearly revealed his weakness as chancellor, and on October 31, 1917, he resigned, to be replaced one day later by Count Georg von Hertling (*q.v.*).

Michaelis finished the war as lord lieutenant of the province of Pomerania; he quit government service in April 1919. Thereafter he devoted his time to church activities and to welfare work on behalf of students. Michaelis died in Bad Saarow in the Mark Brandenburg on July 24, 1936. He had been appointed chancellor as a compromise candidate because neither of the army's two top choices, Bernard von Bülow and Alfred von Tirpitz (*q.v.*), was acceptable to the kaiser; as chancellor, Michaelis simply proved unable to tack an independent course between generals and parliamentary majority. His pious statement of July 1917, "with God's help I will give it a try!" fully summed up his modest political talents.

Fischer, *Griff nach der Weltmacht*; Kitchen, *Silent Dictatorship*; Michaelis, *Für Volk und Staat*; *Biographisches Wörterbuch zur Deutschen Geschichte*, II.

MICHELER, Joseph Alfred (*France, General*), was born in Phalsbourg, France, in 1861. By 1916 he commanded the French Tenth Army at the battle of the Somme. His performance there earned him promotion to army group commander.

At the start of 1917 General Robert Nivelle (*q.v.*), newly appointed commander in chief of the French army, was preparing an offensive northward against the Germans on the Chemin des Dames. Micheler took charge of the Reserve Army Group, which consisted of the Fifth, Sixth, and Tenth armies and was charged with penetrating the German position, driving into open country, and bringing the war to a quick conclusion. Micheler soon developed doubts about Nivelle's prospects for success. The rugged terrain, the poor access roads, the bad weather all militated against a victory at tolerable cost, even a lesser victory than the one Nivelle pledged. At the same time, Micheler was unwilling to confront Nivelle directly with his doubts; although these doubts were shared by the army's other group commanders and many of the rest of the ranking field officers involved in planning the operation.

To add to the dim prospects for the coming campaign, Micheler found he was not, in fact, commander over the Sixth Army. There, General Charles Mangin (*q.v.*), Nivelle's friend and protégé, operated on his own: he set unrealistic objectives for his army in the coming assault and, when challenged by Micheler, appealed directly to Nivelle.

Micheler's only solution to this tangle was to send covert messages to political leaders. War Minister Paul Painlevé (*q.v.*), for example, was made clearly aware of the army's doubts about the coming offensive. From late March until the climactic gathering of civil and military leaders at Compiègne on April 6, the issue hung in doubt. But Nivelle met Micheler's silence at Compiègne by renewed pledges of victory joined to a threat to resign if his plans were countermanded.

The Nivelle fiasco hurt, but did not destroy, Micheler's career. The Reserve Army Group was dissolved and Micheler reverted to command the Fifth Army. There, in December 1917, he criticized General Pétain (*q.v.*), the new French commander in chief, for excessive caution in arranging French defenses! Micheler spent his last days in the field in the spring of 1918. On the old battleground of the Chemin des Dames, German troops smashed the French defenses and drove southward toward the Marne in late May. Micheler and his neighbor at the Sixth Army, General Duchêne, both of whom had ignored Pétain's call for a defense in depth, were both dismissed.

Micheler died in Nice in 1931.

Beaufre, *La France de la Grande Guerre*; King, *Generals and Politicians*; Ryan, *Pétain the Soldier*; Spears, *Prelude to Victory*.

MILIUKOV, Paul Nikolaevich (*Russia, Minister of Foreign Affairs*), was born in Moscow on January 27, 1859, son of a prominent architect. Trained as a historian, he seemed destined for a brilliant academic career when a government order in 1895 barred him from all educational employment in Russia. Penalized in this fashion for his political liberalism, Miliukov responded by spending most of the following decade abroad, teaching in the Balkans, Britain, and the United States. During these years he won a place as a major figure in Russian liberal politics. He was a founding father of the Constitutional Democratic party (the so-called Kadets) in 1905, and he became the leading policymaker for the Kadet delegation in the Duma, the quasi-parliament established in 1906. Barred from running in the first two elections to the Duma, Miliukov finally became a Duma deputy in 1907.

Although the Kadet program included sweeping proposals for land reform, Miliukov put his most enthusiastic efforts behind the push for political change. He hoped and expected Russia's autocracy to evolve into a constitutional monarchy similar to Britain's. Frustrated in his efforts to attain such reform in domestic affairs, Miliukov, between 1907 and 1914, developed a strong interest in foreign policy.

With the outbreak of hostilities in 1914, Miliukov became an ardent supporter of the war effort. Military victory, he hoped, would enhance Russia's status as a great power, specifically by the acquisition of the Turkish Straits and the city of Constantinople. Moreover, he expected the wartime alliance with Britain and France to help bend Russia's autocratic government toward liberal reform. In 1915 he began to criticize the government's inept prosecution of the war, and he led in the formation of the Progressive Bloc, a loose association of Duma liberals and conservatives who called for more capable ministerial leadership. Miliukov's attacks on the regime reached a climax in a bitter speech in the Duma in November 1916 in which he obliquely attacked the Empress Alexandra as well as Prime Minister Sturmer (*qq.v.*).

Following the March 1917 Revolution, Miliukov took the post of foreign minister and dominated the provisional government during its early months. He was unable to perceive or accept the need for sweeping social reforms or shifts in Russian foreign policy. Instead, he urged that Russia fight the war to a victorious conclusion and collect the prize of the Turkish Straits. Miliukov's foreign policy became the first important cause of friction between the provisional government and the more radical Petrograd Soviet. Unyielding in his commitment to war aims and political ideals that antedated the March Revolution, Miliukov was pushed aside by events. Soviet pressure, given weight by massive street demonstrations, forced his resignation in May 1917. Russia began to depart from its wartime alliance.

Miliukov maintained his role as a pillar of moderate liberalism. He led the Kadets in their effort to limit the scope of the revolution, and vigorously opposed Lenin (*q.v.*) and the Bolsheviks. After the November Revolution, he was threatened with arrest and fled to the Don, where White opposition to the new Bolshevik regime was gathering. His final role in wartime Russia was a futile attempt in the summer of 1918 to ally German occupation forces in the Ukraine with the White army of General Alekseev (*q.v.*). He emigrated to France in 1919, where he lived and worked as a writer and journalist until his death on March 31, 1943.

Miliukov, *Political Memoirs, 1905-1917*; Pearson, *The Russian Moderates and the Crisis of Tsarism*; Riha, *A Russian European*; Rosenberg, *Liberals in the Russian Revolution*.

MILLERAND, Alexandre (*France, Minister of War*), was born in Paris, February 9, 1859. His father was a Catholic wine merchant; his mother came from the Jewish bourgeoisie, a shopkeeper's family originally settled in Alsace. Millerand studied at the law faculty of the University of Paris; a friend at school and during his early years of practice was Raymond Poincaré (*q.v.*). The future war minister found his year of military service in 1879/1880 a pleasant and satisfying break from the law student's grind. As a young attorney, Millerand defended striking miners and Socialists, was elected to the Paris Municipal Council in 1884, and reached the Chamber of Deputies at the age of twenty-six. Originally tied to the Radicals, he drifted to the Left, and was reelected in 1889 after running as an independent. Millerand was drawn to socialism in the early 1880s, but, as one historian, Philip M. Williams, has put it, he became "the pioneer on the well-travelled road to fame and power which winds its tortuous way from Left to Right." During the Dreyfus affair, he advised President Loubet to include a Socialist in the projected cabinet of republican concentration. Millerand offered the name of René Viviani (*q.v.*), but he clearly knew himself to be the logical choice. His acceptance of the Ministry of Commerce in 1899 sparked a crisis that extended beyond French socialism to disrupt the entire Second International.

Millerand was an active and reforming minister of commerce, but he increasingly omitted the rhetoric of the class struggle cherished by Socialist militants and instead stressed the role of government activism on behalf of the working class. In 1903 he came out against international disarmament and further alienated his old comrades. Expelled from several French Socialist organizations in 1904, he was a man without a party. As minister of public works under Aristide Briand (*q.v.*) in 1909/1910, he opposed the premier's rough-and-ready device of conscripting railway workers into the army to halt their strike. Briand removed him from the government in 1910. That same year, he joined the loosely tied "Republican-Socialist" party in the Chamber of Deputies.

In 1912 Millerand entered Poincaré's cabinet as minister of war, a post he occupied for over a year. His most recent biographer, Leslie Derfler, has held that "the year [1912] may be taken to mark his ideological passage into the nationalist camp." It clearly set the tenor for his wartime role in the Cabinet. Millerand placed full confidence in the military High Command to run its own affairs, and his first act was to destroy the political dossiers that previous war ministers had used to guide promotions. By abolishing the post of army chief of staff, he placed authority to run the military's daily affairs and to plan for future war in the hands of General Joffre (*q.v.*), the recently appointed chief of the General Staff. Millerand supported Joffre's intention to limit the use of reservists in the early stages of a future war, and generally expressed satisfaction with the army's readiness for whatever external challenge France might face.

During 1913 Millerand strongly supported the three-year service law. With the outbreak of the war, his administrative talents and experience made him a logical candidate for a cabinet post. He joined the *union sacrée* government in late August in his old post of war minister, serving for over a year. Millerand differed from his several successors in making no substantial effort to enter the realm of military strategy and operations; he administered the civilian war effort and left the direction of the fighting to Joffre. The controversy that swirled around him in 1914/1915 had to do with his determination to shield Joffre from those who criticized him, to permit the High Command to function without close civilian control. Historians have been harsh on Millerand, who has been characterized as Joffre's "echo," "mouthpiece," and "sentry."

On August 30, 1914, Millerand urged the government to depart Paris for a safer location. This reflected Joffre's position, and thenceforth Millerand stood guard between Joffre and the government. Millerand refrained from passing to his cabinet colleagues the information he received from General

Gallieni (q.v.) during the battle of the Marne. At the close of 1914 he stood against the return of the government to Paris. It was only a short drive from Paris to Joffre's headquarters; Millerand feared proximity meant a surge in civilian interference in the military conduct of the war. His major achievement in 1914 stemmed from the shell crisis. The French army was down to a scant one month reserve of artillery ammunition by mid-September. Millerand and leading manufacturers met at Bordeaux on September 20 to work out a new production system. A massive buying program abroad, largely in the United States, helped, and by December, the output of artillery shells had tripled.

The start of 1915 brought even greater strains between leaders in the National Assembly and the generals. Millerand again stood with the army. The claimed right of parliamentary committees to visit the combat zone stirred intense feeling in both camps. Millerand did his best to keep civilian leaders away from the War Ministry; Poincaré himself was rebuked for an unauthorized visit! Even Millerand had to bend under the predictable outcry on this issue and on the right of parliamentary committees to visit the factories that were producing military equipment.

Millerand parted company with Joffre on only one major issue: the commander in chief bluntly refused to designate two of his divisions to serve in the eastern Mediterranean to support the planned naval attack on the Dardanelles. Millerand drew them in February from rear area depots and North African garrisons outside Joffre's jurisdiction. It was a significant step: major units of the French army were in the field but, for the first time, not under Joffre's control.

Millerand's fall nearly came in the summer of 1915. Angry at his position on parliamentary inspections of the combat zone, leaders in the National Assembly moved to dilute his power: allegedly to keep him from being overtaxed, they set up undersecretaries in the War Ministry who took over several of Millerand's functions. Prime Minister Viviani saw his position endangered by Millerand and considered firing him. The need to preserve the union sacrée helped protect Millerand; moreover, the army High Command made it clear it opposed such a change. Viviani vacillated, then subsided.

Millerand stood alone in the Cabinet in backing Joffre's ouster of General Sarrail (q.v.), the darling of the Left, in July. As tempers rose in the Chamber of Deputies, the war minister strained to hasten Sarrail's departure for the Dardanelles. He was more successful in shielding Joffre's fall offensive in Champagne from moves to divert several divisions for Sar-

rail. The Left rejected the view Sarrail must wait for reinforcements. In a bitter Chamber debate in late August, Millerand alluded publicly to the Sarrail controversy. It was a serious breach of the civil-military etiquette of the war, in which the Chamber avoided open references to differences on the conduct of the war. The government barely survived as Viviani begged for unity. In October Viviani gave way to Briand, and Millerand to Gallieni.

Millerand was appointed commissioner general for Alsace-Lorraine in 1919. He held the premiership briefly in 1920, then served as president of France, 1920-1924. After long service in the Senate, he died in Versailles, April 7, 1943.

Cassar, *The French and the Dardanelles*; Derfler, *Alexandre Millerand: The Socialist Years*; Goldberg, *The Life of Jean Jaurès*; King, *Generals and Politicians*; Ralston, *The Army of the Republic*; Tanenbaum, *General Maurice Sarrail*; *Dictionnaire des parlementaires français*, VI.

MILNE, Sir Archibald Berkeley (*Great Britain, Admiral*), second baronet, was born at the Admiralty on June 2, 1855, the son of Admiral of the Fleet Sir Alexander Milne. After a short stint at Wellington College, Milne entered the Royal Navy in 1869. For the next thirteen years he served on various units of the fleet and took part in expeditions to put down native uprisings in Africa. In 1882 Arky Barky, as he was known in the service, was assigned to the royal yacht *Victoria and Albert*; he was promoted to the grades of commander in 1884, captain in 1891, rear admiral in 1904, vice admiral in 1908, and admiral three years later. From 1905 to 1912 Milne was second in command of the Atlantic Fleet, then of the Channel Fleet, and finally of the Home Fleet. In November 1912, he was appointed commander in chief in the Mediterranean—a post that came his way primarily owing to court influence. It is generally conceded that Milne was of inferior caliber, utterly lacking in vigor and imagination, and that he owed his various appointments to high favor.

In all fairness, it must be stated that the situation in the Mediterranean in the fall of 1914 was extremely muddled. Would Austria-Hungary go to war at once? Would Italy uphold the Triple Alliance? What would Turkey do? The Admiralty in London initially ordered Arky Barky to assist the French navy in ferrying African troops to France and to bring to action the German ships stationed in the Mediterranean Sea: the battle cruiser *Goeben* and the light cruiser *Breslau*, commanded by Rear Admiral Wilhelm Souchon (q.v.). Unfortunately, the French did not bother to inform Milne of their plans, with the result that the Admiralty ordered the British commander to

Malta. In the ensuing confusion, the *Goeben* and the *Breslau*, after taking on coal at neutral Messina, turned east instead of west as expected, and owing to superior speed outran Admiral Troubridge's (*q.v.*) cruiser squadron to the Dardanelles and to Constantinople, thereby encouraging Turkey's entry into the war on the side of the Central Powers.

While the Admiralty officially "approved measures taken by him in all respects," Milne nevertheless was severely criticized in the press and certain naval circles for his failure to engage the two enemy cruisers. Admiral John Fisher (*q.v.*), who as early as 1909 had depicted Milne as "a serpent of the lowest type," was livid when he heard of the escape of the German vessels. "Personally I should have shot Sir Berkeley Milne for the *Goeben*." Somewhat more subdued, Admiral David Beatty (*q.v.*) was nonetheless equally shocked: "God, it makes me sick." These negative reactions partly account for the fact that the navy apparently found no further opportunity of employment for Milne after his return to London on August 18, 1914; he was placed on the retirement list at the end of the war and spent his remaining days at his ancestral residence of Inveresk Gate, Musselburgh.

Milne in 1921 rather ably defended his actions in the Mediterranean against Sir Julian Corbett's account of the affair in the official *History of the Great War: Naval Operations* and the implied censure of Milne's conduct. More recent investigation by Ulrich Trumpener has partly vindicated Milne's actions by pointing out the confused state of Admiralty thinking on the Mediterranean in August 1914, and the resulting lack of clear directives to the commander at Malta. Yet in the final analysis Marder was right in stating that "Milne was not much good."

Corbett, *Naval Operations*, I; Marder, *Dreadnought to Scapa Flow*, II; Milne, *Flight of the "Goeben" and "Breslau"*; Trumpener, "Escape of the *Goeben* and *Breslau*"; *Dictionary of National Biography 1931-1940*.

MILNE, George Francis (*Great Britain, Field Marshal*), first Baron Milne, was born in Aberdeen on November 5, 1866, the son of a banker. Milne went to the Royal Military Academy at Woolwich and in 1885 was gazetted to the Royal Artillery. Twelve years later he attended the Staff College, Camberley, and, that same year, accompanied Sir H. H. Kitchener (*q.v.*) up the Nile and directed artillery fire at the battle of Omdurman. Milne was attached to Kitchener's intelligence staff during the Boer War as brevet lieutenant colonel. In 1913 he became commander of the artillery of the Fourth Division (Woolwich), and led this unit in France in August 1914 during the bat-

tles of Le Cateau, the Marne, and the Aisne. When Sir John French (*q.v.*) transferred the British Expeditionary Force to Flanders in October, Milne was promoted brigadier general; the next year promotion to major general on the General Staff of the Second Army followed.

Milne's career shifted radically when he was given command of the Twenty-seventh Division and ordered to Salonika: he was chosen for this post primarily because it was believed that he was sufficiently strong of character to resist the blandishments of the French General Maurice Sarrail (*q.v.*), the overall Allied field commander in Greece. In January 1916, Milne was entrusted with command of the XVI Corps, and later that year with all British forces at Salonika under General Sarrail, and then those under General Franchet d'Esperey (*q.v.*).

The story of the British at Salonika is one of frustration: Milne possessed insufficient troops, his units suffered from disease, and they labored under the difficulty of the terrain. The chief of the Imperial General Staff, Sir William Robertson (*q.v.*), opted for a cautious stance in Greece against the Bulgars. It was not until April 24, 1917, that Milne was finally ordered to go on the attack near Lake Dorain, and he was repulsed with heavy losses. French and Serbian forces were finally able to advance against Bulgaria in 1918 and, after the collapse of the Sofia government, Milne advanced to the Turkish frontier, eventually occupying Constantinople after the fall of the Ottoman Empire.

Milne remained at the Porte until November 1920, being promoted general that same year. Two years later he was given the Eastern Command at home, and in 1926 was appointed chief of the Imperial General Staff. He was promoted field marshal in 1928 and five years later retired as Baron Milne, of Salonika and Rubislaw, county of Aberdeen. Milne spent the Second World War enrolled in the Home Guard, and died in London on March 23, 1948. He was known for his keen wit, immense energy, and penetrating intellect.

Falls, *History of the Great War. Military Operations: Macedonia*, 2 vols.; Guinn, *British Strategy and Politics*; *Dictionary of National Biography 1941-1950*.

MILNER, Alfred (*Great Britain, Secretary of State for War*), Viscount Milner, was born in Giessen, Hesse-Darmstadt, on March 23, 1854, the son of a British physician. After high school in Tübingen, Germany, Milner was educated at King's College, London, and at Balliol College, Oxford, where he struck up friendships with H. H. Asquith (*q.v.*) and Arnold Toynbee. After a brief fling at journalism with the *Pall Mall Gazette*, Milner helped found a new university settlement in East London, Toynbee Hall. Later he secured a post in the financial administration of Egypt; he came home in 1892 to take over the chairmanship of the Board of Inland Revenue.

In the spring of 1897, two years after the notorious Jameson Raid, Milner was sent to South Africa in order to resolve the dispute between the Boers and the Britons. The new high commissioner quickly came to realize that "there is no way out of the political troubles . . . except reform in the Transvaal, or war." After a series of tortuous negotiations with the Boer leader Paul Kruger as well as with the government in London, South Africa, in October 1899, plunged into war. The British were ill prepared and it was not until one year later that Lord Roberts was able to put the Boers on the defense; a further eighteen months were required to subdue their guerrilla tactics. In 1900 Milner was appointed administrator of the Orange River Colony and the Transvaal; King Edward VII raised him to the peerage as Baron Milner, of St. James's, London, and Cape Town. The war was finally concluded through the Treaty of Vereeniging on May 31, 1902, and Milner was advanced to a viscountcy. He at once ended the nefarious system of concentration camps and brought to the Cape a host of former friends from Oxford or from Toynbee Hall, commonly called "Milner's kindergarten." Unfortunately for Milner, he agreed to staff the Rand gold mines by importing laborers under indenture from China, a policy that led to the great Liberal victory in the general election of 1906.

After his return in 1905 Milner avoided politics and worked on behalf of the Rio Tinto Company and the Rhodes Trust. He opposed the Liberal budget of 1909 and the resulting Parliamentary Bill of 1911, and he abhorred home rule, allying himself with Sir Edward Carson (*q.v.*) as well as organizing an English league of "Covenanters." The outbreak of war in August 1914 brought Milner back into politics, initially as head of a committee to increase food producton and later to enhance coal output.

On December 9, 1916, Prime Minister David Lloyd George (*q.v.*) created a small War Cabinet of five men to run the war; Lord Milner quickly became the mainstay of the War Cabinet, which he saw as a vehicle with which to restore the New Imperialism. He brought members of his famous "kindergarten" from Pretoria to London and made no secret of his disdain for "that mob . . . this rotten assembly at Westminster," preferring instead that policy be pursued by the gentlemen from Balliol College.

Milner accompanied the prime minister to Rome in January 1917, and helped establish the Supreme War Council against the express wish of Sir William Robertson (*q.v.*), chief of the Imperial General Staff. One month later, Milner was sent to Petrograd to arrange the munitions supply to Russia, but the immediate outbreak of revolution in the Russian capital obfuscated his efforts. Milner objected to General Douglas Haig's (*q.v.*) attritional tactics in Flanders in 1917, and he actively worked behind the scenes to remove Wully Robertson from the Imperial General Staff. When the German Michael offensive broke the French and British front near Amiens, Milner on March 24, 1918, crossed the Channel and two days later at Doullens convinced Premier Georges Clemenceau, an old friend, that Marshal Ferdinand Foch (*qq.v.*) be appointed commander in chief of Allied armies in France. It was to be Milner's last major act as a member of the War Council; on April 19, 1918, he replaced Lord Derby (*q.v.*) as secretary of state for war. It was in this new capacity that Milner advocated Allied intervention in Russia in order, as he put it, to prevent "Germany like a *boa constrictor*, gradually swallowing Russia." Once the tide of war had been turned in the west, Milner favored the abolition of Prussian militarism and the Hohenzollern dynasty, but in October he warned against "denouncing the whole German nation as monsters of iniquity."

After the war, Milner accepted the post of secretary of the Colonial Office but retired from public service in February 1921 after vituperative attacks by Alfred Harmsworth, Lord Northcliffe's (*q.v.*) press. He died at Sturry Court on May 13, 1925, in the knowledge that he had been accepted as chancellor-elect of Oxford University. In his posthumously published papers ("Credo"), Milner's concept of empire was perhaps most clearly stated: "I am an Imperialist and not a Little Englander, because I am a British Race Patriot."

Guinn, *British Strategy and Politics*; Hankey, *Supreme Command*, 2 vols.; Wrench, *Alfred Lord Milner*; *Dictionary of National Biography 1922-1930*.

MIŠIĆ, Živojin (*Serbia, Field Marshal*), was born in the village of Struganik near Valjevo in western Serbia in July 1855. The son of a peasant family, Mišić trained to become an artillery officer, and in 1876-1878, while still a cadet, first saw combat in Serbia's war with Turkey; he fought as a battalion commander in the brief war with Bulgaria in 1885. Marked as a rising young talent, Mišić studied in Austria in 1887, joined the General Staff in 1891, and went on to succeed Radomir Putnik (*q.v.*) as its deputy chief. While with the General Staff, he taught strategy at the Belgrade military academy.

The military revolt of 1903 temporarily halted Mišić's promising career. Serbia's new leaders considered Mišić hostile to their regime and pensioned him off. The Bosnian crisis of 1909 and the intercession of Mišić's patron, General Putnik, brought him back to active duty as deputy chief of staff. Under Putnik, he worked to reorganize and modernize the Serbian army, and during the Balkan Wars of 1912/1913 saw his achievements put successfully to the test. Mišić advanced to the rank of general after assisting Putnik to victory over the Turks at Kumanovo in October 1912; his reputation was bolstered in July 1913 at the battle of Bregalnitsa against the Bulgarians. Nonetheless, he was returned to inactive status that September.

Mišić renewed active service at the start of the First World War and took up his familiar position as deputy to Putnik, the chief of staff and de facto commander in chief. Mišić commanded the First Army during the difficult month-long retreat in November 1914, then took the leading role in December's counteroffensive. The First Army smashed the Austrian right, drove the enemy across the Kolubara, and led the victorious Serbs all the way back to the Save. For this feat, Mišić was elevated to the rank of field marshal (*voivode*).

Mišić's fierce aggressiveness came to the fore again during the grim fall campaign of 1915. As Bulgarian forces pressed in from the east, and as powerful Austro-German columns under Field Marshal von Mackensen (*q.v.*) drove down from the north, Mišić became the leading dissenter from Putnik's policy of retreat. When Putnik, in late November, ordered his trapped armies to march westward across the Albanian mountains to the Adriatic, his prickly subordinate twice took the case for a new offensive to a council of war. Twice he was voted down.

Mišić fell seriously ill during the freezing march to the sea. He recuperated in France, and in September 1916 reassumed command of the First Army. By then, the shattered Serbian forces had rested, refitted, retrained with French help, and formed part of General Sarrail's (*q.v.*) Army of the Orient on the Salonika front. Almost immediately, Mišić led the First Army back to Serbian soil in the advance on Monastir: taking the strategic heights of Kajmakcalan on September 19 from the Bulgarians, Mišić promptly faced an enemy counterattack, but rallied his forces with word that any retreat would be viewed as an act of treason.

On July 1, 1918, Mišić was promoted chief of staff. Under the nominal command of Crown Prince Alexander (*q.v.*), Mišić was leader of the Serbian armed forces. By this time, he had become convinced that a properly prepared attack could break the long stalemate in the Balkans, and he pictured the Serbian army breaking the Bulgarian front at Dobro Pole, then driving into the upper Vardar valley. The *voivode* first convinced Alexander, then took his case to the new French commander, Franchet d'Esperey (*q.v.*). The latter, a kindred soul who felt a decisive assault could indeed unhinge the Bulgarian line, gave Mišić the go-ahead and placed local French forces at his disposal.

Mišić pushed his troops forward on September 15; two days later, he held a salient twenty miles wide and six miles deep, all the while lashing his troops onward. A string of impressive victories followed, and Bulgaria capitulated on September 29. Nish and the road northward to the Danube fell in mid-October, taken in a bold advance by Mišić's old First Army despite d'Esperey's doubts. The Serbian army returned to Belgrade on November 1.

Afterward Mišić became a leading actor in the creation of a united South Slav state. Word arrived from Prime Minister Pašić (*q.v.*) in Paris calling on Mišić to move Serbian forces as rapidly as possible into the southern provinces of the crumbling Austro-Hungarian Empire. Mišić complied with enthusiasm, thus helping to shape the borders of the new kingdom of the Serbs, Croats, and Slovenes.

But Serbia's most distinguished surviving general spent barely two years in the new country he had helped bring into existence. Mišić died in Belgrade on January 20, 1921. His mentor Putnik, who passed from the scene in late 1915, is perhaps his only rival for the title Cyril Falls has awarded Mišić: "the ablest soldier of the Balkan countries."

Adams, *Flight in Winter*; Falls, *History of the Great War. Military Operations: Macedonia*, 2 vols.; Krizman, "The Belgrade Armistice of 13 November 1918"; Palmer, *Gardeners of Salonika*; *Vojna enciklopedija*, 2nd ed., V.

MITCHELL, William (*United States, General*), was born the son of a financier, railroad magnate, and congressman from Wisconsin on December 29, 1879, in Nice, France, where his parents were residing temporarily. Mitchell was in Cuba with the Army of Occupation after the Spanish-American War, and later saw duty in the Philippines. In 1901 he received a commission in the regular army, and after tours of duty in Alaska as well as at various continental posts, was assigned to the General Staff in 1912.

Early in 1914/1915 Mitchell became convinced of the potentials of aviation; he learned to fly in 1916. Airplanes were then assigned to the Signal Corps and

Mitchell for a while commanded its tiny aviation section. He was sent to Spain early in 1917 as military observer, and when the United States entered the European war he transferred to Paris. Mitchell visited the front on his own initiative and learned tactics, organization, and supply problems from Major General Trenchard of the Royal Flying Corps. He apparently influenced French Premier Ribot's request to President Wilson (qq.v.) in May 1917 for an American force of 4,500 airplanes. The energetic flyer met General Pershing (q.v.) upon the latter's arrival in France, and by July 1917, helped frame the American Expeditionary Forces' aviation program. Mitchell next received command of the Air Service of the Zone of the Advance, placed first under the I Corps of the First Army, and later of the First Army Group; in the process he rose in grade from major to brigadier general. In September 1918, he commanded a force of 842 airplanes during the American army's reduction of the St. Mihiel salient, and in October supported the Meuse-Argonne offensive by striking at German land forces with more than 500 bombers. Mitchell viewed the armistice on November 11, 1918, as an untimely interruption in his ambitious plans for strategic bombardment of Germany and large-scale deployment of paratroops.

After the Great War, Mitchell was thwarted in his endeavors to create an "independent" air force through normal service channels, and he appealed instead to the American public. In a series of spectacular aerial displays he demonstrated in the mid-1920s that the airplane had rendered the battleship obsolete, but this "lesson" was to await fruition almost two decades. Further criticism of the war and navy departments resulted in a spectacular court-martial trial and Mitchell's resignation on February 1, 1926. The impatient pioneer of martial aviation died on February 19, 1936, in New York City; Admirals Andrew Browne Cunningham at Taranto and Isoroku Yamamoto at Pearl Harbor were to vindicate Mitchell's courageous prognostications.

Levine, *Mitchell: Pioneer of Air Power*; Mitchell, *Memories of World War I*; *Dictionary of American Biography*, XXII Supplement Two.

MOLTKE, Helmuth von "the Younger" (*Germany, General*), was born in Gersdorf, Mecklenburg, on May 23, 1848, the nephew of the victor of Königgrätz and Sedan. Young Moltke joined the army in 1869 and one year later went to war against France. In 1882 he was promoted captain and appointed adjutant to his illustrious uncle; nine years later he served Wilhelm II (q.v.) in the same capacity, was promoted colonel in 1895 and major general in 1899. The

following year, Lieutenant General von Moltke commanded the prestigious First Guards Division and in 1904 was appointed quartermaster general. Two years later he succeeded Count Alfred von Schlieffen as chief of the General Staff, even though he asked not to be given this post because of his serious doubts about his ability to meet its rigorous demands.

For nearly thirty years Moltke had served as adjutant either to his uncle or to his emperor. His military mind was weaker than and inferior to that of Schlieffen, but it must be stated in his defense that Moltke at times managed to bridle the kaiser's vanity and in the end proved less pliant than was widely assumed; on occasion he even managed to curb Wilhelm's pervasive command interference. At the so-called war council in December 1912, Moltke demanded "an immediate attack against the Entente" and saw the war as unavoidable, "the sooner the better." Unfortunately, Moltke lacked total confidence in Germany's contingency war plan, named after the legendary Schlieffen. He opposed the notion that Liège could be bypassed and rejected the planned dash through the Dutch Maastricht Appendix; instead, he opted to reduce Liège forts and to avoid the possibility of war with the Dutch. And whereas Schlieffen steadfastly counseled utmost strengthening of the right wing even at the cost of baring the left wing in Lorraine, Moltke shrank from total commitment to the right wing and instead used reserves to bolster the left.

Moltke at least proved forceful during the July 1914 crisis. When Wilhelm desired a war only with Russia, the general grew impatient: "The deployment of a host of millions of men cannot be improvised." To which the kaiser acidly replied: "Your uncle would have given me a different answer." Indeed, in August 1914, Moltke critically weakened the right wing of his armies wheeling through Belgium by detaching divisions to guard and eventually to reduce the fortresses of Antwerp, Givet, and Maubeuge. Moreover, on August 25 he panicked over the unexpectedly rapid deployment of Russians in East Prussia and dispatched six divisions from Belgium to the eastern front. Above all, Moltke remained far distant from the main theater of the war, first at Koblenz and then at Luxembourg.

By early September, as the armies of Generals Alexander von Kluck and Karl von Bülow (qq.v.) approached the Marne River, Moltke grew timid and became mentally depressed. Every report of enemy movements conjured up in his mind deep, dark visions of defeat and disaster. At the critical stage of the First Battle of the Marne, from September 5 to 9, Moltke issued no orders whatsoever to army commanders; the latter replied in kind, and from

September 7 to 9 sent headquarters no reports. Given this utter breakdown in communications, Moltke dispatched Colonel Richard Hentsch (*q.v.*) on a 400-mile tour of the front on September 5. The Saxon staff officer had full powers to dispose of German armies and by September 9 had ordered the German retreat from the Marne. A beaten man, Moltke on September 14 yielded to General Erich von Falkenhayn (*q.v.*), even though the change of command was not made public until November 3, 1914. On December 30 Moltke was given the post of deputy chief of staff at Berlin.

Early in 1915 Moltke regained some of his confidence and attempted through the empress and General Paul von Hindenburg (*q.v.*) to undermine Falkenhayn's position with the kaiser. But to no avail. The wily Falkenhayn expertly checked Moltke's crass power play by spreading the news that Moltke's physician considered him unfit for highest command. The younger Moltke died of a heart attack on June 18, 1916, in the Reichstag following burial services for the fallen General Colmar von der Goltz (*q.v.*).

Groener, *Feldherr wider Willen*; Liddell Hart, *Reputations*; Moltke, *Erinnerungen*; Röhl, *1914*; *Geschichte der Ritter des Ordens*, II.

MONRO, Sir Charles Carmichael (*Great Britain, General*), baronet, was born at sea on June 15, 1860, to an ancient Edinburgh family well known in the medical profession. Monro was gazetted from Sandhurst in August 1879 into the Second Foot Regiment, and attended the Staff College ten years later, being best known for his cricket play. In 1898 after duty at Malta, India, and Guernsey, he was promoted major and in 1900 took the Sixth Division to South Africa in time to take part in Lord Roberts' march on Pretoria. From 1901 to 1907 he served at the Hythe School of Musketry, being promoted colonel in 1903. Thereafter came command of the Thirteenth Infantry Brigade in Ireland and promotion to major general in 1910; two years later he was given the Second London Division of the Territorial Forces.

On August 12, 1914, Monroe proceeded to France with the British Expeditionary Force as commander of the Second Division of the I Corps under Sir Douglas Haig (*q.v.*). He took part in the British retreat from Mons as well as in the subsequent advance form the River Marne to the River Aisne. Late in October 1914, after Sir John French (*q.v.*) had transferred the British forces to Flanders, Monro led the Second Division during the First Battle of Ypres; at the end of that year he succeeded Haig as head of the I Corps. In the summer of 1915, Lieutenant General Monro led the I Corps at the bloody battles of Aubers ridge, Festubert, and Givenchy, and in July he was promoted general and given command of the new Third Army. But in October he was ordered to Gallipoli to succeed Sir Ian Hamilton (*q.v.*) as commander of the Mediterranean Expeditionary Force.

Monro, a cool and capable infantry specialist, arrived at Gallipoli on October 27, 1917, and in one morning visited all three landing sites at Cape Helles, Suvla Bay, and Anzac Cove, and recommended immediate evacuation. Winston Churchill (*q.v.*) put it simply: "He came, he saw, he capitulated." Lord H. H. Kitchener (*q.v.*), then secretary of state for war, refused to accept this recommendation, fearing that it would be disastrous for Egypt; but after a personal inspection of the situation at the Straits, Kitchener concurred, and on November 23 the Cabinet ordered the evacuation of the peninsula. This operation was completed by January 1916, after a severe blizzard had mercilessly pounded the more than 100,000 men on the beaches. Ironically, Monro, who took no active part in the evacuation, was decorated for this brilliant action.

Returning to the western front from January to August 1916, as head of the First Army, Monro was perfectly happy with the relative inaction of this army, rightly decrying the senseless slaughter of men at the Somme that year. On October 1, 1916, he was appointed commander in chief in India. In this capacity he increased the Indian military contingent fighting in France, Africa, Mesopotamia, and Palestine nearly fourfold; by November 1918, 600,000 Indian troops were at the various fronts.

Monro remained in India until August 1920, a time when that subcontinent was racked with serious native revolts, the third Afghan War, and the Waziristan campaign. Thereafter, he served from 1923 to 1928 as governor of Gibraltar; he died in London on December 7, 1929. Monro had been created a baronet in 1921, and had from 1918 to 1922 served as aide-de-camp-general to the king. His cool common sense served him well at all posts.

Barrow, *Life of General Monro*; Guinn, *British Strategy and Politics*; *Dictionary of National Biography 1922-1930*.

MONTECUCCOLI degli ERRI, Rudolf Count von (*Austria-Hungary, Admiral*), was born to an ancient patrician family in Modena, Emilia-Romagna, on February 22, 1843. Montecuccoli entered the Austrian navy in 1859 after graduating from the Naval Academy at Trieste-Barcala and later Fiume. He was promoted captain in 1892, rear admiral in 1897, vice admiral six years later, and admiral in

1905. Montecuccoli took part in the naval battle at Lissa on the frigate *Adria* in 1866, but was retired for the next two years in the wake of Austria's defeat at the hands of Prussia. After reinstatement in 1869 Montecuccoli served in various capacities on a variety of warships and visited Spain, Ceylon, and East Africa. In July 1900 Monte, as he was commonly called, was placed in charge of three Austro-Hungarian cruisers dispatched to China as a result of the so-called Boxer Rebellion. Upon his return the following year Montecuccoli was appointed president of the Military Technical Comité, and two years later to the head of the Naval Section in the War Ministry. On October 5, 1904, Monte was proclaimed commander of the navy and chief of the Naval Section.

In perhaps his most famous memorandum on July 6, 1905, Montecuccoli pointed to Italy as the Dual Monarchy's foremost naval opponent. He arranged several visits to Trieste, Pola, and Fiume by Reichsrat deputies in order to convince them of the need for naval expansion. At first Montecuccoli was content with building three ships of the *Radetzky* class for the battle fleet, but in 1909 he flatly demanded 150 million Austrian crowns in order to lay down four new dreadnoughts—an announcement that precipitated the great naval scare of 1909/1910. Over the next two years Monte managed to wring from the Reichsrat 312 and 426 million crowns per annum for the construction of a fleet consisting of sixteen battleships, twelve cruisers, twenty-four destroyers, seventy-two torpedo-boats, and twelve submarines. Montecuccoli was regarded as a stern taskmaster, earning the nicknames Iron Count and later Iron Admiral. His career spanned an exciting era in naval development: as a cadet he had been taught that ships had to be built of wood as steel could not possibly float; as admiral he attended the launching of Austria-Hungary's first dreadnought, the *Viribus Unitis* (1912-1914). On March 1, 1913, at the age of seventy, Montecuccoli retired to make room for younger men; Admiral Anton von Haus (*q.v.*) succeeded him. In retirement, Monte turned down an offer of the title of prince, and in 1917 he advised Emperor Charles to entrust command of the fleet to Rear Admiral Miklós Horthy (*qq.v.*). Montecuccoli died on May 16, 1922, at Baden, near Vienna. He can rightly be regarded as the father of the modern Austro-Hungarian navy.

Marder, *Dreadnought to Scapa Flow*, I; *Neue Österreichische Biographie*, XIV.

MÜLLER, Georg Alexander von (*Germany, Admiral*), was born in Chemnitz on March 24, 1854, the son of an agricultural chemist. Müller grew up in

Sweden, but in 1871 entered the new Imperial German Navy. Eight years later he worked under Alfred Tirpitz (*q.v.*) in the torpedo service, and thereafter received several overseas cruiser commands. In 1889 Müller was first appointed to the Navy Cabinet; two years later he commanded a gunboat in China and in 1895 served Prince Henry (*q.v.*) as adjutant, accompanying the kaiser's brother to the Far East two years later. At the turn of the century, Captain Müller returned to the Navy Cabinet and was ennobled. In 1902 he commanded the battleship *Wettin* and, after a brief stint as naval adjutant to Wilhelm II (*q.v.*) in the grade of rear admiral, was appointed chief of the Navy Cabinet in 1908. Vice Admiral von Müller worked diligently to recruit the officers to staff Tirpitz's rapidly expanding fleet. He campaigned against alcoholism and bachelorhood; his social gatherings ("milk circles") were widely feared by young officers. And to the dismay of most senior admirals, Müller along with the kaiser championed education rather than birth as sole criterion for entrance and promotion in the officer corps. He was promoted admiral in 1910.

At the outbreak of war in August 1914, Müller was calm and resigned. He had long considered war with England as "unavoidable" and considered the timing propitious: "The mood is brilliant." When by Christmas the French had not been overrun and German naval disasters (Helgoland Bight, Falkland, Dogger Bank) increased, Müller grew more pessimistic about the war. Above all, he saw no prospects in a suicide sortie by the numerically inferior High Sea Fleet against the British Grand Fleet, a stance which netted him the disdain of aggressive younger officers and the nickname Rasputin. Being constantly in the vicinity of the kaiser, Müller was accused by his enemies of surrounding the Supreme War Lord with a Chinese Wall. Nor did Müller's opposition to the introduction of unrestricted submarine warfare throughout the period 1914-1916 endear him to naval hawks. Worse yet, the admiral's turnaround on January 9, 1917, at Pless in supporting the resumption of unrestricted submarine warfare and in convincing Chancellor Theobald von Bethmann Hollweg (*q.v.*) to support this bold initiative earned Müller the charge of duplicity from opponents of the U-boat gamble. Admirals Reinhard Scheer and Adolf von Trotha as well as Captain Magnus von Levetzow (*qq.v.*) continued to look on the head of the Navy Cabinet with distrust as Müller steadfastly refused to condone an all-out naval engagement with the British in the North Sea. In attempting to maintain a balance between the views of Bethmann Hollweg and Tirpitz, Müller earned the confidence and trust of neither. Both chancellor and state secretary were removed from office during the course of the war, and the new naval leadership of Scheer, Trotha, and Levetzow agreed in the summer of 1918 to dislodge Müller from the Navy Cabinet. Indeed, after the naval reorganization of August 11, which brought Scheer to power as head of a new Supreme Command of the Navy, Müller was scheduled for retirement and replacement by Trotha as soon as the transition in commands could be completed. Instead, rebellion and revolution in the wake of the planned suicide sortie on October 30, 1918, brought an inglorious end to the Imperial German Navy. Müller retired to Hagelsberg in the Mark to work on his diaries; he died there along the banks of the Spree River on April 19, 1940.

Gemzell, *Organization, Conflict, and Innovation*; Herwig, *"Luxury" Fleet*; Müller, *The Kaiser and His Court*; *Geschichte der Ritter des Ordens*, II.

MURRAY, Sir Archibald James (*Great Britain, General*), was born in Woodhouse, near Kingsclere, Hampshire, on April 21, 1860, the son of a landed proprietor. Murray passed the Royal Military College, Sandhurst, and in 1879 was gazetted to the Twenty-seventh Regiment. He served in Hong Kong, Singapore, and the Cape Colony (Zulu campaign 1888 as captain), before returning to attend the Staff College in 1897; his fellow students included the future field marshals William Robertson, Douglas Haig, and Edmund Allenby (*qq.v.*). Murray was dispatched to Natal in 1899 and to India two years later. Next came staff appointments at Aldershot and at the War Office, promotion to major general in 1910, and two years later appointment as inspector of infantry. His outlook was conventional and narrow; his personality was regarded as chill and reserved.

In August 1914, Murray surrendered command of the Second Division in order to accompany Sir John French (*q.v.*) and the British Expeditionary Force to France as chief of staff. He took part in the retreat from Mons, the battle of Le Cateau, and the retreat on Paris. During these critical days, Murray was seemingly immobilized by the frequent absence of General French from the front. Early in September Murray led his forces to advance from the River Marne, and in October supervised the transfer of the British to Flanders. The heavy losses suffered in the First Battle of Ypres stunned him, and French claims in his book *1914* that his chief of staff was a sick man at the end of that year. It was widely known at the time that Murray had fainted at an inn in St. Quentin on August 26, the day of the battle of Le Cateau. In any case, the French, irritated at what they con-

sidered his obstructionism, applied pressure on General French who yielded, sending his staff chief home in 1915 to be replaced by General Robertson.

The secretary of state for war, Lord H. H. Kitchener (*q.v.*), in February 1915 appointed Murray deputy chief of the Imperial General Staff and in September permanent chief with responsibility for training the New Army then being recruited. However, in the general reorganization of December 1915, Haig replaced French as British commander in chief in France and Murray was offered the command in Egypt and replaced as chief of the Imperial General Staff by Wully Robertson.

Murray's tenure in Egypt was not to be a productive one. Nine of the fourteen divisions stationed there were sent to France before the opening of the Somme offensive; it is a small wonder that with the remaining forces he managed to defeat the Turks at Romani, Magdhaba, and Rafa in the autumn of 1916. Unfortunately, Murray proved overanxious and his thrust into Palestine early in 1917, after the fall of Baghdad, was ill planned. Abandoning the previous policy of merely guarding the Suez Canal, on March 26 he attacked Gaza and nearly took the town; however, a premature victory dispatch to London trapped him into making a second attempt to take the gateway to Palestine, and though launched in a grand manner with tanks and gas, it, too, failed by April 19. Murray had pressed the attack despite feeling understaffed by two divisions, and it cost him his command. On June 29, 1917, General Allenby succeeded him and six months later entered Jerusalem.

Coming home, Murray was given the Aldershot Command to November 1919, having been promoted general in August of that year. He retired from the army in 1922 and died at Makepeace, Reigate, on January 23, 1945.

Falls, *History of the Great War. Military Operations: Egypt and Palestine*, 2 vols.; French, *1914*; Guinn, *British Strategy and Politics*; Murray, *Murray's Despatches*; *Dictionary of National Biography 1941-1950*.

NICHOLAS II (*Russia, Tsar*), was born on May 18, 1868, at the suburban palace of Tsarskoe Selo outside St. Petersburg. In 1881 his father took the throne as Tsar Alexander III. Nicholas' mother was a Danish princess, and his royal cousins included the future King George V of Great Britain and Kaiser Wilhelm II of Germany (*qq.v.*). Nicholas received the standard education for one marked to become the ruler of Russia. Private tutors, notably Konstantin Pobedonostsev of the law faculty at Moscow University, instructed him in his duties as supreme ruler supported by the weight of the church and free of the constitutional restraints that polluted Western European governments. Nicholas served in a regiment of the Imperial Guards, also not an experience designed to prepare him to cope with the twentieth century. He toured the Far East in 1891, narrowly escaping assassination at the hands of a Japanese student, and he returned to marry Princess Alix of Hesse-Darmstadt, the future Empress Alexandra (q.v.). On November 1, 1894, Alexander III suddenly died at the age of fifty. Nicholas, surprised at this rapid turn of events, ascended to the throne, the ruler of a vast, diverse, and volatile empire.

The young tsar found a turbulent domestic scene awaiting him. Peasant revolutionary parties were reviving after the repressive era of the 1880s. Revolutionary groups of another persuasion were taking shape, nourished by the arrival of Marxism and its faith in an inevitable revolution spearheaded by the new class of factory workers. The creaky inefficiency of the imperial government was painfully evident in the wake of the terrible famines that had struck the nation in the early 1890s. Most disturbing of all to any devotee of order and stability was the government's commitment to promote industrial growth. This effort had largely been undertaken at the urging of Finance Minister Sergei Witte, who kept Nicholas convinced of the need to keep Russian economic (and hence military) strength abreast of the other powers of Europe. But the price for this growth was an inevitable interlude—no one knew how long it might last—of social stress. Factory workers, the soldiers of a future Marxist revolution, soon numbered 3 million. Restless and overburdened peasants found their tax obligations expanded to help finance industrial growth. Nicholas might tolerate this necessary change, reminding himself that Russia had often been reformed "from above"; but he had no patience with calls for change from below, even the mild pleas of local government bodies dominated by conservative noblemen for some voice in setting national policy.

In foreign affairs the tsar was the ultimate decision maker, although enough latitude went to a succession of foreign ministers to make Russian intentions seem not only confused but also fundamentally expansionist. A series of clumsy efforts (partly involving the court cronies of the tsar and their business interests) to expand Russian power into Northern China, Manchuria, and Korea had led to the Russo-Japanese War, 1904/1905. In the midst of the calamity, Nicholas was enticed into personal diplomacy by Kaiser Wilhelm II, the result being the stillborn Björkö agreement of July 1905. Foreign Minister Lamsdorff convinced the monarch that this pact was incompatible with Russia's alliance with France. The catastrophe in the Far East brought a thunderous echo in domestic affairs. The revolution of 1905 compelled the tsar, against all his instincts, to grant his subjects guarantees of civil liberty and a limited legislative body, the Duma.

Given the enormous authority the tsar held, his personal life could throw a long shadow over Russian affairs. Here too problems abounded. Acquaintances found Nicholas a modest and affable individual, but also a vacillating personality hiding behind a public posture of inflexibility. The empress exerted a substantial influence over her spouse; she seemed to stiffen the tsar's view of his powers, which, she reminded him, were subject to no limit. Alexandra herself introduced a measure of chaos into the imperial household. After bearing four daughters, in 1904 she gave birth to a son, Alexis. This child suffered from hemophilia, and in her search for a means to treat him, Alexandra was drawn into the orbit of the self-proclaimed holy man Rasputin (q.v.). This unsavory character had views, generally reactionary in character, which had an important influence on the imperial family; they were swayed, for example, by his utter hostility to the Duma. More important, his entrée into the imperial family circle eroded much of the popular affection for the monarchy that had survived the revolution of 1905.

In the July crisis of 1914, a bewildered Nicholas stood at the center of the storm, pushed against his better judgment to make decisions that terrified him. By July 30, bombarded by Foreign Minister Sazonov (q.v.) as well as the nation's senior military leaders, the tsar reluctantly signed the order for general mobilization. In between he had been on the receiving end of personal pleas from Kaiser Wilhelm II to hold back, which he had answered by assuring his German relative that Russia did not really want to go to war.

The tsar's characteristic indecision made itself felt in the first days of hostilities. He wavered before the responsibility of taking direct command of the armed forces, welcomed his ministers' advice to stay home, then chose his uncle, Grand Duke Nikolai Nikolaevich (q.v.), to fill the post. The tsar would hardly have been an improvement over his uncle in the subsequent year of combat, but the nation's command system had been drawn up under the assumption that the tsar would indeed be commander in chief. Without the tsar to bridge the gap, the military system and civil government began to go their separate ways. The direction of military operations devolved into the hands of the army's deputy chief of staff, General Yury Danilov (q.v.). In the larger responsibility of guiding the nation through the trauma of the war, Nicholas proved to be utterly inadequate. He remained most comfortable with a series of ineffectual and reactionary cabinet ministers. Brighter lights like Sazonov and War Minister Polivanov (q.v.) were sooner or later removed. Nicholas viewed the hopes of Duma and industrial leaders of aiding the war effort with deep suspicion. Although he was willing to oust Premier Ivan Goremykin (q.v.) in early 1916 to please the Duma, he replaced the aged reactionary with a slightly younger model of the same breed. In all, he continued to view social and political change, even under the stress of an unprecedented war effort, as something to be resisted at all costs. Given the monarch's central role in government, such an attitude guaranteed that change would come in the extreme form of revolution unless the war was short and successful.

From August 1914 to August 1915, the tsar remained in his suburban palace near St. Petersburg (now renamed Petrograd), except for occasional visits to the front. The early months of 1915 saw him bend slightly under pressure from Duma leaders like Chairman Rodzianko (q.v.); he permitted the formation of war industries committees, with Duma and industrial leaders organizing to aid the military effort. In the wake of the Russian retreat from Poland after the Gorlice breakthrough (May 1915), the tsar reshuffled his cabinet and ousted some of the more visible reactionaries. But, as even a sympathetic biographer like Oldenburg puts it, Nicholas insisted that basic change must not take place; new ministers must share his view of the monarchy's predominant role in the government.

In August 1915, Nicholas took the momentous decision of firing his uncle and assuming direct charge of the field armies. In practice, this meant transferring direction of military operations to General Mikhail Alekseev (q.v.), the new chief of staff. But the change had serious consequences. Almost to a man, the monarch's council of ministers opposed the change; the tsar responded by purging the cabinet's most vocal moderates. Tension with the Duma grew; most of that body's parties coalesced into a "Progressive Bloc." Few Duma members raised a demand for a British-style parliamentary monarchy, but the drift in that direction was evident. Most important of all, much of the power of the monarchy fell into the hands of Empress Alexandra, then irretrievably under the influence of Rasputin. The tsar returned to Petrograd each month, and major decisions remained his to make. But the Duma and much of the educated public perceived the government to be the plaything of the tsar's pro-German wife and her unsavory entourage.

There was a marked deterioration of domestic order in 1916. The government began to disintegrate. Fuel shortages, the collapse of the nation's railroad system, and inflation combined to create a national crisis. Such a situation called for the energy and imagination of Peter the Great. Nicholas offered only business as usual. He presented the Duma with the cosmetic change of Boris Sturmer (q.v.) as premier in place of Goremykin. The tsar made a dramatic appearance at the opening session of the Duma in February 1916, but he curtly rejected Rodzianko's plea for a responsible government. News of military victories arrived. General Yudenich (q.v.) captured a series of Turkish strongholds, and General Brusilov (q.v.) launched a promising spring offensive in Galicia. But the domestic crisis worsened. In the summer Nicholas considered appointing a so-called civil dictator to run the home front. In the end Sturmer received the title, but took no real authority to make it meaningful. Meanwhile, reactionary figures like the empress persuaded the tsar to fire Sazonov, who had dared to suggest offering the Poles postwar autonomy. The empress' hand was also evident in the appointment of Aleksandr Protopopov (q.v.) as minister of the interior in the fall; he turned out to be the last cabinet strongman of the tsarist era. Nicholas objected to Protopopov—whose most evident characteristics included a mental capacity diminished by advanced syphilis and a reputation for being pro-German—but in the end the empress persuaded her husband to go along.

The tsar returned to Petrograd in late December to console his wife over Rasputin's assassination. While still at the front, the tsar had met with Grand Duke Nikolai Nikolaevich, who urged immediate government reforms to head off a political explosion. At Petrograd in early 1917, Rodzianko had offered the same advice. To both of them Nicholas delivered a flat refusal.

Shortly after the tsar returned to supreme military headquarters at Mogilev in late February 1917, news arrived of bread riots in Petrograd. These seemed merely the latest in a series of grim signs of popular discontent; similar incidents in October 1916 had been successfully repressed. The tsar relied on local authorities in Petrograd to put the new unrest down with military force. When Rodzianko telegraphed to plead once again for the establishment of a constitutional monarchy, Nicholas dismissed the request as "nonsense." General Nikolai Ivanov (q.v.), whom the tsar had relieved from an important field command in 1916 for incompetence, was dispatched with

800 decorated combat veterans to restore order in the imperial capital. The tsar himself left for Petrograd (March 13) only to be stranded at Pskov, the headquarters of the northern front. There he received the crushing news that the army's front commanders would not support his effort to remain as monarch. Fearing that his sickly son could not stand the strain of ruling, even under a regency, the tsar abdicated in favor of his brother, the Grand Duke Michael. When Michael refused to accept the crown, the monarchy itself came to an end.

Nicholas was then arrested along with the rest of his immediate family. Half-hearted efforts by the new provisional government to find sanctuary for the imperial family in Britain failed. Just before the Bolshevik Revolution in November, Nicholas, Alexandra, and their tiny entourage were sent to the Siberian city of Ekaterinburg for safekeeping. Civil War doomed them. In the hands of the Czech legion or other anti-Bolshevik elements, the tsar and his family were certain to stand as a rallying point for all varieties of Russian conservatives. Nicholas and his then pathetic family were executed in Ekaterinburg on the night of July 16/17, 1918.

The last tsar was the ultimate victim of nineteenth-century Russian history. He inherited a centralized political system that could work only with a ruler of supreme energy and decisiveness. Even a political genius, which Nicholas could not be, might not have been able to meet the supreme crisis of World War I. At the same time, Nicholas had been imbued with a perilously static view of his authority: to share imperial power meant to destroy all imperial power. But even a more flexible attitude toward the Duma, including the establishment of parliamentary government, offered no certain solution. By 1914 the fissures in Russian society had become so deep and the available paths for moderate change had become so constricted that Nicholas seemed destined to preside over an internal cataclysm. World War I was catalyst, not cause. The tsar was as much the victim as the villain of the Russian tragedy, 1914-1917.

Albertini, *The Origins of the War of 1914*, 3 vols.; Frankland, *Imperial Tragedy: Nicholas II*; Nicholas II, *Dnevnik* and *The Nicky-Sunny Letters*; Oldenburg, *Last Tsar*, 4 vols.; Pearson, *The Russian Moderates and the Crisis of Tsarism*; Stavrou, ed., *Russia under the Last Tsar*; Stone, *The Eastern Front*; Thomson, "Boris Stürmer and the Imperial Russian Government"; *Sovetskaia istoricheskaia entsiklopediia*, X.

NICHOLAS PETROVIĆ-NJEGOŠ (Montenegro, King of Montenegro),

was born in Njegoš in southwestern Montenegro on October 7, 1841. The nephew of reigning Prince Danilo II, Nicholas received a traditional warrior's training in his youth, then left the mountains for schooling in Trieste and Paris. He returned in 1860 to take the crown after his uncle's assassination and personally led his country's armies against the Turks in the unsuccessful war of 1862. Thereafter, he directed Montenegro's recovery, seeking at once to modernize the country's economy, strengthen its military power, and end the diplomatic isolation that had contributed to the recent defeat. In 1868 Nicholas forged a lasting tie with Russia. He dreamed of freeing those of his fellow Serbs still under Turkish control and creating a "Greater Serbia" under Montenegrin leadership.

In 1876, alongside Serbia, the other free Serbian state, Nicholas again marched against the Turks. Russian intervention now helped to overcome new Montenegrin military defeats, so that by 1880 Nicholas found himself ruling a state doubled in size and firmly established on the Adriatic coast. Once again, he led his people through a period of postwar recovery and modernization.

A line of marital alliances provided links to the ruling houses of Italy and Russia. In 1883 Nicholas' eldest daughter Zorka married Peter Karadjordjević of Serbia (q.v.), the exiled prince whom a military revolt brought to the throne in Belgrade twenty years later. Nicholas took the title of king in 1910 on the fiftieth anniversary of his coronation. This nominal elevation could not mask his growing political difficulties, as educated Montenegrins were increasingly restive under a nominally constitutional system that, in fact, left most power in the king's hands. Nicholas' hopes of directing the formation of a united Serbian state faded: Serbia under Peter, larger and more powerful than Montenegro, soon assumed that role after 1903. Friction between Serbia and Montenegro intensified as Montenegrin dissidents used Serbia as a base for plots against Nicholas. The weakness of Montenegro's still primitive armed forces stood out clearly in the Balkan Wars, 1912/1913. Finally, the old monarch's widespread reputation for personal avarice received new emphasis resulting from word of his wartime stock market speculations.

In the July 1914 crisis Nicholas was tempted to remain neutral. Austria offered Montenegro territorial concessions in Albania and the Sanjak of Novibazar. But heated interventionist sentiment in the National Assembly at Cetinje convinced Nicholas to stand by Serbia or to risk being pushed off his throne. Nonetheless, Nicholas' wartime role remained deliberately small. An early offensive northward against Austrian territory failed by October 1914. Thereafter, Montenegrin troops besieged the port of

Scutari in the Turkish dependency of Albania, but this operation betrayed Nicholas' long-time ambitions and drew Montenegro's small army away from the increasingly desperate Serbs.

On January 8, 1916, after Serbia's fall, Nicholas faced unaided the full weight of an Austrian offensive. The Cetinje cabinet had resigned four days earlier, possibly in protest against rumors that Nicholas was angling for a separate peace with Vienna. If so, Nicholas deceived the Austrians; with Montenegro still a belligerent, the old king left for exile in Italy.

Nicholas then faced a new and more serious threat from Serbia. His grandson, Crown Prince Alexander Karadjordjević, and Prime Minister Pašić (*qq.v.*) prepared to absorb Montenegro once the war had ended. Starting in mid-1916 Serbia encouraged Montenegrin political leaders to call publicly for Nicholas' abdication. The successful Allied offensive in the Balkans in September/October 1918 brought the quarrel to a climax, and the advancing Serbian army was ordered to move into Montenegro. Meanwhile, French authorities obliged Serbia by refusing to let Nicholas leave his place of exile in Bordeaux. Stained by his less than heroic role in January 1916 and weakened by persistent rumors thereafter that he was seeking an accommodation with the Central Powers, Nicholas was helpless as the Serbs whipped up prounionist sentiment in Montenegro. The first postwar election in his kingdom found Nicholas' supporters soundly defeated. The old king was deposed on November 26, 1918, and Montenegro became part of a united South Slav state under Serbian hegemony. Nicholas left for a second and final exile in France and Italy. He died in Antibes on March 1, 1921.

Adams, *Flight in Winter*; Albertini, *The Origins of the War of 1914*, 3 vols.; Palmer, "Montenegro: The Smallest Ally"; Petrovich, *History of Modern Serbia*, 2 vols.; Vucinich, *Serbia between East and West; Larousse mensuel*, V.

NIKITA PETROVIĆ-NJEGOŠ (1841-1921). See NICHOLAS PETROVIĆ-NJEGOŠ.

NIKOLA PETROVIĆ-NJEGOŠ (1841-1921). See NICHOLAS PETROVIĆ-NJEGOŠ.

NIKOLAI NIKOLAEVICH "the Younger" (*Russia, General of Cavalry*), was born in St. Petersburg, November 18, 1856. As a member of the Russian imperial family, he received the customary military education followed by rapid promotion. He completed the Nikolaevsky Engineering School in 1873 and graduated from the General Staff Academy three years later. The young aristocrat served in the Russo-Turkish War, 1877/1878, first as aide to his father, Grand Duke Nikolai Nikolaevich "the Elder," the Russian field commander, then in the Guards Cavalry. He was a major general at the age of twenty-nine, by which time his brother had taken the throne as Tsar Alexander III. Nikolai Nikolaevich served as the army's inspector general of cavalry from 1895 to 1905; and in 1901 under his nephew, Tsar Nicholas II (*q.v.*), he was promoted to general of cavalry. During the 1905 revolution the tsar offered his uncle the opportunity to crush national unrest in the role of government dictator; the grand duke refused, helping to push the monarch into constitutional reform instead. He thereby acquired a lasting, albeit exaggerated, reputation as a political liberal.

In the period between the disaster of the Russo-Japanese War and the outbreak of World War I, the grand duke developed the reputation of military reformer. From 1905 to 1908 he led the Council on State Defense, with the charge of coordinating the activities of the army and navy so as to avoid repeating the confusion that had marked military operations in the Far East. Young military reformers were attracted to the imperial uncle, although perhaps more for his commitment to a strengthened military establishment than for his feel for a modern army. Compared to the other guiding star for military reformers, War Minister Sukhomlinov (*q.v.*), the grand duke enjoyed a reputation for reassuring personal honesty. Nonetheless, he was identified by leading members of the Duma with the clique of grand dukes, that is, members of the imperial family who allegedly enjoyed limitless power and were barring the way to necessary military modernization. He responded to criticism in the Duma by resigning from the Council on State Defense in 1908 and busied himself with his work as inspector general of the cavalry and commander of the St. Petersburg Military District.

On August 2, 1914, the tsar suddenly appointed his uncle commander in chief. The old general had anticipated the lesser responsibility of directing the Sixth Army at St. Petersburg. Stone suggests that the monarch and Sukhomlinov declined the supreme command, assuming that real power would rest elsewhere, and thus Grand Duke Nikolai was picked to fill the need for an attractive figurehead, "a great poster." General Yury Danilov (*q.v.*), the grand duke's deputy chief of staff, argues, more plausibly, that the tsar intended to command the armies, but developed cold feet at the last moment. In any case, Nikolai Nikolaevich found himself hoisted to a post he had not anticipated, to carry out war plans with which he was barely familiar.

On August 14 the new generalissimo reached his headquarters at Baranovichi to begin a series of sweeping offensives; these continued for over three months. The grand duke's unwavering offensive preferences stand as his chief contribution to the 1914 campaign. There was no way he could effectively control operations. The Russian army's system of command, based on the premise that the tsar would command in the field, called for two fronts, in effect army groups. The northwestern front faced Germany; the southwestern front faced Austria-Hungary. Such a system certainly avoided burdening a militarily uninformed monarch with excessive responsibility, but it delivered effective authority into the hands of the front commanders. Grand Duke Nikolai became a distant spectator—and critic after the fact—for much of the army's work.

Thus, the generalissimo insisted on an early thrust into East Prussia, in response to cries from Paris for immediate efforts to weaken the German drive into France. The Second Army under General Samsonov (q.v.) was annihilated in late August at Tannenberg, and the First Army under General Rennenkampf (q.v.) was subsequently mauled in the battle of the Masurian Lakes. The grand duke could react to this glaring example of military mismanagement only by dismissing General Zhilinsky (q.v.), the commander of the northwestern front. The simultaneous Galician victories by General Ivanov and his chief of staff, General Alekseev (qq.v.), against the Austrians were equally beyond the generalissimo's reach.

The offensives continued as General Joffre (q.v.) badgered the Russians to press Germany at any cost. Russian armies advanced against Silesia in late September and early October, only to be thrown back by a German counterattack launched from Cracow northward toward Warsaw. In November the grand duke again pointed his armies westward, and again a well-found German offensive, this time from Thorn southeastward toward Lodz, rocked him back on his heels. An ominous pattern became evident: using their superb rail system, German armies could move easily along a north-south axis to halt the Russian "steamroller" over and over. The Russian taste for the offensive combined with unlimited—but poorly equipped and inadequately led—hordes of troops merely produced huge casualty lists. By late November the grand duke and his armies welcomed the onset of winter. Slow, deliberate, and stubborn, Nikolai Nikolaevich had no strategic answer for Russia's military dilemma.

As Russia's supreme commander, the grand duke was drawn into questions beyond the purely military sphere. In August 1914, urged on by Foreign Minister Sergei Sazonov (q.v.), he proclaimed Russia's intention to restore Polish unity under the Russian crown. Such pledges answered Nikolai Nikolaevich's concern about keeping the loyalty of the population in Russian Poland and thus securing the areas immediately to the rear of the fighting front. But the grand duke's reputation as a "liberal" swelled—not necessarily to his advantage—back at Petrograd. Moreover, the tsar was persuaded by conservatives like Minister of the Interior Maklakov (q.v.) not to endorse the action officially, for fear that all of Russia's numerous minorities lodge similar claims. When the Turks launched an offensive in the Caucasus in late December, the grand duke played Joffre's part and called on his allies to divert the foe by offensive operations. This action reinforced the views of such "Easterners" as Winston Churchill and Aristide Briand (qq.v.) and helped create the imbroglio at Gallipoli.

The new year began with the grand duke playing his accustomed role of mediator between his front commanders. When the forces of the northwestern front came to grief in February at the Masurian Lakes—another example of a timely German offensive shattering Russian hopes—the generalissimo gave Ivanov and the southwestern front the main task for 1915. This opened the way to calamity. Already stretched thinly to cover the perimeter of the huge Polish salient, the Russian army could advance only at the cost of further lengthening its line. By spring Ivanov had been able to push into the Carpathians and threatened to penetrate the plains of Hungary, which was sufficient to persuade General von Falkenhayn (q.v.) to reinforce the hard-pressed Austrians. General von Mackensen (q.v.) crashed through the Russian front at Gorlice in early May 1915. The grand duke stirred the French to strike on the western front, but nothing could hold back the Austro-German tide for fully three months. By late August all of Poland was lost, and the enemy stood at the gates of territory inhabited by ethnic Russians. The High Command itself was compelled to retreat from Baranovichi to Mogilev.

Grand Duke Nikolai's critics then had a clear field of fire. The old cavalryman could be castigated for failing to foresee the Gorlice offensive, for mismanaging the flow of reserves, and for refusing, until nearly too late, to withdraw his exposed forces from Warsaw. Indeed, by late August, eight of the eleven field armies had gathered under Alekseev, then commander of the northwestern front, and the grand duke's star was evidently setting. Even more telling was the political attack on the tsar's uncle. His questionable reputation as a liberal had received a dangerous boost during summer riots in Moscow: crowds called on him to take power in place of the hapless tsar. By September the monarch had taken over direct control of Russia's field armies and packed his uncle off to the Caucasus.

As governor general of the Caucasus, Grand Duke Nikolai could bask in the glow of military victories, provided with regularity by his able military commander, General Yudenich (q.v.). During 1916 the grand duke was approached by liberal political leaders, as opposition elements in the Duma and military circles sought a means to oust the tsar and revive the Russian war effort. In this political shadow play, the grand duke apparently refused to join in action against his nephew; but neither did he pass word of the plots to the tsar. Rather, in November 1916, he saw the monarch at Mogilev and demanded constitutional reforms as the only way to avoid political upheaval.

When the March Revolution struck, Grand Duke Nikolai joined the other front commanders in urging the tsar to abdicate. The monarch attempted to restore his uncle to the post of supreme military commander, as a final link between the imperial family and postrevolutionary Russia, but the provisional government would have none of that.

The retired grand duke settled in the Crimea, and in March 1919 went into exile. He quietly lived out his last years in Italy and France. He refused to play an active political role but remained for the White émigré community the pretender to the Russian throne until his death in Antibes, January 5, 1929.

Danilov, *Velikii kniaz' Nikolai Nikolaevich*; Heyman, "Gorlice-Tarnow"; Katkov, *Russia 1917*; Rutherford, *The Russian Army in World War I*; Smith, *The Russian Struggle for Power*; Stone, *The Eastern Front*; Wilfong, "Rebuilding the Russian Army"; *Sovetskaia istoricheskaia entsiklopediia*, X; *Sovetskaia voennaia entsiklopediia*, V.

NITTI, Francesco Saverio (*Italy, Politician*), was born on July 19, 1868, in Melfi in southern Italy. He taught economics at the University of Naples, making his specialty the study of the roots of poverty in his home region. Nitti entered the Chamber of Deputies in 1904 as a Radical. In 1911 he entered the government of Giovanni Giolitti (q.v.) as minister of agriculture, industry, and commerce. He remained until 1914 a staunch supporter of Giolitti, the dominant figure in Italian parliamentary life in the early twentieth century.

World War I altered the course of Nitti's political career. Unlike Giolitti he favored Italian participation in the conflict, although he protested the way in which a vocal minority had maneuvered the country into becoming a belligerent one. Unlike such interventionist leaders as Premier Salandra (q.v.), Nitti saw the war in an ideological framework, as a protection for European democracy against the threat of German militarism rather than as a vehicle for Italian territorial expansion. Nitti remained on the back benches during Italy's first two years in the conflict. He busied himself drawing plans for his homeland's future: he pictured Italy developing, with foreign assistance, into a modern industrial democracy closely linked with Great Britain and France.

In mid-1917 Nitti visited the United States to obtain economic and financial help from the war's newest participant. He returned to find his own stature enhanced. While he had been away, the cabinet of Paolo Boselli (q.v.) was cracking as a result of the crisis precipitated by the enemy victory at Caporetto (October 24). There was talk that Nitti might succeed Boselli. In the end he became instead minister of the treasury in the cabinet of Vittorio Orlando (q.v.), but his stature in the cabinet was second only to Orlando's. His field of responsibility soon embraced the entire war effort.

Nitti became a whirlwind of activity. He considered it essential to mobilize the entire nation and its resources in order to fight the war to a successful conclusion. To meet the nation's economic crises, he persuaded Rome's allies to send in food and fuel supplies to tide Italy over the last year of the war. He obtained financial credits as well, telling the Allies that he had first tapped Italy's meager resources with a successful domestic loan drive.

Nitti also played a significant role in the formation of Italian military policy. He backed the new commander of the Italian army, General Diaz (q.v.), who wished to put off offensive action as long as possible in order to let the army recover from the strain of Caporetto. He also supported Diaz in his vain requests to General Foch (q.v.), the Allied supreme commander, not to draw French and British forces out of Italy for use in blocking Germany's spring 1918 offensives in France.

Disgruntled at the course of events immediately following the armistice, Nitti resigned from his post in January 1919. His bitterness at the failure of the government to adopt his economic demobilization plan precipitated his departure, but, unlike other members of the wartime cabinet such as Leonida Bissolati (q.v.) who resigned with loud words of condemnation for their former colleagues, Nitti went quietly and kept the goodwill of useful political allies.

By June 1919, he had returned to lead his own cabinet. His term in office was marred by domestic discontent and by lingering quarrels over the disappointing territorial gains Italy had been awarded at the Versailles Peace Conference. Nitti tried to present the picture of moderation to his countrymen. He refused to crack down on domestic unrest, and he did not wish to fight useless battles to hang on to the chunks of Italian territory in the Adriatic that had not been awarded to his country in the postwar settlement. He saw his main task as dealing with his country's massive economic problems: to do this successfully meant staying on good terms with powers like the United States, which played a leading role in blocking Italy from obtaining its maximum territorial goals in the Adriatic.

In September 1919, a band of freebooters under the warrior-poet Gabriele D'Annunzio (q.v.) seized Fiume, the most emotionally charged of the disputed chunks of territory. Nitti was crippled by the knowledge that Italy's military establishment was likely to support D'Annunzio rather than the government if the issue came to armed clash. In the immediate confrontation between the moderate economist-politician and the romantic poet, the former was at a hopeless disadvantage. Wanting only to concentrate on domestic issues, Nitti found himself burdened throughout the remainder of his term in office by this bizarre development in the realm of foreign policy.

Nitti left office in June 1920. He maintained a brief alliance with Mussolini, the rising Fascist leader, in the hope that Mussolini's extraparliamentary movement could be toned down and brought within the conventional political system. This pious hope was soon blown away as Mussolini consolidated his hold on Italian life, and Nitti went into exile in 1924.

During World War II Nitti, living in France, was taken into custody by the Germans. He was freed by the Allies at the close of the war and returned from his internment in Germany to his home in Italy. He reentered Italian politics and was elected to the Senate in 1948. He played the role of elder statesman during his last years and died in Rome, February 20, 1953.

Alatri, *Nitti, D'Annunzio e la questione adriatica*; Lowe and Marzari, *Italian Foreign Policy 1870-1940*; Mayer, *Politics and Diplomacy of Peacemaking*; Monticone, *Nitti e la grande guerra*; Seton-Watson, *Italy from Liberalism to Fascism*; Whittam, *Politics of the Italian Army, 1861-1918*.

NIVELLE, Robert (*France, General*), was born in Tulle, October 15, 1856. The son of a French army officer and an English mother, Nivelle graduated from the École polytechnique in 1878 and entered the artillery. He saw action in repressing the Boxer Rebellion in 1900, and in 1908 as a lieutenant colonel he served a tour in North Africa.

When World War I broke out, Colonel Nivelle stood at the head of the Fourth Artillery Regiment, a unit he had commanded since 1911. The first weeks of the war brought him a reputation for daring and imaginative leadership both outside Mulhouse and in the battle of the Marne. In the latter engagement, he lined up his batteries well in front of his infantry to surprise the advancing Germans with a shower of artillery fire from close range. By October he was a brigadier general and in early February 1915 received a division. At the close of the second year of the war, Major General Nivelle commanded the III Corps.

Verdun made the dashing artilleryman a national hero. He took the III Corps, with General Charles Mangin's (q.v.) Fifth Division as its spearpoint, to the beleaguered fortress. In April Nivelle was elevated to command the Second Army, and by the autumn he was organizing effective counterattacks against the Germans with the aid of new artillery techniques. Nivelle's "creeping barrage" allowed the infantry and artillery to stage a coordinated advance, with continuous shell fire pinning down the enemy as the French infantry marched forward. A vast improvement over the futile slaughter in Artois and Champagne in 1915, the new method seemed to mark Nivelle, the artilleryman, as the soldier who understood how the war could be won. On October 24 Fort Douaumont fell to Nivelle and Mangin; they could then recount how the very symbol of the ten-month struggle at Verdun had yielded to Nivelle's tactical vision.

Barely two months later, on December 13, Nivelle catapulted from command of the Second Army to replace General Joffre (q.v.) as France's commander in chief. Joffre's reputation had by then been shattered; the futile offensives of 1915 had begun his decline and the foe's surprise attack on Verdun had completed it. General Pétain (q.v.), the director of the defense of Verdun, seemed the most likely candidate to move to the top. But he was vocally cautious about prospects for a speedy end to the war. Only after long, defensive battles in which France managed to wear the enemy down could victory come. By contrast Nivelle pledged quick success.

Citing his new artillery techniques, Nivelle inspired political leaders like President Raymond Poincaré (q.v.) with visions of a Napoleonic breakthrough that would win the war in a flash. He pictured a spring offensive against the gigantic German salient that stretched from Arras southward to Soissons and then eastward to Reims. The BEF was to hammer against the western edge of the bulge near Arras and the French to follow by striking the southern flank of the enemy on the Chemin des Dames. Artillery techniques that had worked well on a small scale at Verdun were to be supported on a larger stage by the full resources of the French army.

The compelling vision of instant victory was soon darkened by harsh realities. The Germans retreated from the most exposed portion of the salient in early March, leaving the British to move forward unopposed until they reached the powerful defensive line named for Field Marshal von Hindenburg (*q.v.*). The Chemin des Dames attack would have to bear nearly the entire weight of the Allied advance; and many French generals thought its prospects were nearly hopeless. Army group commanders like Pétain, Franchet d'Esperey, and Micheler (*qq.v.*) were not enthusiastic. Micheler, whose Reserve Army Group was designated to conduct the main assault on the Chemin des Dames, was nearly despondent. He could not stand up to Nivelle, and he sent his doubts in the form of letters to politicians like Paul Painlevé (*q.v.*), the new war minister. In late March a series of hasty conferences began, extending through the first week of April. In the end Nivelle triumphed in the conference room. Neither the German retreat nor the entry of the United States into the war nor the sudden collapse of the monarchy in Russia—all unsettling events that prompted cooler heads to call for a policy of wait and see—pulled Nivelle from his path. Supremely confident of success, he threatened to resign on April 6 when army and civilian leaders met at Compiègne to make the final decision. With the glow of Verdun behind him he found no general, not even the terrified Micheler, ready to challenge the offensive's prospects directly. With the promise of victory on Nivelle's lips, no government leader could choose instead another prolonged year of slaughter on the model of 1916. Nivelle's sole concession was to pledge to suspend his attack if it failed to produce the desired results.

It failed. His attack on April 16 did not get beyond the German first line. Casualties were enormous; Nivelle had predicted 10,000 on the first day. The actual number was more than ten times as great. Within four days Nivelle was shifting to a strategy of attrition, little different from the 1916 bloodbath on the Somme. His political allure made it impossible to fire him out of hand. Instead, Pétain moved alongside him as chief of the General Staff and restrained Nivelle for a few weeks. Then, on May 15, Nivelle handed over his responsibilities to Pétain. Portions of the French army were already in a state of open mutiny.

Nivelle faced a military court of inquiry in October 1917, which somehow managed to clear him of serious misconduct. He sat out the rest of the war in the military backwater of North Africa, and, after a brief term of postwar service, died in Paris on March 23, 1924.

Beaufre, *La France de la Grande Guerre*; Griffiths, *Pétain*; Horne, *Price of Glory: Verdun*; King, *Generals and Politicians*; Ratinaud, *1917 ou la révolte des poilus*; Spears, *Prelude to Victory*; *Larousse mensuel*, VI.

NIXON, Sir John Eccles (*Great Britain, General*), was born in Brentford on August 16, 1857, the son of an army captain. He was educated at Wellington College and Sandhurst, and in 1875 joined the Seventy-fifth Foot. Nixon saw duty in the Afghanistan War 1879/1880, was promoted captain in 1888, and major seven years later. At the end of 1901 he was dispatched to South Africa where he fought to the conclusion of the Boer War; thereafter came service in India, and in 1912 he was given command of the Southern Army of India. Nixon had been promoted major general in 1904, lieutenant general five years later, and general in 1914. The following year he was entrusted with the Northern Army of India.

On April 9, 1915, Nixon received command of all British forces in Mesopotamia. His instructions were to secure the oil fields and the pipeline to the east, to control the Basra *vilayet*, or administrative district, and to develop a plan for an eventual advance on Baghdad. London cautioned: "In Mesopotamia a safe game must be played." Nixon at first proved successful: on June 3, 1915, the British took Amara in what is known as General Charles Townshend's (*q.v.*) "regatta" up the Tigris; Townshend quickly exploited this success by pushing almost 200 miles further into the interior, taking Kut el Amara on September 29, 1915. This brilliant little victory was viewed in London as "the one bright spot on the military horizon," and, in order to overcome the loss of prestige in the eyes of the empire's Moslem subjects over Gallipoli, Nixon was permitted on October 23 to march on Baghdad, provided that it could be held. London promised two divisions of Indian troops from France. Townshend, however, did not wait for these reinforcements, and on November 22 began the march on Baghdad. Checked by the Turks near the ancient arch of Ctesiphon, Townshend fell back on Kut el Amara, which the Turks besieged on December 8, 1915. The imminent starvation of his force compelled Townshend to surrender on April 29, 1916; the two divisions promised him from France still had not arrived. Baghdad was finally taken by Sir Frederick Stanley Maude (q.v.) with a numerical superiority of four-to-one over the Turks in March 1917.

Nixon laid down his command ostensibly owing to ill health in January 1916, but in August was summoned home to testify before the Mesopotamia Commission of Inquiry. The latter's verdict was damning: "The weightiest share of responsibility lies with Sir John Nixon, whose confident optimism was the main cause of the decision to advance." Fortunately for Nixon, plans to haul him before a special army court of inquiry were dropped by October 1918, but Nixon's career by then had been utterly dashed. He died in St. Raphael, France, on December 15, 1921.

Guinn, *British Strategy and Politics*; Liddell Hart, *The Real War*; *Dictionary of National Biography 1912-1921*, Third Supplement.

NJEGOVAN, Maximilian (*Austria-Hungary, Admiral*), was born in Agram on October 31, 1858. He entered the navy in 1877 after graduating from the Naval Academy in Fiume. Thereafter Njegovan served at several posts and undertook excursions to the coast of West Africa and to Brazil. After 1893 he commanded various units of the fleet, including the armored vessel *Budapest* in 1906/1907. Njegovan was promoted captain in 1907, and for the next two years served as squadron commander. In 1909/1910 he was appointed a commanding naval adjutant and chief of the operations chancellery in the Naval Section of the War Ministry. In the summer of 1913 in the grade of rear admiral, Njegovan commanded units of the Austro-Hungarian navy during the international blockade of Montenegro; he then served as royal representative in the admiralty council in Skutari.

At the outbreak of the war Njegovan commanded the First Squadron of the battle fleet at Pola, and in this capacity undertook the naval bombardment of Ancona in May 1915. Following the death of Admiral Anton von Haus (q.v.) on February 8, 1917, Vice Admiral Njegovan was entrusted with command of the fleet. Later that year he was promoted full admiral, given complete command of the navy, and made chief of the Naval Section. His brother Viktor served the Habsburg army in the grade of general during the First World War.

Njegovan's tenure as head of the navy was not a particularly successful one. He inherited a service that was exhausted after two and one-half years of fighting, that was desperately short on almost all supplies, and that was racked by political and nationalist propaganda. Moreover, it was a service that

had surrendered the belief in victory. Njegovan made great strides in expanding the port facilities at Cattaro (today called Boka Kotorska) for use by submarines. After serious mutinies had rocked the navy in October 1917 and February 1918, especially in Cattaro, Njegovan was replaced on March 1, 1918, as fleet commander by Rear Admiral Miklós Horthy and as chief of the Naval Section by Vice Admiral Franz von Holub (qq.v.). Vice Admiral Franz von Keil at the same time was made naval adviser to the new Emperor Charles (qq.v.), whose permission was then required before major naval operations could be undertaken. Thus Njegovan's period as head of the navy ended with the fragmentation of command. Njegovan died in Agram on July 1, 1930.

Sokol, *Österreich-Ungarns Seekrieg 1914-1918*, 4 vols.; *Österreichisches Biographisches Lexikon 1815-1950*, VII.

NORTHCLIFFE, Lord (1865-1922). See HARMSWORTH, Alfred Charles William.

NOSKE, Gustav (*Germany, Politician*), was born in Brandenburg on July 9, 1868, the son of a weaver. Noske worked as a basket maker in Halle, Frankfurt, Amsterdam, and Liegnitz, unsuccessfully attempting to organize this trade as an artisan industry. In 1893 he entered the publishing world and four years later was appointed editor of the *Königsberger Volkstribüne*; in 1902 he edited the revisionist *Volksstimme* in Chemnitz. Throughout his life Noske remained a gradualist or revisionist and claimed that he never read Karl Marx's *Kapital* until in retirement. His political career began as city councillor in Königsberg in 1899; in February 1906 he entered the Reichstag as Social Democratic (SPD) deputy from Chemnitz. Noske quickly became an expert in military and colonial matters and in April 1907 publicly revealed the SPD's stance that the workers had a duty to defend their homeland against aggression. Moreover, Noske called on the Prussian army to reform its aristocratic officer corps and to evolve into a genuine people's army. A moderate and party bureaucrat, he opposed the notion of the general strike in 1913 as the workers' principal political weapon. "When blood flows," he said, "it is the German working class that suffers."

The SPD planned to send Noske on an inspection tour of the German colony in East Africa in 1914, but the war obviated this plan. Russian mobilization and the kaiser's proclamation of the *Burgfrieden* ("internal peace") on August 4 turned Noske into an ardent supporter of the war. For the next few years he served as Socialist war correspondent, visiting both fronts as well as the fleet. In the summer of 1917 he welcomed the Reichstag's peace resolution and called for reform of the Prussian suffrage; he hailed the Bolshevik Revolution in November as the end of tsarist autocracy. Noske's career took a decided turn on November 4, 1918, when he was dispatched by the government of Prince Max von Baden (*q.v.*) to quiet rebellious sailors in Kiel. As governor of the port, Noske quickly discerned the nonrevolutionary mood of the sailors, seeing that war weariness had prompted the violent outbursts against Admiral Wilhelm Souchon (*q.v.*). In the meantime, the new government of Friedrich Ebert (*q.v.*) faced rebellious sailors in Berlin, and Noske was recalled to the capital on December 27 as member of the Council of People's Commissars. His previous military expertise in parliament prompted Ebert to entrust army matters to the tireless Noske who, with the aid of Colonel Walther Reinhardt, Prussian war minister, set about to rebuild the army. Noske pressed about 40,000 Free Corps veterans into service, "not unlike the days of Wallenstein." From January 5 to 13, 1919, this right radical force brutally suppressed the Spartacist workers rebellion in Berlin, in the course of which both Rosa Luxemburg and Karl Liebknecht were murdered. This action, undertaken by right-wing troops on the orders of a Socialist minister, effectively divided the German labor movement until 1933.

Noske was appointed defense minister in February 1919 by Chancellor Philipp Scheidemann (*q.v.*); in March he suppressed another bloody workers' uprising in Berlin, and in May his freebooters overthrew the Bavarian Soviet Republic. These acts earned him the sobriquet Bloodhound of the Revolution from Winston Churchill (*q.v.*). Noske proved woefully unprepared in March 1920 to deal with the threat of a right-wing *Putsch*, however, and on March 13 the head of the army, General Hans von Seeckt (*q.v.*), declined to order regular units to fire upon the rebellious Ehrhardt brigade as it occupied the capital. The cabinet subsequently fled Berlin, first to Dresden and then to Stuttgart, from where it directed a successful general strike against the so-called Kapp government. Noske was forced to tender his resignation as defense minister on March 18, 1920.

Noske served as lord lieutenant of the province of Hanover from 1920 until 1933, when the Hitler regime ousted him from office. He was implicated in the July 20, 1944, plot against Hitler and arrested, but somehow managed to avoid execution. Noske died in Hanover on November 30, 1946.

Czisnik, *Gustav Noske*; Noske, *Erlebtes* and *Von Kiel bis Kapp*; Ritter and Miller, *Die deutsche Revolution*; *Biographisches Wörterbuch zur Deutschen Geschichte*, II.

ORLANDO, Vittorio Emanuele (*Italy, Prime Minister*), was born in Palermo, May 19, 1860. He chose a career as an attorney and professor of law. In 1897 Orlando entered the Chamber of Deputies and rose quickly to cabinet positions. He served as minister of education, 1903-1905, and minister of justice, 1907-1909, on both occasions in cabinets led by Giovanni Giolitti (*q.v.*), the dominant figure of Italy's pre-World War I parliamentary system.

In November 1914, Orlando took up his former portfolio as minister of justice, this time under Premier Antonio Salandra (*q.v.*). Orlando favored Italy's intervention in World War I, and he remained minister of justice after Italy became a belligerent (May 1915). Salandra's unsuccessful direction of the war effort brought a broad national government to power in June 1916 under Paolo Boselli (*q.v.*). Orlando supported Boselli and received the important post of minister of the interior.

Orlando rapidly emerged as one of the most controversial members of the cabinet. Domestic opposition to the war was rising, notwithstanding a flash of military victory at Gorizia on the Isonzo in August 1916, and Orlando rejected demands to crack down on domestic dissent. His policy of persuasion not repression had Boselli's approval and was designed in part to keep the government backed by a majority in the Chamber of Deputies. Neutralist feeling still ran strong there. By the fall of 1917 Orlando bent under the weight of criticism: he purged his ministry of assistants alleged to be soft on wartime subversion. The interior minister declared Turin, where riots in August saw police stations ransacked and streets shut down by workers' barricades, a "war zone." Nonetheless, Orlando sought to walk a middle line. On October 16, as Boselli seemed destined to fall from office, the interior minister spoke in the Chamber of Deputies to stress that he stood for both a reinvigorated war effort and a continued respect for constitutional liberties.

The enemy breakthrough at Caporetto (October 24, 1917) and the ensuing retreat demolished the Boselli cabinet. On October 30 Orlando assumed the post of premier. Despite the widespread criticism he had faced—the collapse of the army was attributed by some to the government's failure to discipline the home front—he remained acceptable to most of the Chamber of Deputies. The new cabinet was spurred forward into sweeping mobilization of the nation's resources by Francesco Nitti (*q.v.*), the activist minister of the treasury. Meanwhile, Foreign Minister Sidney Sonnino (*q.v.*), who had been in office since late 1914, tried to maintain continuity in the conduct of Italy's external affairs.

Orlando's Churchillian oratory helped restore the deteriorating situation after Caporetto. At the Rapallo conference (November 5), he asked French and British delegates for fifteen combat divisions, adding that he would continue to wage the war even if he was driven back as far as Sicily. In late December, as dissent began to rise in the Chamber of Deputies, Orlando produced an overwhelming vote of confidence by proclaiming a policy of "resist, nothing but resist."

The army High Command was reordered. The failed General Cadorna (q.v.) was ousted as chief of staff. Orlando consulted with King Victor Emmanuel III and installed the younger and more robust General Armando Diaz (qq.v.), thought to be suited to work in close cooperation with the Cabinet. Orlando instituted close civil-military relations, notably lacking in the Cadorna era, by setting up a permanent War Council of generals and cabinet members in early 1918.

Premier Orlando struck off in several other new directions. He conciliated the neutralist bloc in the Chamber by consenting to an investigation of Caporetto, a sharp slap at Cadorna and the old military High Command. The Socialists and other opponents of the war he had treated gently as minister of the interior then found themselves facing trials for inciting riots. In June Orlando accepted the authority of General Foch (q.v.), the Allied generalissimo, to "coordinate" operations on the Italian front. As the Allied offensives in France and the Balkans gained momentum, Orlando stood ready to fire General Diaz if the Italian military commander persisted in delaying a large-scale offensive. In response, Diaz finally launched the Vittorio Veneto campaign in late October. Sonnino found, much to his discomfort, that Orlando was willing to meet South Slav representatives like Ante Trumbić (q.v.), and to hint to them that Italy was not rigidly opposed to the emergence of a unified South Slav state along the eastern shore of the Adriatic.

The postwar era pulled Orlando into a set of problems far less manageable than those he had faced in the wake of Caporetto. As prime minister and leader of Italy's delegation to the Versailles Peace Conference, Orlando found himself at the center of a tangle of conflicting claims. Sonnino insisted on receiving for Italy every inch of territory promised by the Treaty of London in 1915, most notably the Dalmatian coast. More impassioned nationalists called for taking Italian-inhabited territory all along the eastern Adriatic regardless of the limits set by the London agreement. The principal bone of contention was the port of Fiume, where Italian and Serb army units confronted each other during the closing weeks of hostilities. Orlando himself was roused to a frenzy of patriotism over the need to answer the call of the Italian population for Fiume. It quickly became evident that even the lines set down by the Treaty of London were not sacrosanct to Italy's allies. In early 1919, for example, President Woodrow Wilson (q.v.) established himself as a firm supporter of Yugoslavia's ambitions, even when these collided with Italian claims.

Faced by Wilson's opposition and aware that his own political support at home was eroding, Orlando dramatically walked out of the peace negotiations on April 24, 1919. The last straw had been Wilson's direct appeal to the Italian people to be conciliatory and moderate regarding rival territorial claims in the Adriatic. Back in Rome, Orlando basked for a time in the glow of his restored popularity. But in the end, he and Sonnino had to return to Versailles without any more hope of budging Wilson than before.

On June 19, 1919, Orlando's government collapsed. The problems of demobilization had proved to be highly disruptive. But most of all, the former premier had found himself saddled with the accusation of accepting the "mutilated victory" handed Italy by its ungrateful allies.

Orlando lingered on in Italian politics. As the domestic situation deteriorated in the early 1920s, he tried on two occasions to form a government, without success. The wartime premier tacitly approved the rise of Mussolini and the Fascist movement, breaking with Mussolini only as the Fascist leader moved to establish an open dictatorship in 1924/1925. Orlando then retired to private life for two decades. He entered politics again only in 1946 as president of the postwar constituent assembly. But he was defeated in his last political contest, running for the presidency of the new Italian republic in 1948. He then retired from public affairs for good and died in Rome, December 1, 1952.

Lowe and Marzari, *Italian Foreign Policy 1870-1940*; Mayer, *Politics and Diplomacy of Peacemaking*; Melograni, *Storia politica della grande guerra*; Orlando, *Memorie (1915-1919)*; Pieri, *L'Italia nella prima guerra mondiale*; Seton-Watson, *Italy from Liberalism to Fascism*; *Enciclopedia italiana*, XXV.

PAGE, Walter Hines (*United States, Ambassador*), was born in Cary, North Carolina, on August 15, 1855, the son of a prosperous farmer. Page graduated from Randolph-Macon College and entered into a career of journalism in St. Joseph, Missouri, New York City, and later Raleigh, North Carolina. He served as editor of the *Forum, Atlantic Monthly*, and

The World's Work. Page supported Woodrow Wilson's (*q.v.*) candidacy for the presidency in 1912, and the following year was rewarded with the ambassadorship to the Court of St. James's.

Page set out in London to promote the Anglo-American ascendancy in world politics; his initial efforts were directed towards resolving the Panama Canal toll issue and the Huerta problem in Mexico. The outbreak of war in Europe in the fall of 1914 brought a rift between the Stoic president in Washington and his impetuous envoy in London. Page disliked Wilson's initial adherence to strict neutrality and saw no need to enforce full observance of U.S. rights by both sides. Moreover, the ambassador agreed with British demands that the United States restrict the flow of goods to Germany's neutral neighbors, and he regarded the basic issue to be one of the assault of Prussian militarism upon democratic civilization. In the fall of 1914 Page threatened to resign if the State Department continued to insist that the British adhere to the Treaty of London (1909), which they had not signed, and end the blockade of the North Sea. Page was frustrated by what he considered to be the president's interminable paper war with Berlin, and after the *Lusitania* incident he counseled severing diplomatic relations with Germany and preparation for war. Early in 1916 the ambassador rejected "Colonel" House's (*q.v.*) peace mission to London, Paris, and Berlin; in December he denounced the president's "peace without victory" formula and instead demanded that Germany be crushed militarily. Page submitted his resignation in November 1916, correctly seeing that his position had become utterly untenable, but by February 1917 when Secretary of State Lansing (*q.v.*) had acted on the request, Germany's decision to resume unrestricted submarine warfare had drastically altered the situation.

Page rejoiced over the American declaration of war on April 6, 1917, seeing it as a vindication of his own policies. He at once urged that the government dispatch to Europe all available merchant and naval vessels to alleviate the shipping shortage of the Allies; he also desired a small expeditionary force, to be followed by a powerful American army. At the height of the U-boat offensive in June 1917, Page warned the president that the submarines might turn the tide: "There is therefore a possibility that the war may become a war between Germany and the United States alone." Wilson, in his glacial way, was not overly alarmed: "Page meddles in things outside his domain." In contrast to President Wilson, General Pershing, and Admiral Benson (*qq.v.*), Page had absolutely no qualms about placing America's land and

sea forces under Allied command. The envoy also urged Washington to make large loans at low interest rates available to the Entente. All this feverish activity led to severe strain and nephritis, forcing Page to resign his post in August 1918. He died on December 21, 1918, in Pinehurst, North Carolina.

Cooper, *Walter Hines Page*; Gregory, *Walter Hines Page*; Hendrick, *Life and Letters of Walter Hines Page*, 3 vols.; Trask, *Captains & Cabinets*; *Dictionary of American Biography*, XIV.

PAINLEVÉ, Paul (*France, Minister of War, Premier*), was born in Paris, December 5, 1863, the son of a draftsman. Painlevé's prodigious gifts in science and mathematics elevated him from his modest background to academic distinction. He graduated with honors from the École normale supérieure, took a doctorate in mathematics at the University of Paris, and received a professorship at Lille in 1887. By 1904, barely forty years old, he reached the summit of French academic achievement as professor of mechanics and mathematics at the École polytechnique. He was elected to the Chamber of Deputies in 1910 and took his place with the Independent Socialists, to the right of the militants of the SFIO (unified Socialist party). Soon he was the leader of the Republican-Socialists, one of several splinter groups that made up the Independent Socialists. Painlevé's political and scientific worlds merged in his early interest in aviation. He flew with Wilbur Wright in 1908 and subsequently led the French Air League. Within the National Assembly he devoted most of his energies to committees on naval and aviation affairs.

Painlevé served on the Chamber's aviation and munitions committee after the war broke out, but his main role during the first year of fighting was that of critic from the political Left. He took up the cause of General Sarrail (*q.v.*) with vehemence: in August 1915, he joined other parliamentary leaders in forcing the government to pledge four divisions for Sarrail's planned campaign at the Dardanelles. But he continued a drumfire attack on the government, pushing for a strong commitment to the Balkans and to Sarrail's plans. With the collapse of Prime Minister Viviani's (*q.v.*) government in October, Painlevé received his first cabinet post: minister of public instruction and military inventions in the government of Aristide Briand (*q.v.*).

Painlevé's fourteen-month tenure in this office was stormy. He continued to act as Sarrail's leading advocate, aiding the Left's favorite general to circumvent War Minister Gallieni (*q.v.*). In January 1916, Painlevé promised Sarrail to support all the needs of the Salonika front and throughout 1916 he blocked efforts by Briand to fire or at least to control Sarrail. Painlevé was drawn by Sarrail's political sympathies, but the minister's visits to the front in France led to a more significant military connection. He soon became closely linked to the politically conservative General Pétain (*q.v.*), whose appeal was his opposition to the prevailing offensive posture by the High Command.

In December 1916, Painlevé rejected Briand's offer of the war minister's post. Painlevé had insisted on bringing with him Pétain as the new commander in chief, a proposal Briand could not accept. Neither could Briand's successor, Alexandre Ribot (*q.v.*). Painlevé became war minister in March 1917 under Ribot only after pledging not to undercut the new commander, General Nivelle (*q.v.*), and his projected offensive. Painlevé soon wavered. Rumors in high military circles indicated Nivelle's plans led to bloodly disaster, and Painlevé took soundings among Nivelle's subordinates. Some gave lukewarm endorsements, while Pétain predicted outright calamity. At the climactic meeting of civil and military leaders at Compiègne (April 6), Painlevé led the criticism of the offensive; he defended the government's right to intervene in operations. Nivelle threatened to resign and President Poincaré (*q.v.*) intervened to turn the meeting in favor of Nivelle; Painlevé gave in, ignominiously, for the moment.

The war minister responded to the debacle at the Chemin des Dames by ignoring his March pledge to Ribot. Pro-Nivelle elements in the cabinet made it impossible simply to fire the failed commander. Engaged at Vimy Ridge, the British also objected to suspending the French offensive. Painlevé eased Nivelle out, and on April 29 he brought in Pétain as the army chief of staff; in reality, Pétain was to serve as Painlevé's restraint on Nivelle. By early May the cabinet was ready to see Nivelle go.

Painlevé's talents saw their best use in the crisis of spring/summer 1917. Sarrail's calls for massive reinforcements for the Balkans went unheard. Instead, Painlevé supported Pétain and the reshaping of military policy on the western front. Large-scale offensives ceased. Pétain directed his efforts to restoring order in the mutinous French army. To that end, Painlevé suspended the soldiers' right of appeal from courts-martial to civilian courts in cases involving mass indiscipline. Meanwhile, Painlevé and Poincaré applied clemency freely in such cases—often to Pétain's dismay. Discipline was to be restored, but not at the cost of a bloodbath.

With the fall of Ribot in September 1917, Painlevé formed a short-lived government while continuing on as war minister. He was the last wartime premier to govern on the basis of national conciliation. Elements of the Left still accepted him as one of their own, the man who stopped the deadly offensives of the Joffre-Nivelle era; the Right respected his links with Pétain. The embittered atmosphere and the national malaise of late 1917, however, exceeded Painlevé's abilities. Wright has judged him the worst prepared of France's wartime premiers; his brief tenure as war minister was his only other cabinet post. Pétain's carefully prepared success in the October Malmaison offensive gave Painlevé a military victory. It did no good. Socialists refused to join his cabinet in protest against Ribot's presence, and the *union sacrée* was broken. The Right fired charges of government softness toward defeatism; the Left lashed out at Painlevé's alleged failure to defend accused radicals such as Minister of the Interior Malvy (*q.v.*) with sufficient fervor. Painlevé could hardly govern in his preferred role of conciliator. He lacked the taste and the ability Georges Clemenceau (*q.v.*) soon displayed to rule as quasi-dictator.

Painlevé's sole achievement was in response to the Caporetto crisis. He used the Italian distress call to press the British for a unified strategy on the western front. Traditional British opposition softened to permit the formation of a political body, with a military secretariat attached. This Supreme War Council was a cautious first step to the inter-Allied unity of 1918.

Painlevé's government fell on November 13, 1917, brought down by the Right over the issue of softness toward subversion. He had no further role to play in the direction of the war. Painlevé returned to political prominence only in the mid-1920s. He served briefly as premier in 1925, then as war minister in several succeeding governments. He died in Paris, October 29, 1933.

Griffiths, *Pétain*; King, *Generals and Politicians*; Painlevé, *Comment j'ai nommé Foch et Pétain*; Tanenbaum, *General Maurice Sarrail*; Wright, *Raymond Poincaré and the French Presidency*; *Dictionnaire des parlementaires français*, VI.

PALÉOLOGUE, Georges Maurice (*France, Ambassador*), was born in Paris on January 13, 1859, the scion of a wealthy family of Greek background; Paléologue's parents claimed to be the descendants of the emperors of Byzantium. The young man abandoned an early interest in a scientific career to enter the French Foreign Office in 1880. Beginning in 1883 he spent four years in distant corners of the world from Tangiers to Korea. In 1887 he returned to Paris to spend two decades at the Quai d'Orsay, rising through the ranks of the French foreign-policy-making apparatus. In 1907 Paléologue was named minister to

Bulgaria; he returned to Paris in 1912 to take over the post director of political affairs at the Foreign Office. By then, his career was advancing under the patronage of Raymond Poincaré (*q.v.*), France's premier. Poincaré used Paléologue as a foreign policy adviser and more; in March 1913, for example, Poincaré, then president of France, called in Paléologue to pressure members of the Chamber of Deputies to pass the law establishing a three-year term of military service.

In January 1914, Paléologue accepted the post of ambassador to St. Petersburg. Reluctant at first to receive the appointment, Paléologue changed his mind at the urging of his old friend and sponsor. The new ambassador explained his mission as twofold: to restrain Russia in diplomatic affairs, and, perhaps more plausibly, to push St. Petersburg into the most active kind of military preparations. Whatever message he claimed to deliver, Paléologue found his known link with Poincaré lent special gravity to his words.

In early June 1914, Paléologue enraged leftists in the French Chamber of Deputies by refusing to return to Russia without assurances that the newly elected Chamber would maintain the three-year service law. This raised a variety of suspicions: Paléologue was perhaps intervening in French domestic affairs as the agent of the Russian government; or, conversely, Paléologue was helping President Poincaré to bend the French constitution to allow the head of state to guide the Chamber.

Controversial even before Sarajevo, Ambassador Paléologue stands at the center of the most bitter of historical controversies, the crisis of July 1914. Between July 23 and July 29 Premier René Viviani (*q.v.*) and President Poincaré were at sea, returning to France from a state visit to Russia. Thus, during the escalation of the crisis, Paléologue had unusual freedom of action. Albertini has constructed a detailed brief that accuses Paléologue of a variety of misdeeds; taken together, they mark him as one of the godfathers of the Great War. Albertini sees Paléologue encouraging Russian Foreign Minister Sergei Sazonov (*q.v.*) to make broad pledges of support to Serbia on July 24, by making equally broad pledges that Russia could rely on French aid. Albertini finds Paléologue concealing from authorities in Paris the rapid escalation of the military crisis as Russia shifted from preparing for partial mobilization to adopting the dangerous general mobilization of July 30. Paléologue should have informed Paris by July 29, according to Albertini, and thus allowed French authorities to restrain the Russians. And most damning of all, Albertini accuses Paléologue of preventing his Russian counterparts from understanding the range and nature of the support that Viviani offered; specifically that Viviani pledged to back Russia if St. Petersburg chose to throw its influence behind a peaceful resolution of the conflict between Austria and Serbia.

The ultimate villain in this bill of particulars against Paléologue the warmonger is Poincaré. The close political association between the two is a matter of record. Albertini strongly suggests that Paléologue's "independent" actions were, in fact, under covert orders from Poincaré to press Russia forward toward war with the Central Powers.

Paléologue served in St. Petersburg, more or less uneventfully, until the March Revolution of 1917. Then he was replaced by the less patrician figure of Albert Thomas (*q.v.*), Socialist and France's minister of munitions. Paléologue retired from the Foreign Office in 1921 to write his memoirs; these are widely considered to be sharply slanted away from any hint of Paléologue's culpability in the tragic days of late July 1914. A novelist, connoisseur of Chinese art, and literary critic, the ex-diplomat was named to the Académie française in 1928. He died in Paris, November 18, 1944.

Albertini, *The Origins of the War of 1914*, 3 vols.; Lee, *Europe's Crucial Years*; Paléologue, *An Ambassador's Memoirs*, 3 vols.; Wright, *Raymond Poincaré and the French Presidency*; *Larousse mensuel*, VIII.

PAŠIĆ, Nikola (*Serbia, Prime Minister*), was born in Zaječar in eastern Serbia, December 18, 1845. Setting out to become an engineer, he studied in Belgrade and Zurich. In Switzerland he entered the orbit of Serbian Socialists like Svetozar Marković; the Russian anarchist Mikhail Bakunin was also a close friend of Pašić's. The young engineer returned to Serbia and participated in the 1876/1877 conflict with Ottoman Turkey. In 1878 he was elected to the Serbian National Assembly (Skupština), beginning a remarkable political career that stretched over five decades.

Pašić was a member of the Radical party, which he helped transform from a program of socialism and republicanism to one of nationalism and monarchism. The major domestic issue during his first two decades of public life was the rivalry between the Obrenović dynasty and the National Assembly for political hegemony. In 1883 the quarrel became particularly stormy. Pašić was forced into exile in Bulgaria, accused of plotting armed rebellion against the crown. He was given amnesty and returned home six years later to serve in a variety of high offices.

In 1891/1892 Pašić served for the first time as prime minister; throughout his career he led twenty-two governments in all. He also held office in the 1890s as mayor of Belgrade and ambassador to

Russia. Clashes between the National Assembly's Radicals and the crown continued, fueled in part by the dynasty's Austrophile sentiments and the Radicals' call for a pro-Russian foreign policy. Pašić was imprisoned in 1897 and again in 1899. During his second incarceration, he was pressed, under threat of death, to implicate himself and his party in an assassination plot against the royal family. Already burdened with a reputation as a "trimmer" and political opportunist by younger Radicals, Pašić faced a dim political future.

The military coup of 1903 and the ascent to the throne of Peter Karadjordjević (q.v.) reversed Pašić's failing fortunes. In 1904 he was chosen prime minister; henceforth, until 1918, he stood as the dominant figure in Serbian politics. Under his direction, Belgrade modernized the nation's military, formed a firm diplomatic partnership with Russia, and in the Balkan Wars of 1912/1913 doubled Serbia's size at the expense of Ottoman Turkey and Bulgaria. But the military conspirators of 1903 proved a thorn in Pašić's side. Their claims to political influence peaked in mid-1914: the issue was whether to establish military or civil authority in recently conquered Macedonia. Peter was forced to step down in favor of his son, Prince Alexander (q.v.), and Pašić had to call new elections. The Sarajevo assassination took place as the election campaign was beginning.

The tie between Pašić and the Sarajevo assassins has been a source of bitter controversy. Did Pašić and the Serbian government encourage the plot? If not, was Pašić aware that Bosnian exiles and Serbian military circles led by Colonel Dimitrijević (q.v.) planned a spectacular political murder? Did Pašić act resolutely to prevent the crime? Relevant Serbian archives remain closed, but most historians absolve Pašić of participation in the plot. Indeed, his innate caution and his consciousness of Serbia's need for a military respite after the Balkan Wars make him an unlikely accomplice for the assassins. On the other hand, he probably knew a plot was afoot, and his attempts to prevent the student murderers from crossing from Serbia to Austria-Hungary were ineffective. Belgrade's warnings to Vienna, perhaps too vague and oblique to be taken seriously, did not put Austrian authorities on guard.

On July 25, 1914, Pašić personally delivered Serbia's answer to the Austrian ultimatum. Belgrade's note was highly conciliatory, but it sought to stop short of surrendering the nation's sovereignty to its northern neighbor. Pašić can have had few doubts of the outcome: the Serbian army was already preparing for combat. Judging from reports of Serbia's ambassador in St. Petersburg, Russian support seemed assured.

Serbian military leaders, notably Field Marshal Putnik (q.v.), held the enemy at bay for a year. In the fall of 1915, however, a combined Austro-German-Bulgarian attack sent Pašić and the government into exile, over the mountains to Albania, and finally on to Corfu. By then, a new threat to Pašić had emerged. Ante Trumbić (q.v.), the Croatian exile, headed a Yugoslav Committee in London that claimed to speak for Austria-Hungary's South Slav population. Pašić's war aims, in all probability centered on slicing border regions away from the Habsburg Empire, seemed threatened by larger claims, such as Trumbić's hopes to unite all South Slavs. Some historians, like Dragnich, see Pašić as a proponent of South Slav unity since early in the twentieth century. The weight of historical opinion, however, is presented by Charles Jelavich, who concedes such a unified state may have been Pašić's ultimate dream, but who also sees Pašić working for the duration of the war toward a more powerful Serbia, aggrandized by annexing only part of the Habsburg Empire.

By early 1917 Pašić found the diplomatic environment increasingly hostile. The collapse of the Russian monarchy deprived him of his staunchest ally, while Trumbić and his colleagues had a growing following in the United States and Britain. Thus, at Corfu, in June/July, Pašić met with Trumbić. The Serbian prime minister fended off calls for a federalist Yugoslavia, but he had to concede that a future united South Slav state be formed. Moreover, the Corfu Declaration stated that all citizens of the prospective political creation were to be treated equally.

The final year of the war saw Pašić working to limit the impact of Corfu. He barred the Yugoslav Committee from receiving formal diplomatic recognition from the Allies, and he continued to push for a profitable peace with Vienna. But a more formidable challenge then arose. Prince Regent Alexander had followed more or less quietly in Pašić's wake throughout the war. A more open partisan of South Slav unity than Pašić, the young prince had steadfastly rebuffed calls from Serbian opposition leaders and Allied friends of the Yugoslavs to oust the old man, but the victorious Balkan offensive of September/October 1918 and the ensuing collapse of Habsburg authority in the empire's southern provinces sealed Pašić's fate. Alexander shunted the old man aside, then dominated the November meetings in Belgrade that led to South Slav unity. Denied the premiership in the new kingdom of the Serbs, Croats, and Slovenes (later renamed Yugoslavia), Pašić was packed off to Paris to lead the peace delegation. In reality, he found himself involved in constant internecine warfare with his old foe Trumbić, then foreign minister of the new kingdom.

Pašić was recalled to power only in 1921. He served as prime minister briefly, then returned for a last stint, 1924-1926. Heavy-handed Serbian authorities who dominated the centralized government of the kingdom found other ethnic groups like the Croats responding with bitter enmity. When Pašić died in Belgrade, December 10, 1926, a royal dictatorship under Alexander was only two years away.

Albertini, *The Origins of the War of 1914*, 3 vols.; Dragnich, *Serbia, Pašić, and Yugoslavia*; Jelavich, "Nikolas P. Pašić: Greater Serbia or Jugoslavia?"; Jelavich and Jelavich, *Establishment of the Balkan National States*; Lederer, *Yugoslavia at the Peace Conference*; May, *Passing of the Hapsburg Monarchy*, 2 vols.; Petrovich, *History of Modern Serbia*, II; Stokes, "Serbian Documents from 1914: A Preview"; *Larousse mensuel*, VII.

PAYER, Friedrich von (*Germany, Vice Chancellor*), was born in Tübingen on June 12, 1847, the son of the local university beadle. After studying jurisprudence, Payer in 1871 practiced law in Stuttgart; however, politics proved to be his real love, and he served in the Reichstag as deputy for the German People's party in 1877/1878, 1880-1887, and 1890-1918. Concurrently, Payer was a member of the Württemberg Lower House from 1894 to 1912, presiding as its president for all but his first year in the Stuttgart Parliament. Ennobled in 1906, Payer four years later was instrumental in bringing about the fusion of various left liberal splinter groups into the Progressive People's party, whose parliamentary delegation he headed in Berlin.

During the Great War Payer hoped to bring about constitutional reform in Prussia and to accord the Rechstag a greater voice in national affairs. His greatest hour came in July 1917. On July 6 he joined Matthias Erzberger and Friedrich Ebert (*qq.v.*) to establish an interparty committee consisting of Centrists, Social Democrats, and Progressives—the forerunner of the later Weimar Coalition. Two weeks later Payer refused to be seduced by General Erich Ludendorff's entreaties to join the plot to depose Chancellor Theobald von Bethmann Hollweg (*qq.v.*), and at the end of the month he worked hard on behalf of the Reichstag's peace resolution, calling for an end to the war on the basis of the *status quo ante bellum*. In fact, Payer gained a reputation for several speeches denouncing the vast annexationist schemes of the Pan-Germans and the Conservatives.

In October 1917, ably assisted by Ebert, Payer was appointed vice chancellor in the new government formed by Count Georg von Hertling (*q.v.*). However, Payer failed to realize any of the reforms he had advocated over his long career. On almost every major issue—suppression of the munitions strikes in January 1918, peace negotiations at Brest Litovsk, and Foreign Secretary Richard von Kühlmann's (*q.v.*) dismissal—Payer in the end bowed to the will of the "silent dictator" Ludendorff. One historian has, therefore, described the Hertling-Payer government as constituting "no more than a constitutional cloak thrown over Ludendorff's dictatorship."

During the final months of the war, Payer stayed in office under Chancellor Prince Max von Baden (*q.v.*) and accepted Ludendorff's verdict on September 29 that the western front could no longer be held. At a dramatic confrontation with the general during the chancellor's illness on October 23, Payer refused to accept Ludendorff's reversal and plea that the struggle be continued at least through the winter of 1918; Prince Rupprecht of Bavaria (*q.v.*) had, in fact, apprised the vice chancellor of the desperate plight of the front. Payer rebuffed Ludendorff's appeal to the honor of the army: "I know nothing of soldier's honor. I am a burgher and civilian pure and simple. I can see only starving people."

Payer retired on November 9, 1918. He served briefly as a member of the German Democratic party in 1919/1920 at the National Assembly at Weimar, but played no major role in postwar politics. Payer died in Stuttgart on July 14, 1931.

Kitchen, *Silent Dictatorship*; Payer, *Mein Lebenslauf* and *Von Bethmann Hollweg bis Ebert*; *Biographisches Wörterbuch zur Deutschen Geschichte*, II.

PERSHING, John Joseph (*United States, General*), was born near Laclede, Missouri, on September 13, 1860, the son of a merchant. Pershing graduated from West Point in 1886, standing thirtieth in a class of seventy-seven, yet recognized as its leader. He served five years with the Sixth Cavalry in New Mexico before taking a post as professor of military science and tactics in 1891 at the University of Nebraska at Lincoln, where he obtained a law degree in his spare time. In 1897 Pershing returned to "the Point" as an instructor. Two years later he was assigned a tour of duty in the Philippines and during the Spanish-American War fought in Cuba with the Tenth (Negro) Cavalry Regiment, which earned him the nickname Black Jack. Pershing attended the Army War College in the grade of captain in 1904/1905, and then served as military attaché to Japan and as American observer during the Russo-Japanese War. President Theodore Roosevelt promoted him to the grade of brigadier general over 800 superiors in 1906, and for the next eight years Pershing again served in the Philippines. In August 1915, a fire took the life of his wife and three daughters, and Black Jack became a stiff, taciturn man. Tough, confident, and experienced, he was selected by Secretary of War Baker (*q.v.*) to track down Pancho Villa after his raid on Columbus, New Mexico, in March 1916; Pershing was not to return from that assignment until February 1917, without having captured Villa, but also without having aroused the Mexican government by his actions.

Pershing's ability to adhere to orders prompted the president to entrust him with command of the American Expeditionary Forces on May 26, 1917. The general's only instructions were to maintain independence of command, and Pershing throughout the war adamantly opposed so-called amalgamation. It was not an easy position. Generals Haig and Pétain (*qq.v.*) constantly badgered Pershing to put his men into existing Allied armies so that they could be trained to hold the trenches; Pershing instead trained his men for open field operations and rejected amalgamation owing to national pride, a thirst for military glory, and deep distrust of Entente efficiency. During the bleak weeks in the spring of 1918 when the western front reeled under General Ludendorff's (*q.v.*) Michael offensive, the American field commander offered his fresh troops to French commanders without restrictions—save the principle of a separate American army.

Pershing had, since June 1917, cherished a major American action, and in August 1918 informed Marshal Foch (*q.v.*) that he wished to reduce the St. Mihiel salient "as an American army and in no other way." General Pétain concurred: the doughboys had already received their baptism of fire at Cantigny, Château-Thierry, and in Belleau Wood. On September 12, 1918, Pershing opened up with 3,000 guns and sent the First Army against the 200-square-mile St. Mihiel salient. The American infantry constituted two sharp pincers of the forceps cutting into each side of the salient (part of the German Michael defense line). Pershing, desiring a victory at all costs, hurled seven double-sized divisions (including four French) against eight war-weary German divisions. The outcome was never in doubt. Since the Germans had, in reality, begun to withdraw their troops from the salient the night before, especially French critics, according to Basil Liddell Hart, have stated that "the Americans relieved the Germans."

The American field commander next shifted his army to hook up with the mighty Allied offensive in the Meuse-Argonne sector; on September 26 the U.S. forces undertook a coordinated infantry thrust, supported by artillery, tanks, and airplanes, near Côte Dame Marie against the Kriemhilde sector of the Hindenburg line. Pershing again was anxious for an

American success and tolerated no mediocre or listless commanders. As Liddell Hart noted, "commanders of all grades fell beneath Pershing's sickle almost as fast as their men beneath the scythe of the German machine-guns." The doughboys advanced slowly, and the French leader Clemenceau (*q.v.*) took this opportunity on October 21 to appeal over Pershing's head directly to President Wilson in a letter denouncing American troops as being not "unusable" but "merely unused." The armistice on November 11 precluded further acrimony.

Pershing had grown fearful of the army's chief of staff in Washington, General March (*q.v.*), over his proposal to exchange staff officers and to determine promotion to general grade. In addition, Black Jack had come out for "unconditional surrender" by the Central Powers—without informing "Colonel" House (*q.v.*) of this decision prior to a meeting of the Supreme War Council. In fact, Pershing wanted to crush the Germans and to occupy Berlin, but the war-weary Allies resented such advice.

Black Jack returned to the United States in September 1919 as general of the armies, a rank once held by George Washington. In 1921 he was appointed chief of staff, a post he retired from on September 13, 1924. His memoirs, published in 1931, won the Pulitzer Prize for history; they also evoked acid criticism from General March. Pershing died on July 15, 1948, in Washington, D.C. He was a master of tactics with a rigid devotion to logistics, not a strategist of grand combinations such as a later American commander in Europe (Dwight D. Eisenhower).

Coffman, *War to End All Wars*; Liddell Hart, *The Real War*; Pershing, *My War Experiences in the World War*; Vandiver, *Black Jack*, 2 vols.; *Dictionary of American Biography*, XXV Supplement Four.

PÉTAIN, Henri-Philippe Benoni Omer Joseph (*France, General*), was born on April 24, 1856, in the village of Cauchy-à-la Tour, near Arras. The son of a modest peasant family, Pétain was soon orphaned. His uncle supervised his education in religious academies. He graduated from St. Cyr in 1878 and began a long career as an infantry officer with the elite Chasseurs Alpins on the Italian frontier. Promoted in strict order of seniority, Pétain rose to captain in 1890 and reached major only ten years later. He avoided service in the colonial army where promotions could come far more rapidly. He graduated from the War College in 1890 and served tours as a staff officer in Marseilles and Paris; but even these moves, helpful to others, did not speed him along. As a quietly nonobservant Catholic but a mild anti-

Dreyfusard, he gained no friends on either side of the political fight that divided the army in the late 1890s. Pétain was noted for a cold, reserved manner; but this was broken at times in the least helpful fashion—by heated disagreements with his superiors. Still a major at age forty-four, Pétain distinguished himself, however, at the head of a battalion at the 1900 maneuvers; by then he was a recognized expert on infantry tactics.

In 1901 Pétain's career became intertwined with the evolution of the War College, the debate over the proper infantry tactics for the French army, as well as the larger issue of shaping military doctrine in an era of expanding firepower. He opposed the influence of colleagues like Ferdinand Foch (q.v.), who saw new weaponry, willpower, and high morale as the tools to make the offensive side unbeatable in a future war. "Firepower kills," Pétain insisted. Only close and continuous artillery support could permit successful infantry advances. Any offensive strategy must depend for its success on first weakening the enemy by defensive operations.

Pétain had some influence. The new infantry regulations adopted in 1904 incorporated many of his ideas; his counterarguments to the concept of offensive warfare in all circumstances received wide circulation. But he did not prevail. He was relieved from the War College in 1907; in return, he got an undesirable command in Brittany. The new infantry regulations of 1914 revised his ideas. On the eve of Europe's greatest war, Pétain was getting ready to retire. He probably expected to be forgotten soon, a fifty-eight-year-old colonel with a controversial but hardly distinguished career. His ideas had offended his superiors; he had no combat record to offset their antagonism. But Pétain had foreseen many of the problems of conducting military operations in the war that was about to break out. As Ryan has put it, unlike most of his peers and superiors, he was intellectually prepared for World War I.

In August 1914 Pétain was in temporary command of an infantry brigade of the Fifth Army under General Lanrezac (q.v.). His leadership at the battle of Charleroi, in which he held the Meuse crossings and protected the army's eastern flank, and at the subsequent battle of Guise made him a brigadier general. Before the war was a month old, Pétain had his own division, which he led at the battle of the Marne. There he attacked. The meticulous preparation and the insistence on massive artillery support that he displayed there reflected his prewar ideas, and they became his trademark. By October Pétain led the XXXIII Corps near Arras.

His rise continued in 1915. More important, his views on the war crystallized. Any lingering expectation that the conflict might perhaps be a brief one, decided by a Napoleonic breakthrough, vanished from Pétain's mind. In early May he led his corps in the Artois offensive. As usual, he insisted on heavy artillery support as the key to successful infantry advances. The artillery must prepare the way; then the infantry was to attack; and then, the artillery must be brought up to prepare the next move forward. He took Vimy Ridge, and, twenty miles away at Lille, the Germans prepared to evacuate their army group headquarters. But Pétain's neighbors did not match his progress and his superiors did not have reserves ready at hand. The Artois attack, so well begun, bogged down. Pétain's reward for the achievements of May was command of the Second Army; taking over the XXXIII Corps was General Fayolle (q.v.), a likeminded commander who remained Pétain's right-hand man throughout the rest of the war. In September Pétain led his new army to attack in Champagne, in the second great French assault of the year on the western front. German defenses had improved after the scare in Artois, making French advances that much more difficult. As the year ended, in a report to his superiors Pétain summarized the lessons learned. The enemy must be worn down gradually, with France paying the price in artillery shells rather than with the blood of its infantry. The decisive thrust, the blow that would bring victory, could only come far in the future. Such views went directly counter to the animating philosophy of General Joffre (q.v.), the French generalissimo. Neither were they what the politicians and the public wished to hear.

Pétain's rise to the top of the military ladder required, first of all, a new example of his skill—at Verdun. Second, it could come only after the Napoleonic hopes had been dashed once and for all. On February 21, 1916, the Germans began to assault Verdun. Their aim was not to capture it but to make the French defend it at prohibitive cost. Pétain was placed in charge of the Verdun sector on February 25. In April he took over command of the Center Army Group, which included the forces at Verdun. Pétain met the German threat with a variety of responses. He began a carefully arranged supply system. The German assault on the Verdun salient could be supported by a number of highways and railroads, but the French were compelled to rely on a single road that must operate at peak efficiency at all times. Pétain kept personal command of heavy artillery groups in his effort to break the enemy assaults using the weapon he always preferred to employ. Finally, he adopted the "noria" system, which meant rotating divisions into the Verdun fighting for short periods of time, then sending them to quieter fronts to recover from their ordeal. Tours lasted two to eight days; casualties sometimes reached 50 percent. Fully sixty-five divisions, two-thirds of the French army, underwent the bloodletting. At such a hideous cost, the army remained intact, or so it seemed.

Although Joffre was obviously losing popularity after being surprised at Verdun, Pétain soon found that defensive successes were not enough to make him the new commander in chief. That role went to one of Pétain's subordinates, the optimistic General Robert Nivelle (q.v.), commander of the Second Army. Nivelle had launched a series of successful offensives at Verdun once the enemy threat had been contained. His brave pledge to employ such methods on a gigantic scale, and thus to end the war quickly and victoriously, brought him the generalissimo's role by the close of 1916.

By then Pétain had friends in high places. If President Poincaré disliked the general's caution and pessimism, Paul Painlevé (qq.v.), appointed minister of war in March 1917, was a staunch supporter. When Nivelle had failed ingloriously in the second half of April, Pétain was brought in. After a brief stint as chief of the General Staff—his main duty was to keep Nivelle out of further trouble—Pétain replaced his luckless former subordinate in May.

The army theatened to collapse. Even in Nivelle's last weeks in command, acts of "collective indiscipline" had begun; troops refused to move from rear positions to the front line, for example. Pétain's greatest achievement may have been to hold the skeleton of the army together while he healed its flesh. All of this, one must remember, took place in the face of a dangerous enemy who could attack any moment. Mutineers were executed, although the exact number shot, rather than condemned and subsequently given a lesser penalty, remains in dispute. Painlevé, as well as Premier Ribot (q.v.), would not sanction Draconian measures even if Pétain had been so inclined.

The new generalissimo placed enormous emphasis on changing the nature of French military operations. The vainglorious offensives, of which Nivelle's had been the latest example, ceased. Meanwhile, Pétain personally visited ninety army divisions to hear complaints. He followed up on what he heard by improvements in the smaller amenities of military life: better rest camps, regular leave, improved food. At the same time, however, Pétain jumped into civilian politics. He pressed Ribot's government to crack down on home-front subversives; in particular, he demanded that French Socialists not be permitted to go to Stockholm to attend the Russian-sponsored international congress of Socialists.

By late August Pétain was ready to fight again. Talented army commanders like General Guillaumat at Verdun and General Maistre (qq.v.) at Malmaison launched meticulously prepared offensives: heavy artillery and, increasingly, the use of tanks were to play the lead in wearing down the enemy. Moreover, these were brief attacks for limited gains. By the close of the "terrible year" of 1917, French casualties per month had been cut in half from their April peak. In preparation for the battles to come, Pétain tried to reverse the standard defense methods of the French army. No longer were troops to be concentrated in front-line positions with orders to hold at all costs. Instead, Pétain called for a defense in depth, stressing flexibility and designed, as usual, to meet the needs of the war with the least cost in French lives.

The final year of the war brought a series of thunderous German offensives lasting from late March until July. In response to Ludendorff's (q.v.) assault of March 21 near Amiens, at the point where the French armies and the BEF linked up, Pétain nearly precipitated a crisis within the alliance. He ordered Fayolle, who was commanding the Reserve Army Group, to consider withdrawing southward toward Paris if it proved impossible to hold the German drive. With the appointment of Foch as Allied generalissimo (April 3, 1918), Pétain found himself only the second-ranking figure on the French side. And Pétain's caution—Foch often considered it undue pessimism—received strong opposition from above. In mid-June Premier Georges Clemenceau (q.v.) told Pétain that he no longer had the right to appeal Foch's orders to the French government!

To compound Pétain's troubles, his well-found defensive concepts met strong opposition from his subordinates. On May 27 the Germans crashed through on the Chemin des Dames line and closed on the Marne. General Duchêne, commanding the Sixth Army, had simply ignored Pétain's defensive instructions. In mid-July however, General Gouraud and the Fourth Army east of Reims gave a classic demonstration of how effective Pétain's defense in depth could be.

From July forward, the Allies were on the offensive. Differences between Pétain and Foch faded. Indeed, by October Pétain had put caution aside and was pushing his troops forward with the same fiery enthusiasm Foch had monopolized earlier in the summer. On December 18, barely a month after the November armistice, Pétain received his baton as a marshal of France. The old general's career, seemingly in its last days in 1914, stretched for decades.

Pétain remained on active duty throughout the 1920s and on into the 1930s. In 1934 he entered the Cabinet as minister of War, and in 1939 he accepted appointment as France's ambassador to Spain. In June 1940, in one of the most grim moments in his nation's history, Pétain, then eighty-four years old, took the lead in forming the Vichy regime under the shadow of Adolf Hitler. For this, he was tried after World War II. Sentenced to death, he was reprieved, like many of the mutineers of 1917, and sent to prison for life. He died on the Isle d'Yeu on July 23, 1951.

During World War II Pétain's performance as France's generalissimo in 1917/1918 came under renewed and heavy criticism. Caution, ineffectiveness, and even a lust for blood in punishing the mutineers were placed at his door. Later accounts from scholars like Ryan and Griffiths have restored the balance. But the best comment of all may have come, in the late 1920s, from B. H. Liddell Hart. He praised Pétain's working motto of "victory at the smallest price" and went on to cite Pétain as one of the small number of individuals in World War I "to understand the mechanism of modern war as it has been developed by industrial nations in arms."

Barnett, *The Swordbearers*; Griffiths, *Pétain*; Liddell Hart, *Reputations*; Pedroncini, *Pétain: général en chef*; Ryan, *Pétain the Soldier*.

PETER KARADJORDJEVIĆ (*Serbia, King of Serbia*), was born in Belgrade, June 29, 1844, the son of the reigning monarch, Prince Alexander. Nineteenth-century Serbian politics revolved around the rivalry between the princely Karadjordjević and Obrenović families and their respective followers. In 1859 the political wheel turned, the Karadjordjević line was deposed, and Peter left for an exile that stretched for forty-five years. Educated in Switzerland and France, Peter fought with distinction in the Franco-Prussian War. He spent most of the next three decades in Switzerland, but Serbian affairs remained his vital interest. In his homeland the exiled prince stood high in public esteem. A volunteer in the Bosnian revolt against the Ottoman Turks in the 1870s, he bolstered his popularity by his marriage in 1883 to the daughter of the reigning Serbian line in Montenegro.

In the 1890s rumors of Peter's likely return circulated widely. Disenchantment with the Obrenović rulers mounted, intensified by their pro-Austrian foreign policy as well as their unsavory domestic affairs. In June 1903, a military conspiracy led to the murder of the young Obrenović ruler. Historians absolve Peter of complicity in the crime, but he was the predictable choice to mount the throne. A steeping in Western political ideas—he had, for example, translated Mill's "On Liberty" into Serbo-Croatian—prepared him to fit comfortably into the role of constitutional monarch. But Peter's reign marked a substantial change in Serbia's foreign policy. Belgrade's friendship with Vienna cooled. Russia emerged as Serbia's link with the great powers. Concern for ethnic Serbs outside the nation's borders deepened. En route to Belgrade in 1903 to accept the Serbian crown, Peter found himself greeted in Vienna as "the Yugoslav King" by a throng of Serbian, Croatian, and Slovenian students. Peter's sympathies pointed instead to an expanded Serbia, and in this he was supported by Serbia's political and military leaders. But he found himself a symbol for larger South Slav aspirations. In 1912, during the First Balkan War, Croatian volunteers rushing to aid Serbia hailed Peter as "our King."

Peter presided over a political system constitutional in form but, in fact, rent by persistent clashes between civil and military authorities. In late June 1914, on the eve of the assassination at Sarajevo, crisis erupted. The immediate issue was the control over Macedonian lands won in the recent Balkan Wars. Peter, old and sick, was compelled to step down in favor of his son, Crown Prince Alexander (*q.v.*), who became prince-regent.

During World War I Peter took the role of front-line soldier and symbol of national resistance. In the face of the Austrian offensive of December 1914, he rose from his sickbed to stand in the trenches with a rifle; a few days later, he led the parade of the victorious Serbian army back into Belgrade. The ultimate attack of the Central Powers, then joined by Bulgaria, in October/November 1915 again brought the old man out of retirement. Serbian and foreign observers were treated to the sight of a crowned monarch fighting as a common soldier.

Peter rode a gun carriage over the mountains during the epic Serbian retreat westward to Albania at the close of 1915, then left for Greece and obscurity. His final retirement was broken only in December 1918 when he was crowned as ruler of the new kingdom of the Serbs, Croats, and Slovenes. He passed the throne at once to Alexander.

The soldier-king died in Belgrade, August 16, 1921.

Adams, *Flight in Winter*; Petrovich, *History of Modern Serbia*, II; Vucinich, *Serbia between East and West*; *Larousse mensuel*, V.

PFLANZER-BALTIN, Karl Baron von (*Austria-Hungary, General*), was born in Pécs, Hungary, on

June 1, 1855, the son of an auditor general. His father was raised to noble status in 1893 and when his mother's uncle, Joseph Baron von Baltin, adopted the young lad in 1898, his name officially became the familiar hyphenated form. Pflanzer graduated from the Theresa Military Academy in 1875 and attended the War Academy in 1879/1880. After a brief stint with the General Staff he was sent to the Ulans in 1889 in the grade of captain, and then returned to the General Staff as major in 1891. Pflanzer was an instructor at the War Academy in 1893/1894, and in 1896 was sent to Lemberg as chief of staff of the XII Army Corps in the grade of colonel. Next came tours of duty in Hermannstadt and Kronstadt, Transylvania, as well as in Brünn, Moravia. By October 1911, Pflanzer-Baltin was in line to receive command of an army corps but was denied this assignment owing to ill health. He was sent instead to Vienna as inspector general of Corps Officer Schools; in June 1914 he requested early retirement.

The outbreak of war found Pflanzer-Baltin in North Africa, but at the urgings of Count István Tisza and General Conrad von Hötzendorf (qq.v.) he was reactivated and on October 1, 1914, was promoted general of cavalry and given command of a hastily assembled Army Corps Pflanzer-Baltin in Transylvania. However, the unexpected rapid Russian advance into Galicia prompted Conrad to transfer this corps to the borders of the Bukovina. Pflanzer-Baltin became a master of improvisation and conducted an unorthodox campaign for much of the war in the Carpathian Mountains. When Conrad's counterattack designed to relieve the fortress at Przemysl in January and February 1915 bogged down in the deep snow, Pflanzer-Baltin's army group alone managed to advance on to Czernowitz, but even it was unable to swing north in order to reach the Third Army (Boroević) or the German South Army (Linsingen). The result was that the great fortress at Przemysl fell on March 23, 1915, with the loss of over 170,000 soldiers.

In May 1915, Pflanzer-Baltin's forces were regrouped as the Seventh Army and they took part in heavy fighting near Chotin during the summer as well as in the bitter New Year's battle of 1915/1916. On June 4, 1916, General Aleksei Brusilov (q.v.) launched his powerful attack against the Dual Monarchy's forces in Galicia. After the initial breakthrough at Ocna on June 10, Brusilov rolled up the Fourth Army at Volhynia and drove Pflanzer-Baltin's Seventh Army, which formed the southern front of the Austro-Hungarian forces, out of east Galicia and the entire Bukovina until additional units hastily brought up from the Italian front halted the

Russian advance on the slopes of the Carpathians in September. Pflanzer-Baltin then had to witness the Seventh Army being placed, as Conrad put it, "under German guardianship" as General Hans von Seeckt (q.v.) was appointed its "supreme chief of staff." In fact, Seeckt informed German headquarters that only with German aid and under German command could the eastern front be stabilized; on September 10, 1916, Pflanzer-Baltin was relieved of command of the Seventh Army.

The new Emperor Charles (q.v.) recalled Pflanzer-Baltin as inspector general of all foot soldiers in March 1917, which meant in effect that the general was entrusted with training new recruits in rear areas. But on July 10, 1918, Pflanzer-Baltin was given command of Austro-Hungarian forces in Albania, and the following month he mounted a limited counteroffensive against French and Italian units that netted him Fjeri and Berat. Cut off from communications in Albania, Pflanzer-Baltin refused to believe that the war was over, even when finally notified on November 5 that an armistice had been signed. His army group still flew the imperial-royal standard as it fought its way to the supposed safety of Cattaro. Only on November 18, 1918, convinced that his troops could no longer be relied upon and that the port did indeed belong to the Yugoslav National Committee, would Pflanzer-Baltin consent to be evacuated by sea on an Allied warship. He died in Vienna on April 8, 1925.

Bardolff, *Militär-Maria Theresien-Orden*; Rothenberg, *Army of Francis Joseph*; Wagner, *Der Erste Weltkrieg*; *Neue Österreichische Biographie*, XVI.

PILSUDSKI, Joseph (*Austria-Hungary, Polish War Minister*), was born in the Vilna district of Russian Poland on December 5, 1867, to a family from the lower gentry. Pilsudski was expelled as a medical student in Kharkov in 1886, and the following year he was arrested in Vilna and sent to Siberia for five years for allegedly planning to assassinate Tsar Alexander III. On his return to Vilna in 1892, he became active in founding the Polish Socialist party, and in 1900 was arrested as editor of the clandestine *Robotnik* ("The Worker"). Friends helped him to escape from St. Petersburg in May 1901, and Pilsudski made his way to Cracow in Austrian Poland. Three years later he traveled to Japan with the quixotic notion of enlisting that country's help to establish an independent Poland. Back in Lvov, Pilsudski by 1908 had begun to collect a "private Polish army" and hoped that an Austro-Hungarian victory over Russia, combined with a French victory over Germany, would enable him to liberate his homeland. Viennese army circles were not reticent to lend their support to these anti-Russian undertakings.

With the outbreak of war about 7,000 of Pilsudski's followers were deployed by Austria-Hungary in the lands of the Crown of St. Stephen, while Pilsudski retained command of his legion of about 3,000 soldiers. On November 5, 1916, the Central Powers proclaimed the independence of Congress Poland and Pilsudski accepted the post of war minister in the new Council of State. However, the grandiose proclamation in effect created a German-Austro-Hungarian satellite that was to serve as a manpower reservoir for the Central Powers, and when his men refused to take an oath of loyalty to the military command of the Central Powers, Pilsudski was arrested by German officials in July 1917. He was released from Magdeburg fortress during the German revolution in the fall of 1918; in Warsaw he was proclaimed head of state and first marshal of Poland.

Pilsudski held off an invasion by the Soviet Red Army with the help of the French General Maxime Weygand (q.v.) in 1919/1920. He resigned as head of state in 1921 and as chief of the army two years later, but in May 1926 marched on Warsaw and again assumed dictatorial powers. Pilsudski died in Cracow on May 12, 1935.

Conze, *Polnische Nation und deutsche Politik im ersten Weltkrieg*; Landau, *Pilsudski and Poland*; *Encyclopedia of World Biography*, VIII.

PLEVE, Pavel Adamovich (*Russia, General of Cavalry*), was born June 11, 1850, to a Russian noble family of German origin. He completed the Nikolaevsky Cavalry College in 1870 and the General Staff Academy in 1877. He was immediately posted to serve in the 1877/1878 war against Turkey. The young officer remained in the Balkans, spending two years as adviser to the Bulgarian army and the Bulgarian War Ministry. Pleve returned to Russia in 1880 to follow the customary career pattern of a *Genshtabist*, or General Staff officer, rotating through a series of progressively more responsible staff and line posts. In 1909 he received the plum assignment of commanding the Moscow Military District.

At the outbreak of World War I, Pleve took command of the Russian Fifth Army. With the Fourth Army, soon in the hands of General Evert (q.v.) on his right, Pleve met the full weight of the Austrian offensive northward from Galicia in the last week of August 1914. At Komarów, August 26-31, Pleve's forces paid with 40 percent casualties for the misjudgments of front commander Ivanov (q.v.). Pleve waited in vain for Ivanov to bring up General Ruzsky (q.v.) and the Third Army to mask his open flank spread over a huge expanse. With the Austrian Fourth Army under Auffenberg (q.v.) curling around Pleve's exposed units, the old Russian cavalryman avoided another Tannenberg by a timely withdrawal.

Such decisiveness was unusual in the hidebound upper reaches of the Russian officer corps. But it was in character for Pleve. Sixty-five years old and in fragile health, he would have been put to pasture in most other armies, not handed a hundred thousand men to march around Poland. But Pleve, whom British General Alfred Knox described as "old and bent" with a sharp mind and an iron will, was miles above the customary Russian mediocrity of advanced years. In two and a half days in mid-November he marched his army seventy miles northward across the Polish plains to help the beleaguered Russian Second Army at Lodz. In early 1915 he received command of the new Twelfth Army. Pleve's orders read to strike East Prussia from the south, while General Sievers and the Tenth Army thrust in from the east. The Germans made a hash of this effort to rerun the 1914 Tannenberg campaign through to a different conclusion. They bloodied Sievers at Augustovo in mid-February, leaving Pleve only the option of launching a subsidiary offensive to ease Sievers' plight.

Pleve played the fireman one last time in September 1915. With Russian Poland safely in hand, General Ludendorff (q.v.) sprang a final offensive eastward and northward from his base in East Prussia. Pleve, then back with the Fifth Army, displayed his usual grit. Holding the crucial sector, from the Gulf of Riga to Kovno, he could hardly fail to note that nothing stood between him and Petrograd but undefended, open space. But Pleve and the Fifth held their line. The old man, in truly precarious health, briefly commanded the northwestern front in the second winter of the war. But his days were numbered. He left active duty in February 1916, and died in Moscow, April 10, 1916.

No strategic virtuoso, the perpetually ailing Pleve was, at the least, calm and tough. He represented the best Russia's senior generals could normally muster in leading their field armies in the calamitous first year and a half of the war.

Rostunov, ed., *Istoriia pervoi mirovoi voiny*, I; Rutherford, *The Russian Army in World War I*; Stone, *The Eastern Front*; *Bol'shaia sovetskaia entsiklopediia*, 3rd ed., XX.

PLUMER, Herbert Charles Onslow (*Great Britain, General*), first Viscount Plumer, of Messines, was born in Torquay on March 13, 1857, to an old Yorkshire family. He was educated at Eton and in 1876 joined the Sixty-fifth Foot. Plumer was promoted captain in 1882 and two years later took part in the Sudan campaign. Next came service in South Africa, to which he returned in 1899 in order to organize the Rhodesian Horse. He came home in March 1902, and was promoted brigadier general the following year. Lord Roberts appointed Major General Plumer quartermaster general of the newly formed Army Council; from 1906 to 1909 Plumer commanded the Fifth Division in Ireland. The following year he was promoted lieutenant general and commander in chief at York.

On Christmas 1914 Plumer was given command of the II Army Corps in France, and he proved to be as popular with his soldiers as General Hubert Gough (*q.v.*) was disliked by his. Plumer advanced to command the Second Army in May 1915, and for nearly two uneventful years held the salient at Ypres, training his regulars and drafts for modern siege warfare. In the meantime, the British field commander in France, Sir Douglas Haig (*q.v.*), had desperately sought to drive the Germans from the high ground at Ypres, and throughout the costly battles of the Somme in 1916 and Arras and Lens in 1917 had almost destroyed his armies in this pursuit.

After the collapse of General Robert Nivelle's (*q.v.*) offensive in April 1917, an Allied conference in Paris decided that the British were to undertake an offensive at once while General Henri Pétain (*q.v.*) attempted to restore order and morale in the French armies. Haig instructed Plumer to mount an attack designed to take the high ground around Messines and Wytschaete, and on June 7, 1917, Plumer commenced operations by exploding nineteen great mines, each containing 600 tons of explosives, under the German trenches. This action was followed up by intensive artillery bombardment by nearly 1,000 guns, and an advance by twelve infantry divisions: the plateau was carried at a cost of one-fifth of the projected casualties.

The Allies decided to follow up this success by sending General Gough on July 31 from Messines toward Passchendaele, where General Henry Rawlinson (*q.v.*) was deployed. The operation was a dismal failure, and on August 25 Haig transferred command from Gough to Plumer; the latter repeated the methods employed at Messines and managed by November 13 to capture the high ground at Passchendaele after eight great battles. However, the British artillery had destroyed the local drainage system and this, compounded by torrential downpours, turned the fields into a morass in which

hundreds of soldiers drowned or were suffocated in the mud. In addition, the Italian collapse at Caporetto in October and the disappearance of Russia from the war vitiated these hard-fought gains.

General Plumer, a capable and cool commander, was hastily dispatched to Italy on November 9 to head an Allied force composed of six French and five British divisions in order to shore up the crumbling Italian front along the River Po. The Montello sector was restored by December, and four months later the Second Army was returned to France. Plumer wisely turned down an offer to become chief of the Imperial General Staff early in 1918, thereby clearing the way for Sir Henry Wilson (*q.v.*) to aspire to this position.

Plumer returned to the western front just in time to absorb the blows of General Erich Ludendorff's (*q.v.*) Michael offensive on March 21, 1918. In rapid succession, Messines was lost, Wytschaete fell, and even Passchendaele was taken by the enemy. Plumer refused to panic, however, and he held the Ypres salient and let the German assault exhaust itself. Thereafter, reinforced by the Americans, the Allies counterattacked; the Second Army advanced rapidly in the north, crossed the River Rhine, and marched in triumph through Cologne. Plumer was appointed commander of occupied German territory.

The popular commander was raised to the peerage as Baron Plumer, of Messines and of Bilton, Yorkshire, given the thanks of Parliament, a grant of £30,000, and promoted field marshal in 1919. He served as governor of Malta from 1919 to 1924, and in 1925 began a three-year tour as high commissioner in Palestine. Plumer was raised to the degree of viscount in 1929. He died in London on July 16, 1932, and was buried in Westminster Abbey.

Plumer was perhaps the best British general of the Great War. He understood modern siege warfare and he was not averse to standing up to general headquarters. Above all, he enjoyed the confidence of those who served under him and did not favor the callous strategy of attrition practiced by Generals Haig, Gough, and Kiggell (*q.v.*). His white moustache, red face, and dumpy figure became the model for David Lowe's caricature, Colonel Blimp.

Edmonds, *Military Operations: France and Belgium*, 13 vols.; Harington, *Plumer of Messines*; Liddell Hart, *The Real War*; *Dictionary of National Biography 1931-1940*.

POINCARÉ, Raymond (*France, President*), was born in Bar-le-Duc, August 20, 1860, the son of a prominent engineer. His birthplace and childhood home in Lorraine was occupied by the Germans for three years during the course and aftermath of the Franco-Prussian War, 1870/1871. It remained close to the new border with Germany; by Poincaré's own claim, his strident nationalism drew upon these bitter experiences from his youth. Trained as a lawyer, he entered politics as *chef de cabinet* to the minister of agriculture, a family friend. Poincaré himself was elected to the Chamber of Deputies in 1887. As a youthful thirty-nine-year-old, he received the post of minister of public instruction in 1893. On his first visit, the staff mistook him for a student. The following year, he rose to the prestigious post of minister of finance. In the decade beginning in 1896, Poincaré withdrew from an active political role and concentrated his talents and energy on becoming a wealthy attorney. Acquaintances were struck by his tremendous capacity for hard work and concentration, as well as by his frigid demeanor.

Poincaré took the post of premier in 1912, when Joseph Caillaux (*q.v.*) fell in the aftermath of the Agadir affair. Poincaré obtained ratification of Caillaux's agreement with Germany, but he never had to face accusations of being pro-German. The new premier had been a vocal advocate of military preparedness since 1911, a position that he restated in his ministerial declaration upon taking office in 1912. His main interest rested in foreign affairs, and his actions in 1912 have drawn criticism for contributing to the deepening international crisis. Speaking in Nantes in October of that year, he rejected the idea of European peace at any price. According to Gordon Wright, Poincaré's attitude was predicated upon doubts that peace could, in fact, be maintained; and he communicated those doubts to listeners on both sides of the Rhine. In Germany he raised anxieties. In France he promoted an acceptance of an inevitable armed conflict.

Late that year Poincaré ran actively for the post of president of the Republic. His intentions remain uncertain. The office had been drained of power since the 1870s; active campaigning for the post was rare. He was elected in January 1913, and this position was the one he held throughout World War I. At once he played a dominant role in the selection of the new premier and his cabinet, a portent that he saw the presidency, not as a sinecure, but as a base for directing national affairs. He pushed hard, for example, to extend the term of service for military conscripts to three years in 1913.

In late July 1914, Poincaré and Premier René Viviani (*q.v.*) visited St. Petersburg, just before Austria-Hungary delivered its ultimatum to Serbia. Clearly Poincaré dominated the talks with the Russians, which likely included speculation about a future confrontation between Austria and Serbia. Albertini has suggested that Poincaré left his ambassador in Russia, Maurice Paléologue (*q.v.*), with instructions to push Russia toward war. Paléologue's behavior during the July crisis doubtless contributed to Russia's decision to mobilize; but one can only speculate, not prove, that he was acting according to some malevolent design of Poincaré's.

Poincaré's wartime role was large, but it eludes precise description. Occupying an office considered to be largely ceremonial and legally separated from the responsibilities of the premier, Poincaré influenced rather than acted. But at times he influenced decisively. He chose premiers without the guidance of national elections; normally without the occasion of adverse votes of confidence. He dealt with emissaries of foreign countries. Elements on the political Right urged him to expand his powers to the level of wartime strongman. They were unheeded. But Poincaré did choose and guide weak, inexperienced premiers. As presiding officer over the Council of Defense, he was able to mediate the incessant quarrels among the generals and the politicians. At the same time, the influential Poincaré was destined to face public obloquy. He was the only major public official to hold the same office for the duration of the war. He represented continuity as defeat and intrigue led cabinets to rise, to be reshuffled, and then to fall.

At the start of the war, Poincaré pushed successfully for a Cabinet representing all shades of the political spectrum. Moderates and Socialists were added to Viviani's Radicals to form the wartime *union sacrée* government. The emergence of an independent military High Command under General Joffre (*q.v.*) proved more resistant to his influence. Poincaré had an early hint of what was in store when Joffre refused to send him word about the course of military operations in September. Poincaré and Viviani could only try to circumvent Joffre's authority by such efforts as opening an independent Balkan front in the fall of 1915.

Perhaps Poincaré's most visible intervention into the military course of the war was his vocal support of General Robert Nivelle's (*q.v.*) spring offensive in 1917. Poincaré's backing of Nivelle at the April 6 conference at Compiègne may have been crucial in letting the attack proceed to disaster.

By late 1917 Poincaré's influence even over the civil government was waning. He reluctantly permitted Georges Clemenceau (*q.v.*) to become premier in November 1917, the alternative being Caillaux and a negotiated peace. But Clemenceau brooked little presidential interference in the running of the war. During the Versailles Peace Conference, Poincaré openly backed Marshal Foch (*q.v.*) in the French military leader's demand for stripping Germany of the left bank of the Rhine. But Clemenceau, not Poincaré, shaped the final peace settlement.

Poincaré continued his political career in the postwar period. He served as premier, 1922/1924, and again from 1926 to 1929. During the first of these terms, he ordered French troops into the Ruhr to force Germany to meet its obligations to pay reparations.

He died in Paris, October 15, 1934.

Albertini, *The Origins of the War of 1914*, 3 vols.; King, *Foch versus Clemenceau* and *Generals and Politicians*; Miquel, *Poincaré*; Poincaré, *Au service de la France*, 10 vols.; Wright, *Raymond Poincaré and the French Presidency*; *Dictionnaire des parlementaires français*, VII.

POLIVANOV, Aleksei Andreevich (*Russia, General of Infantry, Minister of War*), was born into an old Russian noble family on March 16, 1855. He graduated from the Nikolaevsky Engineering School in 1874, saw action in the Russo-Turkish War during 1877/1878, and completed the General Staff Academy in 1888. He was an exemplary *Genshtabist* ("General Staff officer"), finishing the academy first in his class. Polivanov began his career as a staff officer in Kiev. In 1899 he reported to General Staff headquarters in St. Petersburg, where he spent the remainder of his military career. He was chief editor of the army's scholarly publications, served as chief of the General Staff in 1905/1906, and, in the latter year, was named assistant minister of war. Polivanov played a major role in the reform movement that preceded World War I. Under General Sukhomlinov (*q.v.*), the minister of war, the crack staff officer worked side by side with leaders in the Duma to obtain funds needed for such necessities as the modernization of the army's artillery. The secretive Sukhomlinov eschewed such contacts; thus, Polivanov soon had a host of friends and supporters in the Duma, notably Aleksandr Guchkov (*q.v.*), the leader of the Octobrists. Polivanov also acquired a reputation for political liberalism. This, plus differences with Sukhomlinov over such shifts in military policy as abandoning the line of antiquated Polish fortresses (which Polivanov opposed), led Sukhomlinov to fire his assistant in 1912. Still popular and ambitious, Polivanov awaited new opportunities while holding the sinecure of a seat on the State Council.

The onset of World War I brought Polivanov his opening. Sukhomlinov found himself the target of heated criticism over the army's lack of preparation for a long war; his critics pointed repeatedly at Russia's shell shortage. No slouch as a political intriguer, Polivanov cleared the way for Sukhomlinov's departure by arranging the trial and execution of Colonel Miasoedov, a friend and protégé of the war minister, as a German spy. In June 1915, Tsar Nicholas II (*q.v.*) reluctantly fired Sukhomlinov and replaced him with Polivanov, now promoted general of infantry.

Along with Duma leaders like Mikhail Rodzianko (*q.v.*), Polivanov favored wide public participation in the war effort. This was accomplished by bringing Duma leaders and captains of industry together in Special Councils to assist the War Ministry. Such measures, which Sukhomlinov had resolutely opposed, aroused the ire of powerful conservatives like Empress Alexandra (*q.v.*). Polivanov rubbed the tsar the wrong way by opposing the monarch's decision to take direct command of the field armies; although, as a serving officer, Polivanov could not sign the Cabinet ministers' petition asking the tsar to reconsider. Nor did it help his cause when Minister of Agriculture Krivoshein (*q.v.*), on the liberal wing of the Cabinet, called in the summer of 1915 for the establishment of a wartime dictatorship. Polivanov was to take over the direction of military operations while Krivoshein himself led the civil government.

By the close of 1915 the tsar had purged Krivoshein and most of the other independent minds in the council of ministers. Polivanov's lone supporter was Foreign Minister Sazonov (*q.v.*), and both of them did not remain in office for long. A serious strike in the Putilov works in Petrograd broke out in early 1916. Polivanov moved to counter it by sequestering the factory and drafting its workers into the military. This energetic response distressed some of his Duma supporters. More important, it brought him into direct conflict with Boris Sturmer (*q.v.*), whom the empress had recently contrived to put in office as prime minister. A petty squabble over the use of military vehicles by Rasputin (*q.v.*), the empress' confidant, brought matters to a head. Alexandra, Sturmer, and Rasputin persuaded the tsar to oust the effective but troublesome war minister in March 1916.

In an interview with British General Alfred Knox in April, Polivanov took pride in having improved the training and the supply of weapons and ammunition to the army. Historians have judged his departure as a calamity: "a triumph of the Empress over rational government" (Thomson) and "an irreparable loss to the war effort" (Pearson).

Polivanov remained a part of the political scene. During the climactic days of the March Revolution, just before the provisional government took power, one Kadet (liberal) leader raised the former minister's name as someone who should be named as "responsible dictator" to restore order. Polivanov never got that call to supreme power. He rallied to the revolution, however, taking over a commission to review military regulations; Guchkov, then war minister, apparently hoped his old friend Polivanov could slow the pace of military democratization. In 1920 the former tsarist general joined the Red Army and urged others to do the same. Like another aristocrat turned revolutionary warrior, Aleksei Brusilov (q.v.), Polivanov never took a combat command. He was serving as military adviser to the Russian delegation at the peace talks with Poland when he died of typhus at Riga on September 25, 1920.

Katkov, *Russia 1917*; Pearson, *The Russian Moderates and the Crisis of Tsarism*; Polivanov, *Memuary*; Rutherford, *The Russian Army in World War I*; Thomson, "Boris Stürmer and the Imperial Russian Government"; Wildman, *The End of the Russian Imperial Army*; Wilfong, "Rebuilding the Russian Army, 1905-1914"; *Bol'shaia sovetskaia entsiklopediia*, XX; *Sovetskaia istoricheskaia entsiklopediia*, XI; *Sovetskaia voennaia entsiklopediia*, VI.

POTIOREK, Oskar (*Austria-Hungary, Field Marshal*), was born in Bleiberg in Kärnten on November 20, 1853. Potiorek quickly climbed up the ladder of military command, becoming deputy chief of the General Staff in December 1902; as such, he was widely rumored to be in line to succeed Baron Friedrich Beck-Rzikowsky as chief of staff, but the appointment instead went in November 1906 to Franz Baron Conrad von Hötenzendorf (q.v.). In 1907 Potiorek commanded the III Army Corps at Graz, but in April 1910 was appointed inspector general of the Habsburg armies; in May 1911 he became governor as well as army inspector in Bosnia and Herzegovina, in the process becoming, like Conrad, convinced of the need for a preemptive strike against Serbia. "Better a defeat on the battlefield," he trumpeted, than submission to Serbian claims to the two provinces. A dapper, dashing soldier, Potiorek ruled the territories with princely powers. On June 28, 1914, he was in charge of security arrangements for the visit to Sarajevo of Archduke Francis Ferdinand (q.v.), but despite one unsuccessful assassination attempt on the life of the heir apparent, Potiorek refused to bring additional troops into the city because none could be found in dress uniform! He was never reprimanded for the slovenly security at Sarajevo.

An ambitious man with intimate ties to the court of Emperor Francis Joseph (q.v.), Potiorek on July 28, 1914, received command of Habsburg forces consisting of nineteen divisions (Fifth and Sixth Armies) for a strike (Plan "B") against Serbia. His nerves badly frayed, his confidence shaken after Sarajevo, and still bitter at having been passed over in favor of

Conrad in 1906, Potiorek not only stayed close to his heavily guarded headquarters but refused to send the Second Army to the east, as requested by Conrad. Above all seeking to restore his tarnished reputation by a victory, he decided on August 12, five days after his formal promotion to supreme commander, Balkan forces, to strike at the twelve Serbian divisions opposing him under General Radomir Putnik (q.v.). Again using his influence at court, Potiorek managed to retain four divisions from the Second Army and to attack the Serbs through a two-pronged drive in the north and south. His optimism was to be badly shaken. At the battle of Jadar his forces were repulsed with heavy losses and had to withdraw behind the Drina River. This notwithstanding, Potiorek yet again managed to rally the support of the emperor as well as of the foreign minister, Count Leopold Berchtold (q.v.), and on September 8 launch a second invasion of Serbia. It fared no better than the first, and Potiorek was forced to withdraw behind the Save River into Hungary; at the same time, Serbian units drove on Sarajevo, forcing the Habsburg Sixth Army on the defensive. Though unable to cope with Putnik's trench warfare, Potiorek managed in October to expel the raiders from Bosnia. For a third time he turned to Schönbrunn, attained the requisite reinforcements, and on November 6 invaded Serbia, also for a third time. Fate seemed at last to favor him: Valjevo fell to the Austrians and the drive to the Kolubara River was crowned with success. Moreover, on December 2 "town and fortress Belgrade" fell to Potiorek, who informed Vienna that he was laying the Serbian capital at "his majesty's feet." This piece of theatrics backfired twenty-four hours later when the enemy, aided by snow in the mountains, rains below, and impassable roads, drove the exhausted and dispirited Habsburg troops out of Belgrade. The Serbs, led by King Peter (q.v.), divided the Austrian Fifth Army at Belgrade from the Sixth at Shabatz by December 9, and six days later hurled them both back behind the Drina-Danube line with heavy losses. In the process, over 200,000 casualties were lost with further tens of thousands suffering from malaria and typhoid fever; however, the Serbs were equally exhausted and plagued by illness, so that thereafter the front fell quiet.

Potiorek's "most igniminious, rankling and derisory defeat" (Churchill) cost him his command on December 22; Archduke Eugene (q.v.) then assumed command of the Serbian front. Potiorek was retired from the army on January 1, 1915, and died a broken soldier at Klagenfurt on December 17, 1933. At the time of his dismissal he had counseled his deputy: "If ever you have the chance again, go in by Belgrade." Instead, it fell to the German Field Marshal August von Mackensen (*q.v.*) to follow this advice in October 1915.

Churchill, *The Unknown War*; Rothenberg, *Army of Francis Joseph*; Strauss Feuerlicht, *The Desperate Act*; Weinwurm, "Feldzeugmeister Oskar Potiorek"; *Der grosse Brockhaus* (1933), XV.

PRATT, William Veazie (*United States, Captain*), was born in Belfast, Maine, on February 28, 1869, the son of a master mariner. Pratt graduated from the Naval Academy in 1889, and for the next two years saw duty with the White Squadron. During the Spanish-American War he was assigned to the Philippines to suppress local insurrections; next came service during the so-called Boxer Rebellion. Pratt was instructor at Annapolis in 1895-1897, 1900-1902, 1905-1906, 1906-1908, and at the Naval War College from 1911 to 1913. For the next two years he commanded the cruiser *Birmingham*.

At the outbreak of war on April 6, 1917, Pratt was at the Army War College. During the opening month of hostilities, Captain Pratt was assigned to the office of the chief of Naval Operations in Washington, and from August 1917 to the end of the Great War he served as assistant chief of Naval Operations. In this capacity he cooperated cloely with Admiral Sims (*q.v.*) in London and was responsible for committing the Navy Department on July 6, 1917, to scrap its long-range "symmetrical" or battleship fleet-building program in order to construct 200 destroyers for antisubmarine warfare. Secretary of the Navy Daniels (*q.v.*) provided Pratt official backing in this endeavor. Although the assistant chief of Naval Operations fully realized that abandoning the capital-ship program "may leave us with our guard down," he nevertheless saw immediate succor in the antisubmarine war as vital "for the future well-being of the Anglo-Saxon race." Sims could hardly have put it better.

In October 1918, Pratt favored moderate naval terms for Germany so that the new state would be "neither autocratic and military nor bolshevik." He accompanied President Wilson (*q.v.*) to the Paris Peace Conference as naval adviser, but his suggestion in November to create a navy for the proposed League of Nations based on the principle of Anglo-American parity found few backers.

After the war Pratt represented the United States at the Washington Conference on Limitation of Armaments in 1921/1922; in 1926 he returned to the Naval War College as its president and two years later was appointed commander in chief of the battle fleet; in 1929 he received the post of commander in chief of the United States Fleet. Pratt again represented the United States at the London Conference on Limitation of Naval Armaments in 1930, and until his retirement in 1933 was chief of Naval Operations. He died on November 25, 1957, in Chelsea, Massachusetts.

Frothingham, *Naval History of the World War*, 3 vols.; Trask, *Captains & Cabinets*; *National Cyclopaedia of American Biography*, XLVI.

PREZAN, Constantine (*Rumania, Lieutenant General*), was born on January 27, 1861. Standard reference works do not record his exact place of birth in Rumania, but he received his secondary education and early military training in Bucharest, attended artillery and engineering courses in France, then returned to his country to serve as a Rumanian army officer. Commissioned a lieutenant in 1880, he distinguished himself as an engineer and received quick promotion. A captain in 1887, he was a major five years later, and became a lieutenant colonel in 1895 at the age of thirty-four. His preparation for high command in the First World War included service on the General Staff and as adjutant to King Ferdinand (*q.v.*).

When Rumania entered the war in August 1916, Major General Prezan took command of the Fourth Army. His forces cut through the Carpathian passes into northern Transylvania. But German-led counterattacks elsewhere (by General von Mackensen in the Dobrudja and then by General von Falkenhayn [*qq.v.*] against the armies on Prezan's southern flank) led Bucharest to order a general halt in Transylvania, then a partial withdrawal. Prezan was overruled when he objected to General Averescu's (*q.v.*) plan to tap the Carpathian forces to form a new army to take Mackensen in the rear. Prezan's fears were well-founded. The poor Rumanian rail system made such lateral transfers difficult. Averescu failed, and the other armies had increasing difficulty holding the line of the Carpathians.

By late November Mackensen and Falkenhayn were converging on Bucharest from the south and west. Prezan took command of a new southern army group. His forces were to present a defensive screen against Falkenhayn, while turning the weight of their attack on Mackensen. This bold Napoleonic concept—it came either from Prezan himself or from the French military adviser, General Berthelot—was beyond the power of Rumania's tired and inexperienced army to execute. Prezan, his reputation intact, led the remnants of the Rumanian forces northeastward to Moldavia.

At the close of 1916 Prezan was promoted lieutenant general and named chief of staff. In early 1917 he directed the painful reconstitution of the Rumanian army, while Averescu's Second Army and a variety of Russian forces held the Sireth River line. Virtually all of Rumania then lay in enemy hands. Prezan accompanied Prime Minister Bratianu (q.v.) to Petrograd in April and received pledges of Russian support for a summer offensive. Rumanian forces fought with success in offensive operations at Marasti (July 1917), then held off a fierce counterattack by Mackensen the next month at Marasesti. But the collapse of the Russians rendered such victories meaningless. In December 1917, King Ferdinand surrendered his titular rank of commander in chief to Prezan to facilitate the inescapable armistice. The peace negotiations of early 1918 led to the partial demobilization of the Rumanian army, but Prezan retained his post at the top, in contrast to many ranking officers who resigned.

During the fall of 1918 Prezan consulted informally with Bratianu to plan Rumania's reentry into the war. That event, which preceded the November armistice by one day, provided Bratianu with invaluable leverage at Versailles the following year.

Prezan commanded the Rumanian army throughout 1919. The presence of Rumanian troops in such areas as Transylvania and the Banat of Temesvar enhanced Bratianu's territorial claims at the peace conference. Prezan's leadership culminated in the capture of Budapest and the collapse of the Communist government of Béla Kun. The brutal behavior of the Rumanian army in seizing all forms of movable wealth from occupied Hungary left a bitter legacy for the postwar era. Prezan was an unconvincing apologist for the conduct of his forces.

General Prezan retired in 1920. The political crisis of 1930, during which King Carol II returned from exile to reclaim his throne, brought Prezan momentarily to prominence. Promoted to the rank of field marshal, he was asked to form a nonparty government. He failed and returned to obscurity. Prezan spent his last years in Italy, but returned to Rumania where he died at his Moldavian estate on August 27, 1943, the anniversary of his country's entry into World War I.

Kiritescu, *La Roumanie dans la guerre mondiale (1916-1919)*; Marie, Queen of Roumania, *The Story of My Life*, 2 vols.; *Enciclopedia Cugetarea* (provided by Professor Glenn Torrey).

PRINCIP, Gavrilo (*Austria-Hungary, Terrorist*), was born in Gornji Obljaj, a small hamlet in Bosnia, on July 13, 1894, the son of a peasant and part-time postman. After grade school Princip entertained a military career, but in the end enrolled in a merchants school at Sarajevo; he left without graduating and attended a high school with thoughts of becoming a poet. In 1911 he joined some Young Bosnian secret societies, however, and as a result of his revolutionary ideas was expelled from high school in 1912. Next Princip migrated to Belgrade, where he volunteered to fight for Serbia in the First Balkan War, only to be rejected as "too small and too weak." When the visit of Archduke Francis Ferdinand (q.v.) to Sarajevo was announced early in 1914, Princip, along with Nedeljko Čabrinović and Trifun Grabeẑ, decided to make an attempt upon the life of the heir presumptive; they were supplied with weapons by Major Vojislav Tankosić of the Serbian organization Union or Death, dubbed the "Black Hand" by its enemies. Colonel Dragutin Dimitrijević (q.v.), who guided the secret organization, supplied the boys with four pistols, six bombs, and some poison.

Disguised as peasants, the armed lads crossed into Bosnia on June 1, reaching the capital three days later. After some initial doubts, they decided to attempt the assassination on June 28, hoping by this violent deed to bring about social, political, and economic reforms for Bosnia and Herzegovina. On June 28 some of the would-be assassins lost courage. Čabrinović threw a bomb, but it failed to find its target. As a result of this attempt upon Francis Ferdinand's life, the route of his motorcade was changed to proceed straight down the Appel Quay, but no one bothered to inform the driver of the car of the change in plans. The reigning military governor, General Oskar Potiorek (q.v.), refused to bring additional troops into the city because they were not in dress uniform. Hence a startled Princip saw the archduke's car suddenly halt before him as Potiorek shouted at the driver to back into the Appel Quay. Princip drew his pistol and fired; within half an hour both Francis Ferdinand and his wife, the Countess Sophie Chotek, were dead.

Princip was arrested and put on trial for his action on October 12, 1914. Sixteen days later the guilty verdicts were handed down, but since under Austro-Hungarian law no youth under the age of twenty could be executed and although Princip's official birthdate in the civil register had initially been noted as June rather than July 1894, the assassin was spared execution and instead sentenced to twenty years at hard labor at the prison in Theresienstadt. Princip died there of tuberculosis on April 28, 1918, at the age of twenty-three. He was buried in an unmarked grave, but exhumed and reburied at Sarajevo in 1920.

Remak, *Sarajevo: The Story of a Political Murder*; Strauss Feuerlicht, *The Desperate Act.*

PRITTWITZ und GAFFRON, Maximilian von (*Germany, General*),

was born in Bernstadt, Silesia, on November 27, 1848, to a thirteenth-century noble clan with a long-standing tradition of military service. Prittwitz enjoyed rapid promotion and a brilliant career: brigade commander in 1897, divisional commander four years later, and head of the XVI Army Corps at Metz in 1906. He was promoted colonel general one year before the Great War broke out and appointed inspector general of the First Army Inspectorate. Among his troops he enjoyed the unflattering nickname of "the rotund soldier."

In August 1914, Prittwitz was entrusted with command of the Eighth Army for the defense of East Prussia. His job was to secure this historical province against the so-called Russian steamroller and, if possible, to lend assistance to the Austro-Hungarian offensive in Galicia. Above all, Prittwitz was to tie down as many Russian forces as possible while the main German thrust would be directed at Paris; once the French had surrendered, succor was promised Prittwitz.

Initially, all went according to plan. On August 17 General Hermann von François, one of Prittwitz's commanders, seized the initiative and attacked the Russians near Stallupönen. Unfortunately, this bold move encouraged Prittwitz three days later to launch a frontal assault against the Russians near Gumbinnen. Vastly outnumbered by General Rennenkampf's (*q.v.*) Niemen Army, Prittwitz panicked at the first repulse and broke off the engagement. Worse, he called military headquarters at Koblenz and informed General Helmuth von Moltke (*q.v.*) that he would have to abandon East Prussia to the Russians, retreat behind the Vistula, and possibly surrender even the Vistula fortresses unless reinforcements arrived at once. Prittwitz's precipitate action had been caused, in part, by the unexpectedly rapid deployment of General Samsonov's (*q.v.*) Narev Army on Prittwitz's southern flank near Neidenburg. In his haste, Prittwitz had not bothered to inform his staff of his call to Moltke. In fact, Lieutenant Colonel Max Hoffmann (*q.v.*) within hours managed to persuade his commander to face the Russian challenge and to deal with Samsonov by shuttling troops south from Gumbinnen—the very plan that was to result in victory at Tannenberg a few days later. However, on August 22 Prittwitz received a curt telegram announcing that a special train was on the way with the new commanders for the east: Generals Paul von Hindenburg and Erich Ludendorff (*qq.v.*). Thus end-ed his career as a result of indecision and half-measures. Prittwitz died a broken man in Berlin on March 29, 1929.

Hoffmann, *Aufzeichnungen*, 2 vols.; Mackensen, *Briefe und Aufzeichnungen*; Wheeler-Bennett, *Wooden Titan*; *Biographisches Wörterbuch zur Deutschen Geschichte*, II.

PROTOPOPOV, Aleksandr Dmitrievich (*Russia, Minister of the Interior*),

was born in Simbirsk province, December 30, 1866. A member of a wealthy family of noble landowners, Protopopov was a prosperous textile manufacturer as well. He served as a leader of the Simbirsk nobility in 1912, but his route to national prominence was through the Duma, the new parliamentary body established in the wake of the revolution of 1905. Protopopov was chosen a representative to the Third Duma in 1907, then reelected to the Fourth Duma in 1912. Politically, he stood on the left of the Octobrist party, a group of industrialists and landowners favoring a gradually evolving constitutional monarchy. In 1914 he was chosen vice chairman of the Duma, and he retained this post during the first two years of World War I.

Protopopov played only a minor role in the first half of the war. As Duma attitudes toward the monarchical regime grew more hostile, Protopopov joined with other moderates in forming a so-called Progressive Bloc, to demand greater Duma influence on government decision making. He also served as chairman of a council of representatives of the metallurgical industry, trying to coordinate the output of Russia's factories with the needs of a wartime economy. In the summer of 1916 he led a group of Duma deputies on an official visit to Great Britain.

In September 1916, it came as an unpleasant surprise to his Duma colleagues and foreign diplomats alike when Protopopov was appointed minister of the interior. Tsarist ministers almost never emerged from the ranks of Duma deputies; and, by autumn 1916, relations between the Duma and the government had become so acrimonious that most deputies felt accepting such an offer called Protopopov's loyalty to the Duma into question. Moreover, his reputation was clouded by an incident that had occurred en route from Britain. The future interior minister had met with an unofficial German representative, a member of the Warburg banking firm, in Stockholm. They discussed possible peace terms. Protopopov had made no commitments, and the conversation was, at most, exploratory. Rumors flew all the same. In Petrograd, and in Allied capitals, one heard that Protopopov, as well as Premier Boris Sturmer (*q.v.*), was maneuvering to betray the Entente by making a separate peace with Germany.

Protopopov's elevation can be attributed to the support of Empress Alexandra and her personal adviser, Grigory Rasputin (qq.v.). Sturmer's inability to run the war effort had become impossible for anyone to ignore. The empress hoped that Protopopov would be capable both in dealing with the large problems of the war (including managing the Duma), and in docilely preserving the prerogatives of the crown. The new minister's qualifications for the most powerful post in the Cabinet were minimal: he lacked administrative experience, and, notwithstanding his obvious taste for high office, he had never demonstrated any notable political abilities. Moreover, his health was ravaged by an advanced case of syphilis; contemporary observers found him physically weak and emotionally erratic. Even Tsar Nicholas (q.v.) had doubts about the appointment; the ability of the empress to sway her husband's crucial political decisions is particularly evident in Protopopov's appointment and his ability to remain in office for seven months.

Sturmer fell in late November, to be succeeded by Aleksandr Trepov and, in January 1917, by Prince Nikolai Golitsyn. Neither of the last premiers played a substantial role in policymaking; thus, the increasingly erratic Protopopov dominated the Cabinet as tsarism went to its grave. The political prospects for Tsar Nicholas and the monarchy were dim by late 1916, but Protopopov managed to make a bad situation hopeless. He moved to expand his ministry's powers, to turn the clock back to the glory days of the 1880s. He wavered between attempts to woo the Duma—at one point he offered to double the members' pay—and a hard line that meant calling elections for a Fifth Duma. Nikolai Maklakov (q.v.), interior minister at the start of the war, was called out of retirement to put his gerrymandering and other gray skills to work to ensure satisfactory election results. Working-class leaders from Petrograd and Moscow were rounded up by the police, while Duma deputies came under tight political surveillance.

When bread riots broke out in Petrograd in early March 1917, Protopopov busied himself setting matches to this revolutionary tinder. He insisted that the city's food supply be directed by the ministry of the interior. He reassured the tsar, hundreds of miles off in Mogilev, that military force would serve to end the unrest. Finally, in the early hours of March 12, he won over his Cabinet colleagues to a call to prorogue the Russian legislative body. Reluctant Duma members were virtually shoved toward participation in the revolution. By that evening, as opposition to the government swelled, Protopopov's colleagues pushed him to resign. The collapse of the entire Cabinet followed at once.

Protopopov was arrested by the new provisional government. The moderates of the March Revolution might have let him off with a lengthy imprisonment, but the Bolshevik Revolution in November sealed his fate. The last, pathetic "strongman" of Tsar Nicholas was executed by firing squad, January 1, 1918.

Florinsky, *The End of the Russian Empire*; Gurko, *Features and Figures of the Past*; Katkov, *Russia 1917*; Pearson, *The Russian Moderates and the Crisis of Tsarism*; Thomson, "Boris Stürmer and the Imperial Russian Government"; *Bol'shaia sovetskaia entsiklopediia*, 3rd ed., XXI; *Sovetskaia istoricheskaia entsiklopediia*, XI.

PUTNIK, Radomir (*Serbia, Field Marshal*), was born in 1847 in the Serbian town of Kragujevac, southeast of Belgrade. Trained as an artillery officer, he fought with distinction in his country's campaigns against Turkey in 1876-1878. A period of study in Russia followed, and in 1884 Putnik joined the Serbian General Staff. After serving in the 1885 war between Serbia and Bulgaria, Putnik was promoted colonel in 1889; the following year he began a term as the army's deputy chief of staff. Meanwhile, he taught tactics at the Belgrade military academy. Putnik's rapid ascent came to a sudden halt in 1895, when his political ties to the Radical party led to his dismissal from active duty. He remained pensioned and without a command for eight years.

The military revolt of 1903 and the ascent of Peter Karadjordjević (q.v.) to the Serbian throne marked a turning point in Putnik's fortunes. He was recalled to service, promoted general, and made chief of staff. Between 1904 and the outbreak of the Great War, Putnik also served three terms as minister of war, leading the way to an improved army by introducing modern rifles and heavy artillery, reorganizing military training, and drawing up careful plans for a future conflict with Turkey. Politics at times intruded: in 1908, Prime Minister Pašić (q.v.) removed Putnik from the post of war minister, a sop to Austrophile circles hostile to Putnik's policy of relying on French suppliers for up-to-date artillery pieces.

As army chief of staff, Putnik displayed the results of his reforms in the Balkan Wars of 1912/1913. His forces defeated the Turks at Kumanovo and Monastir in the First Balkan War, and the victorious general received the signal honor of promotion to field marshal (*voivode*). In June 1913, Putnik wisely held his army in readiness for an attack by Serbia's erstwhile ally, Bulgaria; when the assault came and set off the brief Second Balkan War, Putnik quickly turned the tide in Serbia's favor.

In July 1914 Putnik, in failing health, was at the Austrian health resort of Bad Gleichenberg. Emperor Francis Joseph (*q.v.*) intervened personally to allow the Serbian hero to return home. Austrian armies paid dearly for this act of generosity. As chief of staff—Crown Prince Alexander (*q.v.*) was the nominal head of the army—Putnik smashed two Austrian attempts to invade Serbia in 1914, the first coming in mid-August from the north and northwest. As the enemy crossed the Drina and Save rivers, Putnik wheeled his reserves westward to counterattack. Critics have questioned the *voivode*'s initial strategy of screening the length of the Austrian frontier; but once the attack came, Putnik's mobile infantry easily outdistanced the enemy in covering rough mountain terrain and massing for a successful counterblow. In September Putnik sent his own forces northward into Bosnia to threaten Sarajevo and keep the Austrians nervous.

When General Potiorek (*q.v.*) launched a second advance in early November over the same ground, Putnik retreated for a full month. Only on December 3, after the Austrians had diverted part of their army in a rash attempt to occupy Belgrade, did Putnik strike: four Serbian field armies broke the Austrian line, throwing Potiorek into headlong retreat.

Putnik and his army were put to the ultimate test in 1915. Bulgaria joined the Central Powers, and on September 22 the government in Sofia began to mobilize against Serbia. Meanwhile, an Austro-German force under Field Marshal von Mackensen (*q.v.*) prepared to strike directly at Belgrade. Allied objections barred Serbia's military leaders from a preemptive attack on the Bulgarians, and Putnik was forced to stretch his small army to the limit to cover his eastern flank.

Mackensen struck on October 6, joined by the Bulgarians five days later. Putnik met the danger with a series of skilled retreats, frustrating the German leader's efforts to force a battle of annihilation; the *voivode* hoped Allied aid might arrive through Salonika before the Bulgarians and Mackensen linked up. Meanwhile, Putnik found himself restraining offensive-minded subordinates like General Mišić (*q.v.*), the commander of the First Army.

By mid-November the situation was nearly beyond repair. Serbian counterblows had failed, and the Bulgarians clung to Skopje and the road to Salonika. On November 25 the aged field marshal, too ill to walk, ordered a final retreat over the Albanian mountains to the Adriatic. Putnik had to be carried in a sedan chair; together with his escort, he reached Scutari on December 7. The Serbian High Command had proved unable to coordinate all of the retreating units, but the initiative of local commanders brought most of the army's columns to safety in accordance with Putnik's plan.

Putnik's health was shattered. He was evacuated immediately and died in Nice on May 17, 1917. Under his fiery subordinate, Mišić, the army went on to play a crucial role in the victorious offensive northward from Macedonia in the autumn of 1918. In a generally lackluster field of Balkan military talent, Putnik was a shining star. In the words of Cyril Falls, Putnik, though ill and often confined in a carefully heated headquarters chamber, was "more formidable than many a mediocrity in the pink of condition dutifully visiting his troops in all weathers."

Adams, *Flight in Winter*; Falls, *The Great War*; Haselsteiner, "Die Affäre Putnik"; Keegan and Wheatcroft, *Who's Who in Military History*; Vucinich, *Serbia between East and West*; *Vojna enciklopedija*, VII.

RADOSLAVOV, Vasil (*Bulgaria, Minister-President*), was born in Loveč in northern Bulgaria, July 15, 1854. He obtained his secondary education at Prague, studied law at Heidelberg, and returned to Bulgaria for a career in journalism and politics. Radoslavov joined the Liberal party, and, at the age of thirty, took office as minister of justice. He led the government from 1899 to 1901. It was a period marked by peasant discontent, to which Radoslavov responded with heavy military force. By the time he left office, his reputation for brutality was coupled with a reputation for corruption. The latter scarcely distinguished him in a notoriously unprincipled circle of peers. The actions and policies of Bulgaria's monarch, Prince Ferdinand (*q.v.*), dominated affairs of state. In R. W. Seton-Watson's stinging phrase, Ferdinand manipulated parties, leaders, and politics by "his skill in calculating the psychological moment for driving each batch of swine from the trough of power."

Radoslavov was distinguished, however, by his pro-German and pro-Austrian views. In the early days of the Second Balkan War (June/July 1913), he publicly called on Ferdinand to break Bulgaria's long-standing tie to Russia. Friendly relations with Austria and Turkey, he maintained, were more appropriate for Bulgaria's territorial ambitions in the Balkans. The suggestion matched Ferdinand's own intentions. The monarch installed Radoslavov and an Austrophile Cabinet. Pro-Russian feeling remained strong in Bulgarian public life, but the common purpose of the monarch and the leader of the government neutralized it. Electoral failures made no difference. Radoslavov missed a majority in the election of December 1913; Ferdinand's support and the fragmentation of the opposition in the National Assembly (*Sobranie*) saved the day. Radoslavov shaped a narrow majority in March 1914 after a typically clouded Bulgarian election: his margin of support came from hastily enfranchised Moslems in territory just won in the Balkan Wars.

On the eve of World War I a loan from Austria and Germany marked Radoslavov's policy of rapprochement with the Central Powers. Formerly, Bulgaria's meager state treasury had been filled with the help of the French. Objections by political opponents were brushed aside. In mid-July Radoslavov declared the loan ratified after a raucous *Sobranie* meeting during which the minister-president had brandished a pistol and ignored cries for a roll call vote.

The outbreak of World War I placed Bulgaria in the position of being courted by both sides. Memories of the military and diplomatic defeats in the Second Balkan War were still fresh; Radoslavov and Ferdinand saw that the new conflict offered vast opportunities. The precise relationship between the monarch and his chief minister remains uncertain. Radoslavov's memoirs, on this issue as on most other controversies, are relentlessly uninformative. It seems likely that Ferdinand determined the direction of Bulgarian foreign policy; Radoslavov, as an influential adviser, implemented it. The two shared a sympathy for the Central Powers, but both were willing to take the Entente's offers seriously. While Radoslavov lacked diplomatic experience, he soon proved himself an adept negotiator.

In early August 1914, Austria began the bidding: Bulgaria's reward for joining the Central Powers was to be territory in Serbian Macedonia. Greece and Rumania quickly expressed their objections to such Bulgarian expansion. Together with Russia, they held Radoslavov's government to a course of neutrality. By late August, on the other hand, it was evident a tie between Bulgaria and the Entente would meet Serbian resistance. The Serbs had thrashed the Austrian invaders and sent them back across the Save and Drina. Belgrade saw no need to sacrifice its Macedonian holdings to entice Bulgaria to fight alongside Britain, France, and Russia.

Bulgaria's actions in the last months of 1914 leaned toward Berlin and Vienna. Radoslavov declared martial law and stifled pro-Russian demonstrations. Sofia permitted military personnel and supplies to pass through from the Central Powers to the Turks. Beyond that, Ferdinand and his chief minister would not go. Radoslavov, described by contemporaries as resembling "a *maître d'hôtel*," showed himself admirably equipped for the world of wartime diplomacy. He pointedly reminded the Austrians in late November 1914 that he was negotiating with the Entente. Such talks, he claimed, were needed to appease his domestic opponents. The implicit threat did not go unheard. By January 1915, Radoslavov obtained written pledges of territorial concessions from the Central Powers in Serbian Macedonia. Bulgaria pledged only to remain neutral. Radoslavov had hinted he would apply military pressure on Serbia by concentrating troops near the Serbian frontier. He quickly found "technical reasons" why this could not be done.

The Allied attack on the Dardanelles threatened to reverse Bulgaria's steady drift toward the Central Powers. But General von Falkenhayn (*q.v.*) underscored the need for Bulgarian aid in crushing Serbia and opening supply routes to the beleaguered Turks. Germany seized the diplomatic initiative from Austria, following which Radoslavov received urgent and generous offers. German victories on the eastern front removed Ferdinand's hesitations. The Gorlice breakthrough in early May 1915, the capture of the major Galician city of Lemberg in late June, and the headlong retreat of the Russian army eastward throughout the summer made a German victory in the entire war seem certain. By early September 1915, the Central Powers concluded a military convention and treaty of alliance with Radoslavov's government. A Bulgaria large enough to dominate the Balkans was to emerge from the final peace settlement. In Silberstein's phrase, under Radoslavov's skilled leadership the Bulgarians "had run an expert race."

The invasion of Serbia (October/November 1915) brought hard fighting but culminated in triumph for the Central Powers. The acquisition of Macedonia temporarily quieted Radoslavov's domestic opponents, and the new year began well. Radoslavov's government even got Germany's consent to occupy Macedonian territory originally assigned to Austrian troops. But the obligations that came with an alliance to Germany soon exacted a toll. Berlin pressed Radoslavov's government to join in war against Rumania, dangling the Dobrudja as compensation. When Radoslavov agreed, he faced strong domestic opposition in the *Sobranie*. The political criticism sharpened when Germany used Bulgarian troops in operations outside the Dobrudja; and the army itself began to show the strain when restive Bulgarian units found themselves crossing the Danube for an advance on Bucharest.

By the close of 1916 new frictions were evident to cast doubt on Radoslavov's policy. German requisitioning detachments depleted Bulgaria's food reserves; seized for the Macedonian front, Bulgarian food went more often to Germany itself while Bulgaria was left hungry. Facing Salonika, the Bulgarian army felt weak and unnoticed, in no condition to deal with burgeoning enemy activity. The fall of Monastir in November 1916 caused little concern in Berlin, but seemed ominous when viewed from Sofia. Meanwhile, the Dobrudja, Bulgaria's reward for helping defeat Rumania, remained in German hands.

Radoslavov found himself taunted at home as a German mercenary. He pleaded his case personally at Berlin in early 1917 but returned empty-handed. Refusing to join Germany in declaring war on the United States had no effect on Berlin; and Radoslavov was too closely bound to an alliance with Germany to make moves for a separate peace with the Entente. A final winter made especially painful by widespread hunger set the stage for Radoslavov's departure. The Bucharest peace treaty between Rumania and the Central Powers (May 7, 1918) eliminated Bulgaria's last hopes for receiving the Dobrudja, thereby dooming Radoslavov's government. In June Ferdinand replaced him with the Ententophile Malinov (q.v.).

Radoslavov's followers continued to dominate the *Sobranie* and to bolster Ferdinand's efforts to continue the war. It took the Macedonian debacle in mid-September and the armistice at the close of the month to sweep both Radoslavov and his monarch to exile in Berlin.

During the postwar period the Agrarian regime of Alexander Stamboliski (q.v.) tried Radoslavov in absentia and condemned him for maneuvering Bulgaria into the war. The fall of Stamboliski in 1923 led to efforts to amnesty the former minister-president, ill in Berlin. A bill allowing Radoslavov to come home passed finally in June 1929. It was too late. The ailing old leader died, still in Berlin, on October 21, 1929.

Buchan, ed., *Nations of Today: Bulgaria and Romania*; Holden, "Bulgaria's Entry into the First World War"; Logio, *Bulgaria: Past and Present*; Mamatey, "United States and Bulgaria in World War I"; Potts, "The Loss of Bulgaria"; Radoslawoff, *Bulgarien und die Weltkrise*; R. W. Seton-Watson, *History of the Roumanians*; Silberstein, *Troubled Alliance* and "Serbian Campaign of 1915"; *Bulgarska Entsiklopediia*.

RASPUTIN, Grigory Efimovich (*Russia, Imperial Confidant and Adviser*), was born into a poor Russian peasant family in Tobolsk Province. The exact date of his birth is unknown; estimates range from 1864 to 1872. The family name was Novykh; Grigory received the name *Rasputin*, meaning "the debauchee" or "the dissolute one," from his fellow villagers as a young man. Rasputin fell into trouble with the law for such offenses as petty theft and making sexual advances to young girls; his life took a more promising direction when he came into the orbit of a Russian religious sect, the *Khlysty* or "Flagellants." Russian tradition accepted the kind of individual Rasputin then became: a self-declared holy man claiming the power to heal the sick. By the early years of the twentieth century, he had made his way to St. Petersburg. Sometime between 1905 and 1907, his contacts in the conventional religious hierarchy and among high-ranking members of the nobility allowed him access to the imperial family.

Rasputin's champion became the Empress Alexandra (q.v.). After ten years of marriage and the birth of four daughters, Alexandra had delivered a male child and heir to the throne; she was soon devastated to learn that he suffered from hemophilia. The early death of her mother and a sister, along with various other family tragedies, had made her mistrust conventional medical treatment. Rasputin was only the latest in a succession of faith healers and mystics who had managed to penetrate the empress' circle. The new holy man's apparent ability to keep Alexis, Alexandra's son, alive in times of medical crisis made him a trusted adviser to the empress and, through her, an influence on Tsar Nicholas II (q.v.).

From 1910 onward Rasputin was understood to have substantial political power. This, plus his dissolute behavior (his religious beliefs stressed the need first to sin in order thereafter to be fully redeemed) made him the target of sharp criticism in the Russian Duma, the newly founded legislative body. In 1911 he was briefly expelled from St. Petersburg by Premier Petr Stolypin. The empress succeeded in arranging his return to the capital. At the close of 1912, Rasputin solidified his place within the imperial circle: Alexis was stricken during a family vacation in Poland; with the child at death's door, Rasputin advised the empress to reject the doctors' intended method of treating the lad, who thereupon recovered. By 1913 Rasputin was actively courted by political conservatives like Boris Sturmer (q.v.). The holy man's view that the Duma formed a threat not only to himself but also to the prerogatives of the monarchy made him a natural ally for the political Right.

Rasputin allegedly opposed Russia's entry into World War I. His influence grew, however, during the course of the war. When Tsar Nicholas left to take command of the field armies in the fall of 1915, the empress, advised by Rasputin, took over the substantial governmental chores of the monarch. The precise extent of Rasputin's authority has given rise to controversy. Maire's biography restates the traditional view that "the peasant became dictator." It is likely that Rasputin had a less substantial role. He influenced high-level appointments, encouraging the tsar and empress to choose arch conservatives whom they preferred in any case. He threw his weight against the political claims of the Duma; once again, he reinforced the desires of the imperial couple. In all, Rasputin's greatest historical importance may rest in the personal and political antagonisms he aroused in the Duma and in informed public opinion. These hostilities, combined with the nation's wartime suffering, inevitably undercut the authority of the monarchy.

In individual cases, historians have found Rasputin directly influential. The rise of Sturmer, a poorly qualified bureaucratic hack, to become premier in February 1916 is attributed to Rasputin and the empress. So too is the disastrous elevation of Aleksandr Protopopov (q.v.) to become minister of the interior and the effective leader of the Cabinet from September 1916 to the March 1917 revolution. The exit of capable individuals also can be blamed in large measure on Rasputin. War Minister Andrei Polivanov (q.v.), for example, was forced from office in March 1916, due in part to a petty quarrel with Rasputin over the holy man's use of government vehicles.

By the close of 1916 Rasputin's supposed power had so besmirched the monarchy that a band of conservative aristocrats undertook the task of assassinating him. During the night of December 29/30, by a combination of poison, pistol fire, and drowning, Rasputin was removed from the Russian scene. Alive he had been a calamity for monarchical authority. His death did not improve matters. The ministers, widely considered to be his lackeys, went on misgoverning the nation; the tsar and empress faced the hostilities of the Duma and public without Rasputin to play the role of lightning rod and shield.

Rasputin's lurid personality and his colorful relationship with Russia's ruling family should not divert attention from the deeper problems afflicting the na-

tion. In the best of circumstances, Russia and the circles from which it was likely to draw its political leaders could hardly be expected to surmount the stresses of World War I. The ambitious and intriguing holy man at most accelerated a political breakdown that had, by late 1915, become inevitable.

Enden, *Raspoutine et le crépuscule de la monarchie en Russie*; Frankland, *Imperial Tragedy: Nicholas II*; Fülöp-Miller, *Rasputin: The Holy Devil*; Gurko, *Features and Figures of the Past*; Maire, *Raspoutine*; Rodzianko, *The Reign of Rasputin*; Thomson, "Boris Stürmer and the Imperial Russian Government"; *Sovetskaia istoricheskaia entsiklopediia*, XI.

RATHENAU, Walther (*Germany, Head, Raw Materials Office*), was born in Berlin on September 29, 1867, the son of an engineer and head of the General Electric Company (AEG). Rathenau studied mathematics, chemistry, and philosophy at Berlin and Strassburg, receiving the doctorate in 1889. After an early career in the aluminum industry, Rathenau in 1899 joined the board of directors of the AEG; from 1902 until 1907 he led the banking consortium of the *Berliner Handelsgesellschaft*. He returned to the AEG in 1907, helping it to become Europe's largest electrical firm. Basically a philosopher, Rathenau shunned public life and never married. Above all, he was a strange mixture of contrasting influences; a fervent admirer of Prussian values, and yet a man of distinct Jewish consciousness; a capitalist who desired social reform; a wealthy entrepreneur more devoted to thought than to business; a monarchist who later embraced a democratic, republican state. The goal most dear to Rathenau was the assimilation of the Jews into the Wilhelmian state, which was, unfortunately, not to be. They were to remain second-class citizens.

On August 9, 1914, Rathenau discussed Germany's supply of raw materials with General Erich von Falkenhayn (q.v.), the Prussian war minister, and shortly thereafter was appointed to head a new raw materials office within the Prussian War Ministry. Ably assisted, especially by Wichard von Moellendorff of the AEG, Rathenau convinced the Bavarian, Saxon, and Württemberg war ministries to inventory their stocks of vital war materials and to distribute them in an orderly manner to the firms requisitioning them. As the British naval blockade took effect, Rathenau convinced the Prussian War Ministry to establish a system of private stock companies (War Raw Materials Corporation) to buy, store, and distribute raw materials. Finally, in early December 1914, he was able to establish price ceilings upon certain items in order to prevent excessive war speculation.

Rathenau resigned his post on April 1, 1915, arguing that the new office was well established within the War Ministry and could run without a civilian head; it appears that army jealousy of civilian control as well as anti-Semitic sentiments also pressured him into resigning. The policies he had employed in requisitioning raw materials in Belgium and deploying Belgian forced labor in German industries were to cause him great difficulties with the Allies at a later date. In June 1915, after the death of his father, Rathenau was appointed president of the AEG.

Walther Rathenau had from the start felt that Germany would win the war, but that it would be a long one. Like Chancellor Theobald von Bethmann Hollweg (q.v.), he foresaw the creation of a German-dominated *Mitteleuropa* after the war and as a result favored annexations in the west. Rathenau became firmly convinced that only General Erich Ludendorff (q.v.) could bring the struggle to a successful conclusion, but he never shared the first quartermaster general's wild annexationist schemes in the east. In time, Rathenau parted ways with Ludendorff over the issue of unrestricted submarine warfare, seeing therein the danger of America's entry into the war. In the summer of 1918 Rathenau promulgated a strange appeal to German youth to carry on the struggle; in September and October he sought a *levée en masse* to harness the last remaining forces to defend the homeland.

After November 1918, Rathenau worked to create a single, broad bourgeois political party, but in the end settled for membership in the German Democratic party. In 1919 he served as an expert during the peace discussions at Paris, and from May until October 1921 joined Chancellor Joseph Wirth's Cabinet as minister for national reconstruction. Rathenau basically endorsed the policy of fulfillment, hoping that German inability to meet the Allies' exorbitant demands would reveal the excessive nature of the demands made upon the Reich; he resigned when the major portion of Upper Silesia was turned over to Poland.

In February 1922, Rathenau rejoined Wirth's Cabinet as foreign minister, leading the German delegation to a reparations conference at Genoa. Rathenau became bitterly disappointed with Prime Minister David Lloyd George's (q.v.) refusal to scale down German reparations payments and, spurred on by Baron Argo von Maltzan, on April 16 signed a treaty with the Russians at Rapallo. A rumor that Lloyd George was conducting secret talks with the Russians precipitated Rathenau's willingness to aban-

don his basic pro-West stance and to come to terms with Moscow. At home, his reactionary opponents added the epithets "Bolshevik" and "Russian agent" to the existing ones of "Jew," "defeatist," and "traitor." He was murdered while on his way to work in Berlin on June 24, 1922, by two right radical officers. Perhaps more than any other, Rathenau's life and career show the pathos and tragedy of German Jewry from Bismarck to Hitler.

Berglar, *Walther Rathenau*; Feldman, *Army, Industry, and Labor in Germany*; Kessler, *Walther Rathenau*; Rathenau, *Gesammelte Schriften*, 6 vols. and *Tagebuch 1907-1922*; *Biographisches Wörterbuch zur Deutschen Geschichte*, II.

RAWLINSON, Sir Henry Seymour (*Great Britain, General*), second baronet and Baron Rawlinson, of Trent, was born at Trent Manor on February 20, 1864, the son of Major General Sir Henry Rawlinson. The younger Rawlinson was educated at Eton and at the Royal Military Academy, Sandhurst, and gazetted to the King's Royal Rifles in India in 1884. He returned in 1889 after a brief tour in Burma, and three years later in the rank of captain obtained a transfer to the Coldstream Guards. Appointments to the Staff College and Aldershot came next, and in 1898 Rawlinson served Sir H. H. Kitchener (q.v.) at the Nile, having succeeded to the baronetcy in 1891. In 1899 Major Rawlinson took part in the siege of Ladysmith and one year later joined Lord Roberts at Bloemfontain. He was promoted brigadier general and appointed commandant of the Staff College, Camberley, in December 1903. Thereafter, posted once more to Aldershot, Rawlinson was promoted major general in 1909, and from 1910 to 1914 commanded the Third Division.

Rawlinson was sent to Belgium early in October 1914 to take command of two divisions being landed at Zeebrugge and Ostend for the relief of Antwerp. He arrived too late, however, and the city fell to the Germans on October 10. Rawlinson could do little but cover the escape of the Belgian Field Army down the Flanders coast, defend the Channel ports, and fall back upon Ypres, where he met Sir John French's (q.v.) British Expeditionary Force. Rawlinson's two divisions were absorbed in the main by Sir Douglas Haig's (q.v.) I Army Corps, with the result that he was given a new unit, the IV Corps, to command. Rawlinson led the IV Corps at the battle of Neuve Chapelle in March 1915, and for the remainder of that year guided it at Aubers Ridge, Festubert, and Loos. When Sir Charles Monro (q.v.) left France for Gallipoli at the end of 1915, Rawlinson was promoted lieutenant general and given command of the Fourth Army. To him fell the unenviable task of distracting the Germans at the Somme in order to relieve the pressure on Verdun. Rawlinson firmly believed in attacks with limited objectives, but he was overruled by Haig who desired to attack "the whole of the enemy's lines of defense." On July 1, 1916, he loyally carried out Haig's prolonged assault all along the Somme, losing 57,000 men on the first day of battle alone. In all, the struggle raged until November when foul weather and mutual exhaustion ended the carnage, but not until Britain had suffered over 300,000 casualties.

Rawlinson was promoted general in January 1917. He was mercifully spared the battles of Messines and Arras, but his plans for a combined naval and military attack on the Belgian coast were shelved in favor of Haig's assault at Ypres in July 1917. He commanded the British left at Passchendaele toward the close of that battle, and at the end of 1917 briefly received command of the Second Army during Sir Herbert Plumer's (q.v.) absence. When Sir Henry Wilson (q.v.) became chief of the Imperial General Staff in February 1918, Rawlinson succeeded him as British military representative on the Supreme War Council. And the following month Rawlinson was entrusted with command of the remnants of the British Fifth Army, shattered by the German Michael offensive of March 21. Rawlinson, supported by the French, made a stand at the important rail link of Amiens and, reconstituting his forces as the Fourth Army, turned the tide by capturing Villers-Brettoneux on April 25.

As early as July 4, Rawlinson had tested the combined use of infantry and tanks at Hamel on a small scale, and on August 8, 1918, in what General Erich Ludendorff (q.v.) termed the "black day in the history of the German Army," Rawlinson threw 456 tanks and massed infantry at the Germans at Cambrai on the Amiens front, breaking the enemy lines. The Fourth Army crossed the Somme, took Péronne on August 31, and by mid-September had driven the Germans back to their Hindenburg line. Reinforced by two American divisions, Rawlinson between September 29 and October 8 broke the Hindenburg defense system near St. Quentin, and on Armistice Day his forces stood southeast of Maubeuge and west of Beaumont, having advanced sixty miles—at a cost of 122,000 casualties.

The Fourth Army remained in Belgium until March 1919. When Rawlinson came home, he was created a baron, received the thanks of Parliament, and was given a grant of £30,000 for his services in the Great War. In the latter part of 1919 he was sent to Archangel and Murmansk in order to conduct the evacuation of Allied forces from northern Russia, and the following year Rawlinson was appointed com-

mander in chief in India. He died in Delhi on March 28, 1925, after a hard game of polo and making twenty-one runs at cricket.

Edmonds, *Military Operations: France and Belgium*, 13 vols.; Liddell Hart, *The Real War*; Maurice, *Soldier, Artist, Sportsman: Life of Lord Rawlinson of Trent*; *Dictionary of National Biography 1922-1930*.

RENNENKAMPF, Pavel Karlovich von (*Russia, General of Cavalry*), was born April 29, 1854, to a Russian noble family of German extraction. He graduated from the Helsingfors Infantry Cadet School in 1873 and completed the General Staff Academy in 1882. Rennenkampf saw combat service in the Boxer Rebellion (1900), then commanded a cavalry division in the Russo-Japanese War. In the postwar period he led a series of punitive expeditions to put down revolutionary activity in eastern Siberia. Such exploits may have helped compensate for Rennenkampf's less than brilliant service against the Japanese. He was promoted general of cavalry in 1910, by which time he was a corps commander, and, in 1913, he was advanced to take charge of the Vilna Military District.

At the outbreak of World War I Rennenkampf received the Russian First Army, along with orders to participate in his nation's first major wartime offensive in 1914. On August 17 Rennenkampf was to cross the German border, moving westward into East Prussia. He was to be joined in his attack by Samsonov (q.v.) and the Second Army, advancing northward from the Warsaw Military District. Under the coordination of General Zhilinsky (q.v.), the commander of the northwestern front, the two armies were to pinch off and annihilate the lone German army standing in East Prussia.

The operation was a disaster for which Zhilinsky and Rennenkampf have received varying shares of the blame. Rennenkampf crossed the border on August 17, won easy victories at Stallupönen and Gumbinnen, then slowed to a crawl. By August 23 the Germans were stripping the front facing Rennenkampf, allowing them to use their rail network to fling most of their forces on Samsonov's isolated forces. Zhilinsky failed to push the First Army leader forward; and Rennenkampf, burdened by supply problems, and perhaps none too anxious to "rush" the Germans into a retreat that would prevent Samsonov from cutting them off, never penetrated the thin forces opposite him. The technical weakness of the Russian army intensified the problem. Russian radio transmissions made it clear to the Germans that Rennenkampf posed no threat; because of a lack of trained operators, Russian radio traffic could not be sent in code!

Unlike Zhilinsky, Rennenkampf survived in command. When the Germans turned on him, he took a heavy toll in the defensive action at the Masurian Lakes in early September, then made a timely retreat. By September 13 he was back over the Russian border. Rutherford suggests, however, that this opportune withdrawal degenerated into a rout. Rennenkampf had one more campaign in him. On November 11 the Germans launched a dangerous attack southeastward from Thorn, cutting between Rennenkampf's First Army facing East Prussia from the south, and the Second Army advancing westward toward Silesia. The ensuing battle of Lodz offered both sides a chance for a great victory. The Germans lost their chance to smash the Second Army when forces under General Pleve (*q.v.*) rushed up from the south to help hold Lodz. But Rennenkampf, again slow and hesitant, cost the Russians their opportunity. His First Army came too late to close the trap on the German XXV Reserve Corps, which had curled around to attack Lodz from the east. The Germans escaped, and Rennenkampf found himself unemployed.

His career at an apparent end, Rennenkampf had to defend himself against a commission of inquiry. It was ostensibly directed to look into his purchase of cavalry supplies, which to some eyes seemed indistinguishable from wartime profiteering. But the inquiry clearly took much of its impetus from the cavalryman's dismal combat performance. His court connections saved him from prison, but no more commands were in sight; Rennenkampf retired from military service.

His death came in the form of a last chance to take up a command. After living out most of the war in obscurity, Rennenkampf found himself in southern Russia in early 1918. The Bolsheviks had taken over the government. The final German offensive at the close of February led the Reds to offer charge of an army to Rennenkampf, who was in Taganrog near the Black Sea. He refused, found himself placed immediately on trial, and in early March 1918, Rennenkampf died in front of a Bolshevik firing squad.

Kenez, *Civil War in South Russia, 1918*; Rostunov, ed., *Istoriia pervoi mirovoi voiny*, I; Rutherford, *The Russian Army in World War I*; Stone, *The Eastern Front*; *Sovetskaia istoricheskaia entsiklopediia*, XI; *Sovetskaia voennaia entsiklopediia*, VII.

RIBOT, Alexandre (*France, Minister of Finance, Premier*), was born in St. Omer, February 6, 1842, the son of a banker. A versatile and brilliant student, he chose law over the equally attractive possibility of a career in science. He obtained his degree in 1863 and soon entered government service as a judge. His poor health prevented him from pursuing a conventional academic career on a law faculty. But he was a founder and sometime teacher at the École libre des sciences politiques.

Ribot was elected to the Chamber of Deputies in 1878, beginning a parliamentary career that spanned forty-five years. An Anglophile and admirer of British political liberalism, Ribot placed himself at the center of the French political spectrum, opposing the violent anticlericalism that dominated national politics during his first years in the Chamber. He focused his interests on government finance and foreign affairs as well. He took a firm stand against General Boulanger's efforts at parliamentary revision, the burning issue of the late 1880s. Polished speaker and brilliant debater, Ribot was considered ministerial timber from his early years as a deputy.

Ribot served twice as premier in the next decade, in 1892/1893 and again in 1895, but his most significant contribution to French political life was as foreign minister, 1890-1892. He played the crucial part in forging France's military alliance with Russia. In the summer of 1892, when negotiations seemed deadlocked, Ribot moved the talks to fruition. He accepted the crucial Russian demand that France mobilize in the event of a confrontation between Russia and Austria. Ribot argued that France could not afford to stand aside in such a crisis; moreover, French security demanded an alliance with Russia at virtually any cost.

The Dreyfus affair seemed to end Ribot's ministerial career. His middle position—expecting the army to correct its judicial "error" and condemning the Left's immoderate attacks on the military—offended partisans on both sides. By the first years of the twentieth century, politically isolated and in poor health, Ribot seemed to be an elder statesman in the making. He refused the ambassadorship to Russia in 1908;. he considered his presence as France's envoy to St. Petersburg would sharpen the existing Balkan crisis. He moved to the Senate in 1909, then tried unsuccessfully to get elected president of the Republic in 1912. His position as a political moderate was reinforced by his support of the three-year service law in 1913 and, the next year, by his acceptance of a direct income tax. When he tried to form a government in June 1914, however, he failed in the face of Radical and Socialist opposition.

The war gave Ribot a new lease on political life. He took the Ministry of Finance in the *union sacrée* government of August 1914. He directed France's finances for more than two difficult years. An apostle of fiscal conservatism, he found the tug of wartime necessity led to sweeping reversals in his ideas. Ribot decided to cover expenses by borrowing rather than instituting new taxes, hoping that the war would be short. In any case, with France's richest areas in enemy hands and with the country's population fully mobilized, he doubted France could tolerate the taxation imposed in other countries.

Paying for essential imports, chiefly from the United States, became Ribot's main problem. By mid-1915 he was presiding over painful changes in France's economic position: gold had to be shipped to Britain and French holdings in the United States liquidated. Britain's reluctance to form a united economic front burdened Ribot. The problem crested in August 1916, when Britain negotiated an American loan without informing Ribot, thereby establishing terms France could match only with growing difficulty.

Ribot became France's third wartime premier on March 20, 1917, succeeding Aristide Briand (q.v.). His health was poor, his working hours had to be severely limited, and he accepted the post only out of a sense of duty. He moved quickly to limit the prerogatives with which President Poincaré (q.v.) had tormented his predecessor, but Ribot could not be a consistently decisive leader when the entire context of the war was changing. Russia's March Revolution and the imminent entry of the United States into the conflict placed in question the long-planned offensive of General Nivelle (q.v.). Ribot had personal doubts but allowed the offensive to proceed to disaster. He was wiser in the aftermath. He allowed Commander in Chief Pétain and War Minister Painlevé (qq.v.) the latitude to restore the army by internal reforms and by the abandonment of large-scale offensives. As the Russian Revolution raised hopes on the Left for a negotiated peace, Ribot stood firmly against French Socialists' demands for passports to attend an international gathering in Stockholm. Pétain insisted that a French delegation at Stockholm would shatter the army's will to fight. Ribot followed this advice; the Left never forgave him. Ribot confronted another by-product of events in Russia when French Socialists revealed France's secret territorial agreement with the tsarist government. Already on record as opposing a war of annexation, Ribot answered that all secret wartime treaties were subject to peacetime revision. The Chamber of Deputies was momentarily pacified. On the perennial Greek question, Ribot acted decisively. He had kept the portfolio of foreign minister for himself, and in June he forced out Greece's pro-German king, then rallied the Italians and Serbs to prevent the British from liquidating their role in the Balkans.

Events at home were harder to control. Ribot had secured the support of the Chamber's Radicals by retaining the long-standing minister of the interior, Louis Jean Malvy (q.v.). By July Malvy was under sharp attack for defeatist sympathies and, more concretely, for failing to close down pacifist newspapers. Ribot hesitated to request Malvy's resignation until late August. Pétain won a victory in the meticulously prepared offensive at Verdun that month, but moderate and conservative support for the government drained away. At the same time, Ribot lost the backing of moderate Socialists like Albert Thomas (q.v.) who were drawn leftward as the Socialist rank and file responded to the Russian Revolution. Ribot fell from the office of premier on September 7, 1917, but he remained on as foreign minister for a month. He had rebuffed the peace overtures of Prince Sixte de Bourbon in April in his early days as premier, and proved equally skeptical as the Germans sought negotiations through the Belgians and Briand.

Ribot spent the remainder of the war quietly in the Senate, but he spoke out with fire in the early postwar years. The damage the Germans had inflicted on his home region in northeastern France appalled him, and he became an outspoken advocate of heavy German reparations. Ever the moderate, however, Ribot was equally emphatic in opposing French hopes for territorial gains or permanent political influence on the left bank of the Rhine, which would create a new Alsace-Lorraine and sow the seeds of another war.

Ribot died in Paris, January 13, 1923.

King, *Generals and Politicans*; Ribot, *Journal d'Alexandre Ribot et correspondances inédites, 1914-1922*; Schmidt, *Alexandre Ribot: Odyssey of a Liberal in the Third Republic*.

RICHTHOFEN, Manfred Baron von (*Germany, Captain*), was born in Breslau on May 2, 1892, the son of an army officer of Silesian nobility. Richthofen joined the cavalry in West Prussia in the spring of 1911 and was promoted lieutenant the following year. In August 1914, he took part in cavalry patrols against the Russians in East Prussia, but he quickly discerned that the glory days of the cavalry were gone forever. Having transferred to the infantry, Richthofen rebelled in April 1915 when ordered to quartermaster duty far removed from the front. "My dear Excellency," he wrote his commanding general, "I have not gone to war to collect cheese and eggs, but for another purpose." That purpose in May turned out to be the Air Corps. After training at Ostend with a bomber squadron ("apple barges") and limited experience in the fall battles at the Champagne, the future "ace of aces" failed his pilot's license! Richthofen quickly transferred to the air base at Döberitz and there received his wings. In the spring of 1916 he was at the western front near Verdun; next came reassignment to the east to bomb Russian units near Kovel.

Richthofen's career was launched in August 1916 when Captain Oswald Boelcke included him in a new fighter squadron at the Somme. On September 17 Boelcke's five planes took to the air for the first time and Richthofen scored his first official "kill" against the British. The war in the air quickly became his passion, his sport. He possessed the courage to kill or be killed, and he flaunted his daring with reckless abandon. At the ancestral manor house at Schweidnitz he had hunted elk, deer, boar, and birds; the war now gave him license to hunt even more precious game.

In January 1917 Richthofen received the coveted order *Pour le mérite* after his sixteenth kill and was promoted commander of Fighter Squadron 11, which scored 100 aerial victories between January 23 and April 22, 1917. Richthofen, by then a national hero, was rapidly promoted first lieutenant and on April 8 captain after his thirty-ninth victory. His British opponents referred to him variously as "the Baron," "the jolly old Baron," and "the dear old Baron." He painted his Fokker plane blood-red, in the process adding the nickname "the red knight," or "diable rouge." In July Richthofen was wounded during aerial combat as head of a new Fighter Wing 1. In the fall of 1917 he was sent to Brest-Litovsk, ostensibly to take part in the peace negotiations with the Russians, but in reality, to force rest upon him.

In March 1918 came his seventieth victory and in April his eightieth; all planes downed had been British. It is only fair to point out that many of these "kills" had been joint efforts, but credited to Richthofen in order to swell his reputation. In fact, his entire "flying circus," so named after the tents and equipment that the squadron moved from base to base, was orchestrated to assuage his avarice for victories. Richthofen seldom fought alone, but preferred to remain above his squadron during a dogfight until he spied his chance to swoop down like a hawk upon an unfortunate straggler. "Everything in the air beneath me is lost," he once boasted. He showed no pity towards his victims, dispatching them in a brutal, pitiless manner that earned from General Erich Ludendorff (*q.v.*) the claim that Richthofen's presence at the front was worth that of three infantry divisions.

Richthofen faced the prospect of death stoically. In June 1916, after the death of a fellow ace, Max Im-

melmann, he had coolly written his mother: "In time, death comes to each of us here." On April 21, 1918, Richthofen was shot down over the Somme River. Accounts of his demise differ: Allied historians generally credit a Canadian aviator, Captain Roy Brown, with downing the "red Baron," while German scholars give credit to Australian ground fire. Whatever the case, his plane was hacked to pieces for souvenirs after one British soldier had recognized the downed ace: "Christ, they got the ruddy baron!" Richthofen was buried by the British with full military honors; his body was brought to Germany for burial in Berlin in November 1925. Captain Hermann Göring commanded Fighter Wing 1 in July 1918 following the death of the legendary "red Baron." Richthofen's tradition is today carefully nurtured in the West German air force.

Bodenschatz, *Jagd in Flanderns Himmel*; Gibbons, *The Red Knight*; Norman, *The Great Air War*; Richthofen, *Der rote Kampfflieger*; *Geschichte der Ritter des Ordens*, II.

ROBERTSON, Sir William Robert (*Great Britain, Field Marshal*), first baronet, was born in Welbourn, Lincolnshire, on January 29, 1860, the son of a village tailor. Robertson entered the ranks of the Sixteenth Lancers in 1877; ten years later he passed the examinations for a commission, and joined the Third Dragoons in India. In 1896 he became the first "ranker" to be admitted to the Staff College, and three years later received appointment to the intelligence staff in South Africa under Lord Roberts. He returned to London as major in 1900, was promoted colonel three years later, and in 1907 was posted brigadier general and assistant quartermaster general of the Aldershot Command, the blue ribbon of home appointments. Wully, as he was commonly called, was promoted major general in 1910 and served as commandant of the Staff College for the next three years; his motto at Camberley was: "Hope for the best, prepare for the worst." His personality was chilling and graceless, yet he was endowed with a native shrewdness and immense energy, two traits that partly account for his incredible rise up the military ladder of command. Robertson was ever cognizant of his humble origins and remained intensely loyal to Sir Douglas Haig (*q.v.*), a "gentleman."

Wully Robertson accompanied the British Expeditionary Force to France in August 1914 as quartermaster general. It was not a happy assignment: Sir John French (*q.v.*), its commander in chief, ignored Robertson in favor of the scheming Sir Henry Wilson (*q.v.*), and even barred Robertson from his personal mess. The result was a total lack of communication between Robertson and French during the retreat from Mons. When French's chief of staff, Sir Archibald Murray (*q.v.*), broke down at St. Quentin under the strains of war and the entire British presence in France seemed to collapse, French had no choice but to accept Robertson in January 1915 as Murray's successor. Robertson basically opposed the concept of a broad attack at Loos, but he was willing to support the French in their desire for an offensive to drive the Germans out of their country. Hence, Robertson from the first became a strong proponent of the "Western" strategy at army headquarters, opposing the "side shows" in Palestine, Gallipoli, and Mesopotamia as needless drains on manpower from the vital front in France. During the general reorganization in December 1915, it was suggested initially that Robertson succeed Sir John French as field commander in France, but since he was no gentleman, command went instead to Haig while Robertson was sent home as chief of the Imperial General Staff. Robertson accepted this post only after wringing from Lord H. H. Kitchener (*q.v.*), then state secretary for war, an agreement that the chief of the Imperial General Staff, through a small war council, issue orders directly to the various commanders in chief without the intervention of the army council.

After his assumption of office on December 23, 1915, Robertson at once ordered evacuation of the Helles sector at Gallipoli: "Retention of Helles means dispersion, not concentration of effort." Above all, he sought "to get every possible man, horse and gun on the Western Front." Robertson fully supported Haig's attritional tactics at the Somme in 1916, where fifty-three British divisions were hurled against enemy machine guns and barbed wire until they had reached by mid-November a state of utter exhaustion. Moreover, Robertson's choice of Sir Stanley Maude (*q.v.*) as commander in chief, Mesopotamia, proved to be a contentious one; this energetic and able officer clamored for reinforcements in order to push on to Baghdad at a time when Robertson continued to funnel men and supplies to the morass at the Somme. And when two of Britain's allies, Serbia and Rumania, fell at the end of 1916, the government of Herbert Asquith (*q.v.*) likewise toppled.

The new Prime Minister, David Lloyd George (*q.v.*), and his chief of the Imperial General Staff had a serious falling out in Rome in January 1917 when Lloyd George, without consulting Robertson, put forth a plan for an Allied assault upon Austria-Hungary. Worse yet, the prime minister supported French General Robert Nivelle's (*q.v.*) proposal for a quick break through the German lines in the west,

and even accorded the French commander in chief operational and administrative control of the British armies for this assault—a proposal headed off by Haig and Robertson at an Allied conference at Calais in February.

The failure of Nivelle's offensive in April 1917 and the imminent collapse of Russia in the east prompted Robertson in June 1917 to recommend yet another attack on the western front and to strengthen Haig by recalling several divisions from Egypt and Salonika. This scheme only awakened in Lloyd George the specter of further bloodletting in France and convinced him that victory could be achieved best in Palestine while the Allies waited in France for the arrival of American forces. Neither Haig nor Robertson had much faith in the ability of the Americans to raise a large army for "a very long time," and in the end won the day: the British offensive in the fields of Flanders, ending with the bloody action at Passchendaele, as well as the Italian collapse at Caporetto in October, severely shook the prime minister's faith in the military. With the connivance of the French premier, Paul Painlevé (*q.v.*), it was decided at Rapallo to create a Supreme War Council composed of the heads of government and one other minister from each Ally, aided by members of the permanent military staff. Robertson stormed out of the Rapallo meeting in disgust at this circumvention of his powers.

At a session of the Supreme War Council at Versailles from January 30 to February 2, 1918, Robertson argued vehemently against a planned offensive in Palestine, but to no avail. Moreover, Robertson's inability to work with the prime minister had convinced him to replace Robertson with the more pliable Sir Henry Wilson. Robertson at first refused to condone this Machiavellian ploy by Lloyd George and reportedly ordered Wilson out of his office on February 16, 1918. Two days later, however, he consented to the change and accepted the Eastern Command at home. In June he became commander in chief, Home Forces, and in April 1919 of the British army on the River Rhine. After the war he received the thanks of Parliament, a grant of £10,000, and was created baronet; the following year he was promoted field marshal, retiring from active service in 1921. Robertson died in London on February 12, 1933.

Wully Robertson had been a diehard "Westerner" from 1915 until 1918, that is, he had supported any and all operations in France rather than in Salonika, Gallipoli, Palestine, or Mesopotamia, in the belief that a breakthrough in France alone could end the war. He had been chased out of office in February

1918 by the leading "Easterner," Prime Minister David Lloyd George. In the process, Robertson as chief of the Imperial General Staff had permitted seventy British divisions to be bloodied over and over again at the Somme and in Flanders in order to vindicate the correctness of his strategy.

Bonham-Carter, *Soldier True*; Guinn, *British Strategy and Politics*; Robertson, *Soldiers and Statesmen,* 2 vols.; *Dictionary of National Biography 1931-1940*.

RODZIANKO, Mikhail Vladimirovich (*Russia, President of the Duma*), was born April 12, 1859. A member of an old noble family in Ekaterinoslav Province, Rodzianko graduated from the aristocratic Corps of Pages, then served as a cavalry officer in a unit of the Imperial Guards, 1877-1882. In 1907, after two decades of activity as a leader in local government, Rodzianko took his seat as an Octobrist deputy in the Third Duma. In 1911 he was elected president of the Duma, and he held this position in the Fourth (and final) Duma chosen in 1912. As spokesman for the Duma, Russia's newly hatched parliamentary body, Rodzianko had direct access to Tsar Nicholas II (*q.v.*). He was willing, although scarcely anxious, to criticize the crown. In February 1912, for example, the Octobrist nobleman informed the tsar of the disastrous effects of the imperial family's connection with the disreputable religious practitioner Grigory Rasputin (*q.v.*). When the Octobrist party split in November 1913 on the issue of joining a bloc in opposition to the tsar's ministers, however, Rodzianko led the deputies who voted to remain loyal to the government.

The outbreak of World War I made Rodzianko a leading figure in Russia's version of the *union sacrée.* He accepted without complaint government efforts to limit the Duma to brief, infrequent sessions. In August 1914, for example, the legislative body met for a single day, then adjourned until early 1915. He also did not strongly protest the unconstitutional arrest (November 1914) of the Duma's five-man Bolshevik delegation.

By the spring of 1915 Rodzianko's meetings with the monarch, along with pressure from industrial leaders and the daily evidence of the nation's inability to supply the army properly, brought results. Nicholas accepted Rodzianko's call for the formation of war industry committees; these united representatives of the Duma and industry to cooperate with the Ministry of War in meeting the country's military needs. But Rodzianko's efforts at reforming the government through personal diplomacy had few other achievements. He opposed, to no avail, the monarch's decision to take direct command of the ar-

mies in the fall of 1915. As the Duma convened in February 1916, Rodzianko made a dramatic plea to the tsar to grant a "responsible ministry." The tsar ignored him.

In July 1916, Nicholas considered meeting the nation's multisided domestic crisis—fuel shortages, inflation, the collapse of the rail system—by installing a civil dictator, possibly Premier Boris Sturmer (*q.v.*). Rodzianko played his accustomed role of spokesman for the moderate opposition; he drew the caustic comment from Nicholas that "Rodzianko has talked a lot of nonsense."

By early 1917 even a Rodzianko was being pushed outside his comfortable middle ground. He kept silent about news that civilian leaders like Aleksandr Guchkov (*q.v.*) were seeking military support for a palace coup. He made a final effort in January to warn the tsar about the misrule Empress Alexandra (*q.v.*) and her circle were visiting on Russia in the tsar's absence. Nicholas simply turned away.

When street riots and military mutinies signaled the collapse of the old order in March 1917, Rodzianko played, for the last time, the thankless role of Russian political moderate. He tried—and failed—to get both the Octobrists and the more liberal Kadets to rally to the government. He tried—and failed—to keep military authorities from ordering their troops to fire on street crowds. He tried—and failed—to get the tsar to recall the newly prorogued Duma and to establish a government led by "some person who enjoys the confidence of the country." Nicholas replied to this last plea with the famous statement (March 12, 1917): "Rodzianko has sent me some nonsense which I won't even bother to answer."

Within a few days, the monarchy Rodzianko had hoped to save was gone. The old nobleman himself was elbowed aside by less reluctant representatives of the new order like Paul Miliukov and Aleksandr Kerensky (*qq.v.*). After the November Revolution, he fled to the Don, where the anti-Bolshevik White movement was forming. In 1920 he emigrated to Yugoslavia where he occupied his final years writing his memoirs. Rodzianko died in his new Balkan home, in dire poverty, on January 19, 1924.

Gurko, *Features and Figures of the Past*; Hosking, *The Russian Constitutional Experiment*; Katkov, *Russia 1917*; Pearson, *The Russian Moderates and the Crisis of Tsarism*; Rodzianko, *The Reign of Rasputin*; *Sovetskaia istoricheskaia entsiklopediia*, XII.

RONARC'H, Pierre Alexis (*France, Vice Admiral*), was born in Quimper, February 22, 1865. He entered the Naval Training College at the age of fifteen and saw his first action as an ensign in the Comoro

Islands off Madagascar. In 1900, in a preview of his World War I exploits, Ronarc'h led an artillery unit in the expedition that lifted the siege of the foreign legations at Peking. Two years later Ronarc'h was advanced to the rank of commander, the youngest officer in the French navy to hold that grade. The Russo-Japanese War aroused Ronarc'h's interest in naval mines, and his superiors encouraged him to become France's leading authority on the subject. He invented a mine-sweeping device that played a significant role in the First World War. Promoted captain in 1908, Ronarc'h commanded a crack combined force of destroyers, submarines, and torpedo boats under Admiral Boué de Lapeyrère (*q.v.*), France's naval commander in the Mediterranean. In the first months of 1914 he was promoted rear admiral.

Ronarc'h's service in the First World War began in the trenches. With a force of 6,000 sailors and marines he helped defend Paris during the battle of the Marne, then entered the northern sector of the western front in mid-October. His two naval regiments helped cover the Belgian army's retreat from Antwerp, then clung to the important Dixmuiden bridgehead on the Yser in savage, house-to-house fighting. When relieved in mid-November, his shattered force had lost nearly all of its original members in helping to deny the Germans possession of the Channel ports.

The submarine threat claimed Ronarc'h's attention next. Promoted vice admiral, he became director of the French antisubmarine effort in November 1915. Ronarc'h drew armed trawlers into service for antisubmarine patrols and shifted torpedo boats and destroyers from the Channel to the Mediterranean, where German and Austrian U-boats were taking a heavy toll of Allied shipping. In cooperation with the British, the Mediterranean was divided into separate zones where each navy could take primary responsibility for protecting passing merchant vessels.

In May 1916, Ronarc'h took charge of the newly formed Naval Zone of the Northern Armies, a stretch of water extending from Nieuport to the outskirts of Le Havre. After having reinforced the Mediterranean at the expense of this region, he had the ironic task of defending the French side of the Channel with only a fraction of his country's naval resources.

Ronarc'h's zone was the scene of numerous small actions. He skillfully deployed his thin force of submarines, destroyers, patrol boats, and aerial units to shield merchant shipping and to prevent enemy raids on the armed trawlers that helped guard the antisubmarine nets. Ronarc'h found much of his work involved close cooperation with the British commanders of the more powerful Dover Patrol. The relationship was a cordial one, but the task of blocking U-boats from passing the Dover Straits lay beyond the combined French and British forces until well into 1918. Ronarc'h provided both advice and combat vessels to support the British raid on Zeebrugge in April 1918. In May Ronarc'h argued successfully against the call of General Haig (*q.v.*) to abandon Dunkirk in the face of the German spring offensive in Flanders. To the admiral, such a withdrawal meant the inevitable loss of Calais and the cross-Channel shipping lanes.

On October 17 along with Admiral Keyes (*q.v.*) of the Dover Patrol, Ronarc'h accompanied the Belgian royal family on their solemn seaborne return to Ostend. The months following the armistice found him sweeping his northern zone clear of mines. He served briefly as chief of France's Naval General Staff, then retired in 1920. Ronarc'h died in Paris, April 1, 1940.

As Thomazi has pointed out, Ronarc'h's role in the years 1916-1918 was unspectacular but essential. Only by assuring the passage of millions of men and thousands of transports across the Channel with miniscule losses were the Allies able to continue the war. The capable French admiral with his extensive experience in fighting the U-boat might well have played a still larger role in the entire war. Ronarc'h was perhaps a superior choice for the large Mediterranean theater, with its international complexities and its continuing war against the submarines, than the succession of Dartige du Fournet and Gauchet (*qq.v.*), the diplomatically unsophisticated battleship admirals who found themselves misplaced on the center stage of France's naval war.

Belot and Reussner, *La Puissance navale dans l'historie*, III; Ratinaud, *La Course à la mer*; Ronarc'h, *Souvenirs de la Guerre*; Thomazi, *La Marine française dans la Grande Guerre*, I, IV; *Larousse mensuel*, V.

ROOSEVELT, Franklin Delano (*United States, Assistant Secretary of the Navy*), was born the son of James Roosevelt, vice-president of the Delaware and Hudson Railroad, at Hyde Park, New York, on January 30, 1882. Roosevelt was raised by a Swiss governess and in 1903 graduated from Harvard in three years. He married Anna Eleanor Roosevelt in March 1905, a distant cousin and the niece of President Theodore Roosevelt. Franklin Delano Roosevelt entered politics in 1910 as state senator from heavily Republican Dutchess County, a rural area that included Hyde Park. Early in 1912 Roosevelt became a spokesman for New York progressives in their fight against Tammany Hall, and his efforts helped to elect Woodrow Wilson (*q.v.*) president; FDR was rewarded the following year with the post of assistant secretary of the navy, a position that the Old Roughrider, Theodore Roosevelt, had used to catapult himself to the White House. For the next seven years FDR worked under the close supervision of Secretary of the Navy Daniels (q.v.). He was often impatient with his chief and did not shrink back from undercutting him, yet he learned from Daniels how to deal with congressional leaders and in time came to develop respect for the "chief." Above all, Roosevelt was an enthusiastic supporter of the president.

The first two years of the European war saw the energetic assistant secretary disgusted with the American inaction; as an advocate of preparedness he joined the likes of Leonard Wood and Henry Cabot Lodge (q.v.) in denouncing the cautious neutrality of Wilson and Daniels. Roosevelt's actions bordered at times on insubordination: in March 1917, he approached the British for official exchanges of naval information, an impetuous and indiscreet action taken without sanction by his superiors. Specifically, the yachtsman from Hyde Park wanted to build fifty-foot plywood sub-chasers and to establish himself as the American civilian leader in Europe in order to coordinate the Anglo-American war effort. In October 1917, the ebullient assistant secretary fully backed the proposed mine barrage of the North Sea waters between Scotland and Norway, and when the General Board concurred, was not above telling Daniels "I told you so." This feverish activity prompted admirers to regard FDR as one of the most capable administrators in the capital ("See young Roosevelt about it. . . ."); on the other hand, it moved his detractors to denounce him as shallow, suggesting that "F. D." stood for "feather-duster."

During the summer of 1918 the president finally granted Roosevelt the chance to travel to Europe, where FDR attempted to bring about unified action in the Mediterranean Sea. "The Italians may not love us, but at least they know that we have no ulterior designs in the Mediterranean." The mission proved to be stillborn. When the assistant secretary inquired of Italy in August 1918 why its fleet did not put out to sea even for training exercises, the reply came that the Austrians also preferred to remain in port. Roosevelt commented: "This is a naval classic which is hard to beat, but which perhaps should not be publicly repeated for a generation or two." Upon returning to the United States, the energetic Roosevelt thought about resigning his post in order to accept a commission in the navy, but the war ended before he could realize this scheme. FDR returned to Europe during the winter of 1918/1919 in order to supervise the disposal of American navy property.

He visited the Peace Conference in Paris and returned with Wilson, who turned him into an ardent public supporter of the League of Nations.

Franklin Delano Roosevelt served as president of the United States from 1932 until his death in 1945, but these eventful and controversial years are beyond the scope of this work and, in any case, are sufficiently well known and reported elsewhere.

Freidel, *Franklin D. Roosevelt: The Apprenticeship*; Kilpatrick, *Roosevelt and Daniels*; Trask, *Captains & Cabinets*; *Dictionary of American Biography*, XXIII Supplement Three.

ROQUES, Pierre (*France, General, Minister of War*), was born in Marseilles, December 28, 1856. He attended the École polytechnique and was commissioned into the engineers. A fellow student at the École was Joseph Joffre (q.v.), and Roques' career was influenced by their continuing ties. Roques served in Algeria in 1880, the first in a series of colonial assignments that stretched for twenty-five years. He volunteered for duty in Tonkin in 1885 and commanded a battalion in Dahomey, where he was wounded, in the 1890s. In the rank of colonel he directed railroad construction in Madagascar, 1897-1905, under General Gallieni (q.v.). Joffre was a comrade in arms for Roques both in Tonkin and Madagascar. Colonel Roques became General Roques in 1906 and advanced to major general four years later. He played an important role in promoting French air power as inspector of military aviation, 1910-1912.

Roques proved himself to be an undistinguished combat leader in the large-scale encounters of 1914. He led a corps into Belgium under Langle de Cary, then fought under Foch (qq.v.) at the battle of the Marne. Neither his performance in the Fourth Army nor in Foch's Ninth was marked by skill or initiative. Nonetheless, Joffre promoted him to command the First Army in early 1915. For over a year Roques fought on the relatively quiet front of the Eastern Army Group under General Dubail (q.v.). Much of Dubail's time and energy was spent in stimulating Roques' lackadaisical leadership.

In March 1916, Roques suddenly rose to become minister of war. Once again, Joffre's hand smoothed the way. With the departure of Gallieni from the War Ministry, the commander in chief needed a reliable and unambitious figure to stand between the High Command and interference from the government. The affable Roques turned out to be an unpleasant surprise. He rejected the role of "a sub-Joffre," criticized the defense of Verdun, and demanded that the upper ranks of the army be purged. One casualty inflicted by the war minister was an outraged General Dubail. In August 1916, Roques clashed with Joffre on the perennial issue of opening the front to parliamentary inspection.

Roques proved equally uncomfortable a subordinate for Premier Briand (q.v.). Dispatched to Salonika in October, Roques was expected to return with a report critical of General Sarrail (q.v.), the French commander in the Balkans. Briand intended to use this document as his excuse to order Sarrail home. Instead, Roques praised Sarrail, suggesting he be reinforced as well as freed from Joffre's supervision. Evidence indicates that Sarrail's parliamentary supporters knew the substance of the Roques report before the war minister left France for the eastern Mediterranean. This link between the war minister and the parliamentary Left gravely embarrassed and weakened Briand. Barely surviving a rebellion in the Chamber of Deputies, he rid himself of the unpredictable Roques in December. In all, Roques' nine months as war minister were marked by the declining prestige of the military High Command and the ascending influence on military policy of a restive National Assembly. In Joffre's memoirs the angry commander in chief cast these events in a different light, recalling his fear of Roques' "lack of character vis-à-vis the parliamentarians."

Roques returned to the command of a field army in 1917, then served as inspector of defensive fortifications on the western front during the last year of the war. He died in Saint-Cloud, February 26, 1920.

Dubail, *Quatre années de commandement, 1914-1918*, 3 vols.; King, *Generals and Politicians*; Tanenbaum, *General Maurice Sarrail*; *Dictionnaire des parlementaires français*, VII.

RUPPRECHT, Crown Prince of Bavaria (*Germany, Field Marshal*), was born in Munich on May 18, 1869, the son of the later King Ludwig III. He embarked on a military career, then took time off to study law, and in 1889 attended the War Academy. Rupprecht was appointed regimental commander in 1899, brigade commander in the grade of major general the following year, and divisional commander as lieutenant general in 1903. The Bavarian crown prince was promoted general of infantry and given command of the Bavarian I Army Corps in 1906 and, after extensive travels in the Balkans, was promoted colonel general as inspector general of the IV Army Inspectorate at Munich in 1912.

Rupprecht, in August 1914, was entrusted with the German Sixth Army in Lorraine, with General Krafft von Dellmensingen (q.v.) as his chief of staff. Under the auspices of the Schlieffen plan, the army in Lorraine was to conduct a yielding defensive; however, General Helmuth von Moltke (q.v.) had greatly reinforced the Lorraine contingent, yet at the same time had left it without specific battle orders. Rupprecht's attack on French positions at Morhange-Sarrebourg forced the enemy to retreat, but his forces were too weak to envelop the fleeing French by a march through the rugged Vosges. Early in September the crown prince's Sixth Army experienced a costly rebuff near Nancy-Epinal. Thereafter, Rupprecht led a new Sixth Army at the Somme, then at Arras and Lille, and finally in trench warfare at Ypres; by December the front had stabilized in Flanders. The Sixth Army fought at Neuve Chapelle in March 1915, and at La Bassée and Arras in May. In the fall of that year, Rupprecht again engaged the enemy at La Bassée and Arras, holding the Artois front; he was rewarded with the order *Pour le mérite*. His experiences during these bloody battles transformed him into an outspoken critic of General Erich von Falkenhayn's (q.v.) attritional tactics, and he predicted, to Chancellor Theobald von Bethmann Hollweg (q.v.), defeat if Falkenhayn remained as chief of the General Staff.

Promoted field marshal in July 1916, the following month Rupprecht surrendered command of the Sixth Army to become chief of a new Army Group Crown Prince Rupprecht (Sixth, First, and Second armies) at the Somme. Early in 1917 the crown prince led this formation into defensive positions in the so-called Hindenburg line, all the while lamenting General Erich Ludendorff's (q.v.) utter devastation of the abandoned territory (Operation Alberich). In April and May Rupprecht repulsed bloodletting British assaults at Arras and began seriously to consider the need for an end to the war; munitions were in short supply and both the quality and quantity of recruits left much to be desired. As a result, a rankling enmity set in between the crown prince and Ludendorff, which was further fueled in July 1917 when army headquarters mobilized German industrialists and politicians to overthrow Bethmann Hollweg and to replace him with the pliant Georg Michaelis (q.v.).

As one of Germany's ablest front-line commanders, Rupprecht daily bore witness to the exhaustion of the troops. Neither was he insensitive to the hunger and deprivation rampant at home. This notwithstanding, the crown prince on March 21, 1918, heroically led his army group during the Michael offensive: his forces broke the enemy line at Gouzeaucourt-Vermand-Cambrai and advanced over the old Somme battlefields of 1916 as far as the line Arras-Albert. The Fourth and Sixth Armies had reached Armentières by April, but Marshal Ferdinand Foch's (q.v.) riposte with fresh American units fell fully upon Army Group Crown Prince Rupprecht between the Ancre and Avre rivers. In desperation, Rupprecht on June 1 informed Chancellor Count Georg von Hertling (*q.v.*), a fellow Bavarian, that Ludendorff no longer believed in victory and that peace negotiations ought to be begun at once; the vast gains scored in the east would more than offset a settlement on the basis of the status quo in the west. Hertling refused to accept this pessimistic prognosis, and Rupprecht had no choice but to continue the dreary retreat on the western front behind the so-called Hermann line of defense. His troops fought their last battles along the shores of the Scheldt and Lys rivers, in the process coining the bitter phrase: "The Prussians will fight on to the last Bavarian." When his father, King Ludwig III, abdicated on November 8, 1918, Rupprecht withdrew from public life to his estate at Chiemsee and became a patron of the arts.

The crown prince was generally hailed as the "secret king" of Bavaria after the war, but he refused to condone a militant restoration of the Wittelsbach monarchy. Specifically, he declined to participate in Adolf Hitler's beerhall *Putsch* in November 1923, partly because of the presence of General Luden-dorff, whose violent attacks on religion in general and Catholicism in particular repulsed him. Only briefly in 1933 did Rupprecht consider a monarchist restoration in Bavaria with the aim of heading off the imminent Nazi seizure of power. Rupprecht took his wife and children to Italy at the start of the Second World War; he returned to Bavaria in 1945 and died in Leutstetten on August 2, 1955.

Kitchen, *Silent Dictatorship*; Liddell Hart, *The Real War*; Rupprecht, *Mein Kriegstagebuch*, 3 vols.; Sendtner, *Rupprecht von Wittelsbach*; *Biographisches Wörterbuch zur Deutschen Geschichte*, II; *Geschichte der Ritter des Ordens*, I.

RUZSKY, Nikolai Vladimirovich (*Russia, General of Infantry*), was born into a Russian noble family, March 18, 1854. He graduated from the Konstantinovsky Military College in 1872 and was posted as an infantry officer to an elite guards regiment. The young officer saw his first combat in the Russo-Turkish War, 1877/1878. In 1881 he graduated from the General Staff Academy, a crucial rung on the ladder of advancement for rising members of the officer corps. During the Russo-Japanese War, Ruzsky served as chief of staff in the Second Manchurian Army. The postwar period brought him command of a corps, 1906-1909; a new round of staff duties followed, and in 1912 Ruzsky was named deputy chief of staff for the Kiev Military District.

Both the military and political facets of Ruzsky's career in World War I have been a source of heated dispute. Stone has accused him of "psychotic prudence" in the Galician campaign during the first weeks of the conflict; and, in general, he dismisses him as a "boneless wonder," resurrected from time to time because of his political connections. Mayzel finds him, in contrast, one of the most respected of the army's elite: along with General Alekseev (*q.v.*), the chief of staff, the natural spokesman for the army in time of crisis. Authorities are equally at odds over the reasons behind his up and down wartime career: poor health (Knox), general ineptitude (Stone), or personal conflicts with Alekseev (Mayzel). Out of this tangle, several points are clear enough. Ruzsky was a poor subordinate. He continually took advantage of the slack lines of authority that characterized the Russian High Command. He was, moreover, an erratic field commander, sometimes imperceptive and slow, sometimes quick and energetic. In high politics during the crucial March Revolution, he was much like the other ranking generals in putting the interests of the army (and the war effort) over those of the monarchy.

Ruzsky was first noted during the free-for-all Galician campaign, August/September 1914. As the main weight of the Austrian offensive struck northward toward Lublin and Cholm, Ruzsky led one of the two field armies capable of striking the Austrians' eastern flank. In this situation, Ruzsky proved a timid and self-centered leader. Despite his numerical advantage, he advanced only with great caution; and he ignored the urgings of the front commander, General Ivanov (*q.v.*), to swing to the north to relieve the imperiled Russian forces taking the brunt of the Austrian offensive. Ruzsky's desire to be the general who captured the Austrian stronghold at Lemberg doubtless played a part in his decision.

Ruzsky marched upward. In mid-September he replaced the luckless Zhilinsky (*q.v.*) as commander of the northwest front. He refused to support Ivanov's efforts in central Poland and, until reined in by the High Command, even considered a deep withdrawal to the east, which would have made Ivanov's front untenable. Nonetheless, he showed his mettle at the battle of Lodz in mid-November. When a German offensive struck southeastward from Thorn, threatening to isolate and annihilate his Second Army, Ruzsky responded with *élan*, aided by such able subordinates as General Pleve (*q.v.*). He wheeled his front to face northward, hastened Pleve to the aid of the endangered Second, and tried, with less success, to move General Rennenkampf (*q.v.*) and the First Army westward to cut off the German line of retreat.

Ruzsky gave up the northwestern front in March 1915, served briefly in the lesser role of Sixth Army commander in the summer of 1915, and by the winter of 1916 found himself in charge of the northern front, stretching from the Gulf of Riga to Lake Narocz. This set the stage for his final moment in the limelight in March 1917.

As disorders in Petrograd seemed to get out of hand, Tsar Nicholas II (*q.v.*) made his way northward from Supreme Headquarters at Mogilev. With Russia's railroads crippled by the war and controlled by workers sympathetic to the revolution, the monarch found himself stranded in Ruzsky's headquarters at Pskov. The field armies stood as the tsar's last hope of restoring imperial authority. Representing the nation's senior generals, Alekseev and Ruzsky pressured the vacillating monarch to abdicate. To Mayzel, Ruzsky acted as spokesman for the entire army and thus as the arbiter of these crucial events. One must add, however, that Alekseev, back at Mogilev, orchestrated the process by which the army's senior leaders abandoned Tsar Nicholas and rallied behind the new provisional government.

Events soon passed Ruzsky by. He was ousted from his position as commander of the northern front soon after the March Revolution, possibly for cooperating too readily for Alekseev's tastes with the revolutionary innovations of elected army committees and political commissars. The old general made his way to the north Caucasus, only to find himself a victim of the rapidly escalating Russian Civil War. Bolshevik forces took him into custody in an indiscriminate purge of potential enemies in the fall of 1918, and Ruzsky was executed at Piatogorsk, October 19, 1918.

Katkov, *Russia 1917*; Kenez, *Civil War in South Russia, 1918*; Knox, *With the Russian Army*, 2 vols.; Mayzel, *Generals and Revolutionaries*; Rostunov, ed., *Istoriia pervoi mirovoi voiny*, 2 vols.; Rutherford, *The Russian Army in World War I*; Stone, *The Eastern Front*; Wildman, *The End of the Russian Imperial Army*; *Bol'shaia sovetskaia entsiklopediia*, XXII.

SALANDRA, Antonio (*Italy, Prime Minister*), was born in Troia in southern Italy, August 13, 1853. The son of a wealthy family of landowners, he was educated as a lawyer, taught at the University of Rome, and entered the Chamber of Deputies to represent Foggia in 1886. Salandra received his first Cabinet post as minister of agriculture in 1899. During the first decade of the twentieth century he was a close political ally of Conservative Sidney Sonnino (*q.v.*), serving as finance minister under him in 1906 and again in 1909. In the wake of the Libyan War, 1911/1912, Salandra shifted his political direction, coming into the orbit of the political kingmaker of the era, Giovanni Giolitti (*q.v.*). In March 1914,

when Giolitti left the post of prime minister, Salandra took over. Giolitti's followers dominated the Chamber of Deputies and Salandra's ministry was expected to be merely a brief interlude until Giolitti decided to return to power.

The summer of 1914 was marked by an upsurge in domestic unrest. During June's "Red Week," Salandra found it necessary to call out the army to deal with massive strikes and urban violence. He had barely recovered his equilibrium from this trial when Italy was confronted with the Sarajevo assassination and the subsequent July crisis.

Salandra's lack of experience in foreign affairs placed enormous authority in the hands of his foreign minister, Antonio Di San Giuliano (*q.v.*). Soon after the latter's death in October 1914, Sidney Sonnino took the reins of foreign affairs into his hands. Under San Giuliano's direction, Salandra led Italy into an initial declaration of neutrality on August 2. The refusal to honor Italy's alliance with Germany and Austria-Hungary was explained on the ground that the Vienna government had proceeded against Serbia without first consulting Rome. In reality, Italian policy reflected a number of concerns: withholding active support could eventually bring Italy long-desired territorial gains from Vienna, such as Trieste and the Trentino. Once Britain had entered the war (August 4) with its powerful navy, a stand on the side of the Central Powers exposed Italy to serious military risks. Moreover, strong irredentist feeling in Italy militated against any effort to stand alongside the hated Austrians on any battlefield.

But prolonged neutrality, as Salandra came to see, also held dangers. A vengeful and victorious Germany was unlikely to deal mildly with a double-dealing former ally who continued to withhold armed support. The Entente was equally unlikely to reward Italy with territorial acquisitions for anything less than direct military assistance. If a majority of the nation's population and political representatives favored neutrality, Salandra faced a vocal minority committed to war against Austria-Hungary. Failure to gain something out of the war might cause sufficient popular unrest to endanger the monarchy, or even the social order itself.

Between December 1914 and April 1915, the Salandra government negotiated with both sides. Austrian reluctance, even under strong German pressure, to make territorial concessions to Rome tipped the scales to the Entente, as did the Allied military activity in the Mediterranean seen at the Dardanelles. After a long round of secretive diplomacy—even the cabinet was left in the dark—Salandra and Sonnino pledged Italy to the Entente in the Treaty of London (April 26, 1915).

Before Salandra could obtain a declaration of war—the Giolittian majority in Parliament remained staunchly in favor of neutrality—the picture changed. The Austro-German success at Gorlice (May 2), Allied failures at the Dardanelles, and Berlin's frantic efforts to push Vienna to give Italy what it wanted in the way of territory seemed to make a declaration of war dangerous and unnecessary. Lacking firm support in the Chamber of Deputies, Salandra resigned on May 13. Interventionist demonstrations and the clear preference of King Victor Emmanuel III (*q.v.*) for joining the Entente helped prevent a neutralist government from forming. Salandra returned to the premier's desk on May 16 and Italy declared war against Austria-Hungary on May 24.

"Salandra's war" turned out to be far different from what the prime minister had anticipated. The short, limited conflict to smash the Austrians bogged down into bloody stalemate on the Isonzo. Salandra's reluctance to mobilize the nation, or to declare war on Germany as the Treaty of London required, antagonized Italy's allies. Italian proponents of total war, like Socialist Deputy Leonida Bissolati (*q.v.*), joined their voices to the criticism coming from abroad. The Italian High Command, led by General Luigi Cadorna (*q.v.*), fended off efforts at civilian control. Cadorna agreed with Salandra's reluctance to upend the nation by resorting to full-scale mobilization. But the general clashed with the prime minister in other areas: Cadorna called, for example, for closer cooperation with Italy's allies, as seen in the quarrel between the general and the civilian leader over sending Italian troops to Salonika.

By mid-May 1916, in the wake of five useless offensives on the Isonzo, Salandra's government found itself confronting the *Strafexpedition*. Austrian forces under Conrad von Hötzendorf (*q.v.*) drove southward through the Trentino passes to threaten the Lombard plains. Italian armies on the Isonzo then had an enemy at their back. Cadorna spoke of a massive retreat to the Piave and refused to meet with civilian leaders. Salandra was appalled, but he lacked the confidence to sack the general.

Neutralists opposed to the war combined with deputies who felt it was not being pursued energetically enough. Salandra's government fell on June 10, 1916. It was replaced by a broad coalition led by Paolo Boselli (*q.v.*), the grand old man of the Chamber of Deputies.

Salandra played no further role in World War I, although he attended the Paris Peace Conference as a member of the Italian delegation. He rallied for a time to support Mussolini's Fascist regime, representing Italy at the League of Nations. But he retired from political life in 1925 and died in Rome on December 9, 1931.

Askew, "Italy and the Great Powers Before the First World War"; Bosworth, *Italy, the Least of the Great Powers*; Lowe and Marzari, *Italian Foreign Policy 1870-1940*; Melograni, *Storia politica della grande guerra*; Salandra, *Il diario di Salandra* and *Italy and the Great War*; Seton-Watson, *Italy from Liberalism to Fascism*; Whittam, *The Politics of the Italian Army, 1861-1918*; Enciclopedia italiana, XXX.

SAMSONOV, Aleksandr Vasilevich (*Russia, General of Cavalry*), was born November 14, 1859. He completed the Nikolaevsky Cavalry College in 1877, just in time to see service in the Russo-Turkish War. Seven years later he graduated from the General Staff Academy. Like many a freshly minted *Genshtabist* ("General Staff officer"), he rose rapidly, reaching the rank of general in 1902. The popular and highly regarded young leader commanded first a cavalry brigade, then a division, in the Russo-Japanese War. Upon the close of the conflict in the Far East, Samsonov served a brief stretch as chief of staff of the Warsaw Military District, 1906/1907, then left for more remote parts of the empire. By 1909 he was governor general of Turkestan and commander of the Turkestan Military District. It was at this prestigious but distant post that Samsonov received his assignment in the first weeks of World War I.

At the urging of French leaders, the Russian High Command ordered an early advance against the lone German Eighth Army in East Prussia. General Rennenkampf (*q.v.*), at the head of the Russian First Army, was to drive in from the east on August 17, while Samsonov's Second Army charged up from the south to cut off the German line of retreat. Samsonov's role in the ensuing tragedy is clear to a point. Urged forward by General Zhilinsky (*q.v.*), commanding the northwestern front, Samsonov crossed the German border on August 20. He pushed forward against stiffening resistance until August 26/27, when he found his main body heavily engaged on both flanks. By August 28 the enemy had cut off communications to the south and the Second Army was surrounded.

Samsonov allegedly had doubts about launching such an offensive into East Prussia; Rennenkampf was fifty miles to the east and the Masurian Lakes stood between the two isolated Russian field armies. Stories abound of bad blood between the two Russian army commanders, dating from their service together in the Russo-Japanese War. But Samsonov was above all the victim of the Russian army's high level of incompetence, jerry-built chain of command,

and technical backwardness. Zhilinsky failed to comprehend the range of German options, specifically, the enemy's ability to use rail transportation to concentrate in the south and strike Samsonov's left flank. This dim view of the unfolding campaign led Zhilinsky to permit Samsonov's neighbor Rennenkampf to amble forward. German aerial reconnaissance and monitoring of Russian radio transmission made all of this clear to Samsonov's opponents in East Prussia. The Russians had no aerial reconnaissance planes, and their poorly trained signal personnel transmitted messages without managing to put them in code!

Accounts differ on Rennenkampf and Zhilinsky's motives. Did they slow the First Army down to prepare a long siege at Königsberg, where the Eighth Army was likely to entrench? Or did they hope, by a deliberate crawl forward, to forestall a German "panic" that would lead the enemy to run westward too quickly to let Samsonov close the trap? In any event, by the close of August the Second Army had been transformed into a horde of prisoners of war, 100,000 in number. Accompanied by a tiny escort, Samsonov rode off into the forest to commit suicide.

Gurko, *Features and Figures of the Past*; Rostunov, *Russkii front pervoi mirovoi voiny*; Rutherford, *The Russian Army in World War I*; Stone, *The Eastern Front*; *Sovetskaia voennaia entsiklopediia*, VII.

SAN GIULIANO, Antonio Paterno Castello , Marquis Di (*Italy, Minister of Foreign Affairs*), was born in Catania in eastern Sicily, December 9, 1852. A member of an old noble family active in national politics, the young San Giuliano received his law degree in 1875, achieved local office in 1879, and, in 1882, became the youngest member of the Chamber of Deputies. His interests there centered on colonization and foreign affairs. In 1899/1900 he obtained his first Cabinet portfolio as minister of posts and telegraphs. In 1904, however, he was defeated for reelection to the Chamber. The marquis then entered on a diplomatic career. He managed to begin at the top; in the winter of 1905/1906 he directed the Foreign Ministry for several months. From 1906 to 1910 San Giuliano was a popular and successful ambassador to London. In early 1910 he was posted to the Paris embassy. San Giuliano barely had time to settle in when, in March, he was called to Rome to lead the Foreign Ministry for the second time. During the next four and a half years, the marquis was Italy's only foreign minister.

The job required a master of cynical caution. Italy's diplomatic shelter against Europe's gathering storms was the Triple Alliance. But membership in that alliance meant association with Germany, whose power Italy not only needed but feared. It also meant a link with Austria-Hungary, and Vienna's expansionist designs on the Balkans continually threatened to spark a war of unpredictable dimensions. The situation was further complicated by growing public hostility in Italy toward Austria-Hungary. Italian irredentists bemoaned the fate of their brothers under Austrian control. San Giuliano was interested in expanding Italian influence in areas like Albania, but since that was likely to encourage Austrian expansionism, he found it desirable to be satisfied with the status quo in the Balkans. He was, in any case, certain that any Austrian gains in that sensitive area must be accompanied by territorial acquisitions by Italy, specifically, Trieste, otherwise Italian public opinion was likely to explode.

San Giuliano's policy in the July crisis of 1914 proceeded along several intertangled lines. To restrain Austria from making demands on Serbia was probably the best hope, but hardly a realistic one. To match Austrian gains with reciprocal gains in territory for Italy was next best. But many Italians were unlikely to accept the sight of Italian soldiers fighting side by side with the Austrian army, and that was the only way to make Austria generous in granting territory to Rome. San Giuliano tried to forestall the worst possibility, which was a set of Austrian gains with no compensation whatsoever to Italy. He hinted until August 1 that Italy might indeed honor the Triple Alliance in this instance, but the Austrians insisted on actions not just words. In the end, San Giuliano chose the expedient of neutrality, which he saw as his country's best stance until the drift of military events became clear.

For the remaining few months of his life, San Giuliano watched the evolution of the war; and he attempted to match his diplomatic maneuvers with the rising and falling prospects of each side. This meant, for example, striving to better relations with the Central Powers in late August, as German armies poured through Belgium toward a likely victory in northern France. Conversely, it meant tilting toward the Entente in the aftermath of the battle of the Marne. San Giuliano got nowhere, however, with his request to bring the Allied navies into the Adriatic so that Italy's war effort could begin in the aftermath of the capture of Trieste by the Anglo-French fleet.

San Giuliano died in Rome on October 16, 1914. The war was less than three months old. But Italy's first wartime foreign minister had set an important pattern: watchful waiting; sizing up the prospects of each side for a quick military victory; weighing the generosity of the two rival alliances in rewarding Italy for its intervention in the conflict.

Askew, "Italy and the Great Powers Before the First World War"; Bosworth, *Italy, the Least of the Great Powers*; Lowe and Marzari, *Italian Foreign Policy 1870-1940*; Seton-Watson, *Italy from Liberalism to Fascism*; *Larousse mensuel*, III.

SARKOTIČ von LOVČEN, Stephan Baron (*Austria-Hungary, General*), was born in Sinac, Croatia, on October 4, 1858, the son of an army officer. He graduated from the Theresa Military Academy in 1879 and three years later took part in quelling a rebellion in South Dalmatia. Sarkotič attended the War Academy in 1882-1884 and thereafter was attached to the General Staff. He served in Esseg, Pola, Hermannstadt, and Linz; Sarkotič was promoted major in 1896, colonel five years later, and major general in 1907. The following year Emperor Francis Joseph (*q.v.*) raised Sarkotič into the Hungarian nobility. While stationed in Tyrol from 1908 to 1912, he developed close ties to Archduke Eugene, and on April 10, 1912, succeeded General Svetozar Boroević (*qq.v.*) as commander of the VI Landwehr district in Agram.

At the outset of the Great War, Sarkotič commanded the so-called Domobranzen-Division (Croatian Forty-second Landwehr) against Serbia, actually crossing the Drina, but as early as September 1914 dysentery forced him to take a leave of absence. After the Serbian army drove General Oskar Potiorek (*q.v.*) out of the country and behind the Save and Drina, Archduke Eugene was given command of the Fifth Army, and he requested that his old friend Sarkotič be appointed his chief of staff. Francis Joseph nominated him, however, to become commanding general in Bosnia, Herzegovina, and Dalmatia on December 22, 1914. In this difficult post Sarkotič was responsible both to the supreme commander of the army and to the Finance Ministry; he adopted an iron-handed rule to restore order after Potiorek's disasters. In January 1916, Sarkotič participated in the conquest of Montenegro, storming the commanding heights at Lovčen. In mid-July 1916, in the wake of the Austro-Hungarian setback at Luck, the emperor's military chancellery contacted Sarkotič to ascertain whether he would accept the post of chief of the General Staff in place of General Conrad von Hötzendorf (*q.v.*), but the ruler of Bosnia declined owing to his poor health.

With regard to the future structure of the Dual Monarchy, Sarkotič favored a union of Croatia and Dalmatia with Bosnia-Herzegovina, but unlike Baron Max Hussarek (*q.v.*) rejected trialism in favor of the direct administration of this new unit by Hungary. At a special crown council in Vienna on December 4, 1917, Sarkotič adamantly rejected the proposed division of the common army into separate Austrian and Hungarian contingents and instead called for a "small unitary army . . . prepared and ready to suppress revolutionary subversions and coups." Earlier that same year, Emperor Charles (*q.v.*) had raised Sarkotič into the Hungarian baronage with the title von Lovčen. In November 1918, the Croat was temporarily arrested at Wagram, but after his release by zealous nationalists settled down to a quiet retirement in Vienna. One of the Dual Monarchy's ablest commanders, Sarkotič combined a love of his native Croatia with loyalty and service to the House of Habsburg. He died in Vienna on October 16, 1939.

E. Bauer, *Zwischen Halbmond und Doppeladler*; Rothenberg, *Army of Francis Joseph*; Veltzé, *Unsere Heerführer*; *Neue Österreichische Biographie*, IX.

SARRAIL, Maurice Paul Emmanuel (*France, General*), was born in Carcassone in southern France, April 6, 1856. He graduated from St. Cyr in 1877 and entered active duty as an infantry officer in North Africa. Sarrail's conventional military career took a highly unconventional turn in the 1890s. As a battalion commander, he became a Radical, a Freemason, and a supporter of Dreyfus, known, both within the army and in political circles, as an outstanding exception to the clerical and sentimentally monarchist officers who dominated the army's leadership.

Between 1900 and 1907 Sarrail served in the War Ministry under the reforming General André, commanded the infantry school at St. Maixent where sergeants were trained to rise to officer's rank, and took charge of the military guard at the Chamber of Deputies. He was the director of infantry at the War Ministry from 1907 to 1911, and in 1914 as a major general entered the war as commander of the VI Corps at Châlons. His advancement depended in part on his recognized organizational skills, but his political sympathies and open ties to the important Radical party in the Chamber of Deputies unquestionably aided his career.

Sarrail's VI Corps, as part of General Ruffey's Third Army, advanced northward in a counterattack against the Germans in the lower Ardennes. After a bitter encounter battle (August 22) at Vitron, Sarrail was forced backward to Verdun. Ruffey's lack of composure led General Joffre (*q.v.*) to replace him with Sarrail. The new commander of the Third Army distinguished himself with a tenacious defense of Verdun, rejecting Joffre's suggestion that the Third Army retreat from the crucial fortress if German pressure grew too great. Verdun became the eastern anchor for the French forces during the battle of the Marne.

Sarrail's role enhanced his popularity among leaders of the political Left who began to present him as a desirable successor to Joffre.

In June and July 1915, Sarrail's Third Army suffered a sudden defeat when the Germans reopened operations in the quiescent Argonne sector. Joffre took the occasion to relieve his politically troublesome subordinate, but Sarrail's political contacts and his symbolic role as the leading republican general in the army made this the occasion for a governmental crisis. Sarrail and his supporters were placated when he was offered command of the French forces at Gallipoli, but in light of the rapidly deteriorating situation in the Balkans in September 1915, Sarrail instead became commander of the French forces in Macedonia. He reached Greece in time to launch an offensive up the Vardar valley in October 1915. It was too late, however, to serve its intended purpose of aiding the Serbs, who were being crushed by invading German and Bulgarian armies.

For the next two years, Sarrail and his Army of the Orient remained a center of political and military controversy, which soon involved France's allies as well. Sarrail stood as the favorite general of the political Left, shielded from repeated attempts by Joffre to control him. The Army of the Orient, for which Sarrail demanded reinforcements, became a bone of contention between Allied political and military leaders like Joffre, who favored concentrating all energies on the western front, and those like Prime Ministers Briand and Lloyd George (qq.v.), who hoped other fronts could provide the key to victory. Moreover, Sarrail took an active role in manipulating the Greek political scene to secure his base of operations at Salonika.

In December 1915, Joffre became commander in chief of all French armies, including the Army of the Orient. His deputy, General de Castelnau (q.v.), was sent to Greece in an unsuccessful effort to assert Joffre's authority over Sarrail. In early 1916 in the face of numerically superior Bulgarian forces Sarrail and his British allies moved to secure their position at Salonika by constructing a fortified perimeter seventy miles long. At the same time, Sarrail gradually took over de facto civil administration of the port of Salonika and its environs despite protests from the Greek government. In France, criticism of Joffre led to a reassessment of French military leadership in a closed session of the Parliament in July 1916; representatives of the political Left combined their attacks on Joffre with praise for Sarrail.

Sharp fighting broke out on the Salonika front in the fall of 1916 as the Bulgarians launched a major attack. Sarrail, reinforced by Serbian and Russian contingents and empowered by the British government to direct British forces in Macedonia, counterattacked with spectacular success. Despite heavy losses, Sarrail's forces pushed through difficult mountain terrain to capture Monastir in southern Serbia on November 19. The first important Allied victory in months, the Monastir offensive failed to help beleaguered Rumania, but it reinforced Sarrail's virtually autonomous position in the French army. During these fall months of 1916 Sarrail encouraged an indigenous revolt against the pro-German King Constantine, which culminated with the establishment of a pro-Allied government led by Prime Minister Venizelos (qq.v.).

In 1917 Sarrail's military career reached its peak, followed by utter collapse. In January the Rome conference of political and military leaders from France and Britain formally designated Sarrail as commander in chief of the Allied Army of the Orient. In a preview of the arrangement established on the western front in 1918, all national commanders in Macedonia and Salonika were placed under his direction, while retaining the right to appeal decisions to their respective governments. Sarrail's spring offensive thus utilized Serbian, Russian, Italian, and British forces as well as French contingents. It failed completely. The poorly coordinated attack was carried out by exhausted and dispirited troops over impossible terrain, and the Bulgarians easily held their position on the Struma River. First Sarrail's Russian troops, then some of his French forces mutinied.

Sarrail was able to restore order, aided by the fact that his troops were not aware of the simultaneous mutinies that had assumed more dangerous proportions on the western front. He retained his position only by virtue of his political links; his military record was badly tarnished. In the summer of 1917 the British began to remove two divisions from Salonika. In November Georges Clemenceau (q.v.) became France's prime minister. He was technically a member of the party that had supported Sarrail for years, but their personal relations had never been cordial. Clemenceau's attack on defeatist elements in France sealed Sarrail's fate; investigations in France uncovered documents from Sarrail's headquarters in the hands of known German collaborators. Sarrail was relieved of his command and recalled to France in December 1917. He had no further military role to play in the war.

Sarrail ran unsuccessfully for the National Assembly in 1919, then occupied himself as a journalist and lecturer of the political Left. In the national elections of 1924, his old political supporters returned to office and he went back on active duty. He became high commissioner in Syria and Lebanon, but his failure in dealing with armed revolts led to his recall in 1925. He returned to private life and died in Paris on March 23, 1929.

Isselin, *Battle of the Marne*; King, *Generals and Politicians*; Palmer, *The Gardeners of Salonika*; Sarrail, *Mon commandement en Orient*; Tanenbaum, *General Maurice Sarrail*.

SAZONOV, Sergei Dmitrievich (*Russia, Minister of Foreign Affairs*), was born on July 29, 1860, to a noble family living in Riazan Province. He entered the Russian diplomatic service in 1883 and served in such choice posts as Paris, Washington, and London. In 1906 Sazonov was appointed Russian minister at the Vatican, but he returned to St. Petersburg in May 1909 to serve as deputy to Minister of Foreign Affairs Aleksandr Izvolsky. Little more than a year later, he took over Izvolsky's Cabinet portfolio.

As minister of foreign affairs Sazonov acquired a reputation for modesty and competence, free of the bent for Cabinet infighting that characterized most of the ministers serving Tsar Nicholas II (*q.v.*); thus, he provided a measure of stability in one of the government's most important positions. But the new foreign minister clearly lacked the experience such responsibilities called for; and many observers remarked at his nervous personality and his frequent unsteadiness in setting policy. Albertini suggests that Izvolsky, discredited by the 1908/1909 crisis over Bosnia-Herzegovina, deliberately chose a weakling as a successor; thus, the former foreign minister, then ambassador to France, could hope to go on guiding Russian foreign policy from abroad.

Sazonov at once made overtures to Germany for better relations, beginning with the question of the two countries' rivalry in Persia. The Agadir crisis of 1911 and the subsequent spurt in German naval expenditures helped solidify Russia's ties to France and, more slowly, to Britain. It was Russia's relations with small powers that gave Sazonov his baptism of fire. He had inherited from Izvolsky a policy of promoting alliances among the Balkan states; this, in turn, was based on the ostensible need to restrain Austria-Hungary after that nation's diplomatic triumph in the Bosnian affair in 1909. Likewise, Sazonov was heir to a Russian corps of diplomats prone to go their own way in dealing with small Balkan states. As a result, by October 1912, a Balkan League had become a reality, but in the form of an offensive alliance that soon marched against Ottoman Turkey. By July 1913, Sazonov found himself watching Serbia and Bulgaria, Russia's erstwhile friends, fighting over the spoils of victory, with the defeated Bulgars soon drifting toward the Central Powers.

A more dangerous threat to Russian interests loomed in the mission of General Liman von Sanders (*q.v.*) to Constantinople (December 1913/January 1914) and Berlin's apparent intention to achieve a predominant role in the Ottoman Empire. To counter that threat from the Central Powers Sazonov strengthened existing ties with France and Serbia (Serbia's Premier Nikola Pašić visited Russia in February 1914) and set out to woo Rumania's Ion Bratianu (*qq.v.*).

The assassination at Sarajevo and the ensuing July crisis of 1914 presented Sazonov with his greatest challenge. Albertini has composed the classic case against the "weak, vacillating, muddleheaded, and impulsive" creature. He wobbled between a desire to avoid war and the conviction that Russia must not seem to back down again, as in 1909, to the Central Powers. He allowed French bellicosity, originating with President Raymond Poincaré and transmitted through Ambassador Maurice Paléologue (*qq.v.*), to push him into dangerous saber rattling. Finally, like a host of contemporary European statesmen, he misread the significance of military mobilization. He saw it as a diplomatic tool, a means of pressuring the Central Powers to back away from their demands on Serbia. Quintessentially mistaken, he failed to understand that once Russia's huge armies began to move to the frontier, St. Petersburg could no longer hope to control the pace of events, most notably in Berlin.

Word of the Austrian ultimatum to Russia's ally Serbia reached Sazonov on July 24; he remarked that this meant "a European war." The pessimistic certainty that no steps could avert catastrophe may thus have been present in Sazonov's actions from the start. He called at once for Russian mobilization against Austria-Hungary. That same day, according to Albertini and (more recently) Gale Stokes, he pledged aid to Serbia and urged Belgrade not to yield unconditionally to Vienna's demands. The crisis swelled. Partial mobilization turned out to be impossible: the army had no plans for it; and to improvise such an operation meant jeopardizing Russia's defense against Germany, Austria's powerful ally. The generals stepped in to convince first Sazonov, then the tsar, to consider full-scale mobilization, which came on July 30; the German declaration of war followed on August 1.

Sazonov proved a competent wartime diplomat, a notable achievement given the small help he received from Russia's military performance. He began by obtaining a Russian pledge (August 1914) to reunite Poland at the close of the war, that is, joining Russian Poland with Polish territories held by Austria-Hungary. Conservative opponents, led by Minister of the Interior Nikolai Maklakov (*q.v.*), prevented Sazonov from drawing a public pledge from the tsar; rather, the sympathetic Russian commander in chief, Grand Duke Nikolai Nikolaevich (*q.v.*), made the promise, hoping to secure the rear of his fighting forces in Poland. Sazonov also saw Rumanian neutrality as essential to Russian military hopes in eastern Europe; certainly, he hoped for active support from Bucharest as well. Sazonov found that Bratianu's price was high—but it had to be paid. In early October Sazonov pledged Austrian Transylvania to Rumania in return for all that Bratianu would give in return, benevolent neutrality.

The entry of Turkey into the war in November 1914 recast Russian diplomacy. An outraged Sazonov expressed his anger by calling for Turkey to be compelled to grant Russia control of the Bosphorus. By March 1915, he had obtained a historic triumph: Britain and (more reluctantly) France consented to St. Petersburg's control over the link between the Mediterranean and the Black seas once the war had been fought to a victorious conclusion.

Sazonov scarcely had time to savor his success. The Gorlice offensive of May 1915 shattered Russia's military position in eastern Europe. Bulgaria tilted toward Berlin and Vienna; indeed, the British took over the task of implementing the Entente's slight hopes of keeping Bulgaria neutral. Russia's ally Serbia fell under the combined blows of Germany, Austria, and Bulgaria in October/November 1915. Sazonov himself nearly left office as he took the side of Cabinet liberals, opposing the tsar's decision to take direct control of the armies, as well as the government's move to prorogue the Duma (August/September 1915).

Sazonov survived but he was a target for ambitious reactionaries like Empress Alexandra, her disreputable confidant Rasputin, and the new premier, Boris Sturmer (*qq.v.*). In 1916 the Polish issue brought Sazonov down. France's government, claiming to be responding to wishes of the French Left, sought to make Poland's future an issue for international discussion. Moreover, all of Poland lay under the control of the Central Powers, and Berlin and Vienna seemed about to appeal to Poland's population by some pledge to restore the country's nominal independence under their aegis. Sazonov found the victorious early days of General Brusilov's (*q.v.*) summer offensive a promising time to woo the tsar into a pledge of constitutional autonomy for Poland under Russia once the war had been won. Sturmer, Rasputin, and the empress jumped into the fray. In July the tsar backed away from embracing a liberal future for Poland. Then, to please Alexandra,

he reluctantly removed Sazonov from office. Sturmer added the foreign minister's portfolio to his other posts.

Sazonov obtained the London embassy as a consolation prize, but the March Revolution intervened before he could make the move. He played a diplomat's role in the Russian Civil War, representing the anti-Bolshevik White movement at the Versailles Peace Conference. He died, still in exile, on Christmas Day, 1927.

Albertini, *The Origins of the War of 1914*, 3 vols.; Bestuzhev, "Russian Foreign Policy, February-June 1914"; Dallin, ed., *Russian Diplomacy and Eastern Europe*; Gurko, *Features and Figures of the Past*; Lee, *Europe's Crucial Years*; Sazonov, *Fateful Years*; Smith, *The Russian Struggle for Power*; Stokes, "Serbian Documents from 1914: A Preview"; *Sovetskaia istoricheskaia entsiklopediia*, XII.

SCHEER, Reinhard (*Germany, Admiral*), was born at Obernkirchen near Kassel on September 30, 1863, the son of a teacher. Scheer entered the navy in 1879 and fought against rebellious natives in the Cameroons and German East Africa in 1884 and 1889. For much of the ensuing decade he was attached to the torpedo service; in 1903 Alfred von Tirpitz (*q.v.*) brought Scheer to the Navy Office. In 1907 Scheer returned to the fleet as captain of the battleship *Elsass*, and two years later Admiral Henning von Holtzendorff (*q.v.*) appointed Scheer chief of staff to the High Sea Fleet. In 1911 Scheer returned to Berlin to head the General Department of the Navy Office, but he transferred back to the fleet in February 1913 as chief of the Second Squadron of battleships. Scheer had been promoted rear admiral in 1910 and vice admiral in 1913. He was widely known as an energetic, stern disciplinarian; his sailors referred to him as the "man with the iron mask."

On Christmas Day 1914, Vice Admiral Scheer became chief of the Third Squadron of the High Sea Fleet, and on January 15, 1916, he replaced Admiral Hugo von Pohl as chief of the High Sea Fleet, selecting Captain Adolf von Trotha (*q.v.*) as his chief of staff. Given greater operative freedom for the fleet by the kaiser, Scheer on May 31, 1916, boarded the *Friedrich der Grosse* and took his sixteen battleships, five battle cruisers and eleven light cruisers out to sea to stand off the Danish peninsula at Skagerrak. Late that afternoon the Scouting Forces under Admiral Franz Hipper on board the *Lützow* contacted their British counterparts with Sir David Beatty (*qq.v.*) on board *Lion*. As Beatty attempted to lure the Germans into the arms of the approaching Grand Fleet of Sir John Jellicoe (*q.v.*), a fierce battle ensued in which the Germans performed well: the British battle cruisers *Indefatigable*, *Queen Mary*, and *Invincible* were destroyed in the mêlée. Scheer's High Sea Fleet and Jellicoe's Grand Fleet were on collision course. At about 7 P.M. the two main fleets encountered each other. Jellicoe enjoyed the advantage of the light and his twenty-four dreadnoughts crossed Scheer's T and inflicted a terrible pounding upon the Germans; the battle cruiser *Moltke* alone remained fully operational. The official German history of the war states: "Suddenly the German van was faced by the belching guns of an interminable line of heavy ships . . . salvo after salvo followed almost without intermission." Facing certain annihilation, Scheer at 7:33 P.M. made a dramatic battle turn away and escaped under a heavy smoke screen. Yet inexplicably, within half an hour Scheer again reversed his position 180 degrees, and by 8:15 P.M. his van was once again under fire by the Grand Fleet. Jellicoe had managed a second time to cross Scheer's T, and he demolished especially the ships of the *König* class. Scheer was forced to undertake a third battle turn away and to hurl all available cruisers and torpedo boats against the British to cover his escape. By 9 P.M. the daylight phase of the only major naval battle of the war in the North Sea was over. Scheer headed for port with Jellicoe close on his heels. The Germans were not aware until the next morning that they had inflicted heavy losses upon the English: fourteen ships of 110,000 tons and 6,784 officers and men against eleven ships of 62,000 tons and 3,058 officers and men for Germany.

For his part in the affair, Scheer was promoted admiral, received the order *Pour le mérite*, and was widely hailed as the Victor of the Skagerrak. To be sure, he had displayed his best qualities that day: great willpower, iron nerves, and lack of self-doubts. Yet in a private moment this man of action confided to fellow admirals: "I came to the thing as the virgin did when she had the baby."

Scheer was fully aware of the strategical significance of the battle of Jutland. On July 4, 1916, he informed Wilhelm II (*q.v.*) "that even the most successful outcome of a fleet action in this war will not *force* England to make peace." Instead, the admiral returned to a theme he had already aired in the fall and winter of 1914: "the defeat of British economic life . . . by using the U-boats against British trade." Hence Scheer welcomed the decision of January 9, 1917, to resume unrestricted submarine warfare regardless of the consequences. With the exception of occasional sorties into the North Sea, the High Sea Fleet remained idle for the rest of the war.

Perhaps because of this inactivity, the sailors of the fleet rebelled in August 1917 and demanded more equitable rations and shore leaves. Scheer was convinced that the sailors had been encouraged by the Independent Socialists (USPD) and in vain demanded official prosecution of this party. The Reichstag refused to set aside parliamentary immunity, and the navy fared badly in the ensuing parliamentary debate. Scheer was more successful in dealing with the leaders of the rebellion, however; on September 5 two ringleaders were executed and numerous other sailors received lengthy prison terms.

In October 1917, Scheer dispatched modern battleships from the fleet for use in the Baltic Sea against the islands Ösel, Moon, and Dagö. On August 11, 1918, Scheer forced the kaiser to accept a reorganization of the navy, with Scheer becoming head of a new independent Supreme Command. He chose Commodore Magnus von Levetzow (*q.v.*) as his chief of staff and entrusted the fleet to Admiral von Hipper. Almost immediately, on October 1, the new *Seekriegsleitung* announced a bold, massive submarine construction effort dubbed the Scheer Program as a parallel to the army's Hindenburg Program. But it was too little, too late. When President Woodrow Wilson (*q.v.*) forced Germany on October 14 to cancel the unrestricted submarine campaign, Scheer readily agreed eight days later and instead prepared a final naval sortie against the Grand Fleet in the North Sea in order to save the honor of the officer corps and to secure the navy a future in German politics. Perhaps Scheer also hoped in the course of Operations Plan Nr. 19 to topple through a heroic sacrifice the "defeatist" government of Prince Max von Baden (*q.v.*). Instead, the sailors mutineed on October 30, and the plan died in port. The kaiser dismissed Scheer on November 9 with the curt comment: "I no longer have a navy." The admiral was officially retired by the republic on December 17, 1918.

Scheer settled at Weimar to write his memoirs, in which he bitterly blamed the lost war on the politicians and the deceitful English. He died in Marktredwitz in Upper Franconia of a heart attack on November 26, 1928, and was laid to rest in Weimar. His reputation at the battle of Jutland has been badly blown out of proportion: on at least two occasions Jellicoe badly outmaneuvered Scheer and brought him to the brink of annihilation. Reputation to the contrary, Reinhard Scheer was not one of the great captains.

Germany. Der Krieg zur See. Nordsee, V; Herwig, *"Luxury" Fleet*; Marder, *Dreadnought to Scapa Flow*, II-V; Scheer, *Deutschlands Hochseeflotte*; *Biographisches Wörterbuch zur Deutschen Geschichte*, III; *Geschichte der Ritter des Ordens*, II.

SCHEIDEMANN, Philipp (*Germany, State Secretary without Portfolio*), was born in Kassel on July 26, 1865, the son of an artisan. A typesetter by trade, Scheidemann joined the Social Democratic party (SPD) in his eighteenth year and later served the party as newspaper editor and journalist. He was elected parliamentary deputy for Solingen in 1903 and was to remain in the Reichstag for the next thirty years; in 1906 he served concurrently as city councillor in Kassel. Scheidemann generally avoided party debates, attending only three party congresses between 1906 and 1911, and specifically refused to become embroiled in the great revisionist debate. He described himself as a radical, perhaps thereby hoping to capture the attention of the party's venerable leader, August Bebel. The great SPD electoral victory in 1912 brought Scheidemann election as vice-president of the Reichstag, but he never occupied the office owing to his refusal to pay the obligatory call at court. A facile agitator, Scheidemann became one of the most effective speakers in Parliament, combining a ready wit with humor and sarcasm; vainly he reveled in his oratorical successes.

The July crisis of 1914 found Scheidemann, like Friedrich Ebert (*q.v.*), on vacation; but on August 3 Scheidemann voted in the SPD caucus for war credits, seeing the looming struggle as primarily one against tsarist autocracy. Scheidemann basked in the limelight accorded him by various tours of the front as well as abroad, and the attention paid him by Chancellor Theobald von Bethmann Hollweg (*q.v.*), who carefully sought to uphold the proclaimed *Burgfrieden* ("internal peace"). While generally opposed to vast German territorial annexations, Scheidemann nevertheless in the great debate of April 5/6, 1916, favored retention of Alsace-Lorraine as well as preservation of the territorial integrity of Turkey and Austria-Hungary. In July 1917, he helped General Erich Ludendorff and Colonel Max Bauer (*qq.v.*) to topple Bethmann Hollweg; in the following days, the Social Democrat actually worked with the general on a draft of a peace resolution specifically designed so that "necessary territorial gains and compensations are not precluded." Scheidemann also stated the SPD's position on the Brest-Litovsk peace in March 1918, announcing that his party would abstain from voting to show that while it did not condone all the terms of the Draconian peace, it nevertheless supported the agreement as it at least brought an end to the war in the east. When compared to the almost limitless annexationist schemes of the military and of the Conservative leader, Count Kuno von Westarp (*q.v.*), Scheidemann's moderation on this issue quickly led those who opposed a peace of indemnities and annex-ations to rally to his side under the political banner of the "Scheidemann peace."

On October 3, 1918, Scheidemann joined Prince Max von Baden's (*q.v.*) caretaker government as state secretary without portfolio. At noon on November 9, against the will of Ebert, he announced from the balcony of the Reichstag the creation of a German republic, thereby effectively ending all speculation concerning a possible regency. With Ebert, he became coleader in the Council of People's Commissars and attended the Weimar National Assembly; in February 1919, he was elected first chancellor of the Weimar Republic. It was to be a short-lived tenure. The harsh terms of the Versailles Treaty on May 11 brought from Scheidemann the fateful comment: "What hand would not wither that joins us in this bondage?" He resigned in June 1919.

Philipp Scheidemann retained his parliamentary seat until 1933; from 1920 until 1925 he served also as lord mayor of Kassel. In 1920 he condemned Gustav Noske's (*q.v.*) forceful suppression of workers' revolts in Berlin and Munich; the following year Scheidemann narrowly escaped an attack with prussic acid. His sensational revelation in the Reichstag in 1926 that the German army was secretly training with the Red Army in the Soviet Union earned him the wrath of the right wing, and in 1933 Scheidemann was forced to leave his homeland, first for Czechoslovakia and then for Denmark. He died in exile in Copenhagen on November 29, 1939.

Gatzke, *Germany's Drive to the West*; Scheidemann, *Der Zusammenbruch* and *Memoiren*, 2 vols.; Schorske, *German Social Democracy*; *Biographisches Wörterbuch zur Deutschen Geschichte*, III.

SCHMIDT von KNOBELSDORF, Constantin (*Germany, General*), was born in Frankfurt on the Oder on December 13, 1860. Schmidt joined the cadet corps, then entered the army in 1878. He attended the War Academy and served in the General Staff, becoming battalion commander in 1901. Three years later Schmidt was assigned chief of staff to the X Army Corps and promoted colonel in this position. By 1908 he commanded the Fourth Guards Regiment and in 1911 in the grade of major general was appointed chief of staff to the prestigious Guards Corps; in 1912 he became deputy chief of the General Staff and in January 1914 was promoted lieutenant general.

In August 1914, Schmidt was attached to Crown Prince Wilhelm's (*q.v.*) Fifth Army at Saarbrücken as staff chief and was largely responsible for the battle of Longwy-Longuyon on August 22. The Fifth Army followed up this initial moderate victory with another at Varennes-Montfaucon on September 2/3, and advanced—despite orders to stand!—as far as Verdun and the Argonnes forest. Schmidt finally withdrew from Louppy to Varennes on September 12 in the wake of the German debacle at the Marne. Around Verdun and in the Argonnes forest, the struggle degenerated into trench warfare. When Crown Prince Wilhelm was given command of the Third Army in September 1915 during the fierce battles in the Champagne, Schmidt temporarily commanded the VIII Reserve Corps in brutal combat at Maison de Champagne, for which he received the order *Pour le mérite*.

Schmidt's career took a fateful turn on February 21, 1916, when as chief of staff of the new Army Group Crown Prince Wilhelm he unleashed the assault on Verdun. The attack was planned by Schmidt initially only against the north and northeast sectors of Verdun, but in time was broadened to include the entire area west of the Meuse River. The crown prince sought to destroy "the heart of France" largely for psychological reasons, and General Henri Pétain (*q.v.*) opted to defend it for similar reasons. Finally, it is still not clear whether General Erich von Falkenhayn (*q.v.*) literally meant to bleed the French white at Verdun or whether he hoped the battle might turn into another Sedan, that is, into a doubled envelopment as attempted in September 1914.

Whatever the case, on February 21, a cold, dry day, the Germans commenced an artillery bombardment so ferocious that it transformed the landscape into a lunar crater lake. Division after division of infantry equipped with flame-throwers was hurled against the historic forts Douaumont, Vaux, Thiaumont, Souville, Height 304, and Fleury, among others. But the French held. Crown Prince Wilhelm early in March was overcome with a "grievous pessimism" and desired to break off the engagement, but Schmidt, supported vociferously by Falkenhayn, pushed for victory at all cost. Throughout the summer of 1916 each side fired about 10 million rounds of artillery in and around Verdun; the Germans used up more than forty divisions in the war of attrition that raged along the Meuse. And still Schmidt refused to abandon the senseless slaughter.

Events elsewhere finally brought the macabre Verdun spectacle to an end. At the end of June 1916, the British and French with more than fifty divisions launched a massive assault along the Somme, while concurrently General Aleksei Brusilov (*q.v.*) caved in the Austro-Hungarian front in Galicia. Falkenhayn was thereby forced to curtail the flow of men and munitions to Verdun—just as Fort Vaux finally fell to the attackers. Crown Prince Wilhelm and Schmidt

von Knobelsdorf bitterly fell out over responsibility for the failure to take Verdun, with the result that Schmidt was removed as chief of staff on August 21 and given the X Army Corps as solace. About 300,000 of Germany's best assault troops had died before Verdun, and the morale of the German armies had been badly shaken by this war of attrition.

Schmidt's X Army Corps was dispatched to halt the Russian advance near Kovel; thereafter his Hanoverians were transferred to Alsace, where they engaged in trench warfare in relative quiet until the end of the war. Schmidt was promoted general of infantry in October 1918; in December he headed the X Army Corps at Hanover during demobilization. He retired from active service in September 1919 and died in 1936. His name will forever be linked to the tragic loss of over 300,000 German troops in the old forts of Verdun.

Liddell Hart, *The Real War*; Crown Prince Wilhelm, *Erinnerungen*; Zwehl, *Falkenhayn*; *Geschichte der Ritter des Ordens*, II.

SCHÖNBURG-HARTENSTEIN, Alois Prince von (*Austria-Hungary, General*), was born in Karlsruhe, Baden, on November 21, 1858. He belonged to the Catholic line of the "Schönburge" family, registered in Saxony since the fourteenth century; a branch of the clan had migrated to Austria early in the nineteenth century. Schönburg-Hartenstein attended cadet school in Dresden, but in May 1878 elected to receive a commission in the Austro-Hungarian army, just in time to see action during the occupation of Bosnia that year. Next came the War Academy, followed by duty with the General Staff from 1886 to 1889; in September 1895, Captain Schönburg-Hartenstein was sent to Berlin as military attaché. Two years later he retired in the grade of major of the reserves in order to manage the family estates in Saxony, Bohemia, and Moravia. That same year he was appointed to the Austrian Upper House and from 1898 until 1918 served as its vice-president.

At the outbreak of war, Schönburg-Hartenstein returned to active duty in the grade of major general and saw action in Galicia. At Christmas 1914, he was given command of the Sixth Infantry Division, which he led first on the Russian and later on the Italian front. In July 1916, the prince succeeded Archduke Charles (*q.v.*) as commander of the prestigious XX (Edelweiss) Corps in the grade of general of cavalry; in August of the following year he led a mixed corps composed of six divisions. In bloody fighting his IV Corps defended Mount Gabriele at the Isonzo front against eleven Italian divisions, helping thereby to prepare the way for the victorious Twelfth Isonzo battle (Caporetto).

Schönburg-Hartenstein was considered by General Arz von Straussenburg as a possible successor to War Minister Baron Alexander Krobatin (*qq.v.*) in April 1917, but in the end the job went to General Rudolf Stöger-Steiner (*q.v.*). The prince instead was appointed commander of the IV Corps, but a wave of strikes radiating out from Vienna to the industrial parts of the empire in January 1918 brought repression by the army (Operations Mogul and Revolver), and Schönburg-Hartenstein's appointment as commander of troops at home. In July 1918, he received command of the Sixth Army along the line of the Piave and was severely wounded in the leg in action. He knew that the war had been lost and wrote his family: "My remaining duty is to preserve discipline and to protect the new Austria."

After the war Schönburg-Hartenstein served the Austrian republic, accepting the post of state secretary of the army in September 1933. The following year he was promoted to war minister and, after suppressing Socialist uprisings that originated in Linz, retired from service under Chancellor Dollfuss in July 1934. The prince died on September 20, 1944, at Hartenstein, Lower Austria, an estate that his family had held since 1406.

Bardolff, *Militär-Maria Theresien-Orden*; Rothenberg, *Army of Francis Joseph*; Veltzé, *Unsere Heerführer*; *Biographisches Wörterbuch zur Deutschen Geschichte*, III.

SCHRÖDER, Ludwig von (*Germany, Admiral*),

was born in Hintzenkamp near Ückermünde on July 17, 1854, the son of an estate owner. Schröder joined the navy in 1871, lectured at the Navy School, and later was attached to the Supreme Command of the Navy. In 1900 he was appointed director of the Navy School in Kiel and thereafter department chief of the Admiralty Staff. In 1903 Captain Schröder commanded the Cruiser Squadron in the West Indies, and two years later as rear admiral was inspector of naval artillery. Schröder was chief of the Second Squadron of the High Sea Fleet in 1907 in the grade of vice admiral, and in 1910/1911 as admiral headed the Baltic Sea naval station at Kiel. He retired from active service in 1912 and was ennobled.

The gruff, aggressive Schröder was reactivated at the end of August 1914 as head of a Naval Division assembled in Kiel for service in Flanders under the command of General Hans von Beseler (*q.v.*). The naval infantry came under fire at Overdevaert and Aerschot on September 9 from troops commanded by King Albert (*q.v.*) of Belgium; after repulsing this attack, Schröder's forces advanced on Antwerp, which fell on October 11. In November the division fought at the North Sea coast along the Yser River. By then it had been expanded to a Navy Corps and

entrusted with defense of the Flanders coast on the right wing of the Fourth Army. Schröder improved existing harbor facilities at Brugge, Ostend, and Zeebrugge for use by German submarines and destroyers; one-third of all Allied shipping destroyed resulted from U-boats stationed in Flanders. In July 1917, the Navy Corps defended the triangle Brugge-Zeebrugge-Ostend against British attacks during the bloody battle of Ypres. Schröder's Corps consisted of three divisions (60-70,000 men) posted along the sixty-kilometer coastline.

At the start of the great German Michael offensive in France in 1918, British forces under Commodore Roger Keyes (*q.v.*) attempted on March 22/23 to block the harbor channels at Ostend and Zeebrugge, but they were repulsed and denied this goal by Schröder's men. At the height of the German offensive, naval long-range guns bombarded Paris. However, as the German assault spent itself by June, Allied counteroffensives in September and October drove the Navy Corps as well as the Fourth Army to the Lys River, and beyond. On November 8 Wilhelm II (*q.v.*) appointed Schröder chief of the Kiel naval station and ordered his Flanders Navy Corps to suppress the rebellion on the High Sea Fleet. Schröder was more than willing to move against the rebellious units, but Chancellor Prince Max von Baden (*q.v.*) quickly vetoed such a mission as being politically "suicidal." Thus ended the military career of the popularly hailed Lion of Flanders. After the war, Schröder headed the National Union of German Officers. He died in Berlin on July 23, 1933.

Herwig, *"Luxury" Fleet*; *Biographisches Wörterbuch zur Deutschen Geschichte*, III; *Geschichte der Ritter des Ordens*, II.

SEECKT, Hans von (*Germany, General*),

was born in Schleswig on April 22, 1866, the son of an army officer. Seeckt entered the Prussian army in 1885, attended the War Academy and, after a tour of India, joined the General Staff as captain in 1899. By 1913 Lieutenant Colonel von Seeckt had risen to staff chief of the III Army Corps at Berlin, and he led this unit into the Great War.

In August 1914, the III Brandenburg Corps fought the British at Mons, forced them to stand again at Le Cateau, and advanced to the banks of the Ourcq before the general retreat from the Marne. In January 1915, Seeckt defeated the enemy at Soissons and was promoted colonel as a result. He was already known as a brilliant staff officer with steady nerves; his inscrutable face was highlighted by steely gray-blue eyes and the inevitable monocle.

Seeckt's career changed radically in March 1915 when he was appointed chief of staff to a new

Eleventh Army hastily dispatched to Galicia under General August von Mackensen (*q.v.*) to halt the Russian advance in the east. On May 2 Seeckt led the Eleventh Army's drive through the Russian line at Gorlice-Tarnów, recapturing the great fortress of Przemysl, occupying Lemberg, and clearing Galicia of all enemy troops. He was promoted major general and awarded the order *Pour le mérite*. At the end of August his units stormed Brest-Litovsk, and thereafter the victorious team of Seeckt and Mackensen was regrouped as Army Group Mackensen on the Serbian border. By September the Germans crossed the Danube, captured Belgrade, and advanced as far as the Greek border. Seeckt planned to pursue the Entente forces into Salonika, but General Erich von Falkenhayn (*q.v.*) vetoed this operation in favor of the planned assault against Verdun.

Despite these outstanding achievements, Seeckt was denied independent command and on July 1, 1916, was placed at the disposal of the chief of the General Staff. The incredible success of General Aleksei Brusilov's June offensive in the east (200,000 Austrian casualties), however, forced Falkenhayn to dispatch this able officer as "supreme staff chief" of General Karl Pflanzer-Baltin's (*qq.v.*) Seventh Army in the Bukovina. Staff chief of Army Group Archduke Charles (*q.v.*) on the southeastern front followed after Rumania's declaration of war against Germany. The new Habsburg Emperor Charles in November 1916 agreed that Seeckt should act in the same capacity to Army Group Archduke Joseph (*qq.v.*) in Transylvania. Finally, on December 2, 1917, Seeckt was sent to Constantinople as staff chief of the Turkish Army Command and as adviser to Enver Paşa (*q.v.*), and from August to November 1918, he acted as chief of Turkish headquarters. This brilliant staff officer was rumored to be in line to succeed General Erich Ludendorff (*q.v.*), but the appointment instead went to a south German, General Wilhelm Groener (*q.v.*).

Returning to Germany in 1919, Seeckt in April was appointed military delegate to the Paris peace talks. In the summer of that year he replaced Field Marshal Paul von Hindenburg (*q.v.*) as the army's chief of staff, and in November became head of a thinly veiled general staff (*Truppenamt*) in the new Defense Ministry. In March 1920, Seeckt remained neutral ("troop does not fire upon troop") during the rightwing Kapp *Putsch* in Berlin and was promoted lieutenant general as head of the 100,000-man army. Seeckt transformed the latter into a state within a state and maintained it on a high level partly by secret maneuvers in Russia (the black Reichswehr). On November 8, 1923, he was appointed virtual

military dictator of Germany in the wake of Communist uprisings in Saxony and Thuringia, and the National Socialist revolt in Bavaria. A monarchist at heart, Seeckt never felt comfortable with the Weimar Republic and when he allowed Crown Prince Wilhelm's (*q.v.*) eldest son to participate in army maneuvers, he was fired on October 9, 1926, for violating the "Locarno spirit." Colonel General von Seeckt next served in the Reichstag as delegate for the German People's party. In the early 1930s he urged friends to vote for Adolf Hitler, but by the time he returned from two military missions to Chiang Kai-Shek's China (1933, 1934/35), Seeckt harbored no illusions about the nature of the Nazi state. He died in Berlin-Spandau on December 25, 1936.

Hans von Seeckt was, along with Max Hoffmann (*q.v.*), perhaps Germany's most brilliant staff officer. While Mackensen received the credit for Gorlice-Tarnów and the Serbian campaign, the genius behind these victories was Seeckt. Perhaps because he lacked a patron, Seeckt throughout the Great War was denied independent command. Moreover, he was shunted to relative obscurity (Transylvania, Turkey) at a time when his services would have been of immeasurable value at the western front.

Meier-Welcker, *Seeckt*; Seeckt, *Aus meinem Leben*, 2 vols.; *Biographisches Wörterbuch zur Deutschen Geschichte*, III; *Geschichte der Ritter des Ordens*, II.

SHCHERBACHEV, Dmitry Grigorevich (*Russia, General of Infantry*),

was born February 6, 1857. He completed the Mikhailovsky Artillery School in 1876 and graduated from the General Staff Academy in 1884. By 1907 he was commandant of the academy, and five years later he received charge of the IX Infantry Corps.

In the early weeks of World War I Shcherbachev fought in the Galician campaign; and the IX Corps led the Russian army into the strategic city of Lemberg. By the close of the year Shcherbachev had been promoted general of infantry. In April 1915, he received the Eleventh Army in time for the long summer retreat. In October he found himself the new commander of the Seventh Army on the southwestern front. He undertook his new duties just in time to participate in the calamitous Strypa offensive under General Ivanov (*q.v.*).

Stone sees Shcherbachev as an example of the limited Russian general who, under the leadership of a Brusilov (*q.v.*), could fight effectively. Shcherbachev was taken with the action of the French on the western front, and he leaned invariably toward attacks on a narrow sector where his artillery had been able to pummel the enemy at great length. The Strypa offensive had seen such an approach bring bloody fiasco. Brusilov took Shcherbachev and other self-willed army commanders like Lechitsky and Sakharov in hand. The Brusilov technique of attacking with little in the way of a preparatory bombardment to awaken the enemy was coupled with other promising innovations. Attacks were to come simultaneously along a broad front. Reserves were carefully—and secretly—to be positioned near the proposed breaks in the enemy line well before the attacks commenced.

With such techniques Brusilov's attack in June 1916 brought stunning results. Shcherbachev crossed the Strypa River, where he had failed with bloody losses only six months earlier. Cutting the line of communications of the South Army under Bothmer (q.v.), Shcherbachev threatened to unhinge the entire enemy line. These Russian successes near the northern rim of the Carpathians helped entice Rumania into the war in August 1916.

In April 1917, after the start of the Russian Revolution, Shcherbachev was named commander of Russian forces on the Rumanian front; with this position came the parallel responsibility of serving as military adviser to Rumania's King Ferdinand (q.v.). The Russian soldiers on the Rumanian line soon became a considerable military and political prize. Their distance from the urban centers of Russia, and hence from the worst effects of the political upheaval on military discipline, made these units a reliable fighting force in a time of scarcity. Following the Bolshevik Revolution in November, Shcherbachev dreamed of organizing his own Ukrainian front; with Allied aid he would take on both the Germans and the Bolsheviks.

Such dreams died quickly. By December the Ukrainian authorities were negotiating peace terms with Germany. In early 1918, fearful of Berlin's wrath, the Rumanians pressured Shcherbachev not to send his troops eastward to join the anti-German and anti-Bolshevik White forces collecting on the Don. Shcherbachev remained in Jassy, however, even after Rumania made peace with the Central Powers in May 1918. He came up with a new scheme: he hoped to bring large French contingents into southern Russia where they would aid the White armies on the Don. After the November armistice, Premier Clemenceau (q.v.) made it clear France saw no reason to follow such a plan.

Finally, in January 1919, Shcherbachev succeeded in making his mark on the rapidly escalating Russian Civil War. He mediated the differences among the motley collection of anti-Bolshevik contingents on the Don; thus he helped form a powerful White army that bedeviled Bolshevik leaders like Lenin and Trot-

sky (qq.v.) for nearly two years.

Shcherbachev went into exile in Western Europe later in 1919. He died in Nice, on January 18, 1932.

Kenez, *Civil War in South Russia, 1918*; Rutherford, *The Russian Army in World War I*; Stone, *The Eastern Front*; *Sovetskaia istoricheskaia entsiklopediia*, XVI.

SIMS, William Sowden (*United States, Admiral*), was born the son of an American civil engineer on October 15, 1858, in Port Hope, Ontario; this Canadian birthplace was later used to buttress charges of Anglophilia. Sims entered Annapolis on his second attempt in 1880; after graduation he saw service during the Sino-Japanese War and was posted as naval attaché in France and Russia. Sims early turned his attention to the deplorable state of gunnery and ship design in the American navy and, after official channels refused to hear his pleas for reform, appealed directly to President Theodore Roosevelt in November 1901; this highly unorthodox action brought him the post of inspector of target practice the following year. Within two years the American ships were second to none in terms of gunnery. This forceful pursuit of policies alienated many superiors, and when Captain Sims assured the British in a Guildhall speech in London in December 1910 that they could count on "every man, every ship, and every dollar from their kinsmen across the sea" if the need ever arose, he received a public reprimand from President William Howard Taft. In January 1917, Sims was appointed president of the Naval War College in the grade of rear admiral, and in April was ordered to London to coordinate Anglo-American naval efforts.

Sims regarded the German submarine menace as paramount: "The issue is and must inevitably be decided at the locus of all lines of communications in the Eastern Atlantic." He had no patience with the cautious chief of Naval Operations, who sought to counteract possible German thrusts against the east coast of the United States and the other Americas. Sims bombarded Admiral Benson (q.v.) with urgent requests to release antisubmarine forces for overseas, and finally persuaded the reluctant Benson to dispatch destroyers to Ireland, dreadnoughts to augment the Grand Fleet in Scapa Flow, and antisubmarine craft to render convoy effective; he opposed the projected North Sea mine barrage in the waters between Scotland and Norway as well as a close-in blockade of German ports as ineffective and detrimental to the major effort in the eastern Atlantic. In June 1917, Sims was named commander, U.S. Naval Forces Operating in European Waters as well as naval attaché to Britain; subsequently he was given a Naval Planning Section and appointed to the Allied Naval Council (November 1917). He attained the grade of vice admiral in June 1917, and full admiral in December 1918. Early in 1918 the energetic Sims demanded "radical steps" by the Allies in the Adriatic Sea against the Austro-Hungarian fleet, but Italian intransigence obfuscated all efforts in this theater of the war.

In contrast to Benson, Sims had abandoned the hallowed doctrine of Alfred Thayer Mahan in behalf of a "symmetrical" fleet in favor of immediate antisubmarine efforts, and unlike General Pershing (q.v.) in France, had from the start favored integrating American forces into the Royal Navy. His intense lobbying for naval succor to the hard-pressed Allies led to charges of Anglophilism, and an exasperated Sims finally exploded to his friend Captain Pratt (q.v.) in August 1917: "If you do not think a pro-ally is the right kind of man for this job, they should have sent a pro-Russian with a trunk full of bombs."

Sims returned to the Naval War College in the spring of 1919. He nurtured reservations about President Wilson's (q.v.) war leadership, and refused the Distinguished Service Medal to publicize his stance. Above all, Sims turned a congressional investigation of the awards matter into a postmortem on the conduct of the war at sea, specifically charging Secretary of the Navy Josephus Daniels (q.v.) and Admiral Benson with having dragged their feet in 1917. Daniels later termed Sims' actions during the war as being "in many respects un-American." Fleet Admiral Ernest J. King clearly recognized Sims' nature: "To him all matters were clear white or dead black."

Admiral Sims retired from the navy on October 15, 1922, after the acrimonious congressional investigation; he died on September 28, 1936, in Boston.

Morison, *Admiral Sims and the Modern American Navy*; Sims, *The Victory at Sea*; Trask, *Captains & Cabinets*; *Dictionary of American Biography*, XXII Supplement Two.

SMITH-DORRIEN, Sir Horace Lockwood (*Great Britain, General*), was born in Haresfoot on May 26, 1858, the son of an army colonel. Educated at Harrow and Sandhurst, Smith-Dorrien was gazetted to the Ninety-fifth Foot in 1877. Next came duty during the Zulu War of 1879 and in Egypt three years later and again in 1884/1885; he was known above all for his prowess on the race course and the polo field. Smith-Dorrien attended the Staff College and in 1889 began a decade of service in India; ten years later he was with Sir H. H. Kitchener (q.v.) at Omdurman and followed the sirdar to Fashoda. For the next two years, Smith-Dorrien fought in the Boer War, being

promoted major general. Lord Roberts dispatched him to India in November 1901 as adjutant general, and later Smith-Dorrien commanded the Fourth Division at Quetta. He came home in 1907 to the Command at Aldershot, and five years later was appointed to the Southern Command at Salisbury.

Given command of the II Army Corps on August 17, 1914, Smith-Dorrien led this unit as part of the British Expeditionary Force under Sir John French (q.v.). The II Corps bore the brunt of the German advance at Mons, while Sir Douglas Haig's (q.v.) I Corps was strangely separated from the main body of British troops. Worse yet, Sir John French was some twenty miles from the front at St. Quentin. The plight of the British Expeditionary Force was critical: out of touch with Haig's I Corps, without instructions from the field commander miles away, Smith-Dorrien for almost one week was left to his own devices. French finally ordered his two corps to retreat southwest, but even this late stratagem failed as Haig and Smith-Dorrien were split into two forces by the forest of Mormal, causing a gap of fifteen miles between their inner flanks. On August 26 the exhaustion of his troops and the nearness of the enemy forced Smith-Dorrien to abandon the ordered retreat and to stand at Le Cateau; that same day French's chief of staff, Sir Archibald Murray (q.v.), fainted at an inn in St. Quentin on hearing of the German advance. French at first praised Smith-Dorrien for this valiant act, but later in his book *1914* denounced what he termed "the shattered condition of the Second Corps" after Le Cateau.

At the end of 1914 French and Smith-Dorrien had another confrontation; the British commander in chief supported the desire of the French to mount a broad offensive the following year, while his corps commander counseled that he husband available regulars and await the eventual build-up of men and munitions. Early in 1915 Smith-Dorrien was given command of the Second Army, and in April relieved French troops in the southern portion of the Ypres salient. This unit took a terrible pounding from German-concentrated fire, and Smith-Dorrien pleaded, to no avail, with French to affect a slight retreat to more defensible positions. Relations between the two men were soon strained to the breaking point. On April 22 the Germans launched the first major gas attack at Ypres, breaking through the northern parts of the salient defended by French and Algerian troops, thereby exposing the left flank of Smith-Dorrien's forces. General French at once ordered British counterattacks over the next five days, and only with heavy losses was Smith-Dorrien able to hold Ypres. By April 27 the corps commander could condone such bloodletting no longer and in a bitter note to headquarters asked for an end to the senseless slaughter and a retreat to more secure positions. That same afternoon, French instructed Smith-Dorrien to hand over command of all forces in the salient to General Herbert Plumer (*q.v.*), and ordered him home on May 6 without "reason or explanation." Smith-Dorrien's diagnosis of the situation at Ypres proved to be correct: British forces thereafter drew back just as the corps commander had recommended.

In England Smith-Dorrien was given command of the First Army for home defense for six months in 1915, but he had to decline an offer to lead an expedition to German East Africa owing to a severe bout of pneumonia, from which he did not fully recover before the end of the war. Smith-Dorrien served as governor at Gibraltar from 1918 to 1923, and he died at Chippenham Hospital as a result of a motor accident on August 12, 1930. He declined to the end to discuss the circumstances of his curt dismissal by Sir John French on May 6, 1915.

Ballard, *Smith-Dorrien*; Edmonds, *Military Operations: France and Belgium*, 13 vols.; French, *1914*; Smith-Dorrien, *Memories of Forty-Eight Years' Service*; *Dictionary of National Biography 1922-1930*.

SMUTS, Jan Christian (*Great Britain, General*), was born near Riebeek in the Cape Colony on May 24, 1870, the son of a farmer. The family, of Dutch origin, had settled at the Cape in the seventeenth century. Educated at Victoria College, Stellenbosch, and Christ's College, Cambridge, Smuts sought a career in law, but the growing conflict between Afrikaners and Britons in the Cape Colony lured him into politics. Smuts fought with the Boers in the rank of general and in the winter of 1901 led a daring raid into the Cape Colony. Thereafter, he served Prime Minister Louis Botha as colonial secretary and minister of education; in 1910 he accepted the Ministry of Mines, Defense, and Interior in the new Union of South Africa. Early in 1914 he used his Defense Force to suppress a miners' strike, thereby earning the indemnification of Parliament.

The outbreak of the war in Europe put an end to Smuts' labor troubles as well as to the thorny issue of settlement and registration of Indians in South Africa; the second, or military, phase of his career began. On September 15, 1914, at the request of London, a contingent of South African troops was sent into German South-West Africa. It was nothing less than an imperial disaster. The troops under Colonel S. G. Marwitz rebelled and joined the Germans, and only by using force were Botha and Smuts able to restore order. Early in 1915 Botha advanced inland

from Swakopmund and Smuts from Lüderitzbucht; and in July the German garrison of 3,370 soldiers surrendered to 43,000 South African troops. Early in 1916 the British bestowed upon Smuts command of all imperialist forces in East Africa and promoted their erstwhile opponent lieutenant general in the British army. To Smuts fell the task of bringing the German forces in East Africa under General Paul von Lettow-Vorbeck (*q.v.*) to bay. Although once again greatly outnumbering the enemy, Smuts this time was not able to defeat, much less capture, Lettow-Vorbeck. In March 1916, he managed to outflank the Germans at Salaita Hill on the slopes of Mount Kilimanjaro, and in January 1917, he pursued them down the Rufiji River, but the climate, exhaustion, and disease exacted a heavy toll on his troops. Smuts was recalled to the Cape in January 1917, and ordered to London as representative on the Imperial War Cabinet; later on, Prime Minister David Lloyd George (*q.v.*) grew to respect Smuts' counsel and invited the Afrikaner to join the British War Cabinet.

General Smuts toured the western front and concurred with Sir Douglas Haig (*q.v.*), the British commander in chief in France, that a major effort at Ypres in the direction of Passchendaele was required. Later that year Smuts declined an offer from Lloyd George to command British forces in Egypt, rightly fearing that he might be "stranded" in Palestine. In October 1917, Smuts was asked by the prime minister to employ his great tact and previous experience to quell strikes in the Welsh coal fields. In January 1918, the Afrikaner was sent out to Egypt in order to report on the situation there. He at once recommended that Sir Edmund Allenby (*q.v.*) "press on to Aleppo at the expense of France." This Allenby did with alacrity: Jericho was captured at the end of February and the road cleared for a push upon Amman and Syria beyond.

The irrepressible Smuts on June 8, 1918, offered his services as commander in chief of the U.S. army in France, believing that the Americans did not possess a sufficiently experienced officer for this post; Lloyd George very prudently declined to pass this offer on to President Woodrow Wilson (*q.v.*). By October Smuts had grown apprehensive about the American presence in the world: "As Europe went down, so America would rise. In time the United States of America would dictate to the world in naval, military, diplomatic, and financial matters." He urged the prime minister to prevent such developments.

At the Paris Peace Conference Smuts joined Wilson as the leading proponent of the League of Nations. He also came out in favor of German war reparations and invented the mandate system under which the victors would hold the former German colonies. Yet at the last moment he almost refused to sign the Versailles Treaty, believing this "Carthaginian peace" to be too severe; perhaps he remembered the peace imposed upon the Boers by the victorious Britons at Vereeniging in 1902.

Upon the death of Botha in August 1919, Smuts became prime minister and began yet another phase of his career. Five years later he was defeated in the elections as a result of his bloody suppression of another miners' strike in the Rand. For much of the next two decades he feuded with J.B.M. Hertzog over Cape politics, perhaps most bitterly in 1939 when Hertzog demanded that South Africa remain neutral in the European war. South African troops eventually saw action in Abyssinia, North Africa, and Italy, and in 1941 Smuts, at age seventy-one, was promoted British field marshal in yet a further turn in his incredible career. At San Francisco in 1945 he helped to create the United Nations. His tempestuous career closed at Irene, near Pretoria, on September 11, 1950.

Hancock, *Smuts: The Sanguine Years*; Hancock and Poel, *Selections from the Smuts Papers*, III; Smuts, *War-time Speeches*; Trask, *Captains & Cabinets*; *Dictionary of National Biography 1941-1950*.

SOLF, Wilhelm (*Germany, Colonial Secretary, Foreign Secretary*), was born in Berlin on October 5, 1862, the son of a wealthy merchant. Solf undertook Oriental studies at Halle University (Ph.D.) and London, and after a brief stint at Calcutta in 1889/1890 returned to Germany to study law. He entered the colonial section of the Foreign Office in 1896, then was posted overseas to Calcutta, Dar-es-Salaam, and Samoa (governor from 1900 to 1910). In 1911, after the second Moroccan crisis, Solf was appointed state secretary of the new Colonial Office, where he sought to reach an understanding with Britain over the future of Portugal's African holdings. Solf was able to win several prominent Social Democrats over to colonialism; above all, he sought to create a German colonial empire in central Africa stretching from the Indian to the Atlantic oceans.

The rapid seizure of most German colonies by, especially, Britain and Japan during the opening months of the Great War basically left Solf without official duties. As a result, he entered the war aims debate, stressing time and again the need for German naval bases and for a colonial empire in Africa. Solf regarded the German-occupied territory in the west as basically a "pawn," to be released at the peace table in exchange for the return of Berlin's colonies and for additional African real estate; as late as September 1918 he expected not only the return of lost colonies but also additional Belgian, French, and Portuguese lands in Africa!

Solf favored reform of the antiquated Prussian three-class franchise, and he adamantly opposed the resumption of unrestricted submarine warfare in January 1917. Early on in the war he saw the need for a negotiated peace, and in October 1917 he was mentioned in parliamentary circles as a possible successor to Chancellor Georg Michaelis (*q.v.*).

Chancellor Prince Max von Baden (*q.v.*) on October 3, 1918, appointed Solf state secretary of the Foreign Office. Solf's actions over the next month were generally weak, vacillating, and poorly defined. On October 2 he had supported Prince Max in cautioning against General Erich Ludendorff's (*q.v.*) demand for an immediate cessation to hostilities; yet a fortnight later, when Ludendorff was again ready to continue the struggle, Solf opposed resuming the bloodbath at the front and instead asked that other military advice be solicited. In the end, it fell to Solf to initiate a series of peace notes with President Woodrow Wilson (*q.v.*), but when rumors were circulated to the effect that the state secretary planned to sabotage the German evacuation of the Ukraine, the American leader lost confidence in the new German government. Apparently, Solf never quite realized in his haste to accept Wilson's Fourteen Points that to do so would entail the loss forever of Germany's former overseas possessions.

Wilhelm Solf stayed at the Wilhelmstrasse until December 1918; he departed from the Colonial Office in February 1919. Solf joined the German Democratic party after the revolution of November 1918, and from 1920 until 1928 served as German envoy to Japan. Upon his return, he headed the Overseas Institute in Stuttgart and attempted to rally the political center in Germany against both right and left extremism. Solf died in Berlin on February 6, 1936. His wife Hanna became an active member of the German resistance and after the unsuccessful attempt upon Adolf Hitler's life in July 1944 was arrested until the end of the war.

Vietsch, *Gegen die Unvernunft* and *Wilhelm Solf*; *Biographisches Wörterbuch zur Deutschen Geschichte*, III.

SONNINO, Giorgio Sidney, Baron (*Italy, Minister of Foreign Affairs*), was born in Pisa, March 11, 1847. On his father's side, Sonnino was descended from a wealthy Jewish family in Tuscany; his mother was a Scot. Sonnino began a career in diplomacy in 1867, serving in Madrid, Vienna, Berlin, and Paris.

But in 1873, he returned to Italy and busied himself in scholarly studies of the nation's rural population. In 1880, after establishing himself as an authority on the peasantry and starting a career in journalism, he was elected to the Chamber of Deputies. He took his seat with the Conservatives. Sonnino's first Cabinet post came in 1893; he served over two years as minister of finance, distinguished by his success in meeting financial crisis by the unpopular but effective device of raising taxes. In 1906 and again in 1909/1910 he briefly held the post of prime minister. But Sonnino's governments were just interim affairs; he was no match for Giovanni Giolitti (*q.v.*), who dominated Italian parliamentary life in the decade before 1914.

At the outbreak of World War I Sonnino was at once in favor of intervention. He was known to be pro-German, and, in fact, wanted Italy to join the Central Powers. In the aftermath of the battle of the Marne, however, he shifted to consider intervention on the side of the Entente. When he became foreign minister in November 1914, following the death of Antonio Di San Giuliano, he convinced Prime Minister Salandra (*qq.v.*) to negotiate with both sides over the winter, while the army patched itself up for a spring campaign.

Sonnino saw that the war offered Italy the chance for substantial territorial expansion. In December 1914, as negotiations were getting under way with the Central Powers, he expanded Italy's foothold in Albania by seizing the port of Valona. In February 1915, when he found Austria reluctant to meet Italian demands for Trieste and the Trentino, Sonnino quickly turned to the Entente. Happy to negotiate with either side, he felt nonetheless that the Dardanelles campaign, just begun, might expand the war in the Mediterranean or perhaps end the entire conflict. In either case, Italy's needs required that it be a belligerent. By April 1915, Sonnino had his agreement. The Treaty of London, negotiated in the face of vigorous Russian opposition, gave Italy notable gains in the Adriatic, such as Istria, central Dalmatia, Valona, as well as the Brenner frontier with Austria and the Dodecanese Islands between Crete and Asia Minor.

As Seton-Watson has put it, Sonnino and Salandra had not sought limitless gains but "strong frontiers, Adriatic security, and a balance of power in the Mediterranean." Portions of the Adriatic, notably the port of Fiume, were left for later assignment to one of the Slavic states of the western Balkans. Sonnino looked to a short and limited conflict that would crown Italy's war efforts without upsetting the status quo completely. His vision of a postwar Europe included a stable, if shrunken, Habsburg Empire and new and cordial diplomatic links with Vienna and Berlin for Italy. Sonnino clung with iron consistency to this policy throughout the war. But consistency did not always serve Italy's interests.

The war was not short. Sonnino had failed to ask economic aid in the London pact, although Italy was destined to need it in large amounts over the terrible years ahead. Italian possession of the Dalmatian coast meant antagonizing the South Slavs, who were already forming a Yugoslav Committee in London to promote their vision of a united postwar state. A limited war against Austria meant antagonizing Italy's allies as well; for example, the Treaty of London required Italy to declare war on all of the enemies of the Entente. Sonnino distrusted public opinion anywhere. He had negotiated the Treaty of London in the utmost secrecy; now, less reasonably, he made no effort to build support in public opinion abroad for what was to be a vastly expanded postwar Italy.

Sonnino was capable of bending before some strong winds. It was the timid Salandra, not he, who held out against declaring war on Germany. Sonnino acceded to the calls of General Luigi Cadorna (*q.v.*), the commander of the Italian army, to send troops for a joint effort with Britain and France in Salonika. But, in general, Sonnino went his own way. He avoided attending Allied conferences; not until March 1916 did he finally go to his first one. The Italian foreign minister refused to ease the critical Balkan situation in the summer of 1915 by pledging territorial compensation to Serbia if Serbia would make concessions to the wavering Bulgarians. As a result, Bulgaria joined the Central Powers and most of the Balkans fell to the enemy. When he heard that Britain and France were planning the partition of the Ottoman Empire (in the Sykes-Picot Agreement of February 1916), Sonnino at once expanded Italian territorial claims to include Smyrna and adjacent territories in Asia Minor.

With the fall of Salandra in June 1916, Sonnino continued on, his position and power unchanged, in the new cabinet of Paolo Boselli (*q.v.*). Fending off Allied attempts to conclude a peace of reconciliation with Vienna kept Sonnino busy in early 1917. At St. Jean de Maurienne, he got the reassurances he demanded; thus, the door remained opened to territorial gains at Austria's expense. By the winter of 1917/1918, Vittorio Orlando (*q.v.*), Italy's new premier, had taken office after the military catastrophe at Caporetto. Sonnino then found his diplomatic designs threatened from a number of sides. Woodrow Wilson's (*q.v.*) Fourteen Points called for the principle of nationality to be applied to Italy's territorial readjustments; this imperiled claims to Dalmatia. The Bolshevik Revolution in Russia led to the publication of the Treaty of London, making clear Italy's designs in the Adriatic. In the aftermath of the Italian defeat at Caporetto, Orlando initiated a more conciliatory attitude toward South Slav representatives. He welcomed the Congress of Oppressed Nationalities that met, without official government status, in April 1918 at Rome.

Sonnino saw two ways to shore up Italy's claims dating from 1915. He resolutely vetoed Allied moves to grant the Yugoslav Committee in London official recognition. At the same time, he pushed reluctant Italian military leaders like General Armando Diaz (q.v.) into a full-scale offensive; thus Italy's allies could not claim that Rome had failed to pull its weight on the battlefield.

The Versailles Peace Conference showed Sonnino's travails to have been in vain. Efforts in January 1919 to trade unconditional Italian support for French claims on the Rhine for French support in the Adriatic drew a quick rebuff. Paris would not choose Italy over its more powerful allies. Sonnino's main goal, possession of the Dalmatian coast, fell victim to Woodrow Wilson's solid opposition. The aristocratic Sonnino found himself engulfed in an uncontrollable tide of national frenzy at home. Fiume, which he had never claimed, became the focal point for Italian nationalist shrieks about a government sellout, a "mutilated victory." Even Premier Orlando, who had followed Salandra and Boselli in permitting Sonnino the utmost latitude in directing foreign policy, was caught up in the hue and cry for Fiume. Worst of all, he was willing to trade Dalmatia to get it.

When Orlando dramatically left the peace talks in April 1919, Sonnino had no choice but to follow him and to endure a heated public welcome in Rome. But the Allies did not budge on the Adriatic question, the moves toward a peace treaty with Germany went forward, and Italy had to return meekly to the conference. Sonnino started off on his own again in May 1919, ordering Italian military forces to expand their small foothold in Asia Minor. This meant that a clash with Greece, whose forces were also in the area, was likely to add to Italy's other problems. But Sonnino did not remain in office long enough to pursue this path.

The Orlando cabinet collapsed on June 19, 1919, fallen victim to growing domestic problems but especially to its lack of success at Paris. Sonnino retired to private life. He died in Rome, November 24, 1922.

Bosworth, *Italy, the Least of the Great Powers*; Lowe and Marzari, *Italian Foreign Policy 1870-1940*; Mayer, *Politics and Diplomacy of Peacemaking*; Seton-Watson, *Italy from Liberalism to Fascism*; Sonnino, *Carteggio, 1914-1922*, 2 vols.; *Enciclopedia italiana*, XXXII.

SOUCHON, Wilhelm (*Germany, Admiral*), was born in Leipzig on June 2, 1864, the son of a portrait painter; the family had originally come from France. Souchon entered the navy in 1881, and in December 1888 saw action on board the *Adler* off Apia, Samoa. From 1896 to 1900 he served with the Supreme Command of the Navy, and from 1902 to 1904 with the Admiralty Staff. Souchon was chief of staff of the East Asian Cruiser Squadron during the Russo-Japanese War. After a brief tour in 1908 as captain of the battleship *Wettin*, he became chief of staff of the Baltic Sea naval station at Kiel in 1909; two years later he was promoted rear admiral in this capacity.

The outbreak of the war found Souchon as chief of the German Mediterranean Squadron, consisting of the battle cruiser *Goeben* and the light cruiser *Breslau*. On August 4 he bombarded the French Algerian ports of Bône and Philippeville and then headed to Messina to recoal. There an Allied force should have intercepted him had it not been for the incredible bungling both at the Foreign Office and at the Admiralty in London. Instead, between August 6 and 10 Souchon managed to evade Allied ships and to break through to Constantinople, despite serious boiler leakages in the *Goeben*. The decision to make for the Porte had been reached on August 3 by Admirals Hugo von Pohl and Alfred von Tirpitz (q.v.) without consulting the kaiser. At Constantinople, the German ships were renamed *Sultan Yavuz Selim* and *Midilli* while Souchon became supreme commander of the Turkish navy on August 16. No doubt influenced by the arrival of the two German ships, Turkey declared for the Central Powers in October 1914. Souchon boldly raided the Russian Black Sea port of Sevastopol on October 29 and clashed with superior Russian naval forces off Balaclava (November 18), Batum (December 10), and in the Bosphorus (December 26). He was promoted vice admiral in January 1915 and awarded the order *Pour le mérite* in October 1916.

Souchon returned to Germany in September 1917 and took command of the Fourth Squadron of the High Sea Fleet. He led these latest dreadnought battleships the following month during the German conquest of the Russian Baltic Sea islands of Ösel, Moon, and Dagö. Promoted admiral on August 11, 1918, he was placed on the inactive list during the overall naval reorganization conducted by Admiral Reinhard Scheer (q.v.) of the new Supreme Command of the Navy in order to make room for younger, more energetic flag officers. On October 30, however, Souchon was reactivated and appointed chief of the Baltic Sea naval station. It was an unfortunate decision: that very day sailors on the fleet rebelled rather than take part in a planned death ride against the British Grand Fleet. Souchon therefore arrived at Kiel at the height of the rebellion; he quickly yielded to the Social Democrat Gustav Noske (*q.v.*), who managed to restore order in the port. Souchon retired on March 17, 1919, to St. Magnus near Bremen until his death in 1946.

Germany. Der Krieg zur See . . . in den türkischen Gewässern, I; Herwig, *"Luxury" Fleet*; Trumpener, "Escape of the *Goeben* and *Breslau*"; *Geschichte der Ritter des Ordens*, II.

SPEE, Maximilian Reichsgraf von (*Germany, Admiral*), was born in Copenhagen on June 22, 1861. The family were registered imperial counts and held estates near Düsseldorf and Mühlheim along the Rhine and Ruhr rivers. Spee entered the navy in 1878; he was promoted rear admiral in 1910, when he became second Admiralty officer of the Scouting Forces of the High Sea Fleet. Two years later he was appointed head of the Cruiser Squadron in East Asia, where his forces consisted of the armored cruisers *Scharnhorst* and *Gneisenau* as well as of the light cruisers *Emden* and *Nürnberg*.

At the outbreak of war in August 1914 Rear Admiral von Spee was at Ponape Island. Japan's belligerency made it clear to him that he could not remain in the Far Pacific and, after dispatching the *Emden* as commerce raider to the Indian Ocean, he set out for Chile. At the same time the light cruisers *Dresden* and *Leipzig* of the West Indies Squadron were ordered to join Spee off South America. Spee's armada on November 1 met a British force under Admiral Sir Christopher Cradock (*q.v.*), consisting of the armored cruisers *Good Hope* and *Monmouth*, the light cruiser *Glasgow*, and the auxiliary cruiser *Otranto* ("the floating haystack"), near the Coronel Islands. Spee used his superior speed to demolish both the *Good Hope* and *Monmouth* at a range of eighteen kilometers; the two British cruisers managed to escape under cover of darkness. Britain lost 1,600 men including Cradock in what Sir John Fisher (*q.v.*) termed "the saddest naval action of the war."

After a brief stop at Valparaiso, Spee decided to make for home. He intended to stop at Port Stanley in the Falkland Islands on the way in order to destroy the enemy's wireless station there. In the meantime, a livid Admiral Fisher had dispatched a powerful squadron to the South Atlantic in order to annihilate Spee's forces: the battle cruisers *Invincible* and *Inflexible*, the armored cruisers *Defence, Kent, Carnarvon,* and *Cornwall,* and the light cruisers *Bristol* and *Glasgow.* The outcome was never in doubt: on December 8, 1914, both *Scharnhorst* and *Gneisenau* were destroyed at Port Stanley; *Nürnberg* and *Leip-*

zig were tracked down and demolished. Alone the *Dresden* made good its escape. Germany lost 2,200 officers and men including Spee and his two sons at the Falkland Islands. The kaiser was understandably "very depressed" over the loss of the cruisers. With the exception of the Black and Baltic seas and the Helgoland Bight, the German flag had been chased from the seas. The pocket battleship *Admiral Graf Spee* was christened in honor of the fallen admiral in 1934.

Germany. Der Krieg zur See. Kreuzerkrieg, I; Herwig, *"Luxury" Fleet*; Marder, *Dreadnought to Scapa Flow*, I; *Biographisches Wörterbuch zur Deutschen Geschichte*, III.

SPRING RICE, Sir Cecil Arthur (*Great Britain, Ambassador*), was born in London on February 27, 1859, the son of a high civil servant. Spring Rice was educated at Eton and at Balliol College, Oxford, and in September 1882 entered the Foreign Office, where he served Lords Granville and Rosebery. He was posted abroad to Washington, Berlin, Constantinople, and Teheran, before becoming British commissioner on the Egyptian Caisse de la Dette Publique in 1901. Thereafter came a brief stint in St. Petersburg, followed by appointment as British minister to Persia. In 1908 Spring Rice was posted as minister to Sweden for five years; in April 1913, he received the ambassadorship to his first post, Washington. The outbreak of the European war in August 1914 found him at home in England on leave.

Back in Washington, Spring Rice ironically signed a document to establish a permanent International Peace Commission to which disputes were to be referred. Overall, the ambassador did not have an enviable task in the United States. American claims to the "freedom of the seas" were compounded by anti-British agitation among certain ethnic groups, especially the Irish-Americans and German-Americans. London's blockade regulations in March 1915 and declarations in August and October defining raw cotton as well as cotton products as contraband greatly exacerbated relations with the United States. Above all, the British blacklisting in February 1916 of firms all over the world under the Trading with the Enemy Act aroused American businessmen against Great Britain. Spring Rice was certain that the U.S. military establishment had been infiltrated by German spies, and he felt frustrated by the American President, Woodrow Wilson (*q.v.*), whom he found to be "an unknown force and the movements of his mind are so mysterious that no one seems to be able to prophecy [*sic*] with certainty what decisions he will arrive at."

All this changed early in February 1917 with Germany's decision to resume unrestricted submarine warfare. On April 3 Spring Rice attended the session of Congress in which Wilson declared a state of war to exist between the United States and Germany; Congress supported this initiative three days later. Spring Rice then strained at the leash to elicit more energetic actions from the Americans: "The realities of the war have not yet reached this country." The ambassador continued to be convinced that the Americans simply were not willing to devote their full vitality towards winning the war in Europe, and the crotchety envoy saw sinister anti-British plots in every nook and cranny: "You will notice," he wrote to Foreign Secretary Arthur James Balfour (*q.v.*) in November 1917, "that there are three sorts of Universalists who seem an especial danger to the Allies. The Catholics, the Socialists, the Jews." Spring Rice especially resented the American navy's refusal immediately to scrap its long-term capital ship-building program in favor of antisubmarine craft and merchant shipping. Yet when the United States finally mounted a financial and military effort to overcome the stalemate in Europe, the acerbic Spring Rice grew apprehensive; he warned London that there existed in Washington "an under current of feeling that, by the end of the war, America will have all the ships and all the gold in the world, and that the hegemony probably of the world, and certainly of the Anglo-Saxon race, will pass across the Atlantic." It was probably this paranoia that prompted the British in January 1918 to replace Spring Rice as ambassador with the more stable marquess of Reading, who had already been sent to Washington to rationalize British financial transactions in the United States.

Spring Rice left the American capital on January 13, and on February 14, 1918, he died in Ottawa, Canada, while waiting for a ship to take him home to England.

Gwynn, *The Letters and Friendships of Spring Rice*, 2 vols.; Trask, *Captains & Cabinets*; *Dictionary of National Biography 1912-1921*.

STAMBOLISKI, Alexander (*Bulgaria, Politician*), was born on March 1, 1879, in the village of Slavovitsa near Pazardzhik in southwestern Bulgaria. The son of a prosperous peasant family, the young Stamboliski was elected to the Bulgarian National Assembly (*Sobranie*) in 1908. By then, he had worked as a schoolmaster, studied briefly in Germany, and had risen to dominate his country's peasant party, the Bulgarian Agrarian National Union (*BANU*). Political leader, newspaper editor, and social theorist, Stamboliski put all his talents into a campaign of opposition against Bulgaria's Tsar Ferdi-

nand (*q.v.*). The Agrarian leader demanded a republic, and he deplored Bulgaria's vast expenditures on the monarch's prized army. He called for the creation of a Balkan federation: in this, not in war, Stamboliski saw a solution to the age-old territorial squabbles of the region.

Stamboliski was stubborn in preserving BANU's independence. In late 1913 he refused to join a parliamentary coalition, thereby aiding Ferdinand's Austrophile protégé Radoslavov (*q.v.*) to retain power. But the monarch remained Stamboliski's *bête noire*. In June 1914, the anniversary of Bulgaria's defeat in the Second Balkan War stirred Stamboliski to demand publicly that Ferdinand be hanged.

Stamboliski stood fast against Bulgaria's entry into World War I. He rightly suspected from the start that Ferdinand and Radoslavov were seeking favorable terms for an alliance with the Central Powers. According to Bell, however, even a radical opponent of the regime like Stamboliski could be moved by irredentist feeling. The Agrarian party leader was willing, in the early months of the war, to see Radoslavov negotiate to obtain Macedonia and the Dobrudja. But these prizes had to come in return for Bulgaria's continued neutrality, not its entry into hostilities.

In September 1915, word came that Bulgaria had reached agreement with Berlin and Vienna and was about to plunge into the war. *Sobranie* leaders met first with Radoslavov, then with Ferdinand. Stamboliski minced no words. In a face-to-face meeting with the monarch, he told Ferdinand this conflict would make the throne feel "the people's wrath." Stamboliski attempted to translate this rhetoric into active subversion of Bulgaria's army. Ferdinand countered with arrest, court-martial, and a death sentence (commuted to life in prison).

Even from behind bars, Stamboliski shaped events. He overturned attempts by the moderate Malinov (*q.v.*) to create a broad coalition government in the summer of 1918. All BANU leaders must first be released from prison, he insisted, and the government had to seek an immediate armistice. The collapse of the Macedonian front (September 1918) led to widespread disorder in the army. Released from prison, Stamboliski met with Ferdinand and agreed to visit the front to try to calm the troops. Ferdinand pledged in return to pull Bulgaria out of the war.

Stamboliski's motive in going to the front remains the subject of controversy. He subsequently claimed that he intended all the while to foment revolution. In any event, when he addressed insurgent troops at Radomir, he found they could not be persuaded to renew their loyalty to the government. The Agrarian leader found himself, possibly to his own dismay, declared president of a revolutionary Bulgarian government. The bubble burst at once. The rebels were defeated outside Sofia by forces loyal to the monarch.

Stamboliski survived this episode and entered the government in early 1919. He formed his own cabinet in the fall of that year. And it was Stamboliski himself who signed the Treaty of Neuilly (November 27, 1919), accepting a Bulgaria reduced in size, limited in its military power, and burdened with reparations payments. He solidified his Agrarian party's hold on power by early 1920 and installed a radical peasant regime that was overthrown by a military coup in June 1923. His foreign policy featured efforts to observe the terms of the peace treaty and to deal amicably with former World War I adversaries, notably the new state of Yugoslavia with its Serbian monarch and government. Seeking to solve the Macedonian issue through cooperation with Bulgaria's neighbors particularly inflamed military and nationalist groups within Bulgaria. It was these elements that brought Stamboliski down. Captured during a coup, then tortured and mutilated, Stamboliski was murdered in his native village of Slavovitsa, June 14, 1923.

Bell, *Peasants in Power*; Genov, *Bulgaria and the Treaty of Neuilly*; Rothschild, *The Communist Party of Bulgaria*; *Bulgarska Entsiklopediia*.

STANLEY, Edward George Villiers (*Great Britain, Secretary of State for War, Ambassador*), seventeenth earl of Derby, was born in London on April 4, 1865, to a family of great wealth that dated from William the Conqueror. Educated at Wellington College, Lord Stanley was gazetted to the Grenadier Guards in 1885. Seven years later he was elected Conservative member to the House of Commons for West Houghton, Lancashire. He was always credited with two ambitions in life: to win the Derby and to become prime minister; twice he realized the former. In 1899 Stanley was at Cape Colony with Lord Roberts; four years later he became postmaster general and gained infamy during a postal strike by referring to his employees as "bloodsuckers" and "blackmailers." He succeeded to the earldom in 1908, in time to vote down David Lloyd George's (*q.v.*) "People's" budget the following year in the House of Lords. In 1911 he became lord mayor of Liverpool.

Derby raised five battalions of the King's Regiment on his estate at Knowsley in August 1914, and perhaps for this effort in October 1915 was appointed director of recruiting. Derby favored voluntary service and on the 500th anniversary of the battle of Agincourt, at which an earlier Lord Derby had recruited soldiers for King Henry V, he announced a system whereby all eligible single men between the ages of eighteen and forty-one were to be enrolled for possible enlistment. The so-called Derby scheme failed miserably by December 1915: only one-half of the eligible 2 million single men ever bothered to attest. Prime Minister Herbert Asquith (*q.v.*) on January 5, 1916, reluctantly agreed to enact the first Military Service Act, calling up single men under the age of forty-one. Only after the debacle at Amiens in March 1918 was the full Conscription Act passed.

In June 1916, the secretary of state for war, Lord H. H. Kitchener (*q.v.*), whom Derby described as his "best friend," was lost in the North Sea when the cruiser *Hampshire* struck a mine. At first it was thought that the congenial Derby might take his place, but the Tory leader, Andrew Bonar Law (*q.v.*), not for the first time, conspired against Asquith to appoint Lloyd George to the War Office; Derby, who was known to be favorable toward the generals, was appointed undersecretary of state for war and president of the Army Council. At the end of that year Derby greatly facilitated Lloyd George's ambitions to relieve Asquith of the land's highest office, and he was rewarded with the post of secretary of state for war in the second coalition government. Lloyd George did not, however, include Derby in the inner War Committee or in his "garden suburb" at No. 10 Downing Street. Neither did the prime minister consult the head of the War Office in February 1917 when he agreed temporarily to place Sir Douglas Haig's British armies in France under the command of the French General Robert Nivelle (*qq.v.*) for a planned offensive on the western front. Derby was furious and threatened to resign; in the end, at a meeting hastily called at Calais on February 26/27, the British generals agreed for the coming operations at Arras and the Aisne to give Nivelle optimum support, and they persuaded Derby to remain at his post.

Sir William "Wully" Robertson (*q.v.*), chief of the Imperial General Staff, in February 1918 posed an even greater problem than Haig. Wully Robertson refused to condone Lloyd George's scheme to create within the Supreme War Council an executive committee to control Allied strategic reserves. Robertson took his case to Derby and the latter, egged on by the Beaverbrook and Northcliffe press as well as by the king, once again supported the generals. The secretary of state for war resigned three times in twenty-four hours over the issue of the Allied reserve. The prime minister, in turn, accused Derby of being a diehard "Westerner" and a tool of Haig and Robertson. In fact, Lloyd George had staked his political career on Robertson's removal from office, and he did not shrink back from threatening George V (*q.v.*), who also wished to retain the chief of the Imperial General Staff. In the end, Derby was persuaded to withdraw his resignations as well as his objections to the Allied reserve when he learned that the prime minister had actually offered the War Office to Austen Chamberlain; Sir Henry Wilson (*q.v.*) replaced Robertson on February 18, 1918, as staff chief.

Derby's days at the War Office were numbered. On April 18 Lloyd George appointed Alfred Lord Milner (*q.v.*) head of the War Office and sent Derby as ambassador to Paris where, as the prime minister put it, "it would not be obvious that his bluffness was only bluff." Derby was not accorded a vital role in the drafting of the terms of peace, but as a member of the ambassadors' conference he was involved in the execution of the provisons of the peace. He was greatly admired in Paris for his wealth, breeding, and manners as *"le type accompli d'un lord fermier"* ("the complete gentleman farmer").

Lord Derby returned to the War Office in 1923/1924 under Bonar Law and Stanley Baldwin, but in 1924 retired from public life as lord lieutenant of Lancashire. He had not brought to the War Office a creative mind, but rather an unfortunate propensity for following the advice of whoever counseled him last. Above all, Derby was a procrastinator, a follower rather than a creator of events. The kindest thing said of him was that he was a "John Bull at the heart of things alike in peace and war." The "King of Lancashire," as his biographer called him, died at Knowsley on February 4, 1948.

Birkenhead, *Contemporary Personalities*; Churchill, *Lord Derby*; Guinn, *British Strategy and Politics*; Hankey, *Supreme Command*, 2 vols.; *Dictionary of National Biography 1941-1950*.

STÖGER-STEINER, Rudolf, Edler von Steinstätten (*Austria-Hungary, War Minister, General*), was born in Pernegg in the Steiermark on April 26, 1861. Stöger-Steiner entered the army in 1879, served with the General Staff, and gained a reputation as a ballistics and artillery expert.

In August 1914, Stöger-Steiner received command of the Fourth Infantry Division, which he led during the successful offensive against the Russians at Krasnik. In the early summer of 1915 he was transferred to the Italian front at the head of the XV Army Corps along the Isonzo. In April 1917, however, the new Emperor Charles chose Stöger-Steiner, "more

the courtier than a hard-fisted soldier," to succeed Baron Alexander Krobatin (*qq.v.*) as war minister. Stöger-Steiner was a compromise candidate acceptable to both the Austrian and Hungarian governments.

The general faced his first major crisis on December 4, 1917, when the Hungarian minister-president, Alexander Wekerle, as well as the Honvéd minister, Alexander Szurmay (*qq.v.*), demanded that Charles honor his previous pledge to establish an independent Hungarian army. Ever the compromiser, Stöger-Steiner argued, on the one hand, that it would be unwise to concede under pressure something that was bound to happen in any event, while recommending, on the other, that the creation of an independent Hungarian army would constitute a "genuine coronation of dualism." Above all, he sided with the majority of Habsburg marshals in stating that any reform would have to await the outcome of the war.

Stöger-Steiner was fully aware of the exhaustion and the lack of supplies that plagued the Dual Monarchy's forces in the field. In August 1917 he had already warned Charles that the army could carry on the struggle only up to May 1918, when replacements could no longer be raised. Moreover, there were severe shortages of food and coal; the rations of industrial workers especially needed to be upgraded. Indeed, in January 1918, serious industrial strikes racked Austria-Hungary and the war minister managed to master the situation only by recalling seven divisions from the front to suppress domestic uprisings. As a result, Stöger-Steiner's belief in ultimate victory was badly shaken: "In Vienna and Budapest great strikes; in Bohemia, Galicia and the South [there is] great unrest." In addition, the army fell out with the war minister over his failure to return the seven divisions to the front. And to make matters worse, Socialist sympathizers had so fully dominated Stöger-Steiner's house and staff, that he claimed as early as June 1918 that he could no longer discuss secret plans in his own home. On November 5, 1918, the last Habsburg minister of war requested Emperor Charles to sign a demobilization decree, reducing the army to the twenty divisions allowed under the armistice. Even this order proved redundant; the Habsburg forces had by then fragmented along ethnic lines and returned to their native homes. Stöger-Steiner died in Graz on May 12, 1921.

Glaise-Horstenau, *Collapse of the Austro-Hungarian Empire*; Rothenberg, *Army of Francis Joseph*; *Der grosse Brockhaus*, XVIII.

STRESEMANN, Gustav (*Germany, Politician*), was born in Berlin on May 10, 1878, the son of a bottled-beer distributor. Educated at Berlin and Leipzig, Stresemann early developed a deep love of art and literature; his politics were liberal and passionately patriotic. He joined the National Liberal party in 1903 after a brief flirtation with Friedrich Naumann's National Socialists, and sat in the Reichstag in 1907-1912 and 1914-1918, quickly becoming Ernst Bassermann's ablest aide. Concurrently, Stresemann worked as legal counsel for a consortium of German chocolate manufacturers and in 1912 created and lobbied on behalf of a Union of Saxon Industrialists as well as other entrepreneurial enterprises. A fervent Pan-German, Stresemann before 1914 was active in both the Navy and Colonial Leagues.

The Great War was for the clever and ambitious Stresemann primarily a titanic economic struggle against Russia on land and Britain at sea. In 1917 he succeeded Bassermann as leader of the National Liberals. Stresemann quickly became a skillful and indefatigable spokesman for the military party of General Erich Ludendorff and Colonel Max Bauer, and in July helped them to overthrow Chancellor Theobald von Bethmann Hollweg (qq.v.) because of the latter's indecisive and vacillating foreign policy; he termed the chancellor's dismissal "the most urgent imperative. . . . Nobody has confidence in him." However, Stresemann was to be disappointed when his candidate for the vacant post, Bernhard von Bülow, was passed over in favor of Georg Michaelis (q.v.). While the National Liberal leader supported Ludendorff's vast annexationist program, he nevertheless differed with the general as to where that expansion lay: "Our future does not lie in the East, and the struggle for world markets we will not give up. . . . The world was our field and will be so in the future." Above all, as a true disciple of Admiral Alfred von Tirpitz (q.v.), Stresemann demanded "access to the sea" and "naval bases in the wide world." He also shared the admiral's dream of German "military, political, and economic supremacy" over Belgium, and desired to annex the French coal fields at Longwy-Briey. Stresemann adamantly opposed the Reichstag's peace resolution of July 1917, and instead wished to see the German flag wave over Calais, "a German Gibraltar on the Atlantic." Again and again, he counseled that Germany must gain "whatever we can get in the way of colonies and sea power."

Throughout 1917 the National Liberals cooperated with the Center, Social Democrats, and Progressives in a Reichstag parliamentary majority, but in January 1918, Stresemann broke with the SPD as a result of munitions strikes in Berlin. He realized in October 1918 that the war had been lost; one

historian has described him as a "political tree frog," jumping whichever way the wind blew.

The revolution of 1918 was a bitter blow for Stresemann. Moreover, his application for membership in the new Democratic party was rejected, and hence in December 1918 he rallied the right wing of the former National Liberals into the German People's party. A devout monarchist, Stresemann on August 13, 1923, became chancellor in the first "grand coalition," created to master the triple crises of Franco-Belgian occupation of the Ruhr, Communist revolts in Saxony and Thuringia, and National Socialist Putsch in Bavaria. On November 23 Stresemann was forced to resign as chancellor when the SPD withdrew its support from the coalition because it felt he had overstepped his constitutional powers in suppressing Communist revolts in central Germany; Stresemann remained Germany's foreign minister until his death. The chancellorship of 100 days was a watershed both for Germany and for Stresemann: the Reich ended the costly passive resistance to foreign occupation and under Hans Luther and Hjalmar Schacht stabilized the Mark; Stresemann, who had voted against acceptance of the Versailles Treaty in 1919, gradually came round to the point of view that fulfillment represented Germany's only hope of regaining its international prestige and independence.

The years 1923 to 1929 saw a series of personal diplomatic successes for Stresemann: in 1924 he accepted the Dawes Plan for reparations at London, as a result of which the French and Belgians left the Ruhr one year later; in 1925, with the help of Lord d'Abernon, Stresemann and Aristide Briand (q.v.) of France signed the Locarno Pact, whereby Germany agreed to accept its borders in the west as final; in 1926 the Reich joined the League of Nations, renewed the link to Moscow established by Walther Rathenau (q.v.) at Rapallo in a new Berlin Treaty, and Stresemann shared the Nobel Peace prize with Briand; finally, in 1929 Stresemann accepted the Young Plan for reparations, as a result of which France agreed to evacuate the Rhineland the following year. Stresemann died at Berlin on October 3, 1929, just days before the Wall Street market collapsed. His widow and two sons were forced to emigrate in 1933 after Adolf Hitler seized power.

Stresemann throughout his life remained first and foremost a German patriot. He was quite willing to revise the borders in the east and sought above all to reestablish German economic domination over central Europe. Rather than the first "European" statesman, he was the last Realpolitiker of the Bismarckian school.

Edwards, *Stresemann and the Greater Germany;* Stresemann, *Reden und Schriften,* 2 vols. and *Vermächtnis,* 3 vols.; Thimme, *Gustav Stresemann; Biographisches Wörterbuch zur Deutschen Geschichte,* III.

STURDEE, Sir Frederick Charles Doveton (*Great Britain, Admiral of the Fleet*), first baronet, was born at Charlton, Kent, on June 9, 1859, the son of a naval captain. Sturdee attended the Royal Naval School at New Cross and in 1871 entered the service as cadet. He quickly became known for his intelligence and charm, but also for his unbridled conceit and lack of leadership qualities. During the summer of 1899 Sturdee commanded British naval units off Samoa during the Anglo-American-German squabble, and was rewarded for his efforts with promotion to the grade of captain. In May 1905, he was appointed chief of staff to Lord Charles Beresford, commander in chief, Mediterranean Fleet. Promotion to the grade of rear admiral followed in 1908 and to that of vice admiral in 1913. Sturdee prided himself on being a student of history and of war—to the point that he believed himself to be the only man who knew anything about war. This attitude, as well as the close tie to Beresford, earned the epithet "pedantic ass" from Admiral John Fisher (*q.v.*).

In July 1914, Sturdee was chief of the war staff under the first sea lord, Prince Louis of Battenberg. However, the destruction of Admiral Cradock's (*q.v.*) cruiser squadron at Coronel on November 1, 1914, prompted Admiral Fisher, Prince Louis' replacement, to dispatch Sturdee to South America as commander in chief of forces in the South Atlantic and South Pacific. Fisher detached the powerful battle cruisers *Invincible* and *Inflexible* from the Grand Fleet for the specific purpose of bringing Admiral Count Spee's (*q.v.*) forces to battle as quickly as possible. Sturdee reached Port Stanley in the Falkland Islands on December 7, 1914, with the two battle cruisers as well as with four other cruising ships, thereby enjoying a crushing superiority over the German forces in the area. The following day, Sturdee sighted Spee's flotilla consisting of two armored and three light cruisers. Conditions were highly favorable: there were a calm sea, excellent visibility, and sufficient daylight remaining. The issue was never in doubt. The armored cruisers *Scharnhorst* and *Gneisenau* as well as the light cruisers *Nürnberg* and *Leipzig* were destroyed; the *Dresden* escaped, only to be caught at a later date. It was a complete triumph: the Germans lost more than 2,000 officers and men, including Spee and his two sons, and their vessels had been swept from all but the narrow seas.

After the victory at the Falklands, Sturdee was rewarded with the fourth battle squadron of the Grand Fleet, which he commanded at Jutland on May 31, 1916, his flag on board the *Benbow*. Sturdee was an able squadron commander, his motto "Damn the staff!" notwithstanding. He was somewhat of a heretic on strategy, however, roundly condemning the prevailing single-line deployment and favoring instead divisional tactics. Admiral John Jellicoe (*q.v.*), his commander, refused to listen to him: "Sturdee often goes off at half cock." Promotion to the grade of admiral came in May 1917, but not before Sturdee had been terribly hurt by being bypassed for fleet command late in 1916 by Admiral David Beatty (*q.v.*). Nonetheless, Sturdee served his new chief ably and loyally throughout the remainder of the war.

Admiral Sturdee was appointed commander in chief at the Nore after the war; he held this post until 1921. He died at Camberley on May 7, 1925.

Marder, *Dreadnought to Scapa Flow,* II, III; Pitt, *Coronel and Falkland; Dictionary of National Biography 1922-1930.*

STÜRGKH, Karl Count von (*Austria-Hungary, Minister-President*), was born in Graz on October 30, 1859, to a noble landowner from Styria. Stürgkh began a long career in the civil service in 1881 with an appointment to the Austrian Ministry of Education; nine years later he was elected to the Reichsrat as well as to the Styrian provincial parliament as deputy for the United German Left party. In 1908 Stürgkh served as minister of education in the cabinet of Baron von Bienerth, and in November 1911 replaced Bienerth as Austrian minister-president. A man of limited vision, Stürgkh overthrew the Bohemian constitution on July 26, 1913, yet never managed to develop a working compromise with moderate Czech leaders. As a bureaucrat of German centralistic tendencies, Stürgkh despised the noisy filibustering in Parliament by the non-German minorities and the Social Democrats: on March 16, 1914, he prorogued the Reichsrat owing to Czech obstructionist tactics, supported by the Social Democrats. Parliament was converted into a hospital and did not meet again until May 1917. Stürgkh ruled with the consent of Emperor Francis Joseph (*q.v.*) by emergency decrees (paragraph 14, or basic statute 141 of 1867) and thereby greatly compounded domestic tensions.

The decision to dissolve parliament (in contrast to Count István Tisza, who kept the assembly in Budapest in session) deprived Austrian politicians of a voice in the events following the assassination of Archduke Francis Ferdinand (*qq.v.*) in June 1914. At a Joint Ministerial Council held on July 7, 1914, Stürgkh favored "such far-reaching demands being made of Serbia as justified the presumption of their rejection, in order to open the path for a radical solution through military intervention," in short, war. The minister-president became the initiator of wartime absolutism in Cisleithanian Austria: unrestricted censorship of the press, prohibition of assemblies, general curtailment of civil rights, and extraconstitutional military courts in political matters. Yet even this did not suffice for the army. In August 1914, General Conrad von Hötzendorf (q.v.) established a special War Supervisory Office to control the schools, purge the state bureaucracy of unreliable elements, and extend the zones under direct military control. Army Supreme Command even attempted to replace Stürgkh with a stronger man in September 1915, but the aged monarch would not hear of such overt military intervention in the administration. But Stürgkh's career was near its end: on October 21, 1916, in the first open act of defiance against the war regime, Friedrich Adler, son of the leader of the Social Democrats, emptied his revolver into Stürgkh, crying "Down with absolutism! We want peace!" Thus died the man generally regarded as the last influential minister-president of Cisleithanian Austria; his successors were caretakers at best, dilletantes at worst. Stürgkh's brother Josef (1862-1945) served in the grade of general of infantry and represented the Dual Monarchy's Supreme Command at German army headquarters.

Führ, *Armeeoberkommando und die Innenpolitik in Österreich*; Macartney, *The Habsburg Empire*; Stürgkh, *Politische und militärische Erinnerungen*; *Biographisches Wörterbuch zur Deutschen Geschichte*, III.

STURMER, Boris Vladimirovich (*Russia, Chairman of the Council of Ministers*), was born in Tver Province in 1848, the scion of a Russian noble family of Austrian origin. A graduate in law from St. Petersburg University, Sturmer followed the normal career path for an ambitious young aristocrat in nineteenth-century Russia. He entered the Ministry of Justice in 1875, served as an official in the tsar's court entourage (1878-1892), and was rewarded with the post of provincial governor: in Novgorod in 1895, then in Yaroslav, 1896-1902. In 1902 his appointment as deputy to the minister of the interior brought him close to the apex of government authority. In 1904, following the assassination of the minister, Sturmer was considered the leading conservative candidate to assume this powerful office. But the political tide was running momentarily in the opposite direction, and Sturmer was disgarded in favor of a more moderate figure. He received the customary sop to the pride of a failed bureaucrat, appointment to the State Council, and left the political limelight for over a decade.

Sturmer's ambitions continued to burn. He went on with his work as a court official, helping to plan the three-hundredth anniversary of the dynasty in 1913. That same year, he established ties with Grigory Rasputin, confidant to Empress Alexandra (qq.v.). At the same time the aging bureaucrat founded a political salon. There Russian conservatives could gather both before and after the outbreak of World War I to lament such dangerous official actions as Grand Duke Nikolai Nikolaevich's (q.v.) pledge, in August 1914, to restore unity to the people of Poland at the close of hostilities.

By late 1915 Russia's many-sided misfortunes operated to give Sturmer his chance. The tsar had departed for Mogilev to take charge at Russian military headquarters. Liberal bureaucrats like Minister of Agriculture Aleksandr Krivoshein (q.v.) were being purged from the council of ministers, paying the penalty for opposing the tsar's decision to take direct control over the field armies. The empress and Rasputin were exercising an increasing degree of influence on political appointments. Finally, the ineptitude of Premier Ivan Goremykin (q.v.) in presiding over the war effort was impossible to ignore; witnessed by inflation, a paucity of goods of all kinds in urban marketplaces, and rising anger in the Duma. Sturmer offered the monarchy a fresh face, behind which stood a record of proven obedience and devotion to the political status quo.

What Sturmer lacked was the ability to lead a major nation caught in the maelstrom of total war. As other nations were drawn to replace weak leaders with the likes of a Lloyd George or Ludendorff (qq.v.), tsarist Russia hoisted a nondescript bureaucrat to the top step of its governmental ladder.

Appointed on February 2, 1916, Sturmer busied himself with courtesy calls on members of the Duma. But it quickly became evident that he lacked any constructive ideas to offer his tormented country. He gathered Cabinet portfolios unceasingly; in addition to his duties as premier, he took on the responsibilities of minister of the interior (March-July) and foreign minister (July-November). To his colleagues, however, he was a younger Goremykin: a sixty-seven-year-old in poor health, with a habit of dozing through Cabinet meetings.

Things fell apart. Sturmer forced able ministers like Aleksei Polivanov at the War Ministry and Sergei Sazonov at the Foreign Ministry (qq.v.) out of office. Polivanov left in March over a jurisdictional quarrel involving the right to repress strikes in war plants;

Sazonov departed in July, after Sturmer had torpedoed the foreign minister's plans for winning over the Poles. But, in both cases, personal friction with Sturmer had exacerbated specific policy differences. Government increasingly became a resting place for the incompetent, the reactionary, and the emotionally unstable.

In June/July, despite the spate of good news brought from the fighting front by the first results of General Aleksei Brusilov's (*q.v.*) offensive, the domestic crisis worsened. The tsar then considered energizing the home front through the creation of a legal dictatorship under Sturmer. The project was stillborn, but it served to bring Duma opposition to the premier to the boiling point. We have no hard evidence to support the rumor, widespread in mid-1916, that Sturmer acted the traitor to the Entente and angled for a separate peace with Germany. But the cordial relationship Sazonov had built with Britain and France then cracked, even as the basic direction of Russian policy went unchanged. One is jolted to realize that Russia's premier and (since July) foreign minister was widely considered a German agent, both at home and abroad.

In July Sturmer temporarily deprived some of his political critics of a forum: he persuaded the tsar to prorogue the Duma. But the parliamentary body reconvened in November, and, by then, Sturmer's position had become untenable. The empress ceased to be his stalwart backer; by assuming the portfolio of foreign minister, Sturmer had roused her suspicion that he might be more ambitious than obedient. A general strike exploded in Petrograd in October, just as a revolt in Russian Central Asia indicated crumbling government control in the provinces. On November 14, Sturmer, and by implication Empress Alexandra, received an unprecedented verbal pummeling in the Duma. Kadet leader Paul Miliukov (*q.v.*) led off with a speech asking whether government failures stemmed from "stupidity or treason." More conservative spokesmen gave vent to similar abuse. The imperial family turned to a new champion in the person of Minister of the Interior Aleksandr Protopopov (*q.v.*). His multitude of flaws were to be exhibited in due course; but in the meantime, on November 22, 1916, Sturmer was told to depart. He had been premier for nine irretrievable months.

Sturmer was arrested by the provisional government following the revolution of March 1917. He languished in a Petrograd prison until his death on September 2, 1917. Had he hung on for a few more months of life, he would likely have stood alongside Protopopov before a Bolshevik firing squad.

Dallin, "The Future of Poland"; Gurko, *Features and Figures of the Past*; Pearson, *The Russian Moderates and the Crisis of Tsarism*; Thomson, "Boris Stürmer and the Imperial Russian Government"; *Sovetskaia istoricheskaia entsiklopediia*, XVI.

SUKHOMLINOV, Vladimir Aleksandrovich (*Russia, General of Cavalry, Minister of War*), was born near Kovno on July 16, 1848; his father was a retired military officer turned civil servant, his mother a member of the local nobility. Sukhomlinov graduated from the Nikolaevsky Cavalry School in 1867, served in a guards regiment, then entered the General Staff Academy from which he graduated in 1874. The young cavalryman was decorated for heroism in the Russo-Turkish War of 1877/1878, then returned to teach at the General Staff Academy. From 1886 to 1898 he commanded at his alma mater, the Nikolaevsky Cavalry School; there he gained a wide reputation for his innovations in the use of mounted troops. It was in this post, in 1890, that Sukhomlinov was promoted to the rank of general. In 1898 he took command of the Tenth Cavalry Division, but he left this station to become chief of staff for the Kiev Military District. Sukhomlinov spent nearly a decade in the Ukrainian capital; he took over as military commander there in 1904 and in 1905 took on the additional responsibilities of governor general for the entire province. Perhaps fortunately, his reputation was not put to the acid test of field duty in the Russo-Japanese War. He was made general of cavalry in 1906; by this time, Tsar Nicholas II (*q.v.*) had begun to consult him on a wide range of military policy matters. In 1908 Sukhomlinov was named chief of the General Staff; the year following, he began a stormy term as minister of war that lasted until June 1915.

Many historians have considered Sukhomlinov's stewardship over the War Ministry a disaster. The war minister himself in Norman Stone's biting phrase has usually been pictured as a "uniformed Rasputin," or an indolent, corrupt, and incompetent bumbler. Beyond doubt, Sukhomlinov was open to taking a timely bribe; no doubt, he established a personal spy system to watch over the officer corps and manipulated army promotions to replace rivals with docile nonentities; clearly, he disregarded the wishes of political figures in the Duma and based his day-to-day behavior on staying in the good graces of the tsar.

But Sukhomlinov also produced a stronger, if still flawed, military system. Russia then prepared to fight either an offensive or a defensive campaign against both of the Central Powers. Sukhomlinov centralized military authority under the Ministry of

War. With the aid of General Yury Danilov (*q.v.*), chief of the General Staff's operations section, he developed plans for a speedier mobilization process than had hitherto existed in Russia. The nation's forces were to be prepared to concentrate in the interior, then to ride to the frontier via the railroads. To these achievements, he joined a revised system of reserves, and a vast expansion in the number of artillery pieces for the field armies. Surveys of Russian industry were a first, but essential, step in linking economic resources to the needs of a wartime military system; anticipating war in the near future, Sukhomlinov commenced such studies. All of this was capped by the so-called Great Program of 1913, a four-year plan for the creation of a military force vastly bigger in size and comparable in equipment to that of Germany, the military pacesetter for the Continent.

Not all went well. Opposition from army leaders in the southwestern provinces compelled Sukhomlinov to alter Russia's military-strategic Plan 19; in this scheme, Danilov had called for most of Russia's military power to concentrate against the Germans in East Prussia at the start of the coming war. The revised plan split Russia's offensive potential in order to launch both a weighty blow at Austria-Hungary and a lesser one as well against Germany. Moreover, Sukhomlinov tried without success to abandon Russia's line of antiquated Polish fortresses. These were indefensible, and they pinned down artillery that could serve a useful function with the field armies. But the proposal aroused a storm of counterblasts from army conservatives, and Sukhomlinov had to give way. Although his popular deputy, General A. Polivanov (*q.v.*), cultivated the friendship of influential members of the Duma, Sukhomlinov nonetheless became the target for the hostility and contempt of Russia's legislative leaders. Finally, his "spurt in military modernization" (Wildman) envisioned only a short war. Like the other belligerents, Russia had no shell supplies capable of meeting the strain of prolonged campaigning; unlike such countries as Britain and Germany, Russia lacked the industrial strength and political flexibility to remedy this flaw quickly.

The July crisis of 1914 placed the controversial minister of war at the center of events. The Austrian ultimatum to Serbia (July 23) and the outbreak of war between the Habsburg Empire and Russia's small Balkan ally (July 28) cried for a military response from St. Petersburg. Foreign Minister Sergei Sazonov (*q.v.*) favored partial mobilization, that is, against Austria-Hungary, but he found himself at once pressed by General Yanushkevich (*q.v.*), Russia's recently appointed young chief of staff, to call for general

mobilization against both of the Central Powers. The most authoritative informed voice was that of General Danilov, who returned to St. Petersburg on July 26 to insist that partial mobilization was impossible. Perhaps swayed by pleas from the French, Sukhomlinov stood alongside Yanushkevich; he persuaded first Sazonov, then the reluctant tsar, to mobilize against both Germany and Austria-Hungary on July 30.

The outbreak of war began Sukhomlinov's slide to oblivion. The tsar turned away from his stated intention to take personal command of the army; Sukhomlinov and his archenemy, Grand Duke Nikolai Nikolaevich (*q.v.*), the tsar's uncle, were the leading candidates then to become generalissimo. The prize went to the grand duke. Stone suggests that Sukhomlinov deliberately let the opportunity slip away; the war minister saw no reason why the anticipated short and decisive war should diminish his authority over the military system. When the war surprisingly dragged on, of course, the center of power shifted to the army's commander in chief, not the desk-bound war minister. The short-war illusion came to haunt Sukhomlinov in a second guise as the shell shortage crippled Russia's fighting forces. Stone grants the war minister partial absolution: the field armies were both wasteful of ammunition and lax in controlling their stockpiles; useless fortress garrisons hoarded millions of rounds of artillery ammunition. The public and the Duma were less charitable.

By early 1915 Sukhomlinov's name had become a watchword for incompetence. By spring, his patriotism itself came under attack. Colonel S. N. Miasoedov, a protégé of Sukhomlinov and the man who had run the war minister's prewar spy system to control the officer corps, was accused of treason. Miasoedov faced a hasty court-martial marked by judicial irregularities. He was found guilty and executed at once. Sukhomlinov was then hopelessly compromised, perhaps the victim of his numerous enemies in the Duma and the officer corps acting in collusion.

In June 1915, Tsar Nicholas reluctantly dismissed Sukhomlinov. The retreat from Poland and the worsening shell shortage combined with growing public accusations that the government was a nest for pro-German elements to make it impossible for the war minister to keep his post. In early 1916 the Duma pressured the minister of justice to arrest and investigate Sukhomlinov for alleged misconduct in office. The imperial family intervened, but Sukhomlinov remained under house arrest until the March Revolution of 1917. The provisional government arrested him again and, in September 1917, sentenced him to hard labor for his failure to prepare the nation adequately for the war's ordeal. In May 1918, then seventy years old, Sukhomlinov was released by the Bolsheviks and went into exile. He lived out his remaining years in Germany, at work on his memoirs and other studies intended to vindicate his reputation. He died in Berlin, February 2, 1926.

Albertini, *The Origins of the War of 1914*, II; Gurko, *Features and Figures of the Past*; Katkov, *Russia 1917*; Stone, *The Eastern Front*; Suchomlinof, *Erinnerungen*; Turner, "The Russian Mobilization in 1914"; Wildman, *The End of the Russian Imperial Army*; Wilfong, "Rebuilding the Russian Army"; *Sovetskaia istoricheskaia entsiklopediia*, XIII; *Sovetskaia voennaia entsiklopediia*, VII.

SZURMAY, Alexander Baron (*Austria-Hungary, General*), was born to a bourgeois family at Boksánybánya in Krassó-Szöreny in 1860. He graduated from the Ludovika Academy in 1884 and joined the Hungarian defense force, the Honvéd. Five years later he attended the War Academy and thereafter was assigned to the General Staff's railroad section. Next came further duty in the Ministry of the Honvéd as well as front service as battalion and regimental commander; from 1907 to 1914 Szurmay served as section chief in the Honvédség Ministry.

The outbreak of war found the Hungarian in command of the Thirty-eighth Honvéd Infantry Division; shortly thereafter he was appointed chief of his own army group consisting of two divisions. With the latter he was stationed in the Ung River valley and entrusted with defense of Lupkov Pass against the invading Russian armies arriving from Galicia. Szurmay fought a number of unorthodox battles in the Carpathian passes, and in December 1914, Army Group Szurmay advanced through the Tylicz Pass in the Carpathians and stormed into Galicia; the Hungarian boldly assisted the Fourth Army in the strategic battle near New Sandez. Early in January 1915, Szurmay was recalled by his native government in Budapest, which was fearful of a Russian invasion, and given command of a new army group with instructions once again to defend the Uzsok Pass. From January to April 1915, Szurmay's troops held the pass in bitter fighting. Thereafter he took part in the general advance of the Austro-Hungarian armies after the breakthrough at Gorlice. Szurmay was then given command of a new "Corps Szurmay" to February 1917 and raised into the Hungarian baronage.

General Szurmay occupied the post of Hungarian Honvédség minister from February 1917 to October 1918. In this capacity he participated in a crucial crown council convened on December 4, 1917, to discuss a possible division of the common army into separate Austrian and Hungarian armies. Szurmay pressed for such a division, asserting that "all groups in Hungary are united on the issue of a Hungarian army." Emperor Charles (*q.v.*) closed the council by stating that no solution to the problem could be found until the end of the war.

From February to August 1919, Szurmay was incarcerated in Budapest as one of the officials held responsible for continuing the war; the subsequent occupation of the capital by Rumanian units resulted in his release. The national government of Admiral Miklós Horthy (*q.v.*) later honored General of Infantry Szurmay von Uzsok as "savior of the fatherland," and voted him into the Hungarian Legion of Honor. This lofty recognition came to him for his deeds in March 1915, when he had been thrice ordered to abandon the Uzsok Pass and when he had an equal number of times rejected the order and held the pass as part of the overall front command under General Alexander von Linsingen (*q.v.*) of the German South Army. Szurmay died in Budapest sometime in 1945.

Bardolff, *Militär-Maria Theresien-Orden*; Rothenberg, *Army of Francis Joseph*.

TALÂT PAŞA, Mehmed (*Turkey, Minister of the Interior, Grand Vizier*), was born near Adrianople in Ottoman Thrace in 1874. The child of a family of poor farmers, by the age of thirty-five this "burly Thracian peasant" was to be one of the leading political figures in the Ottoman Empire. Talât's hopes of becoming an army officer ended with his father's death and the family's total impoverishment. With only a limited education, the young man began a career in the local postal service as a telegraph operator. Talât became one of the first members of the Young Turk revolutionary organization. His modest position in the postal system made him a useful cog in the revolutionary machine. His native intelligence and determination—many diplomats came to see him as "the most astute of the Young Turks"—led him quickly to the party's inner circle, a domain of officers where civilians were rarely welcomed.

Along with the young Major Enver (*q.v.*), Talât played a large part in the Revolution of 1908. Unlike Enver, Talât immediately undertook a substantial political role in Ottoman affairs. In the revolution's aftermath he was elected to represent Adrianople in the Parliament at Constantinople. He served as minister of the interior, 1909-1911. When the Young Turk policy of centralizing control over outlying provinces aroused a storm in Parliament, Talât stepped down to ease the crisis. In early 1913, however, the Young Turks began to establish their dictatorship. In 1914 Talât returned to his old Cabinet post, and it remained his main power base until the close of his career.

The precise lines of authority in the Young Turk party remain a source of controversy. The view that Talât, Enver, along with Cemal Paşa (q.v.), formed a dictatorial triumvirate has been replaced by a picture of power more widely diffused. Nonetheless, by the outbreak of World War I, Talât and Enver appeared to most observers to be the key figures in the party. Ruthless men, out to create a secular and modern state, they were not likely to be docile allies in international affairs. They found the memory of the empire's nineteenth-century subservience to the great powers and its still impaired sovereignty to be intolerable.

Enver took the lead in drawing close to the Central Powers after July 1914, but Talât's support was essential to make Turkey a belligerent. He vacillated well into October. Finally, his support for Enver's pro-German policy at the close of October decisively undercut pro-Entente leaders like Finance Minister Cavid Bey (q.v.). In Talât and Cemal, Enver found his indispensable allies.

To keep internal order was Talât's first and most controversial wartime role. In April 1915, anti-Turkish rioting broke out in the Armenian city of Van. Less than four months earlier, Russian forces had crippled Enver's effort to lead a bold Turkish advance in the nearby Caucasus. The government in Constantinople made the decision to deport Armenians en masse from Van and the rest of eastern Anatolia. Both contemporary observers and present-day historians place the burden of the ensuing horrors on Talât and Enver. Trumpener calls the Van fighting a mere pretext for a preplanned policy of genocide. In the face of international protests, including criticism from the German ambassador, Talât pleaded first military necessity, then he pointed to the savagery of uncontrollable subordinates on the scene in Armenia. With the notable exception of Stanford Shaw, western historians have rejected these alibis.

Talât also emerged as one of Turkey's spokesmen in dealing with its allies. Germany found him, like the other Young Turks, a difficult comrade in arms. In September 1916, for example, Talât claimed that Turkey's willingness to accept Berlin's military leadership deserved suitable reward. At the peace conferences ahead, Talât expected Germany to barter away gains in Europe, if need be, to help the Porte recover Turkish losses. Parts of Flanders and Poland

might have to be sacrificed to restore Iraq and Syria to the Turks.

In February 1917, Said Halim Paşa, who had played a largely ornamental role as wartime grand vizier, stepped down. Talât took over as head of the government. The war was going badly. While British columns pushed into Palestine and Mesopotamia, the United States stood on the verge of joining Turkey's opponents. Food shortages in the empire's cities were provoking unrest. Only the disintegration of Russia's war effort provided cause for optimism. There, Talât's career reached its zenith. In April he succeeded in maintaining the facade of unity over the issue of breaking relations with the Americans. In fact, the question had badly divided the Young Turks. That same month, Talât visited Berlin. He returned with the strongest German pledges to date for Turkish territorial gains, and even for additional military aid to Turkey, after the war had been won. Meanwhile, Talât promoted peace feelers to the beleaguered Russian provisional government.

Within a few months, Talât's power and prestige began a terminal decline. The peace initiatives to Petrograd failed. To meet a growing domestic crisis, Talât assumed direct control over his country's food supply, only to find he could no longer manage to improve conditions. Unrest swelled, with Talât the leading target for public fury.

In the final year of the war, Talât's work centered on reshaping Turkey's explosive relationship with Germany. The main issue was the clash of rival interests over Russian Transcaucasia. With Russian military power sinking, Enver took the initiative in calling for Turkish expansion eastward. Talât followed Enver's lead, and by mid-1918 the German-Turkish alliance threatened to dissolve. In August the grand vizier hinted that continued German advances into Transcaucasia might lead Turkey to open the Straits and the Black Sea to Allied warships. An ugly side issue arose. As Enver's armies thrust into Russian Armenia, the Turks once again began the mass murder of Armenians.

By late September Talât returned from Berlin defeated. The collapse of Bulgaria, the British advance through Palestine, and the deepening food crisis at home made compromise with the Germans inevitable. Talât pledged a Turkish pullback, leaving the Germans in effective control of such vital prizes as the Baku oil fields. But had the war not ended so quickly, a renewal of the quarrel seemed assured.

The Young Turk government led by Talât resigned on October 14, 1918. The former interior minister escaped with most of the other leaders of the wartime government early the next month. A German ship spirited him away to the Ukraine; from there he made his way to Germany. Like many of his colleagues, Talât tried to play the role of diplomatic middleman in the postwar years, forming diplomatic connections between Turkey and the Soviet Union. In interviews and in his writings, he disclaimed responsibility for the Armenian massacres with which he was identified in the public mind. Despite these disclaimers and his efforts to conceal his whereabouts, he died at the hand of an Armenian assassin in a Berlin suburb, March 16, 1921. The young Armenian was charged by a German court, tried, and then acquitted. Evidence introduced at the trial indicated that Talât had indeed directed the 1915 massacres. On that basis, his assassin went free.

Ahmad, *Young Turks*; Hovannisian, *Armenia on the Road to Independence, 1918*; Kinross, *Atatürk*; Shaw and Shaw, *History of the Ottoman Empire and Modern Turkey*, II; Silberstein, *Troubled Alliance*; Talât Paşa, "Posthumous Memoirs"; Trumpener, *Germany and the Ottoman Empire*; Weber, *Eagles on the Crescent*; *Larousse mensuel*, V.

THAON DI REVEL, Paolo (*Italy, Admiral*), was born in Turin, June 10, 1859, the son of a cabinet minister in the kingdom of Piedmont. Revel received his commission in the Italian navy in 1877. He served as aide-de-camp to King Umberto (1896-1900), distinguished himself in rescue operations following the Sicilian earthquake of 1908, and, during the Libyan War, was decorated for his exploits while in command of the Second Naval Squadron.

In April 1913, as a rear admiral, Revel became the navy's chief of staff. In the period before World War I, he wisely built up the Italian navy's force of destroyers and submarines, seeing them as the weapons most likely to dominate Italian operations in a future war.

Admiral di Revel remained at his post of chief of staff during the course of World War I and, in February 1917, also assumed the duties of naval commander in chief. During the negotiations leading to the Treaty of London (May 1915), Revel successfully advocated that Allied naval operations in the Adriatic be left under Italian control. He coupled this insistence on Italian naval autonomy with firmly held defensive ideas. By early 1918 this Italian naval posture roused bitter hostility among British and American naval leaders, concerned with the possibility of a German sortie from the Dardanelles using the ships that had formed the Russian Black Sea fleet. Revel was willing to transfer some Italian naval units to Corfu to help guard against this danger, but he firmly rejected calls to place them under a non-Italian commander.

Promoted admiral in November 1918, Revel remained on active duty and entered Mussolini's Cabinet in 1922 as minister of marine. He held this post for over two years before retiring to private life. He died in Rome in March 1948.

Halpern, "The Anglo-French-Italian Naval Convention of 1915" and *The Mediterranean Naval Situation, 1908-1914*; Trask, *Captains & Cabinets*; *Enciclopedia italiana*, XXVIII.

THOMAS, Albert (*France, Minister of Munitions, Ambassador*), was born in Champigny, near Paris, on June 16, 1878. The baker's son proved to be a brilliant student, entering the prestigious École normale supérieure in 1899. He graduated in 1902 with distinction in history and geography, took a teaching position, and produced a succession of notable works on the history of education and the history of syndicalism. Like a number of men of his generation at the École normale, Thomas was attracted to Socialist politics. He joined the French Socialist party (SFIO) and, with his mentor Jean Jaurès, edited several Socialist journals. Elected to the Chamber of Deputies in 1910, Thomas called for the SFIO to abandon its refusal to participate in bourgeois government coalitions. A decade before, while studying at the University of Berlin, Thomas had defended the Socialist "renegade" Alexandre Millerand (*q.v.*) against German Socialists who condemned such participants in bourgeois cabinets. Militant colleagues accused Deputy Thomas of personal ambition in seeking such changes.

The outbreak of World War I produced the political opportunity Thomas had sought. Premier René Viviani (*q.v.*) formed a *union sacrée* government in which Socialists took Cabinet positions; and Thomas called on French workers to rally to the defense of the nation. In May 1915, Thomas himself—still under police surveillance as a potential subversive—accepted the post of undersecretary of state for munitions. His appointment came at a time when all of the belligerents were facing shortages of ammunition. Moreover, it reflected the National Assembly's desire to limit the authority of Minister of War Millerand, who seemed too willing to defer to military desires on all matters concerning the war.

From the first, Thomas vowed "to organize and use to the maximum all of the resources of the country" to achieve victory. He met France's labor shortage by importing workers from France's empire and from foreign countries; he also drew large numbers of women into the work force. Despite the opposition of military leaders, Thomas shielded male workers in vital industries against conscription.

Thomas was alive both to the immediate needs of the war effort and to the possibilities wartime conditions offered to set the stage for future reform. His policy of paying high wages helped prevent industrial unrest, and it also furthered Thomas' long-held desire to better the conditions of France's factory workers. He welcomed the wartime consolidation of French industry under state supervision; this too seemed a step toward a restructured postwar society.

In December 1916, Thomas was appointed to the new post of minister of munitions, which merely reflected the importance of duties he had been performing since May 1915. In early 1917, however, Thomas saw his wartime service take a new turn: he was appointed special ambassador to Russia, replacing Maurice Paléologue (*q.v.*). Thomas was charged with solidifying the wartime alliance and, if possible, promoting a new Russian offensive. He found an ally for the latter goal in Aleksandr Kerensky (*q.v.*), who was emerging as the strongman of the provisional government in Petrograd. But otherwise his mission brought failure. The Russian government's call for peace "without annexations or indemnities" clashed with France's determination to recover Alsace-Lorraine. Soviet leaders sought to gather Socialists from all the warring countries at Stockholm to press the belligerent governments to make peace. Thomas tried, without success, to substitute a meeting of Socialists from the Allied nations alone.

Thomas' moderation was out of step with events in France as well. French Socialists were splitting over the refusal of Alexandre Ribot's (*q.v.*) government to permit them to attend the Stockholm gathering; this, in turn, reflected the larger strains on the *union sacrée* brought on by the horrors of the war and the example of the Russian Revolution. Thomas returned to France to find his party unwilling to see him continue as minister of munitions. He reluctantly resigned on September 12, 1917, rather than serve alongside Ribot. Two months later Thomas hoped to form a new government and to return Socialists to the Cabinet. But the premiership went instead to Georges Clemenceau (*q.v.*).

Thomas participated in the Peace Conference at Versailles, where he drafted the now forgotten portions of the peace treaty that dealt with labor organizations and the rights of workers. He abandoned his seat in the Chamber of Deputies in 1921 to direct the International Labor Bureau of the newly founded League of Nations. Thomas was the epitome of the moderate Socialists in many European nations who rallied to meet the needs of the war effort only to find themselves at odds with more militant elements on the political Left. He died in Paris, May 7, 1932.

Fridenson, ed., *1914-1918: L'Autre front*; King, *Generals and Politicians*; Mayer, *Politics and Diplomacy of Peacemaking*; Schaper, *Albert Thomas*; Wade, *The Russian Search for Peace*; *Dictionnaire des parlementaires français*, I; *Larousse mensuel*, IX.

TIRPITZ, Alfred von (*Germany, Grand Admiral*), was born at Küstrin on March 19, 1849, the son of a jurist. Tirpitz entered the Prussian navy in 1865, and from 1877 to 1888 headed the torpedo service in the Imperial German Navy. His great faith in torpedo boats, his so-called black host, was to be shattered in the First World War. In 1892 Tirpitz served as staff chief in the Supreme Command of the Navy, and four years later as head of the Cruiser Squadron in East Asia he helped to select Shantung Peninsula as the site of a German base. Promoted rear admiral in 1895, Tirpitz was appointed state secretary of the Navy Office in June 1897; he held this post until March 1916. Tirpitz's subsequent career was meteoric: he was promoted vice admiral in 1899, admiral in 1903, and the first grand admiral of Germany in 1911; in 1900 he was raised into the Prussian nobility; and in 1908 he became a member of the Prussian House of Lords.

Stout of figure and sporting the famous two-pronged beard, Tirpitz proved a stern leader, demanding the utmost of a coterie of aides with whom he prepared in detail the annual naval estimates. Future naval leaders such as Eduard von Capelle, Adolf von Trotha, and Reinhard Scheer (*qq.v.*) served apprenticeships in this manner. Above all, Tirpitz was a master manipulator of men and of public opinion. He cleverly prepared the way for naval expansion by serializing sea novels and A. T. Mahan's *The Influence of Seapower Upon History*; he deployed pastors and university professors to spread the naval gospel to the remotest corners of the land; he plied parliamentary delegates with tours and information; he ruthlessly exploited every foreign development on behalf of navalism; and he totally captivated the kaiser through flattery, firmness, and, when needed, the threat of resignation.

Wilhelm II (*q.v.*) was no match for these tactics. Neither was the Reichstag. In 1898 it passed the First Navy Bill calling for a fleet of seventeen battleships and thirty-five cruisers, designed for limited offensives in a war against France and Russia. A radical change occurred, however, with the Second Navy Bill of June 1900, later augmented by Supplementary Bills of 1904, 1906, 1908, and 1912, which constituted a unilateral challenge to British control of the seas. The fleet, scheduled for completion by 1920/1921, would consist of forty-one battleships, twenty large and forty light cruisers. Moreover, there is sufficient evidence to suggest that Tirpitz was not content even with this force and that he was planning on the eve of the Great War a further increase to sixty capital ships. It should not be overlooked that under the Tirpitz plan, the ships were to be automatically replaced every twenty years, thereby removing, as Tirpitz promised the kaiser, "the disturbing influence of the Reichstag on Your Majesty's intentions."

There is no question that the fleet was designed first and foremost for a clash with England in the south-central North Sea, "between Helgoland and the Thames." To camouflage his intentions, Tirpitz developed the so-called risk theory, that is, he argued that he could create a navy of sufficient strength against which war would endanger the superiority of even the greatest fleet. Not only did the risk theory prove utterly fallacious in the Great War, but it was never intended to be more than a subterfuge. To trusted acquaintances, Tirpitz confided that his ultimate goal "really cannot be written down"; when pressed as to why he did not push harder for colonial expansion, the state secretary once replied that one could not "divide the bearskin" until the "bear had been slain." In short, as one historian has stated, the German fleet of sixty capital ships stationed in the North Sea was to constitute a "gleaming dagger" held ready at the jugular vein of Britain.

The Tirpitz plan ultimately, however, suffered shipwreck. The British introduction of dreadnought battleships in 1905/1906 erased the German matériel advantage, and by 1909 it was not England but Germany that faced bankruptcy by the horrendous expenditures on naval building. Parliament became concerned over Tirpitz's anti-British policy and the Prussian army clamored for priority in German defense expenditures as the likelihood of war on two fronts became increasingly clearer by 1910-1912. Finally, engineer officers for the fleet became increasingly difficult to find, and German shipyards in 1914 were eight battleships and thirteen cruisers behind schedule.

It is, therefore, little wonder that Tirpitz desperately worked for peace during the crisis of July 1914. His fleet was at least seven years from completion and war with England at that time would jeopardize his life's work. Moreover, the army brusquely brushed aside naval considerations in August 1914, instructing the junior force not to attempt to interrupt English troop transports across the Channel as the army would mop these units up in the great Cannae around Paris. When victory faded early in September at the Marne, Tirpitz planned feverishly to regain control of naval affairs. He hoped to create a supreme command of the navy around himself or,

failing that, to take charge of the fleet personally; he was denied both goals, partly because he had not commanded a squadron at sea for nearly two decades. In addition, the war also proved Tirpitz's inadequacies as a strategist. The British did not immediately descend into the Helgoland Bight, as German planners had stated they would owing to their mentality and tradition. And the distant blockade at Dover-Calais and Scotland-Norway finally revealed that Mahan's theories on navalism had as prerequisite free access to the world's major maritime arteries, a condition that Tirpitz either never learned or overlooked.

In 1915/1916 the grand admiral's position rapidly deteriorated. The kaiser blamed him for the lack of overseas cruisers and the loss of German ships at Falkland and at the Dogger Bank. In time, Tirpitz was removed from general headquarters and denied influence in major strategy decisions. His frantic efforts on behalf of unrestricted submarine warfare—coming after years of ignoring this weapon and refusing to create what he termed a "museum of experiments"—only earned him further distrust with the supreme war lord. And on March 15, 1916, Tirpitz used the old strategem of threatening to resign once too often in the wake of yet another sharp protest note by President Woodrow Wilson (q.v.) over German U-boat warfare: Wilhelm II accepted his naval architect's resignation with the terse comment, "He is leaving the sinking ship."

In retirement, Tirpitz continued to exert influence on the navy through Admiral von Trotha and Captain Magnus von Levetzow (q.v.), two fervent followers, and through the creation in September 1917 of the million-member right-wing Fatherland party, which called for vast annexations and indemnities as a sine qua non for a German peace.

Tirpitz became a parliamentary deputy for the German National People's party from 1924 to 1928; in 1925 he was instrumental in convincing Field Marshal Paul von Hindenburg (q.v.) to make his successful bid for the presidency. Tirpitz died of heart failure in Ebenhausen, near Munich, on March 6, 1930. His *Memoirs* as well as a two-volume edition of *Political Documents* revealed him to be a bitter, vindictive, and shallow leader.

Tirpitz's role in German history was at once fateful and fatal. The naval race initiated by the Second Navy Bill was the single most decisive act in poisoning Anglo-German relations and assuring British membership in the Entente. And through a score of carefully chosen aides, Tirpitz's construction policies and strategy, especially his overemphasis on battleships, permeated also the navy of Adolf Hitler's

Third Reich. Last but not least, Tirpitz's simple "friend-foe" mentality with regard to fellow naval officers deprived Germany of independent critics and first-rate minds.

Berghahn, *Der Tirpitz-Plan*; Herwig, *"Luxury" Fleet*; Steinberg, *Yesterday's Deterrent*; Tirpitz, *Erinnerungen* and *Politische Dokumente*, 2 vols.; *Biographisches Wörterbuch zur Deutschen Geschichte*, III; *Geschichte der Ritter des Ordens*, II.

TISZA de BOROS-JËNO, István Count (*Austria-Hungary, Prime Minister*), was born to Prime Minister Kálmán Tisza on April 22, 1861, in Budapest. After studies in Berlin and Heidelberg, Tisza returned to Budapest and entered parliament in 1886. Hungary was then on the brink of civil war. An army bill introduced in 1889 triggered a crisis between the Liberal party, which supported the Compromise of 1867, and the parties of "1848," which sought to restore the Hungary of Louis Kossuth. In September 1903, Emperor Francis Joseph (*q.v.*) issued the famous order at Chlopy upholding the principle of a unitary army, but the following month he began negotiations with Tisza, head of the Liberal Party Committee of Nine, to allay an open rift. Tisza, a stubborn and courageous man, was made of sterner stuff than his father, yet had to endure defeat at the polls in January 1905 by the 6 percent of the population that could vote over the issue of magyarization of the army. Tisza firmly believed in the Compromise of 1867; in fact, he viewed it as the supreme guarantor of Magyar-Hungary against Germans, Slavs, and Rumanians, to whom he was unwilling to make concessions. He also opposed the introduction of general suffrage.

Tisza returned as prime minister in June 1913 and, against the will of the heir presumptive, Archduke Francis Ferdinand (*q.v.*), received virtually dictatorial powers. He devoted his efforts to maintaining the privileged position of the Magyars against the demands of other ethnic groups for representation. Unlike Minister-President Karl von Stürgkh (*q.v.*) in Austria, Tisza maintained parliament in session in Budapest throughout the war, and he ruled it with an iron hand. In the July crisis of 1914 Tisza sought a diplomatic rebuff of Serbia, but opposed the desires of Count Leopold von Berchtold and General Conrad von Hötzendorf (*qq.v.*) for war with Belgrade at any cost. At a crucial meeting of the joint Austro-Hungarian Council of Ministers on July 14, Tisza persuaded Berchtold to dispatch an ultimatum to Serbia and to desist from plans to invade at once; later the prime minister added the caveat that the Dual Monarchy would under no circumstances annex Serbian territory. Tisza desired no additional Slav subjects in the empire, and he hoped that such a declaration might in the future constitute a bridge towards Russia.

Early in 1915 Tisza managed to have his friend Burian von Rajecz (*q.v.*) appointed foreign minister and worked hard to ward off the entry of Italy and Rumania into the war on the side of the Entente by suggesting territorial compensations for them, to no avail. Tisza rushed to Vienna in November 1916 upon the death of Emperor Francis Joseph and obtained from the new Emperor Charles (*q.v.*) an agreement for an early coronation in Budapest, which committed Charles to uphold Dualism. But the honeymoon was short-lived: in May 1917, Charles dismissed Tisza, whose pride, stubbornness, and Calvinist creed he disliked. Tisza had also bitterly quarreled with Count Mihály Károlyi (*q.v.*), whom he regarded as a traitor to his class, over the frondeur's demands to introduce universal suffrage, to grant national autonomy to Hungary, and to break up the large estates. After a brief tour of duty at the front as Honvéd colonel, Tisza was murdered by Red Guards in Budapest on October 31, 1918, the very day of Károlyi's appointment as Hungarian prime minister. Ironically, Tisza's stance at the council meeting on July 14, 1914, had been kept such a well-guarded secret that he was viewed by many throughout the war as the driving force behind it. Robert Kann has depicted Tisza as "an incorruptible man of determination, ability, and political blindness."

Erényi, *Graf Tisza*; Kann, *History of the Habsburg Empire*; Rothenberg, *Army of Francis Joseph*; *Neue Österreichische Biographie*, I.

TOWNSHEND, Sir Charles Vere Ferrers (*Great Britain, General*), was born in Southwark on February 21, 1861. He was raised in humble circumstances, his father, for a time heir presumptive to the marquessate, having worked as a minor railway official. Young Townshend joined the Royal Marines in 1881 and three years later took part in the campaign to relieve General Gordon at Khartoum; in 1886 he joined the Indian army. Townshend became an unabashed careerist, changing units and armies as opportunity afforded. Over the next quarter century, he wrangled no fewer than four appointments to India, four at home in England, two in South Africa, and one in Egypt. In 1905 he even undertook a stint as military attaché in France, becoming an ardent admirer of the French military in general, and of Ferdinand Foch (*q.v.*) in particular. Townshend was promoted major in 1895, brevet colonel a decade later, and brigadier general in 1911. War found him at Pindi in August 1914.

Major General Townshend fired off countless entreaties for front command, and in April 1915 he was given the Sixth (Indian) Division under Sir John E. Nixon (*q.v.*). The two commanders intended to seize Basra, drive 2,000 kilometers up the Euphrates River to Baghdad, and take over the oil wells in the region. Somehow, they "forgot" that there were no docks at Basra, no railways to transport their supplies, no hospital facilities, and that it was the hottest time of the year. Undaunted, in May Townshend embarked upon his famous "regatta" up the flooded Tigris to Amara. After a brief rest owing to illness, on September 29 he led his forces into Kut el Amara, taking almost 2,000 Turkish casualties. The Cabinet in London, desperate for some success in the Moslem world after the disastrous Dardanelles expedition, decided that a side show in Mesopotamia might restore its prestige; Nixon was promised reinforcements and encouraged to advance on Baghdad. Townshend declined to await succor and instead marched ahead on his own. The Turks fought a rearguard action at Ctesiphon, covering Baghdad. With supplies running low as the waters in the Tigris fell rapidly, Townshend was forced to halt at Azizieh, sixty miles beyond Kut. The two divisions promised by London never arrived; Nixon awaited supplies at Basra. Superior Turkish forces, commanded by the German Field Marshal Colmar von der Goltz (*q.v.*), drove Townshend back to Kut where, after repulsing three assaults by General Nur-ed-Din, he was invested by December 8. Various attempts at rescue were repulsed with the loss of 24,000 casualties, and the Turks declined a British bribe of £2 million for the release of Townshend's army at Kut. With many soldiers actually dying of starvation, the egotistical Townshend finally capitulated on April 29, 1916.

Nearly 10,000 Anglo-Indian soldiers were marched through the desert heat to Baghdad, then paraded around the Holy City and publicly caned and whipped. Many of them were never heard from again. Townshend fared much better, being interned on Prinkipo Island, near Constantinople. He was knighted in absentia in October 1917 for his "dash" at Kut el Amara. One year later, the Turks released him so that he could act as their "intermediary" at Mudros, where an armistice was signed on October 30, 1918.

Townshend failed to obtain further military command and in November 1920 turned to politics, being elected as independent conservative from the Wrekin district of Shropshire. He proved ineffective and did not stand for reelection. Two trips to Angora in 1922 and 1923 brought him into contact with Kemal Paşa (*q.v.*), but the Cabinet had no need of his services as

an "expert" on Turkey. Townshend died in Paris on May 18, 1924.

Ferro, *The Great War*; Liddell Hart, *The Real War*; Townshend, *My Campaign in Mesopotamia*; *Dictionary of National Biography 1922-1930*.

TROTHA, Adolf von (*Germany, Admiral*), was born in Koblenz on March 1, 1868, the son of an army officer later killed in the Franco-Prussian War of 1870/1871; the family was of ancient noble stock from the Saale River region around Merseburg. Trotha entered the navy in 1886, served in the torpedo branch under Alfred Tirpitz (*q.v.*), and attended the Navy Academy in the winters of 1897/1898 and 1898/1899. Next came duty with the Cruiser Squadron in the Far East under Prince Henry of Prussia (*q.v.*), and from 1901 to 1906 a post in the Central Department of the Navy Office, again under Tirpitz. Thereafter Trotha returned to the fleet on board the *Elsass* and later the *Königsberg*; from 1910 to 1913 he was attached to the Navy Cabinet, but in 1913 Captain von Trotha was given command of the modern dreadnought *Kaiser*.

Trotha commanded the *Kaiser* at the outbreak of the war and had under him one of the kaiser's sons, Prince Adalbert. Trotha as well as Tirpitz lost no opportunity to impress upon this member of the imperial family his views on the need for a naval battle with Britain and for unrestricted submarine warfare. In January 1916, Trotha was appointed chief of staff to Vice Admiral Reinhard Scheer (*q.v.*), the new chief of the High Sea Fleet. In this capacity Trotha was with Scheer on the battleship *Friedrich der Grosse* at Jutland on May 31/June 1, 1916; he received the order *Pour le mérite* for his efforts and in December 1916 was promoted rear admiral.

Trotha was a prime mover in the reorganization of the navy in August 1918, which brought Scheer command of a new *Seekriegsleitung*. Trotha was scheduled to succeed Admiral Georg A. von Müller (*q.v.*) as head of the Navy Cabinet, but he agreed to remain as chief of staff with the fleet in order to accord the new commander, Admiral Franz von Hipper (*q.v.*), a smooth transition period. It was the duumvirate of Trotha and Hipper that was responsible for Operations Plan Nr. 19, which on October 30 sought to hurl the entire High Sea Fleet against the British in an abortive attempt to save the honor of the naval officer corps.

Throughout the war, Trotha had stood solid with Tirpitz on the major issues: in more than seventy letters, the two men coordinated their views. Both continued to place faith in battleships as the loci of naval power, though both also favored unrestricted submarine warfare. Both officers desired the annexation of Belgium and the coast of Flanders, German bases in at least Denmark and the Netherlands, and a host of foreign acquisitions in Africa, South America, Asia, and Asia Minor. Both admirals opposed parliamentary government and both pressed for closer relations with the so-called silent dictators Hindenburg and Ludendorff (*qq.v.*). And when Tirpitz in the fall of 1917 founded the right-wing Fatherland party, Trotha did his best to rally support in the navy for this pressure group.

In November 1918, Trotha became head of the Personnel Office within the Navy Office; in November 1919, he was promoted vice admiral and navy chief within the new Defense Ministry. In this capacity Trotha became deeply embroiled in the reactionary Kapp *Putsch* in March 1920, and in October he was forced to resign as a result. Trotha continued his political career by becoming active in the youth movement. In August 1933, Hermann Göring appointed the admiral to the Prussian Council of State; in July 1934, Trotha assumed the leadership of the German Navy League. He died in Berlin on October 11, 1940.

Adolf von Trotha is perhaps the crassest example of the German officer in politics. No issue was too trivial for his interest, no person too sacred for attack, and no sacrifice too great when it came to furthering the cause of the navy—and of Adolf von Trotha. He served both kaiser and Führer equally well, and partly owing to his influence, the generation of officers reared under Tirpitz was to march blindly to Cannae under Raeder and Dönitz.

Gemzell, *Organization, Conflict, and Innovation*; Herwig, *"Luxury" Fleet*; Trotha, *Grossdeutsches Wollen*; *Geschichte der Ritter des Ordens*, II.

TROTSKY, Leon (*Russia, Politician*), was born on November 7, 1879, in the village of Yanovka, in Kherson Province, north of the Black Sea. The son of a prosperous Jewish peasant farmer, the child's name was Lev Davidovich Bronstein; he took his famous pseudonym Trotsky after he had begun his career as a revolutionary, possibly borrowing it from a guard in one of the first prisons in which he was held. As a young man, Trotsky passed through a career cycle shared by scores of Russian radicals. An interest in revolutionary politics in his late teens led to abandoning higher education—Trotsky had shown great promise as a mathematician—for a life underground. Populist ideology, which saw the peasant masses as the driving force behind a future revolution, gave way to Marxism, with its faith in the political potential of the factory worker. Trotsky was picked up by the Russian police at the age of nineteen and shipped off to Siberia. There he read deeply, displayed his

native talent as a writer, and acquired a wide-ranging reputation as a promising political newcomer. In 1902 the young man escaped from his place of captivity and made his way to London, there to present himself to Vladimir Lenin (*q.v.*), whose work Trotsky had admired in Siberia. Lenin was impressed by the flamboyant novice revolutionary: Trotsky brilliantly displayed his forensic talents in the mass meetings and debates that played a major role in Russian exile life.

Trotsky quickly slipped away from Lenin to establish an independent reputation. He rejected Lenin's rigid model for a professional revolutionary party at the Second Congress of Russian Marxists in London (1903). In the Russian Revolution of 1905, it was Trotsky rather than Lenin who hastened back to lead the St. Petersburg Soviet and to dominate events during the massive general strike in the autumn. Trotsky was arrested, sent to Siberia for a second time, and once again escaped. He spent the next decade as a political writer, journalist, and war correspondent, and a free-lance revolutionary. During the Balkan Wars of 1912/1913, he trailed after the Serbian and Bulgarian armies, acquiring a useful grounding in military affairs.

At the start of World War I, Trotsky moved from Vienna to Zurich and then to Paris. The military side of the war intrigued him, but he devoted the bulk of his energies to a denunciation of the belligerent governments. At Socialist gatherings in Switzerland (Zimmerwald in September 1915 and Kienthal in April 1916) Trotsky stopped short of endorsing Lenin's calls for Russian military defeat as the quickest route to revolution. The two men remained rivals within the disorderly ranks of Russian Marxism, but the March Revolution of 1917 set them on converging paths.

Trotsky heard of the revolution while living in New York; he returned to Petrograd only in May, after a period of internment at the hands of British naval police in Canada. He arrived to find himself in full agreement with Lenin that the provisional government must be overthrown; both men anticipated that a radical Marxist revolution in Russia would quickly spread to the other belligerent nations of Europe. Trotsky joined Lenin's Bolshevik faction shortly after returning to Russia and served as Lenin's chief lieutenant in the political and propaganda campaign that led to the successful November Revolution.

Trotsky then took the post of minister of foreign affairs, with the title changed to "people's commissar for foreign affairs." Attempts to call a peace conference attended by all the warring nations met a wall of indifference; so did parallel appeals to the populations of the belligerent nations to turn on their governments. The pledge of peace had, more than any other element in the Bolshevik program, appealed to large numbers of Russians. Trotsky was reluctantly drawn to an armistice (signed December 15), followed by a peace conference with the Central Powers alone. Unable to accept a victors' peace designed in Berlin, Trotsky tried stalling; then, with Lenin's cautious assent, the people's commissar confronted the Germans with his startling declaration (on February 10) of "no war, no peace"; Russia would neither accept German peace terms nor agree to continue the war. Debo suggests that this shocker aroused interest in German diplomatic circles; but the generals who called the tune in German foreign policy simply recovered their composure and renewed the military drive to the east. Trotsky left office, permitting Lenin to persuade Bolshevik party leaders to accept the humiliating German peace terms.

Trotsky resumed an active role in the revolution in March 1918 as commissar of war. He took the lead in creating the Red Army, rejecting party ideologues' objections to a conventional military force replete with officers, saluting, and harsh discipline. He proved a talented military organizer, and his fiery rhetoric stirred Russian soldiers to fight in 1918 and 1919, just as a year or so before it had helped hasten the breakdown of the tsar's army.

The postwar years were a dismal experience for the brilliant and successful revolutionary leader and military commissar. The loss of Lenin's support (the party chief suffered a series of strokes starting in early 1922, and he died in January 1924) and the rise of skilled rivals, notably Joseph Stalin, led to Trotsky's political demise. He was forced from his posts in the party, then expelled from the party itself in 1927. In 1929 he began a life of exile that ended in Mexico City. There he was assassinated by a Stalinist agent on August 21, 1940.

Debo, *Revolution and Survival*; Deutscher, *The Prophet Armed*; Heyman, "Leon Trotsky's Military Education"; Trotsky, *My Life* and *Voina i revoliutsiia*, 2 vols; Warth, *Leon Trotsky*.

TROUBRIDGE, Sir Ernest Charles Thomas (*Great Britain, Admiral*), was born in Hempstead on July 15, 1862, the son of an army officer. His ancestors had fought at Cape St. Vincent, at the Nile, and at Copenhagen. Troubridge entered the Royal Navy in 1875, after a brief stint at Wellington College. He was promoted to the grade of commander in 1895, and to that of captain in 1901. As naval attaché to Tokyo, he took part in 1904 in the battles of Chemulpo and Port Arthur, and duly reported home on these. That same year he accompanied King Edward VII to Kiel. Three years later Troubridge was entrusted with

command of the battleship *Queen*. In 1910, however, he returned to shore duty as private secretary to the first lord of the Admiralty; at Whitehall he served both Reginald McKenna and Winston Churchill (*q.v.*) well. Two years before the outbreak of the Great War Troubridge was appointed chief of the Naval War Staff. A born leader, he possessed unfortunately no creativity.

Perhaps as a result, Troubridge in January 1913 was given command of the Mediterranean cruiser squadron under the overall British commander in that region, Admiral Archibald "Arky Barky" Milne (*q.v.*). It was in this capacity that Troubridge in August 1914 was blamed by the British public as well as by certain naval leaders of having permitted the German cruisers *Goeben* and *Breslau* to elude him at Messina and thus to enter the Dardanelles, thereby encouraging Turkey to enter the war as Germany's ally. A Court of Inquiry on September 9, 1914, found Troubridge's failure to engage especially the *Goeben* "deplorable and contrary to the tradition of the British Navy." A formal court-martial held between November 5 and 9, 1914, charged Troubridge that "from negligence or default he did on 7 August forbear to chase H.I.G.M.'s *Goeben*, being an enemy then flying." Troubridge was acquitted on the technicality that the *Goeben* constituted a "superior force," and that the Admiralty had specifically ordered him on August 4, 1914, not to engage any "superior force." Thus, although exonerated "fully and honorably," the affair nevertheless greatly damaged Troubridge's career; he was never again employed afloat.

In January 1915, Troubridge was appointed head of a British naval mission to Serbia to evacuate the Serbian army and refugees, and in September 1916, was attached to the personal staff of the crown prince of Serbia, where he remained until June 1919. Troubridge represented Great Britain at the International Danube Commission from 1920 to 1924. He had been promoted to the grades of vice admiral in 1916 and to admiral in 1919, before retiring from active service in 1921. Troubridge died of a heart attack in Biarritz on January 28, 1926. There is no cause to quarrel with Arthur Marder's balanced verdict that Troubridge's fault in August 1914, if any, had been erroneous judgment in not giving chase to the flying German cruisers, and no more.

Corbett and Newbolt, *Naval Operations*, IV; Marder, *Dreadnought to Scapa Flow*, II; Troubridge, *Memories and Reflections*; Trumpener, "Escape of the *Goeben* and *Breslau*"; *Dictionary of National Biography 1922-1930*.

TRUMBIĆ, Ante (*Austria-Hungary, Politician*), was born in 1864 in Split in Austrian Dalmatia. Following legal training at Agram, Vienna, and Graz, Trumbić returned to practice in his native city. He soon emerged as a leader of the Croatian nationalist movement, elected to the Dalmatian Diet in 1895 and the Austrian Parliament two years later. In 1905 he won election as mayor of Split. A Croat living in the relatively benign political circumstances in the Austrian half of the Habsburg Empire, Trumbić only gradually moved away from moderation. He came late to the cause of Croatian separatism and to the parallel movement for a South Slav state combining the southern provinces of Austria-Hungary with the kingdom of Serbia. In 1905, for example, despite the harsh conditions under which Croats had to live in the Hungarian half of the Dual Monarchy, Trumbić launched a futile attempt to bring together Croatian and local Serb leaders to meet with Hungarian political figures.

By the eve of World War I, Trumbić was convinced of the need to escape Habsburg control entirely. In early August 1914, he fled to Rome, where, along with Frano Supilo, he came to lead the community of South Slav exiles from the Habsburg Empire. While Supilo traveled widely, Trumbić maintained links with dissidents back home. In May Trumbić and Supilo set up a Yugoslav Committee in London, with Trumbić serving as chairman. The group claimed to represent the true wishes of the repressed South Slav peoples of the Dual Monarchy. Official Allied policy, however, did not yet envision the end of Austria-Hungary, and the Serbian government under Premier Nikola Pašić (q.v.) viewed the Yugoslav Committee with alarm. Pašić insisted Serbia spoke for all the South Slavs, and he looked to a postwar Serbia strengthened by the annexation of southern provinces of the Habsburg Empire. Trumbić's committee nonetheless began a propaganda campaign picturing Austria-Hungary as a jail for oppressed Slavs. Financial support from South Slav émigrés in North and South America made the Yugoslav Committee, despite its unofficial status, hard to ignore.

The intractable problem of policy toward Pašić's Serbia led to a split between Trumbić and Supilo. Trumbić was willing to defer a clear agreement with the Serbian premier over the form a future Yugoslavia might take. In mid-1916 the issue became critical. Supilo insisted on a clear Serbian commitment to a federalist state; disappointed, he left the Yugoslav Committee to work for an independent Croatia. Trumbić was hardly more optimistic. In the winter of 1916/1917 he prepared to give up the struggle and to emigrate to Latin America. There he intended to drive a taxicab!

The Russian Revolution changed the picture. Pašić had lost his firmest foreign ally. The United States entered the war, raising hopes—or in Pašić's case, fears—American influence would promote the formation of a united South Slav state. Trumbić and other exile leaders were invited to meet Pašić on Corfu to sketch out a compromise plan for future unity: Trumbić gained Serbian agreement to a united country in which all citizens would be equal. But he failed to move Pašić to pledge clearly to form a federation, and Croatian nationalist historians still condemn Trumbić for this omission.

The Croatian leader found Pašić lukewarm in implementing the Corfu agreement. The premier pursued the dream of outright territorial gains for Serbia, even though he had to appease Entente circles friendly to Trumbić's position. Trumbić found his other major problem in Rome. Italian foreign policy looked to territorial gains along the Adriatic coast. Trumbić spent much of the final year of the war trying to win Italian agreement to the creation of Yugoslavia. Following the debacle at Caporetto, Premier Vittorio Orlando (q.v.) met Trumbić halfway. At Orlando's suggestion an anti-Habsburg gathering of refugee leaders, the Congress of Oppressed Nationalities, met in Rome during April 1918. Trumbić was persuaded not to raise the explosive issue of the future border between Italy and Yugoslavia. Meanwhile, he appealed with some success to South Slav troops to refuse to fight in the Austrian army; Italian planes dropped Trumbić's leaflets calling for an independent Yugoslavia over the southern provinces of the Dual Monarchy.

As the war rushed to a close Trumbić found his efforts to gain official recognition for the Yugoslav Committee stymied by Pašić. Despite Pašić's declining role in Serbian affairs in November 1918, the new kingdom of the Serbs, Croats, and Slovenes did not meet Trumbić's hopes for a federation. Appointed the nation's first foreign minister, Trumbić left at once for the Paris Peace Conference, where the issue of the Yugoslav frontier with Italy—evaded during the war—had to be faced.

At Paris, Trumbić clashed repeatedly with Pašić, also a member of the Yugoslav delegation. Trumbić proved an effective emissary; carefully timed and skillful appeals to Woodrow Wilson (q.v.) bolstered the Yugoslav position against the Italians. By early 1920, however, Wilson was gone; the French and the British were supporting the Italian demands; and Trumbić's health was collapsing. In the end, he negotiated the Treaty of Rapallo with the Italians; it was signed on November 12, 1920. Trumbić at least succeeded in limiting Rome's claims, notably in regard to Dalmatia.

Trumbić then turned to domestic affairs. He served in the Yugoslav Parliament in the 1920s. Like many other Croats, he found himself disillusioned by the workings of a Serb-dominated central government, far distant from his wartime hopes. By 1929 Yugoslavia was under a royal dictatorship and Trumbić's career was in shambles. He bitterly expressed doubts about the wisdom of breaking from the shelter of the Habsburg Empire in 1918. Trumbić died in Zagreb (formerly Agram), November 18, 1938.

Eterovich and Spalatin, eds., *Croatia*, II; Grlica, "Trumbić's Policy and Croatian National Interests"; Lederer, *Yugoslavia at the Peace Conference*; Mamatey, *United States and East Central Europe*; May, *Passing of the Hapsburg Monarchy*, 2 vols.; Petrovich, *History of Modern Serbia*, II; Zeman, *Break-up of the Hapsburg Empire*; *Enciklopedija Jugoslavije*, VIII.

TYRWHITT, Sir Reginald Yorke (*Great Britain, Admiral*), first baronet, was born in Oxford on May 10, 1870, the son of a vicar. Tyrwhitt entered the navy in 1883 and received his first destroyer command in 1896. He was promoted to the grade of commander in 1903 and to that of captain in 1908 as head of the fourth destroyer flotilla at Portsmouth. A "grand fighter," Tyrwhitt became a member of the "Fishpond," that is, a favorite of Admiral John A. "Jacky" Fisher (*q.v.*), who regarded the vicar's son as the personification of pugnacity. Later in life, Fisher fondly reminisced about "those glorious reforming years in which we . . . produced men like Commodore Tyrwhitt." Tyrwhitt was utterly without conceit and happily developed no propensity for intrigue. In 1910 he accepted duty in the Mediterranean, returning home two years later as captain of the second destroyer flotilla of the Home Fleet. In 1914 he was promoted to the grade of commodore in charge of all destroyer flotillas in the fleet. He also became a strong backer of naval air development.

The outbreak of war in August 1914 found him at Harwich on board the light cruiser *Amethyst* with the first and third destroyer flotillas. Tyrwhitt remained in charge of the Harwich Force throughout the war—a high tribute of recognition to his unique skills. He was appalled by Germany's "distinctly barbaric" mining of the North Sea, which deeply offended his sporting nature: "It will be months before the North Sea is safe for yachting!" With a natural gift for leadership, a creative mind, and an indomitable offensive spirit, Tyrwhitt was the right man for the job at Harwich. On August 5, 1914, his units were the first in action as they destroyed the German minelayer *Königin Luise* off the Thames estuary. Twenty-three days later, in an action planned by Tyrwhitt in conjunction with Roger Keyes, commander of submarines, Admiral David Beatty's (*qq.v.*) battle cruiser squadron surprised and destroyed three German light cruisers (*Ariadne, Köln, Mainz*) off Helgoland Island. And although the *Amethyst* was severely damaged during the engagement, Tyrwhitt brought it safely to Sheerness, where the commodore recalled, Winston Churchill (*q.v.*) "fairly slobbered over me."

During the German raid on Scarborough and Hartlepool on December 16, 1914, the sea proved too rough for Tyrwhitt's destroyers; his light cruisers barely avoided contact with the German units that day. On Christmas Day 1914, the Harwich Force covered the naval seaplane raid on Zeppelin sheds at Cuxhaven, and in January 1915, the same force played a decisive role along with Beatty's battle cruisers in destroying the German armored cruiser *Blücher* at the Dogger Bank. But the commodore was not pleased with what he regarded to be the leisurely pace of the war at sea. "We are not overworked! In fact, at times I am very bored, as I don't see any prospect of doing business at present."

Relief came in April 1916, when the Harwich Force, consisting of three light cruisers and thirty-five destroyers, encountered the Germans near Lowestoft on yet another so-called tip-and-run raid by the enemy. Tyrwhitt's characteristic doggedness allowed the Harwich Force to maintain contact with the German raiders while Beatty rushed down from Rosyth with his battle cruisers, but to no avail. The German commander, Admiral Friedrich Boedicker, broke off the engagement before either Beatty or Admiral John Jellicoe (*q.v.*) could arrive on the scene.

Perhaps Tyrwhitt's greatest frustration came on May 31, 1916, during the encounter of the two fleets at Jutland. Once the enemy's movements had become known, Tyrwhitt was ready to put out to sea at once, but the Admiralty kept the Harwich Force at one hour's notice, or, as Tyrwhitt put it, "straining at their leash." By the time he was ordered out to sea it was too late: his five light cruisers and eighteen destroyers were thus denied Jellicoe at Jutland by Whitehall's indecision.

In August 1916, Tyrwhitt's forces were the only ones out at sea during yet another German raid, this one on Sunderland. Tyrwhitt gave chase until nightfall on August 19, but then broke contact with Admiral Reinhard Scheer's (*q.v.*) units. Some criticized the commodore for the latter action, but, obviously, it would have been suicidal to engage German heavy ships with only light cruisers and destroyers. Moreover, Jellicoe fully supported Tyrwhitt's actions on that occasion. Throughout 1917 and 1918 Tyrwhitt argued eloquently for naval operations against the German captured ports in Belgium by the Dover Patrol as well as covered naval air attacks on German harbors. As early as October 1916, he had advised operations to block the entrances to the locks at Zeebrugge and Commodore Keyes' dashing attempt to accomplish just that in April 1918 brought this scheme to fruition. Tyrwhitt was promoted to the grade of rear admiral in 1918 and after the armistice accepted the surrender of German U-boats at Harwich.

Tyrwhitt was created a baronet in 1919 and granted £10,000 by Parliament for his wartime service. He was promoted to the grade of vice admiral in 1925, and to that of admiral four years later. He served as commander in chief, China Station, and in 1934 in the grade of admiral of the fleet became the principal naval aide-de-camp to the king. Tyrwhitt died at Sandhurst, Kent, on May 30, 1951. Arthur Marder calls him simply "the outstanding British sea officer of the war."

Corbett and Newbolt, *Naval Operations*, IV, V; Marder, *Dreadnought to Scapa Flow*, II, III, V; *Dictionary of National Biography 1951-1960*.

VALENTINI, Rudolf von (*Germany, Civil Cabinet Chief*), was born in Crussow near Angermünde on October 1, 1855, the son of a Prussian army officer and estate owner of ancient Hessian stock. After studying jurisprudence at Strassburg, Valentini briefly entered the Prussian judicial branch but then transferred to the civil administration; by 1888 he had reached the office of district magistrate (*Landrat*) at Hameln, and eleven years later became privy councillor in the kaiser's civil cabinet. Valentini served as lord lieutenant at Frankfurt on the Oder from 1906 until 1908, when he was appointed Wilhelm II's (*q.v.*) chief of the civil cabinet: as such, Valentini for the next decade was to be closely associated with the monarch's so-called *camarilla* ("coterie"). The new civil cabinet chief was instrumental in 1909 in securing the appointment of Theobald von Bethmann Hollweg (*q.v.*) as chancellor, and quickly became Bethmann Hollweg's closest collaborator; both men decried the fleet policy directed against Britain and instead unsuccessfully sought to evade confrontations with London.

Valentini's first major action during the Great War was to bring about the dismissal of General Erich von Falkenhayn and his replacement with the duumvirate of Field Marshal Paul von Hindenburg and General Erich Ludendorff (*qq.v.*) in the fall of 1916. It was Valentini who convinced a panicked Wilhelm in August 1916 that Germany had no choice but to fight the war to the bitter end, that peace would mean the loss of Alsace-Lorraine, Belgium, occupied France,

and the Reich's "colonial possessions" in the east. Indeed, Valentini as early as 1915 argued that a military decision could be reached only in the east. He opposed the resumption of unrestricted submarine warfare in January 1917 as a blatant attempt by the navy to cover up its erroneous fleet policy; he noted in his diary on January 9: *"finis Germaniae!"*

In May 1917, Valentini, although as a staunch conservative opposed to parliamentarization of the Reich, firmly stood up against Hindenburg-Ludendorff's schemes to dismiss Bethmann Hollweg, informing the kaiser that such a step would be political folly. But in the end the military clique carried the day and Wilhelm sadly noted to Valentini: "I am supposed to dismiss that man who stands head and shoulders above all the others." Valentini, for his part, managed with the help of General Hans von Plessen to secure the candidacy of Georg Michaelis (*q.v.*) as chancellor.

With Bethmann Hollweg's dismissal, the military next trained its guns on Valentini. When Michaelis' successor, Count Georg von Hertling, appointed the liberal parliamentarian Friedrich von Payer (*qq.v.*) as vice chancellor, the court was outraged and convinced that Valentini was the prime mover behind the apparent creeping parliamentarization. In January 1918, Hindenburg and Ludendorff joined the attack on Valentini. Still the kaiser refused to dismiss the civil cabinet chief. Crown Prince Wilhelm (*q.v.*) referred to Valentini as the "evil spirit of the monarchy," but again Wilhelm stood fast. Finally, Hindenburg and Ludendorff planted articles in the press to the effect that Valentini was a traitor because he had reputedly commented that the naval battle at the Skagerrak in May 1916 had precluded any separate peace with Britain. By January 15, 1918, the two generals as well as the crown prince confronted the kaiser with a cruel choice: either Valentini went or Hindenburg and Ludendorff would resign. Valentini yielded the next day rather than force such a brutal decision on the monarch, and a bitter Wilhelm informed the army's candidate as Valentini's replacement, Friedrich Wilhelm von Berg: "I have been asked to make you chief of the civil cabinet." It was the bitter truth; not the monarch but rather the two generals were the arbiters of the Hohenzollern Reich. Valentini died at Hameln on December 18, 1925.

Kitchen, *Silent Dictatorship*; Schwertfeger, *Kaiser und Kabinettschef*; *Biographisches Wörterbuch zur Deutschen Geschichte*, III.

VENIZELOS, Eleutherios (*Greece, Prime Minister*), was born in Mournies, a town on the Turkish-held island of Crete, on August 23, 1864. Venizelos' father, a merchant who had fled to Greece after an unsuccessful rebellion against the Turks, returned from exile with Greek citizenship. Thus, in addition to his Greek ethnic origins, the younger Venizelos held dual Greek and Cretan citizenship during the first half of his life. He received his secondary education in Athens, where he also trained as a lawyer, returning home in the late 1880s to plunge into the Cretan struggle for independence. From his earliest years in politics, Venizelos was a proponent of the Great Idea in Greek affairs. This was the fiery irredentist demand that all ethnic Greeks under Turkish overlordship be reunited with the homeland. Cretan independence was one milestone on this ambitious road.

Venizelos first sprung to prominence in the role of Cretan revolutionary. By 1908 he had become the first prime minister of an independent Crete. Great power objections still prevented union with Greece, but the flamboyant rebel had acquired a reputation that extended beyond his small island. Georges Clemenceau (q.v.) returned from a visit to Crete to say of Venizelos that "the whole of Europe will be speaking of him in a few years." The prophecy proved correct.

The disintegration of the Greek political system at the start of the twentieth century gave Venizelos his larger stage. Diplomatic, military, and financial humiliations led to a revolt by a league of military officers in 1909. Recognizing their inability to handle the full range of government responsibilities, they called on Venizelos. The Cretan firebrand, formerly only a student and visitor in Greece, became prime minister in October 1910.

The dynamic new arrival first made his mark in domestic affairs. The army and navy, for example, were thoroughly overhauled with the help of British and French military missions. Next, Venizelos took the lead in constructing the Balkan coalition that crushed Turkey in 1912/1913. From this First Balkan War and the subsequent Second Balkan War against Bulgaria (June/July 1913), Venizelos drew gains that doubled Greece's territory.

The outbreak of European-wide hostilities in August 1914 placed Venizelos' country in a difficult position. Greece's only ally Serbia entered the war at once. Their 1913 mutual defense pact was aimed at Bulgaria; thus Greece could manage to stay neutral. But Bulgaria and Turkey both coveted Greece's newly gained territory in Macedonia and Thrace. Besides the peril of standing alone against Balkan neighbors in an era of spreading international war, there was also the complex problem of dealing with the great powers. Germany's Kaiser Wilhelm II was the brother-in-law of King Constantine I of Greece (qq.v.). The dynastic tie was hardened by Constan-

tine's conviction Germany would win the war. Thus he saw Greek interests dictating benevolent neutrality toward the Central Powers—and perhaps even an active alliance. This view was consistently endorsed by the monarch's personal entourage, composed largely of German-trained military men. On the other hand, British sea power, for Greece as for Italy, limited the possibility of standing alongside the Central Powers.

Venizelos saw the Entente as the likely winner in the war. Moreover, war between Greece and Turkey was inescapable: their relations had deteriorated rapidly since the Balkan Wars. Thus, once Turkey entered the war in November 1914, Venizelos thought that Greece had the opportunity to fight the inevitable war against the Turks in the ranks of a powerful coalition. To complete Venizelos' view that standing with the Entente served Greek interests, rumors spread that the Great War meant the partition of the Ottoman Empire. The full realization of the Great Idea was at hand. Venizelos, in sharp contrast to the Greek king, saw the war bringing opportunity as well as danger.

Differences in policy between Venizelos and Constantine derived in part from internal divisions existing in Greek affairs before the outbreak of World War I. Given new force by the war years, these internecine conflicts persisted long after 1918. The constitutional powers of the monarch, the supporting role of the military High Command, the contrary challenge of Venizelos and his moderate, reformist style of parliamentary liberalism—such elements collided with increasing violence after July 1914. For Venizelos it meant making policy in a country that first split apart into royalist and Venizelist factions, then slipped into open civil war.

August and September 1914 saw Venizelos, with Constantine's reluctant consent, making approaches to Britain and France. The Greek premier went unheard. With Turkey still neutral, London and Paris perceived Bulgaria as the most promising potential ally in the Balkans; their diplomatic overtures went to the leaders in Sofia, not Athens. By the start of 1915 a new diplomatic state of affairs formed in the Mediterranean. Turkey had joined the Central Powers; an Entente attack on the Dardanelles was about to start. Britain saw the need to offer generous rewards in Asia Minor in return for Greek military aid. Venizelos pictured a Greek army corps helping to seize Gallipoli. Constantine would not agree, and Venizelos resigned from the government in early March. His departure raised the broad constitutional question of where power to make foreign policy lay: with the monarch, or with a premier commanding a parliamentary majority.

Venizelos' existing majority was overwhelmingly reaffirmed in new elections in June 1915. By then, Constantine and his military circle had formed, in Leon's words, "a state within a state." Venizelos returned to power in August, the appointment of his Cabinet having been delayed as long as possible by Constantine's alleged ill health. Bulgaria was on the verge of entering the war. Sofia's order to mobilize came in late September; it seemed to give Venizelos the lever with which Greece could be moved into the ranks of the Entente. A Bulgarian attack on Serbia meant activating the 1913 Greco-Serbian defense pact. Since Serbia was in no position to send 150,000 troops to the Bulgarian frontier as the pact required, Venizelos sought to get Britain and France to send in the required forces.

The Greek premier's hopes crumbled quickly. Allied forces were unavailable in the numbers Venizelos had named. Constantine gave only grudging consent to Greek mobilization: it remains hotly disputed whether he ever consented to the Allied landing in Salonika. Popular support for Venizelos eroded as young Greeks were called to the colors and a foreign army landed at Salonika. Venizelos himself seems to have had second thoughts when he heard rumors that the Entente meant to seize Greek Macedonia only to trade it off for an alliance with Bulgaria. To deepen the muddle, the Allied contingent landed just as Constantine forced Venizelos from office on October 5. Venizelos found himself faced with a pro-German neutralist government. A series of docile nonentities served as premiers in what was then a royal autocracy.

Still deeper fissures in Greek life came in 1916. The presence of an Allied army at Salonika led the Entente ever deeper into Greek affairs. In May Constantine and the General Staff permitted the Bulgarian army to seize the border outpost of Fort Rupel, exposing the Allied position in eastern Macedonia. In August a new Bulgarian assault met no Greek resistance and took the strategic Aegean port of Kavalla, a new blow to Anglo-French security. Rival paramilitary groups, drawn from army reservists, sprang up. Some supported the king, others the Venizelist faction.

In late August Venizelos made a final appeal to Constantine to reestablish a constitutional form of government. The ex-premier's supporters were already in motion. A local coup took place in Salonika in August. Venizelos slipped away to Crete on September 26 to set up a provisional government; then, in October, he established himself at Salonika. He called on Greeks to fight alongside the Entente against Bulgaria. Conspicuously missing in his speeches and proclamations were attacks on the dynasty—in deference to the monarchies that formed the core of the Entente as well as to Greek monarchists. Venizelos probably hoped to dethrone Constantine; his attitude toward the monarchy as a whole is less clear.

A Venizelist regime in northern Greece and a royalist government in the south heated the ingredients for civil war. Skirmishes began between rival Greek forces in early November. Constantine destroyed his last credit with the Allies when his forces fired on Anglo-French landing parties in Athens on December 1. Venizelos declared the king deposed; on December 19 the Salonika regime got British diplomatic recognition. Only Allied reluctance to see open civil war kept the provisional government from moving on Athens. But the Russian Revolution and America's entry into the war diluted the monarchist character of the Entente. In France the fall of Aristide Briand (q.v.) removed a long-time friend of the Greek royal family from the scene. British objections to full support for Venizelos faded when he pledged to maintain the dynasty in the person of Constantine's son Alexander.

Venizelos entered Athens in June 1917. By the start of July he had formed a national government. He brought Greece into the war at once. The fractures in Greek political life remained dangerous, but the Greek leader was able to raise a respectable army. It got its baptism of fire in the spring of 1918 in Macedonia. In September it joined in the climactic breakthrough there that drove Bulgaria from the war. Venizelos was able to go to Versailles as the leader of a victorious and well-armed regional power.

Historians judge Venizelos as a diplomatic virtuoso in the service of a small power on a par with Rumania's Ion Bratianu (q.v.) at Versailles. The Peace Conference brought rich rewards: Western Thrace from Bulgaria; Eastern Thrace and strategic islands in the Aegean from Turkey. The Treaty of Sèvres (August 10, 1920) with Turkey in which the city of Smyrna and adjacent territories came under temporary Greek administration also gave Greece a foothold in Asia Minor. Backed by Britain's Lloyd George (q.v.), who saw Greek ambitions in Asia Minor as a useful counterweight to Italian expansion, Venizelos seemed about to realize the Great Idea.

The dream slipped away. By late 1920 Greece had been at war, almost without pause, for eight years. Venizelos, the diplomat at Versailles, had been an absentee prime minister as well—to the disenchantment of the Greek electorate. He returned in the afterglow of the triumph at Sèvres to find himself rejected by the voters in December 1920, an event historians liken to the fall of Winston Churchill (q.v.) in 1945. Other leaders were unable to achieve the

Great Idea. A triumphant Turkey drove Greek armies from Anatolia, pushing them into the sea at Smyrna in September 1922.

The Greek political scene remained fragmented by wartime quarrels. Venizelos served briefly as prime minister in 1924, then returned for his last turn in office from 1928 to 1933. His diplomatic skills were still sharp. But the domestic situation, bitter to begin with, became unmanageable in the era of the depression. Venizelos fell in early 1933, never to regain power. He died in exile in Paris, March 18, 1936.

Like Constantine, Venizelos and his stewardship of Greek affairs in World War I have given rise to heated debate among Greek and foreign historians. In the service of Greek interests, Venizelos was willing to take his country into a destructive conflict—and to do so at the cost of civil war. The rewards came, only to vanish at once. Accused by his biographer Alastos of megalomania in the service of Greek nationalism, Venizelos has collected few neutral judgments from anyone. Perhaps the most useful of these came from a British historian who called him simply "the most dynamic figure in modern Greek history."

Alastos, *Venizelos*; Helmreich, *From Paris to Sèvres*; Leon, *Greece and the Great Powers*; Palmer, *Gardeners of Salonika*; Stavrianos, *Balkans since 1453*; Theodoulou, *Greece and the Entente*; Woodhouse, *Short History of Modern Greece*.

VICTOR EMMANUEL III (*Italy, King*), also VITTORIO EMANUELE III, was born in Naples, November 11, 1869. The son of King Humbert (or Umberto) I, Victor Emmanuel was educated by military tutors and entered the army as a lieutenant in 1886. His rise was predictably meteoric, and, by the age of twenty-eight, he was at least in name the commander of an army corps. In 1896 the young prince married the daughter of King Nicholas of Montenegro (*q.v.*). Four years later, an anarchist's bullet cut down King Humbert and elevated Victor Emmanuel to the throne.

The young monarch played a comparatively minor role in national affairs over the next fourteen years, an era of relatively peaceful domestic politics and rising prosperity dominated by Liberal political leader Giovanni Giolitti (*q.v.*). The king was apparently comfortable in a constitutional monarchy, despite his family's traditional interest in the nation's foreign and military affairs. He was thought by some to be an ardent irredentist, anxious to reclaim from Austria-Hungary lands inhabited by Italians. But his warlike instincts, if any, were muted. In 1911 it was Giolitti and Foreign Minister San Giuliano (*q.v.*) who led the nation into war with the Ottoman Empire.

The outbreak of World War I and the question of Italian intervention made the king's wishes and influence matters of national importance. Once Italy had refused to honor its alliance with Germany and Austria-Hungary, Premier Salandra and Foreign Minister Sonnino (*qq.v.*), the latter having replaced the deceased San Giuliano in November 1914, negotiated carefully over the next five months, expecting to join the Entente if Austria-Hungary failed to satisfy Italy's territorial demands. The king, along with a few senior officials in the Foreign Office, were aware of the negotiations and the resulting Treaty of London (April 26, 1915). His influence rose to decisive importance in May. On May 4 Italy denounced its alliance with Germany and Austria-Hungary. But Salandra found he lacked a parliamentary majority willing to vote for war, and he resigned on May 13. As massive demonstrations rocked Italy's major cities, especially in the north, led by such flamboyant interventionists as Gabriele D'Annunzio (*q.v.*), the king looked for a new premier. But his own desire to uphold the Treaty of London and to bring Salandra back to office was clear. Perhaps aware that such street speakers and warmongering journalists as young Benito Mussolini were threatening revolution if Italy failed to strike at Austria, the king spoke of abdicating if the nation did not keep its word to its new allies. On May 16, after other candidates had refused the call to form a new government, the monarch enthusiastically summoned Salandra back. War was declared on May 24.

The king spent most of the war years near the front, as nominal commander in chief. His cousin, the duke of Genoa, remained in Rome as regent. In general, Victor Emmanuel's direct intervention in leading the nation remained rare. Some bones of contention between the military High Command, led by General Cadorna (*q.v.*), and the government had to go to the king for his mediation. Such was the case in the spring of 1916 when Cadorna quarreled with Sonnino's growing involvement in Albania. Sonnino used the king's name to fend off Anglo-French moves to work for a separate peace with Vienna; this meant, he said, the renunciation of territorial gains pledged to Italy and that would besmirch the royal honor. In the tumultuous weeks after the enemy breakthrough at Caporetto (October 1917), the king consulted with Premier Vittorio Orlando to help choose General Diaz (*qq.v.*) to replace the discredited Cadorna. The king also urged that the army retreat go no further than the Piave; and his speech reassuring English and French diplomats that this would be the limit of the Italian withdrawal probably helped sway London and Paris to send troops from the western front to prop up the Italians.

Victor Emmanuel had over twenty-eight years left on the throne when World War I ended. He presided passively over Italy's drift into Fascist dictatorship, and he saw his own role diminished by Mussolini. Then, in 1943, anti-Fascist groups like the army rallied to him in a vain effort to oust Mussolini. The post-World War II years put the fate of the monarchy itself in doubt. Facing a plebiscite on the question of keeping the monarchy or establishing a republic, the old king tried to make the first alternative more attractive to the voters by abdicating in favor of his son in May 1946. The next month's elections saw the monarchy defeated by a narrow margin. The last king of Italy went into exile and died in Alexandria, Egypt, on December 28, 1947.

Bertoldi, *Vittorio Emanuele III*; Bosworth, *Italy, The Least of the Great Powers*; Melograni, *Storia politica della grande guerra*; Seton-Watson, *Italy from Liberalism to Fascism*; *Enciclopedia italiana*, XXXV; *Larousse mensuel*, XII.

VIVIANI, René (*France, Premier*), was born in Sidi-Bel-Abbès, Algeria, November 8, 1862, the son of a government official. Educated as an attorney in Paris and admitted to the bar in 1887, he practiced briefly in Algeria, but returned to make his career in metropolitan France. Viviani was drawn to socialism as a young man, making an early reputation for himself as a fiery anticlerical speaker and journalist. Much of his legal work he devoted to representing striking workers. He became secretary to the Socialist deputy Alexandre Millerand (*q.v.*), forming a lasting political and personal link. In 1893 Viviani himself entered the Chamber of Deputies.

By 1899 Viviani's doctrinaire views had cooled visibly. He was considered open to an invitation to join a bourgeois government—an unheard of action for a Socialist up to that time—but the offer went to the more experienced Millerand. Viviani was defeated in the election of 1902 and returned to the Chamber only in 1906. In the interim, he broke with the newly unified and militant French Socialist party, the SFIO, becoming one of a score of former Socialists to form a loose bloc of "Independents," to the right of the SFIO but to the left of the Radicals. Viviani joined the cabinet of Georges Clemenceau, then that of Aristide Briand (*qq.v.*), to serve as France's first minister of labor, 1906-1910.

By 1914 Viviani had established himself as one of France's most talented orators and as a flexible and moderate member of the parliamentary Left. Chosen to be premier by Raymond Poincaré (*q.v.*), he failed to get the necessary majority from the Radical-dominated Chamber of Deputies on his first try in early June 1914. After a brief interlude during which France had no Cabinet, Viviani received the Chamber's tepid approval. His skills notwithstanding, he had a reputation for both laziness and excitability. He lacked the administrative and political experience customarily offered by would-be premiers: he had been neither minister of finance nor minister of foreign affairs. He was probably chosen by Poincaré precisely because he could be swayed on crucial issues. A nominal member of the political Left open to Poincaré's ideas on three-year military service and the broader issues of a vigorous nationalist style in foreign affairs, Viviani constituted a valuable find.

On July 15, 1914, Viviani and Poincaré left for a long-planned visit to St. Petersburg. Viviani found himself in a subordinate position as Poincaré assumed control of the negotiations. On July 26, en route home by way of Scandinavia, the party received messages from Paris that made the gravity of the international situation clear. Viviani agreed to Poincaré's suggestion for an immediate return to France; he also sent a restrained note to the Russians pledging support in the interest of a general peace. The French ambassador to Russia, Maurice Paléologue (*q.v.*), possibly under Poincaré's instructions, ignored the message. Throughout the crisis, Paléologue urged the Russians forward and concealed from Paris such events as the rapid progress of Russian mobilization.

Viviani turned to Poincaré repeatedly during the development of the July crisis. Crucial messages to the Russians and the British were drafted under Poincaré's direction. According to Albertini, during July 30 and July 31, Viviani and his colleagues accepted the strength of prowar feeling in Paris and gave up efforts to block the outbreak of hostilities. With a view to opinion in Britain, they pulled French troops back a short distance from the frontier. Germany was to have the opportunity and the onus of opening hostilities. Viviani's war message of August 4 to the National Assembly was accurate in its main lines; however, it ignored the crucial factor of Russia's general mobilization and France's contribution thereto as elements leading to war.

Indecisive and overly reliant on others in the prewar crisis, Viviani played the same role during the war. Strong pressure from Poincaré overcame the premier's objections and led in late August 1914 to the broadened *union sacrée* government. Viviani found himself helpless in the face of General Joffre's (*q.v.*) insistence on a free hand in running the war. He was reduced to complaining to the commander in chief about a lack of information concerning military operations before the battle of the Marne. By October Viviani found himself barred from touring the war zone on the deadlocked western front; he was being treated like any other member of the National Assembly. His old colleague Millerand, minister of war in the *union sacrée* government, became one of his principal burdens: a parliamentary spokesman for Joffre's quasi-dictatorship over the direction of the war.

In 1915 Viviani presided ineffectually over the bloody stalemate in the west: Joffre conducted fruitless major offensives in March and September. Unrest in the National Assembly grew. It centered on the immediate issue of visits to the front but soon encompassed the entire direction of the war. Ready to oust Millerand, Viviani gave in to Poincaré's objection that such steps would fracture the *union sacrée*.

Viviani also contributed to the birth of France's commitment in the Balkans. He enthusiastically accepted Poincaré's suggestion (January 1915) that a Balkan front be opened. Joffre turned the idea down, but later that month Viviani took the first step toward Salonika. He accepted a British plan, seconded by his Navy Minister Victor Augagneur (*q.v.*), that France join a maritime expedition to force the Dardanelles. When it failed in mid-March, France like Britain geared up for a larger effort. By midsummer Viviani's shaky government needed a victory somehow, somewhere. Meanwhile, the Radicals demanded a suitable post for their hero, General Maurice Sarrail (*q.v.*), recently dismissed from his command in France by Joffre, and the course seemed set for a major French effort at the Dardanelles. Events merely moved the landing westward. Austro-German forces invaded Serbia from the north in early October; a Bulgarian assault on France's lone Balkan ally from the east followed within a week. The need for a rescue mission to bolster the Serbs led to an Anglo-French landing at Salonika.

The plunge into the Balkans came too late to save Viviani. Joffre's fall offensive in the Champagne had failed. Parliamentary commissions had voiced concern over Serbia's exposed position for months—without catching Viviani's attention. Bulgaria's entry into the war on the enemy side brought the government down in late October. Pressed between the millstones of a restless National Assembly and a jealously self-contained High Command, Viviani had never been able to provide a clear direction for the war effort. He remained in the Cabinet, but his days at the center of power were over; he undertook missions to Russia in 1916 and the United States in early 1917.

In the postwar period Viviani represented France at the Washington Naval Conference of 1921 and at the Council of the League of Nations. He died outside Paris, September 6, 1925.

Albertini, *The Origins of the War of 1914*, 3 vols.; Cassar, *The French and the Dardanelles*; Goldberg, *Life of Jean Jaurès*; King, *Generals and Politicians*; Wright, *Raymond Poincaré and the French Presidency*; *Dictionnaire des parlementaires français*, VIII.

WALDSTÄTTEN, Alfred Baron von (*Austria-Hungary, General*), was born in Vienna on November 9, 1872. Waldstätten graduated first in his class from the Theresa Military Academy in 1892, and in the same position from the War Academy five years later. The promising young officer was skipped one grade to the rank of captain and assigned to the General Staff and subsequently to the prestigious Infantry Regiment Kaiser Nr. 1. At the turn of the century he was with the V Army Corps in Pressburg and later served as chief of staff of the Twenty-eighth Infantry Division at Laibach.

At the outbreak of the war Waldstätten was instructor at the War Academy. In August 1914, he assumed the post of chief of staff for Army Group Dankl (*q.v.*) in time to take part in the Russian defeat at Krasnik; thereafter, Waldstätten planned the strategic withdrawals behind the Tanev and San rivers. During the winter of 1914 Army Group Dankl generally assisted the German Ninth Army in blunting Russian offensives emanating from Warsaw and Ivangorod, finally halting the Russian "steamroller" at the line of the Nida River. When General Viktor Dankl was appointed chief of the Tyrolean Defense Command in May 1915, he assigned Colonel von Waldstätten as chief of staff of the famous XX (Edelweiss) Corps, entrusted to Archduke Charles (*q.v.*), the heir to the throne. The heavy Russian incursions into the Bukovina that summer brought about yet another transfer for both Archduke Charles and Waldstätten, this time to the eastern front. In the fall of 1915 Waldstätten was assigned to the Seventh Army of General Hermann Kövess (*q.v.*).

In March 1917, General Arz von Straussenburg replaced Conrad von Hötzendorf (*qq.v.*) as chief of the General Staff of the army and Waldstätten, at the express desire of Emperor Charles, was promoted major general and assigned to Arz as deputy chief of the General Staff. At the new army headquarters at Baden, near Vienna, Waldstätten assumed responsibility for most operational planning while the pliable Arz accompanied Charles on his numerous tours of the fronts. Waldstätten unfortunately was not always up to this demanding task. A case in point was the planned Austro-Hungarian offensive against Italy in May and June 1918. While Conrad favored a thrust from the South Tyrolean Alps into the Venetian plain, taking the Italian army in the flank,

General Svetozar Boroević (*q.v.*), when pressed, came out for a frontal assault across the Piave River; Arz and Waldstätten were in a dither and finally supported strong attacks on both extreme flanks. This inability of headquarters to settle upon a bold plan of action encompassing the keys of surprise and concentration opened the doors for Emperor Charles, who in the end gave both his field commanders equal forces and equal authority to conduct operations. The result was hardly surprising: by June 20 the Dual Monarchy's offensive had been blunted, especially by British and French forces stationed in Italy. The cohesion of the army was shattered and this moral defeat was to have far-reaching repercussions. On November 2, 1918, Waldstätten agreed to return the soldiers of Hungary to their homeland from all fronts. The war had been lost. The general died in Mauerbach, Lower Austria, on January 12, 1952.

Rothenberg, *Army of Francis Joseph*; Veltzé, *Unsere Heerführer*.

WEKERLE, Alexander (*Austria-Hungary, Minister-President*), was born in Mór, Hungary, on November 14, 1848, into an old German Swabian family. Wekerle served most of his career in the Hungarian civil service: secretary of state in the Finance Ministry in 1886, liberal parliamentary delegate the following year, minister of finance from 1889 to 1895, and, concurrently, from 1892 to 1895, minister-president. In the latter year, Wekerle legalized mixed marriages among Catholics, Protestants, and Jews in Hungary and introduced obligatory civil marriage, a measure adamantly opposed by the Conservatives and one that caused his fall from power. An old-line Liberal, Wekerle returned to head a coalition government in 1906; he basically favored upholding the Compromise of 1867 in the face of demands for revision and for the creation of an independent Hungarian army. However, the minister-president in 1906 clashed with Archduke Francis Ferdinand (*q.v.*), the heir presumptive, in his call for introducing the Hungarian language into the joint army. The archduke, in fact, informed Wekerle that once he acceded to the throne, he would seek to revoke Hungary's special position in Habsburg military affairs. An opportunist and able parliamentary tactician, Wekerle managed to cling to office until 1910, surviving numerous Cabinet reorganizations and enduring the verbal diatribes of Hungarian Independence delegates anxious to sever the tie to Vienna.

On August 20, 1917, at nearly seventy years of age, Wekerle again resumed the minister-presidency under the exigencies of wartime exhaustion. Without a solid party base, the staunch Magyar at first op-

posed all attempts to reform the Dual Monarchy along federalist lines; deep down he desired to annex Dalmatia and Bosnia (the *corpus separatum*) to Hungary. However, his greatest undertaking proved to be the reform of the restricted Hungarian suffrage in November 1917 by 40 percent beyond the existing 1.8 million voters. In the end, this measure died in Parliament in the face of stiff Magyar opposition. Perhaps to compensate for this obstruction, Wekerle, supported by his war minister, Alexander Szurmay, that same November pushed Emperor Charles (*qq.v.*) into honoring an earlier pledge to create a separate Hungarian army after the war. This proposal to divide the joint army into separate Austrian and Hungarian armies was not only unrealistic by the end of 1917 but also met with the determined opposition of most Habsburg marshals the following month; this notwithstanding, the Hungarians as late as September 12, 1918, sought to implement such a scheme.

In the field of foreign policies, Wekerle in July 1918 defended Foreign Minister Ottokar Czernin (*q.v.*) against attacks for the "Sixtus letter," in which the Viennese diplomat had suggested that Alsace-Lorraine be returned by Germany to France as a precondition for a general European peace. Early in 1918 widespread strikes especially in Budapest forced Wekerle to promise once again the creation of an independent Hungarian army after the war. His greatest hour, however, came shortly before the end of the war. On October 15, 1918, Wekerle opposed Emperor Charles' decision to promulgate the conversion of Cisleithanian Austria into a federation of independent states; specifically, the Hungarian leader threatened to curtail all food shipments to Austria unless Charles exempted Hungary from this order. In the end, Wekerle carried the day, and Charles promised to maintain the integrity of the lands of the Crown of St. Stephen—at the cost of Croat, German, Rumanian, Ruthenian, and Serb national groups.

But the dissolution of the Dual Monarchy could not be checked, and on October 19 Wekerle officially announced the independence of Hungary, disavowing the *Realunion* of 1867 and clinging only to the fiction of a personal union under the Habsburgs as a last tie. Yet even this action came too late, and the shrewd compromiser on October 23 yielded to the aristocratic frondeur, M. Károlyi (*q.v.*), as minister-president. Well remembered by his political opponents as the man who had squelched the Independence party insurgency in 1906, Wekerle was left out of the mainstream of Hungarian politics in the immediate postwar period; he died in Budapest on August 26, 1921.

Kann, *History of the Habsburg Monarchy*; May, *Passing of the Hapsburg Monarchy*, II; Rothenberg, *Army of Francis Joseph*; *Der grosse Brockhaus* (1935), XX.

WEMYSS, Rosslyn Erskine (*Great Britain, Admiral of the Fleet*), Baron Wester Wemyss, was born in London on April 12, 1864, to James Hay Erskine Wemyss of Wemyss Castle, Fife. Wemyss entered the navy in 1877 along with his third cousin, the Royal Prince George (later King George V [*q.v.*]). Duty in the Mediterranean under Lord Charles Beresford and on board the royal yacht *Osborne* brought out his charm, tact, and abundant common sense. In 1898 in the grade of commander he was in charge of the *Niobe* on special assignment at the Cape Colony during the Boer War; three years later Wemyss joined the duke of York on a tour of the Dominions and received promotion to the grade of captain. In August 1903, Admiral John A. "Jacky" Fisher (*q.v.*) selected Wemyss as first commander of the new cadets' college at Osborne; thereafter came service on several warships as well as the post of naval equerry to King George V in 1910. Two years later Wemyss was promoted to the grade of rear admiral.

The outbreak of war in August 1914 found him in command of the twelfth cruiser squadron with his flag on the *Charybdis* with instructions to act in concert with the French for the western patrol of the English Channel, and to protect the transport of the British Expeditionary Force to France. In September Wemyss escorted the first contingent of Canadian troops to England. In February 1915, his steady character and cool composure made him the right man to govern Lemnos Island and to head the naval station at Mudros, which was to serve as base for the proposed naval assault upon the Dardanelles. On his arrival Wemyss found no water supply, no native labor, and no staff. When Admiral Sackville Carden became ill in March 1915 in the wake of the first round of failure at the Straits, Rosy Wemyss, as he was called, unselfishly recommended that a junior officer, Rear Admiral John De Robeck (*qq.v.*), succeed Carden, remaining at Mudros himself.

In April 1916, Wemyss commanded the first naval squadron in the Helles section with his flag on the *Euryalus*; in November, during De Robeck's absence, he was appointed acting vice admiral. In this capacity Wemyss supported Commodore Roger Keyes' proposal for yet another naval attempt to force the Straits, and Wemyss badgered the first lord of the Admiralty, Arthur James Balfour, as well as General Charles Monro (*qq.v.*) to this end, but to no avail. Moreover, Wemyss opposed the evacuation of Allied troops from Gallipoli. Though disgruntled, he never-

theless threw himself into the evacuation with vigor at Suvla and Anzac.

Wemyss was next appointed commander in chief, East Indies and Egypt Station in January 1916, and supported General Edmund Allenby's (*q.v.*) advance into Palestine in August. That same year he was promoted to the grade of vice admiral. In 1917 Wemyss accepted the newly created office of deputy sea lord, being entrusted by Sir Eric Geddes with reorganizing and expanding the war staff created in 1912 by Winston Churchill (*qq.v.*). Admiral John Jellicoe's (*q.v.*) opposition to this proposal to create a "general staff of the navy" as well as the sea commander's personal differences with both Geddes and the prime minister, David Lloyd George (*q.v.*), resulted in Jellicoe's abrupt dismissal by Geddes near the end of that year and his replacement as first sea lord by Rosy Wemyss.

This turn of events was not received well in the service. Jellicoe complained that he had been "kicked out" for no reason at all, and many senior officers regarded Wemyss as a "Court sailor." On the other hand, Wemyss worked well throughout 1918 with Geddes and helped to plan the daring Zeebrugge operation in April 1918. By August he supported the American plan for a northern mine barrage of the waters between Scotland and Norway. Wemyss represented the Allied navies at the German capitulation at Compiègne on November 11, 1918, and Britain at the Paris Peace Conference in 1919. That year he was promoted to the grade of admiral.

After the war Wemyss was deeply offended by repeated calls for his replacement by Admiral David Beatty (*q.v.*) and by being overlooked from the list of peerages and money awards to the principal war leaders; he left office in November 1919. Thereafter he was specially promoted admiral of the fleet and raised to the peerage as Baron Wester Wemyss. He died at Cannes on May 24, 1933, disappointed that he was never offered employment as a governor or as an ambassador. Arthur Marder states that Wemyss served as first sea lord with distinction and that he conducted himself as a "broad-minded, shrewd man of the world."

Corbett & Newbolt, *Naval Operations*, IV; Marder, *Dreadnought to Scapa Flow*, II, IV, V; Lady Wemyss, *The Life and Letters of Lord Wester Wemyss*; Wemyss, *The Navy in the Dardanelles Campaign*; *Dictionary of National Biography 1931-1940*.

WESTARP, Kuno Count von (*Germany, Politician*), was born in Ludom, Posen, on August 12, 1864, the son of a head forester. After studying law, Westarp joined the Prussian civil service, becoming district magistrate in Bomst, Posen, in 1893 and seven years later in Randow, near Stettin. From 1903 until 1908 he served as police director and finally as president of police in Berlin-Schöneberg; from 1908 until 1920 he sat as justice of the Supreme Court in Berlin. Westarp joined the Reichstag in 1908, and four years later was appointed head of the Conservative party's parliamentary caucus. In fact, since the party's leader, Ernst von Heydebrand und der Lasa, the "uncrowned king of Prussia," concentrated his efforts on defending the three-class franchise in Prussia, Westarp effectively became the leading Conservative spokesman on the national level. An uncompromising Conservative, Westarp was sharp and cutting in his speeches, hard and cold towards any and all critics of Prussia.

At the outset of the Great War Westarp demanded sweeping German annexations as well as indemnities. With regard to Belgium, he sought "occupation of the whole country and complete economic domination"; the Longwy-Briey coal fields were to become German, and a large colonial empire in Central Africa was to be carved out of French, Belgian, and Portuguese holdings there. "Free access to the sea" would be accorded the German navy. And as the agrarian party, the Conservatives demanded immense territorial gains in Poland, the Baltic states, and Russia. Westarp never wavered in his radical annexationist stance. In 1916 he rejected President Woodrow Wilson's (q.v.) peace initiative as "intolerable" to Germany; in August 1917, he refused to define his position on Belgium, thereby undermining Pope Benedict XV's (q.v.) peace proposals; in 1918 Westarp denounced the peace accords of Brest-Litovsk and Bucharest as being too moderate. By the end of September 1918, the Conservative leader still demanded German annexation of Belgium and large indemnities as prerequisites for a general peace.

At home Westarp aimed his sights on Chancellor Theobald von Bethmann Hollweg (q.v.). When, in September 1916, the chancellor hinted at postwar domestic reforms, Westarp vehemently denounced any tinkering with the Bismarckian constitutional system; he viewed the three-class suffrage as "an internal affair of Prussia." In July 1917, he conspired with General Erich Ludendorff, Colonel Max Bauer (qq.v.), and other parliamentary leaders to topple Bethmann Hollweg, whom he considered "utterly unfit for the chancellorship." Westarp that same month denounced the Reichstag's peace resolution: "We would rather win ourselves to death than to succumb cowardly." And when Foreign Secretary Richard von Kühlmann (q.v.) on June 24, 1918, informed Parliament that military victory was no longer attainable,

Westarp promptly apprised army leaders of this revelation and then delivered a blistering attack on the foreign secretary, whom he accused of defeatism. Kühlmann was forced to resign, and Westarp enjoyed his last political triumph in imperial Germany.

Kuno von Westarp, like many right-wing politicians, submerged in November 1918, only to reappear two years later as one of the leaders of the German National People's party, whose parliamentary caucus he led from 1920 until 1925. Although Westarp in 1926 was elected head of the party, he frequently clashed with Alfred Hugenberg, who demanded unbending opposition to all Weimar governments, and four years later quit the party. With Gottfried Treviranus, Westarp in 1930 founded the Conservative People's party, which he represented in the Reichstag for the next two years. A diehard monarchist and Prussian, Westarp played no major role in German politics after 1933; in June 1945, the Russians arrested him, but he died shortly thereafter, on July 30, 1945, in Berlin.

Gatzke, *Germany's Drive to the West*; Kitchen, *Silent Dictatorship*; Westarp, *Konservative Politik*, 2 vols.; *Biographisches Wörterbuch zur Deutschen Geschichte*, III.

WEYGAND, Maxime (*France, General*), was born in Brussels, Belgium, on January 21, 1867. His parentage has remained a mystery to the present day, with speculation rife that he was the illegitimate offspring of the Habsburgs or of the Belgian royal family. He moved to Paris in 1873, entered St. Cyr as a foreigner with the special dispensation of the Ministry of War in 1885, and graduated in 1888 as a cavalry officer, having become a French citizen.

Weygand rose steadily despite an official reprimand for his anti-Dreyfus opinions and statements. He distinguished himself as a cavalry instructor at Saumur and as a troop commander. General Joffre (q.v.), hunting for talented younger officers, was impressed by Weygand's performance in the army's 1912 maneuvers and by the cavalryman's distinguished record in his studies at the Centre des hautes études militaires, newly established to train picked officers for senior commands in the future.

Weygand fought in 1914 in the battle of Morhange as a lieutenant colonel of Hussars in the Fourth Army. Joffre assigned him as chief of staff to General Foch (q.v.), whose performance in the Lorraine campaign led to the command of the newly formed Ninth Army on the Marne. From that time forward, Weygand's career during the war was intertwined with that of Foch.

Weygand distinguished himself at the Marne when Foch placed him in direct charge of the crucial Fère-

Champenoise sector. He followed Foch in the post of chief of staff from 1914 to the close of 1917: the winter campaigns of 1914 at Ypres and the Yser, the 1915 offensive in Artois, the Somme in 1916, and Foch's period of eclipse during most of 1917.

Foch and Weygand constituted a distinguished and smoothly functioning military team. Weygand could take Foch's compressed and often opaque orders and transform them into directives of perfect clarity. The precise boundaries of this symbiotic and effective relationship remain uncertain, but Weygand apparently stimulated and contributed to Foch's ideas as well as seeing to their execution.

In November 1917, the Allied powers took their first step toward a unified command with the formation of a Supreme War Council of political leaders and their permanent military representatives. Foch was initially named as the French representative but his simultaneous role as chief of staff of the French army led to Allied objections. Foch was replaced in December 1917 by Weygand, then a major general, who functioned as his alter ego. When Foch became supreme Allied commander in April 1918, Weygand returned to the role he had never really left, that of Foch's chief of staff and main military collaborator. Foch's skeleton staff, led by Weygand, was never adequate to give detailed direction to the Allied armies, and during the last six months of the war the Foch-Weygand team served mainly as coordinators and inspirers of the armies on the western front.

Weygand's service in the First World War was merely the start of an elaborate military career. He served as high commissioner in Syria in 1924, and during the early 1930s he was chief of staff and wartime commander designate of the French army. Weygand was the French military commander in the eastern Mediterranean during the first months of the Second World War. Recalled by Prime Minister Reynaud to command in France in May 1940, he found a situation he deemed hopeless and recommended French capitulation to the Germans. He was imprisoned by the Germans in 1942 and liberated in 1945; Weygand died in Paris on January 18, 1965.

Bankwitz, *Weygand and Civil-Military Relations*; Foch, *Memoirs*; Hunter, *Marshal Foch*; Weygand, *Foch* and *Mémoires*, 3 vols.

WILHELM, Crown Prince of Prussia and of Germany (*Germany, General*), was born in Potsdam on May 6, 1882, the eldest son of Kaiser Wilhelm II (*q.v.*). Following Hohenzollern tradition, Wilhelm became a lieutenant in the First Foot Guards on his tenth birthday. From 1901 to 1903 he attended Bonn University and in 1905 married Cecilia of Mecklenburg-Schwerin. The crown prince traveled extensively in the Mideast and in Asia Minor, and in 1911, after a grand tour of India, became commander of the First Guards Cavalry Regiment in Danzig. Wilhelm frequently interfered in domestic politics, most notably in defending army officers during the infamous Zabern (Saverne) affair in 1913. Arrogant and haughty beyond the royal norm, Wilhelm rivaled his father in arousing antagonism especially in civilian circles. His private life was hardly a model, and shortly before the Great War he dispatched his wife to virtual exile in a lovely Tudor mansion named after her in Potsdam.

On August 1, 1914, without being in the least qualified for high command, Wilhelm was given the Fifth Army in place of the recently injured General Hermann von Eichhorn (*q.v.*). The Fifth Army was stationed near Diedenhofen-Metz as the pivotal point for the great wheeling movement through Belgium. Ignoring orders to stand, however, Wilhelm attacked the French at Longwy-Longuyon and marched as far west as the very gates of Verdun, where he finally consented to halt. At the Marne on September 5, the Fifth Army formed the outside wing and eventually retreated behind the Aisne as part of the overall withdrawal ordered by Colonel Richard Hentsch (*q.v.*).

Crown Prince Wilhelm's historic hour came on February 21, 1916, when he was nominally placed in charge of the German assault on Verdun. General Erich von Falkenhayn of the General Staff as well as Wilhelm's chief of staff, General Schmidt von Knobelsdorf, pressed the attack regardless of cost; French Marshal Joseph Joffre and General Henri Pétain (*qq.v.*) were equally determined to hold the stone forts and to transform Verdun into the symbol of national determination. By the fall, after the loss of about 300,000 of the finest assault troops, the attack on Verdun had to be broken off and Forts Douaumont and Vaux abandoned. Schmidt von Knobelsdorf was summarily dismissed as Wilhelm's chief of staff as a result.

At the end of September 1916, Wilhelm was appointed chief of a new Army Group Crown Prince Wilhelm and given General Friedrich von der Schulenburg as chief of staff. For much of the next year this army group stood in the sector Verdun-Laon; Wilhelm was promoted general of infantry in January 1917. In April/May his forces, and especially the Seventh Army, fought bloody engagements at the Aisne-Champagne front, while in August/September it was the Fifth Army's turn to hold off violent French assaults near Verdun. The crown prince, always close to the annexationist Pan-

Germans, willingly became a spokesman for all who wished a victorious end to the war with large-scale territorial acquisitions in Belgium and in the east. Specifically, Wilhelm allowed Colonel Max Bauer to use his name in order to topple Chancellor Theobald von Bethmann Hollweg (qq.v.) on July 13, 1917, about which Wilhelm said, "This is the happiest day of my life." At the same time, it should be noted that the crown prince lacked decisive influence on his father during these years. To his credit, Wilhelm refused, in February 1918, to condone Bauer's crude attempt to force the kaiser to abdicate in favor of his eldest son.

On March 21, 1918, Crown Prince Wilhelm's Eighteenth Army stormed British positions at St. Quentin-La Fère as part of the Michael offensive, advancing over the old Somme battlefields of 1916 as far as the line Montdidier-Noyon. On May 27 his Seventh Army took the Chemin des Dames and raced to the Marne River; June 9 saw the Eighteenth Army at Noyon. However, the Allies held, and on July 15 the crown prince led the last attack in the sector Marne-Champagne. Marshal Ferdinand Foch (q.v.) counterattacked from Villers-Cotterêts against the exposed German flank, and once again the Marne had to be abandoned and a retreat behind Aisne and Vesle undertaken. Toward the end of September, Army Group Crown Prince Wilhelm fought pitched battles in the Champagne and along the Meuse against Franco-American units. At Spa on November 9, Wilhelm stood with Schulenburg in opposing all suggestions that he or his father renounce the throne; indeed, for a moment he toyed with the notion that the rebellion at home be suppressed with loyal troops. In the end, Wilhelm II fled to the Netherlands and the crown prince resigned his commission on November 11 after the government of Prince Max von Baden (q.v.) had rejected his offer to bring the armies home. On November 15, 1918, the crown prince fled to Wieringen Island in the Dutch Zuider Zee and on January 1, 1919, renounced all claims to both the German and the Prussian thrones. His wife and children remained at Potsdam.

In November 1923, the crown prince caused a stir when he abandoned his exile and returned to his Silesian estate at Oels. In 1932 the old kaiser forbade his son's candidacy for the office of president of the Weimar Republic, and the crown prince instead urged Berlin to vote for Adolf Hitler. In 1933 Wilhelm joined the Nazi motorized corps and generally supported the Hitler movement. In 1944 he left Oels to avoid the Russians and, after a brief stay at the Cecilienhof in Potsdam, settled at Lindau, Bavaria, where the French eventually seized him. Wilhelm died at Castle Hohenzollern near Hechingen on July 20, 1951.

Herre, *Kronprinz Wilhelm*; Jonas, *Kronprinz Wilhelm*; Wilhelm, *Meine Erinnerungen*; *Biographisches Wörterbuch zur Deutschen Geschichte*, III; *Geschichte der Ritter des Ordens*, II.

WILHELM II (*Germany, Emperor-King*), was born in Potsdam on January 27, 1859, the eldest son of Prince Frederick William of Prussia and Princess Victoria of England. From the start, the lad was weighed down by physical and psychological handicaps: a withered left arm, incurred during birth, caused him discomfort later in life; and the conflict between his grandfather's Prussian conservatism and his parents' English liberalism tugged at his conscience. His mother remained cold and imperious, despising all she saw in a foreign land; her bitter feud with Otto von Bismarck placed the future ruler in an unenviable position between parent and chancellor. Victoria sent her son to high school at Kassel, where he was educated by the Calvinist Georg Hinzpeter. Wilhelm graduated in 1877 and after a brief stint in the guards, which in accordance with Hohenzollern tradition he had entered at age ten, he attended Bonn University, joining the Borussen Corps. Two years later Wilhelm returned to Potsdam and to primarily a military life. In 1881 he married Princess Augusta Victoria of Schleswig-Holstein-Augustenburg, and they had six sons and one daughter.

The death in 1888 of both Emperors Wilhelm I and Frederick III brought Wilhelm II to the thrones of Prussia and Germany on June 15, before his thirtieth birthday. He was ill prepared for the task: his closest associations had been with aristocratic officers in the guards and he had never developed a penchant for sustained work. This notwithstanding, the new ruler desired to be his "own Bismarck." Moreover, for the next two years he wished to appear socially progressive, determined not to renew Bismarck's anti-Socialist laws and also to disavow the secret tie established with Russia in 1887. On March 17, 1890, Wilhelm asked for and the next day received Bismarck's resignation, thus "dropping the pilot," as *Punch* put it.

No steady counselors emerged to guide the ship of state. The earlier favorites such as Adolf Stöcker and Alfred von Waldersee were cast aside; Philipp Eulenburg for a time was the imperial favorite until he became involved in a moral scandal. The new chancellor, General Leo von Caprivi, was a devoted officer, but hardly the man to inherit Bismarck's mantle; he fell from power in 1894 over tariff reform and a bill to meet agitation against the existing order with penal servitude. Prince Hohenlohe, who succeeded Caprivi, fared little better and remained largely a caretaker in office. Wilhelm, for his part, firmly believed in divine right monarchy, never read the constitution, detested journalists and parliamentarians, and developed an intense dislike for democracy in direct proportion to the votes collected by the Social Democrats and the Catholic Center party. On the other hand, he became a champion of the new industrial age, sponsoring technical colleges and scientific societies; he showered his favors upon a new commercial and industrial elite, men such as Ballin, Krupp, Stumm, and Wiegand.

Under the influence of Friedrich von Holstein at the Foreign Office, the kaiser canceled the Reinsurance Treaty with Russia, then failed to offset the loss of the Russian connection with a new link to London. His support of China against Japan in 1894 and his seizure of a base at Kiaochow three years later greatly alarmed the British. Above all, the appointment of Bernhard von Bülow as foreign secretary and Alfred Tirpitz (*q.v.*) as naval secretary in 1897 truly ushered in a New Course in German affairs, one of *Weltpolitik* and conflict with Britain for world empire. In various navy bills passed between 1898 and 1912, Tirpitz, with the rabid support of Wilhelm, sought to create a fleet of sixty capital ships, to be replaced automatically every twenty years, stationed in the North Sea. By the early 1920s this fleet was to be ready to force colonial concessions from London; should Whitehall refuse to bow to pressure, Tirpitz was willing to wage Germany's future on a single naval battle "between Helgoland and the Thames." During the Boer War, Wilhelm greatly exacerbated the British, first by offering President Kruger assistance against them, and later by claiming that his General Staff had devised their blueprint for victory. While bound to England through deep affection and sympathy and to Russia through old family ties, Wilhelm could never make up his mind which nation to court; his advisers, especially Bülow and Holstein, on the other hand, opted to seek an alliance with neither, to play one off against the other, and to sell Germany's support to the highest bidder.

The years after about 1905 revealed the bankruptcy of Wilhelmian diplomacy. Already during the Boer War, the kaiser's idea of creating a sort of Continental League against the Anglo-Saxon powers had been shipwrecked by Chancellor von Bülow and Holstein as well as by the aggressive naval policy. Wilhelm's dramatic landing at Tangier in March 1905, implemented by Bülow against the monarch's better knowledge, mainly served to drive the British closer to France; the resulting conference at Algeciras showed only Austria-Hungary to be solidly in the German camp. Moreover, Wilhelm's attempted diplomatic revolution at Björkö in July 1905 proved

stillborn as the tsar's ministers quickly informed Nicholas II (*q.v.*) that such an offensive and defensive alliance was incompatible with the Franco-Russian treaty of 1894. And in 1907 Russia formally joined the Anglo-French entente of 1904, thereby completing Germany's self-imposed isolation, or encirclement, as it was popularly called in Berlin. That same year the monarch's indiscretions in the *Daily Telegraph* resulted in a state crisis and a vote of censure against him in the Reichstag; Wilhelm temporarily thought of abdicating.

By 1906 Tirpitz's master plan had foundered on Germany's inability to finance vast shipbuilding programs as well as on Britain's decision to build superior quality dreadnought battleships. The financial crisis led to Bülow's fall in 1909 and Britain's resolve to meet the German naval challenge head-on led to a retrenchment on the Continent on the part of the German army's chief of the General Staff, Helmuth von Moltke, the Younger (*q.v.*). At the time of Vienna's annexation of Bosnia and Herzegovina, Wilhelm felt betrayed by the Austrians, who did not even apprise him beforehand of their actions, but both his political and military leaders were determined, regardless of the cost, to support their last remaining ally. Under the new chancellor, Theobald von Bethmann Hollweg (*q.v.*), Germany more and more turned its attention to southeastern Europe and Turkey; the Berlin to Baghdad Railroad and the military mission of General Otto Liman von Sanders (*q.v.*) to the Porte were the most obvious manifestations of this development. Unhappily for Germany, Foreign Secretary Alfred von Kiderlen-Wächter in 1911 decided against the kaiser's wishes to test the French in Morocco again, mainly in the hope of thereby splitting the Entente, or at least acquiring all or part of the French Congo. Wilhelm agreed to dispatch the gunboat *Panther* to Morocco, but Germany failed to gain support in Europe beyond Austria-Hungary. Finally, in February 1912, Bethmann Hollweg sought to defuse the Anglo-German naval rivalry by bringing the British war minister, Lord Haldane of Cloan, to Berlin for direct talks with Wilhelm and Tirpitz; this last attempt at *rapprochement* failed as the day before Haldane left London, a new German navy bill was placed before the Reichstag.

The assassination of Archduke Francis Ferdinand (*q.v.*) at Sarajevo on June 28, 1914, shocked Wilhelm deeply, and on July 2 he declared, "The Serbs must be disposed of, and very soon." It was a question of "now or never." To Krupp, Wilhelm confided that this time he "would not cave in," and on July 6 he issued the famous blank check to Austria-Hungary, assuring it of Germany's support in any action taken against Serbia. But when he received a copy of Belgrade's conciliatory reply to a Viennese ultimatum on July 28, the kaiser was delighted, saying, "A great moral victory for Vienna, and with it every reason for war disappears." But it was not to be. Wilhelm drifted for the next week as mobilization orders and cancellations, partly or wholly, were heaped one atop the other; in the end, he continued to hope that the British would stay out of the fray, but by July 30 he realized that this "mean crew of shopkeepers" would stand by its ties to France and Russia. Not even a frantic burst of telegrams to the tsar, his Cousin Nicky, in Russia could avert the calamity upon which Europe was resolved to embark.

As supreme war lord in the Great War, Wilhelm proved to be a dismal failure. Devoid of deeper strategic insight and unable to lead the nation in time of emergency, he staggered from one crisis to the next until in the end his powers were usurped by two generals. Deep down, the monarch could never sustain a consistent policy, either in peace or in war. As one biographer (Balfour) has noted, Wilhelm's "alternation between dark, suspicious moments of frustration and confident assertions of imminent triumph remained the most marked characteristic" of his personality throughout the war. According to Prussian tradition, the kaiser was to be with his troops during the war, and hence he spent much of the period 1914-1918 at army headquarters: first at Koblenz and Luxembourg, then at Charleville, Spa, and Pless. By and large he remained a spectator; personnel decisions alone remained his prerogative.

The German failure at the Marne in September 1914 prompted Wilhelm to appoint the Prussian war minister, Erich von Falkenhayn (q.v.), as Moltke's successor. Perhaps the kaiser's being "terrified at the thought of a long war" prompted him to permit Falkenhayn to attempt to "bleed the French forces white" before Verdun on February 21, 1916. For thirty-five days the German Fifth Army lost men at the rate of one every forty-five seconds. On the other hand, the kaiser worked hard to prevent an all-out naval battle in the North Sea, rightly fearing that this would result in the end of the High Sea Fleet. And while he favored a separate peace with Russia, he could not bring himself to initiate talks with Nicholas II that might have led to this. Wilhelm despised President Woodrow Wilson (q.v.), and steadfastly refused the American leader's mediation offers, stating "I and my cousins George and Nicholas will make peace when the proper time has come."

By July 1916, Falkenhayn's offensive before Verdun had spent itself, General Aleksei Brusilov (q.v.) attacked in full force in Galicia, and Rumania entered the war against Germany. As a result, Falkenhayn was dismissed in August 1916, in favor of the victors of Tannenberg, Field Marshal Paul von Hindenburg and General Erich Ludendorff (qq.v.). The new duumvirate at once stabilized the western front through a strategic withdrawal and attempted to bolster their land forces with Polish volunteers by agreeing in November to create an independent Polish nation after the war. And whereas in March 1915 Wilhelm had accepted Tirpitz's resignation rather than permit unrestricted submarine warfare against neutral passenger liners, on January 9, 1917, at Pless he concurred with Admiral Henning von Holtzendorff (q.v.) and other naval leaders that Germany needed to play its last "trump" against Britain. The kaiser "fully expected America's entry into the war" as a result of this decision, but he assured his entourage that such a turn of events was "irrelevant" to the outcome of the war.

At home, 1917 proved to be a critical year. Bethmann Hollweg on April 8, Easter Day, wrung from Wilhelm a proclamation stating that after the war there would be franchise reform in Prussia and an overhaul of the Bismarckian constitutional system. While the Easter message delighted many liberals, it solidified the military and its right-wing civilian backers in the belief that the chancellor was an obstacle to a victorious German peace, which alone could uphold the conservative social order of the Reich. On July 13 Wilhelm yielded in the face of threats of resignation from Hindenburg and Ludendorff and dismissed Bethmann Hollweg; Crown Prince Wilhelm, Colonel Max Bauer, and the political leaders Matthias Erzberger, Gustav Stresemann, and Kuno von Westarp (qq.v.) had been eager to assist the military in its political intrigue. The kaiser showed little interest in the next chancellors, Georg Michaelis and Georg von Hertling (qq.v.), and instead occupied his time with schemes to place either his sons or other German princes on the thrones of German-controlled Belgium, Courland, Finland, Poland, and Rumania.

Wilhelm's influence on German affairs remained marginal throughout 1918. He was forced to consent to the ousters of chief of the Civil Cabinet Rudolf von Valentini and Foreign Secretary Richard von Kühlmann (qq.v.), again at the insistence of Hindenburg and Ludendorff. The peace treaties with Russia (Brest-Litovsk) and Rumania (Bucharest) in the spring and summer were dictated largely without his direction. In fact, the army dispatched the kaiser on a whirlwind tour of occupied countries. When at headquarters, he proved to be morose and discursive, often rambling on about President Wilson and his supporters among "international Jewry and Freemasons." Alone the great Michael offensive in France on March 21 captured his attention, but when Marshal Ferdinand Foch (*q.v.*) counterattacked on July 18, Wilhelm knew that the game was up; in the wake of the Allied push around Amiens on August 8, he confided to Ludendorff that the war had been lost. On October 2, in a last desperate attempt to save his throne, Wilhelm appointed Prince Max von Baden (*q.v.*), his second cousin, chancellor and authorized sweeping constitutional changes designed to accord both chancellor and Parliament a greater voice in German affairs.

But it was too little, too late. The Allied and Associated Powers would not tolerate a Hohenzollern on the throne, and when the fleet rebelled on October 30 rather than undertake a suicide sortie against the combined British and American fleets in the North Sea, revolution broke out and spread from port to port in the north. Still, Wilhelm wavered; "A successor of Frederick the Great does not abdicate." Yet he declined suggestions that he seek death in battle at the front or with the fleet. General Wilhelm Groener (*q.v.*) finally informed the monarch that the army "no longer stands behind Your Majesty," and Prince Max, pressured by the Social Democrats Friedrich Ebert and Philipp Scheidemann (*qq.v.*), at last seized the initiative on November 9 and simply announced Wilhelm's abdication. The kaiser denounced this "barefaced treason" by a fellow prince, but within twenty-four hours he was on his way into exile in the Netherlands, thus ending 504 years of Hohenzollern rule in northern Germany.

Wilhelm enjoyed a quiet, tranquil life first at Amerongen and then at Doorn. Queen Wilhelmina's government refused to turn him over to the Allies to be tried as a "war criminal" under Section 227 of the Versailles Treaty; on November 28, 1918, Wilhelm formally renounced all claims to both the Prussian and the German thrones. While he hoped that the German people would one day call him back to rule, he deplored Emperor Charles' (*q.v.*) two abortive attempts to recover his throne in Hungary. Empress Augusta Victoria died in Doorn in March 1921 and was interred at Potsdam, and in November 1922, the kaiser married Princess Hermine (born Reuss). While Wilhelm admired the patriotism of the Nazis, he nevertheless, unlike several of his sons, never fully embraced them as he was disgusted by their racial persecutions and pagan nihilism. Adolf Hitler's crushing defeat of France in May/June 1940 elated Wilhelm: "The German flag over Versailles. Thus is the pernicious entente cordiale of Uncle Edward VII brought to nought." But in the end he remained an exile at Doorn, where he died on June 4, 1941, and was buried.

Wilhelm was a tragic example of a ruler who could not accept and live within his limited talents. From the start he desired to be his "own Bismarck," yet he proved weak and vacillating whenever nerves of steel and inner strength were demanded of him. He was intelligent, yet unable to undertake sustained work. He believed in Prussian virtues such as frugality, but spent outrageous sums of money on the court and his yachts. He basically admired England, but sought to challenge it with a superior fleet. He desired to become *"le roi des gueux,"* as Frederick the Great before him, yet in the end became as reactionary as Bismarck. He constantly rattled the saber, yet was unable in the decisive weeks of July 1914 to steer a consistent course. He prided himself on being the last *"roi connetable,"* but for much of the Great War he was sidelined by the "silent dictatorship" of Hindenburg and Ludendorff. In the last analysis, King Edward VII proved accurate in assessing his nephew as "the most brilliant failure in history."

Balfour, *The Kaiser and His Times*; Cowles, *The Kaiser*; Eyck, *Das persönliche Regiment Wilhelms II.*; Ilsemann, *Der Kaiser in Holland*, 2 vols.; Ludwig, *Kaiser Wilhelm II*; Palmer, *The Kaiser*; Wilhelm II, *My Memoirs*; *Biographisches Wörterbuch zur Deutschen Geschichte*, III.

WILSON, Sir Henry Hughes (*Great Britain, Field Marshal*), baronet, was born in Edgeworthstown, county Longford, Ireland, on March 5, 1864. After failing twice to gain admission into Woolwich and three times into Sandhurst, Wilson in 1882 obtained a commission without examination into the Longford Militia. After a brief tour in Burma, he attended the Staff College in 1892/1893, and was promoted captain. In 1899 he took the Third Infantry Brigade to Natal and later served on Lord Roberts' staff until 1901. Wilson was assigned to the War Office in 1903 and four years later as brigadier general became commandant at Camberley. For three years at the Staff College he advocated close ties with France and established friendly relations with Ferdinand Foch (*q.v.*), head of the French École supérieure de guerre. It was also here that Wilson developed the notion that the British army be at the disposal of France in case of war. In 1910 he returned to the War Office as director of military operations and drew up plans for the deployment of a British Expeditionary Force on the left wing of the French army in the event of war with Germany; three years later he was promoted major general. But in the spring of 1914 Wilson became deeply embroiled in the Curragh incident. When British cavalry officers outside Dublin declared that they would rather resign than compel Ulster to accept home rule, Wilson, a Protestant Irishman, supported the mutiny, but, unlike Sir John French (q.v.), chief of the Imperial General Staff, suffered no consequences as a result of this notorious incident.

When Lord H. H. Kitchener (q.v.) became secretary of state for war in August 1914, Wilson receded into the background as he adamantly opposed Kitchener's independent stance for the British Expeditionary Force in France; indeed, Wilson had been so Francophilic that Paris referred to Sir John French's troops as "L'armee 'W'." Wilson accompanied French to the Continent as deputy chief of the General Staff, and as the fighting around Mons increased and as French's chief of staff, Sir Archibald Murray (q.v.), broke down, Wilson virtually directed the British Expeditionary Force. He lost his nerve after Mons, ordering his soldiers to burn their baggage and to retreat at full speed, but the situation was saved by the calm displayed by the two corps commanders, Sir Douglas Haig and H. L. Smith-Dorrien (qq.v.), as well as by Kitchener. And when the French turned the tide at the River Marne on September 6, Wilson grew so optimistic as to predict that the British would enter Germany within four weeks.

In November 1914, it was debated whether Wilson should replace Murray as French's chief of staff, but on January 25, 1915, Sir William Robertson (q.v.) received this assignment. Wilson became chief liaison officer with French headquarters and was promoted lieutenant general. He denounced Kitchener's "ridiculous and preposterous army of twenty-five corps," depicting it as "the laughingstock of every soldier in Europe." Wilson believed fully in the infallibility of French military judgment.

In December 1915, Wilson was given command of the IV Army Corps, but saw little action throughout 1916 as the IV Corps was denuded of troops for the Somme offensive. Wilson was sent to Russia on December 1 as head of a mission to discuss the supply of war materials; he returned, in March 1917, to his old post as liaison officer with the French, but their new commander in chief, General Henri Pétain (q.v.), loathed Wilson and had him sent home. After a period on half pay, Wilson in September was given the Eastern Command. He used this opportunity to cultivate David Lloyd George (q.v.) and after the Italian collapse at Caporetto in October, Wilson quite unofficially accompanied the prime minister to Rapallo on November 7. There, to the dismay of Robertson, then chief of the Imperial General Staff, it was agreed by prior accord to create a Supreme War Council to coordinate the various Allied war strategies; on December 1, 1917, the glib, voluble Wilson assembled his staff at Versailles as British military representative. The fourteenth, and last, note of the Supreme War Council called for the creation of a general reserve of troops for the entire western front; it had been drafted by Wilson, but foundered on the combined opposition of the various Allied commanders, most notably Haig.

On February 18, 1918, Robertson yielded to Wilson as chief of the Imperial General Staff at the express desire of Lloyd George. Almost immediately, the great German Michael offensive in France on March 21 drove the British back and broke their point of contact with the French at Amiens. Wilson departed for France at once and at an Allied conference at Doullens on March 26 agreed to confer overall military command of the combined Allied armies on his old friend General Foch. The tide was turned by July 18, and the Germans accepted an armistice on November 11, 1918. Ironically, Wilson favored a continuation of the war in the belief that it might finally prompt the prime minister to impose conscription upon Ireland.

Wilson drifted away from Lloyd George after the Paris Peace Conference in 1919, opposing British participation in the League of Nations and the British pro-Greek stance in the Mediterranean. At home Wilson clamored for rigorous measures against Ireland. He was created a baronet, promoted field marshal, given the thanks of Parliament, and a grant of £10,000 for his war services. He retired from the army in 1922 as a staunch foe of the Sinn Fein in Ireland and the Bolsheviks in Russia. In February 1922, he was elected Conservative member of Parliament for North Dawn, Ireland, but on June 22 two Sinn Feiners shot down the mutineer of 1914 on his doorstep at Eaton Place, London. He received a public funeral and was buried in St. Paul's Cathedral.

Henry Wilson was not a great captain, much less a great field commander. Instead, his love of intrigue turned him into a politician rather than a soldier. It was said of him during the Great War that "he got into a state of sexual excitement whenever he saw a politician." Wilson's diary, published in 1927, revealed him to have been full of prejudice and mistaken opinions.

Callwell, *Field-Marshal Sir Henry Wilson*, 2 vols.; Collier, *Brasshat*; Guinn, *British Strategy and Politics*; Keegan and Wheatcroft, *Who's Who in Military History*; *Dictionary of National Biography 1922-1930*.

WILSON, Woodrow (*United States, President*), was born in Staunton, Virginia, on December 28, 1856, the son of a Presbyterian minister. Wilson graduated from the College of New Jersey (Princeton) in 1879, studied law at the University of Virginia, entered graduate school at Johns Hopkins University in 1883, and three years later received the Ph.D. degree with a published thesis on *Congressional Government*. He taught at Bryn Mawr College and Wesleyan University before accepting a post at Princeton as professor of jurisprudence and political economy in 1890; in January 1902 Wilson was appointed president of Princeton University.

The Princeton professor was elected governor of New Jersey in November 1910, and in the autumn of 1911 met "Colonel" Edward House (*q.v.*), who viewed Wilson as an eastern reformer with presidential timber. In June 1912, at the Democratic party's convention in Baltimore, Wilson was nominated as the party's presidential nominee on the forty-sixth ballot; he was fairly certain of victory owing to the bitter Roosevelt-Taft split in the Republican party. On November 5, 1912, Wilson was elected to the nation's highest office.

Woodrow Wilson proved to be a cautious, conservative reformer and an anti-imperialist in the White House. On April 8, 1913, he addressed both houses of Congress, a practice that had lapsed since Jefferson disbanded it. Wilson's immediate concern lay in the realm of foreign policy. He refused to recognize the Huerta regime and when the Mexican leader failed to salute the American flag and to make a public apology for having arrested unwarrantedly several sailors under Admiral Mayo's (*q.v.*) command at Tampico, the president on April 21 ordered U.S. forces to seize Veracruz in order to prevent the unloading of German munitions ships. Only the timely intervention of Argentina, Brazil, and Chile presented Wilson with what he termed an exit from a blind alley. But in the spring he was compelled by the guerrilla leader Francisco "Pancho" Villa's raid on Columbus, New Mexico, to send a punitive expedition under General John J. Pershing (*q.v.*), which compounded the already tense situation by clashing with General Carranza's troops in June 1916. With the aid of House and Ambassador Walter H. Page (*q.v.*), Wilson persuaded the British foreign secretary, Sir Edward Grey (*q.v.*), to withdraw support of Huerta.

In the meantime, the war in Europe rested heavily on the president's mind. Wilson's basic posture was one of strict neutrality while favoring the Allies. He discerned two distinct threats: the British methods of maritime search and control and the German declaration of submarine warfare on February 4, 1915, against belligerent as well as neutral ships in a war zone around the British Isles. This German action tipped the scales against them in Washington. On February 10 the president warned Berlin that destruction of American vessels would constitute "an indefensible violation of neutral rights" and that the United States would hold Germany "to a strict accountability for such acts." After the torpedoing of the *Lusitania* (May) and *Arabic* (August), the German Ambassador Count Bernstorff (*q.v.*) agreed that "liners" would no longer be destroyed; when the *Sussex* was torpedoed in the spring of 1916, Berlin canceled unrestricted submarine warfare after a sharp protest note in which Wilson threatened to sever diplomatic relations with the Reich.

The president won a close reelection in the fall of 1916 over Charles E. Hughes primarily owing to the western vote ("He has kept us out of the war"). In fact, Wilson had tried already in 1915 through "Colonel" House to enforce mediation of the European war with a threat that he would join the side that refused mediation; this heavy-handed ploy failed when the British government refused to act on it. In December 1916, Wilson publicly suggested "an interchange of views" among the belligerents, but again the Allies ignored his pleas. As late as January 4, 1917, the president assured his countrymen: "There will be no war . . . it would be a crime against civilization for us to go in." Eighteen days later he presented the Senate with his famous formula for "a peace without victory." But it was all in vain. On January 9, 1917, German leaders opted to resume unrestricted submarine warfare; when Ambassador Gerard (*q.v.*) was informed of this decision on January 31, Wilson replied by handing Ambassador Bernstorff his passports. Berlin exacerbated this charged atmosphere when Foreign Secretary Arthur Zimmermann (*q.v.*) cabled an offer to Mexico, suggesting a German-Mexican-Japanese alliance alluding to a Mexican reconquest of Texas, New Mexico, and Arizona. Then when four American ships were destroyed by German U-boats on March 22, the president decided to go to war owing to these "actual overt acts." On April 2, 1917, he asked Congress for a declaration of war against Germany; he received his wish four days later.

Wilson's basic diplomatic posture was to render all possible succor to the Allies to assure the military and naval defeat of the Central Powers while avoiding diplomatic entanglements that could lessen his ability to influence the postwar peace settlement. He expressed the feeling to House that "England and France have not the same views with regard to peace that we have by any means," but he felt that the United States would persevere at the peace table because by then the Allies would be "financially in our hands." In the end, the United States preferred to enter the war as an "Associated" rather than as an "Allied" power.

Wilson gave the nation the feeling that this was a people's war. He instituted the army draft, supervised and controlled production through a War Industries Board, inaugurated food and fuel controls, and established a national administration of the railroads. At home, the president gave full backing to Secretary of War Newton D. Baker (q.v.), while overseas he granted General Pershing a free hand to develop the American Expeditionary Forces as the field commander saw fit. Pershing was asked simply to coordinate his war efforts with those of the Entente without thereby surrendering U.S. independence. In November 1917, a U.S. war mission to Europe established a Supreme War Council designed to streamline the war efforts of the Allied and Associated Powers. On January 8, 1918, Wilson, in an effort to counter the Bolshevik peace drive and to strengthen the morale of the Allies, rendered his famous Fourteen Points speech to Congress. The six general points called for open diplomacy, freedom of the seas, removal of trade barriers, reduction of armaments, impartial adjustments of colonial claims, and a League of Nations. On October 23, 1918, the German government of Prince Max von Baden (q.v.) turned to Wilson for an armistice based upon the Fourteen Points; the president accepted the German bid on November 5, and six days later the war ended. French Premier Clemenceau's (q.v.) boast that he had never read the Fourteen Points did not bode well for the postwar peace deliberations.

Most historians agree that Wilson made three major mistakes in the peace settlement. He closely identified himself with the Democrats up for reelection in November 1918, and the subsequent Republican gains at the polls caused him to lose face abroad. The president stubbornly refused to take to Europe either leaders of the Senate or of the Republican party. Finally, by coming in person to Paris he lost the Olympian stature of the past two years. Yet by sheer force Wilson managed by February 1919 to cajole the Paris Conference to accept the Covenant of the League of Nations. In April 1919, however, he suffered a severe setback when the Japanese departed from Paris owing to Wilson's refusal to give them a free hand in Shantung Province in China. An ill-advised appeal to the Italian people over the head of Prime Minister Orlando (q.v.) in behalf of the Fourteen Points greatly strained relations with that country. In the end, the secret treaties negotiated by the Allies in 1915 and 1916 simply could not be squared with Wilsonian idealism.

At home, suffering from paralysis, the president refused any and all conciliatory gestures emanating from the Senate, and especially from the chairman of the foreign relations committee, Senator Henry Cabot Lodge (q.v.). Not even a nationwide tour in September 1919 rallied support to the president; in March 1920, the Senate rejected by seven votes the Versailles Treaty, which incorporated the League of Nations as well as a treaty with France. A deeply disappointed Woodrow Wilson died on February 3, 1924, in Washington, D.C.

Baker, *Woodrow Wilson: Life and Letters*, VII, VIII; DeWeerd, *President Wilson Fights His War*; Livermore, *Politics Is Adjourned*; Trask, *Captains & Cabinets*; *Dictionary of American Biography*, XX.

WOYRSCH, Remus von (*Germany, Field Marshal*), was born in Pilsnitz near Breslau on February 4, 1847, into a Protestant family that in the seventeenth century had moved from Bohemia to Silesia; his mother was the wealthy daughter of the industrialist Websky. Woyrsch entered the army in 1860, fought in the wars of 1866 and 1870/1871, and then transferred to the General Staff; he was promoted colonel in 1896, major general and brigade commander the following year, and lieutenant general in 1901 as chief of the Twelfth Division at Neisse. Woyrsch headed the VI Army Corps at Breslau in 1903/1904, was promoted general of infantry in 1905, and retired six years later at the age of sixty-four.

Reactivated on August 1, 1914, as commander of his native Silesian Landwehr Corps, Woyrsch was ordered to advance against Ivangorod. Early in September the Austro-Hungarian army was heavily engaged at Krasnik and Woyrsch's troops were thrown in to turn an apparent defeat into a modest victory. The Silesians were thereafter deployed as part of the Austro-Hungarian army near Tarnavka against the Moscow Grenadier Corps; after a severe defeat of the alliance partner on September 9, Woyrsch's forces covered the Austrian retreat near Tarnów, losing 8,000 men but saving the Austro-Hungarian First Army from certain annihilation. Only a hastily planned German offensive by the new commanders in the east, Generals Paul von Hindenburg and Erich Ludendorff (qq.v.), drove the Russians behind the Vistula and saved Silesia from occupation.

Woyrsch then returned to German command and from October 1914 until the end of 1917 commanded Army Section Woyrsch in the east. Specifically, early in November 1914 he halted the Russians once again near the Silesian borders at Czentochau; Woyrsch managed to tie down the enemy long enough for Ludendorff to cave in the Russian flank at Thorn. Woyrsch's units, which then included the Austro-Hungarian Second Army, participated in the final victory at Thorn. Woyrsch was rewarded with the coveted *Pour le mérite* and promoted colonel general.

In May 1915, General August von Mackensen's (*q.v.*) Eleventh Army broke through the Russian line at Gorlice-Tarnów, ushering in a series of German offensives all along the eastern front. Woyrsch's units on June 17 defeated the enemy at Sienno, took Ivangorod on July 21/22, and thereafter crossed both the Vistula and Bug rivers; in one month, Woyrsch advanced over 400 kilometers as far as Baranovichi, which in June and July he held against repeated Russian attempts to recapture the city. On August 29, 1916, this capable Silesian officer was entrusted with command of Army Group Woyrsch in southern Poland; the unit was disbanded on December 31, 1917, following the collapse of the Russian front. By then over seventy years of age, Woyrsch requested retirement and was promoted field marshal for his steadfast efforts in the east. After the war Woyrsch assumed command of the southern wing of the German border guards in the east and died at Pilsnitz near Breslau on August 6, 1920.

Clemenz, *Woyrsch*; *Biographisches Wörterbuch zur Deutschen Geschichte*, III; *Geschichte der Ritter des Ordens*, II.

YANUSHKEVICH, Nikolai Nikolaevich (*Russia, General of Infantry*), was born in May 1868. He graduated from the Mikhailovsky Artillery School in 1888 and completed the General Staff Academy in 1896. Most of his service for the next decade and a half took place in the bureaucracy of the Ministry of War. He became a professor of military administration at the General Staff Academy in 1910, left for duty with the ministry of war briefly, then returned to command the General Staff Academy in 1913. Early in 1914, promoted general of infantry, Yanushkevich was appointed chief of staff of the Russian army.

The appointment occasioned surprise within Russian military circles as well as among foreign observers. The new chief of staff was only forty-six years old, he had seen no field service, and much of his work in the Ministry of War had concerned only questions of military supply. Nothing in his activities had indicated exceptional military talent. To most observers, his rapid rise was a credit to his adroitness as a courtier and owed much to the patronage of Grand Duke Nikolai Nikolaevich and Tsar Nicholas II (*qq.v.*).

As chief of staff Yanushkevich played a significant role in the crisis of July 1914. Along with Minister of War Sukhomlinov (*q.v.*), he was an early advocate of general Russian military mobilization. On July 28, after the announcement of Austria's declaration of war on Serbia, Yanushkevich urged Foreign Minister Sazonov (*q.v.*) to persuade the tsar to declare general mobilization. That evening Yanushkevich, on his own authority, ordered general mobilization to begin on July 30. He presumably expected the tsar to be won over to such a move within two days. The tsar wavered on July 29, then reluctantly accepted Yanushkevich's proposals the following day.

With the outbreak of war, Yanushkevich became chief of staff to the new supreme commander, Grand Duke Nikolai Nikolaevich. The inexperienced chief of staff, facing a role patently beyond his talents, left military matters to subordinates like General Yury Danilov (*q.v.*), the chief of operations, and concentrated on the civil administration of the vast geographic area placed under the army's wartime jurisdiction. Russia's initial military defeats prevented him from implementing his plan to deport all able-bodied German males from East Prussia to the Russian interior. Other groups were not so lucky. Yanushkevich led the effort to purge Russian territory of what he saw as unreliable elements. The tsar's Jewish subjects in large areas near the fighting front suffered systematic harassment and mass deportation. Yanushkevich summarily rejected criticism of the course voiced by the tsar's council of ministers.

During the retreat from Poland following the German breakthrough at Gorlice (May 1915), Yanushkevich directed a massive scorched-earth policy. The routine destruction of homes, crops, and industrial resources led at once to mass popular migrations eastward. Yanushkevich's refugee policies unquestionably served to alienate large segments of the population from the army and the regime. Moreover, the influx of refugees placed heavy burdens on the urban centers of Russia where many of the displaced had to settle.

Yanushkevich was relieved as chief of staff in August 1915, and followed Grand Duke Nikolai Nikolaevich to obscurity in the Caucasus for the rest of the war. Yanushkevich retired from the army following the March Revolution in 1917, and he was killed in the Caucasus in unknown circumstances sometime the following year.

Albertini, *Origins of the War of 1914*, II; Graf, "Military Rule Behind the Russian Front, 1914-1917"; Gurko, *Features and Figures of the Past*; Rutherford, *The Russian Army in World War I*; Stone, *The Eastern Front*; Turner,

"The Russian Mobilization in 1914"; *Sovetskaia istoricheskaia entsiklopediia*, XVI.

YUDENICH, Nikolai Nikolaevich (*Russia, General of Infantry*), was born July 30, 1862, into a family of hereditary noblemen in Minsk Province. He graduated from the Aleksandrovsky Military College in 1881; his first assignment was to the elite Litovsky Guards Regiment in Poland. After completing the General Staff Academy with honors in 1887, Yudenich filled a series of staff assignments in Poland and Turkestan, 1887-1904. During the Russo-Japanese War, then a colonel, he distinguished himself as a combat leader, fighting at the head of a regiment, then a brigade, of infantry. His coolness under fire and, in particular, his initiative in the fighting at Sandep and Mukden, marked him off from most of his contemporaries.

Rewarded by promotion to major general, Yudenich began a tour in the Caucasus that lasted from 1907 throughout most of World War I. Deputy chief of staff of the Caucasus Army in 1907, he was promoted lieutenant general and made chief of staff in 1912. He was serving in that capacity when war broke out between Russia and Turkey in early November 1914. Isolated from the large-scale fighting against the Central Powers, the Caucasus front was drained of its best units and relegated to a defensive posture. The entire front was endangered in December when a flanking maneuver by the Turkish Third Army reached Sarikamish; large portions of the Caucasus Army were isolated from their base at Tbilisi.

Yudenich became the man of the hour. He resisted the efforts of the commander of the Caucasus Army, General Myshlaevsky, to order a precipitate general retreat, successfully defended Sarikamish, and administered a stinging defeat to the Turkish Third Army. Yudenich, then elevated to general of infantry, took official command of the Caucasus Army in January 1915. Unflappable, innovative, and daring, he transformed his subordinate and distant front into a source of continual good news and made himself a popular hero. In July/August 1915, the IV Caucasian Corps on the Russian left was defeated west of Lake Van and driven into headlong retreat northward across the Plain of Eleskirt. Contrary to the customary practice of the Russian army, Yudenich refused to reinforce these broken units. Instead he secretly formed a strategic reserve, held it back for the opportune moment, then crushed the advancing Turks with a flank attack.

The defeat of Serbia in October 1915 and the impending Allied withdrawal from Gallipoli threatened to confront Yudenich with powerful, well-equipped Turkish reinforcements. He blocked this danger by a series of spoiling operations in 1916: the Caucasus Army struck at Erzurum (January/February), Trebizond (April), and Erzincan (July). The fall of Erzurum, allegedly an impregnable stronghold, brought Yudenich lasting popular and professional esteem. Nonetheless, his main goal was to weaken and disconcert his opponents, not to seize Turkish territory.

In March 1917, Yudenich replaced Grand Duke Nikolai Nikolaevich (*q.v.*) as supreme civil and military commander in the Caucasus. Yudenich himself was soon relieved by the provisional government and recalled to Petrograd. There he resided until the November Revolution caused him to go into hiding. He left for Finland in November 1918 to join the anti-Bolshevik White movement. The hero of the Caucasus participated in the Russian Civil War in 1919 as commander of the northwestern front. His miniscule White force reached the suburbs of Petrograd in October 1919 before being compelled to retreat to Estonia in the face of the enemy's massive numerical superiority.

Yudenich went into exile in France in 1920. He died in Nice, October 5, 1933. Two years before his death, the fiftieth anniversary of his graduation from the Aleksandrovsky Military College occasioned celebrations in Russian émigré communities from Shanghai to Paris: Yudenich was hailed as the only undefeated Russian general of World War I.

Allen and Muratoff, *Caucasian Battlefields*; Maslovskii, "General Nikolai Nikolaevich IUdenich"; Rutherford, *The Russian Army in World War I*; *General-ot-infanterii N. N. IUdenich k 50-letnemu iubileiu*; *Sovetskaia istoricheskaia entsiklopediia*, XVI.

ZAIONCHKOVSKY, Andrei Medardovich (*Russia, General of Infantry*), was born on December 20, 1862, to a Russian noble family in the province of Orel. He completed the Nikolaevsky Engineering School in 1883 and, five years later, graduated from the General Staff Academy. Zaionchkovsky saw combat in the Russo-Japanese War in command of a regiment, then a brigade, of infantry. In 1912 he was promoted to the command of the Thirty-seventh Infantry Division. It was in this role that he entered World War I. By early 1915 he led a corps.

The Rumanian campaign of 1916 brought Zaionchkovsky into the limelight. Russian military leaders like General Mikhail Alekseev (*q.v.*), the chief of staff, had long considered it useless, and perhaps dangerous, to draw Rumania into the war. The Balkan nation's weak army and indefensible strategic situation made it inevitable that it would draw away Russian resources. Alekseev was determined to avoid this, and all the more so in the summer of 1916, when Russia was conducting a promising offensive under General Brusilov (q.v.) north of the Carpathians.

French cajoling brought Rumania into the war in August 1916. Alekseev grudgingly gave his new ally a token force of three divisions. These were to occupy the border province of Dobrudja; it was hoped their presence might deter Bulgaria, Rumania's unfriendly southern neighbor, from declaring war on it. Zaionchkovsky received the thankless task of commanding this so-called Dobrudja Detachment.

The situation seemed to Zaionchkovsky to promise disaster. His force was too small to be effective. The Bulgarians might hesitate to make war on Russia, which many Bulgarians saw as a traditional friend; but Zaionchkovsky's scratch force included a Serbian division, and the Bulgarians and the Serbs were historic antagonists. After voicing these concerns to Alekseev, Zaionchkovsky heard himself called a coward and received orders to get on with his assignment.

Calamity struck soon after Zaionchkovsky reached the Dobrudja. Bulgaria declared war on Rumania in early September. A motley force of German, Bulgarian, Austrian, and Turkish troops under Field Marshal von Mackensen (q.v.) invaded the Dobrudja at once. Zaionchkovsky found his Rumanian allies prone to leave his flanks open at moments of maximum danger. The Rumanian authorities, in turn, saw their Russian comrades in arms all too willing to ravage the countryside in their spare moments. Despite Mackensen's numerical disadvantage, Zaionchkovsky found himself pushed out of the important port of Constanza by late October. Meanwhile, the German Ninth Army under General von Falkenhayn (q.v.) was sweeping into Rumania from the west. As the Russo-Rumanian alliance buckled under the strain of repeated military failures, Zaionchkovsky was relieved. All the same, Alekseev found himself drawn deeper into the quagmire. By year's end, thirty-six Russian divisions had been dispatched to help the Rumanians hold at least the corner of their country bordering on Russia.

Zaionchkovsky survived the debacle. On his return to Russia, he received command of the XVIII Corps. In 1917 he was promoted general of infantry; then, in the wake of the March Revolution, he was pensioned off. A final chapter in Zaionchkovsky's military career began in 1918, however, when he joined the Red Army. He served as chief of staff for the Thirteenth Army against the White forces led by General Denikin. At the conclusion of the Civil War,

he immersed himself in military history. He had written widely on the subject even before 1914; he was then given the task of leading the Red Army commission studying the lessons of World War I. He himself wrote prolifically on the subject, while teaching at the Red Army Military Academy. His works on the war in which he had played such an uncomfortable role in 1916 are still considered valuable contributions to historical scholarship. Zaionchkovsky died in Moscow, March 22, 1926.

Knox, *With the Russian Army*, 2 vols.; Rostunov, ed., *Istoriia pervoi mirovoi voiny*, II; Rutherford, *The Russian Army in World War I*; Stone, *The Eastern Front*; Zaionchkovskii, *Mirovaia voina*; *Sovetskaia istoricheskaia entsiklopediia*, V; *Sovetskaia voennaia entsiklopediia*, III.

ZECKOFF, Nicholas (1864-1946). See ZHEKOV, Nikola Todorov.

ZHEKOV, Nikola Todorov (*Bulgaria, General*), was born in Sliven, a town in eastern Bulgaria, December 25, 1864. A cobbler's apprentice in his youth, Zhekov graduated from the Military Academy in Sofia and first saw combat in the 1885 war against Serbia. He went to Italy for advanced study, returning to Bulgaria to command a regiment and then a division. During the Balkan Wars of 1912/1913, Zhekov was chief of staff of the Second Army.

World War I brought Zhekov to the top of his country's military ladder. He first served as war minister in the Cabinet of Vasil Radoslavov (q.v.), August-October 1915. His chief responsibility was to ready the Bulgarian army for combat as Radoslavov hardened Sofia's ties to Berlin and Vienna and prepared to enter the conflict. When war came on October 11, Zhekov took direct command of the army.

Zhekov's forces helped shatter Serbia's defense in late 1915, but his important First Army campaigned under direct German control in the person of Field Marshal von Mackensen (q.v.). The Serbian operations set an uncomfortable wartime pattern for Zhekov and his forces. Not only were substantial numbers of Bulgarian troops incorporated into Army Group Mackensen, Zhekov's concerns about Anglo-French landings in Salonika were curtly brushed aside. His call for an offensive to crush the Allied base in eastern Greece before it became a dangerous threat was vetoed by the German High Command. Bulgarian forces were left to hold most of the long Macedonian front with only minimal aid from their allies. The Bulgarians conducted a skillful offensive in August/September 1916; the defensive line was shortened and the Bulgarians took the Aegean port of

Kavalla. But Zhekov also saw more of his forces abruptly detached. Once again they went to Mackensen, this time to bolster the Central Powers' offensive against Rumania in the fall of 1916.

Zhekov's conflict with the Bulgarian government over its inability to keep the Macedonian armies supplied became an open secret. So much so that opposition leaders approached the general in the fall of 1917 for aid in ousting Radoslavov and pulling Bulgaria out of the war. The move apparently struck Zhekov as premature. He betrayed the plotters to the government. But by the spring of 1918, alarmed by the internal disintegration of the army, Zhekov joined in a new effort to oust Radoslavov. The Germanophile premier fell in June, but by then the military balance in the southern Balkans had tipped perilously in favor of Bulgaria's enemies. Only Zhekov's departure for medical treatment in Germany saved him from direct responsibility for the ensuing disaster. Even so, historians have criticized him for faulty defensive positions in Macedonia during the final phase of the war. The decline of the army and unrest on the home front, however, left no one any room for optimism. Allied forces under Franchet d'Esperey (q.v.) burst through the Bulgarian lines at Dobro Pole in mid-September. With its fighting front broken and its army moving toward mutiny, the Sofia government hastened to conclude an armistice.

Zhekov lived in exile in the immediate postwar years. In 1923 he returned to Bulgaria to defend his wartime career. Sentenced to a long prison term, he was given amnesty after three years.

The last years of his life were devoted to quasi-Fascist politics. He led one of several ardently pro-German groups in Bulgaria before and during World War II. Zhekov hoped to come to power with the assistance of Hitler, and Berlin encouraged him with generous treatment. Zhekov was invited to tour France in 1940 to inspect the scenes of Wehrmacht victories; he also received a German pension. But the Germans refused to support Zhekov's dreams of forming his own government. The old soldier left Bulgaria at the close of World War II and died in Füssen, Germany, October 6, 1949.

Bell, *Peasants in Power*; Germany: Reichsarchiv, *Der Weltkrieg*, IX, X, XI, XII; Logio, *Bulgaria: Past and Present*; Nédeff, *Les Opérations en Macedoine*; Palmer, *Gardeners of Salonika*; Stoichev, *Builders and Military Leaders of the Bulgarian Army* (through the courtesy of Professor Frederick B. Chary); *Bulgarska Entsiklopediia*.

ZHILINSKY, Yakov Grigorevich (*Russia, General*), was born in the city of Mikhailov, Riazan Province, on March 27, 1853. He was commissioned upon completion of the Nikolaevsky Cavalry School in 1876. Zhilinsky graduated from the General Staff Academy in 1883 and served in a series of increasingly responsible staff positions over the next two decades. In 1898, in the rank of colonel, he was dispatched to Cuba as a military observer with the Spanish army during the Spanish-American War. The following year he became a member of the Russian delegation to the Hague Peace Conference.

Zhilinsky was promoted to the rank of major general in 1900, and he served as chief of the field staff in the Far East during the first half of the Russo-Japanese War. He rose rapidly in the years following: commander of a cavalry division 1906/1907; commander of the Tenth Army 1907-1910; promotion to the rank of general of cavalry in 1910. He held the post of chief of staff of the Russian army in the years 1911-1913. In this capacity he represented Russia in a three-year series of conferences with the French High Command to work out the specifics of Franco-Russian military cooperation against Germany in the event of war. Zhilinsky committed Russia to deploy 800,000 troops along the German frontier; the Russian forces would undertake offensive operations by the fifteenth day of mobilization. The French, who anticipated a German invasion of their country to follow on the heels of a declaration of hostility, were then assured Germany would face an early invasion as well. Zhilinsky pledged that Russian armies would invade East Prussia or strike across the Vistula near Thorn.

The outbreak of war made Zhilinsky executor of his own pledges. As commander of the Warsaw Military District in 1914, he assumed, according to the Russian war plan, command of the northwestern front. His mission in August 1914 was to coordinate the invasion of East Prussia. The Russian First Army attacked from the east under the command of General Rennenkampf (q.v.). The Second Army under General Samsonov (q.v.) advanced from the south. The two armies were separated by several days' hard marching and by the geographical barrier of the Masurian Lakes. In effect, Zhilinsky served as the main link between the Russian government, pressed by the French for a rapid offensive at any cost, and the scattered armies in the field against Germany.

Zhilinsky's leadership, a model of ineptitude, has received universal and well-deserved condemnation. He misinterpreted Rennenkampf's victory at Gumbinnen on August 20 to mean that the German Eighth Army was in full flight westward toward the Vistula. He bombarded Samsonov to advance northward at maximum speed to cut off the supposedly routed

Germans. Zhilinsky completed Samsonov's perilous isolation by permitting Rennenkampf to conduct a leisurely advance and to divert much of the First Army northwestward toward the fortress of Königsberg. The result was a Russian disaster: the Germans concentrated against Samsonov, smashed his Second Army, then turned on Rennenkampf.

Zhilinsky was relieved of his command in September 1914. Only in late 1915 did he receive a new position: senior Russian representative to the French High Command. The unsuccessful field commander became an unsuccessful military diplomat. His year in France was a stormy one, marked by poor relations with the French commander in chief, General Joffre (q.v.). Joffre accused Zhilinsky, who did not visit the front, of distorting the reports of more serious Russian observers with the French army. The French also criticized Zhilinsky for misrepresenting his personal views as official Russian policy. He was replaced at Joffre's request and returned to Russia at the close of 1916. Zhilinsky retired following the March 1917 Revolution. He joined the Whites in the aftermath of the November Revolution and died in southern Russia sometime in 1918.

Joffre, *Personal Memoirs*, I; Rutherford, *The Russian Army in World War I*; Stone, *The Eastern Front*; Strokov, *Vooruzhennye sily i voennoe iskusstvo v pervoi mirovoi voine*; Williamson, *The Politics of Grand Strategy*; *Sovetskaia istoricheskaia entsiklopediia*, V; *Sovetskaia voennaia entsiklopediia*, III; *Voennaia entsiklopediia*, X.

ZIMMERMANN, Arthur (*Germany, Foreign Secretary*), was born in Marggrobowa in East Prussia on October 5, 1864, the son of a middle-class merchant. Zimmermann studied law at Königsberg and Leipzig and in 1893 joined the consular service as a legal clerk. He served at Shanghai, Canton, and Tientsin before returning to the Foreign Office in 1902 as legation counselor. Five years later he was promoted privy councillor; in 1910 he became department director and in 1911 undersecretary at the Wilhelmstrasse. He was essentially an "unobtrusive administrative functionary" rather than a policy maker. It was widely rumored that he was considered for the top post in January 1913, but the job went instead to the colorless Gottlieb von Jagow (q.v.), perhaps because of Zimmermann's health, his inadequacy in foreign languages, and his nonnoble origins. A stout, ruddy, earthy bachelor, Zimmermann personified middle-class respectability and diligence.

On November 25, 1916, Zimmermann became the first commoner to be state secretary of the Foreign Office in Germany; he was also the first diplomat from the consular service to reach this lofty position. His appointment came about largely because he was known to favor unrestricted submarine warfare, then demanded by Admiral Henning von Holtzendorff, Field Marshal Paul von Hindenburg, and General Erich Ludendorff (qq.v.), among others. Jagow called his successor a "fanatical U-boat warrior" who could always "swim with the stream and with those who shouted loudest." On January 9, 1917, at a crown council in Pless, Germany's military and political leaders gambled the future on the U-boat card. Zimmermann thereafter began to prepare for the expected entry of the United States into the war. Apart from a quixotic plan to incite German-Americans to join Irish-Americans against President Woodrow Wilson (q.v.), the foreign secretary toyed with a possible Japanese-Mexican combination against the United States.

On January 16, 1917, Zimmermann cabled Ambassador von Bernstorff (q.v.) of the decision to resume unrestricted submarine warfare on February 1, and he added the following tantalizing item to be passed on to the Reich's envoy in Mexico: "We make Mexico a proposal of alliance on the following basis: make war together, make peace together, generous financial support, and an understanding on our part that Mexico is to reconquer the lost territory in Texas, New Mexico, and Arizona." Japan was invited to join the alliance. The telegram, as well as several subsequent cables to Bernstorff, was sent via the Scandinavian submarine cable to America and intercepted both by the U.S. State Department and the British Admiralty; on February 24 it was handed to President Wilson in decoded form, and on March 1 it broke in the newspapers. For reasons still unknown, Zimmermann confirmed the authenticity of the wire forty-eight hours later. He successfully defended his action in the Reichstag on March 29, claiming ignorance of how the Americans had intercepted the dispatch; on April 6 Washington declared war against Berlin.

Thereafter, Zimmermann disappeared from the stage of world politics. He resigned as foreign secretary on August 5, 1917, and died in Berlin on June 7, 1940. His telegraphic blunder unquestionably helped to bring the United States into the war as it convinced many American noninterventionists of Germany's continued territorial aspirations in the Western Hemisphere.

Cecil, *German Diplomatic Service*; Kahn, *Codebreakers*; Tuchman, *Zimmermann Telegram*; *Biographisches Wörterbuch zur Deutschen Geschichte*, III.

APPENDIXES

I

CHRONOLOGY
OF EVENTS

1914

June	28	Assassination of Archduke Francis Ferdinand at Sarajevo
July	6	Germany issues "blank check" to Austria-Hungary
	23	Austro-Hungarian ultimatum to Serbia; all points but one accepted by Serbia on July 25
	28	Austria-Hungary declares war on Serbia

August	1	Germany declares war on Russia
	2	Italy announces its neutrality
	3	Germany declares war on France
	4	Germany declares war on Belgium
		Britain declares war on Germany
	6	Austria-Hungary declares war on Russia
		Serbia declares war on Germany
	7	Montenegro declares war on Austria-Hungary
	10	German cruisers *Goeben* and *Breslau* enter Dardanelles
	11	Montenegro declares war on Germany
	13	France declares war on Austria-Hungary
		Britain declares war on Austria-Hungary
	15–17	British Expeditionary Force (BEF) shuttled to France
	17–21	Serbs under Putnik defeat Austro-Hungarians at Jadar
	19/20	Battle of Gumbinnen: Rennenkampf defeats Prittwitz in East Prussia
	20	Germans capture Brussels
		French defeated at Morhange-Sarrebourg in Lorraine
	23	Germany and Japan in state of war
	23–25	Austrian victory at Krasnik by Army Group Dankl
	25	Austria-Hungary and Japan at war
		Moltke transfers four divisions from west to east

	26	BEF retreats after battle of Le Cateau
	26–29	Russian Second Army annihilated at Tannenberg
	27	Austria-Hungary declares war on Belgium
	28	German cruisers *Ariadne*, *Köln*, and *Mainz* lost off Helgoland
	29/30	Austrian advance to Komarów; Russian counterattack drives Austrians beyond Lemberg

September	6–11	Battle of the Marne
	9–11	Russian Niemen Army defeated at the Masurian Lakes
	11	Austrians driven back almost to Cracow
	15	Australians seize New Guinea, Bismarck Archipelago
	22	British cruisers *Aboukir*, *Cressy*, *Hogue* sunk by U-9

October	10	Germans seize Antwerp
	14	Battle of Flanders; "race to the sea" begins
	29	Fisher replaces Marquis of Milford Haven as first sea lord in Britain

November	1	Graf Spee defeats Cradock at Coronel
	3	Montenegro declares war on Turkey
	5	Britain declares war on Turkey
	6	France declares war on Turkey
	7	Japanese storm Tsingtao (Kiaochow) in China
	11	Battle of Ypres; German drive to the sea halted; German offensive against Lodz in the east
	14	Turkey declares holy war against Entente

| December | 3–6 | Serbs defeat Austrians at battle of Kolubara |
| | 8 | Sturdee defeats Spee at the Falkland Islands |

	16	German fleet raid on Scarborough and Hartlepool
	29	Russians smash Turkish offensive at Sarikamish (to January 2, 1915)

1915

January	18	Japan presents Twenty-one Demands to China
	24	Battle of Dogger Bank; Germans lose cruiser *Blücher*; Pohl replaces Ingenohl as German fleet chief
February	1	Germany announces submarine warfare at Pless
	7–15	Winter battle of the Masurian Lakes; Russians defeated at Augustov forest
	16	Winter battle in the Champagne (to March 10)
	17	Germany declares "war zone" around British Isles
	19	Anglo-French naval bombardment of Dardanelles begins
March	10–14	British First Army under Haig launches battle of Neuve Chapelle
	18	Second bombardment of Dardanelles
	22	Austrian fortress Przemysl capitulates
	29	General Liman von Sanders appointed commander of Turko-German forces at Dardanelles
April	22	Second Battle of Ypres (to May 25); first use of chlorine gas by Germans
	25–29	Anglo-French troops landed at Gallipoli
May	2	Mackensen offensive at Gorlice-Tarnów (to June 22)
	7	Liner *Lusitania* torpedoed by Germans
	9	Allied offensive in Artois (to July 23)
	12	South Slav Committee established in London; First Manifesto issued to British
	14	Cabinet crisis in London leads to resignations of Fisher and Churchill
	23/24	Italy declares war on Austria-Hungary, its former ally
	27	Turks begin deportation of Armenians
June	3	Mackensen recaptures Przemysl
	15	Asquith creates coalition government in London
	22	Central Powers retake Lemberg
	29	Italy launches first of twelve battles along the Isonzo River (to July 5)
July	13	German offensive into Courland and Poland

August	5	Germans occupy Warsaw
	6/7	Allied troops land at Suvla Bay and Gaba Tepe
	18	Progressive Bloc formed by majority of Deputies in Russian Duma
	19	Liner *Arabic* sunk off Ireland Germans storm fortress Novo-Georgievsk
	21	Italy declares war against Turkey
	25/26	Mackensen captures Brest-Litovsk
	27	German–Austro-Hungarian offensive in Galicia
September	4–5	Nicholas II replaces Grand Duke Nikolai as army and navy commander in Russia; General Alekseev promoted chief of staff
	8	International Socialist Peace Conference at Zimmerwald, Switzerland
	9	Ludendorff launches offensive against Dvinsk, Vilna
	15	Germans capture Pinsk
	18	Germany halts submarine offensive after *Sussex* incident
	22	General Joffre begins fall battle in the Champagne (to November 3)
	25	Anglo-French campaign in Artois (to October 13); Battle of Loos against Crown Prince Rupprecht
	29	British forces enter Kut el Amara in Mesopotamia
October	5	Anglo-French forces land at Salonika under General Sarrail; Venizelos Cabinet falls in Greece
	6	German-Austro-Hungarian forces under Mackensen cross Danube and Drina into Serbia
	8/9	Central Powers capture Belgrade
	11	War between Bulgaria and Serbia
	29	Premier Viviani replaced by Briand in France
November	27	Serbia occupied by Mackensen Austro-Hungarian naval raid on Durazzo
December	3	General Joffre appointed commander of French forces
	8	Kut el Amara invested by Turkish armies
	9/10	United States expels German attachés Papen, Boy-Ed
	15	Haig replaces French as British commander in France
	18/19	Anglo-French troops evacuated at Gaba Tepe, Suvla Bay

1916

January	8	Austro-Hungarian offensive against Montenegro
	8–9	Allied troops evacuated from Cape Helles
	11	French occupy Corfu as base for Serbian army
	16	Montenegro capitulates to Central Powers (signed January 25)
	24	Scheer replaces Pohl as German fleet chief
February	13	Allies agree to restore Belgium after the war
	21	German offensive at Verdun (to September 9)
	22	British Ministry of Blockade created
	23	Germans resume submarine warfare (to April 20)
	28	German Cameroons capitulate in Africa
	29	First "blacklist" drawn up in London
March	2	Germany resumes submarine warfare (to March 4)
	9	Germany declares war on Portugal
	10	Tirpitz resigns over submarine policy; replaced by Capelle on 15th
	14	War Minister Gallieni resigns in France
April	23	Easter Rebellion in Dublin, Ireland
	24	German fleet raid on Yarmouth, Lowestoft
	29	General Townshend surrenders at Kut el Amara
May	10	*Strafexpedition*: Austro-Hungarian offensive in Trentino against Italy (to July 9)
	17	House of Commons in London passes conscription bill
	22	Germany creates War Food Office; Delbrück replaced by Helfferich as interior secretary
	31	Naval battle at Jutland, or Skagerrak (to June 1)
June	4	General Brusilov offensive in Volhynia against Austria; Luck seized and Bukovina occupied
	5/6	*Hampshire* mined off Orkneys; Kitchener lost at sea
	6/7	Germans storm Fort Vaux at Verdun
	10	Salandra falls in Italy; replaced by Boselli coalition government
	17	Russians capture Czernowitz and storm Carpathian slopes
	24	British artillery battle at Somme commences
July	1	British Fourth Army opens Somme offensive (to November 26)
	7	France and Britain renounce Declaration of London 1909
	28	Hindenburg appointed German supreme commander, east
August	26	Italy declares war against Germany
	27	Rumania declares war against Austria-Hungary
	28	Germany declares war against Rumania
	29	General von Falkenhayn replaced as German chief of staff by team of Hindenburg and Ludendorff
	30	Turkey declares war against Rumania
	31	Germany cancels submarine warfare
September	1	Bulgaria declares war against Rumania
	2	German-Bulgarian units under Mackensen cross Danube River at Turtucaia and invade Dobrudja in Rumania
	6	Central Powers create a united supreme command
	15	First use of tanks by British at the Somme
	18	Greek Army IV Corps voluntarily surrenders Kavalla to Bulgars
	26–29	Falkenhayn seizes Hermannstadt in Rumania
	29	Venizelos establishes provisional government in Crete; moves to Salonika on October 9
October	15	Germany resumes U-war according to "prize" (search and destroy) rules
	21	Austrian Minister-President Stürgkh murdered; replaced by Körber on 31st
	24	Mangin's Corps retakes Fort Douaumont at Verdun
	29	Australia refuses to pass conscription bill
November	1	Ninth Isonzo battle resumes Germans evacuate Fort Vaux at Verdun
	3	General Groener establishes German War Office
	5	Germany announces creation of a Polish kingdom after the war
	7	President Wilson reelected in the United States

14 Miliukov in Duma speech indicts Russian government for "stupidity or treason"

19 French-Russian-Serbian forces capture Monastir

21 Emperor Francis Joseph dies in Vienna; Charles ascends Habsburg throne

23 Mackensen crosses the Danube near Bucharest

Venizelist provisional government declares war on Germany and Bulgaria

24 Minister-President Sturmer replaced by Trepov in Russia

25 Foreign Secretary von Jagow yields to Zimmermann in Berlin

Beatty replaces Jellicoe as British fleet chief; Jellicoe first sea lord

December 1 German military government established in Rumania

Greek royalists attack Anglo-French forces in Athens

2 Reichstag in Berlin passes Auxiliary Service Law

Emperor Charles assumes personal command of Habsburg units

5 Prime Minister Asquith resigns in London

6 Germans occupy Bucharest

10/11 Lloyd George forms Cabinet in London

12 New Cabinet under Briand formed in France

Central Powers send peace note to Allies

13 General Nivelle replaces Joffre as French army chief

Körber Cabinet resigns in Vienna; Clam-Martinic Cabinet formed on 20th

18 President Wilson's peace note

22 Czernin replaces Burian as Habsburg foreign minister

30 Rasputin murdered

1917

January 9 Germany decides to resume unrestricted submarine warfare

Golitsyn replaces Trepov as Russian minister-president

February 1 Germany resumes unrestricted submarine warfare

4 Cabinet under Talât Paşa formed in Turkey

23/24 Kut el Amara retaken by British troops

March 1 Arz von Straussenburg replaces Conrad von Hötzendorf as Habsburg chief of staff

11 Russian Revolution: formation of the Petrograd Council on the 12th

Baghdad captured by British General Maude

14 War Minister Lyautey resigns in Paris

Russian provisional government formed under Lvov, Miliukov, Kerensky

15 Tsar Nicholas II abdicates

16 German strategic withdrawal from Aisne to Siegfried line

17 Briand Cabinet resigns in France; replaced by Ribot on 19th

April 6 French offensive along Aisne and in Champagne (to May 27)

United States declares war on Germany

Independent Social Democratic party formed in Germany

7 Emperor Wilhelm II Easter message promising Prussian franchise reform after the war

8 War Minister Krobatin resigns in Vienna; replaced by Stöger-Steiner

Panama and Germany in state of war

9 Austria-Hungary and United States sever diplomatic ties

British Third Army attacks at Arras (to May 20)

10 Germany and Brazil sever diplomatic relations

Germany and Cuba at war

14 Germany and Bolivia sever diplomatic relations

16 French Nivelle assault near Reims; 16 corps mutiny

Lenin returns to Russia

20 Turkey and United States sever diplomatic relations

28 Germany and Guatemala sever diplomatic relations

May 8 Germany and Liberia sever diplomatic relations

14 Collapse of first provisional government in Russia

Tenth Isonzo battle in Italy

14/15 Austro-Hungarian naval raid into Straits of Otranto

15 Pétain replaces Nivelle as French army chief

17 Germany and Honduras sever diplomatic relations

18 Congress passes draft bill

	19	Germany and Nicaragua sever diplomatic relations
	23	Tisza Cabinet resigns in Hungary; replaced by Esterházy Cabinet on June 15
June	4	Brusilov replaces Alekseev as Russian army chief
	6	Naval revolt in German fleet begins
	7	British offensive in Flanders (to July 21)
		Germany and Haiti sever diplomatic relations
	11	Germany and Santo Domingo sever diplomatic relations
	12	King Constantine of Greece abdicates in favor of his second son, Alexander
	16	First All-Russian Congress of Workers' and Soldiers' Councils
	21	Cabinet Clam-Martinic falls in Vienna; Seidler succeeds on 23rd
	26	Colonel Dimitrijević-Apis executed by Serbian authorities in Salonika
	27	Cabinet Venizelos formed in Greece
	30	Greece and Central Powers sever diplomatic relations
July	1	Brusilov offensive in East Galicia
	3	First American troops landed at Brest
	13/14	German Chancellor von Bethmann Hollweg resigns; replaced by Michaelis
	16-18	July Days: Bolsheviks attempt to seize power in Petrograd
	19	Central Powers launch counteroffensive in Galicia
		German Reichstag passes Peace Resolution 212-126
	20	Pact of Corfu signed by Serbian government and representatives of Habsburg South Slavs
	21	Kerensky becomes minister-president as well as war and navy minister in Russia
	22	Rumanian offensive against Austrians at Marasti (to August 1)
		Siam at war with Central Powers
	24	Canada adopts compulsory service bill
	31	Second Flanders assault launched by Haig in direction of Passchendaele (to September 17)
August	1	Pope Benedict XV mounts peace initiative
	2	General Kornilov replaces Brusilov as Russian army chief

	3	Czernowitz retaken by Central Powers for third time
	4	Liberia and Germany at war
	5	Kühlmann replaces Zimmermann as German foreign secretary
	6-20	Battle of Marasesti: Rumanians hold Marasti salient against Austro-German attacks
	14	China at war with Central Powers
	19	Eleventh Isonzo battle in Italy
	20	French offensive near Verdun (to October 9)
		Esterházy Cabinet falls in Budapest; replaced by Wekerle
September	1	German offensive in the Baltic states; Riga seized by the Eighth Army on the 3rd
	5	Third Zimmerwald peace conference planned in Stockholm
	7	Cabinet Ribot resigns in France; Painlevé succeeds on the 13th
	8	Kornilov's attempted coup in Russia; Kerensky appointed generalissimo
	20	Third British offensive in Flanders near Passchendaele (to December 3)
	26	Germany and Costa Rica sever diplomatic relations
October	6	Germany and Peru sever diplomatic relations
	7	Germany and Uruguay sever diplomatic relations
	12	German navy seizes islands Ösel, Moon, and Dagö in Gulf of Riga (to October 21)
	23	Barthou replaces Ribot as French foreign minister
		French offensive at Chemin des Dames
	24	Twelfth Isonzo battle in Italy: Central Powers rout Italians at Caporetto (to mid-November)
	26	Germany and Brazil at war
		Cabinet Boselli replaced by Orlando in Italy
	31	General Allenby leads British into Beersheba
November	1	German Chancellor Michaelis replaced by Hertling
	5	Allies at Rapallo establish an Allied Supreme Council at Versailles
	7	Provisional government overthrown in Petrograd; Second All-Russian Congress of Workers' and Soldiers' Councils
		British seize Gaza

	8	Government Lenin-Trotsky formed in Russia
	9	Helfferich yields to Payer as vice chancellor in Berlin
		General Diaz replaces Cadorna as Italian army chief
	13	Cabinet Painlevé resigns in Paris; succeeded by Clemenceau on the 16th
	20	Ukrainian Republic proclaimed
		British tank assault at Cambrai (to November 29)
	26	Russia demands an armistice
	27/28	Finland votes to break from Russia
	30	German counteroffensive at Cambrai (to December 7)
December	3	Armistice talks between Russia and the Central Powers at Brest-Litovsk
	7	Austria-Hungary and United States at war
	9	Armistice at Focsani between Rumania and the Central Powers
		Germany and Ecuador sever diplomatic relations
	11	Austria-Hungary and Panama at war
		Allenby enters Jerusalem
	16	Austria-Hungary and Cuba at war
	20	Australia again rejects conscription bill
	22	Central Powers and Russia begin peace negotiations at Brest-Litovsk

1918

January	4	Russia recognizes independence of Finland
	8	President Wilson presents Fourteen Points to Congress
	14	Former Premier Caillaux arrested in France
		Workers strike in Austria-Hungary
	18/19	Russian National Assembly dissolved by Bolsheviks
	28	Munitions workers strike in Berlin
		Russia severs diplomatic ties with Rumania
February	1	Austro-Hungarian naval mutiny at Cattaro
	9	German-Ukrainian peace treaty signed at Brest-Litovsk
		Cabinet Bratianu yields to Averescu in Rumania
	10	Trotsky's "no war, no peace" declaration
	18	Armistice expires in east; German forces advance

	21	British capture Jericho
	25	Germans seize Reval and Pskov
	28	Finland requests German military help
March	1	Brest-Litovsk peace negotiations resume
		Germans storm Kiev
	3	Central Powers and Russia sign peace at Brest-Litovsk
	7	German-Finnish peace treaty signed
	13	German forces enter Odessa
	19	Cabinet Marghiloman formed in Rumania
	21	German Operation Michael launched on western front by Ludendorff with 62 divisions (to March 30)
	23	German guns shell Paris
	26	Foch appointed Allied supreme commander
April	2	Czernin in Vienna reveals Sixtus affair
	3	German troops under Goltz land in Finland
	5	Japanese forces land at Vladivostok
	8	German troops occupy Kharkov
	9	Rumania annexes Bessarabia
		German St. Georg assault (to April 29)
	13	Germans occupy Helsingfors (Helsinki)
	14	Foreign Minister Czernin yields to Burian at Vienna
	20	German armies enter the Crimea
	22-23	British attempt to blockade Ostend and Zeebrugge
		Austro-Hungarian destroyer raid near Valona
	29	Skoropadsky appointed Ukrainian hetman
	30	Guatemala declares war against Germany
May	1	Germans seize Sevastopol
	7	Rumania signs peace treaty with Central Powers at Bucharest
	8	Nicaragua declares war against Central Powers
	23	Costa Rica declares war against Central Powers
	27	Third German offensive (Blücher) under Crown Prince Wilhelm (to June 13)
		Allies land 9,000 troops at Archangel, supported by five warships
June	9	German assault between Montdidier and Noyon
	15	Austro-Hungarian offensive along Piave River (to 23rd)

	16	Cabinet Radoslavov replaced by Malinov in Bulgaria
	18	Allied counteroffensive at Villers-Cotterêts under Foch
July	3	Sultan Mohammed V succeeded by Mohammed VI at Porte
	9	German foreign secretary Kühlmann yields to Hintze
	15	German counterattack near Reims
		Conrad von Hötzendorf retired as Habsburg commander
	16	Tsar Nicholas II and family murdered
		Haiti declares war against Germany
	18	Allied offensive between Aisne and Marne, the so-called Second Battle of the Marne; battle of Château-Thierry
	19	Honduras declares war against Germany
	22	Cabinet Seidler yields to Hussarek (on 25th) in Vienna
	30	German Field Marshal von Eichhorn murdered in Kiev
	31	Scheer replaces Holtzendorff as chief of German Admiralty Staff; creates navy supreme command on September 15
August	8	Allied offensive between Ancre and Avre; "black day of the German army" (Ludendorff)
	11	Allied forces landed at Vladivostok
	20	French offensive between Oise and Aisne
September	12	Franco-American attack between Meuse and Moselle; American thrust into St. Mihiel salient
	15	Allied offensive in Salonika under General Franchet d'Esperey
	18/19	British drive to Haifa, Nazareth; battle of Megiddo
	25	Bulgaria seeks armistice
	26–28	Marshal Foch's grand assault:
		Pershing and Americans at Meuse-Argonne to Mezières
		Franco-Belgian drive into Flanders to Maubeuge
		British storm Siegfried line to Ghent
	27	President Wilson's League of Nations speech in New York
	28/29	Ludendorff/Hindenburg demand an armistice
	29	Allies and Bulgaria sign armistice at Salonika
October	1	British forces enter Damascus
	3	King Ferdinand of Bulgaria abdicates in favor of his son, Boris III

		Max von Baden replaces Hertling as German chancellor
	3/4	Germany appeals to Wilson for an armistice
	4	Austria-Hungary appeals to Wilson for an armistice
	5	Turkey appeals to Wilson for an armistice
		Haig's British troops breach the Siegfried line
	9	Allies seize Cambrai
		Friedrich Karl of Hesse elected king of Finland
	14	Talât Paşa Cabinet resigns in Turkey
	21	Germany ends unrestricted submarine warfare
	23	Wekerle Cabinet resigns in Hungary
	24	Foreign Minister Burian yields to Andrássy in Vienna
	26	Ludendorff replaced with Groener in Germany
	27	Lammasch Cabinet replaces Hussarek in Vienna
		Austro-Hungarian naval mutiny at Pola
	28	Galicia severed from Austria-Hungary
	29/30	Italian "victory" at Vittorio Veneto; Vienna requests an armistice
	30	Allies and Turkey sign armistice at Mudros
	31	Austro-Hungarian fleet turned over to Yugoslavia
		Belgrade evacuated by Central Powers
		Tisza murdered in Budapest; Károlyi minister-president
		Planned "death ride" of German fleet; naval rebellion in Wilhelmshaven
November	2	Foreign Minister Andrássy resigns in Vienna
	3	Sailors' rebellion spreads to Kiel in Germany
		Republic of Poland proclaimed
		Allies and Austria-Hungary sign armistice at Padua
	7/8	Revolution in Munich, Germany
	8/9	Rumania declares war against Germany
	9	Max von Baden resigns in favor of Ebert in Berlin
		Abdication of Wilhelm II announced by Max von Baden
		Scheidemann proclaims German republic in Berlin
		Revolts in Baden, Saxony, and Württemberg
	10	Wilhelm II enters Holland as exile; Crown Prince Wilhelm arrives two days later

	11	Armistice signed in forest of Compiègne
		Emperor Charles gives up all government functions
	12	Austria proclaimed a republic; seeks union with Germany
		Allied fleet enters the Dardanelles
	13	Hungary and Allies sign armistice at Belgrade
	14	Czechoslovakian republic proclaimed under Masaryk
		Lettow-Vorbeck surrenders in northeast Rhodesia
		German U-boats interned at Harwich (in all 122)
	21	German High Sea Fleet interned by Admiral Beatty
		Americans enter Luxembourg
		Germans evacuate Alsace-Lorraine
	26	King Nicholas of Montenegro deposed by Montenegrin National Assembly
	27	Germans evacuate Belgium
	28	Wilhelm II officially renounces claims to thrones of Prussia and Germany
December	1	Yugoslavia officially proclaimed an independent state consisting of Serbia, Montenegro, and Croatia
	13	General Mannerheim becomes regent of Finland
	14	Hetman Skoropadsky toppled in Ukraine
	19	Bratianu Cabinet formed in Bucharest

1919

June	21	German fleet interned at Scapa Flow scuttled
	28	Treaty of Versailles signed
July	9	Germany ratifies Treaty of Versailles
	21	House of Commons ratifies Treaty of Versailles
	31	Poland ratifies Treaty of Versailles
August	8	Belgium ratifies Treaty of Versailles
September	5	New Zealand ratifies Treaty of Versailles
	10	Allies and Austria sign Treaty of St. Germain
	11	South Africa ratifies Treaty of Versailles
	12	Canada ratifies Treaty of Versailles
	21	Australia ratifies Treaty of Versailles
October	2	France ratifies Treaty of Versailles
	6	Italy ratifies Treaty of Versailles
	17	Austria ratifies Treaty of St. Germain
	26	Uruguay ratifies Treaty of Versailles
	30	Japan ratifies Treaty of Versailles
November	7	Czechoslovakia ratifies treaties of Versailles and St. Germain
	12	Brazil ratifies Treaty of Versailles
	19	U.S. Senate refuses to ratify Treaty of Versailles
	27	Allies and Bulgaria sign Treaty of Neuilly
December	9	Rumania ratifies treaties of Versailles and St. Germain

Major source:

Schulthess' Europäischer Geschichtskalender. Neue Folge, vols. 30-35 (Munich 1914-1923).

PRINCIPAL OCCUPATIONS: PREWAR, WARTIME, POSTWAR

A bewildering plethora of titles and occupations greet the reader of European political, diplomatic, and military history. Hence, for the sake of clarity, we have decided to streamline some of these and to render them uniform as far as possible. The word *Deputy* will denote parliamentary delegates in all countries save Britain, where *M.P.* (Member of Parliament) will be used instead. The word *Cabinet* will refer to all cabinet positions except the very important ones of foreign affairs and war; in the case of Britain, Germany, and the United States, the latter two will be referred to as *Secretary*. And with regard to Germany, military leaders will be identified in the Prewar column by the state in which they served (Bavaria, Prussia, Saxony, Würt-temberg). During the Great War they all became part of a federal German army.

When a leader died during the war or too soon thereafter (1919/1920) to resume an old career or to start a new one, an asterisk (*) will so indicate. A dash (—) denotes that a leader either retired fully after the war or that insufficient evidence of a postwar career exists. Parenthetical notations in the Postwar column will identify a career taken up in a new nation created at the Paris Peace Conference. In the case of Russia, these will indicate service with Red or White forces in 1917/1918; an asterisk there will further reveal that the leader died during the ensuing civil war. Finally, specific posts listed will generally depict the highest office attained by a leader.

NAME	PREWAR	WARTIME	POSTWAR
AUSTRIA-HUNGARY			
Adler, Viktor	Physician Journalist Deputy	Deputy Foreign Minister	*
Andrássy, Julius	Deputy Cabinet	Deputy Foreign Minister	Deputy Conspirator (Hungary)
Arz von Straussenburg, Arthur	Military	Military Chief, General Staff	—
Auffenberg, Moritz	Military War Minister	Military	Publicist
Bardolff, Carl	Lawyer Military	Military	Lawyer Deputy (Austria)
Bauer, Otto	Industrialist Deputy Editor	Military Bureaucrat	Foreign Minister Deputy Exile (Austria)
Beneš, Eduard	Lawyer Professor Radical	Radical Journalist	Foreign Minister Prime Minister (Czechoslovakia)
Berchtold, Leopold von	Diplomat Foreign Minister	Foreign Minister	Estate Owner

NAME	PREWAR	WARTIME	POSTWAR
Böhm-Ermolli, Eduard von	Military	Military	—
Bolfras, Arthur von	Military Chancery Head	Military Chancery Head	—
Boroević, Svetozar	Military	Military	—
Burian, István	Diplomat Cabinet	Foreign Minister	—
Charles I	Military Heir Apparent	Military Emperor-King	Conspirator Exile
Clam-Martinic, Heinrich von	Deputy	Military Minister-President	—
Conrad von Hötzendorf, Franz	Military Chief, General Staff	Military Chief, General Staff	Publicist
Czernin, Ottokar	Diplomat Deputy	Diplomat Foreign Minister	Deputy (Austria)
Dankl, Viktor	Military	Military	—
Eugene, Archduke	Military	Military	Exile
Francis Ferdinand, Archduke	Military Heir Apparent	*	
Francis Joseph I	Emperor-King	Emperor-King	*
Frederick, Archduke	Military	Military	Exile
Haus, Anton von	Navy Chief, Naval Section	Navy Fleet Chief	*
Hohenlohe-Schillingsfürst, Gottfried zu	Military	Diplomat	—
Holub, Franz	Navy	Navy Chief, Naval Section	—
Horthy, Miklós	Navy	Navy Fleet Chief	Army Chief Regent (Hungary)
Hussarek, Max	Lawyer Professor Cabinet	Cabinet Minister-President	Professor
Joseph, Archduke	Military	Military	Regent Exile (Hungary)
Joseph Ferdinand, Archduke	Military	Military Air Service	—
Károlyi, Mihály	Deputy	Deputy Premier	President Exile (Hungary)
Keil, Franz von	Navy	Navy	—
Körber, Ernst von	Bureaucrat Minister-President	Cabinet Minister-President	*

NAME	PREWAR	WARTIME	POSTWAR
Kövess, Hermann	Military	Military Army Head	—
Kramář, Karel	Lawyer Deputy	Deputy Radical	Diplomat Premier Deputy (Czechoslovakia)
Krauss, Alfred	Military	Military	Writer
Krobatin, Alexander von	Military War Minister	War Minister Military	—
Kummer von Falkenfeld, Heinrich	Military	Military	—
Lammasch, Heinrich	Lawyer Deputy	Deputy Minister-President	*
Marterer, Ferdinand von	Military	Military	*
Masaryk, T. G.	Professor Deputy	Exile Radical	President (Czechoslovakia)
Montecuccoli, Rudolf von	Navy Chief, Naval Section	—	—
Njegovan, Maximilian	Navy	Navy Fleet Chief	—
Pflanzer-Baltin, Karl von	Military	Military	—
Pilsudski, Joseph	Radical Exile Editor	Military (Polish Legion)	Marshal Dictator (Poland)
Potiorek, Oskar	Military Governor	Military	—
Princip, Gavrilo	Student Terrorist	—	*
Sarkotič von Lovčen, Stephan	Military	Military	—
Schönburg-Hartenstein, Alois von	Military Deputy	Military	Cabinet War Minister (Austria)
Stöger-Steiner, Rudolf	Military	Military War Minister	—
Stürgkh, Karl von	Deputy Minister-President	Minister-President	*
Szurmay, Alexander	Military	Military Honvéd Minister	Military (Hungary)
Tisza, István	Deputy Premier	Premier	*
Trumbić, Ante	Lawyer Deputy Mayor	Exile Radical	Foreign Minister Deputy (Yugoslavia)
Waldstätten, Alfred von	Military	Military	—
Wekerle, Alexander	Bureaucrat Premier	Premier	—

NAME	PREWAR	WARTIME	POSTWAR
BELGIUM			
Albert I	King	King Army Head	King
Broqueville, Charles de	Deputy Premier	Premier	Cabinet Premier
Hymans, Paul	Professor Deputy	Diplomat Cabinet	Cabinet Diplomat Exile
Mercier, Désiré Joseph	Priest Professor Cardinal	Cardinal National Spokesman	Cardinal
BULGARIA			
Ferdinand	Austrian Military King	King	Exile
Malinov, Alexander	Lawyer Deputy Premier	Deputy Premier	Deputy Premier
Radoslavov, Vasil	Journalist Deputy Premier	Premier	Exile
Stamboliski, Alexander	Deputy Editor	Deputy	Premier
Zhekov, Nikola T.	Military	War Minister Army Head	Exile
FRANCE			
Augagneur, Victor	Physician Cabinet	Navy Minister	Civil Servant Deputy
Boué de Lapeyrère, Auguste	Navy Navy Minister	Navy	*
Briand, Aristide	Lawyer Deputy Cabinet Premier	Cabinet Premier	Premier Cabinet
Caillaux, Joseph	Lawyer Deputy Cabinet Premier	Deputy	Cabinet Senator
Castelnau, Edouard de	Military	Military	Deputy
Clemenceau, Georges	Physician Deputy Senator Cabinet Premier	Deputy Premier	Premier
Dartige du Fournet, Louis-René	Navy	Navy	—
Delcassé, Théophile	Journalist Deputy Foreign Minister Diplomat	Foreign Minister	*

NAME	PREWAR	WARTIME	POSTWAR
Dubail, Yvon	Military	Military	Military
Fayolle, Émile	Military	Military	Military
Foch, Ferdinand	Military	Military Generalissimo	Military
Franchet d'Esperey, Louis	Military	Military	Military
Gallieni, Joseph Simon	Military	Military War Minister	*
Gauchet, Dominique Marie	Navy	Navy	—
Guépratte, Émile	Navy	Navy	Deputy
Guillaumat, Adolfe	Military	Military	Military War Minister
Joffre, Joseph	Military Chief, General Staff	Military Chief, General Staff	—
Lacaze, Lucien	Navy	Navy Navy Minister	Navy
Langle de Cary, Fernand	Military	Military	Writer
Lanrezac, Charles	Military	Military	Writer
Lyautey, Hubert	Military Administrator	Military Administrator War Minister	Military Administrator
Maistre, Paul	Military	Military	Military
Malvy, Louis Jean	Lawyer Deputy Cabinet	Cabinet	Exile Deputy Cabinet
Mangin, Charles	Military	Military	Military
Maunoury, Michel	Military	Military	—
Micheler, Joseph Alfred	Military	Military	—
Millerand, Alexandre	Editor Deputy Cabinet War Minister	War Minister	Premier President Senator
Nivelle, Robert	Military	Military Chief, General Staff	Military
Painlevé, Paul	Professor Deputy	Deputy Cabinet Premier	Premier Cabinet
Paléologue, Maurice	Diplomat	Diplomat	Diplomat Writer

NAME	PREWAR	WARTIME	POSTWAR
Pétain, Henri-Philippe	Military	Military Chief, General Staff	Military Cabinet Head of State
Poincaré, Raymond	Lawyer Deputy Cabinet Premier President	President	President Premier Cabinet
Ribot, Alexandre	Lawyer Deputy Cabinet Premier	Cabinet Premier	Senator
Ronarc'h, Pierre A.	Navy	Navy	Navy
Roques, Pierre Auguste	Military	Military War Minister	—
Sarrail, Maurice	Military	Military	Journalist Military Administrator
Thomas, Albert	Teacher Deputy Editor	Cabinet Diplomat	Deputy Bureaucrat
Viviani, René	Lawyer Deputy Cabinet Premier	Premier Cabinet	Deputy Senator Diplomat
Weygand, Maxime	Military	Military	Military Chief, General Staff

GERMANY

NAME	PREWAR	WARTIME	POSTWAR
Albrecht, Duke	Württemberg Military	Military	Head, House of Württemberg
Bachmann, Gustav	Navy	Navy Chief, Admiralty Staff	—
Bauer, Max	Prussian Military	Military Intriguer	Conspirator Military Adviser
Below, Otto von	Prussian Military	Military	Military Veterans Leader
Bernstorff, Johann H. von	Military Diplomat	Diplomat	Deputy Exile
Beseler, H. H. von	Prussian Military	Military Governor General	—
Bethmann Hollweg, Theobald von	Bureaucrat Cabinet Chancellor	Chancellor	—
Bothmer, Felix von	Bavarian Military	Military	—
Bülow, Karl von	Prussian Military	Military	—

NAME	PREWAR	WARTIME	POSTWAR
Capelle, Eduard von	Navy	Navy Navy Secretary	—
Delbrück, Clemens von	Bureaucrat Cabinet	Cabinet	Deputy
Ebert, Friedrich	Editor Deputy	Deputy	Chancellor President
Eichhorn, Hermann von	Prussian Military	Military	*
Einem, Karl von	Prussian Military War Minister	Military	Military
Erzberger, Matthias	Teacher Editor Deputy	Deputy State Secretary	Deputy Chancellor Cabinet Deputy
Falkenhayn, Erich von	Prussian Military War Minister	War Minister Chief, General Staff	Military
Gallwitz, Max von	Prussian Military	Military	Deputy
Goltz, Colmar von der	Prussian Military Adviser	Governor General Military	*
Goltz, Rüdiger von der	Prussian Military	Military	Military Free Corps
Groener, Wilhelm	Württemberg Military	Military First Quartermaster General	Military Cabinet
Haase, Hugo	Lawyer Deputy	Deputy Party Head	Coalition Cabinet
Helfferich, Karl	Professor Bureaucrat Businessman	Cabinet Diplomat	Deputy
Henry, Prince	Navy Fleet Chief	Navy	—
Hentsch, Richard	Saxon Military	Military	*
Hertling, Georg von	Professor Deputy Bavarian Prime Minister	Bavarian Prime Minister Chancellor	*
Hindenburg, Paul von	Prussian Military	Military Chief, General Staff	Military President
Hintze, Paul von	Navy Diplomat	Diplomat Foreign Secretary	Deputy Bureaucrat
Hipper, Franz	Navy	Navy Fleet Chief	—
Hoffmann, Max	Prussian Military	Military	Military Publicist
Holtzendorff, Henning von	Navy Fleet Chief	Navy Chief, Admiralty Staff	*
Jagow, Gottlieb von	Bureaucrat Diplomat Foreign Secretary	Foreign Secretary	—
Kluck, Alexander von	Prussian Military	Military	—

NAME	PREWAR	WARTIME	POSTWAR
Krafft von Dellmensingen, Konrad	Bavarian Military Chief, General Staff	Military	—
Kühlmann, Richard von	Diplomat	Diplomat Foreign Secretary	Businessman
Leopold, Prince	Bavarian Military	Military	—
Lettow-Vorbeck, Paul von	Prussian Military	Military	Military Deputy
Levetzow, Magnus von	Navy	Navy	Navy Police President
Liman von Sanders, Otto	Prussian Military	Military	P.O.W. Publicist
Linsingen, Alexander von	Prussian Military	Military	—
Ludendorff, Erich	Prussian Military	Military First Quartermaster General	Deputy Intriguer
Mackensen, August von	Prussian Military	Military	P.O.W. Military
Marwitz, Georg von der	Prussian Military	Military	Veterans Leader
Max, Prince	Military Baden Heir Presumptive	Chancellor	—
Michaelis, Georg	Lawyer Bureaucrat	Bureaucrat Chancellor	Church, Welfare Leader
Moltke, Helmuth von	Prussian Military Chief, General Staff	Military Chief, General Staff	*
Müller, G. A. von	Navy Chief, Navy Cabinet	Navy Chief, Navy Cabinet	—
Noske, Gustav	Editor Deputy	Deputy	Cabinet Administrator
Payer, Friedrich von	Lawyer Deputy	Deputy Vice-Chancellor	Deputy
Prittwitz und Gaffron, Maximilian von	Prussian Military	Military	—
Rathenau, Walther	Businessman	Administrator Businessman	Foreign Minister
Richthofen, Manfred von	Prussian Military	Military Air Corps	*
Rupprecht, Crown Prince	Bavarian Military	Military	Retired Exile
Scheer, Reinhard	Navy	Navy Fleet Chief	—
Scheidemann, Philipp	Printer Editor Deputy	Deputy Cabinet	Chancellor Deputy Mayor Exile
Schmidt von Knobelsdorf, Constantin	Prussian Military	Military	Military
Schröder, Ludwig von	Navy	Navy	Veterans Leader

NAME	PREWAR	WARTIME	POSTWAR
Seeckt, Hans von	Prussian Military	Military	Military Adviser Deputy
Solf, Wilhelm	Diplomat Colonial Secretary	Colonial Secretary Foreign Secretary	Deputy Diplomat
Souchon, Wilhelm	Navy	Navy	—
Spee, Maximilian von	Navy	Navy	*
Stresemann, Gustav	Deputy Legal Counsel	Deputy	Chancellor Foreign Minister
Tirpitz, Alfred von	Navy Navy Secretary	Navy Secretary Politician	Publicist Deputy
Trotha, Adolf von	Navy	Navy	Navy, Admiralty Chief Veterans and Youth Leader
Valentini, Rudolf von	Bureaucrat Chief, Civil Cabinet	Chief, Civil Cabinet	—
Westarp, Kuno von	Bureaucrat Deputy	Deputy	Deputy
Wilhelm, Crown Prince	Prussian Military	Military	Exile National Socialist
Wilhelm II	Emperor-King	Emperor-King Supreme War Lord	Exile
Woyrsch, Remus von	Prussian Military	Military	Border Guards
Zimmermann, Arthur	Consul Bureaucrat	Foreign Secretary	—

GREAT BRITAIN

NAME	PREWAR	WARTIME	POSTWAR
Aitken, William M.	Financier Businessman	Cabinet	Publisher Cabinet
Allenby, Edmund	Military	Military	High Commissioner
Asquith, Herbert H.	Lawyer Prime Minister	Prime Minister M.P.	M.P. Lord
Balfour, Arthur J.	M.P. Cabinet Prime Minister	First Lord, Admiralty Foreign Secretary	Foreign Secretary Diplomat
Beatty, David	Navy	Navy Fleet Chief	Fleet Chief First Sea Lord
Bonar Law, Andrew	Businessman M.P.	Cabinet	Cabinet Prime Minister
Byng, Julian H.	Military	Military	Governor General Police Chief
Carden, Sackville H.	Navy	Navy	*
Carson, Edward H.	Lawyer M.P.	Cabinet First Lord, Admiralty	Jurist M.P.

NAME	PREWAR	WARTIME	POSTWAR
Churchill, Winston S.	Military Journalist M.P. Cabinet	First Lord, Admiralty Military Cabinet	Cabinet Prime Minister Writer
Cradock, Christopher	Navy	Navy	*
Curzon, George N.	Viceroy Lord	Cabinet	Foreign Secretary Lord
De Robeck, John M.	Navy	Navy	Navy
Fisher, John A.	Navy First Sea Lord	First Sea Lord	*
French, John	Navy Military Chief, Imperial General Staff	Military Chief, BEF France	Lord Lieutenant, Ireland
Geddes, Eric C.	Businessman	Businessman Adviser First Lord, Admiralty	Cabinet Diplomat Businessman
George V	Navy King-Emperor	King-Emperor	King-Emperor
Gough, Hubert	Military	Military	Military Businessman
Grey, Edward	M.P. Foreign Secretary	Foreign Secretary	Envoy Author
Haig, Douglas	Military	Military Chief, BEF France	Military Veterans Leader
Hamilton, Ian	Military	Military	Publicist
Harmsworth, Alfred	Journalist Publisher Businessman	Publisher Envoy Bureaucrat	Publisher
Jackson, Henry B.	Navy	Navy First Lord, Admiralty	Navy
Jellicoe, John R.	Navy	Navy Fleet Chief First Sea Lord	Governor General
Keyes, Roger	Navy	Navy	Navy M.P.
Kiggell, Launcelot	Military	Military Chief of Staff	—
Kitchener, H. H.	Military Governor General	War Secretary	*
Lawrence, T. E.	Explorer Archaeologist	Adviser Military	Publicist Military
Lloyd George, David	Lawyer M.P. Cabinet	Cabinet Prime Minister	Prime Minister
Marshall, William R.	Military	Military	Military
Maude, Stanley	Military	Military	*

NAME	PREWAR	WARTIME	POSTWAR
Milne, Archibald B.	Navy	Navy	—
Milne, George F.	Military	Military	Military Chief, Imperial General Staff
Milner, Alfred	Journalist Administrator Businessman	War Secretary	Cabinet
Monro, Charles C.	Military	Military	Military Governor
Murray, Archibald J.	Military	Military	Military
Nixon, John E.	Military	Military	—
Plumer, Herbert	Military	Military	Military Governor High Commissioner
Rawlinson, Henry S.	Military	Military	Military Army Head, India
Robertson, William R.	Military	Military Chief, Imperial General Staff	Military
Smith-Dorrien, Horace L.	Military	Military	Governor
Smuts, Jan C.	Military Cabinet	Military Cabinet	Prime Minister Cabinet (South Africa)
Spring Rice, Cecil A.	Diplomat	Diplomat	*
Stanley, Edward	Military M.P. Cabinet Mayor	Cabinet War Secretary	War Secretary Diplomat
Sturdee, Frederick	Navy	Navy	Navy
Townshend, Charles	Military	Military	M.P.
Troubridge, Ernest	Navy	Navy	Navy
Tyrwhitt, Reginald Y.	Navy	Navy	Navy Chief, China Station
Wemyss, Rosslyn E.	Navy	Navy First Sea Lord	Navy
Wilson, Henry H.	Military	Military Chief, Imperial General Staff	Military M.P.

GREECE

NAME	PREWAR	WARTIME	POSTWAR
Constantine I	Crown Prince Military Exile King	King Exile	King Exile

NAME	PREWAR	WARTIME	POSTWAR
Metaxas, John	Military	Military Chief, General Staff Exile	Military Exile Cabinet Premier Dictator
Venizelos, Eleutherios	Revolutionary Prime Minister	Prime Minister	Prime Minister Exile

ITALY

NAME	PREWAR	WARTIME	POSTWAR
Bissolati, Leonida	Editor Deputy	Military Deputy Cabinet	*
Boselli, Paolo	Lawyer Professor Deputy Cabinet	Deputy Prime Minister	Fascist Senator
Cadorna, Luigi	Military Chief, General Staff	Military Chief, General Staff	Military
Capello, Luigi A.	Military	Military	Military Fascist Conspirator
Dallolio, Alfredo	Military	Military Cabinet	Military Bureaucrat
D'Annunzio, Gabriele	Writer Deputy Exile	Political Agitator Soldier	Political Agitator Writer
Diaz, Armando	Military	Military Chief, General Staff	Military War Minister
Giolitti, Giovanni	Deputy Cabinet Prime Minister	Deputy	Prime Minister
Nitti, Francesco S.	Professor Deputy Cabinet	Deputy Cabinet	Cabinet Prime Minister Exile Senator
Orlando, Vittorio	Professor Deputy Cabinet	Cabinet Prime Minister	Prime Minister Deputy
Salandra, Antonio	Professor Deputy Cabinet Prime Minister	Prime Minister	Deputy Diplomat Fascist Senator
San Giuliano, Antonio Di	Deputy Cabinet Diplomat Foreign Minister	Foreign Minister	*
Sonnino, Giorgio Sidney	Diplomat Deputy Cabinet Prime Minister	Foreign Minister	Foreign Minister
Thaon di Revel, Paolo	Navy	Navy	Navy Navy Minister

NAME	PREWAR	WARTIME	POSTWAR
Victor Emmanuel III	Military King	King	King-Emperor Exile

JAPAN

NAME	PREWAR	WARTIME	POSTWAR
Gotō, Shimpei	Physician Bureaucrat Cabinet	Cabinet Foreign Minister	Mayor Cabinet
Kamio, Mitsuomi	Military	Military	Military
Katō, Takaaki	Businessman Diplomat Foreign Minister	Foreign Minister	Prime Minister

MONTENEGRO

NAME	PREWAR	WARTIME	POSTWAR
Nicholas Petrović-Njegoš	Military King	King Exile	Exile

RUMANIA

NAME	PREWAR	WARTIME	POSTWAR
Averescu, Alexandru	Military War Minister Chief, General Staff	Military Prime Minister	Prime Minister Deputy
Bratianu, Ion or Ionel	Engineer Deputy Cabinet Prime Minister	Prime Minister	Prime Minister Deputy
Carol I or Charles I	Prince King	King	*
Ferdinand	Military Crown Prince	King	King
Marghiloman, Alexandru	Lawyer Deputy	Deputy Prime Minister	Deputy
Prezan, Constantine	Military	Military Chief, General Staff	Military

RUSSIA

NAME	PREWAR	WARTIME	POSTWAR
Alekseev, Mikhail V.	Military	Military Chief, General Staff	Military (White) *
Alexandra	Empress	Empress Intriguer	*
Brusilov, Aleksei A.	Military	Military Army Head	Military (Red)
Danilov, Yury N.	Military	Military	Exile Writer
Dukhonin, Nikolai N.	Military	Military Chief, General Staff	*
Eberhardt, Andrei A.	Navy	Navy	*
Essen, Nikolai O.	Navy	Navy	*

NAME	PREWAR	WARTIME	POSTWAR
Evert, Aleksei E.	Military	Military	*
Goremykin, Ivan L.	Lawyer Bureaucrat Cabinet Premier	Premier	*
Grigorovich, Ivan K.	Navy Navy Minister	Navy Minister	Exile
Guchkov, Aleksandr I.	Businessman Deputy	Businessman Conspirator War Minister	Exile
Gurko, Vasily I.	Military	Military Chief of Staff	Exile
Ivanov, Nikolai Y.	Military	Military	Military (White) *
Kerensky, Aleksandr F.	Lawyer Deputy	Deputy Cabinet War Minister Premier	Exile Writer
Kolchak, Aleksandr V.	Navy	Navy	Military (White) *
Kornilov, Lavr G.	Military	Military White Leader	Military (White) *
Krivoshein, Aleksandr V.	Bureaucrat Cabinet	Cabinet	Politician (White) Exile
Kuropatkin, Aleksei N.	Military War Minister	Military Administrator	Teacher
Lenin, V. I.	Revolutionary Publicist Editor, Exile	Exile Premier	Premier
Maklakov, Nikolai A.	Bureaucrat Cabinet	Cabinet	*
Miliukov, Paul N.	Professor Deputy	Deputy Foreign Minister	Politician (White) Exile Writer
Nicholas II	Emperor	Emperor Army Head	*
Nikolai Nikolaevich, Grand Duke	Military	Military Army Head	Exile
Pleve, Pavel A.	Military	Military	*
Polivanov, Aleksei A.	Military	Military War Minister	Military (Red)
Protopopov, Aleksandr D.	Businessman Deputy	Deputy Cabinet	*
Rasputin, Grigory E.	Religious Figure Imperial Adviser	Imperial Adviser	*
Rennenkampf, Pavel K.	Military	Military	*
Rodzianko, Mikhail V.	Deputy	Deputy Duma Leader	Exile Writer

NAME	PREWAR	WARTIME	POSTWAR
Ruzsky, Nikolai V.	Military	Military	*
Samsonov, Aleksandr V.	Military	Military	*
Sazonov, Sergei D.	Diplomat Foreign Minister	Foreign Minister	Diplomat (White) Exile
Shcherbachev, Dmitry G.	Military	Military	Military (White) Exile
Sturmer, Boris V.	Bureaucrat	Premier	*
Sukhomlinov, Vladimir A.	Military Chief, General Staff War Minister	War Minister	Exile
Trotsky, Leon	Revolutionary Exile Writer	Exile Foreign Affairs Commissar	War Commissar Exile
Yanushkevich, Nikolai N.	Military Chief, General Staff	Chief, General Staff Military	*
Yudenich, Nikolai N.	Military	Military	Military (White) Exile
Zaionchkovsky, Andrei M.	Military	Military	Military (Red)
Zhilinsky, Yakov G.	Military Chief, General Staff	Military White Leader	*

SERBIA

NAME	PREWAR	WARTIME	POSTWAR
Alexander Karadjordjević	Crown Prince Prince Regent	Military Army Head Prince Regent	King (Yugoslavia)
Dimitrijević-Apis, Dragutin	Military Conspirator	Military	*
Mišić, Živojin	Military	Military Chief, General Staff	Chief, General Staff (Yugoslavia)
Pašić, Nikola	Engineer Deputy Prime Minister	Prime Minister Exile	Diplomat Prime Minister (Yugoslavia)
Peter Karadjordjević	Exile Military King	King Army Head	King (Yugoslavia)
Putnik, Radomir	Military Chief, General Staff	Chief, General Staff	*

TURKEY

NAME	PREWAR	WARTIME	POSTWAR
Cavid Bey, Mehmed	Bureaucrat Teacher Deputy Cabinet	Cabinet	Exile Conspirator
Cemal Paşa, Ahmed	Military Navy Minister	Navy Minister Military Administrator	Exile Military Diplomat

NAME	PREWAR	WARTIME	POSTWAR
Enver Paşa (Enver Bey)	Military War Minister	War Minister Military	Exile Military
Izzet Paşa, Ahmed	Military Chief, General Staff War Minister	Military Grand Vizier	Cabinet
Kemal Paşa, Mustafa	Military	Military	Military President Dictator
Talât Paşa, Mehmed	Bureaucrat Deputy Cabinet	Cabinet Grand Vizier	Exile

UNITED STATES

NAME	PREWAR	WARTIME	POSTWAR
Baker, Newton D.	Lawyer Mayor	Secretary of War	Lawyer Judge
Benson, William S.	Navy	Navy Chief, Naval Operations	Navy Businessman
Bliss, Tasker H.	Military	Military Chief of Staff	Military Diplomat Editor
Bullard, Robert L.	Military	Military	Military
Daniels, Josephus	Journalist Editor Secretary of the Navy	Secretary of the Navy	Journalist Diplomat
Drum, Hugh A.	Military	Military	Military
Gerard, James W.	Lawyer Judge Diplomat	Diplomat	Lawyer Fund Raiser
Graves, William S.	Military	Military	Head, AEF Siberia Military
Harbord, James G.	Military	Military Chief of Staff, AEF France	Military Businessman
House, Edward M.	Planter Politician	Presidential Adviser	Presidential Adviser
Lansing, Robert	Lawyer Secretary of State	Secretary of State	Secretary of State Lawyer
Liggett, Hunter	Military	Military	Military
Lodge, Henry Cabot	Writer Congressman Senator	Senator	Senator
McAdoo, William G.	Lawyer Businessman Secretary of the Treasury	Secretary of the Treasury	Secretary of the Treasury Senator
March, Peyton C.	Military	Military Chief of Staff	Military Publicist
Mayo, Henry T.	Navy	Navy Chief, Atlantic Fleet	Navy Fleet Chief

NAME	PREWAR	WARTIME	POSTWAR
Mitchell, William	Military	Air Service (AEF)	Aviation Pioneer Writer
Page, Walter H.	Editor Diplomat	Diplomat	*
Pershing, John J.	Military	Military Commander, AEF France	Military Chief of Staff
Pratt, William V.	Navy	Navy	Navy Fleet Chief
Roosevelt, Franklin D.	Politician Bureaucrat	Bureaucrat	Governor President
Sims, William S.	Navy	Navy Commander, European Waters	Navy
Wilson, Woodrow	Professor Governor President	President	President

VATICAN

Benedict XV	Priest Papal Nuncio Archbishop	Cardinal Pope	Pope

BIBLIOGRAPHY

Adams, John Clinton. *Flight in Winter*. Princeton, 1942.

Ahmad, Feroz. *The Young Turks: The Committee of Union and Progress in Turkish Politics, 1908-1914*. Oxford, 1969.

Alastos, Doros. *Venizelos: Patriot, Statesman, Revolutionary*. London, 1942.

Alatri, Paolo. *Nitti, D'Annunzio e la questione adriatica (1919-1920)*. Milan, 1959.

Albert I. *Les Carnets de guerre*. Brussels, 1953.

Albertini, Luigi. *The Origins of the War of 1914*. 3 vols. Oxford, 1952.

Alekseev, M. V. "Iz dnevnika Generala M. V. Alekseeva." *Russkii istoricheskii arkhiv*, Sbornik 1. Prague, 1929.

Allen, W.E.D., and Muratoff, Paul. *Caucasian Battlefields: A History of the Wars on the Turco-Caucasian Border, 1828-1921*. Cambridge, 1953.

Allmayer-Beck, J. C., and Lessing, E. *Die K. (u.) K.-Armee 1848-1914*. Munich, 1977.

Althann, Robert. "Papal Mediation during the First World War." *Studies: An Irish Quarterly Review* 61, no. 243.

Andrássy, G. *Diplomatie und Weltkrieg*. Vienna, 1920.

Aronson, Theo. *Defiant Dynasty: The Coburgs of Belgium*. Indianapolis and New York, 1968.

Arz von Straussenburg, A. *Kampf und Sturz der Mittelmächte*. Vienna, 1935.

_____. *Zur Geschichte des Grossen Krieges 1914-1918*. Vienna/Leipzig/Munich, 1924.

Askew, William C. "Italy and the Great Powers Before the First World War." In Edward R. Tannenbaum and Emiliana P. Noether, eds., *Modern Italy: A Topical History since 1861*. New York, 1974.

Aspinall-Oglander, Cecil F. *History of the Great War. Military Operations: Gallipoli*. 2 vols. London, 1929.

_____. *Roger Keyes*. London, 1951.

Asquith, Earl of Oxford and. *Memories and Reflections, 1852-1927*. 2 vols. Boston, 1928.

Auffenberg-Komarów, M. von. *Aus Österreichs Höhe und Niedergang*. Munich, 1921.

Azan, Paul. *Franchet D'Esperey*. Paris, 1949.

Baden, Prince Max von. *Erinnerungen und Dokumente*. Stuttgart, 1968.

Baker, Newton D. *Why We Went to War*. New York, 1936.

Baker, R. S. *Woodrow Wilson: Life and Letters*. Vols. VII, VIII. New York, 1939.

Balfour, Michael. *The Kaiser and His Times*. London, 1964.

Ballard, Colin R. *Smith-Dorrien*. London, 1931.

Bankwitz, Philip Charles Farwell. *Maxime Weygand and Civil-Military Relations in Modern France*. Cambridge, Mass., 1967.

Bardolff, C. von. *Soldat im alten Österreich*. Jena, 1938.

_____. *Der Militär-Maria Theresien-Orden. Die Auszeichnungen im Weltkrieg 1914-1918*. Vienna, 1944.

Barnes, John, ed. *The Beatty Papers: I (1908-1919)*. London, 1970.

Barnett, Correlli. *The Swordbearers: Supreme Command in the First World War*. New York, 1964.

Barrow, Edmund G. *The Life of General Sir Charles Carmichael Monro*. London, 1931.

Bauer, E. *Zwischen Halbmond und Doppeladler*. Vienna, 1971.

Bauer, Max. *Der Grosse Krieg in Feld und Heimat: Erinnerungen und Betrachtungen*. Tübingen, 1921.

Bauer, O. *Die österreichische Revolution*. Vienna, 1923.

Baumgart, Winfried. *Deutsche Ostpolitik 1918: Von Brest-Litowsk bis zum Ende des Ersten Weltkrieges*. Vienna and Munich, 1966.

Baumgarten-Crusius, Artur. *Deutsche Heerführung im Marnefeldzug, 1914*. Berlin, 1921.

Beauduin, Édouard. *Le Cardinal Mercier*. [Paris], 1966.

Beaufre, General [André]. *La France de la Grande Guerre, 1914/1919*. Paris, 1971.

Beaver, Daniel. *Newton D. Baker and the American War Effort, 1917-1919*. Lincoln, Nebr., 1966.

Beaverbrook, W.M.A. *Men and Power, 1917-1918*. New York, 1957.

_____. *Politicians and the War, 1914-1916*. New York, 1928.

Bell, John D. *Peasants in Power: Alexander Stamboliski and the Bulgarian National Union, 1899-1923*. Princeton, 1977.

Belot, Rear Admiral R. de, and Reussner, André. *La Puissance navale dans l'histoire*. Vol. III. Paris, 1958.

Beneš, E. *My War Memoirs*. London, 1928.

Berghahn, Volker R. *Der Tirpitz-Plan: Genesis und Verfall einer innenpolitischen Krisenstrategie unter Wilhelm II*. Düsseldorf, 1971.

Berglar, Peter. *Walther Rathenau: Seine Zeit. Sein Werk. Seine Persönlichkeit*. Bremen, 1970.

Bernstorff, Johann Heinrich von. *Deutschland und Amerika: Erinnerungen aus dem fünfjährigen Kriege.* Berlin, 1920.

———. *Erinnerungen und Briefe.* Zurich, 1936.

Bertoldi, Silvio. *Vittorio Emanuele III.* Turin, 1970.

Bestuzhev, I. V. "Russian Foreign Policy, February-June 1914." *Journal of Contemporary History* 1 (1966).

Bethmann Hollweg, Theobald von. *Betrachtungen zum Weltkrieg.* 2 vols. Berlin, 1921.

Binion, Rudolph. *Defeated Leaders: The Political Fate of Caillaux, Jouvenel, and Tardieu.* New York, 1960.

Biographical Dictionary of Japanese History. Tokyo, 1978.

Biographie nationale. Académie des sciences, des lettres et des beaux-arts de Belgique. 33 vols. to date. Brussels, 1866-.

Biographisches Lexikon zur Geschichte Südosteuropas. 4 vols. Munich, 1974-1980.

Biographisches Wörterbuch zur Deutschen Geschichte. 3 vols. Munich, 1973-1975.

Birkenhead, Earl of. *Contemporary Personalities.* London, 1924.

Bissolati, Leonida. *Diario di guerra.* Turin, 1935.

Blake, Robert. *Unrepentant Tory: The Life and Times of Andrew Bonar Law, 1858-1923, Prime Minister of the United Kingdom.* New York, 1956.

Bodenschatz, Karl. *Jagd in Flanderns Himmel.* Munich, 1938.

Bol'shaia sovetskaia entsiklopediia. 30 vols. Moscow, 1970-1978.

Bonham-Carter, Victor. *Soldier True: The Life and Times of Field-Marshal Sir William Robertson.* London, 1963.

Borton, Hugh. *Japan's Modern Century: From Perry to 1970.* New York, 1970.

Bosworth, R.J.B. *Italy, the Least of the Great Powers: Italian Foreign Policy before the First World War.* London, 1979.

Broesamle, J. J. *William Gibbs McAdoo: A Passion for Change, 1863-1917.* Port Washington, N.Y., 1973.

Bronne, Carlo. *Albert Ier: Le Roi sans terre.* Paris, 1965.

Brown, Victoria F. "The Movement for Reform in Rumania after World War I: The Parliamentary Bloc Government of 1919-1920." *Slavic Review* 38 (1979).

Brusilov, General A.A. *Moi vospominaniia.* 5th ed. Moscow, 1963.

Bruun, Geoffrey. *Clemenceau.* Hamden, Conn., 1968.

Buchan, John, ed. *The Nations of Today: Bulgaria and Romania.* Boston and New York, 1924.

Bulgarska Entsiklopediia. Sofia, 1936.

Bullard, Robert L. *Personalities and Reminiscenses of the War.* Garden City, N.Y., 1925.

Bülow, Karl von. *Mein Bericht zur Marneschlacht.* Berlin, 1919.

Burdick, Charles B. *The Japanese Siege of Tsingtau: World War I in Asia.* Hamden, Conn., 1976.

Burian, S. *Drei Jahre: Aus der Zeit meiner Amtsführung im Kriege.* Berlin, 1923.

Buxhoeveden, Sophie. *The Life and Tragedy of Alexandra Feodorovna, Empress of Russia.* London, 1929.

Cadorna, Luigi. *Altre pagine sulla grande guerra.* Milan, [1925].

Caillaux, Joseph. *Mes mémoires.* 3 vols. Paris, 1942-1947.

Callwell, Charles E. *Field-Marshal Sir Henry Wilson: His Life and Diaries.* 2 vols. London, 1927.

———. *Life of Sir Stanley Maude.* London, 1920.

Capello, Luigi. *Caporetto, perché? La 2ª armata e gli avvenimenti dell'ottobre 1917.* Turin, 1967.

Carson, Edward Henry. *The War on German Submarines.* London, 1917.

Cassar, George H. *The French and the Dardanelles: A Study of Failure in the Conduct of War.* London, 1971.

Cecil, Lamar. *The German Diplomatic Service 1871-1914.* Princeton, 1976.

Chamberlin, William Henry. *The Russian Revolution, 1917-1921.* 2 vols. New York, 1965.

Chasovoi (Paris and Brussels), 1929-1941.

Chastenet, Jacques. *Histoire de la troisième république.* Vol. IV. Paris, 1955.

———, and Renouvin, Pierre, et al. *Clemenceau.* Paris, 1974.

Chi, Madeleine. *China Diplomacy, 1914-1918.* Cambridge, Mass., 1970.

Chi é? Rome, 1940.

Chirikov, N. S. "Admiral A. A. Ebergard." *Morskiia zapiski* 19 and 21 (1961, 1963).

———. "Verkhovnyi pravitel' admiral A. V. Kolchak." *Morskiia zapiski* 20 (1962).

Churchill, Randolph S. *Lord Derby, King of Lancashire: The Official Life of Edward, Seventeenth Earl of Derby, 1865-1948.* London, 1959.

Churchill, Winston S. *Great Contemporaries.* New York, 1937.

———. *The Unknown War: The Eastern Front.* London, 1931.

———. *The World Crisis.* 6 vols. London, 1923-1931.

Clemenceau, Georges. *Grandeur and Misery of Victory.* New York, 1930.

Clemenz, Bruno. *Generalfeldmarschall von Woyrsch und seine Schlesier.* Berlin, 1919.

Clough, Shepard B. *The Economic History of Modern Italy.* New York, 1964.

Coffman, Edward M. *The Hilt of the Sword: The Career of Peyton C. March.* Madison, Wis., 1966.

———. *The War to End All Wars: The American Military Experience in World War I.* New York, 1968.

Colapietra, Raffaele. *Leonida Bissolati.* Milan, 1958.

Collier, Basil. *Brasshat: A Biography of Field-Marshal Sir Henry Wilson.* London, 1961.

Colombo, John R. *Colombo's Canadian References.* Toronto, 1976.

Colvin, Ian. *The Life of Lord Carson.* 3 vols. London, 1932-1936.

Conrad von Hötzendorf, Franz. *Aus meiner Dienstzeit.* 5 vols. Vienna, 1921-1925.

Contamine, Henry. *La Revanche, 1871-1914.* Paris, 1957.

Conze, Werner S. *Polnische Nation und deutsche Politik im ersten Weltkrieg.* Graz and Cologne, 1958.

Cooper, John Milton, Jr. *Walter Hines Page: The South-*

erner as American, 1855-1918. Chapel Hill, N.C., 1977.

Corbett, Julian S., and Newbolt, Henry. History of the Great War: Naval Operations. 5 vols. London, 1920-31.

Cowles, Virginia. The Kaiser. London, 1963.

Cronon, E. David, ed. The Cabinet Diaries of Josephus Daniels, 1913-1921. Lincoln, Nebr., 1963.

Current Biography. 40 vols. New York, 1940-80.

Czernin, O. Im Weltkrieg. Berlin, 1919.

Czisnik, Ulrich. Gustav Noske: Ein Sozialdemokratischer Staatsmann. Göttingen, 1969.

Dallin, Alexander. "The Future of Poland." In Alexander Dallin, ed. Russian Diplomacy and Eastern Europe, 1914-1917. New York, 1963.

Daniels, J. The Wilson Era: Years of War and After, 1917-1923. Chapel Hill, N.C., 1946.

Danilov, IUrii N. La Russie dans la guerre mondiale (1914-1917). Paris, 1927.

_____. Velikii kniaz' Nikolai Nikolaevich. Paris, 1930.

Dartige du Fournet, Louis. Souvenirs de guerre d'un amiral, 1914-1916. Paris, 1920.

Debo, Richard K. Revolution and Survival: The Foreign Policy of Soviet Russia, 1917-18. Toronto and Buffalo, 1979.

Dedijer, Vladimir. The Road to Sarajevo. New York, 1966.

Delbrück, Clemens von. Reden 1900-16. Berlin, 1917.

_____. Die wirtschaftliche Mobilmachung in Deutschland 1914. Munich, 1924.

Der grosse Brockhaus. 21 vols. Leipzig, 1928-35.

Der Krieg zur See: see Germany: Marinearchiv. Der Krieg zur See 1914-18.

Derfler, Leslie. Alexandre Millerand: The Socialist Years. The Hague, 1977.

Deutscher, Isaac. The Prophet Armed: Trotsky, 1879-1921. New York, 1954.

DeWeerd, H. A. President Wilson Fights His War: World War I and the American Intervention. New York, 1968.

Dictionary of American Biography. 20 vols. and 5 supplements. New York, 1928-1936 and 1944-1977.

Dictionary of National Biography. 63 vols. and 7 supplements. London, 1885-1900 and 1901-1971.

Dictionnaire de biographie française. 14 vols. to date. Paris, 1933-.

Dictionnaire des parlementaires français; notices biographiques sur les ministres, députés et sénateurs français de 1889 à 1940. 8 vols. Paris, 1960-1977.

Dizionario biografico degli italiani. 22 vols. to date. Rome, 1960-.

Dizionario storico politico italiano. Florence, 1971.

Djemal Pasha. Memories of a Turkish Statesman 1913-1919. London, 1922.

Dragnich, Alex N. Serbia, Nikola Pašić, and Yugoslavia. New Brunswick, N.J., 1974.

Dubail, Auguste. Quatre années de commandement, 1914-1918: Journal de campagne. 3 vols. Paris, 1920-1921.

Dugdale, Blanche E. C. Arthur James Balfour, First Earl Balfour. 2 vols. London, 1936.

Duus, Peter. Party Rivalry and Political Change in Taishō Japan. Cambridge, Mass., 1968.

Ebert, Friedrich. Schriften, Aufzeichnungen, Reden. 2 vols. Dresden, 1926.

Edmonds, Sir James E. History of the Great War. Military Operations: France and Belgium 1914-1918. 13 vols. London, 1922-1948.

_____, and Davies, H. R. History of the Great War. Military Operations: Italy, 1915-1919. London, 1949.

Edwards, Marvin L. Stresemann and the Greater Germany, 1914-1918. New York, 1963.

Einem, Günther von. Otto von Below, ein deutscher Heerführer. Munich, 1929.

Einem, Karl von. Ein Armeeführer erlebt den Weltkrieg: Persönliche Aufzeichnungen. Leipzig, 1938.

_____. Erinnerungen eines Soldaten 1853-1933. Berlin, 1933.

Enciclopedia Cugetarea. Bucharest [1941?].

Enciclopedia italiana di scienze, lettere ed arti. 35 vols. Rome, 1949-1952.

Enciklopedija Jugoslavije. 8 vols. Zagreb, 1955-1971.

Encyclopedia of Islam, The. 4 vols. to date. Leiden, 1960-.

Encyclopedia of World Biography. 12 vols. New York, 1973.

Enden, Michel de. Raspoutine et le crépuscule de la monarchie en Russie. Paris, 1976.

Epstein, Klaus. Matthias Erzberger and the Dilemma of German Democracy. Princeton, 1959.

Erényi, G. Graf Tisza. Vienna, 1935.

Erzberger, Matthias. Erlebnisse im Weltkrieg. Stuttgart, 1920.

Esmenard, Jean d'. Galliéni, destin hors série. Paris, 1965.

Eterovich, Francis H., and Spalatin, Christopher, eds. Croatia: Land, People, Culture. Vol. II. Toronto and Buffalo, 1970.

Eyck, Erich. Das persönliche Regiment Wilhelms II. Zurich, 1948.

Faldella, Emilio. La grande guerra. 2 vols. Milan, 1965.

Falkenhayn, Erich von. Der Feldzug der 9: Armee gegen die Rumänen und Russen 1916/17. Berlin, 1921.

_____. Die Oberste Heeresleitung 1914-1916 in ihren wichtigsten Entschliessungen. Berlin, 1920.

Falls, Cyril. Armageddon: 1918. Philadelphia and New York, 1964.

_____. The Battle of Caporetto. Philadelphia and New York, 1966.

_____. The Great War. New York, 1959.

_____. History of the Great War. Military Operations: Egypt and Palestine. 2 vols. London, 1928-1930.

_____. History of the Great War. Military Operations: Macedonia. 2 vols. London, 1933-1935.

Fayolle, Marie-Émile. Cahiers secrets de la Grande Guerre. Paris, 1964.

Feldman, Gerald D. Army, Industry, and Labor in Germany 1914-1918. Princeton, 1966.

Feldman, Robert S. "The Russian General Staff and the June 1917 Offensive." Soviet Studies 19 (1968).

Fenaux, Robert. Paul Hymans: Un homme, un temps, 1865-1941. Brussels [1946].

Ferro, Marc. The Great War 1914-1918. London, 1973.

Fischer, Fritz. Griff nach der Weltmacht: Die Kriegsziel-

politik des Kaiserlichen Deutschland 1914-1918. Düsseldorf, 1961.

———. *Krieg der Illusionen: Die deutsche Politik von 1911 bis 1914.* Düsseldorf, 1969.

Fischer, Louis. *The Life of Lenin.* New York, 1964.

Fischer, Rudolf. *Karl Helfferich.* Berlin, 1932.

Fisher, John A. *Memories.* London, 1919.

———. *Records.* London, 1919.

Florinsky, Michael T. *The End of the Russian Empire.* New York, 1961.

Foch, Ferdinand. *The Memoirs of Marshal Foch.* London, 1931.

Foerster, Wolfgang. *Der Feldherr Ludendorff im Unglück: Eine Studie über seine seelische Haltung in der Endphase des ersten Weltkrieges.* Wiesbaden, 1952.

Fontenot, Michael James. "Alexander F. Kerensky: The Political Career of a Russian Nationalist." Ph.D. diss., Louisiana State University, 1976.

Footman, David. *Civil War in Russia.* New York, 1962.

François, Hermann von. *Gorlice, 1915.* Leipzig, 1922.

Frankland, Noble. *Imperial Tragedy: Nicholas II, Last of the Tsars.* New York, 1961.

Franzius, Enno. *Caillaux: Statesman of Peace.* Stanford, Calif., 1976.

Freidel, F. *Franklin D. Roosevelt: The Apprenticeship.* Boston, 1952.

French, John Denton. *1914.* Boston and New York, 1919.

Fridenson, Patrick, ed. *1914-1918: L'Autre front.* Paris, 1977.

Frothingham, T. G. *The Naval History of the World War.* 3 vols. Cambridge, Mass., 1924-1926.

Frye, B. *Erzberger and German Politics, 1914-1921.* Ann Arbor, Mich., 1954.

Führ, C. *Das K.u.K. Armeeoberkommando und die Innenpolitik in Österreich 1914-1917.* Graz/Vienna/Cologne, 1968.

Fülöp-Miller, Rene. *Rasputin: The Holy Devil.* Garden City, N.Y., 1928.

Gade, John A. *The Life of Cardinal Mercier.* New York and London, 1934.

Galet, Émile Joseph. *Albert, King of the Belgians, in the Great War.* Boston, 1931.

Gallieni, Joseph. *Les Carnets de Galliéni.* Paris, 1932.

———. *Mémoires: Defense de Paris.* Paris, 1920.

Gallwitz, Max von. *Erleben im Westen 1916-18.* Berlin, 1932.

———. *Meine Führertätigkeit im Weltkriege 1914/16.* Berlin, 1929.

Gardner, Brian. *Allenby of Arabia: Lawrence's General.* New York, 1966.

Garraty, J. A. *Henry Cabot Lodge: A Biography.* New York, 1953.

Gatzke, Hans W. *Germany's Drive to the West: A Study of Germany's Western War Aims During the First World War.* Baltimore, Md., 1950.

Geiss, Imanuel. *Julikrise und Kriegsausbruch 1914.* 2 vols. Hanover, 1963-1964.

Gemzell, Carl-Axel. *Organization, Conflict, and Innova-tion: A Study of German Naval Strategic Planning, 1888-1940.* Lund, 1973.

General-ot-infanterii N. N. IUdenich k 50-letnemu iubileiu. Paris, 1932.

Genov, G. P. *Bulgaria and the Treaty of Neuilly.* Sofia, 1935.

Gerard, J. W. *My Four Years in Germany.* New York, 1917.

Germany: Marinearchiv. Der Krieg zur See 1914-18. 18 vols. Berlin and Frankfurt, 1922-1966.

Germany: Reichsarchiv. Der Weltkrieg, 1914 bis 1918. 14 vols. Berlin, 1925-1944.

Gerua, General B. "General-rytsar'." *Chasovoi*, no. 187 (1937).

Geschichte der Ritter des Ordens "pour le mérite" im Weltkrieg. Edited by Hanns Möller. 2 vols. Berlin, 1935.

Gibbons, Floyd. *The Red Knight of Germany.* London, 1927.

Giolitti, Giovanni. *Memoirs of My Life.* New York, 1973.

Glaise-Horstenau, Edmund von. *The Collapse of the Austro-Hungarian Empire.* London and Toronto, 1930.

———. *Die Katastrophe: Die Zertrümmerung Österreich-Ungarns.* Vienna, 1929.

Glaise-Horstenau, Edmund von, and Kiszling, R., eds. *Österreich-Ungarns Letzter Krieg, 1914-1918.* 7 vols. Vienna, 1931-1938.

Goldberg, Harvey. *The Life of Jean Jaurès.* Madison, Wis., 1962.

Golovin, N. N. *The Russian Army in the World War.* New Haven, Conn., 1931.

Goltz, Colmar von der. *Denkwürdigkeiten.* Berlin, 1929.

Goltz, Rüdiger von der. *Als Politischer General im Osten 1918-1919.* Leipzig, 1936.

———. *Meine Sendung in Finnland und im Baltikum.* Leipzig, 1920.

Gooch, John. *The Plans of War: The General Staff and British Military Strategy c. 1900-1916.* New York, 1974.

Goodspeed, D. J. *Ludendorff: Genius of World War I.* Boston, 1966.

Görlitz, Walter. *Hindenburg: Ein Lebensbild.* Bonn, 1953.

Gough, Hubert. *The Fifth Army.* London, 1931.

Graf, Daniel W. "Military Rule Behind the Russian Front, 1914-1917: The Political Ramifications." *Jahrbücher für die Geschichte Osteuropas* 22 (1974).

Graves, W. S. *America's Siberian Adventure, 1918-1920.* New York, 1931.

Great Britain: History of the Great War: Military Operations. 23 vols. London, 1922-1948.

Great Britain: History of the Great War: Naval Operations. 5 vols. London, 1920-1931.

Gregory, R. *Walter Hines Page: Ambassador to the Court of St. James's.* Lexington, Ky., 1970.

Gretton, Sir Peter. *Former Naval Person: Winston Churchill and the Royal Navy.* London, 1968.

Grey, Sir Edward. *Twenty-five Years, 1892-1916.* 2 vols. New York, 1925.

Griffiths, Richard. *Pétain: A Biography of Marshal Philippe*

Pétain of Vichy. Garden City, N.Y., 1972.

Grlica, George. "Trumbic's Policy and Croatian National Interests from 1914 to the Beginning of 1918." *Journal of Croatian Studies* 14, 15 (1973-1974).

Groener, Wilhelm. *Der Feldherr wider Willen*. Berlin, 1930.

_____. *Lebenserinnerungen: Jugend. Generalstab. Weltkrieg*. Göttingen, 1957.

_____. *Politik und Kriegführung, ein Rückblick auf den Weltkrieg*. Berlin, 1920.

Groener-Geyer, Dorothea. *General Groener: Soldat und Staatsmann*. Frankfurt, 1955.

Groh, Dieter. *Negative Integration und revolutionärer Attentismus: Die deutsche Sozialdemokratie am Vorabend des Ersten Weltkrieges*. Frankfurt and Berlin, 1973.

Guépratte, Paul Émile. *L'Expédition des Dardanelles, 1914-1915*. Paris, 1935.

Guinn, Paul. *British Strategy and Politics 1914 to 1918*. Oxford, 1965.

Gurko, Vasilii [Basil Gourko]. *War and Revolution in Russia 1914-1917*. New York, 1919.

Gurko, Vladimir I. *Features and Figures of the Past: Government and Opinion in the Reign of Nicholas II*. Stanford, Calif., 1939.

Gwynn, Stephen, ed. *The Letters and Friendships of Sir Cecil Spring Rice: A Record*. 2 vols. Boston and New York, 1929.

Haase, Ernst. *Hugo Haase: Sein Leben und Wirken*. Berlin, 1929.

Halpern, Paul G. "The Anglo-French-Italian Naval Convention of 1915." *The Historical Journal* 13 (1970).

_____. *The Mediterranean Naval Situation, 1908-1914*. Cambridge, Mass., 1971.

_____, ed. *The Keyes Papers*. 3 vols. London, 1979-1981.

Hamilton, Sir Ian. *Gallipoli Diary*. 2 vols. London, 1920.

Hancock, W. K. *Smuts: The Sanguine Years 1870-1919*. Cambridge, 1962.

_____, and Poel, Jean van der, eds. *Selections from the Smuts Papers*. 7 vols. Cambridge, Eng., 1966-1973.

Hankey, Lord. *The Supreme Command*. 2 vols. London, 1961.

Hantsch, Hugo. *Die Geschichte Österreichs*. 2 vols. Graz, 1951-1953.

_____. *Leopold, Graf Berchtold: Grand Seigneur und Staatsmann*. 2 vols. Graz, 1963.

Harbord, J. G. *The American Army in France, 1917-1919*. Boston, 1936.

_____. *Leaves From a War Diary*. New York, 1925.

Harington, Charles. *Plumer of Messines*. London, 1935.

Haselsteiner, Horst. "Die Affäre Putnik." *Österreichische Osthefte* 16 (1974).

Hayase, Yukiko. "The Career of Gotō Shinpei: Japan's Statesman of Research, 1857-1929." Ph.D. diss., Florida State University, 1974.

Helfferich, Karl. *Der Weltkrieg*. 3 vols. Berlin, 1919.

Helmreich, Ernst Christian. *The Diplomacy of the Balkan Wars, 1912-1913*. London, 1938.

Helmreich, Jonathan E. *Belgium and Europe: A Study in Small Power Diplomacy*. The Hague and Paris, 1976.

Helmreich, Paul C. *From Paris to Sèvres: The Partition of the Ottoman Empire at the Peace Conference of 1919-1920*. Columbus, Ohio, 1974.

Hendrick, B. J. *The Life and Letters of Walter Hines Page*. 3 vols. Garden City, N.Y., 1922.

Herben, Jan. *T. G. Masaryk*. Prague, 1923.

Herre, P. *Kronprinz Wilhelm: Seine Rolle in der deutschen Politik*. Munich, 1954.

Hertling, Karl von. *Ein Jahr in der Reichskanzlei: Erinnerungen an die Kanzlerschaft meines Vaters*. Freiburg, 1919.

Herwig, Holger H. "Admirals *versus* Generals: The War Aims of the Imperial German Navy 1914-1918." *Central European History* 5 (1972).

_____. "From Kaiser to Führer: The Political Road of a German Admiral 1923-1933." *Journal of Contemporary History* 9 (1974).

_____. *"Luxury" Fleet: The Imperial German Navy 1888-1918*. London, 1980.

Heyman, Neil M. "Gorlice-Tarnow: The Eastern Front in 1915." *Army Quarterly and Defence Journal* 109 (1979).

_____. "Leon Trotsky's Military Education: From the Russo-Japanese War to 1917." *Journal of Modern History* 48 (1976).

Hindenburg, Paul von. *Aus meinem Leben*. Leipzig, 1927.

Hoffmann, Max. *Die Aufzeichnungen des General-Majors Max Hoffmann*. 2 vols. Berlin, 1930.

_____. *Der Krieg der versäumten Gelegenheiten*. Munich, 1923.

_____. *Tannenberg, wie es wirklich war*. Berlin, 1926.

Höglinger, F. *Minister Präsident Graf Clam-Martinic*. Graz and Cologne, 1964.

Holden, Anne. "Bulgaria's Entry into the First World War: A Diplomatic Study, 1913-1915." Ph.D. diss., University of Illinois at Urbana-Champaign, 1976.

Horne, Alistair. *The Price of Glory: Verdun 1916*. London, 1962.

Horthy, N. *Memoirs*. New York, 1957.

Hosking, Geoffrey A. *The Russian Constitutional Experiment: Government and Duma, 1907-1914*. Cambridge, 1973.

Hovannisian, Richard G. *Armenia on the Road to Independence, 1918*. Berkeley, Calif., 1967.

Hunter, T. M. *Marshal Foch: A Study in Leadership*. Ottawa, 1961.

Hyde, H. Montgomery. *Carson*. London, 1953.

Hymans, Paul. *Mémoires*. 2 vols. Brussels, 1958.

Ilsemann, Sigurd von. *Der Kaiser in Holland*. 2 vols. Munich, 1967-1968.

Isselin, Henri. *The Battle of the Marne*. Garden City, N.Y., 1966.

Jagow, Gottlieb von. *Ursachen und Ausbruch des Weltkrieges*. Berlin, 1919.

James, Robert Rhodes. *Gallipoli*. New York, 1965.

Janssen, K.-H. *Der Kanzler und der General: Die Führungskrise um Bethmann Hollweg und Falkenhayn*. Göttingen, 1966.

Jarausch, Konrad H. *The Enigmatic Chancellor: Bethmann*

Hollweg and the Hubris of Imperial Germany. New Haven, Conn., 1973.

Jelavich, Charles. "Nikolas P. Pašić: Greater Serbia or Jugoslavia?" *Journal of Central European Affairs 11* (1951).

_____, and Jelavich, Barbara. *The Establishment of the Balkan National States, 1804-1920.* Seattle and London, 1977.

Jellicoe, Admiral of the Fleet Earl. *The Grand Fleet, 1914-16: Its Creation, Development and Work.* London, 1919.

Jenkins, Roy. *Asquith.* London, 1964.

Joffre, Marshal Joseph. *The Personal Memoirs of Joffre.* 2 vols. New York, 1932.

Jonas, Klaus W. *Der Kronprinz Wilhelm.* Frankfurt, 1962.

Kahn, David. *The Codebreakers: The Story of Secret Writing.* New York, 1973.

Kann, Robert A. *A History of the Habsburg Empire 1526-1918.* Berkeley, Calif., 1974.

_____. *Die Sixtusaffäre und die geheimen Friedensverhandlungen Österreich-Ungarns im ersten Weltkrieg.* Vienna, 1966.

Károlyi, M. *Fighting the World.* London, 1925.

Katkov, George. *Russia 1917: The February Revolution.* New York, 1967.

Keegan, John, and Wheatcroft, Andrew. *Who's Who in Military History: From 1453 to the Present Day.* London, 1976.

Kenez, Peter. *Civil War in South Russia, 1918: The First Year of the Volunteer Army.* Berkeley, Calif., 1971.

Kennan, George F. *Soviet-American Relations, 1917-1920.* Vol. I. Princeton, 1956.

Kennedy, Paul M. *The Rise and Fall of British Naval Mastery.* New York, 1976.

Kerensky, Alexander. *Russia and History's Turning Point.* New York, 1965.

Kessler, Harry Graf von. *Walther Rathenau: His Life and Work.* New York, 1930.

Keyes, Admiral Sir Roger. *The Naval Memoirs of Admiral of the Fleet Sir Roger Keyes.* 2 vols. London, 1934-1935.

Khoroshavin, A. "Admiral A. V. Kolchak." *Morskiia zapiski 9* (1951).

Kilpatrick, C., ed. *Roosevelt and Daniels: A Friendship in Politics.* Chapel Hill, N.C., 1952.

King, Jere Clemens. *Foch versus Clemenceau: France and German Dismemberment, 1918-1919.* Cambridge, Mass., 1960.

_____. *Generals and Politicians: Conflict between France's High Command, Parliament and Government, 1914-1918.* Berkeley, Calif., 1951.

Kinross, Lord [Patrick Balfour]. *Atatürk: A Biography of Mustafa Kemal, Father of Modern Turkey.* New York, 1965.

Kiritescu [Kiritzesco], Constantin. *La Roumanie dans la guerre mondiale (1916-1919).* Paris, 1934.

Kiszling, R. *Erzherzog Franz Ferdinand von Österreich-Este.* Graz and Cologne, 1953.

Kitchen, Martin. "Hindenburg, Ludendorff and Rumania."

Slavonic and East European Review 54 (1976).

_____. *The Silent Dictatorship: The Politics of the German High Command under Hindenburg and Ludendorff, 1916-1918.* New York, 1976.

Kluck, Alexander von. *Der Marsch auf Paris und die Marneschlacht, 1914.* Berlin, 1920.

Knox, Alfred W. F. *With the Russian Army, 1914-1917.* 2 vols. New York, 1971.

Kossmann, E. H. *The Low Countries, 1780-1940.* Oxford, 1978.

Kotowski, Georg. *Friedrich Ebert: Eine politische Biographie.* Vol. I. Wiesbaden, 1963.

Krack, Otto. *Generalfeldmarschall von Bülow.* Berlin, 1916.

Krafft von Dellmensingen, K. *Der Durchbruch am Isonzo.* Berlin, 1926.

Krauss, A. *Die Ursachen unserer Niederlage.* Munich, 1920.

_____. *Das Wunder von Karfreit.* Munich, 1926.

Krivoshein, K. A. *A. V. Krivoshein (1857-1921). Ego znachenie v istorii Rossii nachala XX veka.* Paris, 1973.

Krizman, Bogdan. "The Belgrade Armistice of 13 November 1918." *Slavonic and East European Review 47* (1970).

Kühlmann, Richard von. *Erinnerungen.* Heidelberg, 1948.

Laffargue, André. *Foch et la bataille de 1918.* Paris, 1967.

Lammasch, H. *Seine Aufzeichnungen, sein Wirken, und seine Politik.* Vienna, 1922.

Landau, Rom. *Pilsudski and Poland.* New York, 1929.

Langle de Cary, Fernand. *Souvenirs de commandement, 1914-1916.* Paris, 1935.

Lanrezac, Charles Louis Marie. *Le Plan de campagne français et le premier mois de la guerre (2 août-3 septembre, 1914).* Paris, 1921.

Lansing, R. *War Memoirs of Robert Lansing.* Indianapolis, Ind., 1935.

Larousse mensuel illustré; revue encyclopédique universelle. 14 vols. Paris, 1907-1959.

Laurens, Adolphe. *Le Commandement naval en Méditerranée, 1914-1918.* Paris, 1931.

Ledeen, Michael A. *The First Duce: D'Annunzio at Fiume.* Baltimore and London, 1977.

Lederer, Ivo J. *Yugoslavia at the Peace Conference: A Study in Frontiermaking.* New Haven, Conn., 1963.

Lee, Dwight E. *Europe's Crucial Years: The Diplomatic Background of World War I, 1902-1914.* Hanover, N.H., 1974.

Lenin, V. I. *O voine, armii i voennoi nauke.* 2 vols. Moscow, 1958.

Leon, George B. *Greece and the Great Powers, 1914-1917.* Thessaloniki, 1974.

_____. "King Constantine's Policy in Exile and the Central Powers, 1917-1918." *Essays in Memory of Basil Laourdas.* Thessaloniki, 1975.

Lettow-Vorbeck, Paul von. *Meine Erinnerungen aus Ostafrika.* Leipzig, 1920.

_____. *Mein Leben.* Bieberach, 1957.

Levine, I. D. *Mitchell: Pioneer of Air Power.* New York, 1943.

Liddell Hart, Basil H. *Reputations: Ten Years After.* Boston, 1928.

_____. *T. E. Lawrence to His Biographers*. New York, 1963.

_____. *The Real War, 1914-1918*. Boston, 1930.

Liggett, H. *A.E.F.: Ten Years Ago in France*. New York, 1928.

Liman von Sanders, Otto. *Five Years in Turkey*. Annapolis, Md., 1927.

Lindenberg, Paul. *König Karl von Rumänien*. 2 vols. Berlin, 1923.

Livermore, S. W. *Politics Is Adjourned: Woodrow Wilson and the War Congress, 1916-1918*. Middletown, Conn., 1966.

Lloyd George, David. *War Memoirs*. 6 vols. London, 1933-1936.

Lodge, Henry Cabot. *The Senate and the League of Nations*. New York, 1925.

Logio, George Clenton. *Bulgaria: Past and Present*. Manchester, 1936.

Lorenz, R. *Kaiser Karl und der Untergang der Donaumonarchie*. Graz, 1959.

Louis, William Roger. *Great Britain and Germany's Lost Colonies 1914-1919*. Oxford, 1967.

Lowe, C. J., and Marzari, F. *Italian Foreign Policy 1870-1940*. London and Boston, 1975.

Lowe, Peter. *Great Britain and Japan, 1911-1914: A Study of British Far Eastern Policy*. London, 1969.

Luckau, Alma. *The German Delegation at the Paris Peace Conference*. New York, 1941.

Ludendorff, Erich. *Kriegführung und Politik*. Berlin, 1921.

_____. *Meine Kriegserinnerungen 1914-1918*. Berlin, 1919.

_____. *Urkunden der Obersten Heeresleitung über ihre Tätigkeit 1916/18*. Berlin, 1919.

Ludwig, Emil. *Kaiser Wilhelm II*. London, 1926.

McAdoo, W. G. *Crowded Years*. Boston, 1931.

Macartney, C. A. *The Habsburg Empire 1790-1918*. New York, 1969.

_____. *Hungary: A History*. Edinburgh, 1962.

Mack, John E. *A Prince of our Disorder: The Life of T. E. Lawrence*. Boston, 1976.

Mackay, Ruddock F. *Fisher of Kilverstone*. Oxford, 1973.

Mackensen, August von. *Briefe und Aufzeichnungen*. Berlin, 1938.

Mackenzie, C. *Dr. Beneš*. London, 1946.

Magnus, Philip. *Kitchener: Portrait of an Imperialist*. London, 1958.

Maire, Gilbert. *Raspoutine*. Paris, 1966.

Malvy, Louis Jean. *Mon crime*. Paris, 1921.

Mamatey, Victor S. "The United States and Bulgaria in World War I." *American Slavic and East European Review* 12 (1953).

_____. *The United States and East Central Europe, 1914-1918: A Study in Wilsonian Diplomacy and Propaganda*. Princeton, 1957.

Mangin, Charles. *Lettres de guerre, 1914-1918*. Paris, 1950.

March, Peyton C. *The Nation at War*. New York, 1932.

Marder, Arthur J. *From the Dreadnought to Scapa Flow: The Royal Navy in the Fisher Era, 1904-1919*. 5 vols. Oxford and London, 1961-1970.

Marie, Queen of Roumania. *The Story of My Life*. 2 vols. New York, 1971.

Marina. Stato maggiore. Uffico storico. *La Marina italiana nella grande guerra*. 8 vols. Florence, 1935-1942.

Marre, Francis. *Le Baron de Broqueville et la défense nationale*. Brussels and Paris, 1918.

Marshall, William R. *Memories of Four Fronts*. London, 1929.

Marshall-Cornwall, Sir James. *Foch as Military Commander*. London, 1972.

_____. *Haig as Military Commander*. New York, 1973.

Masaryk, T. G. *Die Weltrevolution*. Berlin, 1925.

Maslovskii, E. "General Nikolai Nikolaevich IUdenich." *Chasovoi* 62 (1931).

Maurice, Frederick B. *Soldier, Artist, Sportsman: The Life of General Lord Rawlinson of Trent*. Boston and New York, 1928.

Mawdsley, Evan. *The Russian Revolution and the Baltic Fleet: War and Politics, February 1917-April 1918*. New York, 1978.

May, Arthur J. *The Passing of the Hapsburg Monarchy, 1914-1918*. 2 vols. Philadelphia, Pa., 1966.

May, Ernest R. *The World War and American Isolation, 1914-1917*. Cambridge, Mass., 1959.

Mayer, Arno J. *Politics and Diplomacy of Peacemaking: Containment and Counterrevolution at Versailles, 1918-1919*. New York, 1967.

Mayer, Émile. *Nos chefs de 1914*. Paris, 1930.

Mayzel, Matitiahu. *Generals and Revolutionaries: The Russian General Staff during the Revolution. A Study in the Transformation of a Military Elite*. Osnabrück, 1979.

Meier-Welcker, Hans. *Seeckt*. Frankfurt, 1967.

Melograni, Piero. *Storia politica della grande guerra 1915-1918*. Bari, 1969.

Menashe, Louis. "A Liberal with Spurs: Alexander Guchkov, A Bourgeois in Politics." *Russian Review* 26 (1967).

Merkushov, V. "Admiral Essen, vozsozdatel' flota." *Chasovoi* 32 (1930).

Michaelis, Georg. *Für Volk und Staat*. Berlin, 1922.

Miliukov, Paul. *Political Memoirs, 1905-1917*. Ann Arbor, Mich., 1967.

Millett, A. R. *The General: Robert L. Bullard and Officership in the United States Army, 1881-1925*. Westport, Conn., 1975.

Milne, Sir A. Berkeley. *The Flight of the "Goeben" and "Breslau."* London, 1921.

Miquel, Pierre. *Poincaré*. Paris, 1961.

Mitchell, Donald W. *A History of Russian and Soviet Sea Power*. New York, 1974.

Mitchell, W. *Memories of World War I: "From Start to Finish of Our Greatest War."* New York, 1960.

Modern Encyclopedia of Russian and Soviet History, The. 22 vols. to date. Gulf Breeze, Fla., 1976-.

Moltke, Helmuth von. *Erinnerungen, Briefe, Dokumente, 1877-1916*. Stuttgart, 1922.

Monticone, Alberto. *Nitti e la grande guerra (1914-1918)*. Milan, 1961.

Morison, E. E. *Admiral Sims and the Modern American Navy*. Boston, 1942.

Morley, James W. *The Japanese Thrust into Siberia, 1918*. New York, 1957.

Morsey, Rudolf, and Matthias, Erich, eds. *Die Regierung des Prinzen Max von Baden*. Düsseldorf, 1962.

Morskiia zapiski (New York), 1943-1965.

Mosley, Leonard O. *Curzon: The End of an Epoch*. London, 1960.

———. *The Glorious Fault: The Life of Lord Curzon*. New York, 1960.

Müller, G. A. von. *The Kaiser and His Court: The Diaries, Note Books and Letters of Admiral Georg Alexander von Müller, Chief of the Naval Cabinet 1914-1918*. New York, 1961.

Murray, Archibald J. *Sir Archibald Murray's Despatches (June 1916-June 1917)*. New York, 1920.

National Cyclopaedia of American Biography. 57 vols. New York and Clifton, N.J., 1893-1977.

Nédeff, Lieutenant Colonel. *Les Opérations en Macédoine: L'Épopée de Doïran*. Sofia, 1927.

Neue Deutsche Biographie. 11 vols. to date. Berlin, 1953-.

Neue Österreichische Biographie ab 1815. 19 vols. to date. Vienna, 1923-.

Nicholas II. *Dnevnik Imperatora Nikolaia II*. Berlin, 1923.

Nicky-Sunny Letters, The. Correspondence of the Tsar and Tsaritsa, 1914-1917. Hattiesburg, Miss., 1970.

Nicolson, Harold. *King George the Fifth: His Life and Reign*. London, 1952.

Niemann, Alfred. *Revolution von Oben—Umsturz von Unten: Entwicklung und Verlauf der Staatsumwälzung in Deutschland 1914-18*. Berlin, 1927.

Nihon Riku-Kaigun no Seido: Soshiki Jinji [The Structure, Organization, and Personnel of the Japanese Army and Navy]. Tokyo, 1971.

Nish, Ian H. *Alliance in Decline: A Study in Anglo-Japanese Relations 1908-23*. London, 1972.

———. *The Anglo-Japanese Alliance: The Diplomacy of Two Island Empires 1894-1907*. London, 1966.

Norman, Aaron. *The Great Air War*. New York, 1968.

Noske, Gustav. *Erlebtes aus Aufstieg und Niedergang einer Demokratie*. Offenbach, 1947.

———. *Von Kiel bis Kapp: Zur Geschichte der deutschen Revolution*. Berlin, 1920.

Oldenburg, S. S. *Last Tsar: Nicholas II, His Reign & His Russia*. 4 vols. Gulf Breeze, Fla., 1975-1978.

Orlando, Vittorio Emanuele. *Memorie (1915-1919)*. Milan, 1960.

Ormesson, N. B. Wladimir d'. *Auprès de Lyautey*. Paris, 1963.

Österreichisches Biographisches Lexikon 1815-1950. 7 vols. to date. Graz and Cologne, 1957-.

Owen, Frank. *Tempestuous Journey: Lloyd George. His Life and Times*. London, 1954.

Painlevé, Paul. *Comment j'ai nommé Foch et Pétain*. Paris, 1923.

Paléologue, Georges Maurice. *An Ambassador's Memoirs*. 3 vols. New York, 1923-1924.

Palmer, Alan. *The Gardeners of Salonika*. New York, 1965.

———. *The Kaiser: Warlord of the Second Reich*. New York, 1978.

———. "Montenegro: The Smallest Ally." *History of the First World War*. Vol. III. London, 1969.

Palo, Michael Frances. "The Diplomacy of Belgian War Aims during the First World War." Ph.D. diss., University of Illinois at Urbana-Champaign, 1977.

Pamlényi, E. *A History of Hungary*. Budapest, 1975.

Pares, Sir Bernard. *The Fall of the Russian Monarchy: A Study of the Evidence*. New York, 1939.

Patterson, A. Temple. *Jellicoe: A Biography*. London and New York, 1969.

Pavlovich, N. B., ed. *The Fleet in the First World War*. Vol. I. Moscow, 1964.

Payer, Friedrich von. *Mein Lebenslauf*. Stuttgart, 1932.

———. *Von Bethmann Hollweg bis Ebert: Erinnerungen und Bilder*. Frankfurt, 1923.

Pearson, Raymond. *The Russian Moderates and the Crisis of Tsarism, 1914-1917*. London, 1977.

Pedroncini, Guy. *Les Mutineries de 1917*. Paris, 1967.

———. *Les Negociations secrètes pendant la Grande Guerre*. Paris, 1969.

———. *Pétain: général en chef, 1917-1918*. Paris, 1974.

Penrose, C. *James G. Harbord (1866-1947)*. New York, 1956.

Pershing, J. J. *My Experiences in the World War*. 2 vols. New York, 1931.

Petrovich, Michael Boro. *A History of Modern Serbia, 1804-1918*. 2 vols. New York and London, 1976.

Pieri, Piero. *L'Italia nella prima guerra mondiale (1915-1918)*. Turin, 1965.

———. "Les relations entre gouvernement et commandement en Italie en 1917." *Revue d'histoire moderne et contemporaine* 15 (1968).

———., and Rochat, Giorgio. *Pietro Badoglio*. Turin, 1974.

Pirenne, Henri. *La Belgique et la guerre mondiale*. New Haven, Conn. [1928].

Pitreich, A. *Der österreich-ungarische Bundesgenosse im Sperrfeuer*. Klagenfurt, 1930.

Pitt, Barrie. *Coronel and Falkland*. London, 1960.

———, and Young, Peter, eds. *History of the First World War*. 8 vols. London, 1969-1971.

Poincaré, Raymond. *Au service de la France—neuf années de souvenirs*. 10 vols. Paris, 1926-1933.

Polivanov, A. A. *Memuary: Iz dnevnikov i vospominanii po dolzhnosti voennogo ministra i ego pomoshchnika (1907-1916)*. Moscow, 1924.

Porter, Charles W. *The Career of Théophile Delcassé*. Philadelphia, Pa., 1936.

Potts, James M. "The Loss of Bulgaria." In Alexander Dallin, ed., *Russian Diplomacy and Eastern Europe, 1914-1917*. New York, 1963.

Pound, Reginald, and Harmsworth, Geoffrey. *Northcliffe*. London, 1959.

Presseisen, Ernst. *Before Aggression: Europeans Prepare the Japanese Army*. Tucson, Ariz., 1965.

Rabinowitch, Alexander. *The Bolsheviks Come to Power: The Revolution of 1917 in Petrograd*. New York, 1976.

_____. *Prelude to Revolution: The Petrograd Bolsheviks and the July 1917 Uprising*. Bloomington, Ind., 1968.

Radoslawoff [Radoslavov], Vasil. *Bulgarien und die Weltkrise*. Berlin, 1923.

Ralston, David B. *The Army of the Republic: The Place of the Military in the Political Evolution of France, 1871-1914*. Cambridge, Mass., and London, 1967.

Rathenau, Walther. *Gesammelte Schriften*. 6 vols. Berlin, 1929.

_____. *Tagebuch 1907-1922*. Düsseldorf, 1967.

Ratinaud, Jean. *La Course à la mer: De la Somme aux Flandres (Septembre 14-Novembre 17, 1914)*. Paris, 1967.

_____. *1917 ou la révolte des poilus*. Paris, 1960.

Redlich, J. *Kaiser Franz Joseph von Österreich*. Berlin, 1928.

Regele, O. *Feldmarschall Conrad*. Vienna, 1955.

Remak, Joachim. *Sarajevo: The Story of a Political Murder*. New York, 1959.

Renouvin, Pierre. *La Crise européenne et la Première Guerre Mondiale*. Paris, 1962.

Rhodes, Anthony. *The Poet as Superman: A Life of Gabriele D'Annunzio*. London, 1959.

Ribot, Alexandre. *Journal d'Alexandre Ribot et correspondances inédites, 1914-1922*. Paris [1936].

Richthofen, Manfred A. *Der rote Kampfflieger*. Berlin, 1917.

Riddell, Lord. *Lord Riddell's War Diary, 1914-1918*. London, 1933.

Rieber, Alfred J. "Russian Diplomacy and Rumania." In Alexander Dallin, ed., *Russian Diplomacy and Eastern Europe, 1914-1917*. New York, 1963.

Riezler, Kurt. *Tagebücher, Aufsätze, Dokumente*. Göttingen, 1972.

Riha, Thomas. *A Russian European: Paul Miliukov in Russian Politics*. Notre Dame and London, 1969.

Ritter, Gerhard. *Staatskunst und Kriegshandwerk: Das Problem des "Militarismus" in Deutschland*. 4 vols. Munich, 1964-1968.

Ritter, Gerhard A., and Miller, Susanne, eds. *Die deutsche Revolution 1918-1919*. Frankfurt, 1968.

Robbins, Keith. *Sir Edward Grey: A Biography of Lord Grey of Falloden*. London, 1971.

Robertson, William R. *Soldiers and Statesmen, 1914-1918*. 2 vols. London, 1926.

Rochat, Giorgio. *L'esercito italiano da Vittorio Veneto a Mussolini*. Bari, 1967.

_____. *L'Italia nella prima guerra mondiale: Problemi di interpretazione e prospettive di ricerca*. Milan, 1976.

Rodzianko, M. V. *The Reign of Rasputin: An Empire's Collapse*. New York [1927].

Rogger, Hans. "Russia in 1914." *Journal of Contemporary History* 1 (1966).

Röhl, John. *1914: Delusion or Design? The Testimony of Two German Diplomats*. London, 1973.

Ronarc'h, Pierre. *Souvenirs de la Guerre*. Vol. I. Paris, 1921.

Rosenberg, William G. *Liberals in the Russian Revolution: The Constitutional Democratic Party, 1917-1921*. Princeton, 1974.

Rostunov, I. I. *General Brusilov*. Moscow, 1964.

_____, ed. *Istoriia pervoi mirovoi voiny, 1914-1918*. 2 vols. Moscow, 1975.

_____. *Russkii front pervoi mirovoi voiny*. Moscow, 1976.

Rothenberg, G. E. *The Army of Francis Joseph*. West Lafayette, Ind., 1976.

Rothschild, Joseph. *The Communist Party of Bulgaria: Origins and Development, 1883-1936*. New York, 1959.

_____. *East Central Europe between the Two World Wars*. Seattle and London, 1974.

Ruedt von Collenberg, Ludwig. *Generalfeldmarschall von Mackensen*. Berlin, 1935.

Rumpler, H. *Max Hussarek*. Vienna, 1965.

Rupprecht von Bayern, Crown Prince. *Mein Kriegstagebuch*. 3 vols. Berlin, 1929.

Rutherford, Ward. *The Russian Army in World War I*. London, 1975.

Ryan, Stephen. *Pétain the Soldier*. London, 1969.

Salandra, Antonio. *Il diario di Salandra*. Milan, 1969.

_____. *Italy and the Great War: From Neutrality to Intervention*. London, 1932.

Sarrail, Maurice. *Mon commandement en Orient (1916-1918)*. Paris, 1920.

Saul, Norman E. *Sailors in Revolt: The Russian Baltic Fleet in 1917*. Lawrence, Kans., 1978.

Sazonov, Serge. *Fateful Years, 1909-1916*. New York, 1928.

Scham, Alan. *Lyautey in Morocco: Protectorate Administration, 1912-1925*. Berkeley, Calif., 1970.

Schaper, B. W. *Albert Thomas: Trente ans de réformisme social*. Assen, 1959.

Schapiro, Leonard, and Reddaway, Peter, eds. *Lenin: The Man, the Theorist, the Leader; A Reappraisal*. New York, 1967.

Scheer, Reinhard. *Deutschlands Hochseeflotte im Weltkrieg: Persönliche Erinnerungen*. Berlin, 1920.

Scheidemann, Philipp. *Memoiren eines Sozialdemokraten*. 2 vols. Dresden, 1928.

_____. *Der Zusammenbruch*. Berlin, 1921.

Schmidt, Martin E. *Alexandre Ribot: Odyssey of a Liberal in the Third Republic*. The Hague, 1974.

Schorske, Carl E. *German Social Democracy 1905-1917: The Development of the Great Schism*. Cambridge, Mass., 1955.

Schulthess' Europäischer Geschichtskalender. Neue Folge. 30-35. Munich, 1914-23.

Schwertfeger, Bernhard H. *Kaiser und Kabinettschef: Nach eigenen Aufzeichnungen und dem Briefwechsel des wirklichen geheimen rats Rudolf von Valentini*. Oldenburg, 1931.

Seeckt, Hans von. *Aus meinem Leben 1866 bis 1917*. 2 vols. Leipzig, 1938.

Sendtner, Kurt. *Rupprecht von Wittelsbach, Kronprinz von Bayern*. Munich, 1954.

Senn, Alfred Erich. *The Russian Revolution in Switzerland, 1914-1917*. Madison, Wis., and London, 1971.

Seth, Ronald. *Caporetto: The Scapegoat Battle*. London, 1965.

Seton-Watson, Christopher. *Italy from Liberalism to Fascism, 1870-1925*. London, 1967.

Seton-Watson, Robert W. *A History of the Roumanians from the Roman Times to the Completion of Unity*. Cambridge, 1934.

Seymour, C. *The Intimate Papers of Colonel House*. 4 vols. Boston, 1926-1928.

Shaw, Stanford J., and Shaw, Ezel Kural. *History of the Ottoman Empire and Modern Turkey*. Vol. II. Cambridge, 1977.

Sheperd, G. B. *The Last Habsburg*. New York, 1968.

Siebert, Ferdinand. *Aristide Briand: Ein Staatsmann zwischen Frankreich und Europa*. Zurich and Stuttgart, 1973.

Siegelbaum, Lewis H. "The War-Industries Committees and the Politics of Industrial Mobilization in Russia, 1915-1917." Ph.D. diss., Oxford University, 1976.

Silberstein, Gerard E. "The Serbian Campaign of 1915: Its Diplomatic Background." *American Historical Review* 71 (1967).

_____. *The Troubled Alliance: German-Austrian Relations, 1914 to 1917*. Lexington, Ky., 1970.

Sims, William S. *The Victory at Sea*. Garden City, N.Y., 1920.

Smith, C. Jay, Jr. *The Russian Struggle for Power, 1914-1917: A Study of Russian Foreign Policy During the First World War*. New York, 1956.

Smith, Dennis Mack. *Italy: A Modern History*. Ann Arbor, Mich., 1969.

Smith-Dorrien, Horace L. *Memories of Forty-Eight Years' Service*. London, 1925.

Smuts, Jan Christian. *War-time Speeches*. New York, 1917.

Sokol, H. H. *Österreich-Ungarns Seekrieg 1914-1918*. 4 vols. Vienna, 1933.

Sonnino, Sidney. *Carteggio, 1914-1922*. 2 vols. Rome and Bari, 1974-1975.

Sovetskaia istoricheskaia entsiklopediia. 16 vols. Moscow, 1961-1976.

Sovetskaia voennaia entsiklopediia. 7 vols. to date. Moscow, 1976-.

Spears, E. L. *Liaison, 1914: A Narrative of the Great Retreat*. London, 1930.

_____. *Prelude to Victory*. London, 1939.

Spector, Sherman David. *Rumania at the Paris Peace Conference: A Study of the Diplomacy of Ioan Bratianu*. New York, 1962.

Spender, J. A., and Asquith, Cyril. *Life of Herbert Henry Asquith, Lord Oxford and Asquith*. 2 vols. London, 1932.

Stallings, L. *The Doughboys: The Story of the A.E.F. 1917-1918*. New York, 1963.

Stavrianos, L. S. *The Balkans since 1453*. New York, 1958.

Stavrou, Theofanis George, ed. *Russia under the Last Tsar*. Minneapolis, Minn., 1969.

Stegemann, Bernd. *Die Deutsche Marinepolitik 1916-1918*. Berlin, 1970.

Steinberg, Jonathan. *Yesterday's Deterrent: Tirpitz and the Birth of the German Battle Fleet*. New York, 1966.

Steiner, Zara. *Britain and the Origins of the First World War*. New York, 1977.

Stoichev, Ivan K. *Builders and Military Leaders of the Bulgarian Army, 1879-1942*. Sofia, 1941.

Stokes, Gale. "The Serbian Documents from 1914: A Preview." *Journal of Modern History* 48 (1976).

Stone, Norman. *The Eastern Front, 1914-1917*. London, 1975.

Strauss Feuerlicht, Roberta. *The Desperate Act: The Assassination of Francis Ferdinand at Sarajevo*. New York, 1968.

Stresemann, Gustav. *Reden und Schriften*. 2 vols. Dresden, 1926.

_____. *Vermächtnis: Der Nachlass in drei Bänden*. 3 vols. Berlin, 1932-1933.

Strokov, A. A. *Vooruzhennye sily i voennoe iskusstvo v pervoi mirovoi voine*. Moscow, 1974.

Stürgkh, J. M. *Politische und militärische Erinnerungen aus meinem Leben*. Leipzig, 1923.

Suarez, Georges. *Briand, sa vie, son oeuvre*. 6 vols. Paris, 1938-1952.

Suchomlinof [Sukhomlinov], W. A. *Erinnerungen*. Berlin, 1924.

Taillemite, Étienne. *Dictionnaire de la Marine*. Paris, 1962.

Talât Paşa. "Posthumous Memoirs of Talaat Pasha." *Current History* 15 (1921).

Tanenbaum, Jan Karl. *General Maurice Sarrail, 1856-1929: The French Army and Left-Wing Politics*. Chapel Hill, N.C., 1974.

Taylor, A.J.P. *Beaverbrook*. London, 1972.

_____. *English History 1914-1945*. Oxford, 1965.

Temperley, H.W.G., ed. *A History of the Peace Conference of Paris*. 6 vols. London, 1920-1924.

Terraine, John. *Douglas Haig: The Educated Soldier*. London, 1963.

_____. *Mons: The Retreat to Victory*. London, 1960.

Thayer, John A. *Italy and the Great War: Politics and Culture, 1870-1915*. Madison, Wis., 1964.

Theodoulou, Christos. *Greece and the Entente, August 1, 1914-September 25, 1916*. Thessaloniki, 1971.

Thimme, Annelise. *Gustav Stresemann*. Hanover and Frankfurt, 1957.

Thomazi, A. *La Marine française dans la Grande Guerre (1914-1918)*. 4 vols. Paris, 1925-1929.

Thomson, Thomas John. "Boris Stürmer and the Imperial Russian Government, February 2-November 22, 1916." Ph.D. diss., Duke University, 1972.

Tirpitz, Alfred von. *Erinnerungen*. Leipzig, 1919.

_____. *Politische Dokumente*. 2 vols. Hamburg/Berlin/Stuttgart, 1924, 1926.

Torrey, Glenn E. "Irredentism and Diplomacy: The Central Powers and Rumania, August-November, 1914." *Südost-Forschungen* 25 (1966).

_____. "Romania and the Belligerents, 1914-1918: Some Observations on the Sarrail Offensive at Salonika, August, 1916." *Revue roumaine d'histoire* 14 (1975).

_____. "Romania's Entry into the First World War: The

Problem of Strategy." *Emporia State Research Studies* 26 (1978).

———. "Rumania and the Belligerents, 1914-1916." *Journal of Contemporary History* 1 (1966).

———. "Rumania's Decision to Intervene: Bratianu and the Entente, June-July 1916." *Rumanian Studies* 3 (1972-1973).

Townshend, C.V.F. *My Campaign in Mesopotamia.* London, 1920.

Trask, David F. *Captains & Cabinets: Anglo-American Naval Relations, 1917-1918.* Columbia, Mo., 1972.

———. *General Tasker Howard Bliss and the "Sessions of the World," 1919.* Philadelphia, Pa., 1966.

———. *The United States in the Supreme War Council: American War Aims and Inter-Allied Strategy, 1917-1918.* Middletown, Conn., 1961.

Trotha, Adolf von. *Grossdeutsches Wollen: Aus den Lebenserfahrungen eines Seeoffiziers.* Berlin, 1924.

Trotsky, Leon. *My Life: An Attempt at an Autobiography.* New York, 1930.

———. *Voina i revoliutsiia.* 2 vols. Moscow and Petrograd, 1922-1923.

Troubridge, Laura. *Memories and Reflections.* London, 1925.

Trumpener, Ulrich. "German Military Aid to Turkey in 1914: An Historical Re-evaluation." *Journal of Modern History* 32 (1960).

———. *Germany and the Ottoman Empire, 1914-1918.* Princeton, N.J., 1968.

———. "The Escape of the *Goeben* and *Breslau*: A Reassessment." *Canadian Journal of History* 6 (1971).

Tschiwitz, Erich von. *General v. d. Marwitz: Weltkriegsbriefe.* Berlin, 1940.

Tuchman, Barbara W. *The Guns of August.* New York, 1962.

———. *The Zimmermann Telegram.* New York, 1958.

Turner, L.C.F. "The Role of the General Staffs in 1914." *The Australian Journal of Politics and History* 9 (1965).

———. "The Russian Mobilization in 1914." In Paul M. Kennedy, ed., *The War Plans of the Great Powers, 1880-1914.* London, 1979.

Ulam, Adam B. *The Bolsheviks: The Intellectual and Political History of the Triumph of Communism in Russia.* New York, 1965.

Valiani, Leo. *The End of Austria-Hungary.* London, 1973.

Vandiver, Frank E. *Black Jack: The Life and Times of John J. Pershing.* 2 vols. College Station, Tex., 1977.

Varillon, Pierre. *Joffre.* Paris, 1956.

Veltzé, Alois. "Unsere Flottenführer." *Donauland. Illustrierte Monatsschrift* 2 (1918-1919).

———. *Unsere Heerführer.* Vienna, 1918.

Vietsch, Eberhard von. *Bethmann Hollweg: Staatsmann zwischen Macht und Ethos.* Boppard, 1969.

———. *Gegen die Unvernunft: Der Briefwechsel zwischen Paul Graf Wolff Metternich und Wilhelm Solf, 1915-1918.* Bremen, 1964.

———. *Wilhelm Solf: Botschafter zwischen den Zeiten.* Tübingen, 1961.

Voennaia entsiklopediia. 18 vols. St. Petersburg, 1911-1915.

Vojna enciklopedija. 11 vols. Belgrade, 1970-1975.

Vucinich, Wayne S. *Serbia between East and West: The Events of 1903-1908.* New York, 1968.

Wade, Rex A. *The Russian Search for Peace, February-October 1917.* Stanford, Calif., 1969.

Wagner, A. *Der Erste Weltkrieg.* Vienna, 1968.

Waldeyer-Hartz, Hugo von. *Admiral v. Hipper.* Leipzig, 1933.

Warth, Robert D. *The Allies and the Russian Revolution: From the Fall of the Monarchy to the Peace of Brest-Litovsk.* Durham, N.C., 1954.

———. *Leon Trotsky.* Boston, 1977.

Watson, David Robin. *Georges Clemenceau: A Political Biography.* New York, 1974.

Weber, Eugen. *Action Française: Royalism and Reaction in Twentieth-Century France.* Stanford, Calif., 1962.

Weber, Frank G. *Eagles on the Crescent: Germany, Austria, and the Diplomacy of the Turkish Alliance, 1914-1918.* Ithaca, N.Y., 1970.

Weinwurm, Franz. "Feldzeugmeister Oskar Potiorek. Leben und Wirken als Chef der Landesregierung für Bosnien und die Herzegowina in Sarajevo 1911-1914." Ph.D. diss., Vienna University, 1964.

Wemyss, Lord Wester. *The Navy in the Dardanelles Campaign.* London, 1924.

Wemyss, Lady Wester. *The Life and Letters of Lord Wester Wemyss.* London, 1935.

Westarp, Graf Kuno von. *Konservative Politik im letzten Jahrzehnt des Kaiserreiches.* 2 vols. Berlin, 1935.

Weygand, Maxime. *Foch.* Paris, 1947.

———. *Mémoires.* 3 vols. Paris, 1950-1957.

Wheeler-Bennett, John. *Wooden Titan: Hindenburg.* London, 1936.

Whittam, John. *The Politics of the Italian Army, 1861-1918.* London, 1977.

Who Was Who 1916-1928. London, 1929.

Wildman, Allan K. *The End of the Russian Imperial Army: The Old Army and the Soldiers' Revolt (March-April 1917).* Princeton, 1980.

Wilfong, W. Thomas. "Rebuilding the Russian Army, 1905-1914: The Question of a Comprehensive Plan for National Defense." Ph.D. diss., Indiana University, 1977.

Wilhelm, Crown Prince. *Meine Erinnerungen an Deutschlands Heldenkampf.* Stuttgart, 1922.

Wilhelm II. *My Memoirs.* London, 1922.

Willequet, Jacques. "Les relations entre le roi commandant en chef de l'armée, et le gouvernement belge, en 1914-1918." *Revue d'histoire moderne et contemporaine* 15 (1968).

Williamson, John G. *Karl Helfferich 1872-1924: Economist, Financier, Politician.* Princeton, 1971.

Williamson, Samuel R., Jr. *The Politics of Grand Strategy: Britain and France Prepare for War, 1904-1914.* Cambridge, Mass., 1969.

Windrow, Martin, and Mason, Francis K. *A Concise Dictionary of Military Biography: Two Hundred of* the Most Significant Names in Land Warfare, 10th-20th Century. Reading, Eng., 1975.

Wolbe, Eugen. *Generalfeldmarschall Prinz Leopold von Bayern: Ein Lebensbild*. Leipzig, 1920.

Woodhouse, C. M. *A Short History of Modern Greece*. New York and Washington, 1968.

Wrench, John Evelyn. *Alfred Lord Milner: The Man with No Illusions*. London, 1958.

Wright, Gordon. *Raymond Poincaré and the French Presidency*. New York, 1967.

Young, Kenneth. *Arthur James Balfour*. London, 1963.

Zaionchkovskii, Andrei Medardovich. *Mirovaia voina 1914-1918 g.g. Obshchii strategicheskii ocherk*. Moscow, 1924.

Zeine, Zeine N. *The Emergence of Arab Nationalism: With a Background Study of Arab-Turkish Relations in the Near East*. New York, 1975.

Zeman, Z.A.B. *The Break-up of the Habsburg Empire 1914-1918*. London, 1961.

———, ed. *Germany and the Revolution in Russia, 1915-1918: Documents from the Archives of the German Foreign Ministry*. London, 1958.

Zetland, Lawrence, and Dundas, J. L. *The Life of Lord Curzon*. 3 vols. New York, 1928.

Zhitkov, K. "Admiral N. O. Fon Essen." *Morskoi sbornik* 388 (1915).

Zmarzlik, Hans-Günther. *Bethmann Hollweg als Reichskanzler, 1909-1914*. Düsseldorf, 1957.

Zwehl, H. von. *Erich von Falkenhayn, General der Infanterie: Eine biographische Studie*. Dresden, 1926.

INDEX

Page numbers set in **bold face** indicate the location of the main entry.

About the Authors

HOLGER H. HERWIG is Associate Professor of History at Vanderbilt University in Nashville, Tennessee. His earlier works include *The German Naval Officer Corps* and *Politics of Frustration: The United States in German Strategic Planning, 1888-1941*.

NEIL M. HEYMAN is Professor of History at San Diego State University in San Diego, California. A specialist in Russian military history, Professor Heyman has published articles in the *Journal of Modern History, Military Affairs, Studies in Comparative Communism*, and the *Army Quarterly and Defense Journal*.